Practical
Financial
Management

Seventh Edition

WILLIAM R. LASHER

Nichols College

SOUTH-WESTERN

Australia • Brazil • Jap ingdom • United States

SOUTH-WESTERN
CENGAGE Learning

**Practical Financial Management,
Seventh Edition, International Edition**

William R. Lasher

Senior Vice President, LRS/Acquisitions &
Solutions Planning: Jack W. Calhoun

Editorial Director, Business & Economics:
Erin Joyner

Editor-in-Chief: Joe Sabatino

Executive Editor: Mike Reynolds

Developmental Editor: Conor Allen

Senior Editorial Assistant: Adele Scholtz

Senior Brand Manager: Robin LeFevre

Senior Market Development Manager:
John Carey

Marketing Program Manager: Erica Glisson

Executive Marketing Communications
Manager: Jason Lachapelle

Marketing Coordinator: Ilyssa Harbatkin

Art and Cover Direction, Production
Management, and Composition:
PreMediaGlobal

Supervising Media Editor: Scott Fidler

Rights Acquisition Director: Audrey
Pettengill

Rights Acquisition Specialist, Text and
Image: Anne Sheroff

Manufacturing Planner: Kevin Kluck

Cover Image: © Bananastock/Thinkstock

Internal Images: optimarc/Shutterstock.com;
Ensuper/Shutterstock.com; Ensuper/
Shutterstock.com

International Edition:

ISBN-13: 978-1-133-59351-5

ISBN-10: 1-133-59351-8

Package Edition ISBN-13: 978-1-133-59352-2

Package Edition ISBN-10: 1-133-59352-6

Cengage Learning International Offices

Asia
www.cengageasia.com
tel: (65) 6410 1200

Australia/New Zealand
www.cengage.com.au
tel: (61) 3 9685 4111

Brazil
www.cengage.com.br
tel: (55) 11 3665 9900

India
www.cengage.co.in
tel: (91) 11 4364 1111

Latin America
www.cengage.com.mx
tel: (52) 55 1500 6000

UK/Europe/Middle East/Africa
www.cengage.co.uk
tel: (44) 0 1264 332 424

**Represented in Canada by
Nelson Education, Ltd.**
www.nelson.com
tel: (416) 752 9100 / (800) 668 0671

Cengage Learning is a leading provider of customized learning solutions
with office locations around the globe, including Singapore, the United
Kingdom, Australia, Mexico, Brazil, and Japan. Locate your local office at:
www.cengage.com/global

For product information and free companion resources:
www.cengage.com/international
Visit your local office: **www.cengage.com/global**
Visit our corporate website: **www.cengage.com**

Printed in Canada
1 2 3 4 5 6 7 16 15 14 13 12

For the lights of my life,
Donna and our Amanda Noel

Brief Contents

Contents

The seventh edition of *Practical Financial Management* is the latest milestone in a more than 35-year journey in education that began when I was a corporate executive teaching finance as an adjunct professor.

Not long after starting down that road, I realized that I might be able to improve on the approach taken by most finance texts. It was true then, and it's still true today, that most finance texts are harder for students to understand than they should be. The issue is relatively unique to the field. No other business discipline seems to have finance's reputation for unfathomable reading material.

I eventually came to the conclusion that the problem lies in the fact that textbook presentations are inconsistent with the background knowledge and abilities of typical business students. That isn't to say that the texts are poorly done. By and large, finance texts are good books. They're logical, well written, and comprehensive. But they're consistently off target in several key areas with respect to the students who read them.

The first problem has to do with student background. Texts tend to introduce topics using a voice that assumes the student already has some grounding in the area to be studied. Even bright students are confused and intimidated by this practice because most don't know anything about the subject when they start a chapter.

The second issue relates to quantitative material. A great deal of finance is grounded in math and statistics, so students have to take prerequisite courses in those areas. But many business students aren't really comfortable with quantitative methods even after they've had the courses. This leads to the biggest pedagogical problem we have. Textbooks assume business students are better at math than they are. As a result, most readers can't follow textbook presentations of quantitative material without an inordinate amount of time and study.

Finally, there is a troubling lack of practicality in much of this literature. For example, texts present techniques like NPV and IRR implying hair-splitting accuracy that doesn't exist in the real world, where results often depend on biased and uncertain inputs. Textbooks are also silent on the behavioral problems that financial managers deal with every day. For example, the conflict between sales and finance over receivables can tear a company apart, but it is rarely mentioned in textbooks.

The result of all this has been that finance professors don't get much help from textbooks in teaching introductory courses. We develop classroom approaches that get the ideas across, but spend a great deal of time explaining the text rather than using it to support our teaching.

Over a period of years, I developed ways around these problems that eventually evolved into *Practical Financial Management*. I began by writing expositions on subjects that gave students the most trouble, starting with time value and portfolio theory. Those explanations really worked! Time value is a good example. Students have difficulties even though they've generally seen it before. After reading my material, students would come in saying, "I never really understood time value when I had it in accounting and math, but I do now!" As you can imagine, that felt pretty good.

Fifteen years later, after serving in a number of corporate financial positions, including chief financial officer (CFO), I changed careers, becoming a full-time educator in order to pursue my first loves: teaching and writing. One of the results is *Practical Financial Management (PFM)*, now in its seventh edition. *PFM* is unique because of its approach to teaching finance. That approach is the result of a combination of classroom and practical experience. The theme is easy to summarize.

We begin every area of study by presenting the heart of the business problem or issue. We start from scratch, assuming students know nothing about the area. That's critical—we bring readers up from absolute zero so there is no confusion and they know exactly where they're going and why. Look at the beginning of Chapter 9 on portfolio theory for an example (pages 396–397). We begin the chapter by explaining why we study "risk and return" in the first place. We also define the investor's goals right away using terms beginning students can understand. After that, key theories are explained clearly and are quickly backed up with practical examples.

Next, wherever math is involved we explain the physical and business relationships between variables before developing or using equations. We discuss what each aspect of a relationship means as we put it together. That gives the equations substance and meaning to students who are less than comfortable in quantitative areas. See the development of IRR in Chapter 10 as an example (pages 456–458).

Then, when we do use math or complex procedures, we carefully explain what we're doing step by step. We assume students have the basic tools of algebra or accounting or statistics, but we don't assume they know that material well. This is another crucial point. Most students aren't really skilled in those areas. But because our systematic presentation recognizes that, students don't get lost or stuck. *PFM* is a resource students can use by themselves as well as under supervision. They can read whole chapters on their own and come to class better prepared than ever before. Look at the first pages in the development of the time value of money in Chapter 6 as an example (pages 236–237). Also see the development of the statement of cash flows in Chapter 3 for the same idea in the context of difficult accounting material rather than math (pages 78–83).

Finally, I've drawn on my years as a financial executive and CFO to present some insights into how things really work. You'll find these explanations throughout the book, identified by a "*From the CFO*" icon in the margin. A prime example deals with the problems associated with estimating cash flows for capital budgeting projects, which is found in Chapter 11 (see Example 11-3, pages 499–502—the people who propose capital projects are usually biased toward acceptance).

PFM's end-of-chapter Business Analysis exercises are another important practical feature. They are mini-cases designed to open students' eyes to the realities of applying financial principles in actual business situations. The questions at the end of Chapter 11 on cash flow estimation are good examples (pages 503–504).

Throughout, I've tried to write this book in a way that's easy to read, enjoyable, and unintimidating. The word that sums that up is "accessible." I think I've been successful, because reviewers have been unanimous in their praise of the work's conversational style and easy readability.

Thank you for using *Practical Financial Management*. I'm absolutely sure you and your students will be pleased with the learning experience they'll have as a result.

CHANGES TO THIS EDITION

Several changes and additions have been made in the seventh edition to keep *PFM* current with new developments in financial practice and changing economic conditions. Here's a summary of the larger changes/additions.

Corporate Governance

The sections dealing with the Financial Crisis of 2008 and the Sarbanes-Oxley Act have been condensed, updated, and reorganized into a single section on Corporate Governance.

Free Cash Flows

An expanded section on Free Cash Flow (FCF) has been added, emphasizing the importance of the technique in merger analysis. The treatment includes a new Concept Connection Example and an end of chapter problem.

IPOs and Investment Banking

In response to the public interest in the recent Facebook IPO, the seventh edition includes a significant new section on the IPO process focusing on the role of investment banks. The treatment includes underwriting, book building, roadshows, pricing, and IPO pops; and ends with an INSIGHTS Box describing how Morgan Stanley took Facebook through its first few days as a public company.

This new section has been placed in Chapter 8 on stock valuation, because it describes the pricing of new securities. A brief reference to IPOs and investment banks remains in Chapter 5 on financial markets.

Risk in Capital Budgeting—Certainty Equivalents

Recognizing the ever increasing importance of risk in financial analysis, we've added another technique of incorporating it into capital budgeting. Certainty equivalent is presented as an alternative to risk adjusted rates, especially where a pure play company isn't available. A new Concept Connection Example and an end-of-chapter problem are included.

Updated Merger Classifications

The seventh edition adds the distinction between strategic and financial mergers and includes the idea of congeneric mergers, in which companies in related businesses combine.

The European Sovereign Debt Crisis

The continuing European debt crisis has had a negative impact on international business since 2008. Indeed as of mid-2012 there's a possibility that one or more countries will leave the Eurozone resulting in a loss of confidence in the zone and a weakening of the Euro. A discussion of the crisis has been added to Chapter 18 on International Finance. The treatment includes the countries at risk, how they got there, the impact of the post 2008 recession, the risk to banks, contagion, and Eurozone attempts at a fix.

Cash Budgeting

Cash budgeting is a receipts and disbursements approach to forecasting external funding needs. A detailed treatment is found in PFM's Chapter 4 on Financial Planning. However, since cash is an element of working capital, a brief summary of the technique has been added to Chapter 16 on working capital with a reference back to the more complete coverage in Chapter 4.

Appendices

In response to requests from a number of adopters, a formula appendix has been added as Appendix C. Financial Tables continue as Appendix A, and Appendix B, answers to selected problems, remains on the text's website.

The following fascinating INSIGHTS Boxes have also been added:

Tax Pass-Through Businesses

An increasing number of business don't pay income tax because profits pass through to owners. People think of pass-throughs as small firms, but some huge companies take advantage of the privilege. The feature costs the government revenue and provides a tax holiday for some wealthy owners. Has the idea backfired on the legislators who designed it help small businesses compete?

Why Are Munis Tax Exempt? Will It Last?

Why has interest on municipal bonds been tax exempt for almost a hundred years? Is the rationale still appropriate? Can high bracket investors and municipal governments expect the free ride to last? The discussion traces the rule's origin, history, and some of the 125 proposals to change it.

Can Interest Rates Be Negative?

We've become accustomed to low interest since 2008, but can rates actually go south of zero? In other words, would any rational investor pay just to park his money, getting back less than he loaned? It turns out that some will, and the reason shouldn't be a big surprise.

Facebook's Rocky IPO

What happened to Facebook on Friday, May 18, 2012? Read the blow by blow account of what was probably the most anticipated and most disappointing IPO ever.

The Modified IRR Technique (MIRR)

IRR comes with two technical flaws: multiple solutions and reinvestment of inflows at the IRR itself. The latter makes projects appear much better than they actually are. Although not widely used, the MIRR method solves both problems.

Share Repurchases Can Be Risky

Share repurchases seem like a good way to make stockholders love CEOs—but they can backfire. Analysts calculate a return on the corporate cash invested in every repurchase.

And if that return isn't positive, it highlights a loss for stockholders who held onto their shares. That places a spotlight on a bad top management decision. Find out how it works, who's doing well, and who should have done something else with the money.

CONTINUING UNIQUE AND IMPORTANT FEATURES

The following special features have been retained from earlier editions.

Concept Connections

A pedagogical feature was added in the sixth edition called CONCEPT CONNECTIONS. The idea has been very popular with users and is being enthusiastically continued into the seventh addition. We'll describe it here for the benefit of new adopters.

Students often have trouble with end of chapter (EOC) problems, because they're overwhelmed with new material and can't identify individual problems with the right material in the chapter. In other words, they don't know how to get started, so they give up.

CONCEPT CONNECTIONS increases learning efficiency by tying end-of-chapter (EOC) problems to the associated in-chapter examples with concept titles and page references. Wherever an EOC problem is the first in a new topic area, it is preceded by a bold-faced heading that identifies the subject, the example number within the chapter, and the page it's on. That lets students focus quickly without the frustration of searching for the right place to begin, which many don't have the patience to do.

A section at the end of Chapter 1 (page 20) explains and illustrates Concept Connections in more detail. Students should be sure to read it before doing their assignments.

From the CFO

This feature highlights material that's based on the author's experience as a CFO. These comments deal with finance in actual practice and offer tips and insights grounded in real-world experience. "From the CFO" material appears throughout the text and is identified by a logo in the margin and italicized print.

Margin Notes

PFM's summarizing margin notes are particularly complete and thorough. They provide students with a convenient summary/outline of the textual material rather than just a list of key words.

Insights: Practical Finance

PFM's Practical Finance boxes provide analysis and understanding of financial principles as applied in practice alongside textual presentations of the underlying concepts.

Insights: Ethics

Our ethics features delve into the moral dilemmas faced by financial managers every day. The issues are presented alongside relevant subject matter and focus on the ethical problems constantly in today's news.

Insights: Real Applications

The Real Applications features provide real world examples that show how chapter subject matter impacts large, well-known companies.

Business Analysis Exercises

A thought-provoking series of exercises has been placed at the end of each chapter. Basically qualitative in nature, Business Analysis scenarios are mini-cases that place students in delicate organizational or political situations and ask them to develop reasonable solutions.

Supplements

Practical Financial Management comes with a full set of supplements, which are available in print and/or on the text Web site, or by online purchase.

CengageNOW for Lasher's *Practical Financial Management,* 7e, is a powerful and fully integrated online teaching and learning system that provides you with flexibility and control. This digital solution offers a comprehensive set of tools to power your course. CengageNOW offers the following:

- Homework, including algorithmic variations
- Integrated ebook
- Course management tools, including a grade book

Thomson ONE—Business School Edition. Use the Thomson ONE academic online database to work Thomson ONE chapter problems. Thomson ONE combines a full range of fundamental financials, earnings estimates, and market data for hundreds of real-world companies. This is an academic version of the same tools used by Wall Street analysts every day. Access to Thomson ONE—Business School Edition is provided by registering a unique serial number that comes with each new book.

Product Support Web Site. To access this book's Web site, go to www.cengagebrain.com and search for this book by its title. There you'll find student and instructor resources, spreadsheet software, and other useful features. Learn about valuable products and services to help with your finance studies, contact the finance editors, and more.

Spreadsheet Software. *PFM* contains two types of computer problems in the end-of-chapter material. Some problems use spreadsheet templates, while others require students to create their own spreadsheet software. The templates, are available on the text Web site to both students and instructors.

PowerPoint Lecture Slides. PowerPoint slides are available to instructors and are designed for classroom presentation, with many illustrative examples summarized, providing a useful lecture tool. Slides for the seventh edition were developed by Tim Liptrap of Nichols College.

Instructor's Manual. The Instructor's Manual is written and maintained by the text's author. It contains chapter-by-chapter focus statements, pedagogical tips, and teaching objectives. All of the discussion questions are answered in detail, and solutions to the problems are fully worked out. The Instructor's Manual is available on the instructor's Web site, where it is password-protected for instructor use only.

Test Bank. The text author personally edits the test bank, ensuring that all questions are consistent with the text's style and notation and that all are clear, readable, and appropriate for students' abilities. It contains over 2,500 insightful questions categorized by topic area. The questions include multiple choice, true/false, fill-in, essays, and problems.

ExamView. The ExamView computerized testing program contains all of the questions in the test bank. ExamView is easy-to-use test creation software that's compatible with Microsoft Windows. In making up tests, instructors can edit questions, add their own questions or instructions, and print out answer sheets. Questions can be selected by number, randomly or through an on-screen preview. Instructors can also create and administer quizzes online, using the Internet, local-area networks, or wide-area networks.

Acknowledgments

We can't say enough in praise of the following reviewers who participated in the writing of each edition of this book. They provided encouragement, criticism, ideas, and enthusiasm, all at the right times.

Ibrahim Affaneh
Indiana University of Pennsylvania

Brian L. Belt
University of Missouri—Kansas City

Omar M. Benkato
Ball State University

Michael A. Bento
Owens Community College

Sheela Bhagat
Rust College

Gilbert W. Bickum
Eastern Kentucky University

Eric Blazer
Millersville University

Gordon R. Bonner
University of Delaware

Karl Borden
University of Nebraska

G. Michael Boyd
Stetson University

Paul Bursik
St. Norbert College

Haiyang Chen
Youngstown State University

Faye Austin Cook
University of North Carolina at Charlotte

Ron Cooley
South Suburban College

John Critchett
Madonna University

Louann Hofheins Cummings
Siena Heights University

Maryanne P. Cunningham
University of Rhode Island

Dennis Debrecht
Carroll College

Gary R. Dokes
University of San Diego

R. Stephen Elliott
Northwestern State University

Soga Ewedemi
Clarion University of Pennsylvania

E. Bruce Fredrikson
Syracuse University

Phillip Fuller
Jackson State University

Robert J. Hartwig
Worcester State College

Delvin D. Hawley
University of Mississippi

Marianne Hite
University of Colorado at Denver

Norbert Jerina
Cuyahoga Community College

Jenna J. Johannpeter
Belleville Area Community College

Larry Johnson
New Hampshire College

Frederick J. Kelly
Roger Williams University

Robert T. Kleiman
Oakland University

Morris Knapp
Miami-Dade Community College

Howard Langer
California State University—Northridge

Tim Liptrap
Nichols College

S. Brooks Marshall
James Madison University

Lee McClain
Western Washington University

Joseph Meredith
Elon University

Stuart Michelson
University of Central Florida

Cynthia Miglietti
Bowling Green State University

Dianne R. Morrison
University of Wisconsin, LaCrosse

Allen D. Morton
Western Connecticut State University

Kenneth F. O'Brien
Farmingdale State University of New York

James M. O'Donnell
Huntington College

Gregory J. Petrakis
University of Missouri—Kansas City

Armand Picou
University of Central Arkansas

Dennis Proffitt
Grand Canyon University

Luis E. Rivera
Dowling College

Michael R. Rouse
University of Massachusetts—Lowell

Andrew Saporoschenko
Clemson University

Atul Saxena
Mercer University

Frederick P. Schadler
East Carolina University

David Schalow
California State University, San Bernadino

Timothy S. Scheppa
Concordia University

Patricia Setlick
William Rainey Harper College

Sandeep Singh
SUNY Brockport

Elliott P. Smith
Boston College

Edward J. Stendardi
St. John Fisher College

Charles W. Strang
Western New Mexico State University

Waymond D. Summers
Oklahoma City Community College

William K. Templeton
Butler University

Clifford F. Thies
Shenandoah University

Bijesh Tolia
Chicago State University

Sanjay B. Varshney
SUNY Institute of Technology at Utica/ Rome

Sarah S. Wells
Columbia College

Fran Wolf
Youngstown State University

Richard Yanow
Massachusetts College of Liberal Arts

Rassoul Yazdipour
California State University, Fresno

Shirley Zaragoza
Borough of Manhattan Community College

Special thanks go to Dianne Morrison (University of Wisconsin, La Crosse) who carefully checked problems and solutions to help ensure accuracy, and Tim Liptrap (Nichols College) who updated the tax problems and Power Point presentations.

In addition, I would like to extend my sincere appreciation to the members of the South-Western Cengage team whose efforts resulted in this seventh edition and all of its supplements: Mike Reynolds, my acquisitions editor, who provided encouragement and guidance; Conor Allen, my developmental editor who tirelessly coordinated the project and kept it on track, Robin LeFevre, the marketing manager, whose enthusiastic contributions to the promotion of the text have helped to make it the success it is today; and Scott Fidler, senior technology project editor, whose work on the technology products for the text continues to improve the package with each edition.

William R. Lasher
Nichols College

Professor Lasher has a unique background that includes extensive experience as an educator and as a corporate financial executive. Prior to entering full-time academics, he worked for Texas Instruments, Harris Corporation, and the Pacific Telesis organization. During those years, he served as a corporate financial planner, a controller, and as a subsidiary CFO. While working in industry, he taught graduate and undergraduate finance and economics as an adjunct professor at the University of Dallas, the University of Texas at Dallas, and Golden Gate University in San Francisco. He moved into education full time when he joined the faculty at Nichols College in Massachusetts.

Professor Lasher has a B.S. and an M.B.A from Columbia University, received his Ph.D. from Southern Methodist University, holds a J.D. from the New England School of Law, and has earned a Certified Public Accountant designation. He has also published books on business planning, franchising, and the strategic management of small firms.

Introduction to Financial Management

1 CHAPTER

Foundations

1.1 An Overview of Finance

Finance is the art and science of handling money. In the modern world, virtually every organization, public and private, runs on money. That includes families, businesses, governments, and nonprofit enterprises like colleges and churches. Money touches everything we do. And finance, the management of money, is behind most everything we see each day. We don't physically observe the financing behind a building or a new car or a house, but it's there, and without it most of the things we do see wouldn't exist.

That's because without money to pay for resources and a financial system to make trading possible, no one could organize more than a few people to work together at one time.

Our study of finance will be broadly divided into two areas: (1) investments and financial markets and (2) the financial management of companies.[1] These are separate but related. A financial system involves flows of money and paper between the two.

To begin our study of finance, we need a few basic terms and ideas. Let's master these before going any further.

1.1a   Financial Assets

A **real asset** is an object or thing, such as a car, a house, a factory, or a piece of machinery. Real assets have value because they provide services of some kind, such as transportation, shelter, or the ability to produce something.

Financial assets, on the other hand, are legal documents, pieces of paper. Their value comes from the fact that they give their owners claim to certain future cash flows. Most financial assets are either stocks or bonds, and their claim to future income is based on ownership or debt, respectively.

Stock ownership means that the holder of a share owns a piece of the company that issued the stock. As a part owner, he or she is entitled to a share of the firm's profits, which may be paid out in dividends or retained to enhance prospects for growth. The shareholder generally expects to sell the share at some time in the future and will then receive the proceeds of that sale in cash. Thus, the owner of a stock certificate can look for two sources of cash in the future: dividends and the eventual selling price of the share.

A **bond** signifies a debt relationship. When a person buys a bond, he or she is actually lending money to the firm issuing that bond. The terminology seems strange—"buying a bond" meaning "lending money." Nevertheless, a bondholder is actually a lender and as such is entitled to interest on the amount lent and the repayment of principal at the end of the loan period.

Companies issue financial assets to raise money. They generally use that money to buy real assets that are used in running their businesses.

Financial assets are purchased by people or other companies to earn income with funds they don't currently need. Buying such an asset is similar to opening a savings account and receiving interest on the money you've put in the bank. In fact, a savings account is another kind of financial asset. Another name for a financial asset like a stock or a bond is a **security**.[2] A person or organization buying a financial asset is said to be **investing** in that asset, and we generally call that buyer an *investor*.

Investments in financial assets can be made directly by buying securities or indirectly by buying shares in a **mutual fund**. A mutual fund pools the contributions of many investors and employs a professional manager to select securities that match a particular set of investment goals.

A **real asset** is an object that provides a service.

A **financial asset** is a legal document representing a claim to income.

Stock represents an **ownership** interest.

Bonds represent a **debt** relationship.

Investing involves buying financial assets in the hope of earning **income**.

A **mutual fund** purchases securities with the pooled resources of many investors.

---

1. The banking system, a third sector of the financial world, is generally covered in an economics course on "Money and Banking" or "Financial Institutions."

2. Securities are financial assets that can be traded among investors. Hence stocks and bonds are securities while savings accounts are not.

1.1b   Financial Markets

Stocks and bonds as well as certain other kinds of financial assets are issued by companies and purchased by investors in *financial markets*. A **financial market** isn't exactly a place; rather, it's a framework or organization in which people can buy and sell securities in accordance with well-defined rules and regulations. The best known financial market is the **stock market**. It is centered in several places around the country, called **stock exchanges**. The largest exchange is the New York Stock Exchange, often referred to as the NYSE.

To participate in the market, you don't have to go to an exchange. You simply establish a relationship with a *stockbroker* in your area and communicate with him or her by phone. A **stockbroker** is a person who is licensed to help investors buy and sell securities for a commission. Local brokers are connected to the various exchanges electronically. The stock market is really the entire network of brokers and exchanges all connected together. Bond markets for trading debt securities operate similarly.

In summary, financial markets are "places" where investors buy financial assets from companies that issue them. Investors also buy and sell the same financial assets among themselves in the same financial markets. In fact, the vast majority of transactions are among investors. That's because a security is issued by a company only once, but it may be traded among investors many times thereafter.

In practice, the term "market" describes the combined actions of investors acting within the marketplace just described. For example, someone might say that the market has placed a price of $25 on a share of Microsoft stock. That would mean the going price among investors buying and selling the stock of the Microsoft corporation within the structure of the stock market is about $25.

Figure 1-1 is a schematic representation of the interaction between companies and the market.

The field of investments involves making decisions about buying and selling stocks and bonds. Decisions about how to raise money and what to do with it are part of the financial management of a firm. These decisions are made on the two sides of Figure 1-1, which represent the two areas in which our study will be focused.

Now let's consider the word "finance" itself. Its use can be a little confusing. It's a noun, as in "the field of finance." It's a verb, as in "to finance something." And it also has an adjective form, as in "financial management." Let's explore these variations in meaning.

> Securities are traded in **financial markets** like the **stock market**.

> A **stockbroker** is licensed to trade securities on behalf of investors.

FIGURE 1-1   Simplified Financial System

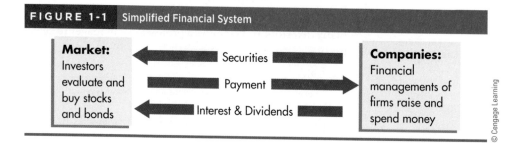

© Cengage Learning

1.1c   Raising Money

The most common application of the term "finance" involves raising money to acquire assets. We've all heard people say they're going to *finance* a car or a house. When they say that, individuals usually mean they're going to borrow money from a bank to buy the item. We can also talk about financing activities like starting a new business or going on vacation.

The word is used similarly in business. Companies *finance assets* when they raise money to acquire those assets. They do that by borrowing, selling stock, or using money they've earned. In recent years, many assets have been acquired through leasing. We say those items are *lease financed*.

A company itself is *financed* when money is raised to get it started or for expansion. Such money can come from borrowing or from selling stock. To the extent the money is borrowed, we say the company is *debt financed*. To the extent it comes from selling stock, we say the firm is *equity financed*. Equity implies financing with an owner's own money.

Looking at Figure 1-1, we see that firms in the box on the right are raising money, financing things. They do that by selling stocks and bonds to investors in the box on the left. The *field of finance* includes both sides of this money-raising transaction. It relates to the concerns of parties raising money and to those of parties providing it. Further, because the money raised flows through financial markets and institutions, their operation is a part of the field as well.

The Changing Focus of Finance   Historically, the field of finance was narrowly limited to activity within financial markets. Today, the perspective has expanded in two directions.

First, in modern finance a great deal of attention is given to the goals and activities of the investor. In the early days, a complete description of a particular security (stock or bond) was considered to be all an investor needed to comfortably make a decision about buying it. Today we've become concerned with the notion of risk in investing and with how investors put together groups of securities called **portfolios** to minimize that risk. We'll examine these concepts at length in Chapter 9.

The second direction of expansion involves the role and function of financial management within firms. Historically, financial managers were told how much money their companies needed for particular projects, and they went outside in pursuit of those funds. They had little to do with deciding how much was needed or what was done with the money after it was raised. Today, financial managers are deeply involved in those related decisions.

1.1d   Financial Management

Financial management means the management and control of money and money-related operations within businesses. Companies have finance departments that are responsible for these functions.

The executive in charge of the finance department is the company's **chief financial officer,** abbreviated **CFO.** The title **vice president of finance** is sometimes used instead of CFO. In either case, the position usually reports to the president of the company.

The term "financial management" refers to the things the CFO and the finance department do. These activities include, among other things, keeping records, paying

---

Financing means raising money to acquire or to do something.

A **portfolio** is a collection of securities.

The corporate executive in charge of the finance department is called the **chief financial officer (CFO).**

employees and suppliers, receiving customer payments, borrowing money, purchasing assets, selling stock, and paying dividends.

It's important to notice that accounting is included in this broad definition of finance and that the accounting function is usually part of the finance department, reporting to the CFO.

Business Decisions   Financial management also refers to the financial input that goes into general business decisions. This extremely important concept is best explained by an example.

Suppose a domestic company is contemplating expanding overseas. That's likely to be a big decision discussed by the firm's key executives over a long period of time. Each executive will have opinions and recommendations related to his or her own area of responsibility, such as marketing or manufacturing. The CFO will similarly have opinions on how to set up the finance function in the new venture, how to do its accounting, and what banks to use. In addition, he or she will probably have to secure funding to support the project, either from a bank or by issuing securities.

Beyond that, however, the CFO must form a judgment about the feasibility of the project in terms of whether it will be profitable enough to justify its own cost. In other words, the bottom line for most projects is money, and the responsibility for assessing that bottom line falls to financial management. (We'll study the techniques used to make this kind of decision, called capital budgeting, in Chapters 10, 11, and 12.)

Oversight   Another important aspect of financial management involves the relationship between finance and other departments in the day-to-day management of the firm. It's important to grasp the fact that finance is responsible for its own activities, but has a responsibility for the operation of other departments as well.

The finance department **oversees** how other departments spend money.

Let's look into that idea a little more deeply. Finance is responsible for money, but other departments deal in money, too. That's because they have to spend it to do their jobs, and their success is defined in terms of money. For example, manufacturing's task may be to produce some quantity of product, but doing the job properly involves keeping costs low and maintaining a reasonable level of inventory.

The finance department generally has an *oversight responsibility* for the effective management of the money other departments spend. Hence, if manufacturing's costs are too high or if it carries too much inventory, finance is responsible for calling attention to those facts and ensuring that corrective action is taken. In other words, *part of finance's job involves looking over everyone else's shoulder to make sure they're using money effectively.*

1.1e   The Price of Securities—A Link Between the Firm and the Market

The two sides of finance, investments and the financial management of the firm, are connected by the fact that companies sell securities to investors in financial markets.

A fundamental truth, which we'll examine in detail later, is that investors buy securities for the future cash flows that come from owning them. Those cash flows depend on the issuing companies' financial performance. Hence, the prices investors are willing to pay for securities depend on their expectations about how well the issuing companies are likely to do in the future in terms of profit. Further, because the future is never guaranteed, the market is also concerned about the risk associated with expected performance. A perception of greater risk tends to lower investor interest and security prices.

The link between company management and investments comes from this relationship between price and expected financial results. Everything firms and their managers do is watched by the market and has an impact on investors' perceptions of likely future performance and risk. Those perceptions, in turn, determine the prices of stocks and bonds.

In other words, the study of investments includes looking at the way companies are managed to estimate future performance. At the same time, the management of companies includes consideration of how business decisions are perceived by investors and the effects those perceptions have on the prices of the firm's stocks and bonds.

1.2   Finance and Accounting

In most industrial companies, the majority of the people involved in money-oriented activities are accountants, so people sometimes get the idea that accounting and finance are synonymous. In fact they're not, and it's important to understand how they fit together.

Accounting is a system of record keeping designed to portray a firm's operations to the world in a fair and unbiased way. The records are used periodically to produce financial statements that present the company's results to anyone who reads them.

However, several other financial functions are performed in most companies. These include raising money, analyzing results, and handling relationships with outsiders such as banks, shareholders, and representatives of the investment community. Most of these functions are performed by the *treasury department.*

> The **controller** is in charge of accounting while the **treasurer** supervises most other financial functions.

The *finance department* normally consists of both the *accounting department* headed by the **controller** and the *treasury department* headed by the **treasurer.** Both of these positions report to the *chief financial officer (CFO).* The typical organization is depicted in Figure 1-2.

In practice, it has become common to think of accounting as an almost separate field and to refer to the other financial functions as finance. For the most part, this means that the treasury functions are called *finance* and the controller functions are called *accounting.*

People tend to have careers in one side of the department or the other, but crossover is possible. It's generally easier for an accountant to move into treasury than the

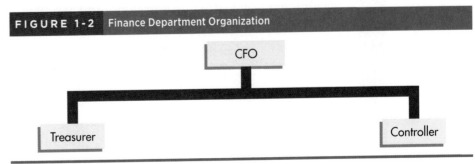

FIGURE 1-2   Finance Department Organization

CFO

Treasurer   Controller

© Cengage Learning

other way around because of the large number of specialized courses required to be a professional accountant. Either controllers or treasurers can become CFOs.

Companies are organized in different ways, and who does what isn't always clear cut. Many of the activities we'll study in this book are done in the accounting department in one company and in the treasury (finance) department in another. Activities such as financial analysis (Chapter 3), financial planning (Chapter 4), and capital budgeting (Chapters 10, 11, and 12) are generally done wherever the resources are available to do the job best.

Finance majors shouldn't be discouraged by the preponderance of accounting jobs in typical industrial companies. The majority of jobs in the investment industry and in financial institutions such as banks and insurance companies are in finance rather than accounting.

1.2a   The Importance of Cash Flow

The relative emphasis placed on cash flow is important in conceptually differentiating between accounting and finance. The accounting system attempts to portray a business's financial results in a way that reflects what is physically going on. In finance we're less interested in such a representative portrayal and tend to concentrate on where cash is coming from and going to. In finance, **"cash is king"**!

> In finance, **cash is king**.

This point can be made clear with a simple example. We'll consider how a typical accounting system represents the acquisition and use of a long-lived asset and contrast that with the way people in finance look at the same event.

The point behind Example 1-1 is that in finance the emphasis is on cash. We're not implying that accountants are ignorant of the cash requirements associated with the

---

CONCEPT CONNECTION   EXAMPLE 1-1

Accounting Records and Cash Flow

Suppose a firm buys a $1,000 asset to be depreciated straight-line over five years at $200 per year. Assume the company pays taxes at a flat rate of 40%. Contrast the accounting portrayal of the asset's life with its cash flow implications.

SOLUTION: The accounting books show the initial addition of the $1,000 asset to a gross assets account. That's followed by yearly depreciation entries, each of which has two parts. Every year $200 of depreciation appears on the income statement to reflect the allocation of one-fifth of the asset's original cost to expense. An addition of $200 is also made to an accumulated depreciation account on the balance sheet, which is subtracted from the asset's original gross value to reflect the wearing out of the item. (We'll review fixed asset accounting in more detail in Chapter 2.) The first year's entries appear as follows.

Income Statement Cost/Expense Entries		Balance Sheet Fixed Assets Account	
		Gross	$1,000
		Accumulated	
Depreciation expense	$200	depreciation	200
		Net	$ 800

In each of the following four years another $200 is recognized as depreciation expense and added to accumulated depreciation on the balance sheet, further reducing the net value of the asset until it reaches zero at the end of the fifth year.

In addition, the tax shown on the income statements will be lower in all five years because depreciation expense reduces profit. That means each year's income tax will be less by 40% of the $200 depreciation expense that comes from having the item. Thinking in terms of tax savings, owning the asset implies:

$$\text{yearly tax saving} = \$200 \times .40 = \$80$$

Notice how much information this set of numbers conveys. The asset originally cost $1,000 and results in an expense of $200 each year that reduces profit. At the same time, the balance sheet indicates how worn out the item is by showing the portion of its original value that's left on the books. The accounting representation thus gives us a portrait of the entire life of the asset and its impact on the business in numbers!

When people in the finance department think about the same asset, their orientation is very different. They're interested in only two numbers: the $1,000 cash outflow needed to acquire the asset and the annual tax saving generated by the depreciation deduction.

The reason for this emphasis is easy to understand. Finance is responsible for raising the initial $1,000, and the future tax saving affects the amount of cash that will have to be raised for other things later on. In fact, a finance person might react that the accounting representation doesn't display the most important piece of financial information about the asset—where the money to buy it came from.

from the
CFO

asset in the example. Their emphasis is simply different, involving a broader portrayal of the business. Finance concentrates on cash flow. We'll keep that in mind throughout our study.

1.2b   The Language of Finance

The practice of finance is closely tied to accounting because financial transactions are recorded within the structure of accounting systems. It's often said that *accounting is the* **language of finance**. Because of this connection, all finance professionals need some knowledge of accounting. However, the level of knowledge required varies significantly depending on one's job.

Accounting is the **language of finance**.

A financial analyst, who investigates companies and makes recommendations about their investment value, needs to know quite a bit of accounting. That's because analysts have to decipher complex financial statements without missing any of the detailed implications that may be buried in the notes and numbers. Stockbrokers, on the other hand, generally sell securities on the basis of a broad knowledge of what's going on in various industries and expectations generated by the reports of analysts. They can get by without much more than an ability to read basic financial statements.

1.3   Financial Theory—The Relationship with Economics

So far we've been examining the practical side of finance and how it fits into the business world. Finance is a field in which millions of people find jobs after they've mastered certain skills that are taught in school. As in any other field, success comes with experience and wisdom after you've learned the basics. In this regard, finance is a lot like accounting—you learn the techniques in school and apply them on the job.

Financial theory has grown out of **economics**.

However, there's also a theoretical aspect to finance. **Financial theory** is a body of thought that is studied and continually developed by highly trained experts, usually professors. In this regard, finance is a lot like economics. Scholars in both fields observe the world of business and government and attempt to model and explain behavior in abstract terms.

In fact, modern financial theory began as a branch of economics during the 1950s. Since that beginning, finance has grown so much that most people now think of it separately, although the term "financial economics" is still used occasionally. The techniques of advanced financial theory are very similar to those of advanced economic theory.

Financial theory has a big impact on practice in some areas and less influence in others. Where the impact is significant, theory influences the direction and approach that people take in practice. As we go forward, we'll identify and explain theoretical elements that have had a noticeable influence on the way the world operates. Theory's most significant impact in recent years has been in the area of investments, which we'll cover in Chapter 9.

The ideas and relationships discussed in this and the last section are portrayed graphically in Figure 1-3.

1.4   Forms of Business Organization and Their Financial Impact

A business can be organized legally in one of three ways: as a sole proprietorship, as a partnership, or as a corporation. Within the third category, there are three possibilities: the regular or C-type corporation, the S-type corporation, and the limited

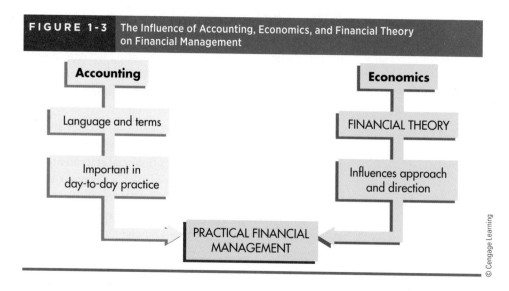

FIGURE 1-3   The Influence of Accounting, Economics, and Financial Theory on Financial Management

© Cengage Learning

liability company known as an LLC. The last two forms are most common among smaller businesses, but are also used by large enterprises from time to time.

The choice of form is important financially because it can have an impact on raising money, taxation, and financial liability. The issue is most relevant in the context of smaller businesses because the vast majority of large companies are organized as C-type corporations.[3]

For financial purposes, a partnership is essentially a sole proprietorship with more than one owner, so we'll concentrate on distinguishing between a proprietorship and a corporation. We'll also begin by ignoring S-type corporations and LLCs and reintroduce them later. We'll explore some of the ideas behind each form through a hypothetical example that stresses the financial advantages and disadvantages of each.

1.4a   The Proprietorship Form

Suppose an entrepreneur wants to open a business, has enough money to get started, and chooses to organize as a sole proprietorship.

Getting Started   Starting a proprietorship is very simple. Because the business is indistinguishable from the entrepreneur, all he has to do to get started is obtain a local permit and declare the business open. That's an advantage of the proprietorship form—it's easy to start.

Taxes   Now suppose the entrepreneur operates for a while and makes a profit. That profit will simply be taxed as personal income to the business owner. That's another advantage of the proprietorship form—the business's profits are taxed only once, and that tax is at personal income tax rates. (We'll see why this is an advantage in a moment.)

Raising Money   Next, suppose the business is successful for six months and the entrepreneur wants to expand but doesn't have enough money to buy the assets required. He therefore looks for outside financing in the form of a loan. Any number of sources are possible, including family, friends, and a bank.

Family and friends might advance some money on the strength of their personal relationship with our entrepreneur, but people who don't know him will always ask two very important questions.

First they'll want to know, "What happens to my money if your business fails?" The honest answer is that the money will be lost.

Next they'll ask, "What happens to me if you're phenomenally successful?" The answer is simply that the lender will get his or her money back with interest.

Now consider the lender's position. Lending to the entrepreneur is a gamble, but not a very good one. The worst possible outcome is a total loss, while the best result imaginable is merely getting back the amount loaned with a few dollars of interest. That might be all right if the chance of loss is very small, but in fact the overwhelming majority of small businesses fail. Of course, lenders know this, so the loan isn't very attractive to them.

For this reason it's almost impossible for a new business to get a loan that isn't fully *collateralized*. A collateralized loan is backed by some asset (the **collateral**) that the lender can take and sell in the event the borrower defaults on paying off the loan.

Assets pledged to guarantee a loan are **collateral**.

3. With the exception of personal service organizations such as law or CPA firms, which are generally partnerships.

Many entrepreneurs use their homes as collateral for start-up loans. In the case we're considering, our business owner's expansion plans would be stopped cold if he didn't have enough collateral to guarantee a loan.

This result is a major disadvantage of the sole proprietorship form. The only way a nonowner can advance money to the business is by lending, and that's a very risky proposition. Therefore, raising start-up or expansion money is difficult while the business is new.

*A major **financial disadvantage** of proprietorship is the difficulty encountered in **raising money**.*

1.4b The Corporate Form

Now let's explore what happens when another entrepreneur starts a similar business using the corporate form.

Getting Started The first thing she'd find is that getting started is somewhat more difficult. She must go through the legal process of incorporation and register with the state, probably using a lawyer to file the papers. The whole thing would take some work and cost a bit of money.

Taxes Once set up, the incorporated business operates in much the same way as the sole proprietorship. When the business makes a profit, however, the tax situation is significantly different.

A corporation is a separate legal entity subject to a *corporate tax* on whatever it earns. What's left over after the corporate tax is paid (earnings after tax or net income) belongs to the corporation.

That's an important point. Even though the entrepreneur owns the business, she doesn't own its earnings directly. The corporation owns them. To get the earnings into her own pocket, the entrepreneur has to declare a dividend that is paid to her as an individual.

However, such a dividend is taxable income to the individual. Hence, our entrepreneur will pay individual taxes on the after (corporate) tax earnings of her company.

*Double taxation of earnings is the major **financial disadvantage** of the traditional **corporate form**.*

In other words, the profits of the business will be taxed twice, once at corporate rates and once at individual rates, before the entrepreneur gets to spend any of the business's earnings. This phenomenon is known as the **double taxation of corporate earnings**. It is the main *financial* **disadvantage** of the **corporate form**.[4]

CONCEPT CONNECTION **EXAMPLE 1-2**

Tax Consequences of Business Form

Ruth Samson owns a business that earns $100,000 before taxes. She wants to take the earnings home and spend them on herself. Assume a simplified tax system in which the relevant rates are 34% for corporations and 30% for individuals on the entire amounts subject to those taxes, including dividends received by individuals[5]. Compare the total tax bills under the sole proprietorship and corporate forms of organization.

Ensuper/Shutterstock.com

---

4. The owner would pay herself a salary, which wouldn't be taxed twice but would have to be reasonable for the value of the work performed. The salary would be part of the business's expenses. Only profit is taxed twice.

5. The tax law in effect through 2012 caps the tax rate on dividends at 15%. It is uncertain whether this unusual tax provision will be continued after that date.

SOLUTION: Under the corporate form, the $100,000 is first subject to a 34% corporate income tax of $34,000, leaving earnings of $66,000. If Ruth wants to take that sum home, she has to declare it as a dividend and pay personal tax on it at 30%, an additional tax of (.30 × $66,000 =) $19,800.

In a sole proprietorship, the $100,000 is taxed once at 30% for a total tax bill of $30,000. The calculations are summarized as follows.

	Corporate	Proprietor
Pretax earnings	$100,000	$100,000
Less:		
Corporate tax (34%)	34,000	—
Earnings/dividend	$ 66,000	$100,000
Less:		
Personal tax (30%)	19,800	30,000
Net	$ 46,200	$ 70,000

Notice that the difference is a very significant $23,800, so the business is paying a lot for the privilege of being a corporation!

Raising Money   Let's assume that our incorporated entrepreneur's business is successful and that she wants to expand, but needs money to do it. If she tries to borrow as an incorporated business, she'll run into the same problems that face the sole proprietor. Lending to a new business is risky, and generally no one will do it. Whether the business is incorporated doesn't make much difference.

However, a corporation has an option that isn't available to a sole proprietor. The incorporated firm can raise money by offering stock to investors. New stockholders will own shares of the business and may have some influence over how it's run. But if less than a 50% interest is sold, effective control can still be maintained by the original owner.

People contemplating buying stock will ask the same two questions that potential lenders ask: "What happens to my investment if the business fails?" and "What happens if it does very well?"

The answer to the first question is the same as it was in the lending case. If the business fails, the stockholder is likely to lose most or all of his or her investment. But the answer to the second question is very different. If the company does extremely well, the stock's price will go up, perhaps multiplying the value of the original investment many times over. In short, the answer to the second question for a stockholder is, "You may get rich!"

Now consider the potential stockholder's position. An investment in the new business is still a gamble in which the worst possible outcome is total loss, but the best result is a very substantial gain. This is a much more attractive gamble than the loan, because the potential reward justifies the risk.

What this means in practical terms is that although people will almost never make uncollateralized loans to start-ups or new companies, they'll frequently buy stock in such ventures. That fact leads us to the *most significant financial advantage of the corporate form:* **ease of raising money** *by selling stock.*

Ease of raising money
by selling stock is the
most significant financial
advantage of the
corporate form.

1.4c   The Truth About Limited Liability

The most frequently cited advantage of the corporate form is limited liability. The concept says that a stockholder cannot be held liable for the debts of the corporation or for damages it may do to others. That in turn implies that all the stockholder can lose is his or her investment in the stock.

Let's state the matter another way. Suppose someone has a valid claim against a business that exceeds its assets. If the business is a proprietorship, the claimant can take the owner's personal property after taking the assets of the business. On the other hand, if the business is a corporation, only the assets of the business can be taken, not the personal assets of the stockholder owners.

The limited liability concept is absolutely valid in the context of owning shares in a company that the investor isn't running. But it doesn't usually work when an entrepreneur is operating his or her own incorporated business. Let's explore why.

Companies generally create liabilities that exceed their assets in two ways: by borrowing money they can't repay and by losing a lawsuit. The first situation is very common. It usually occurs when a firm takes out a loan in the expectation of good business in the near future. The plan is to pay off the debt with the profits from the anticipated business. Trouble arises when the expected sales don't materialize and the firm can't make its loan payments. If things get bad enough, the company goes bankrupt, and the value of the unpaid loan along with other debts exceeds the value of its assets.

Theoretically, incorporation protects business owners from having their personal assets seized as a result of such unpaid loans. In practice, however, lenders circumvent this feature of incorporation by demanding **personal guarantees** from small business owners before making loans to their companies.

Personal guarantees
make entrepreneurs liable
for loans made to their
businesses.

Personal guarantees are side agreements signed along with loan papers that make owners personally responsible for repayment should their businesses fail to meet loan obligations. This device virtually destroys the value of limited liability where loans to small businesses are concerned.

In the second situation, the entrepreneur or an employee damages some outside party. For example, suppose an auto repair shop fixes a customer's brakes negligently and thereby causes an accident. In such a case, the injured party can sue *both* the business and the negligent individuals, bypassing the limited liability of the corporate form.

The limited liability feature of corporations is largely a myth for owner-operated small businesses. However, it is real for stockholders who don't participate in the business themselves.

1.4d   Limited Liability Companies (LLCs) and S-Type Corporations

We've seen that the major financial advantage and disadvantage of the corporate form are the ability to raise money through the sale of stock and the double taxation of earnings, respectively. It's difficult to expand a company that's not a corporation, and double taxation makes it hard to accumulate earnings if a company is a corporation.

However, the government generally favors small businesses because of the jobs they create. To encourage the formation and expansion of new businesses, Congress created some devices that give small firms the best of both worlds. These include **limited liability companies (LLCs)** and the **S-type corporations**.

Both are corporations in the sense of limited liability and the ability to sell stock, but their earnings are not subject to corporate income tax. Earnings pass through the business directly to the personal income of the owners and are taxed only once at personal rates. Essentially, the tax system treats LLCs and S-type corporations as partnerships. That feature makes them a significant incentive to small business formation. Business forms with this feature are called "pass-throughs."

> **LLCs** and **S-type corporations** let small businesses avoid double taxation.

INSIGHTS   Real Applications

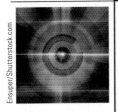

Ensuper/Shutterstock.com

Did the Pass-Through Concept Backfire?
Are There Too Many Pass-Throughs, and Are Some Too Big?

Subchapter S corporations and LLCs are prominent examples of *pass-through* business forms, but there are several others with names like Master Limited Partnership, and Limited Liability Partnership. They all pass profits through to owners before being taxed. Traditional partnerships have always been pass-throughs.

The pass-through privilege was first extended to corporations in the 1950s when congress created Subchapter S companies and broadened in the 1980s when LLCs were authorized. The goal was always to encourage entrepreneurship and to give smaller businesses a chance to compete with corporate giants.

But it's unlikely that government officials expected pass-throughs to be as popular as they turned out to be. Indeed, this entrepreneurial stimulus may have led to a significant shortfall in tax collections.

By 2008, 69% of U.S. businesses weren't paying federal income tax. That's up from 24% in 1986, the year before LLCs were authorized. It's further estimated that 60% of U.S. businesses earning more than $1 million in profits don't pay tax. This is one reason corporate tax collections were a meager 1.7% of GDP in 2010, down from

2.7% in 2006, and far below the 6% levels of the 1950s.

Another problem is that all pass-throughs aren't the small entrepreneurial ventures the program was designed to help. Some are huge. For example, construction giant the Bechtel Group is a tax pass-through, although it's the largest engineering company in the United States, has annual revenues of about $30 billion, and employs approximately 49,000 people.

Pass-throughs can be large, but they're typically owned by relatively few people. That's because in 1987 Congress declared that, with a few exceptions, publically traded companies, typically owned by thousands of stockholders, had to pay taxes. This implies that at the large end, pass-throughs are gifts to the wealthy.

In light of all this, is Congress likely to end the pass-through party any time soon? Probably not, but there have been a number of proposals circulated that include limiting the privilege to reasonably small companies.

SOURCE: "More Firms Enjoy Tax-Free Status," John D. McKinnon, *The Wall Street Journal*, January 10, 2012, A1, A10.

1.5   The Goals of Management

To run a company, management needs a goal or an objective against which to measure the implications of its decisions. In the study of economics, theorists assume that the goal of the firm is profit maximization. The concept works in theory but is unmanageable in the real world. Truly maximizing profit today (in the short run) is likely to cause serious problems tomorrow (in the long run).

For example, the work of most research and development (R&D) departments has little effect on current business, because their efforts are focused on developing products that won't be marketed for years. If a firm fires its R&D staff, today's business won't be affected and profits will increase immediately because of the expenses saved. However, in two or three years, the firm won't have any new products to sell and will probably be in trouble. From that example, we can deduce that simply maximizing short run profit isn't a very good goal for a real company.

Fortunately, financial markets provide an easy-to-state yet realistic goal for management. Because stockholders own the company and have invested for financial gain, and because management works for those stockholders, the appropriate managerial goal is the *maximization of shareholder wealth*. That's generally taken to be equivalent to *maximizing the price of the company's stock.*[6]

Shareholder wealth maximization is a practical goal for corporate management.

This idea gets around the short-run/long-run problem just described. Remember that stock market investors watch everything the company does and reflect those actions in their expectations about the firm's future performance. Those expectations determine the price of the stock today. Current profits also affect the price of the stock, but only as an indicator of future profit.

If a real company fired its R&D department and thereby increased current profits, its stock price wouldn't go up. The market would recognize the long-run folly of the move, and the stock price would drop like a stone.

As our study of finance proceeds, we will run into situations in which a management decision has an impact on stock price. In such cases, we'll assume that the best decision is the one that results in the highest stock price.

1.5a   Stakeholders and Conflicts of Interest

In any company, several groups of people have special interests in the way the firm is run. These groups include the following:

Stockholders	Management
Employees	Creditors
Customers	Suppliers
Local community	

Such interested groups can be called *stakeholders* in or *constituencies* of the company. We'll use the term "stakeholder," meaning that each group has a stake or vested interest in the way the firm is operated. Various conflicts of interest are possible between stakeholder groups. A conflict of interest occurs when something that benefits one group takes away from another.

---

6. We're assuming here that management doesn't keep stock price high fraudulently by lying to investors about the company's performance and its future prospects.

1.5b   Conflicts of Interest—An Illustration

Suppose an employee group at a manufacturing company comes to management with a request. They want the company to build an athletic complex on the factory site so employees can exercise before and after work and during lunch hours. They argue that, although this project will cost money, it will lead to a happier and healthier employee population that will be more effective on the job.

Management agrees that happy, healthy workers are good workers, but also sees a possibility that employees will spend time at the gym at the expense of their jobs or that they will be exhausted on the job after working out. Therefore, they aren't sure whether the facility would help or hurt productivity. On balance, management feels the net efficiency effect will be more or less neutral.

It's important to recognize that this situation reflects a conflict of interest between two stakeholder groups, employees and stockholders. If the athletic facility is built, the money will come out of profits that belong to shareholders. Hence, making the employees a little happier entails making shareholders a little poorer and presumably less happy. In this case, management is effectively an arbitrator and has to make a decision in favor of one group or the other.

In this hypothetical example, the employees' request is something of a luxury, so the decision doesn't generate a lot of emotion when we read about it. But what if working conditions were really terrible at the plant, and employees were asking for money to create a clean, safe work environment? The conflict of interest would still be there, but we would be more likely to favor the employees on an emotional or ethical basis.

1.6   Management—A Privileged Stakeholder Group

> The ownership of a **widely held company** is dispersed so no one has enough control to influence management.

Management usually has a special position among stakeholder groups. Although top managers theoretically work for the company's stockholders, they often have little accountability to that group. If ownership is widely dispersed and no one holds more than 1% or 2% of the company, stockholders have limited influence because no one can muster enough power to force a change in the management team.

In such cases, top managers become entrenched in positions controlling vast company resources and are able to use those resources for their own benefit rather than for the benefit of shareholders.

1.6a   The Agency Problem

> The conflict of interest between stockholders and management is known as the **agency problem**.

The special position of management in widely held companies leads to a particularly onerous conflict of interest known as the **agency problem**. The term is derived from the legal concept of agency.

> An **agent** is hired by a **principal** and given **decision-making** authority.

An *agency relationship* is created when a person hires another and gives him or her decision-making authority over something. For example, if Smith hires Jones to run his business, Jones is the **agent** of Smith, who is called the **principal**. Conversely, if Smith hires Jones to sweep the floor, no agency relationship is created, because no **decision-making authority** is involved. The agency relationship creates an opportunity for abuse by the agent who has control over the assets of the principal. In general, corporate managers are the agents of the firm's stockholders.

The Abuse of Agency   The most common example of abuse of the agency relationship is the practice in which companies pay top executives excessive compensation (compensation includes salary, bonuses, and special deals on buying the company's stock called stock options). The conflict is with stockholders because the excess pay would otherwise be profit, which belongs to them.

Executive compensation levels in excess of $200 million per year are not unusual. Stockholders have a right to ask whether anyone can be worth that much. Perhaps even more outrageous is the fact that high levels of compensation for top executives aren't necessarily connected to good performance by the company.

Compensation isn't the only way in which managers can feather their own nests. The use of company-owned assets such as boats, airplanes, and vacation retreats is common, as are such benefits as expense account meals, chauffeur-driven limousines, and paid country club memberships. These benefits are called **perquisites** ("perks" for short) and have become a way of life among top corporate executives.

> Privileges and luxuries provided to executives are called **perquisites** (or "perks").

Controlling the Agency Problem   Efforts to manage the agency problem generally involve monitoring what the agent is doing. For example, principals can employ auditors to periodically review company books to make sure funds aren't being diverted to questionable uses. Such measures involve costs known as *agency costs*.

Another way to manage the agency problem is to pay a good part of managers' compensation in the form of a bonus tied to company profit. This approach reduces the incentive to spend money on company-owned assets that are used by executives. For example, buying a vacation retreat for executive use will reduce profit by the cost of the facility. If the president's bonus goes up or down with the size of profits, he or she will be less inclined to approve the expenditure for the retreat.

The government has gotten into the act by limiting the corporate tax deductibility of certain expenses such as luxurious meals and executive compensation exceeding $1 million per year. However, the effect of these efforts has been minimal, and the agency problem remains a major issue in the efficient functioning of the American economy. We'll discuss the issue again in Chapter 5 when we consider corporate governance.

1.7   Creditors Versus Stockholders—A Financially Important Conflict of Interest

The conflict of interest between creditors and stockholders is important at this point because it will begin to develop your concept of risk in finance. Let's explore the idea through an illustration.

Suppose Smith starts a business with $1,000 of his own money and convinces Jones to lend the business another $1,000 without a personal guarantee. The business now has cash of $2,000, which comes from debt of $1,000 and equity of $1,000. Smith is the sole owner and decision maker. Jones is a **creditor**.

> A **creditor** is anyone owed money by a business, including lenders, vendors, employees, or the government.

Now suppose Smith decides to use the business to take on some very risky venture. Imagine that the venture has a high probability of total failure, say 50%, in which case all invested funds would be lost. However, if the venture is successful, it will double invested money in a few months. Smith puts the entire $2,000 into the risky enterprise.

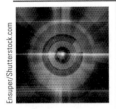

INSIGHTS | Ethics

Ethics and Ethical Investing

Investors buy stocks and bonds expecting to get back more than they spend. That's called earning a **return** on the investment. People are generally interested in the size of the return and the risk associated with it. But is that all they should be concerned about?

Earlier we said companies sold securities to raise money to finance assets. But suppose the assets are to be used in some project or business that's unethical or immoral. Doesn't that mean the investor is indirectly participating in the unethical activity? Should investors be concerned about that? Should they refuse to invest in companies whose activities they feel are unethical?

Let's be precise about what we mean by unethical. It's important not to get ethics mixed up with legality. Most illegal activities are also unethical, so there's no question that we should not participate. Ethics comes up when an activity is morally wrong but is technically legal.

Unethical activities generally involve at least two groups of people. One typically has some power over the other and uses it to gain a benefit at the other's expense.

The tobacco industry provides a good example. People smoke by choice, and the production and sale of cigarettes are legal activities. But the American Lung Association tells us that smoking accounts for an estimated 443,000 deaths per year and drains more than $193 billion per year from the economy in health-care costs and lost productivity.* Further, media reports allege that tobacco companies have kept sales up by targeting children in advertising and manipulating nicotine levels to promote addiction.

Some people consider the making and selling of tobacco products to be a legal but unethical business activity. Under this view, the groups that benefit are the managements and stockholders of tobacco companies who enjoy lucrative jobs and profits. The injured group is smokers who become sick and may die. The power of the benefited group is seen as coming from advertising and the addictive properties of smoking.

On the other hand, some people feel that smokers are aware of the health risks of tobacco and make their own decisions about using it, and that there's nothing morally wrong with providing the product to those who want it.

The question is whether ethics should keep investors who do morally condemn the industry from buying tobacco stocks in pursuit of financial returns. Or should the financial market act as a veil that legally and morally separates investors from what is eventually done with their money?

What do you think? Is it okay to invest in the stocks of tobacco companies?

Ethical investing is a growing practice in which people concern themselves with what the companies whose securities they buy do. Also known as socially responsible investing, it generally takes the form of avoiding the securities of firms that engage in activities considered questionable by the investor.

Ethical mutual funds exist which avoid the stocks of companies that engage in certain activities. For example, the Calvert Group Ltd offers a variety of funds that avoid investing in companies associated with unhealthful products and practices or that have poor records on labor relations, human rights, and the environment.

Ethical issues can be hard to analyze. They're usually charged with emotion and involve costs and benefits that are difficult to see. To keep your thinking clear, go through the following steps when analyzing an ethical problem.

1. Clearly identify the unethical practice. Is it all or part of what the firm is doing? In the tobacco illustration, is it wrong to make cigarettes at all or just to advertise to children?
2. Separate legal and ethical issues. Something may not be OK just because it's legal.
3. Identify the benefited party or group and describe the benefit.
4. Identify the injured party or group and describe the injury or cost.
5. Identify the nature and source of the power of the benefited group. Do they have the ability to manipulate and preserve their power? How did the power come about? Did they do something to create it?
6. State any alternatives the injured group has. How difficult are they to use?
7. State the opposing view. What argument will someone who doesn't feel there's a problem make?

As we continue with our study, we'll highlight ethical issues in finance from time to time.

*Source: American Lung Association, General Smoking Facts, June 2011, www.lungusa.org.

It's important to recognize that this is a very unfair deal between Smith and Jones. It is an abuse of the creditor by the stockholder. To see this, consider what happens if the venture fails versus what happens if it is successful.

In the event of failure, both investors lose equally—their entire $1,000 investments. If the venture succeeds, the company will have $4,000 in cash. However, Jones's claim against that sum will still be $1,000, representing the unpaid loan balance (plus a little interest). The remaining $3,000 will belong entirely to Smith.

To put it another way, the venture is a gamble. The losses are shared equally between the stockholder and the creditor, but the profits all belong to the stockholder. That's not a very good deal for the creditor.

This situation occurs in practice when companies that have borrowed money take on ventures that are riskier than those they took on before borrowing. To prevent this from happening, lenders generally put clauses in loan agreements that preclude the borrowing company from becoming more of a risk taker.

from the **CFO**

1.8   Concept Connections

Concept Connections describes an approach we're using in this text to make learning easier by explicitly connecting concepts presented within chapters to related end-of-chapter problems. In most cases, the concept is illustrated with an in-chapter example like the two you've already seen in this first chapter. Look back at those examples on pages 8 and 12 now. Notice that each has a Concept Connection Example number (1-1 or 1-2) and a subject title.

Now glance ahead at the end-of-chapter problems beginning on page 23. Notice that Problems 1 and 2 are preceded by boldface headings that identify their subjects and refer to the Concept Connection Examples on those subjects. This allows readers to easily find and review appropriate text sections and examples before attempting to solve end-of-chapter problems.

The end-of-chapter problems are arranged roughly in the order in which their subjects are covered in the chapter. The Concept Connection heading appears before the first problem on each subject. Most subjects are supported by several problems, so problems after the first in a subject area don't have headings.

In Chapter 1, there's only one problem on the first subject, Accounting Records and Cash Flow, so the Concept Connection heading for the second subject appears just before Problem 2. The absence of a heading before Problem 3 means that it too deals with the second subject, Tax Consequences of Business Form.

The first problem after each Concept Connection heading is introductory and very similar to the referenced Concept Connection Example in the text. Subsequent problems vary in structure and become more difficult.

It's generally a good idea to try a problem or two immediately after you finish reading about a subject. It's easy to do that with Concept Connections. Just flip to the end-of-chapter problems and scan the Concept Connection headings until you find the subject that matches the Concept Connection Example you've just read. The first problem will usually be easy if you follow the Concept Connection Example as a model.

In a few cases, end-of-chapter problems refer to text sections rather than to examples.

Concept Connections is designed to make your study of finance easier, more engaging, and fun. We're betting you'll like it if you give it a try.

1.9   Securities Analysis and Thomson ONE—Business School Edition

A large part of financial practice involves valuing securities, especially stocks. Valuation means estimating the price a knowledgeable investor *should* be willing to pay for financial assets. Once such a price is determined, it can be compared to the asset's current market price in order to make a buy–sell decision. For example, if we think a stock *should* be worth more than its current market price, buying it will probably lead to a profit as other investors recognize its value and bid its price up.[7]

The process of estimating the value of particular stocks and bonds is called Securities Analysis. It's impossible to overemphasize the importance of Securities Analysis in financial practice. It's critical because most investment decisions are based on the results of analyses done by either investors themselves or professional analysts who issue reports and recommendations that investors read.

A security analysis begins by gathering information about the issuing company. That information is used to forecast the amount and reliability of the future cash flows that are likely to come from owning that stock or bond. The information of interest for an analysis includes general material about what the company does and its prospects for the future, as well as financial detail about its past performance.

---

7. It's important to understand that all movement in the prices of securities comes from the fact that investors have different opinions about the value of individual securities and that those opinions change frequently.

This text will introduce you to securities analysis through a series of exercises based on Thomson ONE—Business School Edition (TO-BSE), which is an educational version of Thomson Financial's professional database. TO-BSE is limited to 500 companies for finance students. As you progress through the book, you will learn to access the TO-BSE system and draw information from it, which you can use in forming your own opinions about companies.

Exercises using Thomson ONE—Business School Edition are included at the end of several chapters and are clearly identified. It's a good idea to have a look at the problem at the end of this first chapter now. You'll find it on page 24. We're confident that you'll thoroughly enjoy the insights into the world of finance these problems provide.

You'll access Thomson ONE—Business School Edition through the text Web site at **www.cengage.com/thomsonone.** Select your book, and click on Companion Web site on the student side of the screen. Instructors click on the faculty side. Click on Thomson ONE—Business School Edition on the menu at the left. Use the Thomson ONE access card packaged with your new textbook to register your serial number and gain access to Thomson ONE. You'll need to create a user name and password.

CONCEPT CONNECTIONS

EXAMPLE 1-1   Accounting Records and Cash Flow, *page 8*

EXAMPLE 1-2   Tax Consequences of Business Form, *page 12*

Ensuper/Shutterstock.com

OlegDoroshin/Shutterstock.com

QUESTIONS

1. Separate the following list of assets into real assets and financial assets. What are the distinguishing characteristics of each type of asset?

   Delivery Truck   Corporate Stock
   Factory Building   Land
   Corporate Bond   Note Receivable
   Inventory   Computer

2. What is the primary factor that determines the price of securities? Can you think of another factor that might significantly affect how investors value the first factor? (Think hard: this second factor isn't mentioned in the chapter.)

3. Discuss the differences, similarities, and ties between finance and accounting.

4. Discuss the relationship between finance and economics.

5. How does the activity of investors in financial markets affect the decisions of executives within the firm?

6. What are the significant financial advantages and disadvantages of the sole proprietorship/partnership form in comparison with the corporate form?

7. Is limited liability a meaningful concept? Why or why not? And if so, for whom?

8. What conflict(s) of interest can you imagine arising between members of the community in which a company operates and some other stakeholders? (*Hint:* Think about pollution.)

9. Is the agency problem an ethical issue or an economic issue?

10. Compare and contrast the terms "stockholder" and "stakeholder."

BUSINESS ANALYSIS

1. Diversified companies are made up of divisions, each of which is a separate business. Large companies have divisions spread over the entire country. In such companies, *most* treasury functions are centralized while *most* accounting functions are carried out in the individual divisions.

   The cash management function controls the collection of revenues and the disbursement of funds from various bank accounts. It makes sure that the company never runs out of cash by monitoring outflows and having lines of bank credit ready in case temporary shortages occur. Today's banking system is linked electronically so that cash can be transferred around the country immediately.

   The credit and collection function decides whether a particular customer can buy the firm's products on credit. After the sale, it is responsible for following up to ensure that the bill is paid. Customers are often reluctant to pay because of problems and misunderstandings with sales or service departments.

   If you were designing the finance department of a diversified company, would you centralize these functions or locate them in the remote divisions? Why? Address each function separately.

2. The company president is reviewing the performance and budget of the marketing department with the vice president of marketing. Should that be a one-on-one meeting, or should the CFO be present? Why? If you feel the CFO should be there, what should be his or her role in the meeting?

PROBLEMS

Accounting Records and Cash Flow: Concept Connection Example 1-1 (page 8)

1. Sussman Industries purchased a drilling machine for $50,000 and paid cash. Sussman expects to use the machine for ten years after which it will have no value. It will be depreciated straight-line over the 10 years. Assume a marginal tax rate of 40%. What are the cash flows associated with the machine

   a. at the time of the purchase?
   b. in each of the following 10 years?

Tax Consequences of Business Form: Concept Connection Example 1-2 (page 12)

2. Harvey Redmond is planning a new business that he expects will grow into a large company within a few years. Harvey's lawyer has advised him that large companies are usually C-type corporations because of stock market considerations, so he's considering that form now to avoid reorganizing later on. However, he's also concerned about the after-tax income he'll be able to take out of the business during the first few years.

   Harvey thinks his business will have pretax earnings (after paying his salary) of about $150,000 per year for the first three years. Does it make sense for him to operate as a proprietorship for three years and then reorganize into a C-type at an estimated cost of $80,000—or to choose the C-type now at essentially no additional cost? Assume a simplified tax system in which the corporate rate is 34% and Harvey's personal tax rate is 28% on all income including dividends.

   Ignore both the fact that the cash flows occur at different times and the possibility of using an S-type corporation or an LLC.

3. Jill Meier is the sole owner of Meier Corp., which provides her only source of income. Jill has always paid herself entirely by drawing dividends from her corporation. A friend suggested that as long as she is earning about what she would have to pay someone else to run the business, she might be better off paying herself a salary instead of dividends because she would avoid the problem of double taxation. If Jill's company earns $120,000, all of which she will pay to herself, how much will she take home under each method? Assume a corporate tax rate of 30% and a personal tax rate of 25% on both salary and dividend income.

THOMSON REUTERS

In this chapter, we'll use Thomson ONE to get a quick overview of several companies that are of investment interest. To do the problem, go to **www.cengage.com/thomsonone**, select your book, click on the Companion Web site and then, on Thomson ONE—Business School Editions. Enter Thomson ONE—Business School Edition by using the user name and password you created when you registered the serial number on your access card. Select the problem for this chapter, and you'll see an expanded version that includes instructions on how to navigate within the Thomson ONE system, as well as some additional explanation of the presentation format.

4. You're a new financial analyst for the brokerage firm of Lodge and Howe. A client has expressed an interest in the following companies:

> Ford Motor Company (F)
> Harley-Davidson (HOG)
> Starbucks (SBUX)
> Microsoft (MSFT)

and you've been asked to provide him with a brief overview of each firm. The letters in parentheses are symbols used to represent company names when security prices are quoted in financial markets. Use either the names or symbols to get to the overview page for each company. Once there, do the following exercises:

a. Briefly summarize the nature of each firm's business.

b. Based on the graph provided on each overview page, write a paragraph discussing the stock's price performance relative to that of the market as a whole. The market is represented by a price index called the S&P 500. Your comments should include statements as to whether the stock's price seems to move up and down with the market or against it, and whether it moves more or less vigorously than the market.

c. How large is the company in terms of annual sales and total assets?

d. How profitable has it been recently? Answer this by stating net income (profits) as a percent of sales. What is the trend of sales and profits over the last three years?

e. What are professional analysts saying about investing in the stock?

f. What is the stock selling for right now? How recent is that quote? What did the stock open at this morning? Is the price moving up or down?

g. Look back at the graph. Does the stock seem *volatile* to you? Think in terms of the range of price movement over the last several months as a percent of an average of the high and low prices.

CHAPTER 2

Financial Background: A Review of Accounting, Financial Statements, and Taxes

Chapter Outline

Accounting Systems and Financial Statements
- The Nature of Financial Statements
- The Accounting System

The Income Statement
- Presentation

The Balance Sheet
- Presentation
- Assets
- Liabilities
- Equity

The Tax Environment
- Taxing Authorities and Tax Bases
- Income Taxes—The Total Effective Tax Rate
- Progressive Tax Systems, Marginal and Average Rates
- Ordinary Income and Capital Gains/Losses

Income Tax Calculations
- Personal Taxes
- Corporate Taxes

Some knowledge of accounting is necessary to appreciate finance. That's because financial transactions are recorded in accounting systems, and financial performance is stated in accounting terms. In other words, if we want to deal with money in business, we have to deal with the system that keeps track of it, and that's accounting. Some knowledge of taxes is also necessary, because tax considerations influence most financial decisions.

Although accounting is generally a prerequisite, finance students have differing levels of knowledge about the subject. Some are quite expert, while others, who may have taken accounting some time ago, don't remember much.

This chapter provides a review of what you need to know about accounting and taxes in a condensed form. If you're not strong in the area, reading the chapter carefully will be a lot quicker than digging the ideas out of your old accounting text. If you are up to speed, you can skim the material and move on.

We'll conduct our review as painlessly as possible, keeping in mind that while financial people need to know something about accounting, they don't have to be accountants. In fact, we won't even have to use debits and credits!

2.1   Accounting Systems and Financial Statements

Virtually everything business enterprises do is recorded as a series of money transactions within the structure of an accounting system. That record and the system itself provide the framework most managements use to control their businesses. Accounting systems produce several standard reports known as financial statements that reflect business performance.

2.1a   The Nature of Financial Statements

Financial statements are numerical representations of a firm's activities for an accounting period.

A business's **financial statements** are numerical representations of what it is physically doing. Keep that concept firmly in mind as we go forward. The idea behind statements is to give a picture of what's happening within the company and between the company and the rest of the world both physically and financially. This excellent idea creates a problem, however, in that it causes statements to be somewhat counterintuitive. That is, they don't necessarily say what a person untrained in accounting is likely to think they're saying. Here's an example.

Is Income "Income"?   Most people think of income as the money they're paid, which, after payroll withholding, is what they take home. In other words, income means cash in your pocket or cash paid to Uncle Sam for your taxes.

The income statement is one of the traditional financial statements. It starts with the dollar amount the company has sold, deducts costs, expenses, and taxes, and winds up with a figure called net income (also called earnings after tax). Most people would expect that figure to represent cash in the pocket of the business or its owner, just like a paycheck. However, it doesn't mean that at all. Several accounting concepts get in the way and give net income a character of its own. We'll describe two major differences between net income and cash flowing into the company's pocket.

Accounts Receivable   It's customary for many businesses to sell most of their products on credit, receiving a promise of later payment rather than immediate cash. Despite the fact that no money is received, accounting theory says that when a credit sale occurs, the firm has done everything it has to do to earn the related income, and that income should therefore be *recognized* in the financial statements.

In fact, however, the firm has less cash than it would have had if it had never made the sale. That's because, although it hasn't collected from the customer, it did supply product and to do so it had to pay for labor and materials.

Uncollected payments for product sold are called *accounts receivable* and represent a big difference between cash and accounting income.

Depreciation   Another idea that seems odd to the uninitiated is the way long-lived assets are handled financially. Suppose a company buys a machine to use in its business, paying $10,000 in cash at the time of purchase. Assume the machine is expected to last five years. How is the cost of the machine recognized as a cost of doing business?

Someone unfamiliar with accounting might think the cost would be recognized along with the outflow of money that pays for the machine—that is, a $10,000 cost in the year of purchase. However, accounting theory says that to properly reflect the workings of the business, we have to match the cost of the machine with the period over which it gives service. Therefore, we prorate the $10,000 cost over the five-year life of the asset.

That's done with a financial device called **depreciation**. If the proration is even over the life of the asset, depreciation allocates $2,000 to cost in the income statement in each of the asset's five years of life. (Evenly prorated depreciation is called *straight line*.)

That convention creates a strange situation in terms of cash in the company's pocket. In the first year, the firm spent $10,000 but could declare only $2,000 as a cost of doing business. In other words, it used a lot more cash than the income statement indicates. In each of the subsequent four years, it didn't spend anything but still got to declare $2,000 in cost. So in those years the income statement indicates that the company used more money than it actually did.

Clearly these practices indicate that accounting income is conceptually different from paycheck income and that financial statements are concerned with more than just the flow of money in and out of the business. They do tell us about that, but they also tell us about what's going on in other ways.

The Three Financial Statements   Three financial statements are of interest to us: the income statement, the balance sheet, and the statement of cash flows. There is a fourth that pertains to changes in owner's equity, but we won't be concerned with it here. The income statement and the balance sheet are the *basic* statements that derive from the books of account. The statement of cash flows is developed from them.

We'll consider the income statement and balance sheet in this chapter and the statement of cash flows in Chapter 3. First, a little background on accounting in general is in order.

2.1b   The Accounting System

An accounting system is an organized set of rules by which every transaction the firm makes is recorded in a set of records. The records are collectively known as the company's "books." Books used to be kept in ledgers that looked like books—hence the name. Today, they're more likely to be records in a computer.

The books are separated into a series of "accounts." An account generally holds records of transactions of a particular type or those related to a particular part of the business. For example, a revenue account receives all transactions involving the sale of product to customers, while a fixed asset account receives records related to the acquisition and disposal of heavy machinery.

Transactions include activities like selling product, buying inventory and equipment, paying wages, building product, borrowing money, paying taxes, and paying dividends. A business transaction is recorded in the books by an *entry*. An entry generally means that we add or subtract a dollar figure to or from the balance in an account.

The Double Entry System   Most accounting systems use the double entry system of keeping records. Double entry means that each entry has two equal parts, called *sides*. Each side of an entry is made to a different account.

The double entry concept is hard to grasp at first. You can get used to the idea by thinking of certain kinds of entries in which the two sides represent where we get money and what we do with it. For example, suppose we bought a machine on credit

Depreciation is the proration of an asset's cost over its service life.

A firm's **financial books** are a collection of records in which money transactions are recorded.

In **double entry** accounting, every entry has two sides that must balance.

for $1,000. That essentially means we bought the machine and took out a loan for the purchase price at the same time. One side of the entry that records this transaction would involve adding $1,000 to the fixed asset account to show that the company now has the machine. The other side would involve adding $1,000 to a payable account to reflect an obligation to pay the money. The asset side of the transaction shows what we did with the money, and the payable side shows where we got it.

The two sides of an entry are called *debits* and *credits*. In any entry, the total debit must equal the total credit. (This is the only time we'll mention debits and credits.)

Consider another example: recording a sale. Suppose we sold an item to a customer for $200. One side of the entry would add $200 to the sales account, but what would the other side be?

The answer depends on the terms of the sale. If the customer paid cash, the other side would simply add $200 to the cash account to reflect that the firm now has that additional money. However, if the customer bought on credit, the $200 would be added to a receivable account to reflect the fact that the company is owed the money.

Every entry must have two equal or *balancing* sides. Hence, it's common to say that correctly kept books are balanced.

Accounting Periods and Closing the Books

Books are **closed** by **updating the period's transactions** in the accounting system and **creating financial statements**.

In business, time is divided into accounting periods, usually months, quarters, and years, during which transactions are accumulated. At the end of each period, all the transactions occurring in the period are totaled and the company's books are brought up to date as of the last day of the period. This process, called *closing the books,* usually takes place in the days immediately following the last day of an accounting period.

Certain procedures are applied to the closed books to generate the financial statements with which we began our discussion. It's important to understand that financial statements are associated with particular accounting periods. The balance sheet is associated with the point in time at the end of the period, while the income statement and statement of cash flows are related to the entire period.

Implications

It's important to keep in mind that last year's financial statements don't say anything about what's going on this year or what will happen next year. They refer only to the past.

Statements can, however, be used as an indication of what is likely to happen in subsequent years. Past financial statements are a little like a person's medical history. If you were sick last year, you're more likely to be sick next year than if you had been healthy. However, a sick person can get well, and a healthy person can get sick and die. Similarly, a firm that was financially sound last year can fail next year if it's mismanaged or if something dramatic happens to its business.

Stocks and Flows

There is a fundamental difference between the two basic financial statements. The income statement reflects *flows* of money *over a period of time.* The balance sheet represents *stocks* of money *at a point in time.*

The income statement shows money flowing in and out of the organization. Revenues flow in while costs and expenses flow out. The difference is profit. The balance sheet makes a statement as of a moment in time. It says at this instant the company owns a particular list of assets and owes a particular list of creditors.

A set of statements includes an income statement that covers an entire accounting period and a balance sheet that can be thought of as a snapshot at the end of that period. The derived statement of cash flows, like the income statement, represents flows over an entire period.

2.2   The Income Statement

An income statement shows how much money a company has earned during the accounting period, commonly a year.

2.2a   Presentation

Most income statements have a form similar to the one shown in Table 2-1. Let's examine each line individually.

Sales   Sales, also called *revenue,* represents the total receipts from selling whatever it is the company is in business to sell. In other words, sales are receipts from normal business operations.

This is an important point. If the company receives money from activities outside its usual form of business, that money should be recorded as other income rather than as sales. For example, a retail business might sell the store in which it operates to move to another. That sale of real estate shouldn't be included in the sales line.

Cost and Expense   Cost of goods sold and expenses are subtracted from sales to arrive at earnings before interest and taxes. Both cost and expense represent money spent to do business, but there's an important distinction between the two. We'll consider cost first and expense a little later.

Cost of Goods Sold (COGS)   COGS (usually just called Cost) represents spending on things that are closely associated with the production of the product or service being sold. For example, in a retail business COGS is usually just the wholesale cost of product plus incoming freight. In a manufacturing business, however, COGS is much more complex. It includes labor and material directly associated with production as well as any peripheral spending in support of production. The peripheral spending is called *overhead* and can be substantial. It includes the cost of such things as factory management, the factory building itself, and depreciation on machinery.

TABLE 2-1	A Conventional Income Statement Format
Sales (Revenue)	$1,000
Cost of goods sold	600
Gross margin	$ 400
Expenses	230
Earnings before interest & taxes	$ 170
Interest expense	20
Earnings before tax	$ 150
Tax	50
Net income	$ 100

© Cengage Learning

In a service business, COGS includes the wages of the people who provide the services, depreciation on their tools and equipment, travel costs of getting to sites requiring service, and the cost of the facilities that house service operations.

Gross Margin   Gross margin, sometimes called *gross profit margin,* is simply sales revenue less COGS. It is a fundamental measure of profitability, getting at what it costs to make the product or service before consideration of the expenses of selling, distributing, or accounting for it.

Expense   Expenses represent spending on things that, although necessary, aren't closely related to production. These include functions like marketing and sales, accounting, human resources, research, and engineering. The money spent in those areas tends to be related to the passage of time rather than to the amount produced.

Depreciation   Although not a separate line on most income statements, depreciation is an important item. We'll study the idea in more detail later. For now, it's important to note that *both* cost and expense usually include some depreciation.

Interest and Earnings Before Interest and Taxes   Most but not all income statement presentations show interest expense separately and give an earnings figure calculated before interest has been paid.

A note on terminology is appropriate here. We often talk in general terms about companies being debt or equity **financed**. This refers to the amounts of debt and equity on the lower right side of the balance sheet. See page 32. All firms have equity financing representing the owner's contribution. But debt financing is a management decision. Some companies have a lot while others use none at all.

Interest   If the firm is partially financed with borrowed money (debt), it has to pay interest on those borrowings. It's important to realize that there's a big difference in the amount of interest various companies pay. If a business is completely financed with the owners' money (equity), there's no interest at all. If part of the financing is borrowed, the firm is burdened with debt and the associated interest payments. A company financed with debt is said to be **leveraged**.

Leverage is the use of **debt** financing.

Earnings Before Interest and Taxes (EBIT)   **Earnings before interest and taxes** is an important line on the income statement, because it shows the profitability of the firm's operations before consideration of how it is financed. The line is also called **operating profit**.

Operating profit (EBIT) is a business's profit **before** consideration of **financing charges**.

To understand the concept of EBIT, imagine that we want to compare the performance of two businesses that are identical except for their financing. Assume one business is entirely equity financed and the other has a significant amount of debt.

If we try to judge the two companies on the basis of net income, we won't get a true picture of the relative strengths of business operations, because the second firm will have its profit reduced by the interest it pays on borrowed money. But the amount borrowed has nothing to do with how well the product sells, the cost of making it, or how well operations are managed.

The problem arises because interest, the payment to creditors, is shown on the income statement, but dividends, the payment to owners, are not. Therefore, a company with debt financing will always look weaker at the net income line than an otherwise identical firm that's equity financed.

To get around this problem, we create the EBIT line. It shows the profitability of business operations *before* results are muddied by the method of financing.

Earnings Before Tax, and Tax   Gross margin less all expenses, including interest, yields earnings before tax. This is conceptually simple: what the business produces before Uncle Sam and the state take out their bites.

Tax   The tax line on the income statement refers to *income* taxes on the amount of earnings before tax. Companies pay other taxes, but those appear as cost or expense items farther up on the income statement.

However, the statutory tax rate applied to earnings before tax doesn't always give the tax shown on the statement. There can be a variety of credits and adjustments behind the final number.

The tax figure also doesn't necessarily reflect the tax actually due, because some items are treated differently for tax and reporting purposes. When the tax due is different from the tax shown, most of the difference is usually taken to a deferred tax account on the balance sheet. Current taxes can be deferred or previously deferred taxes can be due now. Some complicated accounting is generally involved.

We won't worry about such complications in this book. We will generally just calculate business taxes based on current earnings before tax.

Net Income   Net income is calculated by subtracting tax from earnings before tax and is the proverbial "bottom line." As we've already said, it is not equivalent to cash in the firm's pocket. In some cases it may be close to cash flow, but in others it's significantly different. It takes the statement of cash flows to figure out how much the company is really making in the short run.

Net income, also called *earnings,* belongs to the company's owners. It can either be paid out as dividends or retained in the business. **Retained earnings** become an addition to owner's equity on the balance sheet.

Retained earnings are those **not paid** out as dividends.

Terminology   The terminology used on the income statement is far from uniform between companies. The words "income," "profit," and "earnings" are generally synonyms, so you may see any of them on the various lines instead of the expressions we've used here.

2.3   The Balance Sheet

The balance sheet lists everything a company owns and everything it owes at a moment in time. Stated another way, it shows where all of the business's money has come from and what it's been used for. The fundamental principle is that all the sources of money and all the uses must be equal.

The firm's money comes from creditors and owners. Creditors have loaned money in one form or another and thereby create **liabilities** for repayment.

A **liability** is an amount a firm must eventually pay.

Owners have invested in the company or let past earnings remain in it rather than drawing them out. In a loose sense, the firm "owes" its owners their equity investments.

A firm uses its money to acquire assets, both tangible and intangible.

2.3a   Presentation

A balance sheet has two sides. One lists all of the company's assets, and the other lists all of its liabilities and equity.

The balance sheet can be thought of as an equation:

$$\text{assets} = \text{liabilities} + \text{equity}$$

On one side we have assets, representing what the company has done with its money. On the other side we have liabilities and equity, representing where the money came from. If everything has been accounted for properly, the two sides must be equal, or "balance"—hence the name balance sheet. The balance sheet is sometimes called the *statement of financial position*.

A typical balance sheet looks like the one shown in Table 2-2. Notice that total assets equals total liabilities plus equity.

This illustration is somewhat simplified, but it will serve to explain the important features of a balance sheet. We'll start on the asset side and work through the entire statement.

> The ease with which an asset **becomes cash** is referred to as **liquidity**.

Both assets and liabilities are arranged in decreasing order of **liquidity**. Liquidity, in this context, means the readiness with which an asset can be turned into cash or a liability will require cash. On the asset side, the most liquid asset is cash itself. Next comes accounts receivable because one expects that, in the normal course of business, receivables will be collected in cash within a few days. Inventory is next because it is normally sold in short order, generating cash or a receivable. Fixed assets are low on the list because they would generally have to be sold on a used equipment market to be turned into money. Similar logic applies on the liabilities side.

TABLE 2-2   A Conventional Balance Sheet Format

Assets		Liabilities	
Cash	$ 1,000	Accounts payable	$ 1,500
Accounts receivable	3,000	Accruals	500
Inventory	2,000	Current liabilities	$2,000
Current assets	$6,000		
Fixed assets		Long-term debt	$5,000
Gross	$4,000	Equity	2,000
Accumulated depreciation	(1,000)	Total capital	$7,000
Net	$3,000		
Total assets	$9,000	Total liabilities and equity	$9,000

© Cengage Learning

2.3b   Assets

In what follows, we'll consider each asset and present the important elements of its financial/accounting treatment.

Cash   Cash is defined as money in bank checking accounts plus currency on hand. Currency is usually a minor amount. Companies keep cash balances in bank accounts to pay bills and as a precaution against unforeseen emergencies.

Larger companies usually hold a near-cash item called **marketable securities** as well as cash itself. Marketable securities are short-term investments that pay a modest return and are very secure. They can be sold almost immediately if the need arises. Thus, they fill the precautionary need for cash but earn a little interest at the same time.

> **Marketable securities** are **liquid** investments that are held **instead of cash**.

Accounts Receivable   Accounts receivable represent credit sales that have not yet been collected. Under normal conditions, these should be paid in cash within a matter of weeks.

Most companies sell on credit terms of approximately 30 days. Customers often push those terms by taking somewhat longer to pay. That means it isn't unusual for a company to have 45 days of credit sales in receivables. That's (45/365=) 12.3% of a year's revenue.

The Bad-Debt Reserve   Receivables are usually stated net of an offsetting account called the *allowance for doubtful accounts* or the *bad-debt reserve*. As the name implies, this offset allows for the fact that most businesses make some credit sales that are never paid. These are usually a small percentage of total sales.

The bad-debt reserve is created and maintained by adding an amount equal to a small percentage of sales to its balance each month. This amount estimates credit sales that will never be collected even though nobody knows which ones will prove to be bad when they are made. The amount added is generally based on experience. The other side of the entry which maintains the reserve is an expense, that is, a reduction in profit.

Writing Off a Receivable   When a receivable is known to be uncollectible (perhaps because the customer is bankrupt), it should be *written off*. Writing off a receivable means reducing the balance in accounts receivable by the uncollected amount. The other side of the entry normally reduces the bad-debt reserve which has been provided regularly each month for that purpose. Hence a write-off doesn't generally affect the net receivables balance.

However, if the lost receivable is unusually large, the other side of the write-off has to go directly to an expense account. That generally represents an unexpected reduction in profit.

Overstated Receivables   *Profit reductions caused by uncollectible receivables are distasteful, so managements sometimes postpone writing off bad debts that should be recognized. This causes the receivables balance to include amounts that will never be collected. Such an account is said to be overstated. The problem is illustrated in Example 2-1.*

CONCEPT CONNECTION EXAMPLE 2-1

Writing off a Large Uncollectable Receivable

Goodguy Inc. has the following receivables balances ($000):

Gross accounts receivable	$5,650
Bad-debt reserve	(290)
Net accounts receivable	$5,360

Notice that the bad-debt reserve is approximately 5% of the gross receivables balance, which is likely to represent normal losses of about 3% of sales plus a little cushion for unexpected problems.

Last year, a customer approved for credit purchases up to only $100,000 placed an order for product costing $435,000. Eager for the business, Goodguy's president accepted the order over the CFO's objections. The customer has just gone out of business without paying any part of the bill. Goodguy's product is not recoverable. What are the financial statement implications of writing off the bad debt? Assume Goodguy's direct cost of goods sold is 60% of sales revenue.

SOLUTION: Goodguy must reduce gross receivables by $435,000. Because of double entry accounting, the entry accomplishing that reduction must be offset with opposing entries totaling the same amount. If Goodguy starts by using the entire bad-debt reserve to offset the loss, the balance sheet accounts will be ($000):

Gross accounts receivable	$5,215
Bad-debt reserve	0
Net accounts receivable	$5,215

That leaves ($435,000 − $290,000 =) $145,000 to be charged to a bad-debt expense account, impacting the income statement with a reduction in earnings before tax (pretax profit).

But notice that now the firm has no reserve against normal bad-debt losses. Reestablishing a 5% reserve will require additional charges to bad-debt expense over the next few months totaling ($5,215,000 × .05 =) $260,750. Thus, the total impact on the current income statement will be a reduction in pretax profit of ($145,000 + $260,750 =) $405,750.

Analysis

If Goodguy's cost of goods sold is 60% of revenue, the sale last year would have contributed ($435,000 × .40 =) $174,000 to earnings before tax. But the $405,750 charge to bad-debt expense this year is not accompanied by a reduction in cost, so it falls entirely to earnings before tax. In other words, the decision to accept the risky order traded a $174,000 pretax income statement profit last year for a $405,750 pretax loss this year.

Now suppose that

1. Management is graded on current profitability.
2. The customer in question isn't quite out of business yet.
3. But the customer is recognized as being very unlikely to ever pay its bill.

Under these conditions, the receivable should be written off, but it's easy to see that management might be motivated to postpone the write-off to protect its performance rating. That leads to an overstated receivables balance.

Writing off a number of smaller bad debts that have been carried too long can have the same effect as a single large write-off.

Inventory   Inventory is product held for sale in the normal course of business. In a manufacturing company, inventory can be in one of three forms: raw materials, work in process (abbreviated WIP), and finished goods. A retailer has only finished goods inventory.

Work-in-Process (WIP) Inventories   The nature of raw materials and finished goods is self-explanatory, but WIP needs a little explanation. As raw materials move through the production process, labor is expended to produce product. We think of that labor as being embodied in the inventory. For example, if in a certain production step a piece of wood costing $10 is worked on for one hour by a worker who makes $20 an hour, we would think of the wood as having a value of $30 when it emerges from that process. Thus, the work-in-process inventory contains the cost of raw materials and the cost of an increasing amount of labor as it moves toward becoming finished product.

Besides labor, most accounting systems add the cost of factory overhead (the building, equipment, heat, electricity, supervision, etc.) to the value of inventory as labor is added.

The Inventory Reserve   Inventory on the balance sheet is assumed to be usable but frequently isn't. A number of things can happen to make inventory worth less than the firm paid for it. Items can be damaged, become spoiled, get stolen (called *shrinkage*), and become obsolete.

Firms conduct periodic physical counts to discover shrinkage, but other damage often goes undetected until an attempt is made to use or sell the item.

Balance sheet inventories are generally stated net of an inventory reserve to allow for a normal amount of problem material. The inventory reserve is conceptually similar to the bad-debt reserve associated with accounts receivable. It is maintained similarly with an addition each month, the other side of which is an expense.

Writing Off Bad Inventory   If inventory is discovered to be missing, damaged, or obsolete, the balance sheet inventory account must be reduced to reflect the loss. The other side of the entry that reduces the recorded inventory balance normally reduces the inventory reserve, so the net inventory balance is unaffected. However, if the loss is large, part of the reduction may have to be offset directly to an expense account, resulting in a reduction in profit.

Overstated Inventory   *Managements usually try to avoid reducing recorded profits. Therefore, they're prone to accept any rationalization to the effect that the inventory is*

from the
CFO

holding its original value. This can lead to an overstatement of the inventory balance. The situation is very similar to that illustrated in Example 2-1 on page 34 for receivables.

Overstatements   The overstatement of receivables and inventories can be a significant problem to users of financial statements, which purport to reflect the value of a company. To the extent that assets are overstated, the firm's value is less than it is being held out to be. Overstatements can also mean that the company isn't managed effectively. Both of these possibilities are of significant concern in valuing the firm's securities.

Current assets become cash within **one year**.

Current Assets   The first three assets on our balance sheet are called **current assets**. The term "current" means that in the normal course of business, these items can be expected to become cash within one year. More complex businesses have a few other current items, but they are of minor importance compared with these.

The current concept is important in financial analysis, because it relates to a company's ability to meet its obligations in the short run. Most of the money the business receives from normal operations flows in through the current asset accounts. In other words, money that isn't in current assets today may be a long time coming in, but money now in current assets can be expected to be realized as cash soon.

Fixed Assets   Longer-lived items are located below the current section of the balance sheet. Although many things can be in this category, the predominant item is usually fixed assets, which can also be called *property, plant, and equipment* (PPE).

The word "fixed" can be a little confusing. It doesn't mean fixed in location, as a truck or a railroad car can be a fixed asset. It simply implies long lived. A fixed asset is something that has a useful life of at least a year. It's important to understand the basics of fixed asset accounting and the associated concept of depreciation.

According to the **matching principle**, recognition of an asset's **cost** should match its **service life**.

Depreciation   Depreciation is an artificial accounting device that spreads the cost of an asset over its estimated useful life regardless of how it is acquired or paid for. If the cost is spread evenly over the life of the asset, we say the depreciation is straight line. The idea behind depreciation is to match the flow of the asset's cost into the income statement with the delivery of its services over time. This **matching principle** is an important accounting concept.

In some cases, an argument is made that cost flows out of an asset more rapidly in the early years of its life than in the later years. Depreciation can be structured to be greater in the early years to reflect that idea. When the depreciation schedule is front loaded like that, it's called **accelerated depreciation**.

Accelerated depreciation recognizes more of an asset's cost in the **early years** of its life.

Financial Statement Presentation   Depreciation appearing on the income statement reflects an asset's cost. The same depreciation also appears on the balance sheet where its cumulative value helps to reflect the remaining worth of the asset.

Recall that every accounting entry has two sides. The entry posting depreciation expense to the income statement posts the same amount to a balance sheet account called *accumulated depreciation*. Accumulated depreciation is carried as an offset to the value of an asset, so at any time the net value of the asset is the difference

TABLE 2-3	Fixed Asset Depreciation			
Year	Income Statement		Balance Sheet	
1	Depreciation expense	$2,500	Gross Accumulated depreciation Net	$ 10,000 (2,500) $ 7,500
2	Depreciation expense	$2,500	Gross Accumulated depreciation Net	$ 10,000 (5,000) $ 5,000
3	Depreciation expense	$2,500	Gross Accumulated depreciation Net	$ 10,000 (7,500) $ 2,500
4	Depreciation expense	$2,500	Gross Accumulated depreciation Net	$ 10,000 (10,000) $ -0-

© Cengage Learning

between its original cost and its accumulated depreciation. An illustration should make the idea clear.

Suppose a firm buys a truck for $10,000 and decides to depreciate it over a useful life of four years at $2,500 each year. During that time, the income statement will include a $2,500 expense item each year. During the same period, each year's balance sheet will carry three numbers related to the asset: its gross value, its accumulated depreciation, and its net value.

It's important to understand the pattern of these numbers over time. The accounts will look like those shown in Table 2-3 at the end of each year. Notice that each year's depreciation expense is the same. That's because the example is using straight line depreciation. If accelerated depreciation were being used, the early years would have larger numbers than the later years. The total depreciation expense, however, would still be equal to the $10,000 cost of the asset.[1] That's an important idea. Total depreciation can never exceed the cost of the asset.

Also notice that accumulated depreciation grows each year by the amount of depreciation expense in that year, but the asset's gross value stays the same. The asset's true value at any point in time is approximated by the net line, which is known as the item's book value or net book value, abbreviated NBV.

Disposing of a Used Asset   Net book value is not market value. The asset may be salable on the used equipment market for an amount that's more or less than its NBV at any time. It's important to understand the accounting treatment if that occurs. The idea is illustrated in Example 2-2.

Notice that the revenue and accounting profit shown in Example 2-2 would not be part of operating revenue and income, because selling used trucks isn't the company's business. They should be recorded as other revenue and other income.

---

1. We're assuming that at the end of its life the asset will have a zero salvage value. If a positive salvage value is assumed, we would depreciate only the difference between the original cost and that value. Otherwise the procedure would be the same.

CONCEPT CONNECTION   EXAMPLE 2-2

Selling a Fixed Asset

Suppose the truck in Table 2-3 is sold after three years for $4,000 paid immediately in cash.

   a. What revenue and profit would the firm recognize on that transaction?
   b. What cash flow would be generated if the firm's tax rate is 30%?

SOLUTION: The revenue from the sale is simply the price received, $4,000. The cost takes a little more thinking. The truck was originally purchased for $10,000, but three-fourths of that amount has already been recognized as cost/expense on the income statement through the depreciation entries on the left side of Table 2-3. After three years, those total $7,500, so only $2,500 of the truck's original cost remains to be recognized. That amount is conveniently available on the balance sheet as the truck's third-year NBV. Hence we have the following:

a. Profit

Revenue	$4,000
Cost (NBV)	2,500
Profit contribution to EBT	$ 1,500

It's important to understand that the $1,500 profit doesn't represent cash flow because it was calculated with an NBV figure that doesn't reflect current cash movement. The $2,500 NBV is part of the $10,000 cost of the truck spent in cash three years ago. It has remained on the balance sheet since then, waiting to be depreciated, and is moving into cost now because the asset is being sold. We'll continue the example, creating separate columns for accounting and cash.

b. Cash Flow

	Accounting	Cash Flow
Revenue	$4,000	$4,000
Cost (NBV)	2,500	
Profit contribution to EBT	$ 1,500	
Tax (30%)	450	450
Contribution to net income	$ 1,050	
Cash flow		$ 3,550

First focus on the accounting column. The $1,500 contribution to EBT is taxable so we subtract a tax line to arrive at a contribution to net income, $1,050.

Now notice that only two figures in the accounting column represent current cash flow. These are revenue and tax. The others come from the accounting idea of spreading an asset's cost over the period in which it is used.

The cash flow column just shows revenue received minus tax paid for a total of $3,550. Keep in mind that it's always necessary to develop accounting profit when calculating the cash flow on the sale of a used asset because it's needed to calculate tax, which is a cash flow item.

The Life Estimate   Depreciation runs over the estimated useful life of an asset. However, it's quite common for things to last beyond their estimated lives. Assets still in use beyond their life estimates are said to be fully depreciated. Such an asset's gross value remains on the books entirely offset by accumulated depreciation. If it is sold after that time, there is zero cost.

Tax Depreciation and Tax Books   The government provides many incentives to business through the tax system. One of the most prominent involves depreciation, which is a tax-deductible expense.

Deductibility implies that higher depreciation in a given year results in lower tax in that year, because taxable profit is lower. That means accelerated depreciation reduces taxes early in the life of an asset. The savings is given back later in the asset's life when depreciation is lower and taxes are higher, but the net effect is to *defer* taxes if accelerated depreciation is used.

Unfortunately, the lower recorded profit in early years caused by accelerated depreciation isn't something management likes to see. It makes the company look less successful in the short run than it would appear if straight-line depreciation were used. To get around this conflict, the government allows businesses to use different depreciation schedules for tax purposes and for financial reporting purposes. The term "tax books" is used to mean financial records and statements generated by using the tax rules, and the term "financial books" or just "books" is used to mean the regular statements that we're talking about here. The difference between the two methods results in an account called *deferred tax* on the financial books.

Depreciation Is a Noncash Expense   Depreciation is a financial fiction; it doesn't represent a current flow of money even though it's treated as a cost or an expense. It has nothing to do with how an asset is acquired or paid for.

Total Assets   The things we've talked about so far constitute most of the left side of the balance sheet for a majority of companies. Their sum is simply total assets.

2.3c   Liabilities

Liabilities represent what the company owes to outsiders.

Accounts Payable   Accounts payable arise when firms buy from vendors on credit (called **trade credit**). Payables and receivables are opposite sides of the same coin. When a credit sale is made, the seller records a receivable and the buyer records a payable. In most companies, the bulk of accounts payable arises from the purchase of inventory.

> Vendors extend **trade credit** when they deliver product without demanding immediate payment.

Terms of Sale   The length of time allowed until payment is due on a credit sale is specified in the **terms of sale**. Common terms involve payment within 30 days and include a discount for prompt payment. Terms of two 10, net 30, written 2/10, n.30, mean that a 2% discount is allowed if payment is received within 10 days or the full amount is due in 30 days. Trade credit is generally free in that no interest is charged if the full amount is paid within the allowed time.

> **Terms of sale** specify when payment is expected for sales made on trade credit.

from the **CFO**

Stretching payables is delaying payment of trade payables.

Vendors become upset if their bills aren't paid in the times specified under the terms of sale. Delaying payment of trade payables is called **stretching payables** or **leaning on the trade**. If a customer abuses a vendor's terms, the credit privilege is likely to be revoked, and the seller will subsequently demand cash in advance before shipping goods.

Understated Payables   When we discussed accounts receivable and inventory, we were concerned about overstatements, conditions in which the balance sheet claims assets the company doesn't have. On the liabilities side, we're concerned about understatements, conditions in which the firm has liabilities that are not reflected on its balance sheet. *For example, it's possible to receive goods from a vendor, use them, and simply not recognize the transaction financially. Eventually, the vendor will demand payment and the issue will be raised, but that may take quite a while.*

Accruals represent **incomplete** transactions.

Accruals   Accruals are poorly understood by most nonfinancial businesspeople. They are an accounting device used to recognize expenses and liabilities associated with transactions that are not entirely complete.

A Payroll Accrual   The best way to understand accruals is to consider a simple example involving payroll. Suppose a company pays its employees every Friday afternoon for work through that day. Then suppose the last day of a particular month falls on a Wednesday, and the books are closed as of that afternoon. Figure 2-1 shows this situation graphically.

As of the close of business on Wednesday, the financial statements have to include two things that aren't reflected by paper transactions. These arise from the fact that employees have worked for three days (Monday, Tuesday, and Wednesday) that are in the first month, but won't be paid for those days until Friday, which is in the second month.

The first issue is that as of the closing date, the firm owes its employees for those days, and the debt (liability) must be reflected on the balance sheet. The second issue is that the work went into the month just closing and should be reflected in that month's costs and expenses.

If we were to simply recognize payroll expense when the cash is paid on Friday, the three days' labor would go into the second month, and there would be no recognition of the liability at month end.

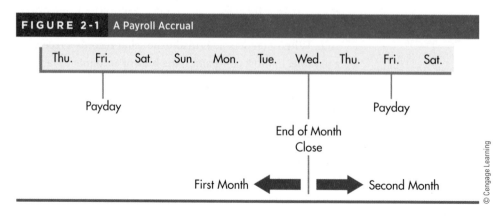

FIGURE 2-1   A Payroll Accrual

The solution is a month-end *accrual* entry in the amount of the three days' wages. One side of the entry increases an accrued wages liability on the balance sheet, while the other side increases wage expense in the closing month. It's important to realize that the liability will be paid in just two days on the next payday.

Other Accruals   There are accruals for any number of things. For example, suppose a company is billed in arrears for property tax at the end of a government fiscal year in June. If the firm closes its books at the end of December, it owes the local government for six months of property tax even though it has received no bill and won't until June. A property tax accrual properly reflects this expense and liability in the meantime.

Current liabilities require cash within **one year**.

Current Liabilities
Current liabilities are defined as items requiring payment within one year; hence, payables and accruals are classified as current. Other current liabilities include notes payable, short-term loans, and any long-term debt that's within a year of its due date.

Net working capital represents the money required to support **day-to-day** activities.

Working Capital
Current assets are collectively referred to as *gross working capital,* while the difference between current assets and current liabilities is known as *net working capital.*

Conceptually, net working capital represents the amount of money a firm needs to carry on its routine day-to-day activities. Formally,

$$\text{net working capital} = \text{current assets} - \text{current liabilities}$$

In practice, people frequently omit the word "net."

Working capital is an important idea to which we'll devote all of Chapter 16.

Long-Term Debt
Typically, the most significant noncurrent liability is long-term debt. It is common practice to refer to it simply as debt, especially if there isn't much short-term debt. Long-term debt usually consists of bonds and long-term loans.

A business financed with **debt** is said to be **leveraged**.

Leverage   A business that is financed with debt is said to be **leveraged**. The word implies that when things are going well, using borrowed money can enhance the return on an entrepreneur's own investment. It works like this.

CONCEPT CONNECTION   EXAMPLE 2-3

Leverage
Sonia Halloran started a business by investing $100,000 of her own capital. The company earned an after-tax profit of $15,000 in the first year, so her return on equity was 15% ($15,000/$100,000). What would her return have been if she had borrowed half of the money, $50,000, at an interest rate that nets to 10% after tax?

SOLUTION: Sonia would have paid $5,000 interest on her loan (10% of $50,000), reducing her profit to $10,000, but the investment of her own money would have been only half as much, $50,000. Hence, her return on investment would be 20% ($10,000/$50,000).

Borrowing money would have *levered* her return up from 15% to 20%. The figures are shown below.

	All Equity	Leveraged
Earnings	$ 15,000	$ 15,000
Interest (after tax)	—	(5,000)
Net Income	$ 15,000	$ 10,000
Debt	—	$ 50,000
Equity	$100,000	50,000
Total capital	$100,000	$100,000
Return	15%	20%

In general, a business is able to produce a higher return on the owner's invested funds by using borrowed money *if* the return on the *total* amount of invested money exceeds the after-tax interest rate being paid on the loan. Otherwise, the effect is in the opposite direction and the return is worse when the business is financed with borrowed money. We'll study the concept of leverage in depth in Chapter 14.

Fixed Financial Charges   The most significant concern about borrowed money is the interest charge. It's important to keep in mind that interest charges are fixed. That means they must be paid regardless of how the business is doing. You can't go to the bank and say, "Sales are down a little this month, so do you mind if I skip the interest payment?" That can be a real problem in tough times. Many businesses have gone bankrupt because of fixed financial obligations.

2.3d   Equity

Equity financing is provided by a business's **owners**.

Equity represents funds supplied to businesses by their owners. These funds are in two forms: direct investment and retained earnings. Direct investment occurs when stock is sold or an entrepreneur puts money into his or her business. Retained earnings occur when profits are kept in the business rather than being paid out to the owners as dividends.

The Representation of Direct Investment by Owners   If a business is incorporated, its direct equity investments are reflected in two stock accounts. One is entitled *common stock* and represents an arbitrary amount called the *par value* of each share times the number of shares outstanding. The other account is usually called *paid in excess* and represents the amount paid for the stock over its par value. The two together represent the total direct equity investment, that is, the money paid for the stock.

It's important to understand that par value is an arbitrary and largely meaningless number. If the business isn't incorporated, the two separate accounts aren't necessary, since there's no stock.

Retained Earnings   A company's profit belongs to its owners, who can either pay it to themselves as dividends or leave it in the business. Earnings paid out are said to be distributed; those kept in the business are said to be retained. If a business is incorporated, the balance sheet will show retained earnings separately from the directly invested money shown in the stock accounts. This may or may not be so in an unincorporated business.

Money retained or "reinvested" in a business is just as much the contribution of its owners as directly invested money. That's because they could have taken it out and used it elsewhere if they wanted to do so.

The retained earnings account is subject to a common misconception. Probably because of the words in the name, people sometimes get the idea that retained earnings represent a reserve of cash on which the firm can draw in times of need. That isn't so. Just like any other invested funds, retained earnings are generally spent on assets shortly after they become available.

The retained earnings account shows all earnings ever retained by the company just as the stock accounts show all money ever invested directly by owners. Neither is generally available as cash at any point in time, because both tend to have been spent on assets to build the business.

Illustration: Equity Accounts   We'll summarize these ideas with a brief illustration. Suppose a firm is started with the sale of 20,000 shares of $2 par value stock at $8 per share and subsequently earns $70,000 of which $15,000 is paid in dividends. The equity accounts will then be as follows.

Common stock ($2 × 20,000)	$ 40,000
Paid in excess ($6 × 20,000)	120,000
Retained earnings ($70,000 − $15,000)	55,000
Total equity	$ 215,000

The Relationship Between Net Income and Retained Earnings   It is very important to understand the interaction between net income and retained earnings in financial statements.

Net income (or earnings after tax) becomes part of retained earnings and therefore part of equity at the end of the accounting period *if* it is not distributed to the owners; that is if no new equity investments are made and nothing is paid out to the owners during an accounting period,

$$\text{beginning equity} + \text{net income} = \text{ending equity}$$

If something is paid out to owners in the form of a dividend, the relation is

$$\text{beginning equity} + \text{net income} - \text{dividends} = \text{ending equity}$$

If new equity is contributed through the sale of additional stock, the relation is

$$\text{beginning equity} + \text{net income} - \text{dividends} + \text{stock} = \text{ending equity}$$

Beginning balance sheet figures, including equity, are those of the balance sheet dated at the end of the prior accounting period. For example, the beginning balance sheet for 2015 is the ending balance sheet for 2014. Therefore, 2015's beginning equity is 2014's ending equity.

Preferred Stock   **Preferred stock** is a security issued by some firms that is effectively a cross between debt and common equity. It's thought of as a hybrid, because it has some of the characteristics of each of the more traditional securities. Legally, however, it is classified as equity and is included in the equity section of the balance sheet *above* the common stock accounts. Total equity is the sum of common and preferred equity. (We'll study preferred stock in Chapter 8.)

Total Capital   The sum of long-term debt and equity is total capital. These funds are generally used to support long-term assets.

Total Liabilities and Equity   The sum of the right side of the balance sheet reflects where all of the company's funds have come from and the obligations it has to outsiders and owners as a result of those advances. Total liabilities and equity must always equal total assets.

2.4   The Tax Environment

In finance, we're primarily concerned with federal income taxes for both individuals and corporations. We will begin, however, with a little background on taxes in general.

2.4a   Taxing Authorities and Tax Bases

Taxes are imposed by various governmental authorities. In this country, we typically think in terms of three taxing levels: federal, state, and local (cities and counties).

Every tax must have a **tax base**, the thing that is taxed. The three common tax bases are income, wealth, and consumption.

Income Tax   The idea of an income tax is straightforward. A taxpayer pays a fraction of her income in a designated time period, generally a year, to the taxing authority. The most important income tax is the federal tax because it typically takes the biggest share of our income. Depending on how much an individual makes, the federal tax (in 2012) can be as much as 35% of the last dollar earned. Most states, but not all, have income taxes, but the rates are much lower—typically from 5% to 10%. Several major cities also have income taxes with rates in the neighborhood of 1%. New York City is a prominent example.

Individuals and corporations are both subject to income taxes, but under different sets of rules, which we'll discuss shortly.

Wealth Tax   Wealth taxes are based on the value of certain types of assets. The most common wealth tax is levied by cities and counties on the value of real estate. The money collected from real estate taxes is typically used to run local school systems and pay for town services such as fire and police departments. Wealth taxes are also called *ad valorem taxes*.

Consumption Tax   Consumption taxes are based on the amount of certain goods we use. The most common consumption tax is a *sales tax* in which the end user of a product pays a tax on its purchase price. It's important to understand that because the tax is on consumption or use, only the end user pays. Therefore, if something is purchased for resale, no sales tax is due.

Sales taxes are imposed by state and local governments. The federal government taxes the consumption of certain items such as alcohol, tobacco, and gasoline. The federal government's consumption taxes are called *excise taxes.*

2.4b   Income Taxes—The Total Effective Tax Rate

Many investment decisions turn on the tax rate that an individual or company will pay on the income from the investment. If there is a state income tax, it should be taken into consideration along with the federal tax. The total effective tax rate is the combined rate to which the taxpayer is subject. It is not simply the sum of the federal and state rates, because state tax is deductible from income in the calculation of federal tax.

For example, suppose a taxpayer is subject to a 30% federal tax and a 10% state tax on income of $100. He or she would pay as follows:

Taxable income for state tax	$ 100
State tax @ 10%	10
Taxable income for federal tax	$ 90
Federal tax @ 30%	27
Net after tax	$ 63
Total tax	$ 37
Total effective tax rate ($37/$100)	37%

Adding the two rates would give 40%. In general, we can calculate the **total effective tax rate (TETR)** using the formula

(2.1) $$\text{TETR} = T_f + T_s(1 - T_f)$$

where T_f is the federal tax rate and T_s is the state tax rate.

2.4c   Progressive Tax Systems, Marginal and Average Rates

A **progressive tax** system is characterized by **higher tax rates** on incrementally higher income.

The U.S. federal income tax system is progressive. In a **progressive tax** system, a taxpayer's tax *rate* increases as income increases. It's important to distinguish that idea from the simpler notion that taxpayers with higher incomes pay higher taxes. The latter statement would be true if everyone paid the same tax rate regardless of their income.

A progressive system might be one in which everyone earning less than $20,000 pays at a 20% rate, but those who earn over $20,000 pay 30% on earnings over $20,000. Because the rate goes up as income increases past $20,000, the system is progressive.

Notice that taxpayers with income over $20,000 don't pay the higher rate on their entire incomes, but only on the amounts over $20,000. For example, a taxpayer earning $25,000 would calculate taxes as follows.

20% of the first $20,000	=	$4,000
30% of the remaining $5,000	=	1,500
Total tax		$5,500

Brackets

Brackets   Tax rates in progressive systems don't increase smoothly as income goes up. Rather, they remain constant over some range of income and then jump abruptly to a higher level for another range. Ranges of income through which the tax rate is constant are called **tax brackets**. Here's a hypothetical progressive tax system with three brackets.

A **tax bracket** is a range of income in which the tax rate is constant.

Bracket	Tax Rate
$0–$5,000	10%
$5,000–$15,000	15%
Over $15,000	25%

This representation of the tax structure is called a *tax table* or a *tax schedule*.

Prior to 1986, the personal tax system had as many as 14 brackets, and many years ago the top rates were as high as 70%. In 2012, there are six brackets, and the highest rate is 35%. We'll discuss the actual rate structure after we illustrate a few ideas using our simplified example.

A taxpayer is often identified by his or her bracket, which is the highest rate at which some of his or her income is taxed. Thus a person earning $10,000 in our example would be said to be in the 15% bracket.

The Marginal and Average Tax Rates   Two tax rate concepts are applicable to every taxpayer. The marginal tax rate is the rate that will be paid on the next dollar of income the person earns. The average tax rate is the percentage of total income the person pays in taxes. The marginal rate is relevant for investment decisions. We'll illustrate why shortly. Now let's calculate some hypothetical taxes as well as some average and marginal rates to get used to the procedure.

Calculations   Using the three-bracket hypothetical tax rate schedule above, we'll calculate the dollar tax and the two rates on incomes of $4,000, $11,000, and $25,000.

At an income of $4,000, a taxpayer is in the lowest bracket and is subject to only one rate. The calculations are very simple. The tax is just 10% of $4,000, or $400, and the average and marginal rates are both clearly 10%.

At $11,000, things are a little more interesting. The tax calculation follows.

$$
\begin{array}{rr}
\text{10\% of the first \$5,000} = & \$\ 500 \\
\text{15\% of the next \$6,000} = & \underline{\ 900} \\
& \$1,400
\end{array}
$$

The average rate is the total tax bill divided by taxable income.

$$\$1,400/\$11,000 = 12.7\%$$

The marginal rate is 15% because that's what would be paid on the eleven-thousand-and-first dollar of income.

Notice that the marginal rate is almost always the bracket rate. Only at the very top of a bracket is it the rate of the next bracket.

At $25,000 the calculation is as follows.

$$
\begin{array}{rcr}
\text{10\% of the first \$5,000} & = & \$\ 500 \\
\text{15\% of the next \$10,000} & = & 1,500 \\
\text{25\% of the last \$10,000} & = & \underline{2,500} \\
& & \$4,500
\end{array}
$$

Notice that each rate is applied to the income within the relevant bracket only. The average tax rate is

$$\$4,500/\$25,000 = 18.0\%$$

The marginal rate is 25%, because that's what would be paid on an additional dollar of earnings.

An important conceptual point in the system we've illustrated is that high-income taxpayers enjoy lower rates on the first part of their earnings. Notice that the taxpayer with a $25,000 income pays only 10% on his or her first $5,000 even though the rest is taxed at much higher rates. You can think of this as a benefit being retained by the high income taxpayer.

In the foregoing examples, we've applied a tax rate schedule to *taxable income*. Taxable income isn't a taxpayer's total or gross income. It must be calculated according to rules within the tax code. We'll cover the basics of those rules shortly.

2.4d   Ordinary Income and Capital Gains/Losses

The tax system recognizes two major types of income: ordinary and capital gain.

Ordinary income is generally the result of normal money-making activity. Examples include salary earned, the profit from an unincorporated business, or interest and dividends received from investments. Salaries, dividends, and interest can only be positive, but business profits can be positive or negative. Hence ordinary income can also be an ordinary loss.

A **capital gain or loss** arises when someone buys something for a particular price, holds it for a while, and then sells it at a different price. If the price at which the object is sold is higher than the price at which it was purchased, the difference represents a capital gain. If the selling price is lower, we have a capital loss. The item involved can be a real or a financial asset.

Ordinary income includes wages, business profits, dividends, and interest.

Capital gain/loss income arises when an asset that's held for investment is sold for more/less than was paid for it.

The Tax Treatment of Capital Gains/Losses and Dividends   Historically, capital gains have received favorable tax treatment. That is, they are taxed at lower rates than ordinary income. The reason behind this treatment lies in the use of the tax system as a means to incentivize desirable economic activity. Investment in assets stimulates the economy, and Congress generally views that as favorable. Taxing profits earned through such investment at lower rates makes projects more attractive and more are undertaken.

The capital gains system is actually very complicated, requiring many rules and explanations of what qualifies for particular treatments. Further, the rules tend to be changed frequently. The most important distinction is the length of time the taxpayer holds an asset before selling it. Currently, if the *holding period* is less than one year, any capital gain on an asset's sale is classified as short-term and isn't eligible for favorable tax treatment. Gains on assets held for more than a year are classified as long-term and usually qualify for favorable tax treatment.

As of 2012, the essence of the system was that the tax rate on long-term capital gains was capped at an unusually low rate of 15% due to legislation passed in the early 2000s. Similar legislation also capped the tax rate on dividend income at 15%. That was an even more dramatic change as dividends have traditionally been taxed as ordinary income. Both changes were passed with the claim that they would stimulate the economy.

Capital losses can be used to offset capital gains. But if gains and losses add up to a net loss, no more than $3,000 of that loss can be used by individual taxpayers to offset ordinary income in any one year. Corporate taxpayers can't use capital losses to offset income statement earnings before tax at all. Thus capital losses receive *unfavorable* tax treatment.

If an individual's capital losses exceed capital gains by more than $3,000 in a given year, the excess can be carried forward into future years as a reduction to ordinary income of up to $3,000 per year. Corporate capital losses can be carried forward to offset future capital gains only.

The Significance of the Tax Treatment   It's important to understand why the treatment of capital gains is a financially significant issue. Many investors buy stock in anticipation of an increase in price rather than to receive dividends. The profit derived from an increase in a stock's price is a capital gain. If it is taxed at substantially lower rates than other profits, buying stock becomes a relatively more attractive proposition to the general investing public. Therefore favorable tax treatment of capital gains makes it easier to raise money by selling stock. Hence the idea is enthusiastically supported by the business community.

2.5   Income Tax Calculations[2]

Income taxes are paid by both people and corporations according to the same basic tax principles. In each case, the tax is levied on a base of taxable income, which is gross income less certain deductions. The tax due is then calculated using a progressive rate schedule. But that's where the similarity ends. The rate schedules for corporations and people are very different as are the rules for determining taxable income. We'll have a look at the basic calculation procedures for both in the following pages.

2.5a   Personal Taxes

Taxes on people are called *personal* or *individual* taxes. The taxpaying unit is a *household,* usually a family of some kind. There are separate schedules for single individuals, married couples filing jointly, married people filing separately, and certain heads of households who aren't married. This last category is largely for single parents. In this book we'll focus on two personal tax schedules, those for single individuals and for married couples filing joint returns. Rates for 2012 are shown in Table 2-4.

Personal tax schedules are adjusted each year to compensate for the effects of inflation. That's done by raising the break points between the brackets each year by a factor that reflects a general increase in prices throughout the economy.

---

2. Disclaimer: The examples and illustrations in this text are intended only to give students a broad overview of the workings of the tax system and therefore omit many details contained in the actual U.S. tax code. They do not constitute tax advice, and are not to be considered training for financial advisors or tax professionals. The procedures outlined herein SHOULD NOT BE USED TO CALCULATE REAL TAXES.

TABLE 2-4	2012 Personal Tax Schedules		
Single Individuals		**Married Couples Filing Jointly**	
Income ($)	Rate (%)	Income ($)	Rate (%)
0–8,700	10	0–17,400	10
8,700–35,350	15	17,400–70,700	15
35,350–85,650	25	70,700–142,700	25
85,650–178,650	28	142,700–217,450	28
178,650–388,350	33	217,450–388,350	33
Over 388,350	35	Over 388,350	35

© Cengage Learning 2014

We'll use the 2012 rate schedules in Table 2-4 for illustrative purposes, but you should realize that the schedules for subsequent years will be somewhat different.

Taxable Income   Items of income such as wages, profits, interest, and dividends are either *taxable* or *exempt*. The most significant exempt item is interest on **municipal bonds**. Municipals, or **munis**, are bonds issued by governmental authorities below the federal level. These include states, counties, and cities. Notice that interest on federal bonds is *not* exempt, but is taxable. Exempt income can also be called an exclusion.

> Interest on **municipal bonds** is **exempt** from federal tax.

Personal taxable income is calculated by adding up all of a taxpayer's income, excluding exempt items, and subtracting amounts known as **deductions and exemptions.**

> **Taxable income** is total non-exempt income less **deductions** and **exemptions**.

Deductions[3]   Deductions are personal expenditures that the tax code permits people to subtract from income before calculating their tax. The most significant deductions for most people are interest on a home mortgage, certain taxes paid to state and local authorities (mainly income and real estate), and donations to recognized charities. If a household hasn't spent much money on these things, a *standard deduction* is allowed.

Exemptions   *Personal and dependency exemptions* are fixed amounts that can be deducted for each person in the household to arrive at taxable income. The exemption amount changes each year to account for inflation. In 2012, it was $3,800. Be careful not to confuse personal exemptions with exempt income; they're two different ideas.

Dividend and Capital Gain Calculations   Although dividends and capital gains are part of taxable income, they had to be handled separately in 2012 as they were taxed at different rates than other income. (This is usually the case with capital gains.) The following example (2–4) should make this idea clear.

---

3. Deductions and exemptions are phased out (limited) for high-income taxpayers.

CONCEPT CONNECTION EXAMPLE 2-4

Calculating Personal Taxes

The Harris family had the following income in 2012

Salaries	Joe	$55,000
	Sue	52,000
Interest on savings account		2,000
Interest on IBM bonds		800
Interest on Boston bonds		1,200
Dividends from General Electric		600

During 2012 they sold an investment property for $50,000 that they had purchased three years earlier for $53,000. They also sold some stock for $14,000 for which they had paid $12,000 five years before. They paid $12,000 interest on their home mortgage and $1,800 in real estate taxes. State income tax of $3,500 was withheld from their paychecks during the year. They contributed $1,200 to their church. They have two children living at home. The exemption rate is $3,800 per person. What is their taxable income and their tax liability? Further, what are their marginal and average tax rates?

SOLUTION: First, add up the Harrises' ordinary income, leaving out the interest on Boston bonds, which is exempt, and dividends, which are currently taxed at their own rate.

Salaries	$107,000
Interest	2,800
	$109,800

Next, calculate the net capital gain or loss.

Loss on investment property	$(3,000)
Gain on stock	2,000
Net capital loss	$ (1,000)

The net capital loss is less than $3,000, so it can be entirely used to offset ordinary income. If the Harrises had had a capital gain, it would require a separate calculation.

Ordinary income (excl. divs.)	$109,800
Capital loss	(1,000)
Income	$108,800

Their deductions are as follows.

Mortgage interest	$ 12,000
Taxes	5,300
Charity	1,200
Total deductions	$ 18,500

Because there are four people in the household, the exemption total is

$$\$3,800 \times 4 = \$15,200$$

Now we can determine their taxable income, excluding dividend income.

Income	$ 108,800
Less:	
Deductions	(18,500)
Exemptions	(15,200)
Taxable income (excl. divs.)	$ 75,100

The Harrises' tax liability on this income can be found using the married filing jointly tax table (see Table 2-4). They are in the 25% tax bracket, so we calculate as follows:

10% of the entire first bracket
$$\$17,400 \times .10 = \$ \ \ 1,740$$
15% of the amount in the second bracket
$$(\$70,700 - \$17,400) \times .15 = \$ \ 7,995$$
25% of the amount in the third bracket
$$(\$75,100 - \$70,700) \times .25 = \underline{\$ \ \ 1,100}$$
Tax on ordinary income $\qquad \$ 10,835$
Next, the tax on dividends at 15% is
$$\$600 \times .15 = \underline{\$ \ \ \ \ \ 90}$$
So the Harrises' total tax liability is $\qquad \$ 10,925$

The Harrises' average tax rate is their total tax liability divided by their taxable income which, including dividends, is $75,100 + $600 = $75,700; so their average rate is

$$10,925/75,700 = 14.4\%$$

Their marginal rate is what they'll pay on incremental income. That's the rate in their current bracket, 25%. Notice, however, that there are really two marginal rates, depending on the nature of the incremental income—25% if it comes from salary or interest, and 15% if it comes from capital gains or from dividends.

Tax Rates and Investment Decisions   A problem arises when an investor wants to choose between a corporate bond and a municipal bond. Both have posted interest rates, but the muni is tax exempt while the corporate issue is not. That means the investor gets to keep all of the interest on the muni but has to pay some of the interest on the corporate bond to the government in tax.

If a muni and a corporate bond are paying the same rate and the risks are similar, the muni is clearly the better deal. However, because of their tax advantage, munis usually don't pay as much interest as similar corporate or federal government bonds.

Investors have to compare the rates offered by competing bonds on an equal basis. Because the stated rate on a muni is after tax, while that of a corporate bond is pretax, one or the other must be restated to get both in the same terms. It's usually easier to restate the corporate. To do that, we just multiply by 1 minus the investor's marginal tax rate.

CONCEPT CONNECTION   EXAMPLE 2-5

Comparing Taxable and Tax Exempt Returns

Suppose the Harris family in the preceding example is offered a choice between an IBM bond paying 11% and a Boston bond paying 9%. Which is better?

SOLUTION: The IBM bond pays 11%, but the Harrises only get to keep

$$11\% \times (1 - .25) = 8:25\%$$

That's their after-tax yield on the bond, and it's less than the 9% offered by Boston. Therefore the Boston bond is the better deal.

What if the Harrises' marginal tax rate was only 15%? Then their after-tax rate on the IBM bond would be

$$11\% \times (1 - .15) = 9.35\%$$

which is more attractive than the Boston bond's 9%.

Notice that high-bracket taxpayers tend to be more interested in tax-exempt bonds than are those with lower incomes.

Ensuper/Shutterstock.com

INSIGHTS   Real Applications

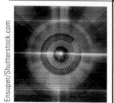

Ensuper/Shutterstock.com

Why Are Municipal Bonds Tax Exempt? Can Investors Expect the Deal to Last?

Tax exempt municipal bonds are a really good deal for both issuers (states, counties and cities) and investors. Indeed, they've been a pillar of the financial/tax system for more than 100 years. Investors benefit from tax free income, which makes *munis* attractive at lower interest rates than those offered by other bonds. That means municipalities can borrow more cheaply than corporations, which is a benefit for local governments and taxpayers. On the other hand, the federal government loses tax revenue from the well-off investors who buy munis.

But why should interest paid by a state, county, or city be tax exempt when interest paid by the federal government on its own bonds is not? Is there something about munis that requires tax exempt status, or is it just a loophole in the tax code? And if the latter, will it survive in the post 2008 crisis environment of recession, out of control federal deficits, and pressure for tax reform?

It turns out the practice is a loophole Congress can easily close. The original policy came from an 1895 Supreme Court decision[1] based on complex constitutional reasoning that prohibited the federal government from taxing certain income from property, in this case bonds. But the constitutional argument only remained valid until 1913 when the 16th Amendment gave the federal government the right to tax any and all income. Since then the Supreme Court has repeatedly affirmed the federal government's right to tax interest from municipal bonds. Nevertheless, interest on most munis has remained tax free.

The issue hasn't been uncontested. There have been about 125 congressional proposals to eliminate the exemption, but none have passed. Several were floating around the capitol in mid-2011.

Most of the suggestions would eliminate the benefit for investors by making muni interest taxable, which implies investors would no longer accept lower rates.

That means issuer's borrowing cost would rise. However, under many proposals, the benefit of low interest borrowing for municipalities would be replaced by a federal subsidy reimbursing up to a third of their interest costs. Bond experts feel there's a good chance one of the current proposals may become law.

Investors, especially smaller ones, are getting worried. Demand for munis has fallen since the financial crisis of 2008,

resulting in a big reduction in new issues and a steady stream of money is being withdrawn from mutual funds that invest in municipal bonds.[2] So it looks like this long time pillar of the financial system may be in danger of collapsing.

---

[1] ***Pollock v. Farmers' Loan & Trust Company***, 157 U.S. 429 (1895).

[2] How Long Will the Tax Break on Municipal Bonds Last?, Jason Zweig, *The Wall Street Journal*, May 7–8, 2011, page B1, B2.

2.5b Corporate Taxes

Corporate taxes are in principle similar to individual taxes. Total income is the business's revenue. Deductions, however, are the charges and expenditures required to run the company. These are essentially the cost and expense items on the income statement. Exemptions don't exist for corporations. The income statement line item earnings before tax (EBT) is a corporation's taxable income. Tax is calculated by taking that figure to the corporate tax table.

Remember from early in this chapter that companies have tax books and financial books that may be somewhat different (page 39). The actual tax liability comes from applying the tax schedule to EBT per the tax books. When we apply the schedule to EBT on the financial books we get a *reported* tax liability. The difference is accounted for through a deferred tax account on the balance sheet. We needn't be too concerned about that difference here, other than to be aware that it often exists. In our examples, we'll assume tax and financial books are the same.

The corporate tax schedule is shown in Table 2-5. Notice that there is something different about the corporate schedule in comparison with the personal schedules. There are obviously eight brackets rather than six, but there's a more significant difference in the pattern of rates. The corporate rates increase to 39% and then decrease back to 34%. Then they rise to 38% before decreasing back to 35%. This pattern seems

TABLE 2-5   Corporate Income Tax Schedule

Income ($)	Rate (%)
0–50,000	15
50,000–75,000	25
75,000–100,000	34
100,000–335,000	39
335,000–10,000,000	34
10,000,000–15,000,000	35
15,000,000–18,333,333	38
Over 18,333,333	35

strange as well as contrary to our notion of a progressive tax system in which higher income means a higher marginal rate.

The ideas behind the system are fairly simple, but implementing them results in the peculiar table. There are basically three goals:

1. A progressive system with income under $10 million taxed at 34% and income over that amount taxed at 35%.

2. Substantially lower rates on incomes up to $75,000.

3. Higher-income taxpayers pay the targeted rates on their *whole* incomes.

The first two goals are easy within a traditional progressive system. It's the third goal that makes things messy.

Recall that in a traditional progressive system, a high-income taxpayer retains the *benefit* of lower tax rates on income in the bottom brackets regardless of how much total income is earned. The corporate system is designed to take away that benefit for wealthy corporate taxpayers so that they pay a constant rate on all of their income.

This is accomplished in two steps. First, the benefit of the 15% and 25% brackets is taken away by putting an additional 5% tax on income between $100,000 and $335,000 to make up for the amount by which the tax rate is below 34% on income up to $75,000. The additional tax is called a *surtax*. (Verify for yourself that the dollar amount of extra tax collected between $100,000 and $335,000 just makes up for the undercollection below $75,000.)

Next, the benefit of a 34% tax on income up to $10 million is taken away with a 3% surtax between $15 million and $18,333,333. Beyond that all income is taxed at a flat 35%.

CONCEPT CONNECTION   EXAMPLE 2-6

Corporate Income Taxes
Calculate the tax liability for corporations with the following EBTs:

a. $280,000
b. $500,000
c. $16,000,000
d. $23,000,000

SOLUTION:

a. Applying the corporate tax table to $280,000 yields the following:

$$\begin{array}{rcl}
\$\ 50,000 \times .15 &=& \$\ \ 7,500 \\
\$\ 25,000 \times .25 &=& 6,250 \\
\$\ 25,000 \times .34 &=& 8,500 \\
\$ 180,000 \times .39 &=& \underline{\$ 70,200} \\
& & \$ 92,450
\end{array}$$

b. Between $335,000 and $10 million the overall tax rate is 34% so the tax on $500,000 is

$$\$500,000 \times .34 = \$170,000$$

c. We don't have to go through the calculations in the bottom brackets because we know that the system recovers those benefits to an overall 34% up to $10 million.

$$\$ 10,000,000 \times .34 = \$ 3,400,000$$
$$\$ 5,000,000 \times .35 = \$ 1,750,000$$
$$\$ 1,000,000 \times .38 = \$ \underline{\quad 380,000}$$
$$\$ 5,530,000$$

d. Over $18,333,333, the tax is a flat 35% of all income starting from nothing, so the tax on $23,000,000 is

$$\$23,000,000 \times .35 = \$8,050,000$$

The corporate tax system favors debt financing.

Taxes and Financing   The U.S. **tax system favors debt financing** of business over equity financing. The reason is that interest payments made to debt investors are tax deductible to the paying company, while dividend payments made to equity investors are not.

To illustrate the point, suppose two companies are identical except that one is financed entirely by debt[4] and one entirely by equity. Assume the payments to the debt and equity investors are the same, say $20, both firms have EBIT of $120, and the tax rate is a uniform 30% (to make the illustration simple).

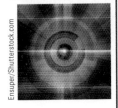

INSIGHTS   Practical Finance

The Other Purpose of the Tax System

The tax system in the United States has two purposes. The first, of course, is to raise money. But the government also uses the system to incentivize what it considers desirable behavior. Sometimes these desirable ends are economic and sometimes they're social. Here are a few examples.

Lower taxes on capital gains and dividends make investment more profitable so people buy more stocks. That makes more funds available for business investment, so companies undertake more new projects. That, in turn, creates jobs and expands the economy.

S-type corporations and LLCs allow small businesses to escape double taxation while enjoying the other benefits of the corporate form. That encourages the formation of new companies, which creates jobs and expands the economy.

Companies get tax credits for employing and training certain types of unskilled, difficult-to-employ people.

Tax Credits are available for money spent on restoring and preserving certain historical buildings.

---

4. In reality, some equity is always required. We're just imagining total debt financing for the sake of the illustration.

To see the point, we have to look beyond net income to the net amount retained by each firm after paying its investors. That is, we have to subtract dividends from net income to arrive at the net addition to retained earnings. The comparison follows.

	Firm Financed by	
	Debt	**Equity**
EBIT	$120	$120
Interest	20	—
EBT	$100	$120
Tax @ 30%	30	36
Net Income	$ 70	$ 84
Dividends	—	20
Net RE addition	$ 70	$ 64

Notice that the firm financed with debt gets to keep $6 more money, about 10% in this case. The difference is in the tax line. The debt-financed firm gets to deduct the payment to its investors before calculating taxes, while the equity financed business has to pay tax on an amount that is not reduced by the dividend payment.

Dividends Paid to Corporations   In Chapter 1, we said that the major financial disadvantage of the corporate form is the double taxation of earnings. Earnings are first taxed as corporate profits and then taxed again as personal income when passed to shareholders in the form of dividends.

But what happens if one corporation owns another that in turn is owned by individuals? Under those conditions, we'd expect *triple taxation.* To see this, consider Figure 2-2 in which corporation B is owned by corporation A, which is owned by individuals.

It's easy to see that a dollar earned by B is taxed as income to B, as dividend income to A, and as dividend income to the shareholders. If B owned corporation C, C's earnings would be subject to quadruple taxation.

The government intends double taxation but not triple taxation and beyond. It therefore gives partial relief by exempting most of the dividends paid by one corporation to another from taxation as income to the receiving company.

Dividends paid **to another corporation** are partially tax exempt.

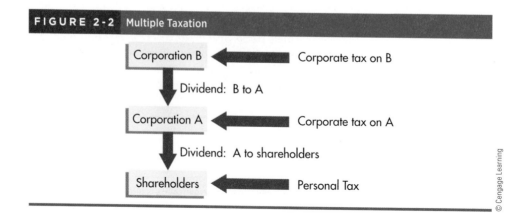

FIGURE 2-2   Multiple Taxation

Corporation B ← Corporate tax on B

Dividend: B to A

Corporation A ← Corporate tax on A

Dividend: A to shareholders

Shareholders ← Personal Tax

The percentage exempted depends on the amount of B's stock owned by A.

Ownership	Exemption
<20%	70%
20%–80%	80%
>80%	100%

In our illustration, this means that if A owns 30% of B and B pays a dividend of $100 to A, A would declare only $20 as income in preparing its taxes. The remaining $80 would be exempt.

Tax Loss Carry Back and Carry Forward
Suppose that over a four-year period a business had three good years and one with a substantial loss. If we consider each year individually, its earnings before tax, tax, and net income might be as shown at the top of Figure 2-3. (We are assuming a flat 30% tax rate to make the illustration simple.)

At first glance, this looks reasonable. The company pays taxes when it has income and no tax when it has a loss. However, the business owner might very well claim that the IRS is putting him or her out of business if the tax system worked like this.

The entrepreneur would point to the total column and claim that over the entire four-year period, the government was trying to make the business pay $90 in tax on $50 of earnings before tax. This would not only be unfair but impossible.

Recognizing this problem, the tax system allows businesses to spread the loss in year 3 among the years before and after. In this case, $100 of the year 3 loss would be carried back into each of years 1 and 2, entirely offsetting income in those years. After the loss year, the company would file amended tax returns for years 1 and 2 and receive refunds of the taxes paid. The remaining $50 of year 3 loss could be carried forward to reduce year 4 EBT. The idea is shown schematically in Figure 2-3.

Losses can be carried back for 2 years and forward for as many as 20 years.

Business **losses** can be **carried backward** or **forward** in time to offset taxes.

FIGURE 2-3 Tax Loss Carry Back and Carry Forward

	Year				
	1	2	3	4	Total
EBT	$100	$100	$(250)	$100	$50
Tax	30	30	—	30	90
Net Inc.	$ 70	$ 70	$(250)	$ 70	$(40)
	$(100)	$(100)		$(50)	
Adjusted EBT	$ 0	$ 0	$ 0	$50	$50
Tax	0	0	0	15	15
Net Inc.	$ 0	$ 0	$ 0	$35	$35

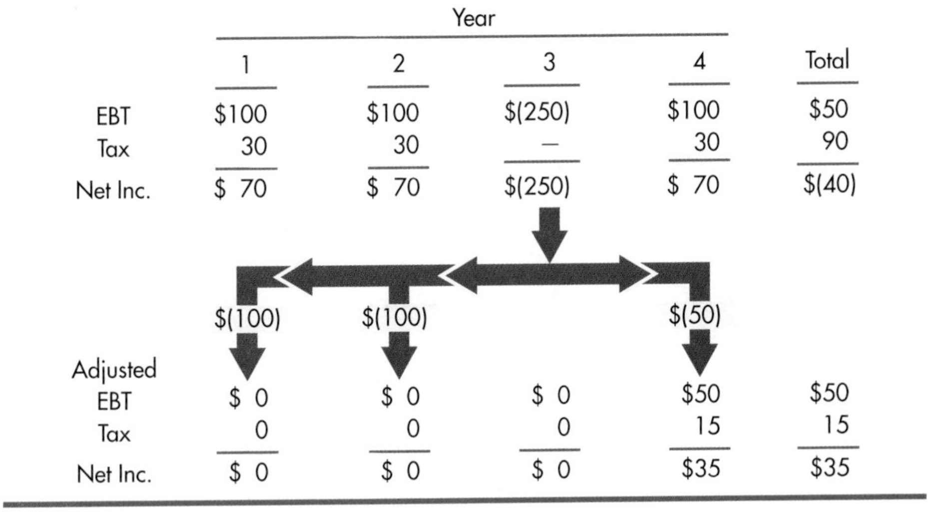

© Cengage Learning 2014

CONCEPT CONNECTIONS

Ensuper/Shutterstock.com

OlegDoroshin/Shutterstock.com

QUESTIONS

1. Why does a financial professional working outside accounting need a knowledge of accounting principles and methods?

2. Discuss the purpose of an accounting system and financial statements in terms of the way the system represents the business.

3. Why is EBIT an important line item in the income statement? What does EBIT show us?

4. What is meant by liquidity in financial statements?

5. What are the common misstatements of balance sheet figures, and why do they present a problem?

6. Do the definitions of current assets and current liabilities suggest a quick way of looking at the firm's ability to meet its financial obligations (pay its bills) over the near term? (*Hint:* Think in terms of ratios.)

7. How are capital and working capital different?

8. What is leverage, and how does it work? What is the main concern about using it?

9. Define the term tax base and discuss common bases. What government units tax on each? What are these taxes commonly called?

10. What is the total effective tax rate?

11. What is taxable income for an individual? How does it differ from taxable income for a corporation?

12. What tax rate is important for investment decisions? Why?

13. Why is the tax treatment of capital gains an important financial issue?

14. Is the corporate tax schedule progressive? Why or why not?

15. What are the tax implications of financing with debt versus equity? If financing with debt is better, why doesn't everyone finance almost entirely with debt?

16. Why are dividends paid from one corporation to another partially tax exempt?

17. Explain the reasoning behind tax loss carry backs and carry forwards.

PROBLEMS

Writing Off a Large Uncollectable Receivable: Concept Connection Example 2-1 (page 34)

1. Canaday Ltd. has the following receivables balances ($M):

Gross accounts receivable	$175
Bad-debt reserve	(3)
Net accounts receivable	$172

Two years ago a customer was approved for an unusually large credit sale of $7M over the objections of the credit and collections department. Shortly after the sale, the customer's business began to deteriorate due to an unexpected recession. To date it has paid only $2M against the order despite the fact that it has consumed all of the material purchased. The collections department has worked diligently to collect the remaining $5M without success. The customer filed for bankruptcy this morning with essentially no assets to pay a large number of creditors. Evaluate the financial statement impact of the bankruptcy on Canaday. Assume Canaday's product cost is 40% of revenue and the bad-debt reserve of $3M will be fully reestablished.

Selling a Fixed Asset: Concept Connection Example 2-2 (page 38)

2. The Johnson Company bought a truck costing $24,000 two and a half years ago. The truck's estimated life was four years at the time of purchase. It was accounted for by using straight line depreciation with zero salvage value. The truck was sold yesterday for $19,000. What taxable gain must be reported on the sale of the truck?

3. If the Johnson Company of Problem 2 is subject to a marginal tax rate of 34%, what is the cash flow associated with the sale of the used truck?

4. Heald and Swenson Inc. purchased a drill press for $850,000 one year and nine months ago. The asset has a six-year life and has been depreciated according to the following accelerated schedule.

Year	Percent of Cost
1	55%
2	20%
3	10%
4	5%
5	5%
6	5%

The press was just sold for $475,000. The firm's marginal tax rate is 35%. Calculate Heald and Swenson's taxable profit and cash flow on the sale. Assume depreciation is spread evenly within each year.

Problems 5 through 13 are numerical exercises intended to develop familiarity with financial statements without actually going through debit and credit accounting entries. They don't follow specific examples in the text, but most provide guidance in the form of hints or instructions.

5. Fred Gowen opened Gowen Retail Sales as a sole proprietorship and recorded the following transactions during his first month in business:
   (1) Purchased $50,000 of fixed assets, putting 10% down and borrowing the remainder.
   (2) Sold 1,000 units of product at an average price of $45 each. Half of the sales were on credit, none of which had been collected as of the end of the month.
   (3) Recorded cost of goods sold of $21,000 related to the above sales.
   (4) Purchased $30,000 worth of inventory and paid cash.
   (5) Incurred other expenses (including the interest from the loan) of $5,000, all of which were paid in cash.
   (6) Fred's tax rate is 40%. (Taxes will be paid in a subsequent period.)
       a. What will the business report as net income for its first month of business? (*Hint:* Write out an income statement and enter revenue, cost, and expense. Then calculate tax and net income.)
       b. List the flows of cash in and out of the business during the month. Show inflows as positives and outflows as negatives (using parentheses). Sum to arrive at a "Net Cash Flow" figure.
       c. Should Fred pay more attention to net income or cash flow? Why?

6. McFadden Corp. reports the following balances on its December 31, 20X2, balance sheet:

	Amounts in Thousands	
Accounts payable	$ 60	
Accounts receivable	120	
Accumulated depreciation	350	
Fixed assets (net)	900	
Inventory	150	
Long-term debt	400	
Paid in excess	160	
Retained earnings	380	
Total assets	1,240	
Total liabilities	500	(long-term debt + current liabilities)

All of the remaining accounts are listed below. Calculate the balance in each.

Accruals	Total current assets
Cash	Total current liabilities
Common stock	Total equity
Fixed assets (gross)	

7. Consider the current asset accounts (Cash, Accounts Receivable, and Inventory) individually and as a group. What impact will the following transactions have on each account and current assets in total (Increase, Decrease, No Change)? (*Hint:* Each transaction has two sides that are equal in amount but opposite in sign. Consider whether the sides offset within current assets or if one side is recorded somewhere else.)

   a. The purchase of a fixed asset for cash
   b. The purchase of a fixed asset on credit
   c. The purchase of inventory for cash
   d. The purchase of inventory on credit
   e. Customer payment of an account receivable
   f. Writing off a customer's bad debt (assume the allowance process is in place)
   g. The sale of a fixed asset for cash
   h. The sale of inventory (at a profit) for cash
   i. The sale of inventory (at a loss) for cash
   j. The sale of inventory (at a profit) on credit

8. On January 1, 20X2, Miller Corp. purchased a milling machine for $400,000. It will be depreciated on a straight line basis over 20 years. On January 1, 20X3, Miller purchased a heavy-duty lathe for $250,000, which will be depreciated on a straight line basis over 40 years.

   a. Compute Miller's depreciation expense for 20X2, 20X3, and 20X4.
   b. Prepare the Fixed Asset portion of the balance sheet (for these two fixed assets) as of the end of 20X2, 20X3, and 20X4. (*Hint:* Subtract *accumulated* depreciation in each year from total original cost. See p. 37.)

9. Becher Industries has three suppliers for its raw materials for manufacturing. The firm purchases $180 million per year from Johnson Corp. and normally takes 30 days to pay these bills. Becher also purchases $150 million per year from Jensen, Inc., and normally pays Jensen in 45 days. Becher's third supplier, Docking Distributors, offers 2/10, n.30 terms. Becher takes advantage of the discount on the $90 million per year that it typically purchases from Docking. Calculate Becher's expected accounts payable balance. (Use a 360-day year for your calculations; for example, calculate Johnson's accounts as $180 million × 30/360.)

10. Belvedere Inc. has an annual payroll of $52 million. The firm pays employees every two weeks on Friday afternoon. Last month, the books were closed on the Tuesday after payday. How much is the payroll accrual at the end of the month? (See page 40.)

11. Sanderson Metals Inc. accrues four liability items: payroll, employee vacation that has been earned but not used, property taxes, and inventory that arrives at its factory dock before an invoice is received from the vendor.

    Payroll: Sanderson pays its employees every other Friday for work performed through that day. The annual payroll is $47 million.

    Property tax: the firm pays the local government $3.6 million per year in property taxes on its factory and office buildings. The tax is paid in arrears* on June 30 at the end of the county's fiscal year.** The firm accrues a liability each month to reflect the fact that it owes the county property tax through that date.

    Vacation: Sanderson's employees get three weeks (15 work days) of vacation each year, which is earned at a rate of (15 ÷ 12 =) 1.25 days per month worked. No vacation can be carried over year end, but an employee can take the current year's vacation before it is actually earned. There are 250 work days each year. The vacation accrual reflects that pay for vacation days earned but not used is a liability of the company.

    Inventory: The accounting department uses vendor (supplier) invoices combined with receiving documents to enter new inventory on the company's books. However, inventory often arrives a few days before the associated invoice is received. The approximate value of material in this received but unbilled status is accrued to reflect that the company is in possession of the goods and has a liability to pay for them.

    Sanderson is currently closing the books on April 20X8. The last day of the month was seven days after a payday. Through the end of April, employees had taken $587,000 of paid vacation time. Five railroad carloads of steel arrived in the last week of April, but invoices for only three of those shipments have been received. An average carload shipment costs $107,000. All prior receipts have been invoiced.

    Calculate Sanderson's April month end accruals balance. (*Hint:* Some accruals, like payroll and inventory, clear a few days after month end. Others, like property tax, build up steadily until cleared at the end of a period like the county's fiscal year. Still others, like vacation, are increased steadily and are decreased when some activity occurs, such as people going on vacation.)

12. In January 20X3, Elliott Industries recorded the following transactions:
    (1) Paid bills from 20X2 totaling $120,000 and collected $150,000 for sales that were made in 20X2.
    (2) Purchased inventory on credit totaling $500,000, 30% of which remained unpaid at the end of January.
    (3) Sold $400,000 of inventory on credit for $600,000, 20% of which remained uncollected at the end of the month.
    (4) Accruals increased by $10,000 during the month.
    (5) Made additional cash payments for expenses incurred during the month totaling $80,000.

    Compute the change in Elliott's working capital for the month of January 20X3. (*Hint:* Each transaction has offsetting entries that sum to zero. If all of the entries are to current accounts, there's no impact on working capital. But if one side is somewhere else, working capital will change.)

---

* A property tax bill paid in arrears is due at the end of the period during which the liability is incurred. The liability for the bill, however, comes from owning the property as time passes. Hence, as each month of the tax year goes by, the company's property tax liability increases by 1/12 of the annual bill until it is paid at the end of the fiscal year.

** A fiscal year is an organization's year for accounting purposes. Many companies and most government units use fiscal years that don't coincide with calendar years. Sanderson's books are kept on a calendar year.

13. The Glavits Company opened for business on Monday, June 1, with inventory of $5,000 and cash in the bank of $7,000. These were its only assets. All start-up financing was provided from the owner's personal funds, and there were no other liabilities. The firm has a line of credit at the bank that enables it to borrow up to $20,000 by writing overdraft checks on its account.

Glavits's terms of sale are net 30, but the new firm must pay its suppliers in 10 days. Employees are the company's only expense. They're paid a total of $1,000 per week each Friday afternoon for the week just ending.

On June 3, the company made a sale of $9,000 out of inventory with a cost of $3,000. On June 10, it received $2,000 of new inventory. There were no other sales or inventory receipts. The company bought a delivery truck, paying with a $6,000 check on June 30. The books were closed for the month on Tuesday, June 30.

Construct Glavits's income statement and balance sheet for June using the worksheet shown. Ignore taxes for this problem. First, enter the beginning balance sheet. Next, enter one number two times in each column to reflect the transaction indicated at the top of the column. Note that sometimes the numbers will be additions and sometimes they will be subtractions. Finally, add across the page to get the statements for June.

Worksheet Rows	Worksheet Columns
1. BALANCE SHEET	1. Opening balance sheet
2. Assets	2. Record sales
3. Cash	3. Record cost of sale
4. Accounts receivable	4. Receive inventory
5. Inventory	5. Pay for inventory
6. Fixed assets (net)	6. Buy truck
7. Total assets	7. Pay employees—first 4 weeks
8. (skip)	8. Pay employees—last 2 days
9. Liabilities	9. Reclassify cash overdraft as loan
10. Accounts payable	10. Record net income as income
11. Accruals	and equity
12. Debt	11. (skip)
13. Equity	12. June statements
14. Total liabilities & equity	
15. (skip)	
16. INCOME STATEMENT	
17. Sales	
18. Cost	
19. Expense	
20. Net income	

Leverage: Concept Connection Example 2-3 (page 41)

14. Jacob Cornwall has a business in which he's invested $250,000 of his own money, which is the firm's only capital. (There are no other equity investors and no debt.) In a recent year, the firm had net income of $20,000 for a return on equity of 8% ($20,000/$250,000). What will the firm's return on equity be next year if net income from business operations remains the same but it borrows $150,000 returning the same amount to Jake from the equity account if:

a. The after tax interest rate is 6%.

b. The after tax interest rate is 10%.

c. Comment on the difference between the results of a and b.

15. Gatwick Ltd. has after-tax profits (net income) of $500,000 and no debt. The owners have a $6 million equity investment in the business. If they borrow $2 million at 10% and use it to retire stock, how will the return on their investment (equity) change if earnings before interest and taxes remain the same? Assume a flat 40% tax rate and that the loan reduces equity dollar for dollar. (A business owner's return on investment or equity is ROI = ROE = Net income/Equity.)

Equity Accounts

See the illustration of the equity accounts on page 43 for problems 16, 17, 18.

16. During the past year, Alpha Co had net income of $150, paid $20 in dividends, and sold new stock for $40. Beginning equity for the year was $700. Calculate ending equity.

17. Mints Entertainment, Inc. had net income of $170,000 and paid dividends of $0.25 per share on its 100,000 shares of outstanding stock in this year. At the end of the year its balance sheet showed retained earnings of $250,000. What was Mints' retained earnings balance at the end of last year?

18. Preston Road Inc. was organized last year when its founders contributed $9 million and issued 3 million shares of $1.25 par value stock. The company earned $750,000 in its first year and paid dividends of $325,000. Construct the equity section of Preston Road's balance sheet as of the end of that year.

19. The Digital Systems Company was organized two years ago to take advantage of an Internet opportunity. Investors paid $12 a share for 2 million shares with a $4 par value. In the next two years, the company had earnings of $2 million and $3 million, respectively. It paid dividends of $1.2 million and $1.3 million, respectively, in those years. At the end of the first year, Digital sold another 500,000 shares of stock at $14 per share. Construct the equity section of Digital's balance sheet initially and at the end of its first and second years in business.

Taxes

20. The Coolidge family had taxable income of $165,000 in 2012. They live in a state in which income over $100,000 is taxed at 11%. What was their total effective (marginal) tax rate? (*Hint:* Use Equation 2.1 on page 45 and Table 2-4 on page 49.)

21. Use the following tax brackets for taxable income:

Bracket	Tax Rate
$0–$10,000	15%
$10,000–$50,000	25%
$50,000–$250,000	30%
Over $250,000	35%

Compute the average tax rate for the following taxable income amounts (see page 46).

a. $20,000

b. $125,000

c. $350,000

d. $1,000,000

22. Joan Petros reported taxable income in 20X2 of $150,000, which included the following transactions:

(1) In June 20X2, Joan sold 100 shares of stock for $40 per share. She had purchased them three months earlier for $35 per share.

(2) In October 20X2, Joan sold 200 shares of stock for $79 per share. She had purchased them three years earlier for $61 per share.

If long-term capital gains are taxed at 15% and *all* ordinary income is taxed at 25%, what is Joan's tax liability for 20X2?

Calculating Personal Taxes: Concept Connection Example 2-4 (page 50)

23. The Lindscomb family had the following income in 2012:

Salaries	Mark	$63,500
	Ashley	57,900

Interest on investments

IBM bonds	$4,750
New York City bond	1,400
Savings account	2,600

The family made home mortgage payments that included interest of $16,480, and paid real estate (property) tax of $4,320 on their home. They also paid state income tax of $5,860 and donated $1,250 to well- known charities. The Lindscombs have three dependent children.

a. Calculate the family's federally taxable income.

b. What is their tax liability assuming they file jointly as a married couple?

c. What are their average and marginal tax rates?

24. The Benjamin family had wage earnings of $185,000 in 2012. They received interest of $4,500 on corporate bonds and $1,500 on bonds issued by the state. Their dividend income was $500, and they had a $1,000 long-term capital gain on the sale of securities.

  They paid real estate taxes of $1,450 and state income tax of $3,000, and they donated $550 to their church. They paid interest of $8,000 on their home mortgage. They have one dependent child. What was their tax liability for 2012?

25. Joan and Harry Leahy both had income in 2012. Harry made $72,500 in wages. Joan has an incorporated small business that paid her a salary of $50,000. In addition, the business had profits of $15,000, which were paid to the Leahys as dividends. They received $5,600 in interest on savings and $350 in interest on a loan made to Harry's brother, Lou. Lou also repaid $2,000 of principal on that loan during the year. The couple had interest income from two bonds, $2,200 on a 20-year IBM issue and $2,700 on a state of Michigan revenue bond.

  They sold some Biotech stock for $14,000 that had been purchased five years before for $4,000. Two years ago, they invested $50,000 in some rural land on the advice of a real estate agent. They sold the property in 2012 for $46,000.

  The Leahys paid $12,500 in mortgage payments of which $9,000 was interest and the rest reduced principal. They paid real estate taxes of $2,750 and state income tax of $6,800 during the year. They contributed $1,500 to their church and $3,000 to the support of Joan's elderly mother. They have two young children. (Joan's mother is not a dependent.)

a. Calculate the Leahy's taxable income.

b. What is their tax liability for 2012?

c. What is their average tax rate?

d. What is their marginal tax rate? Can there be more than one marginal rate? Explain.

Comparing Taxable and Tax-Exempt Returns: Concept Connection Example 2-5 (page 52)

26. Harry Swartz wants to invest in a bond and has narrowed his choices down to two issues. The first is offered by Microsoft Corp. and pays an interest rate of 8%. The second option is offered by the city of Springfield, Massachusetts, and offers a return of 6%. Harry feels that the risk levels inherent in the two bonds are similar. They both mature in 10 years. Harry is single, has taxable income of $125,000 in 2012 and lives in a state that has no personal income tax. Which bond should Harry choose?

27. Dick Dowen is considering three investment opportunities:
    (1) A 4.5% city of Chicago bond that is tax exempt at both state and federal levels.
    (2) A 4.75% state of Illinois bond that is tax exempt at the federal level but taxable at the state level.
    (3) A 6.7% McDonald's corporate bond that is taxable at both the state and federal levels.
        (*Hint:* Use the TETR.)

    If the Illinois state tax rate is 6% and Dick's marginal federal tax rate is 30%, which investment yields the highest after-tax return?

Corporate Income Taxes: Concept Connection Example 2-6 (page 54)

28. Calculate the corporate tax on earnings before tax (EBT) of the following amounts:
    a. $37,000
    b. $57,000
    c. $88,500
    d. $110,000
    e. $5,375,000
    f. $14,000,000
    g. $17,350,000
    h. $23,500,000

29. Ed Fletcher is planning to start a business in corporate form that requires an investment of $500,000. He has that much money, but he can also borrow virtually the whole amount from a rich relative. (This is very unusual.) Ed feels that after the business is started, it will be important to retain as much money in the company as possible to fund growth. Nevertheless, he plans to pay the investor, either himself or his relative, a $50,000 return (10% of the amount invested) each year. That's about as much as could be earned elsewhere. Considering cash retention only, should Ed borrow or invest his own money? That is, which option will result in keeping more money in the company available to grow the business? How much more? The company's total effective tax rate will be 40% (*Hint:* See Taxes and Financing, page 55).

30. Microchip Inc. had the following profits and losses in the years indicated.

2010	$5,000,000
2011	350,000
2012	(3,450,000)

    How much federal tax will it eventually pay for 2010? The corporate tax schedule on page 53 is the same for all three years. (*Hint:* See tax loss carry back and carry forward, page 57.)

31. Inky Inc. reported the following financial information in 2012.

Operating income (EBIT)	$650,000
Interest	$430,000
Dividends from Printers Inc. not included in operating income (Inky owns 3% of Printers)	$ 20,000
Dividends paid to Inky's stockholders	$ 50,000

    a. What is Inky's tax liability? (Use the corporate tax schedule on page 53.) (*Hint:* See dividends paid to corporations, page 56.)
    b. What is Inky's marginal tax rate?
    c. What is Inky's average tax rate?
    d. Explain why only one of the rates in b and c is relevant for financial decisions.

32. The Snyder Corporation had the following income and expense items.

Sales	$180,870,000
Cost	110,450,000
Expenses	65,560,000

In addition, it received both interest and dividends from the Bevins Corp., of which it owns 30%. The interest received from Bevins was $2,430,000, and the dividends were $4,700,000.

Calculate Snyder's tax liability. (*Hint:* See dividends paid to corporations, page 56.)

COMPUTER PROBLEMS

33. Rachel and Harry are planning to get married. Both have successful careers and expect to earn the following this year.

	Rachel	Harry
Salary	$155,380	$146,200
Interest income (taxable)	6,750	45,325
Long-term capital gain/(loss)	5,798	—
Total income	$ 167,928	$ 191,525
Itemized deductions	$ 28,763	$ 15,271

a. Use the PERSTAX program to calculate their total tax bill as single individuals and determine whether getting married will cost or save them money and how much. Assume that getting married during a year subjects the entire year's income to the married filing jointly rate schedule. Assume there are no state taxes.

b. Duncan and Angela are also considering getting married but have considerably lower incomes as follows.

	Duncan	Angela
Salary	$56,450	$37,829
Itemized deductions	6,048	3,224

What will it cost or save them to get married?

34. You've been hired by the nation of Utopia to computerize its approach to calculating taxes. Utopia's progressive tax system contains only two brackets that are applicable to all households. These are as follows.

Income	Rate
Under $30,000	20%
Over $30,000	30%

The treatment of personal exemptions and itemized deductions is similar to the U.S. system, but the exemption amount is permanently fixed at $2,550 per person. No special consideration is given to capital gains and losses or dividends.

Write a spreadsheet program to compute taxes for a typical Utopian household. Test your program with the following cases.

Income	$28,950	$96,250
Number of people	1	5
Deductions	$ 2,800	$ 14,457

Verify that your program works by calculating the Utopian taxes manually. (*Hint:* Use a single conditional instruction [IF statement] to identify which bracket the taxpayer is in *and* make the tax calculation.)

CHAPTER 3

Cash Flows and Financial Analysis

In Chapter 1 we made the point that the orientation of finance is toward cash flows rather than accounting results. Because of the importance of cash flow, we need to understand the concept thoroughly and be familiar with the construction of the statement of cash flows as one of a firm's financial statements. We'll develop that understanding in the first half of this chapter.

Then we'll turn our attention to financial analysis, a technique designed to get practical information about business operations out of financial statements. Before attacking either of these topics, however, we need a little background on financial information in general.

3.1 Financial Information—Where Does It Come From, Who Uses It, and What Are We Looking For?

The term "financial information" refers to the results of business operations stated in money terms. The idea largely implies the material in financial statements but isn't entirely limited to those documents. Financial information about a company is important because people inside and outside use it as a basis for making decisions about the firm and their relationships with it.

Financial information is the responsibility of management. It is created by accountants within the company and reviewed by auditors, but neither accountants nor auditors guarantee its correctness.[1] This creates a conflict of interest, because managements invariably want to portray results as favorably as possible. We'll discuss this idea shortly.

Once prepared, financial information is published to a variety of audiences, who use it to make decisions about the company. Let's begin our study by looking at these users in a little more detail.

3.1a   Users of Financial Information

Financial statements are a report on the issuing company's performance. The main user groups are investors, creditors, and management itself.

Investors and Financial Analysts   The most important function of financial statements is to convey information to outside investors. These are people or organizations that might be interested in buying the company's stock or might be asked to lend it money. Lenders are concerned with the firm's stability and cash flows. The primary focus of stockholders is more likely to be its prospects for growth.

Investors sometimes analyze financial statements themselves, but more often rely on the reports of **financial analysts** who usually work for large brokerage firms or other financial institutions. Their job is to know as much about a particular company and its industry as an outsider can and to use that knowledge to predict the firm's performance. They then make recommendations about its investment value, including whether to buy or sell its stock and whether its debt is safe. Because of their pivotal advisory role, financial analysts can be considered the main audience for investor-oriented information.

A major part of the analyst's job is a careful study of the company's recent financial statements. It's important to realize that published financial statements relate to the past, and the analyst is interested in the future. However, the past factored by current information is usually the best available indicator of the future. In this chapter, we'll have a look at the basic tools used by financial analysts and sophisticated investors.

Vendors/Creditors   Vendors asked to do business with the firm on credit are another important group of statement users. Because they're advancing funds in the form of products and services, they tend to be interested in most of the same things that

> **Financial analysts**
> interpret information about companies and make recommendations to investors.

---

1. Auditors make certain observations and tests which provide a *reasonable level of assurance* that statements are prepared in the proper manner and that all relevant details are disclosed.

concern lenders. The main issue is whether the firm is likely to have cash available to pay its debts in the immediate future.

Management   The final group of statement users is the firm's own management. Financial results show successes and failures in each of the many facets of running a business. Management can study those results to pinpoint relative strengths and weaknesses in operations. This process shows where to put effort to correct problems and improve performance.

3.1b   Sources of Financial Information

The primary source of financial information about any publicly traded company is its own **annual report**. Annual reports are required of companies that sell their stock to the general public, and typically include several years of historical financial information along with a great deal of verbiage about the firm and its business.

The financial information in an annual report must be audited by an independent accounting firm. That process doesn't guarantee complete accuracy, but it usually gives a fair level of assurance that the numbers are presented with reasonable objectivity and in accordance with **generally accepted accounting principles (GAAP)**. However, there's a lot more latitude in the nature of the information presented in the verbiage.

In fact, there's something of a problem with annual reports. They tend to portray past performance and future prospects in a very favorable light. That is, they're biased toward reporting that the firm has done as well as could be expected in the past year and that it will do even better in the future. Reports tend to minimize or ignore mistakes and failures, exaggerate successes, and build up future opportunities in unrealistically optimistic terms.

The annual report is actually a report to stockholders prepared by the company's management. But management works for the stockholders, so they are in effect writing their own report cards. Naturally the result is biased in favor of the people running the firm.

Along these lines, most annual reports have become advertising vehicles and are prepared to be very visually appealing. They're done on glossy paper, in multicolored inks, and are filled with professional quality photographs. They frequently look more like upscale magazines than business documents.

All this isn't necessarily bad as long as readers understand the biases and don't take everything in reports as strictly true. Outright lies are rare, but the truth can be told more or less attractively, and annual reports tend to present things in a rosy glow.

Companies file a more businesslike document called the 10-K with the Securities and Exchange Commission each year. It gives more detailed information than the annual report. Most companies will send you an annual report and a 10-K for the asking.

Brokerage firms and investment advisory services provide reports on most large companies. These reports are the result of the work of their financial analysts. Brokerage firms provide the information free as a service to clients and prospective clients, while investment advisory services publish it for a fee. The best known advisory service is Value Line which provides information on approximately 1,700 stocks. Advisory services provide information to paid subscribers, but it is often available free in libraries.

A firm's **annual report** is the **primary source** of financial information about it.

Value Line's August 2011 report on Microsoft is shown in Figure 3-1. Study the layout of the information it contains for a few minutes. The chart at the top shows the stock's price performance for the last 12 years. Below that 10 to 15 years of history are shown for a variety of financial line items. Notice that some items are stated on a per-share basis.

Moving down the page, there's a short summary of the nature of the company's business followed by a verbal analysis of its current situation and prospects for the future. This section is the heart of the report. It tells investors what the analyst thinks is likely to happen to Microsoft's business and by implication the price of its stock.

At the time this report was written the nation was struggling through the lingering effects of a recession following the financial crisis of 2008. Although the recession was officially over in June 2009, unemployment remained high and business was depressed. Nevertheless, the analyst gives Microsoft a mildly upbeat review. He opens with the statement that the firm should continue to perform well in the coming year and describes two healthy business areas. Two less successful areas are mentioned dismissively, even though one is operating at a loss. The report continues by naming two developing products, but concludes that they will face tough competition. The commentary ends by making some positive comments about cash flow, but then admits that the weak spots mentioned earlier could be challenging. In closing, the analyst recommends the stock to investors with an intermediate time horizon. That generally means those willing to hold the stock for five or more years.

It's worth noting that analysts generally try to tell mediocre or even bad news attractively.

The issues addressed in this descriptive section aren't always purely financial. They can be about any area of business that's crucial, such as markets, products, competition, or mergers. In other words, a lot of "financial information" isn't exactly financial. It might be better described as marketing or strategic information. Keep in mind that financial results are numerical representations of what is physically going on in a business. Thus, deciding whether a firm is a good financial investment begins with a judgment about how it's doing in the market for its products. Notice that Value Line ends the discussion by saying that it has a positive opinion of the stock's investment potential if it's held for an intermediate period.

3.1c   The Orientation of Financial Analysis

Much of the information in the rest of this chapter may seem similar to material you've studied in accounting. However, our orientation is different here. In accounting we're concerned with creating financial statements. In finance we're concerned with using them to evaluate businesses and their prospects for the future. *In particular, financial analysis looks for problems, places where things may not be as they seem, or where results indicate the firm may be heading for trouble.*

from the
CFO

For example, a statement of cash flows might indicate that a firm borrowed a lot of money last year. Accounting per se stops with the presentation of that fact along with information on the things money was spent on during the period. The financial analyst, however, must go further and ask why the borrowing occurred and what it implies for the future.

FIGURE 3-1   Value Line's August 2011 Report on Microsoft

MICROSOFT NDQ-MSFT | RECENT PRICE **25.58** | P/E RATIO **9.1** (Trailing: 9.5 Median: 20.0) | RELATIVE P/E RATIO **0.66** | DIV'D YLD **2.5%** | VALUE LINE **2585**

	High	Low
	58.6 / 20.1	38.1 / 21.4	35.3 / 20.7	30.0 / 22.5	30.2 / 24.0	28.3 / 23.8	30.3 / 21.5	37.5 / 26.6	36.0 / 17.5	31.5 / 14.9	31.6 / 22.7	29.5 / 23.7

TIMELINESS **1** Raised 7/15/11
SAFETY **1** Raised 5/26/06
TECHNICAL **3** Lowered 7/29/11
BETA .80 (1.00 = Market)

LEGENDS
— 11.0 x "Cash Flow" p sh
.... Relative Price Strength
2-for-1 split 2/98
2-for-1 split 3/99
2-for-1 split 2/03
Options: Yes
Shaded areas indicate recessions

2014-16 PROJECTIONS
	Price	Gain	Ann'l Total Return
High	55	(+115%)	23%
Low	45	(+75%)	17%

Target Price Range 2014 2015 2016

Insider Decisions
	S	O	N	D	J	F	M	A	M
to Buy	0	0	0	0	0	0	0	0	0
Options	0	0	1	5	2	2	0	0	2
to Sell	3	0	6	5	2	5	0	0	3

Institutional Decisions
	3Q2010	4Q2010	1Q2011
to Buy	808	841	889
to Sell	801	858	810
Hld's(000)	5225168	4938020	5275039

| Percent shares traded | 21 / 14 / 7 |

% TOT. RETURN 7/11
	THIS STOCK	VL ARITH.* INDEX
1 yr.	8.7	21.2
3 yr.	13.9	42.7
5 yr.	25.7	48.6

1995	1996	1997	1998	1999	2000	2001	2002	2003	2004	2005	2006	2007	2008	2009	2010	2011	2012		© VALUE LINE PUB. LLC	14-16
.63	.92	1.18	1.47	1.93	2.25	2.39	2.65	3.00	3.39	3.72	4.40	5.45	6.60	6.56	7.21	8.35	9.30	Revenues per sh A	12.75
.18	.28	.41	.59	.84	.99	1.09	1.07	1.12	1.15	1.27	1.34	1.65	2.16	1.92	2.47	3.09	3.25	"Cash Flow" per sh	4.25
.15	.21	.33	.45	.70	.85	.90	.94	.97	1.04	1.16	1.20	1.42	1.87	1.62	2.10	2.69	2.80	Earnings per sh B	3.75
--	--	--	--	--	--	--	--	.08	.16	.32	.34	.40	.44	.52	.52	.64	.76	Div'ds Decl'd per sh E■	1.24
--	--	--	--	--	--	--	--	--	--	--	.16	.24	.35	.23	.28	.28	.30	Cap'l Spending per sh	.35
.05	.05	.05	.07	.06	.09	.10	.07	.08	.10	.08	.16	.24	.35	.23	.28	.28	.30		.35
.57	.73	1.02	1.58	2.69	4.05	4.48	4.87	5.69	6.89	4.49	3.99	3.32	3.97	4.44	5.33	6.82	7.90	Book Value per sh D	11.50
9408.0	9408.0	9632.0	9880.0	10218	10218	10566	10718	10718	10862	10710	10062	9380.0	9151.0	8908.0	8668.0	8376.0	8000	Common Shs Outst'g C	7000
28.2	29.1	33.0	42.8	49.8	NMF	35.3	32.4	26.1	25.8	22.9	21.7	19.9	16.3	13.4	13.1	9.6		Avg Ann'l P/E Ratio	13.0
1.89	1.82	1.90	2.23	2.84	NMF	1.81	1.77	1.49	1.36	1.22	1.17	1.06	.98	.89	.83	.59		Relative P/E Ratio	.85
--	--	--	--	--	--	--	--	.3%	.6%	1.2%	1.3%	1.4%	1.4%	2.4%	1.9%	2.5%		Avg Ann'l Div'd Yield	2.5%

CAPITAL STRUCTURE as of 6/30/11
Total Debt $11921 mill. Due in 5 Yrs $6750 mill.
LT Debt $11921 mill. LT Interest $345 mill.
(17% of Cap'l)
Leases, Uncapitalized $481.0 mill. (6/30/2011)

No defined benefit pension plan
Pfd Stock None

Common Stock 8,376,000,000 shs.

MARKET CAP: $214 billion (Large Cap)

	25296	28365	32187	36835	39788	44282	51122	60420	58437	62484	69943	74500	Revenues ($mill) A	90000
	52.4%	45.8%	48.0%	40.6%	44.0%	39.2%	39.1%	40.6%	39.2%	42.9%	42.8%	44.0%	Operating Margin	42.5%
	1536.0	1084.0	1439.0	1186.0	855.0	903.0	1440.0	2056.0	2562.0	2673.0	2766	2900	Depreciation ($mill)	3200
	10003	10384	10526	11330	12715	12599	14065	17681	14569	18760	23150	23150	Net Profit ($mill)	27250
	33.5%	32.0%	32.2%	33.1%	32.0%	31.0%	30.0%	25.8%	26.5%	25.0%	17.5%	24.0%	Income Tax Rate	24.0%
	39.5%	36.6%	32.7%	30.8%	32.0%	28.5%	27.5%	29.3%	24.9%	30.0%	33.1%	31.1%	Net Profit Margin	30.3%
	28505	35832	44999	55597	31860	26568	16414	13356	22246	29529	46144	45000	Working Cap'l ($mill)	50000
	--	--	--	--	--	--	--	--	3746.0	4939.0	11921	12000	Long-Term Debt ($mill)	12000
	47289	52180	61020	74825	48115	40104	31097	36286	39558	46175	57083	63325	Shr. Equity ($mill) D	80500
	21.2%	19.9%	17.3%	15.1%	26.4%	31.4%	45.2%	48.7%	33.6%	36.8%	33.8%	31.0%	Return on Total Cap'l	29.5%
	21.2%	19.9%	17.3%	15.1%	26.4%	31.4%	45.2%	48.7%	36.8%	40.6%	40.6%	36.5%	Return on Shr. Equity	34.0%
	21.2%	19.9%	15.8%	12.8%	19.2%	22.6%	33.0%	37.7%	25.5%	30.7%	31.5%	26.5%	Retained to Com Eq	22.5%
	--	--	8%	15%	27%	28%	27%	23%	31%	24%	22%	27%	All Div'ds to Net Prof	33%

CURRENT POSITION ($MILL.)
	2009	2010	6/30/11
Cash Assets	31447	36788	52772
Receivables	11192	13014	14987
Inventory (Avg Cst)	717	740	1372
Other	5924	5134	5787
Current Assets	49280	55676	74918
Accts Payable	3324	4025	4197
Debt Due	2000	1000	--
Unearned Revenue	13003	13652	15722
Other	8707	7470	8855
Current Liab.	27034	26147	28774

ANNUAL RATES of change (per sh)
	Past 10 Yrs.	Past 5 Yrs.	Est'd '09-'11 to '14-'16
Revenues	13.5%	15.0%	11.5%
"Cash Flow"	10.5%	13.0%	11.0%
Earnings	11.0%	12.0%	12.0%
Dividends	--	21.5%	17.0%
Book Value	5.0%	-4.5%	16.0%

Fiscal Year Ends	QUARTERLY REVENUES ($ mill.) A				Full Fiscal Year
	Sep.30	Dec.31	Mar.31	Jun.30	
2008	13762	16367	14454	15837	60420
2009	15061	16629	13648	13099	58437
2010	12920	19022	14503	16039	62484
2011	16195	19953	16428	17367	69943
2012	17500	20500	17750	18750	74500

Fiscal Year Ends	EARNINGS PER SHARE AB				Full Fiscal Year
	Sep.30	Dec.31	Mar.31	Jun.30	
2008	.45	.50	.47	.45	1.87
2009	.48	.47	.33	.34	1.62
2010	.40	.74	.45	.51	2.10
2011	.62	.77	.61	.69	2.69
2012	.67	.83	.63	.67	2.80

Cal-endar	QUARTERLY DIVIDENDS PAID E■				Full Year
	Mar.31	Jun.30	Sep.30	Dec.31	
2007	.10	.10	.10	.11	.41
2008	.11	.11	.11	.13	.46
2009	.13	.13	.13	.13	.52
2010	.13	.13	.16	.16	.58
2011	.16	.16			

BUSINESS: Microsoft Corp. is the largest independent maker of software. It develops and sells software products for a wide range of computing devices. Also sells the *Xbox* video game console. Revenue sources in fiscal 2011: Microsoft Business, 31.7% of total; Windows & Windows Live, 27.2%; Server and Tools, 24.4%; Entertainment & Devices, 12.7%; Online Services, 3.6%; Other, .4%. Research and development: 12.9% of 2011 sales. Employed 90,000 at 6/30/11. Stock owners: William H. Gates, 7.2%;, other offs. & dirs., 4.9%; BlackRock, Inc. 5.2% (9/10 proxy). Chairman: William H. Gates. CEO: Steven A. Ballmer. Incorporated: Washington. Address: One Microsoft Way, Redmond, Washington 98052-6399. Telephone: 425-882-8080. Internet: www.microsoft.com.

Microsoft should continue performing well in fiscal 2012. (Years end June 30th.) The Microsoft Business Division and the Server and Tools group scored well last year, reflecting the uptake of *Office 2010* and the health of corporate IT spending, and both should hold forth in 2012. Meanwhile, *Windows 7* remains popular, with most corporate customers either having upgraded or in the process of doing so. Still, the well-chronicled shift in the PC market (from desktops and laptops to tablets and smartphones) held the Windows and Windows Live division largely in check in 2011. Nonetheless, the business PC upgrade cycle is alive and well, and should be a positive in fiscal 2012. Meanwhile, the *Xbox/Kinect* duo powered the performance of the Entertainment and Devices group last year, with its popularity with game players likely to remain in force in 2012. Finally, despite progress with *Bing* and respectable prospects for Internet ad placements at the Online Services Division, the group seems set to continue operating deeply in the red this year. In brief, our revenue and earnings estimates for 2012 are unchanged.

The latest version of *Windows Phone* (*Mango*) should be released soon. *Mango* made its smartphone debut in late July in Tokyo, and it appears that Microsoft has brought its mobile operating system up to speed with its competition from Apple and Google, *iOS* and *Android*. Still, Apple and Google are releasing new versions of their systems this fall, so the hill is likely to remain quite steep for Microsoft. Meanwhile, *Windows 8* is on the distant horizon. Its release will extend Microsoft's support to computing platforms other than Intel's. The move should spread its reach in the consumer market, where tablets and other form factors are popular. **Our take on Microsoft shares has not changed since our May report.** The company is running well, and it should continue to generate tremendous cash flow, supporting further share repurchases and a rising dividend payout. Nonetheless, Microsoft's challenges in the Internet search business and in mobile computing remain. Accordingly, these timely shares may be of most interest to investors with an intermediate time horizon.
Charles Clark   *August 19, 2011*

(A) Fiscal year ends June 30th. (B) Primary earnings through fiscal '97, then diluted. Quarters may not add to total. Excl. nonrec. items: '98, d3¢; '99, 1¢ '01, d26¢; '02, d23¢; '03, d5¢; '04, d29¢; '05, d4¢. Next earnings report due late Oct. (C) In millions, adjusted for stock splits. (D) Includes intangibles. In 2011: $12.6 billion, $1.50 a share.
(E) Dividends historically paid in March, June, Sept., and Dec. ■Dividend reinvestment plan available. Special dividend of $3.00 a share paid December 2, 2004.

Company's Financial Strength	A++
Stock's Price Stability	90
Price Growth Persistence	25
Earnings Predictability	85

To subscribe call 1-800-833-0046.

Source: Copyright © 2013 Value Line Publishing LLC. All Rights Reserved Worldwide. "Value Line" is a registered trademark of Value Line Inc.

INSIGHTS   Real Applications

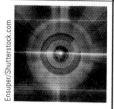

Ensuper/Shutterstock.com

The Devil Is in the Details. . .

Annual reports are a leading source of information for investors. But since they're prepared by management, they tend to be very favorably biased. The bias takes the form of exaggerating successes and down-playing problems and threats. Since we've just had a look at Value Line's current report on Microsoft, the world's largest software developer, let's look at the high-tech giant's annual report from a few years back as an example.

In the late 1990s and early 2000s, Microsoft was under legal attack by the U.S. Justice Department for alleged violation of the Sherman Act, a law that makes certain business behavior illegal if it reduces competition and puts the violator in a monopoly position. The federal government and nineteen states sued Microsoft and demanded, among other things, that it be broken up into two companies to compensate for the alleged anticompetitive effects of its previous behavior.

During one year, the pending lawsuit was in the news constantly, and was undoubtedly a major factor in the investment community's perception of Microsoft stock. Indeed the threat it posed to the company's future probably depressed its stock price considerably. It seems reasonable to expect that a professional analysis of the firm's prospects would have included a thorough

discussion of the lawsuit and an assessment of the likelihood that the firm would be damaged by it.

Yet Microsoft's annual report barely mentioned the suit, even though it was still pending when the report was issued. The litigation was given only six lines in the president's discussion of results which is read carefully by most serious investors. It was mentioned in somewhat more detail in the notes to the financial statements where statements about pending litigation are required by law. But many investors don't read the notes, which are similar to "the fine print" in a contract.

Companies defend their minimal mention of such lawsuits in annual reports saying that management believes the suits are groundless, the companies will eventually win, and that investors therefore shouldn't worry about them. That's the way this case turned out. In the end, Microsoft wasn't hurt by the suit. But while the outcomes of such suits are in doubt, aren't investors entitled to fair and thorough disclosure of their risks, and a discussion of both management's and the other side's arguments? Perhaps, but it would be unusual to find it in an annual report.

Source: Microsoft Corporation Annual Report 2000.

Perhaps the borrowing was to finance expansion into an exciting new venture. That might seem great, but the analyst wants to know if the firm will be able to support the interest payments and whether the venture will need more borrowing later before it starts to generate a profit. On the other hand, the borrowing might be because the firm isn't collecting its receivables or is holding significant useless inventory. In that case, the analyst will want to know how the problem will be resolved and what its impact on long-run profitability will be.

Keep this **orientation** in mind. *In finance our attitude is critical and investigative.*

The **orientation** of the financial analyst is **critical** and **investigative**.

3.2   The Statement of Cash Flows

We've made the point that income as reported in the income statement does not equal cash in the pocket of the business or its owner. Accounting income includes things like depreciation, which is one of several artificial devices designed to make the income statement a representation of the long-run condition of the enterprise. Businesses, however, are run with cold, hard cash on a day-to-day basis. Therefore, another statement is needed to give users information detailing the actual movement of cash in and out of the company. That document is the **statement of cash flows**. It shows a reader where the firm's money came from and what it was spent on during the period covered.

Terminology   A more formal name for the statement of cash flows is the statement of changes in financial position, but people rarely use that awkward title. It comes from the fact that the balance sheet can be called the statement of financial position, and technically the cash statement analyzes changes in the balance sheet. Common usage involves the words "cash flow" or "funds flow." Sources and uses or sources and applications of cash or funds are also ways of referring to what we will call the statement of cash flows.

Cash statements report inflows and outflows of money. Inflows are usually represented by positive numbers while outflows are negative. Negative numbers are shown in parentheses. Naming an inflow describes where money comes from—selling something, for example. Naming an outflow describes how money is used—buying something, for example.

Where the Statement of Cash Flows Comes From   The income statement and balance sheet emerge directly from closing the books. The statement of cash flows does not; it is constructed from the other two statements after they're produced.

3.2a   How the Statement of Cash Flows Works—Preliminary Illustrations

The best way to gain an understanding of the role of cash in financial statements is to appreciate how the statement of cash flows is put together from the balance sheet and income statement. The pages that follow will develop a working knowledge of the principles as well as the calculations involved.

It takes two balance sheets and an income statement to build a statement of cash flows for an accounting period. The income statement is from the period and the balance sheets are as of its beginning and end. (A beginning balance sheet is the ending balance sheet of the previous period.)

The cash statement analyzes where money has come from and gone to by doing two things. First, it takes net income for the period and adjusts it for some of the items that make it different from the everyday concept of income as cash in one's pocket. Second, it takes the two consecutive balance sheets and analyzes the *changes* in everything the company has and everything it owes to determine how those changes have affected the cash balance.

TABLE 3-1	Cash Flow Rules

Asset increase	→	Use
Liability increase	→	Source
Asset decrease	→	Source
Liability decrease	→	Use

© Cengage Learning

This second idea is critically important and can be a little bit tricky. Changes in balance sheet accounts represent cash inflows or outflows, i.e., sources or uses. For example, an account that changes by $5,000 represents a $5,000 cash flow. But, whether the change reflects a source or a use depends on whether the account is an asset or a liability and whether the change is an increase or a decrease. To analyze a change, we apply the four simple rules listed in Table 3-1.

In other words, the second step in developing a statement of cash flows involves looking at the change in each balance sheet account, deciding whether it's a source or use of cash, and then organizing the results in a prescribed way.

Applying these ideas can be a little difficult if we jump right into a business example. It helps to first consider personal examples involving familiar assets and liabilities. The following illustrations will help you understand the rules and their application.

Buying a Car on Credit—The First Two Rules

Suppose Joe Jones had after-tax income of $50,000 and spent $40,000 on normal living expenses during a year. Also assume that at the beginning of the year he had a bank balance of $10,000 and no other assets or liabilities. Further assume that during the year he bought a new car costing $30,000, financing $25,000 with a car loan. At the end of the year he had $15,000 in the bank.

Joe's personal income statement and balance sheets are shown below. Reread the preceding paragraph and make sure that you understand the representation of Joe's activities on his financial statements, especially the beginning and ending balance sheets.

Income Statement—J. Jones

Income	$50,000
Expenses	40,000
Net	$10,000

Balance Sheets—J. Jones

	Beginning	Ending
Assets		
Cash in bank	$10,000	$15,000
Car	0	30,000
Total assets	$10,000	$45,000
Liabilities and Equity		
Car loan	0	$25,000
Equity	$10,000	20,000
Total liab. + eq.	$10,000	$45,000

Now we'll examine Joe's activities in terms of cash flow. We'll write the resulting cash flow statement now and then analyze each line. The sources and uses appear in the far right column.

Statement of Cash Flows—J. Jones

Cash income	$ 50,000	
Cash used for living expenses	(40,000)	
Net source of cash from income		$ 10,000
Use of cash to buy car		(30,000)
Source of cash from loan		25,000
Net cash flow		$ 5,000

Reconciliation

Beginning cash balance	$10,000
Net cash flow	5,000
Ending cash balance	$15,000

Joe had after-tax cash income of $50,000 and expenses of $40,000 for a net of $10,000. That's clearly a source of cash and is shown as a positive number. Next we'll turn to balance sheet changes.

First consider the car loan. (Don't combine the purchase and the loan in your thinking; they're two separate transactions.) When Joe borrowed $25,000, he received the money from the lender, clearly a *source*. But the borrowing also *increased* a loan liability on his balance sheet, in this case from zero to $25,000. The transaction illustrates our second rule: a *liability increase* is associated with a *source* of cash. This is also logical—when you borrow money, the lender is giving you cash.

Next, Joe *used* $30,000 to buy an automobile, which *increased* the car asset account from zero to $30,000 on his balance sheet. This illustrates our first rule: cash is *used* any time an *asset increases.* That too is easy to visualize in this case; you have to spend money to buy a car.

Having written down all of Joe's sources and uses, we combine them into a summarized result called *net cash flow,* in this case equal to $5,000.

To finish the statement, we *reconcile* Joe's net cash flow with his bank account. Assuming all of his money is in the bank, his beginning balance plus his net cash flow must equal his ending bank balance. If it doesn't, we've made a mistake. Here's a slightly more complicated illustration.

Buying and Selling Cars—The Third and Fourth Rules
Suppose at the beginning of the year Sally Smith had a three-year-old luxury car valued at $20,000 that was subject to a $14,000 loan. At the same time, her bank balance was $6,000. During the year she had after-tax income of $60,000 but spent $62,000 on living expenses. In an effort to economize, she sold her car for $20,000 and bought an economy model for $9,000 cash (no loan). When she sold the old car, she paid off the $14,000 loan. At the end of the year her bank balance was $1,000.

Verify that this information is reflected in the following income statement and balance sheets.

Statement—S. Smith

Income	$60,000
Expenses	62,000
Net	$ (2,000)

Balance Sheets—S. Smith

	Beginning	Ending
Assets		
Cash in bank	$ 6,000	$ 1,000
Cars: luxury	20,000	0
economy	0	9,000
Total assets	$26,000	$10,000
Liabilities and Equity		
Car loan	$14,000	0
Equity	$12,000	10,000
Total liab. + eq.	$26,000	$10,000

Now let's consider the cash flow implications of Sally's activities. Once again we'll write the resulting cash flow statement and then analyze each line.

Statement of Cash Flows—S. Smith

Cash income	$ 60,000	
Cash used for living expenses	(62,000)	
Net source of cash from income		$ (2,000)
Source of cash from selling old car		$ 20,000
Use of cash to pay off old car loan		(14,000)
Use of cash to buy new car		(9,000)
Net cash flow		$ (5,000)
Beginning cash balance	$ 6,000	
Net cash flow	(5,000)	
Ending cash balance	$ 1,000	

Sally had negative income during the year because she spent more than she made. Anyone can do that by either drawing down a bank account or borrowing. We'll characterize the overspending as a negative source of cash rather than as a use simply because income is usually a source.

The first thing Sally did was sell her old car for $20,000. That clearly represents a source of cash because she received money for the car. But giving up the car removed it from her balance sheet reducing the luxury car asset account from $20,000 to zero. This illustrates our third rule: an *asset decrease* represents a *source* of cash.

When Sally sold her car she also paid off her car loan. That required giving the lender cash, clearly a use. But the transaction also reduced the loan liability on her balance sheet from $14,000 to zero. This illustrates our fourth rule: a *liability decrease* is a *use* of cash.

Using the Cash Flow Rules   It's easy to see in the preceding illustrations why each transaction is a source or a use of cash. Clearly buying a car requires a use of cash—as does paying off a loan. Similarly, selling a tangible asset like a car generates cash—as does borrowing.

Things are more complicated when we get into business balance sheets because they contain *intangible* assets and liabilities such as receivables and accruals. For most people, it isn't easy to visualize why an increase in accounts receivable is a use of cash or why an increase in accruals is a source.

Fortunately, because of the rules, we don't have to think every balance-sheet change through to construct a statement of cash flows. All we have to do is use Table 3-1 to apply the asset rules to every asset and the liability rules to every liability. In other words, we should treat every asset as a car and every liability as a loan without thinking about why every increase or decrease is a source or a use of cash.[2]

3.2b   Business Cash Flows

In a business, income is represented by adjusting net income from the income statement for noncash items like depreciation. Assets and liabilities are conveniently listed on balance sheets as of the beginning and end of the year, so changes in each account can be calculated easily.

> ■ The **statement of cash flows** presents **operating, investing,** and **financing** activities separately.

Standard Presentation   A business's statement of cash flows is organized to show cash flows from three different kinds of activities: operating, investing, and financing.

Operating activities have to do with running the business on a day-to-day basis.

Investing activities occur when the firm buys (invests in) or sells things such as fixed assets that enable it to do business. Investing activities also include long-term purchases and sales of financial assets.[3]

Financing activities occur when the company borrows money, pays off loans, sells stock, or pays dividends. They have to do with raising money and servicing the obligations that come along with it.

Graphic Portrayal   Before tackling a numerical example, let's fix these ideas in mind by looking at a graphic representation of cash flow in a business.

---

2.   On exams, it may help to memorize the rules and write them down on a corner of your paper as soon as you start so you don't get confused once you've begun a problem.

3.   The term "invest" generally means buying something that is expected to return more than its cost in the future. When individuals say "invest", they usually mean buying a financial asset. However, we sometimes use the term with physical things (investing in a house) or even intangibles (investing in an education). When we talk about investment by companies we generally mean buying the equipment used in doing business such as machinery, vehicles, and real estate.

FIGURE 3-2 Business Cash Flows

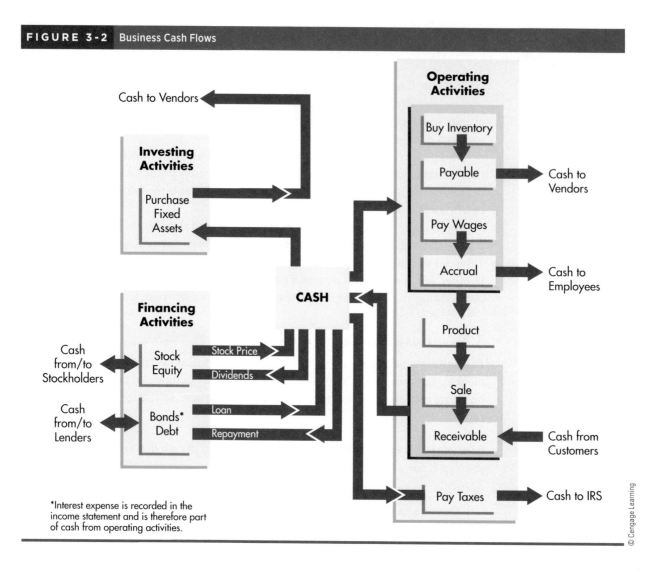

*Interest expense is recorded in the income statement and is therefore part of cash from operating activities.

© Cengage Learning

Figure 3-2 shows how cash flows in and out of a company. Notice that operating activities shown on the right have to do with the normal course of business and the current accounts of the balance sheet. Investing activities generally have to do with buying long-lived assets, either real or financial. Financing activities are concerned with debt and equity.

3.2c   Constructing the Statement of Cash Flows

Now we can look at putting together a statement of cash flows for a business. The best way to do that is to work through a numerical illustration such as the one shown in Example 3-1. The process requires balance sheets at the beginning and end of the period under consideration and an income statement for that period.

CONCEPT CONNECTION   EXAMPLE 3-1

A Business Statement of Cash Flows

Consider the following financial statements for the hypothetical Belfry Company in which the balance sheets are arranged vertically, assets above liabilities.

BELFRY COMPANY BALANCE SHEET FOR THE PERIOD ENDED 12/31/X2 ($000)

ASSETS		
	12/31/X1	12/31/X2
Cash	$ 1,000	$ 1,400
Accounts receivable	3,000	2,900
Inventory	2,000	3,200
CURRENT ASSETS	$6,000	$ 7,500
Fixed assets		
Gross	$4,000	$ 6,000
Accumulated depreciation	(1,000)	(1,500)
Net	$3,000	$ 4,500
TOTAL ASSETS	$9,000	$12,000
LIABILITIES		
Accounts payable	$ 1,500	$ 2,100
Accruals	500	400
CURRENT LIABILITIES	$2,000	$ 2,500
Long-term debt	$5,000	$ 6,200
Equity	2,000	3,300
TOTAL CAPITAL	$7,000	$ 9,500
TOTAL LIABILITIES		
AND EQUITY	$9,000	$12,000

BELFRY COMPANY INCOME STATEMENT FOR
THE PERIOD ENDED 12/31/X2 ($000)

Sales	$10,000
COGS	6,000
Gross margin	$ 4,000
Expense	$ 1,600
Depreciation	500
EBIT	$ 1,900
Interest	400
EBT	$ 1,500
Tax	500
Net income	$ 1,000

In addition, the company sold stock for $800,000 during the year and paid dividends of $500,000.

Operating activities involve the **income statement** and **current** balance sheet accounts.

(Notice that depreciation is shown separately in the income statement for convenience. Most presentations don't do that.)

Develop the statement of cash flows for Belfry one activity at a time and draw some conclusions about the firm's financial condition from the result.

SOLUTION: Operating Activities ($000)

Operating activities are the things a company does on a day-to-day basis to conduct its business. Typically they include buying inventory, producing and selling product, paying expenses and taxes, and collecting on credit sales. The focus of these activities is the production of net income, so we start the cash statement with that figure.

However, net income includes items that don't represent cash flows in the current period. Our next step is therefore to adjust those out. The result is called *operating income*.

In Belfry's case, the only adjustment necessary to calculate operating income is to add back depreciation, which was subtracted in the calculation of net income.

Net income	$1,000
Depreciation	500
Operating income	$1,500

Next we recognize that the money from operating transactions runs through the current balance sheet accounts. Therefore changes in those accounts are part of operating cash flow. We analyze the balances *other than cash* and classify the changes as sources or uses of cash according to the cash flow rules in Table 3-1 on page 74. The cash account is handled separately later.

In Belfry's case, accounts receivable decreased from $3,000 to $2,900, providing a $100 source of cash because, according to the third rule, an asset decrease is a source. Similarly, inventory increased from $2,000 to $3,200 for a use of $1,200 according to the first rule.

Apply the second and fourth rules to the changes in accounts payable and accruals to get the following sources and uses.

Account	Source/(Use)
Receivables	$ 100
Inventory	(1,200)
Payables	600
Accruals	(100)
	$ (600)

The sum of the current account changes and operating income is cash from operating activities. The typical presentation is illustrated for Belfry as follows.

Net income	$1,000
Depreciation	500
Net changes in current accounts	(600)
Cash from operating activities	$ 900

Investing activities typically include purchasing **fixed assets**.

Investing Activities ($000)

Cash from investing activities is simple in this example. The only entry comes from an increase in Belfry's fixed assets of $2,000. This is reflected by the increase in gross fixed assets from $4,000 to $6,000, which is a use of cash according to the first rule.

Notice that we use the gross fixed assets account for this calculation rather than the net. That's because the net figure includes a reduction for accumulated depreciation, the change in which is the other side of the entry that put depreciation on the income statement. That depreciation is already included in the cash flow statement in the operating section, and we don't want to repeat it here.

Hence, cash from investing activities is

Purchase of fixed assets	($2,000)

Financing Activities ($000)

There are three financing activities in this example. The first is an increase in long-term debt—a source according to the second rule. The company appears to have taken out another loan. The second is a sale of stock, and the third a dividend payment. The sale of stock results in an increase in equity, a liability,[4] and is a source according to the second rule. The dividend payment is clearly a use of money. It reduces equity and is therefore a use according to the fourth rule. (The source or use classifications of stock sales and dividends should be obvious. When stock is sold, the company receives money for paper certificates, clearly a cash inflow. Dividends are always paid *by* the company *to* stockholders so they clearly represent outflows.)

Financing activities deal with the **capital accounts, long-term debt** and **equity**.

Cash from financing activities is then calculated as follows.

Increase in long-term debt	$1,200
Sale of stock	800
Dividend paid	(500)
Cash from financing activities	$1,500

The Equity and Cash Accounts

Notice that we haven't calculated the change in equity and classified it as a source or a use of cash. That's because the procedure breaks that change into three parts and includes them individually in two parts of the statement of cash flows. Let's lay the pieces out. The change in equity from the beginning of a period to the end is the sum of net income and the sale of new stock less the dividend paid (see page 43). These are as follows for Belfry.

Net income	$1,000
Stock sale	800
Dividend	(500)
Total change in equity	$1,300

The stock sale and the dividend are included under financing activities, while net income shows up under operating activities.

---

4. Equity is a "liability" of the company to its owners. We treat it as a liability with respect to the cash flow rules.

Also notice that we haven't done anything with the cash account. It's been omitted because the cash flow total of the three activities we've presented so far must equal the change in the cash account. That's shown as a reconciliation at the end of the statement.

Net Cash Flow, the sum of operating, investing, and financing activities, is a positive ($900 − $2,000 + $1,500 =) $400, so we have the following reconciliation, which ties to the balance sheet cash account:

Beginning cash balance	$1,000
Net cash flow	400
Ending cash balance	$1,400

The entire statement of cash flows for Belfry is shown below in the standard, accepted format.

BELFRY COMPANY STATEMENT OF CASH FLOWS FOR THE PERIOD ENDED 12/31/X2 ($000)

CASH FROM OPERATING ACTIVITIES	
Net income	$ 1,000
Depreciation	500
Net changes in current accounts	(600)
Cash from operating activities	$ 900
RECONCILIATION	
CASH FROM INVESTING ACTIVITIES	
Purchase of fixed assets	$(2,000)
CASH FROM FINANCING ACTIVITIES	
Increase in long-term debt	$ 1,200
Sale of stock	800
Dividend paid	(500)
Cash from financing activities	$ 1,500
NET CASH FLOW	$ 400
Beginning cash balance	$ 1,000
Net cash flow	400
Ending cash balance	$ 1,400

To summarize, the statement of cash flows takes information from the income statement and balance sheet and displays it in a manner that highlights the movement of cash. No new information is created; what is already there is simply rearranged in a way that's more usable in the day-to-day running of the business.

Conclusions

In this case, examination of the statement of cash flows leads to some concern about the Belfry Company. The firm is quite profitable, earning 10% on sales, but still had to borrow substantially during the year. Clearly the fixed asset purchase had something to do with the additional funds required. One must ask whether that expenditure was entirely necessary. Another concern is the sudden increase in inventory. Does it mean that some of the existing inventory isn't good? If so, this could imply a big write-off in the future.

You should always keep in mind the fact that it's cash that really counts in business, not net income.

To drive that point home, let's ask another question about Belfry. Notice that during the year it had to borrow an additional $1,200,000 from the bank. Would a bank have been likely to extend that additional credit?

In fact, a bank might have been reluctant to advance more money to this company. Notice that the firm's capital (long-term debt plus equity) is in the neighborhood of 70% debt. We'll see later that such a high proportion of debt is beyond the comfort level of most lenders. The bank could have refused further advances, putting the company in a cash bind. If that had caused Belfry to fail to make its payroll, the company could have been out of business overnight.

Yet Belfry is earning great profits in terms of net income, 10% of sales. Take the lesson to heart: A firm can go broke profitably. Small businesses do it all the time, and it happens to big companies with surprising frequency.

optimarc/Shutterstock.com

from the **CFO**

A firm that manages cash poorly can **go out of business** while making an **accounting profit**.

3.3　Free Cash Flow

Investors often acquire (buy) whole companies. Candidates for acquisition are usually profitable businesses with a history of steady growth. One of the questions potential buyers ask about such companies involves their ability to generate cash.

Some businesses generate enough cash from routine operations to replace worn out equipment and buy new assets to support growth. Others may earn a profit, but need additional cash to stay competitive and grow. In the first, case buyers can expect to receive cash distributions from a newly acquired company, but in the second, they have to invest more equity or borrow to keep the firm growing.

Cash generated **beyond reinvestment** needs is **free cash flow**.

The concept of **free cash flow (FCF)** allows us to estimate whether a company will provide cash or require it in the future. If FCF is positive, business operations are likely to fund their own growth and upkeep and money is available to pay interest and/or dividends. If it's negative, just continuing will require cash contributions from outside the business.

In other words, **free cash flow** is cash generated by operations that's available for distribution to investors.

3.3a　Calculating Free Cash Flow

The FCF idea starts with **earnings before interest and taxes (EBIT)**. (See the review of the income statement, Chapter 2, page 30.) Recall that **EBIT** is calculated by subtracting all costs and expenses except interest and tax from revenue.

Since EBIT is above interest on the income statement, it's not influenced by how the company is financed. As a result, it's also called **Operating Profit**, where the word operating refers to the physical activities of the business exclusive of financing.

We'll think about EBIT on an after tax basis by subtracting a hypothetical tax calculated by multiplying it by the tax rate. The resulting measure of profitability is called **net operating profit**, usually referred to as **NOPAT**. If T is the tax rate

(3.1)   **NOPAT = EBIT − (T)(EBIT) = EBIT (1 − T)**

Notice that if there is no debt, NOPAT equals net income.

Depreciation is one of the items subtracted from revenue when calculating EBIT. But depreciation is a noncash charge, so EBIT understates cash flow by at least that amount. Adding back depreciation gives a figure that's closer to cash flow called **operating cash flow:**

(3.2)   **Operating Cash Flow = NOPAT + Depreciation**

Free cash flow is operating cash flow plus the assumption that the firm will remain competitive and continue growing. Remaining competitive means continually replacing worn out equipment. Since depreciation represents the wearing out of long-lived (fixed) assets, new fixed asset purchases of at least that amount must be made continually. And since an expanding company needs an increasing asset base, fixed asset purchases must exceed depreciation to keep up with growth. Further, since a larger business requires more cash, inventory, and receivables, growth must be supported by continuing increases in the current accounts.

Hence Free cash flow, the money available to investors can be written as

(3.3)   **FCF = Operating Cash Flow**
                         − Increase in Gross Fixed Assets
                              − Increase in Current Accounts

If FCF is positive, operating cash flow provides enough cash for asset growth and leaves something for investors. But if FCF is negative, investors have to make up the shortfall just to keep the firm performing as it has been.

(It's important to notice a difference in *current accounts* in equation (3.3) and in the operating activities section of the statement of cash flows. Here we include changes in the cash account; there we did not.)

3.3b   Free Cash Flow to Equity (FCFE)

An extension of the free cash flow concept focuses on the likelihood that the company will be able to distribute cash to stockholders while continuing to perform as it has if the company is acquired subject to its existing debt. This is accomplished by subtracting the after-tax cost of interest on existing debt and any required principal repayments from FCF. If the tax rate is T, the after-tax cost of interest is interest multiplied by $(1 − T)$ and equation (3.3) becomes

(3.3a)   **FCFE = Operating Cash Flow**
                         − Increase in Gross Fixed Assets
                              − Increase in Current Accounts
                                   − (1 − T)Interest − Principal Reduction

If we calculate FCF for a company that appears to be doing well, we can tell if it's supporting its own performance or if it has a continuing need for new funds.

CONCEPT CONNECTION   EXAMPLE 3-2

A Free Cash Flow Business Analysis

A group of investors is considering buying the Belfry Company of Example 3-1. They're enthusiastic about acquiring the company, and plan to make further investments with the cash they believe it may distribute to them after the purchase.

Analyze Belfry's financial statements using free cash flow principles and comment on the wisdom of the idea. Ignore last year's payment of dividends and sale of stock. Belfry's tax rate is 33%.

SOLUTION: First calculate Belfry's net operating profit and operating cash flow from Equations 3.1 and 3.2 ($000)

$$\text{NOPAT} = \text{EBIT} (1 - T) = \$1{,}900 (1 - .33) = \$1{,}273$$

and

$$\text{Operating Cash Flow} = \text{NOPAT} + \text{Depreciation} = \$1{,}273 + \$500 = \$1{,}773$$

Then subtract increases in gross fixed assets and net current accounts to arrive at free cash flow, the money available for debt and equity investors (lenders and stockholders). The current account detail is the figure calculated in Example 3-1 (page 79) plus an increase in cash of $400,000.

$$\begin{aligned}
\text{FCF} &= \text{Operating Cash Flow} - \text{Increase in Fixed Assets} - \text{Increase in Current Accounts} \\
&= \$1{,}773 - \$2{,}000 - \$1{,}000 \\
&= -\$1{,}227
\end{aligned}$$

If we assume Belfry is acquired subject to its current debt, which can be maintained without net principal reduction, the relevant calculation for our investors is FCFE, free cash flow to equity.

$$\text{FCFE} = -\$1{,}227 - \$400(1 - .33) = -\$1{,}227 - \$267 = -\$1{,}494$$

These negative values for free cash flow and free cash flow to equity should make the potential buyers rather uncomfortable. It implies that Belfry will need an infusion of approximately $1.5 million per year to continue its current operating performance. This means the new owners will either have to contribute more of their own money, sell new stock to others, or borrow to keep the company performing as it has been. Since their plan was to take cash out of the business, they should probably look for another candidate.

It's important to understand that negative free cash flow isn't necessarily a bad thing. If the firm's cash use is due to strategically sound growth which will make it more valuable in the long run, buyers who don't need current cash income may be willing to invest for some time.

3.3c   The Cash Conversion Cycle (Racetrack Diagram)

An alternative and insightful way of looking at business activity in general involves the idea of converting cash into materials and labor that produce products and/or services that are converted back into cash through sale. The idea is illustrated in Figure 3-3, which is usually called the **cash conversion cycle**. However, the term *racetrack diagram* is a little more colorful and tends to fix it in mind better. Starting at the bottom of the

Product is **converted** into cash, which is transformed into more product, creating the **cash conversion cycle**.

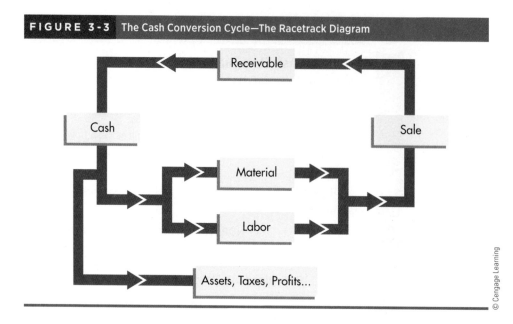

FIGURE 3-3   The Cash Conversion Cycle—The Racetrack Diagram

© Cengage Learning

track, a business uses cash to purchase materials and labor to produce a product. That product is sold, resulting in a receivable. When the receivable is collected, the firm once again has cash in hand that it uses to buy more inventory and labor to produce more product and so on.

In a sense, the company is running around a racetrack, converting cash to product and product to cash. You can think of the firm continually doing this equipped with some level of assets.

Given a level of assets, the firm goes around the track faster by making more sales in the period. Clearly the faster it can go around, the better off it is as long as it doesn't damage something else by going too fast. In other words, it's important to get a lot of sales per dollar of assets employed in the business. That's one of several measures of success.

However, a firm that just runs around the track putting all its money back into product wouldn't be doing its owners much good. A successful business has to pull something out each time around to buy new assets for growth and to replace old ones that wear out, to pay taxes, and for profit. Clearly, the larger the slice that can be taken out of cash flow each time around the track, the better off the firm is. This idea is simply profitability and is shown in the lower part of the figure.

Summarizing, the diagram illustrates that a business has to do two things for success: sell a lot for its level of assets and sell at a reasonable profit margin given its costs and expenses.

Notice that the two things work against each other. The business can always sell more if it charges less, but then it will have less profit. Conversely, a higher price yields more profit but lower sales. We'll come back to this idea toward the end of the chapter.

3.4   Ratio Analysis

People who make judgments about businesses by reading financial statements have developed some relatively standard methods by which they analyze information. The general technique is known as **ratio analysis**. Its use is virtually universal among financial professionals. It is therefore important that you be familiar with the basic technique and a few of the more commonly used ratios.

Ratio analysis involves taking sets of numbers out of the financial statements and forming ratios with them. The numbers are chosen so that each ratio has a particular meaning to the operation of the business.

An example will make the idea clear. There's a ratio that gives a quick indication of whether the company will have the means to pay its bills during the next year. It's called the **current ratio** and is based on the definitions of current assets and current liabilities.

Recall from Chapter 2 that most of the money coming into a firm from normal operations passes through current assets. Similarly, outgoing money normally passes through current liabilities. Further, the definition of "current" is that cash will be generated or required within a year.

It's clear that to remain solvent, a company must have at least as much money coming in as it has going out. This fact suggests that comparing the sizes of current assets and current liabilities at a point in time will give an indication of whether operating cash flows will be positive or negative in the near future. The current ratio does just that. It's formed by dividing current assets by current liabilities, and must exceed 1.0 or the firm can expect to run short of cash within the next year.[5] The current ratio measures **liquidity**, which in this context refers to the company's ability to pay its bills in the short run.

Numerous ratios have been devised, each having a special significance like the current ratio. We'll cover several of the most commonly used ratios in the remainder of this chapter.

> **Financial ratios** are formed from sets of financial statement figures. Ratios **highlight** different aspects of **performance**.

> For a business, **liquidity** refers to its **ability to pay its bills** in the short run.

3.4a   Comparisons

Ratios by themselves have some value, but not nearly as much as they have when they're compared with other similar figures. For example, a current ratio of 1.8 in a particular business might seem all right by itself, but it could cause concern if competing firms have current ratios in excess of 3.0. In such a case, we would suspect that some characteristic of the business requires great liquidity and that the firm we are analyzing doesn't have it.

Ratio analysis is usually conducted in the context of one or more of three comparisons. Comparisons are made with respect to history, the competition, and budget.

History   Comparison with history means looking at a ratio next to the same figure calculated for the same organization in one or more immediately preceding accounting

---

5.   The current ratio generally needs to be quite a bit greater than 1.0. If future inflows and outflows are just equal, timing problems can be expected if the outflows come first.

periods. The idea is to look for trends. If a firm's current ratio is seen to be decreasing steadily over a number of periods, the analyst would ask why.

The Competition   The performance of other companies in the same field is always a good yardstick for evaluating a firm's performance. If a particular measure is substantially off what others are doing, it's a good idea to find out why. Industry average data are often available through trade associations, government publications, banking publications, and the publications of investment analysts.

Budget   Most businesses of any size develop financial plans for the future. We'll study business planning in Chapter 4. For now it's enough to understand that a plan involves a projected set of financial statements from which ratios can be developed. When financial performance is being evaluated, what the organization really did is always compared with what management said it would do in their plan (budget) for the period. Comparing planned and actual ratios highlights where management needs to put its attention in running the business.

> Ratios are typically compared with similar figures from **history**, the **competition**, and **budget**.

3.4b   Common Size Statements

The first step in a financial analysis is usually the calculation of a set of ratios known as **common size statements**. The common size income statement is the most frequently used. The idea can best be understood with an example.

> A **common size income statement** presents each line item as a **percent of revenue**.

Suppose we're interested in comparing the financial performance of two companies in the same line of business that are substantially different in size. For example, consider the income statements of Alpha and Beta.

	Alpha	Beta
Sales revenue	$2,187,460	$150,845
Cost of sales	1,203,103	72,406
Gross margin	$ 984,357	$ 78,439
Expenses	505,303	39,974
EBIT	$ 479,054	$ 38,465
Interest	131,248	15,386
EBT	$ 347,806	$ 23,079
Tax	118,254	3,462
Net income	$ 229,552	$ 19,617

It's hard to tell which company is doing a better job of controlling costs and expenses by looking at the dollar figures because Alpha is so much larger than Beta.

The comparison is made much easier by creating a *common size* statement for each company to abstract away from absolute dollars and state things in relative terms. A common size income statement is formed by stating each line as a percentage of revenue. The percentages are usually stated to the first decimal place and displayed next to the dollar figures.

CONCEPT CONNECTION EXAMPLE 3-3

Common Size Statements

Compare the factory performance of Alpha and Beta with the aid of common size statements.

SOLUTION:

	Alpha		Beta	
	$	**%**	**$**	**%**
Sales revenue	$2,187,460	100.0	$150,845	100.0
Cost of sales	1,203,103	55.0	72,406	48.0
Gross margin	$ 984,357	45.0	$ 78,439	52.0
Expenses	505,303	23.1	39,974	26.5
EBIT	$ 479,054	21.9	$ 38,465	25.5
Interest	131,248	6.0	15,386	10.2
EBT	$ 347,806	15.9	$ 23,079	15.3
Tax	118,254	5.4	3,462	2.3
Net income	$ 229,552	10.5	$ 19,617	13.0

Each percentage figure below sales is a ratio of that line's dollars to revenue dollars. The ratio of cost of sales (or cost of goods sold) to sales revenue is generally called the *cost ratio,* while expenses as a percentage of revenue can be called the *expense ratio.* Net income as a percentage of sales has a name of its own, *return on sales,* and is one of the ratios we'll look at later.

Comparing the two columns of ratios, we can immediately see significant differences in the way the two companies are operating. Alpha's cost is 55% of revenues while Beta's is only 48%. This is unusual because one would expect the larger company to have economies of scale in production that would make it more efficient than the smaller firm.

Several explanations are possible. Alpha might have some production problems, Beta might be particularly good at what it does, or there may be a difference in what they're making. In the last situation Alpha might be producing a simple bottom-of-the-line product that sells at a minimal markup while Beta might be making a fancy customized version of the same thing that's marked up much higher.

from the
CFO

Notice that we don't have a definite answer about the differences in the two firms' factory operations, but the common size analysis leads us to ask the right questions. It doesn't give us the answers, but it gets our investigation of problems started in the right direction.

Common size analysis is particularly useful in comparing a firm's performance with its own history. Unfavorable trends in cost or expense ratios from this year to last and the year before are signals to management that should never be overlooked or taken lightly.

A set of common size statements is generally the first thing an analyst prepares when starting a project.

Common size balance sheets can also be constructed that state everything as a percentage of total assets. They can be useful in determining whether a firm has relatively too much money tied up in inventory or receivables, or whether it uses more equipment than it should.

3.4c Ratios

In the following pages, we'll present some of the more commonly used ratios of financial analysis. Each ratio is designed to illuminate some aspect of how the business is doing. In each case, we'll illustrate how the ratio is calculated, discuss the rationale behind its use, and explain what it's telling the analyst.

Remember that ratios are most meaningful when used in comparisons. For that reason it's difficult to make a generalization about what a good or an acceptable value is for any particular figure. For example, one of the ratios we'll be talking about measures how effectively the firm uses inventory. With respect to that ratio, a good number for a manufacturing company would be terrible for a retailer.

After we've discussed each ratio, we'll calculate its value for the Belfry Company, using the financial statements shown on page 79. We'll continue to show dollar figures to the nearest $1000 (000 omitted) except when per share figures are calculated (pages 99–100).

A Note on Average Versus Ending Values

Notice that we have a beginning and an ending balance sheet for the Belfry Company, which brings up a computational question. When a ratio calls for a balance sheet figure, should we use the beginning, the ending, or an average value?

The answer depends on what the ratio is measuring. If it pertains to a position or status at the end of the year, ending values are appropriate. On the other hand, if the ratio measures an activity that goes on during the entire period, average balance sheet figures better reflect performance. Beginning values alone are never appropriate.

The difference between average and ending values isn't very important if the company is relatively stable and account balances aren't changing much. However, it can be significant if the firm is growing or shrinking rapidly.

Sophisticated analysts always use average balances where appropriate. However, in order to keep the computations in our illustrations and problems simple, we will consistently use ending balances. You should just be aware that the issue exists.

Categories of Ratios

Ratios can be categorized according to the kinds of issues they address. The ones we'll discuss fit into five classifications: liquidity, asset management, debt management, profitability, and market value.

Liquidity ratios indicate the firm's ability to pay its bills in the short run. **Asset management** ratios show how the company uses its resources to generate revenue and profit and to avoid cost. **Debt management** ratios show how effectively the firm uses other people's money and whether it's using too much borrowed money. **Profitability** ratios give us several measures by which to assess the success of the whole venture in making money. **Market value** ratios give an indication of how investors feel about the company's financial future.

Ratios fall into five categories: **liquidity, asset management, debt management, profitability,** and **market value**.

3.4d   Liquidity Ratios

Liquidity ratios measure the ability to meet short-term **financial obligations**.

Liquidity ratios are of particular concern to lenders and suppliers who provide products and services to the firm on credit. They want to be sure the company has the ability to pay its debts.

The Current Ratio   The current ratio is the primary measure of a company's liquidity—that is, its ability to meet its financial obligations in the near future. The calculation is

$$\text{current ratio} = \frac{\text{current assets}}{\text{current liabilities}}$$

The reasoning behind the ratio was discussed earlier as an example. If most everything coming into the firm in the near future is a current asset today, and most everything to be paid out in the near future is a current liability today, then current assets should be substantially above current liabilities to ensure solvency. That means the current ratio has to exceed 1.0. In general, a figure greater than 1.5 or 2.0 is required for comfort.

Having said that, we should point out two anomalies that occur with respect to this ratio. If you look at the balance sheets of large, sophisticated companies that are doing well, you'll often see current ratios in the neighborhood of 1.0. Does this mean these firms are in danger of insolvency?

The answer is generally no, in spite of the low current ratio. The reason is that the firms are being managed very well. Holding current assets like receivables and inventory ties up money that could be used elsewhere. Hence, firms try to operate with as few current assets as possible. Companies which do that well can have relatively low current ratios if they have a line of credit with a bank to cover temporary cash shortages.

It's also important to be aware that a high current ratio can be misleading. Inventories and receivables can be overstated, meaning some items in those accounts are valueless and will never turn into cash. If those items remain on the balance sheet, they can result in an inflated current assets figure and a falsely comforting current ratio.

Belfry's current ratio is

$$\text{current ratio} = \frac{\$7,500}{\$2,500} = 3.0$$

The current ratio is a pure number and is generally not referred to in units of any kind.

The Quick Ratio or Acid Test   The **quick ratio** is conceptually similar to the current ratio. The calculation is

$$\text{quick ratio} = \frac{\text{current assets} - \text{inventory}}{\text{current liabilities}}$$

The liquidity measure provided by the current ratio depends on the conversion of inventory to cash in a reasonable time. However, as we described in Chapter 2, inventory is particularly subject to valuation problems and is often overstated. Inventory also takes more time to convert to cash than other current items.

As a result of these problems, analysts look for a liquidity measure that does not depend on inventory. The quick ratio simply takes it out of current assets in the calculation. The quick ratio is also called the *acid test,* which implies a particularly tough, discerning test.

Current assets sometimes contain minor items such as prepaid expenses that never become cash; they, too, should be subtracted when calculating the quick ratio. In Belfry's case we have

$$\text{quick ratio} = \frac{\$7,500 - \$3,200}{\$2,500} = 1.7$$

Like the current ratio, the quick ratio isn't stated in any particular units.

3.4e   Asset Management Ratios

Asset management ratios address the fundamental efficiency with which a company is run. They help an analyst understand the firm's basic competitiveness.

> The **ACP** measures the time it takes to **collect** on credit sales.

The Average Collection Period (ACP)   The **average collection period (ACP)** represents the average number of days the firm takes to collect its receivables. That is, how long does it take to get paid on credit sales? The ACP is also known as the DSO for *days sales outstanding,* or the receivables cycle. The ACP is stated in *days* and is calculated as follows.

$$\text{ACP} = \frac{\text{accounts receivable}}{\text{average daily sales}}$$

where average daily sales is sales/360. Multiplying the numerator and denominator by 360 gives a more convenient formulation.

$$\text{ACP} = \frac{\text{accounts receivable}}{\text{sales}} \times 360$$

It is common practice to use a 360-day year made up of twelve 30-day months in these calculations.[6]

Clearly, the longer a firm takes to collect its money the worse off it is. Although there are significant exceptions, most credit business is done on terms of 30 days. Frequently, a discount is offered for faster payment on the order of 10 days.

Customers often stretch credit terms by paying a few days late, and sellers, who are anxious to keep their business, don't complain over minor delays. That means it's not unusual to see ACPs of 35 to 45 days in the normal course of business in some industries. However, if the ACP exceeds the company's terms of sale by more than 50%, there are probably serious credit problems.

Collection problems have several important implications. The most apparent is that the firm may be granting credit to customers that lack either the ability or the intent to pay. Another possibility, however, is that customers are finding something wrong with the company's product. Customer dissatisfaction frequently results in a reluctance to pay the bill.

from the
CFO

optimarc/Shutterstock.com

---

6.   The 360-day year is common, but so is the use of a 365-day year. We'll use both conventions from time to time.

The proper interpretation of a high ACP is very important. Although the ACP represents an average collection period, a high figure doesn't usually mean that the average customer is paying excessively slowly. It may imply that while most receivables are being collected fairly promptly, a few are very old, as much as six months or a year. These are unlikely ever to be realized in cash.

Remember from our discussion in Chapter 2 that management is sometimes reluctant to write off questionable receivables because doing so reduces profit. The result of that tendency is an overstated receivables account, which means that the firm's balance sheet is worth less than it purports to be.

Old receivables should be written off without delay or at least reserved through an addition to the allowance for doubtful accounts.

The value of the receivables balance net of the allowance for doubtful accounts should be used in the calculation. For Belfry we have the following ACP.

$$\text{ACP} = \frac{\$2,900}{\$10,000} \times 360 = 104.4 \text{ days}$$

This is not a good result. Belfry clearly has a problem collecting money from at least some of its credit customers.

The Inventory Turnover   The **inventory turnover ratio** is an attempt to measure whether the firm has excess funds tied up in inventory. The ratio is calculated as follows.

Inventory turnover gives an indication of the **quality** of inventory as well as **how well it is managed**.

$$\text{inventory turnover} = \frac{\text{cost of goods sold}}{\text{inventory}}$$

Holding inventory costs money. Inventory costs include interest, storage, insurance, and taxes. In addition, the more inventory a company holds, the more it has at risk of spoiling and becoming obsolete. The inventory turnover measures how many times a year the firm uses up an average stock of goods. A higher turnover is better in that it implies doing business with less tied up in inventory.

A low turnover figure can mean some old inventory is on the books that isn't being used. What is being used may be turning over adequately, but some material can just be dead weight. Such old stock should be disposed of for whatever can be gotten for it.

Operating with too little inventory can create problems, too. Excessively low inventory levels cause stockouts—running out of raw material in the factory or not having the product a customer wants on hand. The result is work stoppages and lost sales. There is definitely a right amount of inventory somewhere between too much and too little. The inventory turnover ratio helps to find it.

An alternate formulation of the inventory turnover ratio involves using sales in the numerator rather than cost of goods sold. In practice the cost of goods sold formulation is preferred because cost and inventory are comparable numbers, whereas sales includes expenses and profit. Either formulation can be used if comparisons are made consistently.

Belfry's inventory turnover using cost of goods sold is

$$\text{inventory turnover} \atop \text{(based on COGS)} = \frac{\$6,000}{\$3,200} = 1.9$$

from the **CFO**

The alternative formulation with sales in the numerator is

$$\text{inventory turnover} \atop \text{(based on Sales)} = \frac{\$10,000}{\$3,200} = 3.1$$

These results would be considered quite bad in most industries. Analysts would immediately want to investigate by looking for obsolete or missing product.

Inventory turnover is a pure number, but it's usually stated in units of "turns" or "times," which are written as "×."

Notice that in this example the results would be considerably different if an average inventory balance was used in the denominator. That's because inventory changed a lot during the year.

Fixed Asset Turnover and Total Asset Turnover   **Fixed and total asset turnovers** measure the relationship of the firm's assets to a year's sales.

$$\text{fixed asset turnover} = \frac{\text{sales}}{\text{fixed assets}}$$

(3.4)
$$\text{total asset turnover} = \frac{\text{sales}}{\text{total assets}}$$

A business can be thought of as using its assets in conjunction with the skills of its employees to generate revenue and profit. These ratios show the relationship between assets and sales. In general, a company that generates more sales with a given level of assets does better than a firm that generates fewer sales with the same assets.

The two ratios allow us to focus on either fixed or total assets. The total assets ratio tends to be more widely used. The ratio using fixed assets is appropriate in industries where significant equipment is required to do business.

These ratios are long-term measures of performance, which are of primary interest to equity investors and stock market analysts. Both asset values are stated net of accumulated depreciation. For the Belfry Company we have the following ratios.

$$\text{fixed asset turnover} = \frac{\$10,000}{\$4,500} = 2.2$$

$$\text{total asset turnover} = \frac{\$10,000}{\$12,000} = .83$$

The units here are generally stated as "times," sometimes with the symbol "×." For example, Belfry's fixed asset turnover might be written as 2.2 × for "2.2 times."

3.4f   Debt Management Ratios

Debt management deals with how the firm uses other people's money to its own advantage. By "other people's money" we mean borrowing as well as trade credit and other liabilities. In financial analysis, we're primarily concerned that a company doesn't use so much of these funds that it assumes excessive risk. This is an important point. The problem with using other people's money is that it requires future cash outflows for interest and/or repayment. If a firm's operations don't supply enough cash for those payments, it can get in big trouble.

Terminology   The term *debt* in ratio analysis requires a little amplification. Some authorities use the word to mean any source of money other than equity. Applied to our examples that definition means *debt* is the sum of long-term debt and current liabilities. Others prefer to restrict the idea of *debt* to interest-bearing obligations, which are generally long-term borrowings.

Theorists tend to prefer the first interpretation. They like to add current liabilities and long-term debt to arrive at a *total debt* figure for use in ratio analysis. Businesspeople, however, are more likely to limit the definition of debt to long-term, interest- bearing borrowing. Clearly this can lead to some confusion.

In this book, we'll simply be careful to say exactly what we mean. We'll call *total debt* the sum of current liabilities and long-term debt. Long-term debt will mean just that, and we'll take the word *debt* by itself to mean formal borrowing regardless of term. Where common usage is different we'll explain.

The Debt Ratio

The **debt ratio** uses the total debt concept and measures the relationship between total debt and equity in supporting the firm's assets. That is, it tells us how much of the firm's assets are supported by other people's money.

$$\text{debt ratio} = \frac{\text{long-term} + \text{current liabilities}}{\text{total assets}}$$

A high debt ratio is viewed as risky by investors, especially lenders. Debt management ratios are generally stated as percentages.

Belfry's debt ratio is

$$\text{debt ratio} = \frac{\$6,200 + 2,500}{\$12,000} = 72.5\%$$

This says that almost three quarters of the company's assets are supported by other people's money. That's high enough to be a concern in most industries.

Debt to Equity Ratio

The **debt to equity ratio** generally uses just long-term debt and is stated somewhat differently than other ratios.

$$\text{debt to equity ratio} = \text{long-term debt : equity}$$

This ratio is a measure of the mix of debt and equity within the firm's total capital. It is an important measure of risk, because a high level of debt can burden the income statement with excessive interest. This makes the firm's profitability fragile in recessionary times. Interest is known as a **fixed financial charge**, and must be paid regardless of whether revenues and profits are healthy. Hence in a business downturn, large interest charges can throw a company into a loss position quickly. The riskiness associated with debt and interest is called **financial risk**.

This ratio is unusual in that it is commonly stated as a proportion rather than as a decimal or a percentage. For example, if capital of $100 includes debt of $33.33, conventional terminology would describe the debt to equity ratio as "one-third—two-thirds," or "33/67." If capital is two-thirds debt, we would say the ratio is "2 to 1 debt to equity."

For Belfry we have

$$\text{debt to equity} = \$6,200 : \$3,300$$

Fixed financial charges like interest increase a firm's **financial risk**.

This would be stated as 1.9 : 1 (1.9 to 1) because $6,200/$3,300 = 1.9. Here again, Belfry is marginal. Two-thirds debt to one-third equity would generally be considered quite risky in most nonfinancial businesses.

Times Interest Earned (TIE)   TIE gets at the idea of burdening the income statement with interest more directly. It measures the number of times interest can be paid out of earnings before interest and taxes (EBIT).

$$\text{TIE} = \frac{\text{EBIT}}{\text{interest}}$$

A high level of **interest coverage** implies safety.

TIE is called a *coverage ratio.* For example, if EBIT is $100 and interest is $10, so TIE is 10, we would say that interest is covered 10 times. Clearly, the more times earnings cover existing interest, the safer it is to lend the firm more money.

For the Belfry Company we have

$$\text{TIE} = \frac{\$1,900}{\$400} = 4.8$$

The appropriate unit is times.

Cash Coverage   There's an obvious problem with the TIE ratio. Interest is a cash payment, but EBIT is not exactly a source of cash. Rather, it's an income statement subtotal that may be considerably different from cash flow. In other words, more or less cash than EBIT may be available in any given year to pay interest. The problem can be partially solved by recognizing that the biggest difference between EBIT and a comparable cash figure is depreciation. It is subtracted as part of cost and expense in the calculation of EBIT.

A better approximation of coverage is available if we form another ratio with depreciation added to EBIT in the numerator. This ratio is called *cash coverage.*

$$\text{cash coverage} = \frac{\text{EBIT} + \text{depreciation}}{\text{interest}}$$

Belfry's cash coverage is

$$\text{cash coverage} = \frac{\$1,900 + \$500}{\$400} = 6.0$$

Fixed Charge Coverage   The TIE and cash coverage ratios recognize interest as a *fixed* financing charge. The term "fixed" implies that interest must be paid regardless of business conditions, unlike dividends, which may be reduced if earnings are poor.

Lease payments are **fixed** financial charges similar to interest.

In recent years, leasing has supplemented debt as a means of acquiring assets. Instead of borrowing to buy equipment, businesses lease the same equipment and make lease instead of interest payments. We'll discuss leasing in Chapter 7.

However, if a company's leased equipment is necessary to stay in business, or if the leases are contractually noncancelable, the payments become fixed charges in the sense that they have to be paid regardless of conditions, just like interest.

We can adjust the TIE ratio to recognize this additional fixed charge. Because lease payments have been subtracted along with other costs and expenses to come to EBIT, they must be added back in the numerator to arrive at a cash figure available to pay all fixed charges. The same amounts must also be added to the denominator as fixed charges equivalent to interest. The resulting ratio is known as *fixed charge coverage.*

$$\text{fixed charge coverage} = \frac{\text{EBIT + lease payments}}{\text{interest + lease payments}}$$

Other fixed charges can be added to the numerator and denominator when appropriate.

We'll assume that the Belfry Company has $700 of lease payments within its cost and expense figures. Its fixed charge coverage is then

$$\text{fixed charge coverage} = \frac{\$1,900 + \$700}{\$400 + \$700} = 2.4$$

Debt management ratios are important to both creditors and stockholders. Creditors want to make sure funds are available to pay interest and principal, and are therefore particularly interested in short-run coverage ratios. Stockholders are concerned about the impact of excessive debt and interest on long-term profitability.

EBITDA and Variations on Coverage Ratios   The idea behind coverage ratios is to compare fixed or obligatory payments with the cash available to pay (cover) them. Thus we add depreciation to EBIT to better approximate cash flow in the cash coverage ratio and recognize lease payments as fixed charges similar to interest in the fixed charge coverage ratio. In many cases, loan principal must repaid regularly, so it's appropriate to add mandatory principle repayments as well. Any combination is possible.

In this context, the term EBITDA has come into use in recent years. EBITDA stands for Earnings Before Interest, Taxes, Depreciation, and Amortization. The last term is an accounting entry that allocates the cost of intangible items over time in a manner similar to depreciation. For example, a company might *amortize* the cost of a patent over time just as it would *depreciate* a fixed asset costing a similar amount.

If a company has depreciation and amortization expense, the numerator of the cash coverage ratio becomes EBIT + Depreciation + Amortization, which leads to the acronym EBITDA. The EBITDA coverage ratio puts all of these ideas together.

$$\text{EBITDA coverage} = \frac{\text{EBITDA + lease payments}}{\text{interest + lease payments + principal repayment}}$$

Notice that principal repayments are not added to the numerator because they aren't expense items and therefore are not subtracted in the calculation of EBIT.

In an effort to keep the Belfry example simple and straightforward, we haven't included amortization, principal repayment, and EBITDA in the example. You should, however, be aware of the EBITDA acronym.

3.4g   Profitability Ratios

The most fundamental measure of a business's success is profit. Without profit there are no dividends, and without dividends or the expectation of them, no one will invest in stock.

Lenders don't like profitless companies either. Firms that are losing money or barely breaking even are perilously close to not being able to repay their loans.

Profitability ratios give us relative measures of the firm's money-making success. That is, they gauge profits per dollar of sales made, assets employed, or equity invested. They're generally stated as percentages.

ROS measures control of the income statement: **revenue, cost,** and **expense**.

Return on Sales (ROS)

Return on sales (ROS) is also called the *profit margin* or *net profit margin*. It is simply net income as a percentage of sales.

(3.5)
$$\text{ROS} = \frac{\text{net income}}{\text{sales}}$$

Notice that this ratio is the bottom line of the common size income statement. It is a fundamental indication of the overall profitability of the business. It gives insight into management's ability to control the income statement items of revenue, cost, and expense.

Belfry's ROS is

$$\text{ROS} = \frac{\$1,000}{\$10,000} = 10\%$$

ROA adds the effectiveness of **asset management** to ROS.

Return on Assets (ROA)

A business uses assets and the skills of its people to earn a profit. **Return on assets (ROA)** quantifies the success of that effort with respect to assets by stating net income as a percentage of total assets.

(3.6)
$$\text{ROA} = \frac{\text{net income}}{\text{total assets}}$$

ROA measures the overall ability of the firm to utilize the assets in which it has invested to earn a profit.

Belfry's ROA is

$$\text{ROA} = \frac{\$1,000}{\$12,000} = 8.3\%$$

ROE adds the effect of **borrowing** to ROA.

Return on Equity (ROE)

Return on equity (ROE) is the most fundamental profitability ratio. It states net income as a percentage of equity.

(3.7)
$$\text{ROE} = \frac{\text{net income}}{\text{equity}}$$

ROE measures the firm's ability to earn a return on the owners' invested capital. It takes the ROA concept one step further by factoring in the effect of borrowed money. If the firm has substantial debt, ROE tends to be higher than ROA in good times and lower in bad times. If there is little or no debt, ROE and ROA are close to the same. We'll talk about the effect of borrowed money, called *leverage,* in detail in Chapter 14. For Belfry we have

$$\text{ROE} = \frac{\$1,000}{\$3,300} = 30.3\%$$

This figure is quite good by most industry standards, and seems in conflict with Belfry's poor performance in the asset management area. The reason is Belfry's liberal use of debt (also called leverage). The company's two-third to one-third debt to equity ratio has leveraged its owner's return up to a heady 30%. In other words, it has turned good results at ROS and ROA into great results at ROE. But a price must be paid for that success and its name is risk. Leverage works both ways. In good times, it makes ordinary results great, but in bad times it makes poor performance terrible and can even cause failure. We'll return to this idea later in this chapter and take a thorough look at leverage in Chapter 14.

3.4h   Market Value Ratios

The ratios we've discussed so far all pertain to the internal management of the firm. As such they are all more or less under the control of management. Another set of ratios compares certain financial statement figures to the value the stock market places on the firm. These ratios are less controllable by management because the perceptions and attitudes of the investing public are imposed on the actions of the company in arriving at market value. Management can influence those perceptions and attitudes, but it doesn't control them.

> A firm's **market capitalization** is the per-share price of stock multiplied by the numbers of shares outstanding.

The market value of a company is reflected in the price of its stock. Multiplying the per-share price by the number of shares outstanding leads to a value for the company as a whole—often called its **market capitalization**. However, it is common practice to think in terms of per-share values.

Price/Earnings Ratio   This ratio compares the market price of the stock to the **earnings per share** calculated from the latest income statement. Earnings per share is simply net income divided by the number of shares of common stock outstanding. It is usually abbreviated as **EPS**, while the price/earnings ratio is referred to as the **P/E ratio**.

> The **P/E ratio** is an indication of the value the **stock market** places on a company.

$$\text{P/E ratio} = \frac{\text{stock price}}{\text{EPS}}$$

The P/E ratio is very important in the stock market. Notice that it tells us how much investors are willing to pay for a dollar of the firm's earnings. For example, if a company's P/E is 10 and earnings per share are $4.50, the stock is selling for $45. Stock market people would say, "The company is selling for 10 times earnings."

Different companies carry different P/Es. Clearly, the higher the P/E, the better because a dollar of earnings translates into more shareholder wealth at higher P/Es. The most significant factor leading to a high P/E ratio is a high expected level of growth by the company.

> A firm's P/E is primarily a function of its **expected growth**.

P/Es must be used with caution. A firm that is losing money doesn't have a meaningful P/E. Further, if profits are very small but the stock has some value, the P/E can be enormous. That isn't meaningful either.

To calculate market value ratios for the Belfry Company, we need the number of shares outstanding and the price of the stock. For the sake of illustration we'll assume that there are 300,000 shares valued at a price of $38 per share. Earnings per share is then (since we're calculating a per-share figure, we'll state net income in dollars rather than thousands of dollars)

$$\text{EPS} = \$1,000,000/300,000 = \$3.33$$

and the P/E ratio is

$$\text{P/E} = \frac{\$38}{\$3.33} = 11.4$$

The P/E ratio is an important indicator of how the investing community feels about a stock. Stocks with promising future earnings are rewarded with high P/Es—meaning that they sell at higher prices than the stocks of other companies with similar per-share earnings.

What constitutes a good P/E ratio varies a great deal over time. The average P/E of widely traded stocks has ranged from less than 10 to more than 40 over the last century. In recent years, Belfry's P/E of about 11 would indicate that investors are unenthusiastic about the company. That could be a result of carrying too much debt and being perceived as a risky investment.

However, P/Es vary tremendously by industry, so a comparison with overall market averages is less meaningful than a comparison with an industry average. In the last 40 years, the highest P/Es have generally been found in high tech fields, where very rapid growth is not unusual.

Market to Book Value Ratio   A company's **book value** is the total value of the equity on its balance sheet. That's equal to the value of assets less liabilities to outsiders. Notice that it may be more or less than the amount the firm could actually realize by selling everything and paying off its debts.

A firm's **book value** is the total value of equity on its balance sheet.

A healthy company is usually expected to have a market value in excess of its book value. This is sometimes known as the **going concern value** of the firm. The idea is that the combination of assets and people that creates an enterprise will generate future earnings that are worth more than the assets alone are worth today.

The market to book value ratio gets at this idea of excess value. Like P/E, it is generally thought of in per-share terms. Market value per share is just the price of the stock, and book value per share is total equity divided by the number of shares outstanding. The calculation is

$$\text{market to book value ratio} = \frac{\text{stock price}}{\text{book value per share}}$$

The market to book value ratio is a broad indicator of what the market thinks of a particular stock. A value below 1.0 indicates grave concern about the company's future. Such a firm is said to be selling *below book.*

Speculative investors sometimes like to gamble on stocks whose market to book value ratio is below 1.0. Situations arise in which a stock's price is depressed because the market has overreacted to bad news about a fundamentally sound company. In such a case, the firm's stock price sometimes rebounds quickly, and an investment at the depressed level can be very profitable. Some investors use the market to book value ratio to identify situations in which this *might* be the case.

Belfry's book value per share is its equity divided by the number of shares outstanding.

$$\text{book value per share} = \$3,300,000/300,000 = \$11$$

The market to book value ratio is then

$$\text{market to book value ratio} = \frac{38}{11} = 3.5$$

Table 3-2 summarizes all of the foregoing ratios.

TABLE 3-2 **Financial Ratios**

Liquidity Ratios

$$\text{current ratio} = \frac{\text{current assets}}{\text{current liabilities}}$$

$$\text{quick ratio} = \frac{\text{current assets} - \text{inventory}}{\text{current liabilities}}$$

*Asset Management Ratios**

$$\text{ACP} = \frac{\text{accounts receivable}}{\text{average daily sales}} = \frac{\text{accounts receivable}}{\text{sales}} \times 360$$

$$\text{inventory turnover} = \frac{\text{cost of goods sold}}{\text{inventory}}$$

$$\text{fixed asset turnover} = \frac{\text{sales}}{\text{fixed assets}}$$

$$\text{total asset turnover} = \frac{\text{sales}}{\text{total assets}}$$

Debt Management Ratios

$$\text{debt ratio} = \frac{\text{long-term debt} + \text{current liabilities}}{\text{total assets}}$$

$$\text{debt to equity ratio} = \text{long-term debt : equity}$$

$$\text{TIE} = \frac{\text{EBIT}}{\text{interest}}$$

$$\text{cash coverage} = \frac{\text{EBIT} + \text{depreciation}}{\text{interest}}$$

$$\text{fixed charge coverage} = \frac{\text{EBIT} + \text{lease payments}}{\text{interest} + \text{lease payments}}$$

$$\text{EBITDA coverage} = \frac{\text{EBITDA} + \text{lease payments}}{\text{interest} + \text{lease payments} + \text{principal repayment}}$$

Profitability Ratios

$$\text{ROS} = \frac{\text{net income}}{\text{sales}}$$

$$\text{ROA*} = \frac{\text{net income}}{\text{total assets}}$$

$$\text{ROE*} = \frac{\text{net income}}{\text{equity}}$$

Market Value Ratios

$$\text{P/E ratio} = \frac{\text{stock price}}{\text{EPS}}$$

$$\text{market to book value ratio} = \frac{\text{stock price}}{\text{book value per share}}$$

Average balance sheet values may be appropriate.

3.4i   Du Pont Equations

Each of the ratios we've been talking about measures a particular aspect of running a company. However, the ratio measures aren't entirely independent, and performance on one is sometimes tied to performance on others.

Two insightful relationships between ratios are captured in the **Du Pont equations**.[7] The first is developed by writing the definition of ROA, Equation 3.6, and multiplying by sales/sales ($=1$, so the multiplication doesn't change the value of the expression).

> The **Du Pont equations** express relationships between ratios that give **insights** into successful operation.

$$\text{ROA} = \frac{\text{net income}}{\text{total assets}} \times \frac{\text{sales}}{\text{sales}}$$

Now reverse the order of the denominators to get

$$\text{ROA} = \frac{\text{net income}}{\text{sales}} \times \frac{\text{sales}}{\text{total assets}}$$

Notice that we've formed two ratios, the product of which is ROA. But we've seen the new ratios before; they're return on sales, Equation 3.5 on page 98, and total asset turnover, Equation 3.4 on page 94. Substituting gives the Du Pont equation:

(3.8)   **ROA = ROS × total asset turnover**

The relationship is an important result. ROA is a fundamental measure of performance, indicating how well a company uses its assets to generate profits. But it is the product of two more elementary measures. The first, ROS, measures how well a firm keeps some of its sales dollars in profit. The second, total asset turnover, measures the company's ability to generate sales with the assets it has.

The Du Pont equation tells us that to run a business well, as measured by ROA, we have to manage costs and expenses well and generate a lot of sales per dollar of assets. This lesson should sound familiar. It's the same message we got from the racetrack diagram (cash conversion cycle, Figure 3-3 on p. 86) earlier in this chapter.

The *extended Du Pont equation* takes the idea one step further by expressing return on equity (ROE) in terms of other ratios. We'll develop that by writing the definition of ROE, Equation 3.7 on page 98, and multiplying by sales/sales and by total assets/total assets.

$$\text{ROE} = \frac{\text{net income}}{\text{equity}} \times \frac{\text{sales}}{\text{sales}} \times \frac{\text{total assets}}{\text{total assets}}$$

Now rearrange the denominators to get

$$\text{ROE} = \frac{\text{net income}}{\text{sales}} \times \frac{\text{sales}}{\text{total assets}} \times \frac{\text{total assets}}{\text{equity}}$$

The last term is called the *equity multiplier*. We'll explain it in a minute, but first notice that the ROE expression is the same as the ROA expression with the last term added.

---

7.   So called because they were developed at the Du Pont corporation.

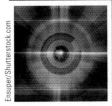

INSIGHTS | Practical Finance

Concepts in Financial Analysis: EVA® and MVA

In recent years, the related ideas of **economic value added (EVA®)** and **market value added (MVA)** have become popular as gauges of business success. The concept behind both measures is the creation of shareholder wealth. We'll consider MVA first.

There are two ways to think about the value of a firm's equity. The *market* value of equity is just stock price times the number of shares outstanding. At the same time, the equity *contributed* by shareholders is reflected in the equity accounts on the company's books (including retained earnings). If market value is greater than book value, some *additional* value has been created by the company acting as an ongoing business. This extra is MVA. It's the cumulative amount management has made for the stockholders over and above dividends since the inception of the firm.

Notice that MVA can be negative if the stock is selling below its book value. Conceptually MVA is similar to the market to book value ratio we discussed earlier. You should be able to see that a negative MVA is equivalent to a market to book ratio of less than 1.0.

The more exciting idea is EVA, economic value added. In theory, it is the amount by which the firm increases or decreases MVA in the current year.

Before defining EVA precisely, it's important to notice something about traditional net income. When we calculate net income we subtract interest from revenues along with other costs and expenses. You can think of interest as the cost the company pays for the use of its debt capital. We do not, however, subtract a payment to stockholders for the use of equity capital.

That means financial analysis based on net income recognizes the cost of debt (interest) but implicitly treats equity as a free source of capital. This presents a problem because equity capital does have a cost, basically the return demanded by stockholders on their investments. Ignoring the cost of equity makes performance seem better than it is. For example, a company with a small positive net income is profitable in an accounting sense but may be an economic failure because it doesn't provide an adequate return to stockholders on their equity investments.

A better measure of overall performance than accounting net income would be produced if we modified the income statement to subtract the cost of both debt and equity capital instead of just the interest cost of debt. This is exactly what EVA does using a concept called the **cost of capital.** We'll study the cost of capital a great deal in a later chapter. For now it's enough to understand that it's a single, average "interest rate" that reflects the rate of return the business pays to the suppliers of its capital, both debt and equity. That rate, stated on an after-tax basis, is the "cost" of the capital funds the firm uses. EVA is defined as follows.

$$EVA = EBIT(1 - T) - (debt + equity)(cost\ of\ capital\ \%)$$

where T is the tax rate.

The first term on the right is EBIT adjusted to an after-tax basis by multiplying by $(1 - T)$. This figure is what the firm's after-tax earnings would be if there were no charges for the use of capital, either debt or equity.

The second term on the right subtracts a charge for the use of capital. Debt + equity is total capital, so the cost of capital percentage times that sum is the dollar amount the firm pays for the use of all of its capital. This term is like the traditional interest charge in the income statement except that it's expanded to include a payment for equity. It's an after-tax figure, because the cost of capital percentage is stated after tax.

Hence, EVA is after-tax earnings less an after-tax charge for all capital. But the charge for capital is simply the minimum amount stockholders and bondholders demand for investing their money. They could make that amount by putting it in any number of alternate investments. Hence, if EVA is positive, the firm is exceeding its investors' expectations. That is, a positive EVA is an extra, an additional contribution to shareholders' wealth made during the year.

This is a very important idea. If EVA is zero, the firm is just earning what investors expect and demand, nothing more and nothing less. That's *adequate* performance. On the other hand, if EVA is positive, management is performing above expectations and contributing some additional value to stockholders. A negative EVA, of course, means the firm is losing ground, making a negative contribution to shareholder wealth.

EVA began to gain popularity about 20 years ago and is one of the hottest ideas in financial management today. More firms seem to be using it with each passing year. Several attribute major gains in market value to a management focus on EVA rather than traditional net income. The EVA and MVA concepts were developed by Stern Stewart & Co., a financial consulting firm. Stern Stewart maintains that its clients who use EVA outperform their peers in the stock market.

Source: www.eva.com.

ROE = ROS × total asset turnover × equity multiplier

Then, substituting Equation 3.8 yields

ROE = ROA × equity multiplier

The equity multiplier has to do with the idea of leverage, using borrowed money instead of your own to work for you. Hence, the extended Du Pont equation says that to measure performance in terms of ROE, we add the concept of leverage to performance in terms of ROA.

To understand the equity multiplier, consider the right side of the balance sheet. It lists all of the places where the firm's money comes from: equity, debt, and other liabilities.[8] These add to total assets because both sides of the balance sheet sum to that figure. Debt and other liabilities are other people's money, while equity is the firm's own money (its owners'). The equity multiplier is related to the proportion to which the firm is financed by other people's money as opposed to owners' money.

For example, suppose a firm has total assets of $100 and equity of $25. That means three quarters of its assets are financed by debt and/or liabilities ($75) and one quarter ($25) is supported by equity. The equity multiplier is ($100/$25 =) 4, and the extended Du Pont equation says that the firm's ROE will be four times its ROA because of the use of other people's money.

That's very good if the business is making a profit and ROA is a positive number. For example, if ROA is 5%, ROE would be a healthy 20%. However, if times get tough, using other people's money is generally bad news. Suppose the business starts to lose

---

8. In our Belfry example, other liabilities are simply current liabilities, but that's not always the case.

money and ROA is −5%. Unfortunately, the multiplier still works the same way, and ROE will be −20%, a pretty dismal figure.

The extended Du Pont equation says something very important about running a business. The operation of the business itself is reflected in ROA. This means managing customers, people, costs, expenses, and equipment. But that result, good or bad, can be *multiplied* by borrowing. In other words, the way you *finance* a business can greatly exaggerate the results of nuts and bolts operations.

Write out the Du Pont equations for Belfry to verify the relationships.

3.4j   Using the Du Pont Equations

Comparing the Du Pont equations between a company and an industry average can give some insights into how a firm is doing in relation to its competitors. For example, suppose we have the following data for Samson Inc. and its industry.

	ROA	=	ROS	×	Total Asset Turnover
Samson Inc.	12%		6%		2×
Industry	15%		5%		3×

The Du Pont equations can be used to **isolate problems**.

If Samson is trying to figure out why its ROA is below average, this display focuses attention in the right direction. It says that Samson's management of income statement items, like cost and expense, is a little better than average, but its use of assets to generate sales, as measured by total asset turnover, is very poor in comparison to the competition.

The turnover problem is probably in one or both of two areas. Perhaps the company has unnecessary or ineffective assets, such as overstated inventory or inefficient machinery. Or maybe its promotional activities are not on target, so sales are lower than they should be. The job is now to find out what's going on and fix the problem.

3.4k   Sources of Comparative Information

The best competitive information for ratio analysis is generally an industry average. These averages are available in several places.

Dun and Bradstreet (D&B) is a credit rating service. Vendors use D&B reports to make decisions about whether or not to sell to customers on credit.

D&B maintains credit files on most businesses in the United States. The files include financial information and comments on a firm's past payment history as reported by other firms that have done business with it. D&B subscribers can order reports on specific companies to help in making the credit decision.

D&B has summarized its data to provide industry average ratios for about 800 lines of business. The information is published in *Industry Norms and Key Business Ratios.*

The Risk Management Association is an association of bank lending officers. It publishes summarized ratio information on 250 industries in *Statement Studies.*

The *U.S. Commerce Department* publishes the *Quarterly Financial Report,* which contains summarized ratio information for a large number of industries. Government reports on industry are usually organized by the Standard Industrial Classification (SIC) Code that provides a systematic segregation and cataloging of industrial activity.

Value Line and similar investment advisory services provide industry profiles as well as reports on individual companies.

3.41   Limitations and Weaknesses of Ratio Analysis

Ratio analysis is **not an exact science** and requires judgment and **experienced interpretation**.

Although ratio analysis is a powerful tool, it has some significant shortcomings. Analysts have to be careful not to apply the techniques blindly with any set of statements they come across. Here are a few of the more significant problems.

Diversified companies, large firms with consolidated operations, create what is probably the biggest analysis problem. Such companies often have divisions operating in significantly different industries. The financial information they publish *consolidates* the results of those different operations into one set of statements. Because the interpretation of ratios is highly dependent on industry norms, this mixing of results from different businesses can greatly reduce the informative value of analysis.

Financial reporting standards set by the accounting profession for diversified businesses require the disclosure of some *segment information,* but it is generally of limited scope and use.

Window dressing refers to practices at year end that make balance sheets look better than they otherwise would through improvements that don't last. Here's a simple example. Imagine a firm with a current ratio that's too low whose business is fundamentally sound so it can borrow long term. Suppose this company takes out a long-term loan a few days before the end of the year, holds the proceeds in cash, a current asset, over year end, and repays the loan a few days later. It thus increases year-end current assets with no impact on current liabilities, thereby improving the reported current ratio.

Accounting principles allow a great deal of latitude in reporting. That means similar companies might report the same thing differently, making their financial results artificially dissimilar. Depreciation is a good example. The choice between accelerated and straight line depreciation is up to the firm, but the difference can double reported depreciation in a given period. That in turn can make a big percentage difference in net income between two essentially identical firms.

Inflation often distorts financial statements. Real estate purchased years ago, for example, will be carried on the balance sheet at its original cost. Yet it may be worth many times that amount in today's market. During periods of rapid inflation, inventory, cost of goods sold, and depreciation can badly distort true results.

The *interpretation* of ratios isn't always clear. Recall our discussion of the current ratio and inventory turnover.

The most important thing to remember with respect to these issues is that *ratio analysis doesn't give answers; it helps you ask the right questions.*

CONCEPT CONNECTIONS

EXAMPLE 3-1   A Business Statement of Cash Flows, *page 79*

EXAMPLE 3-2   A Free Cash Flow Business Analysis, *page 85*

EXAMPLE 3-3   Common Size Statements, *page 89*

Note: Seventeen financial ratios are defined and explained on pages 90–100. Each is illustrated using values from the financial statements of Example 3-1. The ratio calculations are not, however, labeled as individual examples.

QUESTIONS

1. List the main user groups of financial information. What are the reasons for their interest?

2. Where do analysts get financial information about companies? What are their concerns about the information?

3. Financial analysts are generally optimists who believe what they're told. Right or wrong? Explain.

4. If a company's cash account increases from the beginning to the end of the year, there's more cash on hand so that must be a source of cash. Yet the cash account is an asset, and the first cash flow rule says that an asset increase is a use of cash. Explain this apparent conflict.

5. Why don't we calculate the difference in the equity account between the beginning and end of the year and consider that difference as a source or use of cash? Why do we similarly exclude the cash account?

6. What are free cash flows? Who is likely to be most interested in them? Why?

7. Outline the thinking behind ratio analysis in brief, general terms (a few lines; don't go into each ratio individually).

8. Financial ratios don't do you much good by themselves. Explain.

9. What is the reasoning behind using the current ratio as a measure of liquidity?

10. Why do we need the quick ratio when we have the current ratio?

11. A company's terms are net 30 and the ACP is 35 days. Is that cause for alarm? Why or why not?

12. Discuss the different definitions of debt in ratio analysis.

13. Why do people view having too much debt as risky? If you were interested in determining whether a company had too much debt, what measure would you use? Why? How much debt do you think would generally be considered too much?

14. It can be argued that the TIE ratio doesn't make much sense. Why? How would you change the measure to be more meaningful? (*Hint:* Think in terms of cash flows.)

15. Can managers affect market value ratios?

16. Can a competent financial analyst always correctly assess a firm's financial health from publicly available information? Explain.

BUSINESS ANALYSIS

1. The present format for the statement of cash flows is organized according to operating activities, investing activities, and financing activities. That format has only been in use since the late 1980s. The previous format first listed all sources and then all uses of cash, giving a subtotal for each. Cash flow was then the difference between the two subtotals. What advantages or disadvantages do you see of the current format in relation to the old one? Which would you prefer if you had a choice?

2. A company has been growing rapidly for the last three years. It was profitable before the growth spurt started. Although this year's revenues are almost three times those of three years ago, the firm is now losing money. What's the first thing you would do to try to pinpoint where the problem(s) may be?

3. The term "liquidity" is used in several ways. What does it mean in the context of an asset or liability, such as those on the balance sheet? What does it mean when applied to an operating company? What does the similar term "liquidate" mean when applied to a company?

4. The industry average inventory turnover ratio is 7 and your company's is 15. This could be good or bad news. Explain each possibility. How would you find out whether it is bad news?

5. You invested $20,000 in the stock of HiFly Inc. two years ago. Since then the stock has done very well—more than doubling in value. You tried to analyze HiFly's financial statements twice in the last two years, but were confused by several of the detailed notes to those statements. You haven't worried about it though, because the statements show a steady growth in revenue and earnings along with an unqualified opinion by the firm's auditors that they were prepared using generally accepted accounting principles (GAAP). While checking the status of your investments online this morning you were shocked to see that HiFly's price had declined by 30% since you checked it a week ago. What may have happened?

PROBLEMS

A Business Statement of Cash Flows—Current Accounts Detail: Concept Connection Example 3-1 (page 79)

1. The Waterford Wax Company had the following current account activity last year.

	Beginning	Ending		Beginning	Ending
Cash	$ 160	$ 333	Accounts payable	$722	$2,084
Accounts receivable	1,875	3,810	Accruals	217	456
Inventory	438	2,676			
Current assets	$2,473	$6,819	Current liabilities	$939	$2,540

a. Calculate and display the current account detail required for the Cash from Operating Activities section of the statement of cash flows.

b. If you also knew that Waterford's revenues had risen by 20% last year, would you be concerned about the firm's financial health? Why? (Words only.)

A Business Statement of Cash Flows—Operating Activities Detail: Concept Connection Example 3-1 (page 80)

2. Timberline Inc. had the following current accounts last year. ($000)

	Beginning	Ending		Beginning	Ending
Cash	$ 175	$ 238	Accounts payable	$ 205	$ 182
Accounts receivable	1,456	2,207	Accruals	95	83
Inventory	943	786			
Current assets	$2,574	$ 3,231	Current liabilities	$300	$265

In addition, the company had sales revenues of $9,453,000 and costs and expenses (including interest and tax) of $7,580,000. Depreciation of $1,462,000 is included in the cost and expense figures.

Construct a statement showing Timberline's Cash from Operating Activities section, including a detail of changes in balance sheet accounts.

A Business Statement of Cash Flows: Concept Connection Example 3-1 (page 79)

3. Latigoe Inc. has the following financial statements for 20X8. In addition, the company paid stockholders dividends of $2.9 million and received $4.8 million from the sale of new stock. No fixed assets were retired during the year. (*Hint:* That implies that fixed asset purchases and depreciation are equal to the changes in the gross fixed asset and accumulated depreciation accounts.)

Latigoe Inc.

Balance Sheet

For the period ended 12/31/X8 ($000)

ASSETS

	12/31/X7	12/31/X8
Cash	$ 3,245	$ 2,647
Accounts receivable	7,943	5,614
Inventory	12,408	13,653
CURRENT ASSETS	$ 23,596	$ 21,914
Fixed assets		
Gross	$66,098	$ 72,166
Accumulated depreciation	(47,040)	(51,308)
Net	$ 19,058	$20,858
TOTAL ASSETS	$ 42,654	$ 42,772

Latigoe Inc.

LIABILITIES

Accounts payable	$ 1,699	$ 2,208
Accruals	950	754
CURRENT LIABILITIES	$ 2,649	$ 2,962
Long-term debt	$ 9,007	$ 1,352
Equity	30,998	38,458
TOTAL CAPITAL	$40,005	$ 39,810
TOTAL LIABLITIES AND EQUITY	$ 42,654	$42,772

Latigoe Inc.

Income Statement

For the period ended 12/31/X8 ($000)

Sales	$ 67,916
COGS	35,281
Gross margin	$32,635
Depreciation	4,268
Expense	$18,004
EBIT	$10,363
Interest	1,096
EBT	$ 9,267
Tax	3,707
Net income	$ 5,560

Construct Latigoe's statement of cash flows for 20X8.

4. Fitch Inc.'s financial statements are as follows:

Fitch Inc.

Balance Sheet

For the period ended 12/31/X1 ($000)

ASSETS

	12/31/X0	12/31/X1
Cash	$ 2,165	$ 2,647
Accounts receivable	4,832	5,614
Inventory	3,217	2,843
CURRENT ASSETS	$ 10,214	$ 11,104
Fixed assets		
Gross	$ 35,183	$39,456
Accumulated depreciation	(22,640)	(24,852)
Net	$ 12,543	$ 14,604
TOTAL ASSETS	$ 22,757	$ 25,708

LIABILITIES

Accounts payable	$ 1,642	$ 1,420
Accruals	438	1,228
CURRENT LIABILITIES	$ 2,080	$ 2,648
Long-term debt	$ 1,823	$ 409
Equity	18,854	22,651
TOTAL CAPITAL	$ 20,677	$23,060
TOTAL LIABILITIES AND EQUITY	$ 22,757	$ 25,708

Fitch Inc.

Income Statement

For the period ended 12/31/X1 ($000)

Sales	$40,506
COGS	14,177
Gross margin	$ 26,329
Expense	19,487
EBIT	$ 6,842
Interest	180
EBT	$ 6,662
Tax	2,265
Net income	$ 4,397

Fitch also sold stock for $2.5 million and paid dividends of $3.1 million. No fixed assets were retired during the year. (*Hint:* That implies fixed asset purchases and depreciation are the only changes in the gross fixed assets and accumulated depreciation accounts.)

Construct Fitch's statement of cash flows for 20X1.

5. Axtel Company has the following financial statements.

Axtel Company

Balance Sheet

For the period ended 12/31/X1 ($000)

ASSETS

	12/31/X0	12/31/X1
Cash	$ 3,514	$ 2,875
Accounts receivable	6,742	5,583
Inventory	2,573	3,220
CURRENT ASSETS	$ 12,829	$ 11,678
Fixed assets		
Gross	$22,478	$24,360
Accumulated depreciation	(12,147)	(13,313)
Net	$ 10,331	$ 11,047
TOTAL ASSETS	$ 23,160	$ 22,725

LIABILITIES

Accounts payable	$ 1,556	$ 1,702
Accruals	268	408
CURRENT LIABILITIES	$ 1,824	$ 2,110
Long-term debt	$ 7,112	$ 6,002
Equity	14,224	14,613
TOTAL CAPITAL	$ 21,336	$ 20,615
TOTAL LIABILITIES		
AND EQUITY	$ 23,160	$ 22,725

Axtel Company

Income Statement

For the period ended 12/31/X1 ($000)

Sales	$36,227
COGS	19,925
Gross margin	$16,302
Expense	10,868
EBIT	$ 5,434
Interest	713
EBT	$ 4,721
Tax	1,605
Net income	$ 3,116

In addition, Axtel *retired* stock for $1,000,000 and paid a dividend of $1,727,000. Depreciation for the year was $1,166,000. Construct a statement of cash flows for Axtel for 20X1. (*Hint:* Retiring stock means buying it back from shareholders. Assume the purchase was made at book value, and treat it like a negative sale of stock.)

6. Fred Klein started his own business recently. He began by depositing $5,000 of his own money (equity) in a business account. Once he'd done that his balance sheet was as follows.

	Assets	Liabilities and Equity	
Cash	$5,000	Equity	$5,000
Total	$5,000	Total	$5,000

During the next month, his first month of business, he completed the following transactions. (All payments were made with checks out of the bank account.)

- Purchased $2,500 worth of inventory, paying $1,500 down and owing the vendor the remainder.
- Used $500 of the inventory in making product.
- Paid employees' wages of $1,100 on the last day of the month.
- Sold all the product made in the first month on credit for $3,000.
- Paid rent of $1,200.

a. Construct a balance sheet for Fred's business at the end of its first month. (*Hint:* Fred's business has only current assets, current liabilities, and an equity account. Calculate the ending balance in each of the current accounts from the information given. The ending equity account balance will be the difference between the current assets and liabilities at month end.)

b. Construct Fred's income statement. (*Hint:* Fred's revenue is the credit sale. His costs/expenses consist of the inventory used in product sold plus the things other than inventory for which he wrote checks. Ignore taxes.)

c. Construct Fred's statement of cash flows for the month. (*Hint:* Fred's beginning balance sheet has only two accounts, cash and equity, each with a $5,000 balance. All other accounts open with zero balances.)

d. Is Fred's business profitable in an accounting sense? In a cash flow sense? (Words only.)

e. Can the business fail while making a profit? How might that happen in the next month or so? (Words only.)

7. The Blandings Home Construction Company purchased a new crane for $350,000 this year. It sold the old crane for $80,000. At the time it had a net book value of $20,000. Assume any profit on the sale of old equipment is taxed at 25%. These were the only transactions that affected investing activities this year. Construct the Cash Flow from Investing Activities section of the statement of cash flows to concisely convey the maximum information to readers of the company's financial statements.

8. Lansing Inc., a profitable food products manufacturer, has undertaken a major expansion that will be financed by new debt and equity issues as well as earnings. During the last year the company borrowed $5 million for a term of 30 years to finance a new building to house the expanded operations. It also sold 60,000 shares of $4 par value stock at $51 per share to pay for new equipment. It also paid off short-term loans that support inventory and receivables totaling $700,000 as they came due and took out new short-term debt for the same purpose of $850,000, which was outstanding at year end. Lansing also made a scheduled payment of $500,000 on an old long-term loan with which it had acquired production equipment several years ago. The payment included interest of $425,000. Finally the firm paid dividends of $2.50 per share on 700,000 shares of outstanding common stock. Calculate and display the Cash from Financing Activities section of Lansing's statement of cash flows.

9. The Seymour Corp. attempted to increase sales rapidly in 20X1 by offering a new, low-cost product line designed to appeal to credit customers in relatively poor financial condition. The company sold no new stock during the year but paid dividends of $3,000,000. Depreciation for the year was $7,851,000, and no fixed assets were retired or sold. The firm had the following financial statements for 20X1.

Seymour Corp.
Balance Sheet
For the period ended 12/31/X1 ($000)

ASSETS

	12/31/X0	12/31/X1
Cash	$ 2,745	$ 1,071
Receivables	19,842	24,691
Inventory	10,045	15,621
CURRENT ASSETS	$ 32,632	$ 41,383
Fixed assets		
Gross	$ 80,128	$ 97,432
Accumulated depreciation	(60,225)	(68,076)
Net	$ 19,903	$ 29,356
TOTAL ASSETS	$ 52,535	$ 70,739

LIABILITIES AND EQUITY

	12/31/X0	12/31/X1
Accts payable	$ 3,114	$ 6,307
Accruals	768	914
CURRENT LIABILITIES	$ 3,882	$ 7,221
Long-term debt	$36,490	$ 48,128
Equity	12,163	15,390
TOTAL CAPITAL	$48,653	$ 63,518
TOTAL LIABILITIES		
AND EQUITY	$ 52,535	$ 70,739

Seymour Corp.
Income Statement
For the period ended 12/31/X1 ($000)

Revenue	$88,765
COGS	39,506
Gross margin	$49,259
Expenses	34,568
EBIT	14,691
Interest	4,312
EBT	$ 10,379
Tax	4,152
EAT	$ 6,227

a. Without preparing a statement of cash flows, examine the changes in each balance sheet account and summarize in rough terms where Seymour got its cash and what it spent the money on. Include the sum of net income and depreciation as a source of cash.

b. Construct a statement of cash flows for Seymour Corp. How does the information available from the statement compare with the results of your analysis in part a?

c. Does it look like Seymour may be headed for financial trouble? Explain the possible implications of the new product and credit strategy on individual accounts. (*Hint:* Consider the implications of two extreme scenarios; the new product is doing very well or very poorly.)

A Free Cash Flow Business Analysis: Concept Connection
Example 3-2 (page 85)

10. A group of investors is considering buying the Wheelwright Corporation, but does not want to contribute to the company's financial support after the purchase. Wheelwright's management has offered the following financial statements covering last year ($M omitted):

Wheelwright Corporation
Balance Sheets

ASSETS		
	Beginning	Ending
Cash	6	9
Accts receivable	13	20
Inventory	12	7
CURRENT ASSETS	31	36
Fixed Assets		
Gross	100	115
Accumulated depreciation	(12)	(18)
Net fixed assets	88	97
TOTAL ASSETS	119	133

LIABILITIES & EQUITY		
Accts payable	17	21
Accruals	6	8
CURRENT LIABILITIES	23	29
Debt	71	59
Equity	25	45
TOTAL LIABILITIES & EQUITY	119	133

Wheelwright Corporation
Income Statement

Sales	100
COGs*	34
Depreciation	6
Gross Margin	60
Expenses	25
EBIT	35
Interest	7
EBT	28
Tax	8
Net income	20

*Cost of Goods Sold

Wheelwright paid no dividends and sold no new stock during the year. The firm's tax rate is 30%.

a. Develop Wheelwright's free cash flow and make a recommendation as to whether it seems to be an appropriate acquisition for the investors.

b. Assume that the investors will purchase the company subject to its existing debt ($59M). Does that change your recommendation?

11. Slattery Industries reported the following financial information for 20X2:

Revenues	$10.0 million
Costs & expenses	
(excluding depreciation)	8.0
Depreciation	0.5
Taxes	0.6
Net income	0.9
Fixed assets (gross)	10.0
Working capital	4.0

The firm expects revenues costs, expenses (excluding depreciation), and working capital to grow at 10% per year for the next three years. It also expects to invest $2 million per year in fixed assets which includes replacing worn out equipment and purchasing enough new equipment to support the projected growth and maintain a competitive position. Assume depreciation is 5% of the gross fixed asset account, the tax rate is 40%, and that Slattery has no debt and therefore pays no interest.

a. Make a rough projection of cash flows for 20X3, 20X4, and 20X5 assuming no new debt or equity is raised. Simply compute an income statement in each year, add depreciation, and subtract increases in working capital and fixed asset purchases.

b. Are your projections free cash flows?

c. What do your projections imply for Slattery's owners/managers?

d. How would you evaluate Slattery's ability to achieve this level of growth (as measured by the increase in fixed assets)?

Common Size Statements: Concept Connection Example 3-3 (page 89)

12. Linden Corp. has a 10% market share in its industry. Below are income statements ($millions) for Linden and for the industry.

	Linden	Industry
Sales	$6,000	$64,000
Cost of goods sold	3,200	33,650
Gross margin	$2,800	$ 30,350
Expenses:		
Sales and marketing	$ 430	$ 3,850
Engineering	225	2,650
Finance and administration	650	4,560
Total expenses	$ 1,305	$ 11,060
EBIT	$ 1,495	$ 19,290
Interest expense	230	4,500
EBT	$ 1,265	$ 14,790
Tax	500	5,620
Net income	$ 765	$ 9,170

a. Develop common size income statements for Linden and the industry as a whole.

b. What areas should management focus on to improve performance, and what kind of issues should be examined or looked for in each area?

RATIO ANALYSIS

Seventeen ratios are presented, explained, and numerically illustrated on pages 90–100 and summarized in Table 3-2 on page 101. Problem 13 just asks you to calculate the ratios for a set of financial statements. The remaining problems ask you to explore the ratios' meanings and the relationships between them. For most problems you'll write a ratio definition, substitute known quantities, and solve algebraically for an unknown. Some of the problems contain hints to help you get started.

13. Calculate all of the ratios discussed in the chapter for Axtel Company in Problem 5. Assume Axtel had leasing costs of $7,267 in 20X1 and had 1,268,000 shares of stock outstanding valued at $28.75 per share at year end.

14. Norton Industries recorded total cost of goods sold for 20X2 of $6.5 million. Norton had the following inventory balances for the months indicated (end of period balances):

In Millions	
December 20X1	$1.20
January 20X2	1.65
February 20X2	1.70
March 20X2	1.38
April 20X2	1.66
May 20X2	1.93
June 20X2	1.41
July 20X2	1.81
August 20X2	1.78
September 20X2	1.26
October 20X2	1.61
November 20X2	1.63
December 20X2	1.19

a. Compute inventory turnover for Norton using the following methods to calculate the inventory figure:
   1. End of year
   2. Average of the beginning and end of year
   3. Average of the ends of quarters (use the five quarter ends)
   4. Average of the ends of months (use the 13 month ends)
b. Which method provides the most accurate picture of Norton's inventory management? Why?
c. Which method do you think Norton is currently using? Why? (*Hint:* See Limitations and Weaknesses of Ratio Analysis, page 106.)

15. Partridge Inc. sells about $45 million a year on credit. Good credit and collections performance in the industry result in a 35-day ACP.
a. What is the maximum receivables balance Partridge can tolerate and still receive a good rating with respect to credit and collections? (*Hint:* Write the equation defining ACP, treat the A/R balance as the unknown, substitute given or target values, and solve.)
b. If Partridge is now collecting an average receivable in 40 days, by how much will it have to lower the receivables balance to achieve a good rating?

16. Epsom Co. manufactures furniture and sells about $40 million a year at a gross margin of 45%.
a. What is the maximum inventory level the firm can carry to maintain an inventory turnover (based on COGS) of 8.0?
b. If the inventory contains $1.2 million of obsolete and damaged goods that don't turn over at all, how fast would the active inventory have to turn over to achieve an overall turnover rate of 8.0?

17. The Nelson Sheet Metal Company has current assets of $2.5 million and current liabilities of $1.0 million. The firm is in need of additional inventory and has an opportunity to borrow money on a short-term note with which it can buy the needed material. However, a previous financing agreement prohibits the company from operating with a current ratio below 1.8. What is the maximum amount of inventory Nelson can obtain in this manner? (*Hint:* The note will be a current liability and the purchased inventory will be a current asset of the same size, X. Form the limiting current ratio in terms of X and solve.)

18. Sweet Tooth Cookies, Inc. has the following ratios.

$$ROE = 15\%$$
$$Total\ asset\ turnover = 1.2$$
$$ROS = 10\%$$

What percentage of its assets are financed by equity? (*Hint:* Substitute into the extended Du Pont equation.)

19. The Paragon Company has sales of $2,000 with a cost ratio of 60%, current ratio of 1.5, inventory turnover ratio (based on cost) of 3.0, and average collection period (ACP) of 45 days. Complete the following current section of the firm's balance sheet.

Cash	$	Accounts payable	$
Accounts receivable		Accruals	60
Inventory			
Current assets	$	Current liabilities	$ 750

20. You are given the following selected financial information for The Blatz Corporation.

Income Statement		Balance Sheet	
COGS	$750	Cash	$250
Net income	$160	Net fixed assets	$850

Ratios	
ROS	10%
Current ratio	2.3
Inventory turnover	6.0X
ACP	45 days
Debt ratio	49.12%

Calculate accounts receivable, inventory, current assets, current liabilities, debt, equity, ROA, and ROE.

21. Companies often use ratios as a basis for planning. The technique is to assume the business being planned will achieve targeted levels of certain ratios and then calculate the financial statement amounts that will result in those ratios. The process always starts with a dollar assumption about sales revenue. Forecast the balance sheet for Lambert Co. using the following projected information ($000). Round all projections to the nearest thousand dollars.

Sales	$10,000
Cash	$500
Accruals	$50
Gross margin	45%
ACP	42 days
Inventory turns	7.0X
Total asset turnover	1.25X
Current ratio	2.0
Debt : equity	1 : 3

ASSETS		LIABILITIES	
Cash		Accounts payable	
Accounts receivable		Accruals	
Inventory		Current liabilities	
Current assets		Debt	
Net fixed assets		Equity	
Total assets		Total liabilities & equity	

22. Tribke Enterprises collected the following data from its financial reports for 20X3:

Stock price	$18.37
Inventory balance	$300,000
Expenses (excluding COGS)	$1,120,000
Shares outstanding	290,000
Average issue price of shares	$5.00
Gross margin %	40%
Interest rate	8%
TIE ratio	8
Inventory turnover	12X
Current ratio	1.5
Quick ratio	.75
Fixed asset turnover	1.5

Complete the following abbreviated financial statements, and calculate per share ratios indicated. (*Hint:* Start by subtracting the formula for the quick ratio from that for the current ratio and equating that to the numerical difference.)

INCOME STATEMENT

Revenue	_____
COGS	_____
GM	_____
Expense	_____
EBIT	_____
Interest	_____
EBT	_____
Tax	_____
EAT	_____

BALANCE SHEET

Current assets	_____	Current liabilities	_____
Fixed assets	_____	Long-term debt	_____
		Equity:	
		Paid-in capital*	_____
		Retained earnings	_____
		Total equity	_____
Total assets	_____	Total liabilities & equity	_____

*Paid-in Capital = Common Stock + Paid-in Excess

RATIOS

Book value per share _____   Market value per share _____

Refer to the INSIGHTS box on EVA®/MVA on pages 103–104 before attempting Problems 23 and 24.

23. Notice that the calculations called for here do not involve cost of capital. William Edwards, Inc. (WEI) had one million shares of common stock outstanding on 12/31/20X0. The stock had been sold for an average of $8.00 per share and had a market price of $13.25 per share on that date.

WEI also had a balance of $5.0 million in its retained earnings account on that date. The following projection has been made for WEI's next five years of operations:

Year	Net Income	Dividends/Share	Shares Issued	Average Issue Price	Stock Price 12/31
20X1	$700,000	$.20	None	NA	$13.75
20X2	840,000	.22	50,000	$14.00	14.25
20X3	750,000	.24	100,000	13.50	13.80
20X4	900,000	.26	50,000	14.50	15.00
20X5	860,000	.28	None	NA	15.40

Compute the MVA as of 12/31/X0, and compute EVA®, the change in MVA, as a result of each subsequent year's activity. (Assume that all shares issued during any given year received the dividends declared that year.) Comment on management's projected performance over the five-year period. What would you do if you represented a majority of the stockholders? Would the result have been different before MVA/EVA® analysis?

24. Prahm & Associates had EBIT of $5M last year. The firm carried an average debt of $15M during the year on which it paid 8% interest. The company paid no dividends and sold no new stock. At the beginning of the year it had equity of $17M. The tax rate is 40%, and Prahm's cost of capital is 11%. Calculate Prahm's EVA® during the year and comment on that performance relative to ROE. Make your calculations using average balances in the capital accounts.

25. The Hardigree Hamburger chain is a closely held corporation with 400,000 shares of common stock outstanding. The owners would like to take the company public by issuing another 600,000 shares and selling them to the general public in an initial public offering (IPO). (IPOs are discussed in Chapter 5.) Benson's Burgers is a similar chain that operates in another part of the country. Its stock is publicly traded at a price earnings (P/E) ratio of 25. Hardigree had net income of $2,500,000 last year.

   a. How much is Hardigree likely to raise with its public offering?

   b. What will the public offering imply about the wealth of the current owners?

26. **Comprehensive Problem.** The Protek Company is a large manufacturer and distributor of electronic components. Because of some successful new products marketed to manufacturers of personal computers, the firm has recently undergone a period of explosive growth, more than doubling its revenues during the last two years. However, the growth has been accompanied by a marked decline in profitability and a precipitous drop in the company's stock price.

   You are a financial consultant who has been retained to analyze the company's performance and find out what's going wrong. Your investigative plan involves conducting a series of in-depth interviews with management and doing some independent research on the industry. However, before starting, you want to focus your thinking to be sure you can ask the right questions. You'll begin by analyzing the firm's financial statements over the last three years, which are shown below.

   The following additional information is provided with the financial statements. Depreciation for 20X1, 20X2, and 20X3 was $200, $250, and $275 million, respectively. No stock was sold or repurchased, and, like many fast-growing companies, Protek paid no dividends. Assume the tax rate is a flat 34%, and the firm pays 10% interest on its debt.

Protek Company Income Statements
For the periods ended 12/31 ($000,000)

	20X1	20X2	20X3
Sales	$1,578	$2,106	$3,265
COGS	631	906	1,502
Gross margin	$ 947	$1,200	$ 1,763

Protek Company Income Statements
For the periods ended 12/31 ($000,000)

Expenses			
Marketing	$ 316	$495	$ 882
R&D	158	211	327
Administration	126	179	294
Total expenses	$600	$885	$1,503
EBIT	$ 347	$ 315	$ 260
Interest	63	95	143
EBT	$ 284	$220	$ 117
Tax	97	75	40
Net income	$ 187	$ 145	$ 77

Protek Company Balance Sheets
For the periods ended 12/31 ($000,000)

ASSETS	20X1	20X2	20X3
Cash	$ 30	$ 40	$ 62
Accounts receivable	175	351	590
Inventory	90	151	300
CURRENT ASSETS	$ 295	$542	$ 952
Fixed assets			
Gross	$1,565	$2,373	$ 2,718
Accumulated depreciation	(610)	(860)	(1,135)
Net	$ 955	$1,513	$1,583
TOTAL ASSETS	$1,250	$2,055	$2,535

LIABILITIES	20X1	20X2	20X3
Accounts payable	$ 56	$ 81	$ 134
Accruals	15	20	30
CURRENT LIABILITIES	$ 71	$ 101	$ 164
Capital			
Long-term debt	$ 630	$1,260	$1,600
Equity	549	694	771
TOTAL LIABILITIES & EQUITY	$1,250	$2,055	$2,535

a. Construct common size income statements for 20X1, 20X2, and 20X3. Analyze the trend in each line. What appears to be happening? (*Hints:* Think in terms of both dollars and percentages. As the company grows, the absolute dollars of cost and expense spending go up. What does it mean if the percentage of revenue represented by the expenditure increases as well? How much of an increase in spending do you think a department could manage efficiently? Could pricing of Protek's products have any effect?)

b. Construct statements of cash flows for 20X2 and 20X3. Where is the company's money going to and coming from? Make a comment about its free cash flows during the period. Is it likely to have positive or negative free cash flows in the future?

c. Calculate the indicated ratios for all three years. Analyze trends in each ratio and compare each with the industry average. What can you infer from this information? Make specific statements about liquidity, asset management, especially receivables and inventories, debt management, and profitability. Do not simply say that ratios are higher or lower than the average or that they are going up or down. Think about what might be going on in the company and propose reasons why the ratios are acting as they are. Use only ending balance sheet figures to calculate your ratios. Do certain specific problems tend to affect more than one ratio? Which ones?

	Industry Average	20X1	20X2	20X3
Current ratio	4.5			
Quick ratio	3.2			
ACP	42 days			
Inventory turnover	7.5X			
Fixed asset turnover	1.6X			
Total asset turnover	1.2X			
Debt ratio	53%			
Debt : equity	1:1			
TIE	4.5			
ROS	9.0%			
ROA	10.8%			
ROE	22.8%			
Equity multiplier	2.1			

d. Construct both Du Pont equations for Protek and the industry. What, if anything, do they tell us?

e. One hundred million shares of stock have been outstanding for the entire period. The price of Protek stock in 20X1, 20X2, and 20X3 was $39.27, $26.10, and $11.55, respectively. Calculate the firm's earnings per share (EPS) and its price/earnings ratio (P/E). What's happening to the P/E? To what things are investors likely to be reacting? How would a slowdown in personal computer sales affect your reasoning?

f. Would you recommend Protek stock as an investment? Why might it be a very bad investment in the near future? Why might it be a very good one?

COMPUTER PROBLEMS

27. At the close of 20X3, the financial statements of Northern Manufacturing were as follows.

Northern Manufacturing Balance Sheet
For the period ended 12/31/X3 ($000)

ASSETS	12/31/X1	12/31/X29
Cash	$ 500	$ 200
Accounts receivable	6,250	7,300
Inventory	5,180	6,470
CURRENT ASSETS	$11,930	$13,970
Fixed assets		
Gross	$ 7,500	$ 9,000
Accumulated depreciation	(2,400)	(3,100)
Net	$ 5,100	$ 5,900
TOTAL ASSETS	$17,030	$19,870

Northern Manufacturing Balance Sheet
For the period ended 12/31/X3 ($000)

	LIABILITIES	
Accounts payable	$ 1,860	$ 2,210
Accruals	850	220
CURRENT LIABILITIES	$ 2,710	$ 2,430
Long-term debt	$ 11,320	$ 12,335
Equity	3,000	5,105
TOTAL CAPITAL	$14,320	$17,440
TOTAL LIABILITIES		
AND EQUITY	$17,030	$19,870

Northern Manufacturing
Income Statement
For the period ended 12/31/X3 ($000)

Sales	$22,560
COGS	11,506
Gross margin	$ 11,054
Expense	5,332
Depreciation	700
EBIT	$ 5,022
Interest	1,180
EBT	$ 3,842
Tax	1,537
Net income	$ 2,305

In addition, Northern paid dividends of $1.2 million and sold new stock valued at $1.0 million in 20X3. Use the CASHFLO program to produce Northern's statement of cash flows for 20X3.

28. Comparative historical financial statements for Northern Manufacturing of the preceeding problem are as follows.

Northern Manufacturing
Income Statements
For the years ended ($000)

	12/31/X1	12/31/X2	12/31/X3
Sales	$17,850	$20,510	$22,560
COGS	9,100	10,665	11,506
Gross margin	$ 8,750	$ 9,845	$ 11,054
Expense	5,180	5,702	5,332
Depreciation	600	650	700
EBIT	$ 2,970	$ 3,493	$ 5,022
Interest	800	910	1,180
EBT	$ 2,170	$ 2,583	$ 3,842
Tax	868	1,033	1,537
Net income	$ 1,302	$ 1,550	$ 2,305
Dividends paid	$ 650	$ 750	$ 1,200
Stock sold	0	0	1,000
Lease payments	$ 500	$ 700	$ 800

Northern Manufacturing
Balance Sheets
For the years ended ($000)

ASSETS

	12/31/X0	12/31/X1	12/31/X2	12/31/X3
Cash	$ 955	$ 980	$ 500	$ 200
Accounts receivable	3,103	3,570	6,250	7,300
Inventory	2,890	3,033	5,180	6,470
CURRENT ASSETS	$6,948	$ 7,583	$ 11,930	$ 13,970
Fixed assets				
Gross	$5,800	$ 6,650	$ 7,500	$ 9,000
Accumulated depreciation	(1,150)	(1,750)	(2,400)	(3,100)
Net	$4,650	$ 4,900	$ 5,100	$ 5,900
TOTAL ASSETS	$11,598	$ 12,483	$ 17,030	$ 19,870

LIABILITIES

	12/31/X0	12/31/X1	12/31/X2	12/31/X3
Accounts payable	$ 1,860	$ 1,650	$ 1,860	$ 2,210
Accruals	385	742	850	220
CURRENT LIABILITIES	$ 2,245	$2,392	$ 2,710	$ 2,430
Long-term debt	$ 7,805	$7,891	$ 11,320	$ 12,335
Equity	1,548	2,200	3,000	5,105
TOTAL CAPITAL	$ 9,353	$ 10,091	$ 14,320	$ 17,440
TOTAL LIABILITIES &				
EQUITY	$11,598	$ 12,483	$ 17,030	$ 19,870
Number of shares		300,000	300,000	315,000
Stock price		$ 78.12	$ 70.00	$ 65.88

a. Use the ANALYS program to prepare common size statements and a set of financial ratios for each of the last three years.

b. Analyze the results of ANALYS for Northern Manufacturing. The firm has been quite successful in terms of revenue and profit growth so far. Do the ratios reveal any disturbing trends that might indicate future problems?

DEVELOPING SOFTWARE

29. Write a program to generate a statement of cash flows yourself. It isn't as hard as you might think.

First set up the income statement and two balance sheets on the spreadsheet just as they appear in Problem 27. Let the amounts in individual accounts such as Cash, A/R, Revenue, COGS, Interest, and Tax be input items, and let the program calculate all the totals and subtotals such as Current Assets, Total Assets, Gross Margin, and Net Income.

Next take a different area of the spreadsheet and set up the changes in the current accounts and the statement of cash flows shown below.

Take all of the items shown in lowercase xxx's from the statements in the first part of your spreadsheet. Some will be single items like net income and depreciation, but most will be differences between beginning and ending balances like the increase or decrease in long-term debt or the change in receivables. Finally, program the spreadsheet to add up the subtotals where the uppercase XXX's appear and display the reconciliation.

The trickiest part is keeping the signs straight in your subtractions for sources and uses.

Once you have your program written, test it with the inputs to the CASHFLO program and see if you get the same results.

30. Write your own analysis program to calculate a common size income statement and the ratios introduced in this chapter. To keep the exercise reasonably simple, just provide for one year of ratios and one common size statement.

    Construct an input area in your spreadsheet in the form of an income statement and a balance sheet. Input the accounts and have the program calculate all totals and subtotals. Define your common size income statement alongside the input income statement by dividing each input line item by revenue. Define your ratios in another area drawing the numerators and denominators from the input statements.

    Test your program using the 20X3 statements for Northern Manufacturing from Problem 28. Compare your results with those of the Analys program.

Northern Manufacturing

Summary of Changes to Current Accounts
For the year ended 12/31/X3 ($000)

ACCOUNT	SOURCE/(USE)
Receivables	$ xxx
Inventory	xxx
Payables	xxx
Accruals	xxx
	$XXX

Northern Manufacturing

Statement of Cash Flows
For the year ended 12/31/X3 ($000)

CASH FROM OPERATING ACTIVITIES	
Net income	$ x,xxx
Depreciation	xxx
Net changes in current accounts	xxx
Cash from operating activities	$ XXX
CASH FROM INVESTING ACTIVITIES	
Purchase of fixed assets	$(x,xxx)
CASH FROM FINANCING ACTIVITIES	
Increase (Decrease) in long-term debt	$ x,xxx
Sale of stock	xxx
Dividend paid	(xxx)
Cash from financing activities	$X,XXX
NET CASH FLOW	$ XXX
RECONCILIATION	
Beginning cash balance	$ x,xxx
Net cash flow	XXX
Ending cash balance	$X,XXX

 THOMSON REUTERS

In this chapter we'll use Thomson ONE to do some financial analysis of the companies we overviewed in Chapter 1. Go to **www.cengage.com/thomsonone**, select your book and click on the Thomson ONE button. Enter Thomson ONE—Business School Edition using the username and password you created when you registered the serial number on your access card. Select a problem for this chapter, and you'll see an expanded version that includes instructions on how to navigate within the Thomson ONE system, as well as some additional explanation of the presentation format.

31. Take a piece of paper and set up a simple five-column chart. Write the following ratios in the left-most column.

PFM Ratio Name	Thomson ONE ratio name
Current ratio	Current ratio
ACP	Receivables days sales
Total asset turnover	Sales/Total assets
Return on sales	Net income/Sales
Return on assets	Net income/Total assets
Return on equity	Net income/Equity
Times interest earned	Times interest earned
P/E ratio	P/E

Now label the other four columns for the four companies we looked at in Chapter 1: Ford, Harley-Davidson, Starbucks, and Microsoft.

a. For each company go to the Thomson ONE page displaying three or more years of history for annual values of a broad range of financial ratios. Examine the trend in each of the ratios we've listed and note its performance on your chart. Is performance improving, declining, stable, or is there something strange going on?

b. Make another chart and write down the most recent ratios for each company and compare them between companies.

Typically ratios within industries or types of industries are similar if companies are performing similarly. For example, companies in heavy manufacturing tend to have high levels of fixed assets (also called property, plant, and equipment), while companies producing services or intellectual products and retailers tend to have fewer fixed assets. That generally makes the total asset turnover figure lower for manufacturers like Ford and Harley than for firms like Starbucks or Microsoft.

Do your ratios show the similarities we've just described? If not, go to the Thomson ONE page displaying the financial statements themselves and look at dollar line items to see if you can find an explanation. Analyze each ratio.

c. How would you rank the four firms in terms of financial performance? Look at ROS, ROA, ROE, and P/E. What economic or market factors might account for big differences in P/E?

d. Compare Ford and Harley. They both make motor vehicles. Why is their financial performance different or similar? (*Hint:* Think in terms of market and economic factors that make the numbers what they are.)

32. Analyze the performance of each of the four companies we've been working with against its competition. This is called a peer analysis in Thomson ONE. The system will show you a variety of ratios arrayed against their average value among a group of competitors. It will also show the performance of individual competitors on the same ratios.

First note who the competitors are. Does the selection of competitors make sense to you? How is each of our companies doing against its competition? Conduct a thorough analysis. Don't just say better or worse on particular ratios. Try to think of reasons why.

CHAPTER 4

Financial Planning

Chapter Outline

Planning is a big part of modern corporate life, especially in large companies. Firms plan their futures constantly, addressing everything from cash flow and short-term profitability to long-run strategy.

Generally, the higher in management people are, the more time they devote to planning. It isn't unusual for top executives to spend 80% of their time thinking about the future. At the same time, some planning functions involve virtually everyone in management. For example, one thing you can be sure you'll do in your first management job is prepare a budget.

This chapter deals primarily with *financial planning*. Simply put, that means projecting a company's financial statements into the future. However, financial planning is a part of a broader activity known as *business planning*. To really appreciate financial planning, we have to understand the nature and purpose of business planning and see how the financial element fits into the broader concept.

4.1   Business Planning

A **business plan** is a model of what management expects a business to become in the future expressed in **words** and **financial projections**.

The easiest way to describe business planning is in terms of its result. The process produces a document called a **business plan**, which can be thought of as a picture or model of what a business unit is expected to become in the future. The business plan generally looks like a magazine (with graphs and diagrams rather than pictures), and consists of a combination of words and numbers that describe the business.

The numbers in a plan are largely projected financial statements. That is, they're estimates of what the firm's statements will look like in the future if the assumptions about the business made by the planners come true. Such statements based on hypothetical circumstances are called *pro forma*, meaning they are cast "as if" the planning assumptions are true.

The words in a business plan describe the operation in a realistic yet concise way. They discuss broad strategic issues, detail the handling of short-term tactical questions, and amplify the financial projections.

The overall image conveyed by a good business plan is very comprehensive. It includes information on products, markets, employees, technology, facilities, capital, revenue, profitability, and anything else that might be relevant in describing the organization and its affairs.

4.1a   Component Parts of a Business Plan

Although the detail within business plans varies a great deal from company to company, most follow a fairly standard overall format. A typical outline follows:

a. Contents
b. Executive Summary
c. Mission and Strategy Statement
d. Market Analysis
e. Operations (of the business)
f. Management and Staffing
g. **Financial Projections**
h. Contingencies

The first two sections are introductory. The table of contents is just that, and the executive summary is a one-page overview of everything that follows.

The mission and strategy section lays out the basic charter of the business and establishes its long-term direction. The market analysis attempts to demonstrate why the business will succeed against its competitors. The chapter on operations describes how the firm creates and distributes its product or service. The management and staffing chapter details the firm's projected personnel needs and in some cases lays out the credentials of key managers.

The financial section of the business plan projects the company's financial results into the future and is the firm's **financial plan**. How that projection is put together will be our main focus in this chapter. The section on contingencies tells what the company will do if things don't go as planned.

4.1b   The Purpose of Planning and Plan Information

The two major audiences for a firm's business plan and the information it contains are the firm's own management and outside investors.

The Managerial Value of Planning   Business planning has several managerial benefits. One has to do with the process of creating the plan, while the others are related to using the finished product.

The Planning Process   The **planning process** can pull a management team into a cohesive unit with common goals. It helps everyone understand what the objectives of the organization are, why they're important, and how the organization intends to achieve them. Creating a plan forces the team to think through everything that has to be done in the coming period, making sure everyone understands what they have to do.

A Road Map for Running the Business   A business plan functions as a **road map** for getting an organization to its goal. Comparing the details of operating performance with the plan and investigating deviations is an important management process. When a business goes off course, such a comparison is the best way to understand the firm's problems and come up with solutions. The idea is illustrated in Figure 4-1.

A Statement of Goals   A business plan is a projection of the future that generally reflects what management would like to see happen. Accordingly, it can be viewed as a set of goals for the company as a whole and for its individual departments.

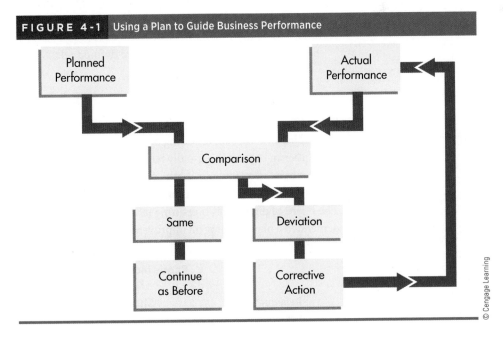

FIGURE 4-1   Using a Plan to Guide Business Performance

© Cengage Learning

A plan contains revenue targets, departmental expense constraints, and various development goals for products and processes. Different people are responsible for different goals, and performance against them can be measured and evaluated.

It's especially common to tie executive compensation to the achievement of goals within business plans. We'll have more to say about goals within plans later in the chapter.

Predicting Financing Needs   **Financial planning** is extremely important for companies that rely on outside financing. Only through accurate financial planning can a corporate treasurer predict when he or she will need to turn to financial markets to raise additional money to support operations.

The financial plan is especially important for anticipating **financing needs**.

Communicating Information to Investors

A **business plan** is management's statement about what the company is going to be in the future, and can be used to communicate those ideas to investors. A plan predicts the future character of the enterprise. It makes an estimate of profitability and cash flow. The financial information tells equity investors what returns they can expect and debt investors where the firm will get the money to repay loans.

The business plan is a vehicle for communicating with potential **investors**.

Small firms use the business plan document itself in dealing with investors. Large companies convey selected plan information to securities analysts who use it and past performance as a basis for recommendations to clients.

Business Planning in Divisions of Large Companies

Large companies are usually organized into decentralized operating divisions that function more or less like independent companies. Most large firms engage in a nearly continuous planning process. Divisions produce their own plans, which are consolidated to create overall corporate plans.

The business planning process is an important vehicle through which divisions communicate with corporate managements. A division's final business plan is a statement of its goals that reflects the parent company's expectations as well as its own. Divisional plans are generally approved by corporate management after lengthy reviews, and nearly everything a division does is compared with its plan.

Success and failure at the division are defined relative to the business plan.

4.1c   Credibility and Supporting Detail

Predictions of the future may not come true. Everyone knows that, so there's always an issue of believability surrounding business plans. Financial plans are especially subject to skepticism because it's usually hard to tell how the planners developed the numbers in the projected statements. Let's consider a simplified example to illustrate the idea.

Suppose Poorly Inc. has revenue of $100 million and profit of $1 million this year. The board of directors is pressuring management for better performance and has demanded a plan showing an improvement. In response, management submits the following:

A good business plan shows enough **supporting detail** to indicate that it is the product of **careful thinking**.

Poorly Inc. Financial Plan

	This Year	*Next Year*
Revenue	$100 million	$120 million
Net income	1 million	12 million

Technically, this projection satisfies the board's request for a plan showing improvement, but the obvious question is why should the board members believe it. In the situation described, they probably would not.

The problem is that this "plan" as presented lacks **supporting detail**. A reader doesn't know whether it's something made up just to satisfy the board's demand or represents the summarized product of a great deal of analysis. In other words, it doesn't tell the reader enough about the thinking behind the financial figures to make them believable.

A competent plan may display summarized financial projections, but the figures are supported by enough detail to show that they're the product of logical thinking. For example, revenue projections are usually supported by schedules showing the products and quantities to be sold, their prices, and which sales organizations are expected to do the selling. These schedules in turn are backed up by reasoning that tells why certain products are expected to sell more than others and why some salespeople will outsell their rivals. The point is that a planner can't just write down a revenue figure that's plucked out of thin air and expect people to believe it.

Supporting detail shows how the numbers in the financial plan were developed. All the detail doesn't have to be included in the plan document itself, but should be available if a reader has questions.

As we proceed, we'll see that financial plans are constructed with varying levels of supporting detail depending on their use. It's important to match the level of detail to the purpose of the plan.

4.1d   Four Kinds of Business Plans

There are as many as four variations on the basic idea of business planning. Each serves a different purpose and results in a separate document. Large, sophisticated companies tend to do all of these different kinds of planning. Small firms usually do only one plan that combines features of the four variations.

The four kinds of planning are (1) strategic planning, (2) operational planning, (3) budgeting, and (4) forecasting.[1,2] They differ according to three attributes: the length of the planning period (the **planning horizon**), the kinds of issues addressed, and the level of financial detail projected.

> The **strategic plan** addresses broad, long-term issues, and contains only summarized, **approximate financial projections**.

Strategic Planning   Strategic planning involves broad, conceptual thinking about the nature of a business, whom it serves, and what it does. It's generally a long-term exercise in which managers try to predict in rough terms what the business will do and become over a period of several years. A five-year horizon is the most common.

Strategic planning begins by questioning the company's very existence. Why is the firm doing what it does? Would it be better off doing something else? What customer

---

1. Planning terminology isn't consistent among companies. In some firms, people talk about an annual operating budget, while others make a long-term forecast. The words "outlook" and "view" are also common. The important distinction is the length of the planning horizon: Multi- (usually five) year—long-term, strategic. One year—intermediate term, operating. Three to six months—short-term, budgetary. Two weeks to three months—very short-term, forecast.

2. Budgets and forecasts are abbreviated business plans and often don't have all the parts described earlier. They are predominantly financial projections.

need does it serve? How? What opportunities are present in the marketplace? What threats? Strategy demands that a company develop a mission and a charter and that it define what it does and why, while stating its loftiest goals.

Once that base is established, strategic planners look forward over several years and consider broad, sweeping issues. At the end of five years, will the firm be in the same lines of business? In the same geographic areas? How large will it have grown? Who will be its competitors, and how will it fight them? And so on.

Strategic planning deals with concepts and ideas expressed mostly with words rather than numbers. The numbers used tend to be simple and approximate. For example, a firm's strategic plan might establish a goal of being the number one or two rated company in its industry based on some measure such as sales or market share. Or a firm might set a sales goal of about $500 million a year, stating that revenue figure without a lot of supporting detail.

Strategic plans include projected financial statements, but they're approximate and ideal, and usually not supported by much detail. The plan's last (usually fifth) year generally shows financial results that reflect the best the business could ever be expected to do.

Strategic plans are often called long-range plans or five-year plans.

In a nutshell, systematic strategic thinking says that a business must first analyze itself, its industry, and the competitive situation. Then it must construct an approach to doing business that takes advantage of its strengths and minimizes the vulnerabilities created by its weaknesses. A strategic plan is a vehicle for documenting this kind of thinking.

Operational Planning

Operational planning involves translating business ideas into concrete, shorter-term projections usually encompassing about a year. Projections are a great deal more detailed here than in strategic planning.

Among other things, operational plans specify how much the company will sell, to whom, and at what prices. They also spell out where the firm will get its inputs and equipment, what those things will cost, and what the firm expects to earn.

The word "operational" or "operating" means having to do with the day-to-day running of the business. Major short-term goals are generally set up in the operating plan. Revenue targets are established along with profit objectives. Sales quotas and product development milestones are laid out. Compensation and bonus systems are also specified. Most companies do an annual plan that is an operational plan and is generally their most important planning exercise.

The **annual operating plan** projects the business **in detail** over a year and is the **most important** planning exercise.

A typical **annual operating plan** is conceptually an almost even mix of words and numbers. The document explains what's going on verbally, but backs the explanation up with financial projections containing substantial supporting detail.

Budgeting

In many industries, business conditions change rapidly and an annual operating plan can be badly out of date by the second half of the year it covers. Budgets are essentially short-term updates of annual plans, typically covering three-month quarters. In addition, they usually contain supporting detail beyond that found in the annual plan.

Budgets are short-term updates of the annual plan when business **conditions change** rapidly.

A **budget** ties down exactly how much money, material, and labor will flow through the organization and fixes responsibility on specific people for making it happen. The budgeting process involves trying to predict exactly how much of which products will be sold and at what cost. Along with that, it attempts a precise estimate of how many dollars will be spent in each department, and on exactly what items: salary, material, travel, and so on.

It's important to realize that the budgetary time frame is too short to make major conceptual changes in the businesses. Policy issues and long-term direction aren't usually discussed, so budgets have relatively fewer words and more financial detail than annual plans. Clearly, a budget can also be considered an operating plan because it details the day-to-day operation of the business.

Forecasting   Forecasts are quick estimates of short-term financial results. They're essentially projections of where the *financial momentum* of a business will carry it over a short period. They usually consist almost entirely of numbers with very little supporting verbiage.

Forecasts are very short-term projections of **profit** and **cash** flow.

Forecasts are generally made either to estimate cash flows or when management gets worried about how the company will close out a period in terms of profits.

Short-term forecasting is especially important with respect to cash requirements. If a company is to pay its bills and make its payroll, it has to have an accurate picture of the cash ins and outs that can be expected over the next few weeks and months. If a temporary shortage is predicted, bank borrowing has to be arranged to keep the firm running until collections catch up with disbursements.

A *cash forecast* is a financial projection made with the explicit purpose of predicting short-term cash needs. Most large firms do *monthly* cash forecasts.[3]

The Business Planning Spectrum   It helps one's understanding of planning to imagine the different kinds of plan arrayed along a spectrum. The broad, conceptual thinking of long-term strategic planning is on one end, while the numerical detail of short-term forecasting is on the other. The idea is illustrated in Figure 4-2. As we move from left to right, the planning horizon (time covered) gets shorter, and the documents progress from qualitative to quantitative—that is, from being mostly words to mostly numbers.

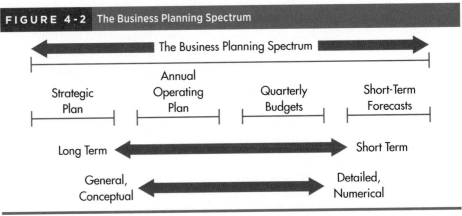

FIGURE 4-2   The Business Planning Spectrum

© Cengage Learning

---

3. The words "plan" and "forecast" have slightly different implications when used as nouns and verbs. A forecast (noun) tends to mean a short-term projection. A plan (noun) has a longer-term implication. The verbs are used more generally and don't tend to be tied to the length of the planning horizon. Hence, we routinely talk about *forecasting* the numbers within a plan or *planning* the numbers within a forecast.

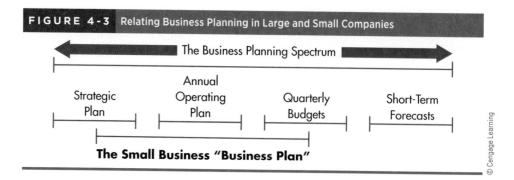

FIGURE 4-3   Relating Business Planning in Large and Small Companies

The Business Planning Spectrum

Strategic Plan   Annual Operating Plan   Quarterly Budgets   Short-Term Forecasts

The Small Business "Business Plan"

© Cengage Learning

Ideally, companies practice the whole spectrum of planning. That's the way most large companies operate, producing all the different documents. In such an environment, the strategic plan and the annual operating plan are each produced once a year about six months apart.[4] In addition, there are usually four quarterly budgets and any number of forecasts.[5]

When in need of funding, **small businesses** tend to do a single **business plan** that contains both strategic and operating elements.

Relating Planning Processes of Small and Large Businesses   In the small business world, the planning spectrum is usually compressed into one document known simply as the company's "business plan." It tends to be produced when the firm is getting started and updated later when money is needed from a bank or another outside source.

The business plan produced by small companies can be related to the full planning spectrum found in larger firms. The idea is illustrated in Figure 4-3. The (small) business plan overlaps three of the exercises along the spectrum. It includes everything we normally think of as operational (annual) planning, as well as elements of both strategic planning and budgeting.

The entrepreneur's plan must do everything the big corporation's annual operating plan does. It has to provide a thorough rationale for the concrete actions planned in the next year and make some fairly detailed projections of quantities, staffing, and dollars over that period.

With respect to strategy, however, the small business plan doesn't need to cover the broadest issues. For example, it doesn't have to discuss why the entrepreneur chose this business over others because that decision has already been made. The plan does have to establish that a market clearly exists and that it can be served by the business. The small business plan must also make longer-term strategic projections of what the business will be three to five years in the future.

Finally, a small business plan has to get under an operating plan and project at least the first year in budget-like detail. Investors generally demand at least this much precision from entrepreneurs.[6]

4. It's important to notice that even though the strategic plan covers five or more years, it is revised annually.

5. Companies in very stable businesses may omit the budget segment of the spectrum. Producers of basic foods and certain regulated utilities are examples. Their revenues don't change much from year to year, so it may not be necessary to rebudget quarterly to keep up with changing business conditions. High-tech industries represent the opposite extreme. Technology and the markets for it change rapidly, and the companies constantly engage in replanning.

6. For a comprehensive treatment of business planning in the context of small business, see *The Perfect Business Plan Made Simple* by William Lasher (New York: Random House 2005).

4.1e   The Financial Plan as a Component of a Business Plan

A financial plan is simply the financial portion of any of the business plans we've been talking about. It is a set of pro forma financial statements projected over the time period covered by the plan.[7]

The **financial plan** is an integral part of the overall **business plan**.

It's important to appreciate the role of the financial plan in each of the four planning documents we discussed earlier. No business plan is complete without a financial projection, but it's of secondary importance in the strategic plan. That document is an exposition of thoughts and ideas that discusses the how and why of a business. The *financials* are pieces of the projection, but generally aren't central to the presentation.

In an annual plan, on the other hand, the financial projection is the centerpiece of the document. In operational terms, a company's financial plan is its business plan.

There are usually a great many words in an annual plan, but they tend to be explanations of how the operating figures are to be achieved rather than discussions that stand by themselves.

Budgets and forecasts, especially the latter, are almost entirely financial planning exercises.

4.2   Making Financial Projections

Projecting financial statements involves translating planned physical and economic activity into dollars. That generally means making a sales forecast first and then developing what the rest of the company needs to do to support the activity implied. Those physical projections lead to the dollar figures in the financial statements.

4.2a   Planning for New and Existing Businesses

Financial plans are constructed for both new and ongoing businesses. The processes are conceptually similar, but as a practical matter it's a good deal harder to plan for an operation that's either very new or has yet to be started.

It's difficult to forecast how much a new business will sell or how much support it will need, because there's no history on which to base projections. That means everything has to be developed from the ground up. Forecasting for an established business is much easier, because recent results and the existing base of assets and liabilities can be used as points of departure for the projection.

The Typical Planning Task   Most financial planning is done for existing businesses. Basically, it involves forecasting changes to what's been going on in the past. The changes are generally referred to as **planning assumptions**. Anything about which an explicit assumption isn't made is implicitly assumed to remain unchanged from the previous year. (For a new business, everything has to be explicitly assumed.)

Most financial planning involves forecasting changes in ongoing businesses based on **planning assumptions**.

---

7.   The terms "financial plan" and "financial planner" have a common meaning that shouldn't be confused with their use in this chapter. Personal financial advisors who set up investment programs (financial plans) for clients are known as "financial planners." The field has nothing to do with business planning or projecting financial statements.

For example, an existing business might plan next year's operations assuming the following changes:

- A 10% growth in unit sales
- A 3% reduction in product price
- A $2 per unit increase in the cost of materials
- Overall labor cost increases of 4%
- An improvement in inventory turnover from 5.3 to 6.3
- An improvement in the ACP from 45 to 40 days
- An increase in interest rates from 7% to 9%
- And so on.

The financial planner's task is to put together a plan, benchmarking from last year's performance, that reflects these changes in the projected financial statements.

4.2b   The General Approach, Assumptions, and the Debt/Interest Problem

In this section, we'll outline how any financial planning problem is tackled and consider the peculiar problem of forecasting debt and interest. We'll begin by establishing exactly what we're trying to forecast and exactly what we have to start with.

What We Have and What We Need to Project   Every financial planning problem involves forecasting future financial statements beginning with the next period, given the results of the last period.[8,9] Only the income statement and balance sheet have to be forecast. The statement of cash flows is developed from those two without any additional projections.

Figure 4-4 shows the planner's task conceptually. The current (this) year's income statement is available, as is the ending balance sheet (which is next year's beginning balance sheet). These items are indicated by $XX in the figure. Using those as references, next year's income statement and ending balance sheet must be forecast, incorporating the physical and economic assumptions made in the plan.

If the plan is for a new business, the $XXs are simply all zeros.

Planning Assumptions   We introduced the idea of an assumption briefly in the last section. At this point we'll define the concept more precisely and illustrate how it works.

A **planning assumption** is some physical or economic condition that is expected to exist during the planning period. Assumptions can reflect any of the forces that influence a firm's financial results. Some things originate outside the company, like interest rates and taxes. Others come from planned management actions, like pricing or cost control. Still others come from customer behavior, like the volume response to a price change.

> A **planning assumption** is an **expected condition** that dictates the size of one or more **financial statement items**.

---

8. For discussion purposes, we'll assume yearly time periods.

9. Most of the time, planning for a particular year is done toward the end of the preceding (current) year. That means planners don't have actual financial results for the current year with which to work. However, because year end is close, they generally have relatively good estimates of the year's actual results.

FIGURE 4-4 The Planning Task

INCOME STATEMENT	This Year	Next Year	BALANCE SHEET	Next Year Begin	End
Revenue	$XX	$?	ASSETS		
COGS	XX	?	Current	$ XX	$?
Gross margin	$XX	?	Fixed	XX	?
Expense	XX	?	Total assets	$ XXX	?
EBIT	$XX	?	LIABILITIES		
Interest	XX	?	Current Liabilities	$ XX	?
EBT	$XX	?	Debt	XX	?
Tax	XX	?	Equity	XX	?
Net income	$XX	?	Total L&E	$ XXX	?

© Cengage Learning

In general, each line on a projected set of financial statements is forecast on the basis of one or more assumptions about the business. Example 4-1 on page 136 illustrates the idea.

The Procedural Approach   Financial plans are built by attacking line items one at a time starting with revenue, doing the kind of thing illustrated in Example 4-1.

The substance of financial planning is the logical translation of assumptions into the forecast figures they imply. It's important to realize that the calculations required for that translation differ, depending on the line item and the nature of the assumption. Some are very simple while others can become involved. We'll go through some more examples shortly.

The procedure moves down the income statement through cost and expense, stopping just *before* the interest expense line. Then the balance sheet projections are addressed. All the asset and liability accounts other than long-term debt and equity are forecast. At that point, the planning procedure encounters a problem.

The Debt/Interest Planning Problem   The next items needed to complete the financial statements are interest expense on the income statement and debt on the balance sheet. The problem is that each depends on the other, so a straightforward forecast is impossible.

It's important to understand the reason for this difficulty, but the explanation can be a little hard to follow. The problem is described in the following paragraphs and illustrated in Figure 4-5. Read the explanation carefully, referring to the illustration at the same time.

Start by examining Figure 4-5. $XXs imply dollar forecasts have already been made and question marks (?) indicate they haven't. Notice that on the income statement we lack a forecast of interest expense and everything below it, including net income. On the balance sheet we have forecasts for all the asset and liability accounts other than debt and equity. Notice that we do have the total liabilities and equity figure because it's equal to total assets.

The **debt/interest** dilemma: Planned **debt** is required to forecast **interest**, but **interest** is required to forecast **debt**.

CONCEPT CONNECTION   EXAMPLE 4-1

Planning Assumptions

This year Crumb Baking Corp. sold 1 million coffee cakes per month to grocery distributors at $1 each for a total of $12 million. The firm had year-end receivables equal to two months of sales or $2 million. Crumb's operating assumptions with respect to sales and receivables for next year are:

1. Price will be decreased by 10% in order to sell more product.

2. As a result of the price decrease, unit sales volume will increase to 15 million coffee cakes.

3. Collection efforts will be increased so that only one month of sales will be in receivables at year end.

Forecast next year's revenue and ending receivables balance on the basis of these assumptions. Assume sales are evenly distributed over the year.

SOLUTION: There are three interrelated planning assumptions in this example. The first reflects a management action with respect to pricing, and the second defines the expected customer response to that action. Together, they establish the revenue forecast: Next year, 15 million coffee cakes will be sold at $.90 each, so total revenue will be

$$\text{revenue} = 15,000,000 \times \$.90 = \$13,500,000$$

The third assumption is that the company's credit and collection activities will be more effective next year. This will be reflected by a decrease from two to one in the number of months of revenue that remain uncollected in accounts receivable at year end.

$$\text{A/R} = \$13,500,000/12 = \$1,125,000$$

Notice that the receivables calculation depends on all three assumptions, because it uses the revenue projection developed from the first two as well as the third assumption about the effectiveness of credit and collections.

To complete the income statement, we need a forecast of interest expense. But interest is calculated by applying the interest rate to the average projected debt balance during the coming year. We know the beginning debt balance, but we have to forecast the ending figure to get an average.

Forecasting ending debt requires that we complete the ending balance sheet, which requires that we forecast ending equity. Ending equity is computed by adding the year's net income from the income statement (less any dividends to be paid plus any new stock that will be sold) to beginning equity. (See page 43.)

But we don't have a forecast for net income because we weren't able to complete the income statement without interest expense, which we don't have because we don't have a forecast for ending debt. In other words, the problem is circular. We need debt to calculate interest, but we have to have interest to calculate debt (through net income and equity).

All this means we can't make a direct forecast of either debt or interest expense. Therefore, we can't complete the financial plan with the direct line-by-line approach we've been using so far. Every financial plan runs into this technical impasse.

FIGURE 4-5 The Debt/Interest Planning Problem

INCOME STATEMENT		BALANCE SHEET		
			Next Year	
			Beginning	Ending
	Next Year			
Revenue	$XX	ASSETS		
COGS	XX	Current	$ XX	$ XX
Gross margin	$XX	Fixed	XX	XX
Expense	XX	Total assets	$XXX	$ XXX
EBIT	$XX	LIABILITIES		
→Interest	?	Current	$ XX	$ XX
EBT	?	Debt	XX	?
Tax	?	Equity	XX	?
Net income	?	Total L&E	$XXX	$ XXX

Net income (less dividends) is added to
beginning equity to arrive at ending equity,
which is required to compute ending debit.

Ending debt is averaged with beginning debt
and multiplied by the interest rate to calculate
interest expense.

© Cengage Learning 2014

An Iterative Numerical Approach

The problem is solved using a numerical technique that begins with a guess at the solution. The guess is usually wrong, but it gives us a starting point from which we can work toward the correct answer.

An **iterative, numerical approach** solves the debt/interest problem.

The procedure works as follows:

1. *Interest:* Guess a value of interest expense.

2. *Net income:* Complete the income statement.

3. *Ending equity:* Calculate ending equity as beginning equity plus net income (less dividends plus new stock to be sold if either of these exist).

4. *Ending debt:* Calculate ending debt as total liabilities and equity (= total assets) less current liabilities less ending equity.

5. *Interest:* Average beginning and ending debt. Calculate interest by multiplying average debt by the interest rate.

6. *Test results:* Compare the calculated interest from step 5 to the original guess in step 1.
   a. If the two are significantly different, return to step 1, replacing the guess at interest with the value just calculated and repeat steps 2 through 6.
   b. If the calculated value of interest is close to the guess, stop.

Procedures like this one that find solutions to problems though a repetitive series of calculations are known as *numerical methods* or *iterative techniques*. Each pass through the procedure is iteration. It rarely takes more than two or three iterations to arrive at an acceptable solution regardless of the initial guess. An example will make the method clear.

CONCEPT CONNECTION   EXAMPLE 4-2

The Debt/Interest Planning Problem

The following partial financial forecast has been done for Hanover Inc. Complete the financial plan, assuming that Hanover pays interest at 10% and has a flat income tax rate of 40% including federal and state taxes. (We'll generally assume a simple, flat tax rate in our examples.) Also assume no dividends are to be paid and no new stock is to be sold.

Financial Plan for Hanover Inc. ($000)

Income Statement		Balance Sheets		
	Next Year		Next Year	
	Next Year		Beginning	Ending
Revenue	$ 10,000	ASSETS		
Cost/Expense	9,000	Total assets	$1,000	$3,000
EBIT	1,000	LIABILITIES		
Interest	?	Current liabilities	$ 300	$ 700
EBT	?	Debt	100	?
Tax	?	Equity	600	?
Net income	?	Total L&E	$1,000	$3,000

SOLUTION: First notice that we're assuming a rather large growth rate in this illustration. Hanover's assets are forecast to triple in one year. That's possible, but unusual. In this case, it will cause the company's debt to increase rather dramatically in the coming year.

We'll complete the forecast using the procedure outlined above, considering each step in turn.

1. *Guess at interest:* In most practical situations, the interest paid last year makes a good starting guess for next year's interest. Since we don't have that here, we'll make an arbitrary guess of $200,000.

The forecast is completed in the next three steps. We'll display the result now, and then show the detail of steps 2 through 4. The bottom of the income statement and the liabilities and equity portion of the balance sheet based on our interest guess are as follows:

First Iteration ($000)

EBIT	$1,000	LIABILITIES & EQUITY		
Interest	200	Current liabilities	$ 300	$ 700
EBT	$ 800	Debt	100	1,220
Tax	320	Equity	600	1,080
Net income	$ 480	Total L&E	$1,000	$3,000

The following steps get us to this result.

2. *Compute net income:* Assuming interest expense of $200,000, net income is $480,000 calculated as follows:

EBIT	$ 1,000,000
Interest	200,000
EBT	$ 800,000
Tax (@ 40%)	320,000
Net income	$ 480,000

3. *Ending equity:* Ending equity is beginning equity plus net income.

Beginning equity	$ 600,000
Net income	480,000
Ending equity	$ 1,080,000

4. *Ending debt:* Ending debt is total L&E less ending equity less ending current liabilities.

Total L&E	$ 3,000,000
Ending equity	(1,080,000)
Current liabilities	(700,000)
Ending debt	$ 1,220,000

At this point we have a set of financial statements based on our guess at interest expense. Next we test to see whether the calculated debt and the implied interest are consistent with that guess.

5. *Interest:* The interest implied by our calculated debt is the product of average debt and the interest rate.

$$\text{average debt} \times \text{interest rate} = \frac{\$100,000 + \$1,220,000}{2} \times .10 = \$66,000$$

6. *Test results:* Our next step is to test the calculated interest from step 5 against the original guess. As is usually the case, the two aren't very close. The original guess of $200,000 is much higher than the calculated interest of $66,000.

We begin the next iteration of the procedure by using the calculated interest figure ($66,000) in place of the guess. Verify that steps 2 through 4 result in the following figures (rounded to the nearest thousand dollars).

Second Iteration ($000)

EBIT	$1,000	LIABILITIES & EQUITY		
Interest	66	Current liabilities	$ 300	$ 700
EBT	$ 934	Debt	100	1,140
Tax	374	Equity	600	1,160
Net income	$ 560	Total L&E	$1,000	$3,000

Given these results, average debt is

$$\frac{\$100,000 + \$1,140,000}{2} = \$620,000$$

and interest is

$$\$620,000 \times .10 = \$62,000$$

Thus, the second guess and the calculated result are off by only $4,000 out of $62,000.

As an exercise, demonstrate that one more iteration with interest of $62,000 gives a result that's accurate to within $150 and ending debt of $1,137,000.

4.2c   Plans with Simple Assumptions

Financial plans can be constructed roughly or with great precision. The difference lies in the amount of thought and detail put into the assumptions on which the plans are based. A rough plan is based on just a few assumptions about the future, while a detailed plan can involve a great many. In this section, we'll look into creating a financial plan for an existing business in simple, rough terms.

Percentage of sales methods assume most financial statement line items **vary directly** with **revenue**.

optimarc/Shutterstock.com

from the
CFO

The Quick Estimate Based On Sales Growth   The **percentage of sales method** is a simple, approximate approach to forecasting financial statements for an existing business. The method involves estimating the company's sales growth rate into the next year and assuming that all income statement and balance sheet line items grow at the same rate. The technique implicitly assumes that the firm's efficiency and all of its operating *ratios* (Chapter 3) stay the same through the growth period.

The assumption that everything varies proportionately with (grows at the same rate as) sales is an oversimplification that's of theoretical interest, but isn't usually applicable in practice. Most of the time, the method is modified to assume that most, but not all, things vary directly with sales. We'll call such an approach the **modified percentage of sales method.** Here's an example illustrating the most common modification, a definite assumption about fixed assets, which are very unlikely to vary directly with sales.

CONCEPT CONNECTION   EXAMPLE 4-3

Plans with Simple Assumptions

The Underhill Manufacturing Company expects next year's revenues to increase by 15% over this year's. The firm has some excess factory capacity, so no new fixed assets beyond normal replacements will be needed to support the growth. This year's income statement and ending balance sheet are estimated as follows:

Underhill Manufacturing Company This Year ($000)

Income Statement		Balance Sheet	
Revenue	$ 13,580	ASSETS	
COGS	7,470	Cash	$ 348
Gross margin	$ 6,110	Accounts receivable	1,698
Expense*	3,395	Inventory	1,494
EBIT	$ 2,715	Current assets	$3,540
Interest	150	Net fixed assets	2,460
EBT	$ 2,565	Total assets	$6,000
Tax	1,077		
Net income	$ 1,488	LIABILITIES & EQUITY	
		Accounts payable	$ 125
		Accruals	45
		Current liabilities	$ 170
		Debt	1,330
		Equity	4,500
		Total L&E	$6,000

*Includes marketing, engineering, and administration.

Assume the firm pays state and federal income taxes at a combined flat rate of 42%, borrows at 12% interest, and does not expect to pay dividends or sell new stock.

Ensuper/Shutterstock.com

Project next year's income statement and balance sheet using the modified percentage of sales method.

SOLUTION: In this problem we'll grow everything except net fixed assets by 15%. That means we'll multiply the following items by 1.15: revenue, COGS, expense, all current assets, and all current liabilities. Then we'll hold net fixed assets constant because of the assumption that the firm has excess capacity and will just replace equipment that wears out. The result is reflected in the following incomplete statements.

Incomplete Statements for Next Year ($000)

Income Statement		Balance Sheet	
Revenue	$15,617	ASSETS	
COGS	8,591	Cash	$ 400
Gross margin	$ 7,026	Accounts receivable	1,953
Expense*	3,904	Inventory	1,718
EBIT	$3,122	Current assets	$4,071
Interest	—	Net fixed assets	2,460
EBT	$ —	Total assets	$6,531
Tax	—		
Net income	$ —	LIABILITIES & EQUITY	
		Accounts payable	$ 144
		Accruals	52
		Current liabilities	$ 196
		Debt	—
		Equity	—
		Total L&E	$6,531

*Includes marketing, engineering, and administration.

At this point we're at the debt/interest impasse. To complete the projection, we have to guess at interest and work through the procedure illustrated in the last section. This time, however, we have last year's interest of $150,000 to use as a starting guess. That and Underhill's other projected figures result in the following first iteration.

Debt/Interest Calculation—First Iteration ($000)

Income Statement		Balance Sheet		
	Next Year		**This Year**	**Next Year**
EBIT	$3,122	ASSETS		
Interest	150	Total assets	$6,000	$6,531
EBT	$2,972			
Tax	1,248	LIABILITIES & EQUITY		
Net income	$1,724	Current liabilities	$ 170	$ 196
		Debt	1,330	111
		Equity	4,500	6,224
		Total L&E	$6,000	$6,531

Taking the average debt at 12% yields a calculated interest of approximately $86,000, which is considerably less than the $150,000 assumed. Two more iterations yield the following complete financial projection.

Underhill Manufacturing Company Next Year ($000)

Income Statement		Balance Sheet	
Revenue	$ 15,617	ASSETS	
COGS	8,591	Cash	$ 400
Gross margin	$ 7,026	Accounts receivable	1,953
Expense*	3,904	Inventory	1,718
EBIT	$ 3,122	Current assets	$ 4,071
Interest	84	Net fixed assets	2,460
EBT	$ 3,038	Total assets	$ 6,531
Tax	1,276		
Net income	$ 1,762	LIABILITIES & EQUITY	
		Accounts payable	$ 144
		Accruals	52
		Current liabilities	$ 196
		Debt	73
		Equity	6,262
		Total L&E	$ 6,531

*Includes marketing, engineering, and administration.

More Accurate but Still Simple Plans   The *modified* percentage of sales method we've just described can be further modified to provide more planning accuracy while still keeping things fairly simple. In Example 4-3 we made an explicit assumption about net fixed assets while letting everything else vary with sales. It's possible to make similar assumptions about anything else we have better knowledge of than a blanket growth assumption.

For example, suppose we've just converted the factory to a new process that's expected to reduce production cost by 10% per unit. In that case, it wouldn't make sense to forecast cost of goods sold to increase at the sales growth rate, as a smaller increase would clearly be more appropriate.

Managers typically have such knowledge about what will happen in a number of business areas that can be put into a plan with one or two simple assumptions. These additions generally improve the plan's credibility without making it significantly more complicated. We'll discuss complex techniques later in the chapter.

4.2d   Forecasting Cash Needs

Recall that a key reason for doing financial projections is to forecast the firm's external financing needs. We can observe that need quickly in the preceding example by comparing Underhill's beginning and ending debt balances for the forecast year. If the balance increases, the plan implies the firm will need more cash than it is generating through operations, and will have to borrow more. A decrease in debt implies that cash will be generated beyond the firm's immediate needs, so debt can be paid down.[10] In this example, Underhill is planning to generate $1,257,000 in cash, enough to pay down its debt from $1,330,000 to $73,000.

When a plan shows increasing debt, the implication is that additional external financing will be needed during the forecast year. Of course, the funds could be acquired by selling additional stock (equity) rather than borrowing. That would be reflected as an increase in the ending equity account beyond the addition of net income to retained earnings, which in turn would reduce the amount of ending debt required to balance the balance sheet.

4.2e   The Percentage of Sales Method—A Formula Approach

In Example 4-3 we used a modified percentage of sales method to create a financial projection based on an assumed growth in revenue and a separate assumption about fixed assets. If we're willing to assume that net fixed assets also grows proportionately with revenue, the percentage of sales method can be condensed into a single formula for the purpose of estimating external funding requirements. We'll call the formula the *EFR* relationship for *external funding requirement.*

The idea behind the EFR relationship is very simple: A growing firm must have enough money on hand to purchase the new assets it needs to support its growth. However, that funding requirement is reduced by two automatic sources, (1) the amount by which current liabilities grow[11] and (2) the amount the firm earns during the year but doesn't pay out in dividends.[12] In other words, for the year being planned (next year):

(4.1)
$$
\begin{aligned}
&\textbf{growth in assets} \\
-\;&\textbf{growth in current liabilities} \\
-\;&\textbf{earnings retained} \\
\hline
=\;&\textbf{external funding requirement}
\end{aligned}
$$

Expression 4.1 is true for any financial projection, but can be written in simple terms when sales, earnings, assets, and current liabilities are all assumed to grow at the same rate, which we'll call g.

We generally define g in terms of sales growth. That is,

$$
g = \frac{\textbf{increase in sales}}{\textbf{sales}_{\text{this year}}}
$$

For example, if this year's sales are $100,000 and next year's are projected to be $115,000, $g = .15$ or 15%.

---

10. A negative figure for ending debt is possible and implies that cash will be generated beyond the firm's beginning debt level. The negative debt would generally be shown as increasing the cash account.

11. Current liabilities are said to provide spontaneous financing because they reflect the acquisition of assets that don't have to be paid for immediately. We will examine this idea in more detail in Chapter 16.

12. In the *unmodified* percentage of sales method, we shortcut the iterative debt/interest procedure by assuming net income grows at the same rate as sales. This is equivalent to assuming that the return on sales ratio (ROS) stays constant.

In terms of expression 4.1, the assumption that assets and current liabilities grow at rate g means

(4.2) $$\text{growth in assets} = g \times \text{assets}_{\text{this year}}$$

and

(4.3) $$\text{growth in current liabilities} = g \times \text{current liabilities}_{\text{this year}}$$

The **EFR** relationship provides an **estimate of funding** needs assuming all financial items **vary directly** with sales.

(The following derivation of the EFR can be skipped without loss of continuity. Just resume reading at Equation 4.6 on page 144.)

To develop an expression for current earnings retained in terms of profits and dividends, begin by recalling the expression for return on sales (ROS) (Chapter 3, page 98).

$$\text{ROS} = \frac{\text{net income}}{\text{sales}}$$

Solve for net income in terms of ROS and sales.

$$\text{net income} = \text{ROS} \times \text{sales}$$

Notice that since we're assuming both net income and sales grow at the same rate, ROS will remain constant from year to year. Then next year's net income can be written as the constant ROS times next year's sales, which are just $(1 + g)$ times this year's sales. So

(4.4) $$\text{net income}_{\text{next year}} = \text{ROS} \times (1 + g)\text{sales}_{\text{this year}}$$

Next write the *dividend payout ratio,* which is defined as the ratio of dividends paid to net income.

$$d = \frac{\text{dividends}}{\text{net income}}$$

From that definition, net income is split between money paid out in dividends, $d(\text{net income})$, and money retained, $(1 - d)\text{net income}$.[13]

Then for next year,

$$\text{earnings retained} = (1 - d)\text{net income}_{\text{next year}}$$

Substituting for net income$_{\text{next year}}$ from expression 4.4 yields

(4.5) $$\text{earnings retained} = (1 - d)\text{ROS} \times (1 + g)\text{sales}_{\text{this year}}$$

Now, to get the EFR relation, rewrite expression 4.1 as an equation, substituting from 4.2, 4.3, and 4.4.

(4.6) $$\begin{aligned}\text{EFR} = &\ g(\text{assets}_{\text{this year}}) \\ &- g(\text{current liabilities}_{\text{this year}}) \\ &- [(1 - d)\text{ROS}][(1 + g)\ \text{sales}_{\text{this year}}]\end{aligned}$$

Although Equation 4.6 looks messy, it's easy to use because everything on the right side comes from this year's financial statements and the growth rate assumption.

13. The expression $(1 - d)$ is called the *retention ratio.*

CONCEPT CONNECTION   **EXAMPLE 4-4**

External Funding Requirement (EFR)

Reforecast the external financing requirements of the Underhill Manufacturing Company of Example 4-3, assuming net fixed assets and net income grow at the same 15% rate as sales. However, also assume the firm plans to pay a dividend equal to 25% of earnings next year.

SOLUTION: First note Underhill's sales, assets, and current liabilities for this year (page 140) as well as its payout ratio. Then calculate its return on sales. (Omit $000 as before.)

$$sales_{this\ year} = \$13,580$$

$$assets_{this\ year} = \$6,000$$

$$current\ liabilities_{this\ year} = \$170$$

$$d = 25.0\%$$

$$ROS = \frac{Net\ income}{sales} = \frac{\$1,488}{\$13,580} = 11.0\%$$

Next write Equation 4.6 and substitute.

$$EFR = g(assets_{this\ year})$$
$$- g(current\ liabilities_{this\ year})$$
$$- [(1 - d)ROS][(1 + g)sales_{this\ year}]$$
$$EFR = .15(\$6,000) - .15(\$170)$$
$$- [(1 - .25)\,(.11)][(1.15)(\$13,580)]$$
$$EFR = -\$413.9$$

This result says that Underhill will generate enough funds during the projected year to reduce its debt by about $414,000.

It's important to keep in mind that the EFR approach and the related unmodified percentage of sales method are of limited value because of the general impracticality of the assumption that everything varies directly with sales. To see that, notice that the $414,000 net cash flow in Example 4-4 is substantially lower than the forecast in Example 4-3 of $1,257,000 (see Forecasting Cash Needs on page 142 immediately following the example). About half of the $843,000 difference comes from the fact that we assumed a dividend in Example 4-4 that wasn't in Example 4-3. The other half, however, comes from the fact that the percentage of sales method forces an assumption of a 15% growth in net fixed assets, which in this case is unrealistic.

4.2f   The Sustainable Growth Rate

> A firm can grow at its **sustainable growth rate** without selling new stock if its financial ratios remain constant.

A firm's **sustainable growth rate** is a theoretical measure of its strength. It is the rate at which the firm can grow if none of its financial ratios change and if it doesn't raise any new equity by selling stock. These conditions are equivalent to the assumptions of the unmodified percentage of sales method.

Sustainable growth is simply the growth in equity created by profits. We can develop an expression for the rate by noticing that business operations create new equity equal to the amount of current earnings retained. That can be written as

$$(1 - d)\text{net income}$$

where d is the dividend payout ratio, the fraction of earnings paid to stockholders as dividends.

This implies a sustainable growth rate in equity, g_s, equal to the amount of new equity created divided by equity itself.

(4.7a)
$$g_s = \frac{\text{net income } (1 - d)}{\text{equity}}$$

from which

(4.7b)
$$g_s = \text{ROE}(1 - d)$$

because ROE = net income/equity.

Notice that although the idea of sustainable growth implies that no new equity is raised through the sale of stock, it does require new borrowing to keep the debt/equity ratio constant as equity grows through retaining earnings.

The value of the sustainable growth concept is largely theoretical. It gives an indication of the determinants of a firm's inherent growth capability. Recall from our study of Du Pont equations (Chapter 3, page 102) that ROE can be written as

$$\text{ROE} = \text{ROS} \times \text{total asset turnover} \times \text{equity multiplier}$$

Substituting this expression for ROE into Equation 4.7b, we have

$$g_s = (1 - d)[\text{ROS} \times \text{total asset turnover} \times \text{equity multiplier}]$$

which can be written more explicitly as

(4.8)
$$g_s = (1 - d) \times \frac{\text{net income}}{\text{sales}} \times \frac{\text{sales}}{\text{assets}} \times \frac{\text{assets}}{\text{equity}}$$

Equation 4.8 says a firm's ability to grow depends on four fundamentals:

1. Its ability to earn profits on sales as measured by its ROS (net income/sales)
2. Its talent at using assets to generate sales as measured by its total asset turnover (sales/assets)
3. Its use of leverage (borrowed money) as measured by the equity multiplier (assets/equity)
4. The percentage of earnings it retains as measured by $(1 - d)$, the *earnings retention ratio*

These ideas can be used to analyze why a particular firm's growth has been good or bad in relation to that of other firms.

CONCEPT CONNECTION   EXAMPLE 4-5

Sustainable Growth Rate

After several years of lower-than-average growth, Slowly Inc. compared its sustainable growth rate with an industry average as follows:

	g_s	=	(1 − d)	×	ROS	×	total asset turnover	×	equity multiplier
Industry	13.5%		.75		6%		1.2		2.5
Slowly Inc.	4.8		.40		8		1.0		1.5

Notice that Slowly's sustainable growth rate is much lower than the average. The question is why. The comparison immediately shows that profitability is not the problem, as Slowly's ROS is better than average. It's also apparent that total asset turnover is a bit low, but not enough to make much difference.

Slowly's growth problem seems to be associated with its modest use of leverage and its dividend policy. The firm's equity multiplier is substantially lower than average, meaning it is financed with proportionately less debt and more equity than other firms. Its *earnings retention ratio,* (1 − d), is also lower than average.

These things may explain why the firm isn't growing rapidly. It's paying most of its earnings out in dividends rather than reinvesting them in growth opportunities. At the same time, it's constrained not to raise much money by borrowing. This is a low-risk strategy but it doesn't lead to rapid growth.

Ensuper/Shutterstock.com

4.2g   Plans with More Complicated Assumptions

The percentage of sales methods (modified and unmodified) are appropriate for quick estimates, but aren't generally used in formal plans because they gloss over too much detail.

It's usually possible to make intelligent estimates of a large number of individual items within a financial plan. Putting those separate pieces of intelligence into the projections clearly makes sense. That's done by incorporating a series of detailed assumptions into the process. Each assumption is worked into the plan in a manner that depends on the way the related item is managed and on its accounting treatment. As an illustration, let's take a closer look at the treatment of fixed assets for the Underhill Manufacturing Company of Example 4-3.

In that example, we made the assumption that the firm had excess factory capacity, which implied that a certain amount of growth could be accommodated in the plant without adding new assets. Hence, net fixed assets could be expected to remain roughly constant. That assumption is reasonable but somewhat simplistic. It would rarely be used in a serious operating plan.

Acquiring fixed assets calls for the commitment of large amounts of money and tends to be analyzed very carefully. That means a great deal of information about fixed assets is usually available.

In fact, the business planning process generally includes a *capital plan,* a list of the assets and projects on which the firm intends to spend money during the coming period.

Real plans generally incorporate **complex assumptions** about important financial items.

In the next example, we'll assume a capital plan has been done for Underhill, and show how some of the information it contains can be worked into the financial plan.

CONCEPT CONNECTION   EXAMPLE 4-6

Planning Fixed Assets

Assume the following for the Underhill Manufacturing Company of Example 4-3.

1. The ending balance sheet for the current year contains the following fixed asset accounts.

Gross	$5,600,000
Accumulated depreciation	(3,140,000)
Net	$2,460,000

2. Next year's depreciation on the assets owned at the end of this year is $450,000, and there are no plans to dispose of old assets.

3. The capital plan indicates that assets will be acquired next year at an estimated total cost of $1.2 million.

4. The average depreciation life of the new equipment will be five years. Straight-line depreciation will be used. Assume one-half year of depreciation will be taken on new assets in the first year to reflect less than a full year's use.

Notice that items 1 and 2 are not planning assumptions. They're financial facts available from the company's accounting records. Items 3 and 4 are planning assumptions summarizing the information contained in Underhill's capital plan.

Forecast Underhill's fixed asset accounts for next year.

SOLUTION: Gross fixed assets will grow by the amount of new capital expenditures.

Beginning gross fixed assets	$5,600,000
Planned additions	1,200,000
Ending gross fixed assets	$6,800,000

Depreciation during the year will come from two sources, the old assets already on board at the beginning of the year and the new additions. We've already established that the old depreciation will be $450,000. New depreciation based on the five-year/straight-line assumption factored down by one half for a partial year of service is

$$\text{depreciation on new assets} = \frac{\$1,200,000}{5} \times \frac{1}{2} = \$120,000$$

Then total depreciation next year is as follows:

Old assets	$450,000
New assets	120,000
Total	$570,000

With this information, the balance sheet fixed asset accounts at year end are forecast as follows. (Review the accounting for fixed assets, Chapter 2, pages 36–37 if necessary.)

Fixed assets are forecast by projecting the **gross** account using the **capital plan** and handling **depreciation** separately.

Ensuper/Shutterstock.com

	Actual Beginning	Planned Additions	Planned Ending
Gross	$5,600,000	$1,200,000	$6,800,000
Accumulated depreciation	(3,140,000)	(570,000)	(3,710,000)
Net	$2,460,000	$ 630,000	$3,090,000

It's important to notice that this approach produces the following fixed-asset-related items for the projected financial statements.

1. The year-end balance sheet account detail

2. An estimate of the use of cash for capital spending for the cash flow statement

3. An estimate of total depreciation for the income statement and the cash flow statement

The approach in Example 4-3, on the other hand, gave us no information beyond the net fixed asset figure, which was not very accurate.

Two Kinds of Planning Assumption—Direct and Indirect—Management by Ratios

A financial planning assumption can be made directly about the financial item to which it's related or indirectly about a derivative of the item, usually a ratio. In Example 4-6, we made direct assumptions about capital expenditures to forecast items related to fixed assets.

Indirect planning assumptions are made about financial **ratios**, which in turn lead to line-item values.

An indirect planning assumption is usually based on the use of financial ratios. Instead of forecasting a particular item, we forecast a related ratio. Accounts receivable is a good example. Managers generally think of receivables in terms of the average time it takes to collect cash from customers rather than in terms of the magnitude of the receivables account on the balance sheet. In other words, receivables are managed through the average collection period (ACP) ratio. (See Chapter 3, page 92.) This means that financial planning assumptions about receivables tend to be made in terms of the ACP. Projected statements are then put together using receivables balances calculated from those assumptions.

CONCEPT CONNECTION   EXAMPLE 4-7

Indirect Planning Assumptions

The Mylar Corporation currently has receivables of $1.2 million on revenues of $7.2 million for an ACP of 60 days calculated as follows:

$$\text{ACP} = \frac{\text{A/R}}{\text{average daily sales}}$$

$$= \frac{\text{A/R}}{\text{sales}} \times 360 = \frac{\$1.2 \text{ million}}{\$7.2 \text{ million}} \times 360 = 60 \text{ days}$$

A review of individual accounts has revealed that there are no very old or plainly uncollectible accounts in the receivables balance.

Management feels that a 60-day ACP represents unacceptably slow payment by customers, and plans to tighten credit and collection policy enough to reduce it to 40 days in the coming year. Next year's revenue projection reflects a growth of approximately 10% to $7.9 million after consideration of the credit and collections policy change.

What balance sheet figure for receivables should be included in the financial plan to reflect this assumption about ACP?

SOLUTION: The indirect planning assumption is that the ACP will be 40 days next year. To put together a financial plan consistent with that assumption, we calculate the year-end receivables balance that results in a 40-day ACP. Begin by rewriting the ACP formula.

Accounts receivable are generally forecast by making an assumption about the **ACP** and calculating the implied balance.

$$ACP = \frac{A/R}{sales} \times 360$$

Then substitute next year's figures, treating A/R as an unknown.

$$40 \text{ days} = \frac{A/R}{\$7,900,000} \times 360$$

Solve this expression for the A/R balance implied by the ACP assumption.

$$A/R = \$877,777 [14]$$

4.2h   A Comprehensive Example—A Complex Plan for an Existing Business

In this section we'll take an ongoing business and make a projection for next year based on a fairly broad set of assumptions. Notice that most of the assumptions are based on changes from last year.

---

14. In practice, the calculation would usually be somewhat more complicated. Most people calculate ACPs on the basis of an average A/R balance over the year using the following formula:

$$ACP = \frac{(\text{beginning A/R} + \text{ending A/R})/2}{sales} \times 360$$

Next year's beginning A/R balance is this year's ending balance, $1.2 million in this case. Substituting yields

$$40 \text{ days} = \frac{(\$1,200,000 + \text{ending A/R})/2}{\$7,900,000} \times 360$$

from which

$$\text{ending A/R} = \$555,556$$

Notice that this figure is unrealistically low because of the inclusion of the high ending balance from last year. If the ACP calculation is based on average A/R balances, the target ACP should be raised in a transitional year to reflect that fact. In this case, a 50-day target over the entire year would be appropriate to get the firm operating at a 40-day level by year end.

CONCEPT CONNECTION   EXAMPLE 4-8

Complex Plans

The Macadam Company is developing its annual plan for next year. The company expects to finish this year with the following financial results.

MACADAM COMPANY INCOME STATEMENT THIS YEAR ($000)

	$	%
Revenue	$14,200	100.0
COGS	7,810	55.0
Gross margin	$ 6,390	45.0
Expenses		
Marketing	$ 2,556	18.0
Engineering	1,065	7.5
Finance & administrative	1,349	9.5
Total expenses	$ 4,970	35.0
EBIT	$ 1,420	10.0
Interest	568	4.0
EBT	$ 852	6.0
Income tax	341	2.4
Net income	$ 511	3.6

MACADAM COMPANY BALANCE SHEET THIS YEAR ($000)

ASSETS		LIABILITIES & EQUITY	
Cash	$ 1,560	Accounts payable	$ 716
Accounts receivable	3,550	Accruals	230
Inventory	2,603	Current liabilities	$ 946
Current assets	$ 7,713	Long-term debt	$4,000
Fixed assets		Equity	
Gross	$12,560	Stock accounts	$6,000
Accumulated depreciation	(3,620)	Retained earnings	5,707
Net	$ 8,940	Total equity	$ 11,707
Total assets	$16,653	Total L&E	$16,653

(The income statement is presented with a common size statement, because certain planning assumptions are commonly based on projected percentages of revenue. See Chapter 3, page 88.)

The current values of Macadam's ACP and inventory turnover ratio can be calculated from the statements.

The ACP is

$$\text{ACP} = \frac{\text{A/R}}{\text{sales}} \times 360 = \frac{\$3,550}{\$14,200} \times 360 = 90 \text{ days}$$

and the inventory turnover based on COGS is

$$\text{inventory turnover} = \frac{\text{COGS}}{\text{inventory}} = \frac{\$7,810}{\$2,603} = 3.0$$

The following facts (not assumptions) are also available about the firm's operations.

Facts

- Virtually all payables are due to inventory purchases, and the COGS is approximately 60% purchased material.
- Assets currently on the firm's books will generate depreciation of $510,000 next year.
- The only balance sheet accrual represents unpaid wages. Preliminary estimates indicate that next year's payroll will be about $6.1 million. Next year's closing balance sheet date will be nine working days after a payday.
- The combined state and federal income tax rate is 40%. (Assume a flat rate.)
- Interest on current and future borrowing will be at a rate of 10%.

The management team has met and agreed upon the following assumptions under which the plan will be developed.

Planning Assumptions

Income, Cost, and Expense

1. During the coming year, the firm will mount a major program to expand sales. The expected result is a 20% growth in revenue. Pricing and product mix will remain unchanged.

2. The revenue growth will be accomplished by increasing efforts in the marketing/sales department. The increased expenses generated will be accommodated by planning marketing department expenses at 19% of the expanded revenue rather than the current 18%.

3. A major cost-reduction effort is under way in the manufacturing department, which is expected to reduce (improve) the *cost ratio* (COGS/revenue) to 53% from its current level of 55%.

4. The engineering department will be unaffected by the expansion in sales. Its dollar expenses will increase by normal inflation at a 4% rate over last year's level.

5. Finance and administrative expenses will need to expand to support the higher volume, but because of scale economies the expansion will be at a lower rate than the growth in sales. A target growth of 10% is planned for those expenses.

Assets and Liabilities

6. A new cash management system[15] will reduce the cash balance by 20%.

7. The current 90-day collection period (ACP) is considered unacceptable. Increased attention to credit and collections in both finance and sales is expected to bring the ACP down to 65 days.

8. Top management feels that the firm is operating with more inventory than it needs. Manufacturing management has been challenged to increase the inventory turnover ratio based on COGS to 5.0 from its present level of 3.0.

---

15. We'll discuss cash management systems in Chapter 16.

9. The capital plan has been put together in preliminary form and indicates capital spending of $5 million. The average depreciation life of the assets to be acquired is 10 years. Straight-line depreciation will be used, and a convention of taking one-half year's depreciation in the first year will be followed.

10. Vendors are complaining because the firm pays its bills in 55 days even though most terms call for payment within 30 days. Fearing that inventory and supplies will be cut off, management has decided to shorten the payment cycle to 45 days.

11. No dividends will be paid next year, and no new stock will be sold.

Construct a financial plan for next year for Macadam based on last year's statements and these assumptions. Assume all balance sheet ratios are calculated using ending balances.

SOLUTION: We'll begin Macadam's plan by projecting each operating line of the income statement and balance sheet. Then we'll complete those statements by iterating for debt and interest. Finally, we'll construct a projected statement of cash flows from the completed income statement and balance sheet.

Notice as we go along that each line item is handled differently. Some are very simple, while others take some calculation. We'll omit the $000 and round all results to the nearest thousand dollars for convenience.

Revenue: Our revenue forecast is based on the direct assumption of a 20% growth rate on last year's figure.

$$\text{revenue} = \$14,200 \times 1.20 = \mathbf{\$17,040}$$

Cost of goods sold (COGS): The forecast of COGS is based on an assumed improvement in manufacturing efficiency, which is reflected in an improvement (lowering) in the *cost ratio* from this year's 55% to 53% next year. The cost ratio is the ratio of COGS to revenue and appears on the COGS line of the common size income statement. Because we know next year's cost ratio as well as its revenue, we can multiply to project COGS.

$$\text{COGS} = \$17,040 \times .53 = \mathbf{\$9,031}$$

Marketing expense: Departmental expenses are frequently managed to a first level of approximation in common size terms. This implies comparing those expenses as percentages of revenue to industry averages to keep them in reasonable ranges. In this case, Macadam's top management is permitting spending in marketing to increase from 18% to 19% of sales to allow for an expanded effort in sales. The figure is easily forecast as 19% of next year's sales.

$$\text{marketing expense} = \$17,040 \times .19 = \mathbf{\$3,238}$$

Notice that this represents a very substantial growth (27%) over last year's spending in dollar terms.

Engineering expense: Engineering is a long-term development function that isn't directly related to the current year's sales. Hence, there's no reason to assume it has to grow a great deal to support the marketing expansion. The assumption of a 4% growth in spending over last year just keeps up with normal inflation.

$$\text{engineering expense} = \$1,065 \times 1.04 = \mathbf{\$1,108}$$

Finance and administrative expense: Finance and administrative expenses pay for things like accounting, treasury, personnel, and executive management. These functions grow with revenue, but economies of scale tend to make them more efficient as size increases, implying that they should grow less rapidly than sales. In this case, management has assumed a growth of 10%, half the rate assumed for sales.

$$\text{finance and administrative expense} = \$1,349 \times 1.10 = \mathbf{\$1,484}$$

The next line on the income statement is interest, which we can't address until we've completed the balance sheet down to debt. Therefore, we'll move on to current assets at this point.

Cash: A new system is forecast to improve Macadam's cash management, resulting in a 20% decrease in the balance from its current level. This assumption is quite aggressive in the face of an increase in business.

$$\text{cash} = \$1,560 \times (1 - .20) = \mathbf{\$1,248}$$

Accounts receivable: Macadam manages its receivables indirectly by addressing the ACP, which it has forecast at 65 days for next year.

Most managements forecast **accounts receivable** indirectly through the **average collection period (ACP)**.

$$\text{ACP} = \frac{\text{A/R}}{\text{sales}} \times 360$$

from which

$$65 = \frac{\text{A/R}}{\$17,040} \times 360$$

and

$$\text{A/R} = \mathbf{\$3,077}$$

Notice that this forecast represents a decrease in A/R in spite of the planned increase in revenue, which would normally be expected to raise receivables. That's because the improvement in collections is forecast to have a bigger effect than the growth in revenue. This too is a very aggressive assumption.

Inventory: Management has assumed an improvement in inventory utilization, which is reflected by an increase in the inventory turnover ratio to 5.0 from its current level of 3.0. This (indirectly) implies an inventory level through the equation defining the turnover ratio.

Inventory is generally forecast **indirectly** through the **inventory turnover** ratio.

$$\text{inventory turnover} = \frac{\text{COGS}}{\text{inventory}}$$

from which

$$5.0 = \frac{\$9,031}{\text{inventory}}$$

and

$$\text{inventory} = \mathbf{\$1,806}$$

Here again it's important to notice the aggressiveness of management's planning assumption. A 20% volume increase would normally lead to larger inventories, but this forecast is for a substantial decline due to the projected efficiency improvement.

Fixed assets: The fixed asset forecast is handled exactly as illustrated in Example 4-6. Additions and depreciation are as follows:

Gross fixed asset additions	$5,000
Depreciation	
New equipment = [$5,000/10] × 1/2 =	250
Old equipment	510
	$ 760

From these and the beginning balances in the fixed asset accounts, the ending balances are forecast as follows:

	Beginning	**Additions**	**Ending**
Gross	$12,560	$5,000	$17,560
Accumulated depreciation	(3,620)	(760)	(4,380)
Net	$ 8,940	$4,240	$13,180

Accounts payable: Macadam is currently slow-paying vendors in 55 days, probably to conserve cash. The practice is an abuse of most credit terms, which demand payment in 30 days, and the firm is getting a bad reputation among its suppliers. That can lead to production problems if suppliers hold up delivery. Management has decided to adjust its policy by paying in 45 days. This is still a violation of most 30-day terms, but it's less flagrant and more likely to be tolerated by vendors over the long run. Our problem is to calculate the payables balance implied by the policy.

Payables are generated almost entirely by inventory purchases, which are 60% of product cost. Hence, the total amount passing through the payables account in a year is 60% of COGS. If bills are paid in 45 days, the unpaid amount at any time is 45/360 of that annual total. This thinking leads to the following calculation.

$$\text{accounts payable} = \text{purchases} \times \frac{45}{360} = .60 \times \text{COGS} \times \frac{45}{360}$$

$$= .60 \times \$9,031 \times \frac{45}{360} = \textbf{\$677}$$

(As an exercise, demonstrate that this year's payables balance represents a 55-day payment policy.)

Accruals: Macadam's only accrual reflects unpaid wages. Recall that the amount of such an accrual represents wages earned between the year's last payday and its closing date. (See Chapter 2, page 40.) The amount can be estimated by examining a calendar to determine the ending date of the year being planned and the date of the immediately preceding payday. The period between the two dates represents the time for which wages have to be accrued. In this case, there are nine working days between the two dates, which represent 1.8 (= 9/5) normal five-day workweeks. Hence, the accrual must be for 1.8/52 of the total amount paid to employees in a year. Next year's annual payroll is estimated at $6,100, so the amount that will be accrued is

$$\text{accruals} = \$6,100 \times \frac{1.8}{52} = \$211[16]$$

This completes the forecast of the operating items in Macadam's income statement and balance sheet. To complete those statements, we have to go through the iterative procedure illustrated previously to determine debt and interest. That's readily accomplished by starting with this year's interest as a guess for next year. Three iterations result in the statements below. The figures that come from the iterative procedure are shown in italics.

---

16. In practice, accrual calculations tend to be more complex than this. Firms often have different payrolls for different types of employees, and everyone isn't always fully paid off as of payday. In addition, a number of things besides wages are generally accrued.

Notice the side-by-side (comparative) format in which the statements are presented. This year and next year are shown together for both statements, and a common size presentation is included for the income statement. This format is highly recommended for planning work because it makes it easy to work with the year-to-year changes that are the essence of most planning exercises.

MACADAM COMPANY PROJECTED INCOME STATEMENT ($000)

	This Year		Next Year	
	$	%	$	%
Revenue	$14,200	100.0	$17,040	100.0
COGS	7,810	55.0	9,031	53.0
Gross margin	$ 6,390	45.0	$ 8,009	47.0
Expenses				
Marketing	$ 2,556	18.0	$ 3,238	19.0
Engineering	1,065	7.5	1,108	6.5
Finance & administrative	1,349	9.5	1,484	8.7
Total expenses	$ 4,970	35.0	$ 5,830	34.2
EBIT	$ 1,420	10.0	$ 2,179	12.8
Interest	568	4.0	485	2.8
EBT	$ 852	6.0	$ 1,694	10.0
Income tax	341	2.4	678	4.0
Net income	$ 511	3.6	$ 1,016	6.0

MACADAM COMPANY PROJECTED BALANCE SHEET ($000)

	This Year	Next Year		This Year	Next Year
ASSETS			**LIABILITIES & EQUITY**		
Cash	$ 1,560	$ 1,248	Accounts payable	$ 716	$ 677
Accounts receivable	3,550	3,077	Accruals	230	211
Inventory	2,603	1,806	Current liabilities	$ 946	$ 888
Current assets	$ 7,713	$ 6,131	Debt	$4,000	$5,700
Fixed assets			Equity		
Gross	$12,560	$17,560	Stock	$6,000	$6,000
Accumulated depreciation	(3,620)	(4,380)	Retained earnings	5,707	6,723
Net	$ 8,940	$13,180	Total equity	$ 11,707	$12,723
Total assets	$16,653	$ 19,311	Total L&E	$16,653	$ 19,311

Macadam's financial plan is completed by constructing a projected statement of cash flows. That is readily done by using the procedures we studied in Chapter 3. No new projecting is required because the cash flow statement comes entirely from the income statement and balance sheet, which have already been forecast. The comparative format we're using makes constructing a cash statement particularly convenient. We begin with a summary of the planned changes in working capital items.

MACADAM COMPANY PROJECTED CHANGES IN WORKING CAPITAL ($000)

	Beginning	Ending	Change
Accounts receivable	$3,550	$3,077	$ 473
Inventory	2,603	1,806	797
Accounts payable	716	677	(39)
Accruals	230	211	(19)
Decrease/(increase) in working capital			$1,212

The projected statement of cash flows follows immediately.

MACADAM COMPANY PROJECTED STATEMENT OF CASH FLOWS ($000)

OPERATING ACTIVITIES	
Net income	$ 1,016
Depreciation	760
Decrease in working capital	1,212
Cash from operating activities	$2,988

MACADAM COMPANY PROJECTED STATEMENT OF CASH FLOWS ($000)

INVESTING ACTIVITIES	
Increase in gross Fixed assets	$(5,000)
Cash from investing activities	$(5,000)
FINANCING ACTIVITIES	
Increase in debt	$ 1,700
Cash from financing activities	$ 1,700
NET CASH FLOW	$ (312)
RECONCILIATION	
Beginning cash	$ 1,560
Net cash flow	(312)
Ending cash	$ 1,248

4.2i   Planning at the Department Level

The financial plan we developed for the Macadam Company in Example 4-8 includes an income statement that shows the total expenses of three major departments: marketing, engineering, and finance/administration.

It's important to understand that in operational plans (annual plans and quarterly budgets) projections of departmental expenses are much more detailed and complex than the single numbers appearing on the income statement. The statement numbers are simply departmental totals. They're *supported* by documentation that details the nature of the expenses and when during the planning period they'll occur.[17]

---

17. In a long-range strategic plan such supporting detail generally doesn't exist.

FIGURE 4-6 Supporting Detail for Annual Planning at the Department Level

Department: Sales Training — Annual Plan 20X1					
Item	**1Qtr**	**2Qtr**	**3Qtr**	**4Qtr**	**Total**
Headcount	35	36	38	38	
Wages	$350K	$360K	$382K	$383K	$1,475K
Overtime	$ 78K	$ 86K	$ 38K	$ 40K	$ 242K
Travel	...	...	...	...	...
Depreciation	...	...	...	...	...
Telephone	...	...	...	...	...
Supplies	...	...	...	...	...
Advertising		...	...	...	...
⋮	⋮				⋮
Misc. Expenses	...	...	...	...	...
Total	$XXX	$XXX	...	...	$X,XXX

© Cengage Learning

Departmental detail supports the expense entries on the planned income statement.

The format for **departmental detail** is usually a spreadsheet with time periods across the top and expense categories down the side. In an annual plan, the time periods are usually quarterly. The idea is illustrated in Figure 4-6.

The illustration shows expense detail for a single subdepartment within the larger marketing department. Every subdepartment has such a sheet, all of which consolidate into a single detail sheet for marketing as a whole. The total expense figure in the lower right corner of the consolidated sheet must match the marketing expense figure on the plan's income statement.

Manufacturing Departments

Spending detail in expense areas like marketing, engineering, and administration is relatively straightforward and easy to understand. In manufacturing departments, the way in which departmental plans are reflected in the income statement is quite a bit more complex.

Spending in manufacturing becomes incorporated in the cost of product through cost accounting procedures. Money spent is absorbed into inventory and then moves onto the income statement as COGS to the extent that product is sold. Therefore, a fully developed manufacturing plan must assume spending levels in factory departments, production quantities, and inventory levels at the beginning and end of the year.

The **cost ratio** assumption summarizes **enormous detail** in manufacturing departments.

Comparing actual manufacturing performance with plan involves breaking variations in product cost into those caused by spending differences and those caused by differences in production quantities, and comparing each with plan. The approach we've taken in the Macadam example is something of a shortcut in that we're working with the overall cost ratio, which is a top-level summary of a great deal of cost detail. The approach is an effective way for senior management to overview factory cost, but has to be backed up by analysis at the department level.

Our purpose here is to give readers an overview of planning processes. For that we can stay at the summary level implied by cost ratios as long as we understand that real business plans are supplemented with considerably more detail.

4.2j   The Cash Budget

Forecasting cash is an especially important part of financial planning. Companies need to be able to predict cash balances accurately, because running out can be a complete disaster. For example, even if everything else is going well, a firm without the cash to meet its payroll is likely to fail quickly. Hence, well-managed companies pay a lot of attention to cash.

There are two ways to forecast cash. We've already looked at the first, which involves forecasting the income statement and balance sheet and deriving a projected statement of cash flows from those documents.

The second approach, known as **cash budgeting**, is more detailed. It involves forecasting cash receipts and disbursements on the dates they're likely to occur. Then the ins and outs are summed in each planning period, usually months, to get net cash flows.

Receipts generally come from making cash sales, collecting receivables, borrowing, and selling stock. Disbursements include paying for purchases, wages, taxes, and other expenses such as rent, utilities, supplies, and outside services.

> The **cash budget** is a detailed projection of **receipts and disbursements** of cash.

Receivables and Payables—Forecasting with Time Lags

Forecasting the collection of receivables is difficult, because it's hard to know exactly when customers will pay their bills. Some pay within the terms of sale, usually 30 days, but others lean on the trade and don't pay for 50 or 60 days. A few never pay at all.

However, firms generally have historical information on the percent of revenues that tend to be collected in each month following sales. For example, on the average a firm's collections may behave according to the following *time lagged* pattern.

Months after sale	1	2	3
% collected	60%	30%	8%

Notice that the total collected is 98%, which recognizes that on the average 2% of sales turn out to be bad debts.

Applying the pattern to each month's forecast of sales revenue lets us build up a projection of collections. Here's an illustration showing how first quarter sales might be collected.

	Jan	Feb	Mar	Apr	May	Jun
Sales	$500	$600	$700			
Collections from sales made in						
Jan		$300	$150	$ 40		
Feb			360	180	$ 48	
Mar				420	210	$56
Total collections		$300	$510	$640	$258	$56

There's an added complication if a prompt payment discount is offered. In that case, first month collections are reduced to reflect some customers taking the discount.

Payables are handled similarly but with more precision, because the firm knows its own payment policy. For example, if a company pays its bills 30 days after receipt of product, it simply lags forecast inventory receipts by one month to predict disbursements. If the policy is to pay in 45 days, split the payment evenly between the first and second month after receipt.

Debt and Interest   Forecasting short-term debt and interest can be a little tricky if a company is funding current cash needs directly by borrowing, which isn't unusual. Under that arrangement the current month's interest payment is based on the loan balance at the end of the last month. But that balance changes depending on whether the month's cash flow is positive or negative. That means we have to work our way through a forecast, month by month, to calculate the interest payments.

Consider the following illustration in which interest is charged at 1% per month. Assume the forecast of everything but interest has been completed and is summarized in the first line, and that there's no debt at the beginning of the year (end of December). Interest is charged/earned on cumulative cash flow, which is debt when negative and money in the bank when positive.

	Dec	Jan	Feb	Mar	Apr
Cash flow before interest		$(500)	$ (800)	$ (700)	$ 900
Interest		0	5	13	20
Net cash flow		$(500)	$ (805)	$ (713)	$ 880
Cumulative cash flow at month end	0	$(500)	$(1,305)	$(2,018)	$(1,138)

Working from left to right, there's no interest payment in January, but cash flow is negative, so there's a $500 debt at the end of the month. Interest of $5 is charged on that balance in February. That adds to the month's negative cash flow making the cumulative debt $1,305. That generates $13 interest in March, which adds to that month's cumulative outflow bringing it to $2,018, and so on.

Other Items   Forecasting most other items is fairly straightforward. Payroll dates are known so wages are easy to forecast. The payment dates for interest and repayment on long-term debt are also generally easy to predict as are big disbursements for things like taxes and projects.

CONCEPT CONNECTION   EXAMPLE 4-9

Cash Budgeting

The Pulmeri Company's revenues tend to go through a quarterly cycle. It's now mid-March and management expects the first quarter's pattern to be repeated in the second quarter. The six-month period is as follows ($000):

	Jan	Feb	Mar	Apr	May	Jun
Revenue	$5,000	$8,000	$9,000	$5,000	$8,000	$9,000

Historically, Pulmeri collects its receivables according to the following pattern.

Months after sale	1	2	3
% collected	65%	25%	10%

No prompt payment discount is offered, and there are virtually no bad debts. The firm purchases and receives inventory one month in advance of sales. Materials cost about half of sales revenue. Invoices for inventory purchases are paid 45 days after receipt of material.

Payroll runs a constant $2.5 million per month, and other expenses such as rent, utilities, and supplies are a fairly steady $1.5 million per month. A $0.5 million tax payment is scheduled for mid-April. Pulmeri has a short-term loan outstanding that is expected to stand at $5 million at the end of March. Monthly interest is 1% of the previous month-end balance.

Prepare Pulmeri's cash budget for the second quarter.

SOLUTION: First lay out revenue and lag in collections according to the historical pattern.

	Jan	Feb	Mar	Apr	May	Jun
Revenue	$5000	$8,000	$9,000	$5,000	$8,000	$9,000
Collections from sales made in						
Jan		$3,250	$ 1,250	$ 500		
Feb			5,200	2,000	$ 800	
Mar				5,850	2,250	$ 900
Apr					3,250	1,250
May						5,200
Second quarter collections				$8,350	$6,300	$ 7,350

Next, lag inventory purchases (half of sales dollars) *back* one month from the date of sale and then lag the payment two months *forward* in two equal parts.

	Jan	Feb	Mar	Apr	May	Jun
Purchases		$4,500	$2,500	$4,000	$4,500	
Payment						
Feb			$2,250	$ 2,250		
Mar				1,250	$ 1,250	
Apr					2,000	$2,000
May						2,250
Payment for materials				$ 3,500	$ 3,250	$4,250

Next, summarize these results along with payroll and other disbursements and work through the interest charges.

Pulmeri Company
Cash Budget
Second Quarter 20X1
($000)

	Jan	Feb	Mar	Apr	May	Jun
Revenue	$5,000	$8,000	$ 9,000	$ 5,000	$8,000	$ 9,000
Collections				8,350	6,300	7,350
Disbursements						
Materials purchases				$ 3,500	$ 3,250	$ 4,250
Payroll				2,500	2,500	2,500
General expenses				1,500	1,500	1,500
Tax payment				500		
Disbursements before interest				$ 8,000	$ 7,250	$ 8,250
Cash flow before interest				$ 350	$ (950)	$ (900)
Interest				(50)	(47)	(57)
Net cash flow				$ 300	$ (997)	$ (957)
Cumulative cash flow (loan)			$(5,000)	$(4,700)	$(5,697)	$(6,654)

4.3   Management Issues in Financial Planning

Financial plans and their use in business create a number of potential managerial problems. It's a good idea to be aware of these problems before you run into them at work.

4.3a   The Financial Plan as a Set of Goals

The Macadam Company of Example 4-8 can be used to illustrate an important practical use of a financial plan. Look back at the way the ACP and the inventory turnover ratio have been used to construct next year's financial statements, and notice the large size of the forecast improvements. In essence, the ratios and the associated balance sheet accounts are set up as targets to be achieved by the responsible managers.

In most companies, executive pay is part salary and part bonus. In well-managed companies, executive bonuses are tied to the achievement of measurable goals like the ACP and inventory turnover in this example. In the Macadam Company, it's quite likely that the CFO's bonus will depend in some part on lowering the ACP to the planned level and that the bonus for the VP of manufacturing will depend on increasing the inventory turnover ratio.

Seen in this context, the financial plan becomes a tool with which to manage the company and motivate desirable performance. It's easy to identify several bonusable features and the responsible departments in the Macadam plan:

- 20% growth in revenue—marketing/sales
- Inventory turnover—manufacturing
- 53% cost ratio—manufacturing
- ACP—finance and marketing/sales[18]
- Reduction in vendor complaints—finance
- Control cash balance—finance
- Overall profitability and cash flow—general manager and staff VPs
- Operating departments within planned expense levels—individual departments

Inherent Conflicts   Financial plans are used as management goals all the time. A problem sometimes arises, however, when top management puts in what may be described as stretch goals. A **stretch goal** serves as a target toward which the organization strives, but isn't likely to be achieved.

In the Macadam example, inventory turnover is probably a stretch goal. Notice that the plan calls for a 67% improvement, from 3× to 5×. In most factories, that would be a Herculean achievement in one year. Top management probably wants the organization to work hard on turnover, but doesn't really expect it to achieve the goal in a year.

A stretch goal can sometimes backfire in terms of motivation. Instead of stretching toward the goal, people may give up on it if they consider it impossible.

from the
CFO

---

18. We will discusses the reasons that marketing/sales share the responsibility for collections and the ACP in Chapter 16.

Another problem arises if someone else uses the plan and assumes it's an accurate estimate of what's going to happen in the future. To understand this issue, let's evaluate the cash flow implication of the assumption that inventory turnover will increase to 5.0.

Notice that in the statement of changes in working capital, the source of cash resulting from the decrease in inventory is $797,000. However, that's after a 20% volume increase. If there were no improvement in turnover, instead of shrinking, inventory would actually grow by $407,000 [($9,031/3) − $2,603]. That means the cash flow effect of the turnover assumption is a *source* of roughly $1.2 million.

Now suppose Macadam uses the plan's cash flow projection as a basis for arranging next year's bank borrowing. If the turnover assumption doesn't come true, the firm will have understated its borrowing requirements by up to $1.2 million. That means the arrangement it makes with the bank is unlikely to provide enough cash to get it through the year.

Obviously, the CFO should take a modified plan to the bank.

4.3b   Risk in Financial Planning in General

Let's pursue this idea a little further. We'll begin by reexamining Macadam's overall plan with an eye toward judging whether it's likely to come true. In doing that, it's important to keep in mind that what a plan says about a business's future flows directly from the *assumptions* made by the planners. Therefore, the impression conveyed may or may not be realistic.

Look back at Macadam's list of assumptions. Everything is marvelously positive. Revenue is going to grow by a whopping 20%, the cost of production will decrease by 2% (that's a lot in an established factory), and asset management will be terrifically successful. We have to ask ourselves if *all* of these positive things are likely to come true without any offsetting negatives. The answer is generally no.

The situation depicted for Macadam is typical of corporate business plans. Everything is routinely forecast to improve in the future, regardless of whether recent performance has been good or bad. The positive assumptions made by managements tend to be a combination of stretch planning and what might be called aggressive optimism. This is a condition in which people allow what they want to happen to overshadow their forecast of what's likely to happen.

from the **CFO**

For example, suppose a business operation is planning for next year after having had sales of $100 million and profits of $6 million last year. The chances are that the performance of the organization's top management is measured primarily by growth in revenue and profit. An "A" report card might be revenue of $120 million and profit of $8 million next year. In such a situation, it is very common for top management to define its expectations about next year's performance in terms of the "A" report card. It is then likely to force the organization into a plan that shows those goals being met even if market conditions are such that they're unrealistic.

The practice is called **top-down planning** because top executives force a plan on the rest of the organization. Middle and lower-level managers often feel that such plans are unrealistic. The risk in financial planning is that a great many plans overstate achievable performance because of the top-down phenomenon.

Excessive optimism in business planning can be a major problem because important operating and investment decisions are based on the information in plans. If an optimistic future is projected, resources tend to be committed in ways that will take advantage of that success. If it doesn't materialize, there is generally considerable loss.

The issue can be stated another way. It's never quite clear whether a company's plan (for periods of a year or longer) is a candid statement of what's likely to happen in the future or a set of desirable goals. All plans are ultimately a little of each, but which idea predominates and the extent of the diversion between the two is generally a bit of a mystery.

Underforecasting—The Other Extreme

The opposite phenomenon can also occur when people know their performance is going to be graded relative to a plan. Underforecasting sets up a goal that's easy to meet and ensures success in the future. The practice is especially common when department managers submit their expense requirements as inputs to the planning process. The philosophy is "ask for more than you need, because you won't get everything you ask for." This is especially true in operational planning where targets are set that are tied to compensation.

Bottom-up planning puts together the requests and forecasts of lower and middle management without judgment by top-level executives. Bottom-up plans have a tendency to understate achievable performance.

Underforecasting is a less serious problem in that it results in plans that are beaten by actual performance. That's a pleasant problem in comparison to significantly underperforming a widely published estimate.

The Ideal Process

Ideally the financial planning process is a combination of top-down and bottom-up elements. Healthy planning begins with a completely bottom-up pass at a plan to which top management applies its judgment in a give-and-take process. The end result is a realistic compromise that stretches the organization's abilities, but can be achieved.

In well-run companies, it's common for financial management to assume an important role in addressing the problem of unrealistic forecasting in either direction. Led by the CFO, the finance staff acts as a voice of reason in reviewing planning assumptions. Unrealistic assumptions should be challenged and sent back to the responsible departments for justification or revision.

Scenario Analysis—"What If"ing

Many companies address the risk issue by producing a number of plans reflecting different *scenarios,* each of which is a variation on the assumptions underlying the plan. The term "what if"ing means the same thing, analyzing what would happen if an assumption takes on one value rather than another.

In scenario analysis, assumptions can be varied singly or several can be changed at a time. In Example 4-8, Macadam's management might be concerned that the assumption of a 20% growth in revenue is too aggressive. It would then be appropriate to construct another plan based on the assumption of only a 10% growth.[19]

Bottom-up plans are consolidated from lower management's inputs, and tend to understate what the firm can do.

Planning ideally **combines** top-down and bottom-up processes.

optimarc/Shutterstock.com
from the
CFO

---

19. It's important to realize that many assumptions are interrelated, so changing one implies some change in others. This is especially true of revenue, which tends to drive the whole plan. For example, the assumption of an improved cost ratio in the Macadam example is probably partially dependent on spreading overhead over the larger production volume implied by the revenue growth assumption. Therefore, changing the revenue assumption downward is likely to require modifying the cost ratio improvement assumption to a less aggressive figure.

On the other hand, there might be concern about several issues. Then a scenario could be constructed varying all of the questionable assumptions at once. For example, the implication of lower revenue growth coupled with a less significant improvement in asset management could be investigated. This might be achieved by constructing a plan based on a 15% revenue growth, an ACP of 75 days, and an inventory turnover ratio of 4.0.

Scenario analysis gives planners a feel for the impact of their assumptions not coming true. It produces a range of values within which the important results of a plan can be expected to fall.

INSIGHTS   Ethics

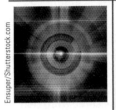

Judgment Calls and Ethics in Business Planning

It's common for the planning system to put financial executives in uncomfortable ethical positions. Plans are vehicles for communications to outsiders and they are usually put together by the finance department. But outside communications are ultimately the responsibility of the chief executive officer (CEO). That means that a CEO who doesn't like what a plan says can apply his or her "judgment" and tell outsiders something else.

Problems arise when CEOs use judgment to further their personal ends or just refuse to accept unpleasant realities. Chief financial officers (CFOs) get caught in the middle, because although they work for CEOs, they're supposed to have an overriding responsibility for truth and fairness in financial representations. They also have to stand up next to the CEO when the message is delivered and at least act as if they support every word.

Here's an illustration. Suppose the planning process at a division of a large corporation reveals that it's likely to lose market share and a great deal of money in the future. If the information is revealed to parent company executives in an upcoming meeting, they're likely to replace the division's president whose strategy is probably responsible for the poor performance. On the other hand, if a falsely optimistic plan is presented, the current president and his policies will continue in place, but the eventual loss is likely to be much larger.

The president plans to present the optimistic version of the plan. The division CFO feels this constitutes misleading corporate management. What is her ethical responsibility?

To appreciate this dilemma, it's crucial to understand that all plans are to some extent matters of opinion. No one can say with certainty that the executive is proposing to lie. He's just supporting a planning position that most people would find very unrealistic if they knew all the details. The fact that it serves his own personal ends makes him suspect, but it doesn't prove he doesn't believe in the better plan. Optimistic people tend to believe what they want to in spite of overwhelming evidence to the contrary all the time!

If the CFO refuses to go along and insists on presenting the more likely plan herself, she'll be setting up a confrontation with her boss in front of senior management. That will probably destroy her relationship with the president forever. And she may not win. Remember that the corporate managers put the president in charge because they valued his judgment above that of others. They may still do that in spite of strong evidence that he's wrong. The fact that the CFO may eventually be proven right doesn't help because the damage will be done, and she'll be long gone by then.

On the other hand, if the CFO doesn't stand up and give her opinion, there's no doubt the unduly optimistic plan will be accepted. That will probably mean deeper losses for the company, which might lead to closing the division and laying off its employees. At that time, the corporate people will probably want to know why the division's management team didn't see the problem coming.

What are the CFO's options? What would you do?

Communication   Perhaps the biggest problem related to risk in planning is communication. A business unit is expected to have a financial plan that management is confident it will achieve. Holding more than a brief discussion with outsiders about how likely the plan is to come true casts doubt on management's confidence in its own ability to steer the company. As a result, a single plan tends to be published with the attendant risks we've been discussing.

4.3c   Financial Planning and Computers

Today, virtually all financial planning is done with the aid of computers. It's important to understand what computers do for planning and what they don't do.

> **Computers** make planning **quicker** and more thorough, but **don't improve the judgments** at the heart of the process.

Computers make repetitive calculations easy, but they don't do our thinking for us. In other words, computers help us create plans once we've made judgments about the underlying business assumptions, but they don't help us with those judgments. It's very important to realize that the heart and substance of financial planning lies in making assumptions, not in cranking out numbers. Hence, computers have made us quicker planners, but not necessarily better planners.

Repetitive Calculations   Repetitive planning calculations come from two sources. One is multiyear forecasts. Calculations beyond one year tend to be repetitive of the first year's.

The second and more important source is change. The normal planning process involves making a set of assumptions, developing a plan from those assumptions, and evaluating its implications. If the plan isn't satisfactory, the assumptions are changed and everything is recomputed and reevaluated. This can go on literally dozens of times until a satisfactory plan is reached.

Before the advent of computers, recomputing a plan was a time-consuming, labor-intensive process that seriously limited the number of things that could be evaluated. Today that's changed. With the help of a personal computer and spreadsheet software, any number of assumption sets can be tried quickly and easily. That's been an enormously positive development in planning.

CONCEPT CONNECTIONS

QUESTIONS

1. A financial plan has to be either a prediction about the future or a statement of goals; it can't be both. Explain this statement and comment on its validity.

2. The following issues are related to the accuracy and reliability of financial plans. Explain the process/issues related to each.

   - Top-down versus bottom-up planning
   - Plans as statements of goals versus plans as predictions of what's going to happen
   - Planning assumptions
   - Aggressive optimism versus underforecasting
   - Scenario analysis

3. Why is it important that physical assumptions precede financial results in the planning process? For example, what's wrong with assuming you want a business that sells $50 million a year earning a profit of $5 million, and then building a revenue and cost plan to fit those goals?

4. Why is planning for a new business harder than planning for an established operation? In which do you have to make more assumptions? Why? What implicit assumption provides a shortcut in one situation?

5. Briefly describe the debt/interest planning problem and the approach that leads to its solution. (Use a few brief sentences. Don't list the procedural steps or give a numerical example.)

6. How are planning assumptions reflected in projected financial statements? Is there a standard computational procedure for incorporating assumptions into planned numbers? What's the difference between simple, estimated plans and more complex, precise plans? Can a plan be precise, complex, and inaccurate at the same time? If so, how?

7. Comment on the value of the formula (EFR) approach to estimating funding requirements. Could it create more problems than it solves?

8. Contrast planning cash requirements, especially borrowing, using the statement of cash flows derived from forecast financial statement with a cash budget. Which is likely to be more useful in running a finance department?

9. Financial planning is no longer a problem in business because of the advent of personal computers. Armed with a computer and the appropriate software, anyone can do a plan for even the largest and most complicated company. Evaluate this statement.

10. You're a new member of the planning staff within the finance department at Bertram Enterprises, a large manufacturer of household goods. The firm does an annual operating plan and a long-range plan every year. You've just received a note from the CFO asking you to help him prepare for a meeting with the firm's investment bankers to discuss issuing new securities in the future. The note asks you to prepare an estimate of the company's funding needs and suggests that you "start with" the most recent annual and long-range plans. You're confused by the term "start with," since the plans clearly indicate future funding needs. What might the CFO be getting at, and how would you approach the assignment?

11. You are developing next year's financial plan for Ajax Inc., a medium-sized manufacturing company that's currently operating at 80% of factory's capacity. The firm is launching a sales promotion that's expected to generate a sudden 20% increase in revenues starting at the beginning of the new year. Unlike current sales which are virtually all on credit, approximately 50% of the new business will be paid in cash. No changes are planned in the company's operations other than acquiring the resources necessary to support the sales growth. Develop some reasonable planning assumptions for the following balance sheet line items and explain your reasoning for each. (*Hint:* Which balance sheet items will be effected by an increase in sales proportionately or less than proportionately. Assume any additional cash needed is borrowed.)

Cash	Accounts Payable
Accounts Receivable	Accruals (wage)
Inventory	
Gross Fixed Assets	Debt
Accumulated Depreciation	Equity

BUSINESS ANALYSIS

1. Ed Perez has always wanted to run his own restaurant. He worked part time in the food service business during high school and college and has worked for a large restaurant chain since graduating from college four years ago. He's now ready to open a franchised family-style restaurant. However, a large investment is required to get started. Ed has saved some money, but will also have to secure a substantial loan.

   Fortunately, Ed's old college roommate, Joe Dixon, is now a loan officer with the local bank. Besides being a good friend, Joe knows that Ed is a stable, hard-working businessman and an excellent credit risk.

   Ed is now meeting with Joe to apply for the loan. After exchanging pleasantries, Joe asks to see Ed's business plan. In response, Ed tells him all about the idea and shows him the written information from the franchisor, which Joe glances at briefly.

   Joe listens politely, leans back in his chair, and says, "Ed, I've known you for years. I'm sure this is a great idea, and that you'll make a terrific restaurateur, but we can't even begin to consider a loan until we see a fully developed business plan that looks at least five years into the future."

   a. Why is Joe (the bank) insisting that Ed prepare a business plan?
      1. What will it show the bank?
         i. List some specific concerns the bank might have that a plan would answer outside of the financial section.
         ii. List several concerns that the financial plan might answer for the bank.
         iii. Why is the bank insisting on such a long planning horizon? Does that imply the bank is looking for a strategic plan?
      2. What will preparing a business plan do for Ed?
         i. Before he gets started.
         ii. After he gets started.
         iii. What will he learn by doing the financial plan?
   b. What kind of thinking is the bank looking for in Ed's plan? That is, should the plan be strategic or operational or short term?

2. You're the CFO of the Ramkin Company, which makes and sells electronic equipment. The firm was originally an independent business, but was acquired by the larger BigTech Inc. 10 years ago and is now operated as a division. BigTech has an elaborate planning system requiring all divisions to produce a strategic plan and an annual operating plan once a year, a budget each quarter, monthly cash forecasts, and several quick forecasts near the end of each quarter.

   The forecasts are done primarily by the finance department and don't require much of anyone else's time. However, the strategic plan takes a good deal of executive effort, while budgets and the annual operating plan demand a great deal of management effort at all levels.

   It's eight o'clock on a morning in mid-October, and the executive team is about to start a meeting to kick off the preparation of the annual operating plan for the next calendar year. As the meeting convenes, Charlie Gogetter, the VP of marketing, is clearly upset. He takes the floor and makes the following statements.

   "I'm tired of spending all this time on these silly plans! We just finished a strategic plan in June that must've taken a month of my time while the western sales region got inself into big trouble. We also did a third quarter budget in June, and a fourth quarter budget in September. Now we're starting another plan that will probably tie up half of my sales managers' time until Christmas.

   "On top of that it seems whenever we're not planning, we're putting together reviews comparing actual performance to plan. Before we were acquired by BigTech, we hardly ever planned and we did just fine! It's true we're a lot larger and more complex now, but I don't think we can spend this much time planning rather than doing!

   "I suggest that the CFO (he gestures toward you) be assigned to throw together something we can submit to BigTech, and that the rest of us get on with our work."

   Other members of the group share Charlie's feelings to some extent, and his comments have created some unrest among the executive team about the company's management style. Prepare a response to his statement and proposal. Don't rule out the possibility that BigTech is overdoing planning.

3. You've just been hired as CFO of the Gatsby Corp., a new company in the high-tech computer business. Shortly after your arrival you were amazed to find that the firm does virtually no planning. An extensive business plan was put together when it was started with venture capital eight years ago, and revised when another round of funding was needed four years later. Other than on those occasions, no planning seems to have been done at all.

The firm was founded by its entrepreneur president, Harvey Gatsby, based on a new technical product he'd invented. Initial demand for the gadget was overwhelming and the firm grew rapidly if chaotically until about a year ago, when competitive devices started to affect its business. The following conditions exist today.

- Sales of the original product are beginning to decline.

- The organization seems to have a number of people and departments whose function and value aren't clear.

- The engineering department is pursuing several new developments that have commercial possibilities, but progress has been haphazard and no one seems to have thought through how any money will be made from the ideas.

- Additional funding is required to get any new products that might be developed to market. Harvey has suggested that you dust off the old business plan for another run at investors.

You feel that the company is in real danger, and that the source of the problem is that management hasn't done any real forward planning in years. In your opinion, the first step toward recovery is to install a competent planning system. Write a memo to Harvey outlining your concerns and suggestions. Include:

a. The problem—why the happy chaos of the past may be about to come to an end, and what that may mean.

b. How management's approach has to change if the firm is to survive. In other words, it will have to do a good deal of forward thinking and structured planning.

c. A statement of how planning systems differ between small and larger companies.

d. The benefits Gatsby can expect to realize by planning in a careful, structured way.

e. The need for a well-defined financial plan.

PROBLEMS

Planning Assumption-Example 4-1 (page 136)

1. The Lineberry Golf Cart Co. sold 7,400 carts this year at an average unit price of $3,000. The firm produced the carts at a 42% cost ratio, which is calculated as cost of goods sold (COGS) divided by revenue. At year end, 50 days of sales remained uncollected in accounts receivable, and three months of inventory was on hand (a month of inventory is 1/12 of the year's COGS).

    The golf cart business is booming and management plans a 10% increase in unit sales despite a 5% price increase. The firm has programs in place to improve production efficiency, inventory management, and the effectiveness of collection efforts. It is assumed that these programs will decrease the cost ratio to 40%, lower year-end inventory to two months, and lower year-end receivables to 40 days of sales.

    Use the format below to develop this year's and next year's revenue and cost of goods sold (COGS) and year ending balance for accounts receivable and inventory. Calculate using a 360-day year and assume sales are evenly distributed over the year.

	This Year	Next Year's plan
Units		
Unit price		
Revenue:		
Cost ratio		
COGS:		
Days sales in A/R		
A/R balance:		
Months of inventory on hand		
Inventory balance		

The Debt/Interest Planning Problem: Concept Connection Example 4-2 (page 138)

2. The Cambridge Cartage Company has partially completed its forecast of next year's financial statements as follows:

Cambridge Cartage Company Financial Plan ($000)

Income Statement		Balance Sheet		
			Next Year	
	Next Year		*Beginning*	*Ending*
Revenue	$ 17,220	ASSETS		
Cost/expenses	14,120	Total assets	$ 12,540	$ 18,330
EBIT	$ 3,100	LIABILITIES & EQUITY		
Interest	?	Current liabilities	$ 410	$ 680
EBT	?	Debt	5,630	?
Tax	?	Equity	6,500	?
Net income	?	Total L&E	$ 12,540	$ 18,330

The firm pays interest at 10% on all borrowings and pays a combined state and federal tax rate of 40%. Complete the forecast income statement and balance sheet. Begin by guessing at interest expense as 10% of beginning debt.

3. Lap Dogs Inc. is planning for next year and has the following summarized results so far ($000):

Income Statement

EBIT	236
Interest	?
EBT	?
Income tax	?
Net income	?

Balance Sheet

	This Year	Next Year
Assets	582	745
Current liabilities	63	80
Debt	275	?
Equity	244	?
Total L&E	582	745

The firm pays interest of 12% on all borrowing and is subject to an overall tax rate of 38%. It paid interest of $20,000 this year and plans a $75,000 dividend next year. Complete Lap Dog's forecast of next year's financial statements. Round all calculations to the nearest $1,000.

4. The Libris Publishing Company had revenues of $200 million this year and expects a 50% growth to $300 million next year. Costs and expenses other than interest are forecast at $250 million. The firm currently has assets of $280 million and current liabilities of $40 million. Its debt to equity ratio is 3:1. (That is, capital is 75% debt and 25% equity.) It pays 12% interest on all of its debt and is subject to federal and state income taxes at a total effective rate of 39%.

Libris expects assets and current liabilities to grow at 40%, 10% less than the revenue growth rate. The company plans to pay dividends of $10 million next year.

a. What is the planned debt to equity ratio at the end of next year?

b. Do these results indicate a problem?

Plans with Simple Assumptions: Concept Connection Example 4-3 (page 140)

5. The management of Coker Corp. is doing a quick forecast of 20X9 using the modified percentage of sales method in preparation for a more detailed planning exercise later in the month. The estimate is to assume a 10% growth in sales. All other line items are to be assumed to grow at the same rate except for fixed assets which is projected to increase by $88,000 due to an expansion program already underway. Approximate financial statements for the current year, 20X8, and a planning worksheet are shown below. The firm pays 9% interest on all of its debt. Assume the tax rate is a flat 25%. There are no plans for dividends or the sale of additional stock next year. Make a forecast of Coker's complete income statement and balance sheet. Work to the nearest thousand dollars. (*Hints:* The easiest way to grow a number by 10% is to multiply it by 1.1 rather than taking 10% and adding. Do not grow subtotals. For example, to grow revenue and COGS by 10%, round each to the nearest thousand and subtract for gross margin. Don't grow interest, debt, or equity; use the debt/interest iteration technique.)

Coker Corp.
Current and Projected Income Statements
($000)

	20X8	20X9
Revenue	$642	
COGS	289	—
Gross Margin	$353	
Expenses	$240	
EBIT	$113	
Interest (9%)	33	—
EBT	$ 80	
Inc Tax (25%)	$ 25	—
Net income	$ 55	

Coker Corp.
Current and Projected Balance Sheets
($000)

	ASSETS			LIABILITIES & EQUITY	
	20X8	20X9		20X8	20X9
C/A	$198		C/L	$ 87	
F/A	552	____	Debt	325	
Total	$750		Equity	338	____
			Total	$750	

6. Larime Corp. is forecasting 20X2 near the end of 20X1. The estimated year-end financial statements and a worksheet for the forecast follow.

Larime Corp. Projected Income Statement ($000)

	20X1		20X2	
	$	%	$	%
Revenue	$ 245,622	100.0		100.0
COGS	142,461	58.0	___	___
Gross margin	$103,161	42.0		
Expenses	$ 49,124	20.0	___	___
EBIT	$ 54,037	22.0		
Interest (12%)	9,642	3.9	___	___
EBT	$ 44,395	18.1		
Income tax (43%)	19,090	7.8	___	___
Net income	$ 25,305	10.3		

Larime Corp. Projected Balance Sheet ($000)

	20X1	20X2		20X1	20X2
ASSETS			**LIABILITIES & EQUITY**		
Current assets	$178,106		Current liabilities	$85,700	
Fixed assets	142,128	___	Debt	78,178	
Total	$320,234		Equity	156,356	___
			Total	$320,234	

Management expects the following next year.

- An 8% increase in revenue.
- Price cutting will cause the cost ratio (COGS/sales) to deteriorate (increase) by 1% (of sales) from its current level.
- Expenses will increase at a rate that is three quarters of that of sales.
- The current accounts will increase proportionately with sales.
- Net fixed assets will increase by $5 million.
- All interest will be paid at 12%.
- Federal and state income taxes will be paid at a combined rate of 43%.

Make a forecast of Larime's complete income statement and balance sheet. Work to the nearest thousand dollars.

7. The Eagle Feather Fabric Company expects to complete the current year with the following financial results ($000).

Income Statement		Balance Sheet	
Revenue	$36,100	Assets	
COGS	14,440	Cash	$ 1,000
GM	$ 21,660	Accounts receivable	5,000
Expenses	12,635	Inventory	2,888
EBIT	$9,025	Current assets	$ 8,888
Interest (11%)	625	Net fixed assets	7,250
EBT	$ 8,400	Total assets	$16,138
Tax (42%)	3,528	Liabilities & equity	
Net income	$ 4,872	Accounts payable	$ 1,550
		Accruals	530
		Current liabilities	$ 2,080
		Debt	5,598
		Equity	8,460
		Total L&E	$16,138

Forecast next year using a modified percentage of sales method assuming no dividends are paid and no new stock is sold along with the following:

a. A 20% growth in sales and a 40% growth in net fixed assets.

b. A 15% growth in sales with a 10% growth in expenses and a 20% growth in net fixed assets (Note that negative debt in a forecast means the business will generate more cash than is currently owed.)

External Funding Requirement (EFR): Concept Connection Example 4-4 (page 145)

8. Fleming, Inc. had a dividend payout ratio of 25% this year, which resulted in a payout of $80,000 in dividends. Return on sales (ROS) was 8% this year and is expected to increase to 9% next year. If Fleming expects to have $305,100 available from next year's retained earnings, what percent increase is it forecasting in revenues?

9. The Dalmation Corporation expects the following summarized financial results this year ($000).

Income Statement		Balance Sheet	
Revenue	$ 10,500	Assets	
Cost/expenses	9,100	Current assets	$ 5,500
Tax	560	Net fixed assets	6,900
Net income	840	Total assets	$12,400
Dividends	420	Liabilities & equity	
		Current	$ 320
		Debt	5,080
		Equity	7,000
		Total L&E	$12,400

Use the EFR relation to estimate Dalmation's external funding requirements under the following conditions:

a. Sales growth of 15%

b. Sales growth of 20% and a reduction in the payout ratio to 25%

c. Sales growth of 25%, elimination of dividends, and a 4% improvement in ROS

10. Lytle Trucking projects a $3.2 million EBIT next year. The firm's marginal tax rate is 40%, and it currently has $8 million in long-term debt on which it pays an average rate of 8%. Management is projecting a requirement for additional assets costing $1.5 million and no change in current liabilities. They plan to maintain a 30% dividend payout ratio. Any additional borrowing required to fund next year's asset growth will carry a 7% coupon rate. Lytle does not plan on issuing additional stock next year. Using the EFR concept rather than the EFR equation, develop an algebraic formula of your own to compute the additional debt needed to support an asset growth of $1.5 million. (*Hint:* Start with the idea that additional debt = new assets internally generated funds. Then write an algebraic expression for internally generated funds based on the income statement from EBIT to net income and the dividend payout ratio.)

Sustainable Growth Rate: Concept Connection Example 4-5 (page 147)

11. The Bubar Building Co. has the following current financial results ($000).

Revenue	$45,000	Assets	$37,000
Net income	3,600	Equity	28,580
Dividends	1,800		

On the average, other building companies pay about one-quarter of their earnings in dividends, earn about six cents on the sales dollar, carry assets worth about six months of sales, and finance one-third of their assets with debt.

Use the sustainable growth rate concept to analyze Bubar's inherent ability to grow without selling new equity versus that of an average building company. Identify weak areas and suggest further analyses.

12. Broxholme Industries has sales of $40 million, equity totaling $27.5 million, and an ROS of 12%. The sustainable growth rate has been calculated at 10.9%. What dividend payout ratio was assumed in this calculation?

Planning Fixed Assets: Concept Connection Example 4-6 (page 148)

13. Livetree Ltd. is developing a detailed financial plan for next year and expects to have the following fixed asset accounts by the end of this year ($000).

Gross	$45,789
Accumulated depreciation	(26,328)
Net fixed assets	$ 19,461

The capital plan already completed calls for expenditures of $7,042,000 on new equipment next year, which will be depreciated straight line over a 10-year period without a half-year convention. Assets currently on the books will depreciate by $4,258,000 next year.

Develop Livetree's ending fixed asset balances for the planned year.

Indirect Planning Assumptions: Concept Connection Example 4-7 (page 149)

14. The Winthrop Company is constructing a five-year plan. The firm's ACP is currently 90 days, while its inventory turnover ratio is 3× based on COGS. The company has forecast aggressive

revenue growth along with efficiency improvements in manufacturing and credit and collections as follows. (Year 0 is the current year.)

	Year					
	0	*1*	*2*	*3*	*4*	*5*
Revenue ($000)	$50.0	$57.5	$66.0	$76.0	$87.5	$100.0
Cost ratio	60%	59%	58%	57%	56%	55%
ACP (days)	90	70	60	50	45	40
Inventory turnover	3×	4×	5×	6×	6.5×	7×

For each planned year:
a. Calculate the COGS.
b. Calculate the A/R balance at year end.
c. Calculate the inventory balance at year end.

15. Assume we're at the end of "this year" planning "next year's" financial statements. Calculate the following using indirect planning assumptions as indicated.

a. Sales are forecast to be $58,400,000. Management wants to plan for a 45-day ACP next year. What ending receivables balance should be planned for next year?

b. What ending inventory should be planned if revenue is expected to be $457,000 and the cost ratio is 53% (cost of goods sold as a percentage of revenue) and management wants to forecast an inventory turnover of 5×.

c. Normal credit terms from suppliers request payment within 30 days. In an effort to conserve cash, management has decided to pay in 50 days. Nearly all payables come from purchases of inventory. Materials make up 60% of the Cost of Goods Sold. Next year's revenue is forecast to be $378 million. The firm's cost ratio is expected to be 56%. What figure should be included in next year's ending balance sheet for accounts payable?

Complex Plans: Concept Connection Example 4-8 (page 151)

16. The Owl Corporation is planning for 20X2. The firm expects to have the following financial result in 20X1 ($000).

INCOME STATEMENT

	$	%
Revenue	$37,483	100.0
COGS	14,807	39.5
Gross margin	$22,676	60.5
Expense	17,721	47.3
EBIT	$ 4,955	13.2
Interest	$ 1,380	3.7
EBT	$ 3,575	9.5
Income tax	1,430	3.8
Net income	$ 2,145	5.7

Balance Sheet

ASSETS		LIABILITIES & EQUITY	
Cash	$ 1,571	Accounts payable	$ 1,388
Accounts receivable	6,247	Accruals	985
Inventory	2,468	Current liabilities	$ 2,373
Current assets	$ 10,286		
Fixed assets		Capital	
Gross	$25,608	Debt	$ 12,390
Accumulated depreciation	(14,936)	Equity	6,195
Net	$ 10,672		$ 18,585
Total assets	$20,958	Total L&E	$20,958

Management has made the following planning assumptions:

INCOME STATEMENT

- Revenue will grow by 10%.
- The cost ratio will improve to 37% of revenues.
- Expenses will be held to 44% of revenues.

BALANCE SHEET

- The year end cash balance will be $1.5 million.
- The ACP will improve to 40 days from the current 60.
- Inventory turnover will improve to 7× from 6×.
- Trade payables will continue to be paid in 45 days.
- New capital spending will be $5 million.
- Newly purchased assets will be depreciated over 10 years using the straight-line method taking a full year's depreciation in the first year.
- The company's payroll will be $13.7 million at the end of 20X2.
- No dividends or new stock sales are planned.

The following facts are also available:

- The firm pays 10% interest on all of its debt.
- The combined state and federal income tax rate is a flat 40%.
- The only significant payables come from inventory purchases, and product cost is 75% purchased materials.
- Existing assets will be depreciated by $1,727,000 next year.
- The only significant accrual is payroll. The last day of 20X2 will be one week after a payday. Forecast Owl's income statement and balance sheet for 20X2. Round all calculations to the nearest $1,000 and use a 360-day year.

17. The Haverly Company expects to finish the current year with the following financial results, and is developing its annual plan for next year.

Haverly Company Income Statement This Year ($000)

	$	%
Revenue	$ 73,820	100.0
COGS	31,743	43.0
Gross margin	$ 42,077	57.0
Expenses		
Marketing	$ 17,422	23.6
Engineering	7,087	9.6
Finance & administrative	7,603	10.3
Total expenses	$32,112	43.5
EBIT	$ 9,965	13.5
Interest	2,805	3.8
EBT	$ 7,160	9.7
Income tax	3,007	4.1
Net income	$ 4,153	5.6

Haverly Company Balance Sheet This Year ($000)

ASSETS		LIABILITIES & EQUITY	
Cash	$ 8,940	Accounts payable	$ 1,984
Accounts receivable	12,303	Accruals	860
Inventory	7,054	Current liabilities	$ 2,844
Current assets	$28,297	Long-term debt	$ 22,630
Fixed assets		Equity	
Gross	$65,223	Stock accounts	$ 18,500
Accumulated depreciation	(23,987)	Retained earnings	25,559
Net	$ 41,236	Total equity	$44,059
Total assets	$69,533	Total L&E	$69,533

The following facts are available.

FACTS

- Payables are almost entirely due to inventory purchases and can be estimated through COGS, which is approximately 45% purchased material.

- Currently owned assets will depreciate an additional $1,840,000 next year.

- There are two balance sheet accruals. The first is for unpaid wages. The current payroll of $32 million is expected to grow by 12% next year. The closing date of the year will be six working days after a payday. The second accrual is an estimate of the cost of purchased items that have arrived in inventory, but for which vendor invoices have not yet been received. This materials accrual is generally about 10% of the payables balance at year end.

- The combined state and federal income tax rate is 42%.

- Interest on current and future borrowing will be at a rate of 12%.

The plan will be based on the following assumptions.

PLANNING ASSUMPTIONS

Income Statement Items

(1) Revenue will grow by 13% with no change in product mix. Competitive pressure, however, is expected to force some reductions in pricing.

(2) The pressure on prices will result in a 1.5% deterioration (increase) in the next year's cost ratio.

(3) Spending in the marketing department is considered excessive and will be held to 21% of revenue next year.

(4) Because of a major development project, expenses in the engineering department will increase by 20%.

(5) Finance and administration expenses will increase by 6%.

Assets and Liabilities

(6) An enhanced cash management system will reduce cash balances by 10%.

(7) The ACP will be reduced by 15 days. (Calculate the current value to arrive at the target.)

(8) The inventory turnover ratio (COGS/inventory) will decrease by .5×.

(9) Capital spending is expected to be $7 million. The average depreciation life of the assets to be acquired is five years. The firm uses straight-line depreciation, and takes a half year in the first year.

(10) Bills are currently paid in 50 days. Plans are to shorten that to 40 days.

(11) A dividend totaling $1.5 million will be paid next year. No new stock will be sold.
Develop next year's financial plan for Haverly on the basis of these assumptions and last year's financial statements. Include a projected income statement, balance sheet, and statement of cash flows.

Cash Budgeting: Concept Connection Example 4-9 (page 160)

18. Lapps Inc. makes a gift product that sells best during the holiday season. Retailers stock up in the fall so Lapps's sales are largest in October and November and drop dramatically in December. The firm expects the following revenue pattern for the second half of this year ($000). The third quarter figures are actual results, while the fourth quarter is a projection.

	Jul	Aug	Sep	Oct	Nov	Dec
Revenue	$5,500	$6,000	$7,500	$8,000	$9,500	$4,000

Historically, Lapps collects its receivables according to the following pattern.

Months after sale	1	2	3
% collected	60%	30%	9%

The firm offers a 2% prompt payment discount, which is taken by about half of the customers that pay in the first month.

Lapps receives inventory one month in advance of sales. The cost of material is 40% of revenue. Invoices are paid 45 days after receipt of material.

The firm uses temporary labor to meet its seasonal production needs, so payroll can be estimated at 35% of the current month's sales. Other expenses are a constant $1.8 million per month. A $.7 million tax payment is scheduled for November, and an expansion project will require cash of $.5 million in October and $.8 million in December. Lapps has a $6 million short-term loan outstanding at the end of September. Monthly interest is 1% of the previous month-end balance. Prepare Lapps's cash budget for the fourth quarter.

19. Blue & Noble is a small law firm that does all of its business through billings (no cash sales). Historically, the firm has collected 40% of its revenue in the month of billing, 50% during the first month after billing, and 8% during the second month after billing. Two percent typically remains uncollectible. Revenue projections for the coming year are $47,500 for January and $50,000 for February. Cash receipts of $50,600 are expected in March. What revenues are projected for March?

CHAPTER 5

The Financial System, Corporate Governance, and Interest

Chapter Outline

In Chapter 1, we touched on the nature of the financial system when we described financial assets and markets. In this chapter, we'll expand on those ideas. We'll have a closer look at the money flows in the economy and gain a better understanding of the manner in which investors, companies, and securities come together in stock and bond markets. Finally, we'll take an in-depth look at interest, the price of money.

5.1 The Financial System

An industrialized economy consists of three sectors: consumption, production, and government. The consumption sector is made up of households buying and consuming products and services that are created in the production sector. The government sector produces services that are used by both consumers and producers, and collects taxes from both.

It's important to understand that the sectors are conceptual, and that individual people are generally in at least two sectors at the same time. For example, when workers are on the job, they're in the production sector, but when they go home they become part of the consumption sector.

With respect to the issues we'll be illustrating here, the government sector acts a great deal like the production sector. It pays its employees wages and creates services that are "purchased" with tax dollars. It also issues debt securities that function much like those of corporations. Therefore, we'll lump government and production together and talk about just two sectors, production and consumption.

5.1a Cash Flows Between the Sectors

Money flows back and forth between the production and consumption sectors every day. The wages workers receive for their roles in the production process represent income to the consumption sector. The money consumers spend on products and services in turn becomes income to the production sector. Producers spend their income on inputs used to produce more product, including wages that flow back to the consumption sector, and so on, creating a cyclical flow of money. These normal, everyday flows are illustrated in Figure 5-1.

5.1b Savings and Investment

Two important features of the system are not included in Figure 5-1. The first involves the consumption sector. People generally don't spend their entire incomes

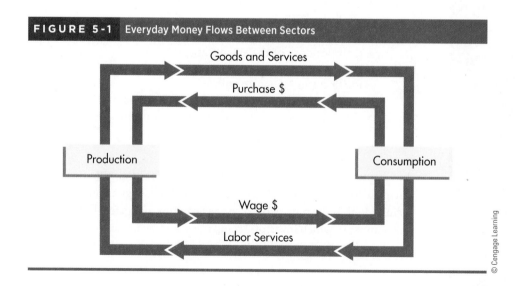

FIGURE 5-1 Everyday Money Flows Between Sectors

Goods and Services

Purchase $

Production

Consumption

Wage $

Labor Services

© Cengage Learning

on consumption. Most save at least a little and need a place to put savings in which a return[1] can be earned.

The second missing feature involves the production sector. In addition to doing everyday business, companies occasionally spend large sums of money on projects such as new factories, additional equipment, and starting new enterprises.

In other words, each sector has a need that isn't pictured in Figure 5-1. Consumers need a way to save the income they don't spend, and companies need a way to obtain extra money for occasional major projects.

These needs are happily coincidental. The economic system contains a source of money in consumer savings and a use for it in funding business projects. All that's lacking is a way to connect the two. That is, we have to put companies' needs for extra money together with the availability of money saved by consumers.

Financial markets
connect production's
need for money with
consumption's available
savings.

The connection is provided by **financial markets** in which buyers and sellers of financial assets meet. Companies that need money issue securities, usually stocks or bonds, which are sold to individuals. Consumers buy the securities with their savings, and companies use the proceeds to do their projects.

Consumers are said to *invest* in the securities, which are expected to generate a *return* on the money invested in their purchase. That return comes in the form of interest on bonds or dividends and price appreciation in the case of stock.

Figure 5-2 shows the financial system redrawn to include the previously omitted features. In short, financial markets provide a conduit for the transfer of savings from

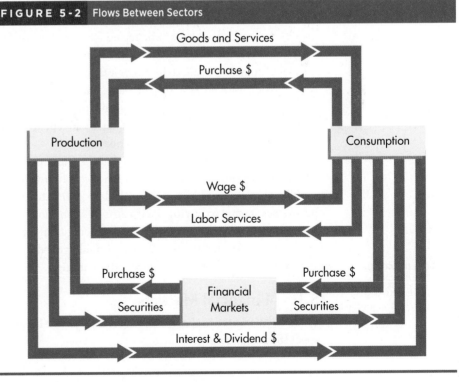

FIGURE 5-2   Flows Between Sectors

Goods and Services

Purchase $

Production

Consumption

Wage $

Labor Services

Purchase $

Securities

Financial
Markets

Purchase $

Securities

Interest & Dividend $

© Cengage Learning

1.   A return is extra income we receive for letting someone else use our money. Interest, for example, is the return lenders receive for letting borrowers use their money.

Consumer **savings equals** industrial **investment**.

the consumption sector to the production sector. When the production sector uses this money it is said to be *investing* in projects, enterprises, and assets. Hence, economists say that **savings equals investment** in the economy.[2]

Financial markets are extremely important to the health of an economy. Their role and function will be a major focus of our study in this book.

Raising and Spending Money in Business   Here's another way to think about the system shown in Figure 5-2. We can think of a company as spending two kinds of money. One kind is the day-to-day funds that come from normal profits and are used to support routine activities. The other kind is the large sums occasionally needed to support major projects and get businesses started. These funds are raised by selling financial assets.

The money flows at the top of Figure 5-2 represent the routine day-to-day activities. The second kind of money, which supports large projects and investments in equipment, generally doesn't come from operating funds. Firms more frequently raise that money as needed through financial markets. This money-raising process is represented in the bottom portion of Figure 5-2.

When money for a project is raised by borrowing, we say the project is *debt financed*. When the money comes from the sale of stock or from the company's earnings, we say the project is *equity financed*.

Term   The word "term" refers to the length of time between the present and the end or *term*ination of something. Both financial investments and physical projects have terms. A long-term project is one that will take a long time to complete. A long-term loan is one that doesn't have to be repaid for several years. The word "maturity" is also used to indicate the term of a loan. Debt *matures* on the day it is to be repaid.

Debt financing is said to be either long or short term depending on the length of time allowed until it has to be paid back. Short term generally means less than a year, intermediate term is one to five years, and long term is more than five years. People frequently leave out the intermediate-term concept and just think of long- and short-term debt as being more or less than one year.

Stocks have an indefinite term in that they have no specified repayment date. Therefore, they're thought of as very long-term financing.

The projects we talked about in the last section tend to be long term, like getting businesses started or buying fixed assets. It's common practice to match the term of a project or asset with the term of the financing that pays for it. For example, funding for a project expected to take 10 years shouldn't need to be repaid in much less than 10 years. The practice is called **maturity matching**.

Maturity matching: A project's duration should match the term of the financing that supports it.

5.1c Financial Markets

Financial markets are classified in several ways. We'll discuss classifications with respect to term and purpose.

---

2. Notice that the term "invest" seems to have two slightly different meanings. Individuals are said to invest in financial assets, while firms invest in production facilities and equipment. What economists actually mean when they say savings equals investment is that investment by consumers in financial assets (savings) equals investment by companies in the means of production.

Capital Markets

Capital markets deal in long-term debt and stock.

Money acquired for long periods is referred to as **capital**, and the financial markets that deal with it are known as **capital markets**. They trade in stocks and in debt securities having terms longer than one year.[3]

Money Markets

Money markets deal in short-term debt.

Markets in which short-term debt is traded are called **money markets**. They play an important role in setting interest rates for the rest of the economy, which we'll get into later in the chapter.

In business, most of the money that supports day-to-day operations is generated by sales. However, companies do borrow short term to cover temporary operating shortages. Most of the time, short-term corporate borrowing is done from banks, but there are financial markets that deal in short-term debt instruments[4] known as *notes, bills, and commercial paper.*

Federal borrowing supports yearly **deficit spending** and the **national debt**.

The federal government is especially active in issuing short-term debt. In the last 50 years, the government consistently spent more than it took in, creating a *federal budget deficit* in nearly every year. The accumulated sum of the annual deficits is the **national debt**. The government borrows to fund yearly deficits and to replace old debt as it matures. More than half of the national debt is short term, so there's a very active market in short-term federal debt.

Primary and Secondary Markets

The basic purpose of financial markets is to facilitate the flow of funds from the saving public to the production sector for investment in business projects. However, most of what goes on in the largest and best known markets has little to do with that transfer.

Funds are actually transferred from individual investors to companies only when securities are issued and purchased for the first time. Immediately after that first sale, securities belong to individual investors who may or may not choose to retain them permanently. In most cases, investors hold onto securities for a while but eventually sell them to others. Security sales subsequent to the first one are *between investors* and don't involve the issuing company at all.

The initial sale of a security is a **primary market** transaction. Subsequent sales between investors are in the **secondary market**.

The first sale of a security, in which the money proceeds go to the issuing company, is called a **primary market** transaction. Subsequent sales of the security, between investors, are called **secondary market** transactions. The vast majority of transactions in traditional financial markets like the stock market are secondary.

Corporate financial managers are concerned about secondary stock market transactions even though there's no immediate cash impact on their companies. The secondary market sets the level of a stock's price and therefore influences how much can be raised in future issues. *In addition, senior managers' compensation is usually tied to the company's stock price, and that tends to generate an intense interest in the secondary market.*

from the
CFO

optimarc/Shutterstock.com

Direct and Indirect Transfers, Financial Intermediaries

Primary market transactions, which transfer money from individual investors to companies, can occur directly or indirectly through a financial intermediary. Let's consider the direct method first.

---

3. The word **capital** (assets) also refers to the long-lived assets generally purchased with capital funds.

4. The term **financial instrument** is another expression for a security or a document evidencing a debt.

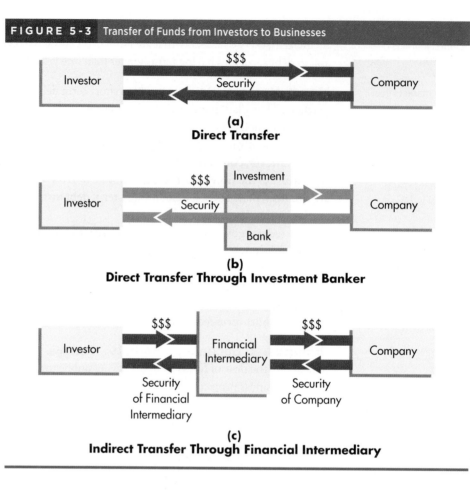

FIGURE 5-3   Transfer of Funds from Investors to Businesses

(a)
Direct Transfer

(b)
Direct Transfer Through Investment Banker

(c)
Indirect Transfer Through Financial Intermediary

© Cengage Learning

In a direct transfer, an investor simply buys the security of a company. That kind of transfer is shown in Figure 5-3(a), but it's a rare occurrence as illustrated. Companies don't usually market new securities to the public by themselves. Rather, they use the services of an **investment bank**, an organization that helps market new securities.

> An **investment bank** helps companies market their securities.

The investment bank typically lines up investors interested in buying a new issue beforehand, and functions as a broker bringing buyers and sellers together. A direct transfer through such an organization is illustrated in Figure 5-3(b). The transfer is direct because, even though the investment bank may take temporary possession of the securities, it actually just passes them through to the buyer.

The indirect transfer is illustrated in Figure 5-3(c). Although the diagram looks similar to 5-3(b), something very different is taking place. In an indirect transfer, a **financial intermediary** collects money from many individuals, pools it, and then makes investments with it. The securities purchased are not passed through to the individual investors. Instead, the financial intermediary holds on to those securities and gives the individual investors a *security of its own*. That is, it gives them some kind of claim upon itself.

> A **financial intermediary** sells shares in itself and invests the funds collectively on behalf of its investors.

A *mutual fund* is a good example. It takes money from many individual investors and uses it to buy a portfolio of stocks and bonds. (A portfolio is a collection of financial assets.) Each investor receives a number of *shares in the fund* proportionate to the size of his or her investment, but none of the individual stocks and bonds from the portfolio.

The important point is that the portfolio is owned *collectively* by individuals who have invested in the fund, but no one can identify any particular stock or bond as his or her own. An important result of this arrangement is that the fund's management controls the pooled resources of many people, which often amounts to a vast sum of money. As a result, funds have a great deal of influence in stock and bond markets.

Mutual funds and similar financial intermediaries are called **institutional investors** and play a major role in today's financial markets. They own about one quarter of the stocks listed on the major exchanges but make about three quarters of the trades. That makes them very influential in setting prices and trends in the secondary market.

Here are some other kinds of financial intermediaries.

> *Pension funds* receive the retirement contributions of workers and employers, and invest the money in stocks, bonds, and real estate. Employees own pension accounts representing their proportionate share of the fund assets.
>
> *Insurance companies* collect premiums from customers and invest the money to provide a pool of assets from which to pay claims.
>
> *Banks* receive deposits from individuals and make loans to companies. The bank's portfolio of financial assets is its loan portfolio, while depositors' accounts represent claims on those assets.

*Financial intermediaries are **institutional investors**.*

5.2   The Stock Market and Stock Exchanges

We briefly described the stock market in Chapter 1. In this section we'll amplify that description and develop an understanding of the market's workings.

5.2a   Overview

The stock market is a financial system or organization embedded within the larger economic system of the nation. It isn't a single place where people go to buy and sell stocks, although many people associate it with the New York Stock Exchange (NYSE).

Rather, the stock market is a network of **exchanges** and **brokers**. An exchange is actually a company that provides a physical marketplace and the administrative capability of transferring stocks from one owner to another. **Brokerage firms**, or **houses**, are also companies. They employ individuals (the brokers) who are licensed by the government to assist people in buying and selling securities. Both the exchanges and the brokers earn a living from commissions and fees charged on transactions made by people who buy and sell securities.

*A **broker** is licensed to assist people in trading securities.*

The government grants the exchange the basic right to make a market in securities. Brokers are *members* of stock exchanges. Each exchange has a limited number of *seats* that are purchased by brokerage firms. Owning a seat makes one a member and confers the right to do business on the exchange.

5.2b   Trading—The Role of Brokers

To trade in stocks, an investor must have a client account with a broker through which buy and/or sell orders are placed. It's common practice to do this by telephone. Major brokerage houses have offices throughout the country, and people usually deal with individual brokers located in a nearby office.

Once a broker has a client order, it's submitted for execution, a process currently undergoing almost constant change. There are two major ways to execute trades, as well as a number of variations. The traditional approach is a face-to-face method involving a **designated market maker**. That approach is being replaced by Electronic Communications Networks (ECNs) that operate with little human intervention beyond the inputting of orders. We'll describe each approach briefly.

In the traditional system, brokerage firms have representatives at exchanges known as **floor brokers**. Local brokers submit customer orders to those representatives. At the exchange, each stock is traded in a particular spot on a large trading floor in an auction-like process supervised by a **designated market maker**. Market makers were formerly called **specialists**. Market makers are responsible for conducting orderly markets in their stocks. To do that they must buy and/or sell on their own accounts when a buyer can't find a seller or a seller can't find a buyer. This process is said to provide liquidity to the market—meaning sales don't stop when the prices of buy and sell orders temporarily don't match. Market makers buy and sell at different prices. They will buy at the **bid** price, which is lower than the **ask** price at which they'll sell. The difference, called the **spread,** is the market makers' profit.

When a floor broker receives an order, he takes it to the location of that stock's market maker along with other floor brokers and makes the trade. Once transactions are done, confirmations are passed back to local brokers and their clients. Actual settlement of the sale and transfer of the stock doesn't happen for a few days.

Figures 5-4 and 5-5 show the impressive exterior and the trading floor of the New York Stock Exchange, the biggest proponent of the market maker system. People do business at various places around the floor. Trading between floor brokers and market makers goes on continually while the exchange is open.

This rather colorful process is steadily being replaced by **ECNs**, which are simply automated systems that use computers to seek matching buy and sell orders from among those submitted by various traders. Once matches are found, trades are executed electronically for a fee.

Figure 5-6 is a representation of the overall trading process.

Floor brokers trade on the floor of the exchange.

Designated market makers maintain orderly markets in specific stocks.

ECNs are replacing traditional methods of trading stocks.

5.2c   Exchanges

There are several stock exchanges in the United States. The largest is the New York Stock Exchange (NYSE) in the downtown financial district of New York City, the area collectively referred to as Wall Street. In 2007, the NYSE merged with Euronext, a fully electronic European stock exchange, to form the world's largest exchange called NYSE Euronext, which lists over 8,000 companies.

The NYSE deals in the securities of about 2,800 American companies. Although there are a few exceptions, these tend to be the nation's largest businesses. Those stocks are said to be *listed* on the exchange.

FIGURE 5-4

The Imposing Exterior of the New York Stock Exchange

FIGURE 5-5   The Trading Floor of the New York Stock Exchange

AP Photo/Richard Drew

FIGURE 5-6   Schematic Representation of a Stock Market Transaction

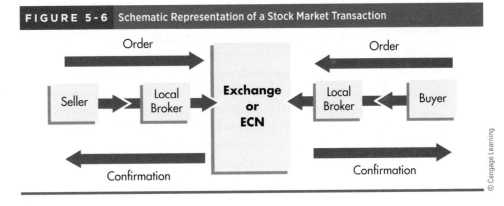

© Cengage Learning

The NYSE handles most of the stock trading activity in the nation. Another exchange, until recently called the American Stock Exchange (AMEX), is located a few blocks away. Historically, the AMEX was very similar to the NYSE expect that it was smaller and tended to list smaller, newer companies. At one time it handled about 15% of the nation's trading volume. However, in recent years the AMEX has been a victim of competition and by 2012 handled only about 1% of national volume. NYSE Euronext purchased AMEX in January 2008 and began calling it NYSE Amex, maintaining the historically significant AMEX title. But in May 2012, the operation's name was changed to NYSE MKT signaling the demise of a name that had been a fixture on Wall Street since 1953.

A third major exchange is called Nasdaq. It was originally organized by the National Association of Securities Dealers and derives its name from their computer system, the National Association of Security Dealers Automated Quotation (NASDAQ) System. Since its beginning in the early 1970s, Nasdaq has grown steadily in size and importance and today is an arch rival of the NYSE for securities trading business.

The big difference between Nasdaq and the NYSE and NYSE MKT exchanges is that the latter two are "physical location" exchanges, while Nasdaq is an electronic exchange. Trading on the NYSE or NYSE MKT takes place on the floors of those exchanges, and brokers have to be there to participate. Trading on the Nasdaq is electronic, and participants can be anywhere.

In addition to the NYSE, the NYSE MKT, and Nasdaq, there are several regional exchanges located in other major cities. They generally list companies of local interest. Today the exchanges are linked electronically, which makes them function for many purposes as one big exchange.

The Market   All the activity we've just described and more make up the *stock market*. Although the exchange represents a physical center for much of what goes on, the term "market" refers to the entire interconnected set of places, organizations, and processes.

Regulation   Securities markets are regulated under both state and federal laws, but the most important rules are federal. The Securities Act of 1933 required companies to disclose certain information to potential investors when promoting new securities in the primary market. The Securities Exchange Act of 1934 extended the disclosure requirements to existing stocks and set up the **Securities and Exchange Commission (SEC)** to oversee financial market activities.

The laws are primarily aimed at disclosure and the prevention of certain kinds of manipulative and deceptive behavior. Disclosure means that investors must be given full and accurate information about the companies and people behind stocks that are offered for sale. Manipulation means taking advantage of an official or privileged position to make profits on fluctuations in the prices of securities.

For example, it's illegal to make short-term profits on **insider information**, which is information available to an executive of a company but not to the general public.[5] Suppose a drug company is about to release information about a powerful new cancer treatment that is expected to be a big money maker in the future. That information release could be expected to drive the stock's price up considerably. It would be illegal for an insider to buy stock just before the announcement and sell it just after, making a short-term profit on the price increase.

Securities law is a large and complex field. For now, all we need to do is be aware that it exists and understand its basic direction.

5.2d   Private, Public, and Listed Companies, and the OTCBB

Suppose you notice a small company in your neighborhood that seems to be doing well and decide to buy some of its stock. Could you do this as easily as you could buy shares of IBM or Microsoft, with a simple call to your broker?

> The sale of securities is regulated by the federal government through the **Securities and Exchange Commission (SEC)**.

> Securities law is primarily aimed at **disclosure**.

---

5. People like accountants and lawyers who have access to privileged information but are not employees are also insiders.

If a company is small, buying its stock might not be easy, and you might not be able to get any at all. That's because not all companies are traded on exchanges, and many aren't for sale to the public. Let's trace the life of a typical business enterprise to see how and when its stock becomes available for investment.

Suppose an entrepreneur starts a small unincorporated business. Because the firm isn't a corporation, it has no stock for outsiders to buy, and ownership is entirely vested in the entrepreneur. If the business is successful and the owner wants to raise money for expansion, he can incorporate in order to sell stock to others. We'll assume he does that.

Privately held companies can't sell securities to the general public.

Privately Held Companies   At this point, the firm is said to be a **privately held**, or **closely held**, **company**. The stock of privately held companies can be sold to other people, but those sales are severely restricted by federal regulations. Generally, there can't be a large number of stockholders, and sales solicitations can't be made across state lines. These regulations are aimed at limiting fraudulent investment schemes in which confidence artists offer bogus securities to unwary and unsophisticated investors.

Suppose our entrepreneur raises money by selling stock to a few people he knows and continues to expand the company. We'll assume that things continue to go well and, after some time, more and bigger growth opportunities present themselves. Taking advantage of such opportunities requires a lot more funding, but the business owner has run out of friends and relatives. To sell a substantial amount of stock, he has to make an offering to a large number of people.

A publicly traded company can sell securities broadly after a prospectus is approved by the SEC.

Public Companies   Offering securities for sale to the general public requires the approval of the SEC and the registration of each security offered with the commission. A firm that has received such approval is known as a *public company* or a **publicly traded company**. The process of obtaining approval and registration is known as *going public*.

Going public requires the assistance of an investment bank. The bank determines whether a market can be expected to exist for the company's stock and the likely price at which a block of stock can be sold. If the estimated price is acceptable to the firm's owners, the registration procedure begins with the preparation of a document known as a **prospectus**.

The prospectus gives detailed information about the firm's business, its financing, and the background of its principal officers. When securities are eventually offered for sale, a copy of the prospectus must be provided to potential investors. However, the prospectus must be submitted to the SEC and approved before anything can be sold.

The purpose of the prospectus is *disclosure*. That is, the document must truly and accurately inform potential investors of the nature of the business and the risks involved. If the president was recently in jail for securities fraud, for example, that fact must be disclosed. Similarly, if the company is depending on the success of some new technological process or the granting of a patent, those facts must be revealed.

The law provides severe penalties for fraud on the part of *anyone* involved in the preparation of a prospectus—not only owners and officers of the company, but accountants, lawyers, and bankers who might have been hired to assist in the process.

An unapproved prospectus is called a **red herring**.

While the SEC is reviewing a prospectus, the firm may not offer its securities for sale to the public. However, it may circulate the prospectus stamped with the word "PRELIMINARY" in red letters. Such a document is known as a **red herring**, indicating it does not yet represent an actual offering.

It's important to understand that approval of a prospectus by the SEC doesn't represent an endorsement of the security as a good investment opportunity. That is, a firm could be in an absolutely terrible business, one almost guaranteed to fail (like selling saltwater at the beach!) and still receive SEC approval because all the appropriate information was disclosed. In fact, SEC approval doesn't even guarantee that everything relevant is disclosed, because the commission doesn't have the resources to check much of the information that's submitted.

The IPO   When a prospectus is approved by the SEC, the securities described may be sold to the public. This initial sale is called an **initial public offering**, abbreviated **IPO**.

> The market for **initial public offerings (IPOs)** is very volatile and risky.

IPOs constitute a subdivision of the general stock market and are considered quite risky. The prices of newly traded companies sometimes advance very rapidly after their IPOs, but can drop dramatically as well.

Investment bankers generally line up buyers for IPOs before the securities are actually released, so the general public doesn't usually get involved right away. Institutional investors such as mutual funds are frequent buyers.

Notice that the initial public offering is a primary market transaction. Once the securities are placed with investors, further trading will involve secondary market transactions. We'll discuss the IPO process in depth in Chapter 8.

If our entrepreneur went through all this, he would probably have retained a majority of the firm's stock for himself. The IPO would have placed a value on the shares of the stock that were sold and thereby would have implicitly valued the shares still held by the entrepreneur. In a successful IPO, that value is far in excess of book value, and the entrepreneur can become a millionaire overnight, at least on paper!

The OTCBB   At this point the company is partially owned by investors who purchased shares in its IPO, and partially owned by the entrepreneur and anyone who bought in before the firm went public. Now suppose any of these investors want to sell some or all of their holdings. How can that be accomplished?

Notice that we haven't as yet said anything about a stock exchange in this scenario. Also recall that stock exchanges trade only in certain stocks that are *listed* on those exchanges. In other words, our firm's securities aren't listed on an exchange, so investors can't buy or sell shares there. A vast number of companies fit this description. They're public and therefore available to be generally traded, but they're not listed on an exchange.

> Smaller public companies are traded on the **OTCBB**.

Such unlisted securities can be traded through a system overseen by the Financial Industry Regulatory Authority (FINRA), that is called the **Over-the-Counter Bulletin Board (OTCBB)**. The OTCBB posts price quotes on new, very small, or infrequently traded issues. That information enables brokers and dealers to buy and sell those stocks on behalf of clients. This is the route through which our entrepreneur's stock would be marketed. (Another organization, OTC markets Group, Inc., informally called "Pink Sheets," competes with the OTCBB.)

It's generally more expensive to trade in the stocks of the smaller firms handled by the OTCBB than in stocks listed on exchanges. Because few investors tend to be interested in any particular small company, brokers have to work hard to match buyers and sellers. For that service they receive higher commissions and fees than those paid for trades in stocks listed on exchanges where there is an active market all the time.

Listing on an Exchange   Now suppose the company we've been talking about continues to grow and becomes popular among investors. It's in the company's interest to make it easy for those investors to trade in the secondary market for the firm's stock even though no money from those trades goes to the company itself. That's because a smoothly operating secondary market in the stock will make further new issues of the firm's securities easier to sell in the future.

Companies **list** themselves on an exchange to make trading their securities easier.

So, if the trading volume warrants, the company can *list* its stock on an exchange. This is a relatively easy process if the exchange's requirements for size and length of time in business are met. After that the firm is a **listed company**.

5.2e   Stock Quotations

Stock quotations summarize recent trading activity in individual stocks. They're used by investors to monitor the progress of shares they own or are thinking about buying. Until a few years ago, the only practical way for most people to get quote information was through newspaper listings, which published prices as of the close of the previous business day. The leading print source was *The Wall Street Journal*. If an investor wanted anything more current than yesterday's close, she had to call her broker.

Of course the Internet has changed that dramatically. Today, most investors get their information from Web sites that give quotes that are only about 20 minutes old.

It's easy to find an online quotation source. Set your browser to search for "stock quotations" and take your pick. Most have a small window on the first page labeled *search* or *quote*. Enter the symbol or name of the company you're interested in and hit "enter" or click "search" or "quote".

Figure 5-7 is a generic representation of some of the information found in a typical online quote for Microsoft Corporation. Most sites display more information including some graphics, but we're just showing basics here. The numerical information in Figure 5-7 was quoted at *finance.yahoo.com* on September 28, 2012, at 11:23 EDT, but the same figures were available on other sites. Let's review the items shown to get an understanding of the kind of information online listings offer. We'll explain the items as we go along.

At the top of the figure we see the company's name followed by Nasdaq and MSFT. This is telling us that Microsoft is traded on the Nasdaq exchange and that its

FIGURE 5-7	Selected Information from a Typical Online Stock Quotation

Microsoft Corporation (Nasdaq: MSFT)

Last Trade	$29.89
Previous Close	$30.16
Change	↓$0.27
52 week Range	$24.26–$32.95
Day's Range	$29.79–$30.26
Volume	18,253,037 shares
Dividend	$0.92
Dividend Yield	3.00%
P/E	14.94
EPS	$2.00

Source: finance.yahoo.com.

symbol is MSFT. The symbol is an abbreviation of the firm's name used in referencing stock market data. All listed companies have symbols.

Below that we see the price quotation, $29.89, which is the price of the most recent (last) trade available. The next two lines show the price of the last trade on the previous business day (the closing price) and the change from that price. The downward arrow means a decrease. Notice that the reader sees the direction of the price's movement at a glance.

The next two lines show two price ranges in which the stock has sold. The first is over the last year and the second is within the current day. The one-year range reflects nearly a 36% change from the lowest to the highest price. That's not unusual for volatile, high tech stocks like Microsoft. The next line is volume which tells us that over 18 million shares had changed hands so far that day. That's a typical morning for Microsoft.

The next two lines show the P/E ratio and EPS we discussed in Chapter 3. It's important to understand that the presence of these ratios in stock quotations is an indication that investors consider them very important.

INSIGHTS | **Practical Finance**

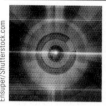
Ensuper/Shutterstock.com

Efficient Financial Markets

In an effort to explain certain characteristics of the behavior of stock prices, theorists have hypothesized that U.S. financial markets are *efficient.* In this context, efficiency means information travels around the market so fast that it's virtually impossible to find a bargain.

The idea is that there's an army of analysts working in the securities industry, and that analysts, brokers, and investors are wired together electronically by phone and computer. When some new piece of information comes out that suggests a stock may be worth more or less than its current price, it's disseminated with lightning speed, and investors bid the price up or down within hours if not minutes.

The implication of efficiency is that an investor can't *consistently* beat the market by studying up on stocks because all available information is already reflected in stock prices. Beating the market means earning above-average returns by consistently finding bargains.

Don't be discouraged. Not everyone agrees that the **efficient market hypothesis** is correct. We'll have more to say about the idea in Chapter 8.

5.3 Corporate Governance

Corporate governance refers to the relationships, rules and procedures under which businesses are organized and run. In recent years, concern over corporate governance has focused on the ethics and legality of financial relationships between top managers and the corporations they serve.

The idea is connected to the **agency problem** (see Chapter 1, page 17), which refers to a conflict of interest between executives and stockholders that occurs because top executives can make their companies do things that enrich those executives at the expense of others, especially stockholders and the investing public.

There have been two major financial crises thus far in the 21st century that have been described as failures of corporate governance. Basically the people in charge of some large companies used their positions of power and confidence to enrich themselves at the expense of average Americans.

The first event occurred in 2000 when a stock market crash was largely caused by the discovery of fraud in the financial reporting of as many as 1,000 large, publicly traded companies. The result was a substantial decline in the stock market, a recession, and ultimately the passage of the Sarbanes Oxley-Act (SOX) aimed at improving corporate governance practices in publicly traded companies.

The second crisis occurred in 2008 when the financial system recognized that trillions of dollars of supposedly high grade securities backed by American home mortgages were riddled with "subprime" mortgage loans that were virtually certain to default. The shock nearly collapsed the American banking system and led the nation into the worst recession in 75 years. The corporate governance issues this time were more ethical than legal and are related to compensation systems and attitudes in the financial industry that motivated executives to take excessive risks with other people's money.

Although the post-crisis recession was officially over in June 2009, the sluggish economy and high unemployment have persisted well into 2012. The federal government's eventual response to the crisis was another law, the Dodd–Frank Act, which increases government regulation of the financial system to prevent a recurrence. The controversial act was passed in July 2010, but implementation has been slow.

In the remainder of this section, we'll review the events leading to both crises in the hope that readers will be more aware of the power and risk involved in the corporate world. We'll begin with a brief look at executive compensation and the idea of a moral hazard.

5.3a   Executive Compensation

The most flagrant abuse of governance/agency occurs when top executives are paid excessively and in ways that motivate illegal/unethical behavior. Excessive executive pay takes several forms. Salaries and bonuses are high, but the really big money is related to stock, usually through executive **stock options**. Under option plans, executives are given the right to purchase blocks of stock at low fixed prices during limited time periods beginning a few years in the future. If the market price of a company's stock rises above the fixed purchase price during the option period, the executive can *exercise* the option by buying at the low fixed price, and then sell the shares for an immediate profit.

An **employee stock option** grants the right to purchase stock at a set price over a limited period.

CONCEPT CONNECTION   EXAMPLE 5-1

Executive Stock Options

Harry Johnson is CEO of Wellbridge Corp. He's paid a salary of $2.5 million and a performance bonus of $1.5 million. In addition, Harry was granted an option on 200,000 shares of stock at $20 per share three years ago. The stock was selling for $19 at the time.

The option period begins two years from the date of issue, which is at the end of June of this year, and expires after three more years. It is now June 15. Wellbridge stock is currently selling for $48.65. If Harry receives his bonus and exercises his stock option at $48.65, how much will he make this year?

Ensuper/Shutterstock.com

SOLUTION: Harry will receive cash compensation consisting of his salary and bonus as follows:

Salary	$ 2,500,000
Bonus	1,500,000
	$4,000,000

Exercising his stock options and selling at the current market price will lead to the following gain:

Proceeds of sale (200,000 × $48.65=)	$9,730,000
Less option payment (200,000 × $20.00=)	(4,000,000)
Gain on option	$5,730,000

Hence Harry's income for the year will be

Cash payments from Company	$4,000,000
Stock option gain	5,730,000
Total	$9,730,000

Notice first that CEO Harry will make more on stock options than he's paid in cash. That isn't unusual. Next notice that Harry's option gain won't exactly be free to the company. The 200,000 new shares could have been sold to investors at or near the $48.65 market price. So Harry's gain is the company's cost.[6] Finally, notice the magnitude of Harry's compensation. It's fair for ordinary stockholders to ask if anyone can be worth that much. Yet Harry's pay isn't unusual for a CEO.

5.3b The Moral Hazard of Stock-Based Compensation

A **moral hazard**[7] is a situation that tempts people to act in immoral or unethical ways. Unfortunately, stock-based compensation plans like Harry's create serious moral hazards. Notice that CEO Harry's compensation is tied to Wellbridge's stock price, and there's a limited period during which it can be exercised. He is therefore motivated to hold the stock's price up by any means as the end of June approaches. For example, suppose Harry has information that, if announced, would cause the stock's price to drop by $10 per share. That would personally cost Harry $2 million if it happened before the end of June. As a result Harry may suppress the information until he's exercised his option and sold his stock.

Even worse, in order to **increase** the stock's price when he exercises his options, Harry might fabricate information that makes the company's future look brighter than it is. He could lie about the success of research projects, the strength of the firm's competitive position, the probable results of lawsuits, and most importantly about the firm's financial results.

Stock options can motivate executives to act **unethically** to hold stock price up.

---

6. Costs that involve forgoing an opportunity rather than paying out money are called *opportunity costs*. They don't appear in accounting records, but are nevertheless real.

7. A moral hazard exists when a person can make money by acting in an unethical or immoral way. For example, if it were possible to insure a $200,000 house for $400,000, the owner would be tempted to burn it down for a profit. That's why you can't insure properly for more than it's worth.

Notice that this situation represents a failure of corporate governance in that the system motivates an illegal/unethical act but does not provide safeguards or procedures to keep it from happening.

The Moral Hazard for Founders   Moral hazards aren't limited to executives who are employees. The temptations for founders can be even worse.

CONCEPT CONNECTION   EXAMPLE 5-2

A Moral Hazard for Founders

Suppose CEO Harry of Example 5-1 is Wellbridge's founder and has retained 20% of its stock. Further suppose the total market value of the firm[8] is $20 billion. That means Harry is worth about ($20 × .2=) $4 billion. What impact would a price decline of $10 have on his personal wealth?

SOLUTION: At a market price of $48.65, a $10 price change represents a value decrease of

$$\$10:00/\$48.65 = .206 = 20.6\%$$

That means our founder/CEO's net worth[9] would decrease by approximately

$$\$4 \text{ billion} \times .206 = \$824 \text{ million}$$

That's a powerful incentive to keep negative information away from the stock market or to create false information that makes the firm look better than it is raising stock price.

Ensuper/Shutterstock.com

5.3c   The Events of the 1990s

The stock market saw an unprecedented boom in the 1990s. Buoyed by the enthusiasm, the top managements of a large number of companies seemed to get the idea that the accounting rules and SEC regulations about financial reporting weren't serious matters. They then undertook to **pump up their stock prices by publishing false or deceptive financial statements.** The deceptions were amazingly widespread, but were eventually exposed contributing to a major stock market decline in 2000.

The first and best known of many to crash was Enron, a petroleum pipeline company that had morphed into a huge energy trader/broker, becoming the seventh largest company in the nation. The firm collapsed into virtually nothing when news of its accounting irregularities hit the financial press.

Almost **1,000 public companies restated** their financial statements because of **questionable reporting** practices.

Altogether about 10% of publicly traded companies, almost 1,000 firms, **restated** their financial statements between 1998 and 2002 to eliminate the effects of questionable reporting. Approximately $6 **trillion** of stock market value disappeared, much of the loss triggered by this fraud-induced phenomenon.

---

8. The market value of a company whose stock is regularly traded is the current stock price multiplied by the number of shares outstanding (held by investors).

9. A person's net worth is her total assets minus her total liabilities. The concept is applicable to companies as well as people, but it's usually called equity in a business context.

The investing public lost confidence in financial markets, and an alarmed Congress took legislative action to prevent a recurrence. The result was the Sarbanes-Oxley Act (SOX).

5.3d   The Sarbanes-Oxley Act[10]

The government investigation into the corporate fraud of the 1990s and early 2000s revealed several key areas that contributed to the overall problem. The three most significant were

- The Public Accounting Industry: Auditors failed to ensure compliance with accounting standards.
- Corporate Governance: Boards of directors failed to control executive fraud.
- Wall Street: Securities analysts issued reports biased in favor of companies that did business with their investment banker employers.

We'll summarize the more important provisions of SOX that address these issues.

Title I: Oversight of the Public Accounting Industry   Public accounting firms are the financial system's first line of defense against fraud. Unfortunately, some firms were not taking this responsibility seriously enough.

Prior to SOX, the industry was self-regulated. Firms reviewed one another's records, but there was no central authority that monitored performance. SOX created the **Public Company Accounting Oversight Board (PCAOB)**, which now monitors the activities of public accounting firms by requiring registration, setting standards of performance, and providing inspection and disciplinary procedures.

> SOX established the **PCAOB to oversee the public accounting** industry.

Title II: Auditor Independence   Auditors are hired and paid by client company executives but may have to prevent them from doing what they want, a tough yet previously manageable task. But during the 1990s, some auditors aligned themselves too closely with clients and lost sight of their mission to protect the investing public. Three problem areas were identified: consulting, reporting, and friendships.

> SOX prohibits consulting by public accounting firms.

Consulting: CPA consulting revenues often exceeded auditing income. In order to protect consulting income, auditors would yield to client pressure regarding presenting questionable financial information. SOX now bans auditing firms from providing clients with management consulting, IT consulting, and most other services. Tax services are still permitted.

Reporting: Auditors were hired by the client's CEO and/or CFO, the people who generally wanted to bend or break the rules. SOX now requires that auditors report to the audit committee of the board of directors, which now must be made up of outside directors and contain at least one financial expert.

Friendships: Auditors were often assigned to client companies indefinitely, leading to personal friendships that made challenging clients difficult. SOX limits the tenure of senior audit managers to five years with one client.

---

10. The material in this section is drawn from Robert Prentice and Dean Bredeson, *A Student Guide to the Sarbanes-Oxley Act*, 2nd ed. (Mason, Ohio: South-Western Cengage Learning, 2010).

Title III: Corporate Responsibility   When fraudulent financial reporting was discovered, CEOs frequently used an "ignorance defense," claiming they knew nothing of the wrongdoing and blaming overzealous underlings. SOX now requires that **CEOs and CFOs certify** that they have reviewed the correctness of financial statements and that they are responsible for internal financial controls.

SOX requires **CEOs to certify** that financial controls are adequate and that financial statements are **not false or misleading.**

Title V: Wall Street Reforms—Pressure on Securities Analysts   Brokerage firms employ analysts to report on companies as investments. But brokerage firms did other business with those companies and pressured analysts to produce favorable reports.

SOX now requires analysts to certify that they believe their own reports and that their pay is not tied to their recommendations.

5.3e   Life After Sarbanes-Oxley

SOX was passed quickly after the market decline of the early 2000s, and critics contended that it was overzealous, having been created in the heat of the moment. The biggest criticism was that complying with SOX might cost more than the value of its benefits, and a softening of the rules seemed a possibility.

However, the perception of SOX's cost/benefit tradeoff improved with time, and by 2008, studies had shown that the savings associated with the better internal controls required by SOX outweighed their cost. As a result, a major softening in SOX rules now seems unlikely.

Once SOX was in effect, the business/financial community seemed to breathe a sigh of relief. People thought the governance problem was fixed and that a sudden market crash followed by a recession was virtually impossible for a really long time. Few recognized the problem already developing in the depths of the financial system that within a few short years would rock the economy to its very foundations, creating a crisis far worse than the one we had just been through.

5.3f   The Financial Crisis of 2008

In 2008 (beginning in mid-2007), an unprecedented financial crisis struck the United States. It was characterized by the sudden failure or near-failure of several "systemically" important financial institutions. *Systemically important* means that the institution is so large that its collapse would jeopardize the nation's entire economic system. The crisis triggered the most severe recession in 75 years and spread to other countries, creating a "global economic crisis." The underlying cause of the crisis was the collapse of certain securities tied to the U.S. real estate market, which we'll review in the next few pages.

Background: Home Ownership, Mortgages, and Risk   Few families can afford to buy a home without a mortgage loan, which provides much of the cash to buy property. The loan is *secured* by the house itself, meaning if the borrower fails to make loan payments, the lender can take the house. Failure to make payments is called *default,* while the lender taking the house is *foreclosure.*

A buyer must "qualify" for a mortgage loan. Traditionally that meant having a 10% to 20% down payment, an adequate monthly income, and a good credit history. Under those conditions, the loan is a relatively safe investment for the lender.[11] The down payment provides an equity cushion for the bank in the event of foreclosure. Equity is the portion of the home's value that exceeds the mortgage. The cushion comes from the fact that expenses and losses in foreclosure are paid out of equity before any of the lender's money is lost. The possibility of losing equity gives homeowners an incentive to avoid default and foreclosure. That's important. When there's little equity, homeowners in financial trouble are more likely to walk away, leaving the bank with a loss.

Another source of bank safety has traditionally been appreciation in the value of property because it adds equity after purchase. Previously, real estate in the U.S. appreciated consistently over the preceding 75 years, especially during the 1990s and early 2000s.

For these reasons, residential mortgage loans were safe investments for banks. Foreclosures averaged only about 2% and the bank's interest was usually protected by equity. The amount of money borrowed for mortgages is enormous, approximately *$12 trillion*.

The Bank's Perspective   Banks and similar financial institutions pay interest on deposits and lend that money to borrowers at higher interest rates. The rate difference is called a *spread* and is how the bank pays its expenses and earns a profit.

Traditionally, banks loaned mortgage money to home buyers, holding the loans until they were paid off. This created two problems—the first was **liquidity**, meaning that most of the money was tied up for 15 or 20 years as a mortgage was slowly paid off. In order to make another loan, a bank had to accumulate more deposits.

The second problem was profitability. The mortgage loans that provided a bank's income were made at fixed rates for as long as 30 years. But a bank's largest expense is interest payments on deposits, which are **short-term** loans made to the bank by its customers.[12] That means the banks' income was fixed by the rates on long term mortgages, while its expenses depended on the short-term rates it paid on deposits, which change constantly.

Banks generally earn profits because mortgage rates are usually higher than short-term deposit rates. But occasionally short-term rates climb above the long-term rates, and the bank is in a loss position. (See pages 222–224.)

Securitization   These problems were addressed by a technique known as securitization. The mortgage is an asset to the bank that can be sold to an investor for a lump sum that recovers the bank's cash plus a fee for originating the loan.[13] After the sale, the loan has been removed from the bank's balance sheet and replaced with cash, which can be used to make another loan. Notice that selling off its mortgage loans rids the bank of

---

11. Traditional mortgages with lower down payments are usually allowed if the borrower purchases private mortgage insurance (PMI), which protects the lender if the buyer defaults.

12. Deposits are short term because money can be withdrawn from savings accounts any time, and certificates of deposit usually mature within a few years.

13. We'll learn how to calculate the value of a stream of payments stretching into the future in Chapter 6.

both problems: It frees up cash to make new loans, and income is no longer tied to the interest rate on old loans, but comes from making new loans.

A Bundle of Loans and Securitization   Typically a bank sells most of its loans to an investment bank that specializes in *issuing* securities and bundles the mortgages into a pool. This issuer receives all of the payments on the mortgages in the pool, creating a cash flow that ideally continues until the loans are paid off. It then **securitizes** the pool by selling securities to investors that give them rights to receive shares of that stream of money. These securities are called **collateralized debt obligations (CDO)**[14] because the cash stream is supported by the collateral value of the homes that underlie the mortgages in the pool.

> **Securitizing** a pool of mortgages means selling **rights** to its cash flow called **CDOs.**

The Attraction of CDOs   CDOs were purchased by institutional investors all over the world. These included investment banks, hedge funds,[15] and insurance companies. The worldwide interest in CDOs is one of the reasons the crisis became global. CDOs were popular because they earned high returns, were liquid, and were perceived as safe.

> **CDOs** are purchased by **institutional** investors.

Returns were high because the underlying investments were mortgages that paid higher rates than short-term investments. It was also possible to boost those rates by accepting more risk. CDOs were also liquid, meaning buyers could get out of their investments by selling their CDOs in a secondary market (see page 183). Finally, CDOs were considered safe, because they were based on the U.S. residential real estate market, which had a history of low default rates and equity protection for lenders.

> **CDOs** were traded on a secondary market.

Risk and the Concept of the CDO Tranche   Even though CDOs were considered safe, people recognized that they did carry some risk because a few homeowners default even in the best of times.

Realizing that CDO buyers had different risk tolerances, issuers devised a way to "slice" the cash flow stream into pieces of different risk called **tranches,** (French for *slice*). Higher-risk tranches sold at lower prices, which increased their return.

The risk allocation technique is important. Suppose the total anticipated cash flow from a mortgage pool is $9M and the issuer wants to slice it into three $3M tranches of increasing risk called A, B, and C. The issuer doesn't know which mortgages will default, so it can't sort weaker homeowners into higher-risk tranches.

> Tranche **risk** is related to a **sequential** cash payout system.

Instead, the revenue stream is applied to the tranches sequentially. That is, all of the money coming in is paid to the holders of tranche A securities until they are completely paid off. Then the stream is used to pay off tranche B, and finally tranche C.

Since defaults reduce the overall stream of payments, they tend to affect only lower (higher risk) tranches that are paid off last; that is, defaults cut the tail off the stream, which will always reduce payments to tranche C's investors, but rarely B's and almost never A's. Lower risk tranches like A are *senior* and those with higher risk (like C) are *junior*.

---

14. Collateral is an asset that's pledged to guarantee the repayment of a loan. The house is collateral for a mortgage loan.

15. A hedge fund is a mutual fund that invests in relatively risky opportunities. Participation is generally limited to wealthy investors.

A Flaw in the Risk Allocation Method   But there's a problem in this method of assigning risk arising from the assumption that only about 2% of mortgages default. If that's true, a sequential distribution of cash virtually guarantees tranches A and B will be fully paid.

But what if a bundle contained so many high-risk loans that 70% or 80% might default? Then even tranche A wouldn't be completely safe, while tranches B and C would be very risky indeed.

The problem was that the 2% default rate was from traditional loans to qualified buyers in stable real estate markets. The situation became completely different when risky subprime loans, which we'll discuss shortly, entered the picture.

The Role of Rating Agencies   Rating agencies study debt securities and rate them on the likelihood of default with letter grades from AAA to C. AAA means very low risk, while C means defaulted. Ratings above BBB are called "investment grade," meaning relatively low risk consistent with prudent, long-term investing.

Rating agencies have been seriously faulted as contributing to the crisis by inflating ratings on CDO tranches that were riddled with high-risk loans. In many cases, AAA ratings were assigned and later downgraded, making the crisis worse.

The CDO Market—Size and Complexity   The foregoing is a simplified description of the formation of and market for CDOs. The actual market is as complicated as it is enormous. The total value of mortgage-based CDOs in mid-2009 was estimated at $9 trillion, most of which were held by financial institutions worldwide. The complexity of CDO market operations and risk assessment is such that valuation (pricing) was always uncertain, and CDOs usually traded at prices based on recent sales of comparable assets. This method of pricing CDOs proved to be an important factor as the crisis developed.

The Subprime Mortgage Market
A period of prosperity ended in 2000, raising concerns about recession. In response, the Federal Reserve lowered interest rates a number of times, reaching a 40-year low by 2003. The rates on CDOs, however, did not drop proportionately, and CDO demand increased quickly. Indeed, many institutions borrowed at low short-term rates to invest in CDOs.

If the increased demand for CDOs was to be met, mortgage lenders had to increase the pace at which they were making new loans. They were eager to do that to earn origination fees, but there weren't enough qualified borrowers applying. Recall that a qualified borrower has a down payment, reliable income, and a good credit history. The industry was running out of that kind of applicant.

Subprime Techniques and Implications
Faced with a demand it couldn't meet with traditional lending rules, the mortgage industry created **subprime loans**. These are simply loans made to unqualified borrowers without a down payment and/or manipulating income qualifications by creating loans with payments that start low and increase with time. The following techniques were common:

Zero-Down Loans   Foregoing a down payment created a pool of homeowners with **no equity and little to lose** in foreclosure who were less motivated to avoid default. It also meant lenders had no equity cushion to protect their investments.

ARM payments can **increase**, leading to **default**.

Adjustable-Rate Mortgages (ARMs)   Adjustable-rate mortgages (ARMs) charge interest at rates that move with financial markets, but *initially* have lower rates than comparable fixed-rate loans. That lowers early monthly payments. The bad news is that ARM borrowers are stuck with increased payments when rates rise increasing default risk, especially if borrowers have no equity in their homes to protect. A very low early rate is called a **teaser rate**.

In **NegAm** loans, the principal **increases** until the rates resets, increasing payments **dramatically**.

Negative Amortization (NegAm) Loans   In a NegAm loan, early payments are lower than the monthly interest charge, and unpaid interest is added to principal which *increases* over time. The low payment period is generally five years. After that, payments are recalculated to pay off the larger principal over the remaining life of the loan at the then existing ARM rate. This generally results in a staggering increase in monthly payments leading to default. NegAm loans are called **option ARMs**, because the borrower chooses the level of early payments. These loans have an enormous default rate.

Lenders qualified subprime borrowers by requiring only enough income to afford the lower early ARM payments. That is, they ignored what would happen if rates rose enough to make it difficult for borrowers to keep up with their payments.

Alt-A Loans—No Documentation   Alt-A loans were extended to borrowers without proof of their incomes or asset and debt positions. That meant that ignorant or dishonest people could borrow money that they had little chance of repaying.

Borrower Rationale   It's fair to ask why borrowers took on loans with payments they knew might increase beyond their ability to pay and why lenders approved such loans. One reason is that some borrowers didn't understand what they were getting into. **Predatory lending** occurred when commission-driven brokers sold loans to people they knew couldn't afford them.

Making loans to people who clearly can't afford them is **predatory lending**.

But there's another reason that seemed reasonable at the time. Real estate prices had been increasing for 10 years and were expected to continue upward. It was a risky but reasonable strategy to buy a house with zero down and a low payment loan for a few years while the house appreciated, giving the homeowner equity in the property. With that, she could qualify for a traditional mortgage and live in the house safely for years. Alternatively, a homeowner could sell the house and pocket the appreciation, a strategy called **flipping**. Unfortunately, flipping created another class of subprime buyers, investors out for a quick profit.

Buying a house for a quick profit on price appreciation is called **flipping**.

Political Pressures   Moderate relaxation of mortgage credit standards has long been perceived as socially desirable because it seemed like a good way to extend home ownership to lower-income families who otherwise couldn't afford it.

The Credit Default Swap (CDS)
The Credit Default Swap (CDS) is a recent financial innovation that added uncertainty to the financial system, *making the crisis worse*. Invented in the 1990s, a CDS is a contract between a buyer and a seller in which the seller agrees to repay losses the buyer suffers on a debt security. In return, the seller receives premium payments over the life of the security.

Credit Default Swaps are agreements to pay another the amount **lost** on a **defaulted** debt security.

For example, suppose A holds a debt security issued by B. A can buy a credit default swap from C in which C agrees to pay A for any loss of value experienced on the security if B defaults. In return, A pays C premiums over the life of the security. A CDS sounds like an insurance policy but it isn't; the most important differences are:

- The CDS buyer (A) doesn't have to own B's debt security or suffer a loss in the event of B's default. Real insurance protects only actual losses.
- The CDS seller (C) is not government regulated as insurance companies are.
- The CDS seller (C), because it is unregulated, is not required to carry cash reserves to pay buyers in the event of large losses.

In addition, CDS contracts can be traded on a secondary market. That means speculators can gamble on whether B will default on its security without investing any money in it themselves.

The existence of a secondary market also means that CDS contracts might be traded many times during their lives. This implies that the original buyer (A) may have had no idea whether the party holding the other side of its contract has the resources to pay off if default occurs. And since some institutions had invested in both sides of CDS contracts prior to the financial crisis, it wasn't clear to what extent they might be called upon to pay off as an insurer on someone else's defaulted debt holding.

CDSs exploded onto the financial system in the early 2000s, reaching a peak volume estimated at $45 trillion by 2007. They were heavily applied to CDOs.

Credit Default Swaps tied the fortunes of financial institutions together so that the failure of one could contribute to the failure of another.

The Scene Is Set   Let's summarize where the economy was on the eve of the crisis.

A new kind of security, called a CDO, has been created based on cash flows from U.S. residential mortgages, which have traditionally been safe investments, so CDOs are considered safe. Institutions worldwide have invested trillions in CDOs. CDOs are difficult to value and are therefore priced on the basis of recent sales.

The subprime home loan market has been operating for about three years creating mortgages in which homeowners have no equity and can barely make their payments. These mortgages are ARMs, so monthly payments will rise dramatically if interest rates increase. Hence subprimes, unlike traditional mortgages, are risky and likely to default.

CDOs are full of subprime loans, but it isn't clear how many support particular CDOs.

A new kind of risk-spreading contract has been created called a credit default swap (CDS) which is seen as "insurance" against losing money on a debt investment. But it isn't insurance, because the insured party often doesn't know who its insurer is or if it can cover a loss. CDSs link financial institutions in a network so complex that no one knows their full exposure to risk.

CDOs are heavily insured with CDSs.

Thousands of **subprime loans** were **foreclosed** in 2004–6.

The Trigger—Interest Rates Rise   In 2004, the Federal Reserve became concerned about inflation and began a series of interest rate increases that raised the Fed funds rate fourfold by July 2006. Mortgage rates also went up, putting an end to rising real estate prices.

As rates rose ARM payments rose, and thousands of subprime borrowers defaulted. Lenders foreclosed and marketed the homes at depressed prices, further slowing the market. Investors dependent on rising prices to flip houses also threw them on the market driving prices down faster and further.

The Effect on the CDO Market and CDO Owners   The increasing number of defaults soon became evident in the cash streams flowing into CDOs, creating a valuation problem. No one knew how secure any CDO was, so no one was willing to set a price at which it could trade. As a result, the secondary CDO market froze, i.e., **trading stopped**.

CDO cash flows declined, creating uncertainty about value, and **trading stopped**.

But if trading on a type of security stops because no one can price them, a problem is created in the financial statements of institutions that own similar securities. That is, at what value should the security be carried on its owner's balance sheet? If the book value of the asset was overstated, it should be written down.[16] This idea was reinforced when debt rating agencies lowered their ratings of CDOs.

But the unanswered question was: How large should that write-down be? CDO prices didn't decline, they just ceased to exist. Did that mean they were zero, or just hiding?

Accounting Losses, Cash Losses, and Withdrawals   Writing down a CDO reduces its asset value on its owner's financial statements as well as profit in the current year, which in turn reduces equity. (See Example 2-1 on page 34.) This happens even though the lower cash flows may not be experienced for years.

CDO write-downs lead to **huge losses** at financial firms that can cause **failure**.

During 2008, staggering losses and equity reductions were recognized by financial institutions that had invested in CDOs. The write-downs reduced assets and equity, but left liabilities untouched. That meant the ratios of assets and equity to liabilities decreased. Unfortunately, those paper changes can be a disaster for financial institutions, which are required to maintain certain ratios at "safe" levels. If they don't, they're deemed to have failed and can be taken over by regulators.

Some financial institutions also have depositors (banks) or shareholders (hedge funds) who can withdraw their funds. When those individuals hear about CDO losses, they tend to lose confidence and try to withdraw their money immediately. Mass withdrawals are called a **run** and can result in the overnight failure of the institution.

A mass investor withdrawal is a **run**.

When financial firms suffered these kinds of losses during the financial crisis, they needed quick injections of cash in the form of or loans to survive. Most weren't able to raise the money privately and were either acquired by other companies that weren't as exposed to subprime CDOs, were bailed out by the federal government, or failed.

---

16. A write-off reduces an asset's value to zero. A write-down is just a partial write-off that leaves some value in the asset account.

The Effect on the Economy   Because of the widespread use of Credit Default Swaps, the CDO octopus had tentacles far beyond those firms that held CDOs. CDSs were everywhere and tied companies together in terms of exposure to CDO risk. As a result, no one knew who would fail next, so everyone was afraid to do business with anyone. Wall Street ground to a halt.

Banks didn't know who would fail next, so they **stopped lending**.

More important to the general economy, banks became fearful of making loans with any risk at all, and lending to nonfinancial businesses almost stopped. That meant companies that depended on bank credit to conduct everyday operations couldn't get loans and found it difficult to stay in business.

Consumer credit also became difficult because banks quickly stiffened credit standards. That forced people to cut back on debt-financed spending that had been a mainstay of the pre-crisis economy.

To make matters worse, consumers were frightened by media reports of what was happening on Wall Street and began to curtail spending to conserve money in case they lost their jobs. That meant less demand for product, less work for producers, fewer jobs, and layoffs. The economy slipped into the worst recession in 75 years. According to the National Bureau of Economic Research, the official start date of the recession was January 2008.

Federal Government Actions in 2008
By the early months of 2008, officials at the U.S. Treasury and the Federal Reserve knew the economy was in serious trouble. The immediate problem was that a number of financial institutions that were "too big to fail" were tottering on the brink of insolvency. *Too big to fail* really means too big for the *government to let fail* because the failure would damage the financial system. An unprecedented number of such firms were at risk in 2008, and the government geared up to preserve the economy. Its intervention took three forms:

- Some firms were taken over by the government under existing federal regulations.

- Officials brokered takeovers (mergers) of at-risk institutions by firms in better condition.

- The federal government "bailed out" several companies, largely banks, with loans and stock purchases.

Two actions were particularly important in the development and ultimate depth of the crisis.

The Failure and Bailout of Bear Stearns   Bear Stearns, a venerable pillar of Wall Street, was one of five large, independent investment banks in the financial industry. In July 2007, two of its hedge funds lost a total of $1.5 billion in client money due to investments in junior CDO tranches. As its asset values plummeted, Bear was beset with withdrawal demands from investors which it couldn't meet and asked the Federal Reserve for a bailout.

The government came to Bear's rescue with a loan and helped broker a deal in which commercial bank JPMorgan Chase bought the firm in March 2008. Morgan paid $10 per share for Bear's stock which had been trading at $160 a year earlier. The agreement was supported by a further government loan and a guarantee that it would absorb any loss beyond $1 billion suffered by Morgan.

The bailout of Bear Stearns met with considerable public criticism. The public characterized it as a giveaway of taxpayer money and charged that it created a situation that encourages Wall Street big shots to take excessive risks by saving them from the consequences of their own bad decisions. As a result, federal officials were wary of bailing out anyone else.

The Non-Bailout of Lehman Brothers   A few months later, Lehman Brothers, a firm that had been a fixture in the financial community for 185 years, found itself in a similar predicament. This time, however, responding to the public concern over the bailout of Bear Stearns, the federal government refused to help. Lehman Brothers filed the largest bankruptcy in U.S. history and virtually disappeared.

Many experts believe the government's refusal to bail out Lehman was an enormous mistake. The lack of federal help had an unexpectedly negative effect on the Wall Street community. Lehman's failure sent the financial industry it into a shocked paralysis that helped to precipitate if not cause the crisis probably driving it to the depths it eventually reached. The nation's largest financial institutions had for years operated under the assumption that the government would shield them from collapse under the *too big to fail* doctrine. When the federal government turned its back on Lehman, the industry felt suddenly stripped of that protection. The result was a virtual freezing of the financial community, putting the entire economy at risk.

The End of the Crisis, the Lingering Recession and Corporate Governance   Although the immediate government actions late in 2008 enabled some important financial institutions to continue functioning, they didn't pull the nation out of the recession, which was nine months old by the end of September 2008. The fundamental problem was that the banking system wasn't lending money.

Banks had stopped lending to each other because risky CDOs and credit default swaps (CDSs) had made it impossible to assess the strength of other financial institutions and no one wanted to make a loan that wouldn't be repaid. But the banks' new fear of risk wasn't confined to financial industry borrowers. That fear drove the banks from lending to virtually anybody to lending to almost no one, including businesses and consumers. This was an especially dramatic change from the prosperous years preceding the crisis when much of the nation's economic activity was debt financed.

The appropriate government policy goal seemed clear: Get banks to start lending again. The question was, how to do it. As it turned out, answering that question proved to be very difficult. The next several years were characterized by government programs which injected hundreds of billions of dollars into the economy aimed at pulling the nation out of the recession triggered by the crisis. The government declared the recession officially over in June 2009, but that optimistic statement hasn't been supported by observation of the economy. In early 2012, unemployment remained unacceptably high, business was still sluggish, and the federal deficit was enormous. Despite all that, the economy did appear to be on the road to recovery.

So, in the end, the government bailouts and a number of very expensive stimulus programs seem to have worked as the financial system didn't fail and slowly began to struggle back to normalcy. It's important to realize, however, that a number of economists think that we would have been better off in the long run without so much federal intervention.

Why is the Financial Crisis of 2008 a Corporate Governance Issue   It may not be clear to the reader at this point why so many people consider the financial crisis of 2008 a failure of corporate governance. A comparison with the events of 2000 may help.

The market decline and ensuing recession that began with the collapse of Enron and led to the Sarbanes-Oxley Act was clearly brought about by fraud at the top of large corporations. Executives promulgated falsified financial statements that made their companies appear more valuable than they were. That caused investors to bid stock prices up making the executives rich because of stock based compensation (see Examples 5-1 and 5-2 on pages 193–195). But when the fraud was discovered, stock prices fell and ordinary investors lost most of their money.

That was clearly a corporate government problem because the system created an incentive for dishonesty by tying executive wealth to stock prices without providing safeguards for detecting false reporting. Hence the governance system encouraged outright fraud.

The situation was rather different in 2008. Then the governance issue was the encouragement of unethical rather than illegal behavior. The idea is that the system incentivized taking risks (gambling) in ways in which the rewards of winning were enjoyed by one group while the pain of loss fell on another.

For example, suppose a mortgage lender makes a subprime ARM loan to a home buyer who can barely make the payments. The lender knows there's a good chance interest rates will rise and the buyer will default, but by the time that happens the loan will have been sold to a CDO investor and be off the bank's books. Notice that the lender got its fee (reward) when the loan was made and sold, but the pain of the default falls on the homeowner and the CDO investor.

Governance issues in the Crisis of 2008 were **ethical** rather than criminal.

It's important to realize that there's generally nothing illegal about the lender's behavior in our example. All mortgage loans have some chance of defaulting, so the lender always passes some risk into the CDO when it sells the loan. And certainly the home buyer in the example isn't guaranteed to default. So the question is an **ethical** one. Just how much risk is it ok to pass into the CDO without calling an investor's attention to it, especially if you know the CDO investor probably thinks all mortgage loans are safe?

There wasn't a legal answer to that question as the crisis took shape. Nevertheless, the banking/financial system incentivized making increasingly risky loans by separating the rewards and consequences of the loan approval decision. That's a failure of governance because top executives at the lender organization and the investment bank that securitized the loan were focused on short term rewards (commissions and bonuses) that come from making lots of loans and collecting lots of origination fees. And they set up corporate cultures and compensation plans that valued and rewarded only making the loans, not worrying about what happened afterward.

We also call this idea a moral hazard. Consider the moral hazard created by the "too big to fail" idea described in the following box.

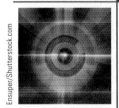

Government bailouts create a moral hazard.

INSIGHTS   Ethics

Government Bailouts as Moral Hazards

A moral hazard exists when people can engage in lopsided gambles (take risks). If they win, they keep the prize, but if they lose, someone else pays. That situation makes it very tempting to gamble in a big way.

Corporate executives gamble with their companies' money by taking on risky projects that include investing in securities like CDOs. Normally, if the projects are successful, the companies prosper and the executives become wealthy. On the other hand, if the projects fail, the companies do poorly and the executives may lose their jobs.

But if the government bails the company out after a risky adventure turns bad, the firm and the decision-making executive just continue on as before—without corporate or personal loss or punishment.

In a bailout, the loss is borne by the government, which means the taxpaying public. In other words, bailouts create situations in which risk takers profit from wins, but don't suffer from losses, which are borne by the public. That encourages executives at "too big to fail" companies to continue to take unreasonable risks.

Should personal ethics limit the risks executive in this position take? Probably, but it doesn't seems to have happened. The Wall Street culture doesn't appear to be moving in that direction, either, as there's a remarkable lack of contrition or remorse being expressed by the authors of the crisis who pocketed billions while it happened.

The Dodd-Frank Act   Once it was generally recognized that the root of the 2008 crisis was in the U.S. financial system, especially the giant "Wall Street" firms, Congress moved to fix the problem with new legislation in much the same way it had acted only a few years earlier in creating SOX. The result was the Dodd-Frank Act—more formally called the Dodd-Frank Wall Street Reform and Consumer Protection Act.

Unfortunately, the financial system behind the 2008 crisis was a great deal more complicated than the scenario faced by Congress in 2002 when it created SOX to regulate corporate fraud. The result is that Dodd-Frank is an extremely complicated act, even by federal government standards. It was signed by the president on July 21, 2010, but few of its provisions were to be implemented immediately. Rather, the implementation was to be phased in over a number of years in accordance with a provision-by-provision schedule. In addition, the Act requires that various federal agencies make up sets of rules governing conduct on over 240 issues and complete more than 65 separate studies to evaluate the impact of the Act's provisions.

Here are a few of Dodd-Frank's major goals:

End too big to fail protection for financial institutions; i.e., no more bailouts.

Provide advance warning when institutions begin to present systematic risks.

Provide an orderly procedure for winding down failing financial firms.

Create an independent Consumer Financial Protection Bureau to examine and regulate banks and credit unions.

Create a financial stability oversight council to identify firms that may become systematically important.

Break up certain existing financial companies that are too large.

Limit certain securities trading practices of banks using their own money.

Require mortgage lenders to ensure that borrowers have the ability to make payments.

Establish penalties for irresponsible lending.

Create an office of credit ratings to ensure that rating agencies are unbiased.

Give shareholders a say (nonbinding) on executive compensation.

Create the Federal Insurance Office to monitor the insurance industry on a federal level.

Regulate securitization (mortgages) by requiring the issuers to retain 5% of the risk.

Obviously, the Dodd-Frank Act has set a very ambitious agenda for itself.

> The **financial industry is resisting** the implementation of Dodd-Frank.

In the meantime, the **financial industry** has been vigorously **resisting implementation** of the Act. It has done that through its substantial and well-funded congressional lobby, by instigating movements to repeal the Act and by filling lawsuits against federal agencies to slow implementation down. For example, several financial industry groups sued the U.S. Commodity Futures Trading Commission in December 2011 to block the implementation of a provision that would limit certain trading positions, based on an allegation that the government had not conducted an adequate cost–benefit analysis of the impact of the provision.

As of early 2012, implementation was behind schedule but moving. Although few doubt that some form of Dodd-Frank will eventually be implemented, the degree to which it will achieve its lofty goals is far from certain.

5.4   Interest

Investing in a security implies entrusting money to the organization that issued the security. The issuer uses the money and pays the investor for the use. The payment is called the *return* on the investment and is usually stated in terms of a percentage of the money invested.

The term **interest** is reserved for the return on a debt investment, meaning the investor lends money to the issuer of the security. The primary vehicle for making debt investments is the **bond**. An investor in a bond is making a loan to the issuing company even though we say he or she buys the bond. Every bond has an associated interest rate that is paid to the investor who holds it.

People often talk about *the* interest rate as though there were only one. In fact, there are many rates depending on the nature of the debt and on the characteristics of the borrowers and lenders. The various interest rates tend to move up and down more or less together. A statement like "the interest rate is moving up" is a reference to an approximate, average level rather than to anything specific.

Debt investments are loans and have **terms**. The term of a loan or a bond is the time from the present until the obligation must be repaid. A bond is said to *mature* at the end of its term on its *maturity date*. The word "maturity" can be synonymous with "term." That is, a bond with a 10-year term can also be said to have a **maturity** of 10 years.

It's important to notice that bonds are *non-amortized* debt. An amortized debt is one in which the principal is paid back regularly along with interest over the life of the loan. Consumer credit, such as home mortgages and car loans, is generally amortized debt. Most business and government debt is non-amortized. Borrowers issuing bonds pay interest only, usually semiannually, until the maturity date, and then must repay the entire principal at once.

5.4a   The Relationship Between Interest and the Stock Market

Returns on stock investments and interest rates on debt are related. Investors always have a choice between investing in debt instruments like **bonds** or savings accounts or in equity securities like **stock**. (When you put money into a savings account you're lending it to the bank.) In other words, stocks (equity) and bonds (debt) compete for investors' dollars.

Debt investments are generally safer than stocks, so people prefer them if the expected return on the stock and the interest on the debt are nearly equal. As a result, stocks have to offer higher returns than debt to induce people to invest in equity. As interest rates on debt move up and down over time, the return on stock investments moves up and down as well, usually remaining somewhat above the interest rate on debt.

This movement has a significant effect on the stock market because of the relationship between the return on a stock investment and the price of a share. *A higher return is associated with a lower price.* This should be clear if you think in terms of bargains. Suppose a particular stock is expected to produce a barely acceptable return over the next year. You're thinking of buying some shares, but you aren't quite sure if it's a good deal. Then imagine that the price is suddenly cut in half, while nothing else changes. That makes the stock a much better deal, a bargain. The return it now offers as a percentage of the lower invested price is much higher.

In general, the market changes the return on a share of stock by changing its price, so if stock returns move up, prices move down, and if returns move down, prices move up. We'll understand this idea much better when we study the material in Chapter 8. For now the basic principle is what's important: **Stock prices and returns move in opposite directions**.

Margin notes:

Bonds are the primary vehicle for making debt investments.

A debt's **term** or **maturity** is the time until it must be repaid.

Stocks (equity) and **bonds** (debt) **compete** for investors' dollars. Stocks offer higher returns but have **more risk**.

Interest rates and security prices **move in opposite directions**.

But remember what we just said about returns and interest rates. Changes in the overall level of stock returns are driven by changes in interest rates on debt investments. That means the general price level of the stock market is driven up and down by changes in interest rates on debt. As interest rates go up, stock prices go down, and as rates go down, prices go up.

That's a very good reason for us to be familiar with the inner workings of interest rates! Interest isn't the only thing that affects the general price level of stocks, but it's very important and more predictable than other influences.

5.4b   Interest and the Economy

The interest rate has a significant effect on the economy in general. High interest rates tend to stifle economic activity, while low rates tend to promote it. That's because both in business and in our personal lives a lot is done on credit.

Consider a family interested in buying a new home. If interest rates are high, their mortgage payments will be high and they may not be able to afford the house they want. Lower interest rates mean lower payments, so houses become more affordable in general and the family is more likely to buy.

When interest rates are low, people buy more houses, cars, refrigerators, and just about everything else. Because someone has to manufacture those products, more sales lead to more jobs and a healthier economy.

The same idea applies to business. Companies often use borrowed money to buy new equipment and undertake new projects. When interest rates are high, borrowing is expensive, and not many projects look good because they don't earn enough to cover their interest cost. When rates are low, more projects are viable and are undertaken. The increased activity in turn leads to a healthier economy.

All this causes the financial community to be very interested in interest rates, and gives us good reason to examine exactly what's in an interest rate and how rates are determined.

Lower interest rates stimulate business and economic activity.

5.4c   Debt Markets

Interest rates are set by the forces of supply and demand in debt markets. To understand how these forces work, we need to review an analytic tool from economics—the supply and demand diagram.

Supply and Demand—A Brief Review   A demand curve is a graph relating price and quantity in the market for a product or service. It reflects the desires and abilities of buyers at a particular point in time. The graph's vertical axis represents price and its horizontal axis indicates the quantity purchased in a period. Figure 5-8 shows a demand curve labeled D.

Virtually all demand curves slope downward to the right. That simply means people will buy more of the product if the price is low and less if it's high.

A supply curve relates prices with quantities supplied by producers. The curve is upsloping, indicating that suppliers are willing to produce and sell more product at higher prices than at lower prices. The supply curve is labeled S in Figure 5-8.

Drawing both curves on the same set of axes shows that there's only one point at which both buyers and sellers are happy: the intersection of the two curves.

FIGURE 5-8 Supply and Demand Curves for a Product or Service

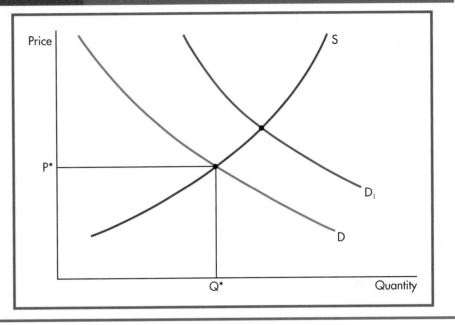

The market tends to operate at that point, and we say it is in equilibrium there. These ideas are depicted in Figure 5-8 where the equilibrium price and quantity are represented by P* and Q*, respectively.

If the conditions of supply or demand change, the curves shift their positions and the market sets a new equilibrium price. Suppose, for example, buyers' preferences change so that they generally want more of the product at any price. Such a change is reflected in the diagram as a shift to the right of the demand curve to D_1. If supply doesn't change at the same time, the new equilibrium point will be higher along the supply curve, resulting in a higher P* and Q*.

> In debt markets **lenders represent supply** and **borrowers represent demand**.

Supply and Demand for Money   In the market for debt, people are borrowing and lending money rather than buying and selling a commodity. Instead of buyers, we have borrowers, and instead of sellers, we have lenders. It's important to understand that point. The supply curve in a debt market represents the willingness of people to lend money, and the demand curve represents people's (companies') desire to borrow.

In the diagram for a debt market, the horizontal (quantity) axis is the amount borrowed in a time period. The vertical axis is the price of borrowing. *That price is interest.* You can think of borrowing as renting a lender's money for a period of time, and interest as the rent payment. It's customary to express this price of borrowing as the percentage of principal required for a one-year rental. That's simply the annual interest rate with which we're all familiar.

> Interest is the **price** of money in a debt market.

A supply and demand graph for a debt market is shown in Figure 5-9. The letter k is used to represent the interest rate. The debt securities in this market are called *bills, notes,* and *bonds,* depending on their term when initially issued. For convenience we'll just refer to them all as bonds.

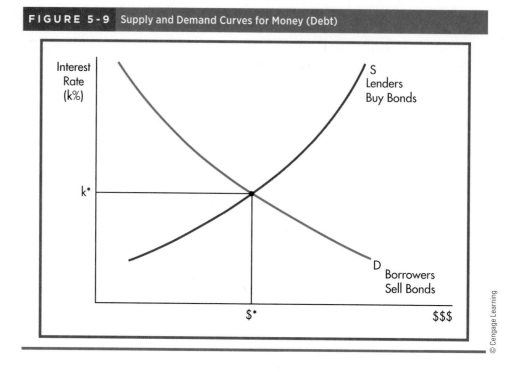

FIGURE 5-9 Supply and Demand Curves for Money (Debt)

© Cengage Learning

Borrowers **sell** bonds
Lenders **buy** bonds.

Borrowers are companies and the government. They **sell** bonds. The downsloping demand curve indicates that they will borrow more (sell more bonds) if interest rates are low. Lenders are individuals and organizations that **buy** bonds. The upsloping supply curve indicates that they are willing to lend more (buy more bonds) when interest rates are high.

Don't be confused by the reversal of the traditional buy and sell roles in the market for debt. In the traditional supply and demand curve depicted in Figure 5-8, demanders do the buying and suppliers do the selling. Here demanders sell (borrow), while suppliers buy (lend). The reversal is just a result of the peculiar terminology of finance in which buying a bond means lending money.

The Determinants of Supply and Demand   When we described the supply and demand picture for a product or service, we said that changes in conditions cause the curves to slide back and forth. The same is true in debt markets.

The demand for borrowed funds depends on the opportunities available to use those funds and the attitudes of people and businesses about doing things on credit. If people feel good about the economy and their futures, they'll be willing to buy houses, cars, vacations, and other things with borrowed money. Similarly, businesses will borrow for expansion and new projects if demand for their products is strong and they have confidence in the future. If these conditions aren't met, they'll borrow only what they have to.

The supply of loanable funds ultimately depends on what economists call the time preference for consumption of individuals. The time preference for consumption refers to whether a person is inclined to spend a dollar of income on current consumption or invest it to grow into something more. Most people have a definite preference for current consumption and spend most of their income as it's earned, saving only a fraction.

Remember that money saved by individuals becomes available for borrowing when people invest their savings in debt securities and savings accounts. So people's time preference for consumption dictates the level of their savings and therefore the supply of loanable funds. A decrease in the preference for current consumption, for example, leads to increased savings and an increase in the supply of debt. This is reflected in a rightward shift in the supply curve in Figure 5-9.

Changes in these conditions occur constantly throughout the economy, causing the supply and demand curves for borrowed money to slide back and forth over time. As a result, the market interest rate is moving up or down most of the time.

For most of the twentieth century, movement was modest. The rates stayed at relatively low levels, about 3% to 6% until the early 1970s, when the fluctuation became much more dramatic. In the early 1980s, some rates exceeded 20%. In the 1990s and 2000s, rates have again been low and stable. The ability to forecast interest rates would clearly be very valuable, but as yet no one has been able to do it with any consistency.

5.5   The Components of an Interest Rate

Any interest rate can be broken into two pieces, each of which can be further subdivided into components. Let's look at the two major pieces first.

> Interest rates include **base rates** and **risk premiums**.

All rates can be thought of as the sum of a **base rate** and a **premium for risk** borne by the lender. We'll represent the interest rate by the letter k, so we can write

$$(5.1) \qquad \textbf{k = base rate + risk premium}$$

5.5a   Components of the Base Rate

> The base rate is **pure interest** plus **expected inflation**.

The base rate is the rate at which people lend money when there's no risk involved in the loan. It has two components, the **pure interest rate** and the **expected rate of inflation** over the life of the loan. The pure interest rate is also called the *earning power of money.* We'll use the symbols k_{PR} to denote that idea and INFL to represent expected inflation. Then we can write

$$(5.2) \qquad \textbf{base rate} = \textbf{k}_{\textbf{PR}} + \textbf{INFL}$$

> The **pure interest rate** is the **earning power of money**.

The Pure Interest Rate   The pure interest rate is more of an abstract concept than anything observable in the real world. It's the rate that would exist in a perfect economy in which there is no inflation, securities can always be sold quickly for their full value, and people always live up to their promises.

In another sense, you can think of the pure rate as the average return that can be earned with money available for investment in business. Again the idea is unadjusted for inflation or risk. This is the sense in which we call the **pure rate** the basic **earning power of money.**

The pure rate can be thought of as compensation to lenders for the loss of the productive power of their money. It's generally taken to be between 2% and 4%.

The Inflation Adjustment   Inflation refers to a general increase in prices. We usually assume that the increase is uniform over all prices and wages, although in reality some things inflate faster than others.

The key notion behind the idea of inflation is the cost of a particular bundle of goods. If the bundle costs $100 at the beginning of a year and prices inflate by 5% during the year, the same bundle will cost $105 at year end. In other words, $100 won't buy as much at the end of the year as it did in the beginning. Money will have lost some of its value.

Now imagine that you loaned someone $100 at 5% interest during a year in which the inflation rate was also 5%. Assume the loan is successfully paid off with interest so you have $105 at year end. Are you any better off than you were at the beginning of the year? The answer, of course, is no, because your year-end $105 won't buy any more than $100 bought before you made the loan. To come out ahead, you have to charge an interest rate that *exceeds* the inflation rate.

In fact, that's exactly what lenders do. Interest rates always include the anticipated inflation rate over the loan period as an add-on to the pure rate. That addition is reflected in the formulation of Equation 5.2. INFL in the equation can be thought of as an inflation adjustment equal to the **average inflation rate** anticipated over the life of the loan.

> Interest rates include **estimates of average annual inflation** over loan periods.

5.5b   Risk Premiums

Risk in lending refers to the chance that a lender will receive less than the full value of the principal advanced plus the agreed interest in return for making a loan. In general, loans have varying degrees of risk. Some are very secure, so the chance of not being fully repaid is virtually zero. Others involve a substantial possibility that the lender will receive less than he or she bargained for.

Most lenders are willing to make loans that involve risk. However, they always demand compensation for bearing higher levels of risk. That simply means they want to be paid more for making a risky loan than for making a safe one. Because the payment lenders receive is interest, they demand more of it in the form of higher rates when making riskier loans.

The difference between the interest rate charged on a given loan and the rate charged on a zero-risk loan is called the loan's **risk premium**. This idea is expressed in Equation 5.1 where the base rate is implied to have zero risk.

> Lenders demand a **risk premium** of extra interest for making risky loans.

Different Kinds of Lending Risk   We'll think of business loans as typically being made through bond issues. In that context, lenders face risks that come from several sources. The simplest to understand is default, which occurs when a borrower doesn't repay the obligation. Other risks are associated with bond prices.

When people lend by buying bonds, they generally terminate their investments long before the bonds mature by selling them to other investors. This involves risk because the price at the time of sale may be different from the amount the investor paid for the bond. If the price is lower, selling will cause a loss. The situation is especially difficult if the lender has an immediate need for funds and has to get out of the investment quickly at whatever price is available.

The important point is that bond lending losses can be associated with fluctuations in the prices of bonds as well as with the failure of borrowers to repay the loans. In what follows, we'll describe three sources of risk and formulate a distinct risk premium for each. The sum of these premiums will be the overall risk premium in Equation 5.1. The three sources of risk are *default, liquidity,* and *maturity.*

Default risk is the chance the borrower won't pay principal or interest.

Default Risk

Default Risk   **Default risk** represents the chance that the borrower won't repay the entire obligation consisting of principal and interest. Losses due to default can be anywhere from the entire amount loaned to a fraction of the interest due. It's important to keep in mind that default isn't solely associated with failure to repay principal at the end of a loan's term. A borrower can default at any time by failing to pay periodic interest.

The size of the *default risk premium* demanded by lenders depends on their perception of the creditworthiness of the borrowing company. That perception is based on the firm's financial condition and its record of paying off its debts in the past. Premiums range from 0% to 6 or 8%. It's important to realize that default premiums don't increase without limit. When a company gets too risky it simply becomes unable to borrow at any interest rate.

Default most commonly occurs when business conditions deteriorate and borrowers don't have funds to service their debt. This doesn't always result in failure or a major loss. Temporarily delayed interest payments are fairly common when companies are in trouble.

Default doesn't actually have to occur for related problems to exist. Suppose a company borrows money through a bond issue and subsequently gets into financial trouble. Assume the loan principal isn't due and the firm continues to make the required interest payments, but financial analysts can tell that each payment is a close call. In other words, the company isn't in default, but its continuing ability to avoid default is in question. New investors would be very reluctant to buy the firm's bonds at full price. To sell, an individual holding such a bond would probably have to reduce its price to get out of the investment.

A time dimension is also involved in the risk of default. Suppose a large, strong company issues a one-year debt instrument. Investors considering the issue won't be concerned about default because a serious deterioration in the firm's financial condition is unlikely to occur in only one year. However, if the issue is a long-term bond, investors will be somewhat concerned because even the strongest companies can get into trouble over a long period.

This kind of thinking indicates that for strong companies, the default risk premium is very small for short-term debt but is significant for longer issues.

Liquidity Risk

Liquidity Risk   Some companies' bonds are more difficult to sell than others even if there's nothing wrong with them. The debt of small firms that are not widely known can be particularly hard to market, because only investors who know the firm or its management will be interested in buying. Such bonds are said to be *illiquid.* The sellers must reduce their prices enough to interest buyers with no previous knowledge of the company. That's likely to mean taking a loss.

Liquidity risk refers to the chance of incurring that kind of loss, and the *liquidity risk premium* is extra interest demanded by lenders as compensation for bearing it.

Liquidity risk is somewhat variable with the term of the security. Very short-term obligations don't generally involve much liquidity risk, because a lender in need of funds can just wait out the period until maturity.

Maturity Risk   The primary reason for changes in bond prices is movement in the interest rate in the debt market. It is a fundamental principle of finance and economics that bond prices and interest rates move in opposite directions. We made a similar statement about stocks earlier, but the relation is more precise and predictable for bonds than for stocks.

At this point in our study, we haven't developed enough knowledge to understand why this relationship between prices and interest rates occurs and exactly how it works. We'll gain a full understanding of the phenomenon when we study Chapter 7. For now we have to accept two things. The first is what we've already said, that prices and rates move against each other. The second is that the price change associated with a given interest rate change is larger for bonds with a longer maturity (time to go until they are due to be repaid) than for bonds with a shorter maturity.

Let's be very clear about that second point. If a bond is due to mature in a short time, a change in the interest rate will have a small effect on its value. On the other hand, if the principal isn't to be repaid for many years, the same interest rate change will have a significant effect on the bond's value. The longer the maturity, the bigger the price change.

Price changes due to interest rate fluctuations are another source of risk for lenders who invest in bonds. If interest rates increase after an investor purchases a bond, its price will decline and the investor will take a loss if he or she has to get out of the investment quickly. If the bond's term is short, the loss is small and can almost be ignored. But if the security has a long maturity, the loss can be significant.

This means longer-term bonds are riskier for investors than shorter-term bonds. We call this idea **maturity risk** because it varies with the term or maturity of the bond. Investors demand a *maturity risk premium,* which ranges from virtually nothing for short-term instruments to 2% or more for longer-term issues. Slight variations on this idea are called **price risk** and **interest rate risk**.

It's important to notice that the loss we're talking about here doesn't occur if the investor holds the bond to maturity. It only happens if he or she has to sell early at a depressed price.

5.5c   Putting the Pieces Together

We can now rewrite Equation 5.1, substituting the elements we've discussed for the base rate and the risk premium.

(5.3) $$k = k_{PR} + INFL + DR + LR + MR$$

where

k_{PR} = pure interest rate

INFL = inflation adjustment (the average expected inflation rate over the life of the loan)

DR = default risk premium

LR = liquidity risk premium

MR = maturity risk premium

This important equation says that an interest rate generally consists of the pure earning power of money, plus an allowance for inflation, plus an adjustment for each of three identifiable sources of risk.

We'll call Equation 5.3 the **interest rate model**, meaning that it's an abstract portrayal of how interest rates work.

People often refer to k on the left side of the equation as the *nominal* or *quoted* interest rate. It's the market rate that we've been talking about all along.

Setting Interest Rates   It's important to understand that Equation 5.3 represents a theoretical construct. People don't actually sit around thinking up how much each of the elements should be and then add them to come up with a rate to charge on a loan. Rates are set by the forces of supply and demand. If a particular lender doesn't feel the going rate is high enough, he or she simply doesn't invest.

The equation is an economic *model* of reality, an *explanation* of what generally has to be behind the interest rate, given the needs of investors. However, like most economic models, it sometimes doesn't seem to be consistent with reality.

For example, at times a reasonable estimate of the pure rate plus the current inflation rate equals or exceeds the prevailing interest rate in some markets. That means the risk premiums in those markets must be zero or negative, which doesn't make a lot of sense.

The model is a way of thinking, a tool to aid our understanding. Occasionally things happen in the real world that aren't included in the model, and during those periods it doesn't quite work. But that's not a reason to condemn it as valueless.

5.5d   Federal Government Securities, Risk-Free and Real Rates

The interest rate model represented by Equation 5.3 enables us to understand three special situations that are important in practical finance. We'll consider each in turn.

Federal Government Securities   Governmental bodies at all levels issue debt securities that are similar to those issued by companies. Cities, states, and the federal government issue long-term bonds, but the federal Treasury also issues a great many short-term securities. Treasury bills have terms from 90 days to a year, while notes mature in 1 to 10 years.[17] The interest rate model, Equation 5.3, can be applied to government debt as well as to corporate debt securities.

However, federal government debt has an important characteristic that isn't shared by anyone else's debt: There's no default risk associated with federal government debt. Therefore, the default risk premium in Equation 5.3 is zero when the model is applied to Treasury securities.

It's tempting to think that the reason behind this confidence on the part of the investors is a belief that there will always be a federal government. (If there isn't, we

---

17. The securities of the federal government are called *Treasury* securities.

won't be worried about money and interest rates anyway!) But the reason is more subtle. For example, as long as there's a federal government, we'd expect state governments to exist. Yet state default risks and the associated premiums are definitely not zero. Think about this for a moment before reading on. Can you figure out why the federal government can never default on a loan?

The answer lies in a power that the federal Treasury keeps to itself. It can print money! No one else can. The federal government could pay off all of its debt by simply printing huge stacks of money. It doesn't do so because such an action would create a massive inflation that would disrupt the economy, but the capability is always there. As a result, there's no chance of federal default.

As a practical matter, liquidity risk is also zero for federal debt. That's because there's always an active market in the federal government's obligations. The chance of being unable to sell a federal bond, note, or bill at the going price is very small. That statement definitely cannot be made for the securities of lower governmental units. In fact, a major problem with the obligations of local governments (cities, counties, etc.) is that they are often illiquid.

Maturity risk is not zero for government securities. It's the same as it is for any other borrower.

> **Treasury (federal government)** securities are default and liquidity **risk free**.

The Risk-Free Rate

The foregoing ideas give rise to the notion of a risk-free interest rate. This rate includes the pure rate and an allowance for inflation, but nothing for any of the risks we've been talking about.

Noting that government debt has no default or liquidity risk, and that maturity risk is insignificantly small for short-term debt, we can surmise that short-term Treasury securities are essentially risk free. In fact, people generally take the 90-day Treasury bill rate to be the current **risk-free rate**.

Notice that the risk-free rate is the same as the base rate we used to introduce the idea of the components of interest (see Equation 5.1 and Equation 5.2). All interest rates are essentially the risk-free rate plus premiums for various risks.

The risk-free rate is an important idea in financial theory. It provides an alternative place for investors to put their money that's always available. In other words, if investors don't like the general opportunities available in debt markets, they can always park their money in short-term government securities until something more attractive comes along. It can also be viewed as a conceptual floor for the structure of interest rates. If investors can always get the risk-free rate without bearing risk, no investment that does have risk can offer a lower rate. When we encounter the risk-free rate, we'll denote it as k_{RF}.

> The **risk-free rate** is approximately the yield on short-term Treasury bills.

The Real Rate of Interest

In economics the term *real* refers to figures and statistics that are adjusted to remove the effects of inflation. The **real interest rate** is the rate that currently exists less the inflation adjustment. In terms of Equation 5.3, INFL is zero.

The real interest rate tells investors if they're actually getting ahead. Suppose, for example, you invest some money in a long-term security at 8% interest. Several years later, you discover that the inflation rate has risen to 10%, and you're actually losing purchasing power on your investment at a rate of 2% per year.

This situation hasn't been unusual in the last 40 years. For that reason, people have become reluctant to make long-term commitments at lower market rates. The

> **Real interest rates** have no adjustment for inflation.

solution has often been to make long-term contracts at variable interest rates that move up and down as the inflation rate and the nominal interest rate change.

There are also occasional periods in which the real interest rate is negative on most investment opportunities. That can happen because we don't really know what the rate of inflation is at a point in time until the government statistics come out several months later. If inflation rises rapidly while supply and demand forces push interest rates down, the actual interest rate can wind up below the inflation rate for some period. Obviously, when that happens the model expressed in Equation 5.3 isn't working very well.

The Real Risk-Free Rate   Putting the last two concepts together results in the idea of a real risk-free rate, a term that is sometimes used in financial circles. "Real" implies the inflation adjustment is zero, and "risk-free" implies that all the risk premiums are also zero.

Looking at the interest rate model, we can immediately see that the real risk-free rate is conceptually identical to the pure interest rate, k_{PR}.

CONCEPT CONNECTION   EXAMPLE 5-3

Using the Interest Rate Model

Sunshine Inc. is planning to borrow money to support a three-year project by issuing bonds (notes) of the same term. The following information is available.

1. The pure interest rate is 2.0%.

2. Inflation will be 3% next year and 4% for several years thereafter.

3. Sunshine's debt generally carries a default risk premium of 1.5%.

4. The firm is fairly well known and carries a liquidity risk premium of .5%.

5. Maturity risk premiums on three-year debt have been about 1.0% lately.

    a. Estimate the interest rate Sunshine will have to offer to sell the bonds (k_s). Round to the nearest tenth of a percent.

    b. Moonlight Ltd., a competitor of about the same size and reputation, recently issued three-year debt paying 11%. What does the interest rate model imply about the investment community's perception of Moonlight's risk relative to Sunshine's?

SOLUTION:

    a. First calculate INFL as the average inflation rate over the life of the loan.

$$INFL = (3 + 4 + 4)/3 = 11/3 = 3.67 = 3.7$$

Then write the interest rate model and substitute for k_s.

$$k_S = k_{PR} + INFL + DR + LR + MR$$
$$= 2.0 + 3.7 + 1.5 + .5 + 1.0$$
$$= 8.7\%$$

b. Write the interest rate model for Moonlight treating DR as an unknown, then substitute, and solve for DR.

$$k_M = k_{PR} + INFL + DR + LR + MR$$
$$11.0 = 2.0 + 3.7 + DR + .5 + 1.0$$
$$DR = 3.8$$

The debt market seems to be assigning Moonlight a default risk premium of 3.8%, which is (3.8/1.5 =) 2.5 times as large as Sunshine's. The implication is that Moonlight is considered quite a bit more risky. It's important to understand, however, that the risk measure implied by DR is not numerically precise, so we can't say that Moonlight is 2 ½ times as risky as Sunshine. We'll learn how the financial world measures risk numerically in Chapter 9.

Next we'll consider a problem in which we'll use the interest rate model to estimate rates for a number of bond terms with variable assumptions about the model's components.

CONCEPT CONNECTION   EXAMPLE 5-4

Using the Interest Rate Model over a Range of Terms

You're a junior analyst in the treasury department of the Bullwork Company. The treasurer is contemplating raising money for a new plant expansion by issuing debt securities, but is unsure of the interest rates the company might have to pay. He has asked you to estimate the interest cost of issues with maturities ranging from 1 to 10 years.

You are aware that rates are actually set by supply and demand forces in the debt market, but feel the interest rate model (Equation 5.3) will provide some reasonable estimates under normal conditions. The following assumptions seem to provide a reasonable starting point.

a. The pure rate of interest is 3%.

b. Inflation is expected to rise in the near future and then subside. Your favorite economist projects the following pattern.

Year	Inflation Rate
1	4%
2	6
3	8
4	6
5–10	5

c. The default risk premium will be zero for one-year debt, but it will increase .2% for each additional year of term to a maximum of 1%.

d. The liquidity premium is zero for one- and two-year debt and .5% for longer issues.

e. The maturity risk premium is zero for a one-year term and increases by .3% for each additional year of term to a maximum of 2.5%.

Prepare a table showing the projected interest rate for loans of various terms and the components of each rate.

SOLUTION:

First we'll calculate the inflation adjustment for securities having terms from 1 to 10 years. That involves taking the average inflation rate over the entire projected term. To calculate the figures in the third column, average the figures on that line and above in the second column. For example, INFL for five years is the average of 4, 6, 8, 6, and 5.

Year	Inflation Rate	Inflation Adjustment
1	4.0%	4.0%
2	6.0	5.0
3	8.0	6.0
4	6.0	6.0
5	5.0	5.8
6	5.0	5.7
7	5.0	5.6
8	5.0	5.5
9	5.0	5.4
10	5.0	5.4

Next we'll create a table with a column for each of the elements of the model and fill in each column according to the assumed behavior of the factor including the INFL we've just calculated. The estimated interest rate is simply the sum of each row across the columns.

Term	k_{PR}	+	INFL	+	DR	+	LR	+	MR	=	k
1	3.0		4.0		0.0		0.0		0.0		7.0%
2	3.0		5.0		0.2		0.0		0.3		8.5
3	3.0		6.0		0.4		0.5		0.6		10.5
4	3.0		6.0		0.6		0.5		0.9		11.0
5	3.0		5.8		0.8		0.5		1.2		11.3
6	3.0		5.7		1.0		0.5		1.5		11.7
7	3.0		5.6		1.0		0.5		1.8		11.9
8	3.0		5.5		1.0		0.5		2.1		12.1
9	3.0		5.4		1.0		0.5		2.4		12.3
10	3.0		5.4		1.0		0.5		2.5		12.4

Notice that the interest rate is higher for longer-term loans. That's normal, although sometimes the reverse is true. In this case, the rising rate can be traced to the action of the risk factors. Each increases with increasing term for its own reason. The inflation factor has an unusual impact in this instance. It first rises and then falls away as the projected annual rates of inflation rise and then subside to a constant level.

5.5e   Yield Curves—The Term Structure of Interest Rates

As the example in the last section illustrates, interest rates generally vary with the term of the debt. The relationship is known as the *term structure of interest rates.*

A graphic portrayal of the term structure is known as a **yield curve. Yield** is simply another term for return or interest. Figure 5-10 shows two yield curves of different shapes.

Most of the time short-term rates are lower than long-term rates and the yield curve is upsloping to the right. This is called a *normal* yield curve because it is the most common. Sometimes, however, long rates are lower than short rates and the curve slopes downward. That's called an *inverted* yield curve.

A great deal of thought has gone into trying to explain the forces that drive the yield curve to take a particular shape. That is, why should long and short rates differ in either direction? Three explanations have emerged, all of which have some appeal.

The Expectations Theory   The **expectations theory** says that the curve slopes up or down on the basis of people's expectations about the general level of future interest rates. For example, suppose on a given day all interest rates are a uniform 5% regardless of term, and everyone expects them to stay there indefinitely. That means the yield curve is flat at 5%. Then imagine something happens to cause everyone to believe interest rates will increase to 10%, but only after remaining at 5% for two more years. Put yourself in the place of a lender under these conditions. You'd be willing to make a loan of up to two years at 5%, because that would be the prevailing rate during that entire period. But would you make a three-year loan at 5%? Clearly you wouldn't, because in the third year you'd be stuck earning 5% on your money while everyone else is making 10%.

> The **yield curve** plots interest against term for otherwise similar loans. The **normal curve** slopes upward reflecting higher rates on longer loans.

> **Expectations theory**: Today's rates rise or fall with term as future rates are expected to rise or fall.

FIGURE 5-10   Yield Curves

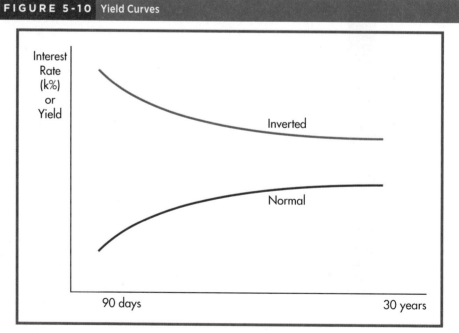

However, you might be willing to make the loan at a rate that reflects an average of two years at 5% and one year at 10%, [(5 + 5 + 10)/3 =] 6.67%. That way your overall yield would be the same as it would be if you'd made three one-year loans.

What if someone wanted to borrow for four years? You'd want a rate that averaged two 5% years and two 10% years for 7.5%. Notice that the average rate is increasing as the term of the loans increases and we get more 10% years into the calculation. That increase is the essence of an upward-sloping normal yield curve.

A variation on the expectations theory says that the shape of the curve depends on people's expectations about inflation. But because the inflation rate is a large part of the interest rate (see Equation 5.3), expectations of increasing inflation are essentially equivalent to expectations of an increasing interest rate.

The Liquidity Preference Theory   The **liquidity preference theory** says that the yield curve should be upward-sloping because lenders generally prefer short-term loans. They're more liquid, making it easier to get invested cash back if you have to. As a result of that preference, there has to be an additional interest inducement to lend long term. Hence, long rates will usually be higher, and the normal yield curve slopes up.

This argument involves two of the ideas we discussed in the development of the interest rate model of Equation 5.3. One is the liquidity risk concept, that short-term loans are better for lenders because people can wait for maturity rather than selling their bonds. The second is the maturity risk idea, that short bonds are better for bond-holders (lenders) because they are less subject to price variation due to interest rate movement. That makes them less risky and perhaps easier to sell.

In a nutshell, liquidity preference means that investors like short-term securities because they're easier to get out of in a hurry. Therefore, longer-term securities have to offer higher rates to attract buyers (lenders).

> **Liquidity preference theory:** Investors prefer shorter-term securities and must be induced to make longer loans.

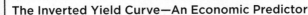

INSIGHTS | Practical Finance

The Inverted Yield Curve—An Economic Predictor

The yield curve inverts only rarely, but when it does, it's usually a signal that a recession or an economic slowdown is ahead. Economists agree that an inverted yield curve isn't a perfect predictor of a weakening economy, but history indicates that it's a fairly good one. There have been nine inversions in the last 58 years and seven of them were followed by downturns, the last beginning in 2007–8. That's a success rate of about 78% which is pretty good for economic indicators. Inversions are defined by comparing the yields on three-month Treasury bills and 10-year Treasury notes. If the 10-year rate is lower, the yield curve is said to be inverted. To count, the inversion has to last for at least a few months.

So why should an inverted yield curve signal trouble? One line of reasoning is based on expectations about interest rates. If bond investors think rates are generally going down, they often lock in the higher rates available before the decline by buying long-term bonds. If enough investors do that, the prices of long-term of long-term bonds are driven up, lowering their yields. (Recall that bond yields and prices move in opposite directions.)

Another rationale is that lower rates are associated with economic downturns because that's when the Federal Reserve puts downward pressure on interest rates to stimulate the economy. Hence, an expectation of lower rates due to government pressure is associated with the end of a boom and the beginning of a slowdown.

The economy began to flirt with a mildly inverted yield curve in 2005 and early 2006. But that inversion wasn't very deep, so many just dismissed it at the time. What's more, there wasn't much of anything else to indicate that a slowdown was coming. In fact, the economy was enjoying an unusually long period of sustained, stable growth at that time.

Economists were definitely puzzled—enough so that a number of articles appeared in financial publications wondering if some fundamental economic change had stripped the yield curve of its predictive power. But then the curve inverted again in July of 2006 and stayed that way into 2007. And we all know what happened then—the financial crisis of 2007-8 which was followed by the worst economic downturn in 75 years.

So it looks like the yield curve was right again, even though it isn't easy to understand why. The factors behind the crisis/recession of 2008 and beyond were unprecedented and largely unexpected before 2007. So was the on again–off again inversion of 2005 through early 2007 truly related to the troubles ahead? If so, how? It's almost spooky, isn't it? Here's a little history to wonder about.

Inversion Period	Recession Date
July 2000–January 2001	March 2001
May 1989–August 1989	July 1990
October 1980–September 1981	July 1981
November 1978–May 1980	January 1980
June 1973–November 1974	November 1973
December 1968–February 1970	December 1969

The Inverted Yield Curve and Banks

An inverted yield curve's effect on banks and banking stocks is more certain. Banks' primary source of income comes from borrowing at low rates and lending the borrowed money at higher rates. That generally means borrowing short term by taking in savings deposits and certificates of deposit (CDs). (These are short term loans to banks because savings deposits can be withdrawn on demand, and CDs typically have terms that vary from six months to a few years.) Banks then make long-term loans to individuals and businesses that can last up to 30 years.

This works fine under a normal yield curve when short rates are substantially below longer rates. But when the yield curve inverts and short rates are higher than long rates, this basic source of banking income evaporates, and industry earnings take a dive. That, of course, drives investors away and banking stock prices fall.

SOURCES: Michael Hudson, "Grading Bonds on Inverted Curve," *The Wall Street Journal* (January 8, 2007); Scott Patterson, "Uncertainty Is Certain Next Year," *The Wall Street Journal* (December 12, 2005); Clint Riley, "Investors Puzzle: Banks and Flat Yield Curve," *The Wall Street Journal* (January 30, 2006); Mark Whitehouse, "Yields on Bonds Invert Reflecting Unease About Economy's Future," *The Wall Street Journal* (December 28, 2005); Mark Whitehouse, "Economists Ask If Bonds Have Lost Their Predictive Power," *The Wall Street Journal* (December 29, 2005).

Market segmentation theory: Loan terms define independent segments of the debt market, which set separate rates.

The Market Segmentation Theory

The **market segmentation theory** goes back to the forces of supply and demand in the market for debt pictured in Figure 5-9. It says that the debt market isn't represented by a single set of supply and demand curves, but by many sets, each representing a separate market for money of a specific term.

When people are interested in borrowing money, they have a definite term in mind that is based on the use they intend to make of the funds. For example, a company interested in building a factory wouldn't want to fund it by borrowing for 90 days; it would be in the market for a very long-term loan. If it couldn't get that, it wouldn't want any loan at all.

Lenders operate similarly. They want to commit their funds for a definite period of time at a known yield. If they have long-term money available, they don't want short-term borrowers.

This results in a debt market that's *segmented* by term. Each segment has its own supply and demand picture with an independent set of forces pushing the curves back and forth. That means the market interest rate in each segment is independently determined, and not related to the market rate in other segments.

This independence leads to a pattern of rates that just happens. Most of the time market forces are such that short rates are lower than long rates and the yield curve takes its normal upward-sloping shape. However, at times independent market forces push short rates higher and the yield curve slopes down.

CONCEPT CONNECTIONS

EXAMPLE 5-1 Executive Stock Options, *page 193*

EXAMPLE 5-2 A Moral Hazard for Founders, *page 195*

EXAMPLE 5-3 Using the Interest Rate Model, *page 219*

EXAMPLE 5-4 Using the Interest Rate Model over a Range of Terms, *page 220*

QUESTIONS

1. Describe the sectors into which economists divide an industrialized economy and outline the financial flows between them.

2. What do we mean when we say businesses spend two kinds of money? Where does each kind come from? How is each used?

3. What is the primary purpose of financial markets?

4. Define the following terms: primary market, secondary market, capital market, and money market.

5. What's the difference between a direct and an indirect transfer of money between investors and firms?

6. Your friend Sally just returned from a trip to New York where she was very impressed by a visit to the stock market. Is it correct to say that she visited the stock market? What exactly did Sally visit? Is there more than one place in New York that she might have visited? Explain exactly what the stock market is and how it's related to what Sally visited.

7. Describe the process that occurs when an investor places an order with a broker to buy or sell stocks under the market maker/specialist system.

8. Your friend Charlie is excited about a newly issued stock. You've looked at the company's prospectus and feel it's a very risky venture. You told Charlie your opinion, and he said he wasn't worried because the stock has been approved by the SEC and therefore must be OK. Write a paragraph to help Charlie out. What is the main thrust of federal securities regulation?

9. Describe insider trading. Why is it illegal?

10. Explain the following terms: privately held company, publicly traded company, listed company, OTCBB, Nasdaq, IPO, prospectus, and red herring.

11. Define term and maturity. Is there a difference?

12. Corporate executives sometimes abuse their positions by overpaying themselves at the expense of stockholders. When that happens, are the executives' gains dollar-for-dollar losses to stockholders or can investors lose more or less than the amounts by which the executives profit? Explain thoroughly.

13. Why does stock-based compensation create a moral hazard for executives?

14. Describe the primary conflict of interest that caused the public accounting industry to fail in its duty to protect the investing public's interests in the 1990s.

15. Why did securities analysts issue biased reports in the 1990s? In what direction were the reports biased?

16. List the traditional qualifications for a mortgage loan and describe how each protects the lender.

17. What bank problems does securitization solve?

18. What is a *tranche* and how was its risk estimated before the crisis?

19. What factors are likely to push the reset payment up in a NegAm loan?

20. Why would a rational borrower take out a NegAm loan?

21. Why did credit default swaps make the crisis worse?

22. What was the trigger that started the crisis? If it hadn't happened, would the crisis have been averted?

23. Interest is said to drive the stock market. But interest is paid on bonds and loans, while stocks pay dividends, never interest. It would seem that interest has nothing to do with the stock market. Explain this apparent contradiction.

24. Discuss the similarities and differences between supply and demand for a good (product or service) and supply and demand in a money (debt) market.

25. Briefly explain the idea of representing an interest rate as a collection of components. What is represented by the base rate? What is the risk premium for? Explain the idea of risk in lending.

26. Why is inflation important to lenders? How do they take it into consideration?

27. Explain the nature of the potential lending losses associated with each of the following: default risk, liquidity risk, and maturity risk.

28. Do all loans have default, liquidity, and maturity risk more or less equally? Are some types of loans relatively free of some risks? Is the debt of a particular organization free of certain risks? If so, explain who, what, and why.

29. Explain the ideas of a risk-free rate and the real rate of interest. Is either of them approximated by anything that exists in the real world?

30. What is a yield curve? Briefly outline three theories that purport to explain its shape. How does the yield curve influence the behavior of lenders?

BUSINESS ANALYSIS

1. Harry, a friend of yours, is taking a course in economics, and has become confused by some of the terminology because of the way people commonly use the same words. The economics professor says investment occurs when companies buy equipment and build factories. Yet Harry has always heard people talk about investing as a method of saving when they put money in the bank or purchase securities. He's confused by these dissimilar uses of the word and has asked you to explain. After asking for your help, Harry happily states that there's one thing he does understand perfectly about what the econ prof says, and that is "savings equals investment." Because investing in stocks and bonds is also saving money, it's obvious that savings equals investment! Write a brief explanation to help out.

2. Brokers and mutual funds do the same thing: invest your money for you. Is that statement true or false? Explain. What kind of financial institution is a mutual fund? What is its distinguishing feature? Describe how savings banks and insurance companies are similar to mutual funds.

3. Sharon Jacobs is CEO of Henderson Industries Inc., a public company. Henderson makes heavy construction equipment like bulldozers and cranes which it sells to small construction companies. These customers are generally in poor financial condition and must finance their purchases with banks or finance companies. Unfortunately lenders have had increasing trouble collecting on their loans. As many as 30% of customers default, requiring the lenders to repossess and resell the equipment. This usually avoids a loss, but it's an administrative hassle. Because of the ups and downs of the construction industry, it is impossible at the time of sale to predict which customers will default.

The economy is going downhill at present and Henderson has been experiencing financial difficulties itself. The company's problems are reflected in its stock price which has declined 40% over the last two years on weakening sales.

In order to boost sales, Henderson would like to sell to new customers that are financially even weaker than its current customers. Unfortunately, the banks and finance companies won't lend to even weaker borrowers. As a result, Henderson is considering offering product to these new customers on deferred payment terms.

That means it will receive a stream of monthly payments over two or three years until the equipment is paid off. Defaults on this new business will probably be worse than the finance companies are now experiencing but no one knows by how much. The good news, however, is that Sharon thinks she can sell a *lot* of equipment to these new customers.

On top of all this, the deferred payment idea presents an accounting issue. Typically when a sale is made, the entire price of the product along with its cost are recognized on the income statement at the time of sale. Any unpaid money is carried as a receivable regardless of how long the customer has to pay.

But if there are serious questions about collecting the deferred payments, it's more appropriate to use the *installment sales method* which recognizes revenue and a pro rata portion of cost only as cash is received from customers.

What ethical issues does Sharon face with respect to disclosure of financial information including but not limited to the income statement?

Suppose Sharon has stock options and/or a bonus package that depend on stock price. How might her compensation plan affect her decisions?

4. Does the so-called risk-free rate actually have some risk? (This is a tough question that isn't discussed in the chapter. Think about what makes up the risk-free rate and what among those pieces is an estimate of the future.)

5. Your Aunt Sally has a large portfolio of corporate bonds of different maturities. She has asked your advice on whether to buy more or get rid of some. You anticipate an increase in interest rates in the near future. How would you advise her? Would your advice depend on the maturity of individual bonds?

PROBLEMS

1. Refer to the Microsoft stock quotation on page 191. Demonstrate that the price earnings (P/E) ratio is consistent with other information in the listing.

Executive Stock Options: Concept Connection Example 5-1 (page 193)

2. Sam Lawson is a vice president at a large communications firm. His compensation includes a salary of $400,000, a bonus of $200,000, and a stock option package that allows him to purchase 30,000 shares of the company's stock at $45 per share. He can exercise the option anytime within a three-year period that starts on the first of next month. The stock is now selling at $62.50 per share. If the current price holds until the first of the month, and Sam exercises his option, how much will he make this year?

3. Read Business Analysis Case 3. Henderson Industries Inc.'s stock is currently selling at $22.40 per share. Sharon Jacobs, the CEO, has options to buy 250,000 shares at $25.50 per share that expire at the end of this year. Sharon feels that if the traditional accounting method is used, implementing the deferred payment sales program will push the stock's price about halfway toward the level it was at two years ago which was about $43. (That method recognizes the entire price and cost of a sold item on the income statement at the time of sale.) If the installment sales technique is used, the price of the stock will probably be unchanged but may even go down a little.

   How much will Sharon make on her stock option if she can pressure Henderson's auditors into allowing the traditional method?

A Moral Hazard for Founders: Concept Connection Example 5-2 (page 195)

4. If Sharon Jacobs of the previous problem is also a founder of the company and has retained 8 million shares of its stock, how much of a difference will the auditor's decision make in her personal wealth outside of the stock option?

Using the Interest Rate Model: Concept Connection Example 5-3 (page 219)

5. Nu-Mode Fashions Inc. manufactures quality women's wear and needs to borrow money to get through a brief cash shortage. Unfortunately, sales are down, and lenders consider the firm risky. The CFO has asked you to estimate the interest rate Nu-Mode should expect to pay on a one-year loan. She's told you to assume a 3% default risk premium, even though the loan is relatively short, and to assume the liquidity and maturity risk premiums are each .5%. Inflation is expected to be 4% over the next 12 months. Economists believe the pure interest rate is currently about 3.5%.

6. Calculate the rate Nu-Mode in the last problem should expect to pay on a two-year loan. Assume a 4% default risk premium and liquidity and maturity risk premiums of .75% due to the longer term. Inflation is expected to be 5% in the loan's second year.

7. Keena is saving money so she can start a two-year graduate school program two years from now. She doesn't want to take any chances on going to grad school, so she's planning to invest her savings in the lowest risk securities available, Treasury notes (short-term bonds). She will need the first year's tuition in two years and the second year's in three. Use the interest rate model to estimate the returns she can expect on two- and three-year notes. The inflation rate is expected to be 4% next year, 5% in the following year, and 6% in the year after that. Maturity risk generally adds .1% to yields on shorter term notes like these for each year of term. Assume the pure rate is 1.5%.

8. Adams Inc. recently borrowed money for one year at 9%. The pure rate is 3%, and Adams's financial condition warrants a default risk premium of 2% and a liquidity risk premium of 1%. There is little or no maturity risk in one-year loans. What inflation rate do lenders expect next year?

9. Mountain Sports Inc. borrowed money for two years last week at 12%. The pure rate is 2%, and Mountain's financial condition warrants a default risk premium of 3% and a liquidity risk premium of 2%. The maturity risk premium for two-year loans is 1%. Inflation is expected to be 3% next year. What does the interest rate model imply the lender expects the inflation rate to be in the following year?

10. The Habender Company just issued a two-year bond at 12%. Inflation is expected to be 4% next year and 6% the year after. Habender estimates its default risk premium at about 1.5% and its maturity risk premium at about .5%. Because it's a relatively small and unknown firm, its liquidity risk premium is about 2% even on relatively short debt like this. What pure interest rate is implied by these assumptions?

11. Charles Jackson, the founder and president of the Jackson Company, is concerned about his firm's image in the financial community. The concern arose when he went to the bank for a one-year loan and was quoted a rate of 12%, which was considerably more than the firm had been paying recently. He has asked you, the treasurer, for an analysis that could shed some light on what might be causing the bank to ask for such a high rate.

     Your research indicates the following. The economy is stable with a 3% inflation rate that isn't expected to change in the near future. The local banking community consistently considers the pure interest rate to be about 4%. Liquidity risk for companies of Jackson's size and reputation is generally not more than 1%, and maturity risk is virtually zero for one-year loans. In the past, Jackson's reputation has warranted a low default risk premium of 2%. The firm's financial condition has been stable for some time. Two months ago Jackson had a major dispute with one of its suppliers. Charles refused to pay for a large shipment due to poor quality. The vendor did not agree and claimed that Jackson was just using the quality issue to avoid paying its bills. (*Hint:* Suppose the vendor reported the dispute to a credit agency.)

12. Use the interest rate model to solve the following problem. One-year treasury securities are yielding 12%, and two-year treasuries yield 14%. The maturity risk premium is zero for one-year debt and 1% for two-year debt. The real risk-free rate is 3%. What are the expected rates of inflation for the next two years? (*Hint:* Set up a separate model for each term with the yearly inflation rates as unknowns.)

13. Inflation is expected to be 5% next year and a steady 7% each year thereafter. Maturity risk premiums are zero for one-year debt but have an increasing value for longer debt. One-year government debt yields 9%, whereas two-year debt yields 11%.

    a. What is the real risk-free rate and the maturity risk premium for two-year debt?

    b. Forecast the nominal yield on one- and two-year government debt issued at the beginning of the second year.

Using the Interest Rate Model over a Range of Terms: Concept Connection Example 5-4 (page 220)

14. Economists have forecast the following yearly inflation rates over the next 10 years:

Year	Inflation Rate
1	3.0
2	2.5
3–6	4.0
7–10	3.0

    Calculate the inflation components of interest rates on new bonds issued today with terms varying from one (1) to ten (10) years.

15. The interest rate outlook for Montrose Inc., a large, financially sound company, is reflected in the following information.

    • The pure rate of interest is 4%.

    • Inflation is expected to increase in the future from its current low level of 2%. Predicted annual inflation rates follow.

Year	Inflation Rate
1	2%
2	3
3	4
4	5
5–20	6

    • The default risk premium will be .1% for one-year debt, but will increase by .1% for each additional year of term to a maximum of 1%.

    • The liquidity premium is zero for one- and two-year debt, .5% for three-, four-, and five-year terms, and 1% for longer issues.

    • The maturity risk premium is zero for a one-year term and increases by .2% for each additional year of term to a maximum of 2%.

    a. Use the interest rate model to estimate market rates on the firm's debt securities of the following terms: 1 to 5 years, 10 years, and 20 years.

    b. Plot a yield curve for the firm's debt.

    c. Using different colors on the same graph, sketch yield curves for

        i. federal government debt and

        ii. Shaky Inc., a firm currently in financial difficulty.

    d. Explain the pattern of deviation from Montrose's yield curve for each of the others.

16. Atkins Company has just issued a series of bonds with 5- through 10-year maturities. The company's default risk is .5% on 5-year bonds, and grows by .2% for each year that's added to the bond's term. Atkins' liquidity risk is 1.0% on 5-year bonds, and grows by .1% for each additional year of term. Maturity risk on all bonds is .2% on one-year bonds, and grows by .1% for each additional

year of term. What is the difference between the interest rates on Atkins' bonds and those on federal government bonds of like terms?

17. Assume that interest rates on federal government bonds are as follows:

1-year	6.5%
2-year	6.3%
3-year	6.0%
4-year	5.8%
5-year	5.5%
10-year	5.2%
15-year	5.0%
20-year	5.0%

Do the theories of the shape of the yield curve offer any insights into this rate pattern? Discuss the expectations, liquidity preference, and market segmentation theories separately.

18. The real risk-free rate is 2.5%. The maturity risk premium is .1% for 1-year maturities, growing by .2% per year up to a maximum of 1.0%. The interest rate on 4-year treasuries (federal government bonds) is 6.2%, 7.5% on 8-year treasuries, and 8.0% on 10-year treasuries. What conclusions can be drawn about expected inflation rates over the 10-year period?

PART

2

Discounted Cash Flow and the Value of Securities

Time Value of Money

The time value of money is based on the idea that a sum of money in your hand today is worth more than the same sum promised at some time in the future, even if you're absolutely certain to receive the future cash.

The idea is pretty easy to grasp if you think in terms of having a bank account and being promised an amount of money a year from now. Money in the bank earns interest, so it grows over time. The value today of the sum promised in one year is an amount that will grow into that sum if deposited in the bank now. In other words, a sum promised in a year is worth only as much as you'd have to put in the bank today to have that sum in a year.

That value obviously depends on the interest rate the bank is paying. The higher the interest rate, the faster money grows, so the less you'd have to deposit today to get a given amount next year.

Let's look at an example using a future amount of $1,000. How much would a promise of $1,000 in one year be worth today if the bank paid 5% interest? That question is equivalent to asking how much money will grow into $1,000 in one year at 5% interest. The answer is $952.38; we'll worry about how we got it a little later. The important thing to understand now is that if we deposit $952.38 for one year, we'll earn interest of 5% of that amount,

$$\$952.38 \times .05 = \$47.62$$

which when added to the original deposit yields $1,000.

$$\$952.38 + \$47.62 = \$1,000.00$$

Therefore, a guaranteed promise of $1,000 in a year is worth $952.38 today *if* the interest rate is 5%.

> The **present value** of a sum at a future time is the amount that must be deposited at interest today to have the sum at that time.

We say that $952.38 is the **present value** of $1,000 in one year at 5%. Alternatively, we say that $1,000 is the **future value** of $952.38 after one year at 5%.

If the interest rate were 7%, the present value of $1,000.00 in one year would be $934.58, a smaller number:

$$\$934.58 \times .07 = \$65.42$$

and

$$\$934.58 + \$65.42 = \$1,000.00$$

In other words, a higher rate of interest makes the present value of a future amount smaller. This makes sense; the bank deposit is earning faster, so you don't have to put as much in to get to the desired amount at the end of the year.

The time value of money is one of the most important principles in finance and economics today. It's based on the simple ideas we've just stated, but the applications can get quite complicated as we'll see later in this chapter.

> The **discounted** value of a sum is its present value.

The subject can also be called **discounted cash flow**, abbreviated as DCF. Using that terminology in our first example, we would say the $952.38 is the *discounted* value of the $1,000.

Here's another way of looking at the same thing. Suppose you have a firm, written contract promising to pay you $1,000 in one year's time, but you need as much cash as you can get today. You could take the contract, called a note, to a bank, which would **discount** it for you at whatever interest rate it charges. If the bank's interest rate was 5%, it would give you $952.38 for the note. If the rate was 7%, the bank would be willing to give you only $934.58.

6.1 Outline of Approach

Our study of time value will involve learning to deal with *amounts* and *annuities.* An amount problem is similar to what we've already been talking about, involving a single amount of money that grows at interest over time into a larger sum. An annuity problem deals with a stream of equal payments, each of which is placed at interest and grows over time.

We'll further divide each of these categories into two more. Within each we'll look at situations dealing with present values and those dealing with future values.

In all we'll be looking at four types of problems.

amount—present value

amount—future value

annuity—present value

annuity—future value

After we've mastered these, we'll put the techniques together and work with some relatively complicated compound problems.

Mathematics   As we approach each of the four categories, we'll develop a formula suited to doing that type of problem. The algebra needed to develop the formula may look a little intimidating to readers who aren't strong in math. Don't be alarmed. The math required to do the financial problems once you accept the formula is quite simple. Developing the formulas is background that's good to know, but you don't have to remember it to do practical work.

Time Lines   Students sometimes find time value problems confusing. The time line is a graphic device that helps keep things straight. Time is divided into periods and portrayed along a horizontal line. Time zero is the present, and we count periods to the right.

A **time line** is a graphic portrayal of a time value problem.

Time 1 is the *end* of the first period, time 2 the end of the second, and so on. We can make notations above and below the time line to keep track of various pieces of the problem we're working on, such as interest rates and amounts. For example, a time line for the illustration we talked about before would look like this.

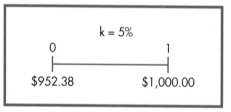

Most people don't need time lines for simple situations like this one, but the devices can help a lot in more complicated problems. We'll use them where appropriate as we go forward. We'll begin with yearly periods, but later we will introduce shorter spans.

A Note About the Examples   Several of the examples in this chapter are used to teach important financial practices as well as to illustrate computational techniques. You should be sure to learn and understand the business situations described in each of these illustrations. The first one you'll encounter is in Example 6-2, which describes the equivalence of deferred payment terms and a cash discount.

6.2   Amount Problems

Amount problems involve a single sum of money that can be thought of as moving back and forth through time under the influence of interest. As it moves into the future, the sum gets larger as it earns interest. Conversely, as it moves back in time, the sum gets smaller. We'll begin with future value-oriented situations.

6.2a   The Future Value of an Amount

To find the future value of an amount, we need a convenient way to calculate how much a sum of money placed at interest will grow into in some period of time. Let's start with a simple situation. Suppose we invest a sum of money in the bank at interest rate k. How much will it be worth at the end of one year?

Call the sum today PV, for present value, and the amount we'll have at the end of the year FV_1, for future value in one year. And call the decimal equivalent of the interest rate k (.05 for 5%).

At the end of a year, we'll have the amount originally invested, PV, plus the interest on that amount, kPV. So we can write

$$FV_1 = PV + kPV$$

Factor PV out of the right side, and we have

(6.1) $$FV_1 = PV(1 + k)$$

Now suppose we leave FV_1 in the bank for another year, and we want to know how much we'll have at the end of that second year. We'll call that FV_2. The second year's calculation will be the same as the one we just did, but we'll use FV_1 instead of PV.

$$FV_2 = FV_1 + kFV_1$$

Factor out FV_1.

$$FV_2 = FV_1(1 + k)$$

Now substitute for FV_1 from Equation 6.1 to get

(6.2) $$FV_2 = PV(1 + k)(1 + k)$$
$$FV_2 = PV(1 + k)^2$$

Notice the similarity between Equations 6.1 and 6.2. FV_1 is equal to PV times $(1 + k)$ to the *first* power, while FV_2 is PV times $(1 + k)$ to the *second* power. It's easy to see that if we performed the same calculation for a third year, FV_3 would be equal to PV times $(1 + k)$ to the *third* power, and so on, for as many years into the future as we'd care to go.

We can *generalize* the relationship and write

(6.3)
$$FV_n = PV(1 + k)^n$$

for any value of n. This expression gives us a very convenient way to calculate the future value of any present amount given that we know the interest rate, k, and the number of years the money is invested, n.

For example, if we deposited $438 at 6% interest for five years, how much would we have? Using Equation 6.3 gives

$$FV_5 = \$438(1.06)^5$$

Raising 1.06 to the fifth power on a calculator gives 1.3382, so

$$FV_5 = \$438(1.3382)$$
$$= \$586.13$$

The only messy part of the calculation is raising 1.06 to the fifth power. Looking at Equation 6.3, we can see that calculating $(1 + k)^n$ will always be tedious, especially for larger values of n.

However, notice that the value of $(1 + k)^n$ depends only on the sizes of k and n, and that in business situations these variables take on a relatively limited number of values. Therefore, it's feasible to make up a table that contains the value of $(1 + k)^n$ for common combinations of k and n. We'll call $(1 + k)^n$ the *future value factor for k and n,* and write it as $FVF_{k,n}$. Table 6-1 is a partial table of values for this factor. A more extensive version is given in Appendix A (Table A-1) for use in solving problems.

We can now rewrite Equation 6.3 in a more convenient form by referring to the table.

(6.4)
$$FV_n = PV[FVF_{k,n}]$$

The **future value factor** for k and n is the calculated value of $(1 + k)^n$.

TABLE 6-1	The Future Value Factor for k and n $FVF_{k,n} = (1 + k)^n$						
				k			
n	1%	2%	3%	4%	5%	6%	...
1	1.0100	1.0200	1.0300	1.0400	1.0500	1.0600	
2	1.0201	1.0404	1.0609	1.0816	1.1025	1.1236	...
3	1.0303	1.0612	1.0927	1.1249	1.1576	1.1910	...
4	1.0406	1.0824	1.1255	1.1699	1.2155	1.2625	...
5	1.0510	1.1041	1.1593	1.2167	1.2763	1.3382	...
6	1.0615	1.1262	1.1941	1.2653	1.3401	1.4185	...
⋮	⋮	⋮	⋮	⋮	⋮	⋮	

CONCEPT CONNECTION   **EXAMPLE 6-1**

Future Value of an Amount

How much will $850 be worth if deposited for three years at 5% interest?

SOLUTION: To solve the problem, write Equation 6.4 and substitute the amounts given.

$$FV_n = PV\left[FVF_{k,n}\right]$$
$$FV_3 = \$850\left[FVF_{5,3}\right]$$

Look up $FVF_{5,3}$ in the three-year row under the 5% column of Table 6-1, getting 1.1576, and substitute.

$$FV_3 = \$850\left[1.1576\right]$$
$$= \$983.96$$

Problem-Solving Techniques   Equation 6.4 is the first of four formulas that you will use to solve a variety of time value problems. Each equation contains four variables. In this case, the variables are PV, FV_n, k, and n. Every problem will give you three of the variables and ask you to find the fourth.

In time value problems, **three** of four variables are **given,** and **we solve for the fourth**.

If you're asked to find PV or FV_n the solution is very easy. Simply look up the factor for the given k,n combination in the table and substitute in the equation along with the given PV or FV_n. The last problem gave us PV and asked for FV_n. Here's one that gives us the future value and requires us to find the present value.

CONCEPT CONNECTION   **EXAMPLE 6-2**

Present Value of an Amount and the Deferred Payment Equivalent of a Cash Discount

Ed Johnson sold 10 acres of land to Harriet Smith for $25,000. The terms of the agreement called for Harriet to pay $15,000 down and $5,000 a year for two years. What was the real purchase price if the interest rate available to Ed on invested money is 6%?

SOLUTION: What Ed is getting today is $15,000 plus the present value of two $5,000 payments, each to be received at different times in the future. The problem is to compute these PVs and add them to the $15,000.

The present value of the payment due at the end of the first year is calculated by writing Equation 6.4 and substituting the known elements.

$$FV_n = PV\left[FVF_{k,n}\right]$$
$$\$5,000 = PV\left[FVF_{6,1}\right]$$

Table 6-1 of Appendix A (Table A-1) gives $FVF_{6,1} = 1.0600$. Substitute and solve for PV.

$$\$5,000 = PV \, [1.0600]$$
$$PV = \$4,716.98$$

The second calculation is the same, but the payment is two years away, so we use $FVF_{6,2} = 1.1236$. That gives a present value of $\$4,449.98$.

In a present value sense, the actual sale amount is the sum of these two PVs and the down payment,

$$\$15,000.00 + \$4,716.98 + \$4,449.98 = \$24,166.96$$

That's $833.04 less than the $25,000 price quoted.

In real estate finance, we would say that the *terms of sale* resulted in an effective price reduction of $833.04, even though the real estate records would indicate a transaction price of $25,000. Terms of sale state when and how the purchase price has to be paid. The seller's willingness to accept part of the price later is worth a specific amount of money. In other words, it is the equivalent of a cash discount.

The Opportunity Cost Rate   Notice that in the last problem, we calculated the present values using the interest rate available to the seller, 6%, even though nothing was actually invested at that or any other rate. We used the 6% rate because if the seller had received the full price at the time of sale, he would have been able to invest the deferred payments at that rate. Therefore, in a sense, he lost the income from that investment by giving the deferred payment terms.

We say that the lost interest income is the **opportunity cost** of giving the discount. In this case, because the seller's alternative is stated as a rate of interest at which he could have invested, we call it the *opportunity cost rate.*

The opportunity cost concept is a bit slippery. For example, you could argue that Ed Johnson might not have been able to sell the property to anyone without giving the deferred terms or an equivalent discount, and therefore there wasn't really any cost to the deferred terms at all. Nevertheless, we still say that the opportunity cost rate from Johnson's viewpoint is 6%.

The opportunity cost rate frequently isn't the same to different parties in the same transaction. In Example 6-2, Ed Johnson's opportunity cost rate is 6%, because that's the rate at which he can invest. But suppose Harriet Smith has to borrow to pay for the land and that she must do so at a rate of 10%. Her opportunity cost rate is then 10%, not 6%. To her the deferred payment terms are worth a discount of $1,322.32, quite a bit more than what they implicitly cost Ed Johnson. (Verify this by calculating the effective price at 10% as we did in the example at 6%.)

In this example the deferred terms are a pretty good deal. They're worth more to the recipient than to the donor!

In general, the opportunity cost of using a resource in some way is the amount it could earn in the next best use.

The **opportunity cost** of a resource is the benefit that would have been available from its next best use.

6.2b   Financial Calculators

Financial calculators take most of the drudgery out of time value problems. They work directly with mathematical relationships like Equation 6.3 rather than with tables.

There's a temptation to skip the mathematical work we've been doing here and go directly to using a calculator without mastering the algebraic approach. That's a big mistake. If you go straight to the calculator, you'll never truly understand what's behind time value or be comfortable with it. Certainly in practice we use calculators almost exclusively, but it's very important to know what's behind the numbers that flash on the display.

In the rest of this chapter, we'll concentrate on the approach we've been developing that uses financial tables, but we'll also show calculator solutions in the page margins.

How to Use a Typical Financial Calculator in Time Value   Recall that there are four variables in any time value problem. Values for three are given, and the fourth is unknown. Financial calculators have a key for each variable. To use a calculator, enter the three known variables, pressing the appropriate key after each input. Then press a compute key, followed by the key for the unknown variable. The calculator responds by displaying the answer.

There are actually five time value keys because annuities require one that isn't used in the amount problems we've looked at so far. When we solve a problem, we use four keys and set to zero, or ignore, the fifth. The keys selected tell the calculator which kind of problem is being done. The time value keys and their meanings are as follows:

> n—Number of time periods
>
> I/Y—Interest rate (other labels. %i, I/YR, I% YR)
>
> PV—Present value
>
> FV—Future value
>
> PMT—Payment

The last key is the periodic payment associated with an annuity. We'll talk about it later when we get to annuities. For now it should be ignored (if you clear the time value registers before starting) or set to zero.

The compute key is usually labeled either CPT or 2nd. On some calculators there isn't a compute key; the calculator just knows the last key hit is the unknown.

Before trying a problem, take a look at your calculator's instruction manual. You may have to get into a particular mode of operation and clear the time value registers before starting. Advanced calculators also have a feature regarding the interest rate that needs to be set properly. They take the interest rate input and automatically divide it by a number of compounding periods per year. The default setting is usually 12, for 12 months a year. We'll get into non-annual compounding periods later. For now, set the calculator for one (1) period per year.

Calculator Solution

Key	Input
n	1
I/Y	6
FV	5,000
PMT	0
Answer	
PV	4,716.98

Now solve Example 6-1, using your calculator. Here's how.

1. The problem runs for three years. Enter 3 and then press n.
2. The interest rate is 5%. Enter 5 and then press I/Y.
3. The present value is $850. Enter 850 and then press PV.
4. Press 2nd or CPT (if necessary) and then press FV.
5. The calculator displays 983.98 or –983.98

Some calculators use a sign convention intended to reflect inflows as positive numbers and outflows as negatives. For example, if PV is entered as a positive, FV shows up as a negative. The idea is that PV is a deposit and FV is a withdrawal.

Notice that a calculator solution may be a little off a table solution because the table only carries four decimal places. The calculator carries 12 or more significant digits. Also notice that the interest rate is generally entered as a whole number even though the equations work with the decimal form.

In the remainder of this chapter, we'll show abbreviated calculator solutions for examples in the margins. Here's an illustration showing the first $5,000 payment in Example 6-2.

6.2c The Expression for the Present Value of an Amount

Either amount equation can be used to solve any amount problem.

Notice that we are able to use Equation 6.4 to solve problems asking for *either* the present value or the future value. However, the expression is set up to make the future value calculation a little easier, because FV_n is isolated on the left side.

For convenience, we can develop another equation that's oriented toward solving the present value problem. We'll begin with Equation 6.3,

$$FV_n = PV(1 + k)^n$$

Now simply solve for PV by dividing through by $(1 + k)^n$ and switching the terms to opposite sides.

(6.5)
$$PV = FV_n \frac{1}{(1 + k)^n}$$

Slightly more sophisticated mathematical notation enables us to write the same thing with a negative exponent.

(6.6)
$$PV = FV_n(1 + k)^{-n}$$

The term $(1 + k)^{-n}$ can be thought of as a factor depending only on k and n that can be tabulated. We'll call that factor the **present value factor for k and n** and write it as $PVF_{k,n}$. The values of $PVF_{k,n}$ are given in Appendix A (Table A-2). We can now re-write Equation 6.6 by using this factor and reference to the table.

(6.7)
$$PV = FV_n[PVF_{k,n}]$$

We use this expression and the associated table just like we used Equation 6.4. It too can be used to solve for either present or future values, but it is more conveniently formulated for present values. Do Example 6-2 on your own using Equation 6.7.

The Relation Between the Future and Present Value Factors

It's important to notice that Equations 6.4 and 6.7 really express the same relationship, since they both come from Equation 6.3. It's also important to realize that the present and future value factors are reciprocals of one another. That is,

The future and present value factors are **reciprocals**.

(6.8)
$$FVF_{k,n} = \frac{1}{PVF_{k,n}}$$

More on Problem-Solving Techniques

Solving for **k or n** involves searching a table.

So far we've looked at problems that ask us to solve for FV_n or PV. When the unknown element in the equation is k or n, the approach is a little different. Notice that in both Equations 6.4 and 6.7, k and n appear as subscripts on the factors referring to table values. That means we can't use traditional algebraic methods to solve for an unknown k or n.

We'll change Example 6-1 a little to illustrate what we mean. In that problem, we asked how much $850 would grow into in three years at 5% interest and got an answer of $983.96.

CONCEPT CONNECTION   EXAMPLE 6-3

Finding the Interest Rate

Suppose instead we were asked what interest rate would grow $850 into $983.96 in three years. In this case we have FV_3, PV, and n, but we don't have k.

Calculator Solution

Key	Input
n	3
PV	850.00
FV	983.96
PMT	0
Answer	
I/Y	5.0

SOLUTION: We'll use Equation 6.7 this time, just for variety. The general approach is to write the equation

$$PV = FV_n[PVF_{k,n}]$$

and substitute what's known,

$$\$850.00 = \$983.96\,[PVF_{k,3}]$$

Notice that this equation can't be solved algebraically for k.

The approach we must take is to solve for the whole factor, $PVF_{k,3}$, and then find its value in the table. Once we've done that, we can read off the unknown value for k from the column heading. Solving for the factor gives

$$PVF_{k,3} = \$850.00/\$983.96 = .8639$$

We have to find .8639 in Appendix A (Table A-2), but we don't have to search the entire table for it. We know that in this problem n = 3, so we can confine our search to the row for three years. Looking along that row we don't find .8639 exactly, but we do find .8638. That's close enough to assume that the difference is due to rounding error. Looking up to the top of the column, we read 5% as the solution to the problem.

Solutions Between Columns and Rows   Most of the time, solutions for k and n don't come out exactly on numbers in the table. That is, the calculated factor is somewhere between the columns or rows. The appropriate approach when that happens depends on the accuracy needed in the solution. For some purposes, it's enough to round the answer to the closest tabulated row or column. If a more accurate answer is necessary and you're using tables like the ones provided here, you have to estimate between columns and rows.

In practice, financial calculators are used to solve time value problems. They give exact results without using tables. Before financial calculators were invented, people used enormously detailed tables that filled entire volumes. For illustrative purposes in what follows, we'll just round to the nearest table value of n or k.

CONCEPT CONNECTION   **EXAMPLE 6-4**

Solving for the Number of Time Periods

How long does it take money invested at 14% to double?

SOLUTION: Don't be confused by the fact that we're not given a present and future value in this case. What we are given is a relation between the two. If the money is to double in value, the future value must be twice the present value. Alternatively, we could ask how long it would take $1 to double into $2. We'll use Equation 6.4 in this case,

$$FV_n = PV \left[FVF_{k,n} \right]$$

Solving for the factor and substituting yields

$$FVF_{14,n} = FV_n / PV = 2.000$$

Next we look for 2.0000 in Appendix A (Table A-1), confining our search to the column for $k = 14\%$. We find the table value is between five and six years.

n	14%
5	1.9254
6	2.1950

Clearly, 2.0000 is closer to 1.9254 than it is to 2.1950; therefore, the nearest whole integer number of years is 5. Notice that the calculator solution gives an exact answer of 5.29 years.

Calculator Solution

Key	Input
I/Y	14
FV	2
PV	1
PMT	0
Answer	
n	5.29

Ensuper/Shutterstock.com

6.3   Annuity Problems

The second major class of time value problems involves streams of payments called *annuities*. These are generally more complex than amount problems and harder to visualize, so using time lines can be important.

6.3a   Annuities

An **annuity** is a stream of equal payments, made or received, separated by equal intervals of time. Hence, $5 a month for a year is an annuity. A stream of monthly payments that alternates from $5 to $10 is not an annuity, nor is a stream of $5 payments that skips an occasional month. Both the amount and the time interval must be constant to have an annuity.

When payments occur at the end of the time periods, we have what's called an *ordinary annuity*. This is the usual situation. If the payments occur at the beginning of each period, we call the stream an *annuity due*. Figures 6-1 and 6-2 show time lines for both cases for a stream of four $1,000 payments.

Annuities have definite beginning and end points in time; they don't go on forever. A stream of equal payments at regular time intervals that does go on forever is called a *perpetuity*. It has to be handled by its own rules, which we'll study later in the chapter.

The Time Value of Annuities   Annuities are common in business and have important time value implications. For example, suppose a long-term contract calls for payments of $5,000 a year for 10 years. A question that arises immediately concerns the value of the agreement today. That is, if the recipient wants to discount all the payments for immediate cash, how much will they be worth in total?

A similar question asks for the future value of the entire annuity if all 10 payments are put in the bank when received and left there until the end of the contract.

Either of these questions can be answered by taking the present or future value of each payment separately and adding the results. That is a tedious process, however, involving 10 separate calculations. It's much more convenient to develop expressions that enable us to calculate the present or future value of the entire annuity at once.

We'll begin with the future value problem.

FIGURE 6-1   Ordinary Annuity

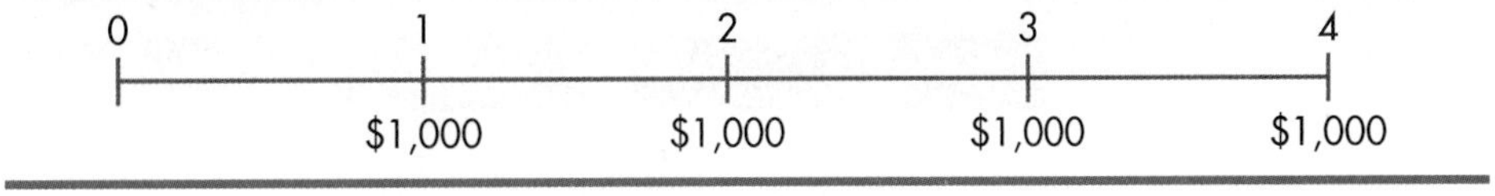

0	1	2	3	4
	$1,000	$1,000	$1,000	$1,000

© Cengage Learning

FIGURE 6-2   Annuity Due

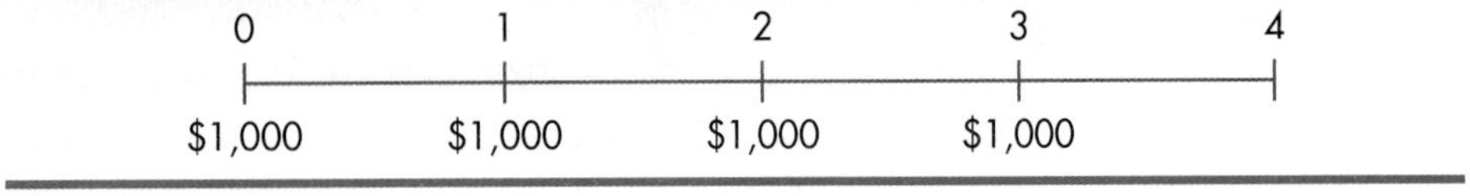

0	1	2	3	4
$1,000	$1,000	$1,000	$1,000	

© Cengage Learning

6.3b   The Future Value of an Annuity—Developing a Formula

We can develop an expression for the future value of an annuity that's similar to the formulas we studied for amounts. We'll approach the task by examining the future value of a three-year ordinary annuity, using the tools we acquired in dealing with amounts.

We'll portray the annuity along a time line and represent the yearly cash payment as a variable called *PMT*, as shown in Figure 6-3.

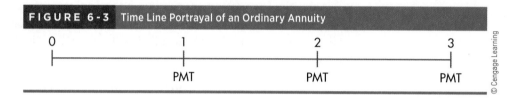

FIGURE 6-3   Time Line Portrayal of an Ordinary Annuity

© Cengage Learning

The Future Value Problem   Precisely stated, the assumption behind the future value of an annuity is that each amount, PMT, earns interest at some rate, k, from the time it appears on the time line until the end of the last period. The **future value of an annuity** is simply the sum of all the payments and all the interest. This is the same as taking the future value of each PMT treated as an amount and adding them.

For example, imagine someone gives you $100 a year for three years and that you put each payment in the bank as soon as you get it. The future value of an annuity problem is to calculate how much you have at the end of the third year. It's clearly more than $300 because of interest earned.

The Future Values of the Individual Payments   We'll develop an expression for the future value of an annuity by projecting the future value of each payment to the end of the stream individually. The approach is illustrated in Figure 6-4. We'll call the end of the third year time 3, the end of the second time 2, and so on.

> The **future value of an annuity** is the sum, at its end, of all payments and all interest if each payment is deposited when received.

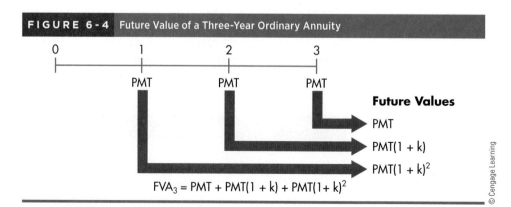

FIGURE 6-4   Future Value of a Three-Year Ordinary Annuity

Future Values

PMT

PMT(1 + k)

PMT(1 + k)^2

$$FVA_3 = PMT + PMT(1 + k) + PMT(1+ k)^2$$

© Cengage Learning

First consider the third payment. It occurs at the end of the annuity, so it spends no time earning interest at all. Therefore, its value at time 3 is simply PMT.

The second payment occurs at time 2, one year before the end of the annuity, and spends one year earning interest. Its value at time 3 is $PMT(1 + k)$. Think of this as the future value of the present amount PMT for one year at interest rate k. This comes from Equation 6.1 with PMT substituted for PV.

Now consider the first payment. It occurs at the end of the first year and spends two years earning interest. Its value by the end of the annuity is $PMT(1 + k)^2$.

All this is portrayed graphically in Figure 6-4, along with the sum of the future values of the three payments which we're calling FVA_3 for future value of an annuity of three periods.

The Three-Year Formula   Let's rewrite the expression for FVA_3 from Figure 6-4 with two changes and then examine what we have. The first change will be to explicitly recognize the exponent of 1 on $(1 + k)$ in the middle term on the right. That is, $(1 + k) = (1 + k)^1$. It's simply common practice not to write an exponent of 1 even though it's there. The second change involves recognizing that anything raised to a zero exponent equals 1. That is, $x^0 = 1$ for any value of x. In this case, we're going to multiply the first term on the right by $(1 + k)^0$. This gives

$$(6.9) \qquad FVA_3 = PMT(1 + k)^0 + PMT(1 + k)^1 + PMT(1 + k)^2$$

Notice the regular progression of the terms on the right side of Equation 6.9. Each contains PMT multiplied by an increasing power of $(1 + k)$ starting from zero. Notice also for this three-year case that there are three terms and that the exponents start with zero and increase to two, one less than the number of years.

Generalizing the Expression   Now imagine we have a four-year annuity, and we want to develop a similar expression for it. How would that expression differ from what we've written here for the three-year case?

In a four-year model, the first payment would earn interest for three years, so its future value would be $PMT(1 + k)^3$. The second payment would earn interest for two years, and the third for one year; the fourth would earn no interest at all. These latter payments would be just like the ones in the three-year case, so the only thing different in the four-year model is the addition of the new term $PMT(1 + k)^3$. That addition fits our progression perfectly. It adds one more term with the next higher exponent.

You should be able to see that this could be done for any number of additional years. Each will add one more term with the next higher exponent of $(1 + k)$. Further, the highest exponent will always be one less than the number of years. Hence, we can *generalize* Equation 6.9 for any number of years, n.

$$(6.10) \qquad FVA_n = PMT(1 + k)^0 + PMT(1 + k)^1 + PMT(1 + k)^2 + \\ \cdots + PMT(1 + k)^{n-1}$$

Equation 6.10 can be written more conveniently by using the mathematical symbol Σ, which implies summation over the values of some index.

(6.11)
$$\text{FVA}_n = \sum_{i=1}^{n} \text{PMT}(1 + k)^{n-i}$$

As i ranges from 1 to n, each of the terms of Equation 6.10 is formed in reverse order. For example, when $i = 1, n - i = n - 1$, and we get the last term. When $i = 2$ we get the next to last term, and so on, until $i = n$ and $n - i = 0$, which gives us the first term.

Because PMT appears identically in every term, we can factor it outside of the summation.

(6.12)
$$\text{FVA}_n = \text{PMT} \sum_{i=1}^{n} (1 + k)^{n-i}$$

The Future Value Factor for an Annuity   Now look at the entire summation term. It depends only on the values of n and k. For example, for $n = 3$ years the summation is

$$(1 + k)^0 + (1 + k)^1 + (1 + k)^2$$

which is equivalent to

$$1 + (1 + k) + (1 + k)^2$$

In general, the summation term for n years is

$$1 + (1 + k) + (1 + k)^2 + \cdots + (1 + k)^{n-1}$$

This expression can be calculated for pairs of values of n and k and placed in a table. The idea is identical to what we did in developing the future value factor for an amount $[\text{FVF}_{k,n} = (1 + k)^n]$, only this expression is more complex.

We'll call the summation in Equation 6.12 the *future value factor for an annuity* and write it as $\text{FVFA}_{k,n}$. Values for ranges of k and n are given in Appendix A (Table A-3).

The Final Formulation   The future value factor for an annuity can replace the summation in Equation 6.12 like this.

$$\text{FVA}_n = \text{PMT} \boxed{\sum_{i=1}^{n} (1 + k)^{n-i}}$$
$$\longrightarrow =\text{FVFA}_{k,n}$$

Rewriting Equation 6.12 using the factor, we get

(6.13)
$$\text{FVA}_n = \text{PMT}[\text{FVFA}_{k,n}]$$

6.3c   The Future Value of an Annuity—Solving Problems

We'll use Equation 6.13 to solve future value problems where annuities are involved. Notice that there are four variables in this equation: FVA_n (the future value itself), PMT (the payment), k (the interest rate), and n (the number of periods). Problems will generally give three of them and ask for the fourth. The first step in problem solution is always writing down the equation and substituting the known elements. Once this is done, the solution procedure is very similar to that used for amount problems.

Annuity problems tend to be a bit more complex than amount problems, so it helps to draw a time line to keep the pieces straight.

CONCEPT CONNECTION   EXAMPLE 6-5

Future Value of an Annuity

The Brock Corporation owns the patent to an industrial process and receives license fees of $100,000 a year on a 10-year contract for its use. Management plans to invest each payment until the end of the contract to provide a fund for development of a new process at that time. If the invested money is expected to earn 7%, how much will Brock have after the last payment is received?

SOLUTION: The time line for this straightforward problem looks like this.[1]

Calculator Solution

Key	Input
n	10
I/Y	7
PMT	100,000
PV	0

Answer	
FV	1,381,645

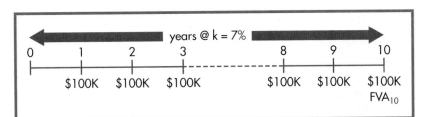

First write Equation 6.13,

$$FVA_n = PMT\left[FVFA_{k,n}\right]$$

and substitute the given information,

$$FVA_{10} = \$100,000\left[FVFA_{7,10}\right]$$

Next look up $FVFA_{7,10}$ in Appendix A (Table A-3), getting 13.8164. Substitute and solve for the future value.

$$FVA_{10} = \$100,000\,[13.8164]$$
$$= \$1,381,640$$

Notice that the actual money received is only $1,000,000; the rest is interest.

---

1. A capital K is frequently used to denote thousands of dollars, replacing a comma and three zeros. M can be used to denote millions.

Calculator Solutions for Annuities   Annuity problems are similar to amount problems in that they have four variables of which three are given and one is unknown. However, the variables are somewhat different.

All amount problems involve both the present and future values of the amount. Annuity problems involve a payment (PMT) and *either* the future value or the present value of the annuity. Hence, in an annuity problem we use the PMT key, and we zero either PV or FV, depending on the nature of the problem.

Example 6-5 is a future value of an annuity problem, so we use the FV key, and we zero the PV key. That, along with putting in a value for PMT, tells the calculator what kind of a problem it's doing. Notice that although we write the future and present values of annuities as FVA and PVA, we just use the FV and PV buttons on the calculator. Also notice that the calculator solution is different by $5 due to rounding.

The Sinking Fund Problem   In Chapter 5, we learned that companies borrow money by issuing bonds for periods as long as 30 or 40 years. Bonds are non-amortizing debt, meaning borrowers make no repayment of principal during bonds' lives. Borrowers pay only interest until maturity and then must repay the entire principal in a lump sum. This means that on the maturity date, a bond-issuing company must either have a great deal of money on hand or must reborrow to pay off the old bonds coming due.

Lenders can become quite concerned about this practice. They may feel that a borrowing company can generally earn enough to pay annual interest, but are worried that it won't have enough cash on hand at maturity to pay off principal, and also may not be able to reborrow. This can spell bankruptcy for the bond-issuing company and a big loss for the investor/lender.

The solution to the problem can be a **sinking fund**. A sinking fund is a series of payments made into an account that's dedicated to paying off a bond's principal at maturity. Deposits are planned so that the amount in the bank on the date the bonds mature will just equal the principal due.

If lenders require a sinking fund for security, it's included as a provision in the bond agreement. The sinking fund problem is to determine the periodic deposit that must be made to ensure that the appropriate amount is available at the bond's maturity. This is a future value of an annuity problem in which the payment is unknown.

from the **CFO**

A **sinking fund** provides cash to pay off a bond's principal at maturity.

CONCEPT CONNECTION   **EXAMPLE 6-6**

Sinking Fund

The Greenville Company issued bonds totaling $15 million for 30 years. The bond agreement specifies that a sinking fund must be maintained after 10 years, which will retire the bonds at maturity. Although no one can accurately predict interest rates, Greenville's bank has estimated that a yield of 6% on deposited funds is realistic for long-term planning. How much should Greenville plan to deposit each year to be able to retire the bonds with the money put aside?

Calculator Solution

Key	Input
n	20
I/Y	6
FV	15,000,000
PV	0
	Answer
PMT	407,768.35

SOLUTION: First recognize that the time period of the annuity is the last 20 years of the bond issue's life, because the bond agreement states that the sinking fund must be maintained only after 10 years. In other words, time zero isn't today but the beginning of the eleventh year in the bond's life.

The problem's time line looks like this.

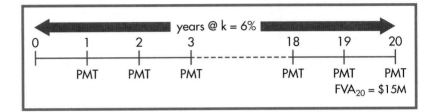

First write the future value of an annuity formula, Equation 6.13.

$$FVA_n = PMT[FVFA_{k,n}]$$

In this case, the future value itself is known. It's the principal amount of the bond issue that will have to be repaid, $15 million. Also, k is 6% and n is 20 years, the duration of the sinking fund according to the contract. Substitute these values.

$$\$15,000,000 = PMT[FVFA_{6,20}]$$

Next look up $FVFA_{6,20}$ in Appendix A (Table A-3), getting 36.7856, and substitute.

$$\$15,000,000 = PMT[36.7856]$$

Finally, solve for PMT.

$$PMT = \$407,768.26$$

Greenville will have to deposit just under $408K per year starting in the eleventh year of the bond issue's life to ensure that the bonds will be retired on schedule without a problem.

At this point we're going to digress from time value problems themselves to study a little more detail about the workings of interest rates.

6.3d   Compound Interest and Non-Annual Compounding

Until now we've been working with annually compounded interest. Although interest rates are always quoted in annual terms, they're usually not compounded annually, and that varies the actual amount of interest paid. Before going any further, let's be sure we know exactly what the term **compound interest** means.

Compounding refers to earning interest on previously earned interest.

Compound Interest   Compounding refers to the idea of earning interest on previously earned interest. Imagine putting $100 in the bank at 10%. We'd earn $10 in the first year and have a balance of $110 at year end. In the second year, we'll earn $11 for a balance of $121, in the third year $12.10, and so on. The interest is larger each year

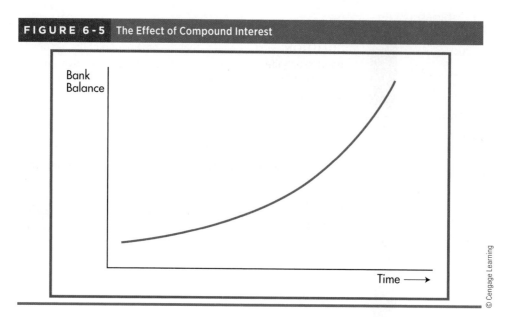

FIGURE 6-5 The Effect of Compound Interest

© Cengage Learning

because it's calculated on a balance that increases with the accumulation of all prior interest.

Under compound interest the balance in the bank grows at an exponential rate. Graphically, an amount placed at compound interest grows as shown in Figure 6-5. The increasing steepness of the curve as time progresses is characteristic of exponential growth.

Compounding Periods   Every interest rate has an associated **compounding period.** Commonly used periods are annual, semiannual, quarterly, and monthly. When none is mentioned, an annual period is implied.

The compounding period associated with an interest rate refers to the frequency with which interest is credited into the recipient's account for the purpose of calculating future interest. The shorter the period, the more frequently interest is credited and the more interest is earned *on interest.*

An example will make the idea clear. If a bank pays 12% interest compounded annually, someone depositing $100 is credited with $12 at the end of a year, and the basis for the second year's interest calculation is $112. A time line portrayal of the year would look like this.

If the 12% is compounded semiannually, the year is divided into two halves and 6% interest is paid in each. However, the first half year's interest is credited to the depositor at midyear and earns additional interest in the second half. The additional interest is 6% of $6 or $0.36. The time line portrayal looks like this.

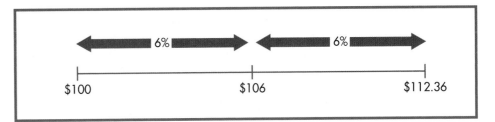

Compounding 12% quarterly involves dividing the year into four quarters, each paying (12%/4 =) 3%. Each quarter's interest is credited at the end of the quarter. The time line looks like this.

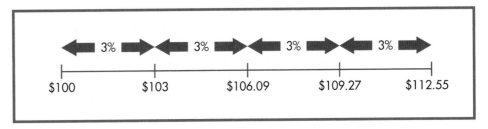

It's easy to get each successive quarter's ending balance by multiplying the previous balance by 1 plus the *quarterly* interest rate in decimal form. That's 1.03 in this case. This is just the $(1 + k)$ idea we've been working with, but k is stated for a quarterly compounding period.

Compounding 12% monthly involves dividing the year into 12 monthly periods, each bearing a 1% interest rate. If $100.00 is initially deposited, the year-end balance will be $112.68.

It's common practice to quote an annual rate and state the compounding period immediately afterward. The quarterly case in our 12% example would be quoted as "12% compounded quarterly." Those words literally mean 3% interest paid on quarterly periods.

The quoted rate, 12% in this case, is called the **nominal interest rate**. We'll write it as k_{nom}. The word "nominal" just means named.

It's possible to pay interest compounded on any time period; however, the periods we've mentioned are the most common in business. Daily compounding is encountered only rarely.

The theoretical limit as periods become shorter is continuous compounding in which interest is instantaneously credited as earned. Continuous compounding takes some special math that we'll discuss later.

> Interest rates are quoted by stating the **nominal rate** followed by the **compounding period**.

The Effective Annual Rate

Notice in the 12% example above that the final bank balance increases with more frequent compounding. Let's summarize those calculations. For an initial deposit of $100 and a nominal rate of 12%, Table 6-2 shows the amounts in the bank at the end of one year.

TABLE 6-2	Year-End Balances at Various Compounding Periods for $100 Initial Deposit and k_{nom} = 12%

Compounding	Final Balance
Annual	$112.00
Semiannual	112.36
Quarterly	112.55
Monthly	112.68

© Cengage Learning

These differences in a depositor's balance mean that although all four rates are quoted as 12%, different amounts of interest are actually being paid. As we've explained, the difference is due to the frequency of compounding.

It's important to quantify the effect of different compounding methods to avoid confusion in financial dealings. That is, people need to know just how much more monthly or quarterly compounding pays than annual compounding at any nominal rate. This need for clarification has led to the idea of an **effective annual rate (EAR)**. It's the rate of annually compounded interest that is just equivalent to the nominal rate compounded more frequently. Stated another way, it's the annually compounded rate that gets the depositor the same account balance after one year that he or she would get under more frequent compounding.

The **effective annual rate (EAR)** is the annually compounded rate that pays the same interest as a lower rate compounded more frequently.

Let's consider 12% compounded monthly as an example. What annually compounded interest rate will get a depositor the same interest? Table 6-2 shows that monthly compounding results in an ending balance of $112.68 on an initial deposit of $100; hence, the total interest paid is $12.68.

The annually compounded rate that pays this much interest is calculated by dividing the interest paid by the principal invested.

$$\$12.68/\$100.00 = .1268 = 12.68\%$$

Hence, 12.68% compounded annually is *effectively* equal to 12% compounded monthly. What are the EARs for semiannual and quarterly compounding at 12%?

Truth in lending legislation requires that lenders disclose the EAR on loans. Watch for it the next time you see an advertisement for a bank.

In general, the EAR can be calculated for any compounding period by using the following formula.

(6.14)
$$EAR = \left(1 + \frac{k_{nom}}{m}\right)^m - 1$$

where m is the number of compounding periods per year (12 for monthly, 4 for quarterly, and 2 for semiannually).

The effect of more frequent compounding is greater at higher interest rates. Table 6-3 illustrates this point. At a nominal rate of 6%, the effective increase in interest due to monthly rather than annual compounding is only .17%, which represents a 2.8% increase in the rate actually paid ($.17/6.00 = .028 = 2.8\%$). At 18%, however, the effective increase is 1.56%, which represents an 8.7% increase in what's actually paid.

TABLE 6-3	Changes in the Effect of Compounding at Different Rates		
Nominal Rate	EAR for Monthly Compounding	Effective Increase	Increase as % of k_{nom}
6%	6.17%	.17%	2.8%
12	12.68	.68	5.7
18	19.56	1.56	8.7

The APR and the EAR　Some credit card companies charge monthly interest on unpaid balances at rates in the neighborhood of 1.5%. This represents a monthly compounding of interest on the cardholder's debt. They advertise that the annual percentage rate, known as the APR, is 18%, 12 times the monthly rate.

> The **annual percentage rate (APR)** associated with credit cards is actually the nominal rate and is less than the **effective annual rate (EAR)**.

Don't confuse the **annual percentage rate (APR)** with the **effective annual rate (EAR)**. The APR is actually the nominal rate. Table 6-3 shows that at a nominal rate of 18% the EAR for monthly compounding is 19.56%, somewhat more than 18%.

Compounding Periods and the Time Value Formulas　Each of the time value formulas contains an interest rate, k, and a number time of periods, n. In using the formulas, the time periods must be compounding periods, and the interest rate must be the rate for a single compounding period.

The problems we've dealt with so far have all involved annual compounding. In that case, the compounding period is a year, and the appropriate interest rate is the nominal rate itself. Things are a little more complicated with non-annual compounding periods. Let's consider quarters as an example.

Suppose we have a time value problem that runs for five years and has an interest rate of 12%. If compounding is annual, k and n are simply 12 and 5, respectively. However, if compounding is quarterly, the appropriate period is one quarter and the rate for that period is (12%/4 =) 3%. Further, the time dimension of the problem needs to be stated as 20 quarters rather than five years (5 years × 4 quarters/year = 20 quarters). Hence, k and n for the problem should be 3 and 20, respectively.

Whenever we run into a problem with non-annual compounding, we have to calculate the appropriate k and n for use in the formulas from the nominal rate and time given in the problem. Some simple rules make that easy to do.

If a problem gives a nominal rate and states time in years, compute k and n for use in the formulas as follows.

$$\text{Semiannual:} \quad k = k_{nom}/2 \quad\quad n = \text{years} \times 2$$
$$\text{Quarterly:} \quad k = k_{nom}/4 \quad\quad n = \text{years} \times 4$$
$$\text{Monthly:} \quad k = k_{nom}/12 \quad\quad n = \text{years} \times 12$$

Recall that some calculators will automatically divide the interest input by a number of compounding periods for you. That feature is convenient if you're working with the same kind of compounding all the time. But because we're switching from one to another, it's better to leave the setting at one (1) and input the interest rate for the compounding period.

Let's try two problems involving the future value of an annuity to get used to these ideas (Examples 6-7 and 6-8).

CONCEPT CONNECTION   EXAMPLE 6-7

Monthly Compounding

You want to buy a car costing $15,000 in 2½ years. You plan to save the money by making equal monthly deposits in your bank account, which pays 12% compounded monthly. How much must you deposit each month?

SOLUTION: In this situation, the future value of a series of payments must accumulate to a known amount, indicating a future value of an annuity problem.

First, calculate the correct k and n. Because compounding is monthly,

$$k = \frac{k_{nom}}{12} = \frac{12\%}{12} = 1\%$$

and

$$n = 2.5 \text{ years} \times 12 \text{ months/year} = 30 \text{ months.}$$

Next, write the future value of an annuity expression and substitute.

$$FVA_n = PMT\left[FVFA_{k,n}\right]$$
$$\$15,000 = PMT\left[FVFA_{1,30}\right]$$

Use Appendix A (Table A-3) to find $FVFA_{1,30} = 34.7849$ and substitute.

$$\$15,000 = PMT\,[34.7849]$$

Finally, solve for PMT.

$$PMT = \$431.22$$

Calculator Solution

Key	Input
n	30
I/Y	1
FV	15,000
PV	0
Answer	
PMT	431.22

Ensuper/Shutterstock.com

CONCEPT CONNECTION   EXAMPLE 6-8

Quarterly Compounding

Jeff and Susan Johnson have a daughter, Molly, just entering high school, and they've started to think about sending her to college. They expect to need about $100,000 in cash when she starts. Although the Johnsons have a good income, they live extravagantly and have little or no savings. Susan analyzed the family budget and decided they could realistically put away $1,500 a month or $4,500 per quarter toward Molly's schooling. They're now searching for an investment vehicle that will provide a return sufficient to grow these savings into $100,000 in four years. If quarterly compounding is assumed, how large a return (interest rate) do the Johnsons have to get to achieve their goal? Is it realistic?

SOLUTION: Once again we recognize this as a future value of an annuity problem because of the stream of payments involved and the fact that the Johnsons are saving for a known future amount.

Because the problem runs for four years and the compounding is quarterly, n is calculated as

$$n = 4 \text{ years} \times 4 \text{ quarters/year} = 16 \text{ quarters}$$

Ensuper/Shutterstock.com

Equation 6.13 gives the future value of an annuity expression.

$$FVA_n = PMT[FVFA_{k,n}]$$

Substituting values from the problem, we have

$$\$100,000 = \$4,500[FVFA_{k,16}]$$

Solving for the factor yields

$$FVFA_{k,n} = 22.2222$$

In Appendix A (Table A-3), we search for this value along the row for 16 periods and find that it lies between 4% and 4.5%. In this case, it's fairly easy to estimate that the factor is about half of the way between 4% and 4.5%.

Hence, the approximate solution is 4.2%, however, that's a quarterly rate. The appropriate nominal rate is

$$4.2\% \times 4 = 16.8\%$$

This is a high rate of return to expect on invested money. Is it reasonable to expect such a rate to be sustained over four years?

There's no definite answer to that question. There have been times when that expectation would have been reasonable, but such a high rate can always be expected to involve substantial risk. Because they probably don't want to risk not being able to send Molly to college, the Johnsons should probably try to save a little more and opt for a more conservative investment.

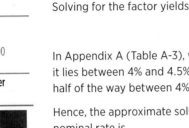

Calculator Solution

Key	Input
n	16
PMT	4,500
FV	100,000
PV	0
Answer	
I/Y	4.225

6.3e The Present Value of an Annuity—Developing a Formula

The present value of an annuity is simply the sum of the present values of all of the annuity's payments. We could always calculate these individually, but it's much easier to develop a formula to do all the calculations in one step as we did with the future value. The method we'll use is similar to that used in developing the future value formula, but we'll proceed more quickly because we've used the approach before.

We begin with a time line portrayal of a three-period annuity and write down the present value of each payment in terms of the interest rate, k. In this case we divide by powers of $(1 + k)$ instead of multiplying as in the future value case. Review Equations 6.5 and 6.6 to see that this gives the present value of an amount. Figure 6-6 is the time line portrayal.

The present value is formed for the first payment by dividing the payment amount by $(1 + k)$, for the second payment by dividing by $(1 + k)^2$, and so forth. Notice that this is equivalent to multiplying by present value factors, because $1/(1 + k)$ is the present value factor for k and one period; $PVF_{k,1}$; $1/(1 + k)^2$ is the present value factor for k and two periods; and so on.

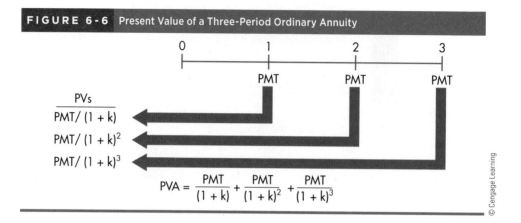

FIGURE 6-6   Present Value of a Three-Period Ordinary Annuity

$$PVA = \frac{PMT}{(1 + k)} + \frac{PMT}{(1 + k)^2} + \frac{PMT}{(1 + k)^3}$$

The present value of the three-period annuity is

(6.15)
$$PVA = \frac{PMT}{(1 + k)} + \frac{PMT}{(1 + k)^2} + \frac{PMT}{(1 + k)^3}$$

which can also be written as

(6.15)
$$PVA = PMT(1 + k)^{-1} + PMT(1 + k)^{-2} + PMT(1 + k)^{-3}$$

with negative exponents to indicate one over the powers of $(1 + k)$.

Notice how regular the expression is. Every payment produces a term involving PMT divided by $(1 + k)$ to a successively larger power beginning with 1.

Examining Figure 6-6, we can easily see that adding more periods to the annuity would just add more terms to the equation. For example, a fourth payment would produce a term $PMT(1 + k)^{-4}$, and so on.

Thus we can generalize Equation 6.15 for any number of periods, n, as follows.

(6.16)
$$PVA = PMT(1 + k)^{-1} + PMT(1 + k)^{-2} + \cdots + PMT(1 + k)^{-n}$$

Next, we can factor PMT out of the right side of Equation 6.16 and use summation notation to represent the terms involving negative powers of $(1 + k)$.

(6.17)
$$PVA = PMT \left[\sum_{i=1}^{n} (1 + k)^{-i} \right]$$

Once again, we notice that the expression in the brackets is a function of only k and n, and can be tabulated for likely values of those variables. This is the present value factor for an annuity and is written as $PVFA_{k,n}$.

(6.18)
$$PVFA_{k,n} = \sum_{i=1}^{n} (1 + k)^{-i}$$

Values of the present value factor for an annuity are tabulated in Appendix A (Table A-4).

Finally, we can rewrite Equation 6.17 by substituting from Equation 6.18. The resulting expression is convenient for use in solving problems when used in conjunction with Appendix A (Table A-4).

(6.19)
$$PVA = PMT[PVFA_{k,n}]$$

6.3f   The Present Value of an Annuity—Solving Problems

Equation 6.19 for the present value of an annuity works just like Equation 6.13 does for the future value of an annuity. There are four variables. PVA (the present value itself), PMT (the payment), k (the interest rate), and n (the number of periods). Problems will generally present three of them as known and ask you to find the fourth. The general approach is similar to what we've already been doing.

Terminology–Discounting   The present value of money expected in the future is always less than the dollar value of that future sum. This is true whether the money expected is one or more amounts or an annuity. In the annuity case, the present value of the annuity is always less than the sum of the payments.

Because of this *less than* relationship, it's common to say that we *discount* a future sum to its present value. Further, the present valuing process itself is commonly called *discounting*.

The expression is especially common in banking. If a company has a reliable expectation of receiving a specified sum of money in the future, say from a contract, it's

---

CONCEPT CONNECTION   EXAMPLE 6-9

Present Value of an Annuity

The Shipson Company has just sold a large machine to Baltimore Inc. on an installment contract. The contract calls for Baltimore to make payments of $5,000 every six months (semiannually) for 10 years. Shipson would like its cash now and asks its bank to discount the contract and pay it the present (discounted) value. Baltimore is a good credit risk, so the bank is willing to discount the contract at 14% compounded semiannually. How much will Shipson receive?

SOLUTION: The contract represents an annuity with payments of $5,000. The bank is willing to buy it for its present value at a relatively high rate of interest. The higher the rate of interest, the lower the price the bank is willing to pay for the contract.

First calculate the appropriate k and n for semiannual compounding.

$$k = k_{nom}/2 = 14\%/2 = 7\%$$
$$n = 10 \text{ years} \times 2 = 20.$$

The time line looks like this.

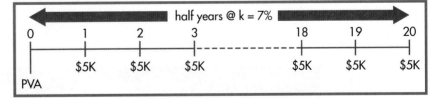

Write Equation 6.19 and substitute the known information.

$$PVA = PMT\left[PVFA_{k,n}\right]$$
$$PVA = \$5,000\left[PVFA_{7,20}\right]$$

Appendix A (Table A-4) gives $PVFA_{7,20} = 10.5940$. Substituting and solving for PVA yields

$$PVA = \$52,970$$

Calculator Solution

Key	Input
n	20
I/Y	7
PMT	5,000
FV	0
Answer	
PV	52,970.07

possible to sell that expectation to a bank for its present value at the bank's interest rate. We then say the bank is *discounting* the contract. The interest rate the bank uses is called the *discount rate* for the transaction.

Spreadsheet Solutions

Time value problems can be solved using spreadsheet programs like Microsoft Excel™. The technique is similar to using a calculator. We'll explain the technique assuming that you're familiar with the basics of spreadsheet software.

Recall that there are four variables in every time value problem, but they're different depending on whether we're dealing with amounts or annuities. In amount problems, we have PV, FV, k, and n, while in annuity problems we have *either* PVA *or* FVA, PMT, k, and n. Also recall that when using a calculator we use the PV and FV keys for both amounts and annuities. We can do this because the calculator is programmed to solve an annuity problem if we input a positive value for PMT and zero for either PV or FV. It solves an amount problem if we input zero for PMT. Hence, there is a total of five possible variables as follows.

k n PV FV PMT

To solve a problem with a calculator, we enter three numbers and zero a fourth. The calculator then gives us the unknown fifth variable.

A spreadsheet program uses similar logic. There are five spreadsheet time value functions. Each is used to calculate one of the five time value variables. Each function takes the *other* four variables as inputs. We'll use Microsoft Excel to illustrate. The five functions are as follows

To Solve For	Use Function
FV	FV(k, n, PMT, PV)
PV	PV(k, n, PMT, FV)
k	RATE(n, PMT, PV, FV)
n	NPER(k, PMT, PV, FV)
PMT	PMT(k, n, PV, FV)

To solve any time value problem, select the function for the unknown variable, put the problem values for the three known variables in the proper order within the parentheses, and input zero for the fourth variable. (Zero PMT for all amount problems, zero PV for future value of an annuity (FVA) problems, and zero FV for present value of an annuity (PVA) problems.)

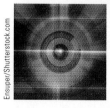

INSIGHTS   Practical Finance

The Lottery: Congratulations, You're Rich—But Not as Rich as You Thought

State lottery jackpots are enormous sums of money, but they're not really as big as they're made out to be. That's because of the time value of money and the way the prizes are paid. Large lottery prizes are typically paid over 25 years, but the lottery authority states the winnings as the sum of the payments without consideration of time value. For example, a $25 million prize is really $1 million a year for 25 years, an annuity.

What the winner really has today is the present value of that annuity. If a lucky player wants her money immediately, she has to accept the discounted value of the stream of payments. Suppose the interest rate is 7%. A calculation using the present value of an annuity formula reveals that the winner's real prize is about $11.7 million. That's nothing to sneeze at, but it is a far cry from $25 million.

To make matters worse, winnings are taxable, largely in the top bracket. Let's be optimistic and assume the winner hires a good tax accountant and only winds up paying about 32% in taxes. That knocks down the immediately available, after-tax winnings to about $8.4 million, a third of the amount advertised.

There are two minor complications in the procedure. The first is simply that interest rates are entered in decimal form rather than as whole numbers, so use .07 for 7%. The second involves the signs of the cash figures. Notice that there are three cash variables—FV, PV, and PMT—one of which is always zero. Hence, in every problem, there are two dollar variables. These must be of opposite signs.

The easiest way to think of this issue is in terms of inflows and outflows. Imagine, for example, a simple problem in which we're depositing a sum of money in a bank today (PV) and withdrawing it with interest (FV) some years later. If we define flows into the bank as positives, then flows out must be negatives. Hence, if PV is positive, FV is negative, whether the figures are inputs or outputs of the calculation. The reverse definition is also OK, as long as the variables have opposite signs.

This convention can create a bit of a problem if you forget it and input only positive figures. In some applications, the program simply gives you the correct answer with a negative sign, but in others the program doesn't work at all. Hence, the first thing to check when you get an error is the sign of your inputs.

Here's an example of the whole process. Suppose we want to calculate the amount we'll have in the bank after six years if we deposit $4,000 today at 7% interest. We're looking for the future value of an amount, so we choose the first function,

$$FV(k, n, PMT, PV)$$

and input as follows.

$$FV(.07, 6, 0, -4000)$$

Notice that we input 0 for PMT because we're not doing an annuity problem, we input the interest rate in decimal form, and we input the PV as a negative.

Now let's change things just a little to illustrate an annuity problem. Suppose we want to know the future value of a $4,000 annual annuity for six years at 7%. We choose the future value (FV) function again and input as follows.

$$FV(.07, 6, -4000, 0)$$

Notice we're now telling the program that it's dealing with an annuity by inputting a nonzero number for PMT. And because there's no present value in a future value of an annuity calculation (see Equation 6.13 on page 246), we input 0 for PV. The cell carrying this function will display the present value of our annuity. Boot up your computer and verify that these examples yield answers of $6,002.92 and $28,613.16, respectively.

CONCEPT CONNECTION

EXAMPLE 6-10

Spreadsheets

The bank in Example 6-9 discounts contracts for customers like Shipson frequently. Contracts can have payments of any constant amount for any number of periods, and the bank's interest rate changes frequently. Write a spreadsheet program for the bank that will calculate the discounted amount that should be paid on any contract like Shipson's after the interest rate, the term of the contract (in payment periods), and the amount of the payment are input into conveniently labeled cells.

SOLUTION: In this case, the bank wants to calculate the present value of an annuity, so we'll use the PV function

$$PV(k, n, PMT, FV)$$

Since this program will only be used for one thing, we can customize the formula by zeroing FV and making the PMT variable negative.

$$PV(k, n, -PMT, 0)$$

Then the banker just has to input the appropriate interest rate, number of periods, and payment as a positive number. Here we'll input .07 for k, one-half of the annual 14% rate, 20 semiannual periods, and payments of $5,000. Notice that we do have to deal with non-annual compounding just as we did using calculators or tables.

Here is a spreadsheet that does the job, along with a note detailing the operative formula. Notice that the input cells are programmed directly into the PV function along with a negative sign for the payment and a zero for the future value variable. The banker inputs the appropriate values into the blue cells, and the discounted amount of the contract appears in the brown cell.

	A	B	C	D	E	F	G
1							
2			**DISCOUNTING A CONTRACT**				
3							
4							
5		**Inputs**					
6							
7		**Interest Rate**			0.07		
8							
9		**Payment Periods**			20		
10							
11		**Payment Amount**			5000		
12							
13							
14		**Discounted Value**			$52,970.07		
15							
16							
17							
18		The formula in E14 is = PV(E7,E9, − E11,0)					
19							
20							

Amortized Loans   The most common application of the present value of an annuity concept is in dealing with amortized loans. Debt is said to be amortized when the principal is paid off gradually during its life. Car loans, home mortgages, and many business loans are amortized.

An **amortized loan** is generally structured so that a *constant* payment is made periodically, usually monthly, over the loan's term. Each payment contains one month's interest and an amount to reduce principal. Interest is charged on the outstanding loan balance at the beginning of each month, so as the loan's principal is reduced, successive interest charges become smaller. Because the monthly payments are equal, successive payments contain larger proportions of principal repayment and smaller proportions of interest.

In applying the present value of an annuity formula to an amortized loan, the amount borrowed is always the present value of the annuity, PVA, and the loan payment is always PMT.

> An **amortized loan's** principal is paid off gradually over its life.

CONCEPT CONNECTION   EXAMPLE 6-11

An Amortized Loan—Finding the Loan Payment, PMT

Suppose you borrow $10,000 over four years at 18% compounded monthly repayable in monthly installments. How much is your loan payment?

SOLUTION: First notice that for monthly compounding, k and n are

$$k = k_{nom}/12 = 18\%/12 = 1.5\%$$
$$n = 4 \text{ years} \times 12 \text{ months/year} = 48 \text{ months.}$$

Then write Equation 6.19 and substitute.

$$PVA = PMT[PVFA_{k,n}]$$
$$\$10,000 = PMT[PVFA_{1.5,48}]$$

Appendix A (Table A-4) gives $PVFA_{1.5,48} = 34.0426$, so

$$\$10,000 = PMT(34.0426)$$

and

$$PMT = \$293.75$$

Calculator Solution

Key	Input
n	48
I/Y	1.5
PV	10,000
FV	0
Answer	
PV	293.75

Ensuper/Shutterstock.com

CONCEPT CONNECTION   EXAMPLE 6-12

An Amortized Loan—Finding the Amount Borrowed, PVA

Suppose you want to buy a car and can afford to make payments of $500 a month. The bank makes three-year car loans at 12% compounded monthly. How much can you borrow toward a new car?

SOLUTION: For monthly compounding,

$$k = k_{nom}/12 = 12\%/12 = 1\%$$
$$n = 3 \text{ years} \times 12 \text{ months/year} = 36 \text{ months.}$$

Calculator Solution

Key	Input
n	36
I/Y	1
PMT	500
FV	0
Answer	
PV	15,053.75

Ensuper/Shutterstock.com

Write Equation 6.19 and substitute.

$$PVA = PMT \left[PVFA_{k,n} \right]$$
$$PVA = \$500 \left[PVFA_{1.36} \right]$$

Appendix A (Table A-4) gives $PVFA_{1,36} = 30.1075$, and

$$PVA = \$500(30.1075)$$
$$PVA = \$15,053.75$$

That is, the bank would lend you $15,053.75.

Loan Amortization Schedules   A loan amortization schedule lists every payment and shows how much of it goes to pay interest and how much reduces principal. It also shows the beginning and ending balances of unpaid principal for each period.

To construct an amortization schedule, we have to know the loan amount, the payment, and the periodic interest rate. That's PVA, PMT, and k. Let's use the loan in the last example as an illustration. Table 6-4 shows the completed computation for the first two lines. Follow the explanation in the next paragraph for the first line, verify the second line, and fill in the third and fourth lines yourself.

The loan amount is $15,053.75. This is the beginning balance for the first monthly period. The payment is a constant $500.00, that amount is entered on every row in the payment column. Although the nominal interest rate in this case is 12%, the monthly interest rate is 1% because compounding is monthly. Therefore, the monthly interest charge is calculated as 1% of the month's beginning loan balance.

Loan amortization schedules detail the interest and principal in each loan payment.

$$\$15,053.75 \times .01 = \$150.54$$

As the payment is $500 and $150.54 goes to interest, the remaining ($500.00 − $150.54 =) $349.46 reduces principal. The ending loan balance is the beginning balance less the principal reduction, ($15,053.75 − $349.46 =) $14,704.29. This amount becomes the beginning balance for the next period, and the process is repeated.

This procedure carried out for 36 monthly periods will bring the ending balance to zero at the end of the last period. It's important to notice what happens to the

TABLE 6-4   A Partial Amortization Schedule

Period	Beginning Balance	Payment	Interest @1%	Principal Reduction	Ending Balance
1	$15,053.75	$500.00	$150.54	$349.46	$14,704.29
2	14,704.29	500.00	147.04	352.96	14,351.33
3	————	500.00	————	————	————
4	————	500.00	————	————	————
.	.	.	.	.	.
.	.	.	.	.	.
.	.	.	.	.	.

© Cengage Learning

composition of the payment as the loan is paid down. The interest charge declines, and the portion devoted to principal reduction increases, while the total payment remains constant.

Mortgage Loans   Loans used to buy real estate are called **mortgage loans** or just *mortgages*. A home mortgage is often the largest single financial transaction in an average person's life. A typical mortgage is an amortized loan with monthly compounding and payments that run for 30 years; that's 360 payments.

CONCEPT CONNECTION   **EXAMPLE 6-13**

Interest Content of Early Loan Payments

What is the interest content of the first payment on a 30-year, $100,000 mortgage loan at 6% (compounded monthly)?

SOLUTION: First calculate k and n for the loan.

$$k = \frac{k_{nom}}{12} = \frac{6\%}{12} = .5\%$$

$$n = 30 \text{ years} \times 12 \text{ months/year} = 360$$

Next write Equation 6.19, substitute, and solve for the monthly PMT.

$$PVA = PMT\left[PVFA_{k,n}\right]$$
$$\$100,000 = PMT\left[PVFA_{.5,360}\right]$$
$$\$100,000 = PMT(166.792)$$
$$PMT = 599.55$$

The first months's interest is .5% of $100,000.

$$\$100,000 \times .005 = \$500$$

So $500 of the first payment goes to interest, leaving $99.55 to reduce principal. Stated another way, the first payment is 83.4% interest.

Calculator Solution

Key	Input
n	360
I/Y	.5
PV	100,000
FV	0
	Answer
PMT	599.55

Ensuper/Shutterstock.com

This situation reverses toward the end of the mortgage when most of the payment is principal. In other words, during the early years of a mortgage, the principal is paid down slowly, but near the end it's amortized quickly.

This payment pattern has two important implications for homeowners. The most important is related to the fact that mortgage interest is tax deductible. Early mortgage payments provide homeowners with a big tax deduction, while later payments don't.

Consider the first payment on the loan in Example 6-13. If the homeowner is in the 25% tax bracket, he or she will save $125 in taxes by making that payment because it contains deductible interest of $500 ($500 × .25 = $125).

Hence, the *effective* loan payment is as follows.

Early mortgage payments are **almost all interest** and provide a big tax savings.

Payment	$599.55
Tax savings	125.00
Net	$474.55

In effect, the government shares the cost of home ownership, especially in the early years. Later on, although equity builds up faster, the tax benefit isn't nearly as great. (In this context, equity means the portion of the home's value that belongs to the homeowner as opposed to being supported by a bank loan.)

The second implication of the mortgage payment pattern is that halfway through a mortgage's life, the homeowner hasn't paid off half the loan.

CONCEPT CONNECTION   EXAMPLE 6-14

Mortgage Balance at Halfway

Calculator Solution

Key	Input
n	180
I/Y	.5
PMT	599.55
FV	0

Answer	
PV	71,048.78

Calculate the unpaid balance of the loan in Example 6-13 after 15 years, i.e., halfway through the mortgage's life. That represents the amount one could borrow making 180 payments of $599.55. Because this is what's left after 15 years, it must represent the remaining loan balance.

SOLUTION: Using Equation 6.19 as before but with n = 180, we have

$$PVA = PMT\left[PVFA_{k,n}\right]$$
$$= \$599.55\left[PVFA_{5,180}\right]$$
$$= \$599.55[118.504]$$
$$= \$71,049.07$$

Thus, halfway through the life of this $100,000 mortgage, roughly $71,000 is still outstanding. In other words, only about 29% of the original loan has been paid off.

Another interesting feature of a long-term amortized loan like a mortgage is the total amount of interest paid over the entire term. Again considering the loan in Example 6-13, at 6% the homeowner pays approximately 87% of the amount of the loan in interest even after considering the tax savings.

Total payments ($599.55 × 360)	$215,838.00
Less original loan	100,000.00
Total interest	$ 115,838.00
Tax savings @ 25%	28,959.50
Net interest cost	$ 86,878.50

Of course, this effect varies dramatically with the interest rate. Over the last 30 years, rates have varied between 3% and 16%. Recently, in the 2000s, they've been on the low end of that range. Verify that the net after-tax interest cost of a $100,000 mortgage loan at 8% is $123,116.28.[2]

Amortized Loans and Tax Planning   Because interest payments on business loans and home mortgages are tax deductible, we're sometimes interested in projecting the total interest and principal payments to be made during a particular future year of a loan's life. If we don't want to write out the entire amortization schedule, we can solve the problem by calculating the loan balance at the beginning and end of the year.

---

2. At 12%, a typical mortgage rate in the 1980s, the first mortgage payment is 97% interest, and the net after-tax interest cost over 30 years is almost twice the amount borrowed.

CONCEPT CONNECTION   EXAMPLE 6-15

Principal and Interest Paid in a Year

Calculate the principal and interest payments in the third year of the $100,000 loan in Example 6-13.

SOLUTION: The loan balance at the beginning of the third year will be the amount left after 24 payments have been made and there are 336 left to go.

We find it by using Equation 6.19 ($PVFA_{.5,336} = 162.569$, and $PVFA_{.5,324} = 160.260$ are not included in Appendix A [Table A-4]).

$$
\begin{aligned}
PVA &= PMT\left[PVFA_{k,n}\right] \\
&= \$599.55\left[PVFA_{.5,336}\right] \\
&= \$599.55[162.569] \\
&= \$97,468.24
\end{aligned}
$$

Similarly, 324 payments will be left after three years.

$$
\begin{aligned}
PVA &= \$599.55\left[PVFA_{.5,324}\right] \\
&= \$599.55[160.260] \\
&= \$96,083.88
\end{aligned}
$$

The difference between these balances, $1,384.36, is the amount paid into principal during the year. There are 12 payments totaling ($599.55 × 12 =) $7,194.60, so the interest portion is this amount less the contribution to equity.

Total payments	$7,194.60
Principal reduction	(1,384.36)
Deductible interest	$5,810.24

Calculator Solution

Key	Input
n	336
I/Y	.5
PMT	599.55
FV	0
Answer	
PV	97,468.15

Calculator Solution

Key	Input
n	324
I/Y	.5
PMT	599.55
FV	0
Answer	
PV	96,083.99

Ensuper/Shutterstock.com

The Adjustable-Rate Mortgage (ARM)   We discussed adjustable-rate mortgages in Chapter 5 in connection with the financial crisis of 2008. An ARM is a mortgage in which the interest rate is periodically reset to remain close to current market rates. The device transfers the risk associated with changing rates from the lender to the borrower.

When an ARM resets, the borrower's monthly payment changes to amortize the outstanding loan balance over the remaining life of the mortgage. In Equation 6.19, PVA becomes the outstanding balance at the time of reset, k is the new monthly interest rate, and n is the remaining life of the loan.

But suppose a borrower wants to evaluate the consequences of an ARM before signing loan papers? That takes a two-step calculation. He must project the loan balance at the estimated time of reset and then calculate a new payment using that and new estimates of k and n. The idea is illustrated in Example 6-16 on page 266.

6.3g   The Annuity Due

So far we've dealt only with ordinary annuities in which payments occur at the ends of time periods. When payments occur at the beginnings of time periods, we have an annuity due, and our formulas need to be modified somewhat.

CONCEPT CONNECTION   EXAMPLE 6-16

Estimating an Arm Reset

Roxanne Smothers is considering buying a new house and has been offered two options on a $200,000, 30-year mortgage. The first is a fixed-rate loan at 7% with constant payments of $1,331 per month. Second is an ARM with an initial rate of 6% and initial payments of $1,199.

Roxanne is concerned that interest rates might rise substantially over the next several years. Calculate her monthly ARM payment if its rate resets to 9% after five years.

SOLUTION: First calculate the projected unpaid ARM balance after five years (60 months). To do that, write Equation 6.19 and substitute PMT = $1,199, k = .5, and n = 300 (remaining term in months) as we did in Examples 6-14 and 6-15.

$$PVA = PMT[PVFA_{k,n}]$$
$$= \$1,199[PVFA_{.5,300}]$$
$$= \$1,199[155.207]$$
$$= \$186,093$$

Next, use Equation 6.19 to calculate the payment required to amortize $186,093 over the remaining 25 years at 9%.

$$k = 9/12 = .75 \ n = 25 \times 12 = 300$$
$$PVA = PMT[PVFA_{k,n}]$$
$$\$186,093 = PMT[PVFA_{.75,300}]$$
$$\$186,093 = PMT[119.162]$$
$$PMT = \$1,562$$

So, if interest rates rise to 9% by the fifth year, Roxanne's ARM payments will jump to $1,562, a 30% increase. That's $231 more than the fixed-rate mortgage payment.

Remember, interest rates may not rise, or they may rise by more than 9%. Which mortgage would you choose?

In an **annuity due**, payments occur at the **beginning** of each period.

The Future Value of an Annuity Due

In an **annuity due**, payments are paid or received at the beginning rather than at the end of each period. Consider the future value of an annuity formula as developed in Figure 6-4. Review that figure on page 244 now. Because the end of one period is the beginning of the next, we can create the annuity due by simply shifting each payment back one period in time. This is shown schematically in Figure 6-7. There is now a payment at time 0, but none at time 3.

Because each payment is received one period earlier, it spends one period longer in the bank earning interest. Therefore, each payment's future value at the end of the annuity will be whatever it was before times $(1 + k)$. The additional $(1 + k)$ is shown in italics in the diagram.

The future value of the annuity due, which we'll call $FVAd_3$, is then

$$FVAd_3 = PMT(1 + k) + PMT(1 + k)(1 + k) + PMT(1 + k)^2(1 + k)$$

which can be rewritten by factoring out the additional $(1 + k)$ as

(6.20) $$FVAd_3 = [PMT + PMT(1 + k) + PMT(1 + k)^2](1 + k)$$

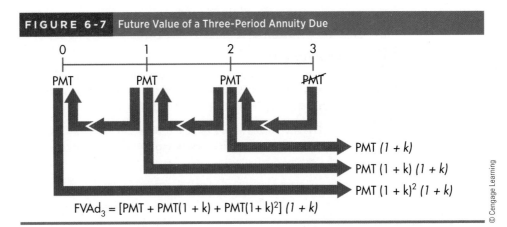

FIGURE 6-7 Future Value of a Three-Period Annuity Due

$$FVAd_3 = [PMT + PMT(1 + k) + PMT(1+ k)^2]\ (1 + k)$$

It's easy to see that no matter how many periods we choose to add, every term in an annuity due will be the same as it is in an ordinary annuity multiplied by an extra $(1 + k)$. Therefore, we can generalize Equation 6.20 to n periods.

(6.21) $$FVAd_3 = [PMT + PMT(1 + k) + \cdots + PMT(1 + k)^{n-1}](1 + k)$$

Once we've done that, the term inside the brackets can be developed into the ordinary annuity formula just as before. The only thing changed is the addition of the $(1 + k)$ factor on the right. Hence, the final formula for an annuity due is just our old formula for an ordinary annuity multiplied by $(1 + k)$.

(6.22) $$FVAd_n = PMT[FVFA_{k,n}](1 + k)$$

Situations in which an annuity due is appropriate can be recognized when words such as "starting now," "starting today," or "starting immediately" are used to describe a payment stream.

Advanced calculators let you set annuity payments at either the beginning or end of periods. If you set the beginning, the calculator takes care of the additional $(1 + k)$ multiplication automatically. However, if you're only doing an occasional annuity due problem, it's just as easy to multiply manually.

The Present Value of an Annuity Due   Applying logic similar to that of Figure 6-7 to the derivation of the present value of an annuity formula yields a similar formula for the present value of an annuity due, which we'll call PVAd.

(6.23) $$PVAd = PMT[PVFA_{k,n}](1 + k)$$

This expression is used in the same way as Equation 6.22. Example 6-17 involves an annuity due sinking fund.

As an optional exercise, work through the development of Equation 6.23.

Recognizing Types of Annuity Problems   The most common student errors in working annuity problems involve confusion over whether to use the present or future value technique. Here's a little guidance on how to keep the two straight.

CONCEPT CONNECTION   EXAMPLE 6-17

Annuity Due

The Baxter Corporation started making sinking fund deposits of $50,000 per quarter today. Baxter's bank pays 8% compounded quarterly, and the payments will be made for 10 years. What will the fund be worth at the end of that time?

SOLUTION: Recall from Example 6-6 on page 248 that a sinking fund is a future value of an annuity problem in which we're saving up money to retire a bond at its maturity. First calculate k and n.

$$k = 8\%/4 = 2\%$$
$$n = 10 \text{ years} \times 4 \text{ quarters/year} = 40 \text{ quarters}$$

Next write Equation 6.22 and substitute known values from the problem.

$$FVAd_n = PMT\left[FVFA_{k,n}\right](1 + k)$$
$$FVAd_{40} = \$50,000\left[FVFA_{2,40}\right](1.02)$$

Get $FVFA_{2,40} = 60.4020$ from Appendix A (Table A-3) and substitute.

$$FVAd_{40} = \$50,000[60.4020](1.02)$$
$$= \$3,080,502$$

It's important to notice that the interest rate, k, is used in two different ways in annuity due problems. It's one of two subscripts on the future value factor for an annuity, $FVFA_{k,n}$ and it appears algebraically in the term $(1 + k)$. Used as a subscript, it represents a column heading in one of the annuity tables in Appendix A, most of which are written as integer numbers. But in the algebraic term $(1 + k)$, it's the decimal form of a percent, in this example .02 for 2%, and $(1 + k)$ is $(1 + .02)$ which is 1.02.

Calculator Solution

Key	Input
n	40
I/Y	2
PMT	50,000
PV	0

	Answer
FV	3,020,099
	×1.02
FV	3,080,501

First, an annuity problem is always recognized by the presence of a *stream* of *equal* payments. Whether the value of the payments is known or unknown, a series of them means an annuity.

Annuity problems always involve some kind of a transaction at one end of the stream of payments or the other. If the transaction is at the end of the stream, you have a future value problem. If the transaction is in the beginning, you have a present value problem. Here's a graphic representation of this idea.

A loan is always a present value of an annuity problem. The annuity itself is the stream of loan payments. The transaction is the transfer of the amount borrowed from the lender to the borrower. That always occurs at the beginning of the payment stream.

Putting aside money to pay for something in the future (saving up) is always a future value of an annuity problem. For example, suppose we're saving up to buy a car by depositing equal sums in the bank each month. The deposits are the payments, and the car purchase is the transaction at the end of the payment stream.

6.3h   Perpetuities

A **perpetuity** is a stream of regular payments that goes on **forever**.

A series of equal payments that occur at equal intervals and go on forever is called a **perpetuity**. You can think of a perpetuity as an infinite annuity although it's not really an annuity because it has no end.

The concept of future value clearly doesn't make sense for perpetuities, because there's no end point in time to which future values can be projected. The present value of a perpetuity, however, does make sense.

The present value of a perpetuity, like that of an annuity, is the sum of the present values of all the individual payments. At first that doesn't seem to make sense either, because you'd think the sum of the present values of an infinite number of payments would be an infinite number itself.

However, the *present value* of each payment in an infinite stream is a diminishing series of numbers. Each payment's PV contribution to the sum is smaller than that of the one before because it's farther out into the future. Mathematically, the sum of such a diminishing series of numbers turns out to be finite. Further, the computation of that finite value is rather simple.

The present value of a perpetuity of payments of amount PMT, at interest rate k, which we'll call PV_p, is just

(6.24)
$$PV_P = \frac{PMT}{k}$$

where k is the interest rate for the period on which the payment is made. For example, if the payment is made quarterly and interest is compounded quarterly, k is the interest rate for quarterly compounding, $k_{nom}/4$.

Notice that the present value of a perpetuity at a given interest rate is a sum that, if deposited at that rate, will just earn the amount of the payment each period without compounding. To see that, just solve Equation 6.24 for PMT.

CONCEPT CONNECTION   EXAMPLE 6-18

Perpetuities—Preferred Stock

The Longhorn Corporation issues a security that promises to pay its holder $5 per quarter indefinitely. Money markets are such that investors can earn about 8% compounded quarterly on their money. How much can Longhorn sell this special security for?

Preferred stock dividends are a perpetuity.

SOLUTION: Longhorn's security represents a perpetuity paid on a quarterly basis. The security is worth the present value of the payments promised at the going interest rate.

$$PV_P = \frac{PMT}{k} = \frac{\$5.00}{.02} = \$250$$

Securities that offer a deal like this are called **preferred stocks.** We'll study preferred stocks in detail in Chapter 8.

CONCEPT CONNECTION   EXAMPLE 6-19

Perpetuities—Capitalization of Earnings

Ebertek is a privately held corporation that is currently being offered for sale. Big Corp. is considering buying the firm. Ebertek's earnings after tax have averaged $2.5 million for the last five years without much variation. Interest rates are about 10%. What is a realistic starting point for price negotiations?

SOLUTION: If the parties agree that Ebertek's earnings stream is stable, a fair price for the company is the present value of a perpetuity of those earnings. In this case, the company should be worth approximately

A steady stream of **earnings** is **capitalized** at its present value as a perpetuity.

$$PV_P = \frac{PMT}{k} = \frac{\$2,500,000}{.10} = \$25,000,000$$

This valuation process is called the *capitalization of earnings,* at the relevant interest rate, which is 10% in this case. In essence, we equate the stream of payments to an amount of capital (money) that would earn an equivalent series of payments at the current interest rate.

Negotiations move up or down from that starting point depending on whether future earnings prospects look better or worse than the recent past.

Continuous Compounding   In the section on compound interest earlier in this chapter, we discussed compounding periods of less than a year. We specifically addressed annual, semiannual, quarterly, and monthly periods.

Compounding periods can theoretically be even shorter than a day. Hours, minutes, or seconds are indeed possible. In the limit, as time periods become infinitesimally short, we have the idea of *continuous compounding* in which interest is instantaneously credited to the recipient's account as it is earned.

The development of formulas for continuous compounding is more mathematically advanced than we want to deal with in this text. Therefore, we'll just present an expression for amount problems without derivation.

(6.25) $$FV_n = PV(e^{kn})$$

where k is the nominal rate *in decimal form,* and n is the number of years in the problem.

The letter e represents a special number in advanced mathematics whose decimal value is 2.71828.... All financial and engineering calculators have an e^x key for calculating exponential values of e. Notice that you can use Equation 6.25 to solve for either the present or future value of an amount. Fractional values for k and/or n can be used directly in this equation. The idea is illustrated in Example 6-20.

A Note on the Similarity of the Equations   Either of the two amount equations can be used to solve any amount problem because both come from Equation 6.3. The four variables are the same, and the time value factors are reciprocals of one another.

The two annuity expressions appear to have the same symmetry, but they don't. The annuity equations are not interchangeable, and each is suited only to its own type of problem. Further, there isn't a reciprocal relationship between the factors. You therefore must choose the correct annuity formula before starting a problem.

CONCEPT CONNECTION   **EXAMPLE 6-20**

Continuous Compounding

The First National Bank of Charleston is offering continuously compounded interest on savings deposits. Such an offering is generally more of a promotional feature than anything else.

    a.   If you deposit $5,000 at 6½% compounded continuously and leave it in the bank for 3½ years, how much will you have?

    b.   What is the equivalent annual rate (EAR) of 12% compounded continuously?

SOLUTION: To solve part (a), write Equation 6.25 and substitute from the problem.

$$FV_n = PV(e^{kn})$$
$$FV_{3.5} = \$5,000(e^{(.065)(3.5)})$$
$$= \$5,000(e^{.2275})$$

Use a calculator to calculate $e^{.2275} = 1.255457$, then multiply.

$$FV_{3.5} = \$6,277.29$$

For part (b), calculate the interest earned on a $100 deposit at 12% compounded continuously in one year.

$$FV_n = PV(e^{kn})$$
$$FV_1 = \$100(e^{(.12)(1)})$$
$$= \$100(e^{.12})$$
$$= \$100(1.1275)$$
$$= \$112.75$$

Because the initial deposit was $100, the interest earned is $12.75, and the EAR is $12.75/\$100 = 12.75\%$.

Compare this result to the year-end balances and resulting EARs for other compounding periods at 12% shown in Table 6-2 on page 252 and the related discussion.

Table 6-5 summarizes all of the time value formulas we've developed.

TABLE 6-5   Time Value Formulas

Equation Number	Formula	Table
	Amounts	
6.4	$FV_n = PV\,[FVF_{k,n}]$	A-1
6.7	$PV = FV_n\,[PVF_{k,n}]$	A-2
	Ordinary Annuities	
6.13	$FVA_n = PMT[FVFA_{k,n}]$	A-3
6.19	$PVA = PMT[PVFA_{k,n}]$	A-4
	Annuities Due	
6.22	$FVAd_n = PMT[FVFA_{k,n}](1 + k)$	A-3
6.23	$PVAd = PMT[PVFA_{k,n}](1 + k)$	A-4
	Perpetuity	
6.24	$PV_P = PMT/k$	
	Continuous Compounding	
6.25	$FV_n = PV(e^{kn})$	

6.3i   Multipart Problems

Real situations often demand putting two or more time value problems together to get a final solution. In such cases, a time line portrayal can be critical to keeping things straight. Here are two examples.

CONCEPT CONNECTION   **EXAMPLE 6-21**

Simple Multipart

Exeter Inc. has $75,000 invested in securities that earn a return of 16% compounded quarterly. The company is developing a new product that it plans to launch in two years at a cost of $500,000. Exeter's cash flow is good now but may not be later, so management would like to bank money from now until the launch to be sure of having the $500,000 in hand at that time. The money currently invested in securities can be used to provide part of the launch fund. Exeter's bank has offered an account that will pay 12% compounded monthly. How much should Exeter deposit with the bank each month to have enough reserved for the product launch?

SOLUTION: Two things are happening at once in this problem. Exeter is saving up money by making monthly deposits (an annuity), and the money invested in securities (an amount) is growing independently at interest.

To figure out how much the firm has to deposit each month, we need to know how much the annuity deposits have to accumulate into by the end of two years. That's not given, but it can be calculated. The stream of annuity deposits must provide an amount equal to $500,000 less whatever the securities investment will grow into.

Thus, we have two problems that must be handled sequentially. First we have an amount problem to find the future value of $75,000. Once we have that figure, we'll subtract it from $500,000 to get the contribution required from the annuity. Then we'll solve a future value of an annuity problem for the payment required to get that amount.

It's important to notice that k and n aren't the same for the two parts of the problem. For the amount problem, we have quarterly compounding over two years at 16%, so k = 4% and n = 8 quarters. In the annuity problem, we have monthly compounding of 12% for two years, so k = 1% and n = 24 months. The two-part time line follows.

Calculator Solution

Key	Input
n	8
I/Y	4
PV	75,000
PMT	0
Answer	
FV	102,643

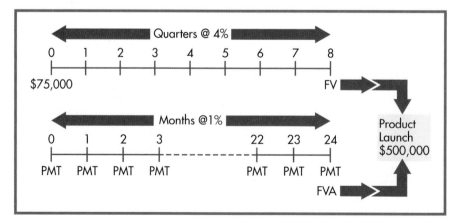

Find the future value of $75,000 by using Equation 6.4.

$$FV_n = PV[FVF_{k,n}]$$
$$FV_8 = \$75,000[FVF_{4,8}]$$
$$= \$75,000[1.3686]$$
$$= \$102,645$$

Calculator Solution

Key	Input
n	24
I/Y	1
FV	397,355
PV	0

	Answer
PMT	14,731

Then the savings annuity must provide

$$\$500,000 - \$102,645 = \$397,355$$

In other words, the future value of the annuity of the savings deposits is $397,355. Use Equation 6.13 to solve for the required payment.

$$FVA_n = PMT[FVFA_{k,n}]$$
$$\$397,355 = PMT[FVFA_{1,24}]$$
$$\$397,355 = PMT[26.9735]$$
$$PMT = \$14,731$$

CONCEPT CONNECTION   EXAMPLE 6-22

Complex Multipart

The Smith family plans to buy a new house three years from now for $400,000. They'll take out a traditional 30-year mortgage at the time of purchase. Mortgage lenders generally base the amount they'll lend on the borrower's gross family income, allowing roughly 25% of income to be applied to the mortgage payment. The Smiths anticipate that their family income will be about $96,000 at the time they'll purchase the house. The mortgage interest rate is expected to be about 9% at that time.

The mortgage alone won't provide enough cash to buy the house, and the family will need to have a down payment saved to make up the difference. They have a bank account that pays 6% compounded quarterly in which they've already saved $20,000. They plan to make quarterly deposits from now until the time of purchase to save the rest. How much must each deposit be?

SOLUTION: We need three time lines to visualize this problem: one for the $20,000 already in the bank, one for the loan, and one for the savings to be made over the next three years. A time line diagram for the problem appears below in this box.

Notice that the problem is focused around the date of purchase of the house. The amount problem and the annuity of the savings end at that time, but that's when the loan begins. That is, time 0 for the loan isn't the present but a time three years in the future. Nevertheless, we'll refer to the loan amount as the present value of the annuity of the payments.

The problem asks us to calculate how much the Smiths need to save each quarter. To do that we have to know how much they need to save up in total. That's the future value of the annuity of their savings, FVA_{12} in the diagram. That sum is going to be $400,000 less the amount that can be borrowed, less the amount that the money already in savings will have grown into. Those amounts are PVA and FV_{12}, respectively, in the diagram.

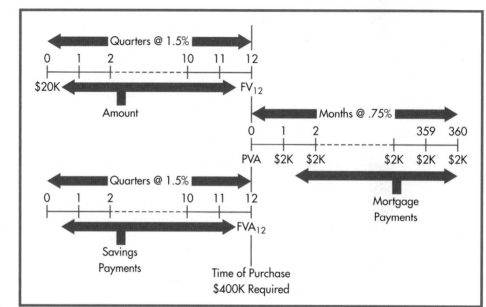

Calculator Solution

Key	Input
n	360
I/Y	.75
PMT	2,000
FV	0

	Answer
PV	248,564

First, calculate the amount that can be borrowed using the present value of an annuity formula (Equation 6.19). A 30-year mortgage at 9% implies k = .75 and n = 360. The Smiths' annual income is $96,000 or $8,000 a month. Generally about 25% of that amount, $2,000, can be used for a mortgage payment.

$$PVA = PMT[PVFA_{k,n}]$$
$$= \$2,000[PVFA_{.75,360}]$$
$$= \$2,000[124.282]$$
$$= \$248,564$$

Calculator Solution

Key	Input
n	12
I/Y	1.5
PV	20,000
PMT	0

	Answer
FV	23,912

Next, calculate the future value of the $20,000 already in the bank using Equation 6.4. Six percent compounded quarterly for three years implies k = 1.5 and n = 12.

$$FV_{12} = \$20,000[FVF_{1.5,12}]$$
$$= \$20,000[1.1956]$$
$$= \$23,912$$

The savings requirement is $400,000 less these amounts; that's $127,524. This sum is the future value of the annuity of the savings deposits. We can solve for the required deposit by using the future value of an annuity formula (Equation 6.13).

Calculator Solution

Key	Input
n	12
I/Y	1.5
FV	127,524
PV	0

	Answer
PMT	9,779

Because this money is going into the same bank account as the previous $20,000, k and n are the same.

$$FVA_n = PMT[FVFA_{k,n}]$$
$$\$127,524 = PMT[FVFA_{1.5,12}]$$
$$\$127,524 = PMT[13.0412]$$
$$PMT = \$9,779$$

Don't be confused by the fact that the savings deposits and the $20,000 already saved are in the same account. For purposes of calculation, they can be treated as though they're in identical but separate accounts.

Our figures show that the Smiths would have to deposit almost $9,800 a quarter, which is about $3,267 a month. That's probably too much to be realistic at their income level.

6.3j   Uneven Streams and Imbedded Annuities

Many real-world problems involve streams of payments that aren't even. When that occurs, we can't use the annuity formulas to calculate present and future values, and generally we must treat each payment as an independent amount problem. For example, consider the payment stream represented by the following time line.[3]

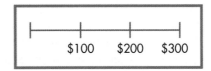

The only way to deal with this stream is to handle each payment as an individual amount. That's not too hard if we're looking for the present or future value, but it's quite difficult if we're looking for an interest rate that yields a particular present or future value.

For example, we might be asked to find the interest rate at which the PVs of the individual amounts just add up to $500.

The correct approach to that question is iterative. That means we guess at an interest rate and calculate the PV of the stream. If the calculated PV isn't $500, we make another, better guess and recalculate. As we'll see shortly, there's a way of making sure the second guess moves us closer to the solution. We'll do this problem as an illustration.

CONCEPT CONNECTION   EXAMPLE 6-23

Present Value of an Uneven Stream of Payments

Calculate the interest rate at which the present value of the stream of payments shown above is $500.

SOLUTION: We'll use the present value of an amount formula for each successive payment and start off by guessing at an interest rate of 12%. The present value of the entire stream is then

$$PV = FV_1 [PVF_{k,1}] + FV_2 [PVF_{k,2}] + FV_3 [PVF_{k,3}]$$
$$= \$100 [PVF_{12,1}] + \$200 [PVF_{12,2}] + \$300 [PVF_{12,3}]$$
$$= \$100(.8929) + \$200(.7972) + \$300(.7118)$$
$$= \$462.27$$

This figure is lower than the $500 we're looking for, so our guess was wrong. Because our guess discounted the figures by too much, and higher interest rates discount amounts more, we conclude that the next guess should be lower.

Using 11% gives $471.77, which is closer but still not high enough. Try a few more iterations to show that the answer is between 8% and 9%.

---

3. Although we haven't shown one here, you should recognize that one or more payments in a stream like this can be negative. A negative payment simply means that money is going the other way. For example, if a series of payments represents projected profits from a business, a negative number would just reflect a loss in some period. It would make a negative contribution to the present or future value calculation.

Imbedded Annuities   Sometimes uneven streams have regular sections, and we can use the annuity formula to reduce the number of calculations required to compute the present or future values.

Consider calculating the present value of the following uneven stream in which the third through sixth payments represent a $3 annuity of four periods.

Instead of calculating the present value of each term, we can recognize the annuity and use the PVA formula for that part. However, we have to remember that the annuity formula gives the present value at the beginning of the annuity. In this case, that's at time 2, not at time 0. Hence, we have to bring the "present" value of the annuity back another two periods as an amount to get its "present" value as of time 0 as indicated schematically in the diagram.

The **"present value"** of an imbedded annuity is moved back in time **as an amount**.

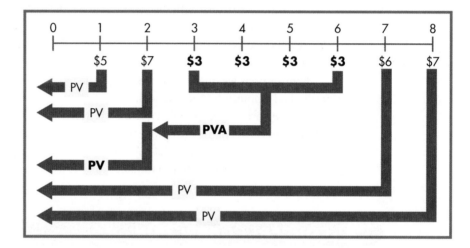

CONCEPT CONNECTION   EXAMPLE 6-24

Imbedded Annuity

Calculate the present value of the uneven stream above at 12%.

SOLUTION: First handle the first two and the last two payments as simple amount problems.

$$\text{Payment 1: PV} = FV_1 [PVF_{12,1}] = \$5(.8929) = \$4.46$$
$$\text{Payment 2: PV} = FV_2 [PVF_{12,2}] = \$7(.7972) = \$5.58$$
$$\text{Payment 7: PV} = FV_7 [PVF_{12,7}] = \$6(.4523) = \$2.71$$
$$\text{Payment 8: PV} = FV_8 [PVF_{12,8}] = \$7(.4039) = \$2.83$$

Next find PVA for the annuity at the beginning of period 3 (end of period 2), and bring it back two years as an amount.

$$\text{PVA} = PMT [PVFA_{12,4}] = \$3(3.0373) = \$9.11$$

and

$$\text{PV} = FV_2 [PVF_{12,2}] = \$9.11(.7972) = \$7.26$$

Now add up all the PVs to get the final answer of $22.84.

Calculator Solutions for Uneven Streams   Financial calculators have the ability to handle uneven streams with a limited number of payments. They're generally programmed to find the present value of the stream given an interest rate or the interest rate that will yield a particular present value. Your calculator's operating manual includes instructions on how to input uneven cash flows and produce these results.

Spreadsheets have functions that do the same thing and are generally easier to use than calculators.

Evaluating uneven streams is a key element of an important financial technique known as capital budgeting which we'll study in great detail in Chapters 10, 11, and 12. We'll look into calculator and spreadsheet solutions at that time.

CONCEPT CONNECTIONS

QUESTIONS

1. Why are time value concepts important in ordinary business dealings, especially those involving contracts?

2. Why are time value concepts crucial in determining what a bond or a share of stock should be worth?

3. In a retail store, a discount is a price reduction. What's a discount in finance? Are the two ideas related?

4. Calculate the present value of one dollar 30 years in the future at 10% interest. What does the result tell you about very long-term contracts?

5. Write a brief verbal description of the logic behind the development of the time value formulas for annuities.

6. Deferred payment terms are equivalent to a cash discount. Discuss and explain this idea.

7. What's an opportunity cost interest rate?

8. What is a sinking fund? How is it related to time value?

9. The amount formulas share a closer relationship than the annuity formulas. Explain and interpret this statement.

10. Describe the underlying meaning of compounding and compounding periods. How does it relate to time value? Include the idea of an effective annual rate (EAR). What is the annual percentage rate (APR)? Is the APR related to the EAR?

11. What information are we likely to be interested in that's contained in a loan amortization schedule?

12. Discuss mortgage loans in terms of the time value of money and loan amortization. What important points should every homeowner know about how mortgages work? (*Hint:* Think about taxes and getting the mortgage paid off.)

13. Discuss the idea of capitalizing a stream of earnings in perpetuity. Where is this idea useful? Is there a financial asset that makes use of this idea?

14. When an annuity begins several time periods into the future, how do we calculate its present value today? Describe the procedure in a few words.

BUSINESS ANALYSIS

1. A business can be valued by capitalizing its earnings stream (see Example 6-19, page 270). How might you use the same idea to value securities, especially the stock of large publicly held companies? Is there a way to calculate a value which could be compared to the stock's market price that would tell an investor whether it's a good buy? (If the market price is lower than the calculated value, the stock is a bargain.) What financial figures associated with shares of stock might be used in the calculation? Consider the per-share figures and ratios discussed in Chapter 3, including EPS, dividends, book value per share, etc. Does one measure make more sense than the others? What factors would make a stock worth more or less than your calculated value?

PROBLEMS

Note: For all problems involving non-annual compounding see pages 249–253 and Concept Connection Examples 6-7 and 6-8, pages 254–255.

Amount Problems

Future Value of an Amount: Concept Connection Example 6-1 (page 237)

1. What will a deposit of $4,500 left in the bank be worth under the following conditions?
   a. Left for nine years at 7% interest
   b. Left for six years at 10% compounded semiannually
   c. Left for five years at 8% compounded quarterly
   d. Left for 10 years at 12% compounded monthly

Present Value of an Amount: Concept Connection Example 6-2 (page 237)

2. The Lexington Property Development Company has a $10,000 note receivable from a customer due in three years. How much is the note worth today if the interest rate is
   a. 9%?
   b. 12% compounded monthly?
   c. 8% compounded quarterly?
   d. 18% compounded monthly?

Finding the Interest Rate: Concept Connection Example 6-3 (page 241)

3. What interest rates are implied by the following lending arrangements?
   a. You borrow $500 and repay $555 in one year.
   b. You lend $1,850 and are repaid $2,078.66 in two years.
   c. You lend $750 and are repaid $1,114.46 in five years with quarterly compounding.
   d. You borrow $12,500 and repay $21,364.24 in three years under monthly compounding.
      (*Note.* In parts c and d, be sure to give your answer as the annual nominal rate.)

Solving for the Number of Time Periods: Concept Connection Example 6-4 (page 242)

4. How long does it take for the following to happen?
   a. $856 grows into $1,122 at 7%
   b. $450 grows into $725.50 at 12% compounded monthly
   c. $5,000 grows into $6,724.44 at 10% compounded quarterly

5. Sally Guthrie is looking for an investment vehicle that will double her money in five years.
   a. What interest rate, to the nearest whole percentage, does she have to receive?
   b. At that rate, how long will it take the money to triple?
   c. If she can't find anything that pays more than 11%, approximately how long will it take to double her investment?
   d. What kind of financial instruments do you think Sally is looking at? Are they risky? What could happen to Sally's investment?

Deferred Payment Equivalent to Cash Discount: Concept Connection Example 6-2 (page 237)

6. Branson Inc. has sold product to the Brandywine Company, a major customer, for $20,000. As a courtesy to Brandywine, Branson has agreed to take a note due in two years for half of the amount due.
   a. What is the effective price of the transaction to Branson if the interest rate is. (1) 6%, (2) 8%, (3) 10%, or (4) 12%?
   b. Under what conditions might the effective price be even less as viewed by Brandywine?

7. Paladin Enterprises manufactures printing presses for small-town newspapers that are often short of cash. To accommodate these customers, Paladin offers the following payment terms.

   1/3 on delivery

   1/3 after six months

   1/3 after 18 months

   The Littleton *Sentinel* is a typically cash-poor newspaper considering one of Paladin's presses.
   a. What discount is implied by the terms from Paladin's point of view if it can invest excess funds at 8% compounded quarterly?
   b. The *Sentinel* can borrow limited amounts of money at 12% compounded monthly. What discount do the payment terms imply to the *Sentinel*?
   c. Reconcile these different views of the same thing in terms of opportunity cost.

8. Charlie owes Joe $8,000 on a note that is due in five years with accumulated interest at 6%. Joe has an investment opportunity now that he thinks will earn 18%. There's a chance, however, that it will earn as little as 4%. A bank has offered to discount the note at 14% and give Joe cash that he can invest today.
   a. How much ahead will Joe be if he takes the bank's offer and the investment does turn out to yield 18%?
   b. How much behind will he be if the investment turns out to yield only 4%?

9. John Cleaver's grandfather died in 2012 and left him a trunk that had been locked in his attic for years. At the bottom of the trunk, John found a packet of 50 U.S. Savings Bonds that had never been cashed in. The bonds were purchased for $11.50 each in 1920 and pay 3% interest as long as they're held. (Assume annual compounding.) (Government savings bonds like these accumulate and compound their interest, unlike corporate bonds which regularly pay out interest to bond holders.) (*Hint:* $[FVF_{k,a+b}] = [FVF_{k,a}] [FVF_{k,b}]$.)
   a. How much were the bonds worth in 2012?
   b. How much would they have been worth if they paid interest at a rate more like that paid during the 1970s and 80s, say 7%?
   c. Comment on the difference between the answers to parts (a) and (b).

Annuity Problems
Future Value of an Annuity: Concept Connection Example 6-5 (page 247)

10. How much will $650 per year be worth in eight years at interest rates of
    a. 12%?
    b. 8%?
    c. 6%?

11. The Wintergreens are planning ahead for their son's education. He's eight now and will start college in 10 years. How much will they have to set aside each year to have $65,000 when he starts if the interest rate is 7%?

12. What interest rate would you need to get to have an annuity of $7,500 per year accumulate to $279,600 in 15 years?

13. How many years will it take for $850 per year to amount to $20,000 if the interest is 8%?

Sinking Fund: Concept Connection Example 6-6 (page 248)

14. Blanchard Inc. would like to borrow $12 million for 20 years through a bond issue but has been having difficulty finding lenders willing to advance that much. The firm's investment banker has advised the CFO that potential bond buyers are not worried about Blanchard's ability to make the periodic interest payments on such a loan. However, they are concerned that it will have enough cash on hand to repay the loan when the principal is due in 20 years. The banker has suggested that a sinking fund might allay their fears; he also said funds deposited in such accounts can be expected to earn about 6% annually.
    How much would Blanchard have to deposit each year if the fund is started
    a. when the bonds are issued.
    b. 5 years after the bonds are issued.
    c. 10 years after the bonds are issued.
    d. 15 years after the bonds are issued.

Effective Annual Rate (EAR) (page 251)

15. Ralph Renner just borrowed $30,000 to pay for a new sports car. He took out a 60-month loan and his car payments are $761.80 per month. What is the effective annual rate (EAR) on Ralph's loan?

Present Value of an Annuity: Concept Connection Example 6-9 (page 257)

16. What would you pay for an annuity of $2,000 paid every six months for 12 years if you could invest your money elsewhere at 10% compounded semiannually?

17. Annuities are attractive investment vehicles for retirement savings, as many people prefer an income stream in retirement to a lump sum in the bank. It's easy to trade one for the another by purchasing an annuity for its discounted value from a bank or an insurance company.

    Lisa Montgomery just retired at age 65 with retirement savings of $750,000. She thinks she'll live to about 85 and would like a guaranteed monthly income until then. Her bank is offering annuity investments discounted at 6% compounded monthly. How much monthly income will Lisa have if she invests the entire sum in an annuity?

An Amortized Loan—Finding the Loan Payment, PMT: Concept Connection Example 6-11 (page 261)

18. Sam Rothstein wants to borrow $15,500 to be repaid in quarterly installments over five years at 16% compounded quarterly. How much will his payment be?

An Amortized Loan—Finding the Amount Borrowed, PVA: Concept Connection Example 6-12 (page 261)

19. Harry Clements would like to buy a new car. He can afford payments of $650 a month. The bank makes four-year car loans at 12% compounded monthly. How much can Harry borrow toward a new car?

20. A $10,000 car loan has payments of $361.52 per month for three years. What is the interest rate? Assume monthly compounding and give the answer in terms of an annual rate.

Amortization Schedule: Table 6-4 (page 262)

21. Construct an amortization schedule for a four-year, $10,000 loan at 6% interest compounded annually.

Mortgage Loans: Concept Connection Example 6-13, 6-14, and 6-15 (page 263–265)

22. Ryan and Laurie Middleton just purchased their first home with a traditional (monthly compounding and payments) 6%, 30-year mortgage loan of $178,000.
    a. How much is their monthly payment?
    b. How much interest will they pay in the first month?
    c. If they make all their payments on time over the 30-year period, how much interest will they have paid?
    d. If Ryan and Laurie decide to move after 7 years, what will the balance of their loan be at that time?
    e. If they finance their home over 15 rather than 30 years at the same interest rate, how much less interest will they pay over the life of the loan?

The next four problems (23–26) deal with a 30-year mortgage loan for $150,000 at 6%.

23. What are the monthly *payments* on the loan? Construct an amortization table for the first six months.

24. Construct an amortization schedule for the last six months of the loan. (*Hint:* What is the unpaid balance at the end of 29½ years?)

25. How soon would the loan be paid off if the borrower made a single additional payment of $33,000 to reduce principal at the end of the fifth year?

26. What are the payments to interest and principal during the 25th year of the loan?

27. Adam Wilson just purchased a home and took out a $250,000 mortgage for 30 years at 8%, compounded monthly.
    a. How much is Adam's monthly mortgage payment?
    b. How much sooner would Adam pay off his mortgage if he made an additional $100 payment each month?

    The financial tables in Appendix A are not sufficiently detailed to do parts (c) and (d). Solve them using a financial calculator.

    c. Assume Adam makes his normal mortgage payments and at the end of five years, he refinances the balance of his loan at 6%. If he continues to make the same mortgage payments, how soon after the first five years will he pay off his mortgage?
    d. How much interest will Adam pay in the 10th year of the loan
        i. If he does not refinance
        ii. If he does refinance

Estimating an ARM Reset: Concept Connection Example 6-16 (page 266)

28. Harrison Conway is choosing between a fixed-rate and an adjustable-rate mortgage (ARM) for $300,000. Both are 30-year mortgages with monthly payments and compounding. The fixed rate is offered at 8%, while the initial rate on the ARM is 6%. Harrison is concerned that inflation may be a problem within 10 years and that rates may return to levels not seen since the mid-1980s, i.e., in the neighborhood of 12%. Compare the payment on the fixed-rate loan to what Harrison would have to pay on the ARM if it reset to 12% after 10 years. For simplicity, assume that just one resetting occurs. Round all calculations to the nearest dollar.

Annuity Due: Concept Connection Example 6-17 (page 268)

29. Joe Ferro's uncle is going to give him $250 a month for the next two years starting today. If Joe banks every payment in an account paying 6% compounded monthly, how much will he have at the end of *three* years?

30. How long will it take payment of $500 per quarter to amortize a loan of $8,000 at 16% compounded quarterly? Approximate your answer in terms of years and months. How much less time will it take if loan payments are made at the beginning of each quarter rather that at the end?

Perpetuities—Capitalization of Earnings: Concept Connection Example 6-19 (page 270)

31. Roper Metals Inc. is in negotiations to acquire the Hanson Sheet Metal Company. Hanson's after-tax earnings have averaged $19 million per year for the last four years without much variation around that average figure. So far, discussions have been about the "business fit" of the two firms and pricing has been conspicuously ignored. Roper's CEO feels the venture is risky and needs to

pay a price that would yield his firm a return of about 20% if no operating improvements come out of the merger.

    a. What offering price should he put on the table to open negotiations?

    b. Hanson's management is sure to want a higher price. Would that imply capitalizing earnings at a higher or lower rate? Why?

    c. What arguments is Hanson likely to use?

Continuous Compounding: Conception Connection Example 6-20 (page 271)

32. Local banks are all offering 6% compounded monthly on five-year Certificates of Deposit. Hanover Bank has offered continuous compounding at the same nominal rate on new CDs hoping to attract additional customers. Sharon Shaker has just received a $50,000 royalty check for a romance novel she wrote last year. She has no immediate need for the money and intends to deposit it for about 5 years at the best interest rate she can get. How much more interest will her deposit earn at Hanover than at another bank?

Multipart Problems
Simple Multipart: Concept Connection Example 6-21 (page 272)

33. The Tower family wants to make a home improvement that is expected to cost $60,000. They want to fund as much of the cost as possible with a home equity loan but can afford payments of only $600 per month. Their bank offers equity loans at 12% compounded monthly for a maximum term of 10 years.

    a. How much cash do they need as a down payment?

    b. Their bank account pays 8% compounded quarterly. If they delay starting the project for two years, how much would they have to save each quarter to make the required down payment if the loan rate and estimated cost remain the same?

Complex Multipart: Concept Connection Example 6-22 (page 273)

34. The Stein family wants to buy a small vacation house in a year and a half. They expect it to cost $75,000 at the time. They have the following sources of money:

    (1) They have $10,000 currently in a bank account that pays 6% compounded monthly.

    (2) Uncle Murray has promised to give them $1,000 a month for 18 months starting today.

    (3) At the time of purchase, they'll take out a mortgage. They anticipate being able to make payments of about $300 a month on a 15-year, 12% loan.

In addition, they plan to make quarterly deposits to an investment account to cover any shortfall in the amount required. How much must those additions be if the investment account pays 8% compounded quarterly?

35. Clyde Atherton wants to buy a car when he graduates from college in two years. He has the following sources of money:

    (1) He has $5,000 now in the bank in an account paying 8% compounded quarterly.

    (2) He will receive $2,000 in one year from a trust.

    (3) He'll take out a car loan at the time of purchase on which he'll make $500 monthly payments at 18% compounded monthly over four years.

    (4) Clyde's uncle is going to give him $1,500 a quarter starting today *for one year.* In addition, Clyde will save up money in a credit union through monthly payroll deductions at is part-time job. The credit union pays 12% compounded monthly. If the car is expected to cost $40,000 (Clyde has expensive tastes!), how much must he save each month?

36. Joe Trenton expects to retire in 15 years and has suddenly realized that he hasn't saved anything toward that goal. After giving the matter some thought, he has decided that he would like to retire

with enough money in savings to withdraw $85,000 per year for 25 years after he retires. Assume a 6% return on investment before and after retirement and that all payments into and withdrawals from savings are at year end.

  a. How much does Joe have to save in each year for the next 15 years to reach this goal?
  b. How much would Joe have needed to save each year if he had started when retirement was 25 years away?
  c. Comment on the difference between the results of parts a and b.

37. Janet Elliott just turned 20 and received a gift of $20,000 from her rich uncle. Janet plans ahead and would like to retire on her 55th birthday. She thinks she'll need to have about $2 million saved by that time in order to maintain her lavish lifestyle. She wants to make a payment at the end of each year until she's 50 into an account she'll open with her uncle's gift. After that she'd like to stop making payments and let the money grow with interest until it reaches $2 million when she turns 55. Assume she can invest at 7% compounded annually. Ignore the effect of taxes.

  a. How much will she have to invest each year in order to achieve her objective?
  b. What percent of the $2 million will have been contributed by Janet (including the $20,000 she got from her uncle)?

38. Merritt Manufacturing needs to accumulate $20 million to retire a bond issue that matures in 13 years. The firm's manufacturing division can contribute $100,000 per quarter to an account that will pay 8%, compounded quarterly. How much will the remaining divisions have to contribute every month to a second account that pays 6% compounded monthly in order to reach the $20 million goal?

39. Carol Pasca just had her fifth birthday. As a birthday present, her uncle promised to contribute $300 per month to her education fund until she turns 18 and starts college. Carol's parents estimate college will cost $2,500 per month for four years, but don't think they'll be able to save anything toward it for eight years. How much will Carol's parents need to contribute to the fund each month starting on her 13th birthday to pay for her college education? Assume the fund earns 6% compounded monthly.

40. Joan Colby is approaching retirement and plans to purchase a condominium in Florida in three years. She now has $40,000 saved toward the purchase in a bank account that pays 8% compounded quarterly. She also has five $1,000 face value corporate bonds that mature in two years. She plans to deposit the bonds' principal repayments in the same account when they're paid. Joan also receives $1,200 per month alimony from her ex-husband which will continue for two more years until he retires (24 checks including one that arrived today). She's decided to put her remaining alimony money toward her condo, depositing it as it is received in a credit union account that pays 8% compounded monthly. She'll make the first deposit today with the check she already has. Joan anticipates buying a $200,000 property. What will her monthly payment be on a 15-year mortgage at 6%? What would the payment be on a 30-year loan at the same interest rate?

Uneven Streams and Imbedded Annuities: Concept Connection Examples 6-23 and 6-24 (page 275–277)

41. Amy's uncle died recently and left her some money in a trust that will pay her $500 per month for five years starting on her 25th birthday. Amy is getting married soon, and she would like to use this money as a down payment on a house now. If the trust allows her to assign its future payments to a bank, and her bank is willing to discount them at 9% compounded monthly, how much will she have toward her down payment on home ownership? Amy just turned 23.

42. Lee Childs is negotiating a contract to do some work for Haas Corp. over the next five years. Hass proposes to pay Lee $10,000 at the end of the third, fourth, and fifth years. No payments will be received prior to that time. If Lee discounts these payments at 8%, what is the contract worth to him today?

43. Use amount and annuity techniques to calculate the present value of the following pattern of annual cash flows at an annual interest rate of 12%. Round to the nearest dollar.

Years	1–4	5–9	10
Cash Flow per year	$20,000	$30,000	$40,000

44. The Orion Corp. is evaluating a proposal for a new project. It will cost $50,000 to get the undertaking started. The project will then generate cash inflows of $20,000 in its first year and $16,000 per year in the next five years, after which it will end. Orion uses an interest rate of 15% compounded annually for such evaluations.
    a. Calculate the "net present value" (NPV) of the project by treating the initial cost as a cash outflow (a negative) in the present, and adding the present value of the subsequent cash inflows as positives.
    b. What is the implication of a positive NPV? (Words only.)
    c. Suppose the inflows were somewhat lower, and the NPV turned out to be negative. What would be the implication of that result? (Words only.)
       (This problem was a preview of a technique called capital budgeting, which we'll study in detail in Chapters 10, 11, and 12.)

COMPUTER PROBLEMS

45. Home mortgage rates are determined by market forces, and individual borrowers can't do much about them. The time it takes to pay off a mortgage loan, however, varies a great deal with the size of the monthly payment, which is under the borrower's control.

    You're a junior loan officer for a large metropolitan bank. The head of the mortgage department is concerned that customers don't appreciate that a relatively small increase in mortgage payments can make a big difference in how long the payments have to be made. She feels homeowners may be passing up an opportunity to make their lives better in the long run by not choosing shorter-term mortgages that they can readily afford.

    To explain the phenomenon to customers, she's asked you to put together a chart that displays the variation in payment size with term at typical interest rates. The starting point for the chart should be the term for a typical 30-year (360-month) loan. Use the TIMEVAL program to construct the following chart.

Mortgage Payments per $100,000 Borrowed as Term Decreases
Mortgage Term in Years

Rates	30	25	20	15
4%				
5%				
6%				
7%				
8%				

Write a paragraph using the chart to explain the point. What happens to the effect as interest rates rise? Why?

46. Amitron Inc. is considering an engineering project that requires an investment of $250,000 and is expected to generate the following stream of payments (income) in the future. Use the TIMEVAL program to determine if the project is a good idea in a present value sense. That is, does the present value of expected cash inflows exceed the value of the investment that has to be made today?

Year	Payment
1	$63,000
2	69,500
3	32,700
4	79,750
5	62,400
6	38,250

a. Answer the question if the relevant interest rate for taking present values is 9%, 10%, 11%, and 12%. In the program, notice that period zero represents a cash flow made at the present time, which isn't discounted. The program will do the entire calculation for you if you input the initial investment as a negative number in this cell.

b. Use trial and error in the program to find the interest rate (to the nearest hundredth of a percent) at which Amitron would be just indifferent to the project.

This problem is a preview of an important method of evaluating projects known as *capital budgeting*. We'll study the topic in detail in Chapters 10, 11, and 12. In part a of this problem, we find the *net present value (NPV)* of the project's cash flows at various interest rates and reason intuitively that the project is a good idea if that figure is positive. In part b, we find the return inherent in the project itself, which is called the *internal rate of return (IRR)*. We'll learn how to use that in Chapter 10.

47. The Centurion Corp. is putting together a financial plan for the company covering the next three years, and it needs to forecast its interest expense and the related tax savings. The firm's most significant liability is a fully amortized mortgage loan on its real estate. The loan was made exactly ten and one-half years ago for $3.2M at 11% compounded monthly for a term of 30 years. Use the AMORTIZ program to forecast the interest expense associated with the real estate mortgage over the next three years. (*Hint:* Run AMORTIZ from the loan's beginning and add up the months in each of the next three years.)

DEVELOPING SOFTWARE

48. Write your own program to amortize a 10-year, $20,000 loan at 10% compounded annually. Input the loan amount, the payment, and the interest rate. Set up your spreadsheet just like Table 6-4 (page 262), and write your program to duplicate the calculation procedure described.

CHAPTER 7

The Valuation and Characteristics of Bonds

Chapter Outline

Valuation is a systematic process through which we establish the price at which a security *should* sell. We can call that price the security's *intrinsic* value.

7.1 The Basis of Value

Securities are pieces of paper or records in a computer file, and unlike real assets, they have no utility of their own. Real assets such as houses and cars have worth because they provide services like shelter and transportation. Paper assets must

rely on something else to make them valuable. That something is the expectation of future income that goes along with owning securities. This is an important point. *Every* financial asset depends for its value on the future cash flows that come with it.

Since money expected in the future is worth its present (discounted) value today, *a security's value is equal to the* **present value of its expected future cash flows.** Further, the security should sell in financial markets for a price very close to that value.

There are often differences of opinion about what the price of a security should be. They arise because people make different assumptions about what the security's cash flows will turn out to be and about the appropriate interest rate to use in taking present values. The most arguable cash flows are associated with stocks because future dividends are never guaranteed and the eventual selling price of a share is always speculative.

The idea of valuation is bound closely to the concept of return on investment. Because of the precise nature of the work we're about to undertake, we need to be very exact in our understanding of what the terms "investment" and "return" mean.

7.1a Investing

Investing means using a resource in a way that generates *future benefits* rather than in a way that results in immediate satisfaction. We say an investor *forgoes current consumption* in order to improve his or her position in the future. In everyday language, that means a person buys securities or puts money in the bank rather than spending it on a new car or going out to dinner.

In finance, investing means putting money to work to earn more money, generally by entrusting it to a person or an organization that uses it and pays the owner for its use. The two most common methods of entrusting money are lending and buying an ownership interest in a business. They are called debt and equity investments, respectively. The vehicle for a debt investment is generally a bond, while for an equity investment it's a share of stock.

7.1b Return

Returns on One-Year Investments **Return** is what an investor receives for making an investment. It can be expressed as a dollar amount or as an annual percentage rate. For investments held for one year, the *rate of return is the money the investor receives divided by the amount he or she invests.*

For debt, that's simply the interest received divided by the amount loaned, which is the interest rate we've been calling k. Let's look at the idea a little more deeply in terms of the time value of money.

An amount PV loaned for one year at interest rate k earns interest of kPV. If the lender receives the principal plus the interest at the end of the year, these are the future cash flows that come from making the original investment of PV. Call these future cash flows FV_1 and write

$$FV_1 = PV + kPV$$

$$FV_1 = PV(1 + k)$$

Securities are worth the present value of the future cash income associated with owning them.

Investing means using a resource to benefit the future rather than for current satisfaction.

Return, expressed as an amount or a percentage is what an investor receives for investing her money.

We recognize this as Equation 6.1 from our study of the time value of money.

Now solve for the original investment.

$$PV = \frac{FV_1}{(1 + k)}$$

Again we recognize this expression from our study of time value. It's the present value of a future amount due in one year, Equation 6.5, with n = 1.

In the context of valuing a security that represents a loan (usually a bond), think of PV as the *price* of the security that returns cash flows FV_1. Then the rate of return, k, can be thought of as the **interest rate that makes the present value of the future cash flows equal to the price.** This is a fundamental definition that applies to any investment held for any length of time. (The term **discount rate** is often used for **interest rate.**)

The details are a bit more involved for equity (stock) investments than for debt because the future cash flows are more complicated. Nevertheless, the basic rule is the same. We'll discuss the returns to equity investments in Chapter 8.

> The rate of return on a security is the interest rate that **equates the present value of its expected future cash flows with its current price**.

> An **interest rate** is often called a **discount rate**.

Returns on Longer-Term Investments   When the holding period is longer and there are a number of cash flows at different times, the concept remains the same. The return is still the discount (interest) rate that makes the present value of the future cash flows equal to the price.

For example, suppose someone offers to sell you an investment that will pay $200 one year from now and $250 two years from now for $363 paid today. If you accept the offer, the return on your investment will be the interest rate at which the present value of the two payments just equals the $363 "price" of the investment today. A time line for the arrangement looks like this.

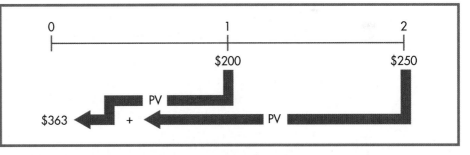

> The terms **yield, return, and interest** mean essentially the same thing.

As an exercise, show that the return on this hypothetical investment would be very close to 15% by adding the present values of the two payments at that rate.

The term "yield" is synonymous with "rate of return." Its use is especially common with debt securities and traditional loans.

In the remainder of this chapter, we'll look closely at the valuation of bonds and then at their institutional[1] characteristics. We'll turn our attention to stocks in Chapter 8.

7.2 Bond Valuation

Bonds represent a debt relationship in which the issuing company borrows and the buyer lends. A bond issue is an arrangement through which one company can borrow

---

1. The term "institutional" refers to the rules and practices according to which things are done in an organized society.

A **bond issue** allows an organization to borrow from many lenders at one time under a single agreement.

from many people at once. For example, suppose a firm wants to borrow $10 million but can't find anyone willing to lend that much. Many people might be willing to lend smaller amounts, however, if the firm's credit reputation is good. If the company issues 10,000 bonds at $1,000 each, as many as 10,000 people could participate in the loan by buying one bond apiece. Bonds enable firms to raise large amounts by spreading a loan among a number of lenders.

Before we get into the valuation of bonds, we need to learn a little about terminology and practice. We've introduced some of these ideas before, but will repeat them here for convenience.

7.2a   Bond Terminology and Practice

A bond's **term** or **maturity** is the time from the present until the principal is to be returned.

A bond's **par** or **face value** is the amount the issuer intends to borrow at the **coupon rate** of interest.

A bond represents a loan made by the buyer to the issuer for a period known as the **term**. The bond itself is a **promissory note** that serves as legal evidence of the debt. Bonds are said to *mature* on the last day of their terms. The word *term* means the bond's lifetime when it's first issued. Thereafter it means the time from the present until the maturity date. For example, a 20-year bond that's five years old has a term of 15 years. Every bond issued has a **par** or **face value**, which is printed on the face of the document. This is the amount the issuing company intends to borrow; in effect, it's the principal of the loan.

Bonds are *non-amortized* debt. That means no repayment of principal is made during the life of the bond. Rather, the face value is repaid in a lump sum on the maturity date. Interest is paid regularly, however, usually semiannually.

Any lender is said to extend *credit* to borrowers. Therefore, bondholders are called *creditors* of the company issuing the bonds. The term "creditor" also applies to banks that make loans to companies and vendors that sell products without receiving immediate payment.

Newly issued bonds are called *new issues,* as one might expect, while older bonds are commonly called **seasoned issues**.

The Coupon Rate   Most bonds pay interest at rates set at the time of issue called **coupon rates**. The coupon rate applied to the face value of a bond yields the dollar amount of interest paid, called the **coupon payment**. Coupon rates and payments are generally fixed throughout the life of a bond regardless of what happens to interest rates in financial markets.

The term "coupon" is outdated but is still in common use. Years ago, bonds were issued with a number of coupons attached that looked something like a sheet of postage stamps. When an interest payment was due, a bond owner would clip off a coupon and send it to the issuing company, which would return a check for the interest. Hence, the term "coupon" became associated with bond interest.

Coupons are rarely used today. Interest payments are now mailed directly to bondholders whose names and addresses are *registered* with the issuing company or its agent. Nevertheless, the term "coupon" is still associated with bond interest.

7.2b   Bond Valuation—Basic Ideas

Now we have enough background to begin studying bond valuation. Keep in mind that valuation simply means determining the price a security should command in the financial market in which it is traded.

Adjusting to Interest Rate Changes   Let's put several facts from our earlier work together with what we've just learned about bonds. First, recall from Chapter 5 that securities including bonds are sold in both primary and secondary markets. A primary market transaction refers to the original sale of the bond by the issuing company, and secondary market transactions are subsequent trades among investors. Second, recall from our discussion of financial markets in Chapter 5 that interest rates change all the time. Finally, we've just learned that most bonds pay interest at coupon rates that are fixed throughout their lives.

All this raises a question. How can a bond that pays a fixed rate be sold in the secondary market if interest rates have changed since it was originally issued? An example will make the idea clear.

Suppose Tom Benning, a typical investor, buys a newly issued 20-year bond directly from the Groton Company for its face value of $1,000. We'll assume that the bond pays interest at a coupon rate of 10%, which is the market rate for bonds of comparable risk at the time. From the discussion we've already had about valuation, we know that Tom has actually purchased a stream of future income. He'll receive interest payments of $100 a year (10% of $1,000) for 20 years and a payment of $1,000 returning principal along with the last interest payment.

Now imagine that a few days after Tom's purchase, interest rates rise to 12%. Also assume that coincidentally something occurs in Tom's financial situation that requires him to get out of the bond investment. That is, he needs the cash he used to buy the bond for something else, perhaps an emergency.

Tom can't go back to Groton, the issuing company, and ask for a refund. The company borrowed the funds expecting to keep them for 20 years, and it would be unwilling to give up those terms. So to get his money back, Tom has to sell the bond to another investor in a secondary market transaction.

Let's suppose Tom approaches Sandra Fuentes, a friend who he knows is in the market for an investment, and asks if she'd like to buy his Groton Company bond. She says she might be interested and asks how much he wants. Tom answers that he bought it only a few days ago for $1,000 and would like to get about that much. What would Sandra's reaction be to Tom's asking price?

Unfortunately for Tom, Sandra wouldn't be willing to pay $1,000. That's because the increase in interest rates has given her better options. New bonds now being issued offer 12%, which means they'll pay $120 a year for 20 years plus the final $1,000. Sandra, as a rational investor, would have to refuse Tom's offer.

But suppose Tom is desperate and really has to sell his bond. What is he to do? Clearly the only way he'll interest a buyer is to lower the price. In fact, he'll have to lower the price until the return to the new buyer on his or her investment is just 12%. It turns out that he'd have to lower the price to exactly $849.51. We'll see how that figure is calculated later in the chapter. For now, the important thing to understand is that the price of bonds on the secondary market *drops* in response to an increase in interest rates.

What would have happened if interest rates had fallen rather than gone up? In that case, new issues would have offered less interest than Tom's bond, and he could have sold it for *more* than $1,000. In general, bond prices *rise* in response to a *drop* in interest rates.

Summarizing, we see that *bond prices and interest rates move in opposite directions*. This phenomenon is a fundamental and critically important law of finance and economics. When interest rates decline, the prices of debt securities go up; when rates increase, prices go down. The price changes are just enough to keep the yields (returns) on investments in seasoned issues equal to the yields on new issues of comparable risk and maturity. In other words, **bonds adjust to changing yields by changing their prices**.

As a result of all this, bonds don't generally sell for their face values. They trade for more or less, depending on where the current interest rate is in relation to their coupon rates. The terminology associated with this phenomenon is important. Bonds selling above their face values are said to be trading at a *premium*, while those selling below face value are said to trade at a *discount*. If at a point in time the market interest rate returns to a bond's coupon rate, the bond sells for its face value at that time. At such a time, we say the bond is trading at *par value*.

> Bond **prices** respond to **changes** in the market rate of **interest** by moving in a direction **opposite** to the change.

7.3c   Determining the Price of a Bond

We made the point earlier that the value and hence the price of any security should be equal to the present value of the expected future cash flows associated with owning that security. In the case of bonds, those future cash flows are quite predictable, because they're specified by the bond agreement.

Bondholders receive interest payments periodically and a lump sum return of principal at the bond's maturity. Yearly interest is determined by applying the coupon rate to the face value of the bond, and the principal is simply the face value itself.

Let's illustrate the pattern of these payments by setting up a time line to display the cash flows coming from a $1,000 bond with a coupon rate of 10% whose maturity date is 10 years off. Most bonds pay interest semiannually, but for illustrative purposes, we'll assume this one pays annually. The time line of cash flows is illustrated in Figure 7-1.

Notice that the amount received in the 10th year is the sum of the last interest payment and the return of principal. Also notice that the interest payments are all the same and occur regularly in time.

It's important to realize that it doesn't matter whether the bond is new at time zero. The picture shown would be valid for a new 10-year bond, a 20-year bond that's currently 10 years old, or any other 10% $1,000 bond that has 10 years to go until maturity. Time zero is now, and the only thing that matters in today's valuation is *future* cash flows. Past cash flows are gone and irrelevant to today's buyer.

Having used Figure 7-1 to visualize bond cash flows in a simple numerical case, let's generalize the idea by showing a time to maturity of n periods, an interest payment represented as PMT, and a face value of FV. Recognize that each of these

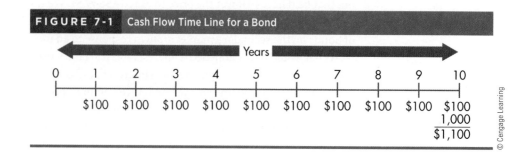

FIGURE 7-1   Cash Flow Time Line for a Bond

© Cengage Learning

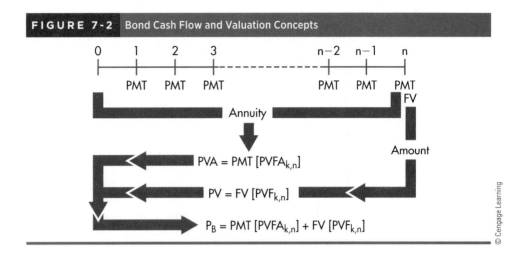

FIGURE 7-2 Bond Cash Flow and Valuation Concepts

elements varies with different bonds. The general case is represented by the time line at the top of Figure 7-2.

In practice, most bonds pay interest semiannually. That means the periods represented along the time line in Figure 7-2 are usually half years. Under those conditions, the interest payment, PMT, is calculated by applying the coupon rate to the face value and dividing by 2. For example, if the bond in Figure 7-2 had 10 years to go until maturity, had a face value of $1,000, and paid 10% interest in two semiannual installments, the time line would contain 20 periods, and each PMT would be $50.

The Bond Valuation Formula   As we've been saying, a security's price should be equal to the present value of all the cash flows expected to come from owning it. In the case of a bond, the expected cash flows consist of a series of interest payments and a single payment returning principal at maturity. Hence, the price of a bond, which we'll write as P_B, is the present value of the stream of interest payments plus the present value of the principal repayment.

(7.1) P_B = PV(interest payments) + PV(principal repayment)

Because the interest payments are made regularly and are constant in amount, they can be treated as an annuity, and we can calculate their present value by using Equation 6.19, the present value of an annuity formula. We'll rewrite that formula here for convenience.

(6.19)   PVA = PMT[$PVFA_{k,n}$]

Applying this formula directly to the bond's interest, we can write

(7.2)   PV(interest payments) = PMT[$PVFA_{k,n}$]

where PMT is the bond's regular interest payment, n is the number of interest-paying periods remaining in the bond's life, and k is the current market interest rate for comparable bonds for the interest-paying period.

A bond's principal is always equal to its face value, so the return of principal is an expected payment of that amount n periods in the future. Its present value can be calculated using Equation 6.7, the present value of an amount formula, which we'll repeat here.

(6.7) $PV = FV_n[PVF_{k,n}]$

We'll drop the subscript on FV_n and think of FV as face value rather than future value in this application. Then we can write

(7.3) $PV \text{ (principal repayment)} = FV[PVFA_{k,n}]$

Substituting Equations 7.2 and 7.3 in 7.1, we get a convenient expression for calculating the price of a bond based on its future cash flows using our familiar time value techniques.

(7.4) $P_B = PMT[PVFA_{k,n}] + FV[PVF_{k,n}]$

The approach is illustrated graphically in Figure 7-2. In essence, pricing a bond involves doing an annuity problem and an amount problem together, and summing the results.

> A bond's value is the sum of the present value of the **annuity of its interest payments** plus the present value of the **return of principal**, both taken at the current **market rate** of interest.

Two Interest Rates and One More

It's important to notice that two interest rates are associated with pricing a bond. The first is the coupon rate, which, when applied to the face value, determines the size of the interest payments made to bondholders. The second is k, the current market yield on comparable bonds at the time the price is being calculated. Don't confuse the two. The rate at which the present value of cash flows is taken is k. The only thing you do with the coupon rate is calculate the interest payment.

The return or yield on the bond investment to the bondholder is k. It is the interest rate that makes the present value of all the payments represented in Figure 7-2 equal to the price of the bond. Because this return considers all payments until the bond's maturity, it's called the **yield to maturity**, abbreviated YTM. When people refer to a bond's yield, they generally mean the YTM.

The third yield associated with a bond is called the *current yield*. This is a summary piece of information used in financial quotations and is not associated with the pricing process. The current yield is the annual interest payment divided by the bond's current price.

As we've been saying, solving bond problems just involves doing two time value problems and adding up the results. The only tricky part of the process is translating from common bond language or terminology into the variables in the bond pricing formula, Equation 7.4. The following example will make the process clear.

Notice that we've included a calculator solution in the margin next to the example as we did in the time value examples in chapter 6. We'll describe how to use a calculator to solve bond problems after you've worked your way through the example and a practice problem.

CONCEPT CONNECTION EXAMPLE 7-1

Finding the Price of a Bond

The Emory Corporation issued an 8%, 25-year bond 15 years ago. At the time of issue, it sold for its par (face) value of $1,000. Comparable bonds are yielding 10% today. What must Emory's bond sell for in today's market to yield 10% (YTM) to the buyer? Assume the bond pays interest semiannually. Also calculate the bond's current yield.

SOLUTION: This is the typical bond problem. We're given a bond's face value, coupon rate, and remaining term, and are asked to find the price at which it must sell to achieve a particular return. Since the return is the market interest rate, we're being asked to find the market price of the bond. The question is equivalent to asking for the present value of the bond's expected cash flows at today's interest rate.

To solve the problem, we first write Equation 7.4, the bond valuation formula.

$$P_B = PMT[PVFA_{k,n}] + FV[PVF_{k,n}]$$

Then we put the information given in the proper form for substitution into the equation.

The interest payment is found by applying the coupon rate to the face value and dividing by two, because payments are semiannual.

$$PMT = [\text{coupon rate} \times \text{face value}]/2$$
$$= (.08 \times \$1,000)/2$$
$$= \$40.00$$

Next we need n, the number of interest-paying periods from now until the end of the bond's term. This bond, like most, pays interest semiannually, so we multiply the number of years until maturity by 2 to get n. Notice that n represents the time from now until maturity. It doesn't matter how long the bond has been in existence previously. In this case, the term was originally 25 years but the bond is now 15 years old and the term is (25 − 15 =) 10 years, so

$$n = 10 \text{ years} \times 2 = 20$$

Next we need k, the current market interest rate. Recall that when using time value formulas for non-annual compounding, we have to state n and k consistently for the compounding period. Here, n represents a number of semiannual periods, so k must be stated for semiannual compounding. That just means dividing the nominal rate by 2,

$$k = 10\%/2 = 5\%$$

Finally, the face value is given directly as $1,000, so

$$FV = \$1,000$$

Substitute these values into the bond equation,

$$P_B = \$40[PVFA_{5,20}] + \$1,000[PVF_{5,20}]$$

and use Appendix A for the factors. Table A-4 gives

$$PVFA_{5,20} = 12.4622$$

while Table A-2 yields

$$PVF_{5,20} = .3769$$

Calculator Solution

Key	Input
n	20
I/Y	5
FV	1,000
PMT	40
Answer	
PV	875.38

Ensuper/Shutterstock.com

Substituting, we get

$$P_B = \$40[12.4622] + \$1{,}000[.3769]$$
$$= \$498.49 + \$376.90$$
$$= \$875.39$$

This is the price at which the Emory bond must sell to yield 10% to the buyer. It won't be competitive with other bonds at any higher price. Notice that it's selling at a discount, a price below its face or par value because the current interest rate is above the coupon rate.

The bond's current yield is calculated as follows.

$$\text{current yield} = \frac{\text{annual interest}}{\text{price}} = \frac{\$80}{\$875.39} = 9.14\%$$

Although using the bond valuation formula is easy once you get used to it, students often have trouble knowing where to put what at first. Here's a self-test example using the method we've just illustrated. It will help your understanding a great deal if you work it yourself, using the last example as a guide, *before* looking at the solution.

CONCEPT CONNECTION   EXAMPLE 7-2

Self-Test

Carstairs Inc. issued a $1,000, 25-year bond 5 years ago at 11% interest. Comparable bonds yield 8% today. What should Carstairs's bond sell for now?

SOLUTION: The variables are as follows (as usual, assume semiannual interest).

$$PMT = (.11 \times \$1{,}000)/2 = \$55$$
$$n = 20 \times 2 = 40$$
$$k = 8\%/2 = 4\% \text{ and}$$
$$FV = \$1{,}000$$

Then, using Equation 7.4,

$$P_B = PMT[PVFA_{k,n}] + FV[PVF_{k,n}]$$
$$= \$55[PVFA_{4,40}] + \$1{,}000[PVF_{4,40}]$$
$$= \$55(19.7928) + \$1{,}000(.2083)$$
$$= \$1{,}088.60 + \$208.30$$
$$= \$1{,}296.90$$
$$\text{current yield} = \$110/\$1{,}296.90 = 8.48\%$$

Calculator Solution

Key	Input
n	40
I/Y	4
FV	1,000
PMT	55

Answer	
PV	1,296.89

Ensuper/Shutterstock.com

Estimating the Answer First   If we think of the bond as having been issued at a time when the market rate was equal to the coupon rate, we can make a rough estimate of the current price before starting the problem. That provides a good reasonableness check on the solution we come up with. We base the estimate on the fact that bond prices and interest rates move in opposite directions.

In Example 7-1, we knew the current price of the bond had to be *below* the face value of $1,000. That's because the market interest rate had *risen* from 8% at the time of the bond's issue to its current value of 10%. Further, the increase was fairly substantial, so we were looking for a significant drop in price, which is what we found.

It doesn't matter whether the interest rate fluctuated up and down past 8% after the bond was issued or moved directly to 10%. The only rates that count for today's price are the original coupon rate and the current rate.[2]

Before starting a bond problem, you should always decide whether the new price will represent a premium or a discount from the face value.

In general, price changes due to a given interest rate change will be larger the more time there is remaining until maturity. We'll see that more clearly in the next section.

Now let's go back and see how Examples 7-1 and 7-2 are solved with a financial calculator.

Solving Bond Problems with a Financial Calculator   In Chapter 6, we noted that financial calculators have five time value keys. When doing amount or annuity problems, we used four of the five keys and zeroed the fifth.

In bond problems, we use all five keys. The calculator is programmed to recognize the five inputs as two problems and add the results together. In a bond problem, the keys have the following meanings:

> n—Number of periods until maturity
>
> I/Y—Market interest rate
>
> PV—Price of the bond—that is, the present value of all the cash flows
>
> FV—Face value of the bond
>
> PMT—Coupon interest payment per period

The unknown is either the price of the bond (PV) or the market interest rate (I/Y), which is equal to the bond's yield to an investor buying at the current price. To solve a problem, we enter the four known variables first, press the compute key, and then press the key for the unknown variable.

If your calculator uses a sign convention, cash flows to and from the bondholder must be of opposite signs. That means PMT and FV, flows to the bondholder, will be of one sign while PV, the price coming from the bondholder, will be of the other sign.

Sophisticated calculators have a "bond mode" that allows you to input exact calendar dates for the present and the bond's maturity as well as some additional details about the payment of principal and interest. This facilitates the exact pricing of bonds sold in the middle of the month and issues with unusual provisions. Traders operating in fast-moving bond markets use such calculating options all the time. The time value keys are sufficient for our purposes, since our goal is simply to gain

---

2. Bonds aren't always issued at coupon rates equal to the current market interest rate, but it helps to understand the pricing process if we imagine that they are. In practice, coupon rates are usually targeted at or near the current market rate. However, the mechanics of printing and issuing cause a delay between the time the rate is chosen and the time the bond actually hits the market. As a result, there's usually a slight difference between coupon rates and current market rates. Bonds issued above or below market rates simply sell at premiums or discounts, respectively, when offered on the primary market. Because market rates change constantly, some discount or premium is almost always associated with a new issue.

a broad understanding of bond operations. Work through the calculator solutions to Examples 7-1 and 7-2 given in the margins.

7.2d   Maturity Risk Revisited

In Chapter 5, we developed an interest rate model in which rates generally consist of a base rate plus premiums for various risks borne by lenders. In particular, the model recognizes *maturity risk*, which is related to the term of the debt. We're now in a position to fully understand this important idea.

Maturity risk arises from the fact that bond prices vary (inversely) with interest rates. When an investor buys a bond, the only way to recover the invested cash before maturity is to sell it to someone else. If interest rates rise and prices fall while the investor is holding the bond, the sale to someone else will be at a loss. (Review page 216 if necessary.)

This is exactly what happened to Tom Benning in our illustration of price adjustments to interest rate changes. The possibility of such a loss viewed at the time of purchase is the risk we're talking about.

Maturity risk has two other names, *price risk* and *interest rate risk*. These terms reflect the fact that bond *prices* move up and down with changes in *interest rates*.

The expression *maturity risk* emphasizes the fact that the *degree* of risk is related to the maturity (term) of the bond. The longer the term (time until maturity), the greater the maturity (price, interest rate) risk. The reason is that the prices of longer-term bonds change more in response to interest rate movements than do the prices of shorter-term bonds.

To see that, let's look again at the bond in Example 7-1. It was issued at 8% and had 10 years to go until maturity. Interest rates rose to 10%, and the price dropped to $875.39. Let's calculate what the price would have become under varying assumptions about the remaining term to maturity without changing anything else in the problem.

Table 7-1 gives the bond's price and the price drop from $1,000 at terms of 2, 5, 10, and 20 years. You might want to verify that these figures are correct as an exercise. Each of the price changes in Table 7-1 is the result of the same increase in interest rates, from 8% to 10%. Notice how much larger the price drop becomes as the term of the bond increases. This is the essence of maturity risk. The possible loss on debt investments due to interest-rate-induced price changes increases with the term of the debt.

Realizing this fact, investors demand a premium to compensate for the additional risk they bear with longer issues. This is the *maturity risk premium*.

As Time Goes By   Let's consider the original Emory Corporation bond in Example 7-1 again. Recall that the interest rate rose from 8% to 10%, and the price fell from $1,000 to $875.39 with 10 years of term to go.

> **Maturity risk** exists because the prices of **longer-term** bonds **fluctuate** more in response to **interest rate** changes than the prices of shorter-term bonds.

TABLE 7-1	Price Changes at Different Terms Due to an Interest Rate Increase from 8% to 10%	
Time to Maturity	**Price**	**Drop from $1,000**
2 years	$964.54	$ 35.46
5	922.77	77.23
10	875.39	124.61
20	828.36	171.64

Let's imagine a very unlikely event just to enhance our understanding of the processes involved in bond pricing.

What would happen to the price of the Emory bond as time goes by *if interest rates didn't change again* for the remainder of the bond's life (a practical impossibility)? Would the price remain at $875.39, or move to something else? Test your understanding by answering the question before reading on.

In fact, the bond's price would slowly rise to $1,000 as maturity approached. If you have trouble seeing that, think of what it would be worth on the day before maturity. Someone buying at that time would be getting virtually no interest, because the last interest payment would be prorated almost entirely to the person who owned the bond during most of the last period. A buyer on the day before maturity would be buying a payment of $1,000 to be made the next day. That would be worth very nearly $1,000. This logic tells us that as we get closer to maturity, the price has to approach the bond's face value of $1,000.

We've already calculated what the price would be at two points along the way to maturity in our hypothetical example. Table 7-1 tells us that with five years to go the price will be $922.77 and when just two years remain, it will be $964.54. Graphically, the progression in prices is shown in Figure 7-3.

7.2e   Finding the Yield at a Given Price

Basically only two questions are asked about the dollars and cents of bonds. We've just explored the first, finding the price at which a bond achieves a specified yield. The second question is the reverse of the first. It asks for the yield on a bond investment if the security sells at a particular price. In the bond valuation formula, Equation 7.4, this question asks us to find the market interest rate, k, given a value for P_B.

Let's rewrite Equation 7.4 for convenient reference.

$$P_B = PMT[PVFA_{k,n}] + FV[PVF_{k,n}]$$

FIGURE 7-3   **Price Progression with Constant Interest Rate**

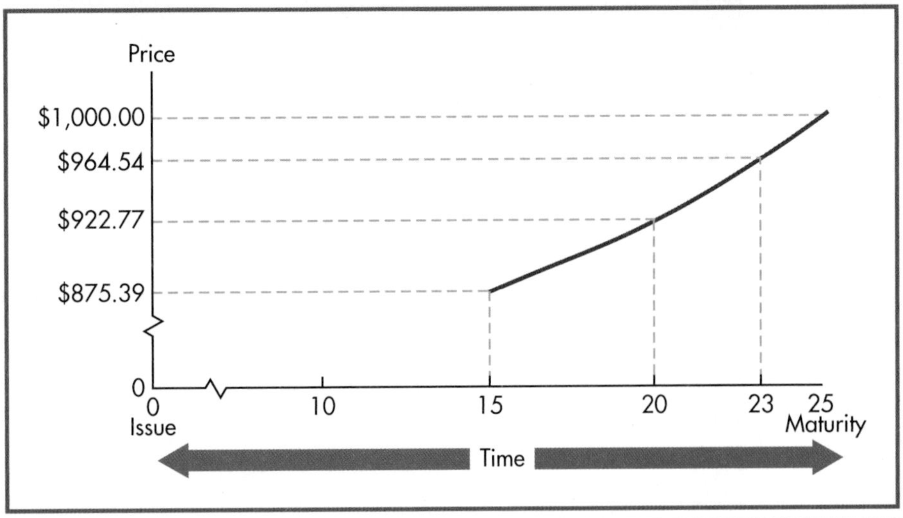

© Cengage Learning

Recall that finding P_B when the market yield is known simply involves doing two time value problems and adding the results together. We do a present value of an annuity problem for the interest payments and a present value of an amount problem for the return of the face value. Finding k when P_B is known is conceptually the same but much more difficult.

Recall the time value problems we studied in Chapter 6. In both amount and annuity problems, we were able to solve for an unknown k quite easily. We did so by solving one of the time value formulas for a factor, and then finding the factor in the table.

Even though the bond formula utilizes present value factors and the same tables we used in Chapter 6, this approach doesn't work. It fails because Equation 7.4 uses two time value factors at the same time. As we have only one equation, we can't solve for both and therefore can't find the right column in each table simultaneously.

This mathematically unfortunate state of affairs means we have to resort to a rather tedious approach to solving the problem—trial and error. We begin by guessing at a solution for k. Then we value the bond at that return using Equation 7.4 and whatever other information we have. That process results in a price we can compare with the price given by the problem. If they're significantly different, we have to guess at the return again and reevaluate for another price. We keep doing that until we get a price that's very close to the one we're looking for.

The trial and error approach isn't as haphazard as it may seem. By applying a little logic, we can usually get close to the answer in a few tries. An example will make the process clear.

CONCEPT CONNECTION   **EXAMPLE 7-3**

Finding the Yield at a Price

The Benson Steel Company issued a 30-year bond 14 years ago with a face value of $1,000 and a coupon rate of 8%. The bond is currently selling for $718. What is the yield to an investor who buys it today at that price? (Assume semiannual compounding.)

SOLUTION: First we make an educated guess at the answer on the basis of our knowledge that interest rates and bond prices move in opposite directions. In this case, the $718 price is substantially below the face value of $1,000, so we know the bond's yield must be quite a bit above the coupon rate. Let's make a first guess at 10%. Evaluating at 10%, we have the following variables.

$$PMT = (.08 \times \$1,000)/2 = \$40$$
$$n = 16 \times 2 = 32$$
$$k = 10\%/2 = 5\%$$
$$FV = \$1,000$$

Then, using equation 7.4, we have

$$P_B = PMT[PVFA_{k,n}] + FV[PVF_{k,n}]$$
$$= \$40[PVFA_{5,32}] + \$1,000[PVF_{5,32}]$$
$$= \$40(15.8027) + \$1,000(.2099)$$
$$= \$632.11 + \$209.90$$
$$= \$842.01$$

Calculator Solution

Key	Input
n	32
I/Y	5
FV	1,000
PMT	40

	Answer
PV	841.97

Calculator Solution

Key	Input
n	32
PV	718.00
FV	1,000
PMT	40
Answer	
I/Y	6 × 2 = 12.0

Note: PV may have to be input with a sign opposite to that of FV and PMT.

Clearly, 10% isn't the solution, because we're looking for the rate that yields a price of $718. Our choice has brought the price down from $1,000, but not far enough. That means we have to bring the rate up quite a bit more. For illustrative purposes, let's jump all the way to 14% (we probably wouldn't go that far if we weren't trying to make a point). The only input that changes from our last try is k, which is now

$$k = 14\% / 2 = 7\%$$

Substitute into Equation 7.4 and verify that the calculation leads to

$$P_B = 620.56$$

This figure is substantially below the target of $718, so we've pushed our interest rate too high. Now we know the answer has to be between 10% and 14%. Let's try a figure right in the middle. Evaluate the bond at 12% to verify that the resulting price is

$$P_B = 718.36$$

This is just a shade higher than the actual selling price, so the true yield is just below 12%. For most purposes, declaring 12% the solution would be close enough.

Financial calculators are programmed to solve bond programs, including finding yields. The internal workings of such calculators do exactly what we've just done, find the solution by trial and error. The calculator solution for yield is shown in the margin.

7.2f   Call Provisions

Circumstances sometimes arise in which bond issuers want to pay off their indebtedness early. This commonly occurs when interest rates drop after bonds are issued.

For example, suppose a company issues a 30-year bond with a 15% coupon rate when interest rates are at about that level. Some years later, suppose rates drop to 7%. The firm will be stuck paying above-market rates on the bond's principal until maturity unless it can somehow get out of the loan arrangement with the bondholders.

Companies that issue bonds anticipate this sort of thing and like to include call provisions in bond agreements to protect themselves. A **call provision** is a clause that gives the issuing organization the right to pay off the bond prior to maturity. In our illustration, the company would like to borrow money at the new lower interest rate of 7% and use it to retire the old bond that pays 15%. The process is called *refunding* the debt.

Investors who buy bonds don't like call provisions because they feel the clauses give firms the opportunity to renege on interest rate obligations. In the example we've just described, the bondholders were getting a 15% return on funds in a market that currently offered only 7%. If the bond is paid off early, they'll lose that 15% and will have to reinvest at 7%.

These conflicting interests are reconciled with a two- or three-part compromise. First, call provisions are generally written to include a *call premium* that must be paid to bondholders if the feature is exercised. This means that if the company chooses to pay a bond off early, it must pay lenders (bondholders) some extra money

Call provisions allow bond issuers to **retire** bonds **before maturity** by paying a premium to bondholders.

as compensation for their loss of the original deal. The premium is usually stated in terms of extra interest at the coupon rate and diminishes as the bond's maturity approaches.

Second, issuers usually agree that the bond won't be called until a certain number of years after the beginning of its life. This initial time is the period of *call protection*. Finally, to attract buyers, a bond with a call provision may have to pay a somewhat higher interest rate than similar bonds without call provisions.

Call provisions are also sometimes exercised to free companies of restrictions imposed by certain agreements associated with bond contracts called *indentures*. For example, a company considering a bond issue may agree to avoid risky ventures partly because none are available. But if an attractive idea comes up later, the only way to participate may be to call the bond to get rid of its indenture. We'll discuss indentures later in the chapter.

Figure 7-4 portrays a declining call premium starting at one year's interest on a 10%, $1,000 bond with a term of 10 years, and a call-protected period of 5 years. Although call premiums often decline, we'll assume they're constant to keep our computations simple.

The call premium is also known as a *call penalty*. This apparent conflict is easily explained by point of view. The payment is a premium to the investor who receives it but a penalty to the company that pays it. Call provisions are also called *call features*.

The Effect of a Call Provision on Price   A special situation arises when a bond with a call provision is in its protected period, but appears certain to be called as soon as that period is over. In such a case, the traditional bond valuation procedure doesn't work because it includes cash flows projected to occur after the protected period. These cash flows aren't likely to be forthcoming because the bond will probably be paid off exactly at the end of the protected period. In such cases, bondholders will actually receive normal interest payments up until call, at which time they'll receive the bond's face value plus the call premium. The situation is illustrated graphically in Figure 7-5.

Examine the diagram carefully. It shows the entire life of a bond that was originally intended to pay interest for 10 semiannual periods. This would normally be a five-year bond. The first three years are call protected in this example. We're assuming the first year has passed, so the present is indicated by "**Now**" at the end of period 2.

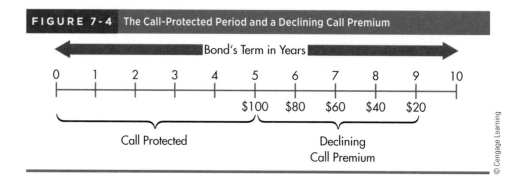

FIGURE 7-4   The Call-Protected Period and a Declining Call Premium

© Cengage Learning

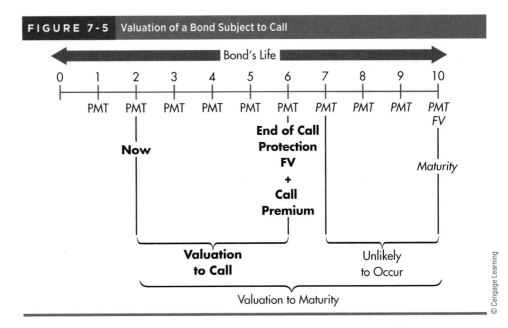

FIGURE 7-5   Valuation of a Bond Subject to Call

We assume the interest rate has dropped substantially or the issuer wants to be free of some restriction in the indenture, so the bond is very likely to be called at the end of the third year, period 6. Cash flows planned after that time probably won't happen. These are shown in italics.

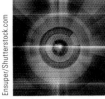

INSIGHTS   Practical Finance

Can a Bond Be a Bond Without Paying Interest?

The answer to that mysterious question is yes; they're called **zero coupon bonds**.

To understand the idea, think about a bond issued at a very low coupon rate—say, half the market rate. It would sell at a deep discount because the interest payments would be less than investors could get elsewhere. But offsetting the low interest payments, investors would receive the bond's face value at maturity, which would be more than they paid for it. In other words, investors who chose the bond would be trading some current income for a capital gain later on. But that capital gain would be unusual in that it wouldn't come from changing market values. It would actually be interest earned on the debt all along but not paid until maturity.

If we take this idea to the extreme, making the coupon interest smaller and smaller until it's gone, we've got a zero coupon bond. Essentially it's just a promise to pay a face amount in the future that sells for the present value of that amount today.

The "zero" has some interesting tax implications. You'd think the investor would pay no tax until maturity because no money is received until then. But that isn't the case. The IRS *imputes* interest during the bond's life and demands tax on the phantom income.

We're all familiar with zeros under another name, U.S. savings bonds. They operate in exactly the same way. We buy a bond for the present value of its face at maturity. They're a popular gift because a $100 bond only costs about $60. There is one big difference, however. The government gives buyers of its own "zeros" a break by not taxing the interest until maturity.

A **zero coupon bond** pays no interest during its life, but imputed interest is still taxable.

We'd normally value this bond by taking the present value of all the payments from Now until maturity, including the return of the face value at maturity. This would mean that in the bond valuation formula we would use n = 8 and substitute the face value for FV.

What's actually going to happen, however, is a shorter series of interest payments ending with the sixth, and a final payment equal to FV *plus* the call premium.

Valuing the Sure-to-Be-Called Bond   We can value this bond with the same formula we've used up until now by making two simple modifications to our inputs. All we have to do to realistically represent what is likely to happen is let n equal the time to call instead of the time to maturity, and add the call premium to the face value when we portray the final payment. The sum of the face value and the call premium is known as the *call price*.

We can express these ideas in a modification of the bond formula as follows.

(7.5) $P_B(call) = PMT[PVFA_{k,m}] + CP[PVF_{k,m}]$

where

$$m = \text{number of periods to call}$$

$$CP = \text{call price} = \text{face value} + \text{call premium}$$

PMT and k are computationally the same as in the problem without a call. However, k is known as the yield to call, abbreviated YTC, because it's used in taking the present value of cash flows only until the call is likely to occur.

CONCEPT CONNECTION   **EXAMPLE 7-4**

Pricing a "Likely to Be Called" Bond

The Northern Timber Co. issued a $1,000, 25-year bond 5 years ago. The bond has a call provision that allows it to be retired any time after the first 10 years with the payment of an additional year's interest at the coupon rate. Interest rates were especially high when the bond was issued, and its coupon rate is 18%. Interest rates on bonds of comparable risk are now 8%. What is the bond worth today? What would it be worth if it didn't have the call feature? Assume interest payments are semiannual.

SOLUTION: This problem asks us to evaluate the price of the bond, first assuming the call feature will be exercised (which is very likely) and then in the normal way. The basic assumption is that the bond must *yield* the current rate of interest in either case. That is, even if the bond is going to be called, the price will adjust to bring the yield to the market rate of 8%. A graphic depiction of the problem follows (the interest payments are omitted).

Notice that the time line shows semiannual periods rather than years. The call premium is 18% of $1,000 or $180, so the call price is ($1,000 + $180 =) $1,180.

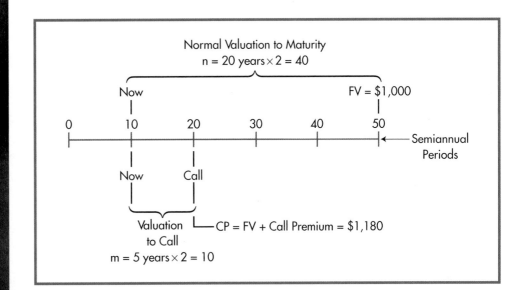

At the top of the diagram, above the time line, we show the period over which the bond would normally be evaluated and the face value to be returned of $1,000. At the bottom, we show the relevant period for a likely call and a call price of $1,180.

First, we'll evaluate to maturity using Equation 7.4.

$$P_B = PMT[PVFA_{k,n}] + FV[PVF_{k,n}]$$

The variables follow.

$$PMT = (.18 \times \$1,000)/2 = \$90$$
$$n = 20 \times 2 = 40$$
$$k = 8\% / 2 = 4\%$$
$$FV = \$1,000$$

Substituting, we have

$$
\begin{aligned}
P_B &= \$90[PVFA_{4,40}] + \$1,000[PVF_{4,40}] \\
&= \$90[19.7928] + \$1,000[.2083] \\
&= \$1,781.35 + \$208.30 \\
&= \$1,989.65
\end{aligned}
$$

Notice how much the price has risen, almost doubling the original $1,000. That's because the drop in the interest rate was very substantial *and* the bond has a long time to go until maturity. This price represents the present value of Northern Timber's (the bond issuer) cash flow commitment if the bond isn't called.

Next we'll evaluate to call using Equation 7.5.

$$P_B(call) = PMT[PVFA_{k,m}] + CP[PVF_{k,m}]$$

The variables follow.

$$PMT = (.18 \times \$1,000)/2 = \$90$$
$$m = 5 \times 2 = 10$$
$$k = 8\% / 2 = 4$$
$$CP = \$1,000 + .18(\$1,000) = \$1,180$$

Calculator Solution

Key	Input
n	40
I/Y	4
FV	1,000
PMT	90

	Answer
PV	1,989.64

Calculator Solution

Key	Input
n	10
I/Y	4
FV	1,180
PMT	90
	Answer
PV	1,527.15

Substituting,

$$P_B(\text{call}) = \$90[PVFA_{4,10}] + \$1,180[PVF_{4,10}]$$
$$= \$90[8.1109] + \$1,180[.6756]$$
$$= \$729.98 + \$797.21$$
$$= \$1,527.19$$

Notice that the price is substantially above $1,000 but is much less than the price without a call. From the point of view of a bond buyer, the only relevant price is $1,527.19, because the likelihood of call is very high. This price represents the value of Northern Timber's cash flow commitment if the bond is called. Notice how much Northern will save if it calls the bond.

The Refunding Decision   Whenever the current interest rate is substantially below a bond's coupon rate and the issue has a call feature, the issuing company has to decide whether or not to exercise the call. The company has to compare the interest savings from calling the bond with the cost of making the call and issuing a new bond to raise the money required to pay the old one off.

The difference in bond prices in the last example shows the interest savings associated with a call and includes a major cost item, the call premium. However, the figure does not include administrative expenses or the cost of issuing a new bond.

The costs incurred in issuing new bonds are known as *flotation costs* and can be rather substantial. They're primarily brokerage fees paid to investment bankers, but they also include administrative expenses and the costs of printing and engraving.

As a result of these costs, interest rates have to drop a lot before it's advisable for a company to refund by calling in one bond issue and floating another.

Dangerous Bonds with Surprising Calls   *Bonds can occasionally have obscure call features buried in their contract terms that can cause unwary investors real grief. These generally take the form of a clause that says if some particular event occurs, the bond will be called at face value.*

The most common of these clauses involves *sinking fund* provisions. Recall that in Chapter 6, we described a sinking fund as a way lenders guarantee that borrowers will have enough money put aside to pay off a bond's principal when it comes due. (Review pages 248–249 if necessary.) There we said that borrowing firms can make deposits in a separate account whose future value will be the amount of the bond's principal.

Another way to provide for an orderly payoff of principal is to require that the individual bonds of an issue be called in and paid off over a series of years rather than all at once. For example, suppose a company borrowed a million dollars for 25 years by issuing 1,000 25-year bonds, each with a face value of $1,000. Repayment could be made a lot more secure if, instead of paying off all the bonds at the maturity date, the company called and retired a few each year during the last five years of the issue's life.

Sinking fund provisions often require companies to do just that, call in and retire a fixed percentage of the issue each year toward the end of the term. Since this procedure is for the benefit of the bondholders (to increase their security), the agreements don't generally include a call premium. The bonds called are usually determined by a *lottery*, so no one knows which bonds will be called early and which will continue to maturity.

Now, suppose a particular bond that's subject to sinking fund provisions like these happens to be selling at a premium because of interest rate changes. An unlucky investor might buy a $1,000 face value bond for, say, $1,100, and in short order receive a call at $1,000 that results in an immediate loss of $100! This does happen, even though bond investments are supposed to be relatively safe.

Here's another example. Government agencies issue bonds that are backed by mortgages on residential real estate. If the mortgages underlying the bonds are held to maturity, the bonds pay interest until maturity. But if the mortgages are paid off early, the funds are used to retire the bonds at face value. Because no one knows how fast people will pay off their home mortgages, you can never be sure the mortgage-backed bonds won't be called early.

Needless to say, it's wise to check the details of bond agreements before investing.

7.2g   Risky Issues

Sometimes bonds sell for prices far below those indicated by the valuation techniques we've described so far in this chapter. For example, suppose we applied Equation 7.4 to a particular $1,000 face value bond and came up with a value of $950. However, suppose we checked and found the bond to be trading at $500.

from the
CFO

This would usually mean the company that issued the bond is in financial trouble, and there is some question about its ability to honor the obligations of the bond agreement. In other words, analysts feel it might default on the payment of interest and/or principal. Obviously such a risk will cause investors to lower their estimates of what any security is worth.

Financial purists argue that in such a situation, Equation 7.4 still gives the right answer if we properly select the interest rate k. The argument is that the increased risk should be reflected in a higher expected return to the investor. Using a higher k, results in a lower calculated price. In other words, the bond has slipped into a lower quality class, which should be reflected by the requirement of a higher yield to compensate for the chance that the investor may lose everything if things go poorly for the company.

However you look at it, a major deterioration in a bond-issuing company's financial performance will substantially depress the price of its securities, including bonds.

7.3   Convertible Bonds

A **convertible bond** is exchangeable for a fixed number of shares of the issuing company's stock at the bondholder's discretion. The number of shares exchanged for the bond is determined by a **conversion ratio** that's set at the time the bond is issued.

For example, a $1,000 par (face) value *convertible* with a 50-to-1 conversion ratio would exchange for 50 shares of stock. Notice that stating the conversion ratio along with the bond's par value implies a **conversion price**. In this case, the bond converts at a stock price of $1,000/50 = $20. In general,

(7.6)
$$\text{conversion ratio} = \frac{\text{bond's par value}}{\text{conversion price}} = \text{shares exchanged}[3]$$

Ordinary bonds are generally safer investments than stock in the same company, but don't offer stock's potential for price appreciation. A *convertible feature* allows bondholders to enjoy some of that price appreciation if the firm is successful.

Conversion prices are usually set 15% to 30% *above* the stock's market price at the time the convertible is issued. Then if stock prices rise above conversion prices, convertible owners make money by converting and selling their shares at the appreciated market price.

In exchange for this potential, investors are generally willing to accept lower yields on convertibles than on ordinary bonds. That means they can be issued at lower coupon rates and cost borrowers less in interest expense.

> Convertibles let **bondholders** participate in **stock price appreciation**.

CONCEPT CONNECTION   EXAMPLE 7-5

Basics: Investing in Convertible Bonds

Harry Jenson purchased one of Algo Corp.'s 9%, 25-year convertible bonds at its $1,000 par value a year ago when the company's common stock was selling for $20. Similar bonds without a conversion feature returned 12% at the time. The bond is convertible into stock at a price of $25. The stock is now selling for $29. Algo pays no dividends. (Notice that this bond's coupon rate was set below the market rate for nonconvertible issues.)

a. Harry exercised the conversion feature today and immediately sold the stock he received. Calculate the total return on his investment.

b. What would Harry's return have been if he had invested $1,000 in Algo's stock instead of the bond?

c. Comment on the difference between the returns in parts (a) and (b) and from investing in a nonconvertible bond.

d. Would the convertible have been a good investment if the stock's price had fallen?

SOLUTION:

a. Use Equation 7.6 to calculate the number of shares exchanged for the bond.

---

3. Convertibles are always *debentures*, unsecured bonds. We'll discuss types of bonds later in the chapter. It is common practice to refer to the face value of a convertible as its par value.

$$\text{shares exchanged} = \frac{\text{par value}}{\text{conversion price}}$$

$$= \frac{\$1,000}{\$25}$$

$$= 40 \text{ shares}$$

The proceeds from selling those shares at the current market price were

$$40 \times \$29 = \$1,160$$

In addition, the bond paid interest during the year of

$$\$1,000 \times .09 = \$90$$

So total receipts from the bond investment were

$$\$1,160 + \$90 = \$1,250$$

The bond cost Harry $1,000, so his gain is

$$\$1,250 - \$1,000 = \$250$$

for a return on the invested cost of

$$\frac{\$250}{\$1,000} = 25\%$$

b. If Harry had invested $1,000 in Algo's stock, he would have purchased

$$\frac{\$1,000}{\$20} = 50 \text{ shares}$$

each of which would have increased in value by

$$\$29 - \$20 = \$9$$

for a total gain of

$$50 \times \$9 = \$450$$

His return would have been

$$\frac{\$450}{\$1,000} = 45\%$$

c. Investing in Algo's ordinary debt would have returned 12%. Investing in its stock returned 45%. The convertible, at 25%, allowed bond investors to participate in some, but not all, of the unusually high return enjoyed by stock investors this year.

d. Convertibles limit risk relative to investing in stock. Had Algo's stock price fallen, an investment in it would have generated a negative return. But Harry's return would have been the convertible's 9% coupon rate unaffected by the stock's poor performance. That's less than the 12% offered by ordinary debt, but substantially better than a loss.

Convertibles are **less risky** than stock.

The Effect of Conversion on the Financial Statements and Cash Flow

When conversion occurs, an accounting entry is made that takes the par value of converted bonds out of long-term debt and places it in the equity accounts as if new shares had been sold at the conversion price. (See page 42–44 for equity accounting.)

It's important to notice that there is no *immediate* cash flow impact from a conversion; the transaction is strictly on the company's books. However, conversion has important ongoing cash flow implications. The original debt is gone, so interest payments stop immediately, but the newly created shares are entitled to dividends if any are paid. But, since many companies that issue convertibles don't pay dividends, conversion usually implies a decrease in cash outflow.

Conversion also strengthens the balance sheet by removing debt and adding equity, which improves all debt management ratios (page 96–97).

Conversion has **no immediate cash flow** impact, but affects **ongoing** cash flow.

Convertibles as Deferred Stock Purchases

Notice that it's possible to look at an investment in a convertible as a **deferred purchase of equity (stock)**. If a substantial increase in stock price is very likely, eventual conversion is virtually assured. That means the bond and associated interest payments can be viewed as temporary, and the long-term effect of the transaction is a sale of stock.

Convertibles can be thought of as **deferred stock purchases**.

7.3a   Advantages of Convertible Bonds

Several advantages can make convertibles attractive to issuing companies and investors:

Advantages to Issuing Companies

Issuing companies may experience these advantages:

1. Convertible debt tends to be offered by risky companies that have problems with conventional borrowing. Risky businesses always pay higher interest rates than more stable firms and sometimes are completely unable to borrow. For these firms, convertible features are *sweeteners* that can induce lenders to accept lower rates or lend where they ordinarily would not.

2. A convertible can be viewed as a way to sell equity at a price above market. In Example 7-5, if Algo's management was sure the firm's stock was undervalued when the convertible was issued and that it would eventually be converted, they were essentially selling stock at the conversion price of $25 when the market price was $20.

3. We'll learn later in this chapter that lenders generally insist on reducing their risk with contracts called bond indentures that limit the activities of borrowers while debt is outstanding. When debt is convertible, lenders view themselves as purchasing equity, so they're less concerned about restrictions. As a result, convertible bonds usually have mild indentures or none at all.

Convertibles:
1. Offer **lower** interest rates.
2. May sell stock **above** market.
3. Have **few restrictions**.

Advantages to Buyers

Convertible bond buyers may see the following advantages.

1. Convertibles offer buyers the chance to participate in the stock price appreciation offered by risky equity investments.

2. At the same time, convertibles offer a way to limit the risk associated with stock investments which can result in big losses as well as big gains.

7.3b   Forced Conversion

Reconsider Example 7-5 and imagine that after Algo's stock has risen to $29, Harry decides to indefinitely delay exercising his bond's conversion feature. He might do that because he expects the stock price to remain at or above $29 and he can collect interest on his bond investment until he's ready to close out his position in Algo altogether. This is better than converting and holding the stock, because Algo doesn't pay dividends.

Algo's management wants its bond converted for two reasons. They'd like to avoid paying further interest, but also want to exchange debt for equity to strengthen the balance sheet. For these reasons, convertibles are virtually always issued with call features that can be used to force conversion. Typically, convertible call features have call premiums of one year's coupon interest. (See page 301 for call features.)

For example, suppose in our continuation of Example 7-5, Algo calls the bond to force conversion. Harry is then faced with a choice. He can either accept the call price of $1,090[4] or convert and sell his shares for a total of $1,160 as calculated in the example. Clearly, a rational investor will do the latter.

> **Conversion** can be forced by a **call feature**.

Issuers generally call convertibles when stock prices have risen to levels that are 10% to 15% above conversion prices.

Overhanging Issues   Recall that the purpose of issuing convertibles may not be to borrow money, but may be to sell equity at a price above market. In those cases, convertibles become problems if stock prices don't increase enough to make the bonds' conversion values more than their call prices (i.e., calls won't force conversion).

> When **stock prices don't rise**, convertibles become **overhanging issues**.

For example, suppose in Example 7-5, Algo's stock price rises to $27 and stops. Conversion at that price yields

$$40 \times 27 = \$1,080$$

which is less than the call price of $1,090, so investors will accept a call rather than convert. Essentially, an overhanging issue means Algo is stuck with debt it doesn't want.[5]

7.3c   Valuing (Pricing) Convertibles

Valuing a convertible is somewhat complicated because the security's value (price) can depend on *either* its value as a traditional bond *or* the market value of the stock into which it can be converted. Let's look at a diagram to illustrate this idea before examining a numerical example. Figure 7-6 graphs the value (price) of a convertible against the underlying stock's price.

We'll assume market interest rates are such that an otherwise identical bond without a conversion feature would sell for its par value of $1,000. *This is the convertible's value as a bond.* On the diagram, it is the horizontal line that intersects the vertical price axis at $1,000. We'll assume interest rates don't change, so this figure remains constant throughout the illustration. It's important to realize that the convertible's

---

4. $1,000 plus one year's interest at 9%.
5. Algo would rather have equity to avoid paying interest and to make its balance sheet stronger.

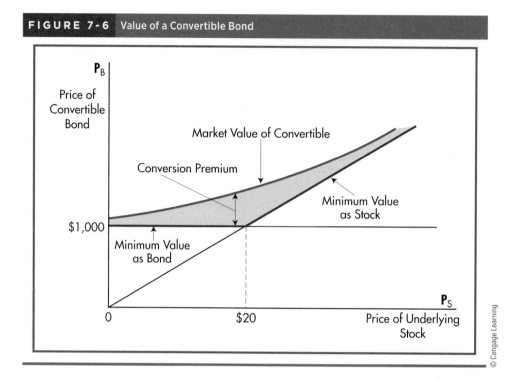

FIGURE 7-6 Value of a Convertible Bond

value as a bond doesn't have to be par. It depends on the interest rate and can be any figure calculated using the bond equation. We'll demonstrate this in an example shortly.

The diagonal line from the origin represents the convertible's value as stock   It is simply the number of shares exchanged for one bond (the conversion ratio) multiplied by the current stock price. Let's assume that this particular bond is convertible into 50 shares of stock, so the equation of the diagonal line is

$$P_B = 50P_S$$

where P_B and P_S are the prices of the bond and the stock, respectively.

Notice that at low stock prices the convertible's value as a bond is higher than its value as stock. At higher prices, it's worth more as stock.

At any stock price, the convertible is worth **at least the larger** of its value as a bond or as stock. That means the higher of the stock and bond value lines represents minimum value of the convertible as a function of stock price. In the diagram, this minimum value path is represented by the boldfaced line running along the horizontal from $1,000 and breaking upward along the value as stock line.

The market value of a convertible lies above the minimum value line because there's always a possibility that the stock's price will go up and improve the return of the bond's owner still further. That possibility gives the convertible a little extra value. In the diagram, market value is shown as a curved line above the bent minimum value line. The difference between market value and the appropriate minimum is the **conversion premium**, indicated in the diagram.

A convertible is worth at least the larger of its value as stock or as a bond.

The **conversion premium** is the excess of a convertible's **market value** over its **value as stock or a bond**.

The minimum values as stock and as a bond are equal at the intersection of the two minimum value lines. That point can be found by substituting the value as a bond into the equation of the diagonal value as stock line. In this illustration we have:

$$P_B = 50P_s$$
$$\$1,000 = 50P_s$$
$$P_s = \$1,000/50$$
$$= \$20$$

CONCEPT CONNECTION   EXAMPLE 7-6

Calculating the Conversion Premium

What was the conversion premium of the Algo convertible in Example 7-5 at the time it was issued?

SOLUTION: A diagram for this problem is shown below. Find the results of the following calculations on it as we move through the solution. Summarizing from Example 7-5, Algo's convertible bond was issued for 25 years at a coupon rate of 9%. The market rate was 12%, and the bond was exchangeable into 40 shares of stock.

To solve this problem, we have to find the breakpoint on the minimum value line and decide whether the stock price was to the right or left of it when the convertible was issued. That will tell us which minimum value formulation to use in calculating the conversion premium.

First, we'll calculate the minimum value of the convertible as a bond by writing Equation 7.4 and substituting the following from the problem.

$$PMT = (.09 \times \$1,000)/2 = \$45$$
$$n = 25 \times 2 = 50$$
$$k = 12\%/2 = 6\%$$
$$FV = \$1,000$$
$$P_B = PMT[PVFA_{k,n}] + FV[PVF_{k,n}]$$
$$= \$45[PVFA_{6,50}] + \$1,000[PVF_{6,50}]$$
$$= \$45(15.7619) + \$1,000(.0543)$$
$$= \$709.29 + \$54.30$$
$$= \$763.59$$

Calculator Solution

Key	Input
n	50
I/Y	6
FV	1,000
PMT	45
Answer	
PV	763.57

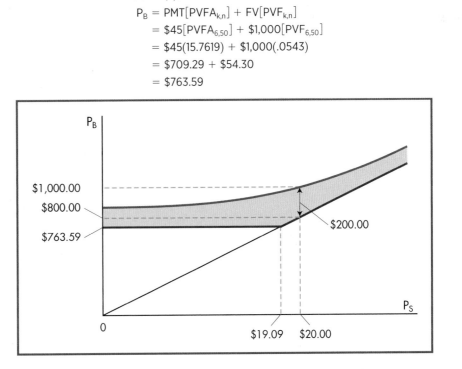

To find the breakpoint, we must find the stock price at which the convertible's minimum value as stock is just equal to this amount. Do that by writing the equation of the minimum value as stock line and substituting the bond price we've just calculated.

Noting that the conversion ratio is ($1,000/$25 =) 40 shares of stock to one bond, the minimum value as stock line is

$$P_B = 40P_S$$

Substitute $P_B = \$763.59$ and solve for P_S.

$$P_B = 40P_S$$
$$\$763.59 = 40P_S$$
$$P_S = \$19.09$$

When the convertible was issued, the market price of the stock was $20, which is to the right of the breakpoint in the diagram. That means the convertible's value as stock is the appropriate minimum. Calculate the bond's minimum value as stock at a stock price of $20 by substituting into the equation for the value as stock line.

$$P_B = 40P_S$$
$$= 40 \times \$20$$
$$= \$800$$

Harry bought the convertible for a market price of $1,000, so our solution is

$$\text{conversion premium} = \text{market price} - \text{minimum}$$
$$= \$1,000 - \$800$$
$$= \$200$$

7.3d   Effect on Earnings Per Share—Diluted EPS

Earnings per share (EPS) is net income (earnings after tax) divided by the number of shares of stock outstanding. Essentially, EPS is a firm's money-making power stated on a per-share basis. We mentioned this idea briefly in Chapter 3 (page 99), and we'll study it again in Chapter 8.

EPS is a key factor in pricing stocks.

In everyday finance, **EPS** is a key factor in determining the value of stocks. Investors decide how much they're willing to pay for shares based in large part on the issuing companies' EPS. A growing EPS is a very positive sign, while one that's stagnant or declining can lead to a depressed stock price. Indeed, EPS is so important that it and the related price earnings ratio (P/E ratio, see page 99) are the first things investors look at when studying potential investments.

Convertible securities have an important impact on EPS, but before we can appreciate, it we have to understand the idea of dilution.

Dilution   Suppose a company with 1,000 shares of stock outstanding has a total value of $100,000, so each share is worth $100. Now suppose the company sells 100 new shares to new investors at $100 each for a total of $10,000. Would the old stock-holders object to the sale?

The answer is no because the additional equity contributed by the new investors would increase the value of the company just enough to keep the value of the old shares constant. After the purchase, there would be 1,100 shares, but the firm would be worth an extra $10,000 and each share would still be worth ($110,000/1,100=) $100.

But suppose the new shares were priced at only $50 for a total of $5,000. The equity contribution would increase the firm's value to only $105,000, but there would still be 1,100 shares outstanding. So the value of each share, new and old, would be ($105,000/1,100=) $95.45.

Notice that the new shareholders get a big gain because their investment of $50 per share is suddenly worth $95.45. But that gain is at the expense of the old shareholders who see a drop of ($100 95.45=) $4.55 in their per-share value. In a situation like this, we would say the old stockholders' interests were **diluted** by the sale of new shares at a price below that of the old ones.

Earnings dilution is an easy extension of the same idea. Suppose the firm earns 10% on the value figures above. Then before the stock sale, EPS is

> **Earnings dilution** is a drop in **EPS** caused by a sale of **stock at** a **below market** price.

$$\text{EPS} = \text{earnings/shares} = (\$100,000 \times .10)/1,000 = \$10$$

The stock sale at $100 per share results in

$$\text{EPS} = \text{earnings/shares} = (\$110,000 \times .10)/1,100 = \$10$$

But the sale at $50 per share yields

$$\text{EPS} = \text{earnings/shares} = (\$105,000 \times .10)/1,100 = \$9.55$$

Here we'd say the existing stockholders had suffered an earnings dilution in that their EPS diminished. Since a drop in EPS generally leads to a drop in stock price, shareholders are very concerned about dilution or potential dilution in earnings.

Convertibles and Dilution   Convertible securities cause dilution. Consider the Algo convertible in Example 7-5. Recall that the bond was convertible into stock at a price of $25 and was exercised when the stock's market price was $29. That means Harry, the convertible owner, received $29 per share when he sold his converted stock, but Algo received an equity injection of only $25 per share in the form of a shift of debt into equity. This has the same dilutive effect as a sale of new stock at $25 when its market value is $29.

> Unexercised **convertibles** represent **potential** dilution.

In other words, dilution just about always happens when a company's stock price rises after a convertible is issued. Because of this phenomenon, the existence of unexercised convertibles always represents a *potential* dilution in a firm's EPS.

Disclosure of the Dilutive Potential of Convertibles   Investors use EPS to help determine the price they're willing to pay for stock. But if there are unexercised convertibles, future EPS may be smaller than expected simply because of their dilutive effect. That's a problem because it could result in investors being misled into paying too much for the stock.

In response to the problem, the accounting profession, acting through the Financial Accounting Standards Board (FASB), created rules requiring that companies report potential dilution from convertible and certain other securities in their financial statements. The rules have been modified several times since they first appeared in 1969. FASB 128, as it is called, requires that companies report two EPS figures, **basic EPS** and **diluted EPS**.

Basic EPS is what you would expect, earnings after tax divided by the number of shares outstanding during the year. If the number of shares isn't constant during the year, an average over time is used.

Diluted EPS is calculated assuming all existing convertibles are exercised creating new shares as of the beginning of the year. Essentially, it shows the worst-case scenario for dilution.

EPS calculations sound simple but can be complicated because of midyear changes in the number of shares outstanding and the effects of the assumed conversions on income. Example 7-7 illustrates the latter complication.

CONCEPT CONNECTION EXAMPLE 7-7

Dilution

Montgomery Inc. is a small manufacturer of men's clothing with operations in southern California. It issued 2,000 convertible bonds three years ago at a coupon rate of 8% and a par value of $1,000. Each bond is convertible into Montgomery's common stock at $25 per share.

Management expected the stock price to rise rapidly after the convertible was issued and to lead to a quick conversion of the bond debt into equity. However, a recessionary climate has prevented that from happening, and the bonds are still outstanding.

Last year, Montgomery had net income of $3 million. One million shares of its stock were outstanding for the entire year, and its marginal tax rate was 40%. Calculate Montgomery's basic and diluted EPS for the year.

SOLUTION:

Basic EPS

The basic EPS calculation is very simple because the number of shares outstanding was constant for the entire year.

$$\text{basic EPS} = \frac{\text{net income}}{\text{shares outstanding}} = \frac{\$3,000,000}{1,000,000} = \$3.00$$

Diluted EPS

Diluted EPS assumes all convertibles are exercised at the beginning of the year. Two adjustments have to be made to the EPS calculation above. The first adds newly converted shares to the denominator, while the second adjusts net income in the numerator for the after-tax effect of the interest saved when the bond debt is eliminated.

Use Equation 7.6 to calculate the number of new shares issued for each bond converted as

$$\text{shares exchanged} = \frac{\text{bond's par value}}{\text{conversion price}} = \frac{\$1,000}{\$25} = 40$$

Then multiply by 2,000 bonds for the total number of new shares issued, and add that to the original number of shares outstanding.

$$\text{shares from conversion} = 2,000 \times 40 = 80,000$$
$$\text{new shares outstanding} = 1,000,000 + 80,000 = 1,080,000$$

The 2,000 bonds pay interest at 8% on a $1,000 par value. Hence, the interest saved by their conversion into equity is

$$\text{interest saved} = .08 \times \$1,000 \times 2,000 = \$160,000$$

But since interest is tax deductible at 40%, paying it saved taxes of

$$\$160,000 \times .40 = \$64,000$$

so the improvement in net income from eliminating the interest is

$$\$160,000 - \$64,000 = \$96,000$$

And net income for calculating diluted EPS is

$$\$3,000,000 + \$96,000 = \$3,096,000$$

Then

$$\text{diluted EPS} = \frac{\$3,096,000}{1,080,000} = \$2.87$$

7.3e   Other Convertible Securities

Convertible features can be associated with certain other securities. The most common is preferred stock. We introduced preferred stock briefly in Example 6-18 (page 269) and will study it in detail in Chapter 8. Convertible preferred shares are similar to convertible bonds in that both are potentially dilutive. They're treated similarly in the calculation of diluted EPS.

Certain securities that are not convertibles can also result in issuing new stock at prices below market. Until exercised, they too represent potential dilution, and the calculation of diluted EPS must be adjusted for them. The most common example is a *warrant*, which gives its owner the right to buy a limited amount of new stock at a fixed price during a specified period. We'll discuss warrants in Chapter 8.

7.4   Institutional Characteristics of Bonds

In the remainder of this chapter, we'll describe some of the more important features of bonds and bond agreements that aren't directly related to pricing. Keep the fundamental definition of a bond in mind as we go forward. A bond is a device that enables an organization (generally a corporation or a government unit) to borrow from a large number of people at the same time under one agreement.

7.4a   Registration, Transfer Agents, and Owners of Record

A record of owners of **registered securities** is kept by a **transfer agent**. Payments are sent to **owners of record** as of the dates the payments are made.

Bonds are classified as either **bearer bonds** or **registered bonds**. Bearer bonds belong to whomever possesses them, a convention that makes them dangerously subject to loss and theft. Bearer bonds have coupons attached for the payment of interest as described earlier.

The owners of registered bonds are recorded with a **transfer agent**. This is an organization, usually a bank, that keeps track of the owners of stocks and bonds for issuing companies. When one investor sells a security to another, the agent *transfers* ownership in its records as of the date of the sale. On any given date, there is a particular **owner of record** on the transfer agent's books for every bond (and share of stock) outstanding. Interest payments are sent directly to the owners of record of registered bonds as of the date the interest is paid.

7.4b Kinds of Bonds

Several distinguishing features, in addition to convertibility which we've already considered, divide bonds into different categories. We'll briefly discuss a few of the more important distinctions.

Secured Bonds and Mortgage Bonds

Secured Bonds and Mortgage Bonds *Secured bonds* are backed by the value of specific assets owned by the issuing company. If the firm defaults, the secured bondholders can take possession of the assets and sell them to recover their claims on the company. The essence of the secured arrangement is that the assets tied to specific debt aren't available to other creditors until that debt is satisfied. When the securing assets are real estate, the bond is called a **mortgage bond**.

> Mortgage bonds are secured by real estate.

Debentures **Debentures** are unsecured bonds. They rely on the general creditworthiness of the issuing company rather than the value of specific assets. Debentures are clearly more risky than the secured debt of the same company. Therefore, they must usually be issued to yield higher returns to investors.

> Unsecured bonds are **debentures**.

Subordinated Debentures and Senior Debt The term "subordinated" means lower in rank or priority. In terms of debt, it means having lower priority than other debt for repayment in the event the issuing company fails. Debentures can be subordinated to specific issues or to all other debentures in general. The debt having priority over a **subordinated debenture** is known as **senior debt**.

Conceptually, subordination arises with the senior debt. For example, suppose a lender is considering making a loan but fears the borrower will take on more debt from other lenders in the future. Then if the borrower failed, whatever assets were available to satisfy unpaid loans would have to be shared among a large number of creditors. Some security is afforded to the first lender by writing a clause into the loan agreement requiring the subordination of all future debt.

> Subordinated debt is lower in priority for payment of principal and interest than senior debt.

Because **subordinated debt** is riskier than senior or unsubordinated debt, it generally requires a higher yield than those issues.

Junk Bonds **Junk bonds** are issued by companies that are not in particularly sound financial condition or are considered risky for some other reason. They generally pay interest rates that are as much as 5% higher than the rates paid by the strongest companies. Hence, they're also called *high-yield* securities.

> Junk bonds are issued by risky companies and pay high interest rates.

Before the mid-1970s it was virtually impossible for risky firms, especially new, small companies, to borrow by issuing unsecured bonds. Investors were simply unwilling to accept the risks associated with such firms at any promised rate of return. At that time, however, a concept of pooling risky bonds arose and seemed to make high-risk, high-yield issues viable in the sense of being reasonably safe investments. For a few years the volume of junk bonds exploded, growing until it represented 10% to 20% of the total domestic bond market.

In the late 1980s and early 1990s, the safety perceived in the pooling technique evaporated when the economy went into a sustained recession. As a result, the junk bond vehicle lost much of its popularity. We'll discuss junk bonds again in Chapter 17.

INSIGHTS   Practical Finance

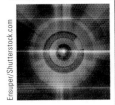

Can a Bond Have a Negative Interest Rate?

Would you pay someone for the privilege of lending them money? That's what a negative interest rate implies. Doesn't sound reasonable—does it? But it actually happens from time to time in the market for short-term debt securities issued by financially strong governments. The securities are called bills rather than bonds, and are usually issued for 90 days. In the United States, they're known as Treasury bills or T-bills. So the question is would you lend your government money if it promised to give you back only, say, 99 cents for every dollar you paid for your T-bills? The answer is sometimes, *Yes!*

The phenomenon generally happens in secondary markets; that is, when investors trade the bills among themselves. But lately it's happened in the primary market (first time the bill is sold) as well in Germany, Switzerland, and the Netherlands.

Of course, there's a logical reason investors are occasionally willing to pay to park their money rather than be paid for

its use. That reason is safety. In early 2012, Europe was in the throes of a monetary crisis in which people feared defaults on the sovereign* debt of several countries including Greece and Spain. Corporate debt and stocks also looked very risky. Indeed, the very survival of the Euro was being questioned. People had gone from looking for better returns to worrying about just hanging onto their money! That made investment in financially strong German short-term debt look good even at small negative returns. The same thing happened in the United States in the depth of the financial crisis.

Matt Phillips and Emese Bartha, "German Yields South of Zero," *The Wall Street Journal* (January 10, 2012).

David Wessel, "Interesting situation: When Rates Turn Negative," *The Wall Street Journal* (August 9, 2012), A2.

*Sovereign debt is the debt of the central (federal) government of a nation. It is supported by the government's authority to tax the nation's population.

7.4c   Bond Ratings—Assessing Default Risk

Recall that in Chapter 5, we discussed several risks associated with bonds, including the risk of default (page 215). In practice, investors and the financial community go to great lengths to assess and control exposure to default risk in bonds.

Bonds are assigned quality ratings that reflect the probability of their going into default. Higher ratings mean lower default probabilities. The **bond ratings** are developed by *rating agencies* that make a business out of staying on top of the things that make bonds and the underlying firms more or less risky. The best known rating agencies are Moody's Corporation (known as Moody's) and Standard & Poor's Corporation (generally called S&P).

The agencies rate bonds by examining the financial and market condition of the issuing companies and the contractual provisions supporting individual bonds. It's important to realize that the analysis has these two parts. A bond's strength is fundamentally dependent on that of the issuing corporation, but some things can make one

Bond ratings gauge the probability that issuers will fail to meet their obligations.

bond safer than another issued by the same company. For example, a mortgage bond backed by real estate will always be stronger than an unsecured debenture issued by the same company. Similarly, senior debt is always superior to subordinated debt.

The process of rating a bond begins with a financial (ratio) analysis of the issuing firm using the kinds of tools we developed in Chapter 3. To that the agencies add any knowledge they have about the company, its markets, and its other dealings. For example, suppose a firm has good financial results and a prosperous market outlook but is threatened by a major lawsuit. If the lawsuit is very serious, it can lower the rating of the firm's bonds.

Bond ratings are not precise in the sense of being the result of a mathematical formula. Although they do rely heavily on standard numerical (ratio) analyses, they also include qualitative judgments made by the rating agencies.

Rating Symbols and Grades

Moody's and S&P use similar scales to describe the bonds they rate. It's important to be generally familiar with the meaning of the terms. Table 7-2 summarizes the symbols used by the two firms and their meanings. The distinction between bonds above and below the Baa/BBB is especially significant. Bonds at or above that level are said to be **investment grade**, while those below are considered substandard. The latter can be called *junk bonds*.

Investment grade Bonds have low default risk.

Why Ratings Are Important

Throughout our study, we've stressed the fact that risk and return are related, and that investors *require* higher returns on riskier investments. Ratings are the primary measure of the default risk associated with bonds. Therefore, they're an important determinant of the interest rates investors demand on the bonds of different companies.

In effect, the rating associated with a firm's bonds determines the rate at which the firm can borrow. A lower rating implies the company has to pay higher interest rates. That generally means it's more difficult for the company to do business and earn a profit, because it's burdened with a higher cost of debt financing. To be precise about what we've just said, the idea is laid out in Figure 7-7.

All bond yields (interest rates) move up and down over time, but there's always a *differential* between the rates required on high- and low-quality issues. The lower

TABLE 7-2	Moody's and S&P Bond Ratings	
Moody's	**S&P**	**Implication**
Aaa	AAA	Highest quality, extremely safe
Aa	AA	High quality
A	A	Good quality
Baa	BBB	"Investment grade," medium quality
Ba	BB	Poor quality
B	B	Low quality, risky
Caa	CCC	Low quality, possible default
Ca	CC	Low quality, default, recovery possible
C	D	Defaulted, or may default

FIGURE 7-7   The Yield Differential Between High- and Low-Quality Bonds

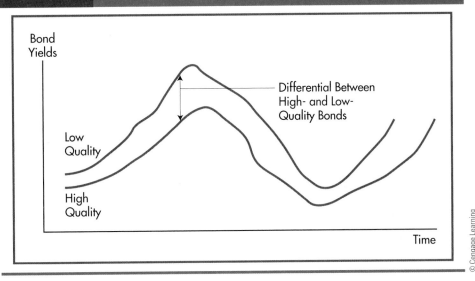

curve associated with high-quality bonds means that the issuing companies can borrow at lower rates (more cheaply) than those associated with risky, low-quality bonds. The safest, highest quality bond is a federal treasury bond, which has no default risk (Chapter 5, page 217). Its yield plotted on a graph like Figure 7-7 would be lower than that of any other bond.

A bond's rating affects the size of the differential between the rate it must pay to borrow and the rate demanded of high-quality issues. It does not affect the overall up and down motion of the rate structure. Clearly, the differential reflects the risk of default perceived to exist with lower-quality bonds. This is the default risk premium we discussed in Chapter 5.

The Differential Over Time   Notice that the quality differential tends to be larger when interest rates are generally high than when they're low. This is an important fact and makes logical sense. High rates tend to be associated with recessions and tough economic times. It's during those periods that marginal companies are prone to fail. In other words, the risk of default associated with weak companies is greater in bad times than in good times. Because it expresses the level of risk, the differential tends to be larger in recessionary periods.

> The **differential** between the yields on high- and low-quality bonds is an indicator of the health of the economy.

In fact, this phenomenon is strong enough to be considered an *economic indicator.* That means a high differential is taken as a signal that harder times are on the way.

The Significance of the Investment Grade Rating   Most bonds are purchased by institutional investors rather than by individuals. These investors include mutual funds, banks, insurance companies, and pension funds. Many such institutions are required by law to make only relatively safe, conservative investments. Therefore, they can deal only in investment grade bonds. This requirement severely limits the market for the debt of companies whose bonds aren't considered investment grade.

10. What is the relationship between bond prices and interest rates? Verbally describe how this relationship comes about. How can we use this relationship to estimate the value of a bond?

11. What is interest rate or price risk? Why is it sometimes called maturity risk? Explain fully.

12. What causes maturity risk? In other words, *why* do long-term bonds respond differently to interest rate changes than short-term bonds? (*Hint:* Think about how the present value formulas work.)

13. Using words only, describe the process of finding a bond's yield at a given selling price.

14. Under what conditions is a bond almost certain to be called at a particular date in the future? How does this condition affect its price?

15. How and why do sinking funds enhance the safety of lenders?

BUSINESS ANALYSIS

1. You're an analyst in the finance department of Flyover Corp., a new firm in a profitable but risky high-tech business. Several growth opportunities have come along recently, but the company doesn't have enough capital to undertake them. Stock prices are down, so it doesn't make sense to try to raise new capital through the sale of equity. The company's bank won't lend it any more money than it already has, and investment bankers have said that debentures are out of the question. The treasurer has asked you to do some research and suggest a few ways in which bonds might be made attractive enough to allow Flyover to borrow. Write a brief memo summarizing your ideas.

2. The Everglo Corp., a manufacturer of cosmetics, is financed with a 50–50 mix of debt and equity. The debt is in the form of debentures that have a relatively weak indenture. Susan Moremoney, the firm's president and principal stockholder, has proposed doubling the firm's debt by issuing new bonds secured by the company's existing assets and using the money raised to attack the lucrative but very risky European market. You're Everglo's treasurer and have been directed by Ms. Moremoney to implement the new financing plan. Is there an ethical problem with the president's proposal? Why? Who is likely to gain at whose expense? (*Hint:* How are the ratings of the existing debentures likely to change?) What would you do if you really found yourself in a position like this?

3. You're the CFO of Nildorf Inc., a maker of luxury consumer goods that, because of its product, is especially sensitive to economic ups and downs (people cut back drastically on luxury items during recessionary times).

In an executive staff meeting this morning, Charlie Suave, the president, proposed a major expansion. You felt the expansion would be feasible if the immediate future looked good, but were concerned that spreading resources too thin in a recessionary period could wreck the company. When you expressed your concern, Charlie said he wasn't worried about the economy because the spread between AAA and B bonds is relatively small, and that's a good sign. You observed, however, that rates seem to have bottomed out recently and are rising along with the differential between strong and weak companies. After some general discussion, the proposal was tabled pending further research. Later in the day, Ed Sliderule, the chief engineer, came into your office and asked, "What in the world were you guys talking about this morning?" Prepare a brief written explanation for Ed.

4. Paliflex Corp. needs new capital, but is having difficulty raising it. The firm's stock price is at a 10-year low, so selling new equity means giving up an interest in the company for a very low price. The debt market is tight and interest rates are unusually high, making borrowing difficult and expensive. In fact, Paliflex isn't certain that anyone will lend to it because it's a fairly risky company.

On the other hand, the firm's long-term prospects are good, and management feels the stock price will recover within a year or two. Ideally, management would like to expand the company's equity base so it can borrow more later on, but at the moment the stock price is just too low.

Suggest a capital strategy that addresses both the short and long run, explaining why it is likely to work.

PROBLEMS

Assume All Bonds Pay Interest Semiannually.
Finding the Price of a Bond: Concept Connection Example 7-1 (page 295)

1. The Altoona Company issued a 25-year bond 5 years ago with a face value of $1,000. The bond pays interest semiannually at a 10% annual rate.
   a. What is the bond's price today if the interest rate on comparable new issues is 12%?
   b. What is the price today if the interest rate is 8%?
   c. Explain the results of parts (a) and (b) in terms of opportunities available to investors.
   d. What is the price today if the interest rate is 10%?
   e. Comment on the answer to part (d).

2. Calculate the market price of a $1,000 face value bond under the following conditions:

	Coupon Rate	Time Until Maturity	Current Market Rate
a.	12%	15 years	10%
b.	7	5	12
c.	9	25	6
d.	14	30	9
e.	5	6	8

3. What is the current yield on each of the bonds in the previous problem?

4. The Sampson Company issued a $1,000 bond 5 years ago with an initial term of 25 years and a coupon rate of 6%. Today's interest rate is 10%.
   a. What is the bond's current price if interest is paid semiannually as it is on most bonds?
   b. What is the price if the bond's interest is paid annually? Comment on the difference between (a) and (b).
   c. What would the price be if interest were paid semiannually and the bond were issued at a face value of $1,500?

5. Fix-It Inc. recently issued 10-year, $1,000 par value bonds at an 8% coupon rate.
   a. Two years later, similar bonds are yielding investors 6%. At what price are Fix-It's bonds selling?
   b. What would the bonds be selling for if yields had risen to 12%?
   c. Assume the conditions in part a. Further assume interest rates remain at 6% for the next 8 years. What would happen to the price of the Fix-It bonds over that time?

6. The Mariposa Co. has two bonds outstanding. One was issued 25 years ago at a coupon rate of 9%. The other was issued 5 years ago at a coupon rate of 9%. Both bonds were originally issued with terms of 30 years and face values of $1,000. The going interest rate is 14% today.
   a. What are the prices of the two bonds at this time?
   b. Discuss the result of part (a) in terms of risk in investing in bonds.

7. Longly Trucking is issuing a 20-year bond with a $2,000 face value tomorrow. The issue is to pay an 8% coupon rate, because that was the interest rate while it was being planned. However, rates increased suddenly and are expected to be 9% when the bond is marketed. What will Longly receive for each bond tomorrow?

8. Daubert, Inc., planned to issue and sell at par 10-year, $1,000 face value bonds totaling $400 million next month. The bonds have been printed with a 6% coupon rate. Since that printing, however, Moody's

downgraded Daubert's bond rating from Aaa to Aa. This means the bonds will have to be offered to yield buyers 7%. How much less than it expected will Daubert collect when the bonds are issued? Ignore administrative costs and commissions.

9. Tutak Industries issued a $1,000 face value bond a number of years ago that will mature in eight years. Similar bonds are yielding 8%, and the Tutak bond is currently selling for $1,291.31. Compute the coupon rate on this bond. (In practice, we generally aren't asked to find coupon rates.) (*Hint*: Substitute and solve for the coupon payment.)

10. John Wilson is a conservative investor who has asked your advice about two bonds he is considering. One is a seasoned issue of the Capri Fashion Company that was first sold 22 years ago at a face value of $1,000, with a 25-year term, paying 6%. The other is a new 30-year issue of the Gantry Elevator Company that is coming out now at a face value of $1,000. Interest rates are now 6%, so both bonds will pay the same coupon rate.
   a. What is each bond worth today? Comment on your result.
   b. If interest rates were to rise to 12% today, estimate without making any calculations what each bond would be worth. Review page 296 on estimating if necessary.
   c. Calculate the prices in part (b) to check your estimating ability. If interest rates are expected to rise, which bond is the better investment?
   d. If interest rates are expected to fall, which bond is better? Are long-term rates likely to fall much lower than 6%? Why or why not? (*Hint*: Think about the interest rate model of Chapter 5 and its components.)

Finding the Yield at a Price: Concept Connection Example 7-3 (page 300)

11. Smithson Co.'s Class A bonds have 10 years to go until maturity. They have a $1,000 face value and carry coupon rates of 8%. Approximately what do the bonds yield at the following prices?
   a. $770
   b. $1,150
   c. $1,000

12. Hoste Corp. issued a $1,000 face value 20-year bond 7 years ago with a 12% coupon rate. The bond is currently selling for $1,143.75. What is its yield to maturity (YTM)?

13. Pam Smith just inherited a $1,000 face value K-S Inc. bond from her grandmother. The bond clearly indicates a 12% coupon rate, but the maturity date has been smudged and can't be read. Pam called a broker and determined that similar bonds are currently returning about 8% and that her bond is selling for $1,326.58. How many more interest payments can Pam expect to receive on her inherited bond? (*Hint*: Use an iterative approach, but solve for n rather than k.)

14. Ernie Griffin just purchased a five-year zero coupon corporate bond for $680.60 and plans to hold it until maturity. Assume Ernie has a marginal tax rate of 25%.
   a. Calculate Ernie's after-tax cash flows from the bond for the first two years. Assume annual compounding.
   b. Describe in words the difference in cash flows between owning Ernie's bond and a five-year U.S. savings bond for the same amount.
   (*Hint*: See the Insights box on page 303 for this problem.)

Pricing a "Likely to Be Called" Bond: Concept Connection Example 7-4 (page 304)

Problems 15 through 17 refer to the bonds of The Apollo Corporation, all of which have a call feature. The call feature allows Apollo to pay off bonds anytime after the first 15 years, but requires that bondholders be compensated with an extra year's interest at the coupon rate if such a payoff is exercised.

15. Apollo's Alpha bond was issued 10 years ago for 30 years with a face value of $1,000. Interest rates were very high at the time, and the bond's coupon rate is 20%. The interest rate is now 10%.
    a. At what price should an Alpha bond sell?
    b. At what price would it sell without the call feature?

16. Apollo's Alpha-1 bond was issued at a time when interest rates were even higher. It has a coupon rate of 22%, a $1,000 face value, an initial term of 30 years, and is now 13 years old. Calculate its price if interest rates are now 12%, compare it with the price that would exist if there were no call feature, and comment on the difference.

17. Apollo's Beta bond has just reached the end of its period of call protection, has 10 years to go until maturity, and has a face value of $1,000. Its coupon rate is 16%, and the interest rate is currently 10%. Should Apollo refund this issue if refunding costs a total of 8% of the value of the debt refunded plus the call penalty? (*Hint*: See the refunding decision page 306.)

18. Snyder Mfg. issued a $1,000 face value 30-year bond 5 years ago with an 8% coupon. The bond is subject to call after 10 years, and the current interest rate is 7%. What call premium will make a bondholder indifferent to the call? (*Hint*: Equate the formulas for the bond's price with and without the call.)

Risky Issues (page 307)

19. Your friend Marvin is excited because he believes he's found an investment bargain. A broker at QuickCash Investments has offered him an opportunity to buy a bond issued by Galveston Galleries Inc. at a very attractive price. The 30-year bond was issued 10 years ago at a face value of $1,000, paying a coupon rate of 8%. Interest rates have risen recently driving bond prices down, but most economists think they'll fall again soon driving prices back up. That makes Marvin and his broker think this bond may be a real money maker if he buys now, holds for a year or two, and then sells. The bonds of companies that were similar to Galveston at the time its bond was issued are now yielding 12%. Galveston's bond is selling at $300 which the broker claims is a fantastic bargain. Marvin knows you're a finance major and has asked your opinion of the opportunity. How would you advise him?

Basics: Investing in Convertible Bonds: Concept Connection Example 7-5 (page 308)

20. Pacheco Inc. issued convertible bonds 10 years ago. Each bond had an initial term of 30 years, had a face value of $1,000, paid a coupon rate of 11%, and was convertible into 20 shares of Pacheco stock, which was selling for $30 per share at the time. Since then the price of Pacheco shares has risen to $65, and the interest rate has dropped to 8%. What is the least that each of the bonds is worth today? Comment on the function of the bond valuation procedure for convertibles.

21. Jake Cornwall just bought a $1,000 par value, 8% coupon rate, 30-year bond issued by Pristine Corp. Interest rates had risen somewhat between the time the coupon rate was set and the bond was issued, so Jake got it at a discount, paying only $950. The bond is convertible into 50 shares of stock at a conversion price of $20 per share. Similar Pristine Corp. bonds without the conversion feature carry 10% coupon rates and are also selling at $950. Pristine's stock is selling at $15 per share. The company consistently pays an annual dividend of $1 per share. Calculate the following at the end of one year:
    a. The return on Jake's investment if the stock's price rises to $25 per share, Jake exercises the conversion, and then he sells immediately.

    b. The one-year return on Jake's investment if he had invested in Pristine's ordinary bonds (no conversion) and if interest rates at the end of the year were the same as they were when he purchased the bond.

    c. Jake's one-year return if he had invested in the company's stock.

    d. What would the returns on the three investments have been if the stock's price hadn't moved?

    e. What would the returns on the three investments have been if the stock's price had declined to $12 and interest rates were the same as on the day he purchased the bond?

    f. What would the return on Jake's investment have been if Pristine had forced conversion at a stock price of $23 a few days before the end of the year?

    g. Comment on the effect of the forced conversion on investors.

Calculating the Conversion Premium and Dilution: Concept Connection Examples 7-6 and 7-7 (pages 313 and 316)

22. The Maritime Engineering Corp. sold 1,500 convertible bonds two years ago at their $1,000 par value. The 20-year bonds carried a coupon rate of 8% and were convertible into stock at $20 per share. At the time, the firm's stock was selling for $15, and similar bonds without a conversion feature were yielding 10%. Maritime's stock is now selling for $25. The firm does not pay dividends.

    a. Calculate the return on investment from buying the bond when it was issued, exercising the conversion today, and immediately selling the stock received.

    b. What would the return on an investment in Maritime's stock have been?

    c. What was the conversion premium of the bond at the time it was issued?

    d. Last year Maritime had net income of $4.5 million and 3 million shares outstanding. The company's marginal tax rate was 34%. Compute Maritime's basic and diluted EPS.

23. Lindstrom Corp. reported earnings after tax of $2,160,000 last year along with basic EPS of $3. All of Lindstrom's bonds are convertible and, if converted, would increase the number of shares of the firm's stock outstanding by 15%. Lindstrom is subject to a total effective tax rate of 40% and has a TIE of 10 (See page 96). Compute Lindstrom's diluted earnings per share.

24. Harvester Inc. has net income of $75,000,000 and 15,000,000 shares of common stock outstanding. Several years ago it issued 10,000, 8% coupon, 30 year convertible debentures at a par value of $1,000. The conversion price was set at $25; the price of the stock at the time was about $18. The company is taxed at a total effective rate of 35% and regularly pays an annual dividend of $0.50 per share. The bond issue included a call feature with a call premium of two years coupon interest and a 5-year period of call protect which has now passed.

    Management thought the stock price would increase steadily over the next few years and anticipated a quick conversion into equity, but that hasn't happened. The stock is now selling for $30, and management is considering a call hopefully to force conversion.

    a. Calculate Harvester's Basic and Fully Diluted EPS.

    b. What is annual the cash flow impact on the company of conversion of all the bonds?

    c. Evaluate a bondholder's position at this time. Why haven't they converted?

    d. Will a call force conversion? Why? That is, what is difference in value for each bond between conversion and call?

    e. Why does management prefer conversion to call? (Words only.)

COMPUTER PROBLEMS

25. You are a securities salesperson. Many of your clients are elderly people who want very secure investments. They remember the days when interest rates were very stable (before the 1970s) and bond prices hardly fluctuated at all regardless of their terms. You've had a hard time convincing some of them that bonds, especially those with longer terms, can be risky during times when interest rates move rapidly.

     Use the BONDVAL program to make up a chart using the format shown to help illustrate your point during discussions with your clients.

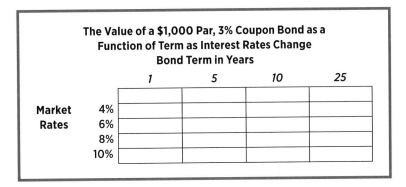

		Bond Term in Years			
		1	5	10	25
Market Rates	4%				
	6%				
	8%				
	10%				

The Value of a $1,000 Par, 3% Coupon Bond as a Function of Term as Interest Rates Change

     Write a brief paragraph outlining your warning about bond price volatility to an elderly customer. Refer to your chart.

26. Use BONDVAL to find the YTM of the following $1,000 par value bonds.

	1	2	3
Market price	$752.57	$1,067.92	$915.05
Coupon rate	6.5%	7.24%	12.5%
Term	15.5 yrs	8.5 yrs	2.5 yrs

Appendix 7A

A7.1   Lease Financing

A "lease" is a contract that gives one party the right to use an asset owned by the other in return for a periodic payment. The owner of the property is called the lessor and the user is the lessee. Leasing is a method of financing assets that is actually similar to debt.

Most of us are familiar with leases in the context of houses and apartments where the lessor is the landlord and the lessee is the tenant[6]. In recent years, leasing automobiles has also become common practice. In business, companies lease equipment of all kinds as well as real estate.

A7.2   The Development of Leasing in Business

Prior to the 1950s, leasing was almost entirely limited to real estate (i.e., leasing office or factory space). Since then the technique has spread to equipment to the extent that today approximately 30% of all equipment acquired by businesses is leased.

A7.2a   Leasing and Financial Statements

The best way to understand the early development of leasing is through an example. Imagine that Textronix Inc. has the following simplified balance sheet.

Textronix Inc. Balance Sheet ($000)

Current assets	$ 10	Current liabilities	$ 5
Fixed assets	90	Long-term debt	45
Total assets	$100	Equity	50
		Total debt & equity	$100

We're interested in the firm's debt management ratios (review pages 94–96 if necessary), recalling that excessive debt is perceived as risky and is generally a negative to investors.[7] For simplicity we'll focus on the debt ratio which is defined as total debt divided by total assets, where total debt is current liabilities plus long-term debt. Notice that Textronix's debt ratio is a fairly high 50%, calculated as follows.

$$\text{debt ratio} = (\text{current liabilities} + \text{long-term debt})/\text{total assets}$$
$$= (\$5 + \$45)/\$100$$
$$= \$50/\$100$$
$$= 50\%$$

---

6. It's important to distinguish between a lease and a rental. Renting implies paying for the temporary use of an asset, but without a longer-term commitment. However, the term "rent" is often used loosely to refer to lease payments as well as rental payments.

7. When debt is high, adding more causes investors to bid the firm's stock price down. It also worries lenders who charge higher interest on new borrowing, and may refuse to extend more credit.

Now suppose management wants to acquire a $50,000 asset, but doesn't want to use equity[8] funds to buy it. One approach is to purchase the equipment with borrowed money using the asset itself as collateral.[9] Doing that would put an additional $50,000 asset on the balance sheet along with another $50,000 in long-term debt. The new balance sheet would appear as follows.

Textronix Inc. Balance Sheet ($000)

Current assets	$ 10	Current liabilities	$ 5
Fixed assets	140	Long-term debt	95
Total assets	$150	Equity	50
		Total debt & equity	$150

Notice that the loan makes the debt ratio considerably worse (higher).

$$\text{debt ratio} = (\$5 + \$95)/\$150$$
$$= \$100/\$150$$
$$= 66.7\%$$

Debt used to acquire assets can cause debt management **ratios** to deteriorate.

Seen in this light, borrowing to buy is a real problem for Textronix. **Deterioration in the debt ratio** would probably mean paying a premium interest rate for the funds and might even make borrowing impossible. It's also likely to have a negative impact on the price of Textronix's stock. Notice that the problem is ownership. Since Textronix owns the asset, it and the associated debt have to go on the balance sheet.

But suppose the asset could be used without ownership. Then Textronix's balance sheet would be unaffected, and its financial ratios would not deteriorate. Originally, leasing allowed a firm to do just that, use something without owning it. Lease payments were recognized as expenses on the income statement, but had no impact on the balance sheet. Hence, in the beginning, leasing avoided the ratio problems that come with borrowing to buy. Recognition of this result in the 1950s and 1960s led to a rapid increase in the amount of *lease financed* equipment in the United States. Leasing became the leading form of **off balance sheet financing**—using an asset without reflecting it or its financing on the balance sheet.

Leases may provide **off balance sheet financing**.

Not recognizing large leases on the balance sheet made financial statements **misleading**.

Misleading Results   It's important to notice that the result we've described made financial statements misleading. The risk in debt comes from the fact that payments are obligatory charges that if missed can cause the firm to fail. Essentially the same is true of lease payments when leases are noncancelable. Noncancelability means that if the lessee returns the equipment during the lease term, the remaining payments are still a legal obligation much the same as an unpaid loan. Since long-term leases on major equipment are virtually always noncancelable, they are effectively debt with all of its problems and risks. But in the early days, they didn't show up on balance sheets. In other words, an investor reading the financial statements of a company that used lease financing could have been misled into thinking the firm was stronger than it was.

By the early 1970s there was substantial concern within the accounting profession over distortions in reported financial results due to leasing. Along with that concern,

---

8. Retained earnings or money raised by selling new stock.

9. If a borrower defaults on a loan, the lender can sell collateral to satisfy the loan obligation.

pressure built to provide accounting rules that would require disclosing long-term leases as the equivalent of debt.

Accounting rules at the time did state that all leases had to be disclosed in notes to the financial statements. Those opposed to change argued that this footnote disclosure was enough. They insisted that sophisticated users of financial statements read the notes and understand exactly what companies are doing in spite of off balance sheet financing. The counterargument, which prevailed, is that not all investors are sophisticated or attentive enough to fully appreciate financial statement notes, and that more explicit disclosure is required to prevent financial statements from being misleading.

A7.3   The Financial Accounting Standards Board and FASB 13

The task of curing the distortion in financial results caused by leasing fell to the Financial Accounting Standards Board (FASB), a professional accounting organization that promulgates rules governing how financial statements are put together. The board issued *Statement of Financial Accounting Standards No. 13* (FASB 13 for short, referred to verbally as "fazbee thirteen") on the subject in November 1976. This standard dictates rules for the financial reporting of leases that are based on economic effects rather than legal technicalities.

The distorting effects of lease financing arose from the fact that asset ownership is crucial to financial reporting, and leasing allows use without ownership. The FASB attacked the problem by redefining ownership.

Prior to FASB 13, ownership for financial-reporting purposes was defined legally. An asset was owned by whoever held its title (usually a bill of sale). It didn't matter that someone else (a lessee) was using the asset. FASB 13 said that concept of ownership didn't reflect economic reality. It maintained that the real owner of an asset is whoever enjoys its benefits and is burdened with its risks and responsibilities.

FASB 13 redefines ownership in an **economic sense**.

Specifically, the standard says that if a lease transfers those benefits and burdens to a lessee for most of an asset's life, then that lessee is the owner **for financial-reporting purposes,** and must account for the asset on its balance sheet.[10]

The FASB also addressed leases that include provisions that pass legal ownership to lessees as the lease ends or provide that lessees can purchase the assets at prices below *fair market value* (called *bargain purchase options*). According to the Board, those leases are just disguised installment sales contracts and must be accounted for as sales. That is, the lessor is really just lending the purchase price to the lessee, and subsequent lease payments are actually loan payments.

A7.3a   Operating and Capital (Financing) Leases

The FASB said that there are essentially two kinds of leases, which it called operating and capital. Capital leases are often called **financing leases**, because they're a method of financing the permanent acquisition of equipment. They effectively transfer economic ownership while operating leases do not.

Financing leases must be **capitalized** on the balance sheet.

---

10. The benefit of ownership is the productive use of the equipment. The burdens include providing for maintenance, insurance, and property taxes.

Under FASB 13, lessees must *capitalize* financing leases. That means they must make accounting entries that put the value of leased assets and the associated liabilities on their balance sheets. The value of a leased asset is usually its fair market value and the associated liability reflects the obligation to make lease payments in the future. The resulting balance sheet accounts are similar to those that would appear if the lessee purchased the asset with borrowed money.

In other words, after FASB 13, operating leases can still be used to provide off balance sheet financing, but financing leases cannot. Naturally lessees strive to interpret leases as operating whenever they can. The Board made it easy to determine the nature of the lease by promulgating four rules, all of which must be met for a lease to qualify as operating.

1. The lease must not transfer legal ownership to the lessee at its end.
2. There must not be a bargain purchase option at the end of the lease.
3. The lease term must be less than 75% of the asset's estimated economic life.[11]
4. The present value of the lease payments must be less than 90% of the asset's fair market value at the beginning of the lease.[12]

Operating leases are not capitalized, but must satisfy *four rules*.

The first two rules exclude disguised installment sales contracts from treatment as operating leases. The third says that if the attributes of ownership are transferred for most of the asset's life, it no longer truly belongs to the lessor and the lease must be treated as a financing lease. The fourth addresses whether the lessor is really selling the equipment through the lease. If the present value of the committed lease payments is close to the asset's value, then the transaction is probably a sale, and ownership should effectively pass to the lessee.

As a practical matter, it's fairly easy to identify operating leases. They're usually relatively short, say one to three years. The lease payments usually include a charge for equipment maintenance, and lessors generally pay for insurance and property taxes. Because these things are included, operating leases are sometimes called *service leases*.

Operating leases are also generally cancelable on short notice (usually 30 days), although a cancellation penalty may be required. Financing leases, on the other hand, are *noncancelable*.

A7.3b   Financial Statement Presentation of Leases by Lessees

The financial statement presentation and accounting for operating and financing leases are very different. Operating leases are simple, while financing leases are complex. We'll discuss both, presenting only the highlights of the financing lease treatment.

Operating Leases   The financial statement treatment of operating leases is straightforward. There are no balance sheet entries, and lease payments are simply treated as an expense on the income statement. There is, however, a requirement that the details of all leases be disclosed in footnotes to the financial statements.

---

11. An asset's economic life is the period over which it will be used. That is generally longer than the period over which it is depreciated.

12. The interest rate used to take this present value is the rate the lessee would pay if it borrowed new money at the time the lease is signed.

Financing (Capital) Leases   At the beginning of a financing lease, the lessee must record an asset on its balance sheet reflecting the leased equipment's value. It must also record an offsetting liability related to its obligation to make lease payments. Both of these amounts are usually taken to be equal to the present value of the stream of committed lease payments, a sum that is usually about equal to the fair market value of the equipment. The liability appears in the debt section of the balance sheet and is normally called lease obligation. The interest rate for the present value calculation is generally the rate the lessee would have to pay if it were borrowing new money at the time the lease begins.

Once these accounts are set up, they are amortized[13] independently. The asset is simply depreciated. The **lease obligation** liability is treated like a loan. An effective interest rate is assumed,[14] and lease payments are divided between interest and principal reduction as if they were loan payments. The technique is identical to the one we studied in Chapter 6 under Loan Amortization Schedules (see page 262).

> Financing leases are usually capitalized at the **present value** of committed **lease payments**.

> Leased **assets are depreciated**. Lease **obligations** are amortized as **loans**.

CONCEPT CONNECTION   EXAMPLE 7A-1

Accounting for a Financing Lease

Emeral Inc. is a moderately sized construction company that operates in upstate New York. Last year it leased a crane from GD Credit Corp. for a term of 15 years at an annual rental of $20,000 payable at the end of each year. The crane is expected to be completely worn out and valueless at the end of the lease. Before the lease agreement was made, other financing sources were willing to lend to Emeral at 5%. Emeral will depreciate the crane using the straight line method over the 15-year life of the lease.

Just before the lease was signed, Emeral's balance sheet was as follows:

Emeral Inc. Balance Sheet ($000)

Current assets	$ 20		Current liabilities	$ 10
Fixed assets	180		Long-term debt	90
Total assets	$200		Equity	100
			Total liabilities & equity	$200

The lease is treated as a financing lease.

a. Construct Emeral's balance sheet after the lease is signed showing the leased asset and lease obligation separately. (We'll work in whole dollars but present balance sheet accounts rounded to the nearest $1,000.)

b. Calculate the firm's debt ratio before and after the lease takes effect, and comment on the difference.

c. (Optional) Reconstruct the balance sheet after the first annual lease payment is made assuming all other accounts are unchanged.

SOLUTION:

a. Emeral will capitalize the lease at an amount equal to the present value of the annuity formed by the contracted lease payments. That amount is calculated using the present value of an annuity formula,

---

13. Amortizing balance sheet accounts means writing them down to zero over time. Assets are amortized through depreciation, while liabilities (think in terms of a loan) are amortized as they are paid off.

14. Usually the same rate used to take the present value of the lease payments.

Equation 6.19 (see page 256).

$$PVA = PMT[PVFA_{k,n}]$$
$$= \$20,000[PVFA_{5,15}]$$
$$= \$20,000(10.3797)$$
$$= \$207,594$$

Hence, the balance sheet immediately after the lease is signed is as follows.

Emeral Inc. Balance Sheet ($000)

Current assets	$ 20	Current liabilities	$ 10
Leased crane	208	Lease obligation	208
Fixed assets	180	Long-term debt	90
Total assets	$408	Equity	100
		Total liabilities & equity	$408

b. Emeral's debt ratio before the lease is ($000)

$$\text{debt ratio} = \frac{\text{current liabilities } + \text{ long-term debt}}{\text{total assets}}$$
$$= (\$10 + \$90)/\$200$$
$$= 50\%$$

After the lease is signed, the lease obligation is included as debt in calculating the debt ratio, which increases substantially.

$$\text{debt ratio} = \frac{\text{current liabilities } + \text{ lease obligation } + \text{ long-term debt}}{\text{total assets}}$$
$$= (\$10 + \$208 + \$90)/\$408$$
$$= \$308/\$408$$
$$= 75\%$$

Comment: The lease creates a major deterioration in Emeral's debt ratio that could jeopardize its viability. It would certainly lessen the firm's ability to borrow from other sources.

c. (Optional) To construct the new balance sheet, we must calculate the first year's amortization of the leased crane and lease obligation accounts. Each of those is then subtracted from the respective beginning account balances. The asset is simply depreciated, while the liability is amortized as if it were a loan at 5%.

First, consider the leased crane account. After the first year, it is reduced by one year's

$$\text{depreciation} = \frac{\$207,594}{15} = \$13,840$$

Next, consider the lease obligation account. It's treated as a loan bearing 5% interest. We'll calculate the first year's ending balance just as we would if we were constructing a loan amortization schedule (see page 262).

Interest in the first year is 5% of the beginning obligation (loan).

$$\text{interest} = \$207,594 \times .05 = \$10,380$$

Subtract this from the lease payment to calculate the portion of the payment that reduces the lease obligation (loan principal).

$$\text{obligation reduction} = \text{lease payment} - \text{interest}$$
$$= \$20,000 - \$10,380$$
$$= \$9,620$$

Subtract the reduction from the beginning obligation (loan) balance to get the first year's ending balance.

$$\text{new lease obligation} = \text{beginning balance} - \text{obligation reduction}$$
$$= \$207,594 - \$9,620$$
$$= \$197,974$$

Finally put the new asset and obligation balances into the balance sheet rounded to the nearest $1,000.

Emeral Inc. Balance Sheet ($000)

Current assets	$ 20	Current liabilities	$ 10
Leased crane	194	Lease obligation	198
Fixed assets	180	Long-term debt	90
Total assets	$394	Lease balancing account	(4)
		Equity	100
		Total liabilities & equity	$394

Leased assets and obligations are **amortized independently** and usually have unequal balances.

Notice that because the leased crane and the lease obligation accounts are amortized using different methods, there's no reason that their balances should be equal until the end of the lease when both will be amortized to zero. For illustrative purposes, we've shown the difference in a small balancing account which would disappear at the end of the lease. In practice, what we're showing in the balancing account would just fall into equity.

A7.4 Leasing from the Perspective of the Lessor

Being a lessor is an investment alternative to lending. It's usually done by financial institutions like banks, finance companies, and insurance companies, rather than individuals. Instead of lending money to a customer company to buy equipment, the finance company buys the equipment and leases it to the customer firm.

Recall from our work on the time value of money in Chapter 6 that the mathematics of lending are governed by the formula for the present value of an annuity, which we presented as Equation 6.19 (see page 256 for the equation and page 259 for its application to lending). We'll renumber that expression and repeat it here for convenience.

(7A.1)
$$\text{PVA} = \text{PMT}[\text{PVFA}_{k,n}]$$

When this expression is applied to loans, PVA is the amount borrowed, PMT is the loan payment (including interest and a return of principal), k is the loan's interest rate, and n is its term. $PVFA_{k,n}$, of course, is a table factor. Keep in mind that the interest rate is the lender's return on its investment in the loan.

If any three of these variables are known, Equation 7A.1 can be solved for the fourth. Specifically, if a lender wants to earn a particular return on an invested amount over some period, the formula lets us calculate the payment it must ask of the borrower.

The **mathematics** of basic leases **and loans** are identical.

Basic financing leases work the same way. Instead of giving a company money to buy equipment, a lessor buys the equipment and delivers it along with a lease contract. Then it collects lease payments instead of loan payments. The lease payments required to provide the lessor with a given return are calculated in exactly the same way as the payments would be on a loan of equal term and amount. In the leasing arrangement, the interest rate is referred to either as the **lessor's return** or the *rate implicit in the lease*.

The **lessor's return** is the rate **implicit in the lease**.

Leasing can be a safe way to invest if the leased assets have a continuing market value. The lessor holds legal title, so if the lessee defaults, it's relatively easy to repossess the assets and recover the lessor's investment by selling or leasing those assets again. Lessors also get better treatment than lenders if the lessee/borrower enters bankruptcy. (We'll discuss bankruptcy in Chapter 17.)

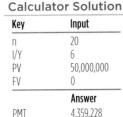

CONCEPT CONNECTION   EXAMPLE 7A-2

Calculating Lease Payments and Returns

Suppose the Prudential Insurance Co. is looking for a safe, long-term investment that will earn 6%. Further assume that Ford Motor Company wants to acquire a number of special purpose railroad cars to transport new automobiles to distribution hubs around the country. Ford wants to buy railroad cars valued at a total of $50 million and expects them to last 20 years after which they will be essentially worthless. Prudential considers the investment relatively safe because there's an active market for used railroad cars. It is therefore willing to buy the cars and lease them to Ford.

a. What annual lease payment should Prudential ask of Ford to achieve its targeted 6% return on a 20-year lease? Assume lease payments will be made at the end of each year.

b. Suppose Ford wants to take the lease but is unwilling to pay more than $4 million per year. What will be Prudential's return if it agrees to Ford's terms?

Calculator Solution

Key	Input
n	20
I/Y	6
PV	50,000,000
FV	0

Answer	
PMT	4,359,228

SOLUTION:

a. The required lease payment is calculated using Equation 7A-1, the present value of an annuity formula.

$$PVA = PMT[PVFA_{k,n}]$$
$$\$50,000,000 = PMT[PVFA_{6,20}]$$
$$\$50,000,000 = PMT(11.4699)$$
$$PMT = \$4,359,236$$

b. Here we're simply asked to solve an annuity problem for the interest rate rather than for the payment. The technique should be familiar from our work in Chapter 6. (See Example 6-3 on page 236.)

$$PVA = PMT[PVFA_{k,n}]$$
$$\$50,000,000 = \$4,000,000[PVFA_{k,20}]$$
$$PVFA_{k,20} = \frac{\$50,000,000}{\$4,000,000}$$
$$= 12.5000$$

Examination of Table A-4 shows the return at this payment level to be just under 5%. A financial calculator gives an exact answer of k = 4.96%.

A7.5   Residual Values

In the examples we've considered so far, the equipment was assumed to have no value at the end of the lease. That essentially means the assets' economic lives were estimated to be equal to the lease terms. In many cases, equipment is expected to have a positive **residual value** at the end of the lease. This makes pricing and return calculations slightly more complex.

A residual value means the lessor can expect an additional cash flow at the end of the lease. The cash can come from one of three sources. The lessee may buy the equipment, the lessor may sell it to someone else, or it may be re-leased to the original or another lessee.

The last alternative is usually associated with operating leases that have relatively short terms. In such cases, lessors may need to lease equipment several times to recover their investments and earn a reasonable return. We'll concentrate on situations in which a relatively small residual is expected at the end of a long-term lease.

It's important to understand that the residual is a very *soft* number. That means it's an inaccurate estimate, largely because it's so far in the future. The actual value of the equipment at the end of 20 years will depend on its condition *and* the market for used railroad cars at that time, both of which are difficult to predict. The residual could turn out to be anything from zero to two or three times the amount estimated.

*The leased asset's estimated **value** at the **end** of the lease is the **residual**.*

*The **present value** of the **residual** is **subtracted** from the lessor's **investment** in payment and return **calculations**.*

*Residuals are **soft** numbers.*

A7.5a   Residuals in General

Residual values are included in most leases and are often important in negotiations between lessors and lessees. A higher residual means lower payments, so lessees argue that the equipment will hold its value over a long time. Lessors want higher payments so their investments will be returned quickly and argue the opposite.

Since the actual residual value of equipment at the end of a lease depends in large part on its condition, lessors often insist on a penalty if residual values turn out to be lower than planned. In theory, such a clause simply asks the lessee to pay for abusing the equipment during the lease. But it can be a trap for lessees, because a weak market for used equipment can depress the value of items coming off lease regardless of condition.

CONCEPT CONNECTION   EXAMPLE 7A-3

Residual Values

Reconsider Example 7A-2 part (a) assuming Prudential estimates that the railroad cars will be worth $3 million at the end of the 20-year lease. Calculate the lease payment that will bring Prudential a 6% return on its investment.

SOLUTION: Even though Prudential will have to spend $50 million to acquire the railroad cars, it doesn't have to recover quite that much from the lease payments. In a present value sense, Prudential's investment is $50 million reduced by the present value of the expected residual.

First, calculate the present value of the $3 million residual over 20 years at 6% using Equation 6-7 for the present value of an amount. (See page 240.)

$$PVA = FV_n[PVF_{k,n}]$$
$$= \$3,000,000[PVF_{6,20}]$$
$$= \$3,000,000(.3118)$$
$$= \$935,400$$

Now, subtract that amount from the $50 million purchase price of the railroad cars.

$$\$50,000,000 - \$935,400 = \$49,064,600$$

Finally, calculate the required lease payment based on this smaller investment and notice that it is slightly reduced.

$$PVA = PMT[PVFA_{k,n}]$$
$$\$49,064,600 = PMT[PVFA_{6,20}]$$
$$\$49,064,600 = PMT(11.4699)$$
$$PMT = \$4,277,683$$

Calculator Solution

Key	Input
n	20
I/Y	6
FV	3,000,000
PMT	0

Answer	
PV	935,414

Calculator Solution

Key	Input
n	20
I/Y	6
PV	49,064,600
FV	0

Answer	
PMT	4,277,675

A **higher residual** means a **lower payment** so residuals are important in **negotiations**.

Automobile leases are notorious for manipulating payments and residuals. Lower lease payments can often be negotiated if the lessee accepts a higher residual. That sounds good when the lease is signed. However, the residual is usually the price the customer will pay if he wants to keep the car when the lease is over. If he doesn't, there can be a penalty if the residual in the contract exceeds the used car value of the vehicle at the end of the lease. So what may seem like a good deal in terms of car payments can lead to a big charge in the longer run.

A7.6   Lease Versus Buy—The Lessee's Perspective

Companies rarely have enough cash on hand to purchase major pieces of equipment or real estate. That means the decision to acquire an asset is usually accompanied by a decision about financing. There are three broad financing possibilities, equity,[15] debt, and leasing. For purposes of this discussion, we'll assume the company doesn't want to use equity, so the choice is between debt (borrowing to buy) and leasing.

---

15. Money from retained earnings or the sale of new stock.

Ensuper/Shutterstock.com

Both lenders and lessors are easy to find if the company needing equipment is a reasonably good credit risk. Firms can borrow through bonds or directly from banks, while lease financing is available from *leasing companies* (lessors) which may be banks or finance companies (General Electric Capital is the nation's largest leasing company). Lessors often work through brokers who match them with equipment users, handle negotiations, and take care of contractual paperwork.

> A **lease–buy** analysis demonstrates whether it's **cheaper** to **lease** or to **borrow** to buy equipment.

It's always appropriate to conduct a **lease–buy analysis** to compare the cost of the two approaches when new assets are being acquired. The analysis involves laying out the cash flows associated with the two financing methods and calculating the present value of each series. The approach with the lowest cost in a present value sense is the best choice.

The interest rate used in taking both present values is the rate the firm is currently paying on new debt adjusted for taxes. The debt rate is used because leasing and borrowing have similar risks, and it is easily ascertained.

The tax adjustment states the debt rate after taxes. The idea is that interest is a tax deductible expense so every dollar spent on it saves taxes of ($1 × T), where T is the tax rate. In general, an after-tax rate is just the pretax rate times (1 − T). For example, if the interest rate is 10% and the tax rate is 40%, the after-tax debt rate is

$$10\%(1 - T) = 10\%(1 - .4) = 10\%(.6) = 6\%$$

We'll discuss after-tax rates at length in a later chapter.

Lease-buy analysis is straightforward, but care must be exercised so that depreciation, taxes, and residual values are treated properly. The best way to understand the technique is through an example.

CONCEPT CONNECTION   EXAMPLE 7A-4

Lease Versus Buy Analysis

Halidane Transfer Inc. is an armored car service that operates in the Chicago area transferring cash between customer locations and various banks. The firm has 22 armored vehicles which are fully utilized serving existing customers. Management recently accepted a new business opportunity that requires two additional vehicles, each of which costs $150,000. Halidane expects to use the new cars for 10 years, but will depreciate them over 5 years for tax purposes. Assume that tax law dictates the allowable depreciation in each year of the vehicles' lives as follows.[16]

Year	Percentage of Original Cost
1	35%
2	25
3	20
4	10
5	10

Halidane can acquire the cars with $300,000 borrowed from its bank at 10%, repayable over five years.

---

16. We're using a simplified tax depreciation schedule to keep the example straightforward. We'll use the actual tax system called MACRS in a problem at the end of this appendix and discuss it in Chapter 11.

Alternately, it can lease both cars for five years from BNI Leasing Inc. for an annual payment of $70,000 with an option to purchase at fair market value at the end of the lease. BNI and Halidane agree that the cars will probably be worth about $30,000 each at that time.

The terms of the lease specify that Halidane will bear the cost of maintenance, property taxes, and insurance on the vehicles. The firm's marginal tax rate is 40%. Should Halidane lease or buy the new armored cars?

SOLUTION: To answer this question, we'll lay out the five-year cash flows implied by the alternatives and calculate the present value of net outflows associated with each. The alternative with the lower present value of net outflows is then preferred.

Since all of the cash flows we'll calculate are after tax, it's appropriate to take present values with an after-tax interest rate. We're using Halidane's 10% cost of debt, so our discount rate for present value calculations is

$$10\%(1 - T) = 10\%(1 - .4) = 6\%$$

> A **lease–buy** analysis compares the **present values** of cash outflows for leasing versus buying equipment.

Notice that Halidane pays for maintenance, taxes, and insurance in both options, so they need not be considered in the analysis. Also recall that parentheses mean negative cash flows (i.e., outflows).

We'll start with borrowing to purchase the assets. The following worksheet develops the appropriate cash flows which are discussed in the subsequent paragraph.

		Year				
Purchase ($000)	**0**	**1**	**2**	**3**	**4**	**5**
(1) Purchase cars	$(300)					
(2) Allowable depreciation %		35%	25%	20%	10%	10%
(3) Tax depreciation [(2) × $300]		$105	$75	$60	$30	$30
(4) Tax savings [(3) × 40%]		$ 42	$30	$24	$12	$12
(5) Net cash flow [(1) + (4)]	$(300)	$ 42	$30	$24	$12	$12

Line (1) reflects the present (time 0) purchase of the cars with borrowed money.[17] The next three lines calculate the cash flow associated with depreciation. Notice that depreciation is not itself a cash expense, but has a cash impact because it is deductible and reduces taxes as shown in line (4). Line (5) reflects net cash flow, the sum of the purchase price and tax savings from depreciation.

The present value of the purchase approach is just the present value of line (5), which is an uneven stream of cash flows. The present value of an uneven stream is taken by treating the flows individually. (See Chapter 6, page 275.)

$$PV = -\$300,000 + FV_1[PVF_{6,1}] + FV_2[PVF_{6,2}] + FV_3[PVF_{6,3}]$$
$$+ FV_4[PVF_{6,4}] + FV_5[PVF_{6,5}]$$
$$= -\$300,000 + \$42,000(.9434) + \$30,000(.8900) + \$24,000(.8396)$$
$$+ \$12,000(.7921) + 12,000(.7473)$$
$$= -\$300,000 + \$104,946 = -\$195,054$$

The lease alternative involves tax deductible lease payments that result in a constant after-tax cash outflow which can be treated as an annuity. However, at the end of the lease, Halidane

---

17. There's no reason to show the loan as an inflow and the payments as outflows because their present values will just cancel one another. This is true because we're discounting using an after-tax interest rate.

won't own the vehicles. Since the plan is to use them for 10 years, it will have to exercise the purchase option at the end of year 5 for an estimated $60,000.

Lease ($000)	0	Year 1	2	3	4	5
(1) Lease payments		$(70)	$(70)	$(70)	$(70)	$ (70)
(2) Tax savings [(1) × 40%]		28	28	28	28	28
(3) After-tax lease payment [(1) − (2)]		$(42)	$(42)	$(42)	$(42)	$ (42)
(4) Purchase option						(60)
(5) Net cash flow [(3) × (4)]		$(42)	$(42)	$(42)	$(42)	$(102)

The easiest way to calculate the present value of the leasing alternative is to treat the annuity and the fifth year purchase separately. The present value of the after-tax annuity is

$$PVA = PMT[PVFA_{6,5}] = -\$42,000(4.2124) = -\$176,921$$

And, the present value of cash outflows associated with the purchase is

$$PV = FV_5[PVF_{6,5}] = -\$60,000(.7473) = -\$44,838$$

Hence, the present value of cash outflows associated with leasing is

$$PV = -\$176,921 - \$44,838 = -\$221,759$$

Comparing the two alternatives, we see that the leasing plan is about 13% more costly. Further, the lease has a small element of risk in that purchasing the cars at its end may turn out to cost more than $60,000.

(Notice that lease–buy calculations have nothing to do with the financial statement presentation of capital leases illustrated in Example 7A-1. Those issues involve the firm's financial books. Lease–buy analysis deals strictly with cash flows.)

Leasing is usually **more expensive** than borrowing to buy, because lessors demand higher returns than borrowers.

The result shown in the preceding example, that lease financing is more expensive than borrowing, is the usual situation. It exists because lessors generally demand higher returns than lenders. Given that, and the fact that FASB 13 takes away much of the benefit of off balance sheet financing, it's fair to ask why leasing is as popular as it is. We'll look into that in the next two sections.

A7.7   The Advantages of Leasing

Leasing often offers several advantages that can make it worth its extra cost. We'll discuss a few issues in this section and a major tax advantage in the next.

A7.7a   No Money Down

Leasing offers several **advantages** other than off balance sheet financing that may **justify its cost**.

Lenders typically won't finance the entire cost of an asset. They require that borrowers put some of their own money into the deal. We're all familiar with this idea in the context of buying cars and houses, where we call the purchaser's contribution a *down payment*. Lessors don't usually require a down payment, essentially offering 100% financing. This can be very attractive to firms that have good prospects, but are cash poor. A great many small businesses are in that position.

A7.7b   Restrictions

Lenders usually put restrictions on the activities of borrowers to ensure they will be able to pay off their debt. These restrictive rules are called indentures when the lending is through bonds and covenants with loans. Typical restrictions limit the amount of dividends the borrower can pay, restrict the types of business it can pursue, and require that it maintain certain financial ratios at acceptable levels. Lessors' restrictions are usually much less stringent or nonexistent.

A7.7c   Easier Credit with Manufacturer/Lessors

Equipment manufacturers sometimes lease their own products. In an effort to place their equipment, they will often lease to marginally creditworthy customers. This may be the only way some financially weak companies can acquire equipment.

A7.7d   Avoiding the Risk of Obsolescence

Certain equipment tends to become obsolete very rapidly. In this context, obsolescence means newer equipment does a job so much better or cheaper that a company using older equipment is at a competitive disadvantage. In certain high-tech businesses, that can happen in a year or two.

Short leases have the effect of transferring that risk to lessors, because lessees can walk away from the obsolete equipment when leases are over. This can be attractive to lessees even though they're paying for the privilege through a higher cost of financing.

A7.7e   Tax Deducting the Cost of Land

Land is not depreciable for either tax or financial-reporting purposes. Hence, if a company owns real estate, the portion of the cost representing land can never be recognized as an expense which when subtracted from income reduces taxes.

However, if real estate is leased, the entire lease payment can be deducted by a lessee regardless of the fact that some of it represents a recovery of the cost of land purchased by the lessor. Hence, leasing effectively allows lessees to depreciate land for tax purposes.

A7.7f   Increasing Liquidity—The Sale and Leaseback

Firms sometimes find themselves short of cash while owning substantial assets that are not encumbered by debt.[18] In that situation, it isn't unusual to sell the asset to a financial institution to generate liquid cash and then lease the asset back from the same institution over a long period of time. The technique is called a *sale and lease-back* and is usually used to free up cash invested in real estate.

A7.7g   Tax Advantages for Marginally Profitable Companies

Under certain conditions, for tax reasons, it doesn't make financial sense to own assets when leasing is available. This usually occurs when companies expect to lose money or be marginally profitable for several years. The technique is called leveraged leasing and is described in the next section.

---

18. The asset is not serving as collateral for a loan.

A7.8   Leveraged Leases

A benefit of owning assets is the ability to deduct depreciation from income in the calculation of taxes. This effectively reduces the cost of those assets in the long run. For example, suppose a piece of equipment costs $100 million and the owner's marginal tax rate is 40%. Then for each dollar of cost that flows into depreciation, the firm saves $0.40 in taxes, and over the asset's life the owner pays $40 million less tax. In essence, the government splits the cost of ownership with taxpayers. If assets are acquired with borrowed money, interest provides a similar benefit because it is also tax deductible.

> The **government splits** the **cost** of **ownership** through **lower taxes** from **depreciation deductions**.

But if a company isn't making a profit, it doesn't pay any tax, and depreciation and interest deductions don't save any money. Situations like that are fairly common; the airline industry provides a good example. The combination of a unionized workforce, federal regulation, and price competition has kept many airlines at or below breakeven profitability for years.

But unprofitable companies still need to acquire new assets. Airlines, for example, must continually acquire new planes to replace old equipment that becomes obsolete. If they don't, they lose the ability to compete.

> In a **leveraged lease**, the **lessor acquires** the equipment with a combination of its own and **borrowed** money.

Leveraged leases (also called *tax leases*) can provide a solution to this problem. In a leveraged lease, a profitable lessor purchases equipment with a combination of its own and borrowed money and enters into a financing lease with a lessee. The lessor generally contributes 20% to 40% of the asset's cost and borrows the rest. The term *leveraged* refers to the use of debt in a transaction. The higher the proportion of debt, the higher is the degree of leverage. A leveraged lease is illustrated in Figure 7A-1.

The lessee treats the transaction as it would any financing lease, but there's a difference in the lessor's treatment on its own books and for tax purposes. Ordinarily, lessors account for financing leases as if they were loans. That means they're not allowed to depreciate the assets and don't get the tax benefits of ownership. But the rules change when assets are purchased with a substantial proportion of borrowed money. Then lessors are permitted to depreciate leased assets and gain the associated tax benefits. They can also tax deduct interest on the borrowed money.

FIGURE 7A-1   Leveraged Lease

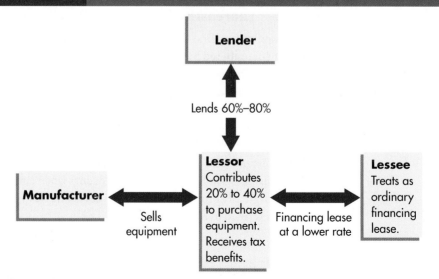

© Cengage Learning

Leveraged leases allow **unprofitable lessees** to enjoy some of the **tax benefits** of **ownership** indirectly.

Internalizing the tax benefits of ownership makes the overall transaction more profitable to the lessor *who shares that extra profit with the lessee through reduced lease payments.* Thus, an unprofitable lessee indirectly gains some of the benefits of ownership through the lower lease payments offered in a leveraged lease.

CONCEPT CONNECTIONS

EXAMPLE 7A-1   Accounting for a Financing Lease, *page 334*

EXAMPLE 7A-2   Calculating Lease Payments and Returns, *page 337*

EXAMPLE 7A-3   Residual Values, *page 339*

EXAMPLE 7A-4   Lease Versus Buy Analysis, *page 340*

QUESTIONS

1. What, in general, is meant by off balance sheet financing?

2. Describe the feature of financial reporting that made leasing popular before FASB 13.

3. What argument was made against adopting FASB 13? (One-line answer.)

4. There's a fundamental difference between rules one, two, and four for qualifying as an operating lease and rule three. What is it?

5. Just what is placed on the balance sheet in a financing lease?

6. In leases with no residuals, lessors calculate the lease payments they must charge as if the lease were a loan. How does the presence of a residual change the calculation?

7. Why are residuals important in negotiations between lessees and lessors?

8. Depreciation is a noncash charge. Why then is it important in lease–buy analysis? (Very short answer.)

9. Leasing is generally more expensive than borrowing to buy, and FASB 13 has reduced the availability of off balance sheet financing. Why then is leasing popular?

10. Leveraged leases offer tax advantages to unprofitable companies.
    a. Why are they called leveraged?
    b. Briefly, how do they work?

BUSINESS ANALYSIS

1. You've just joined SeaCraft Inc., a manufacturer of fiberglass boats, as its CFO. When you took the job, you knew that the company was not in the best financial condition. Profits are adequate, but the firm is carrying substantial debt. To make matters worse, the company's largest fiberglass molding machine is almost completely worn out and needs to be replaced. SeaCraft can't pay for a new machine out of operating profit, and the owner, Sam Alston, doesn't want to sell any new stock which would dilute his interest.

    You've looked into borrowing money to acquire the machine and can get a deal with practically no down payment and a favorable interest rate through some banking contacts. But Sam is concerned about taking on more debt. He would like to sell the company and retire, but he's afraid that a heavier debt load will depress the price he might get. You agree that his concern is well founded.

    Sam rushed into your office this morning with what he described as a great idea. He'd read an article that said just about anything could be leased and also knew that SeaCraft already leased a number of copying machines. On his way to see you, he stopped into the accounting department and found that neither the copying equipment nor any associated liability was on SeaCraft's balance sheet.

Ensuper/Shutterstock.com

Storming into your office, he declared, "Leasing the molding machine is going to solve my debt problems! You're supposed to be the financial expert, why didn't you think of it? Why do I have to think of everything? Get on this quick! I want to see a lease deal on my desk by the end of the week." Before you could answer, he rushed out for a meeting with the marketing department.

Prepare a tactful memo to Sam explaining a little more about leasing and why it may not be as wonderful for SeaCraft as he thinks. Write the memo for a reader who is not a financial person (i.e., avoid using technical jargon like FASB, capitalize, equity, annuity, and present value). Talking about financing, balance sheets, assets, and debt is OK.

PROBLEMS

1. Caruthers Inc. is a small manufacturing firm and has the following summarized balance sheet.

Caruthers Inc. Balance Sheet ($000)

Current assets	$ 20	Current liabilities	$ 15
Fixed assets	130	Long-term debt	65
Total assets	$150	Equity	70
		Total liabilities & equity	$150

The firm is interested in acquiring a fleet of 10 company cars for its sales staff. The cars have an economic life of seven years, but Caruthers plans to keep them for only three because it doesn't want its salespeople driving around in old vehicles. The cars cost $20,000 each, and Caruthers is considering borrowing to purchase them.

a. Restate Caruthers's balance sheet after the loan is made.

b. Calculate the firm's debt ratio now and immediately after the loan is made.

c. Comment on the change in part (b). (Words only.)

d. Suggest a solution and explain why it will qualify for accounting treatment that will avoid the problem highlighted in part (b). (Words only.)

2. Henderson Engineering Ltd. just leased a computer-aided design system for five years with annual payments of $12,000 payable at the end of each year. The lease contains a provision that allows Henderson to purchase the machine at its fair market value as used equipment when the lease expires. Industry data indicate that systems like these normally last for about eight years. Henderson could have purchased the machine for $50,000 with money borrowed at 9%.

Does Henderson have to capitalize the lease on its balance sheet? Why?

Accounting for a Financing Lease: Concept Connection Example 7A-1 (page 334)

3. Taunton Manufacturing Inc. is a machine shop in Taunton, Massachusetts. The firm recently leased a drill press for a 20-year term at payments of $9,000 per year payable at year end. No residual value was assumed in the lease which is clearly a financing lease. Taunton can borrow at 8% and will depreciate the press straight line over 20 years.

Shortly before the lease became effective, Taunton's balance sheet was as follows:

Taunton Manufacturing Inc. Balance Sheet ($000)

Current assets	$ 35	Current liabilities	$ 25
Fixed assets	315	Long-term debt	95
Total assets	$350	Equity	230
		Total liabilities & equity	$350

Answer the following questions working in whole dollars but present balance sheet accounts rounded to the nearest $1,000.

    a. Construct Taunton's balance sheet showing the capitalized lease and the related lease obligation.

    b. Calculate the firm's debt ratio before and after the lease, and comment on the difference.

    c. (Optional) Reconstruct the balance sheet at the end of the first year assuming the other accounts remain the same.

Calculating Lease Payments and Returns: Concept Connection 7A-2 (page 337)

4. Wings Inc. is a commuter airline that serves the Boston area. Wings plans to lease a new plane through Nantucket Capital Inc. The lease term is 15 years, and no residual value is expected at its end.

    a. What *monthly* lease payment must Nantucket charge to earn a 12% return on its investment if the plane Wings wants costs $1.5 million?

    b. What would Nantucket's return be if it agreed to accept *annual* payments of $200,000?

Residual Values: Concept Connection Example 7A-3 (page 339)

5. Suppose Wings and Nantucket of the previous problem agreed to assume a $300,000 residual value for the plane at the end of the lease. How much will Wings have to pay monthly to give Nantucket its 12% return?

Lease Versus Buy Analysis: Concept Connection Example 7A-4 (page 340)

6. Paxton Sheet Metal Works Inc. is about to acquire a new stamping press that costs $400,000. It is considering purchasing the asset with money it can borrow at 10% repayable in annual, year-end installments over six years. It has also been offered an opportunity to lease the machine for payments of $86,500 per year, payable at year end, also over six years. The machine is depreciable for tax purposes over six years according to the following schedule. (This is the actual tax schedule for five-year life assets; "a half-year convention" takes a half year's depreciation in the first and last years; see page 498.)

Year	Percentage of Original Cost
1	20.0%
2	32.0
3	19.2
4	11.5
5	11.5
6	5.8

The lease contains a purchase option at its end at fair market value which is estimated to be $100,000. It also stipulates that Paxton will be responsible for paying for maintenance, taxes, and insurance. Paxton's marginal tax rate is 30%. Conduct a lease–buy analysis to determine which option is preferable from a purely financial point of view.

8 CHAPTER

The Valuation and Characteristics of Stock

Chapter Outline

Common Stock
- The Return on an Investment in Common Stock
- The Nature of Cash Flows from Common Stock Ownership
- The Basis of Value

Growth Models of Common Stock Valuation
- Developing Growth-Based Models
- The Constant Growth Model
- The Expected Return
- Two-Stage Growth
- Practical Limitations of Pricing Models

Valuing New Stocks—Investment Banking and the Initial Public Offering (IPO)
- IPOs for Different Securities
- Investment Banking
- Promoting and Pricing the IPO
- Book Building and the Road Show
- Prices After the IPO

Some Institutional Characteristics of Common Stock
- Corporate Organization and Control
- Voting Rights and Issues
- Stockholders' Claims on Income and Assets

Preferred Stock
- Valuation of Preferred Stock
- Characteristics of Preferred Stock

Securities Analysis

Options and Warrants
- Options in General
- Stock Options
- Call Options
- Intrinsic Value
- Options and Leverage
- Trading in Options
- Writing Options
- Put Options
- Option Pricing Models
- Warrants
- Employee Stock Options

In this chapter, we'll be concerned with determining the value of equity securities, including common and preferred stock. We'll find the process is much less precise than the procedures we studied for bonds because of the nature of equity cash flows.

8.1 Common Stock

Corporations are owned by the holders of their common stock. Stockholders choose directors, who in turn appoint managers to run the company. In theory, this means that stockholders have a voice in running the company through the board of directors.

However, most large companies are *widely held,* meaning that stock ownership is spread among a large number of people with no individuals or groups controlling more than a few percent. Under those conditions, stockholders have little power to influence corporate decisions, and stock ownership is simply an investment.

In other words, we don't tend to think of having any role as *owners* when we buy stock. We're just interested in the future cash flows that come from owning shares. In that sense, *equity* (stock) investments are just like *debt* (bond) investments; the only thing we're interested in is money. (An exception occurs when institutional investors acquire large blocks of stock.)

Most **equity** investors aren't interested in a role as **owners**.

8.1a   The Return on an Investment in Common Stock

In a stock investment, income comes in two forms. Investors receive dividends and realize a gain or loss on the difference between the price they pay for stock and the price at which they eventually sell it. This last part is called a *capital gain* or *loss.*

The **future cash flow** associated with stock ownership consists of **dividends** and the eventual **selling price** of the shares.

It pays to be precise about this idea and write it as an equation. Suppose we buy a share of stock, hold it for one year, and then sell it. Call the price we pay today P_0 and the price at the end of one year P_1. If we receive a dividend during the year, call that D_1. Then our income is the dividend, D_1, plus the difference in prices, $(P_1 - P_0)$, and our investment is the original price, P_0. The return, k, can be written as

(8.1)
$$k = \frac{D_1 + (P_1 - P_0)}{P_0}$$

Notice that the return on a stock investment can be a negative number if the stock's price decreases while the investor holds it. In the equation, this means $P_1 < P_0$.

Next we'll solve Equation 8.1 for P_0, the stock's price today. To do that, multiply through by P_0,

$$kP_0 = D_1 + (P_1 - P_0)$$

add P_0 to each side, and then factor it out on the left.

$$P_0 + kP_0 = D_1 + P_1$$
$$(1 + k)P_0 = D_1 + P_1$$

Finally, divide through by $(1 + k)$ to get

(8.2)
$$P_0 = \frac{D_1 + P_1}{(1 + k)}$$

Notice that D_1 and P_1 are the future cash flows that come from buying the stock today at price P_0. Further notice that division by $(1 + k)$ is equivalent to multiplying by the present value factor for interest rate k and one year. (See page 240.)

Therefore, Equation 8.2 says that *the return on our stock investment is the interest rate that equates the present value of the investment's expected future cash flows to the amount invested today, the price P_0.*

This result is fundamental. The return on any stock investment is the rate that makes the present value of future cash flows equal to the price paid for the investment today. This principle also holds for investments held for more than one year.

Dividend and Capital Gain Yields   The return on a stock investment can be broken into two parts related to the two sources of income associated with stock ownership. Rewrite Equation 8.1 as two fractions.

(8.3)
$$k = \frac{D_1}{P_0} + \frac{(P_1 - P_0)}{P_0}$$

The first part, D_1/P_0, is known as the **dividend yield**, and the second part, $(P_1 - P_0)/P_0$, is called the **capital gains yield**. Recall that yield and return mean the same thing.

The **return** on a stock investment comes from **dividends** and **capital gains**.

8.1b   The Nature of Cash Flows from Common Stock Ownership

As we've said, an investor who buys stock can expect two forms of future cash flow: a stream of dividends and the proceeds of the eventual sale of the shares.

Figure 8-1 is a time line reflecting these ideas for an investment made today and held for n years. In our work with stock valuation, we'll use annual time periods[1] and indicate payments in a particular year by subscripting the symbol for the payment with the number of the year.

For example, D_1 and D_2 will mean the dividends paid in the first and second years, respectively, and P_n will mean the price of the stock at the end of the nth year. We'll indicate the present with a zero subscript, so P_0 means the price today and D_0 means today's dividend or the most recent one paid.

We'll assume an investor buying today pays P_0, but does not receive D_0, which went to the last owner.

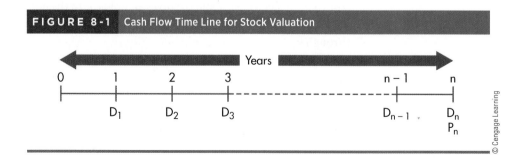

FIGURE 8-1   Cash Flow Time Line for Stock Valuation

© Cengage Learning

---

1. Dividends are generally paid quarterly, but for valuation purposes, things are simplified by working in annual terms.

Comparison of Cash Flows from Stocks and Bonds   Notice that the cash flow pattern for stocks appears similar to the one associated with bonds. In both cases, a series of regular payments is followed by a single larger payment that can be thought of as the return of the original investment. That is, dividends seem analogous to interest payments, while the final sale of stock appears to be like the return of a bond's principal.

In fact, however, the similarity is rather superficial because of the differing natures of the cash flows in the two cases. It's worthwhile to explore those differences rather carefully. We'll begin by comparing interest and dividends.

A bond's interest payments are guaranteed by the borrower, and are therefore fairly certain to be received. Companies have to be very close to failure before they default on bond interest. Dividends, on the other hand, carry no such guarantee. This is an important point. There's no agreement associated with common stock that makes any representation about the payment of dividends. Investors depend on them for value, but nothing is committed, promised, or guaranteed by the company. Indeed, a firm with a long history of paying dividends can stop at any time, especially if business turns bad.

Next, recall that the interest payments associated with a bond are constant in amount. That makes it easy to develop a formula to value bonds, because interest can be represented as an annuity. Dividends, on the other hand, are rarely constant. In fact, people generally expect dividends to increase over time as the company grows.

Things are equally imprecise with respect to the final payments received by stockholders versus bondholders. With a bond, the payment is the contractually promised loan principal equal to the bond's face value. A stockholder, on the other hand, has to sell his or her shares at the prevailing market price to realize a final payment. This price can be higher or lower than the price originally paid.

Let's emphasize that last point even further. There's no provision in a common stock investment for the repurchase of shares or for any return of the investor's capital by the company. That means the money for the final payment comes from another investor rather than from the issuing company as it does with a bond.[2]

In summary, the cash flows associated with stock ownership are dividends and the proceeds of the eventual sale of the shares. Both are distinctly imprecise and difficult to forecast.

8.1c   The Basis of Value

The **basis for stock value** is the **present value** of expected **cash inflows** even though dividends and stock prices are difficult to forecast.

In spite of the imprecision of forecasted dividends and prices, the value of stock depends on the present value of those future cash flows. In terms of the portrayal in Figure 8-1, the stock's value is the sum of the present value of the n dividend payments and the present value of the selling price in the nth period. Keep in mind that the successive dividends generally have different values, so we have to distinguish between them by carrying the subscripts in D_1, D_2, through D_n.

Valuing a stock involves making some *assumptions* about what its future dividends and its eventual selling price will be. Once this has been done, we take the present

---

2. If a bond isn't held until maturity, it too must be sold to another investor, but the bondholder always has the option of holding it until maturity and receiving face value.

value of the *assumed* (projected) cash flows at an appropriate interest rate to estimate the share's current price. Contrast this with bond valuation. There we had no need to make any assumptions about the future cash flows because they were spelled out by the bond contract.

We can write a generalized stock valuation formula from these ideas by treating the dividends and the selling price as a series of independent amounts to be received at various times in the future.

Equation 6.7 on page 240 gave us an expression for the present value of an amount to be received n periods in the future at interest rate k. We'll repeat that expression here for convenience.

(6.7) $$PV = FV_n[PVF_{k,n}]$$

Now, think of each dividend and the eventual selling price shown in Figure 8-1 as an FV_n, where n is the number of periods into the future until that particular amount is received. The present value of the first dividend can be written as $D_1[PVF_{k,1}]$. The second is $D_2[PVF_{k,2}]$, and so on through the nth dividend and the price in the nth period.

P_0, the value of the stock today, is the sum of all these amounts, and can be written as follows.

(8.4) $$P_0 = D_1[PVF_{k,1}] + D_2[PVF_{k,2}] + \cdots + D_n[PVF_{k,n}] + P_n[PVF_{k,n}]$$

CONCEPT CONNECTION EXAMPLE 8-1

Stock Valuation Based on Projected Cash Flows

Joe Simmons is interested in the stock of Teltex Corp. He feels it is going to have two very good years because of a government contract, but may not do well after that. Joe thinks the stock will pay a dividend of $2 next year and $3.50 the year after. By then he believes it will be selling for $75 a share, at which price he'll sell anything he buys now. People who have invested in stocks like Teltex are currently earning returns of 12%. What is the most Joe should be willing to pay for a share of Teltex?

SOLUTION: Joe shouldn't pay any more than the present value of the cash flows he expects. Those are $2 at the end of one year and $3.50 plus $75 at the end of two years. Writing Equation 8.4 for two years, we have

$$P_0 = D_1[PVF_{k,1}] + D_2[PVF_{k,2}] + P_2[PVF_{k,2}]$$
$$= \$2.00[PVF_{12,1}] + \$3.50[PVF_{12,2}] + \$75.00[PVF_{12,2}]$$
$$= \$2.00[.8929] + \$3.50[.7972] + \$75.00[.7972]$$
$$= \$64.37$$

If the market price of Teltex is below about $64, Joe should buy; if not, he shouldn't invest.

The Intrinsic (Calculated) Value and Market Price Example 8-1 illustrates a basic principle of securities analysis. Joe's research led him to forecast the future dividends and price given in the example. According to his analysis, the present value of those cash flows is fundamentally what the stock is worth. We call that the stock's intrinsic value (according to Joe).

> A stock's **intrinsic value** is based on **assumptions** about future cash flows made from **fundamental analyses** of the firm and its industry.

However, if other investors don't agree with Joe's dividend and price estimates, their ideas of Teltex's intrinsic value will differ from his. The firm's market price is generally thought to be a consensus of the intrinsic values calculated by everyone watching the stock. If Joe's value is higher than the consensus, and if he's right, he'll be getting a bargain if he buys.

The process of developing intrinsic values and comparing them with market prices is known as **fundamental analysis**. We'll come back to the idea later in the chapter.

8.2   Growth Models of Common Stock Valuation

Equation 8.4 is a convenient way to look at stock valuation when we have a relatively short planning horizon and some reason to make specific assumptions about future prices and dividends. Generally, however, we can't forecast the future in that much detail. We're more likely to look at a company and simply forecast a *growth rate* of earnings and dividends into the future starting from wherever they are now.

> Stock valuation models are based on **predicted growth rates** because forecasting exact future prices and dividends is very difficult.

For example, suppose a company has grown at an average rate of 5% per year over the last three or four years, and we expect its condition to improve slightly in the short run. The future being as uncertain as it is, it's difficult to make the detailed forecast of dividends and future prices needed to use Equation 8.4. However, most of us would be comfortable in saying that the company and its dividends are likely to grow at 6% into the indefinite future.

Because that's the best we can often do in predicting the future, we'll find it useful to develop expressions that value stocks on the basis of only their present positions and assumptions about growth rates.

8.2a   Developing Growth-Based Models

Notice that Equation 8.4 treats the stock's dividends and eventual selling price as separate amounts in the present valuing process. Each is multiplied by the present value factor for the appropriate interest rate and time, which is represented in the equation as $PVF_{k,i}$, where i takes values from 1 to n.

In Chapter 6, we developed the formulation of any $PVF_{k,i}$, which we'll repeat here for convenience.

$$(6.5) \qquad PVF_{k,i} = \frac{1}{(1 + k)^i}$$

Clearly, multiplying by $PVF_{k,i}$ is equivalent to dividing by $(1 + k)^i$. Review Equation 6.5 on page 240 if this isn't familiar.

In what follows, we'll find it convenient to represent present values of amounts by dividing by $(1 + k)^i$ instead of multiplying by the factor of $PVF_{k,i}$. Rewriting

> A stock's **value today** is the sum of the **present values** of the **dividends** received while the investor holds it and the **price** for which it is eventually sold.

Equation 8.4 to reflect this change in notation, we have

$$(8.5) \qquad P_0 = \frac{D_1}{(1 + k)} + \frac{D_2}{(1 + k)^2} + \cdots + \frac{D_n}{(1 + k)^n} + \frac{P_n}{(1 + k)^n}$$

An Infinite Stream of Dividends   Notice again that our stock valuation formula, now represented by Equation 8.5, involves a stream of dividends followed by a final selling price. This portrayal fits well with our concept of stock ownership: buy, hold for a while, and then sell. However, it's not convenient to work with in terms of valuation.

Think about P_n, the price at the end of the holding period. At that time, the nth period, it will represent the current price just as P_0 represents the current price today. Therefore, its value then will involve a stream of dividends that starts in period $n + 1$ and a selling price at some point further into the future, say period m. In other words, the person who buys the stock in period n will hold it until period m and then sell it. That person's valuation model will look like this.

$$P_n = \frac{D_{n+1}}{(1 + k)} + \cdots + \frac{D_m}{(1 + k)^{m-n}} + \frac{P_m}{(1 + k)^{m-n}}$$

Conceptually, we can replace P_n in Equation 8.5 with this expression and wind up with a revised expression containing a longer stream of dividends and a final price further away in the future.

We can conceptually do the same thing again in period m. That is, we can think about the next sale and replace P_m with another series of dividends followed by a price in the still more distant future. We can do that as many times as we like and push the eventual selling price as far into the future as we like. Indeed, we can conceptually push the final P infinitely far into the future!

However, the present value of any amount that is infinitely far away in time is clearly zero, so Equation 8.5 becomes the present value of an infinitely long stream of dividends and nothing else.

In short, we've replaced the final selling price with the rest of the dividends forever. This more useful valuation expression is written as follows by using summation notation.

Conceptually, it's possible to **replace** the final selling price with an **infinite series of dividends**.

(8.6)

$$P_0 = \sum_{i=1}^{\infty} \frac{D_i}{(1 + k)^i}$$

A Market-Based Argument If shifting from Equation 8.5 to Equation 8.6 seems strange, here's another way to convince yourself that it makes sense.

Imagine that we're pricing a primary market transaction, one in which the firm is initially offering its stock to the investing public. Think of the investment community *as a whole* setting the stock's price. In other words, ignore the fact that individual investors will subsequently trade the stock back and forth among themselves, and think of them as one unified body setting a price for the stock when it's issued. In fact, that's exactly what the market process does.

This price, set by the market acting collectively, must be based on the present value of future cash flows moving from the company to the investing community. But there's only one kind of payment that moves from the company to investors, and that's dividends. So the only basis for valuation by the community as a whole is the entire future stream of dividends; there's nothing else available. This leads directly to Equation 8.6.

Working with Growth Rates

Growth rates work just like interest rates. If we're told that something whose value is $100 today will grow at 6% next year, the amount of the growth is

$$\$100 \times .06 = \$6$$

and the new size of the variable is

$$\$100 \times 1.06 = \$106$$

We usually represent growth rates with the letter g, which takes the decimal value of the percentage rate. For example, a 6% growth rate implies $g = .06$.

Growth rates are usually used to predict future values of variables whose values are known today. For example, if today's dividend is D_0 and we want to forecast year 1's dividend, D_1, assuming growth rate g, we can write

$$D_1 = D_0 + gD_0$$
$$= D_0(1 + g)$$

Year 2's dividend is just year 1's multiplied by $(1 + g)$ again.

$$D_2 = D_1(1 + g)$$

Noticing the expression for D_1 just above, we can substitute and write

$$D_2 = D_0(1 + g)^2$$

D_3 is this expression multiplied by $(1 + g)$ again, and so on for as many subsequent D's as we need. In general, the ith dividend is

(8.7) $$D_i = D_0(1 + g)^i$$

When successive values of a growing dividend are needed, we just multiply by $(1 + g)$ repeatedly.

CONCEPT CONNECTION   EXAMPLE 8-2

Growth Rates

Apex Corp. paid a dividend of $3.50 this year. What are its next three dividends if it is expected to grow at 7%?

SOLUTION: In this case $D_0 = \$3.50$ and $g = .07$, so $(1 + g) = 1.07$. Then

$$D_1 = D_0(1 + g) = \$3.50(1.07) = \$3.75,$$
$$D_2 = D_1(1 + g) = \$3.75(1.07) = \$4.01, \text{ and}$$
$$D_3 = D_2(1 + g) = \$4.01(1.07) = \$4.29.$$

8.2b   The Constant Growth Model

Equation 8.6 says that the value of a stock is the present value of an infinite stream of dividends but makes no statement about what those dividends are. In other words, the $D_1, D_2, \ldots, D_n$ can have any values, randomly chosen or a regular progression of numbers.

When we know D_0, the last dividend paid, and we assume dividends will grow at some constant rate in the future, Equation 8.7 gives us a convenient way to forecast any particular dividend.

We can put these two ideas together by substituting Equation 8.7 into Equation 8.6 and rewriting as follows.

(8.8)
$$P_0 = \sum_{i=1}^{\infty} \frac{D_0(1 + g)^i}{(1 + k)^i}$$

This expression is the basis of the constant growth model. It represents the sum of an infinite series of fractions as follows.

$$P_0 = \frac{D_0(1 + g)}{(1 + k)} + \frac{D_0(1 + g)^2}{(1 + k)^2} + \frac{D_0(1 + g)^3}{(1 + k)^3} + \cdots \infty$$

Notice that the numerators represent a series of dividends, each of which is larger than the last because of multiplication by the factor $(1 + g)$. The denominators reflect the present value factors for successive years into the future. These, too, get successively larger because of multiplication by $(1 + k)$.

Because D_0 appears in each term of the series, it can be factored out, and we have

(8.9)
$$P_0 = D_0 \left[\frac{(1 + g)}{(1 + k)} + \frac{(1 + g)^2}{(1 + k)^2} + \frac{(1 + g)^3}{(1 + k)^3} + \cdots \infty \right]$$

Now, *if k is larger than g,* the fractions in the brackets get smaller as the exponents get larger. Both the numerators and denominators become larger numbers as the exponents grow, but if k is bigger than g, the denominators get large faster. Any fraction whose denominator is much larger than its numerator is a very small number. In this case, the successive fractions approach zero as the exponents get big.

As a result, the entire expression in brackets is a *finite* number when k is larger than g. This leads to a finite value for P_0 even though we're summing an infinite stream of numbers to get it.

When k is larger than g, we say we're forecasting **normal growth**. When g is greater than k, we say we have *super normal growth*. Super normal growth can occur in business, but lasts for limited periods. We'll consider it in detail later. For now we'll concentrate on normal growth situations.

In stock valuation, **normal growth** occurs when **k > g**.

Constant Normal Growth—The Gordon Model

Equations 8.8 and 8.9 look pretty intimidating, but can be reduced to something simple with a little mathematics that we needn't worry about here. We'll just accept the result.

The simplified form of Equation 8.8 is

(8.10)
$$P_0 = \frac{D_0(1 + g)}{k - g} = \frac{D_1}{k - g}$$

This expression is known as the *constant growth model,* because it assumes that the stock's dividends are going to grow at the constant rate, g, into the indefinite future. It is also called the **Gordon model** after Myron J. Gordon, a scholar who was behind its development and popularization.

The **Gordon model** is a simple expression for forecasting the **price** of a stock that's expected to **grow at a constant, normal rate**.

Notice that the equation makes sense only if growth is normal—that is, if k > g. Otherwise the denominator is negative (or zero), leading to a negative (or undefined) price which isn't meaningful.

Also notice that the numerator can be expressed either as $D_0(1 + g)$ or as D_1. Keep in mind that D_0 is the most recent dividend paid to the stock's former owner. D_1 is the next dividend. It is the first one that will be received by someone who buys the stock today. Think of D_1 as the *first dividend into the period of normal growth*. That image will help your understanding later in the chapter.

The constant growth model is easy to use. Here's a straightforward example.

CONCEPT CONNECTION   EXAMPLE 8-3

The Constant Growth (Gordon) Model

Atlas Motors is expected to grow at a constant rate of 6% a year into the indefinite future. It recently paid a dividend of $2.25 a share. The rate of return on stocks similar to Atlas is about 11%. What should a share of Atlas Motors sell for today?

SOLUTION: Write Equation 8.10 and substitute D_0 = $2.25, k = .11, and g = .06.

$$P_0 = \frac{D_0(1 + g)}{k - g} = \frac{\$2.25(1.06)}{.11 - .06} = \$47.70$$

This price includes the value of all dividends to be paid after time zero, but does not include D_0, which has already been paid to the stock's current owner.

The Zero Growth Rate Case—A Constant Dividend   It is of interest to value a stock that's expected to pay a constant, never-changing dividend. In that case, we don't need a subscript on the variable representing the dividends because they're all the same. We'll call each dividend D.

This case can be represented by Equation 8.10 if we let g equal zero, and then $D_0 = D_1 = D$ and 8.10 becomes

(8.11)
$$P_0 = \frac{D}{k}$$

A **zero growth** stock is a **perpetuity** to the investor.

You should recognize Equation 8.11 as the expression for the present value of a perpetuity from our work in Chapter 6. (See page 269.) A perpetuity is an unchanging payment made regularly for an indefinite period of time. That's exactly what we're describing in the constant dividend model.

CONCEPT CONNECTION   EXAMPLE 8-4

Constant Dividend

Lexington Corp. is in a stagnant market, and analysts foresee a long period of zero growth for the firm. It's been paying a yearly dividend of $5 for some time, which is expected to continue indefinitely. The yield on the stock of similar firms is 8%. What should Lexington's stock sell for?

SOLUTION: Write Equation 8.11 and substitute.

$$P_0 = \frac{D}{k} = \frac{\$5}{.08} = \$62.50$$

People don't usually assume that common stock will pay the same dividend forever. It's more usual to assume some positive growth rate. There is, however, a security known as *preferred stock* that does pay the same dividend year after year with no expectation of increase or decrease. We'll study it later in the chapter.

Ensuper/Shutterstock.com

8.2c   The Expected Return

The Gordon model can be recast to focus on the return on the stock investment implied by the constant growth assumption. This is easily done by solving Equation 8.10 for k. In this formulation, k represents an **expected return**, and is often written as k_e.

(8.12)
$$k_e = \frac{D_1}{P_0} + g$$

The concept of expected return will be important in the next chapter. In this case, it says that if an investor's knowledge and predictions about a company's stock are rolled up into a forecast growth rate, the return implied by the forecast is given by Equation 8.12.

If we take $D_1 = D_0(1 + g)$ and assume that D_0 and P_0 are actual values of the latest dividend and the current price, the equation gives an estimate of the return to be had by investing in the stock at price P_0.

It's worthwhile to compare Equation 8.12 with Equation 8.1, which we'll repeat here for convenience.

(8.1)
$$k = \frac{D_1}{P_0} + \frac{(P_1 - P_0)}{P_0}$$

Recall that the two terms on the right side of Equation 8.1 are the dividend yield and the capital gains yield. Compare Equation 8.12 with Equation 8.1 and notice that they're identical in all but the second term on the right. This implies that those terms have the same meaning in both equations. In other words, the capital gains yield in the Gordon model is nothing but the growth rate. That makes intuitive sense because the whole company, including dividends and stock prices, is assumed to be growing at rate g.

8.2d   Two-Stage Growth

Situations sometimes arise in which a firm's future growth isn't expected to be constant. Specifically, we often know something about the near-term future that can be expected to have a *temporary* effect on the firm's prospects. For example, the release of a new product might create a period of rapidly expanding demand after which further growth slows to normal.

The usual *two-stage* forecast involves a rapid, *super normal* growth rate for one, two, or even three years and a *normal* rate thereafter. Recall that super normal means a rate in excess of k, the return on the stock. Our task is to use the tools we've developed thus far to value a stock that's expected to behave in this way.

First, let's look at a time line picture of such an investment opportunity. The top of Figure 8-2 shows a general case in which the firm grows at rate g_1, the super normal rate, for two years and then grows indefinitely at rate g_2, the slower normal rate.

We can value this stock using the constant growth model, but we have to apply it carefully. The model gives us a value for a share of stock *at the beginning of an infinite period of constant, normal growth*.

In Figure 8-2 we have constant, normal growth, but it doesn't start at time zero. It starts at the end of the second year. Therefore, we have to apply the Gordon model at that point in time.

When we do that, the result is a price for the stock at the end of the second year, or equivalently at the beginning of the third. We'll call that price P_2. It includes the value

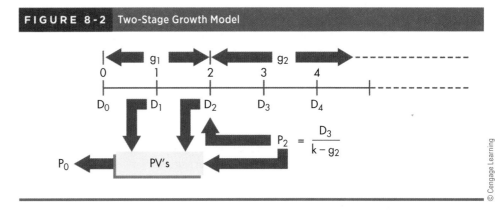

FIGURE 8-2   Two-Stage Growth Model

© Cengage Learning

of all dividends to be paid subsequent to year 2, but not the dividend of year 2 itself, D_2. In other words, it takes into account D_3, D_4, D_5, and so on.

Using the Gordon model at the end of the second year requires a modification of the notation we used before. Look back at Equation 8.10. Notice that the numerator in that expression is D_1, which is *the first dividend into the period of normal growth*. In the model we're working with now, that's D_3, because the growth rate changes at the end of year 2.

In addition, the denominator of Equation 8.10 contains the normal growth rate g. In this case, we have two growth rates, but the normal one that continues indefinitely is g_2, so that's the one we must use. The correct way to formulate the constant growth model in this application is

$$P_2 = \frac{D_3}{k - g_2}$$

This expression is portrayed in Figure 8-2 along with its position along the time line.

A person buying this stock today gets three things in the future: D_1, D_2, and P_2. The two dividends are clearly cash flows forecast at the ends of years 1 and 2. P_2, on the other hand, is an actual cash flow only if the purchaser sells the stock at the end of the second year. Nevertheless, we'll treat P_2 just as though it were a cash flow expected two years in the future.

The value of a security today is the present value of future cash that comes from owning it, so the value of the stock represented in Figure 8-2 is the sum of the present values of D_1, D_2, and P_2. This is indicated schematically in the diagram.

> **The two-stage growth model** allows us to value a stock that's expected to grow at an unusual rate for a **limited time**.

Ensuper/Shutterstock.com

CONCEPT CONNECTION   EXAMPLE 8-5

Valuation Based on Two-Stage Growth

Zylon Corporation's stock is selling for $48 a share. We've heard a rumor that the firm will make an exciting new product announcement next week. By studying the industry, we've concluded that this new product will support an overall company growth rate of 20% for about two years. After that, we feel growth will slow rapidly and level off at about 6%. The firm currently pays an annual dividend of $2, which can be expected to grow with the company. The rate of return on stocks like Zylon is approximately 10%. Is Zylon a good buy at $48?

SOLUTION: To determine whether Zylon is a good buy, we'll estimate what it *should* be worth on the basis of the present value of future cash flows, and compare that result with the market price. If our valuation is higher, we might conclude that the stock is a bargain and buy it.

Drawing a diagram similar to Figure 8-2 generally helps in problems like this. The time line below shows the growth rates and dividends.

The dividend paid recently, D_0, is given as $2.00. The first future dividend is forecast by growing $2.00 at the first year's growth rate. That's accomplished by multiplying by 1 plus the growth rate in that year.

$$D_1 = D_0(1 + g_1) = \$2.00(1.20) = \$2.40$$

To get the second year's dividend, we multiply by $(1 + g_1)$ again.

$$D_2 = D_1(1 + g_1) = \$2.40(1.20) = \$2.88$$

We do *nearly* the same thing for D_3. The firm is now growing at rate g_2, which is 6% in this example. Hence,

$$D_3 = D_2(1 + g_2) = \$2.88(1.06) = \$3.05$$

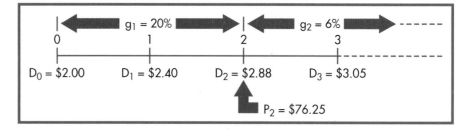

Next, we use the Gordon model *at the point in time where the growth rate changes and constant growth begins.* That's year 2 in this case, so

$$P_2 = \frac{D_3}{k - g_2} = \frac{\$3.05}{.10 - .06} = \$76.25$$

This result is also indicated in the diagram.

All that remains in calculating a price is to take the present value of each of the elements to which a buyer at time zero is entitled and add them up; these are D_1, D_2, and P_2.

$$P_0 = D_1[PVF_{k,1}] + D2[PVF_{k,2}] + P_2[PVF_{k,2}]$$
$$P_0 = \$2.40[PVF_{10,1}] + \$2.88[PVF_{10,2}] + \$76.25[PVF_{10,2}]$$
$$P_0 = \$2.40[.9091] + \$2.88[.8264] + \$76.25[.8264]$$
$$P_0 = \$67.57$$

Now we compare $67.57 with the listed price of $48.00. Clearly our valuation is larger. If our assumptions are correct, the stock should be worth almost $20 more than its current market price. If we're right, the price will rise substantially in a relatively short time, so we would be wise to buy.

8.2e   Practical Limitations of Pricing Models

optimarc/Shutterstock.com

from the
CFO

It's important to remember that the growth rate models we've been studying are abstractions of reality. They're simplified representations of the real world that at best can give us only approximations of what's likely to occur in the future. We have to be careful not to view them as being accurate to the penny even though our calculations result in figures like the $67.57 in the last example.

It's especially important to understand that our results can never be any more accurate than the inputs that go into the model. In this case, those inputs are the projected growth rates and the interest rate.

Growth rate estimates are guesses that can be off by quite a bit. For example, in the case we've just illustrated, the predicted 20% growth rate could actually turn out to be anything from 15% to 25%. Rates at either end of this range will make a big difference in the figure we finally get for P_0.

The exact interest rate isn't always known either. The rates of return that people require to invest in stocks vary according to the risk they perceive in any particular company. Different investors have different perceptions, so our 10% rate might easily be 9% or 11%.

Another big source of inaccuracy comes from the denominator of the Gordon model. Notice that it's the difference between two of our estimated inputs, the interest rate and a growth rate. If those numbers are estimated to be close together, their difference is small and the calculated price blows up because a small denominator makes the value of a fraction large.

Look at the calculation of P_2 in Example 8-5. The denominator of the fraction, $k - g_2$, is $(.10 - .06 =)$ .04. But suppose our estimates of k and g_2 were a little off, and k should have been 9% and g_2 more like 7%. Then the denominator would have been $(.09 - .07 =)$ .02 and P_2 would have been $154.08. [The numerator would also change to $($2.88 \times 1.07 =)$ $3.08.] This would have made P_0 $131.89 rather than $67.57. That's a 95% difference in the estimated value of the stock coming from input errors that are relatively much smaller (10% for k and 17% for g_2)!

The point is that when it comes to estimating stock prices, finance is not engineering! Our numbers just aren't all that accurate. Keep that in mind when using the results the way we did in the last example. The estimated value of the stock turned out to be $67.57, which looked very good in comparison with the $48 market price. But suppose the stock had been selling for $62 instead of the example's $48. Could we have concluded that it was still a bargain, although not as big a one? In other words, could we expect to make $5.57 on the purchase of a share?

The answer to that question is probably no. The difference of about $5 out of $67 isn't large enough to overcome the margin for error inherent in the estimating process. At a market price of $48, we'd be pretty sure we had something, but at $62 we really can't say much at all. Basically, the result would be saying the stock is worth in the neighborhood of $65 or $70. Any finer estimates than that are meaningless.

Stock valuation models give **approximate** results because the inputs are approximations of reality. **Bond** valuation is **precise** because the inputs are exact.

Comparison with Bond Valuation   The comments about inaccuracy in the last section refer only to stock valuation; bonds are a completely different story. The bond pricing model gives a precise valuation for the security, because the future cash flows are contractually guaranteed in amount and time. Unless a borrowing company defaults on its obligation, which is rare among higher grade issues, we can predict the exact pattern of future interest and principal payments. Having that, we can determine the price exactly for any yield. Yields in turn are established quite accurately by market forces influenced by the stability of the issuing company and the term of the debt.

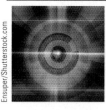

Ensuper/Shutterstock.com

INSIGHTS   Practical Finance

Reconciling Valuation Theory and Practice

People who work with stock investing day in and day out aren't likely to think of valuation in terms of present value models. Brokers and frequent investors are more likely to work with earnings per share and price/earnings ratios to predict short-term price movements. The EPS model is expressed by the following relation.

(a)
$$P_0 = EPS \times P/E$$

where P_0 is the stock's price, EPS is earnings per share, and P/E is the price/earnings ratio.

According to this view, to the extent that companies have different P/E ratios, the market values their earnings differently. For example, if two firms each earn $1 per share and their P/Es are 10 and 20, their stocks will sell for $10 and $20 regardless of the fact that their earnings are the same. In other words, the market puts a different value on a dollar of earnings depending on who makes it.

This doesn't seem consistent with the valuation models we've been studying, which say price is based on the present value of *dollar* earnings *only*.

Things get more confusing if you look at the relationship expressed in equation (a) closely. Mathematically, it's just an identity because P/E is just price over EPS. Hence, it reduces to

$$P_0 = EPS \times \frac{P_0}{EPS}$$

or

$$P_0 = P_0$$

which doesn't have much value for anything.

But in fact there's more to it than that. The stock market tends to fix short-run P/E ratios within ranges by industry. And within industries, better performers get higher P/Es than poor performers. In other words, certain favored industries and certain favored companies are rewarded with higher than normal P/Es. That is, in the short run, the P/E ratio is relatively stable, so price changes depend mainly on changes in recent earnings, EPS.

That still doesn't seem to reconcile well with the models that value stocks according to the present value of *future* cash flows until you realize two things. First, recent earnings are predictors of future earnings, so a higher EPS today means more earnings and dividends in the future. Second, countless studies have shown that the primary determinant of who gets what P/E is expected growth. The higher a company's expected growth, the higher its P/E.

That means equation (a) works like a crude Gordon model in which higher growth rates and higher current earnings both imply a higher current stock price. In other words, the seat-of-the-pants approach used by rough-and-tumble practitioners is very consistent with sophisticated valuation theory. That should give us all a sense of calm and well-being.

Stocks That Don't Pay Dividends   Some companies pay no dividends even when their profits are high. Further, many openly state their intention never to pay dividends. Nevertheless, the stocks of such firms can have substantial value.

The growth models we've been working with base stock values solely on the present value of a dividend stream. How can such a model be valid if there are stocks with value that pay no dividends?

The answer to this puzzling question lies in understanding when and why firms pay no dividends to stockholders. Firms that don't pay dividends even when their earnings are good are usually in an early period of their development and growing rapidly. Growth requires cash, and managements feel it's futile to pay out dividends only to turn around and borrow or issue more stock to raise money to support that growth. Stockholders agree because they hope to own a piece of a much larger company if growth continues.

However, most people understand that rapid growth doesn't go on forever. When growth in the industry and firm slows down, even the most vocal non-dividend payers eventually begin paying. In other words, stocks that don't pay dividends today are expected to pay large dividends at some time in the future. It's those distant dividends that impart value.

If a company truly never paid a dividend, there would be no way for the investing community as a whole to *ever* get a return on its investment. And that doesn't make much sense.

Stocks that **don't pay dividends** have value because there's a general expectation that **some day they will**.

8.3 Valuing New Stocks—Investment Banking and the Initial Public Offering (IPO)

Our discussion so far has focused on valuing stocks that have been available for some time. In this section, we'll look at emerging stocks that are being sold to the public for the time. Are these **Initial Public Offering (IPOs)** valued any differently than stocks that have been around for a while? In theory shouldn't be, but as a practical matter, things are less rational in this segment of the equity market.

We mentioned IPOs briefly in Chapter 5, stressing the requirements for registration with the SEC (page 190). Here we'll focus on promoting and bringing new issues to market where they can emerge in a frenzy of enthusiastic bidding or slide into the market with a disappointing thud. We'll have a look at this fascinating and complex process in the next few pages.

8.3a   IPOs for Different Securities

The IPOs that generate the most excitement sell the stocks of new companies, but there are IPOs for other new securities, notably bonds. There are actually more IPOs for bonds than stocks because new bonds can be issued to replace older, maturing bonds as well as to raise new money.

The sale of new shares of an existing stock is handled like an IPO but is actually a **seasoned equity offering (SEO)** or a **secondary equity offering**. These aren't especially interesting from a pricing perspective, because the market value of the old shares determines the price of the new. (The new shares may be offered slightly below market to ensure their sale.)

The IPOs we're concerned with here are the first public sales of new company stocks, that is, the first time people other than founders and private investors have an opportunity to buy in. That happens when the founding group wants to raise a lot of money, usually to support growth.

The shares sold in an **IPO** are new, but the offering usually includes some existing shares that were previously issued to founders and early investors. Although these shares are sold within the IPO process, they actually constitute a secondary offering. (Recall from Chapter 5 that the sale of newly issued securities is a primary market transaction while subsequent sales between investors are secondary market transactions. See page 183.)

IPOs may include shares owned by founders and early investors.

8.3b   Investment Banking

The first step a new company takes toward an IPO is establishing a relationship with an **investment bank**, which is an organization that specializes in marketing new securities.[3] Investment banks tend to specialize in different business areas. For example, Morgan Stanley has been the leading bank for high tech and Internet companies for some time. The investment bank does a study of the new company and its prospects to determine whether it's likely to attract enough investors to raise the money its management wants. If the bank feels it can be done, the firm is accepted as client.

An **investment bank** sells new securities to investors.

Syndication   Most IPOs are too big and carry too much risk for a single investment bank, so a **lead bank** recruits others forming a **syndicate** which shares the process. The lead bank, also called the principal or managing investment bank, is in charge. Larger syndicates can include over fifty banks.

Most IPOs are handled by **syndicates** of investment banks.

Registration   An early step in the IPO process is filing a registration statement, called Form S-1, with the Securities and Exchange Commission (SEC). The statement calls for a great deal of financial and technical information, and may be over 100 pages long. A summary of the information, known as a **Prospectus,** is part of the S-1 document. The prospectus is intended for distribution to potential investors. The lead investment bank generally advises the client company during the preparation of its registration statement.

Underwriting   There's a good deal of risk in an IPO, because no one knows how much value the market will place on the new stock before trading begins. For example, suppose a company wants to raise $20 million through an IPO by selling one million shares at $20 each. If enough buyers don't come forward at that price, either

---

3. The term investment *bank* seems strange here since we don't generally think of banks as marketing organizations. But distributing new securities is a banking function, although its history in the United States is a little disjointed. During the depression of the 1930s, a large number of bank failures led Congress to pass a board Banking Reform Act. Part of that legislation, the Glass–Steagall Act of 1933, prohibited commercial banks from participating in investment banking. As a result, investment banks were separate organizations until Glass–Steagall was repealed by the Gramm–Leach–Bliley Act in 1999. Some economists feel that the repeal of Glass–Steagall was a major cause of the financial crisis of 2008.

the firm won't raise its $20 million or it will have to reduce the offering price to sell more shares. But more shares at a lower price will reduce the percentage of the post IPO stock held by the original owners. In essence, they'd be giving up more of the company than they intended. Indeed they might even regret the IPO if the price turns out to be too low.

In the majority of cases investment banks solve this problem by **underwriting** IPOs. In an underwritten issue the investment bank makes a **firm commitment** to buy the stock from the new company at a fixed price and is then responsible for reselling the shares to investors. Of course, the bank sells the shares at a higher price than it paid. The difference is the **underwriting spread**, and is how investment banks earn a profit. The client company understands that the spread is part of the fee it pays the bank for its services. The investment bank syndicate is also called an **underwriting syndicate** and the investment bank is often just called the **underwriter.**

Underwriting spreads range from as little as 2% to as much as 10% of the money raised. Generally, the bigger the deal, the lower the spread percentage. Other IPO costs include accounting and legal fees, printing and engraving costs and fees for listing on stock exchanges. Overall, the issuing company generally pays between 3% and 15% of the money raised in fees and charges. Once again, the larger the deal, the lower is the overall percentage cost. The 3% range isn't reached until the IPO approaches $50 million.

Best Efforts   In smaller deals, investment banks may be reluctant to assume the risk of underwriting, but may accept the placement on a **best efforts** basis. That simply means the issuing company gets whatever the bank is able to sell the new shares for, less expenses and a commission.

8.3c   Promoting and Pricing the IPO

Quiet Period   A **quiet period** begins when the registration statement is filed and continues until the SEC accepts the statement by declaring it effective. This is generally within 20 days of filing. During the quiet period, company executives and representatives of the investment bank may show potential investors copies of the prospectus conspicuously stamped in red ink with the word "preliminary", but may not share any other information about the company or finalize any orders for stock. A preliminary prospectus is known as a **red herring**. The prospectus contains a *price range* for the IPO stock, but not the exact offering price which has not yet been determined.

A second quiet period lasts for 40 calendar days after trading begins. During this time, no one associated with the company or the IPO can issue any forecast or analysis of the company's projected performance. This is to make sure that all investors have equal access to information about the business during the early days of trading.

8.3d   Book Building and the Road Show

At this point, the company and the bank need to decide on the price and the number of shares that will be offered in the IPO. In order to do that, they need an estimate of the level of investor demand that exists for the stock. That's done in a process called **book building**, conducted during a **road show**. It's important to understand that investment banks have long-standing relationships with institutional investors, such as

Investment banks **underwrite** IPOs by making **firm commitments** to buy new stock.

During the **quiet period,** the preliminary prospectus **(red herring)** is distributed, but no stock may be sold.

IPOs are promoted during **road shows.**

pension funds, insurance companies, mutual funds, college endowments, and hedge funds',[4] as well as with certain wealthy individuals.

The road show is a fast, intense trip to major cities around the country made by the issuing company's executives and their investment bankers. The purpose of the trip is to make promotional presentations on the new company and the IPO to potential investors, most of whom are the investment bank's institutional clients. The team generally makes two or three presentations a day for about two weeks leading up to the IPO date. After each presentation the bank asks the investor clients in the audience how many shares they're willing to buy based on the price range in the prospectus. The responses constitute the **book** which builds into an order list as the road show progresses.

The road show generally ends at about the same time the SEC approves the registration statement which is shortly before the IPO date. At this time, company executives and their bankers have a good sense of investor demand for the stock. The final price and number of shares is set after the market closes on the evening before trading begins.

The bank then allocates the IPO shares among the investor who expressed interest during the road show. In most cases, the investment bank places the majority of the IPO stock with these large, special relationship investors rather than with the general public who are called **retail investors**. Hence IPO buyers tend to be large, powerful organizations that are "insiders" in the financial system. Another way of saying it is that small, individual (retail) investors rarely have an opportunity to buy into an IPO.

> Most IPO stock is allocated to **institutional investors**.

> Ordinary people who buy stocks are **retail investors**.

It's important to understand that the sale of the IPO shares is an *off market* transaction, meaning it isn't the result of an auction-like process as are ordinary stock trades. The price is set by the investment bank and the issuing company, usually based on information from the book building process, and all shares are sold at that price. Traditional trading begins shortly after the IPO transaction.

8.3e   Prices After the IPO

The Investment Bank in the Middle

> The issuing company and investors are both clients of the investment bank.

The investment bank is in the center of the IPO process. It stands between the issuing company and the investors who buy the new shares. Both of these are the bank's clients and have put their trust in the banker, but their interests conflict. The company wants to get as much as it can for its stock, while the investors want a very high return on their money, which only happens when securities are acquired for less than full value.

It's important to understand that when an investment bank prices an IPO it's estimating the price at which the market will value the stock in open trading. But in spite of careful analysis and the book building process, no one knows for sure what that market value of new stock will be until the IPO is over and trading begins. Nevertheless the bank's estimate becomes the price IPO investors pay and the company receives (less costs and the spread).

So immediately after the IPO, when the entire market is able to bid the stock's price up or down, someone is bound to be unhappy. If the price goes up, the company's

---

4. A hedge fund is an investment fund that makes high risk investments in search of significantly high returns. Participation is generally limited to wealthy individuals.

owners will feel they should have gotten more for the portion of the firm they sold. They will have "left money on the table." But the buyers will be happy because they'll see a big return on their investment. On the other hand, if the price remains constant or goes down, the company's founders will feel good because they got as much cash as possible, but the investors will be upset because they'll either see no gain or a loss from taking the banker's advice.

Underpricing and IPO Pops   Faced with this dilemma, there seems to be a strong tendency to **underprice** IPOs to make the stock's price go up right after the IPO. The phenomenon is called the **IPO Pop**, and it happens in most IPOs, especially if the company is in an exciting hi-tech field and the IPO has been substantially "hyped."

Underpricing may happen because investment bankers know they're likely to be marketing shares in another IPO to the same investors before long and want to keep their good will. But conversely, some observers argue that underpricing only *seems* to occur. And that's because the investing public becomes too enthusiastic about new companies and bids their price up unrealistically immediately following IPOs. Then after only a short while the overpriced shares fall back down, often below the original IPO price.

A Little Big Pop History   IPO pops are measured by the percentage increase in the stock's price over the IPO price at the close of the first day of trading. Unfortunately, the stock's price is sometimes already falling by then. The classic IPO pop was VA Linux Systems Inc., a hi-tech firm that went public in December 1999. After an IPO at $30, the stock closed its first day of trading at $239.25, up 698%. Earlier in the day, it had peaked at $320, up 967%. But the ride didn't last. A year later the stock was selling for $8.50, and its price was in the neighborhood of fifty cents by the middle of 2002.

Linux went public at the height of a stock market "bubble" that burst in 2000 with a serious market crash followed by a recession. December of 1999 was in the middle of a six-month period in which 96 IPOs closed up 100% or more on their first day.

Here are a few big pops[5] that occurred at various times:

TheGlobe.com	606%
Foundry Networks	525%
Akamai	458%
Linkedin	109%

Pop Strategies   Whatever its cause, the IPO Pop phenomenon has generated a strategy among the privileged investors that have access to IPOs. The idea is to participate in the IPO by purchasing shares, hold them while the price increases quickly, and then sell after only a few days before the price falls again. Wall Street jargon calls an investor who uses the strategy a **stag** and the gain a **stag profit**.

A pop-based strategy available to less privileged investors is simply to buy as soon as possible after trading starts, watch the rising price very carefully, and sell the moment it starts down.

IPOs seem to be underpriced to reward investors.

A rapid increase in price when trading begins is an **IPO Pop**.

---

5.   Source: Spencer Jakab, "Ahead of the Tape," *The Wall Street Journal* (May 18, 2012) C1.

Investment banks **support** the new stock's price to keep it above the IPO price.

Market Stabilization   The lead investment bank is actually committed to supporting at least a small pop by keeping the price of the stock above the IPO price during the first few days of trading. It does that by purchasing shares if the market for the issue is weak. Of course, if demand is very weak, stabilization may be impossible.

Most IPO pops don't last, and the stocks usually underperform for years.

Price in the Longer Run and the Retail Investor   Unfortunately, the result of underpricing and the pop phenomenon, intentional or not, is generally bad for retail investors. Enthused about the company but unable to participate in the IPO, they buy at pop-inflated prices only to lose out when the stock drops and stays down. The majority of IPO stocks enjoy a brief pop, fall back to or below the IPO price, and then underperform the overall market for several years.

INSIGHTS | **Practical Finance**

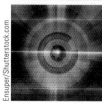
Ensuper/Shutterstock.com

Facebook's IPO: How to Feel Bad About Raising $16B

Facebook, by far the brightest star in the social networking sky and probably the most anticipated IPO in history, went public on Friday, May 18, 2012. And promptly fell on its face.

The IPO price was set the night before at a heady $38, up $3 from the top of the original range quoted in the prospectus. Trading opened late at 11:30 AM due to serious technical problems with Nasdaq's computers that confused the entire day. The opening price was $42, which sounds like a good start, but after a brief jump, the stock went nowhere but down. Shares closed up a shade at $38.23, but only because of active support from Morgan Stanley, the IPO's lead investment bank. The first day's bottom line: A 23 cent "IPO Pop" is pretty embarrassing performance.

Things got even worse after the first day of trading. Earlier, the IPO analysts had been predicting the stock would settle in the $44 range, but by late August, it was trading below $20, having dipped as low as $18.75. That's a decline of almost 50% from the IPO price. Needless to say investors were upset.

On the other hand, the IPO's money raising performance was nothing less than outstanding. Morgan Stanley placed 421.2 million Facebook shares at $38 raising just over $16 billion. That makes Facebook the largest tech company IPO ever, the fourth largest American IPO in history, and the sixth largest worldwide.

So was May 18th a good day or a bad day for Facebook? It's hard to say. It raised a lot of money. The founders and early investors cashed out some of their own stock at what turned out to be a premium price. But investor relations will probably be dismal for some time. And Morgan Stanley's relationship with its institutional investors may be severely damaged.

Let's look at a few of the reasons investors may not be as excited about Facebook as they had been.

Nasdaq's technical problems made the first day trading chaos. After a delayed opening, volume overwhelmed the system. Orders weren't confirmed for hours, so investors cancelled and/or resubmitted, creating doubled or voided orders. Some people didn't know how much stock they held until Monday afternoon. The confusion caused millions of dollars in losses.

Facebook's business is based on advertising revenue, which is showing signs of weakening. Some analysts say that's because users aren't in a shopping mode when they're on the site, so advertising isn't effective. Indeed, on May 15, General Motors announced it was discontinuing Facebook advertising because it doesn't help sales.

Another concern is that Facebook users are migrating from desktops and laptops to mobile devices with small screens that make visual advertising difficult. And, Facebook isn't set up to provide its full range of services to mobile devices. In particular, it can't provide mobile apps such as games. This means the company needs to do a fast technical catch up.

Yet another issue involves lawsuits and regulations regarding privacy, which could limit the services Facebook can offer and its ability to sell information about user behavior.

Finally, the prospectus contains 23 pages of warnings about potential risks as well as a statement about the role of the 28-year-old founder, Mark Zuckerberg, who owns 57% of the voting stocks, entirely controlling the company:

> "As a stockholder . . . Mr. Zuckerberg is entitled to vote
> his shares . . . in his own interests, which may not
> always be in the interests of our stockholders generally."

Sort of makes you think twice about investing, doesn't it? Remember, even a great company with a popular product isn't a good investment if it's overpriced.

Sources: Geoffrey Fowler and Shayndi Raice, "Facebook Gets Religion on Revenue," *The Wall Street Journal* (May 18, 2012); Shayndi Raice, Anupreeta Das, and John Letzing, "Facebook Prices IPO at Record Value," *The Wall Street Journal* (May 18, 2012); Shayndi Raice, Ryan Dezember, and Jocob Bunge, "Facebook's Launch Sputters," *The Wall Street Journal* (May 19–20, 2012); Jenny Strasburg, Jacob Bunge and Gina Chon, "Nasdaq's Facebook Problem," *The Wall Street Journal* (May 21, 2012); L. Gordon Crovitz, "Will Regulators Unfriend Facebook?" *The Wall Street Journal* (May 21, 2012); Jacob Bunger, Aaron Lucchetti, and Gina Chon, "Investors Pummel Facebook," *The Wall Street Journal* (May 22, 2012); Michelle kung, and Ryan Dezember, "Facebook's Mobile Miscalculation," *The Wall Street Journal* (May 22, 2012); Shayndi Raice, Anupreeta Das, and Gina Chon, "Inside Fumbled Facebook Offering," *The Wall Street Journal* (May 23, 2012); The Motley Fool, "Caution is the Word for Facebook," *Sunday Telegram* (Week of June10, 2012).

8.4   Some Institutional Characteristics of Common Stock

Common stock represents an investment in equity (ownership) that theoretically implies control of the company. That is, it's logical to assume that an ownership interest means a stockholder has some influence on the way the company is run.

As a practical matter, however, influence depends on how much stock is held by any one person or group. Because most management issues are decided by a majority vote, stockholders owning minority interests have little power when someone else has a clear majority or when no one owns a substantial percentage of the firm. To understand how all of this works, we have to look at how companies are run.

8.4a   Corporate Organization and Control

Corporations are controlled by **boards of directors** whose members are elected by stockholders.

Corporations are controlled by **boards of directors** whose members are elected by stockholders. The board appoints the firm's senior management, which in turn appoints middle and lower management and runs the company on a day-to-day basis. Major strategic decisions are considered by the board, but only a few really big issues, like mergers, must be voted on by the stockholders.

Corporate boards are generally made up of the company's top managers and a number of *outside directors*. Board members may be major stockholders, but they don't have to be.

Companies are said to be widely held when stock ownership is distributed among a large number of people and no single party or group has a significantly large share. When that happens, it is very difficult to make a change in the board because it's hard to organize voting stockholders against the incumbent members. In such situations, members of top management on the board have effective control of the company with little accountability to stockholders. (There have been a few exceptions to this rule in which institutional investors owning large blocks of stock became dissatisfied with performance and were able to force changes in management and the board.)

Top **managers** effectively **control widely held companies**, because no stockholder group has enough power to remove them.

The outside directors are supposed to be a restraint on this autonomy of management, but generally don't do much along those lines.[6] Of course, when a substantial percentage of stock is under the control of a single group, that group has effective control of the company because it can elect board members. In widely held companies, 15% to 25% is generally enough for effective control if no one else has more than a few percent.

The Role of the Equity Investor   As we said early in the chapter, most of the investors who buy stock in sizable companies don't look for a role in running the company. They're simply interested in the cash flows that come from stock ownership.

Preemptive rights allow stockholders to maintain their proportionate ownership.

Preemptive Rights   Preemptive rights allow stockholders to maintain their proportionate ownership of corporations. When new shares are issued, common stockholders have the right to purchase a portion of the new issue equal to the percentage of the outstanding shares they already own. If preemptive rights exist, current stockholders must be offered this option before the new shares can be sold to anyone else.

Preemptive rights are common, but there's generally no law requiring them. Hence, if stockholders have preemptive rights, it's because they were written into the company's rules of operation (called its charter, articles, or bylaws) by the people who originally formed the corporation.

8.4b   Voting Rights and Issues

Most common stock comes with voting rights. That means each share gets an equal vote in the election of directors and on major issues. Voting issues are usually limited to changes in the company's charter, which broadly defines what it does, and questions about mergers.

Each share of **common** stock has one vote in the election of directors, which is usually cast by **proxy**.

Stockholders vote on directors and other items at an *annual stockholders' meeting* that corporations are required by law to hold. Most shareholders don't attend, however, and vote by **proxy** if at all. Proxies give the authority to vote shares to a designated party. Generally, the current board members solicit shareholders by mail for their proxies. If the firm's performance has been reasonably good, the proxies are given and the board is reelected.

A **proxy fight** occurs if parties with conflicting interests solicit proxies at the same time. This usually happens when a stockholder group is unhappy with management and tries to take over the board. We'll talk about proxy fights more in Chapter 17.

---

6. There have been a few notable exceptions in recent years in which CEOs have been removed by groups led by outside directors.

Majority and Cumulative Voting   Suppose a company's stock is held by two groups of stockholders with differing interests. Also assume one group has a clear majority of the shares outstanding. Traditional *majority voting* gives the larger group control of the company to the virtual exclusion of the minority group. This is because each director is chosen in a separate election, so the majority group can win every seat.

Cumulative voting is a way to get some minority representation on the board. Under the cumulative method, each share of stock gets one vote for every seat being elected. Minority stockholders can then cast all their votes for one seat or split them up among several elections. This means the minority interest can concentrate its votes on one or two seats and be likely to win, thereby getting some representation on the board.

<aside>**Cumulative voting** gives minority interests a chance at some representation on the board.</aside>

Shares with Different Voting Rights   It's possible to issue more than one class of stock with different rights associated with each class. Along these lines, a practice that affects control involves issuing a class of stock with limited voting rights or with no votes at all. If such an issue receives the same dividends as traditional voting stock, it may be attractive to the typical investor who has no interest in control anyway.

Nonvoting stock was fairly common in the early part of this century, but has been unusual since the 1930s. At that time, there was a general resistance to it from the government, the stock exchanges, and investors. The idea has reemerged recently, however, in association with mergers and acquisitions.

8.4c   Stockholders' Claims on Income and Assets

Stockholders have a **residual claim** on both income and assets. That means they are the last in line among all the claimants on the firm's resources.

With respect to income, stockholders own what's left after all operating costs and expenses are paid, after bondholders receive their interest and any principal due, and after preferred stockholders get their dividends. That doesn't sound like a very good deal, but it often is.

When business is bad, stockholders are in the worst position of all because the company's money is more likely to run out before they're paid than before other claimants are paid. That's why common stock is considered the riskiest investment.

When business is good, however, the residual after everyone else is paid can be enormous, and it all belongs to the stockholders. Essentially, the "upside" potential in stock ownership is limitless.

The residual income belonging to stockholders is essentially the net income line on the income statement. It is either paid out to them in dividends or retained and reinvested in the business. Both options are clearly beneficial to stockholders. Dividends are immediate money in their pockets, while retained earnings contribute to growth that makes the stock more valuable.

With respect to assets, the residual position means that if the corporation fails and is liquidated, stockholders don't get anything until everyone else is paid. That often means they don't get anything at all.

<aside>Common stockholders are **last in line** to receive income or assets, and so bear **more risk** than other investors. But their **residual** interest is large when the firm does well.</aside>

8.5 Preferred Stock

Preferred stock is a security that has some of the characteristics of common stock and some of those of bonds. It's often referred to as a *hybrid* of the two—that is, a cross between common stock and bonds.

Preferred stock pays a constant dividend forever. When a share is initially issued, two things are specified: the initial selling price in the primary market called the stock's par value, and the dividend. The ratio between the two reflects the current return on investments of similar risk, the market interest rate.

For example, if the interest rate is 10% and a company wants to issue preferred shares at $100 each, it would offer a dividend of $10. This would be referred to as a $10 preferred issue rather than a 10% preferred issue.

You can think of the 10% rate as being similar to the coupon rate on a bond. The preferred's initial selling price (issue price) is conceptually similar to a bond's face value. Preferred stock is generally issued at prices (par values) of $25, $50, and $100.

It's important to notice that, like common stock, preferred stock, carries no provision for the return of capital to the investor. That is, the issuing company never has to pay the initial selling price back.

8.5a Valuation of Preferred Stock

An investor who purchases a share of preferred stock receives a constant dividend forever. Because all securities are worth the present value of their future cash flows, a share of preferred is worth the present value of that infinitely long stream of dividend payments.

In Chapter 6, we said that a constant stream of payments stretching into the indefinite future is a *perpetuity* (page 269). We also learned a simple formula to calculate a perpetuity's present value, which we'll repeat here for convenience.

(6.24)
$$PV_p = \frac{PMT}{k}$$

Preferred stock pays a constant dividend and is valued as a **perpetuity**.

We'll use this basic equation for **preferred stock**, but will change the variable names to more appropriately reflect the application. The perpetuity's payment (PMT) is the preferred dividend, which we'll call D_p. The present value of the perpetuity (PV_p) must equal the security's price, which we'll call P_p. The interest rate will remain k. Then the expression for the price of a preferred share is

(8.13)
$$P_p = \frac{D_p}{k}$$

Notice that the valuation of a preferred share is conceptually identical to that of a zero growth common share discussed earlier in this chapter (page 357).

Like bonds, preferred stock is issued to yield approximately the current rate of interest. When interest rates change, preferred shares have to offer competitive yields to new secondary market buyers. This is accomplished through price changes.

Prices of preferred stocks, like those of bonds, move inversely with interest rates. However, calculating new preferred prices is much easier than calculating bond prices. We simply insert the new interest rate into Equation 8.13 and solve for P_p.

CONCEPT CONNECTION   **EXAMPLE 8-6**

Pricing Preferred Stock

Roman Industries's $6 preferred originally sold for $50. Interest rates on similar issues are now 9%. What should Roman's preferred sell for today?

SOLUTION: Just substitute the new market interest rate into Equation 8.13 for today's price.

$$P_p = \frac{D_p}{k} = \frac{\$6.00}{.09} = \$66.67$$

Notice that the original yield on the issue was ($6/$50 =) 12%. Because the interest rate dropped from 12% to 9%, we know the price has to be above its original value of $50. This gives a reasonableness check on our answer.

8.5b Characteristics of Preferred Stock

As a security, preferred stock has some unique characteristics relative to traditional debt and equity. We'll summarize a few issues.

The Cumulative Feature   Nearly all preferred stock comes with a **cumulative feature** designed to enhance its safety for investors. The cumulative feature generally states that if preferred dividends are passed (not paid) in any year or series of years, no common dividends can be paid until the preferred dividends in arrears are caught up.

> Common dividends can't be paid unless the dividends on **cumulative preferred** are current.

For example, if a firm gets into financial trouble and doesn't pay dividends on a $5 preferred for three years, no common dividends can be paid until each preferred shareholder has received the cumulative total of $15 per share.

Comparing Preferred Stock with Common Stock and Bonds   Some of the features of preferred stock are like those of bonds, while some are more like those of common stock. Some are in between. Let's consider a few specifics.

Payments to Investors   The fact that preferred dividends are constant and don't increase even if the company grows makes them similar to the constant interest payments of a bond. They're unlike the dividends on common stock, which are usually expected to grow with the firm.

> The features of **preferred stock** allow it to be characterized as a **cross between common stock and bonds**.

Maturity and Return of Principal   A bond has a maturity date on which the principal is returned. Preferred stock has no maturity and never returns principal. In that respect, it's like common stock, which never returns principal either.

Assurance of Payment   Interest must be paid or bondholders can force a company into bankruptcy. Common stock dividends can be passed indefinitely. Preferred dividends can be passed, but are subject to a cumulative feature. In this respect, it is somewhere between bonds and common stock.

Priority in Bankruptcy   In the event of bankruptcy, bondholders have a claim on the company's assets to the extent of the unpaid principal of the bonds. Common stockholders are entitled only to what's left after all other claimants have been paid.

Preferred stockholders are again in between. They have a claim in the amount of the original selling price of the stock, but it is subordinate to the claims of all bondholders. That is, it comes before the interests of common stockholders but after those of bondholders.

Voting Rights   Common stockholders have voting rights, while preferred stockholders do not. In that respect, preferred stock is like bonds.

Tax Deductibility of Payments to Investors   Interest is tax deductible to the paying company, while dividends, common or preferred, are not. In this respect, preferred stock is very much equity.

Preferred stock is legally equity, but from what we've just said, it's clearly more like debt in many ways. For that reason, it's generally treated separately in financial analysis.

The Order of Risk   The features we've been talking about create an ordering of risk associated with the three securities. Bonds are the safest, common stock is the most risky, and preferred is in the middle. The compensation for the risk in common stock is that the return—through dividend increases and price appreciation—can be very high if the company does exceptionally well. That possibility doesn't exist with either of the other two.

The name "preferred" stock comes from the idea that of the two types of equity, you'd rather have preferred stock if the firm does poorly or fails.

Taxes and Preferred Stock Investors   The U.S. tax code treats preferred dividends just like common dividends in that they're not tax deductible to the company paying them. That makes preferred stock a relatively expensive source of financing.

Like common dividends, preferred dividends received by another corporation are 70% or more exempt from taxation. (See Chapter 2, page 57.) This partial tax exemption, coupled with preferred stock's relatively low risk, makes it especially attractive to some institutional investors. Hence, those investors bid up preferred prices until they're not attractive to individual investors who don't have the tax exemption. The result is that not many *people* invest in preferred stock.

8.6   Securities Analysis

Securities analysis is the art and science of selecting investments.

Valuation is part of a broader process aimed at selecting investments known as **securities analysis**. The term is applied to both stocks and bonds, but most of the activity relates to selecting stocks. There are two basic approaches to analysis; we'll briefly describe each.

Fundamental analysis looks at a company and its business to forecast value.

Fundamental Analysis   **Fundamental analysis** involves doing research to discover everything possible about a firm, its business, and its industry (the firm's fundamentals). Once analysts become expert in a company's field, they forecast its sales and expenses over the coming years. From that they project earnings and then a stream of dividends based on the firm's stated or implied dividend policy. The forecast dividend stream is used as input to the valuation models we've been discussing.

The Thomson One database provided with this text is a powerful tool in fundamental analysis.

Technical Analysis

Technical analysts take a different approach. Technicians believe market forces dictate prices and, more importantly, price movements. They also believe movement patterns tend to repeat themselves over time. By studying past price changes, technicians believe they can recognize patterns that precede major up or down movements in the prices of individual stocks.

Technicians prepare elaborate charts displaying the prices and volumes[7] of virtually all stocks traded. These are examined in an effort to discern patterns that precede major moves. Because of this technique, technical analysts are also called *chartists*.

Technicians feel one doesn't have to know *why* a firm's stock has value in terms of underlying cash flows. Rather, they believe it's enough to accept that it does have value, and rely on predictable market phenomena to make investment decisions.

Fundamentalists Versus Technicians

The two schools of thought are rather vocally opposed to one another, although many people use ideas from both camps. Scholars are almost universally fundamentalists. Nevertheless, the technical school of thought has a significant following.

A number of statistical studies have been done in attempts to prove or disprove the validity of technical analysis once and for all. To date no one has definitely proven anything to the satisfaction of the other side.

The Efficient Market Hypothesis (EMH)

The **efficient market hypothesis (EMH)** pertains to information flows within financial markets in the United States. It says that financial markets are efficient in that new information is disseminated with lightning speed.

The theory asserts that information moves so fast around the thousands of analysts, brokers, and investors who make up the stock market that prices adjust to new information virtually immediately. In other words, when some new knowledge about a stock becomes available, it is analyzed and disseminated so fast that the market price adjusts to reflect the information in a matter of hours or less.

For example, suppose a pharmaceutical company announced that it had discovered a cure for cancer. That would certainly raise the price of the firm's stock. The EMH says that the price rise will happen immediately because analysts will be on the phone right away telling client investors the news, and they'll bid the price up as fast as they can.

The implication is that at any time, all available information is already reflected in stock prices, and studying historical patterns of price movement can't consistently do an investor any good. Hence, the EMH is a direct refutation of the validity of technical analysis.

However, the EMH implies that we won't find many bargains using fundamental analysis and valuation models either. That's because an army of professionals is doing fundamental analysis all the time, and they will have already discovered and disseminated anything an individual can figure out.

---

7. "Volume" refers to the number of shares traded in a period. A price change at a low volume of trading isn't generally as significant as the same change accompanied by a higher volume.

The validity of the EMH is subject to dispute. It will probably never be proven to be either right or wrong. At this point in your study, you should just be aware of its existence and have a basic grasp of what it says.

8.7   Options and Warrants

Options are securities that make it possible to invest in stocks without actually holding shares. Warrants are similar but less common. We'll discuss options in some detail and then briefly describe warrants.

An option is a contract that gives one party a **temporary right to buy** an asset from the other at a fixed price. (Alternatively, an option contract may grant the right to sell.) It's a good idea to understand a little about the general concept before we get into financial options.

8.7a   Options in General

Options are used in business all the time. An option to buy real estate will familiarize us with the way they work and lead us into options on stocks. Suppose a company is interested in building a new factory and has identified a desirable site but will need six months to make a final decision on the project. How can it hold onto the right to buy the land without making a commitment now?

The solution can be an option contract granting the firm the right to buy the site within six months at a stipulated price. That locks in the land's availability and price but leaves management free to not make the purchase. Of course, the company has to pay the landowner for that privilege, but this cost is a small fraction of the value of the real estate. The option is a purchase contract that's suspended at the discretion of the buyer for a limited time after which it expires. Now consider the following possibility that will help us move into financial options.

Suppose after almost six months, the firm decides it's not going to build the factory but notices that the price of real estate has gone up 30%. What should it do?

Clearly, it should exercise the option to buy the land and then sell it for a profit, which will be made *without owning the land* while it appreciated. This is possible with any asset on which options are sold. The big advantage of options is that they cost far less than the underlying assets. That advantage is what financial options are all about.

8.7b   Stock Options

Options on stock are conceptually similar to real estate options, but they aren't purchased to acquire stock. Rather, they're bought to speculate (gamble) on price movement. Stock options are themselves securities and can be traded in financial markets. An option to **buy** a stock is known as a **call option** or just a **call**. Options to sell real assets are unusual, but options to sell stock are common. They're known as **put options** or just **puts**. We'll discuss calls and puts separately in the sections that follow.

Options are the most important example of a class of financial assets known as **derivative securities**. A derivative is so named because it derives its value from the price of another **underlying security**, in this case the optioned stock.

Leverage amplifies the
return on an investment.

Investors are interested in stock options because they provide speculative **leverage**, a term applied to any technique that **amplifies the return** on an investment. Option leverage comes from the fact that the return on an investment in options can be many times larger than the return on the underlying stock. We'll describe how that works shortly.

8.7c   Call Options

Imagine that a stock is selling for $55 and someone offers you a contract under which he agrees to sell you a share for $60 anytime during the next three months. This is a basic call option. It grants its owner the right to *buy* a share at a fixed price for a specified period, typically three, six, or nine months. At the end of that time, the option expires and can no longer be *exercised*.

The price the option holder pays for the contract is the **option price**, which we'll call P_{Op}. It's always a great deal less than the stock's price. An option on a stock worth $55 might sell for $2 or $3.

This idea is portrayed graphically in Figure 8-3. The stock's current price is called just that, but the $60 is known as the option's **strike price**, **striking price**, or **exercise price**.

An option to **buy** a stock at a **strike price** sells for the **option price**.

Ask yourself the following questions. Would you pay anything for this option contract? Why? And if you would pay for the deal, what factors would make you pay more or less? Think about these questions before reading on.

An investor might be willing to buy this option, because there's a chance the stock's price will exceed $60 within the next three months. If that happens, an option owner can buy at $60 and immediately sell for the higher market price. For example, suppose an investor paid $1 for the option and the stock's price went to $63. She would exercise at $60 and immediately sell for $63, making the $3 difference less the $1 paid for the option contract.

Notice that the $2 profit is a 200% return on the $1 investment in the option. But also notice that if the stock's price doesn't pass $60 in three months, the option expires and the $1 is lost. That's a 100% loss on the investment.

FIGURE 8-3   Basic Call Option Concepts

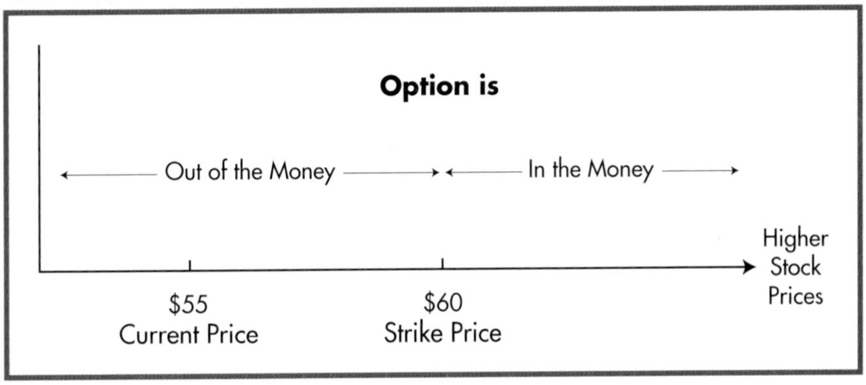

© Cengage Learning

Two factors make options more or less appealing. An option on a volatile stock is worth more than one on a stable issue, because a volatile stock's price is more likely to go above the strike price in the allotted time. People also pay more for options with more time until expiration, because that gives the stock's price more time to move past the strike price.

The Call Option Writer   There are two parties to an option contract, a buyer and a seller. Don't confuse buying and selling the option contract with buying and selling the optioned stock. Until now we've focused on option buyers who have the right to buy stock at the strike price.

Terminology with respect to option sellers can be a little tricky. The first person to sell an option contract is the person who creates it by agreeing to sell the stock at the strike price. He is said to *write* the option. Once it's written, the option contract becomes a security and the writer sells it to the first buyer who may sell it to someone else later on. No matter how many times the option is sold, the writer remains bound by the contract to sell the underlying stock to the current option owner at the strike price if she exercises.

A call option writer hopes the underlying stock's price will remain stable. If it does, he will have a gain from the receipt of the option price. We'll talk about writing options in more detail later.

> Option **originators** are said to **write** options.

8.7d   Intrinsic Value

If a stock's current price is below the strike price of a call option, as we've shown in Figure 8-3, we say the option is *out of the money*. If the stock's price is above the strike price, we say the option is *in the money*.

When an option is in the money, it has an immediate minimum value that doesn't depend on the underlying stock's price moving higher. We call that the option's **intrinsic value**. For example, suppose the stock underlying the option in Figure 8-3 is selling for $65. Then the option to buy at $60 must be worth at least $5, because an option owner can exercise at $60 and immediately sell at $65 for a $5 gain (less the option price).

In general, a call option's intrinsic value is the difference between the underlying stock's current price and the option's strike price. The relationship is reflected in Equation 8.14.

> **Intrinsic value** is the **difference** between the stock's **current price** and the **strike price**.

(8.14)
$$V_{IC} = P_S - P_{Strk}$$

where V_{IC} = Intrinsic value of a call option,
P_S = current price of the underlying stock, and
P_{Strk} = the option's strike price.

V_{IC} is simply zero when the stock's price is less than the strike price (i.e., when the option is out of the money and $P_S < P_{Strk}$).

It's apparent from Equation 8.14 that the intrinsic value of an option is a linear function of the price of the underlying stock, P_S. A graph of the value of an option with a $60 strike price, called *an option at $60,* is shown in Figure 8-4. Notice that the intrinsic value is horizontal at zero to the left of the strike price and slopes upward to the right of the strike price.

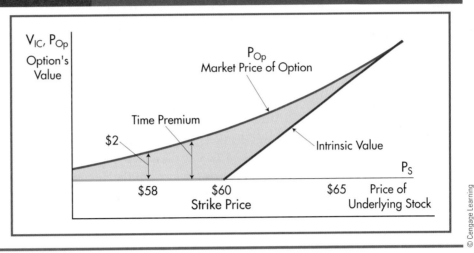

FIGURE 8-4 The Value of a Call Option

Figure 8-4 also shows the actual market price of the option, P_{Op}, the curved line lying above the intrinsic value. It's important to notice that the option always sells for a price that's at or above its intrinsic value. The difference between the intrinsic value and the option price is called the option's **time premium**, the lighter space in Figure 8-4.

Investors are willing to pay premiums over intrinsic value for options because of the chance that they will profit if the underlying stock's price goes higher. The exact shape of the graph of a particular option's premium depends on the stock's volatility, the time until expiration, and the attitude of the market about the underlying company. The general shape is shown in Figure 8-4. The premium is generally largest when a stock's price is near but a little below the option's strike price; it diminishes as the stock price rises.

This characteristic shape is a result of the way the leverage offered by the option varies with the price of the underlying stock. It's important to understand why that shape takes the form it does.

8.7e   Options and Leverage

Leverage amplifies return on investment.

Financial **leverage** is a term used to describe any technique that amplifies return on investment (ROI). For example, suppose a traditional stock investment results in a 10% return. Then a leveraged investment in the same stock might result in a 40% or 50% return over the same period. Unfortunately, leverage works on losses too, so if the stock's return turned out to be −10%, the leveraged investment would have produced −40% or −50%.

Options represent one of a number of leveraging techniques. We'll refer to Figure 8-4 to see how they work. In the diagram, imagine that the underlying stock is trading at $58 and that the time premium on a call option is $2.[8] (The option price is also $2 because

---

8. We're just assuming this premium for illustrative purposes. The actual premium would depend on factors such as the underlying stock's volatility and the time until expiration as well as the demand for options at the time. A reasonable value is $2.

its intrinsic value is zero at that stock price.) Now imagine that the stock's price increases to $65, the option is exercised, and the optioned share is sold. We'll ignore brokerage commissions for simplicity.

First, let's look at an investment in the stock over the same period. It would have been purchased at $58 and sold at $65 for a $7 profit and a return on investment (ROI) of

$$\text{ROI} = \frac{\$7}{\$58} = 12.1\%$$

Now consider investing in the option. The buyer initially paid $2 for the option. Then he exercised, buying the underlying stock at $60 and immediately selling at $65 for a $5 gain, which was reduced by the $2 option price. Hence, the option buyer's net gain is $3. *But* he had only the $2 option price tied up in the transaction. Hence, his ROI is

$$\text{ROI} = \frac{\$3}{\$2} = 150\%$$

Options offer a great deal of **leverage**.

Notice the tremendous power of the option to multiply the investor's return. The option's ROI is $(150/12.1=)$ 12 times that of a traditional stock investment. The potential for this kind of return contributes a great deal to the option's value when the stock's price is just below the strike price.

The option isn't quite as good a deal when the stock is trading above the strike price. There are two reasons for that. The stock price has to rise higher to make a given profit, and the buyer has to pay a positive intrinsic value in addition to the time premium for the option. That makes his investment larger, which decreases the leverage effect. These factors make the time premium diminish as the stock's price increases over the strike price. A numerical example is provided in the footnote.[9]

The time premium is smaller farther to the left of the strike price in Figure 8-4 simply because it becomes less likely that the stock will ever move into the money.

Options That Expire   It's important to keep in mind that options are exercisable only over limited periods at the end of which they expire and become worthless. That makes option investing very risky. For example, if an option is purchased

---

9. Suppose the premium is $1 when the stock's price is $65. That means an option buyer pays the intrinsic value of ($65 − $60 =) $5 plus the $1 premium, or $6 for the option. Then suppose the stock's price goes up by another $7 to $72.

First consider the return on an investment in the stock. It would be purchased at $65 and sold at $72 for a $7 profit and a return on investment (ROI) of

$$\text{ROI} = \$7/\$65 = 10.8\%$$

Now consider the return on the option. The buyer exercises at $60 and sells his share at $72 for a $12 gain. But the option cost $6, so his profit on the whole transaction is ($12 − $6 =) $6. And his ROI is

$$\text{ROI} = \$6/\$6 = 100\%$$

That's considerably less than the 150% generated by the same price movement from a lower starting point. As a result, the option is less attractive and the premium is lower.

Options become
worthless when they
expire.

out of the money and the underlying stock's value never exceeds the strike price, the option expires and the buyer loses the price paid for it. It's important to realize that's a 100% loss.

If an option is purchased at a price that includes a positive intrinsic value (to the right of $60 in Figure 8-4) and the underlying stock goes down in value, the option buyer's loss at expiration is the time premium paid plus the decrease in intrinsic value. That will only be a 100% loss if the stock's price declines all the way to the strike price.

As its expiration date approaches, any option's time premium shrinks to virtually zero as the time remaining for the stock's price to change diminishes. Notice that anyone owning an option with a positive intrinsic value just before expiration must act quickly to avoid losing that value.

8.7f   Trading in Options

Up until now, we've spoken as if buyers always hold options until they are either exercised or expire. In fact, that's not the case. Options can be bought and sold between investors at any time until they expire. Options on selected stocks are traded on a number of exchanges throughout the country. The largest, oldest, and best known is the **Chicago Board Options Exchange,** abbreviated CBOE.

The largest options
exchange is the **Chicago
Board Options Exchange
(CBOE)**.

Price Volatility in the Options Market   Option prices move up and down with the prices of the underlying securities, but the relative movement is much greater for options. For example, in Figure 8-4, we said the option might sell for $2 when the underlying stock's price is $58. Now suppose the stock's price goes up to $65 while there's still some time until expiration. Observe from the graph that the option sells for a price which includes its intrinsic value of ($65 − $60 =) $5 and a smaller time premium. Assume that premium is $1 (not shown), so the option's price is $6.

Option **prices move** very
rapidly.

The stock's $7 price movement from $58 to $65 is a 12.1% increase, but it has driven the option's price to triple in value from $2 to $6 (a 200% increase). As a result of this phenomenon, prices in options markets are extremely volatile and fast moving.

Options Are Rarely Exercised Before Expiration   In the situation just described, suppose the option owner believes further increases in the underlying stock's price are unlikely and wants to close out his investment even though there's a good deal of time left until expiration. In that case, virtually all traders would sell the option to another investor rather than exercise it. That's because exercising brings only ($65 − $60 =) $5, which is less than the $6 option price.

Options are **rarely
exercised** until
immediately before
expiration.

Exercising requires throwing away whatever value is in the time premium, in this case $1. As a result, options are rarely exercised before expiration when the time premium shrinks to zero.

The Downside and Risk   It's important to think about the upside and downside of option trading at the same time. There's a chance of a very high return through leverage, but there's also a good chance of a total loss. That's another way of saying leverage

Speculating in **options**
involves a good **chance of
total loss**.

works both ways, amplifying losses as well as gains. It's a big mistake to get so caught up in the potential gains that you lose sight of the losses that are also possible.

8.7g   Writing Options

Investors can issue or *write* option contracts which are bought by other investors. People write options for the premium income received when they're sold. But option writers give up whatever profits their buyers make. Option writers and buyers essentially take opposite sides of bets on which way underlying stock prices will move.

An option is written either covered or naked. In a **covered** option, the writer owns the underlying stock at the time the option is written. If the stock's price goes up and a call option buyer exercises, the writer must sell at the strike price. The option writer isn't out any additional cash, but he missed out on the price appreciation he would have had if he hadn't written the option.

For example, suppose an investor has a share of stock purchased some time ago for $40 that's currently selling for $55, and he writes a call option on it at a striking price of $60. Then suppose the stock goes to $70 and the buyer exercises. The investor must sell the share for $60 even though it's now worth $70. In a sense, he has had an "opportunity loss" of $10 by not being able to sell at $70. In reality, he realizes a gain of $20 plus the option price over his original $40 cost.

Someone who writes an option **naked** doesn't own the underlying stock at the time she writes the option. She therefore faces more risk. In the situation described in the last paragraph, if the option had been written naked, the writer would have had to buy a share at $70 and sell it at $60, losing $10 less the option price received earlier.

An option is written **covered** when the **writer owns** the optioned stock.

An option is written **naked** when the **writer does not own** the optioned stock.

CONCEPT CONNECTION   EXAMPLE 8-7

Stock Options

The following information refers to a three-month call option on the stock of Oxbow Inc.

Price of underlying stock	$30
Strike price of three-month call	25
Market price of the option	8

a. What is the intrinsic value of the option?
b. What is the option's time premium at this price?
c. Is the call in or out of the money?
d. If an investor writes and sells a covered call option, acquiring the covering stock now, how much has he invested?
e. What is the most the buyer of the call can lose?
f. What is the most the writer of the call naked can lose?
    Just before the option's expiration, Oxbow is selling for $32
g. What is the profit or loss from buying the call?
h. What is the profit or loss from writing the call naked?
i. What is the profit or loss from writing the call covered if the covering stock was acquired at the time the call was written?

SOLUTION:

a. Write Equation 8.14 and substitute.

$$V_{IC} = P_S - P_{Strk}$$
$$V_{IC} = \$30 - \$25 = \$5$$

b. The time premium is the difference between the option's price and its intrinsic value.

$$\text{time premium} = P_{Op} - V_{IC}$$
$$= \$8 - \$5 = \$3$$

c. The call option is in the money because it has a positive intrinsic value.

d. To establish a covered call, the investor buys the stock at its market price and sells an option immediately. The option's price therefore offsets the investment in the stock.

$$\text{investment} = \text{price of stock} - \text{price of call option}$$
$$= P_S - P_{Op}$$
$$= \$30 - \$8$$
$$= \$22$$

e. The most any option buyer can lose is the option price, $8 in this case.

f. A writer of a call naked has to buy the stock on the open market if his buyer exercises the option. In theory, the stock can rise to any price, so the naked call writer can lose an infinite amount. In practice, a prudent investor would limit her losses by purchasing the share when it started to move up.

g. The call owner exercises the option, paying the strike price, and simultaneously sells the share at market price. Any resulting gain (loss) is reduced (made worse) by the price paid for the call.

Market price of stock at time of exercise			$32
Less:	Strike Price	$(25)	
	Price of option	(8)	(33)
Loss			$ (1)

h. An investor who wrote a call naked buys the stock at market price when the option is exercised and sells at the strike price. The result is improved by the price received for the option.

Market price of stock at time of exercise			$(32)
Plus:	Strike price	$25	
	Price of option	8	33
Gain			$ 1

i. An investor who wrote a call covered bought the stock at market price when the option was written and sells it at the strike price. The result is improved by the price received for the option.

Market price of stock at time of exercise			$(30)
Plus:	Strike price	$25	
	Price of option	8	33
Gain			$ 3

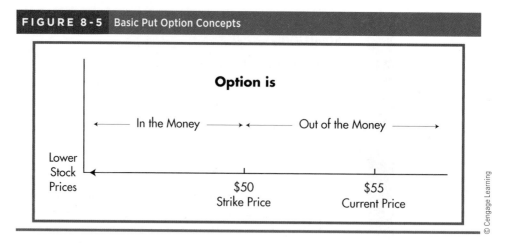

FIGURE 8-5 Basic Put Option Concepts

© Cengage Learning

8.7h Put Options

A **put** is an option to **sell**.

A **put option,** or just a *put,* is an option to sell at a specified price. Investors buy puts if they think the price of the underlying security is going to fall.

For example, suppose a stock currently has a market price of $55 and a put option is available to sell at a strike price of $50. The option buyer makes money if the stock's price drops to $45 by buying a share at that price and selling it to the option writer for $50.

A **put buyer profits** if the optioned stock's **price falls**.

Put options are in the money when the stock is selling below the strike price, $50 in this case. This idea is shown graphically in Figure 8-5.

The intrinsic value of a put is the difference between the strike price and the current price of the stock when that difference is a positive number; otherwise, it is zero. This relationship is expressed in Equation 8.15.

(8.15)
$$V_{IP} = P_{Strk} - P_S$$

where V_{IP} = Intrinsic value of a put option,
P_S = current price of the underlying stock, and
P_{Strk} = the option's strike price.

When the stock is trading above the strike price, the intrinsic value is just zero (i.e., when the option is out of the money and $P_S > P_{Strk}$). As with call options, puts sell for a time premium over their intrinsic values. This idea is shown in Figure 8-6.

8.7i Option Pricing Models

When we discussed stocks earlier in this chapter and bonds in Chapter 7, we studied pricing models that allowed us to predict the prices those securities should command in financial markets. (See the bond equation on page 294 and the Gordon model on page 356.) Options, like stocks and bonds, are traded securities, so it's logical to ask if a similar pricing model exists for them. The modeling problem is more difficult for options than for stocks and bonds, because it's hard to express an option's value as the present value of a stream of future cash flows.

FIGURE 8-6　The Value of a Put Option

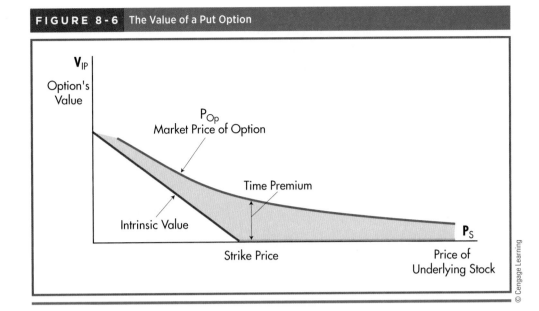

A viable option pricing model was developed some years ago by two well-known financial scholars, Fischer Black and Myron Scholes.[10] The **Black-Scholes Option Pricing Model** has achieved significant popularity despite the fact that it is extremely complex mathematically. This is possible because calculators and spreadsheets have been programmed to carry out the complex math after being given a few straightforward inputs. As a result, real-world practitioners use the model frequently.

> Option prices can be estimated using the **Black-Scholes Option Pricing Model**.

The Black-Scholes model determines option prices as a function of the following variables:

　　Underlying stock's current price

　　Option's strike price

　　Time remaining until the option's expiration

　　Volatility of the market price of the underlying stock

　　Risk-free interest rate

At this point in your study, you should just be aware that the Black-Scholes model exists and that it gives reasonable but not precisely accurate results similar to those of stock pricing models.

8.7j　Warrants

> Options are **secondary market** activities. The underlying **companies** are **not involved**.

It's important to notice that the options we've been discussing up until now are strictly secondary market phenomena (see page 183). That is, they're traded *between investors,* and the companies that issue the underlying stocks are not involved. Specifically, those companies don't get any money when options are written or exercised.

Warrants are similar to call options but are issued by the underlying companies themselves. When a warrant is exercised, the company issues new stock in return for the exercise price. Warrants are therefore primary market instruments.

---

10. "The Pricing of Options and Corporate Liabilities," *Journal of Political Economy* 81 (May–June 1973): 637–654.

Warrants are like options but are **issued by companies** which receive **equity** at exercise.

Warrants are **sweeteners attached** to other securities.

Warrants are like call options in that they give their owners the right to buy stock at a designated price over a specified period. They differ in that the time period is generally much longer, typically several years.

Warrants are usually issued in conjunction with other financing instruments as "sweeteners" to make the primary security more attractive. For example, suppose Jones Inc. wants to borrow, but isn't in good financial condition, so lenders (bond buyers) have rejected its bonds. Assume Jones has good long-term prospects, and its stock is selling for $40.

Under these conditions, lenders may be induced to take Jones's bonds if the firm *attaches* one or more warrants to each bond giving the owner the right to buy a share at $50 within the next five years. The warrants provide an incentive to buy the bonds if people think the stock is likely to go over $50 before five years have passed.

Warrants are generally **detachable** and traded independently.

Warrants can generally be *detached* and sold independently at a market value of their own. That effectively reduces the price of the bonds and increases their yield to the investor. Alternatively, bondholders can keep the warrants and exercise them for a quick gain if the stock's price rises above $50.

Notice that if the warrants are exercised, the company receives an equity infusion based on a price of $50 rather than the higher market price. The bonds are unaffected by the exercise of the warrants.

8.7k   Employee Stock Options

For many years, American companies have given certain employees stock options as part of their compensation. Employee options are actually more like warrants than traded options because they don't expire for several years and strike prices are always set well above current stock prices. Employees who receive options generally get less in salary than they otherwise would.

Stock options are often used **instead of** a portion of **salary**.

Workers like being paid with options if the firm has a bright future, because even a few options can be worth more than the salary forgone. For example, many ordinary employees at high-tech firms like Microsoft became millionaires during the 1980s and 1990s because of employee stock options.

Employee stock options **don't cost the company anything in cash** when issued.

Companies favor paying people with options because they don't cost anything in cash when issued. Since employees who receive options get lower salaries, the practice improves financial results by lowering payroll costs. Beyond that, supporters argue that the practice has an important role in keeping the United States a leader in innovation. They maintain that the chance of getting rich through options attracts the best and brightest people with innovative ideas to new companies. Without options, struggling new firms couldn't afford that kind of talent and would not prosper.

Employee options have a dilutive effect (see pages 314–317), on the interests of other shareholders, but historically most investors have been willing to accept that.

Senior executives are the **biggest recipients** of employee **stock options**.

The Executive Stock Option Problem   Recipients of the biggest employee stock options are senior executives. In larger companies, pay packages of top people typically include salary in the millions of dollars and options that can generate income in the tens of millions of dollars.

In recent years, a great deal of criticism has been leveled at option-rich packages for top management. It is argued that such pay structures give executives too much incentive to maximize stock prices. In other words, since the personal wealth of CEOs and CFOs is directly tied to stock price through options, they may be tempted to take extreme measures to keep prices up at the expense of others. We discussed this idea in Chapter 5 when we studied corporate governance and the Sarbanes–Oxley Act. We'll recap those ideas here for readers who may not have covered that section.

To understand this danger, we have to recognize that financial results drive stock prices and that top executives can manipulate financial results. The situation is a classic conflict of interest in that someone in control of a system that determines his own pay has an incentive to manipulate that system to the detriment of others. In other words, there are a number of unethical ways to make financial results seem better than they are, and the decision to use them rests with senior executives.

Stock options provide an **incentive** for executives **to misstate financial statements** to keep **stock prices up**.

If the methods are used, overstated financial results are interpreted favorably by investors who bid stock prices up. Stocks remain overvalued until the investment community discovers what has been going on. Then prices crash, rapidly destroying value for shareholders. But by then, high-flying executives have exercised their options, sold the shares, and pocketed enormous sums of cash. Essentially, executive teams get rich on money contributed by investors who were deceived into paying too much for stock.

Pension funds are an even more startling problem. Company-controlled retirement plans are often heavily invested in the company's own stock, the value of which evaporates when deceptive reporting is uncovered. The result is that top executives effectively steal their employees' retirement savings.

For years, the investing community wasn't overly concerned about this deception, because everyone assumed auditors would keep financial results reasonably accurate. In other words, people knew overstatements existed but didn't believe they were excessive.

Misstatements of financial results **uncovered** in the early 2000s **undermined confidence** in the **honesty** of corporate **management**.

But in the early 2000s, it became apparent that auditors couldn't always be counted on to police corporate financial reporting, because they were caught up in a conflict of interest of their own. Since auditors are paid by the companies they audit, they're likely to accede to the wishes of the senior executives they're supposed to be watching. They do that by interpreting accounting rules liberally and signing off on financial statements that are deceptive and likely to mislead investors.

In the early 2000s, the stock prices of several major corporations collapsed when the investing community learned that their financial statements contained major misrepresentations. The best-known cases were Enron, a leading player in energy; WorldCom, the telecommunications giant that owned MCI; and Tyco, a conglomerate that participates in a wide variety of businesses. In addition, Arthur Andersen, Enron's auditor and one of the world's largest accounting firms, went out of business as a result of its role in the Enron debacle.

These collapses led to a loss of confidence in corporate management by the investing public. Option-based compensation wasn't the only problem uncovered, but many feel the system sets up a climate that encourages management to focus on short-term financial results and inevitably leads to less than honest reporting.

The executive stock option system sets up a **conflict of interest** that can **lead to dishonest** reporting.

The scandal led to a major review of financial reporting and auditing procedures by the accounting profession as well as congressional legislation aimed at punishing knowing deception by senior executives. A major issue within the overhaul was a requirement that companies recognize employee stock options as expenses at the time they're issued even though no cash is actually disbursed. Doing that makes giving executives overly generous option packages less attractive to issuing companies, because expense recognized on the income statement lowers profits, and that generally has an adverse effect on investor enthusiasm.

Expensing options also presents a technical valuation problem, because at the time of issue, no one knows how much an option will eventually be worth. That's because it's impossible to say how high the price of the underlying stock will rise. Hence it's hard to know how much to charge to expense when an option is granted.

Nevertheless, as we've learned in this section, options do have market value when they're issued even if the underlying stock is trading below the striking price. Hence it's quite reasonable, and definitely conservative, to recognize some expense at that time. Further, the valuation problem can be handled, at least approximately, using sophisticated option pricing techniques such as the Black-Scholes model we discussed earlier (page 385).

The Accounting Profession's Response to Expensing Options upon Issue

Accounting rules and conventions are created and disseminated by the Financial Accounting Standards Board (FASB). That body issued a statement regarding the financial treatment of options given as compensation in 1995. The statement was promulgated as FASB 123, and recommended that companies expense options. Unfortunately, the statement was vague on the method of calculating the amounts that should be expensed. It also left the decision on whether to expense up to individual companies. As might be expected, virtually no one chose to recognize expense when options were issued as a result of FASB 123.

The board revisited the question in response to the events of the early 2000s, issuing a revised statement in 2004, FASB 123(R). The revision made expensing options mandatory for public companies beginning in 2005. It also gave more guidance on how to value them. The Black-Scholes model is still available but so are other slightly less involved techniques known as lattice models.

The high-tech companies that make liberal use of options as compensation argued vigorously against an expensing requirement right up until the time it was implemented. They claimed it would put them at a competitive disadvantage and drive venture capital out of the country. So far, however, the practice hasn't seemed to have had much effect on investors or the high-tech industry.

CONCEPT CONNECTIONS

EXAMPLE 8-1   Stock Valuation Based on Projected Cash Flows, *page 352*

EXAMPLE 8-2   Growth Rates, *page 355*

EXAMPLE 8-3   The Constant Growth (Gordon) Model, *page 357*

EXAMPLE 8-5   Valuation Based on Two-Stage Growth, *page 359*

EXAMPLE 8-6   Pricing Preferred Stock, *page 373*

EXAMPLE 8-7   Stock Options, *page 382*

QUESTIONS

1. Discuss the nature of stock as an investment. Do most stockholders play large roles in the management of the firms in which they invest? Why or why not?

2. Compare and contrast the nature of cash flows stemming from an investment in stock with those coming from bonds.

3. Verbally rationalize the validity of a stock valuation model that doesn't contain a selling price as a source of cash flow to the investor. Give two independent arguments.

4. Why are growth rate models practical and convenient ways to look at stock valuation?

5. What is meant by normal growth? Contrast normal and super normal growth. How long can each last? Why?

6. Describe the approach to valuing a stock that is expected to grow at more than one rate in the future. Can there be more than two rates? What two things have to be true of the last rate?

7. Discuss the accuracy of stock valuation, and compare it with that of bond valuation.

8. Do stocks that don't pay dividends have value? Why?

9. How is the IPO price of a stock determined? Is that price likely to be the stock's intrinsic value?

10. Is the IPO Pop experienced by most new stocks likely to be a reflection of market forces driving shares toward their intrinsic values?

11. Preferred stock is said to be a hybrid of common stock and bonds. Explain fully. Describe the cash flows associated with preferred and their valuation.

12. Discuss the relative riskiness of investment in bonds, common stock, and preferred stock.

13. Compare fundamental analysis and technical analysis. Which makes more sense to you?

14. What does the efficient market hypothesis say? What is its implication for stock analysis?

15. Options are more exciting than investing in the underlying stocks because they offer leverage. Explain this statement.

16. Is investing in options really investing, or is it more like gambling?

BUSINESS ANALYSIS

1. Your cousin Charlie came into a large inheritance last year and invested the entire amount in the common stock of IBD Inc., a large computer company. Subsequently, he's been very interested in the company and watches it closely. Recently the newspaper carried a story about major strategic changes at IBD, including massive layoffs and business realignments. Charlie was devastated. He doesn't understand how the firm could have made such changes without the knowledge or approval of its stockholders. Write a brief letter to Charlie explaining how things really work.

PROBLEMS

Dividend and Capital Gain Yields, page 350

1. Paul Dargis has analyzed five stocks and estimated the dividends they will pay next year as well as their prices at the end of the year. His projections are shown below.

Stock	Current Price	Projected Dividend	Projected Price
A	$37.50	$1.45	$43.00
B	24.50	.90	26.50
C	57.80	2.10	63.50
D	74.35	None	81.00
E	64.80	3.15	63.00

Compute the dividend yield, capital gain yield, and total one-year return implied by Paul's estimates for each stock.

Stock Valuation Based on Projected Cash Flows: Concept Connection Example 8-1 (page 352)

2. The stock of Sedly Inc. is expected to pay the following dividends.

	Year			
	1	**2**	**3**	**4**
Dividend	$2.25	$3.50	$1.75	$2.00

At the end of the fourth year its value is expected to be $37.50. What should Sedly sell for today if the return on stocks of similar risk is 12%?

3. Fred Tibbits has made a detailed study of the denim clothing industry. He's particularly interested in a company called Denhart Fashions that makes stylish denim apparel for children and teenagers. Fred has done a forecast of Denhart's earnings and looked at its dividend payment record. He's come to the conclusion that the firm will pay a dividend of $5.00 for the next two years followed by a year of $6.50. Fred's investment plan is to buy Denhart now, hold it for three years, and then sell. He thinks the price will be about $75 when he sells. What is the most Fred should be willing to pay for a share of Denhart if he can earn 10% on investments of similar risk?

Growth Rates: Concept Connection Example 8-2 (page 355)

4. Mitech Corp's stock price has been growing at approximately 8% for several years and is now $30. Based on past growth rate performance, what would you expect the stock's price to be in five years?

The Constant Growth (Gordon) Model: Concept Connection Example 8-3 (page 357)

5. The Spinnaker Company has paid an annual dividend of $2 per share for some time. Recently, the board of directors voted to grow the dividend by 6% per year from now on. What is the most you would be willing to pay for a share of Spinnaker if you expect a 10% return on your stock investments?

6. The Pancake Corporation recently paid a $3 dividend and is expected to grow at 5% forever. Investors generally require an expected return of at least 9% before they'll buy stocks similar to those of Pancake.

   a. What is Pancake's intrinsic value?

   b. Is it a bargain if it's selling at $76 a share?

7. Tyler Inc.'s most recent annual dividend was $3.55 a share. The firm has been growing at a consistent 4% rate for several years, but analysts generally believe better times are ahead and future growth will be in the neighborhood of 5%. The stock is currently selling for $75. Stocks similar to Tyler earn returns ranging from 8% to 10%.

   a. Calculate values for a share of Tyler at interest rates of 8%, 9%, and 10%.

   b. Do you think Tyler is a good investment for the long run—that is, for someone planning to hold onto it for 10 or more years?

   c. Do you think it's a good investment for the short term? That is, should you buy it with the expectation of selling in a relatively short period, say a year or less?

   d. Repeat the calculations in part (a) assuming that instead of rising, Tyler's growth rate (1) remains at 4% or (2) declines to 3%.

   e. Comment on the range of prices that you've calculated in parts (a) and (d).

8. The Anderson Pipe Co. just paid an annual dividend of $3.75 and is expected to grow at 8% for the foreseeable future. Harley Bevins generally demands a return of 9% when he invests in companies similar to Anderson.

   a. What is the most Harley should be willing to pay for a share of Anderson?

   b. Is your answer reasonable? What's going on here? What should Harley do with this result?

9. Cavanaugh Construction specializes in designing and building custom homes. Business has been excellent, and Cavanaugh projects a 10% growth rate for the foreseeable future. The company just paid a $3.75 dividend. Comparable stocks are returning 11%.

   a. What is the intrinsic value of Cavanaugh stock?

   b. Does this seem reasonable? Why or why not?

   c. If Cavanaugh's growth rate is only 8.5% and comparable stocks are really returning 12%, what is Cavanaugh's intrinsic value?

   d. Do these relatively small changes in assumptions justify the change in the intrinsic value? Why or why not?

Valuation Based on Two-Stage Growth: Concept Connection Example 8-5 (page 359)

10. The Miller Milk Company has just come up with a new lactose-free dessert product for people who can't eat or drink ordinary dairy products. Management expects the new product to fuel sales growth at 30% for about two years. After that, competitors will copy the idea and produce similar products, and growth will return to about 3%, which is normal for the dairy industry in the area. Miller recently paid an annual dividend of $2.60, which will grow with the company. The return on stocks similar to Miller's is typically around 10%. What is the most you would pay for a share of Miller?

     Problems 11 through 13 refer to Softek Inc., a leader in the computer software field. Softek has two potentially big-selling products under development. Alpha, the first new product, seems very likely to catch on and is expected to drive the firm's growth rate to 25% for the next two years. However, software products have short lives, and growth can be expected to return to a more normal rate of 6% after that period if something new isn't launched immediately.

     Beta, the second product, is a logical follow-on, but management isn't as confident about its success as it is about Alpha's. Softek's most recent yearly dividend was $4, and firms in the industry typically return 14% on stockholder investments.

11. You are an investment analyst for a brokerage firm and have been asked to develop a recommendation about Softek for the firm's clients. You've studied the fundamentals of the industry and the firm, and are now ready to determine what the stock should sell for based on the present value of future cash flows.

    a. Calculate a value for Softek's stock assuming product Alpha is successful but Beta isn't. In other words, assume two years of growth at 25% followed by 6% growth lasting indefinitely.

    b. Calculate a price assuming Beta is also successful and holds Softek's growth rate at 25% for two additional years.

12. Calculate a price for Softek assuming Alpha is successful and Beta is also successful but doesn't do quite as well as Alpha. Assume Softek grows at 25% for two years and then at 18% for two more. After that it continues to grow at 6%. (*Hint:* Don't be confused by the fact that there are now three growth periods. Just calculate successive dividends, multiplying by one plus the growth rate in effect until you get the first dividend into the period of normal growth. Then apply the Gordon model. A time line is a must for this problem.)

13. How would you advise clients about Softek stock as an investment under the following conditions? Give reasons for your advice. (No calculations.)

    a. Softek is currently selling at a price very near that calculated in part (a) of Problem 11.

    b. It is selling near the price calculated in Problem 12.

    c. It is selling at a price slightly above that calculated in part (b) of Problem 11.

14. Garrett Corp. has been going through a difficult financial period. Over the past three years, its stock price has dropped from $50 to $18 per share. Throughout this downturn, Garrett has

managed to pay a $1 dividend each year. Management feels the worst is over but intends to maintain the $1 dividend for three more years, after which they plan to increase it by 6% per year indefinitely. Comparable stocks are returning 11%.

a. If these projections are accurate, is Garrett stock a good buy at $18?

b. How do you think the market feels about Garrett's management?

15. General Machine Works Inc. (GMW) has been losing money for some time but has managed to maintain an annual dividend of $1. The company's strategy is to restructure by getting smaller while working on labor and product-line problems at the same time. Once that's done, management feels the firm will return to profitability and begin a long period of growth at about 3% per year. GMW's stock price has been declining steadily for some time and is now the neighborhood of $20 per share.

   You're an analyst for Barnstead and Heath, a small brokerage firm that employs a number of financial consultants who advise clients on stock investments. Some of the consultants feel that GMW's strategy will work as planned and have asked you if they should tell their clients that this is a good time to buy GMW stock. How would you advise them? Assume clients demand a return of about 10%, and dividends will shrink by 10% per year for three years.

16. Sudsy Inc. recently paid an annual dividend of $1.00 per share. Analysts expect that amount to be paid for three years after which dividends will grow at a constant 5% per year indefinitely. The stock is currently trading at $20, and investors require a 15% return on similar issues. Has the stock market properly priced Sudsy's stock?

Pricing Preferred Stock: Concept Connection Example 8-6 (page 373)

17. Blackstone Corporation's $7 preferred was issued five years ago. The risk-appropriate interest rate for the issue is currently 11%. What is this preferred selling for today?

18. Fox Woodworking Inc. issued preferred shares at a face value of $50 to yield 9% 10 years ago. The shares are currently selling at $60. What return are they earning for investors who buy them today?

19. The following preferred stocks are returning 8.5% to their owners who purchased the shares when they were issued:

Stock	Dividend	Current Price
A	5%	$14.71
B	7	41.18
C	11	129.41

   Calculate the prices at which they were issued.

20. Koski and Hass Inc. (K&H) just paid a $2 dividend, which is expected to grow at 5% indefinitely. The return on comparable stocks is 9%. What percent of the intrinsic value of K&H stock is attributable to dividends paid more than 20 years in the future?

Stock Options: Concept Connection Example 8-7 (page 382)

21. Seth Harris is an avid investor who likes to speculate on stock price changes. Lately, he's become bored with the slow movement of most stock prices and thinks options might be more exciting. He has been following the stock of Chelsea Club Inc., a women's apparel manufacturer. Chelsea's stock price has been stable for more than a year, but Seth is convinced it will increase in the near future but probably not rapidly.

   Amanda Johnson owns 1,000 shares of Chelsea Club purchased a year ago at $37. She thinks the stock's price will continue in the upper $30s indefinitely and may even fall a little. Her broker has recommended writing options as a source of income on stagnant stocks.

   Chelsea is selling for $38, and six-month call options at a $36 strike price sell for $4.

This morning Amanda wrote call options on her 1,000 shares, which Seth bought through an options exchange. At the time of that transaction:

a. What was the intrinsic value of an option?

b. What was the option's time premium?

c. Was the call in or out of the money?

d. How much has Amanda invested?

e. What is the most Seth can make or lose?

f. What is the most Amanda can make or lose?

It's almost six months later, Chelsea is selling for $44, Amanda's options are about to expire, and Seth exercises.

g. What is Seth's profit or loss?

h. What is Amanda's profit or loss?

i. Does Amanda incur an "opportunity loss"? If so, how much is it?

j. What would Amanda's profit or loss have been if her call had been written naked?

COMPUTER PROBLEMS

22. The Rollins Metal Company is engaged in a long-term planning process and is trying to choose among several strategic options that imply different future growth rates for the company. Management feels that the main benefit of higher growth is that it enhances the firm's current stock price. However, high growth strategies have a cost in that they generally involve considerable risk. Higher risk means that investors demand higher returns, which tends to depress current stock price.

    Management is having a hard time evaluating this cost–benefit trade-off because growth and risk are conceptual abstractions. In other words, it's hard to visualize how growth and risk interact with each other as well as with other things to produce stock prices. Management can, however, intuitively associate each strategy option with a growth rate and a required rate of return implied by risk.

    You are a financial consultant who's been hired to help make some sense out of the situation. You feel your best approach is to develop a systematic relationship between return, growth, and stock price that you can show to management visually.

    Use the STCKVAL program to develop the following chart assuming the strategic options result in different constant growth rates that start immediately. The firm's last dividend was $2.35 per share.

    The Price of Rollins Stock as a Function of Growth Rate and the Return Required by Investors

	Growth Rates (g)			
Required Returns (k)	6%	8%	10%	12%
7%		—	—	—
9%			—	—
11%				—
13%				

    Can you make any general comments about the risk-return trade-off based on your chart?

23. Suppose the strategic options available to the Rollins company in the last problem result in *temporarily* enhanced growth. Each option can be associated with a super normal growth rate that lasts for some period after which growth returns to the firm's normal 5%. Further suppose the duration of the super normal growth is a variable which can also be affected by strategic policy. Use the STCKVAL program for two-stage growth to develop the following chart assuming a required return of 10%.

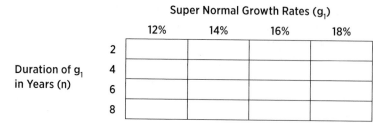

The Price of Rollins Stock as a Function of Temporary Growth Rate
and Duration at a Required Return Rate of 10%

| | | Super Normal Growth Rates (g_1) | | | |
		12%	14%	16%	18%
	2				
Duration of g_1	4				
in Years (n)	6				
	8				

Can you use your chart to make any general comments about the risk-return trade-off under this assumption about the nature of the strategic options?

DEVELOPING SOFTWARE

24. Program your own two-stage growth model for two years of super normal growth (g_1) followed by normal growth (g_2) lasting forever. Treat both growth rates, the last dividend (D_0), and the required rate of return (k) as inputs. Here's how to do it. (Refer to Figure 8-2 and Example 8-5 on pages 359–360. You'll be programming exactly that procedure.)

   1. Lay out four cells horizontally in your spreadsheet (to represent a time line starting with time zero).
   2. Put D_0 in the first cell.
   3. Form the next two cells by multiplying the one before by $(1 + g_1)$.
   4. Form the fourth cell by multiplying the third by $(1 + g_2)$.
   5. Calculate P_2 in another cell using the Gordon model with the fourth cell in the numerator and $(k - g_2)$ in the denominator.
   6. Form P_0 as the sum of the present values of the middle two cells in the time line and the present value of the cell carrying P_2.

25. Program a model for three years of super normal growth.

 THOMSON REUTERS

Go to **www.cengage.com/thomsonone**, select your book and click on the Thomson ONE button. Enter Thomson ONE—Business School Edition by using the username and password you created when you registered the serial number on your access card. Select a problem for this chapter, and you'll see an expanded version that includes instructions on how to navigate within the Thomson ONE system, as well as some additional explanation of the presentation format.

26. We can use Thomson ONE to value stocks with the Gordon Model. We'll illustrate with Sherwin Williams (SHW), a stable paint manufacturer.

   Access Sherwin in Thomson ONE and calculate growth rates for dividends, earnings per share, and revenues. Select a rate you think reflects the company's potential. Use it and the most recent dividend to estimate intrinsic value assuming a modest 7% or 8% return. Find Sherwin's current stock price. Is it a good buy? Vary your assumptions about growth rate and return. What does it take to get an intrinsic value in line with the market's thinking?

   Now try to do the same thing for the companies we worked on before. Summarize the problems you encounter. Do you think a two-stage Gordon model might work for Harley-Davidson?

27. We can also use a stock's price earnings ratio (P/E) to gauge whether it is over- or undervalued. Reread the Insights box on page 362, and make a chart listing the companies we've been working with down the left side along with column headings for the current P/E, six years of history, and the P/E ratios of a few peers. Access the Thomson ONE and record these ratios on your chart.

    A firm's P/E ratio can be low in its historical range or relative to its peers because it has poor prospects, in which case the market correctly bids down price. However, the market often temporarily overreacts to bad news by driving a stock's price down. Then a low P/E can be a buying opportunity.

    Combine your P/E information with any general information about these companies or the economy you have and make a judgment as to whether their stocks are undervalued, overvalued, or priced about right.

Risk and Return

Chapter Outline

This chapter explores the relationship between risk and return inherent in investing in securities, especially stocks. In what follows, we'll define risk and return precisely, investigate the nature of their relationship, and find that there are ways to limit exposure to investment risk.

The body of thought we'll be working with is known as *portfolio theory.* The ideas behind the theory were motivated by observations of the returns on various investments over many years. We'll begin by reviewing those observations.

9.1 Why Study Risk and Return?

As we've said before, there are fundamentally two ways to invest: debt and equity. Debt involves lending by buying bonds or putting money into savings accounts. Equity means buying stock.

People are constantly looking at the relative returns on these two investment vehicles. It has always been apparent that long-run average returns on equity investments are much higher than those available on debt. Indeed, over most of the twentieth century, equity returns averaged between 9% and 10% while debt returns averaged between 3% and 4%. At the same time, inflation averaged about 3%, so debt investors didn't get ahead by much!

The period from 2000 to the middle of 2012 seems to contradict what we've just said about equity (stock) investments returning 9% or 10% in the long run. Indeed, the return on the overall stock market (measured by the S&P 500) between 2000 and 2010 was virtually zero. That performance led to calling the period a "lost decade."

But in fact there have been other "lost decades" in the last 100 years. The 1930s actually saw overall negative returns, while the market was more or less stagnant in the late sixties and seventies. More important in terms of averages is the observation that equity returns immediately following such periods of poor performance has generally been good enough to make up for the lost time. So, although ten years seems like a long time, economically it isn't the long run, and most experts think high average returns to equity will persist.

But average returns aren't the whole story. Although equity returns tend to be much higher than debt returns in the long run, they are subject to huge swings during shorter periods. In a given one- or two-year period, for example, the annual return on stock investments can be as high as 30% or as low as −30%. The high side of this range is great news, but the low side is a disaster to most investors.

The short-term variability of equity returns is a very important observation because few people invest for really long periods, say 75 years. Most everyone has a much shorter time horizon of 2, 10, or perhaps 20 years. The variability of equity returns means that if you invest in stock today with a goal of putting a child through college in five years, there's a good chance that you'll lose money instead of making it. That's a frightening possibility to most people.

As a result of these observations, people began to wonder if there wasn't some way to invest in equities (stocks) that would take advantage of their high average rate of return but minimize their risk at the same time.

Thinking about that question resulted in the development of some techniques that enable investors to control and manage the risk to which they subject themselves while searching for high returns. These techniques involve investing in combinations of stocks called **portfolios**.

In the rest of this chapter, we'll gain a better understanding of the concept of risk and see how it fits into the portfolio idea. Keep in mind throughout that the reason we do this is to *capture the high average returns of equity investing while limiting the associated risk as much as possible.*

The **return on equity (stock)** investments has historically been **much higher** than the **return on debt** investments.

Equity is historically much **riskier** than debt.

Portfolios are collections of financial assets held by investors.

9.1a   The General Relationship Between Risk and Return

People usually use the word "risk" when referring to the probability that something bad will happen. For example, we often talk about the risk of having an accident or of losing a job.

In financial dealings, risk tends to be thought of as the probability of losing some or all of the money we put into a deal. For example, we talked about the risk of default on a loan in Chapter 5, meaning the probability that the loan wouldn't be paid back and the lender would lose his or her investment. Similarly, an investment in a share of stock results in a loss if the price drops before an investor sells. The probability of that happening is what most people think of as risk in stock investments.

In general, investment opportunities that offer higher returns also entail higher risks. Let's consider a hypothetical example to illustrate this central idea.

Suppose you could invest in a stock that will do one of two things. It will either return 15% on your investment or become valueless, resulting in a total loss of your money. Imagine for the sake of illustration that there's no middle ground; you either make 15% or lose everything. Suppose the chance of total loss is 1% and the chance of a 15% return is 99%. The *risk* associated with investing in this stock can be thought of as a 1% chance of total loss.

Let's further assume that all stocks behave in this peculiar way and offer only two possible outcomes, some positive return or a total loss. However, the level of positive return and the probability of total loss can be different for each stock.

It's important to visualize this hypothetical world. Every stock has a positive level of return that's quite likely to occur. *Investors more or less expect to receive that return,* yet they realize that every stock investment also carries some risk, the probability that they'll lose their entire investment instead.

Now, suppose you're not happy with the 15% return offered by the stock we started with, so you look around for an issue that offers a higher rate. **As a general rule, you'd find that stocks offering higher likely returns also come with higher probabilities of total loss**. For example, an issue offering a 20% return might entail a 3% chance of total loss, while something offering a 25% return might have a 10% chance of loss, and so on.

This relationship is the financial expression of a simple fact of business life. Higher profit business opportunities are generally untried ventures that have a good chance of doing poorly or failing altogether. As a result, higher likely return goes hand in hand with higher risk.

Of course, in the real world there aren't just two possible outcomes associated with each investment opportunity. The actual return on a stock investment can be more or less than the most likely value by any amount. The illustration's total loss is in fact a worst-case situation. The real definition of risk therefore has to be more complex than the one in the illustration. Nevertheless, the general rule remains the same: Higher financial rewards (returns) come with higher risks.

Unfortunately, it isn't easy to understand how the real risk–return relationship works—that is, to predict just how much risk is associated with a given level of return. Understanding the real risk–return relationship involves two things. First we have to define risk in a measurable way, and then we have to relate that measurement to return according to some formula that can be written down.

It's important to realize that the true definition of risk isn't simple and easily measurable the way it was in the illustration. There we had only one bad outcome, total loss, so risk was just the probability of that outcome. In reality, there are any number of outcomes that are less favorable than we'd like, and each has a probability of happening. Some outcomes are very bad, like losing everything, while others are just mildly unpleasant, like earning a return that's a little less than we expected. Somehow we have to define risk to include all of these possibilities.

Portfolio Theory—Modern Thinking About Risk and Return   Recent thinking in theoretical finance, known as **portfolio theory**, grapples with this issue. The theory defines investment risk in a way that can be measured, and then relates the

Stocks with **higher likely returns** generally also have **higher risks of loss**.

measurable risk in any investment to the level of return that can be expected from that investment in a predictable way.

Portfolio theory has had a major impact on the practical activities of the real world. The theory has important implications for how the securities industry functions every day, and its terminology is in use by practitioners all the time. Because of the central role played by this piece of thinking, it's important that students of finance develop a working familiarity with its principles and terminology. We'll develop that knowledge in this chapter.

9.1b   The Return on an Investment

We developed the idea of a return on an investment rather carefully in the last two chapters. Recall that investments could be made in securities that represent either debt or equity, and that the return was the discount (interest) rate that equated the present value of the future cash flows coming from an investment to its current price.

In simpler terms, you can think about the return associated with an investment as a rate of interest that the present valuing process makes a lot like the interest rate on a bank account. In effect, the rate of return ties all of an investment's future cash flows into a neat bundle, which can then be compared with the return on other investments.

One-Year Investments   In what follows, we'll use the idea of returns on investments held for just one year to illustrate points, so it's a good idea to keep those definitions in mind in formula form. We developed the expressions in Chapters 7 and 8, but will repeat them here for convenience.

A debt investment is a loan, and the return is just the loan's interest rate. This is simply the ratio of the interest paid to the loan principal.

(9.1)
$$k = \frac{\text{interest paid}}{\text{loan amount}}$$

This formulation leads to the convenient idea that a return is what the investor receives divided by what he or she invests. A stock investment involves the receipt of dividends and a capital gain (loss). If a stock investment is held for one year, the return can be written as

(9.2)
$$k = \frac{D_1 + (P_1 - P_0)}{P_0}$$

Here P_0 is the price today, while P_1 and D_1 are respectively the price and dividend at the end of the year. This is Equation 8.1, which we developed on page 349.

Returns, Expected and Required   Whenever people make an investment, we'll assume they have some expectation of what the rate of return will be. In the case of a bank account, that's simply the interest rate quoted by the bank. In the case of a stock investment, the return we expect depends on the dividends we think the company is going to pay and what we think the future price of the stock will be. This anticipated return is simply called the **expected return**. It's based on whatever information the investor has available about the nature of the security at the time he or she buys it. In other words, the expected return is based on Equation 9.2 with *projected* values inserted for P_1 and D_1.

The **expected return** on a stock is the return investors feel is most likely to occur based on currently available information.

It's important to realize that *no rational person makes any investment without some expectation of return*. People understand that in stock investments the actual return probably won't turn out to be exactly what they expected when they made the investment because future prices and dividends are uncertain. Nevertheless, they have some expectation of what the return is most likely to be.

At the same time, investors have a notion about what return they must receive in order to make particular investments. We call this concept the **required return** on the stock.

The required return is related to the perceived risk of the investment. People have different ideas about the safety of investments in different stocks. If there's a good chance that a company will get into trouble, causing a low return or a loss on an investment in its stock, people will require a higher expected return to make the investment.

A person might say, "I won't put money into IBM stock unless the expected return is at least 9%." That percentage is the person's *required return* for an investment in IBM. Each individual will have a different required return for every stock offered. Exactly how people form required returns is a central subject of this chapter. The important point is that *substantial investment will take place in a particular stock only if the generally expected return exceeds most people's required return for that stock*. In other words, people won't buy an issue unless they think it will return at least as much as they require.

> The **required return** on a stock is the minimum rate at which investors will purchase or hold a stock based on their perceptions of its risk.

> Significant investment in a stock occurs only if the **expected return exceeds the required return** for a substantial number of investors.

9.1c   Risk—A Preliminary Definition

We talked about risk earlier, and alluded to the fact that its definition in finance is somewhat complicated. The definition we'll eventually work with is a little different from the way we normally use the word. We'll need to develop the idea slowly, so we'll begin with a simple definition that we'll modify and add to as we progress. The simple definition is consistent with our everyday notion of risk as the chance that something bad will happen to us.

For now, **risk** *for an investor is the chance (probability) that the return on an investment will turn out to be less than he or she expected when the investment was made*. Notice that this definition includes more than just losing money. If someone makes an investment expecting a return of 10%, risk includes the probability that the return will turn out to be 9%, even though that's a positive return. Let's look at this definition of risk in the context of two different kinds of investment.

> A preliminary definition of investment **risk** is the **probability that return will be less than expected**.

First consider investing in a bank account. What's the chance that a depositor will receive less interest than the bank promised when the account was opened? Today that chance is very small, because most bank accounts are insured by the federal government. Even if the bank goes out of business, depositors get their money, so we're virtually guaranteed the promised return. A bank account has virtually zero risk because there's little or no chance that the investor won't get the expected return.

Now consider an investment in stock. Looking at Equation 9.2, we can see that the return is determined by the future price of the stock and its future dividend. Because there are no guarantees about what those future amounts will be, the return on a stock investment may turn out to be different from what was expected at the time the stock was purchased. It may be more than what was anticipated or it may be less. Risk is just the probability that it's anything less.

Feelings About Risk   Most people have negative feelings about bearing risk in their investment activities. For example, if investors are offered a choice between a bank account that pays 8% and a stock investment with an expected return of 8%, almost everyone would choose the bank account because it has less risk. People prefer lower risk if the expected return is the same. We call this characteristic **risk aversion**, meaning that most of us don't like bearing risk.

Risk averse investors prefer lower risk when expected returns are equal.

At the same time, most people see a trade-off between risk and return. If offered a choice between the 8% bank account and a stock whose expected return is 10%, some will still choose the bank account, but many will now choose the stock.

It's important to understand that risk aversion doesn't mean that risk is to be avoided at all costs. It is simply a negative that can be offset with more anticipated money—in other words, with a higher expected return.

We're now armed with sufficient background material to attempt an excursion into portfolio theory.

9.2 Portfolio Theory

Portfolio theory is a statistical model of the investment world. We'll develop the ideas using some statistical terms and concepts, but will avoid most of the advanced mathematics. We'll begin with a brief review of a few statistical concepts.

9.2a Review of the Concept of a Random Variable

A **random variable** is the outcome of a chance process and has a probability distribution.

In statistics, a **random variable** is the outcome of a chance process. Such variables can be either *discrete* or *continuous.* Discrete variables can take only specific values whereas continuous variables can take any value within a specified range.

CONCEPT CONNECTION   **EXAMPLE 9-1**

Discrete Probability Distributions

Suppose you toss a coin four times, count the number of heads, and call the result X. Then X, the number of heads, is a random variable that can take any of five values: 0, 1, 2, 3, or 4. For any series of four tosses, there's a probability of getting each value of X [written P(X)] as follows.[1]

X	P(X)
0	.0625
1	.2500
2	.3750
3	.2500
4	.0625
	1.0000

Ensuper/Shutterstock.com

---

1. The probabilities can be calculated by enumerating all of the 16 possible head-tail sequences in four coin tosses and counting the number of heads in each. Each sequence has an equal one-sixteenth probability (.0625) of happening. The probability of any number of heads is one-sixteenth times the number of sequences containing that number of heads.

Such a representation of all the possible outcomes along with the probability of each is called the *probability distribution for the random variable X.* Notice that the probabilities of all the possible outcomes have to sum to 1.0. The probability distribution can be shown in tabular form like this or graphically, as in Figure 9-1.

The number of heads in a series of coin tosses is a *discrete* random variable because it can take on only a limited number of discrete values, each of which has a distinct probability. In our example, the only outcomes possible are 0, 1, 2, 3, and 4. There can't be more than four heads or fewer than zero, nor can there be a fractional number of heads.

The Mean or Expected Value   The value that the random variable is most likely to take is an important statistical concept. In symmetrical probability distributions with only one peak like the one in Figure 9-1, it's at the center of the distribution under its highest point. We call this most likely outcome the *mean* or the *expected value* of the distribution, and write it by placing a bar over the variable. In the coin toss illustration, the mean is written as

$$\overline{X} = 2$$

Thinking of the mean as the value of the random variable at the highest point of the distribution makes intuitive sense, but the statistical definition is more precise.

> The **mean** or **expected value** of a distribution is the most likely outcome for the random variable.

FIGURE 9-1   **Discrete Probability Distribution**

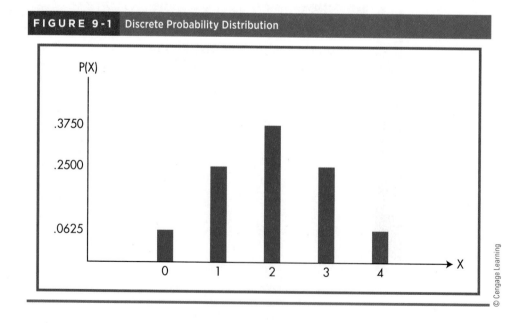

The mean is actually the weighted average of all possible outcomes where each outcome is weighted by its probability. This is written as

$$\bar{X} = \sum_{i=1}^{n} X_i P(X_i)$$

where X_i is the value of each outcome and $P(X_i)$ is its probability. The summation sign means that we add this figure for each of the n possible outcomes.

CONCEPT CONNECTION   EXAMPLE 9-2

Calculating the Mean of a Discrete Distribution

Calculating the mean for discrete distributions is relatively easy. For the coin toss illustration, we just list each possible outcome along with its probability, multiply, and sum.

X	P(X)	X * P(X)
0	.0625	.00
1	.2500	.25
2	.3750	.75
3	.2500	.75
4	.0625	.25
	1.0000	$\bar{X}$ = 2.00

The mean is simply the mathematical expression of the everyday idea of an average. That is, if we repeat the *series* of coin tosses a number of times, the average outcome will be 2. Notice that the process of multiplying something related to an outcome (in this case the outcome itself) by the probability of the outcome and summing gives an average value. We'll use the technique again shortly.

The Variance and Standard Deviation   A second important characteristic of a random variable is its variability. The idea gets at how far a typical observation of the variable is likely to deviate from the mean. Here's an example.

Suppose we define a random variable by estimating the heights of randomly selected buildings in a city. Allow 12 feet per story. The results might range from 12 feet for one-story structures to more than 1,000 feet for skyscrapers. Suppose the average height turned out to be 30 stories or 360 feet. It's easy to see that a typical building would have a height that's very different from that average. Some office buildings would be hundreds of feet higher, while all private homes would be hundreds shorter.

Now, suppose we did the same thing for telephone poles, measuring to the nearest foot, and got an average height of 30 feet. Unlike buildings, we'd find that telephone poles don't vary much around 30 feet. Some might be 31 feet and some 29, but not very many of them would be far out of that range.

The point is that there's a great deal of difference in *variability around the mean* in different distributions. Telephone pole heights are closely clustered around their average, while building heights are widely dispersed around theirs.

In statistics, this notion of how far a typical observation is likely to be from the mean is described by the **standard deviation** of the distribution, usually written as the Greek letter sigma, σ. You can think of the standard deviation as the average (standard) distance (deviation) between an outcome and the mean. For example, in our building illustration the "average" (typical) building might be 20 stories different in height than the mean height of all buildings. As we'll explain shortly, that interpretation isn't quite right because of the way standard deviations are calculated, but it's a good way to visualize the concept.

The standard deviation idea intuitively begins as an average distance from the mean. One would think that could be calculated in the same way as the mean itself. That is, by taking the distance of each possible outcome from the mean, multiplying it by the probability of the outcome, and summing over all outcomes. Mathematically that would look like this:

$$\sum_{i=1}^{n}(X_i - \overline{X})P(X_i)$$

The problem with this formulation is that the deviations [the $(X_i - \overline{X})$'s] are of different signs depending on the side of the mean on which each outcome (X_i) is located. Hence, they cancel each other when summed. Statisticians avoid the problem by squaring the deviations before multiplying by the probabilities and summing. This leads to a statistic called the *variance* written as

$$\text{Var } X = \sigma_X^2 = \sum_{i=1}^{n}[(X_i - \overline{X})^2]P(X_i)$$

In words, the variance is the average *squared* deviation from the mean. The *standard deviation* is the square root of the variance.

Intuitively, taking the square root of the variance reverses the effect of the earlier squaring to get rid of the sign differences. Unfortunately, it doesn't quite work. The square root of the sum of squares isn't equal to the sum of the original amounts. Hence, the standard deviation isn't an average distance from the mean, but it's *conceptually* close. This is why we use the term *standard* deviation instead of average deviation. In any event, standard deviation and variance are the traditional measures of variability in probability distributions and are used extensively in financial theory.

For a discrete distribution like our coin toss, we calculate the variance and then the standard deviation by (1) measuring each possible outcome's distance from the mean, (2) squaring it, (3) multiplying by the probability of the outcome, (4) summing the result over all possible outcomes for the variance, and then (5) taking the square root for the standard deviation. Of course, the mean has to be calculated first. The computations are laid out in Example 9-3.

The **standard deviation** gives an indication of how far from the mean a typical observation is likely to fall.

CONCEPT CONNECTION   **EXAMPLE 9-3**

Calculating the Variance and Standard Deviation of a Discrete Distribution
Calculate the variance and standard deviation of the number of heads in four tosses of a coin

X_i	$(X_i - \bar{X})$	$(X_i - \bar{X})^2$	$P(X_i)$	$(X_i - \bar{X})^2 * P(X_i)$
0	−2	4	.0625	0.25
1	−1	1	.2500	0.25
2	0	0	.3750	0.00
3	1	1	.2500	0.25
4	2	4	.0625	0.25

$$\text{Var X} = \sigma_x^2 = \overline{1.00}$$
$$\text{Std Dev} = \sqrt{\text{Var X}} = \sigma^2 = 1.00$$

This example is unusual in that the variance is exactly 1, so the standard deviation turns out to be the same number.

Keep in mind that the terms "variance" and "standard deviation" are both used to characterize variability around the mean.

The Coefficient of Variation   The *coefficient of variation,* CV, is a *relative* measure of variation. It is the ratio of the standard deviation of a distribution to its mean.

$$CV = \frac{\sigma_X}{\bar{X}}$$

It is essentially variability as a fraction of the average value of the variable. In our coin toss example, the mean outcome is two heads in a series of four tosses. The standard deviation is one head, meaning a typical series will vary by one from the mean of two. The coefficient of variation is then $(\frac{1}{2} =)$ .5, meaning the typical variation is one half the size of the mean.

Continuous Random Variables   Other random variables are continuous, meaning they can take any numerical value within some range. For example, if we choose people at random and measure their height, that measurement could be considered a random variable called H. A graphic representation of the probability distribution of H is shown in Figure 9-2. In this graph, probability is represented by the area under the curve and above the horizontal axis. That entire area is taken to be 1.0.

When the random variable is continuous, we talk about the probability of an actual outcome being *within a range* of values rather than turning out to be an exact amount. For example, it isn't meaningful to state the probability of finding a person whose height is *exactly* 5′2″ because the chance of doing that is virtually zero. However, it is meaningful to state a probability of finding a person whose height is between 5′1⅞″ and 5′2⅛″. In the distribution, that probability is represented by the area under the curve directly above and between those values on the horizontal axis.

Calculating the mean and variance of a continuous distribution is mathematically more complex than in the discrete case, but the idea is the same. The mean is the

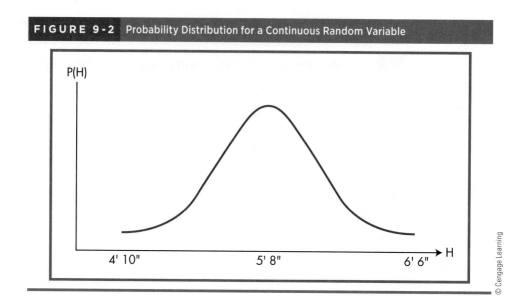

FIGURE 9-2   Probability Distribution for a Continuous Random Variable

average of all possible outcomes, each weighted by its probability. When the distribution is symmetrical and has only one peak, the mean is found under that peak.

9.2b   The Return on a Stock Investment as a Random Variable

In portfolio theory, the return on an investment in stock is considered a **random variable**. This makes sense because return is influenced by a significant number of uncertainties. Consider Equation 9.2. In that expression, the value of the return depends on the future market price of the stock, P_1, and a future dividend, D_1. Both of these amounts are influenced by the multitude of events that make up the business environment in which the company that issued the stock operates. The price is further affected by all the forces that influence financial markets. In other words, there's an element of uncertainty or randomness in both the future price and the future dividend. It follows that there's an uncertainty or randomness to the value of k, and we can consider it a random variable.

Return is a continuous random variable whose values are generally expressed as percentages. Equation 9.2 calculates the decimal form of those percentages (e.g., .10 for 10%). In straightforward stock investments, the lowest return possible is −100%, a total loss of invested money, but there's technically no limit to the amount of positive return that's possible.

Like any random variable, the return on a stock investment has an associated probability distribution. Figure 9-3 is a graphic depiction of a probability distribution for the return on a stock we'll call X. The return on X is called k_X. The values the return can take appear along the horizontal axis, and the probabilities of those values appear on the vertical axis. The shape of the distribution depicts the likelihood of all possible actual values of k_X according to areas under the curve.

The total area under the curve is 1.0, and the proportionate area under any section represents the probability that an actual return will fall along the horizontal axis in that area. For example, the shaded area in the diagram represents the probability that in any

FIGURE 9-3   The Probability Distribution of the Return on an Investment in Stock X

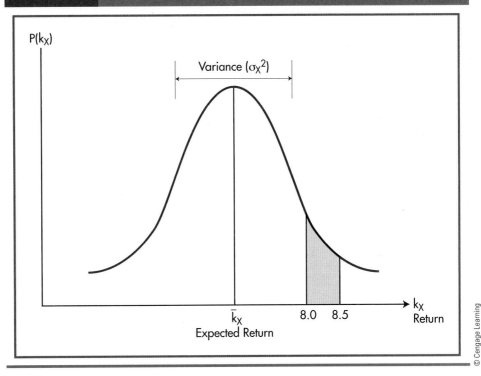

© Cengage Learning

particular year the actual return on an investment in stock X will turn out to be between 8.0% and 8.5%. If that area is .1 or 10% of the total area under the curve, the probability of the actual return being between 8.0% and 8.5% in any year would be 10%.

The mean or expected value (the most likely outcome) is usually found under the highest point of the curve. It's indicated as $\bar{k}_X$ in the diagram.

The **mean** is the statistical representation of the average investor's **expected return** that we talked about earlier. This is an important point. Portfolio theory assumes that all of the knowledge the investment community has about the future performance of a stock is reflected in the probability distribution of returns perceived by the investors. In particular, the mean of that perceived distribution is the expected return investors plan on receiving when they buy.

The variance and standard deviation of the distribution show how likely it is that an actual return will be some distance away from the expected value. A distribution with a large variance is more likely to produce actual outcomes that are substantially away from the expected value than one with a small variance.

Figure 9-3 shows the variance conceptually as the width of the distribution. We'll use σ_X^2 to indicate that we're talking about the distribution of returns for stock X. Similarly, σ_X will be the standard deviation for stock X. A large variance implies a wide distribution with gently sloping sides and a low peak. A narrow distribution with steeply sloping sides and a high peak has a small variance and standard deviation. Figure 9-4 shows distributions with large and small variances.

Notice that the large variance distribution has more area under the curve farther away from the mean than the small variance distribution. This pattern means that

> The **mean** of the distribution of returns is the stock's **expected return**.

FIGURE 9-4 Probability Distributions with Large and Small Variances

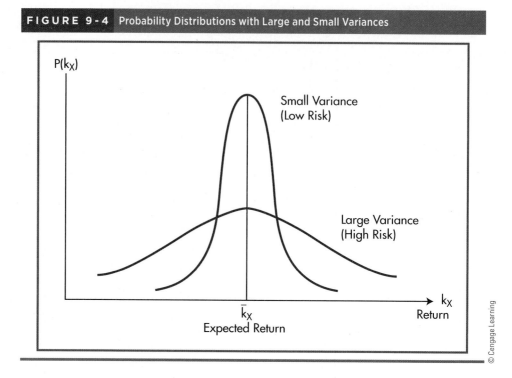

more actual observations of the return are likely to be far away from the mean when the distribution's variance is large. Stated another way, returns will tend to be more different, or more variable, from year to year when the variance is large. When the variance is small, actual returns in successive years are more likely to cluster closely around the mean or expected value.

9.2c   Risk Redefined as Variability

The meaning of risk in portfolio theory differs from the definition we gave earlier. Before we said that risk is the probability that return will be less than expected. In portfolio theory, risk is **variability**. That is, a stock whose return is likely to be significantly different from one year to the next is risky, while one whose returns are likely to cluster tightly is less risky. Stated another way, a risky stock has a high probability of producing a return that's substantially away from the mean of the distribution of returns, while a low-risk stock is unlikely to produce a return that differs from the expected return by very much.

But this is exactly the idea of variance and standard deviation that we've been talking about, so in portfolio theory, *a stock investment's risk is defined as the standard deviation of the probability distribution of its return.* A large standard deviation implies high risk and a small one means low risk. In practical terms, high risk implies *variability* in return, meaning that returns in successive years are likely to be considerably different from one another.

Figure 9-4 can be interpreted as showing a risky stock and a low-risk stock with the same expected return. The difference is in the variances, which can be visually observed as the widths of the distributions.

This definition is somewhat inconsistent with the earlier version in which we said risk was the probability that return would be *less than* what was expected. One would think that a more appropriate definition in statistical terms would equate risk with only the left side of the probability distribution because in that area return is less than expected. Defining risk as the entire standard deviation includes the probability that the return turns out to be more than expected, and we're certainly not concerned if that happens.

Indeed, a left-side-only definition would make more intuitive sense. However, it would be very difficult to work with mathematically. Theorists solved the problem by noticing that return distributions are usually relatively symmetrical. This means that a large left side always implies a large right side as well. Why not therefore define risk for mathematical convenience as total variability, understanding that we're really only concerned with the probability of lower than expected returns (those on the left)? Indeed, this is what was done. The resulting technical definition of risk is a little strange in that it includes good news as well as bad news, but that doesn't bother us if we keep the reason in mind.

So we actually have two definitions of risk that are both correct. In practical terms, risk is the probability that return will be less than expected. In financial theory, risk is the variability of the probability distribution of returns.

Terminology isn't entirely consistent. When talking conceptually about risk, people are likely to use the terms "variance" or "variability." But when a precise value is needed to represent risk in a mathematical equation, it's more common to use σ, the standard deviation.

Notice also that defining risk as the probability that return will be less than expected doesn't tell us much. For more or less symmetrical distributions of returns, that probability will always be about 50%. But for some investments the return is never below the expected value by very much, while for others it can be below by a lot. The variance definition gets right at this distinction. If the distribution has a large variance, the return can be below the expected value by a substantial amount, and an investor can be hurt badly.

An Alternate View   There's another way to visualize risk that many students find helpful. Imagine plotting the historical values of return on a particular stock over time. When we do that, we get an up-and-down graph like one of those shown in Figure 9-5. Over time, the stock's return is seen to oscillate around its average value, $\bar{k}_x$. The more the stock's return moves up and down over time, the more risky we say it is as an investment. That is, the greater the amplitude of the swings, the riskier the stock. This view is simply a graphic result of the variance of the distribution. In the diagram, stock A is relatively high risk and stock B is relatively low risk. We will use this representation again shortly.

9.2d   Risk Aversion

Now we're in a position to define **risk aversion** more precisely. The axiom simply states that people prefer investments with less risk to those with more risk **if the expected returns are equal**. Figure 9-6a illustrates the idea with probability distributions. The narrower distribution has less risk and will be preferred to the wider, riskier distribution.

Risk aversion means investors prefer lower risk when **expected returns are equal**.

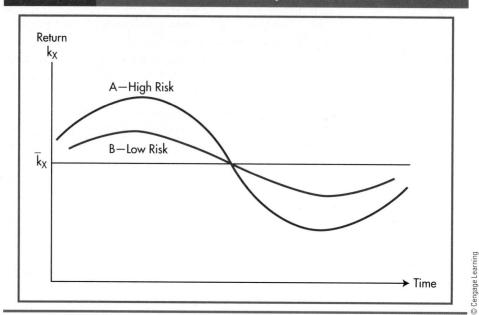

FIGURE 9-5 Investment Risk Viewed as Variability of Return over Time

© Cengage Learning

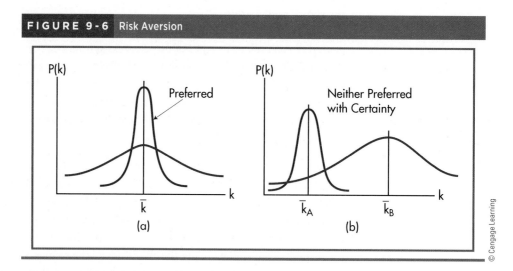

FIGURE 9-6 Risk Aversion

© Cengage Learning

It's important to understand that this preference is assumed to hold universally only in cases where the expected returns are exactly equal. When the choice is as illustrated in Figure 9-6b, the principle of risk aversion tells us nothing. There, investment A is preferred on the basis of risk, while investment B is preferred on the basis of expected return. Which will be chosen depends on the individual investor's tolerance for risk.

CONCEPT CONNECTION   EXAMPLE 9-4

Evaluating Stand-Alone Risk

Stand-alone risk is variation independent of portfolio considerations.

The notions of risk we've just developed are associated with owning shares of a single stock by itself. That can be characterized as **stand-alone risk** because the stock's variability stands alone independent of anything happening in the owner's portfolio.

Harold MacGregor is considering buying stocks for the first time and is looking for a single company in which he'll make a substantial investment. He has narrowed his search to two firms, Evanston Water Inc. and Astro Tech Corp. Evanston is a public utility supplying water to the county, and Astro is a relatively new high-tech company in the computer field.

Public utilities are classic examples of low-risk stocks because they're *regulated monopolies*. That means the government gives them the exclusive right to sell their products in an area but also controls pricing so they can't take advantage of the public by charging excessively. The *utility commission* usually sets prices aimed at achieving a reasonable return for the company's stockholders.

On the other hand, young high-tech firms are classic examples of high-risk companies. That's because new technical ideas can be enormously profitable, complete failures, or anything in between.

Harold has studied the history and prospects of both firms and their industries, and with the help of his broker has made a discrete estimate of the probability distribution of returns for each stock as follows.

Evanston Water		Astro Tech	
k_E	$P(k_E)$	k_A	$P(k_A)$
6%	.05	−100%	.15
8	.15	0	.20
10	.60	15	.30
12	.15	30	.20
14	.05	130	.15

Evaluate Harold's options in terms of statistical concepts of risk and return.

SOLUTION: First calculate the expected return for each stock. That's the mean of each distribution.

Evanston Water			Astro Tech		
k_E	$P(k_E)$	$k_E * P(k_E)$	k_A	$P(k_A)$	$k_A * P(k_A)$
6%	.05	0.3%	−100%	.15	−15.0%
8	.15	1.2	0	.20	0.0
10	.60	6.0	15	.30	4.5
12	.15	1.8	30	.20	6.0
14	.05	0.7	130	.15	19.5
		$\overline{k}_E = 10.0\%$			$\overline{k}_A = 15.0\%$

Next calculate the variance and standard deviation of the return on each stock.

Evanston Water

k_E	$k_E - \bar{k}_E$	$(k_E - \bar{k}_E)^2$	$P(k_E)$	$(k_E - \bar{k}_E)^2 * P(k_E)$
6%	−4%	16	.05	0.8
8	−2%	4	.15	0.6
10	0	0	.60	0.0
12	2	4	.15	0.6
14	4	16	.05	0.8

$$\text{Variance } \sigma_E^2 = \overline{2.8}$$
$$\text{Standard Deviation } \sigma_E = 1.7\%$$

Astro Tech

k_A	$k_A - \bar{k}_A$	$(k_A - \bar{k}_A)^2$	$P(k_A)$	$(k_A - \bar{k}_A)^2 * P(k_A)$
−100%	−115%	13,225	.15	1,984
0	−15	225	.20	45
15	0	0	.30	0
30	15	225	.20	45
130	115	13,225	.15	1,984

$$\text{Variance } \sigma_A^2 = \overline{4,058}$$
$$\text{Standard Deviation } \sigma_A = 63.7\%$$

Finally, calculate the coefficient of variation for each stock's return.

$$CV_E = \frac{\sigma_E}{\bar{k}_E} = \frac{1.7}{10.0} = .17$$

$$CV_A = \frac{\sigma_A}{\bar{k}_E} = \frac{63.7\%}{15\%} = 4.25$$

DISCUSSION: If Harold considers only the expected returns on his investment options, he'll certainly choose Astro. It's most likely return is half again as high as Evanston's. But a glance at the distributions reveals that's not the whole story. With Evanston, Harold's investment is relatively safe, because the worst he's likely to do is a return of 6% rather than the expected 10%.

Investing in Astro is a completely different story. While Harold's most likely return there is 15%, a substantial chance (15%) exists that he'll lose everything. There's also a 20% chance he'll earn a zero return. Possibilities like these give people concerns about investing in this kind of stock.

It's also important to appreciate the high side of the two distributions. With Evanston, Harold isn't likely to do much better than the expected return, because the highest yield available is only 14%. The utility commission's pricing regulations guarantee that. But with Astro there's a chance of more than doubling invested money in a relatively short time. That's reflected in the 15% chance of a 130% return. That tends to offset the depressing loss possibilities in the minds of some investors.

It should be clear that on a stand-alone basis, Astro is a relatively risky stock, while Evanston is relatively safe. Astro's risk and Evanston's lack of it come from the *variation* in the distributions of their returns, which we just observed by examining the distributions in detail. But the idea is also available in summarized form from the standard deviations and coefficients of variation.

First notice that Astro's standard deviation is 63.7%. That means a "typical" return has a good chance of being about 64% above or below the expected return of 15%. That's an enormous range for return, from −49% to 79%. On the other hand, Evanston's standard deviation is only 1.7%, meaning a typical return will probably be less than two percentage points off the expected return.

It's tempting to compare the two companies by saying Astro's risk is (63.7/1.7=) 37 times that of Evanston. But that's not quite fair because Astro has a higher expected return. It makes more sense to compare the coefficients of variation, which state the standard deviations in units of their respective means. Evanston's CV is .17 while Astro's is 4.25, so it's more reasonable to say that Astro is (4.25/.17=) 25 times as risky as Evanston.

A picture is even more telling. Continuous approximations of the two distributions are plotted as follows:

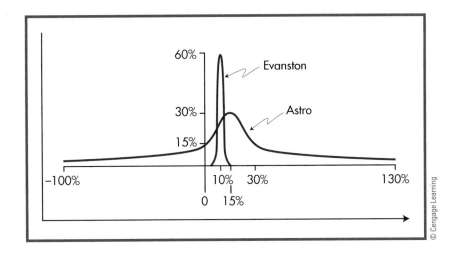

So, after having said all that, which stock should Harold choose?

Although our analysis has laid out the solution clearly, no one but Harold can answer that question. That's because his choice depends on his degree of *risk aversion*. Evanston is the better choice with respect to risk, but Astro is better with respect to expected return. Which dominates is a personal choice that only the investor can make.

9.2e Decomposing Risk—Systematic (Market) and Unsystematic (Business-Specific) Risk

The **returns** on securities tend to **move** up and down **together**.

A fundamental truth of the investment world is that the returns offered on various securities tend to move up and down together. They don't move exactly together, or even proportionately, but for the most part, stocks tend to go up and down at the same times.

Events and Conditions Causing Movement in Returns   Returns on stock investments move up and down in response to various events and conditions that affect the environment. Some things influence all stocks, while others affect only specific companies. News of politics, inflation, interest rates, war, and economic events tend to move most stocks in the same direction at the same time. A labor dispute in a particular industry, on the other hand, tends to affect only the stocks of firms in that industry.

Although certain events affect the returns of all stocks, some returns tend to respond more than others to particular things. Suppose news of an impending recession hits the market. The return on most stocks can be expected to decline, but not by the same amount. The return on a public utility like a water company isn't likely to change much. That's because people's demand for water doesn't change much in hard times, and the utility is a regulated monopoly whose profitability is more or less guaranteed by the government. On the other hand, the return on the stock of a luxury goods manufacturer may drop sharply, because recession signals a drying up of demand for the company's product.

In short, there's a general but disproportionate movement together upon which is superimposed a fair amount of individual movement.

Movement in Return as Risk   Remember that one way to look at a stock's risk is to consider the up-and-down movement of its return over time as equivalent to that risk (Figure 9-5). Think of that total movement as the total risk inherent in the stock.

Separating Movement/Risk into Two Parts   It's conceptually possible to separate the total up-and-down movement of a stock's return into two parts. The first part is the movement that occurs along with that of all other stocks in response to events affecting them all. That movement is known as *systematic risk*. It affects the entire economic system.

The second part is whatever movement is left over after the first part has been removed. This movement is a result of events that are specific to particular companies and industries. Strikes, good or bad weather, good or bad management, and demand conditions are examples of things that affect particular firms. This remaining movement is called *unsystematic risk*. It affects specific companies.

Systematic and unsystematic risk can also be called **market risk** and **business-specific risk**, respectively.

*A stock's risk can be separated into **systematic or market** risk and **unsystematic or business-specific** risk.*

9.2f   Portfolios

Most equity investors hold stock in a number of companies rather than putting all of their funds in one firm's securities. We refer to an investor's total stock holding as his or her *portfolio*.

*Portfolios have **their own** risks and returns.*

Risk and Return for a Portfolio   Each stock in a **portfolio** has its own expected return and its own risk. These are the mean and standard deviation of the probability distribution of the stock's return. As might be expected, the total portfolio also has its own risk and return.

The return (actual or expected) on a portfolio is simply the average of the returns of the stocks in it, where the average is weighted by the proportionate dollars invested in each stock.

CONCEPT CONNECTION   **EXAMPLE 9-5**

Portfolio Return

Suppose we have the following three-stock portfolio.

Stock	$ Invested	Return
A	$ 6,000	5%
B	9,000	9
C	15,000	11
	$30,000	

The return on the portfolio, expected or actual, is

$$k_p = w_A k_A + w_B k_B + w_C k_C$$

where k_p is the portfolio's return and the w's are the fractions of its total value invested in each asset. The weighted average calculation is as follows.

$$k_p = \frac{\$6K}{\$30K}(5\%) + \frac{\$9K}{\$30K}(9\%) + \frac{\$15K}{\$30K}(11\%)$$
$$= (.2)(.05) + (.3)(.09) + (.5)(.11)$$
$$= 9.2\%$$

The risk of a portfolio is the variance or standard deviation of the probability distribution of the portfolio's return. That depends on the variances (risks) of the returns on the stocks in the portfolio, but not in a simple way. We'll understand more about this relationship of portfolio risk to stock risk as we move on.

The Goal of the Investor/Portfolio Owner   As we said earlier, the goal of investors is to capture the high average returns of equities while avoiding as much of their risk as possible. *That's generally done by constructing diversified portfolios to minimize portfolio risk for a given return.*

Investment theory is based on the premise that portfolio owners care only about the financial performance of their whole portfolios and not about the stand-alone characteristics of the individual stocks in the portfolios.

In other words, an investor evaluates the risk and return characteristics of a new stock only in terms of how that stock will affect the performance of his or her portfolio and not on the stand-alone merits of the stock. How a stock's characteristics can be different in and out of a portfolio will become clear shortly.

Investors are concerned with how stocks **impact portfolio performance** and not with their stand-alone characteristics.

9.2g   Diversification—How Portfolio Risk Is Affected When Stocks are Added

Diversification means holding many **different** stocks to reduce risk.

Our basic goal in investing, to capture a high portfolio return while avoiding as much risk as possible, is accomplished through diversification. **Diversification** means adding different, or diverse, stocks to a portfolio. It's the investor's most basic tool for managing risk. Properly employed, diversification can reduce but not eliminate risk (variation in return) in a portfolio. To achieve the goal, however, we have to be careful about how we go about diversifying. We'll need to address unsystematic (business-specific) risk and systematic (market) risk separately.

Business-Specific Risk and Diversification

If we diversify by forming a portfolio of the stocks of a fairly large number of different companies, we can imagine business-specific risk as a series of essentially random events that push the returns on individual stocks up or down. The stimuli that affect individual companies are separate events that occur across the country. Some are good and some are bad.

Because events causing **business-specific risk** are random from the investor's point of view, their effects simply cancel when added together over a substantial number of stocks. Therefore, we say that business-specific risk can be "**diversified away**" in a fairly large portfolio. In other words, the good events offset the bad ones, and if there are enough events the net result tends to be about zero.

However, a word of caution is in order. For this idea to work, the stocks in the portfolio have to be from companies in fundamentally different industries. For example, if all the companies in a portfolio were agricultural, the effect of a drought wouldn't be random. It would hit all of the stocks. Therefore, the business-specific risk wouldn't be diversified away.

This is an easy but powerful concept. For investors who hold numerous stocks, business-specific risk simply doesn't exist at the aggregate level because it's "washed out" statistically. Individual stocks still have it, but portfolios do not, and the portfolio is all the investor cares about.

> **Business-specific risk** is essentially random and can be **diversified away**.

Systematic (Market) Risk and Diversification

Reducing market risk in a portfolio calls for more complicated thinking than does handling business-specific risk. It should be intuitively clear that if the returns of all stocks move up and down more or less together, we're unlikely to be able to eliminate all of the movement in a portfolio's return by adding more stocks. In fact, systematic or market risk in a portfolio can be reduced but never entirely eliminated through diversification. However, even the reduction of market risk requires careful attention to the risk characteristics of the stocks added to the portfolio.

The Portfolio   To appreciate the issue, imagine we have a portfolio of stocks that has an expected return $\bar{k}_p$. In what follows, we'll assume for simplicity that all the stocks have the same expected return. It's all right to make this unrealistic assumption for illustrative purposes, because the points we're getting at involve the interplay of risk among stocks and not of returns.

Our portfolio will have its own risk or variation in return, which is determined by the stocks in it. We'll assume the portfolio has been put together to mirror exactly the makeup of the overall stock market. That is, if the prices of the stocks in the overall market are such that Microsoft makes up 2% of the market's value, we'll spend 2% of our money on Microsoft stock, and so on through all the stocks listed on the market. If the portfolio is constituted in this way, its return will move up and down just as the market's return does. In other words, the portfolio's risk will just equal the market's risk. The behavior of the portfolio's return over time is illustrated in Figure 9-7 by the green line labeled P.

The Impact on Portfolio Risk of Adding New Stocks   We now want to consider the impact on the portfolio's risk of adding a little of *either* of two new stocks to it. We'll call these stocks A and B. The special behavior of the return on each is shown in

FIGURE 9-7   Risk In and Out of a Portfolio

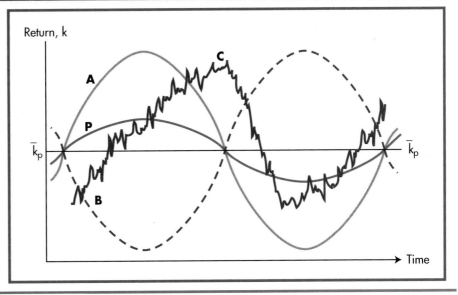

Figure 9-7. Notice that we're not talking about adding both stocks A and B at the same time. Rather the idea is to assess the impact on the risk of the resulting portfolio of adding a little of A **or** a little of B to the original portfolio.

First consider stock A. What happens to the risk of the portfolio if we add a few shares of A? Notice that A's return achieves its highs and lows at exactly the same times as does the portfolio's, and that its peaks and troughs are higher and lower, respectively, than the portfolio's. It should be clear that the inclusion of a little A will tend to heighten the portfolio's peak returns and depress its lowest returns. In other words, it will make the swings in the portfolio's return larger. That means it will add risk to the portfolio.

In statistical terms, A's return is said to be perfectly positively correlated with the portfolio's return. That means the two returns move up and down at exactly the same times. Such stocks will generally add risk to a diversified portfolio.

Now consider the pattern of returns on stock B over time. Its peaks occur with the portfolio's valleys, and its valleys coincide with the portfolio's peaks. The return on stock B is always moving up or down in a direction opposite the movement of the return on the portfolio.

What will happen to the pattern of returns of the portfolio if we add a few shares of B? Clearly, the peaks will be lower and the valleys will be higher—that is, the swings won't be as wide. According to our definitions, that means the risk will be lowered by adding some B. In statistical terms, B's return is said to be perfectly negatively correlated with the portfolio's return. That means the returns move in opposite directions. Such stocks will always lower the portfolio's risk.

In short, A adds risk to a portfolio while B reduces the portfolio's risk.

The Risk of the New Additions by Themselves and in Portfolios   Now consider the relative riskiness of stocks A and B without reference to a portfolio. That is, how risky is each one standing alone? Figure 9-7 shows that A's and B's returns have about the same level of variation. That is, their peaks and troughs are about the same height. Therefore, their stand-alone risks as individual stocks are about the same.

However, in a portfolio sense, A is risky and B is safe in that A adds and B subtracts risk. This is a central and critically important concept. *Although A and B are equally risky on a stand-alone basis, they have completely opposite risk impacts on a portfolio.*

The portfolio definition of a stock's risk is related to the **timing** of the variability of the stock's return rather than to the magnitude of the variation. It has to do with the way the new stock's return changes when the portfolio's return changes. Or, if the portfolio is constituted like the market as we've assumed, it has to do with the **way the stock's return changes with the return on the market**.

However, the degree to which a stock's return moves with the market is what we've called market risk. Hence, we can say that *a stock's risk in a portfolio sense is its market risk.*

Choosing Stocks to Diversify for Market Risk   How do we diversify to reduce market risk in a portfolio? Figure 9-7 might imply that it's easy: Just add stocks like B until the movement of the portfolio is virtually dampened out. Unfortunately, stocks like B that move countercyclically with the market are few and far between.

The classic example of such a stock involves shares in a gold mine. When returns on most stocks are down, people flee from paper investments and put money in tangible assets, notably gold. That drives the price of gold up. A higher price for gold means a gold mine becomes more profitable, which elevates the return on its stock. Hence, when the return on most stocks is down, the return on gold mine stocks tends to be up. The reverse happens when stock returns are generally high.

Although people do diversify with gold mine stocks to stabilize portfolios, there aren't enough of them to do the job thoroughly. There simply aren't many stocks around that are negatively correlated with the market.

However, a great number of stocks are available whose returns behave in a manner somewhere between those of A and B in the diagram. In terms of the behavior of return, that kind of stock can be thought of as a combination of A and B. Such a stock is illustrated by line C in Figure 9-7. Stocks like C are said to be *not* perfectly positively correlated with the portfolio.

Adding some C to the portfolio will generally reduce its risk somewhat. If we think of C as a hybrid or cross between A and B, its addition is a way to get a little B into the portfolio indirectly. An intuitive way to put it is to say that C contains a little of the "risk personality" of B.

In summary, market risk generally can be reduced but not eliminated by diversifying with stocks like C that are not perfectly positively correlated with the portfolio.

The Importance of Market Risk

Let's return to stocks A and B in Figure 9-7 for a moment. The illustration is constructed to point out two different concepts of risk. Considered individually, the stocks are equally risky, yet in a portfolio one is risky and the other is not. Which interpretation is appropriate and when?

The relative risk attributes of the two stocks are entirely changed if we assume investors focus on portfolios rather than on individual stocks. Modern portfolio theory is based on that assumption. *What matters is how stocks affect portfolios rather than how they behave when considered alone. And how they affect portfolios depends only on market risk because business risk has been diversified away.*

Margin notes:

Stocks with **equal stand-alone risk** can have **opposite risk impacts on a portfolio** because of the **timing** of the variations in their returns.

Market risk in a portfolio can be reduced but not eliminated by diversifying with stocks that are **not perfectly positively correlated** with the portfolio.

Caution: The concepts of risk associated with portfolio theory **may not be appropriate for individual** investors.

This is a fundamental result of portfolio theory. According to the theory, what matters in the investment world is market risk alone. *It is also a dangerous result.* Business-specific risk is truly diversified away only in large portfolios. For the small investor with a limited portfolio, that doesn't occur. An individual business reversal can devastate an investment program if the stock represents a significant portion of a small portfolio. Hence, while the thinking behind portfolio theory may be appropriate for running a mutual fund, it should not be applied blindly to managing one's personal assets.

9.2h   Measuring Market Risk—The Concept of Beta

A stock's **beta** measures its **market risk**.

Because market risk is of such central importance to investing, it's appropriate to look for a way to measure it for individual stocks.

A statistic known as a stock's **beta** coefficient has been developed that is commonly considered to be the measure of a stock's **market risk**. Essentially, beta captures the variation in a stock's return which *accompanies* variation in the return on the market.

A stock's **characteristic line** reflects the average relationship between its return and the market's. **Beta is the slope of the characteristic line.**

Developing Beta   A stock's beta coefficient is developed by plotting the historical relationship between the return on the stock and the return on the market.[2] Figure 9-8 shows such a plot. Each point represents a past time period for which we plot the stock's return, k_X, on the vertical axis and the market's return, k_M, on the horizontal axis. Doing this for a number of past periods results in a "scatter diagram" of historical

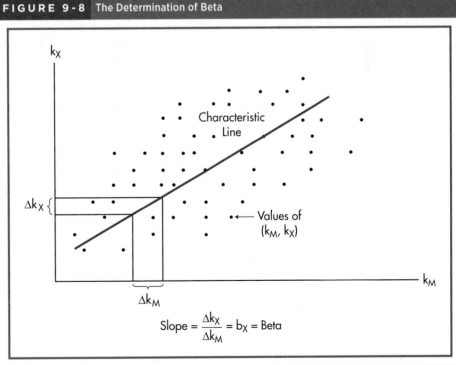

FIGURE 9-8   The Determination of Beta

$$\text{Slope} = \frac{\Delta k_X}{\Delta k_M} = b_X = \text{Beta}$$

© Cengage Learning

---

2. The return on the market is estimated by calculating the return on a market index such as the Standard & Poor's 500.

observations. A regression line fitted to these data points is known as the **characteristic line** for the stock.

The characteristic line represents the average relationship between the stock's return and the market's return. Its slope is particularly rich in information. The slope tells us *on the average* how much of a change in k_X has come about with a given change in k_M. This is exactly what we're looking for in terms of measuring market risk. The slope is an indication of how much variation in the return on the stock goes along with variation in the return on the market.

To see this, notice that as we move along the characteristic line, a change in k_M, Δk_M, comes with a change in k_X, Δk_X. The relationship between these changes is reflected in the slope of the line.

$$(9.3) \qquad \textbf{Slope} = \frac{\textbf{rise}}{\textbf{run}} = \frac{\Delta k_X}{\Delta k_M} = b_X = \textbf{beta}$$

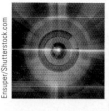

INSIGHTS | Practical Finance

Is It Investing or Gambling?

Investing is putting money at risk in the hope of earning more money—a return. But isn't that also a definition of gambling? Certainly it is, so what's the difference between investing and gambling, and why do we have such different moral and ethical attitudes about them?

Investing has economic value to the society that gambling doesn't. But, aside from that, from an individual's perspective, it's fair to ask about the distinction between playing the stock market and taking a trip to Las Vegas.

Viewing both processes in terms of the probability distributions of their returns provides some insight. Investing tends to be characterized by probability distributions with positive expected values (means) and relatively small probabilities of very large gains or losses. Gambling, on the other hand, generally has a zero or negative expected value and offers a good chance of losing everything placed at risk. The attraction of gambling is that there's also a visible chance of winning many times the amount risked along with its entertainment value. Think of playing roulette in a Las Vegas casino. It's no secret that the odds are stacked slightly in favor of the house, and that many visitors leave town with empty pockets. But there are also a few well-publicized examples of people who hit the jackpot. Graphically, the distributions might look something like this.

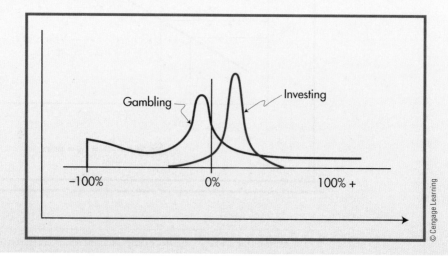

This view leads to another logical question. Are there activities that people normally call investing that are more like gambling? The answer is a resounding yes. Buying the stock of a high-risk new venture might be an example. There are also some financial markets that are risky to the point of bordering on gambling (e.g., commodities and futures markets, which are beyond the scope of this book).

In fact, the whole idea of portfolio theory is to move the investor's exposure toward the investment profile we've just described and away from the gambling profile.

The important thing to take away from this discussion is that something isn't "investing" just because it happens through the financial industry. Brokers like to characterize all their offerings as investing because it has a nobler image. But, in fact, some financial "investments" are really more like gambles.

Market risk is defined as the degree to which the return on the stock moves with the return on the market. That idea is summarized perfectly by the slope of the characteristic line. The slope can therefore be *defined* as the measure of market risk for the stock. This measure is called the beta coefficient, or simply *beta,* for the stock.

Projecting Returns with Beta   Knowing a stock's beta enables us to estimate changes in its return given changes in the market's return.

CONCEPT CONNECTION   **EXAMPLE 9-6**

Projecting Returns with Beta

Conroy Corp. has a beta of 1.8 and is currently earning its owners a return of 14%. The stock market in general is reacting negatively to a new crisis in the Middle East that threatens world oil supplies. Experts estimate that the return on an average stock will drop from 12% to 8% because of investor concerns over the economic impact of a potential oil shortage as well as the threat of war. Estimate the change in the return on Conroy shares and its new return.

SOLUTION: Beta represents the past average change in Conroy's return relative to changes in the market's return.

$$b_{Conroy} = \frac{\Delta k_{Conroy}}{\Delta k_M}$$

Substituting,

$$1.8 = \frac{\Delta k_{Conroy}}{4\%}$$

$$\Delta k_{Conroy} = 7.2\%$$

The new return can be estimated as

$$k_{Conroy} = 14\% - 7.2\% = 6.8\%$$

Understanding Beta It's important to understand that beta represents an average relationship based on past history. To appreciate this, consider the movement from one data point to the next in Figure 9-8.

The change between any two successive values of k_X represents movement caused by the combination of market risk forces and business-specific risk forces. In other words, such a change is part of the stock's total risk. By regressing k_X versus k_M, we're making the assumption that movement along the line representing an average relationship between the variables reflects only market-related changes. In this view, movement from one data point to the next has two components, movement to and from the line and movement along the line. Movement to and from the line represents business-specific risk, while movement along the line represents market risk.

Forecasting with beta, as in the last example, uses only the average relationship between the returns, which is assumed to be market related. It says nothing about business-specific risk factors.

CONCEPT CONNECTION EXAMPLE 9-7

The Effect of Business-Specific Risk

Suppose Conroy Corp. in Example 9-6 is a defense contractor that makes sophisticated anti-missile systems. Would the estimate of return done in that example be valid? What if Conroy were in the orange juice business?

SOLUTION: It's unlikely that the estimate would be much good if Conroy were a defense contractor. The threat of war could be expected to have a positive impact on the company because of its defense-related line of business. In other words, such a threat is likely to have a major business-specific risk impact on the firm's return that would act in a direction opposite the market-related decline.

If Conroy made orange juice, we wouldn't expect a business-specific risk change due to the Middle East crisis, so the market-related estimate would be more realistic.

Betas are developed from **historical data** and **may not be accurate** if a **fundamental change** in the business environment occurs.

Beta over Time Any firm's beta is derived from observation of the behavior of its return in the past relative to the return on the market. Use of the statistic implicitly assumes that the relationship between the two returns is going to remain constant over time. In other words, using beta assumes the stock's return will behave in the same way in the future that it did in the past relative to the market's return. This assumption is usually reasonable, but at times it may not be.

CONCEPT CONNECTION EXAMPLE 9-8

The Effect of a Changing Business Environment

Let's consider the Conroy Corp. of the last two examples once more, again assuming that it is a defense contractor. Think of the early 1990s when the Cold War was ending and military budgets were being reduced dramatically. Would a projection using beta have been valid at that time?

SOLUTION: In this situation, the value of Conroy's beta is uncertain. The data from which the firm's characteristic line was developed would have been from earlier periods during the Cold War when military spending and lucrative defense contracts were considered a way of life that was likely to continue forever. The early 1990s were characterized by a climate of reduced defense budgets which made high-technology defense production look a lot more risky. Therefore, the future beta was likely to have been different from the past value at that time.

Volatility   Beta measures volatility in relation to market changes. In other words, it tells us whether the stock's return moves around more or less than the return of an average stock.

A beta of 1.0 means the stock's return moves on average just as much as the market's return. Beta > 1.0 implies the stock moves more than the market. Beta < 1.0 means the stock tends to move with the market but less. Beta < 0 (negative) means the stock tends to move against the market, that is, in the opposite direction. Such stocks are rare. Stock B of Figure 9-7 is a negative beta stock. Gold mines are the primary real-world example of such stocks.

The idea of beta immediately suggests an investment strategy. When the market is moving up, hold high-beta stocks because they move up more. When the market is moving down, switch to low-beta stocks because they move down less!

> Small investors should remember that **beta doesn't measure total risk**.

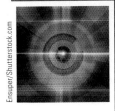

INSIGHTS   Practical Finance

Just How Risky Is AT&T—Really? A Problem with Betas

Calculating beta is a pretty simple procedure. It's just a straightforward linear regression of a stock's return versus the market's. Unfortunately, in some cases several problems can make calculated betas unreliable. One of the biggest involves the evolution of the company whose risk is being assessed. If the firm has changed significantly during the period from which the historical return data comes, beta may be virtually meaningless. That's because the company as it stands today isn't the same business that generated the returns used in the regression analysis. AT&T provides an excellent example.

Before 1983, AT&T was "the" phone company in the United States. It supplied all long distance service and local service in most metropolitan areas, and operated Bell Laboratories, which handled communications technology and manufacturing. But AT&T was sued by the Justice Department for violation of antitrust laws that prohibit monopolies. As a result, the firm agreed to break into eight separate companies. Long distance service and Bell Labs continued to operate under the AT&T name, while local service was divided among seven regional firms collectively referred to as "Baby Bells."

AT&T continued to provide long distance service and technology through the late 1980s and early 90s, but acquired NCR, a major computer manufacturer, in 1991. It operated these three businesses for five years until 1996, when it again split, this time along the lines of those businesses. The AT&T name stayed with long distance operations, while technology and computers were split off as Lucent Technologies and NCR, respectively.

In 2001, AT&T split into four pieces: AT&T Business, AT&T Wireless, AT&T Broadband, and AT&T Consumer. These represent several new lines AT&T developed after the 1996 split, including cable television, Internet service, cell phone service, and local phone service. The broadband unit was sold in 2002.

In 2005, AT&T was acquired by SBC, one of the baby bells spun off in 1983 (SBC owns BellSouth, an original baby bell). The combined company renamed itself AT&T Inc. in a move that seems to take the firm a step back toward its pre-1983 composition. There haven't been any major corporate structure changes since 2005.

Making all this even more complicated is the fact that the nature of the telephone business was changing dramatically during much of this time. Before 1983 phone companies were regulated monopolies and cell phones didn't exist. But since the early eighties the business has been a competitive free-for-all, and wireless phones have permanently altered the way people communicate. These changes are significant because the risk characteristics of regulated and competitive industries are different, as are those of the fast-moving cellular phone business.

So how meaningful is AT&T's beta today? Probably not very meaningful, because the company hasn't been a consistently defined enterprise over any period from which data on returns can be collected.

SOURCE: History Timeline, www.Att.com

Beta for a Portfolio   Because beta measures market risk, the degree to which a stock moves with the market, it makes sense to think about market risk and beta for an entire portfolio. In fact, the concept is rather simple. Beta for a portfolio of stocks is just the weighted average of the betas of the individual stocks where the weights are the dollar amounts invested in each stock. Consider the two stock portfolios in Example 9-9.

CONCEPT CONNECTION   EXAMPLE 9-9

Portfolio Beta

Stock	Beta	Current Dollar Value	Portion of Value
A	.7	800	.8
B	1.1	200	.2
		1,000	1.0

Then the portfolio's beta, written b_p, is calculated as follows.

$$b_p = .8b_A + .2b_B = .8(.7) + .2(1.1) = .78$$

A Note on Decimal Accuracy   Notice that the portfolio beta we just calculated is expressed to two decimal places. You'll sometimes see betas calculated to three decimal places. However, if you think about the nature of beta and the way it's derived for individual stocks, it's apparent that such accuracy is meaningless. Rounding off to one decimal place is generally sufficient.

9.2i   Using Beta—The Capital Asset Pricing Model (CAPM)

The **CAPM** attempts to explain **stock prices** by explaining how investors' **required returns** are determined.

The things we've been discussing in this chapter are inputs to a sophisticated mathematical model of the financial world called the **capital asset pricing model**, abbreviated as **CAPM**. The terminology can be a little confusing. A "capital asset" is a share of stock, and "pricing model" implies an attempt to explain how stock prices are set in the market.

The CAPM has been around for some time. It was developed during the 1950s and 1960s by economists Harry Markowitz and William F. Sharpe, who shared the 1990 Nobel Prize in economics for their work.

The CAPM's Approach   The model's approach to determining how prices are set is to explain how the required rate of return on a stock comes about. Recall that the required rate of return is the return that just holds investors in the stock. It's the amount an individual has to expect to get in order to be willing to put his or her money in a particular company's stock. It's related to the riskiness of the issue as perceived by the investor. (Review page 399 if necessary.) People won't invest unless the expected return is at least equal to their required return.

Price Depends on Return   In general, once a required rate of return is specified, price follows. For example, consider Equation 9.2, our definition of the return on a stock investment (page 399). If we solve that equation for the current price, P_0, we get

$$P_0 = \frac{D_1 + P_1}{(1 + k)}$$

where we can think of k as the required rate of return.

If we make assumptions about the future price and dividend, P_1 and D_1, the current price of the stock, P_0, depends on knowing k.

Another approach involves the Gordon model, Equation 8.10 (Page 356) from Chapter 8, on stock valuation. We'll repeat that expression here for convenience, considering k a required rate of return.

(8.10)
$$P_0 = \frac{D_0 (1 + g)}{k - g}$$

Notice that if the last dividend, D_0, is known and an assumption is made about the growth rate, g, the current price again depends on knowing k. We'll use this relationship in some problems shortly.

All this says that if we understand how required returns are set, we'll understand a great deal about how prices are established.

Rates of Return, the Risk-Free Rate, and Risk Premiums   At this time, we have to make a few points about rates of return in general. First, interest is the rate of return on debt and is conceptually identical to the rate of return on an equity investment. Therefore, we can mix the two ideas as we like. Specifically, we can have both interest rates and rates of return on stock investments within the same equation.

Next we need to recall the concept of a risk-free rate of return from Chapter 5. (Review page 219 if necessary.) A risk-free investment is one in which there is no possibility of receiving less than the expected return. Federally insured bank accounts are essentially risk free, as are investments in short-term Treasury debt. The current rate of interest paid on three-month Treasury bills is generally taken to be the prevailing risk-free rate, written as k_{RF}.

The rate of return on any other investment involves some allowance for bearing risk added to the risk-free rate. The allowance is known as the *risk premium* for the investment. If we call some investment Y, we can write the return on Y as

$$k_Y = k_{RF} + k_{RPY}$$

where k_{RPY} is the risk premium on investment Y. Solving for the risk premium, we have

$$k_{RPY} = k_Y - k_{RF}$$

That is, Y's risk premium is the difference between the return on Y and the risk-free rate. Hold onto that idea for a moment along with the idea that the required rate of return on an investment in a stock is the risk-free rate plus some *premium* for bearing the risk associated with that stock.

The mystery is to try to explain just what that **risk premium** depends on. This is what the capital asset pricing model purports to do.

> The **CAPM** purports to explain how the **risk premiums** in required rates of return are formed.

Putting the Pieces Together
Each of the concepts we've talked about so far, including return as a random variable, risk defined as variance, risk aversion, all the portfolio ideas, and beta, is a necessary assumption undergirding the CAPM.

All of these ideas can be stated in mathematical terms. When they are, some advanced math can be used to derive a single, simple equation that defines the required return on a stock in terms of its risk. That equation, called the **security market line, SML**, is the heart of the CAPM.

> The **SML** is the heart of the **CAPM**.

The beauty of the model and probably a reason for its wide acceptance is the simplicity of this result.

The Security Market Line (SML)
The security market line proposes that required rates of return are determined by the following equation.

(9.4)

$$\underbrace{k_X = k_{RF} + \overbrace{(k_M - k_{RF})}^{\text{Stock X's Risk Premium}} b_X}_{}$$

Market Risk Premium

where:
  k_X is the required return on stock X
  k_{RF} is the risk-free rate
  k_M is the return on the market
  b_X is stock X's beta coefficient

First notice that the right side of the equation is in two parts: the risk-free rate and a risk premium for stock X. This is consistent with the ideas we expressed earlier about rates of return in general.

Next we'll consider the risk premium in detail. It's made up of two parts, the expression in parentheses and beta. Beta, of course, is our measure of market risk for stock X. The expression in parentheses is the difference between the return on the market and the risk-free rate.

The Market Risk Premium   In the section before last, we said that the difference between the return on an investment and the risk-free rate is the risk premium for that investment. Therefore, the term in parentheses in Equation 9.4 is the risk premium for an investment in the market as a whole. That can be interpreted as an investment in an "average" stock or in a portfolio constituted to mirror the market.

The **market risk premium** reflects the average tolerance for risk of all investors at a point in time. In other words, it's indicative of the degree of **risk aversion** felt by the investing community.

The **market risk premium**, $(k_M - k_{RF})$, is a reflection of the investment community's level of **risk aversion**.

The Risk Premium for Stock X   The risk premium for stock X is just the market, or "average," risk premium multiplied by stock X's own beta, the measure of its market risk.

What the SML is saying is simple and yet profound. It alleges that a stock's risk premium is determined only by the market risk premium factored by the stock's beta.

Notice that the only thing in the equation that relates specifically to company X is b_X, the measure of X's *market risk*! So if management wants to influence stock price, an important way to try to do so is by changing the volatility of the firm's return and thereby its beta.

The **CAPM** asserts that the only **company-specific** thing affecting required return is **market risk**.

The important implication of the SML is that *only market risk counts*. Business-specific risk doesn't enter the equation; market risk does through beta. Put another way, **investors are rewarded with extra return only for bearing market risk**, not for bearing business-specific risk. This makes sense because we've assumed that business-specific risk is diversified away for portfolio investors.

The SML holds for the stock of any company. That's why we've used the generic "X" to represent the company's name. The model says that any firm's required rate of return, as generally perceived by most investors, can be found by just putting that company's beta into Equation 9.4.

The SML as a Portrayal of the Securities Market   The SML can be thought of as representing the entire securities market, most notably the stock market. To show this we'll plot the line in *risk–return space*. That simply means the graph will have return on the vertical axis and risk along the horizontal axis. The variable representing risk will be beta. The SML is portrayed graphically in Figure 9-9, where it's seen as a straight line.

Recall the standard formulation for plotting a straight line from algebra.

(9.5) $$Y = mx + b$$

Here y is traditionally the vertical axis variable and x is the horizontal axis variable. When the equation of a straight line is in this form, m is the slope of the line and b is its y-intercept.

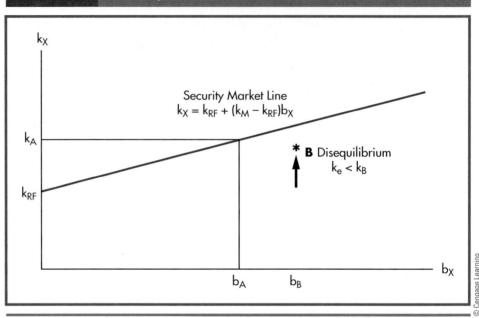

FIGURE 9-9   The Security Market Line

In our graph of the SML, the variable on the vertical axis is k_X and the variable on the horizontal axis is b_X. We can write Equation 9.4 in the same form as Equation 9.5 and compare the two.

$$k_X = \underbrace{(k_M - k_{RF})}_{m} \underbrace{b_x}_{x} + \underbrace{k_{RF}}_{b}$$
$$y = \qquad m \qquad\quad x \ + \ b$$

(Don't confuse the X's and b's in the two equations. In the first, X represents the generic name of a company. In the second, x refers to the variable on the horizontal axis. In the first equation b represents beta, a variable, but b is a constant, the y intercept, in the second equation.)

The comparison shows that the slope of the SML is the market risk premium $(k_M - k_{RF})$. Thus, the slope of the SML is a reflection of the risk tolerance or level of risk aversion felt by investors in general. If investors become more risk averse, the spread between k_M and k_{RF} will increase because people will demand a larger premium for bearing any level of risk. When that happens, the SML will get steeper. Conversely, if people become less concerned about risk, the market risk premium will shrink and the SML will become flatter.

The slope of the **SML** plotted in **risk–return space** reflects the general level of risk aversion.

It's important to understand that attitudes about risk do change, and that those changes are reflected in real differences between k_M and k_{RF}.

The **vertical intercept** of the SML represents investment in short-term government securities.

Next consider the intercept of the SML with the vertical axis. This is the y-intercept in the traditional equation. The value of k_X at the intercept point is clearly k_{RF}. This makes sense because risk, represented by beta, is zero at the left side of the graph. The intercept point is saying that an investor always has the option of putting money into government securities earning k_{RF} with no risk.

© Cengage Learning

The SML portrays the market in terms of risk and return in that any stock can be thought of as occupying a point along the line determined by its level of risk. For instance, stock A is shown on the diagram. If we enter the graph at A's beta, b_A, we can find A's required return by moving up to the line and then over to the vertical axis at k_A.

The SML as a Line of Market Equilibrium

A system is said to be in *equilibrium* if it tends to remain in a constant state over time. The equilibrium condition is said to be *stable* if, when the system is displaced, forces are created that tend to push it back into the equilibrium position.

The SML represents an equilibrium situation if, for every stock along the line, the expected rate of return is equal to the required rate of return. In that case, investors holding stocks are happy because their expected and required rates of return are at least equal. There is no excess of either buyers or sellers, and in theory the market remains where it is.

Now suppose conditions change in such a way that the expected return on some stock becomes less than its required return. This situation is represented by point B in the diagram, where the expected return, shown as k_e, is less than the required return for stock B, which is on the SML above b_B.

In this case, people who own the stock will be inclined to sell because the anticipated return no longer meets their needs. That is, it is below their required return, which is on the SML. However, potential buyers will not be interested in purchasing the stock because the expected return is also lower than their required returns. In other words, we have would-be sellers but no interested buyers. When that happens in the market for anything, there's only one solution if trading is to take place—sellers must lower their asking prices. In other words, the market price falls.

Now examine Equation 9.2 once again which we'll repeat here for convenience.

(9.2)
$$k = \frac{D_1 + (P_1 - P_0)}{P_0}$$

Notice that the current market price is represented as P_0. If P_0 falls while D_1 and P_1 remain unchanged, the value of k on the left side of the equation *increases*. That means the expected return becomes higher as new investors have to spend less for the same future cash flows.

> The SML represents a condition of **stable equilibrium**.

In Figure 9-9, this means market forces drive the expected return back up toward the equilibrium line of the SML. Hence, the stock market equilibrium is stable, because when some external occurrence displaces a return away from the equilibrium line, forces are created to push it back.

In reality, the market is never quietly in equilibrium, because things are always happening that move stock prices and returns around. The important point of the theory is that market forces are constantly being created that tend to push things back *toward* an equilibrium position with respect to risk and return.

Valuation Using Risk-Return Concepts

We can use the ideas of the capital asset pricing model in another approach to stock valuation. The method assumes that the marginal investor buys and sells the stock at the return determined by the SML, and that those sales determine market price.

The SML and the Gordon model provide a two-step **approach to valuation**.

Given that assumption, we can calculate the price in two steps. First we use the SML to calculate a required rate of return. Then we use that return in the Gordon model to arrive at a price.

CONCEPT CONNECTION   EXAMPLE 9-10

Valuing (Pricing) a Stock with CAPM

The Kelvin Company paid an annual dividend of $1.50 recently and is expected to grow at 7% into the indefinite future. Short-term Treasury bills are currently yielding 6%, and an average stock yields its owner 10%. Kelvin stock is relatively volatile. Its return tends to move in response to political and economic changes about twice as much as does the return on the average stock. What should Kelvin sell for today?

SOLUTION: First write the SML for Kelvin from Equation 9.4.

$$k_{Kelvin} = k_{RF} + (k_M - k_{RF})b_{Kelvin}$$

Next, notice that the inputs to the SML have been specified in the problem description without being named. The return on short-term Treasury bills reflects the current risk-free rate, k_{RF}, and the return on the "average stock" is equivalent to the return on the market, k_M. Finally, recognize that we've been given beta in rather cryptic terms. Political and economic changes are things that tend to affect all stocks, and the response to them relates to market risk. Therefore, saying Kelvin's return responds twice as much as the average to those things implies that Kelvin's beta is 2.0.

Substituting for Kelvin's required return we have

$$k_{Kelvin} = 6 + (10 - 6)2.0 = 14\%$$

Next, write the Gordon model and substitute using k_{Kelvin} for k in the denominator.

$$P_0 = \frac{D_0(1 + g)}{k - g}$$

$$= \frac{\$1.50(1.07)}{.14 - .07}$$

$$= \$22.93$$

The Impact of Management Decisions on Stock Prices   The fact that management decisions can affect both beta and likely future growth rates makes the SML approach to valuation relevant for policy decisions.

CONCEPT CONNECTION   EXAMPLE 9-11

Strategic Decisions Based on CAPM

The Kelvin Company described in the last example has an exciting new opportunity. The firm has identified a new field into which it can expand using technology it already possesses. The venture promises to increase the firm's growth rate to 9% from the current 7%. However, the project is new and unproven, so there's a chance it will fail and cause a considerable loss. As a result, there's some concern that the stock market won't react favorably to the additional risk. Management estimates that undertaking the venture will raise the firm's beta to 2.3 from its current level of 2.0. Should Kelvin undertake the new project?

SOLUTION: A strategic decision such as this should be based on the primary objective of the firm's management, maximizing shareholder wealth. That's equivalent to maximizing the price of the company's stock.

An increased growth rate will have a positive effect on stock price. Convince yourself of this by examining how the growth rate, g, influences the value of P_0 in the Gordon model in the last example. A bigger g makes the numerator larger and the denominator smaller, both of which contribute to an increase in P_0. (Remember that g must remain less than k.)

On the other hand, examining the SML of Equation 9.4, we see that a larger beta results in a larger risk premium and therefore a larger required rate of return. That in turn goes into the denominator of the Gordon model as k, and a larger k in the Gordon denominator results in a smaller price.

Hence, taking on the new project involves two things that tend to move the stock's price in opposite directions. Faster growth will increase stock price, while higher risk will decrease it. The question is which effect will dominate. We can find out by calculating an estimated price assuming the project is undertaken.

First, recalculate the required rate of return.

$$k_{Kelvin} = 6 + (10 - 6)\,2.3 = 15.2\%$$

Then, recalculate the price using the Gordon model with the new return and the new estimated growth rate.

$$P_0 = \frac{D_0(1 + g)}{k - g} = \frac{\$1.50(1.09)}{.152 - .09} = \$26.37$$

The resulting price of $26.37 is higher than the $22.93 price before the project (from Example 9-10). This indicates that the positive effect of the increased growth rate outweighs the negative effect of increased risk. Therefore, the venture looks like a good idea.

In actual practice it would be difficult to make accurate estimates of the effect of a project like this on a firm's growth rate and beta. Such estimates would be subjective guesses at best. The impact on beta would be particularly vague. Nevertheless an exercise like this would give management a valuable insight into the potential effects of their actions on stock price.

from the
CFO

Adjustments to Changing Market Conditions   As the securities market changes over time, the equilibrium of the SML accommodates to the altered conditions by shifting its position. We'll consider two such movements.

The SML shifts **parallel** to itself in response to changes in the **risk-free rate**.

The Response to a Change in the Risk-Free Rate   When the **risk-free rate** changes, all other things held equal, the SML simply shifts up or down **parallel** to itself. The new

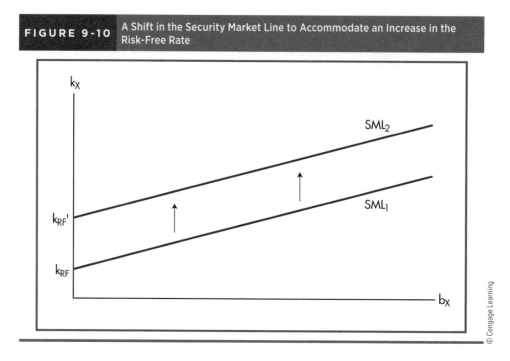

FIGURE 9-10 A Shift in the Security Market Line to Accommodate an Increase in the Risk-Free Rate

equilibrium position is determined by the new rate at the vertical axis intercept. The idea is illustrated in Figure 9-10 for an increase in the risk-free rate from k_{RF} to k_{RF}'.

The shift illustrated in Figure 9-10 contains a subtlety. The parallel shift of the SML implies that its slope remains the same. Recall that the slope of the SML is the market risk premium $(k_M - k_{RF})$, which reflects the general degree of investors' risk aversion.

If the slope of the SML doesn't change when k_{RF} changes, k_M must also increase or decrease by the amount of the change in k_{RF}. This makes sense because the market rate, like any other rate, consists of the risk-free rate plus a risk premium.

The Response to a Change in Risk Aversion A change in the general sensitivity of investors to risk will be reflected in a change in the market risk premium, represented as $(k_M - k_{RF})$ and as the *slope* of the SML in the diagram. We'll assume that k_M changes with no accompanying change in k_{RF}.

Changes in **attitudes toward risk** are reflected by **rotations of the SML** around its vertical intercept.

A change in slope alone is reflected by a **rotation of the SML** around the constant vertical intercept point at k_{RF}. The idea is illustrated in Figure 9-11.

In the illustration, SML_1 rotates to SML_2 in response to an *increase* in risk aversion. In other words, the average investor demands a higher risk premium on any investment to compensate for his or her increased aversion to risk. The higher premium is reflected in a steeper slope for the resulting SML. These ideas are illustrated in Example 9-12.

9.2j The Validity and Acceptance of the CAPM and its SML

The capital asset pricing model is like the other models we've discussed in that it is an abstraction of reality. It's a simplification of the complex securities world, designed to help in making predictions about what stock prices and returns will do. Such predictions can then be used to make various investment decisions.

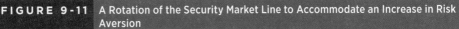

FIGURE 9-11 A Rotation of the Security Market Line to Accommodate an Increase in Risk Aversion

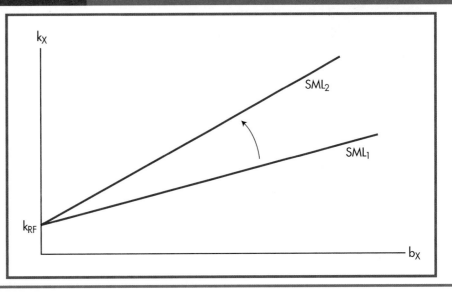

© Cengage Learning

CONCEPT CONNECTION   **EXAMPLE 9-12**

The SML and Changing Market Conditions

The Sidel Company has a beta of 1.25. The risk-free rate is currently 6%, and the market is returning 10%. According to the SML, Sidel's required rate of return is

$$k_S = k_{RF} + (k_M - k_{RF})b_S = 6 + (10 - 6)1.25 = 11.0$$

a. **A Change in the Risk-Free Rate:** Calculate Sidel's new required rate of return if the risk-free rate increases to 8% and investors' risk aversion remains unchanged.

b. **A Change in Risk Aversion:** Calculate the new required rate if the return on the market increases to 11% with the risk-free rate remaining at the original 6%.

SOLUTION:

a. If the risk-free rate changes with no change in risk aversion, the market return has to change with it, so the difference between the two remains constant. Substituting into the SML, we have

$$k_S = k_{RF} + (k_M - k_{RF})b_S = 8 + (12 - 8)1.25 = 13.0\%$$

In this case, interest rates in general will rise by the increase in the risk-free rate.

b. If the market return changes by itself, simply substitute the new value into the SML as follows.

$$k_S = k_{RF} + (k_M - k_{RF})b_S = 6 + (11 - 6)1.25 = 12.25\%$$

Here the increase in the market return reflects a higher risk premium, meaning people are more concerned about bearing risk. As a result, the rate on all risky investments will rise.

In both cases, the price of Sidel stock will fall.

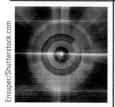

Ensuper/Shutterstock.com

INSIGHTS   Practical Finance

Beta in Practice

The concept of beta as a measurement of risk is probably the most widely used piece of stock market theory today. Investment advisory services publish betas for all heavily traded stocks, and people in the securities industry talk about beta all the time.

However, it's quite likely that many of the people who use the term aren't aware of exactly what it means. Beta measures risk, and risk means volatility of return, both up and down. Most people are aware of that much. But beta measures market-related volatility, not total volatility. That's what the average person forgets.

Beta means market risk only, and that's the relevant measure only if you're dealing with a well-diversified portfolio. If you're a moderate or small investor, beta tells only part of the story, and you can get hurt pretty badly by the part it doesn't tell.

The main reason for CAPM's popularity is probably its simplicity. The model's operative equation, the SML, is short and easy to understand. This is unusual among mathematical and statistical models, which are typically very difficult.

In addition, CAPM provides something that's very relevant in finance, a tangible statement of the relationship between risk and return. Everyone intuitively feels there's a relation between the two, and that higher risk goes along with higher return. But until CAPM came along, no one had a usable handle on the idea. In other words, there wasn't anything that said *this* much risk is appropriate for *that* much return, and therefore I'll invest, but otherwise I won't.

Unfortunately, because models that simplify the real world have to leave a lot out, they don't always work. CAPM is no exception to that general rule. Scholars are deeply divided on its validity and usefulness. Many question whether there is any real predictive value in the SML at all, while others feel the equation is sound but that people tend to apply it incorrectly. Staunch proponents maintain that the model is entirely valid and works under most conditions.

> The CAPM is **not universally accepted**, and a continuing debate exists as to its relevance and usefulness.

The most important attack on the CAPM has come from the work of two well-known scholars, Eugene Fama and Kenneth French. They found no historical relationship between the returns on stocks and their betas.[3] The CAPM, of course, assumes that a relationship does exist as expressed by the SML. If Fama and French are right, the CAPM isn't worth much. Other researchers, however, have challenged their work on both empirical and theoretical grounds. A lively controversy continues in the scholarly literature that is as yet inconclusive.

It's unlikely that the leading scholars in this area will come to an agreement any time soon. CAPM and beta, the associated measure of risk, are part of the framework of theoretical finance and will probably remain so for the foreseeable future.

For our purposes, you should understand the ideas and assumptions leading up to the SML and appreciate what the equation is saying in terms of the relation between risk and return. We'll assume that it's a pretty good representation of reality most of the time.

---

3. Eugene Fama and Kenneth French, "The Cross-Section of Expected Stock Returns," *Journal of Finance* 47, No. 2 (June 1992): 427–65.

It is important, however, to keep one important limitation in mind. The model's risk as measured by beta is market risk only, and not a stock's total risk. As we said earlier, that limits the concept substantially.

CONCEPT CONNECTIONS

Ensuper/Shutterstock.com

OlegDoroshin/Shutterstock.com

QUESTIONS

1. What is the fundamental motivation behind portfolio theory? That is, what are people trying to achieve by investing in portfolios of stocks rather than in a few individual stocks or in debt? What observations prompted this view?

2. What is the general (in words) relationship between risk and return?

3. Define and discuss (words only, no equations) the concepts of expected return and required return.

4. Give a verbal definition of "risk" that's consistent with the way we use the word in everyday life. Discuss the weaknesses of that definition for financial theory.

5. Define risk aversion in words without reference to probability distributions. If people are risk averse, why are lotteries so popular? Why are trips to Las Vegas popular? (*Hint:* Think in terms of the size of the amount risked and entertainment value.)

6. The following definition applies to both investing and gambling: putting money at risk in the hope of earning more money. In spite of this similarity, society has very different moral views of the two activities.

   a. Develop an argument reconciling the differences and similarities between the two concepts. That is, why do people generally feel good about investing and bad about gambling? (*Hint:* Think of where the money goes and what part of a person's income is used.)

   b. Discuss the difference between investing and gambling by referring to the probability distributions shown on page 420. Identify the representations of a total loss, a big win, and likely outcomes.

7. Why does it make sense to think of the return on a stock investment as a random variable? Does it make sense to think of the return on a bond investment that way? How about an investment in a savings account?

8. In everyday language, "risk" means the probability of something bad happening. "Risk" in finance, however, is defined as the standard deviation of the probability distribution of returns.

   a. Why do these definitions seem contradictory?

   b. Reconcile the two ideas.

9. Analyze the shape of the probability distribution for a high-risk stock versus that of a low-risk stock. (*Hint:* Think in terms of where the area under the curve lies.)

10. Describe risk in finance as up-and-down movement of return. Does this idea make sense in terms of the variance definition?

11. Define and discuss the idea of separating risk into two parts. Describe each part carefully.

12. Describe the goal of a portfolio owner in terms of risk and return. How does he or she evaluate the risk characteristics of stocks being considered for addition to the portfolio?

13. Discuss lowering portfolio risk through diversification. Consider
    a. Unsystematic (business-specific) risk.
    b. Systematic (market) risk.

14. Describe the concept of beta. Include what it measures and how it's developed.

15. Describe the SML in words. What is it saying about how investors form required rates of return? Thoroughly evaluate the implications of the SML's message.

16. How does the SML determine the price of a security?

17. How is risk aversion reflected in the SML?

18. The CAPM purports to explain how management decisions about risk can influence the well-being of stockholders. Describe in words the mechanism through which this works.

19. Is the CAPM a true and accurate representation of the securities world?

BUSINESS ANALYSIS

1. You've just begun work at the brokerage firm of Dewey, Cheatam, and Howe as a stock analyst. This morning you read an article in the paper that said a large-scale reduction in defense spending is imminent. Fred Fastbuck, a broker at the firm, has several clients who are elderly retirees. You recently learned that he's actively putting those clients into several defense industry stocks he describes as low risk. Fred has told you that he feels the stocks are low risk because they have betas of 1.0 or less. How would you advise Fred? Consider the real meaning of beta and its constancy over time.

PROBLEMS

Expected and Required Returns, Equation 9.2 (page 399)

1. The Duncan Company's stock is currently selling for $15. People generally expect its price to rise to $18 by the end of next year. They also expect that it will pay a dividend of $.50 per share during the year. (*Hint:* Apply Equation 9.2 page 399.)
    a. What is the expected return on an investment in Duncan's stock?
    b. Recalculate the expected return if next year's price is forecast to be only $17 and the dividend $.25.
    c. Calculate the actual return on Duncan if at the end of the year the price turns out to be $13 and the dividend actually paid was just $.10.

2. The Rapscallion Company's stock is selling for $43.75. Dave Jones has done some research on the firm and its industry, and he thinks it will pay dividends of $5 next year and $7 the following year. After those two years, Dave thinks its market price will peak at $50. His strategy is to buy now, hold for the two years, and then sell at the peak price. If Dave is confident about his financial projections but requires a return of 25% before investing in stocks like Rapscallion, should he invest in this opportunity? (*Hint:* Approximate the answer by extending Equation 9.2 to two years and taking half of the result.)

Calculating the Mean and Standard Deviation of a Discrete Probability Distribution: Concept Connection Examples 9-1, 9-2, and 9-3 (pages 401, 403, and 405)

3. Wayne Merritt drives from Cleveland to Chicago frequently and has noticed that traffic and weather make a big difference in the time it takes to make the trip. As a result, he has a hard time planning activities around his arrival time. To better plan his business, Wayne wants to calculate

his average driving time as well as a measure of how much an actual trip is likely to vary from that average. To do that, he clocked 10 trips with the following results:

Driving Time	Number of trips
6 hrs, 0 min	1
6 hrs, 15 min	1
6 hrs, 30 min	2
6 hrs, 45 min	3
7 hrs, 0 min	1
7 hrs, 30 min	1
9 hrs, 20 min	1

a. Calculate the mean, standard deviation, and coefficient of variation of Wayne's driving time to Chicago. (*Hint:* Treat the 10 trips as the 10 possible outcomes of a discrete probability distribution, each of which has a probability of .1. Work in total minutes for each trip.)

b. Calculate the average variation in driving time. Compare the standard and average variations. Is the difference significant? Which is more meaningful to Wayne?

Discrete Probability Distributions: Concept Connection Example 9-1 and Footnote 1 (page 401)

4. Suppose dice had four sides instead of six, so rolling a single die would produce equally likely numbers from 1 to 4, and rolling two dice would produce numbers from 2 to 8.

a. Compute the probability distribution of outcomes from rolling two dice.

Mean and Standard Deviation: Concept Connection Examples 9-2 and 9-3 (page 403 and 405)

b. Calculate the mean, standard deviation, and coefficient of variation of the distribution.

***Note:* For Problems 5–8, assume discrete probability distributions for the returns on stocks to keep the computations simple.**

Evaluating Stand-Alone Risk: Concept Connection Example 9-4 (page 411)

5. Conestoga Ltd. has the following estimated probability distribution of returns.

Return	Probability
4%	.20
12	.50
14	.30

Calculate Conestoga's expected return, the variance and standard deviation of its expected return, and the return's coefficient of variation.

6. The probability distribution of the return on an investment in Omega Inc.'s common stock follows.

Return	Probability
5%	.05
8	.25
10	.40
12	.25
15	.05

Graph the probability distribution. Calculate the expected return, the standard deviation of the return, and the coefficient of variation.

7. Calculate the expected return on an investment in Delta Inc.'s stock if the probability distribution of returns is as follows.

Return	Probability
−5%	.10
5	.25
10	.30
15	.25
25	.10

Plot the distribution on the axes with Omega Inc. in the previous problem. Looking at the graph, which company has the lower risk/variance? If offered the choice between making an investment in Delta and in Omega Inc., which would most investors choose? Why?

8. The Manning Company's stock is currently selling for $23. It has the following prospects for next year.

Next Year's		
Stock Price	Dividend	Probability
$25	$1.00	.25
30	1.50	.50
35	2.00	.25

Calculate Manning's expected return for a one-year holding period.

Risk Aversion: Figure 9-6 (page 410)

9. Imagine making choices in the following situation to test your degree of risk aversion. Someone offers you the choice between the following game and a sure thing.

  The game: A coin is tossed. If it turns up heads, you get a million dollars. If tails, you get nothing.

  The sure thing: You're given $500,000.

  a. What is the expected value of each option?

  c. Which option would you choose?

  d. Viewing the options as probability distributions, which has the larger variance? What is the variance of the sure thing? (No calculations.)

  e. Suppose the game is changed to offer a payoff of $1.2 million for a head but still offers nothing for a tail. The sure thing remains $500,000. What is the expected value of each option now? Which option would you choose now?

  f. Most people will have chosen the sure thing in part (d). Assuming you did too, how much would the game's payoff have to increase before you would choose it over the sure thing?

  g. Relate this exercise to Figure 9-6 on page 410.

Portfolio Return: Concept Connection Example 9-5 (page 415)

10. A portfolio consists of the following four stocks:

Stock	Current Market Value	Expected Return
A	$ 180,000	8%
B	145,000	10
C	452,000	12
D	223,000	5
	$1,000,000	

What is the expected return of the portfolio?

11. Laurel Wilson has a portfolio of five stocks. The stocks' actual investment performance last year is given below along with an estimate of this year's performance.

	Last Year		This Year	
Stock	Investment	Return	Investment	Return
A	$50,000	8.0%	$55,000	8.5%
B	40,000	6.0	40,000	7.0
C	80,000	4.0	60,000	4.5
D	20,000	12.0	45,000	9.0
E	60,000	3.0	50,000	5.0

Compute the actual return on Laurel's overall portfolio last year and its expected return this year.

Projecting Returns with Beta: Concept Connection Example 9-6 (page 421)

12. Threads Inc. manufactures stylish clothing for teenagers. The firm has a beta of 1.4 and earned a return on equity of 20% last year. However, a new financial crisis has just hit the stock market and Wall Street experts think the return on an average stock will be cut in half this year. The market has been producing equity returns of about 18% lately. Estimate this year's return on an equity investment in Threads.

Portfolio Beta: Concept Connection Example 9-9 (page 424)

13. The stocks in Problem 11 have the following betas.

Stock	Beta
A	1.1
B	0.6
C	1.0
D	1.6
E	0.8

Calculate Laurel's portfolio beta for last year and for this year. Assume that the changes in investment (value) come from changing stock prices rather than buying and selling shares. What has happened to the riskiness of Laurel's portfolio? Should she be concerned?

14. A four-stock portfolio is made up as follows.

Stock	Current Value	Beta
A	$4,500	.8
B	2,900	.6
C	6,800	1.3
D	1,200	1.8

Calculate the portfolio's beta.

The Determination of Beta: Figure 9-8 (page 423)

15. Charming Co. manufactures decorating products. Treasury bills currently yield 5.4% and the market is returning 8.1%.

   a. Calculate Charming Co.'s beta from its characteristic line as depicted below.

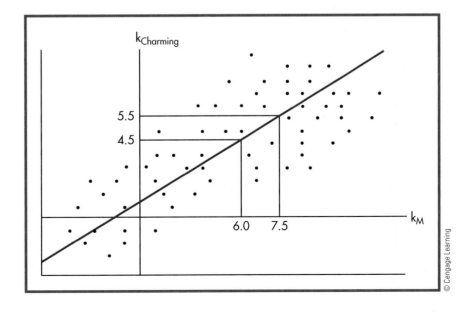

b. What expected return would an average investor require to buy shares of Charming?

c. Would the answer to part (b) be a "fair" return? Why? (*Hint:* Think in terms of whether the investor has a diversified portfolio or just a few stocks and the risk she faces in each case.)

16. The return on Holland-Wilson Inc. (HWI) stock over the last three years is shown below along with the market's return for the same period.

Year	HWI	Market
1	4.0%	3.0%
2	9.0	6.0
3	12.0	10.0

Plot HWI's return against that of the market in each of the three years. Make three estimates of HWI's beta by drawing characteristic lines between pairs of data points (1 and 2; 1 and 3; 2 and 3). What does this range of betas imply about the stock's risk relative to an average stock?

17. You have recently purchased stock in Topical Inc. which has returned between 7% and 9% over the last three years. Your friend, Bob, has criticized your purchase and insists that you should have invested in Combs Inc., as he did, because it's been returning between 10% and 12% in the last three years. Bob knows nothing about financial theory. Topical's beta is 0.7 and Comb's is 1.2. Treasury bills are currently yielding the risk-free rate of 4.2%, while the stock market is returning an average rate of 9.4%.

a. What return should you expect from Topical? What return should Bob expect from Combs?

b. Write a few words explaining to Bob why these expected returns aren't the whole story.

18. Erin Behlen has a three-stock portfolio and is interested in estimating its overall return next year. She has $25,000 invested in Forms Corp., which has a beta of 1.3; $75,000 in Crete Corp. with a beta of .8; and $20,000 in Stalls Corp, which has a beta of 1.45. The stock market is currently returning 10.2% and Treasury securities are yielding the risk-free rate of 4.6%. What return should Erin anticipate on her portfolio? (*Hint:* Calculate the portfolio beta and then apply the SML.)

19. The CFO of Ramekin Pottery Inc. is concerned about holding up the price of the company's stock. He's asked you to do an analysis starting with an estimate of the return investors are likely to require before they will invest in the firm. The overall stock market is currently returning 16%, 90-day treasury bills yield 6%, and the return on Ramekin's stock typically responds to changes in the political and economic environment only about 60% as vigorously as does that of the average stock.

a. Prepare an estimate of the firm's required return using the CAPM.

b. Is a higher or lower required return good for the company? Why?

c. Suppose the CFO asks you what management can do to improve the required return. How will you respond?

d. What will you tell him if he wants it done within the next three months?

20. You are a junior treasury analyst at the Palantine Corporation. The treasurer believes the CAPM gives a good estimate of the company's return to equity investors at any time and has asked you to prepare an estimate of that return using the SML. Treasury bills currently yield 6% but may go up or down by 1%. The S&P 500 shows a return of 10% but may vary from that figure up to 12%. Palantine's beta is .8. Construct a table showing all possible values of $k_{Palantine}$ for 1% increments of k_{RF} and k_M (nine entries). For this problem treat k_M and k_{RF} separately. That is, do not assume an increase in k_M when k_{RF} changes.

Valuing (Pricing) a Stock with CAPM: Concept Connection Example 9-10 (page 430)

21. The Framingham Company expects to grow at 4% indefinitely. Economists are currently asserting that investment opportunities in short-term government securities (Treasury bills) are readily

available at a risk-free rate of 5%. The stock market is returning an average rate of 9%. Framingham's beta has recently been calculated at 1.4. The firm recently paid an annual dividend of $ 1.68 per share. At what price should shares of Framingham stock be selling?

22. Whole Foods Inc. paid a quarterly dividend of $0.47 recently. Treasury bills are yielding 4%, and the average stock is returning about 11%. Whole Foods is a stable company. The return on its stock responds to changes in the political and economic environment only about 70% as vigorously as that of the average stock. Analysts expect the firm to grow at an annual rate of 3.5% into the indefinite future. Calculate a reasonable price that investors should be willing to pay for Whole Foods stock.

23. Seattle Software Inc. recently paid an annual dividend of $1.95 per share and is expected to grow at a 15% rate indefinitely. Short-term federal government securities are paying 4%, while an average stock is earning its owner 11%. Seattle is a very volatile stock, responding to the economic climate two and a half times as violently as an average stock. This is, however, typical of the software industry.
    a. How much should a share of Seattle be worth?
    b. Do you see any problems with this estimate? Change one assumption to something more reasonable and compare the results.

24. The Aldridge Co. is expected to grow at 6% into the indefinite future. Its latest annual dividend was $2.50. Treasury bills currently earn 7% and the S&P 500 yields 11%.
    a. What price should Aldridge shares command in the market if its beta is 1.3?
    b. Evaluate the sensitivity of Aldridge's price to changes in expected growth and risk by recalculating the price while varying the growth rate between 5% and 7% (increments of 1%) and varying beta between 1.2 and 1.4 (increments of .1).

25. Bergman Corp. has experienced zero growth over the last seven years paying an annual dividend of $2.00 per share. Investors generally expect this performance to continue. Bergman stock is currently selling for $24.39. The risk-free rate is 3.0%, and Bergman's beta is 1.3.
    a. Calculate the return investors require on Bergman's stock.
    b. Calculate the market return.
    c. Suppose you think Bergman is about to announce plans to grow at 3.0% into the foreseeable future. You also believe investors will accept that prediction and continue to require the same return on its stock. How much should you be willing to pay for a share of Bergman's stock?

26. Weisman Electronics just paid a $1.00 dividend, the market yield is yielding 10%, the risk-free rate is 4%, and Weisman's beta is 1.5. How fast do investors expect the company to grow in the future if its stock is selling for $27.25?

Strategic Decisions Based on CAPM: Concept Connection Example 9-11 (page 430)

27. Weisman Electronics from the previous problem is considering acquiring an unrelated business. Management thinks the move could change the firm's stock price by moving its beta up or down and decreasing its growth rate. A consultant has estimated that Weisman's beta after the acquisition could be anywhere between 1.3 and 1.7 while the growth rate could remain at 9% or decline to as little as 5%. Calculate a range of values for Weisman's stock based on best-and-worst case scenarios.

28. Broken Wing Airlines just paid an annual dividend of $2, has a beta of 1.3, and a growth rate of 6% for the foreseeable future. The current return on the market is 10%, and Treasury bills earn 4%. If the rate on Treasury bills drops by 0.5% and the market risk premium $[(k_M - k_{RF})]$ increases by 1.0%, what growth rate would keep Broken Wing's stock price constant? (*Hint:* Calculate the price before rates change, then use it as P_0 in a problem with the changed rates and solve for g.)

29. Lipson Ltd. expects a constant growth rate of 5% in the future. Treasury bills yield 8% and the market is returning 13% on an average issue. Lipson's last annual dividend was $1.35. The company's beta has historically been .9. The introduction of a new line of business would increase the expected growth rate to 7% while increasing its risk substantially. Management estimates the firm's beta would increase to 1.2 if the new line were undertaken. Should Lipson undertake the new line of business?

The SML and Changing Market Conditions: Concept Connection Example 9-12 (page 433)

30. The Picante Corp.'s beta is .7. Treasury bills yield 5% and an average stock yields 10%.

   a. Write and sketch the SML and locate Picante on it. Calculate Picante's required rate of return and show it on the graph.

   b. Assume the yield on Treasury bills suddenly increases to 7% with no other changes in the financial environment. Write and sketch the new SML, calculate Picante's new required rate, and show it on the new line.

   c. Now assume that besides the change in part (b), investors' risk aversion increases so that the market risk premium is 7%. Write and sketch the resulting SML, calculate Picante's required return, and show it on the last line.

COMPUTER PROBLEM

31. Problem 22 in Chapter 8 concerned the Rollins Metal Company, which is engaged in long-term planning. The firm is trying to choose among several strategic options that imply different future growth rates and risk levels. Reread that problem on page 393 now.

   The CAPM gives some additional insight into the relation between risk and required return. We can now define risk as beta and evaluate its effect on stock price by constructing a chart similar to the one called for in Problem 22 of Chapter 8, replacing k on the left side with beta (b).

   Rollins's beta calculated from historical data is .8. However, the risky strategies being considered could influence that figure significantly. Management feels beta could rise to as much as 2.0 under certain strategic options. Treasury bills currently yield 3%, while the S&P index is showing a return of 8%. Recall that Rollins's last dividend was $2.35.

   a. Use the CAPMVAL program to construct the following chart.

The Price of Rollins Stock as a Function of Growth Rate and Beta

	Growth Rates (g)			
Beta (b)	6%	8%	10%	12%
.8				
1.2				
1.6				
2.0				

   b. The effect of beta on required return and price is influenced by the general level of risk aversion, which in the CAPM is represented by $(k_M - k_{RF})$, which is also the market risk premium and the slope of the SML. In part (a) of this problem, the market risk premium is $(8\% - 3\% =)$ 5%. Economists, however, predict a recession that could sharply increase risk aversion. Reconstruct the chart above assuming the market risk premium increases to 7% (k_M rises to 10% with no change in k_{RF}).

   c. Do your charts give any new insights into the risk-return-growth relationship? (i.e., how does the reward for bearing more risk in terms of stock price change in recessionary times?) Write the implied required return on your charts next to the values of beta. Then compare the charts with the one from Problem 22 of Chapter 8.

d. Does the inclusion of beta and the CAPM really make management's planning job any less intuitive? In other words, is it any easier to associate a strategy's risk level with a beta than directly with a required return?

DEVELOPING SOFTWARE

32. Write a spreadsheet program to calculate the expected return and beta for a portfolio of 10 stocks given the expected returns and betas of the stocks in the portfolio and their dollar values.

    The calculation involves taking a weighted average of the individual stocks' expected returns and betas where the weights are based on the dollar values invested in each stock.

    Set up your spreadsheet like this:

	Stock	Value	Weight	Beta	Factor	k_e	Factor
1.	ABC	$ 5,530	.0645	.93	.0600	8.0%	.5160
2.	EFG	2,745	.0320	1.25	.0400	12.2%	.3904
		:	:	:	:	:	:
10.	XYZ	9,046	.1055	1.12	.1182	11.5%	1.2133
		$85,715	1.0000		XXX		XXX

Sum columns for: Portfolio beta ——
Portfolio k_e ——

The computational procedure is as follows.

1. Input the names of the stocks, their dollar values, their betas, and their k_e's.
2. Sum the value column.
3. Calculate the weight column by dividing each row's value cell by the cell carrying the sum of the values.
4. Calculate the beta and k_e factors by multiplying the individual beta and k_e cells by the cells in the weight column on the same row.
5. Sum the two factor columns for the results indicated.

Is your program general in that it will handle a portfolio of *up to* 10 stocks, or will it only work for exactly 10? If it is general, what do you have to be careful about with respect to inputs?

Extra: Assume you have $1 million to invest in stocks. Look up several stocks' betas in Value Line and estimate k_e for each. Look up the current price of each stock online and form a hypothetical portfolio by allocating your money among the stocks. Find your portfolio's expected return and beta using your program.

THOMSON REUTERS

Go to **www.cengage.com/thomsonone,** select your book and click on the Thomson ONE button. Enter Thomson ONE—Business School Edition by using the user name and password you created when you registered the serial number on your access card. Select a problem for this chapter, and you'll see an expanded version that includes instructions on how to navigate within the Thomson ONE system, as well as some additional explanation of the presentation format.

33. In this exercise we'll explore beta, portfolio theory's measure of risk, and its theoretical impact on stock prices.

    Enter Thomson ONE for each of the five companies we've been working with, Sherwin Williams (SHW), Ford (F), Harley-Davidson (HOG), Starbucks (SBUX), and Microsoft (MSFT). Find and record each company's beta. Also look up and record the betas of General Mills (GIS), a large food processing company with a low beta, and Yahoo (YHOO), a provider of Internet services with a high beta.

Computations with Beta

Evaluate the impact of different betas by calculating the required return on each company using the SML (Equation 9.4 on page 426). Assume k_M is 6% and k_{RF} is 2%. How large is the variation between the smallest and largest required return?

Now make a hypothetical price calculation using the Gordon model (see page 430) and the returns you've just calculated. In each case, assume the last dividend paid was $1, and the expected growth rate is 4%. You should see that the price difference generated by real betas under the assumption that dividends and growth rates are equal is very large.

But these things generally are not equal. Companies that issue high-risk stocks are often expected to grow rapidly and pay small or no dividends. Using your Gordon Model results, find the growth rate assumption about the highest beta stock that will equate its price with that of the lowest beta stock. *(Write the Gordon Model still assuming a $1 dividend, substitute the high beta return for k, and set the resulting expression equal to the low beta price. Then solve for g.)*

What growth rate assumption would result in the same price for the highest beta stock if it paid a dividend of $.50 instead of $1?

Beta as Volatility Relative to the Market

Beta is not a precise measure of risk. Indeed, some authorities don't feel it has much validity at all. Recall that beta measures only market risk, which is the degree to which a stock's return moves with the market's. The market is generally represented by the S&P 500 index, which is based on the average price of 500 selected stocks. In the following exercise, we'll use a graphic representation of price performance as an approximation of return to help you develop your own sense of the beta technique.

Enter Thomson ONE and examine the three-year stock price history compared with the S&P 500 graph for each company.

Notice the degree to which each stock has historically moved with the market. Do this by looking for periods in which the market represented by the S&P 500 line is trending up or down. Then observe whether the stock is trending in the same direction. Is the stock's movement more or less vigorous in the same direction as the market's? (This is usually easiest to see with high beta stocks.) Work your way down the list of stocks as betas decrease. Are there periods when certain stocks don't seem to move with the market or move against it? Are these periods frequent or unusual? You may want to experiment with five- and ten-year graphs.

From your observations, does beta seem to predict movement relative to the market's? Is that a worthwhile measure of risk if we don't know where the market is going from one week to the next? Why or why not? After these observations, do you feel like an investor really appreciates a stock's risk if she knows its beta? In what context is beta most meaningful?

Business Investment Decisions—Capital Budgeting

Capital Budgeting

Chapter Outline

Characteristics of Business Projects
- Project Types and Risk
- Stand-Alone and Mutually Exclusive Projects
- Project Cash Flows
- The Cost of Capital

Capital Budgeting Techniques
- Payback Period
- Net Present Value (NPV)
- Internal Rate of Return (IRR)
- Comparing IRR and NPV
- NPV and IRR Solutions Using Financial Calculators and Spreadsheets
- Projects with a Single Outflow and Regular Inflows
- Profitability Index (PI)
- Comparing Projects with Unequal Lives
- Capital Rationing

The money companies spend in the normal course of business can be divided into two categories. Funds are expended on an everyday basis to buy inventory, pay expenses, and compensate employees. These expenditures can be thought of as short term in that they support daily activity.

In addition to such short-term expenditures, firms spend large sums on special projects from time to time. For example, machines normally wear out and need to be replaced every few years. The replacement expenditures tend to be relatively large, but they are infrequent. New business ventures provide a second example because they generally require initial spending to get started. Start-up amounts are usually large, but the opportunities don't come along often. Spending on things like these is long term because the projects involved tend to last for long periods. As a general rule, money spent on long-term projects is called *capital*.

The field known as **capital budgeting** *involves planning and justifying how capital dollars are spent on long-term projects.* It provides methods through which projects are evaluated to decide whether they make sense for a particular business at a point in time. It also provides a basis for choosing between projects when more than one is under consideration at the same time.

10.1 Characteristics of Business Projects

10.1a Project Types and Risk

Projects fit into three general categories: **replacement, expansion**, and **new venture**. We've already used the first and the last of these as examples in the opening section. Expansion simply involves doing something the firm already does on a larger scale. It usually requires investing money in additional resources and equipment similar to that already on hand.

A risk is associated with investing money in any project. For now we'll define that risk simply as the chance of making less on the project than management expects when the decision to go ahead is made.

Broadly speaking, risk varies with project type, increasing as we move from replacement to expansion to new venture. A replacement is the safest endeavor because we're doing something that's already being done. Expansion projects are riskier because they're based on a forecast increase in demand for the company's product that may not materialize. Finally, the riskiest project is a new venture, something the company hasn't done before. No one ever knows whether they'll be successful at something they haven't tried.

10.1b Stand-Alone and Mutually Exclusive Projects

Projects can be evaluated in either of two contexts. The first involves a proposal without a competing alternative. For example, suppose an old machine is wearing out and there's only one replacement product on the market. The choice is simply whether to buy the new machine (the project) or to do nothing.

This single-project situation is known as a **stand-alone project**. We need to decide on a project's viability by itself, standing alone. Is it a good deal for the company or not? Another way to think of it is to say that no other project is currently competing for the resources required to do this one.

The second situation involves choosing between projects. It occurs either when there's more than one way to do something, or when two different things are proposed but there's only enough money to do one of them. As an example of the first circumstance, assume the worn-out machine can be replaced by either of two new ones. Suppose the first option is relatively cheap to buy but is expensive to operate and produces low-quality output. The second costs more initially but runs less expensively and produces better product. Which should the firm choose? Notice that it must choose one or the other, because only one replacement is required. In this context, the alternatives are said to be **mutually exclusive**, since choosing either excludes the other.

Sometimes projects can be mutually exclusive even if they're totally different physically. That occurs when a firm has only enough resources to do one project at a time. For example, suppose an electronics firm has new venture opportunities in computer technology and radio transmission, but it has only enough money to undertake one new idea. The projects are mutually exclusive because doing one precludes doing the other, even though from business and technical viewpoints they're entirely separate. Further, the limiting resource doesn't have to be money. It might be trained personnel, plant capacity, or management's time.

10.1c   Project Cash Flows

The first step in the capital budgeting process requires that any project under consideration be represented as a series of cash flows that is incremental to the business.

> The first and usually most difficult step in capital budgeting is **reducing projects to a series of cash flows**.

This requirement is easiest to picture in the context of a new venture. Imagine that such a new business will take an initial investment of $50,000, will lose $10,000 in the first year, and is expected to generate $15,000 in cash each year for the next five years before being shut down. For capital budgeting purposes, the project can be summarized as just that series of yearly cash outflows and inflows. If we call the cash flow in the ith year C_i, and let C_0 be the initial investment at the beginning of year 1, we can represent the project as follows, where the numbers in parentheses are negative and represent outflows.

C_0	$(50,000)
C_1	(10,000)
C_2	15,000
C_3	15,000
C_4	15,000
C_5	15,000
C_6	15,000

> Business projects involve **early cash outflows** and later inflows. The **initial outlay** is required to get started.

It's important to notice the pattern of cash flows shown here. Projects nearly always involve an initial outflow of funds followed by inflows at later dates. C_0 is virtually always negative because it represents the **initial outlay** necessary to get a project started. The remaining figures tend to be positive, although they may include some negatives as in the example.

It's conceptually easy to identify incremental cash flows for a new venture. The representation can be more difficult to see when we're talking about a replacement project. The incremental cash flows in replacement projects are things like savings on fuel and maintenance or improved profitability due to higher quality product. That kind of incremental cash flow can be hard to quantify.

In fact, the most difficult and inaccurate part of capital budgeting is estimating project cash flows. For the time being we'll proceed by assuming the estimates are given for the projects we'll be talking about. In the next chapter, we'll return to the issue and consider cash flow estimation in more detail.

10.1d   The Cost of Capital

> A firm's **cost of capital** is the **average rate it pays its investors** for the use of their money.

Capital budgeting theory is based on the time value of money and the idea of return on investment. A central concept in the theory is the idea of a firm's **cost of capital**. This is the rate of return the firm pays to its long-term investors for the use of their money.

The purpose of the concept is intuitively obvious: An investment makes sense only if it earns more than the cost of funds put into it.

For example, suppose you want to start a business in which you expect to earn a return of 15% on invested money. Further suppose you have no money of your own, but you can borrow from a relative who demands 18% interest. Does it make sense to start the business? Of course not; you'd be losing money from the outset because you'd have to pay more for your funds than you could earn using them. It would make sense to begin the business only if you could borrow the start-up money at *less than* 15%. In this illustration, the cost of capital is the rate at which you can borrow to undertake the venture.

In general, firms have two sources of capital—equity and debt—and pay different rates of return to the investors who supply each. In practice, the cost of capital is a single rate that reflects the average of the rates for those two sources.

Here's a simple example. Suppose the total dollar amount of a firm's capital is 75% equity and 25% debt. Assume the stockholders (equity) are receiving a 10% return, while the creditors (debt) are getting 8% interest. The cost of capital is the *weighted average* of the two returns, where the weights are the proportionate amounts of money invested in each of the two kinds of capital. The calculation follows:

	Portion		**Return**	
Equity	.75	×	10%	= 7.5%
Debt	.25	×	8	= 2.0
Weighted average cost of capital				= 9.5%

In other words, the cost of capital is a blending of the rates the company provides to its investors. The idea seems simple enough, but can get very complicated in practice.[1] It's an important concept, and we'll devote an entire chapter to it later in the book. For now we'll assume that every firm knows what its cost of capital is and measures opportunities against it.

10.2   Capital Budgeting Techniques

In what follows, we'll look at four capital budgeting techniques. Each consists of a series of calculations and a set of decision rules. Using any technique involves calculating a number that the technique associates with a project and then applying the decision rules to that number. Each technique has slightly different decision rules for stand-alone and mutually exclusive situations.

10.2a   Payback Period

The simplest capital budgeting technique is the payback period. In it we calculate the amount of time it takes for a project's planned cash flows to "pay back" the initial outlay. In other words, we measure the time it takes for the project to break even. This time period is the parameter used for making comparisons. Payback is most meaningful when there's just one cash outflow at the beginning of the project. The technique is most easily understood through a numerical example as illustrated in Concept Connection Example 10-1 at the top of the next page.

---

1. We've oversimplified for the sake of this preliminary illustration. As we'll see in Chapter 13, the cost of debt must take into account the tax deductibility of interest.

CONCEPT CONNECTION   EXAMPLE 10-1

Payback Period

The project represented in the following table consists of an initial outlay of $200,000 followed by four inflows of $60,000. The payback period is easily visualized by displaying the cumulative cash flow below the yearly cash flows.

	Year				
	0	**1**	**2**	**3**	**4**
Cash flow (C_i)	$(200,000)	$ 60,000	$ 60,000	$ 60,000	$60,000
Cumulative cash flow	(200,000)	(140,000)	(80,000)	(20,000)	40,000

Payback period = 3.33 years

Notice that the cumulative cash flow is negative by $20,000 after three years and positive by $40,000 after four years. If cash is assumed to flow evenly throughout the year, breakeven occurs after 3.33 years—that is, after three years and four months. This length of time is the **payback period** for the project.

> The **payback period** is the time it takes to recover early cash outflows. **Shorter** paybacks are preferred.

Payback Decision Rules

Stand-Alone Projects   Decision rules in the payback technique are based on the idea that it's better to recover invested money sooner than later. Companies that use the technique generally have stated policies for the maximum time allowable for capital recovery. The stand-alone decision rule is simply that an acceptable project's payback period must be less than that policy maximum, which is typically about three years for small projects. We can state that rule conveniently as follows.

$$\text{payback period} < \text{policy maximum} \longrightarrow \text{accept}$$
$$\text{payback period} > \text{policy maximum} \longrightarrow \text{reject}$$

Mutually Exclusive Projects   By the same reasoning, we generally prefer a project that pays back sooner to one that pays back later. Therefore, the mutually exclusive decision rule for payback is simply ***shorter is better***. If P/B_A and P/B_B represent the payback periods for projects A and B, respectively, we can write the decision rule like this.

$$P/B_A < P/B_B \longrightarrow \text{choose project A over project B}$$

Weaknesses of the Payback Method

Payback is a generally unsophisticated approach to capital budgeting that is criticized for two major shortcomings. First, it ignores the time value of money. Thus, future dollars are weighted equally with current dollars in the calculations. Notice in the example that money spent on the initial outlay at the beginning of the project is offset dollar for dollar by cash coming in as much as four years later. This is clearly a distortion of values as the correct offset would involve the present values at time 0 of the projected cash inflows.

Second, the technique ignores cash flows after the payback period. This second deficiency can lead to the wrong answer even in simple cases. The idea is illustrated in Concept Connection Example 10-2 below.

CONCEPT CONNECTION   EXAMPLE 10-2

Weakness of the Payback Technique

Use the payback period technique to choose between mutually exclusive projects A and B.

	Project A	Project B
C_0	$(1,200)	$(1,200)
C_1	400	400
C_2	400	400
C_3	400	350
C_4	200	800
C_5	200	800

SOLUTION: Project A's payback period is clearly three years because its initial $1,200 investment is entirely recovered in that time. Project B is identical to A for the first two years and only slightly different in the third year, when the cash inflow is just $50 lower. However, that slightly lower payment in year 3 means that B's payback isn't complete until sometime in the fourth year. In other words, the payback period is a little longer for project B than for project A. The payback decision rule therefore chooses A over B. But B is clearly the better project because of what goes on after year 3 when B receives much larger cash inflows. The differences in years 4 and 5 overwhelm the minor difference in year 3 but are ignored by the method.

Why Use the Payback Method?   It's reasonable to ask why anyone uses the payback method given these weaknesses. The answer is that the method is quick and easy to apply, and it serves as a rough screening device.

If a project flunks payback, it's likely to be dismissed without further consideration. If it passes, one of the more sophisticated methods will be applied in further analysis.

The Present Value Payback Method   A variation on the method attempts to correct one of its deficiencies: the fact that it ignores time value. In this approach, the payback calculation is made after taking the present value of all the cash flows at an appropriate discount rate.

This approach makes logical sense but still leaves the second deficiency unaddressed while losing the method's "quick and dirty" simplicity. As a result, it's rarely used.

10.2b   Net Present Value (NPV)

A project's **NPV** is the sum of the present values of its cash inflows and outflows at the **cost of capital**.

A fundamental principle of finance and economics is that the *present value* of future cash flows is what counts when making decisions based on value. The **net present value (NPV)** technique applies this idea to the analysis of projects.

In the net present value technique, we calculate the present value of each of a project's cash flows and add them together. The result is the net present value of the project, usually referred to as the **NPV**. The word "net" implies an offsetting of pluses against minuses which reflects the fact that some flows are positive (inflows) and others are negative (outflows). Decisions about which projects to undertake are then based on project NPVs.

The present value calculations are made using the firm's *cost of capital* as an interest rate. This is an important point; the appropriate discount rate for most NPV calculations is the firm's cost of capital as described earlier in this chapter.

We can represent a project's NPV with the following equation:

(10.1) $$NPV = C_0 + C_1[PVF_{k,1}] + C_2[PVF_{k,2}] + \cdots + C_n[PVF_{k,n}]$$

where C_i through C_n are the project's forecast cash flows, and C_0 is the initial outlay. The $[PVF_{k,i}]$ are, of course, the present value factors we studied in Chapter 6. Notice that C_0 isn't multiplied by a present value factor. That's because the initial cash flow is assumed to occur immediately, in the present.

We'll digress for just a moment to write an alternate, more algebraic formulation of Equation 10.1. If we recall that $[PVF_{k,i}]$ is defined as $1/(1 + k)^i$ (see page 240), we can write:

(10.1a) $$NPV = C_0 + \frac{C_1}{(1 + k)} + \frac{C_2}{(1 + k)^2} + \cdots + \frac{C_n}{(1 + k)^n}$$

Here division by $(1 + k)^i$ is equivalent to multiplying C_i by a present value table factor.[2] We'll need this formulation to make a point later on, but won't use it for computation. For now it's important to simply understand the equivalence of the two expressions while keeping in mind that we will *always use Equation 10.1 for computations.*

It's important to think about the signs of the C's in Equation 10.1, remembering that negatives are cash outflows and positives are inflows. As we said earlier, the negatives tend to occur first, followed by the positives. Equation 10.1 says that the NPV is the difference between the present values of all the positives and all the negatives. If the present value of the inflows (positives) is greater, NPV is a positive number. NPV is negative if the present value of the outflows is larger.

NPV and Shareholder Wealth

An insightful way to look at capital spending projects involves their impact on shareholder wealth. A project's net present value is the net effect that the undertaking is expected to have on the value of the firm. If a positive-NPV project is taken on and successfully completed, the economic value of the firm should be increased by exactly the amount of the project's NPV. Conversely, a negative NPV project will decrease the value of the firm by the amount of the negative NPV.

Therefore, a capital spending program that maximizes the NPV of projects undertaken will contribute to maximizing shareholder wealth, the ideal goal of management. This direct link to shareholder wealth maximization makes NPV the most theoretically correct capital budgeting technique.

---

2. Review Equations 6.5 through 6.7 on page 240 if it isn't clear to you that this is equivalent to multiplying by the present value factors $PVF_{k,1}$, $PVF_{k,2}$, and so on.

So far we've been discussing NPVs for projects to be undertaken in the future. It's important to realize that cash flows may not actually turn out as expected. So a project that has a high *planned* NPV may turn out to have a very different impact on shareholder wealth after it's completed. Nevertheless, before the fact, the planned NPV is our best estimate of the future outcome.

Decision Rules

A **positive NPV** implies an acceptable project on a **stand-alone** basis.

Stand-Alone Projects　　Clearly, a project in which the present value of planned cash inflows exceeds the present value of outflows is desirable. Conversely, one in which the outflows are larger is undesirable. These situations correspond to projects with positive and negative NPVs, respectively. This logic leads to the *stand-alone decision rule.*

$$\text{NPV} > 0 \longrightarrow \text{accept}$$
$$\text{NPV} < 0 \longrightarrow \text{reject}$$

CONCEPT CONNECTION　　　　　　　　　　**EXAMPLE 10-3**

Net Present Value (NPV)

Project Alpha has the following cash flows:

C_0	C_1	C_2	C_3
$(5,000)	$1,000	$2,000	$3,000

If the firm considering Alpha has a cost of capital of 12%, should the project be undertaken?

SOLUTION: Project Alpha's NPV is found by summing the present value of each of the cash flows at the firm's cost of capital. We'll calculate the present values by multiplying each cash flow by the present value factor for 12% and one, two, or three years, respectively. Remember that C_0 isn't factored because it's a present cash flow. Applying Equation 10.1 we have:

$$\text{NPV} = C_0 + C_1[\text{PVF}_{k,1}] + C_2[\text{PVF}_{k,2}] + C_3[\text{PVF}_{k,3}]$$

$$= -\$5{,}000 + \$1{,}000[\text{PVF}_{12,1}] + \$2{,}000[\text{PVF}_{12,2}] + \$3{,}000[\text{PVF}_{12,3}]$$

$$= -\$5{,}000 + \$1{,}000(.8929) + \$2{,}000(.7972) + \$3{,}000(.7118)$$

$$= -\$5{,}000 + \$892.90 + \$1{,}594.40 + \$2{,}135.40$$

$$= -\$377.30$$

Hence project Alpha's NPV is negative at the firm's cost of capital, so it should not be undertaken.

In what follows, we'll generally organize calculations like these in a tabular format as follows:

Year	Cash Flow	PV Factor	PV of Cash Flow
0	$(5,000)	1.0000	$(5,000.00)
1	1,000	.8929	892.90
2	2,000	.7972	1,594.40
3	3,000	.7118	2,135.40
			NPV = $ (377.30)

It's important to notice that even though a project's total inflows exceed its outflows, it can still have a negative NPV. The reason is that the inflows are generally further in the future, so the present valuing process diminishes their value more than it does that of the outflows. In the example, the undiscounted value of the inflows adds to $6,000, while the single outflow is only $5,000. Nevertheless, on a present value basis, the inflows are less than the outflows.

In a **mutually exclusive** context, projects with **larger NPVs** are **preferred**.

Mutually Exclusive Projects   The larger the amount by which the present value of cash inflows exceeds the present value of outflows, the larger is a project's NPV and the more it can be expected to contribute to shareholder wealth. In other words, *a bigger NPV is better than a smaller NPV.* This leads to the *mutually exclusive decision rule:*

$$\text{NPV}_A > \text{NPV}_B \longrightarrow \text{choose project A over B}$$

where NPV_A and NPV_B are the net present values of projects A and B, respectively.

The idea is straightforward on its face: Choose the project with the largest NPV. However, several questions come up in actual practice. The following example provides another drill on calculating NPVs and applying the decision rules; at the same time, it raises some issues related to the practical application of the method.

CONCEPT CONNECTION   EXAMPLE 10-4

Mutually Exclusive Decisions and Judgment Issues

The Xavier Motor Company makes outdoor power equipment including lawn mowers and garden tractors and is considering two diversification ventures. The first involves manufacturing a larger, more powerful tractor. The second opportunity involves building snowblowers.[3] The manufacturing and engineering technology required for making snowblowers is very similar to that needed for garden equipment, but Xavier has never made snowblowers before.

Management wants to make a decision based on only five years of projected cash flows because of the uncertainty of the distant future. In other words, if a project isn't expected to earn enough to justify itself in five years, management considers it too risky.

Working with representatives from marketing, engineering, and manufacturing, a financial analyst has put together a set of projected incremental cash flows for each project. Xavier's cost of capital is 9%.

XAVIER MOTOR COMPANY PROJECT ESTIMATES ($000)		
Year	**Tractor**	**Snowblower**
0	$(3,000)	$(3,500)
1	(250)	(700)
2	500	800
3	1,000	1,200
4	1,500	2,000
5	1,500	2,000

3. For the benefit of our Southern readers, we should explain that a snowblower (or snow thrower) is essentially a power snow shovel. It operates like a lawn mower but instead of cutting grass it throws snow off of sidewalks and driveways.

Ensuper/Shutterstock.com

A financial analysis of the projects should provide answers to the following questions.

a. If the projects were being considered on a stand-alone basis, would they be acceptable?

b. If Xavier can spend no more than $4 million on new projects, which should be chosen?

c. If Xavier's management is willing to consider two more years of projected cash flow at the level of the last two years, which project should be chosen?

d. Are any additional risk considerations relevant?

SOLUTION: We begin by calculating the NPV for each project. We'll show these calculations in tabular form, multiplying the yearly cash flows by the present value factor for 9% and the appropriate year ($PVF_{9,i}$).

XAVIER MOTOR COMPANY NPV PROJECT ANALYSIS ($000)

Year	Factor	Cash Flows Tractor	Cash Flows Snowblower	PV of Cash Flows Tractor	PV of Cash Flows Snowblower
0	1.0000	$(3,000)	$(3,500)	$(3,000)	$(3,500)
1	.9174	(250)	(700)	(229)	(642)
2	.8417	500	800	421	673
3	.7722	1,000	1,200	772	927
4	.7084	1,500	2,000	1,063	1,417
5	.6499	1,500	2,000	975	1,300
				NPV = $ 2	$ 175

We can answer the first two questions immediately.

a. Both projects have positive NPVs and therefore are technically acceptable on a stand-alone basis. However, neither is positive by very much in relation to the size of the investments involved. The tractor project is especially marginal. This result is bound to raise some questions about the advisability of the projects. For now we'll just note that the projects are acceptable in accordance with the NPV method and return to the issue of accuracy later.

b. The projects are mutually exclusive because their initial outlays total $6.5 million and the company only has $4.0 million available for capital projects. In the mutually exclusive situation, the snowblower appears to have the edge, but not by much.

The next two questions require a few more calculations and a lot more judgment.

c. The distant future is always hard to pin down. It's easy to forecast great sales and profitability six or more years in the future. Exuberant sales and marketing people do it all the time. The question is, how many of those forecasts should a reasonably prudent financial manager accept when making decisions about the commitment of substantial amounts of money? Let's calculate the impact of another two years on the NPV analysis.

XAVIER MOTOR COMPANY NPV PROJECT ANALYSIS ($000)

| Year | Factor | Cash Flows | | PV of Cash Flows | |
		Tractor	Snowblower	Tractor	Snowblower
6	.5963	$1,500	$2,000	$ 894	$ 1,193
7	.5470	1,500	2,000	821	1,094
			Addition to NPVs	1,715	2,287
			Previous NPVs	2	175
			New NPVs	$1,717	$2,462

Notice how the entire complexion of the problem has changed. Both projects now clearly appear favorable on a stand-alone basis. That is, the NPVs are substantially positive relative to the size of the early investments. Further, the snowblower now seems to be an obvious choice with a substantial NPV advantage. (It's possible to make virtually any project look good by forecasting positive cash flows in the distant future.)

d. *This question raises another big issue: Are the forecasts for the two projects equally reliable? There's a strong argument that they are not. Snowblowers are a new business for Xavier, while the tractor is an extension of something it's already doing. The implication is that the snowblower project may be much riskier than the tractor project. If that's the case, is a simple comparison of the NPVs valid? Probably not.* We'll study some approaches to incorporating risk into capital budgeting analyses in Chapter 12.

For now you should concentrate on being sure you understand the mechanics of the NPV method—that is, how to calculate NPVs and how to apply the decision rules. However, keep the concerns brought up by this problem in mind. We'll return to them in the next two chapters.

10.2c   Internal Rate of Return (IRR)

Instead of comparing present value dollar amounts, the **internal rate of return (IRR)** technique focuses on rates of return. The IRR concept can be defined in two ways. In fundamental terms, a project's IRR is just the return it earns on invested funds. However, the concept can also be defined in terms of the NPV Equation written in the form of 10.1a. We'll have a close look at both approaches.

The Project as an Investment   In the IRR method we view a project as an investment of the company's money, which in principle is similar to the purchase of a financial asset. In this view, the cash outlay at the beginning of a project is like an investor paying cash to purchase a stock or a bond. Subsequent cash inflows from the project are similar to interest or dividend payments received by the investor.

The analogy is easy to visualize when a project has only one cash outflow occurring at its beginning, time zero. Consider the project in Example 10-3; we'll repeat those cash flows here for convenience.

C_0	C_1	C_2	C_3
$(5,000)	$1,000	$2,000	$3,000

Notice that the project calls for one cash outflow, or payment, followed by three inflows. The initial $5,000 outlay can be thought of as the "price" of receiving the subsequent inflows. In other words, accepting the project financially amounts to putting up the initial $5,000 in return for which the investing company receives the later inflows.

Recall that in Chapters 7 and 8 we defined the return on an investment as the interest rate at which the discounted value of the future cash flows just equals the price of the investment (see pages 289 and 350). The same idea applies here. The IRR is the interest rate at which the present value of the three inflows just equals the $5,000 outflow (price).

In this view, the IRR is analogous to the yield on a bond. Recall that purchasing a bond entitles the owner to a series of interest payments and a repayment of principal. These are cash inflows for which the investor pays the bond's price. The interest rate that equates the present value of the investor's inflows to the price of the bond (outflow) is the bond's yield. Similarly, the rate that equates the present value of a project's inflows to the initial outlay is the IRR.

The idea is a little harder to see when there's more than one outflow—for example, if there are two negative cash flows before the inflows start. In such a case, the IRR is the interest rate that equates the present value of all inflows with the present value of all outflows. In other words, the IRR is just the return on the investment of the outflows.

Defining IRR Through the NPV Equation   We can gain additional insight by relating the IRR concept to the NPV method. The two approaches are closely related in that both NPV and IRR can be defined by essentially the same equation.

In the last section, we defined a project's NPV with Equation 10.1, but said that we would use an alternate formulation, Equation 10.1a, later on. Referring to that alternate expression, IRR is simply the value of the interest rate, k, at which NPV equals zero. This occurs when the present value of all the inflows is just equal to the present value of all the outflows, and they offset one another. This means IRR is the solution to the NPV equation with the interest rate treated as the unknown and NPV set to zero. This is the same as saying that *the IRR is the interest rate at which a project's NPV equals zero.*

Rewriting Equation 10.1a with NPV = 0 and using IRR in place of k yields the expression that defines IRR.

The **IRR** is the interest rate that **makes a project's NPV zero.**

(10.2)
$$0 = C_0 + \frac{C_1}{(1 + IRR)} + \frac{C_2}{(1 + IRR)^2} + \cdots + \frac{C_n}{(1 + IRR)^n}$$

When the C_i are given for a particular project, Equation 10.2 is one equation in one unknown, IRR. The solution is *the* IRR for the project. Every project of practical interest has an IRR just as every project has an NPV.

Decision Rules   IRR decision rules follow directly from thinking in terms of a return on an investment.

Stand-Alone Projects   In the stand-alone case, we're asking whether investment in a project is a good use of the company's money. The answer depends on the rate the firm pays to use that money. We described that rate as the company's *cost of capital* earlier in this chapter.

A project is acceptable on a stand-alone basis if its **IRR exceeds the cost of capital**.

Recalling the illustration given there (starting a business with borrowed money, page 449), we can generalize by saying that no one should invest in anything unless the return on the investment is expected to exceed the rate paid for the use of the money invested.

Because a project's IRR is the return on funds invested in the project, and the cost of capital reflects the average rate the company pays for the use of long-term money, the stand-alone decision rule follows from this generalization: *Invest in a project only if its IRR exceeds the firm's cost of capital.* Or,

$$\text{IRR} > k \longrightarrow \text{accept}$$
$$\text{IRR} < k \longrightarrow \text{reject}$$

where k is the firm's cost of capital.

In a **mutually exclusive** context, projects with **larger IRRs** are **preferred**.

Mutually Exclusive Projects   The decision rule for mutually exclusive projects also follows from the definition of IRR as a return on an investment. We prefer investments with higher rates of return to those with lower rates. Hence, *a bigger IRR is better.* Or, if IRR_A and IRR_B relate to projects A and B, respectively,

$$\text{IRR}_A > \text{IRR}_B \longrightarrow \text{choose project A over project B}[4]$$

Calculating IRRs   Examination of Equation 10.2 shows that calculating internal rates of return for a general series of cash flows isn't easy. A project's IRR is the solution to that equation when a fixed set of numbers has been substituted for the C_i. Notice that the equation is a polynomial of order n in the variable IRR. Further, it's a very messy polynomial because the powers of the unknown appear in the denominators of the fractions on the right. In general, such an equation can't be solved algebraically for values of n greater than 2.

We get around this difficulty by using an iterative, numerical approach to solving the equation. In fact, we actually use Equation 10.1 to find a solution to Equation 10.2.

Equation 10.1 defines a project's NPV and enables us to calculate that figure for any interest rate, k, given a set of cash flows (the C_i). To find a project's IRR, we simply try different values for k in Equation 10.1 until we find one at which the NPV is zero. That value of k is the IRR.

Finding IRRs usually requires an **iterative**, trial-and-error technique.

To solve a problem, we guess at the project's IRR and calculate an NPV using the guess as the interest rate in Equation 10.1. If the NPV doesn't come out to be zero, the first guess was incorrect, and we guess again. However, the result of the first calculation contains information that indicates the direction in which the second guess should be made. The following example will make the procedure clear.

---

4.   We'll see shortly that the IRR decision rule can occasionally lead to the wrong choice in mutually exclusive situations.

CONCEPT CONNECTION   EXAMPLE 10-5

Internal Rate of Return (IRR)—Iterative Procedure

Find the IRR for the series of cash flows in Example 10-3.

C_0	C_1	C_2	C_3
$(5,000)	$1,000	$2,000	$3,000

If the firm's cost of capital is 8%, is the project a good idea? What if the cost of capital is 10%?

SOLUTION: We'll start by guessing that the IRR is 12% and calculating the project's NPV at that rate. As it happens, we've already done that calculation in Example 10-3. Review that calculation on page 453 now and see that the resulting NPV is ($377.30).

Clearly, the project's NPV at 12% is not zero, so we have to make another guess. To focus that guess, look at the problem's pattern of cash flows. The positive numbers are in the future, displayed on the right. These positives are affected by the discounting process when we take present values. In effect, they're shrunk by their respective present value factors before being combined with the negative $5,000 to form the NPV. *Notice that a larger interest rate shrinks the positive numbers more than a smaller rate does, but doesn't affect the initial outlay, because it isn't discounted.*

Our first guess of 12% shrank the positive numbers too much, so that they became less than the negative outlay of $5,000 by $377.30. We'd like our next guess to shrink the positive cash flows less, so we'll choose a *smaller* interest rate.

We can summarize this thinking by saying that the magnitude of a project's NPV moves inversely with the interest rate used in its calculation. This relationship is portrayed graphically in Figure 10-1.

FIGURE 10-1
NPV Profile

A project's **NPV profile** is a graph of its NPV versus the cost of capital. It **crosses** the horizontal axis at the **IRR**.

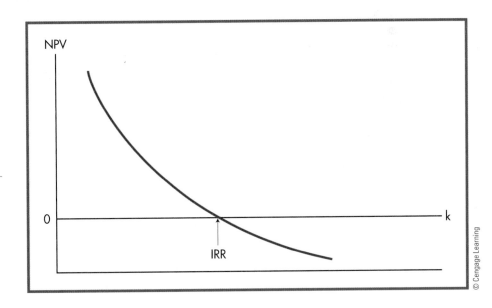

© Cengage Learning

The graph depicted is known as an **NPV profile**. Every project with a defined set of cash flows (the C_i) has an NPV profile that appears as a line on the graph. The lines will generally be downsloping to the right and cross the horizontal axis at some point. The IRR is the point at which the project's NPV is zero. That occurs where the NPV profile crosses the k axis as shown in the graph.

It's important to realize that the NPV profiles of capital budgeting projects slope downward to the right, because the pattern of cash flows generally involves outflows first (negative numbers) and inflows later (positive numbers). A higher discount rate therefore affects the positives more than the negatives and has the net effect of shrinking the NPV. The analysis of unusual patterns is left as an exercise.

Finding a project's IRR is equivalent to locating the crossover point of the NPV profile and the horizontal axis by testing points on either side. In the current problem, our first guess has taken us to the right of the crossover. Our next guess must be a lower interest rate to move the NPV up and get closer to the IRR.

We'll keep track of our calculations by setting up a two-column table to portray each interest rate choice and the NPV calculated to go along with it. Use the calculation method shown in Example 10-3 to verify that the entries shown below are correct. NPVs are shown rounded to the nearest whole dollar.

Interest Rate Guess	Calculated NPV
12%	$(377)
10	(184)
9	(83)
8	22
7	130

The calculated NPV changes sign between 9% and 8%, which means the IRR is between those interest rates.

If the firm's cost of capital is 8%, the project is marginally favorable. If the cost of capital is 9%, it's unfavorable.

Notice that this technique is similar to the iterative approach we used to find the yield on a bond given its price in Chapter 7 (pages 299–301).

Financial calculators are programmed to find the IRR for a general set of cash flows. Internally, such machines are going through the iterative process we've just illustrated.

Technical Problems with IRR   Two technical problems are associated with the IRR method. They *rarely* present practical difficulties, but anyone using the technique should be aware that they exist.

Multiple Solutions   The IRR for a project is defined as the solution to Equation 10.2 with the project's cash flows substituted for the C_i and IRR treated as the unknown. The expression comes from the NPV equation operating at the point where NPV equals zero.

A problem arises because Equation 10.2 is an nth-order equation in the variable IRR, where n is the number of years the project lasts. That means it can have as many as n solutions. How do we know which one is correct? At first glance, this seems like a fatal problem for the IRR method, but in reality it isn't.

Solutions to the equation can be either positive, negative, or what mathematicians call imaginary.[5]

Unusual projects can have **more than one IRR**, but they rarely present practical difficulties.

It turns out that the number of positive solutions to Equation 10.2 depends on the pattern of the project's cash flows. There can be no more positive solutions than there are *sign reversals* in the cash flow stream. A sign reversal occurs when the C_i change from negative to positive or from positive to negative.

The normal pattern of project cash flows involves only one sign change. There's almost always a negative initial outlay, C_0, followed by a series of periods with positive cash flows. C_0 is sometimes followed immediately by a few negative flows before the inflows start, but even then there's only one sign change from negative to positive. That means there's only one positive solution for IRR, which is the correct one.

In the occasional project with one or two negative cash flow years interspersed among the positives, there can be more than one IRR solution. However, in practical problems there's generally only one solution within a reasonable range of values for an interest rate, say, between 0% and 50%. That's the one we're looking for. When other positive solutions exist, they tend to be figures like 300% or 400%, or are the result of very unlikely cash flow patterns.

As a practical matter, the multiple-solution issue can be all but ignored.

The Reinvestment Assumption   Examine Equation 10.2 once again. Suppose we have a typical case with a negative C_0 followed by a long series of cash inflows. The IRR method makes an implicit assumption about what happens to those cash inflows after they're received. It assumes that inflows are *reinvested* at the IRR until the end of the project's life.

The reinvestment assumption presents a problem in the case of especially profitable ventures. Suppose a project has an IRR of 50%. The company is unlikely to find other opportunities with returns that high in which to reinvest the funds thrown off by the project. Therefore, the reinvestment assumption is unlikely to be satisfied. But that casts a doubt on the reality of the 50% solution. In other words, the return rate is very high, but it may not truly be 50%.

Contrast IRR with the NPV method in such a situation. A project with a very high IRR would also have a high NPV, but the reinvestment assumption in that method requires only that cash flows be reinvested at the cost of capital. That's because the discount rate in the NPV technique is just k, the cost of capital, as shown in Equation 10.1 and Equation 10.1a. Such investments are virtually always available.

The reinvestment problem is also somewhat academic—that is, not a practical concern. When returns on projects are in the 50% neighborhood, people don't worry about *exactly* how high they are. In other words, if a project computes to a 50% IRR, people don't argue about whether it's 50% or only 40%. In either case, if the projected cash flows are correct, they indicate a very good opportunity.

---

5. Imaginary numbers are functions of the square root of minus one (−1). They are the subject of an entire branch of advanced mathematics.

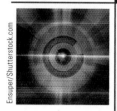

INSIGHTS Practical Applications

The Modified Internal Rate of Return (MIRR)

The technical difficulties with IRR have motivated the development of a technique called the Modified Internal Rate of Return (MIRR) that eliminates both the reinvestment and multiple solutions problems. IRR assumes cash inflows are reinvested at the IRR, which is unrealistic if the IRR is high (say > 25%) because other opportunities at such rates are usually not available. MIRR simply forces reinvestment at the cost of capital, a more available rate.

The technique is relatively simple. Consider a project that runs for n years with an initial outlay, C_0, at the beginning and later cash flows, C_1 through C_n. Most of the later flows will be positive inflows, but some may be negative outflows. The MIRR is calculated in three steps. First, the future values of all the positive cash inflows are calculated at the end of the project (period n) and added together. Second, all of the negative cash outflows are discounted to their present values at time 0 and added to the initial outlay, C_0. Both time value calculations are done at the cost of capital.

At this point, the project is represented by just two numbers, a single present outflow and a single future inflow at its end. These calculations create a project with an initial outlay, one big cash inflow at its end, and nothing in between. MIRR is then the interest rate that makes this project's NPV zero. That's the interest rate at which the present value of the big future inflow is equal to the initial outlay. Finding that rate is a time value problem in which the interest rate is the unknown.

Consider the following three-year example. Project Zebra requires an initial outlay of $500 and an additional outlay of $100 in year 2. It is expected to generate cash inflows of $300 in year 1 and $600 in year 3. The cost of capital is 12%. The timeline below includes a schematic representation of the project's MIRR calculations.

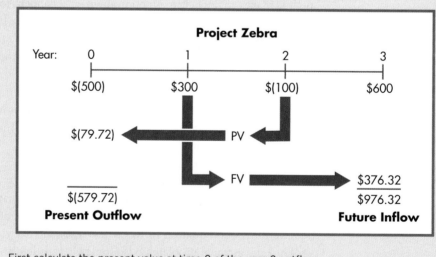

First calculate the present value at time 0 of the year 2 outflow:

$$PV = FV\,[PVF_{12,2}]$$
$$= -\$100(.7972)$$
$$= -\$79.72$$

Combine that with the initial outlay for the total present outflow

$$\text{Present Outflow} = -\$500.00 - \$79.72 = -\$579.72$$

Next calculate the future value at time 3 of the year 1 inflow

$$FV = PV \, [FVF_{12,2}]$$
$$= \$300(1.2544)$$
$$= \$376.32$$

Add that to the cash flow in year 3 to get the total future inflow. (Both present and future values are taken at the cost of capital.)

$$\text{Future Inflow} = \$600.00 + \$376.32 = \$976.32$$

Finally, find the interest rate that makes the present value of the future inflow equal to the present outflow. Using the future value of an amount formula, Equation 6.4 from page 236, we have

$$FV = PV \, [FVF_{k,n}]$$
$$\$976.32 = \$579.72 \, [FVF_{MIRR,3}]$$
$$[FVF_{MIRR,3}] = \$976.32/\$579.72 = 1.6841$$

Calculator Solution	
Key	**Input**
n	3
PV	579.72
FV	976.32
PMT	0
	Answer
I/Y	18.98%

Table A-1 in Appendix A yields an MIRR of approximately 19%.

Hence, project Zebra should be accepted because its MIRR is above the 12% cost of capital.

It's important to appreciate why MIRR is better than the regular IRR. The cash flows are projected to the end of the project at the cost of capital, not at the IRR. That means MIRRs will generally be lower and more realistic than artificially inflated IRRs. Project Zebra's IRR, for example, is 23.0% while its MIRR is a more conservative and realistic 19%.

10.2d   Comparing IRR and NPV

The internal rate of return and the net present value methods are the two major approaches to evaluating capital budgeting projects. It's logical to ask whether they always give the same solutions to problems. Surprisingly, the answer to that question is no. Let's explore why with the aid of the NPV profile that we introduced earlier.

The NPV profile *for a project* is a graphic representation of the relationship between a project's NPV and the interest rate at which it's calculated. It is simply the graph of Equations 10.1 or 10.1a for a particular set of cash flows (the C_i).

Look back at the NPV profile in Figure 10-1 (page 459). The related discussion demonstrated that the line of the profile slopes downward to the right for projects that involve early cash outflows and later cash inflows. Because that is invariably the case for business projects, all profiles of interest to us slope downward to the right. However, their shapes aren't identical, and they cross the horizontal axis at different points. In addition, the profiles of different projects *may* cross one another, as illustrated in Figure 10-2.

We can use the NPV profiles depicted there to show how the NPV and IRR methods can give conflicting directions when we're choosing among mutually exclusive projects.

Notice in Figure 10-2 that project A's profile crosses the k axis to the right of project B's. That means $IRR_A > IRR_B$. Therefore, the IRR method chooses project A

FIGURE 10-2 Projects for Which IRR and NPV Can Give Different Solutions

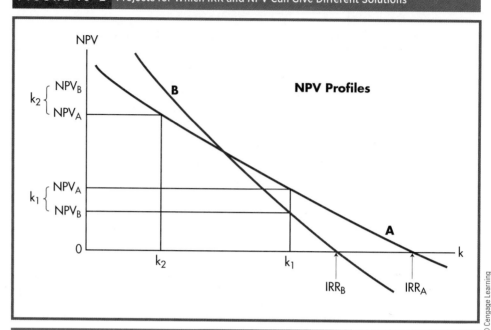

over project B. Does the NPV method also choose project A? It depends on the cost of capital. We'll demonstrate by graphically evaluating the two projects against each other using the NPV method at different values of k.

To determine graphically any project's NPV at a particular cost of capital, we find k on the horizontal axis and move vertically to the project's NPV profile. From there we move left to the vertical axis and read the value of NPV.

First choose cost of capital k_1 and locate NPV_A and NPV_B, the NPVs for projects A and B, respectively. These are shown toward the bottom of the vertical axis in the diagram. Notice that NPV_A is above (is larger than) NPV_B, indicating that the NPV method chooses project A just as the IRR method does.

Now do the same thing for cost of capital k_2, which is to the left of the point at which the two profiles cross. The resulting NPVs are shown toward the top of the vertical axis. Notice that the result is reversed. This time the NPV method chooses project B over A, a result opposite that of the IRR method.

Examination of the diagram provides some insight into when this phenomenon may occur. To give conflicting results, the NPV profiles have to cross in the first quadrant of the graph at interest rates that are of practical interest. That doesn't happen often. Even when it does, we can generally expect the two methods to agree when the cost of capital isn't too far below the project IRRs.

> The NPV and IRR methods can occasionally give **conflicting results** in mutually exclusive decisions.

The Preferred Method in Case of Conflict

As a practical matter, conflicts between the IRR and NPV methods are rare. When they do occur, *the NPV method is preferred,* because its *reinvestment assumption* is more easily satisfied, and NPV is tied directly to wealth maximization.

10.2e NPV and IRR Solutions Using Financial Calculators and Spreadsheets

Modern financial calculators and spreadsheet software take most of the drudgery out of calculating NPVs and IRRs. The technology is especially convenient when we need to find an IRR because it allows us to avoid the tedious iterative process described earlier. We'll outline how to solve problems using a Texas Instruments BAII PLUS™ calculator and Microsoft's Excel® spreadsheet. Inputting to the calculator can be a little tricky, so you'll probably have to refer to its user's manual as well.

Calculators A calculator will find a project's NPV or IRR quickly once the associated cash flows are entered. To enter cash flows on the BAII PLUS, begin by pressing the CF button to enter the cash flow mode, and then clear the working memory by pressing 2nd and then CLR Work.

The calculator is programmed to prompt the user for the cash flows one at a time, starting with the initial outlay which it calls CFo (we've called this figure C_0). Type in the value, make it negative (an outflow) by hitting the $+/-$ key, and then press ENTER. (After entering a number, press the $\downarrow$ key to move to the prompt for the next input item.)

The machine then prompts for up to 24 *different* cash flows, referred to as C01, C02, . . . , C24. However, after each of these cash flows is entered, the machine prompts for a "frequency" displayed as F01, F02, . . . , F24. The frequency allows you to repeat the last cash flow entered up to 9,999 times before moving on to the next *different* cash flow. If you don't enter a frequency, the machine assumes 1. For example, the series

$$-500 \ 100 \ 200 \ 200 \ 200 \ 800$$

can be entered with the following inputs:

Prompt	Entry
CFo	−500
C01	100
F01	
C02	200
F02	3
C03	800

You can move back and forth through the cash flow and frequency figures you've entered using the $\uparrow \downarrow$ keys. Cash flows can also be inserted, deleted, or changed using procedures outlined in the user's manual.

NPV and IRR Once a project's cash flows are in the machine, calculating NPV and IRR is easy. To find the NPV, begin by pressing the NPV button. The machine will prompt for I, the interest rate at which you want to do the present value calculation (this is generally the cost of capital we've called k). Type the interest rate as a whole number (e.g., 12 for 12%) and press ENTER. Now press $\downarrow$ and then CPT (for compute). The project's NPV will appear on the screen. To get IRR, just press IRR and then CPT.

As an exercise, use your calculator to compute NPVs and IRRs for the project cash flows in Examples 10-3 and 10-4.

Spreadsheets   Spreadsheet solutions for NPV and IRR are easy to do. We simply arrange the project's cash flows in a series of consecutive cells along a row or column and use the spreadsheet software's NPV and IRR functions. Here's an example using Microsoft Excel™ and the cash flows from Example 10-3.

	A	B	C	D	E
1	Project Cash Flows:				
2		−$5,000	$1,000	$2,000	$3,000
3					
4	Cost of Capital: k =		0.12		
5					
6	NPV =	($377.41)			
7					
8	IRR =	8.2%			

The formula in cell B6 is

$$= B2 + NPV(C4, C2:E2)$$

Let's first focus on the NPV function. Its first argument is an interest rate—the cost of capital in this case—which we've put in cell C4. Notice that we input interest rates (cell C4) in decimal form in spreadsheets rather than as whole numbers as we do when using calculators. The other argument is the range of cells containing the project's *future* cash flows, C2 to E2. Notice that the NPV function calculates the present value of the *future* cash flows only. That means we have to add the initial outlay separately, which we do by including B2 in the formula.

The IRR function, on the other hand, takes the whole series of cash flows including the initial outlay. The formula in cell B8 is simply

$$= IRR (B2:E2)$$

10.2f   Projects with a Single Outflow and Regular Inflows

Many projects are characterized by a single initial cash outflow followed by a finite number of equal inflows coming at regular time intervals. As an illustration, take the project in our last example and shift $1,000 from the third year to the first.

C_0	C_1	C_2	C_3
$(5,000)	$2,000	$2,000	$2,000

This pattern is much easier to work with because the inflows can be treated as an annuity. In such cases, we can rewrite the equations, defining NPV and IRR using the present value of an annuity formula.[6]

Equation 10.1 defining NPV becomes

(10.3) $$NPV = C_0 + C[PVFA_{k,n}]$$

where C is the constant annual inflow, k is the cost of capital, n is the project's life in years, and C_0 is the initial outlay. Remember that C_0 is a negative number.

> **Annuity formulas** can be used to calculate NPV and IRR when projects have **single outlays and regular inflows**.

---

6.   We're using the present value of an annuity from Chapter 6, page 246, but replacing PMT with C just to be more consistent with our present notation, which represents cash flows as Cs.

The second term on the right is the present value of the annuity formed by the project's positive cash flows over a period of n years at interest rate k.

Similarly, Equation 10.2 defining IRR becomes

(10.4) $0 = C_0 + C[PVFA_{IRR,n}]$

Equation 10.4 is especially convenient, because it lets us avoid the iterative procedure otherwise necessary to find IRRs.

CONCEPT CONNECTION   EXAMPLE 10-6

Finding NPV and IRR When Inflows Are Regular

Find the NPV and IRR for the project used as an illustration immediately above. Assume the cost of capital is 12%.

SOLUTION: To calculate NPV, write Equation 10.3 and substitute from the cash flow pattern.

$$NPV = C_0 + C[PVF_{k,n}]$$
$$NPV = -\$5.000 + \$2,000[PVFA_{12,3}]$$

Find the present value factor for an annuity for 12% and 3 years in Appendix A (Table A-4) and substitute

$$NPV = -\$5.000 + \$2.000(2.4018)$$
$$NPV = -\$196.40$$

To calculate the IRR, write Equation 10.4 and substitute

$$0 = C_0 + C[PVFA_{IRR,n}]$$
$$0 = -\$5.000 + \$2,000[PVFA_{IRR,3}]$$

Notice that this is a time value problem in which the interest rate is the unknown. Recall that our procedure for solving such problems involves solving for the factor, $PVFA_{IRR,3}$, finding that value along the third row in Table A-4 and reading the interest rate at the top of the table.

Solve for the factor.

$$PVFA_{IRR,3} = \$5.000/\$2.000$$
$$= 2.5000$$

Now search for 2.5000 in Appendix A (Table A-4) along the row for three periods. The solution is between 9% and 10%.

Compare these results for NPV and IRR with those we calculated in Examples 10-3 and 10-5. Did shifting the $1,000 forward by two years make a big difference?

10.2g   Profitability Index (PI)

IRR and NPV are the most widely used capital budgeting techniques. Payback is used frequently but generally as a preliminary screening device before one or both of the other methods. Although new approaches are proposed from time to time, none has caught on in a big way. One approach, however, is used often enough to make it worth mentioning briefly. The **profitability index (PI)** is essentially a variation on the NPV method. We'll define it by referring to Equation 10.1a.

The PI compares the present value of a project's *future* cash flows with the initial outlay required to get the project started, making the comparison in the form of a ratio.

The **profitability index (PI)** is the ratio of the present value of inflows to the initial outlay. Projects are **acceptable if PI > 1**. **Larger PIs are preferred**.

Recall that the initial outlay is C_0. Hence, PI is defined as the sum of all the terms to the right of C_0 in Equation 10.1a divided by C_0.

$$(10.5) \qquad PI = \frac{\dfrac{C_1}{(1+k)} + \dfrac{C_2}{(1+k)^2} + \cdots + \dfrac{C_n}{(1+k)^n}}{C_0}$$

The PI is also known as the benefit/cost ratio, reflecting the idea that the positive cash flows expected in the future are benefits, while the initial outlay is a cost.

The concept is poorly defined if some of the early C_is after C_0 are negative. In such a case, it isn't clear whether those should be considered costs and added to the denominator, or negative benefits and subtracted from the numerator. The idea works best when the initial outlay, C_0, is the only negative cash flow, which is a fairly common situation. (We should really write $-C_0$ in the formula, but generally don't.)

Essentially, the PI is the ratio

$$\frac{\text{present value of inflows}}{\text{present value of outflows}}$$

NPV, by way of contrast, is the *difference* between the present value of inflows and the present value of outflows.

When the present value of inflows exceeds the present value of outflows, the PI will be greater than 1.0. This condition is equivalent to a positive NPV. Further, a larger PI is preferable to a smaller PI, because it implies more inflows relative to outflows in a present value sense. This is equivalent to preferring a larger to a smaller NPV.

Decision Rules   All this leads to the decision rules for the profitability index.

Stand-Alone Projects

$$PI > 1.0 \longrightarrow \text{accept}$$
$$PI < 1.0 \longrightarrow \text{reject}$$

Mutually Exclusive Projects

$$PI_A > PI_B \longrightarrow \text{choose project A over project B}$$

where PI_A and PI_B are the profitability indices for projects A and B, respectively.

Comparison with NPV   The comparison with NPV decision rules isn't exact. In the stand-alone case, a $PI > 1.0$ always coincides with $NPV > 0$. However, the two methods may compute the relative desirability of projects differently and may not make the same choices among competing options.

CONCEPT CONNECTION — EXAMPLE 10-7

Profitability Index (PI)

Compute the profitability index for a project with the following cash flows if the cost of capital is 9%. Is the project acceptable on a stand-alone basis?

C_0	C_1	C_2	C_3
$(4,500)	$1,500	$2,000	$1,600

SOLUTION: The present value of future cash flows is computed as follows:

Year (i)	C_i	$PVF_{9,i}$	PV
1	$1,500	.9174	$ 1,376
2	2,000	.8417	1,683
3	1,600	.7722	1,236
			$4,295

Then, from Equation 10.5, the PI is

$$PI = \frac{\$4,295}{\$4,500} = .95$$

Because the profitability index is less than 1.0, the project is not acceptable.

10.2h   Comparing Projects with Unequal Lives

Projects with substantially **unequal lives** aren't directly comparable.

Mutually exclusive decisions are sometimes complicated by the fact that the competing projects don't extend over the same period of time. When the disparity is significant, it can make a direct comparison of the projects meaningless.

For example, suppose a manufacturing company is replacing a production machine and must choose between two new models that have different lives. Assume both new machines save $750 per year in cost, but the longer-lived model is expected to last six years, while the other will be good for only three years. Of course, the more durable replacement will be more expensive. Assume the costs of the machines are $2,600 and $1,500, respectively. A comparison of IRRs and NPVs is shown in Figure 10-3 for an 8% cost of capital. (Figures 10-3 and 10-4 taken together are shown as Example 10-8.)

INSIGHTS | Practical Finance

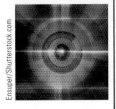

Which Methods Do Businesses Prefer?

Big Companies

Virtually all large companies do capital budgeting using sophisticated, time value-based methods. However, although NPV is theoretically the best technique, companies use IRR just as frequently. That's probably because people are more comfortable with rates of return than with sums of present valued dollars. We're all familiar with interest rates on savings accounts from childhood. We learn about returns on stock investments early in our adult lives, and businesspeople talk about returns on sales, assets, and equities all the time.

NPV, on the other hand, is a little abstract. Most people don't learn about it until college, and you can't hold the present value of a dollar in your hand. Executives understand NPV, but the concept is a little alien. As a result many gravitate toward IRR or use both methods.

Small Companies

Things are very different in smaller businesses. Studies indicate that smaller businesses tend to commit capital on the basis of the payback method or don't do any formal analysis at all.

There are probably two reasons for that finding. First, it's likely that most small firm managers simply haven't been educated in finance and don't know how to apply the more sophisticated techniques. Second, the small firm focus is just about always on very short-term cash flow. In the very short run, payback does a creditable job, so entrepreneurs may feel they don't need anything else.

SOURCE: L. R. Runyon, "Capital Budgeting Decision Making in Small Firms," *Journal of Business Research* 11 (September 1983): 389–97; John R. Graham and Campbell R. Harvey, "Capital Budgeting Methods Preferred by CFOs," *Journal of Financial Economics* 60(2001): 187–243.

Notice that the shorter project has a better IRR, but the longer has a superior NPV. This conflict is due to the disparity in the project's lives.

The problem arises mainly with the NPV method. To visualize the difficulty, think of a replacement machine as having an annual benefit during its entire life. The problem is that the NPV method adds up six years of benefits for one project and only three years for the other. Therefore, the longer-lived machine usually winds up with a higher NPV.

Putting it another way, the fact that one machine has a six-year life forces us to look at a six-year time horizon, and the shorter-lived project is implicitly assumed to have nothing going on in the last three years.

The **replacement chain method** extends projects until a common time horizon is reached.

The Replacement Chain Method   To solve the dilemma we have to realize that if the company buys the cheaper machine, it will have to buy another replacement at the end of the first three years.

In theory, any pair of projects with different lives can be compared using the *replacement chain method* by chaining both until a common time period is reached. For example, a 3- and a 4-year project could be compared by chaining both to 12 years.

CONCEPT CONNECTION   EXAMPLE 10-8

Replacement Chain

The correct way to compare the two projects in Figure 10-3 is to explicitly include a replacement for the short-lived machine at the end of its life. In essence, we *chain* two of the short projects together to cover the same time span as the longer project. The idea is portrayed graphically in Figure 10-4. The time line pictured there should replace the short line in Figure 10-3.

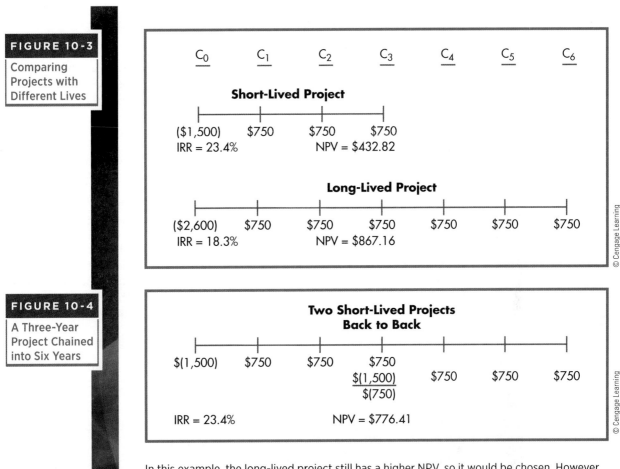

FIGURE 10-3

Comparing Projects with Different Lives

FIGURE 10-4

A Three-Year Project Chained into Six Years

In this example, the long-lived project still has a higher NPV, so it would be chosen. However, the NPV comparison is more reasonable now that the second three-year period is considered in the short-lived case. Notice that the IRR of the short-lived project is not affected by chaining.

The approach has a significant drawback in that a large number of replacements may be necessary to get equal time horizons for the competing projects. For example, if one option lasts 5 years and the other 8, we'd have to look at 40 years of replacements to make the comparison, and that isn't realistic.

> The **equivalent annual annuity** method replaces each project with an equivalent perpetuity.

The Equivalent Annual Annuity (EAA) Method   Turning each project into an **equivalent annual annuity (EAA)** is the easiest way to solve the time disparity problem. To understand the method, think in terms of chaining projects the way we did in the last section. However, replace each project link in the chain by its NPV. Then replace that with an annuity of the same length whose NPV is equal to the project's NPV. Example 10-9 on the next page will make the idea clear.

Notice, after reading the example, that we can also compare EAAs on the basis of their present values by using the present value of a perpetuity formula. This simply amounts to dividing the EAA by the decimal value of the relevant interest rate. Because the cost of capital is the same for both projects, this will result in the same choice.

CONCEPT CONNECTION EXAMPLE 10-9

Equivalent Annual Annuity (EAA)

The shorter-lived project we've been working with has a life of three years and an NPV of $432.82 (Figure 10-3). The equivalent three-year annuity is found by substituting that amount into the present value of an annuity formula along with three years and the appropriate interest rate as follows.

$$PVA = PMT[PVFA_{k,n}]$$
$$\$432.82 = PMT[PVFA_{8,3}]$$

Now find the factor in Appendix A Table A-4, substitute, and solve for the annuity payment, which is the EAA.

$$\$432.82 = PMT(2.5771)$$
$$PMT = \$167.95$$
$$= EAA$$

The idea is illustrated in Figure 10-5 for the three-year project shown chained in Figure 10-4. As the diagram indicates, we make two conceptual steps. First we replace the project with its NPV. Then we replace that with an annuity of the same length which has the same NPV. In this way, we replace the project with an equivalent stream of equal benefits.

FIGURE 10-5

Replacing a Project with Its NPV and EAA

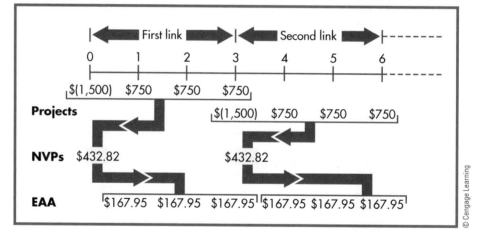

Because we can chain the project forward through time as long as we like, we can represent it by an indefinitely long stream of payments equal to the EAA. It's important to realize that this is true even though the EAA calculation is based on the number of years in the life of the original project.

Further, we can calculate an EAA for *any* project regardless of its life. And because all EAAs are infinite annuities, we can choose among projects by comparing their annuity payments.

The longer-lived project in our illustration has an NPV of $867.16 and a life of six years. Its EAA is calculated as follows:

$$PVA = PMT[PVFA_{k,n}]$$
$$\$867.16 = PMT[PVFA_{8,6}]$$
$$\$867.16 = PMT(4.6229)$$
$$PMT = \$187.58$$
$$= EAA$$

This is larger than the shorter project's EAA of $167.95, so we again come to the conclusion that the longer project is better.

10.2i   Capital Rationing

A firm's *capital budget* is the total amount of money to be spent on capital projects in a period of time, usually a year. How large should that amount of money be?

In theory, the answer to that question is easy. Every project with a positive NPV is expected to increase shareholder wealth and should be undertaken. Therefore, the optimal capital budget would be large enough to undertake all available projects with positive NPVs or equivalently with IRRs that exceed the cost of capital.

We'll illustrate the idea by considering a company with the following projects available, sorted in decreasing order of IRR:

Project	IRR	C_0
A	16%	$8M
B	14	5M
C	12	6M
D	11	3M
E	8	6M
F	6	7M

Figure 10-6 plots the projects on a graph that displays interest rates against cumulative capital spending. Each lettered block represents a proposed project. The blocks' heights are the project IRRs while their widths are the amounts of capital each requires to get started. Usually that's the project's initial outlay, C_0.

FIGURE 10-6   Capital Rationing

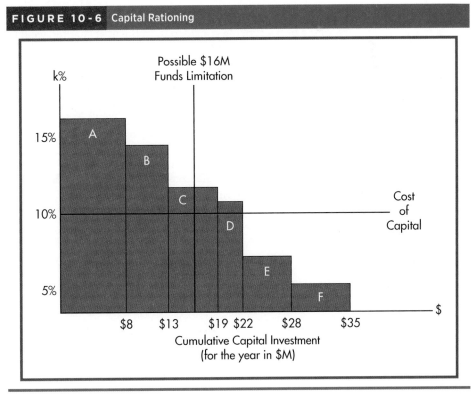

Notice again that the projects are arranged in decreasing order of IRR, and that the firm's 10% cost of capital is shown as a horizontal line. The projects are either stand-alone opportunities or the best choice among mutually exclusive options.

This portrayal makes it easy to see which projects have IRRs that exceed the cost of capital and therefore should be done. In this case, if there is no funds limitation, the firm will maximize shareholder wealth by undertaking projects A, B, C, and D while forgoing projects E and F.

In practice, however, there is rarely enough money available to do all proposed projects that appear to have positive NPVs. Some capital constraint is likely to be imposed like the one shown in the diagram at $16M. When such a constraint is imposed, we have **capital rationing**—in that available capital dollars have to be rationed among projects.

> **Capital rationing** involves selecting projects subject to a funding limitation.

Capital rationing creates a problem because projects are generally not divisible. In this case, we can't do part of project C, so we can't do it at all. That leaves some unused money within the budget between the end of project B and the constraint. The rationing problem is to choose the best set of projects that fits into the capital constraint. By "best" we mean the set that maximizes NPV. In the illustration, the choice appears to be easy because D, the next best project, just fits into the $3M space available. In some cases, however, the choice isn't so obvious. It's possible that the selection of projects that maximizes NPV could omit one of the higher-rated projects in favor of one or more lower-rated projects that fit better within the constraint.

Finding the best possible solution to a capital rationing problem involves using techniques from a field of mathematics known as constrained maximization. The subject is quite complex and beyond the scope of this book, but you should be aware of its existence.

Using sophisticated mathematics to find a precise solution to capital rationing problems implies attributing a great deal of accuracy to the NPV and IRR estimates of the projects being considered. In the next chapter, we'll learn that such accuracy frequently isn't possible.

In practice, managers ration capital intuitively, choosing among projects for a variety of reasons, not all of which are strictly financial. In that way, they make choices that are usually close to the best, but not exactly optimal.

from the
CFO

CONCEPT CONNECTIONS

QUESTIONS

1. Define "mutual exclusivity" and describe ways in which projects can be mutually exclusive.

2. Capital budgeting is based on the idea of identifying incremental cash flows, so overheads aren't generally included. Does this practice create a problem for a firm which, over a long period of time, takes on a large number of projects that are just barely acceptable under capital budgeting rules?

3. Relate the idea of cost of capital to the opportunity cost concept (pages 237–238). Is the cost of capital the opportunity cost of project money?

4. The payback technique is criticized for not using discounted cash flows. Under what conditions will this matter most? That is, under what patterns of cash flow will payback and NPV or IRR be likely to give different answers?

5. Explain the rationale behind the NPV method in your own words. Why is a higher NPV conceptually better than a lower one?

6. Projects A and B have approximately the same NPV. Their initial outlays are similar in size. Project A has early positive cash flows, and little or nothing is expected to come in later on. Project B has much larger positive cash flows than A, but they're further in the future. Can you make any general statement about which project might be better?

7. Suppose the present value of cash ins and outs is very close to balanced for a project to build a new $50 million factory, so that the NPV is $25,000. The same company is thinking about buying a new trailer truck for $150,000. The NPV of projected cash flows associated with the truck is also about $25,000. Does this mean that the two projects are comparable? Is one more desirable than the other? If the cash flows have similar risks, are the projects equally risky? (*Hint:* Think in terms of the size of the investment placed at risk in relation to the financial rewards expected.)

8. Think about the cash flows associated with putting $100,000 in the bank for five years, assuming you draw out the interest each year and then close the account. Now think about a set of hypothetical cash flows associated with putting the same money in a business, operating for five years, and then selling out. Write an explanation of why the IRR on the business project is like the bank's interest rate. How are the investments different?

9. What is it about the cash flows associated with business projects that makes the NPV profile slope downward to the right? Would the NPV profile of any randomly selected set of positive and negative flows necessarily slope one way or the other? Why?

10. The following set of cash flows changes sign twice and has two IRR solutions. Identify the sign changes. Demonstrate mathematically that 25% and 400% are both solutions to the IRR equation.

C_0	C_1	C_2
$(320)	$2,000	$(2,000)

On the basis of this example, why would you expect multiple solutions to be an unusual problem in practice?

11. Under what conditions will the IRR and NPV methods give conflicting results for mutually exclusive decisions? Will they ever give conflicting results for stand-alone decisions? Why?

12. Why is the profitability index more appropriately described as a variation on the NPV technique than as a variation on the IRR technique?

13. Show that the profitability index (PI), the initial outlay (C_0), and the net present value (NPV) of a project are related by the following equation.

$$NPV = C_0(1 - PI)$$

(*Hint:* State both the NPV and the PI in terms of C_0 and the sum of all other cash flows.)

BUSINESS ANALYSIS

1. You are a financial analyst for the Ajax Company, which uses about $1 million of inventory per month. The purchasing manager has come to you for help with a buying decision. He can get a big discount on $15 million of inventory by buying it all at once. However, there is some risk of obsolescence when buying that far in advance. He understands that large purchases are frequently analyzed by means of capital budgeting techniques, and he asks for your help in deciding whether to buy the specially priced inventory. How would you advise him? Is capital budgeting appropriate?

2. Risk in capital projects is the probability that a project will earn less than expected. Make up and describe one hypothetical project in each of the replacement,

expansion, and new venture categories. List a few ways that each might go wrong and cause the cash flows to be less favorable than expected. Can you think of situations in which projects could result in losses? Could the losses exceed the initial investment (C_0)?

3. Charlie Brown is thinking about starting Wing-It Airlines to fly a commuter route in and out of a major city. Four planes are on the market that will do the job, but each has different flight, load, and operating characteristics. Charlie is unsure of the demand for his service and feels that it may depend to some extent on the type of plane chosen. Whether the business is feasible may depend on which airplane is used in conjunction with the demand estimate assumed. Are capital budgeting techniques appropriate for analysis of this problem? If so, is the issue a stand-alone or mutually exclusive decision?

4. The Budwell & Son Oil Company is looking at two drilling proposals. One project lasts for three years, costs $20 million to start, pays back quickly, and has

an NPV of $15 million. The other project also costs about $20 million to start, but has an expected life of seven years, takes much longer to pay back, and has an NPV of $17 million. Mr. Budwell, the company's founder, favors the shorter project because of the quick investment recovery. His son Billy, however, has taken finance in college and insists that the only way to judge projects is on NPV. He therefore favors the longer project. They've engaged you as their financial advisor to settle the issue. How would you advise them?

5. Webley Corp. has a capital budget limited to $20 million. Five relatively high IRR projects are available that have initial investments totaling $15 million. They are all roughly the same size. A sixth project has an IRR only slightly lower than those of the first five but requires an $8 million investment. Several other smaller projects are available with IRRs quite a bit lower than the sixth. The president has stated that it's too bad the firm has to pass up the sixth project, but it just doesn't fit into the budget. How would you advise him?

PROBLEMS

Payback Period: Concept Connection Example 10-1 (page 450)

1. Gander, Inc. is considering two projects with the following cash flows:

Year	Project X	Project Y
0	($100,000)	($100,000)
1	40,000	50,000
2	40,000	0
3	40,000	0
4	40,000	0
5	40,000	250,000

Gander uses the payback period method of capital budgeting and accepts only projects with payback periods of 3 years or less.

a. If the projects are presented as stand-alone opportunities, which one(s) would Gander accept? If they were mutually exclusive and Gander disregarded its three year rule, which project would be chosen?

b. Is there a flaw in the thinking behind the correct answers to part (a)?

Net Present Value (NPV): Concept Connection Example 10-3 (page 453)
Profitability Index (PI): Concept Connection Example 10-7 (page 469)

2. A project has the following cash flows:

C_0	C_1	C_2	C_3
$(700)	$200	$500	$244

a. What is the project's payback period?

b. Calculate the project's NPV at 12%.

c. Calculate the project's PI at 12%.

3. Calculate the NPV for the following projects:

   a. An outflow of $7,000 followed by inflows of $3,000, $2,500, and $3,500 at one-year intervals at a cost of capital of 7%.

   b. An initial outlay of $35,400 followed by inflows of $6,500 for three years and then a single inflow in the fourth year of $18,000 at a cost of capital of 9%. (Recognize the first three inflows as an annuity in your calculations.)

   c. An initial outlay of $27,500 followed by an inflow of $3,000 followed by five years of inflows of $5,500 at a cost of capital of 10%. (Recognize the last five inflows as an annuity, but notice that it requires a treatment different from the annuity in part (b). See "Imbedded Annuities," Chapter 6, page 275).

4. Clancy Inc. is considering a project with the following cash flows:

C_0	C_1	C_2	C_3
$(7,800)	$2,300	$3,500	$4,153

   a. Clancy has a policy of rejecting all projects that don't pay back within three years and analyzing those that do more carefully with time value based methods. Does this project warrant further consideration?

   b. Should Clancy accept the project based on its NPV if the company's cost of capital is 8%? Is the recommendation definite or marginal?

   c. What conclusion will the firm reach based on PI and an 8% cost of capital? Is the conclusion definite or marginal?

Internal Rate of Return (IRR)—Iterative Procedure: Concept Connection Example 10-5 (page 459)

5. Should the project being considered in the previous problem be accepted or rejected based on IRR? (*Hint:* Start by guessing 11% for IRR.) Does the IRR method seem to give a more definite result? If so, would your recommendation after considering all four methods be strong or cautious?

6. Calculate an IRR for the project in problem 2 using an iterative technique. (*Hint:* Start by guessing 15%.)

7. Calculate the IRR for the following projects:

   a. An initial outflow of $15,220 followed by inflows of $5,000, $6,000, and $6,500.

   b. An initial outflow of $47,104 followed by inflows of $16,000, $17,000, and $18,000.

8. Calculate the NPV at 9% and the IRR for the following projects:

   a. An initial outlay of $69,724 and an inflow of $15,000 followed by four consecutive inflows of $17,000.

   b. An initial outlay of $25,424 followed by two zero cash years and then four years of inflows at $10,500. (*Hint:* See "Imbedded Annuities," page 275 for parts b&c.)

   c. An outlay of $10,672 followed by another outlay of $5,000 followed by five inflows of $5,000.

9. Calculate the NPV at 12% and the IRR for the following projects. Find IRRs to the nearest whole percent.

   a. An initial outflow of $10,000 followed by three inflows of $4,000.

   b. An initial outflow of $10,000 followed by inflows of $3,000, $4,000, and $5,000.

   c. An initial outflow of $10,000 followed by inflows of $5,000, $4,000, and $3,000.

   d. Notice that in parts (a), (b), and (c), a total of $12,000 is received over three years. Compare the NPVs and IRRs to see the impact of shifting $2,000 between years one and three.

10. Grand Banks Mining Inc. plans a project to strip-mine a wilderness area. Setting up operations and initial digging will cost $5 million. The first year's operations are expected to be slow and to net a positive cash flow of only $500,000. Then there will be four years of $2 million cash flows after which the ore will run out. Closing the mine and restoring the environment in the sixth year will cost $1 million.

   a. Calculate the project's NPV at a cost of capital of 12%.

   b. Calculate the project's IRR to the nearest whole percent.

11. Hamstring Inc. is considering a project with the following cash flows:

C_0	C_1	C_2	C_3	C_4
$(25,000)	$10,000	$12,000	$5,000	$8,000

The company is reluctant to consider projects with paybacks of more than three years. If projects pass the payback screen, they are considered further by means of the NPV and IRR methods. The firm's cost of capital is 9%.

   a. What is the project's payback period? Should the project be considered further?

   b. What is the project's NPV? Does NPV indicate acceptance on a stand-alone basis?

   c. Calculate the project's IRR by using an iterative approach. Start with the cost of capital and the NPV calculation from part (b). Does IRR indicate acceptance on a stand-alone basis?

   d. What is the project's PI? Does PI indicate acceptance on a stand-alone basis?

12. Project Alpha requires an initial outlay of $35,000 and results in a single cash inflow of $56,367.50 after five years.

   a. If the cost of capital is 8%, what are Alpha's NPV and PI? Is the project acceptable under each of these techniques?

   b. What is project Alpha's IRR? Is it acceptable under IRR?

   c. What are Alpha's NPV and PI if the cost of capital is 12%? Is the project acceptable under that condition?

   d. What is Alpha's payback period? Does payback make much sense for a project like Alpha? Why or why not?

Finding NPV and IRR When Inflows Are Regular: Concept Connection Example 10-6 (page 467)

13. The Sampson Company is considering a project that requires an initial outlay of $75,000 and produces cash inflows of $20,806 each year for five years. Sampson's cost of capital is 10%.

   a. Calculate the project's payback period by making a single division rather than accumulating cash inflows. Why is this possible in this case?

   b. Calculate the project's IRR, recognizing the fact that the cash inflows are an annuity. Is the project acceptable? Did your calculation in this part result in any number(s) that were also calculated in part (a)? What is it about this problem that creates this similarity? Will this always happen in such cases?

   c. What is the project's NPV? Is the project acceptable according to NPV rules?

14. Calculate the IRR, NPV, and PI for projects with the following cash flows. Do each NPV and PI calculation at costs of capital of 8% and 12%. Calculate IRRs to the nearest whole percent.

   a. An initial outlay of $5,000 and inflows of $1,050 for seven years.

   b. An initial outlay of $43,500 and inflows of $14,100 for four years.

   c. An investment of $78,000 followed by 12 years of income of $11,500.

   d. An outlay of $36,423 followed by receipts of $8,900 for six years.

Mutually Exclusive Decisions and Judgment Issues: Concept Connection Example 10-4 (page 454)

15. Island Airlines Inc. needs to replace a short-haul commuter plane on one of its busier routes. Two aircraft are on the market that satisfy the general requirements of the route. One is more expensive than the other but has better fuel efficiency and load-bearing characteristics, which result in better long-term profitability. The useful life of both planes is expected to be about seven years, after which time both are assumed to have no value. Cash flow projections for the two aircraft follow:

	Low Cost	High Cost
Initial cost	$775,000	$950,000
Cash inflows, years 1 through 7	154,000	176,275

  a. Calculate the payback period for each plane and select the best choice.
  b. Calculate the IRR for each plane and select the best option. Use the fact that all the inflows can be represented by an annuity.
  c. Compare the results of parts (a) and (b). Both should select the same option, but does one method result in a clearer choice than the other based on the relative sizes of the two payback periods versus the relative sizes of the two IRRs?
  d. Calculate the NPV and PI of each project assuming a cost of capital of 6%. Use annuity methods. Which plane is selected by NPV? By PI?
  e. Calculate the NPV and PI of each project, assuming the following costs of capital: 2%, 4%, 6%, 8%, and 10%. Use annuity methods. Is the same plane selected by NPV and PI at every level of cost of capital? Investigate the relative attractiveness of the two planes under each method.
  f. Use the results of parts (b) and (e) to sketch the NPV profiles of the two proposed planes on the same set of axes. Show the IRRs on the graph. Would NPV and IRR ever give conflicting results? Why?

Replacement Chain and Equivalent Annual Annuity (EAA): Concept Connection Examples 10-8 and 10-9 (pages 470–472)

16. Bagel Pantry Inc. is considering two mutually exclusive projects with widely differing lives. The company's cost of capital is 12%. The project cash flows are summarized as follows:

	Project A	Project B
C_0	$(25,000)	$(23,000)
C_1	14,742	6,641
C_2	14,742	6,641
C_3	14,742	6,641
C_4		6,641
C_5		6,641
C_6		6,641
C_7		6,641
C_8		6,641
C_9		6,641

  a. Compare the projects using payback.
  b. Compare the projects using NPV.
  c. Compare the projects using IRR.
  d. Compare the projects using the replacement chain approach.
  e. Compare the projects using the EAA method.
  f. Choose a project and justify your choice.

CALCULATOR PROBLEMS

The problems in this section should be solved using a financial calculator. See pages 465–466.

17. Callaway Associates, Inc. is considering the following mutually exclusive projects. Callaway's Cost of capital is 12%.

Year	Project A	Project B
0	($80,000)	($80,000)
1	$44,000	$65,000
2	$34,000	$30,000
3	$ 14,000	$ 0
4	$ 14,000	$ 5,000

a. Calculate each project's NPV and IRR.

b. Which project should be undertaken? Why?

18. Tutak Industries is considering a project requiring an initial investment of $200,000 followed by annual cash inflows of $45,000 for the next six years. A second six-year project has an initial outlay of $325,000.

a. How much would the second project have to generate in annual cash flows to have the same IRR as the first?

b. If Tutak's cost of capital is 8%, how much would the second project have to generate in annual cash flows to have the same NPV as the first project?

19. Provide the missing information for the following projects using the present value of an annuity function [time value of money (TVM) keys rather than the cash flow (CF) function keys]. (*Hint:* The present value of the annuity of the annual cash flows minus the initial outlay must equal the NPV. For example, for Project A, calculate the present value of five $35,000 cash inflows and subtract the initial outlay (C_0) to get the project's NPV.)

Project	Initial Outlay (CO)	Length (in years)	Annual Cash Flow	Cost of Capital	NPV
A	$100,000	5	$35,000	8%	?
B	200,000	4	?	13	$35,000
C	300,000	7	50,000	?	15,000
D	400,000	?	56,098	9	20,000
E	?	6	75,000	10	25,000

20. Calculate IRRs for the projects in the previous problem.

21. Huron Valley Homes is considering a project requiring a $1 million initial investment. Expected cash inflows will be $25,000 in the first year, $100,000 in the second year, and $200,000 per year for the next six years.

a. Calculate the project's IRR and the NPV assuming an 8% cost of capital.

b. How much would each of the last six payments have to be to make the project's NPV $100,000?

22. Consider two mutually exclusive projects, A and B. Project A requires an initial cash outlay of $100,000 followed by five years of $30,000 cash inflows. Project B requires an initial cash outlay of $240,000 with cash inflows of $40,000 in the first two years, $80,000 in the next two years, and $100,000 in the fifth year.

a. Compute the IRR for each project.

b. Compute the NPV for each project for each of the following costs of capital: 0%, 4%, 8%, 12%, and 16%, and record your results in a table.

  c. For which costs of capital do the IRR and NPV methods select the same project?
  d. Examine the table created in part (b) and determine the costs of capital between which the methods begin to select different projects. Is your answer consistent with the result of part (a)? Explain your answer in terms of NPV profiles.

Mutually Exclusive Decisions and Judgment Issues: Concept Connection Example 10-4 (page 454)

23. Kneelson and Botes Inc. (K&B) is a construction company that does road and bridge work for the state highway authority. The state government solicits bids on construction projects from private contractors. The winning contractor is chosen based on its bid price as well as its perceived ability to do the work.

    Sophisticated contractors develop bids using capital budgeting techniques because most projects require cash outlays for hiring, equipment, and materials before getting started (C_0). After that the state makes progress payments to cover costs and profits until the job is finished $(C_1 \ldots C_n)$.

    Contractors know that even after they've won a bid, realizing the planned profits and cash flows isn't assured in part because government budgets can change while construction progresses. If funding is up, officials tend to add to the work originally ordered leading to increased profits and cash flows. But if funding is down, officials start to nitpick the contract looking for cost savings, which generally leads to lower cash inflows. State budget projections are fairly good for a year or two, but tend to be inaccurate over longer periods.

    K&B has been offered two, four-year contracts, but doesn't have enough cash or management depth to take on both (mutually exclusive because of resource limitations). One project involves road repair, most of which will be done and paid quickly. The other requires working on a new bridge. The bulk of the cash inflows on bridge projects generally occur near completion.

    K&B's estimating department has put together the following projections of the two projects' cash flows:

	($000)	
	Road Repair	**Bridge Work**
C0	($3,000)	($4,500)
C1	3,000	100
C2	2,000	2,000
C3	1,000	3,000
C4	100	4,500

    K&B doesn't know its exact cost of capital, but feels it's between 10 and 15%. This is not uncommon in smaller companies. (In Chapter 13, we'll learn that estimating the cost of capital can be difficult and less than precise for firms of any size.)

    The company has hired you as a financial consultant to make a recommendation as to which project to accept.

    a. Calculate the payback period for both projects. Which does payback choose?
    b. Calculate the IRR for both projects. Which does the IRR method choose? Is the choice clear or is it a close decision? Is the choice consistent with the result of the payback method?
    c. Calculate NPVs for both projects for costs of capital from 10 to 15% in 1% increments. Then plot both projects' NPV profiles on a graph similar to that shown in Figure 10-2 on page 464. Does the NPV method give a meaningful result? If so, is it consistent with the results of the payback and IRR methods? Which method is theoretically the best? Does that help in this situation?

    d. You must make a recommendation to K&B's management regardless of any technical difficulties you've encountered. Provide another, less quantitative argument that tends to support one project over the other. (*Hint:* See Business Analysis 4 on page 476.)

    e. What is your recommendation and why?

Replacement Chain and Equivalent Annual Annuity (EAA): Concept Connection Example 10-8 and 10-9 (pages 470–472)

24. Haley Motors is considering a maintenance contract for its heavy equipment. One firm has offered Haley a four-year contract for $100,000, to be paid in advance. Another firm has offered an eight-year contract for $165,000, also to be paid in advance. Haley will be able to save $34,000 per year under either contract because its employees will no longer have to do the work themselves.

    a. If Haley's cost of capital is 10%, which project should be selected? Use both the replacement chain and the equivalent annual annuity (EAA) method to justify your answer.

    b. If Haley's cost of capital is 12%, does it change the decision? What about 14%?

25. Cassidy and Sons is reviewing a project with an initial cash outflow of $250,000. An additional $100,000 will have to be invested after the first year, followed by an additional investment of $50,000 at the end of the second year. Beginning at the end of year 3, the project is expected to generate cash flows of $90,000 per year for the next eight years.

    a. Calculate the project's payback period, IRR, and its NPV and PI at a cost of capital of 8%.

    b. What concerns might Cassidy have regarding this project beyond the financial calculations from part (a)?

26. Zuker Distributors handles the warehousing of perishable foods and is considering replacing one of its primary cold storage units. One supplier has offered a unit for $250,000 with an expected life of 10 years. The unit is projected to reduce electricity costs by $50,000 per year. However, it requires a $20,000 refurbishing every two years, beginning two years after purchase. Another supplier has offered a cold storage unit with similar capabilities for $300,000. It will produce the same savings in electricity costs, but requires refurbishing every five years at a cost of $40,000. Zuker's cost of capital is 8.5%. Use NPV to determine which cold storage unit Zuker should select.

Capital Rationing: Figure 10.6 (page 473)

27. Griffin-Kornberg is reviewing the following projects for next year's capital program:

Project	Initial Investment	Length in Years	Annual Cash Flow
A	$3.0 million	6	$ 719,374
B	3.5 million	5	970,934
C	4.0 million	7	904,443
D	5.0 million	4	1,716,024
E	6.0 million	6	1,500,919
F	7.0 million	5	1,941,868
G	8.0 million	7	1,725,240

Projects A and B are mutually exclusive and so are Projects D and E. Griffin-Kornberg has a 9% cost of capital and a maximum of $14 million to spend on capital projects next year. Use capital rationing to determine which projects should be included in Griffin-Kornberg's capital program.

Modified Internal Rate of Return (MIRR): Insights Box (page 462)

28. Find the MIRR and the IRR for the following capital budgeting project and comment on the difference between the two. The cost of capital is 12%.

Year:	0	1	2	3
	$(800)	$550	$(150)	$700

COMPUTER PROBLEMS

Developing Software

29. Write a spreadsheet program to calculate the NPV of a project with an irregular pattern of cash flows for up to 10 periods without using the spreadsheet software's NPV function. Essentially, the task is to program Equation 10.1a with n = 10.

    First, input the interest rate (k) in a single cell.

    Next, set up three horizontal rows of 11 cells (including C_0). The top row will receive the cash flows as inputs.

    Program the present value factor for each period into the second row of cells using the interest rate you input earlier as follows:

Period	0	1	2	...	...	10
Factor	1	$\dfrac{1}{1 + k}$	$\dfrac{1}{(1 + k)^2}$	...	...	$\dfrac{1}{(1 + k)^{10}}$

Note that we're calling the interest rate k, but it will appear as a cell name in your program.

Next, form the third row by multiplying the top two cells in each column together. This makes the third row the present value of each cash flow.

Finally, sum the values along the third row in another cell to form the project's NPV.

Notice that your program will handle a project of less than 10 periods if you simply input zero (or leave blank) the cash flow cells from n11 to 10.

Also notice that you can easily extend your program to any reasonable number of periods by extending the horizontal rows and the programming logic. Test your program on the data in Example 10-4 on pages 454–456 to make sure it works correctly.

30. The Tallahassee Motor Company is thinking of automating one of its production facilities. The equipment required will cost a total of $10 million and is expected to last 10 years.

The company's cost of capital is 9%. The project's benefits include labor savings and a quality improvement that will lower warranty costs. Savings are estimated as follows:

Year	Cost Savings ($000)
1	$ 574
2	864
3	1,246
4	2,748
5	3,367
6	2,437
7	2,276
8	1,839
9	1,264
10	623

a. Use the program developed in the previous problem to find the project's NPV. Is the project acceptable?

b. Use the program to develop the data for an NPV profile. Evaluate the NPV for interest rates (costs of capital) from 6% to 14%.

c. Use the program to iteratively find the project's IRR to one-tenth of a percent.

CHAPTER 11

Cash Flow Estimation

Early in the last chapter we said that any project to be analyzed by capital budgeting techniques must be represented as a series of estimated cash flows. We portrayed the flows for a typical project as $C_0, C_1, \ldots, C_n$, and assumed that they were readily available. In this chapter, we'll consider exactly how such cash flow estimates are developed. In the next chapter, we'll look into some modern developments in capital budgeting that deal with incorporating risk into the analysis.

11.1 Cash Flow Estimation

We'll begin by placing cash flow estimation within the overall capital budgeting process and making some important observations about people's perceptions.

11.1a Capital Budgeting Processes

Capital budgeting consists of two distinct processes. The first is estimation of the cash flows associated with projects. The second is evaluation of the estimates using techniques like NPV and IRR. There is a tendency to take the forecast cash flows for granted and to overlook the difficulties involved in their estimation. Further, once a set of projections is made, people tend to treat it as a concrete fact not subject to error.

The same tendency leads to associating the capital budgeting concept solely with the evaluation techniques, especially NPV and IRR, and becoming caught up in an incorrect perception of the accuracy and precision of the whole process. Indeed, the

techniques we studied in the last chapter seem like "financial engineering" in their direct and unambiguous approach to the task of choosing among projects. Problem solutions come out to what seems like hair-splitting accuracy, and it's easy to get a feeling of comfort and security in the correctness of the method.

However, this secure feeling of great accuracy is misplaced. The results of an NPV or IRR analysis are only as accurate as the cash flow estimates used as inputs. And those estimates are forecasts of the *future,* which are always difficult to make and subject to considerable error.

In practice, forecasting accurate project cash flows is the more difficult and arbitrary of the two capital budgeting processes. In a sense, it's the more important because it's where error and bias can creep into the analysis. Applying NPV and/or IRR is a straightforward task that isn't likely to result in error or misinterpretation. The calculation may be complicated, but it's easy in the sense that we don't have to make any judgments about what we're doing. Making cash flow estimates, on the other hand, requires the exercise of a good deal of judgment about what to include, what to leave out, and how heavily to weight things in relation to one another. As a result, a particular set of estimated flows may be very good or very bad depending on the nature of the project and who's doing the estimating.

This is an important point that's often overlooked. Anyone can make the right capital budgeting decisions with NPV and IRR *given* a set of cash flows. It's developing the right set of cash flows that's tough.

In this chapter, we'll take a close look at what goes into estimating cash flows. We'll be especially concerned with the practical matter of ambiguities, uncertainties, and biases in the process.

> **Estimating** project **cash flows** is the **most difficult** and error-prone part of capital budgeting.

11.2   Project Cash Flows—An Overview and Some Specifics

First we'll sketch a broad approach to the estimating process, then we'll consider a few issues that require special treatment, and finally we'll look into some detailed examples.

11.2a   The General Approach to Cash Flow Estimation

Cash flow estimation can be a messy calculation, but it's conceptually quite simple. We just think through all the events a project is expected to bring about and write down the financial implications of each event in the future time period in which we expect it to occur. Then we add up everything in each time period.

We generally use a spreadsheet format for our estimations. The sheet's columns are time periods starting with the present and extending into the future over the project's life. The rows are financial items that will either generate or require cash.

> Cash estimates are done on **spreadsheets** by enumerating the issues that impact cash and forecasting each over time.

For example, a sales forecast leads to an estimate of cash inflows from customers, while an expense projection leads to a pattern of outflows to employees and vendors. When everything is enumerated, we add up each column to arrive at a forecast of each future period.

It will help your perspective if you look ahead at Table 11-1 on page 492 to get an idea of what the finished product looks like.

Forecasts for new ventures tend to be the most complex, so we'll consider them before talking briefly about expansion and replacement projects. For those projects we generally just leave out some of the issues considered for new ventures. It helps to organize our thinking if we consider things in several separate categories. A general outline for estimating new venture cash flows follows.

Pre–Start-Up, the Initial Outlay   Enumerate everything that has to be spent before the project is truly started. Include expenses and assets that have to be purchased. Also include the tax impact of expense items. The sum of these things is C_0, the *initial outlay*.

The Sales Forecast, Units and Revenues   The incremental business expected from the project is laid out in spreadsheet form (on paper or in a computer) over future time periods. It's best to forecast in terms of units and then multiply by projected prices to arrive at sales dollars.

Cost of Sales and Expenses   Plan for costs directly related to the new sales forecast as well as expenses necessary for indirect support of the increased activity level. To do that, assume relationships between sales and cost and between sales and expense based on the nature of the business being analyzed.

Assets   New assets to be acquired with cash are planned over the project's life whenever they're expected to be acquired. Most are needed during the initial, pre–start-up period. It's important not to neglect working capital, which requires cash like any other asset.

Depreciation   When planning for physical assets, it's important to forecast depreciation because it affects taxes even though it's a noncash expense.

Taxes and Earnings   Summarizing the taxable and tax deductible items in each period lets us calculate the project's impact on earnings and taxes. Calculate incremental taxes and treat them like any other cash flow item.

Summarize and Combine   Adjust earnings for depreciation and combine it with the balance sheet items to arrive at a cash flow estimate in each forecast period.

Expansion projects tend to require the same elements as new ventures, but generally require less new equipment and facilities.

Replacement projects are generally expected to save costs without generating new revenue, so the estimating process tends to be somewhat less elaborate. The expected dollar savings are planned over future periods along with the assets required to realize those savings. Depreciation and tax calculations are necessary in most cases.

We'll look at some examples after the next section.

11.2b   A Few Specific Issues

It helps to keep a few specific items in mind when making cash flow estimates. We'll consider several before moving on to examples.

The Typical Pattern   Nearly all business projects require an *initial outlay* of funds before getting started. Subsequently, flows tend to be positive (inflows) with some notable exceptions. The typical pattern is characterized by early outflows followed by later inflows.

A replacement project is generally fairly simple in this respect. The initial outlay is the cost of the new equipment less any salvage value available for the old. Future cash flows are the savings or benefits of using the new, more efficient machinery. They start immediately and are generally relatively stable.

Other kinds of projects can have several negative cash flow periods. New ventures, for example, typically lose money for the first few years after an initial outlay, so there are several negative periods at the outset. More complex projects can require infusions of cash at different times, so it's possible to have negative flows at any time. For example, a cleanup requirement at the end can make the last flow of a project negative.

Project Cash Flows Are Incremental
The most fundamental concept about project cash flows is that they are **incremental** to the company's normal business. "Incremental" means *in addition to* and, at least conceptually, *separate from*. In other words, we must answer the following question: What cash flows will occur if we undertake this project that wouldn't occur if we left it undone and continued business as before?

Sunk Costs
Some expenditures associated with a project should not be included in capital budgeting cash flows. **Sunk costs** are monies that have already been spent at the time of the analysis. The fact that sunk money is gone cannot be changed by decisions about the project.

For example, suppose a company spends money to study a new area of business and later conducts an analysis to decide whether to enter the field. The cost of the study should *not* be included in the project's cash flow stream for capital budgeting analysis, because at the time of the analysis the money has already been spent.

The analysis of a decision must include only *future* costs that are dependent on the decision. The study money is gone and won't be recovered whether the new field is entered or not, so it's irrelevant to the decision.

Opportunity Cost
Resources aren't free even though they sometimes seem to be. Suppose a firm has an idle production facility and is evaluating a project that requires a similar resource. The idle factory will be used if the project is undertaken and won't require a cash outlay. Does that mean the facility is a zero cost item in the project's capital budgeting analysis?

It's tempting to say yes, especially if there are no other plans for the building. However, that's not the right way to look at the problem. The appropriate cost of any resource is whatever has to be *given up* to use it, in other words, its value in the next best use.

In this example, suppose the firm has no other production use for the idle factory, but can sell it for $1 million (the next most lucrative use). In such a case we'd say $1 million is the **opportunity cost** of the factory and use that amount as a cash outflow in the analysis. In effect, the company is forgoing a $1 million cash inflow by using the facility in the project. The factory would be free only if it had no market value and no other use by the company.

Impacts on Other Parts of the Company
Projects sometimes have impacts on other parts of the company that have to be considered. Suppose a company sells a

Margin notes:

Most cash **outflows** occur **early**; inflows happen **later**.

Only **incremental** cash flows count.

Sunk costs have already been spent and are ignored.

The **opportunity cost** of a resource is its value in its best alternative use and is included in capital budgeting analyses.

family model product and is considering introducing a luxury model. Some customers who buy the family model will probably switch to the luxury line. The result will be a loss of income in the family line that should be reflected as a negative cash flow in the analysis of the new proposal.

Overhead Levels   Basic overheads are usually considered fixed and left out of project analysis. There are times, however, when overhead changes have to be considered.

For example, suppose a company has a central human resources department that is considered overhead by operating departments. Most capital budgeting projects involve the addition of only a few new people in operating departments, so the workload of the human resources department isn't increased significantly by the larger staff. But suppose a particular project calls for so many new employees that an additional human resources administrator is required for their support. In such a case, the increased cost *in the human resources department* must be reflected as a cost of the project. In other words, the project has an *incremental overhead effect* that should be reflected in its projected cash flows.

Taxes   Capital projects are generally expected to improve profitability, but more profit usually means more taxes. It's important to calculate incremental cash flows net of any additional taxes caused by the project.

To do that we have to calculate the incremental impact of the project on earnings before tax and then calculate the extra tax and include it as a cash outflow. In other words, we deal with **after-tax cash flows** in capital budgeting.

All capital budgeting cash flows are stated **after tax**.

Cash Versus Accounting Results   It's important to keep the distinction between earnings and cash flows in mind when doing project projections. Capital budgeting deals only with cash flows, so in theory we hardly need mention accounting net income at all. However, business managers invariably want to know the *net income impact* of projects as well as the results of the capital budgeting analysis. It's therefore important to keep both available although separate.

Projects generally require new **working capital**, which requires cash.

Working Capital   Projects that involve increased sales normally also require increases in receivables and inventories (partially offset by payables). In other words, higher revenue demands more **working capital**, which builds up during the project's early years along with revenue. It's important to recognize that increases in working capital have to be funded with cash outflows just like the acquisition of any other asset, and that these flows have to be included in the project's forecast.

Ignore Financing Costs   When project cash flows are projected, we do *not* include the interest expense of carrying a cumulative outflow over time. This is a significant difference between cash flow estimation and the financial forecasting associated with business planning (Chapter 4). Cash flow estimation is concerned with the value of projects regardless of how they're financed, so we look only at operating cash flows.

Ignore interest **expense** when estimating incremental cash flows.

This is not to say that the capital budgeting concept ignores interest expenses or the time value of money. The time cost of money is explicitly accounted for in the evaluation process when the NPV and/or IRR techniques are applied. Because it's taken into account there, we don't need to consider it when estimating cash flows.

Old Equipment   Some projects, especially replacements, involve discarding old equipment. That equipment can sometimes be sold on a secondhand market, providing a cash inflow that partially offsets the expense of the new equipment.

It's important to consider this source of funds in cash flow estimation. It's also important to recognize that the income from the sale of old equipment may be reduced by taxes on an accounting profit on the sale.

11.3   Estimating New Venture Cash Flows

New venture projects tend to be larger and more elaborate than expansions or replacements. However, incremental cash flows can be easier to isolate with new ventures, because the whole project is easily seen as distinct and separate from the rest of the company. The best way to understand the process is through a detailed example.

CONCEPT CONNECTION   EXAMPLE 11-1

New Venture Cash Flows

The Wilmont Bicycle Company manufactures a line of traditional multispeed road bicycles. Management is considering a new business proposal to produce a line of off-road mountain bikes. The proposal has been studied carefully and the following information is forecast.

Cost of new production equipment and machinery including freight and setup		$200,000
Expense of hiring and training new employees		125,000
Pre-start-up advertising and other miscellaneous expenses		20,000
Additional selling and administrative expense per year after start-up		120,000
Unit sales forecast		
Year 1	200	
Year 2	600	
Year 3	1,200	
Year 4 and beyond	1,500	
Unit price		600
Unit cost to manufacture (60% of revenue)		360

Last year, anticipating an interest in off-road bicycles, the company bought the rights to a new gearshift design for $50,000.

Wilmont's production facilities are currently being utilized to capacity, so a new shop has to be acquired for incremental production. The company owns a lot near the present facility on which a new building can be constructed for $60,000. The land was purchased 10 years ago for $30,700, and now has an estimated market value of $150,000.

If Wilmont produces off-road bicycles, it expects to lose some of its current sales to the new product. Three percent of the new unit forecast is expected to come out of sales that would have been made in the old line. Prices and direct costs are about the same in the old line as in the new.

Wilmont's general overhead includes human resources, finance, and executive functions, and runs about 5% of revenue. Small one-time increments in business don't affect overhead spending, but a major continuing increase in volume would require additional support. Management estimates that additional spending in overhead areas will amount to about 2% of the new project's revenues.

New revenues are expected to be collected in 30 days. Incremental inventories are estimated at $12,000 at start-up and for the first year. After that an inventory turnover of 12 times based on cost of sales is expected. Incremental payables are estimated to be 25% of inventories.

Wilmont's current business is profitable, so losses in the new line will result in tax credits. The company's marginal tax rate is 34%.

SOLUTION: The Initial Outlay. First we'll consider cash flows required before start-up, which comprise the initial outlay, C_0. We'll work in thousands of dollars and carry one decimal place. That amounts to forecasting to the nearest $100, which provides more than enough detail for estimating purposes.

Expenses of an operating nature will be tax deductible against other income before start-up. These include the cost of hiring, training, advertising, and other miscellaneous items.

Hiring and training	$125.0
Advertising and miscellaneous	20.0
Deductible expense	$145.0
Tax credit @ 34%	49.3
Net after-tax expenses	$ 95.7

Next add the cash needed for physical assets necessary to get started.

Equipment	$200.0
New construction	60.0
Initial inventory	12.0
Assets subtotal	$ 272.0

Add the operating items and the physical assets to get the total, actual pre–start-up outlay.

Net after-tax expenses	$ 95.7
Assets subtotal	272.0
Actual pre–start-up outlay	$367.7

Next we have to recognize the opportunity cost of the land. The property has a market value of $150,000, but if it were to be sold for that amount, a capital gains tax would be due on the increase in value over its original cost. Corporations don't get favorable capital gains rates, so the tax rate would be 34%.

	Capital Gain	Cash
Sales price	$150.0	$150.0
Cost	30.7	
Capital gain	$ 119.3	
Tax on gain @ 34%		40.6
Cash forgone (price − tax)		$109.4

Summarizing, we obtain a figure for C_0.

Actual pre–start-up cash outlay	$367.7
Opportunity cost of land	109.4
C_0 (initial outlay for analysis)	$477.1

Cash Flows After Start-Up

Incremental sales forecasts often begin small, grow for a few years, and then level off. Other forecast elements commonly do the same thing, change for a few years and then remain constant. When that happens, we have to forecast out in time only until the numbers stop changing from year to year. Subsequent years are then repetitive.

In this case, sales are forecast to grow for four years before leveling off. However, a change in depreciation after the fifth year affects taxes. Hence, the annual cash flow estimate changes each year until the sixth year and then remains constant. We'll therefore estimate only the first six years, understanding that for a longer forecast we just need to repeat the last year as many times as we like. The calculations are laid out in Table 11-1 and discussed in the following paragraphs. **Follow Table 11-1 as you continue to read this example.**

TABLE 11-1   Cash Flow Estimation

Wilmont Bicycle Company
Estimated Cash Flows
Mountain Bike Project ($000)

	Year					
	1	2	3	4	5	6+
Revenue and Gross Margin						
Units	200	600	1,200	1,500	1,500	1,500
Revenue	$120.0	$360.0	$ 720.0	$ 900.0	$ 900.0	$ 900.0
Cost	72.0	216.0	432.0	540.0	540.0	540.0
Gross margin	$ 48.0	$ 144.0	$ 288.0	$ 360.0	$ 360.0	$ 360.0
Tax Deductible Expenses						
SG&A expense	$120.0	$ 120.0	$ 120.0	$ 120.0	$ 120.0	$ 120.0
Depreciation	41.5	41.5	41.5	41.5	41.5	1.5
General overhead	2.4	7.2	14.4	18.0	18.0	18.0
Loss on old line	1.4	4.3	8.6	10.8	10.8	10.8
Total	$165.3	$ 173.0	$ 184.5	$ 190.3	$ 190.3	$ 150.3
Profit Impact and Tax						
EBT impact	$(117.3)	$ (29.0)	$ 103.5	$ 169.7	$ 169.7	$ 209.7
Tax	(39.9)	(9.9)	35.2	57.7	57.7	71.3
Net income impact	$ (77.4)	$ (19.1)	$ 68.3	$ 112.0	$ 112.0	$ 138.4
Add depreciation	41.5	41.5	41.5	41.5	41.5	1.5
Subtotal	$(35.9)	$ 22.4	$ 109.8	$ 153.5	$ 153.5	$ 139.9
Working Capital						
Accounts receivable	$ 20.0	$ 45.0	$ 67.5	$ 75.5	$ 75.5	$ 75.5
Inventory	12.0	18.0	36.0	45.0	45.0	45.0
Payables	(3.0)	(4.5)	(9.0)	(11.3)	(11.3)	(11.3)
Working capital	$ 29.0	$ 58.5	$ 94.5	$ 109.2	$ 109.2	$ 109.2
Change in working capital	$ (17.0)	$ (29.5)	$ (36.0)	$ (14.7)	—	—
Net Cash Flow						
Net cash flow	$(52.9)	$ (7.1)	$ 73.8	$ 138.8	$ 153.5	$ 139.9

It's generally best to forecast revenue with **unit and price** detail.

Revenue

The revenue forecast at the top of the table is developed by laying out the unit sales projection and multiplying by the projected price of $600. It's important to forecast both physical units and future prices rather than just total revenue. Maintaining unit-price detail makes it easier to alter the forecast to reflect different assumptions as well as check the reasonability of the entire estimate.

Cost and Gross Margin

Production cost can be built up from components or forecast as a percentage of revenue consistent with previous experience in the same or similar businesses. In this case, Wilmont is experienced in making bicycles and feels that a *cost ratio* of 60% will be appropriate for the new line. Applying this ratio to the revenue figures yields the projected cost line. Gross margin follows by subtracting cost from revenue.

SG&A

Next we calculate items that affect pretax income, beginning with selling, general and administrative (SG&A) expense estimated at $120,000 per year.

Depreciation

Deductible depreciation is in two separate pieces because equipment and buildings are depreciated over different lives. Equipment can be written off over 5 years for tax purposes, while the building has to be amortized over 39 years. We'll assume straight-line depreciation for both and ignore partial-year conventions for convenience. Then the annual depreciation is as follows.

Equipment ($200,000/5)	$40,000
Building ($60,000/39)	1,538
Depreciation, first five years	$ 41,538
Thereafter	1,538

It's important to understand why and how depreciation is included in the cash flow estimate even though it's a noncash expense. The reason is that depreciation is subtracted from revenue in calculating earnings before tax on which income taxes are paid. Once taxes and net income are calculated, we add depreciation back in a separate line.

Overhead

The next line represents the expected increase in general overhead calculated at 2% of incremental revenues.

Loss in Old Line

Following overhead is an allowance for the lost business expected in the old product line. It was estimated that 3% of the unit forecast would come from the old line. Assuming the cost and price relationships are about the same in the old line as in the new, we can estimate the profit impact of this loss as 3% of the new gross margin forecast and include it as an expense.

EBT, Tax, and Net Income

Add these expense items and subtract the total from gross margin for the impact on earnings before tax (EBT). The tax calculation is just 34% of EBT, which leads to the impact of the

from the

CFO

project on net income. *Although this figure isn't relevant for capital budgeting purposes, it's invariably important to operating managers and should therefore be calculated and displayed as part of the analysis.*

Add-Back Depreciation

The cash impact of the operating items above is calculated by adding back depreciation, the only noncash charge in this example.

Working Capital

Finally, we calculate the cash required to build up the working capital necessary to support the project. This means estimating the year-end balances for accounts receivable, inventories, and accounts payable.

Receivables

We're assuming that receivables are collected in 30 days, meaning there's one month of uncollected revenue in accounts receivable (A/R) all the time. The average level during each year is therefore one-twelfth of that year's revenue. Having the average figure in two successive years, we can average them to get the year-end figure for the first of the years. The calculations for the first two years are shown below. Year 1's average monthly revenue is $10,000; in year 2 that figure builds to $30,000. On the way between the two levels, assuming the growth is smooth, it passes through $20,000 at year end.

Year	Revenue	Average A/R	Year-End A/R
1	$120,000	$10,000	$20,000
2	360,000	30,000	45,000
3	720,000	60,000	

Inventory

Inventory is estimated as one month's cost of goods sold, so take the annual cost figure divided by 12 except in the first year where a $12,000 level has been explicitly assumed.

Payables

Payables are 25% of inventory.

Summarize these items and calculate the year-to-year **change** in working capital, which reflects the cash required to fund it over the project's life. In the first year, the change in working capital is $17,000 rather than $29,000 because an initial inventory of $12,000 is assumed to have been acquired before start-up.

The after-tax cash flow estimates for years 1 through 6 are calculated by adding the working capital requirements to the subtotal just above the working capital section. These figures along with the initial outlay calculated earlier represent the cash flows estimated for the off-road bike project.

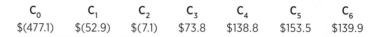

C_0	C_1	C_2	C_3	C_4	C_5	C_6
$(477.1)	$(52.9)	$(7.1)	$73.8	$138.8	$153.5	$139.9

Notice that the cash forecasts for subsequent years will be repetitions of the sixth year if sales remain at a steady 1,500 units. Therefore, in this case, we can extend the forecast by just adding more inflows of $139,900.

It's important to notice two things that are not in the calculations above.

Sunk Costs and Interest

There is no provision for the $50,000 already spent for the new gearshift design. That money is gone whether the mountain bike project is accepted or not and is therefore irrelevant. Only *future* flows that depend on the decision to go ahead should be considered in the project's analysis. Past or **sunk** costs that can't be changed or recovered aren't considered even though they're related to the project.

Second, there's no allowance for interest on accumulated cash flows as a cost or income of the project. The cost of funds is explicitly included in capital budgeting when the NPV and IRR techniques are applied. Therefore, it doesn't need to be considered in the estimation of project cash flows.

11.3a Terminal Values

It's possible to assume the incremental cash flows associated with a project go on forever. The assumption is especially common with respect to new ventures that are expected to continue as businesses indefinitely. For example, in the Wilmont Bicycle Company problem we've just completed, it's not unreasonable to assume that the year 6 cash flow of approximately $140,000 continues into the indefinite future.

There's a convenient way to reflect this assumption in the cash flow stream that Wilmont will use in capital budgeting. The repetitive cash flow starting in period 7 is a perpetuity whose "present" value at the beginning of period 7 (end of period 6) is C_7/k, where k is the cost of capital (see perpetuities on pages 269–270). This amount, known as the project's **terminal value,** is added to the *period* 6 cash flow to reflect the continuation of the project.

Cash flows forecast to continue forever are compressed into finite **terminal values** using perpetuity formulas.

CONCEPT CONNECTION   EXAMPLE 11-2

Terminal Values
If Wilmont's cost of capital is 10%, the project's terminal value would be

$$\frac{\$140,000}{.10} = \$1,400,000$$

It's also possible to assume a perpetual cash flow that grows at some rate, g. In that case, the terminal value is calculated by dividing the first ongoing cash flow by (k − g) instead of k. Suppose Wilmont forecasts a 3% growth in the mountain bike project's cash flows starting with $140,000 in period 7. The project's terminal value would then be

$$\frac{\$140,000}{.10 - .03} = \$2,000,000$$

Ensuper/Shutterstock.com

Notice how large the terminal value cash flow is relative to the project's earlier flows. Indeed the terminal value assumption overwhelms everything else in the projection. Also notice that the magnitude of the terminal value is very sensitive to the growth rate assumed.

Terminal Values are a big problem with respect to the accuracy of capital budgeting analyses. An optimistic long-run forecast can make a project look good on an NPV basis even if the short-run projections are poor. Since the terminal period doesn't start for some time, it's hard to disprove the assumptions behind it. Hence, people who propose projects tend to portray them as growing rapidly into the indefinite future. **It's generally up to the finance department to keep such projections reasonable and conservative.**

There's a strong argument that infinite projections shouldn't be used at all because of the uncertainty of the distant future. This position maintains that if a project can't be justified in a reasonably long time—say, 10 years—it shouldn't be undertaken. We'll discuss terminal values in more detail in Chapter 17.

11.3b   Accuracy and Estimates

Now that we've had a look at the estimating process, we need to revisit the important point about precision that we discussed briefly at the beginning of the chapter.

The NPV and IRR techniques give the impression of great accuracy, since NPVs and IRRs are easily calculated to several decimal places. Such precision isn't real. Although IRR and NPV calculations are very exact, they're based on the cash flows input to the capital budgeting model. Those flows are *estimates* of the future and, like all estimates, are subject to error and bias.

In Example 11-1, Wilmont's cash flow estimates were built on the unit sales forecast. But for a new product, that forecast could easily be off by 20%. Such variability implies that it usually doesn't pay to expend a great deal of effort to make other elements of the estimate precise. For example, an estimator might spend a lot of time determining whether the appropriate cost ratio for the mountain bike project is 60 or 61%. That would be a waste of time given the inaccuracy of the underlying sales forecast. Notice that we worked in tenths of thousands of dollars in Table 11-1 and could easily have rounded to thousands without loss of substance.

Estimating inaccuracies come from any number of sources, but unintentional biases are probably the biggest problem in capital budgeting. Projects are usually proposed by people who have an interest in their approval, and it's generally those same individuals who provide the technical input for the estimated cash flows used in capital budgeting. This creates an inherent conflict of interest.

For example, suppose a company's manufacturing department has proposed buying a new, state-of-the-art production machine to replace an old machine that's beginning to wear out. If the new machine is purchased, product quality will be consistently higher, and there will be fewer equipment breakdowns that cause production stoppages. Such problems create the most stress in manufacturing managers' lives and significantly affect their performance ratings. Therefore, manufacturing managers are likely to perceive the new machine as a way to make their lives easier and better.

It is true that the manufacturing department will be charged with the cost of the new machine, but if that cost is included in the department's budget, it won't create an overrun that requires explaining. All things considered, manufacturing executives are likely to perceive the machine in an entirely positive light.

---

from the **CFO**

from the **CFO**

Capital budgeting results are **no more accurate** than the **projections of the future** used as inputs.

Representing the new machine as a series of cash flows requires putting a dollar value on the improved quality of output and on the machine's higher reliability. The implication is that the increased quality will result in higher customer satisfaction and fewer complaints. The better reliability will presumably result in less lost time on the production floor.

Making financial estimates of effects like these is a very subjective affair. We can generally say that the new machine will have a positive effect, but exactly how large it will be is hard to pin down. The results are difficult to identify even after the project is implemented. The effects of happier customers and fewer breakdowns rarely show up clearly on a financial statement. If they happen at all, they're just rolled into the normal financial results of operations.

As a result of all this, estimating the financial impact of such a project often turns out to be little more than educated guesswork that can never be proven right or wrong. But the people making the guesses are probably going to be members of the manufacturing team who proposed the project in the first place and feel that it's a terrific idea. Therefore, their tendency will be to overestimate the benefits and underestimate the costs. We'll consider some of these issues in an example shortly.

11.3c   MACRS—A Note on Depreciation

The U.S. government lets companies use *accelerated depreciation* when computing income for tax purposes. Under an accelerated method, depreciation is shifted forward in an asset's life, so more is taken in the early years and less later on with no change in the total. This means taxable income and taxes due are lower in the early years and higher later on. In essence, the scheme *defers* taxes.

This is an advantage because of the time value of money. To understand that, think of taking a dollar of deferred tax and putting it in the bank until it has to be paid several years later, and keeping the interest earned in the meantime.

Accelerated depreciation creates a problem, however, because companies don't like to show lower profits in the short run even if they'll be made up later on. As a result companies generally don't use accelerated depreciation to calculate the earnings shown to stockholders and the public. It's important to understand that it's perfectly legitimate to use two sets of accounting rules like this, one for *tax* purposes and one for *financial reporting* purposes.

Recall that depreciation is a noncash expense item. It represents a fictitious allocation of cost over time intended to make financial results match physical activity. It doesn't represent actual spending. Also recall that in capital budgeting we're interested in cash flow, not accounting results. Hence, the only reason we include depreciation in capital budgeting calculations is because of its effect on taxes, which are real cash flow items.

Therefore, if a firm uses accelerated depreciation for tax purposes, it should use that depreciation in capital budgeting calculations. We haven't shown this detail in our examples to keep things simple for illustrative purposes, but you should be aware of how this feature of the tax system works.

Modified Accelerated Cost Recovery System. Many accelerated methods are available to spread depreciation over an asset's life. The tax code, however, dictates exactly how it's to be done. The method is called the **Modified Accelerated Cost Recovery System**, generally abbreviated **MACRS**. First the system classifies assets into different categories and specifies a depreciation life for each. Then it provides a table showing the percentage of the asset's cost that can be taken in depreciation during each year of life. The classification rules are fairly extensive as are the tables, so we'll just show a representative sample consisting of three-, five-, and seven-year assets as follows.

Class	Representative Equipment
3-year	Research equipment
5-year	Automobiles and computers
7-year	Furniture and equipment

	Depreciation as a Percentage of Cost Property Class		
Year in Life	3-year	5-year	7-year
1	33.3%	20.0%	14.3%
2	44.4	32.0	24.5
3	14.8	19.2	17.5
4	7.5	11.5	12.5
5		11.5	8.9
6		5.8	8.9
7			8.9
8			4.5

Notice that there's depreciation in an extra year in each column, and the first entry in each column is smaller than the second. Both oddities are due to the *half-year convention,* which assumes assets are placed in service in the middle of the year in which they're acquired. Hence, the first entry in each column represents a half year of service and leaves another half year to be recognized at the end of the class life period.

MACRS applies only to equipment. Buildings (real estate) are depreciated straight-line over 27.5 years if they're residential and over 39 years otherwise. (31.5 for some older properties.) Land isn't depreciated.

11.3d   Expansion Projects

Expansion projects are similar to new ventures in that they usually involve incremental revenue and cost, new assets that have to be acquired and depreciated, and a variety of new expenses. Therefore, the cash flow estimating format we've just used for a new venture, as illustrated in Table 11-1, is generally applicable to expansions as well. Replacement projects have a somewhat different structure as we'll see in the next section.

11.4   Estimating Cash Flows for Replacement Projects

Replacement projects generally have fewer elements to consider than new ventures, but identifying what is incremental can be trickier. It can be especially hard to specify what will happen if you don't do the project. For example, suppose a production machine is getting old and needs to be replaced. Do we compare the performance of the new machine with the current performance of the old one, or assume that the old one will continue to deteriorate? If the latter, how much additional cost will the deterioration bring about? Tax effects are also complicated in replacement projects.

CONCEPT CONNECTION   EXAMPLE 11-3

Replacement Projects

Harrington Metals Inc. purchased a large stamping machine five years ago for $160,000. To keep the example simple, we'll assume that the tax laws at the time permitted straight-line depreciation over eight years and that machinery purchased today can be depreciated straight-line over five years. The machine has not performed well, and management is considering replacing it with a new one that will cost $300,000. If the new machine is purchased, it is estimated that the old one can be sold for $90,000. The quoted costs include all freight, installation, and setup.

The old machine requires three operators, each of whom earns $50,000 a year including all benefits and payroll costs. The new machine is more efficiently designed and will require only two operators, each earning the same amount.

The old machine has the following history of high maintenance cost and significant downtime.[1]

	Year				
	1	2	3	4	5
Hours down	40	60	100	130	128
Maintenance expense ($000)	In warranty	$20	$ 70	$ 84	$ 90

Downtime on the machine is a major inconvenience, but it doesn't usually stop production unless it lasts for an extended period. This is because the company maintains an emergency inventory of stamped pieces and has been able to temporarily reroute production without much notice. Manufacturing managers estimate that every hour of downtime costs the company $1,000, but have no hard data backing up that figure.

The makers of the replacement machine have said that Harrington will spend about $30,000 a year maintaining their product and that an average of only 30 hours of downtime a year should be expected. However, they're not willing to guarantee those estimates after the one-year warranty runs out.

The new machine is expected to produce higher quality output than the old one. The result is expected to be better customer satisfaction and possibly more sales in the future. Management would like to include some benefit for this effect in the analysis, but is unsure of how to quantify it.

PROBLEM: Estimate the incremental cash flows over the next five years associated with buying the new machine. Assume Harrington's marginal tax rate is 34% and that the company is currently profitable so that changes in taxable income result in tax changes at 34% whether positive or negative. Assume any gain on the sale of the old machine is also taxed at 34%.

SOLUTION: There are two kinds of cash flow items in this problem: those that can be estimated fairly objectively and those that require some degree of subjective guesswork. Let's consider the objective items first.[2]

---

1. "Downtime" refers to periods during which the machine isn't operable, usually due to maintenance or repair.

2. *Objective* means measurable or determinable without bias. A *subjective* item, on the other hand, cannot be measured precisely, and estimates of its value are subject to distortion due to the estimator's biases and opinions. For example, a person's height and weight are objective; good looks are subjective.

Initial Outlay Including the Sale of an Old Asset

The new machine will cost $300,000 less whatever proceeds come from the sale of the old one.

The old machine has a market value of $90,000, but sale at that price will result in a taxable gain. The proceeds of its sale will be the cash received less any tax paid on that gain.

The unit was originally purchased for $160,000 and is being depreciated straight-line over eight years at $20,000 per year. It's now five years old, so the remaining book value is $60,000. The after-tax proceeds of the sale are calculated as follows ($000):

	Accounting	Cash
Sale price	$90.0	$90.0
Book value	60.0	
Gain on sale	$30.0	
Tax @ 34%	$ 10.2	(10.2)
Net cash proceeds of sale		$ 79.8

The project's initial outlay is as follows.

Cost of new machine	$300.0
Less proceeds from sale of old machine	79.8
Initial outlay	$220.2

Now we'll consider incremental cash flows during the five-year planning period. The straight-forward items are the tax implications of a new depreciation pattern and the labor savings due to requiring one less operator.

Depreciation

Purchasing the new machine will alter the depreciation tax shield as follows ($000):

	Year				
	1	2	3	4	5
New depreciation	$60.0	$60.0	$60.0	$60.0	$60.0
Old depreciation	20.0	20.0	20.0		
Net increase in depreciation	$40.0	$40.0	$40.0	$60.0	$60.0
Cash tax savings @ 34%	$ 13.6	$ 13.6	$ 13.6	$20.4	$20.4

Labor

The labor savings come from just the cost of one employee.

	Year				
	1	2	3	4	5
Labor savings	$50.0	$50.0	$50.0	$50.0	$50.0

Subjective benefits based on opinions are hard to quantify and lead to biases when estimated by people who want project approval.

Now we have to deal with the **subjective** items in the estimate. Three effects have to be considered. These are the differences between the new machine and the old in maintenance expense, downtime, and product quality. Each clearly has a value, but it's hard to say how much.

from the
CFO

The **financial analyst** should ensure that only **reasonable estimates** of unprovable benefits are used.

It is at this stage of the analysis that the role of the financial analyst is most crucial. The people putting together the proposal to buy the new machine are likely to be very optimistic about the subjective benefits. It's the job of the finance department to be the voice of reason in the decision-making process and to make sure that only realistic estimates of subjective benefits are included.

Let's consider the issues in this example one at a time.

Maintenance Cost

The most concrete issue is the maintenance cost. We have to forecast the *difference* in the cost of maintenance on the new machine and on the old one. Looking at the record, we can see that the old machine's cost increased steadily for several years, but has recently leveled off at about $90,000. The question is whether to assume it will stay there or resume its increase as the machine gets older.

The new machine offers a one-year warranty and promises a cost of $30,000 a year thereafter. However, that figure is not guaranteed. The issue is whether to believe the $30,000 or assume a higher number. We'll lay out a set of maintenance cost figures that reflects maintenance on the old machine continuing at $90,000 and the new machine performing as promised.

	Year				
	1	2	3	4	5
Old machine	$90.0	$90.0	$90.0	$90.0	$90.0
New machine	In warranty	30.0	30.0	30.0	30.0
Savings	$90.0	$60.0	$60.0	$60.0	$60.0

The difference between the two maintenance estimates represents the cash savings due to replacing the machine. Notice that it's possible to manipulate the analysis by varying the assumptions about either or both estimates. If we want to make the project look good, we can assume the old machine's costs will get worse and the new one's will hold at $30,000. If we assume the new machine will cost more while the old one holds at $90,000, the project looks worse.

The point is that there's a great deal of latitude in the forecast, and reasonable estimates of the maintenance cost savings can vary by quite a bit. For purposes of the example, we'll use the one shown here.

Downtime

Next let's look at the downtime estimate. Here two variables are considered: how much downtime will actually be saved by the new machine and how much each hour is worth. The questions involved in estimating the hours saved are similar to those asked in dealing with the maintenance cost. The old machine has been experiencing about 130 hours of downtime a year, while the new one promises 30 for a saving of 100 hours. Good arguments can be made for raising or lowering that figure by quite a bit.

The compounding question, however, is how much an hour of saved downtime is worth. It clearly should have some value, but it's difficult to say how much. This is a very common problem. We know there's a cost or benefit to something, but we're not able to estimate its value with any precision.

optimarc/Shutterstock.com

from the
CFO

Manufacturing management's subjective estimate of $1000 is likely to be on the high side because of the biases we discussed earlier. *A conservative approach, on the other hand, might be to refuse to include anything in the analysis for the saved downtime because its value can't be documented. Anything in between is also possible.*

In situations like this, most people favor a middle-of-the-road approach. That implies giving some value to the saved downtime, but choosing a value substantially lower than that recommended by manufacturing. In this case, $400 per hour is probably reasonable. Combining that figure with the saved time estimate of 100 hours yields an estimated cash flow savings of $40,000 per year.

Quality

Next we'll examine the most subjective claim in favor of the new machine, increased quality of output. Once again, this issue is very common when people are trying to justify a project. The issue isn't whether the output actually will be of higher quality. That should be ascertainable by testing the output of a demo machine against the output of the old one. The question is whether an increase in the quality of certain component parts will significantly increase customer satisfaction, and whether that will translate into more future sales.

Several scenarios are possible. If customers or service technicians have been actively complaining about the parts from the old machine, it's easier to argue that higher quality will have a future sales impact than if the old parts weren't a problem. But even then, the impact is likely to be very difficult to estimate. As a general rule, when the connection between a project and the claimed cash flow impact is this tenuous, financial people tend to want to leave it out of the analysis. That's what we'll do in this case.

Now we can summarize the estimated cash flows in the years after installation of the new machine.

	Year				
	1	**2**	**3**	**4**	**5**
Labor savings	$ 50.0	$ 50.0	$ 50.0	$ 50.0	$ 50.0
Maintenance savings	90.0	60.0	60.0	60.0	60.0
Downtime savings	40.0	40.0	40.0	40.0	40.0
Total	$180.0	$150.0	$150.0	$150.0	$150.0
Tax	61.2	51.0	51.0	51.0	51.0
Net after tax	$ 118.8	$ 99.0	$ 99.0	$ 99.0	$ 99.0
Tax savings on depreciation	13.6	13.6	13.6	20.4	20.4
Cash flow	$132.4	$ 112.6	$ 112.6	$ 119.4	$ 119.4

Combining these with the initial outlay yields the project's estimated cash flow stream.

C_0	C_1	C_2	C_3	C_4	C_5
$(220.2)	$ 132.4	$ 112.6	$ 112.6	$ 119.4	$ 119.4

Ethics in Cash Flow Estimation

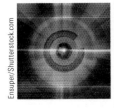

We've just seen that strong departmental interests can attach to capital budgeting decisions, and that wide ranges of inputs can be accepted in making those decisions. It's also true that people stretch the truth to get what they want. What are the ethical issues of knowingly providing biased information to a decision-making process to get an outcome that's favorable to your own department?

In answering, recall that in ethical situations one group often has power over another (page 19). Is information power? Who benefits and who gets hurt if the company buys the new machine in Example 11-3 based on manufacturing's claims if those claims are exaggerated?

Here's another interesting situation. Imagine that an executive puts together a proposal for a new venture. It's common for the person proposing something like that to get to run the start-up. Then, if it's successful he or she moves up the management ladder rapidly and makes a lot of money. Do you see a motivation for the executive to overstate the project's benefits and understate its negatives? Is the executive's gamble one sided in that he or she has a lot to gain and little to lose? Who loses if the project is undertaken and fails?

CONCEPT CONNECTIONS

EXAMPLE 11-1 New Venture Cash Flows, *page 490*

EXAMPLE 11-2 Terminal Values, *page 495*

EXAMPLE 11-3 Replacement Projects, *page 499*

OlegDoroshin/Shutterstock.com

QUESTIONS

1. The typical cash flow pattern for business projects involves cash outflows first, and then inflows. However, it's possible to imagine a project in which the pattern is reversed. For example, we might receive inflows now in return for guaranteeing to make payments later. Would the payback, NPV, and IRR methods work for such a project? What would the NPV profile look like? Could the NPV and IRR methods give conflicting results?

BUSINESS ANALYSIS

1. You are a new financial analyst at Belvedere Corp., a large manufacturing firm that is currently looking into diversification opportunities. The vice president of marketing is particularly interested in a venture that is only marginally connected with what the firm does now. Other managers have suggested enterprises in more closely related fields. The proponents of the various ideas have all provided you with business forecasts from which you have developed financial projections, including project cash flows. You have also calculated each project's IRR with the following results.

Project	IRR	Comments
A	19.67%	Marketing's project, an almost totally new field
B	19.25	Proposed by manufacturing, also a very different field
C	18.05	Proposed by engineering, a familiar field

You are now in a meeting with senior managers that was called to discuss the options. You have just presented your analysis, ending your talk with the preceding information.

After your presentation, the vice president of marketing stands, congratulates you on a fine job, and states that the figures clearly show that project A is the best option. He also says that your financial analysis shows that project A has the full backing of the finance department. All eyes, including the CFO's, turn to you. How do you respond?

2. Most top executives are graded primarily on their results in terms of net income rather than net cash flow. Why, then, is capital budgeting done with incremental cash flows rather than with incremental net income?

3. Creighton Inc. is preparing a bid to sell a large telephone communications system to a major business customer. It is characteristic of the telephone business that the vendor selling a system gets substantial follow-on business in later years by making changes and alterations to that system. The marketing department wants to take an *incremental* approach to the bid, basically treating it as a capital budgeting project. They propose selling the system at or below its direct cost in labor and materials (the incremental cost) to ensure getting the follow-on business. They've projected the value of that business by treating future sales less direct costs as cash inflows.

They maintain that the initial outlay is the direct cost to install the system, which is almost immediately paid back by the price. Future cash flows are then the net inflows from the follow-on sales. These calculations have led to an enormous NPV and IRR for the sale viewed as a project.

Both support and criticize this approach. (*Hint:* What would happen if Creighton did most of its business this way?)

4. Webley Motors, a manufacturer of small gas engines, has been working on a new design for several years. It's now considering going into the market with the new product and has projected future sales and cash flows. The marketing and finance departments are putting together a joint presentation for the board of directors that they hope will gain approval for the new venture. Part of the presentation is a capital budgeting analysis of the project that includes only estimated future costs and revenues. Dan Eyeshade, the head of investor relations, insists that calculations shown to the board include the money spent on research in the past several years. He says that to ignore or omit those costs would be deceiving the board about the true cost of the project, which would be both unethical and legally dangerous. Comment on Dan's position. If you disagree, prepare an argument that will convince him to change his mind, and suggest an alternative presentation that will satisfy you both.

5. The Capricorn Company is launching a new venture in a field related to but separate from its present business. Management is proposing that financing for the new enterprise be supplied by a local bank, which it has approached for a loan. Capricorn's finance department has done a capital budgeting analysis of the venture, projecting reasonable cash flows and calculating an NPV and an IRR that both look very favorable.

The bank's loan officer, however, isn't satisfied with the analysis. She insists on seeing a financial projection that calculates interest on cumulative cash flows, incorporates that interest as a cost of the project, and shows the buildup and decline of the debt necessary to accomplish the proposal. She essentially wants a business plan complete with projected financial statements. Reconcile the bank officer's position with capital budgeting theory.

6. Wilson Petroleum is a local distributor of home heating oil. The firm also installs and services furnaces and heating systems in homes and small commercial buildings. The customer service department maintains sales and service records on current customers, who number about 400. Detailed customer records are kept manually in file cabinets, and a small computer system holds all customer names and addresses for mailing and billing purposes. One full-time clerk maintains all the records and handles all billing and customer inquiries. Customers occasionally complain if delivery or service is late, but only one or two mild complaints are received each month. Delays are primarily a result of problems in the field rather than problems in assigning calls in the service department.

A consultant has proposed a new computer system that will completely automate the customer service function. It will provide online billing and immediate access to all customer records. The cost of the proposed system is $50,000 initially plus about $7,000 a year for maintenance and support. It will still take a person to run it. The consultant says the new system will provide faster service and superior insight into the needs of the customer base, which will result in better customer relations and more sales in the long run.

Discuss the pros and cons of the consultant's proposal. What further justification should management demand before buying? Could the consultant have made the proposal for reasons that aren't in Wilson's best interest? Could the consultant be well meaning yet biased? Explain.

PROBLEMS

New Venture Cash Flows—Depreciation: Concept Connection Example 11-1 (page 490)

1. A project that is expected to last six years will generate incremental profit and cash flow before taxes and depreciation of $23,000 per year. It requires the initial purchase of equipment costing $60,000, which will be depreciated over four years. The relevant tax rate is 25%. Calculate the project's cash flows. Round all figures within your computations to the nearest thousand dollars.

2. Auburn Concrete Inc. is considering the purchase of a new concrete mixer to replace an inefficient older model that is completely worn out. If purchased, the new machine will cost $90,000 and is expected to generate savings of $40,000 per year for five years at the end of which it will be sold for $20,000. The mixer will be depreciated to a zero salvage value over three years using the straight-line method. Develop a five-year cash flow estimate for the proposal. Auburn's marginal tax rate is 30%. Work to the nearest thousand dollars.

Replacement Projects—Sale of an Old Asset: Concept Connection Example 11-3 (page 499)

3. Flextech Inc. is considering a project that will require new equipment costing $150,000. It will replace old equipment with a book value of $35,000 that can be sold on the secondhand market for $75,000. The company's marginal tax rate is 35%. Calculate the project's initial outlay.

Replacement Projects—Initial Outlay: Concept Connection Example 11-3 (page 499)

4. Tomatoes Inc. is planning a project that involves machinery purchases of $100,000. The new equipment will be depreciated over five years straight-line. It will replace old machinery that will be sold for an estimated $36,000 and has a book value of $22,000. The project will also require hiring and training 10 new people at a cost of about $12,000 each. All of this must happen before the project is actually started. The firm's marginal tax rate is 40%. Calculate C_0, the project's initial cash outlay.

5. The Olson Company plans to replace an old machine with a new one costing $85,000. The old machine originally cost $55,000 and has six years of its expected 11-year life remaining. It has been depreciated straight-line assuming zero salvage value and has a current market value of $24,000. Olson's effective tax rate is 36%. Calculate the initial outlay associated with selling the old machine and acquiring the new one.

6. A four-year project has cash flows before taxes and depreciation of $12,000 per year. The project requires the purchase of a $50,000 asset that will be depreciated over five years straight-line. At the end of the fourth year the asset will be sold for $18,000. The firm's marginal tax rate is 35%. Calculate the cash flows associated with the project.

7. Voxland Industries purchased a computer for $10,000, which it will depreciate straight-line over five years to a $1,000 salvage value. The computer will then be sold at that price. The company's marginal tax rate is 40%. Calculate the cash flows associated with the computer from its purchase to its eventual sale including the years in between. (*Hint:* Depreciate the difference between the cost of the computer and the salvage value. At the end of the depreciation life, a net book value remains that is equal to the salvage value.)

8. Resolve the previous problem assuming Voxland uses the five-year Modified Accelerated Cost Recovery System (MACRS) with no salvage value to depreciate the computer. Continue to assume the machine is sold after five years for $1,000. (*Hint:* Apply the MACRS rules for computers on pages 497–498 to the entire cost of the computer. Notice, however, that there will be a positive net

book value after five years because MACRS takes five years of depreciation over six years due to the half-year convention.)

9. Shelton Pharmaceuticals Inc. is planning to develop and introduce a new drug for pain relief. Management expects to sell 3 million units in the first year at $8.50 each and anticipates 10% growth in sales per year thereafter. Operating costs are estimated at 70% of revenues. Shelton will invest $20 million in depreciable equipment to develop and produce this product. The equipment will be depreciated straight-line over 15 years to a salvage value of $2.0 million. Shelton's marginal tax rate is 40%. Calculate the project's operating cash flows in its third year.

New Venture Cash Flows: Concept Connection Example 11-1 (page 490)

10. Harry and Flo Simone are planning to start a restaurant. Stoves, refrigerators, other kitchen equipment, and furniture are expected to cost $50,000, all of which will be depreciated straight-line over five years. Construction and other costs of getting started will be $30,000. The Simones expect the following revenue stream ($000):

Year	1	2	3	4	5	6	7
Sales	$60	$90	$140	$160	$180	$200	$200

Food costs are expected to be 35% of revenues, while other variable expenses are forecast at 25% of revenues. Fixed overhead will be $40,000 per year. All operating expenses will be paid in cash, revenues will be collected immediately, and inventory is negligible, so working capital need not be considered. Assume the combined state and federal tax rate is 25%. Do not assume a tax credit in loss years, and ignore tax loss carry forwards. (Taxes are simply zero when EBT is a loss.) Develop a cash flow forecast for the Simones' restaurant.

Terminal Values: Concept Connection Example 11-2 (page 495)

11. Oxbow Inc. is contemplating a new venture project and has done a detailed five-year cash flow estimate with the following result ($000):

C_0	C_1	C_2	C_3	C_4	C_5
(257)	(65)	50	90	130	170

The Firm's cost of capital is 12%.

a. Use a financial calculator to compute the project's NPV and IRR, and make the appropriate recommendation to management. (If you don't have a financial calculator just calculate NPV.)

b. Charles Dunn, Oxbow's Marketing VP, has argued that it's unreasonable to exclude cash flows past year 5 from the analysis. Calculate the project's terminal value assuming that year 5's cash flow goes on forever. Recalculate the project's NPV and IRR under Charles's assumption.

c. Charles further argues that the most appropriate assumption is that cash flows beyond the fifth year incorporate a 3% long-run growth rate. Calculate the terminal value, NPV, and IRR implied by this assumption.

d. Comment on the results implied by the use of aggressive terminal value assumptions.

12. Sam Dozier, a very bright computer scientist, has come up with an idea for a new product. He plans to form a corporation to develop the idea and market the resulting product. He has estimated that it will take him and one employee about a year to develop a prototype and another year to bring a working model to market. There will be no income during those years. After that he expects sales to grow rapidly, estimating revenues of $700,000, $1,500,000, and $5,000,000 in the third, fourth, and fifth years, respectively.

Starting the project will require *research equipment* costing about $500,000 which will be depreciated for federal tax purposes under the MACRS system (see page 497). Beyond that it will take another $400,000 in tax deducible expenses to get going.

Sam thinks he can fund the development work including supporting himself and paying an employee with about $200,000 per year. Once sales begin in the third year, direct costs will be 40% of revenues and indirect costs, including salaries for Sam and all employees, will be $300,000, $500,000, and $1,800,000 in the third, fourth, and fifth years, respectively. The nature of the business is such that working capital requirements are minimal. A net investment of $200,000 in the third year is expected to provide for working capital needs. Sam has $1,500,000 saved which he thinks is enough to launch and operate the business until it begins to generate income.

Sam plans to sell the business at the end of the fifth year. He thinks it will be worth $2,500,000 at that time.

The business will be a C-type corporation subject to federal corporate income taxes (see page 53). Sam will be the sole stockholder and will be subject to federal (personal) capital gains tax when he sells the company (assume the top capital gains rate discussed on pages 47–48). Ignore state taxes.

a. Develop a cash flow estimate for Sam's business. Include the effect of tax loss carry forwards as well as any capital gains taxes he will pay on its sale. Does Sam have enough cash to fund this venture without contributions from outside investors?

b. Calculate the project's NPV and IRR (a financial calculator is recommended). Assume the cost of capital is 12%. Is the venture a good investment of Sam's time and money?

13. The Leventhal Baking Company is thinking of expanding its operations into a new line of pastries. The firm expects to sell $350,000 of the new product in the first year and $500,000 each year thereafter. Direct costs including labor and materials will be 60% of sales. Indirect incremental costs are estimated at $40,000 a year. The project will require several new ovens that will cost a total of $500,000 and be depreciated straight-line over five years. The current plant is underutilized, so space is available that cannot be otherwise sold or rented. The firm's marginal tax rate is 35% and its cost of capital is 12%. Assume revenue is collected immediately and inventory is bought and paid for every day, so no additional working capital is required.

a. Prepare a statement showing the incremental cash flows for this project over an eight-year period. (Structure as a new venture.)

b. Calculate the payback period, NPV, and PI.

c. Recommend either acceptance or rejection.

d. If the space to be used could otherwise be rented out for $30,000 a year, how would you put that fact into the calculation? Would the project be acceptable in that case?

New Venture Cash Flows—Working Capital: Concept Connection Example 11-1 (page 490)

14. Harrington Inc. is introducing a new product in its line of household appliances. Household products generally have 10-year life cycles and are viewed as capital budgeting projects over that period. Harrington's working capital forecast for the project is as follows:

- $1.0 million will be invested in inventory before the project begins.
- Inventory will increase by $100,000 in each of the first six years.
- Accounts receivable will increase by $150,000 in each of the first four years and by $100,000 in each of the next two years.
- Accounts payable will increase by $110,000 in each of the first six years.
- During the last four years, the balance in each of these accounts will return to zero in four equal increments.
- Accruals are negligible.

Calculate the cash flows associated with working capital from the initial outlay to the end of the project's life.

Replacement Projects: Concept Connection Example 11-3 (page 499)

15. Meade Metals Inc. plans to start doing its own deliveries instead of using an outside service for which it has been paying $150,000 per year. To make the change, Meade will purchase a $200,000 truck that will depreciate straight-line over 10 years to a $40,000 salvage value. Annual operating expenses are estimated at $80,000, including insurance, fuel, and maintenance on the truck, as well as the cost of a driver. Management plans to sell the truck after five years for $100,000. Develop the project's five-year cash flows. Meade's tax rate is 40%. (*Hint:* Treat as a replacement project. Savings are the difference in the contractor's cost and that of operating the truck with an old asset sale in the last year.)

16. Assume that Meade Metals Inc. of the previous problem is replacing an old truck with a new one instead of replacing an outside delivery service. The old truck was purchased eight years ago for $120,000. It has been depreciated straightline based on a 10-year life and a $20,000 salvage value. The old truck's annual operating expenses are $110,000, and it has a market value of $40,000. Develop a five-year cash flow projection for this replacement project.

17. Olson-Jackson Corp. (OJC) is considering replacing a machine that was purchased only two years ago because of dramatic improvements in new models. The old machine has been depreciated straight-line, anticipating a 10-year life based on a cost of $240,000 and an expected salvage value of $20,000. It currently has a market value of $180,000. If the old machine is kept five more years, it would have a market value of $60,000 at the end of that time. A new machine would cost $350,000 and would be depreciated straight-line over five years to a salvage value of $50,000, at which time it would be sold at that price. Develop a cash flow projection showing the difference between keeping the old machine and acquiring the new one. Assume the tax rate = 40%. (*Note:* A complete cash flow projection for the project would include the financial benefits of the better performance of the new machine as well as a comparison of the operating costs of the two models. In this problem, we're just focusing on the cost of the equipment.)

18. The Catseye Marble Co. is thinking of replacing a manual production process with a machine. The manual process requires three relatively unskilled workers and a supervisor. Each worker makes $17,500 a year and the supervisor earns $24,500. The new machine can be run with only one skilled operator who will earn $41,000. Payroll taxes and fringe benefits are an additional third of all wages and salaries.

    The machine costs $150,000 and has a tax depreciation life of five years. Catseye elects straight-line depreciation for tax purposes. A service contract covers all maintenance for $5,000 a year. The machine is expected to last six years, at which time it will have no salvage value. The machine's output will be virtually indistinguishable from that of the manual process in both quality and quantity. There are no other operating differences between the manual and the machine processes. Catseye's marginal tax rate is 35%, and its cost of capital is 10%.

    a. Calculate the incremental cash flows associated with the project to acquire the machine.

    b. Calculate the project's payback and NPV. Would you accept or reject the project?

    c. Suppose there is no alternative but to lay off the displaced employees, and the cost of severance is about three months' wages. How would you factor this information into the analysis? Does it change the project's acceptability?

    d. How would you characterize this project's risk?

Replacement Projects—Subjective Issues: Concept Connection Example 11-3 (page 499)

19. Blackstone Inc. manufactures western boots and saddles. The company is considering replacing an outmoded leather processing machine with a new, more efficient model. The old machine was purchased for $48,000 six years ago and was expected to have an eight-year life. It has been depreciated on a straight-line basis (ignore partial-year conventions). The used machine has an estimated

market value of $15,323. The new machine will cost $60,000 and will be depreciated straight-line over five years. All depreciation assumes zero salvage.

The new machine is expected to last eight years (its economic life), and then will have to be replaced. Assume it has no actual salvage value at that time.

Assume Blackstone's marginal tax rate is 35%.

Operating cost savings are summarized as follows:

	Old	**New**
Annual maintenance cost	$2,000 increasing $200 in each future year	None for two years, $1,500 thereafter
Cost of fixing production defects	$3,000	$1,000
Operators	2 @ $20,000	1.5 @ $24,000

The shop supervisor feels the new machine will produce a higher quality output and thus affect customer satisfaction and repeat sales. She thinks that benefit should be worth at least $5,000 a year, but doesn't have a way to document the figure. Losses generate tax credits.

a. Calculate the relatively certain incremental cash flows associated with the new machine over its projected economic life of eight years and the NPV at a cost of capital of 12% based on those cash flows. (Round to whole dollar.)

b. Suppose the foreman's $5,000 quality improvement estimate were to be included. How big an impact would it have in relation to the other numbers? Comment.

New Venture/Expansion—Terminal Values: Concept Connection Examples 11-1 and Example 11-2 (pages 490 and 495)

20. The Ebitts Field Corp. manufactures baseball gloves. Charlie Botz, the company's top salesman, has recommended expanding into the baseball bat business. He has put together a project proposal including the following information in support of his idea.

- New production equipment will cost $75,000 and will be depreciated straight-line over five years.
- Overheads and expenses associated with the project are estimated at $20,000 per year during the first two years and $40,000 per year thereafter.
- There is enough unused space in the factory for the bat project. The space has no alternative use or value.
- Setting up production and establishing distribution channels before getting started will cost $300,000 (tax deductible).
- Aluminum and wood bats will be produced and sold to sporting goods retailers. Wholesale prices and incremental costs per unit (direct labor and materials) are as follows:

	Aluminum	**Wood**
Price	$18	$12
Cost	11	9
Gross margin	$ 7	$ 3

- Charlie provides the following unit sales forecast (000):

	Year					
	1	2	3	4	5	6
Aluminum	6	9	15	18	20	22
Wood	8	12	14	20	22	24

The sixth year sales level is expected to hold indefinitely.

- Receivables will be collected in 30 days, inventories will be the cost of one month's production, and payables are expected to be half of inventories. Assume no additional cash in the bank or accruals are necessary. (Use one-twelfth of the current year's revenue and cost for receivables and inventories, respectively.)
- Ebitts Field's marginal tax rate is 35%, and its cost of capital is 12%.

a. Develop a six-year cash flow estimate for Charlie's proposal. Work to the nearest $1,000.

b. Calculate the payback period for the project.

c. Calculate the project's NPV assuming a six-year life. Is the project acceptable?

d. Is the cost of capital an appropriate discount rate for the project considering its likely risk relative to that of the rest of the business? Why?

e. What is the project's NPV if the planning horizon is extended to eight years? (Add the incremental PV from two more years at year 6's cash flow.)

f. What is the NPV if management is willing to look at an indefinitely long time horizon? (*Hint:* Think of the cash flows in year 6 and beyond as a perpetuity.)

g. Comment on the results of parts (e) and (f).

21. Segwick Corp. manufactures men's shoes, which it sells through its own chain of retail stores. The firm is considering adding a line of women's shoes. Management considers the project a new venture because there are substantial differences in marketing and manufacturing processes between men's and women's footwear.

The project will involve setting up a manufacturing facility as well as expanding or modifying the retail stores to carry two products. The stores are leased, so modification will involve leasing larger spaces, installing new leasehold improvements, and writing off some old leasehold improvements.[3]

The expected costs are summarized as follows:

Asset Items

New manufacturing equipment, depreciated over five years (straight-line)	$750,000
Acquisition of a facility for design and manufacturing	
Land (no depreciation)	480,000
Building, depreciated over 31.5 years straight-line	630,000
	$1,110,000
Leased retail space	
Net new lease expense, per year	$ 40,000
New leasehold improvements depreciated over the next five years straight-line	200,000
Write-off of old improvements	90,000
Depreciation reduction due to written off improvements per year for three more years	30,000

Expense Items

Cost of hiring and training new people	150,000
Initial advertising and promotion	200,000
Yearly advertising and promotion	50,000
Yearly sales salaries	900,000
Additional corporate overhead ($000/yr)	$20, $42, $60, $80, $80, $80

Revenue and Cost

The unit sales forecast is as follows in thousands:

Year	Units	Average Price
1	30	$65
2	40	68
3	50	70
4 and on	60	75

Direct cost excluding depreciation is 40% of sales.

---

3. Leasehold improvements are assets added to leased premises by the tenant. They are generally depreciated over the remaining life of the lease.

Working Capital

Sales are to retail customers who pay with checks or credit cards. It takes about 10 days to clear both of these and actually receive cash.

Inventories are estimated to be approximately the direct cost of two months' sales.

Payables are estimated as one quarter of inventories.

Assume incremental cash is required equal to 2% of revenues.

Accruals are insignificant.

Estimate the current accounts based on the current year's sales and cost levels.

Other Items

Management expects a few of the company's current male customers to be lost because they won't want to shop in a store that doesn't exclusively sell men's shoes. The gross margin impact of these lost sales is estimated to be $60,000 per year.

The company has already purchased designs for certain styles of ladies' shoes for $60,000.

Segwick's cost of capital is 10%. Its marginal tax rate is 35%.

a. Develop a six-year forecast of after-tax cash flows for Segwick.

b. Calculate the project's payback period, NPV, IRR, and PI, and make a recommendation about acceptance.

c. Assume you are told that the men's shoe industry is very stable, being served by the same manufacturers year after year. However, firms enter and leave the ladies' shoe business regularly. Would this knowledge make you more or less comfortable with the analysis you've done of this project? Why?

COMPUTER PROBLEM

22. The Paxton Homes Co. is a successful builder of moderate to high-priced houses. The firm is currently considering an expansion into light commercial construction in which it would build shopping centers and small office buildings. Management considers the idea a new venture because of the major differences between commercial and residential construction.

    Getting into the new line of business will require an investment of $12.5 million in equipment and $3 million in expenses. The equipment will be depreciated over five years. Part of the start-up money will come from the sale of some old trucks and cranes. These have a total market value of $1.8 million and an NBV of $600 million. Selling the equipment will result in a depreciation reduction of $200 million per year for three years.

    Revenue from the commercial line is expected to be $6 million in the first year and to grow by $2 million in each succeeding year until it reaches $20 million. After that, growth is uncertain and may be anywhere from 0% to 6% per year. Costs and expenses, including incremental overhead, will be 110% of revenues in the first year, 85% in the next two years, and 70% thereafter. Economies of scale in materials purchasing are expected to save the residential business about $250,000 per year but not until the fourth year. Net working capital requirements are estimated at 10% of revenue. The combined federal and state tax rate on the incremental business will be 40%. Losses can be offset against other profits and can therefore be viewed as earning a tax credit at the same rate. Paxton's cost of capital is 12%.

    You are a financial analyst assigned to evaluate the commercial construction proposal. Use the CAPBUD program to analyze the project and prepare a presentation in which you will make a recommendation either favoring or opposing its undertaking. Here are some ideas for approaches to your presentation.

    a. Establish a base case using the information given. Forecast into the future until the numbers stop changing (eight years). Assume a terminal value based on a continuation of the eighth year's cash flows with no further growth. Is the project acceptable based on NPV and IRR given these assumptions?

b. Test the sensitivity of the base case analysis to the terminal value assumption by varying the growth rate to 3% and 6%.

1. Comment on the difference the terminal growth rate assumption makes.

2. Construction is a cyclical industry in that it is very subject to the ups and downs of the economy. In good times growth is enormous, but in bad times the industry and the firms in it shrink rapidly. Given that fact, how do you feel about the terminal value assumption?

3. Evaluate the project's NPV and IRR assuming a 10-year planning horizon—that is, assuming zero cash flows after the tenth year. Does this approach make more or less sense to you than the terminal value assumptions used in part (a)?

c. Test the sensitivity of the analysis to changes in revenue growth. For example, suppose revenue grows by only $1 million per year instead of two until the eighth year. Is the project a good idea then? What if cost/expense is a higher percentage of revenue than anticipated?

CHAPTER 12

Risk Topics and Real Options in Capital Budgeting

Chapter Outline

Risk in Capital Budgeting—General Considerations
- Cash Flows as Random Variables
- The Importance of Risk in Capital Budgeting

Incorporating Risk into Capital Budgeting—Numerical and Computer Methods
- Scenario/Sensitivity Analysis
- Computer (Monte Carlo) Simulation
- Decision Tree Analysis

Real Options
- Real Options in Capital Budgeting
- Valuing Real Options
- Designing Real Options into Projects

Incorporating Risk into Capital Budgeting—The Theoretical Approach and Risk-Adjusted Rates of Return
- Estimating Risk-Adjusted Rates Using CAPM
- Problems with the Theoretical Approach—Finding the Right Beta and Concerns About the Appropriate Risk Definition
- Certainty Equivalents

12.1 Risk in Capital Budgeting—General Considerations

In our discussions in the last chapter, we emphasized the idea that cash flow estimates are subject to a good deal of error. Different people will make different estimates of the same thing, and actual flows are apt to vary substantially from anybody's estimates. A more concise way to put the same thing is just to say that cash flow estimates are *risky*.

In recent years, the subject of risk has been given a great deal of attention in finance, especially in the area of portfolio theory (Chapter 9). In this section, we'll look at some approaches to incorporating risk into capital budgeting, including one that applies elements of portfolio theory to capital budgeting problems.

12.1a   Cash Flows as Random Variables

In everyday usage, the term "risk" is associated with the probability that something bad will happen. In financial theory, however, we associate risk with random variables and their probability distributions. Risk is the chance that a random variable will take a value significantly different from the one we expect, regardless of whether the deviation is favorable or unfavorable. In terms of a probability distribution, the value we expect is the mean (expected value), and the chance that an observation will be significantly different from the mean is related to the variance or standard deviation. (Recall that standard deviation is the square root of variance).

Recall that in portfolio theory (Chapter 9) the return on an investment is viewed as a random variable with an associated probability distribution, and "risk" is defined as the variance or standard deviation of that distribution. In capital budgeting, the risk inherent in estimated cash flows can be defined in a similar way. Each future **cash flow** can be thought of as a separate **random variable** with its own probability distribution. In each case, the risk associated with the flow is related to the variance of the distribution. The idea is illustrated in Figure 12-1, in which the random variable C_i is the cash flow in the ith period.

When cash flows are viewed like this, the **NPVs** and **IRRs** of projects are also **random variables** with their own probability distributions. That's because they're calculated as functions of the various cash flows in a project, which are random variables themselves. The idea is conceptually illustrated in Figure 12-2.

This view makes explicit the idea that estimated cash flows as well as the resulting NPVs and IRRs have most likely (expected, mean) values, but will probably turn out to be somewhat different from those values. The amount by which the actual

> In capital budgeting each future period's **cash flow** is a **random variable**.

> The **NPV** and **IRR** of any project are **random variables** with expected values and variances that reflect **risk**.

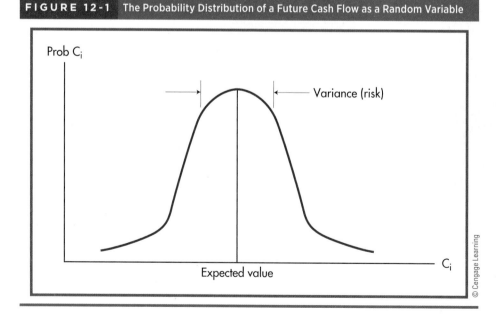

FIGURE 12-1   The Probability Distribution of a Future Cash Flow as a Random Variable

© Cengage Learning

FIGURE 12-2   Risk in Estimated Cash Flows

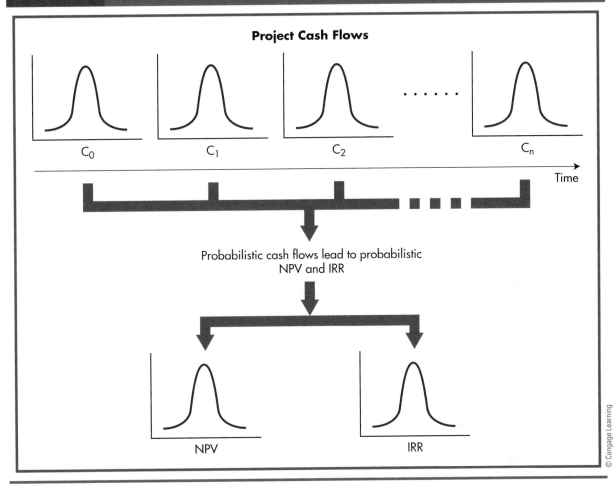

value is likely to differ from the expected value is related to the distribution's variance or standard deviation, which can be visualized intuitively as the width of the bell-shaped curve.

12.1b   The Importance of Risk in Capital Budgeting

Up until now we've thought of each cash flow as a *point estimate*. That's a single number rather than a range of possibilities with a probability distribution attached. When we do that, we're computing NPVs and IRRs that are also point estimates, and ignoring the possibility that the true NPV or IRR could turn out to be higher or lower. That means there's a good chance we'll be making *wrong decisions* by using NPVs and IRRs that come from risky cash flow estimates.

For example, suppose we're making a capital investment decision that involves a choice between two projects with NPVs that look like those shown in Figure 12-3. Notice that NPV_B has a higher expected value than NPV_A, but is also more risky.

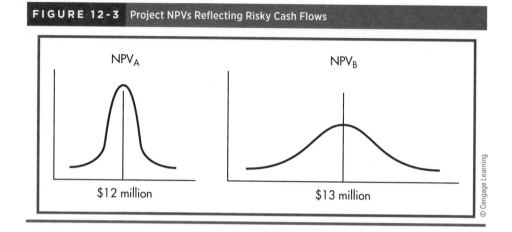

FIGURE 12-3 Project NPVs Reflecting Risky Cash Flows

NPV$_A$

$12 million

NPV$_B$

$13 million

© Cengage Learning

The capital budgeting techniques we considered in Chapter 10 will invariably choose project B over project A because it has a higher expected NPV and the methods ignore risk. But there's a good chance that project B's NPV (and IRR) will actually turn out to be less than project A's, perhaps by quite a bit. If that happens, we will have made the wrong decision at a potential cost of millions.

Risk Aversion   The principle of risk aversion that we studied in portfolio theory applies to capital budgeting just as it does to investing. All other things being equal, we prefer less risky capital projects to those with more risk.

To make the point plainer, imagine that projects A and B in Figure 12-3 have exactly the same expected NPV. The NPV technique would be indifferent between them, yet any rational manager would prefer the one with the lower risk.

Changing the Nature of the Company   Another dimension to the risk issue goes beyond individual projects and relates to the fundamental nature of the firm as an investment. Companies are characterized by investors largely in terms of risk. That was the point of our study of portfolio theory in Chapter 9. When people buy stocks and bonds, expected returns matter, but risk matters just as much.

In capital budgeting, we think of projects as incremental to the normal business of the firm. We view them as sort of *stuck onto* the larger body of what goes on every day. Yet every project affects the totality of the company, just as every stock added to a portfolio changes the nature of that portfolio. In the long run, a company is no more than a collection of all the projects it has undertaken that are still going on. In a very real sense, *a company is a portfolio of projects.*

Hence, if a firm takes on new projects without regard for risk, it's in danger of changing its fundamental nature as perceived by investors. A firm that starts to adopt riskier projects than it has in the past will slowly become a riskier company. The higher risk will be reflected in a more volatile movement of the firm's return, which in turn will result in a higher beta. And that higher beta can generally be expected to have a negative impact on the price of the company's stock.

We can conclude that some consideration of risk *should* be included in capital project analysis. If it isn't, the full impact of projects simply isn't understood at the time they're chosen and implemented.

Ignoring risk in capital budgeting can lead to **incorrect decisions** and **change the risk character** of the firm.

12.2 Incorporating Risk into Capital Budgeting— Numerical and Computer Methods

Once the idea that risk *should* be incorporated in the capital budgeting process is accepted, the question of *how* to do it has to be addressed. Considering the capital budgeting techniques we studied in the last chapter, it's not at all obvious how we ought to go about factoring in risk-related ideas.

Quite a bit of thought has been given to the subject and several approaches have been developed. We'll look at some numerical methods and then examine more theoretical approaches.

12.2a Scenario/Sensitivity Analysis

The fundamental idea behind risk in capital budgeting is that cash flows aren't likely to turn out exactly as estimated. Therefore, actual NPVs and IRRs are likely to be different from those based on estimated cash flows. The management question is just *how much* an NPV or an IRR will change given some deviation in cash flows. A good idea of the relationship between the two changes is available with a procedure called scenario analysis.

In the following discussion we'll refer only to NPV, understanding that the comments also apply to IRR and other capital budgeting techniques.

Suppose a project is represented by a number of estimated future cash flows, each of which can actually take a range of values around the estimate. Also suppose we have an idea of what the best, worst, and most likely values of each cash flow are. Graphically the idea involves a picture like this for *each* cash flow.

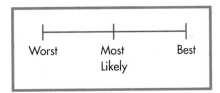

The most likely value of each cash flow is the estimate we've been working with up until now, sometimes called a *point estimate.*

If we calculate the project's NPV using the most likely value of each cash flow, we generally get the most likely NPV for the project. If we do the calculation with the worst possible value of each C_i, we'll get the worst possible NPV. Similarly, we'll get the best NPV if we use all the best cash flows. Notice that we can calculate an NPV with *any* combination of cash flows. That is, we could pick a worst case for C_1, a best case for C_2, something in between for C_3, and so on. All we have to do to calculate an NPV is to choose one value for each cash flow.

Every time we choose a value for every one of the project's cash flows, we define what is called a *scenario,* one of the many possible outcomes of the project. When we calculate the NPV of several scenarios we're performing a **scenario analysis**.

This procedure results in a range of values for NPV along with a good estimate of the most likely value. But it doesn't give a very good notion of the probability of various values within the range. We can choose as many scenarios as we like, however, by selecting any number of different sets of outcomes for the cash flows. Evaluating a number of scenarios gives a subjective feel for the variability of the NPV to changes in our assumptions about what the cash flows will turn out to be.

Evaluating outcomes under a variety of assumptions about cash flows is **scenario analysis**.

CONCEPT CONNECTION   EXAMPLE 12-1

Scenario/Sensitivity Analysis

Project A has an initial outflow of $1,400 and three variable cash inflows defined as follows:

	C_1	C_2	C_3
Worst case	$450	$400	$700
Most likely	550	450	800
Best case	650	500	900

a. Analyze project A's NPV range and its sensitivity to a worst-case result in year 3.

b. Suppose that in each year the worst cash flow has a probability of .2, the best of .3, and the most likely of .5. What are the probabilities of the worst, best, and most likely scenarios? What is the probability of most likely cash flows in the first two years followed by worst in the third year?

SOLUTION:

a. The worst possible NPV will result if the three lowest cash flows all occur. Assume the cost of capital is 9%. Then the worst NPV is

$$NPV = -\$1,400 + \$450[PVF_{9,1}] + \$400[PVF_{9,2}] + \$700[PVF_{9,3}]$$
$$= -\$1,400 + \$450[.9174] + \$400[.8417] + \$700[.7722]$$
$$= -\$109.95$$

Similar calculations lead to a best-case scenario with an NPV of $312.14, and an NPV of $101.10 for the scenario involving the most likely cash flow for every C_i, which is the project's traditional NPV.

Now suppose management feels pretty good about the most likely estimates in the first two years, but is uncomfortable with the high cash flow numbers forecast for year 3. They essentially want to know what will happen to the traditional NPV if year 3 turns out badly.

To answer that question, we form a scenario including the most likely flows from years 1 and 2 and the worst case from year 3. Verify that the NPV from that scenario is $23.88. Notice that management's concern is well founded, as a worst case in the third year alone yields a marginally positive NPV.

b. The probability of the worst-case scenario is

$$.2 \times .2 \times .2 = .008$$

The probability of the best-case scenario is

$$.3 \times .3 \times .3 = .027$$

The probability of the most likely scenario is

$$.5 \times .5 \times .5 = .125$$

The probability of two most likely cash flows followed by a worst is

$$.5 \times .5 \times .2 = .05$$

Another name for essentially the same process is **sensitivity analysis**. That is, we investigate the *sensitivity* of the traditionally calculated NPV to changes in the C_i. In the last part of part (a) in the last example, we saw that a change of $100 in the year 3 cash flow led to a change of ($101.10 − $23.88 =) $77.22 in the project's NPV. In other words, the NPV changed by about 77% of the change in year 3 cash flow. The mathematically astute will recognize that in this simple example 77% is just the present value factor for 9% and three years.

> **Scenario/sensitivity analysis** selects worst, middle, and best outcomes for each cash flow and computes NPV for a variety of combinations.

12.2b   Computer (Monte Carlo) Simulation

The power of the computer can help to incorporate risk into capital budgeting through a technique called *Monte Carlo* simulation. The term "Monte Carlo" implies that the approach involves the use of numbers drawn randomly from probability distributions.[1]

Figure 12-2 intuitively suggests the approach. Reexamine that illustration (Figure 12-2) on page 515. Notice that each cash flow is itself a random variable with a probability distribution, and that all combine to create the probability distributions of the project's NPV (and IRR).

Monte Carlo simulation involves making assumptions that specify the shapes of the probability distributions for *each* future cash flow in a capital budgeting project. These assumed distributions are put into a computer model so that random observations[2] can be drawn from each.[3]

Once all the probability distributions are specified, the computer simulates the project by drawing one observation from the distribution of each cash flow. Having those, it calculates the project's NPV and records the resulting value. Then it draws a new set of random observations for each of the cash flows, discards the old set, and calculates and records another value for NPV. Notice that the second NPV will probably be different from the first because it is based on a different set of randomly drawn cash flows.

The computer goes through this process many times, generating a thousand or more values (observations) for NPV. The calculated values are sorted into ranges and displayed as histograms reflecting the number of observations in each range. Figure 12-4 is a sample of the resulting display, where the numbers along the horizontal axis represent the centers of ranges of values for the calculated NPVs. For example, the value of 600 over the NPV value of $100 means that 600 simulation calculations resulted in NPVs between $50 and $150.

If the height of each column is restated as a percentage of the total number of observations, the histogram becomes a good approximation of the probability

---

1.   Monte Carlo is the site of a famous gambling casino in Monaco.

2.   In this context, the term "observation" refers to a number drawn from a probability distribution or to the result of calculations made from such numbers.

3.   In more detailed models, a probability distribution can be assumed for *each* of the elements that *goes into* the periodic cash flow estimates. For example, if period cash flows are the difference between revenue and cost, one might specify distributions for both, and calculate cash flow as the difference between an observation on revenue and one on cost.

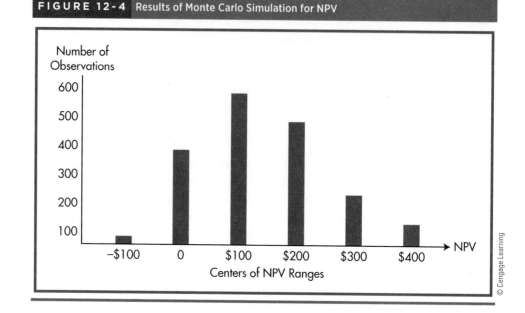

FIGURE 12-4 Results of Monte Carlo Simulation for NPV

distribution of the project's NPV *given the assumptions made about the distributions of the individual cash flows.*

Armed with this risk-related information, managers can make better choices among projects. For example, look back at Figure 12-3 on page 516. **Simulation** would give us approximations of the shapes of the distributions shown, as well as the most likely values of NPV. In the case illustrated, decision makers might well choose project A over project B in spite of B's NPV advantage because of A's lower risk.

Simulation models cash flows as random variables and **repeatedly calculates NPV**, building its distribution.

Drawbacks   Using the simulation approach has a few drawbacks. An obvious problem is that the probability distributions of the cash flows have to be estimated subjectively. This can be difficult. However, it's always easier to estimate a distribution for a simple element of a problem, like a single cash flow, than for a more complex element, like the final NPV or IRR.

A related issue is that the distributions of the individual cash flows generally aren't independent. Project cash flows tend to be positively *correlated* so that if early flows are low, later flows are also likely to be low. Unfortunately, it's hard to estimate the extent of that correlation.

Another problem is the interpretation of the simulated probability distributions. There aren't any decision rules for choosing among projects with respect to risk. Just how much risk is too much or how much variance is needed to overcome a certain NPV advantage isn't written down anywhere. Such judgments are subjective, and depend on the wisdom and experience of the decision makers.

In spite of these problems, simulation can be a relatively practical approach to incorporating risk into capital budgeting analyses.

12.2c   Decision Tree Analysis

We made the point earlier that scenario analysis gives us a feel for the possible variation in NPV (and IRR) in a capital budgeting project, but doesn't tell us much about the probability distribution of the NPV outcome. Decision tree analysis lets us approximate the NPV distribution if we can estimate the probability of certain events within the project. A **decision tree** is essentially an expanded time line that "branches" into alternate paths wherever an event can turn out in more than one way.

For example, suppose a capital budgeting project involves some engineering work with an uncertain outcome that won't be completed until the project has been underway for a year. If the engineering turns out well, subsequent cash flows will be higher than if it doesn't. The situation is captured in the decision tree diagram shown in Figure 12-5.

> **A decision tree** is a graphic representation of a business project in which events have multiple outcomes, each of which is assigned a probability.

FIGURE 12-5   A Simple Decision Tree

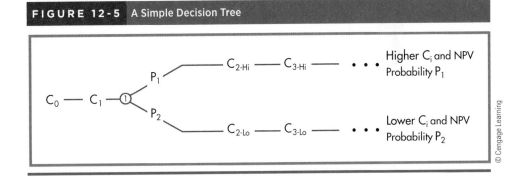

© Cengage Learning

The project starts with initial outlay, C_0, followed by cash flow C_1, but after that there are two possibilities depending on the success of the engineering work. Each of the two possible outcomes is represented by a *branch* of the decision tree. The place at which the branches separate is called a *node* and is commonly shown as a small numbered circle to help keep track of complex projects.

The estimated probability that a branch will occur is indicated (P_1, P_2) just after the node at which it starts. In this case, the upper branch represents an engineering success, which results in high cash flows indicated by C_{2-Hi}, C_{3-Hi} .... The lower branch represents less success and lower cash flows C_{2-Lo}, C_{3-Lo} ....

Any number of branches can emanate from a node, but their probabilities must sum to 1.0, indicating that one of the branches *must* be taken.

A *path* through the tree starts on the left at C_0 and progresses through node 1 along one branch or the other. There are obviously just two possible paths in Figure 12-5. An overall NPV outcome is associated with each path. In this case, the more favorable outcome is along the upper path and has cash flows C_0, C_1, C_{2-Hi}, C_{3-Hi} ..., while the less favorable lower path has cash flows C_0, C_1, C_{2-Lo}, C_{3-Lo} ....

Evaluating a project involves calculating NPVs along all possible paths and associating each with a probability. From that a **probability distribution for NPV** can be developed. The technique is best understood through an example. (We're working with NPV, but everything we say is equally applicable to IRR. Read the following example carefully; we will build on it throughout the rest of this section and the next.)

> **A probability distribution** of a project's **NPV** can be developed using **decision tree** analysis.

CONCEPT CONNECTION   EXAMPLE 12-2

Decision Tree Analysis

The Wing Foot Shoe Company is considering a three-year project to market a running shoe based on new technology. Success depends on how well consumers accept the new idea and demand the product. Demand can vary from great to terrible, but for planning purposes, management has collapsed that variation into just two possibilities: good and poor. A market study indicates a 60% probability that demand will be good and a 40% chance that it will be poor.

It will cost $5 million to bring the new shoe to market. Cash flow estimates indicate inflows of $3 million per year for three years *at full manufacturing capacity* if demand is good, but just $1.5 million per year if it's poor. Wing Foot's cost of capital is 10%. Analyze the project and develop a rough probability distribution for NPV.

SOLUTION: First draw a decision tree diagram for the project ($000).

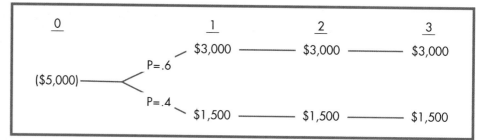

Next calculate the NPV along each path, using Equation 10.3 (page 466), which we'll repeat here for convenience ($000).

(10.3) $$NPV = C_0 + C[PVFA_{k,n}]$$

Good consumer demand:

$$NPV = -\$5,000 + \$3,000[PVFA_{10,3}]$$
$$NPV = -\$5,000 + \$3,000(2.4869)$$
$$NPV = -\$5,000 + \$7,461$$
$$NPV = \$2,461$$

Poor consumer demand:

$$NPV = -\$5,000 + \$1,500(2.4869)$$
$$NPV = -\$5,000 + \$3,730$$
$$NPV = -\$1,270$$

Notice that we now have the elements of a probability distribution for the project's NPV. We know there's a 60% chance of an NPV of $2,461,000 along the upper path and a 40% chance of an NPV of −$1,270,000 along the lower path.

The expected NPV (the mean or expected value of the probability distribution of values for NPV) is calculated by multiplying every possible NPV by its probability and summing the results ($000). (See the review of statistics at the beginning of Chapter 9 if necessary.)

Demand	NPV	Probability	Product
Good	$2,461	.60	$1,477
Poor	(1,270)	.40	(508)
		Expected NPV =	$969

Summarizing, we can say that the project's most likely NPV outcome is approximately $1.0 million, and that there's a good chance (60%) of making about $2.5 million, *but* there's also a substantial chance (40%) of losing about $1.3 million.

Notice that Wing Foot's management gets a much better idea of the new running shoe project's risk from this analysis than it would from a projection of a single value of $1.0 million for NPV. The decision tree result explicitly calls out the fact that a big loss is quite possible. That information is important because a loss of that size could ruin a small company. It could also damage the reputation of whoever is recommending the project.

The analysis also shows that if things turn out well, the reward for bearing the risk will probably be about half the size of the initial investment. That's also an important observation, because people are less likely to take substantial risks for modest returns than for outcomes that multiply their investment many times over.

The end result of the analysis in this case might well be a rejection of the project on the basis of risk even though the expected NPV is positive.

More Complex Decision Trees and Conditional Probabilities

Most processes represented by decision trees involve more than one uncertain event that can be characterized by probabilities. Each such event is represented by a node from which two or more new branches emerge, and the tree widens quickly toward the right. A more typical tree is illustrated in Figure 12-6.

Notice that there are additional nodes along the branches that emanate from node 1, each splitting the original branch into two or three more. In this diagram, there are five paths from left to right through the tree. Each starts at C_0 and ends along one of the branches on the far right. Each path has an NPV calculated using all of the cash flows along that path.

The probability of a path is the product of all of the branch probabilities along it. These are known as **conditional** probabilities, meaning that the probabilities coming out of node 2 are conditional on the upper branch out of node 1 happening.[4] Keep in mind that the probabilities out of each node must sum to 1.0. For example, $P_1 + P_2 = 1.0$ and $P_3 + P_4 + P_5 = 1.0$.

> Probabilities out of later nodes are **conditional** upon the outcome at earlier nodes along the same path.

> The **probabilities emerging** from any decision tree **node** must **sum to 1.0.**

FIGURE 12-6   A More Complex Decision Tree

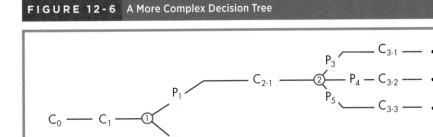

© Cengage Learning

---

4. The probability of a path is also called the *joint* probability of the individual branches along that path.

CONCEPT CONNECTION   EXAMPLE 12-3

More Complex Decision Trees

The Wing Foot Shoe Company of Example 12-2 has refined its market study and has some additional information about potential customer acceptance of the new product. Management now feels that there are two possibilities along the upper branch. Consumer response can be good, or it may be excellent. The study indicates that *if* demand is good during the first year, there's a 30% chance it will grow and be excellent in the second and third years. Of course, this also means there's a 70% chance that demand in years 2 and 3 won't change.

If consumer response to the product turns out to be excellent, an additional investment of $1 million in a factory expansion will allow the firm to make and sell enough product to generate cash inflows of $5 million rather than $3 million in both years 2 and 3. Hence, the net cash inflows for the project will be ($5 million − $1 million =) $4 million in year 2 and $5 million in year 3. (The expansion is necessary to achieve the better financial results because Example 12-2 stated that the factory was at capacity along the upper path.) A decision tree for the project with this additional possibility is as follows:

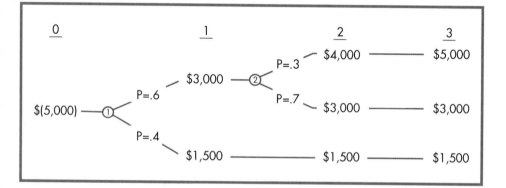

The probabilities coming out of node 2 are conditional probabilities, meaning that they exist only along the good demand path. In other words, they are *conditional upon* good demand happening out of node 1, which itself has a probability of .6. The probability of arriving at the end of any path through the decision tree is calculated by multiplying all of the probabilities along the path. Hence, the probability of the upper path is (.6 × .3 =) .18, the middle path is (.6 × .7 =) .42, and the lower path is just .40 as it was before. It's important to notice that these probabilities sum to 1.0, indicating that all possible outcomes are achieved by routes through the tree.

The NPV along each path is calculated in the traditional manner using all of the cash flows along the path. The middle and lower paths have the same cash flows as the paths in Example 12-2, so we've already calculated those NPVs. The NPV for the new upper path is just the sum of three present value of an amount calculations added to the initial outlay ($000).

$$
\begin{aligned}
\text{NPV} &= -\$5,000 + \$3,000[\text{PVF}_{10,1}] + \$4,000[\text{PVF}_{10,2}] + \$5,000[\text{PVF}_{10,3}] \\
&= -\$5,000 + \$3,000(.9091) + \$4,000(.8264) + \$5,000(.7513) \\
&= -\$5,000 + \$2,727 + \$3,306 + \$3,757 \\
&= \$4,790
\end{aligned}
$$

Then the probability distribution for the project and the calculation of the expected return are as follows:

Acceptance	NPV	Probability	Product
Excellent	$4,790	.18	$ 862
Good	2,461	.42	1,034
Poor	(1,270)	.40	(508)
		Expected NPV =	$1,388

The distribution is shown graphically as follows:

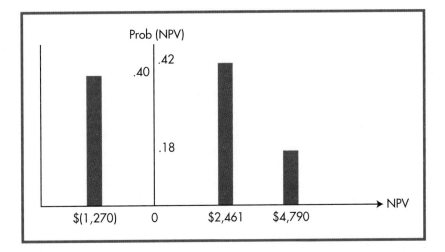

Once again it's important to notice how much more information is available through decision tree analysis than would be from a single point estimate of NPV. In this case, the additional information tells us there's a fairly good chance (18%) of doing very well on the project. But there's still a substantial chance (40%) of losing money. As in Example 12-2, that outcome could be ruinous, and a prudent management might still avoid the project even though the expected value of the NPV is somewhat more positive than before.

12.3   Real Options

An option is the ability or right to take a certain course of action, which in business situations generally leads to a financially favorable result.

Here's an example. Suppose a business sells sports apparel in a shopping mall and specializes in jackets and sweatshirts bearing the insignia of professional football teams. Also, suppose the business depends on bank credit to support routine operations, meaning it generally needs to have a loan outstanding just to keep going.[5] Assume its typical loan is $1 million. Now suppose the local pro football team has a chance at the Super Bowl this year. If the team makes it, the demand for football

---

5.   That in itself doesn't mean the business is weak or in danger of failing. We'll learn about this kind of financing in Chapter 16 when we study working capital.

jackets will double, and the business will need $2 million in bank credit. But if the extra credit isn't available, the additional sales will be lost.

The situation puts the business owner in a dilemma. He doesn't want to borrow the extra $1 million and pay interest on it all year because he isn't sure the additional sales will materialize. But he also knows that if he goes to the bank for an incremental loan at the last minute, he may not get it because the bank may be short of funds at that time.

The solution may be an arrangement with the bank in which it makes a *commitment* to lend the extra money in return for a *commitment fee,* which is usually about 1/4% per year of the committed but unborrowed amount. If the business does borrow the money, the bank just charges its normal interest rate while the loan is outstanding. If it doesn't, the business just pays the commitment fee, ($1 million × .0025 =) $2,500 in this case.

The arrangement gives the business owner the ability to take advantage of the potential increase in demand for football apparel in that he has the *option* of borrowing the extra money to support the increased sales. We call that ability a **real option.** The word *real* means the option exists in a real, physical business sense. It's inserted to distinguish real options from financial options.[6]

Notice that the real option has a value to the business owner. It's worth at least as much as the commitment fee he pays the bank, and it may be worth a lot more depending on the probability of the local team getting into the Super Bowl and the profit he'd make on the additional sales if that happened.

12.3a   Real Options in Capital Budgeting

Real options frequently occur in capital budgeting projects. Their impact is best seen when the project is analyzed using a probabilistic approach such as decision tree analysis. A real option's presence generally increases the expected NPV of a project. That increase is often a good estimate of the option's value.

> A **real option** is a course of action that **can be made available**, usually at a cost, which **improves financial results** under certain conditions.

> The **value** of a **real option** can be **estimated** as the **increase in project NPV** that its inclusion brings about.

CONCEPT CONNECTION   EXAMPLE 12-4

Real Options

Consider the Wing Foot Shoe Company's situation after the possibility of excellent demand is introduced as described in Example 12-3.

a. Is a real option present?

b. Suppose space at Wing Foot's plant is scarce, and room for an expansion is available only at $.5 million cost at the project's outset. This is in addition to the $1 million the expansion will cost in year 2 if it's done. In other words, the project's initial outlay will increase by $.5 million if the expansion option is included. If demand isn't excellent, that money will be wasted. Should the expansion space be purchased under the conditions presented in Example 12-3?

---

6. The most common financial option is the right to purchase stock at a fixed price for a specified period. That right is known as a *call option* and is for sale at an *option price.* If the stock's market price rises above the fixed price during the period, the option holder buys the stock and immediately sells it for a profit. If the market price doesn't exceed the fixed price during the period, the option expires, and the investor loses what she paid for it. Stock options were treated in detail in Chapter 8.

SOLUTION:

a. Notice that in Example 12-2, Wing's factory is at full capacity at a sales level consistent with good consumer acceptance of the new product (page 522). This is shown along the top branch of the decision tree. If capacity expansion isn't possible, there's nothing management can do to take advantage of higher than expected demand. The situation differs in Example 12-3 because the firm has the option of investing an additional $1 million in an expansion if larger demand is experienced. Then the project could generate more sales and increased cash flows that might more than offset the cost of the new capacity.

The opportunity to respond to the realization that consumer acceptance is excellent by expanding the plant is a real option. In other words, management has the *option* of expanding capacity at an incremental cost to meet higher than expected demand. There's no cost associated with this real option as described so far. We'll consider the implications of a real option with a cost in part b.

b. Having the extra space from the beginning of the running shoe project gives management the real option to expand. Without it, management doesn't have that choice. Hence, in order to decide whether it's wise to purchase extra space, we have to place a value on the ability to expand capacity. We'll then compare that value with the cost of the option which is $.5 million.

It's relatively easy to make a first approximation of the value of the real option in this case. It's just the difference in the *expected values* of the project's NPV calculated with and without the option. That makes sense because expected NPV is the basic measure of the project's value to the firm.

We calculated the expected NPV without the option in Example 12-2 and with it in Example 12-3. The option was the only difference in those situations. From those examples we have the following:

Expected NPV with option	$1,388
Expected NPV without option	969
Value of expansion option	$ 419[7]

Since the value of the real option is less than its $.5 million cost, it seems that management shouldn't buy the space for the potential expansion ahead of time. However, we'll see shortly that there may be another reason to consider keeping the expansion option alive.

---

7. It's important not to confuse the value of the option in an expected value sense and with what it's worth if the expansion actually happens. Look at the calculation of the expected value of the project's NPV in Example 12-3. If demand is excellent and the expansion happens, NPV is $4,790 along the top path. If demand is just good, NPV is $2,461 along the middle path. The difference between those figures is $2,329. That's the amount the expansion capability contributes *if* demand actually turns out to be excellent.

   However, at the beginning of the project, when we're doing capital budgeting, we don't know whether that will happen. At that time we just know there's an 18% chance of excellent demand. Recognizing this, the expected value calculation adds 18% of $2,329 to the project's expected NPV, which, within rounding error, is $419 ($2,329 × .18 = $419.22).

The Abandonment Option

Look at the decision tree in Example 12-3 (pages 524–525) once again. Notice that the lower path representing poor demand has a negative NPV of $(1,270), indicating the project will be a money-losing failure if customers are reluctant to buy the new design. Once management realizes demand is poor, say after the first year, does it make sense to continue producing the running shoes in years 2 and 3, earning inflows of just $1,500? It does if there are no alternate uses for the resources involved in making the shoes, since a positive cash contribution of $1,500 per year is better than nothing.

But suppose the facilities and equipment used to make the new shoe can be redeployed into something else. Under those conditions it may make sense to abandon the project altogether.

CONCEPT CONNECTION   EXAMPLE 12-5

Abandonment Options

Wing Foot has other lines of shoes in which most of the equipment purchased for the running shoe project can be used if the new idea is abandoned. Management estimates that at the end of the first year the equipment's value in those other uses will be $4.5 million. How does this information impact the analysis of the running shoe project?

SOLUTION: If the project is abandoned and the equipment is redeployed at the end of the first year, cash flows along the bottom path of the decision tree in Example 12-3 (page 524) would be ($1,500 + $4,500 =) $6,000 in the first year and zero in years 2 and 3. The NPV along the bottom path would then be as follows:

$$\begin{aligned} NPV &= -\$5,000 + \$6,000[PVF_{10,1}] \\ &= -\$5,000 + \$6,000(.9091) \\ &= -\$5,000 + \$5,455 \\ &= \$455 \end{aligned}$$

Recalculate the project's expected NPV, assuming the bottom path is replaced by abandonment. To do that, repeat the calculation in Example 12-3 replacing the NPV of $(1,270) along the bottom path with $455.

Acceptance	NPV	Probability	Product
Excellent	$4,790	.18	$ 862
Good	2,461	.42	1,034
Poor	455	.40	182
		Expected NPV =	$2,078

Notice that the expected NPV has increased from $1,388 to $2,078.

It's very important to appreciate two things about the calculations we've just done. First, abandonment is a course of action available to management that improves the project's expected NPV. Therefore, if abandonment is possible, it's a real option.

Second, the existence of the abandonment option lowers the project's risk substantially. We can see that by looking at the diagram in Example 12-3 that graphically displays the probability distribution of the project's NPV (page 524). Notice that the project as originally presented has a 40% probability of a negative NPV of $(1,270). This is essentially a loss of that amount. We commented earlier that such a loss could ruin a small firm and might be a reason to avoid the project altogether.

But if the abandonment option exists as we've described it, that outcome is pushed to the right and becomes a 40% probability of a small gain of $455. That makes the project taken as a whole a lot less risky. Indeed, it's unlikely that a firm would need to avoid the project because of the risk of ruin if this abandonment option exists.

12.3b   Valuing Real Options

The **value** of a real option is **at least** the **increase in NPV** it brings about.

In Example 12-4, we calculated the value of a real option as the increase it created in the NPV of the project in which it is embedded. That's a good starting point for valuation, but it doesn't capture the whole story because of the risk reduction we've just described.

In fact, real options are generally worth more than their expected NPV impact because of the effect they have on risk. Recall that individuals and managers are *risk averse*, meaning they prefer less risky undertakings when expected returns or NPVs are equal. That preference generally means people are willing to pay something for risk reduction over and above the amount by which a real option increases expected NPV. Unfortunately it's difficult to say just how much more, because neither a precise measure of risk nor a relationship between risk and value exists in the capital budgeting context. In other words, we know the value of real options may be enhanced by their effect on risk, but we can't say by how much.

A real option may be **worth more** than the increase it causes in NPV, because it also **reduces project risk**.

An Approach Through Rates of Return   One possible approach to valuing real options involves *risk-adjusted rates* of return. We'll discuss the idea in detail in the next section. For now it's enough to understand that lower risk should be associated with a lower rate of return in our NPV calculations. Hence, if a real option lowers a project's risk, it may be appropriate to recalculate its NPV using a lower interest rate than the firm's cost of capital. Since lower interest rates produce higher present values, this procedure makes the recalculated NPV larger, thereby assigning a higher value to the real option. The difficult question is choosing the right risk-adjusted rate.

The Risk Effect Is Tricky   Consider the expansion option of Example 12-4 in which we indicated that the expected benefit of the option may not be worth its cost. (Recall that the expected NPV increase was $419,000 while the cost of preserving the option was $500,000.) We arrived at that tentative conclusion without considering the option's effect on risk. We just said that the risk reduction properties of real options lend them extra value. If that's the case isn't it possible that the option to expand is worth more than $419,000?

Pause for a moment and answer that question before reading on. (*Hint:* Compare the effect of the abandonment option and the expansion option on the probability distribution of NPV for the project.)

Although real options often reduce risk, the risk effect of the expansion option probably doesn't help to enhance its value. We can see that by carefully comparing its effect with that of the abandonment option. The risk-reducing effect of the abandonment option is significant because it eliminates the risk of a substantial loss. The expansion option, on the other hand, makes a larger profit available if things go really well, but doesn't change the fact that there's a 40% chance of a large loss which might ruin the firm. Since that large, high probability loss is the key risk issue, there's little or no risk-reducing value in the expansion option.

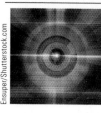

INSIGHTS   Real Applications

Volatile Energy Prices and Real Options Thinking Can Lead to Big Profits on Inefficient Facilities

Real options thinking has become especially popular in industries that require big investments in capital equipment. Classic examples are air transportation, which requires giant jet planes with enormous price tags, and the electric power industry, in which providers build costly power plants. Prior to its descent into disgrace and bankruptcy in 2001, Enron Corp. was a large energy company whose base business involved building and running electric power plants as well as natural gas pipelines. The firm's application of real options thinking to power plants in the late 1990s provides a fascinating example of the scope of the technique.

Real options reasoning was used to justify building three electric power plants in Mississippi and Tennessee that were inefficient by design. They're so inefficient that the electricity they produce costs 50% to 70% more than the industry standard. The plants cost a lot less to build than state-of-the-art facilities, but that's not the reason they were put in place.

At the time deregulation in the electric utility industry had led to amazingly volatile wholesale prices for electric power. Indeed the price of power varied from a normal level per megawatt hour of about $40 to an unbelievable $7,000. That volatility coupled with real options thinking made the inefficient plants not only feasible, but a great idea.

The plants weren't intended to operate all the time. They were to be fired up only when energy rates spiked to levels so high that production costs didn't matter. For example, if a megawatt hour of electricity was selling for $1,000, it didn't matter much whether it cost $20 or $30 to produce.

The inefficient power plants gave their owner the option to generate and sell more electricity when rates peaked. At other times they were simply left idle. The cost of building the plants was the cost of having that option. This is a classic real options situation. If the probability of peak prices is fairly high, the expected value of the extra profits the plants bring in exceeds the cost of building those plants, and having them increases the expected NPV of power-generating operations.

Under these conditions the plants may have had to operate only a week or two each year to more than pay for themselves. The plants represented a *flexibility option,* because they gave their owner the flexibility to respond to high electricity prices with expanded output.

SOURCE: "Exploiting Uncertainty," *Business Week* (June 7, 1999)

All of this says that the value of real options has to be considered carefully on a case-by-case basis. A good deal of advanced theoretical work is currently being done in the area.

12.3c   Designing Real Options into Projects

It makes sense to design projects so that they contain beneficial real options whenever possible. We've already seen two examples in which thinking about real options at the beginning of a project might make a big difference later on.

The **abandonment option** discussed in Example 12-5 increased expected NPV and lowered risk at the same time. Hence, the example illustrates that it's a good idea to design the ability to quit into projects. Unfortunately that isn't always easy. Contractual obligations, for example, can make abandonment tough. In our illustration, suppose Wing Foot guaranteed retailers the new shoes for three years, signed a lease for factory space, and entered long-term purchasing contracts with suppliers. Then stopping after one year would require breaking the contracts, which could be difficult and costly. Prudent managers should always try to avoid entanglements that make exit hard.

Expansion options like the one illustrated in Example 12-4 are very common. When the ability to expand costs extra money early in the project's life, a careful financial analysis is necessary, as we've indicated. However, the option frequently requires little or no early commitment and should be planned in whenever possible.

Investment timing options also come up frequently. Here's an example. Suppose a company is looking at a project to build a new factory, and has identified an unusually good site, but it can't make a final decision for six months. Management doesn't want to buy the property now, because there's a chance the firm won't build the factory. But management doesn't want to lose out to another buyer because if it does decide to build later on, it would then have to start looking for a site all over again.

The solution can be a *land option contract* in which the landowner grants the company the right to buy the site at any time in the next six months at a fixed price in return for a nonrefundable fee called the *option price.*

The option is a purchase contract between a buyer and a seller that's suspended at the discretion of the buyer for a limited time. If the buyer doesn't *exercise* the option by the end of that time, it just expires. The land option lets the firm delay its investment in the land until it's sure about other relevant issues and problems.

Flexibility options let companies respond more easily to changes in business conditions. For example, suppose a firm buys the same part from two suppliers for $1 per unit. If it gives all of its business to one supplier, the price would be $.90 per unit. But if that single supplier fails, the firm's business will suffer while it's unable to get the part. Hence, the flexibility of having both suppliers available may be worth the extra $.10 per unit.

12.4   Incorporating Risk into Capital Budgeting—The Theoretical Approach and Risk-Adjusted Rates of Return

The theoretical approach to incorporating risk into capital budgeting focuses on rates of return. Recall that an *interest rate* plays a central role in both the NPV and IRR methods. Until now we've taken that key rate to be the firm's cost of capital. Let's briefly review how it is used in both techniques.

The **cost of capital** plays a **key role** in both NPV and IRR.

In the NPV method, we calculate the present value of cash flows using the cost of capital as the discount rate. A higher discount rate produces a lower NPV, which reduces the chances of project acceptance. In the IRR method, the decision rule involves comparing a project's return on invested funds with the cost of capital. A higher cost of capital means a higher IRR is required for acceptance, which also lowers the chance of the project being qualified.

In summary, the acceptance or rejection of projects depends on this key interest rate in both methods, with higher rates implying less likely acceptance. In what follows, we'll investigate the implications of doing the calculations with an interest rate other than the cost of capital.

Using a higher, **risk-adjusted rate** for **risky** projects **lowers their chance of acceptance**.

Riskier Projects Should Be Less Acceptable

The idea behind incorporating risk into capital budgeting is to make particularly risky projects less acceptable than others with similar *expected* cash flows. Notice that this is exactly what happens under capital budgeting rules if projects are evaluated using higher interest rates. A higher discount rate lowers the calculated NPV for any given set of cash flows, while a higher threshold rate means calculated IRRs have to be larger to qualify projects.

Therefore, a logical way to incorporate risk into capital budgeting is to devise an approach that uses the NPV and IRR methods, but analyzes riskier projects using higher interest rates in place of the cost of capital. Logically, the higher the risk, the higher the interest rate that should be used. This approach will automatically create a bias against accepting higher-risk projects. Higher rates used to compensate for riskiness in financial analysis are called **risk-adjusted rates**.

Projects with **risk** consistent with **current** operations should be evaluated using the **cost of capital**.

The Starting Point for Risk-Adjusted Rates

Earlier in this chapter, we said that in the long run a company can be viewed as a collection of projects, and that adopting a large number of relatively risky endeavors can change its fundamental nature to that of a more risky enterprise.

It makes sense to take the current status of a firm as the starting point for risk measurement and to let the cost of capital be the interest rate representing that point. Then it's logical to analyze projects that are consistent with the current riskiness of the company using the cost of capital and to use higher rates for riskier projects.

Relating Interest Rates to Risk

These ideas are consistent with the interest rate fundamentals we studied in Chapter 5. Recall that every interest rate is made up of two parts: a base rate and a premium for risk. The idea was expressed as an equation that we'll repeat here for convenience.

$$(5.1) \qquad k = \text{base rate} + \text{risk premium}$$

This equation says that investors demand a higher risk premium and consequently a higher interest rate if they are to bear increased risk. In capital budgeting, the company is investing in the project being analyzed, and the interest rate used in the analysis is analogous to the rate of return demanded by an investor from a security.

If the project's risk is about the same as the company's overall risk, using the firm's **cost of capital** is appropriate. If the project's risk is higher, a rate with a higher risk premium is needed.

Choosing the Risk-Adjusted Rate for Various Projects   The ideas we've described in this section make logical sense, but run into practical problems when they're implemented. The stumbling block is the arbitrariness of choosing the appropriate risk-adjusted rate for a particular project.

Projects are generally presented with point estimates of future cash flows. Assessing the riskiness or variability of those cash flows is usually a subjective affair, so there's little on which to base the choice of a risk-adjusted rate. However, some logical thinking can help.

Recall that projects fit into three categories of generally increasing risk: replacement, expansion, and new venture. Replacements are usually a continuation of what was being done before, but with new equipment. Because the function is already part of the business, its risk will be consistent with that of the present business. Therefore, the cost of capital is nearly always the appropriate discount rate for analyzing replacement projects.

Expansion projects involve doing more of the same thing in some business area. They're more risky than the current level, but usually not very much more. In such cases, a rule of thumb of adding one to three percentage points to the cost of capital is usually appropriate.[8]

New venture projects are the big problem. They usually involve a great deal more risk than current operations, but it's hard to quantify exactly how much. So choosing a risk-adjusted rate is difficult and arbitrary. However, *sometimes* we can get help from portfolio theory.

12.4a   Estimating Risk-Adjusted Rates Using CAPM

Portfolio theory and the capital asset pricing model (Chapter 9) deal with assigning risk to investments. Under certain circumstances, the techniques developed there can be used to generate risk-adjusted rates for capital budgeting.

The Project As a Diversification   When a company undertakes a new venture, the project can be viewed as a diversification similar to adding a new stock to a portfolio. We can look at this idea in two ways.

The first involves seeing the firm as a collection of projects. A new venture simply adds another enterprise to the company's project portfolio, which then becomes more diversified. In the second view, the project diversifies the investment portfolios of the firm's shareholders into the new line of business.

This second idea is important and profound; let's explore it more deeply. Suppose a firm is in the food processing business. Stockholders have chosen to invest in the company because they're comfortable with the risks and rewards of that business. Now suppose the firm takes on a venture in electronics. To the extent of the new project, stockholders are now subject to the risks and rewards of the electronics business. They could have accomplished the same thing by selling off some of their food processing company stock and buying stock in an electronics firm. In essence, the company has done that for them, probably without their permission.

A new venture **diversifies** the company and its shareholders.

---

8. If the expansion is very large, a bigger adjustment may be necessary.

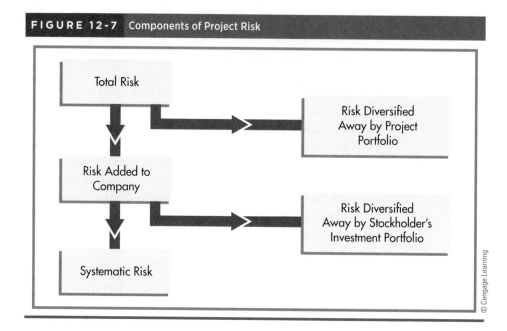

FIGURE 12-7 Components of Project Risk

© Cengage Learning

Diversifiable and Nondiversifiable Risk for Projects

In Chapter 9, we separated investment risk into systematic and unsystematic components. Unsystematic (business-specific) risk is specific to individual firms or industries and can be diversified away by having a wide variety of stocks in a portfolio. Systematic (market) risk, on the other hand, is related to movement with the entire market and can't be entirely eliminated through diversification.

Projects viewed as investments have two levels of diversifiable risk because they're effectively in two portfolios at the same time. Some risk is diversified away within the firm's portfolio of projects, and some is diversified away by the stockholders' investment portfolios.

These ideas lead to an additional, intermediate concept of risk, the undiversified risk added to a company by the addition of a project. The idea is illustrated in Figure 12-7.

Notice that the risk left over after the two kinds of diversifiable risk are removed is systematic (market) risk. This is the same concept of systematic (market) risk used in portfolio theory, but here it's associated with a project rather than a company.

Estimating the Risk-Adjusted Rate Through Beta

The capital asset pricing model we studied in Chapter 9 gives us an approach to measuring *systematic risk* for *companies* by using the security market line (SML). The SML (Equation 9.4 on page 426.) defines the firm's required rate of return in terms of a base rate and a risk premium. We'll repeat it here for convenience.

(9.4)
$$k_X = k_{RF} + (k_M - k_{RF})b_X$$

where k_X is the required rate of return for company X, k_{RF} is the risk-free rate, k_M is the return on the market, and b_X is company X's beta.

The term

$$(k_M - k_{RF})b_X$$

is the risk premium for company X's stock, which is a function of b_X, the company's beta. Beta in turn measures only systematic (market) risk. But the bottom block

Under certain conditions the **SML** can be used to determine a **risk-adjusted rate** for a **new venture project**.

in Figure 12-7 also represents systematic (market) risk. In other words, the SML gives us a risk-adjusted interest rate related to a particular kind of risk for the stock of a company, and we find that same kind of risk in the analysis of projects.

> *If a capital budgeting project is viewed as a business in a particular field, it may make sense to use a beta common to that field in the SML to estimate a risk-adjusted rate for analysis of the project.*

A **pure play** company is in only one line of business.

Recall, for example, the food processing company that takes on a venture in electronics. It might be appropriate to use a beta typical of electronics companies in the SML to arrive at a risk-adjusted rate to analyze the project. This line of thinking is especially appropriate when an independent, publicly traded company whose beta is known can be found in the same business as the venture. The approach is known as the **pure play** method of establishing a risk-adjusted rate. The **pure play company** has to be solely in the business of the venture; otherwise its beta won't be truly appropriate.

CONCEPT CONNECTION   EXAMPLE 12-6

Risk-Adjusted Rates—SML

Orion Inc. is a successful manufacturer of radio communications equipment sold in consumer and commercial markets. Management is considering producing a sophisticated tactical radio for sale to the Army, but is concerned because the military market is known to be quite risky. The military radio market is dominated by Milrad Inc., which holds a 60% market share. Antex Radio Corp. is another established competitor with a 20% share. Both Milrad and Antex make only military radios. Milrad's beta is 1.4 and Antex's is 2.0. Orion's beta is 1.1. The return on an average publicly traded stock (k_M) is about 10%. The yield on short-term treasury bills (k_{RF}) is currently 5%. Orion's cost of capital is 8%.

The military radio project is expected to require an initial outlay of $10 million. Subsequent cash inflows are expected to be $3 million per year over a five-year contract.

On the basis of a five-year evaluation, should Orion undertake the project?

SOLUTION: The military business is clearly riskier than Orion's radio communications equipment business judging by the relative betas of Orion and its potential rivals. Therefore, a CAPM-based risk-adjusted rate is appropriate for the analysis. Milrad and Antex are both pure play companies, but the fact that Milrad is the market leader probably reduces its risk. If Orion enters the field it will be in a position similar to Antex's, so a risk-adjusted rate based on that firm's beta is most appropriate.

First we calculate the risk-adjusted rate using the SML and Antex's beta.

$$k = k_{RF} + (k_M - k_{RF})b_{Antex}$$
$$= 5\% + (10\% - 5\%)2.0$$
$$= 15.0\%$$

Notice that this rate is considerably higher than Orion's cost of capital (8%).

Ensuper/Shutterstock.com

Next calculate the proposed project's NPV using the risk-adjusted rate ($ millions).

$$\begin{aligned} NPV &= C_0 + C[PVFA_{k,n}] \\ &= -\$10.0 + \$3[PVFA_{15,5}] \\ &= \$10.0 + \$3(3.3522) \\ &= \$0.1 \end{aligned}$$

Notice that the risk-adjusted NPV is barely positive, indicating that the project is marginal.

If Orion's 8% cost of capital had been used in the analysis, the result would have been as follows ($ millions):

$$\begin{aligned} NPV &= -\$10.0 + \$3[PVFA_{8,5}] \\ &= -\$10.0 + \$3(3.9927) \\ &= -\$10.0 + \$12.0 \\ &= \$2.0 \end{aligned}$$

Compare these two results. The capital budgeting rule unadjusted for risk would clearly have accepted the project, but consideration of risk has shown it to be a very marginal undertaking. This can be a crucial managerial insight! However, in the next section, we'll see that there are more questions lurking about.

12.4b   Problems with the Theoretical Approach—Finding the Right Beta and Concerns About the Appropriate Risk Definition

Using the CAPM to estimate risk-adjusted rates as illustrated in the last section appears straightforward and unambiguous. However, it would be rather unusual for the technique to fit into the real world as neatly as it did in the example. Generally, the biggest problem is finding a pure play company from which to get an appropriate beta. For example, if Milrad and Antex were divisions of larger companies, their separate betas wouldn't be available, and the betas of their parent companies would be influenced by the operations of divisions in other fields. As a result, we're usually reduced to estimating betas based on those of firms in similar rather than exactly the same businesses. This reduces the credibility of the technique by quite a bit.

However, there's another, more basic problem. Look back at Figure 12-7. Notice that three levels of risk are attached to projects, and that the CAPM technique uses the last level, systematic risk. But systematic risk is a concept that's really only relevant in the context of a well-diversified portfolio of financial assets. It excludes all unsystematic risks that may be associated with the project itself or with the company. In the context of a firm making day-to-day business decisions, disregarding unsystematic risk may not be appropriate.

For example, suppose the military radio project in Example 12-6 fails because Orion's management doesn't know how to deal with the government.[9] That risk isn't

---

9. This is a very real problem. Government and commercial markets are entirely different worlds.

included in systematic risk because it's related specifically to Orion. But shouldn't Orion be concerned about risks like that when considering the project? Most people would agree that it should.

This reasoning suggests that total risk as pictured in Figure 12-7 is the more appropriate measure for capital budgeting. But CAPM doesn't give us an estimate of that. All we can say is that total risk is higher than systematic risk.

Let's look at Example 12-6 again in that light. The military radio project is marginal at a risk-adjusted rate reflecting only systematic risk. If a broader definition of risk is appropriate, the risk-adjusted rate should be even higher, which would lower NPV and make the project clearly undesirable.

Projects in Divisions—The Accounting Beta Method   Sometimes a large company has divisions in different businesses, each of which has substantially different risk characteristics. In such cases, the cost of capital for the entire firm can't be associated with any particular division, so some kind of a proxy rate has to be found for capital budgeting within divisions.

The pure play method just described might be used if pure play companies can be found in the right businesses, but that's often not possible. If an appropriate surrogate can't be found, and a division has separate accounting records, an approximate approach can be used. The approximation involves developing a beta for the division from its accounting records rather than from stock market performance. This is accomplished by regressing historical values of the division's return on equity against the return on a major stock market index like the S&P 500. The slope of the regression line is then the division's approximate beta and the SML can be used to estimate a risk-adjusted rate. This approach is called the *accounting beta method.*

12.4c   Certainty Equivalents

We've just examined risk adjusted rates, a popular approach to incorporating risk into capital budgeting. It works by raising the rate at which risky future cash flows are discounted in calculating a project's NPV. This makes the present value of each cash flow lower resulting in lower NPV and less likely acceptance. Notice that the method works on cash flows indirectly through the interest rate. The certainty equivalent approach is more direct in that it makes risky projects less acceptable by simply lowering the cash flow estimates themselves.

The method asks the decision maker(s) to consider each forecast cash flow individually and come up with a lower, risk free cash flow that they would consider equally as attractive as the risky cash flow that's been forecast.

Here's an example. Suppose someone offers you pay you a sum of money in one year that depends on a random (risky) process with five equally probable outcomes as follows:

Outcome	1	2	3	4	5
Payment ($)	$0	$50	$100	$150	$200

What single, certain payment, to be received in one year's time, would you accept in return for giving up that risky payment. The certain amount you would trade for the risky process is your *certainty equivalent* for the process. We also say you're *indifferent* between the certain payment and the risky process.

Now imagine that the process above represents a cash flow in a capital budgeting project. In that case, all we would see projected is the most likely (expected) payment of $100. But a business decision maker would know that the actual cash flow could turn out to be anywhere from zero to $200.

The certainty equivalent technique involves having decision makers select a certainty equivalent for every cash flow in the project. That's usually done by picking a *certainty equivalent factor* between zero and 1.0 for each cash flow and multiplying the cash flow by the factor to arrive at the certainty equivalent figure. Certainty equivalent factors usually decline as they proceed into the future simply because the distant future is harder to forecast that the nearer term. But the technique also allows the decision maker to recognize particularly risky years and put in lower factors for those years.

Once the stream of certainty equivalent cash flows is developed, the risk adjusted NPV is calculated by discounting the stream back to the present. However, the cost of capital is not the appropriate interest rate for that calculation because it reflects the company's average risk, which is not zero. In theory, certainty equivalents imply zero risk, so the risk free rate is more appropriate for the NPV calculation.

CONCEPT CONNECTION   EXAMPLE 12-7

Certainty Equivalents

Bluefin Inc.'s cost of capital is 10% while the risk free rate is currently 5%. The company has a project under consideration for which a set of cash flows have been forecast by the group proposing the project. Senior management is somewhat concerned that the projected cash flows may be upwardly biased by the proposers' enthusiasm for the idea. They have therefore developed a set of certainty equivalent (CE) factors to be applied to the proposed figures. The original cash flow estimate, the CE factors and the resulting certainty equivalent estimates are as follows ($000):

Year	0	1	2	3	4	5
Cash Flow	(200)	60	60	60	60	60
CE Factor	1.0	.90	.80	.75	.70	.65
CE Cash Flow	(200)	54	48	45	42	39

Calculate the project's traditional NPV and the certainty equivalent NPV and make a recommendation on acceptance or rejection. Round calculations to the nearest thousand dollars.

SOLUTION: The traditional NPV can be calculated using Equation 10.3 for projects with regular inflows and discounting with the cost of capital ($000):

$$NPV = C_0 + C[PVFA_{k,n}] = -\$200 + \$60[PVFA_{10,5}]$$
$$= -\$200 + \$60(3.7908) = -\$200 + \$227$$
$$= \$27$$

Since NPV > 0 by an amount that is significant with respect to the size of the $200,000 initial outlay, we would traditionally (without consideration of risk) accept the project.

Now calculate the certainty equivalent NPV discounting at the risk free rate.

$$NPV = C_0 + C_1[PVF_{k,1}] + C_2[PVF_{k,2}] + \cdots\cdots + C_n[PVF_{k,n}]$$

$$NPV = -\$200 + \$54[PVF_{5,1}] + \$48[PVF_{5,2}] + \$45[PVF_{5,3}] + \$42[PVF_{5,4}] + 39[PVF_{5,5}]$$

$$= -\$200 + \$54(.9524) + \$48(.9070) + \$45(.8638) + \$42(.8227) + 39(.7835)$$

$$= -\$200 + \$199$$

$$= -\$1$$

Hence the project is marginally unacceptable after consideration of risk.

There's no doubt that the certainty equivalent technique is highly subjective in that the CE factors are nothing more than decision makers' judgments. But the same is true of the risk adjusted rate approach if there's no pure play company available, which is more often than not the case. In that situation, the manager makes a subjective guess at an interest rate which compensates for the project's risk.

The question is, at which process is the business decision maker likely to be better. Selecting an interest rate that *indirectly* lowers NPV through a complex time value calculation, or *directly* lowering NPV by judging down the cash flows themselves. Although theorists seem to prefer risk adjusted rates, a good argument can be made that business people are more comfortable working directly with the dollar projections.

A Final Comment on Risk in Capital Budgeting   Adjusting capital budgeting procedures to recognize risk makes a great deal of sense. However, the methods available to implement the concept are less than precise. As a result, risk-adjusted capital budgeting remains more in the province of the theorist than of the financial manager.

To put it another way, virtually everyone uses capital budgeting techniques, but only a few overtly try to incorporate risk. Business managers do recognize risk, but they do it through judgments overlaid on the results of analysis when decisions are finally made.

Nevertheless, it's important that students understand the risk issue because it's a very real part of decision making. Recognizing risk is a major step toward bringing theory in line with the real world. Even though we can't precisely put the idea that cash flows are subject to probability distributions into our analysis, we'll make better decisions for having thought about it.

CONCEPT CONNECTIONS

optimarc/Shutterstock.com

Ensuper/Shutterstock.com

QUESTIONS

1. In 1983, the Bell telephone system, which operated as AT&T, was broken up, resulting in the creation of seven regional telephone companies. AT&T stockholders received shares of the new companies and the continuing AT&T, which handled long distance services. Prior to the breakup, telephone service was a regulated public utility. That meant AT&T had a monopoly on the sale of its service, but couldn't charge excessive prices due to government regulation. Regulated utilities are classic examples of low risk–modest return companies. After the breakup, the "Baby Bells," as they were called, were freed from many of the regulatory constraints under which the Bell system had operated, and at the same time had a great deal of money. The managements of these young giants were determined to make them more than the staid, old-line telephone companies they'd been in the past. They were quite vocal in declaring their intentions to undertake ventures in any number of new fields, despite the fact that virtually all of their experience was in the regulated environment of the old telephone system. Many stockholders were alarmed and concerned by these statements. Comment on what their concerns may have been.

2. A "random variable" is defined as the outcome of one or more chance processes. Imagine that you're forecasting the cash flows associated with a new business venture. List some of the things that come together to produce cash flows in future periods. Describe how they might be considered to be outcomes of chance processes and therefore random variables. Cash flow forecasts for a project are used in Equations 10.1 and 10.2 to calculate the project's NPV and IRR. That makes NPV and IRR random variables as well. Is their variability likely to be greater or less than the variability of the individual cash flows making them up?

3. One of the problems of using simulations to incorporate risk in capital budgeting is related to the idea that the probability distributions of successive cash flows usually are not independent. If the first period's cash flow is at the high end of its range, for example, flows in subsequent periods are more likely to be high than low. Why do you think this is generally the case? Describe an approach through which the computer might adjust for this phenomenon to portray risk better.

4. Why is it desirable to construct capital budgeting rules so that higher-risk projects become less acceptable than lower-risk projects?

5. Rationalize the appropriateness of using the cost of capital to analyze normally risky projects and higher rates for those with more risk.

6. Evaluate the conceptual merits of applying CAPM theory to the problem of determining risk-adjusted interest rates for capital budgeting purposes. Form your own opinion based on your study of CAPM (Chapter 9) and the knowledge of capital budgeting you're now developing. The issue is concisely summarized by Figure 12-7. Is the special concept of risk developed in portfolio theory applicable here? Don't be intimidated into thinking that because the idea is presented in textbooks, it's necessarily correct. Many scholars and practitioners feel this application stretches theory too far. On the other hand, others feel it has a great deal of merit. What do you think and why?

BUSINESS ANALYSIS

1. Ed Draycutt is the engineering manager of Airway Technologies, a firm that makes computer systems for air traffic control installations at airports. He has proposed a new device whose success depends on two separate events. First, the Federal Aviation Administration (FAA) must adopt a recent proposal for a new procedural approach to handling in-flight calls from planes experiencing emergencies. Everyone thinks the probability of the FAA accepting the new method is at least 98%, but it will take a year to happen. If the new approach is adopted, radio makers will have to respond within another year with one of two possible changes in their technology. These can simply be called A and B. The A response is far more likely, also having a probability of about 98%. Ed's device works with the A system and is a stroke of engineering genius. If the A system becomes the industry standard and Airway has Ed's product, it will make a fortune before anyone else can market a similar device. On the other hand, if the A system isn't adopted, Airway will lose whatever it has put into the new device's development.

Developing Ed's device will cost about $20 million, which is a very substantial investment for a small company like Airway. In fact, a loss of $20 million would put the firm in danger of failing.

Ed just presented his idea to the executive committee as a capital budgeting project with a $20 million investment and a huge NPV and IRR reflecting the adoption of the A system. Everyone on the committee is very excited. You're the CFO and are a lot less excited. You asked Ed how he reflected the admittedly remote possibility that the A system would never be put in place. Ed, obviously proud of his business sophistication, said he'd taken care of that with a statistical calculation. He said adoption of the A system required the occurrence of two events, each of which has a 98% probability. The probability of both happening is (.98 × .98 = .96) 96%. He therefore reduced all of his cash inflow estimates by 4%. He maintains this correctly accounts for risk in the project.

Does Ed have the right expected NPV? What's wrong with his analysis? Suggest an approach that will give a more insightful result. Why might the firm consider passing on the proposal in spite of the tremendous NPV and IRR Ed has calculated?

2. Might Ed's case in the preceding problem be helped by a real option? If so, what kind? How would it help?

3. Charlie Henderson, a senior manager in the Bartok Company, is known for taking risks. He recently proposed that the company expand its operations into a new and untried field. He put together a set of cash flow projections and calculated an IRR of 25% for the project. The firm's cost of capital is about 10%. Charlie maintains that the favorability of the calculated IRR relative to the cost of capital makes the project an easy choice for acceptance, and urges management to move forward immediately.

Several knowledgeable people have looked at the proposal and feel Charlie's projections represent an optimistic scenario that has about one chance in three of happening. They think the project also has about one chance in three of failing miserably. An important consideration is that the project is large enough to bankrupt the company if it fails really badly.

Charlie doesn't want to talk about these issues, claiming the others are being "negative" and that he has a history of success with risky ventures like this. When challenged, he falls back on the 25% IRR versus the 10% cost of capital as justification for his idea.

The company president has asked you for your comments on the situation. Specifically address the issue of the 25% IRR versus the 10% cost of capital. Should this project be evaluated using different standards? How does the possibility of bankruptcy as a result of the project affect the analysis? Are capital budgeting rules still appropriate? How should Charlie's successful record be factored into the president's thinking?

4. In evaluating the situation presented in the previous problem, you've found a pure play company in the proposed industry whose beta is 2.5. The rate of return on short-term treasury bills is currently 8% and a typical stock investment returns 14%. Explain how this information might affect the acceptability of Charlie's proposal.

What practical concerns would you overlay on top of the theory you've just described? Do they make the project more or less acceptable? Does the fact that Bartok has never done this kind of business before matter? How would you adjust for that inexperience? Is the risk of bankruptcy still important? What would you advise doing about that? All things considered, would you advise the president to take on the project or not?

PROBLEMS

Scenario/Sensitivity Analysis: Concept Connection Example 12-1 (page 518)

1. The Glendale Corp. is considering a real estate development project that will cost $5 million to undertake and is expected to produce annual inflows between $1 million and $4 million for two years. Management feels that if the project turns out really well the inflows will be $3 million in the first year and $4 million in the second. If things go very poorly, on the other hand, inflows of $1 million followed by $2.5 million are more likely. Develop a range of NPVs for the project if Glendale's cost of capital is 12%.

2. If Glendale's management in the previous problem attaches a probability of .7 to the better outcome, what is the project's most likely (expected) NPV? Comment on the result of your calculations.

3. Keener Clothiers Inc. is considering investing $2 million in an automatic sewing machine to pro-
duce a newly designed line of dresses. The dresses will be priced at $200, and management expects
to sell 12,000 per year for six years. There is, however, some uncertainty about production costs associated with the new machine. The production department has estimated operating costs at 70%
of revenues, but senior management realizes that this figure could turn out to be as low as 65% or
as high as 75%. The new machine will be depreciated at a rate of $200,000 per year (straight line,
zero salvage). Keener's cost of capital is 14%, and its marginal tax rate is 35%. Calculate a point estimate along with best- and worst-case scenarios for the project's NPV.

4. Assume that Keener Clothiers of the previous problem assigns the following probabilities to production cost as a percent of revenue.

% of Revenue	Probability
65%	.30
70	.50
75%	.20

Sketch a probability distribution (histogram) for the project's NPV, and compute its expected NPV.

5. The Blazingame Corporation is considering a three-year project that has an initial cash outlay (C_0)
of $175,000 and three cash inflows that are defined by the following independent probability dis-
tributions. All dollar figures are in thousands. Blazingame's cost of capital is 10%.

C_1	C_2	C_3	Probability
$50	$40	$75	.25
60	80	80	.50
70	120	85	.25

a. Estimate the project's most likely NPV using a point estimate of each cash flow. What is its
probability?
b. What are the best and worst possible NPVs? What are their probabilities?
c. Choose a few outcomes at random, calculate their NPVs and the associated probabilities, and
sketch the probability distribution of the project's NPV.

[Hint: The project has 27 possible cash flow patterns (3 × 3 × 3), each of which is obtained by
selecting one cash flow from each column and combining with the initial outlay. The probability
of any pattern is the product of the probabilities of its three uncertain cash flows. For example, a
particular pattern might be as follows:

	C_0	C_1	C_2	C_3
C_i	$(175)	$50	$120	$80
Probability	1.0	.25	.25	.50

The probability of this pattern would be

$$.25 \times .25 \times .50 = .03125.]$$

6. Sanville Quarries is considering acquiring a new drilling machine that is expected to be more efficient than the current machine. The project is to be evaluated over four years. The initial outlay
required to get the new machine operating is $675,000. Incremental cash flows associated with
the machine are uncertain, so management developed the following probabilistic forecast of cash
flows by year ($000). Sanville's cost of capital is 10%.

Year 1	Prob	Year 2	Prob	Year 3	Prob	Year 4	Prob
$150	.30	$200	.35	$350	.30	$300	.25
175	.40	210	.45	370	.25	360	.35
300	.30	250	.20	400	.45	375	.40

a. Calculate the project's best and worst NPV's and their probabilities.

b. What are the value and probability of the most likely NPV outcome? [*Hint:* Don't use the middle value for each year. Rather, calculate the expected value of each year's cash flow.]

c. What are the probabilities of the best and worst cases?

7. Using the information from the previous problem, randomly select four NPV outcomes from the data. (Select one cash flow from each year and compute the project NPV and the probability of that NPV implied by those selections.) Do your selections give a sense of where NPV outcomes are likely to cluster?

Decision Tree Analysis: Concept Connection Example 12-2 (page 522)

8. Northwest Entertainment Inc. operates a multiplex cinema that has nine small theaters in one building. Business has been good lately and management is considering a project that will add five screens at an estimated cost of $3 million. The success of the expansion depends on whether local demand over the next two years will support the additional capacity. Demand is believed to depend on the local economy. An economist at a nearby university has predicted a 90% probability of continued prosperity in the area and a 10% chance of a moderate downturn. Management feels that if prosperity continues, the new theaters will generate a profit margin of $2 million in the first year and $3 million in the second. A moderate downturn would produce contributions of $1.5 and $2 million. Northwest's cost of capital is 12%.

a. Draw a decision tree for the project.

b. Calculate the NPV along each path.

c. Develop the probability distribution of the project's NPV.

d. Calculate the project's expected NPV.

e. Make a recommendation on the project with an appropriate comment on risk.

More Complex Decision Trees: Concept Connection Example 12-2 and 12-3 (pages 522 and 524)

9. Work Station Inc. manufactures office furniture. The firm is interested in "ergonomic" products that are designed to be easier on the bodies of office workers who suffer from ailments such as back and neck pain due to sitting for long periods. Unfortunately customer acceptance of ergonomic furniture tends to be unpredictable, so a wide range of market response is possible. Management has made the following two-year probabilistic estimate of the cash flows associated with the project arranged in decision tree format ($000).

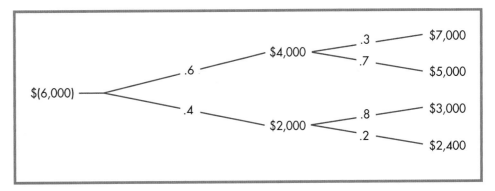

Work Station is a relatively small company and would be seriously damaged by any project that lost more than $1.5 million. The firm's cost of capital is 14%.

a. Develop a probability distribution for NPV based on the forecast. In other words, calculate the project's NPV along each path of the decision tree and the associated probability.

b. Calculate the project's expected NPV.

c. Analyze your results and make a recommendation about the project's advisability considering both expected NPV and risk.

Abandonment Options: Concept Connection Example 12-5 (page 528)

10. Resolve the last problem assuming Work Station Inc. has an abandonment option at the end of the first year under which it will recover $5 million of the initial investment in year 2. What is the value of the ability to abandon the project? How does your overall recommendation change?

11. Vaughn Clothing is considering refurbishing its store at a cost of $1.4 million. Management is concerned about the economy and whether a competitor, Viola Apparel, will open a store in the neighborhood. Vaughn estimates that there is a 60% chance that Viola will open a store nearby next year. The state of the economy probably won't affect Vaughn until the second year of the plan. Management thinks there is a 40% chance of a strong economy and a 60% chance of a downturn in the second year. Incremental cash flows are as follows:

Year 1:

Viola opens a store—$700,000

Viola doesn't open a store—$900,000

Year 2:

Viola opens a store, strong economy—$850,000

Viola opens a store, weak economy—$700,000

Viola doesn't open a store, strong economy—$1,500,000

Viola doesn't open a store, weak economy—$1,200,000

Perform a decision tree analysis of the refurbishment project. Draw the decision tree diagram, and calculate the probabilities and NPVs along each of its four paths. Then calculate the overall expected NPV. Assume that Vaughn's cost of capital is 10%.

Real Options: Concept Connection Example 12-4 (page 526)

12. Vaughn Clothing of the previous problem has a real option possibility. Carlson Flooring has expressed an interest in trading buildings with Vaughn after Vaughn is refurbished. Carlson has offered to reimburse Vaughn for 70% of its refurbishment costs at the end of the first year if they make the trade. Vaughn would then forgo all incremental cash flows for the second year. Carlson is willing to keep the option open for one year in return for a non-refundable payment of $150,000 now. Should Vaughn pay the $150,000 to keep the option available?

13. Spitfire Aviation Inc. manufactures small, private aircraft. Management is evaluating a proposal to introduce a new high-performance plane. High-performance aviation is an expensive sport undertaken largely by people who are both young and wealthy. Spitfire sees its target market as affluent professionals under 35 who have made a lot of money in the stock market in recent years.

Stock prices have been rising rapidly for some time, so investment profits have been very handsome, but lately there are serious concerns about a market downturn. If the market remains strong, Spitfire estimates it will sell 50 of the new planes a year for five years, each of which will result in a net cash flow contribution of $200,000. If the market turns down, however, only about 20 units a year will be sold. Economists think there's about a 40% chance the market will turn down in the near future.

There are also some concerns about the design of the new plane. Not everyone is convinced it will perform as well as the engineering department thinks. Indeed, the engineers have sometimes been too optimistic about their projects in the past. If performance is below the engineering estimate, word-of- mouth communication among fliers will erode the product's reputation, and unit sales *after the first year* will be 50% of the preceding forecasts. Management thinks there's a 30% chance the plane won't perform as well as the engineers think it will. The cost to bring the plane through design and into production is estimated at $15 million. Spitfire's cost of capital is 12%.

a. Draw and fully label the decision tree diagram for the project.

b. Calculate the NPV and probability along each path.

c. Calculate the project's expected NPV.

d. Sketch a probability distribution for NPV.

e. Describe the risk situation in words compared to a point estimate of NPV.

14. If Spitfire elects to do the project, what is an abandonment option at the end of year 1 worth if Spitfire can recover $8 million of the initial investment into other uses at that time? If the recovery is $13 million?

15. The New England Brewing Company produces a super premium beer using a recipe that's been in the owner's family since colonial times. Surprisingly, the firm doesn't own its brewing facilities, but rents time on the equipment of large brewers who have excess capacity. Other small brewers have been doing the same thing lately, so capacity has become difficult to find and must be contracted several years in advance.

New England's sales have been increasing steadily, and marketing consultants think there's a possibility that demand will really take off soon. Last year's sales generated net cash flows after all costs and taxes of $5 million. The consultants predict that sales will probably be at a level that will produce net cash flows of $6 million per year for the next three years, but they also see a 20% probability that sales could be high enough to generate net cash inflows of $8 million per year.

Meeting such an increase in demand presents a problem because of the advance contracting requirements for brewing capacity. Unless New England arranges for extra facilities now, there's a 70% chance that brewing capacity won't be available if the increased demand materializes. An option arrangement is available with one of the large brewers under which it will hold capacity for New England until the last minute for an immediate, nonrefundable payment of $1 million. New England's cost of capital is 9%.

a. Draw a decision tree reflecting New England's cash flows for the next three years without the option, and calculate the expected NPV of operating cash flows. (Note that there's no need to include an initial outlay because we're dealing with ongoing operations.)

b. Redraw the decision tree to include the capacity option as a real option in your calculations. What is its value? Should it be purchased?

c. Does the real option reduce New England's risk in any way?

Risk-Adjusted Rates—SML: Concept Connection Example 12-6 (page 535)

16. Hudson Furniture specializes in office furniture for self-employed individuals who work at home. Hudson's furniture emphasizes style rather than utility and has been quite successful. The firm is now considering entering the more competitive industrial furniture market where volumes are higher but pricing is more competitive. A $10 million investment is required to enter the new market. Management anticipates positive cash flows of $1.7 million annually for eight years if Hudson enters the field. An average stock currently earns 8%, and the return on treasury bills is 4%. Hudson's beta is .5, while that of an important competitor who operates solely in the industrial market is 1.5. Should Hudson consider entering the industrial furniture market?

17. Crest Concrete Inc. has been building basements and slab foundations for new homes in La Crosse, Wisconsin, for more than 20 years. However, new home sales have slowed recently and residential construction work is hard to get. As a result, management is considering a venture into commercial construction. Although Crest would still be pouring concrete in commercial building,

almost everything else about the business differs substantially from homebuilding, which is all the firm has done until now.

The local commercial concrete business is dominated by two firms: Readi-Mix Inc. and Toddy Concrete Inc. Readi-Mix has been in business for 50 years, has a market share of 70%, and a beta of 1.3. Toddy has been in the area for only five years and has a beta of 2.4. Crest's own beta is .9, and its cost of capital is 9.3%. Both of these were developed during a long period in which the housing market was prosperous and growing steadily. The stock market is currently returning 11% and treasury bills are yielding 4.2%.

Crest will have to spend $950,000 to get started in the commercial field and expects net cash inflows of $250,000 in the first year $400,000 in the second year, and $700,000 in the third.

Should Crest give commercial construction a try?

18. Illinois Fabrics Inc. makes upholstery that's used in high-quality furniture, largely chairs and sofas. Illinois has traditionally sold their fabric to manufacturers who use it to cover furniture frames they produce. These manufacturers then wholesale the finished product to furniture stores. Management has analyzed the finished chairs and sofas of several manufacturers and found that the highest value element they contain is the Illinois fabric. They further found that generally the frames were shoddily produced.

Illinois' VP of Manufacturing, Harrison Flatley, has proposed starting a new business called Illinois Furniture which will produce and market the end product using the fabric the firm already manufactures. Harrison has put together a proposal to start such a venture which results in a steady stream of cash income of $5 million per year after an initial investment of $25 million to be spent on manufacturing facilities and the development of a sales relationship with retailers. The analysis comes up with an NPV for the project assuming the income stream is a perpetuity and taking its present value at Illinois' 10% cost of capital.

$$\text{NPV} = -\$25M + \$5M/.10 = -\$25M + \$50M = \$25M$$

Top management likes the idea but is concerned about risk in two areas. First, furniture manufacturing seems to be a riskier business than making fabric as manufacturing firms are always entering and leaving the industry. The average beta of the publicly traded end product manufacturers is a relatively high 1.9. By contrast, Illinois' beta is .9.

Second, management fears that an economic downturn would impact a new business more seriously than it would the existing competitors. Management fears that there's a 40% chance of a downturn in the near future which would reduce Harrison's income projections by 20%.

Re-analyze Harrison's proposal and make a recommendation to management. Treasury bills are yielding 4% and the S&P 500 index is yielding 10%.

Certainty Equivalents: Concept Connection Example 12-7 (page 538)

19. The Brown Owl Corporation manufactures high quality outdoor equipment for adventurous people who enjoy hiking, hunting, climbing, and trekking under extreme conditions. The firm has been very successful with things like cold weather clothing, boots, mountain climbing equipment, and camping gear. However, all of their products support land based activities, they've never done anything involving boating or deep water fishing. Yesterday Tim Woods, the vice president of marketing, made a proposal to the executive committee for entry into the water sports field beginning with a new and radically designed kayak. The proposal treats the venture as a capital budgeting project and includes an initial outlay along with five years of projected cash flows as follows ($M):

Year	0	1	2	3	4	5
Cash Flow	(5.5)	1.5	3.0	5.0	6.0	6.5

Tim admits his projection is optimistic but insists the water sport field is easily accessible because of Brown Owl's reputation and the innovative genius of the new kayak design. The president of the company thinks Tim is a terrific marketing VP but isn't so sure about his financial ability. He has asked you to do some risk related analysis of the idea and make a recommendation to the committee. Brown Owl's cost of capital is 12% and the risk free rate is 5%.

a. Calculate the kayak project's traditional NPV based on Tim's forecast.
b. Apply the certainty equivalent technique to the proposal assuming the CE factors start with 1.0 for C_0 and fall off by .1 each year thereafter.
c. Assume the factors fall off by .15 each year.
d. Comment on the advisability of the project including risk considerations.

13 CHAPTER

Cost of Capital

Chapter Outline

The Purpose of the Cost of Capital

Cost of Capital Concepts
- Capital Components
- Capital Structure
- Returns on Investments and the Costs of Capital Components
- The Weighted Average Calculation—The WACC
- Capital Structure and Cost—Book Versus Market Value

Calculating the WACC
- Developing Market Value Based Capital Structures
- Calculating Component Costs of Capital
- Putting the Weights and Costs Together

The Marginal Cost of Capital (MCC)
- The Break in MCC When Retained Earnings Run Out

The Cost of Capital—A Comprehensive Example

A Potential Mistake—Handling Separately Funded Projects

We introduced the cost of capital briefly in Chapter 10 because we needed some appreciation of the concept to grasp the rationale behind capital budgeting. In this chapter, we'll explore the idea in more detail and learn how to calculate a firm's cost of capital.

13.1 The Purpose of the Cost of Capital

A company's cost of capital is the average rate it pays for the use of its capital funds. That rate provides a benchmark against which to measure investment opportunities in the context of capital budgeting.

The idea is very straightforward. No one should invest in any project that will return less than the cost of invested funds. Because a firm's cost of capital is the best estimate of the cost of any money it invests, it should never take on a project that doesn't return at least that rate.

This is equivalent to saying that to be accepted, a project must either have an IRR that exceeds the cost of capital or an NPV that is positive when computed at that rate. These ideas were developed in Chapter 10 where we used the symbol k to represent the cost of capital. Review pages 448–449 if necessary.

The **cost of capital** is the average rate paid for the use of capital funds. It is used **primarily** in **capital budgeting**.

It's quite important to the effective management of a company that its cost of capital be estimated accurately. Otherwise the firm is likely to make incorrect investment decisions that can jeopardize its profitability and long-run survival.

The cost of capital concept is similar to an idea we've already studied: an individual investor's required return for a particular stock. In Chapter 9 (pages 399–400), we said that an investor wouldn't buy a stock unless its expected return was higher than his or her required return for that company. Further, we said that people base required returns on risk.

A company's cost of capital can be thought of as its required return for all capital budgeting projects that have risk levels approximately equal to its own risk. A project's expected return is its IRR. Hence, a firm won't invest in a project unless its IRR (expected return) exceeds that firm's cost of capital (required return).

13.2   Cost of Capital Concepts

"Capital" refers to money acquired for use over long periods of time. The funds are generally used for getting businesses started, acquiring long-lived assets, and otherwise doing the kinds of projects we studied in Chapters 10 through 12 under the topic of capital budgeting. On a firm's financial statements, capital appears on the lower right side of the balance sheet.

13.2a   Capital Components

The **components** of a firm's capital are **debt**, **common equity**, and **preferred stock**.

Capital can be divided into **components** according to the way the money was raised. The two basic classifications are **debt** and **common equity**. Debt is borrowed money raised through loans or the sale of bonds. Common equity indicates an ownership interest, and comes from the sale of common stock or from retaining earnings.

A third kind of capital comes from the sale of **preferred stock.** (Review pages 372–374 if necessary.) Preferred can be thought of as a cross between debt and equity because it has some of the characteristics of each. Legally, it's a kind of equity, but for many financial purposes it behaves more like debt. Because of this hybrid nature, preferred is sometimes combined with one of the other components for purposes of analysis.

However, preferred stock offers investors a return which is generally different from that of either debt or common equity. Therefore, in the context of the cost of capital, it's handled separately as a third component.

In the rest of this chapter, we'll refer to common equity simply as equity, and preferred equity as preferred stock or just preferred. Hence the three capital components are debt, preferred stock, and equity.

13.2b   Capital Structure

Capital structure is the mix of the three **capital components**.

The mix of capital components in use by a company at a point in time is its **capital structure.** We generally describe capital structure in percentage terms referring to the relative sizes of the components. For example, a firm that has the following capital components can be described as 30% debt, 10% preferred stock, and 60% equity.

Debt	$ 30,000,000	30%
Preferred stock	10,000,000	10
Equity	60,000,000	60
Total capital	$100,000,000	100%

The Target Capital Structure

A great deal of importance is sometimes placed on operating with the "right" capital structure. However, the determination of what's right is the subject of some debate. We'll address this issue in Chapter 14. In the meantime, we'll assume that the management of a firm may have a particular mix of capital components that it considers more desirable than any other. We'll call that mix the firm's **target capital structure**, and assume that management strives to maintain it as money is raised.

Where a target capital structure has been designated, we'll see that it can be used in place of the actual capital structure for certain calculations.

A firm's **target capital structure** is a mix of components that management **considers optimal** and strives to maintain.

Raising Money in the Proportions of the Capital Structure

As a practical matter, an exact capital structure can't be maintained continuously, because money tends to be acquired in finite amounts by issuing securities of one kind or another, one at a time.

For example, suppose a firm had the capital structure just illustrated and that mix was also its target. Further suppose the company needed to raise an additional $1 million. To do that, it would generally issue and sell $1 million of either debt, preferred stock, or common stock. Trying to sell some of each security in the proportion of 30–10–60 wouldn't be practical.

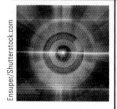

INSIGHTS   Practical Finance

The Cost of Capital—Intuitively

Suppose an entrepreneur plans to open a business that will earn 12% on invested money. If he has no money of his own, but can borrow at 15%, does it make sense to start the business?

Clearly it doesn't. The enterprise is certain to lose money, because it will pay more for funds than it will earn using them. The business makes sense only if the entrepreneur can borrow at a rate below 12%.

This is the idea behind the cost of capital. We shouldn't pay more for a resource than it earns. In this simple case, the cost of capital is just the rate at which borrowed funds are available. In reality, firms have more than one kind of capital, and each has a different cost. The cost of capital is a single rate that represents an average of those costs.

Issuing one security for the additional money would throw the proportions in the capital structure off target. Then the next time it raised capital, the company could try to move back toward the target mix.

In spite of this practical difficulty, cost of capital **calculations** are generally based on the assumption that money is **raised in the exact proportions** of some capital structure. In this case, we would assume the firm raised its $1 million by selling $300,000 in new bonds and $100,000 in new preferred stock, along with $600,000 of equity. The equity would come from a combination of retained earnings and the sale of

Cost of capital **calculations** assume that capital is **raised in the exact proportions** of some capital structure.

new common stock. The assumption isn't very realistic, but the distortion it produces is generally small.

13.2c Returns on Investments and the Costs of Capital Components

The **return earned** by investors on the security underlying a capital component is its **unadjusted cost**.

Investors provide capital to companies by purchasing their securities. The investors' returns are paid out by the companies, so those returns are costs to the firms in which the investments are made. This is a fundamental point. The return received by an investor on a particular type of security (debt, preferred, or equity) and the cost to the company of the funds raised through that security are opposite sides of the same coin.

For a particular company, investments in the securities underlying the three capital components offer different returns because each type of security has different risk characteristics. Thus, each capital component has a distinct cost that's related to the return earned by the investors who provide that component. And because the returns are different, so are the costs.

Because component securities have **different risks**, they offer **different returns** and have **different costs**. Equity is **highest**, debt is **lowest**, and preferred is **between**.

Generally the return on an equity investment is higher than the return on debt or preferred because the risk is higher. Hence, the firm's cost of equity capital is higher than its cost of debt or preferred stock. The return/cost of debt tends to be the lowest of the three because debt is the least risky investment. The cost of preferred is usually between the cost of debt and that of equity.

Although the cost paid out by the company is the investor's return, there are some adjustments that keep the *effective* cost and return from being exactly the same. Hence, we say that cost and return are related rather than equal. We'll describe the adjustments later.

For now, the important point is that there are separate component costs of capital for debt, preferred stock, and equity. And each component cost is related to the return earned by investors owning the security underlying that component.

13.2d The Weighted Average Calculation—The WACC

Calculating the cost of capital is conceptually quite simple. Firms raise capital from several sources, each of which has its own cost. A firm's overall cost of capital is the average of the costs of its separate sources weighted by the proportion of each source used. The separate sources are the capital components we've been talking about, and the proportions are the percentages of each component in the firm's capital structure.

The WACC is a **weighted average** of component costs where the weights reflect the amount of each component used.

The procedure has led to the term **weighted average cost of capital**, abbreviated **WACC**. The expression has exactly the same meaning as the simpler "cost of capital" we've been using until now. It's customary to use the expression WACC in discussions of the subject, because it avoids confusion with the cost of capital for an individual component.

Computing the WACC—An Example   To compute a WACC, we need two things: the mix of the capital components in use and the cost of each component. We'll get into how we arrive at each shortly, but first let's preview what we'll do once we have them. An example is the easiest way to understand the procedure.

CONCEPT CONNECTION   EXAMPLE 13-1

WACC Calculations

Calculate the WACC for the Zodiac Company given the following information about its capital structure:

Capital Component	Value	Cost
Debt	$ 60,000	9%
Preferred stock	50,000	11
Common stock	90,000	14
	$200,000	

SOLUTION: First we compute the capital structure weights on the basis of the dollar values given. This involves adding up the dollar amounts and stating each as a percentage of the total. That calculation results in the first two numerical columns below. The weight of the debt component, for example, is

$$\frac{\$60,000}{\$200,000} = .30 = 30\%$$

Notice that the weights have to add up to 1.00 or 100%, and that they are the decimal equivalents of the percentages in the firm's capital structure.

Next multiply the cost of each component by its weight and sum the results as shown. The result is the WACC.

Capital Component	Value	Weight		Cost		
Debt	$ 60,000	.30	×	9%	=	2.70%
Preferred stock	50,000	.25	×	11	=	2.75
Common stock	90,000	×	×	14	=	6.30
	$200,000	1.00		WACC	=	11.75%

13.2e   Capital Structure and Cost—Book Versus Market Value

A major source of confusion about the WACC stems from the fact that both capital structure and component costs can be viewed in terms of either the book or market value of the underlying capital. We'll talk about structure first and then about component costs.

Capital Structure—Book Versus Market   The book values of a firm's capital accounts reflect the prices at which the securities that raised its capital were originally sold, and are embodied in the capital section of its balance sheet. Market values reflect the current market prices of those same securities. The firm's capital structure can be based on either. We'll illustrate the difference with a case in which there's only debt and equity capital (no preferred stock).

Assume the Diplomat Corporation, a new firm, raises $100,000 in equity by selling 10,000 shares of common stock at $10 each. It also borrows $100,000 by selling 100 bonds at a par value of $1,000. Immediately after those transactions, Diplomat has the capital structure shown in Table 13-1, which reflects both book and market values.

> The **value of capital** can be stated based on the **book or market prices** of the underlying securities.

TABLE 13-1	The Diplomat Corporation's Initial Capital Structure—Book and Market Equal			
Equity	10,000 shares × $10	=	$100,000	50.0%
Debt	100 bonds × $1,000	=	100,000	50.0
		Total	$200,000	100.0%

Now imagine that Diplomat's stock price increases to $12, while interest rates climb and drive the price of its bonds down to $850. These market adjustments do not change the capital entries on the company's books. Therefore, the book value based structure remains as shown in Table 13-1. However, the market value based structure does change significantly. The result is shown in Table 13-2.

TABLE 13-2	The Diplomat Corporation's Market Value Based Capital Structure			
Equity	10,000 shares × $ 12	=	$ 120,000	58.5%
Debt	100 bonds × $850	=	85,000	41.5
		Total	$205,000	100.0%

Capital structures based on book and market values are generally different because the market values of securities change all the time, and those changes are not reflected on company books. Our question is which basis for structure is appropriate for calculating the WACC?

Component Returns/Costs—Book Versus Market   Investors' returns and the related component costs of capital can also be thought of in either book or market terms. We'll illustrate with a bond.

Suppose a firm sells a 10% coupon rate bond at its face value. Initially an investor buying the bond earns a 10% return, and the company pays the same 10% interest on the borrowed money. Suppose the market interest rate later falls to 8%.

After the market rate change, two returns can be associated with the bond. The original investor is still receiving 10% on his or her investment, and the company is still paying 10% on the original amount borrowed. However, a new investor buying the bond will have to pay a higher price and will therefore earn a return of only 8%. Hence, either an 8% market rate or a 10% book rate can be associated with the debt.

Once again, our question is which should be reflected in the component cost of debt in the WACC calculation.

The Appropriate Perspective for the WACC Calculation   Which view—book or market—is more appropriate for calculating the WACC? To answer that question we have to understand exactly what the use of each implies in the context of capital budgeting.

Book values relate to capital the company already has. It was raised in the past to support past projects. Using those values to calculate the WACC results in a figure that reflects the composite cost of existing capital that's already committed.

Market values relate to the current state of capital markets. Using market values to calculate the WACC gives a figure that reflects an average of what capital would cost if it were raised today.

We use the WACC in techniques like IRR and NPV to evaluate newly proposed projects. Old capital isn't available to fund these undertakings because it has already been spent. Hence, firms generally have to fund projects with new capital they have yet to raise. It therefore makes sense to evaluate those new projects against the likely cost of the new capital that will support them.

That means it's appropriate that the WACC reflect current market conditions, because those conditions are the best estimate of what capital will cost during the coming period. Hence, we should use market values throughout the WACC calculation.

The Customary Approach   The customary approach is to assume that in the future, the firm will either maintain its present capital structure based on market prices or will strive to achieve some target structure also based on market prices. Either of these structures is combined with market-based component costs of capital to develop the WACC.

People are generally less concerned with the precision of the capital structure in the calculation than with the accuracy of the component costs of capital. In practice, it turns out that calculating the present structure at market prices is somewhat tedious. Further, the market-based structure is constantly changing. A reasonable target structure is often used for simplicity as much as for any other reason. The error implied is generally very small.

13.3   Calculating the WACC

Calculating a real WACC involves three distinct steps. First we develop a market value based capital structure. Then we *adjust* the market returns on the securities underlying the capital components to reflect the company's true component costs of capital. Finally, we put these together to calculate a WACC.

13.3a   Developing Market Value Based Capital Structures

Developing a capital structure involves stating the dollar amounts of the capital components in use by the firm, adding them up, and then restating each as a percentage of the total. A book value structure is easy to calculate because the book values of debt, preferred stock, and equity are readily available on the balance sheet. Developing a market value based structure is more difficult. It requires that we compute the current market value of all the securities underlying each category of balance sheet capital, and then develop a structure from those values. The best way to understand the procedure is through an example.

CONCEPT CONNECTION   EXAMPLE 13-2

Market Value Based Capital Structure

The Wachusett Corporation has the following capital situation:

Debt: 2,000 bonds were issued 5 years ago at a coupon rate of 12%. They had 30-year terms and $1,000 face values. They are now selling to yield 10%.

Preferred stock: 4,000 shares of preferred are outstanding, each of which pays an annual dividend of $7.50. They originally sold to yield 15% of their $50 face value. They're now selling to yield 13%.

Equity: Wachusett has 200,000 shares of common stock outstanding, currently selling at $15 per share.

Develop Wachusett's market value based capital structure.

SOLUTION: The market value of each capital component is the market price of the underlying security multiplied by the number of those securities outstanding. We can use the valuation concepts from Chapters 7 and 8 to arrive at prices for the bonds and preferred stock. The price of the common stock is given.

Debt: The price of Wachusett's bonds is calculated using the bond formula developed in Chapter 7, Equation 7.4. In this case, k = 5%, n = 50, PMT = $60, and FV = $1,000. (See page 294.)

$$P_b = PMT[PVFA_{k,n}] + FV[PVF_{k,n}]$$
$$= \$60[PVFA_{5,50}] + \$1,000[PVF_{5,50}]$$
$$= \$60(18.2559) + \$1,000(.0872)$$
$$= \$1,182.55$$

Because there are 2,000 bonds outstanding, the market value of the debt is

$$\$1,182.55 \times 2,000 = \$2,365,100$$

Preferred stock: The preferred shares pay a $7.50 dividend and currently yield 13%. Each preferred share is valued as follows (see Chapter 8, Equation 8.13, page 372).

$$P_p = \frac{D_p}{k} = \frac{\$7.50}{.13} = \$57.69$$

Because there are 4,000 preferred shares outstanding, their total market value is

$$\$57.69 \times 4,000 = \$230,760$$

Common equity: The market value of Wachusett's common stock is just the market price times the number of shares outstanding.

$$\$15.00 \times 200,000 = \$3,000,000$$

Market value based weights: Next we summarize and compute the capital component weights based on market values.

Debt	$ 2,365,100	42.3%
Preferred	230,760	4.1
Equity	3,000,000	53.6
	$5,595,860	100.0%

13.3b   Calculating Component Costs of Capital

In this section, we'll look into procedures for calculating the component costs of capital for debt, preferred stock, and equity. In each case, we'll start by considering the market return currently received by *new* investors on the securities underlying the component. Then we'll make certain adjustments to those returns that are necessary to reflect practical reality. We'll describe the adjustments before getting into the individual component costs.

Adjustments—The Effect of Financial Markets and Taxes   Although the returns received by investors and the costs paid out by companies are the same money, the amounts *effectively* paid and received can be different because of taxes and certain transaction costs associated with doing business in financial markets.

The returns paid to new investors are **adjusted** to arrive at **effective** costs to the company.

Taxes   The tax effect applies only to debt and stems from the fact that interest payments are tax deductible to the paying firm. That effectively makes debt cheaper than it would be if interest weren't deductible.

For example, if the firm's marginal tax rate is 40%,[1] the payment of $1 in interest reduces taxable income by $1, and the firm pays $.40 less tax even though the investor gets the full dollar of interest. By way of contrast, $1 paid as a dividend is not deductible and results in no tax savings.

The dollar cost of paying an amount of interest, I, is

$$I(1 - T)$$

The **tax deductibility of interest** makes debt an even **cheaper** source of capital than it is due to low risk.

where T is the tax rate. The same rule applies when interest is expressed as a rate of return. If the firm pays interest at a rate k_d, the effective after-tax cost of paying that rate is

$$k_d(1 - T)$$

For example, if the interest rate is 10% and the tax rate is 40%, the cost of debt adjusted for taxes would be

$$k_d(1 - T) = 10\%(1 - .4) = 6\%$$

Recall that the return paid to investors on debt is the lowest of the three capital components because debt is the least risky investment. The tax effect reduces the cost of debt even further in relation to the cost of the other components, making it a real bargain.

Flotation costs lower the amount received when a security is issued, **increasing the cost** of the capital raised.

Flotation Costs   Flotation costs are administrative fees and expenses incurred in the process of issuing and selling (floating) securities. You can think of flotation cost as a commission paid to firms in the investment banking industry for services performed in raising capital.

If flotation costs are f percent of the proceeds of a security issue that raises an amount P paid by investors, the amount received by the issuing company is

$$P - fP = P(1 - f)$$

---

1.   The marginal federal income tax rate for most firms is 35%. However, most companies are also subject to state income taxes, so 40% is a reasonable approximation of an average total rate.

where f is in decimal form in the equation. Clearly, flotation costs lower the amount of money a firm receives when it sells securities. They have the effect of making the cost of the issue higher than the return received by investors. In general we can write

$$\text{component cost of capital} = \frac{\text{investor's return}}{(1-f)} = \frac{k}{(1-f)}$$

In words, the component cost of capital is higher than the investor's return by the ratio of $1/(1-f)$.[2]

For example, if the return on a particular security is 10% and flotation costs are 20%, the component cost of capital is

$$\text{component cost of capital} = \frac{k}{(1-f)} = \frac{10\%}{(1-.20)} = 12.5\%$$

The Cost of Debt   To calculate the component cost of debt based on market returns, we take the return received by investors currently purchasing the firm's bonds and adjust it for the effects of taxes. Most debt isn't initially sold to the general public, but is *privately placed* with large investors. Therefore, flotation costs are minimal, and we needn't adjust for them.

The market return on business debt is generally well known for the firm's own securities or for issues of similar risk. We'll call that return k_d. Then the cost of debt is

(13.1) $$\text{cost of debt} = k_d(1-T)$$

where $(1-T)$ adjusts for the fact that interest is tax deductible to the paying firm.

> The **cost of debt** is the investor's return adjusted for the **tax deductibility of interest** payments.

CONCEPT CONNECTION   EXAMPLE 13-3

Cost of Debt

Blackstone Inc. has 12% coupon rate bonds outstanding that yield 8% to investors buying them now. Blackstone's marginal tax rate including federal and state taxes is 37%. What is Blackstone's cost of debt?

SOLUTION: First notice that k_d is the current market yield of 8%, not the coupon rate. To calculate the cost of debt we simply write Equation 13.1 and substitute from the information given.

$$\begin{aligned}
\text{cost of debt} &= k_d(1-T) \\
&= 8\%(1-.37) \\
&= 5.04\%
\end{aligned}$$

Ensuper/Shutterstock.com

---

2. This relationship is strictly true only when the investment is expected to generate an infinite stream of cash flows. If the stream is finite, as in a bond investment, it is an approximation.

The Cost of Preferred Stock   Preferred stock provides an investor with a constant dividend as long as the share remains outstanding. Recall from our work in Chapters 6 and 8 that such an arrangement is known as a *perpetuity.*

The price of a preferred share is the present value of the perpetuity of the dividend stream, and is given by the expression

(13.2)
$$P_p = \frac{D_p}{k_p}$$

where P_p is the current price of a share, D_p is the preferred dividend, and k_p is the return on the investment in preferred stock. (See Chapter 6, page 269 and Chapter 8, page 372.)

Solving Equation 13.2 for the investor's return yields

(13.3)
$$k_p = \frac{D_p}{P_p}$$

The **cost of preferred stock** is the investor's return adjusted for **flotation costs**.

Preferred dividends are not tax deductible to the issuing firm, so no tax adjustment needs to be made. However, flotation costs must be incorporated by multiplying Equation 13.3 by $1/(1 - f)$. Rewriting, we have

(13.4)
$$\text{cost of preferred stock} = \frac{D_p}{(1 - f)P_p} = \frac{k_p}{(1 - f)}$$

CONCEPT CONNECTION   EXAMPLE 13-4

Cost of Preferred Stock

The preferred stock of the Francis Corporation was issued several years ago with each share paying 6% of a $100 par value. Flotation costs on new preferred are expected to average 11% of the funds raised.

    a.   What is Francis's cost of preferred capital if the interest rate on similar preferred stock is 9% today?

    b.   Calculate Francis's cost of preferred if the stock is selling at $75 per share today.

SOLUTION: Notice that parts (a) and (b) of this problem pose the same question with slightly different given information. In part (a), we have the market return directly, and in part (b), we have the information needed to calculate it.

    a.   Write Equation 13.4 using only the last term on the right, and adjust the market return for flotation costs directly.

$$\text{cost of preferred stock} = \frac{k_p}{(1 - f)} = \frac{9\%}{1 - .11} = 10.1\%$$

    b.   In this case, instead of having the yield, we're told that the stock is currently selling for $75. We also know it pays an annual dividend of 6% of $100 or $6. Write Equation 13.4 using the middle term and substitute.

$$\text{cost of preferred stock} = \frac{D_p}{(1 - f)P_p} = \frac{\$6}{(1 - .11)\$75} = 9.0\%$$

The Cost of Common Equity

The market return available on an equity investment isn't as easy to come up with as the market return on debt or preferred stock. Those securities give an investor known streams of future payments in return for the prices paid, so calculating the return is easy. The anticipated return on a stock investment, on the other hand, depends on *estimates* of future dividends and prices, which are much less certain than interest payments and preferred dividends.

As a result of this uncertainty, the market return on an equity investment has to be estimated. To do that we can use some of the ideas we've developed in earlier chapters. We'll look at three approaches involving the CAPM, the constant growth (Gordon) model, and risk premiums.

Another complication arises from the fact that equity comes from **two sources**, retained earnings and the sale of new stock. These have to be treated separately because they turn out to have **different costs**. We'll look at each in turn, beginning with retained earnings.

> The **cost of equity** is imprecise because of the **uncertainty** of future cash flows.

The Cost of Retained Earnings

It's tempting to think of retained earnings as free to the company, because they come from its own internal operations. However, all earnings belong to the firm's stockholders whether they're paid out as dividends or retained. To the extent that management retains earnings, they reinvest shareholders' money in the company for them.

In other words, retained earnings represents money stockholders could have spent if it had been paid out in dividends. Therefore, those stockholders deserve a return on the funds just as though the money had been paid out and reinvested through the purchase of new shares. By this logic, the market return on new shares is the appropriate starting point for estimating the cost of retained earnings.

> New equity comes from **two sources**, stock sales and retained earnings, which have **different costs**.

No Adjustments Between Return and Cost for Retained Earnings

It's important to notice that retained earnings are the only *internally generated* capital source. They aren't raised through financial markets, so they don't incur flotation costs. They're also not tax deductible. Hence, no adjustments are necessary to convert return to cost.

> The cost of **retained earnings** is equal to the **unadjusted** return earned by new buyers of the firm's stock.

The CAPM Approach—The Required Rate of Return

We studied the capital asset pricing model (CAPM) in Chapter 9. The model is a theory purporting to explain how investors set required rates of return for particular stocks. Recall that the required rate is the return that just induces investors to purchase a stock, and is generally assumed to be a function of the stock's risk. The expected rate of return, on the other hand, is the return investors expect in the future given the knowledge currently available about a particular stock.

Under normal market conditions stock prices are more or less *in equilibrium,* meaning that expected and required rates of return are about equal. Hence, the market return on a particular stock can be approximated by estimating either the required return or the expected return. The CAPM allows us to estimate the required return; we'll look at estimating with the expected return in the next section.

The CAPM's expression for the required rate of return is the security market line (SML). It was presented in Chapter 9 as Equation 9.4. We'll relabel the expression and repeat it here for convenience.

Ensuper/Shutterstock.com

(13.5)

$$k_X = k_{RF} + (k_M - k_{RF})b_X$$

where: k_X is the required return on stock X

k_{RF} is the risk-free rate, usually taken to be the current return on three-month treasury bills

k_M is the return on the market or on an "average" stock, usually estimated through a market index like the S&P 500

b_X is stock X's beta coefficient, the measure of company X's market risk

Equation 13.5 provides a direct estimate of the current market return available to investors on the equity of company X. It is therefore also a direct estimate of the cost of equity acquired through retained earnings, because no tax or market adjustments are necessary.

CONCEPT CONNECTION   **EXAMPLE 13-5**

Cost of Retained Earnings—SML

The return on the Strand Corporation's stock is relatively volatile as reflected by the company's beta of 1.8. The return on the S&P 500 is currently 12% and is expected to remain at that level. Treasury bills are yielding 6.5%. Estimate Strand's cost of retained earnings.

SOLUTION: Write Equation 13.5 and substitute directly, using the return on the S&P 500 as k_M and the Treasury bill yield as k_{RF}.

$$\text{cost of RE} = k_X = k_{RF} + (k_M - k_{RF})b_X$$
$$= 6.5\% + (12\% - 6.5\%)1.8$$
$$= 16.4\%$$

The Dividend Growth Approach—The Expected Rate of Return   In Chapter 8, we developed an expression for pricing a stock that is expected to grow at a constant rate into the indefinite future. The model is alternatively called the *dividend growth model* or the *Gordon model* after the scholar who developed it. The expression was presented as Equation 8.10. We'll relabel and repeat it here with one minor change in notation. We'll replace k in the denominator with k_e to emphasize the idea that the rate is the expected return on an investment in the stock.

(13.6)

$$P_0 = \frac{D_0(1 + g)}{k_e - g}$$

where: P_0 is the current price of the stock

D_0 is the most recent annual dividend paid by the company

k_e is the expected return on an investment in the stock

g is the anticipated, constant growth rate of the company and its dividend stream

Solving Equation 13.6 for k_e gives a direct estimate of the cost of equity capital obtained through retained earnings. The result is Equation 13.7.[3]

(13.7)
$$\text{cost of RE} = k_e = \frac{D_0(1 + g)}{P_0} + g$$

CONCEPT CONNECTION   EXAMPLE 13-6

Cost of Retained Earnings—Constant Growth (Gordon) Model

Periwinkle Inc. paid a dividend of $1.65 last year, and its stock is currently selling for $33.60 a share. The company is expected to grow at 7.5% indefinitely. Estimate the firm's cost of retained earnings.

SOLUTION: Write Equation 13.7 and substitute for Periwinkle's expected return and the cost of RE.

$$\text{cost of RE} = k_e = \frac{D_0(1 + g)}{P_0} + g$$
$$= \frac{\$1.65(1.075)}{\$33.60} + .075$$
$$= .053 + .075 = 12.8\%$$

The **cost of retained earnings** can be estimated using the **CAPM**, the **dividend growth (Gordon) model**, or a **risk premium**.

The Risk Premium Approach   Since beginning our study of interest in Chapter 5, we've recognized that any return can be thought of as the sum of a base rate and premiums for bearing risk.

Investment risk and the associated risk premiums vary among companies, but they also vary between the kinds of securities offered by a single company. Debt is the safest investment, while equity has considerably more risk.

The relationship between the risk of debt and the risk of equity is relatively constant among companies. In other words, the *increment* in risk between debt and equity is about the same for high-risk and low-risk firms. That increment tends to command an additional risk premium of between 3% and 5%.

As a result, it's feasible to estimate the return on a firm's equity by adding three to five percentage points to the market return on its debt, which is generally easy to get. We can formalize the relationship as

(13.8)
$$k_e = k_d + rp_e$$

where k_d and k_e are the respective market returns on debt and equity, and rp_e is the additional risk premium on equity. The cost of retained earnings is then equal to this estimate of k_e.

---

3. Recall that in the Gordon model the *next* dividend is $D_1 = D_0 (1 + g)$. Hence, Equations 13.6 and 13.7 can also be written with D_1 in the numerators of the fractions.

CONCEPT CONNECTION   EXAMPLE 13-7

Cost of Retained Earnings—Risk Premium

The Carter Company's long-term bonds are currently yielding 12%. Estimate Carter's cost of retained earnings.

SOLUTION: Simply write Equation 13.8 and substitute, using 4% for the incremental risk premium.

$$\text{cost of RE} = k_e = k_d + rp_e$$
$$= 12\% + 4\%$$
$$= 16\%$$

The Cost of New Common Stock   So far, we've been talking about equity capital from retained earnings. Firms often need to raise more equity capital than is available from earnings and do so by selling new common stock.

Equity from new stock is just like equity from retained earnings, with the exception that raising it involves incurring flotation costs. Therefore, the expressions we've used so far to estimate the cost of equity have to be adjusted to reflect those costs. This is easiest to do in Equation 13.7, the dividend growth model, because the price of the stock appears explicitly in that expression. The adjustment simply involves substituting $(1 - f)P_0$ for P_0, where f represents the fraction of the price going to flotation cost. The result is as follows.

The cost of **new common stock** includes an adjustment for **flotation** costs.

(13.9) $$\textbf{cost of new equity} \ = \ \mathbf{k_e} = \frac{\mathbf{D_0(1 + g)}}{\mathbf{(1 - f)P_0}} + \mathbf{g}$$

CONCEPT CONNECTION   EXAMPLE 13-8

Cost of New Common Stock

Suppose Periwinkle Inc. of Example 13-6 had to raise capital beyond that available from retained earnings. What would be its cost of equity from new stock if flotation costs were 12% of money raised?

SOLUTION: Write Equation 13.9 and substitute from Example 13-6, including a 12% flotation cost.

$$\text{cost of new equity} \ = \ k_e = \frac{D_0(1 + g)}{(1 - f)P_0} + g$$

$$= \frac{\$1.65(1.075)}{(.88)\$33.60} + .075$$

$$= .06 \ + \ .075 \ = 13.5\%$$

13.3c   Putting the Weights and Costs Together

Once we've calculated a market value based capital structure and a series of component costs based on market returns, the weighted average calculation for the WACC is a simple matter. The procedure is identical to the one we illustrated in Example 13-1 using the appropriate weights and costs. We'll forgo presenting the same computation here.

A comprehensive example presented after the next section includes the weighted average calculation in its proper sequence.

13.4   The Marginal Cost of Capital (MCC)

The **MCC** is a graph of the WACC showing **abrupt increases** as larger amounts of capital are raised in a planning period.

A firm's WACC is not independent of the amount of capital raised. In fact, it tends to increase abruptly from time to time as funding requirements are increased. Changes in the WACC are reflected in the **marginal cost of capital (MCC) schedule**, which is a graph showing how the WACC changes as a firm raises more capital during a planning period, usually a year. Glance ahead to Figure 13-1 on page 565 to see the idea expressed graphically.

The WACC/MCC terminology is a little confusing. The MCC schedule is a graph showing the values the WACC goes through as larger amounts of money are raised. We could just as easily call it a graph of the WACC. The term "marginal cost of capital" (MCC) itself means the cost of the next dollar of capital to be raised.

Notice that the WACC starts out at one level and jumps to a higher level as the total amount of capital raised passes a certain point. If still more capital were to be raised, the MCC would have more step-function jumps like the one shown. The first jump or break is of particular interest.

13.4a   The Break in MCC When Retained Earnings Run Out

The first increase in the MCC usually occurs when the firm runs out of retained earnings and starts raising external equity by selling stock. The WACC increases at that point because the cost of equity increases. We can see this phenomenon clearly by comparing two of the examples in the last section.

The MCC **breaks** when **retained earnings are exhausted**, and the cost of equity increases due to **flotation** costs.

Example 13-6 and Example 13-8 both involve the cost of equity for Periwinkle Inc. In the first example, we calculated the cost of retained earnings, and in the second, we dealt with the cost of equity from new stock. Notice that the 13.5% cost of new equity is higher than the 12.8% cost of retained earnings. The difference is due to the flotation costs associated with selling the new shares.

We generally assume firms use all the money available from retained earnings before selling new stock, so the cost of equity capital increases abruptly as the firm moves into externally raised money. But if the cost of equity increases at some point, the WACC must also increase at the same point because equity is an element in the weighted average calculation. A numerical illustration will make these ideas clear.

CONCEPT CONNECTION EXAMPLE 13-9

The MCC

Assume the information in Table 13-3 about the Brighton Company, and develop its MCC schedule.

TABLE 13-3

The Brighton Company's Capital Structure, Component Costs, and Capital Requirements

	Capital Structure	Component Cost
Debt	40%	8%
Equity	60%	From RE 10%
		From new stock 12%
Expected retained earnings		$3 million
Total capital requirement		10 million

SOLUTION: Calculate the WACC, first using the cost of retained earnings and then using the cost of new equity. These are the WACCs before and after the retained earnings breakpoint. The two computations are shown in Table 13-4. Notice that the only difference between them is the cost of equity.

TABLE 13-4

The Brighton Company's WACC Calculations

	Capital Structure Weights		Capital Component Cost		
With equity from RE					
Debt	.4	×	8%	=	3.2%
Equity	.6	×	10	=	6.0
				WACC =	9.2%
With equity from new stock					
Debt	.4	×	8%	=	3.2%
Equity	.6	×	12	=	7.2
				WACC =	10.4%

Table 13-4 shows that Brighton's WACC will increase by 1.2% as the firm uses up retained earnings and moves into new equity.

Locating the Break

The next question involves locating the break in terms of total funding. In other words, how much capital will have been raised when the WACC increases?

This turns out to be a simple matter. Recall that we assumed capital will be raised in the proportions of some capital structure. In this case, the structure is 60% equity, so every dollar raised will be 60% equity. We also expect to have $3 million of retained earnings to use up before turning to new stock. Hence, our question is equivalent to asking for the total funding level when 60% of that total is $3 million. In other words, $3 million is 60% of what number?

The calculation answering that question is division by .6. Brighton will have raised a total of

$$\$3 \text{ million}/.60 = \$5 \text{ million}$$

when it runs out of retained earnings. Therefore, the WACC *breaks* at $5 million.

This is an important calculation. The first breakpoint of the WACC/MCC is always found by dividing the amount of retained earnings available by the fractional proportion of equity in the capital structure.

Find the **MCC break** by dividing **available RE** by the **proportion of equity** in the capital structure.

The MCC Schedule

Brighton's results are shown graphically in Figure 13-1. The graph shows the WACC at various funding levels. As we said earlier, the overall portrayal is referred to as the marginal cost of capital (MCC) schedule. Notice how the schedule makes a definitive break at the point where retained earnings are exhausted. Also notice that the break occurs at the level of total capital that has been raised when retained earnings run out ($5 million), not at the level of available retained earnings, $3 million in this case.

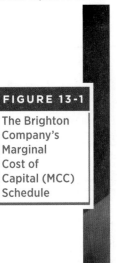

FIGURE 13-1

The Brighton Company's Marginal Cost of Capital (MCC) Schedule

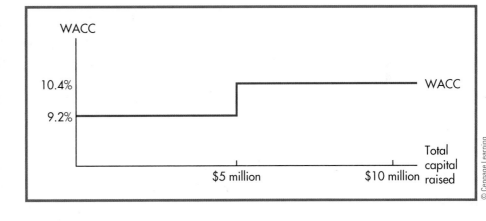

Other Breaks in the MCC Schedule   For most companies, the WACC is reasonably constant, aside from the break into external equity, as long as moderate levels of capital are raised. However, low-cost funds cannot be raised at or near the initial WACC without limit. The internal workings of capital markets tend to put restrictions on the amount of new money available to companies in any time period.

For example, suppose Brighton attempted to raise $20 million instead of $10 million. Perceiving such a large capital program as risky, investors would be likely to demand higher returns for further investments in both debt and equity. That means Brighton would have to pay higher interest rates to borrow more and accept a lower price to sell additional stock. Effectively, the MCC would have more upward steps to the right on the graph between $10 million and $20 million.[4]

Combining the MCC and the IOS   A firm's available capital budgeting projects can be sorted into descending order of IRR and displayed on the same set of axes as the MCC. The idea is shown in Figure 13-2 for the Brighton Company of Example 13-9. Each block represents a project. The heights and widths of the blocks are, respectively, the

---

4. Occasionally the cost of debt or preferred increases *before* the shift from retained earnings to outside equity. Then that point isn't the *first* break in the MCC as we've described.

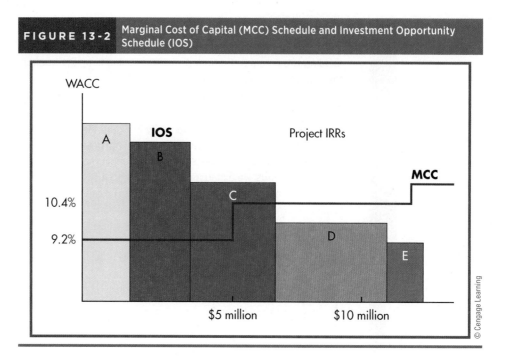

FIGURE 13-2 Marginal Cost of Capital (MCC) Schedule and Investment Opportunity Schedule (IOS)

© Cengage Learning

The **investment opportunity schedule (IOS)** is a plot of the IRRs of available projects arranged in descending order.

projects' IRRs and the amounts of capital they require. The pattern traced by the upper rightward boundary of the projects is known as the **investment opportunity schedule (IOS)**. The horizontal segments of the IOS are the IRRs of the respective projects.

This portrayal makes clear which projects should be undertaken and which should not. Brighton should accept projects as long as the IOS (IRR) is above the MCC. Figure 13-2 shows that projects A, B, and C should be undertaken, but projects D and E should not. Notice that the first break in the MCC makes projects D and E unacceptable. If the WACC continued at 9.2% indefinitely, both of these projects would have IRRs equal to or above the cost of capital. Because the MCC breaks as new equity has to come from the sale of stock, they don't.

The **MCC and IOS plotted together** show which projects should be undertaken.

Interpreting the MCC The portrayal in Figure 13-2 seems to imply that Brighton should evaluate the first $5 million of capital projects with a WACC of 9.2% and projects using the next $5 million with a WACC of 10.4%. However, this approach is cumbersome in that it requires keeping track of more than one WACC. The same effect is achieved by taking a marginal approach and defining the WACC as the rate at which the IOS and the MCC intersect, 10.4% in the illustration.

The firm's WACC for the planning period is at the **intersection** of the **MCC** and the **IOS**.

This is an important point. A firm's WACC for a planning period (usually a year) is determined by the availability of financial resources *and* the pattern of investment opportunities projected during that period.

13.5 The Cost of Capital—A Comprehensive Example

In this section, we'll work through a comprehensive example of the calculations necessary to develop a firm's WACC and the MCC curve. We'll also comment on practice as we go along.

CONCEPT CONNECTION   EXAMPLE 13-10

Cost of Capital Comprehensive Example

Baxter Metalworks Inc. has the following elements of capital.

Debt: Baxter issued $1,000 30-year bonds 10 years ago at a coupon rate of 9%. Five thousand bonds were sold at par. Similar bonds are now selling to yield 12%.

Preferred stock: 20,000 shares of 10% preferred stock were sold 5 years ago at their $100 par value. Similar securities now yield 13%.

Equity: The company was originally financed with the sale of 1 million shares of common stock at $10 a share. Accumulated retained earnings are currently $3 million. The stock is now selling at $12.50.

Target capital structure: We won't get into the reasoning behind the idea that one mix of capital components might be better than another until Chapter 14. For now, assume that Baxter has chosen the following target capital structure.

Debt	20%
Preferred stock	10
Equity	70
	100%

This means management attempts to keep the market values of the capital components reasonably close to these proportions over time as money is raised.

Other information:

- Baxter's marginal income tax rate including federal and state rates is 40%.
- Flotation costs average 10% in the sale of common and preferred stock.
- Short-term Treasury bills currently yield 7%.
- An average stock currently yields 13.5%.
- Baxter's beta is 1.4.
- The firm is expected to grow at 6.5% indefinitely.
- The annual dividend paid last year was $1.10 per share.
- Next year's business plan includes earnings of $3 million, of which $1.4 million will be retained.

Calculate Baxter's capital structure, capital component weights, and its WACC before and after the retained earnings break. Sketch the firm's MCC.

SOLUTION: We'll solve this problem and illustrate some important points along the way with the following steps.

1. Book values and weights (for reference only).
2. Market values and weights.
3. Compare target, book, and market weights, and comment on practice.
4. Capital component costs.
5. Computation of WACCs.
6. Sketch MCC.

1. Book Values and Weights of Baxter's Capital Components

First we'll recreate the capital section of Baxter's balance sheet.

Debt (5,000 bonds @ $1,000).		$ 5,000,000
Preferred stock (20,000 shares @ $100).		2,000,000
Equity		
Common stock (1 million shares @ $10).	$10,000,000	
Retained earnings	3,000,000	13,000,000
Total capital.		$20,000,000

Now calculate the book weights by stating debt, preferred equity, and common equity as percentages of total capital. This calculation is made for reference only, because we don't use book values to calculate WACC.

Debt	$ 5,000,000	25%
Preferred	2,000,000	10
Equity	13,000,000	65
	$20,000,000	100%

2. Market Values and Weights

To calculate capital component weights based on market values, we have to find the current market value of the securities underlying each component.

Debt: The market value of Baxter's debt is based on the current price of its outstanding bonds. That price is different from face value, because the market interest rate is no longer equal to the bond's coupon rate. The calculation is made using the bond formula developed in Chapter 7, Equation 7.4. In this case k = 6%, n = 40, PMT = $45, and FV = $1,000. Review pages 295–296 if this procedure is unfamiliar to you.

$$
\begin{aligned}
P_p &= PMT[PVFA_{k,n}] + FV[PVF_{k,n}] \\
&= \$45[PVFA_{6,40}] + \$1,000[PVF_{6,40}] \\
&= \$45(15.0463) + \$1,000(.0972) \\
&= \$774.28
\end{aligned}
$$

Because 5,000 bonds are outstanding, the market value of the debt is

$$\$774.28 \times 5,000 = \$3,871,400$$

Preferred stock: The preferred shares were issued to yield 10% at a $100 par value. Therefore, the preferred dividend is $10. The market yield is now 13%, so each preferred share is valued as follows (see Chapter 8, Equation 8.13, page 372).

$$P_p = \frac{D_p}{k} = \frac{\$10}{.13} = \$76.92$$

For the 20,000 preferred shares outstanding, their total market value is

$$\$76.92 \times 20,000 = \$1,538,400$$

Common equity: The market value of Baxter's common stock is easy to calculate. The shares are selling at $12.50 and there are 1 million outstanding, so their value is

$$\$12.50 \times 1,000,000 = \$12,500,000$$

Market value based weights: Next we summarize and compute the capital component weights based on market values.

Debt	$ 3,871,400	21.6%
Preferred	1,538,400	8.6
Equity	12,500,000	69.8
	$17,909,800	100.0%

As you can see, calculating market value weights is somewhat tedious. This is especially true if a number of different classifications of stocks and bonds are all outstanding at the same time.

3. Book, Market, and Target Capital Structures

At this point, it's appropriate to stop and compare the alternative capital structures we've talked about. These are the target structure and structures based on book and market values. The results are summarized as follows.

	Book	Market	Target
Debt	25%	21.6%	20%
Preferred stock	10	8.6	10
Common equity	65	69.8	70
	100%	100.0%	100%

Notice that in this example, the weights aren't very different from one another. Of course, that's not always the case, but it does happen quite a bit. It's especially true that the market value based weights and the target structure are quite similar.

In the rest of this example, we'll use the market value weights, noticing that they're very close to the target structure.

4. Capital Component Costs

Next we'll calculate the cost of each capital component using the rules developed earlier.

Debt: The cost of debt is given by Equation 13.1. It's equal to the return being received by debt investors adjusted for taxes.

$$\text{cost of debt} = k_d(1 - T)$$
$$= 12\%(1 - .40)$$
$$= 7.2\%$$

Preferred stock: Equation 13.4 gives us the cost of preferred either through consideration of the preferred dividend relative to its market price or by directly adjusting the market yield for flotation costs. Because we're given a market yield of 13% in this case, we'll do the latter.

$$\text{cost of preferred stock} = \frac{k_p}{(1 - f)} = \frac{13\%}{(1 - .10)} = 14.4\%$$

Equity: We'll deal with the cost of equity in two steps. First we'll estimate the cost of retained earnings, and then the cost of new stock.

Retained earnings: We'll approach the cost of retained earnings in the three ways we've considered and then reconcile the results.

CAPM: Equation 13.5 gives the return required on Baxter's stock by a typical investor in terms of the risk-free rate, the market return, and Baxter's beta.

$$\text{cost of RE} = k_B = k_{RF} + (k_M - k_{RF})b_B$$
$$= 7.0\% + (13.5\% - 7.0\%)1.4$$
$$= 16.1\%$$

Dividend growth: Equation 13.7 gives the expected return on Baxter's stock given its current price, recent dividend history, and anticipated growth rate.

$$\text{cost of RE} = k_e = \frac{D_0(1 + g)}{P_0} + g$$
$$= \frac{\$1.10(1.065)}{\$12.50} + .065$$
$$= .094 + .065$$
$$= 15.9\%$$

Risk premium: The risk premium approach adds a premium of 3% to 5% to the return on a firm's debt to allow for the extra risk involved in an equity investment. Using Equation 13.8 and a middle value of 4% for the additional premium, we have

$$\text{cost of RE} = k_e = k_d + rp_e$$
$$= 12\% + 4\%$$
$$= 16\%$$

Some **judgment** is required in **reconciling** the results of the different approaches to the **cost of equity**.

Reconciliation: In this case the three approaches give similar results, which are summarized as follows.

CAPM	16.1%
Dividend growth	15.9
Risk premium	16.0

Hence, using 16.0% for the cost of retained earnings seems reasonable. When the estimates vary considerably, some judgment is required to select an appropriate rate.

New stock: The return on equity raised through the sale of new stock is estimated using the dividend growth model adjusted for flotation costs. Equation 13.9 yields

$$\text{cost of new equity} = k_e = \frac{D_0(1 + g)}{(1 - f)P_0} + g$$
$$= \frac{\$1.10(1.065)}{(.90)\$12.50} + .065$$
$$= .104 + .065$$
$$= 16.9\%$$

Notice that the cost of newly sold stock is .9% higher than the cost of retained earnings.

A note on accuracy: As we've said before, it's important to realize that return/cost calculations with respect to equity are not as accurate as our tenth of a percent figures seem to imply. An estimate that's good to about half of a percent is generally the best we can hope for.

5. Computation of the WACCs

Deriving the WACC is now a straightforward weighted average calculation. We'll use weights based on market values. The calculation has to be done twice because of the two different costs of equity for retained earnings and new stock. The results will be the WACCs before and after the retained earnings breakpoint.

The computation is laid out in the following table. The entries in the weight column are the decimal equivalents of the percentages of each component in the capital structure based on market values. Treat the pre-break and after-break pairs of columns separately. Multiply the cost of each component by the number in the weight column to get the factor column. Then add the factors for the WACC. We use results rounded to the nearest tenth of a percent in applications.

Capital Component	Weight	Pre-Break		After-Break	
		Cost	*Factor*	*Cost*	*Factor*
Debt	.216	7.2%	1.56	7.2%	1.56
Preferred stock	.086	14.4	1.24	14.4	1.24
Equity	.698	16.0	11.17	16.9	11.80
	1.000	WACC =	13.97%	WACC =	14.60%
		Use rounded values: 14.0%			14.6%

6. The MCC

The MCC schedule shows the WACC before and after the retained earnings breakpoint. To plot it we have to know how much capital will have been raised when the break occurs.

Baxter expects to generate $1.4 million in retained earnings next year, and every dollar raised is assumed to be 69.8% equity—either retained earnings or new stock. To locate the break-point we have to answer the following question: $1.4 million is 69.8% of what total capital amount? To get the answer, simply divide $1.4 million by .698, the fractional component of equity in the capital structure.

The calculation is

$$\$1,400,000/.698 = \$2,005,731$$

For practical purposes, we'll round this result and assume the retained earnings breakpoint is $2 million. The plot of Baxter's MCC can then be drawn as follows.

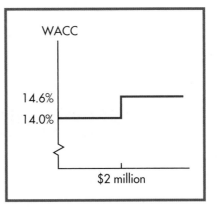

At some point to the right, the MCC would step upward again as Baxter approaches the limits of its money-raising capability and the various capital components become more expensive. However, we can't predict exactly where those steps will be the way we can forecast the breakpoint due to running out of retained earnings.

13.6 A Potential Mistake—Handling Separately Funded Projects

Sometimes a project is proposed that is to be funded entirely by a single source of capital. This situation can create some confusion about the application of the WACC in practice.

For example, a firm might float a bond issue and use the proceeds entirely to fund just one project. It's logical to ask whether the cost of capital used to evaluate the project should be the cost of the bond issue and not the firm's WACC. Because debt tends to be the cheapest form of capital, such an approach would make the project more likely to be accepted.

Although it seems that a close matching of a source of funds with its use would be appropriate whenever possible, it's a mistake in capital budgeting which has to be conducted within the context of the firm's overall capital-raising capability. Firms cannot continue to raise low-cost debt indefinitely without from time to time raising higher cost equity. In other words, firms have a limited debt capacity that can be used up until a further infusion of equity is made.

Let's consider an illustration in which the firm is borrowing exclusively to fund a project to see what can happen if we base the accept/reject decision on the cost of debt alone. For simplicity, we'll assume the firm has no preferred stock. Imagine that its cost of debt and cost of equity are 8% and 12%, respectively, and that the capital structure is half debt and half equity, so the WACC is 10%. Suppose the project proposed has an IRR of 9%, is evaluated against the 8% cost of debt, and is therefore accepted. Notice that it would have been rejected if evaluated against the WACC of 10%.

> **All projects** should be evaluated against the **WACC including** those with **dedicated funding**.

Now suppose that sometime later another project comes along with an IRR of 11%, and the firm tries to borrow to fund it. However, lenders say the company's debt capacity is exhausted and refuse to advance funds.

Suppose equity money is available to fund the project, but its cost is 12%. Using the same rationale of measuring a project against the cost of the specific capital component funding it, the firm evaluates the second project against the 12% cost of equity and rejects it.

Notice what has happened. The company has accepted a project with an IRR of 9% and rejected one with an IRR of 11%. This obvious error is a result of trying to match funding sources and uses within the constraint of one firm's capital-raising capability. Had the firm evaluated both projects at the WACC of 10%, the correct accept/reject decisions would have been made. The implication is clearly that *all* projects (which are risk consistent with the firm's operations) should be evaluated at the WACC.

INSIGHTS | **Practical Finance**

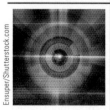

Ensuper/Shutterstock.com

Revisiting EVA

Recall that at the end of our study of ratio analysis in Chapter 3 (pages 103–104) we introduced two new performance measurement concepts, market value added (MVA) and economic value added (EVA®). We're now in a better position to appreciate EVA.

EVA is important because of a shortcoming in the concept of net income, the traditional measure of financial performance. Net income begins with revenue and subtracts costs and expenses *including interest* to arrive at the so-called "bottom line." Hence, the traditional income statement charges operations with the cost of debt, but *ignores the cost of equity and preferred stock.* That means net income implicitly treats equity and preferred as free resources which, of course, they aren't. EVA corrects that problem by charging for the use of all capital instead of just debt. The charge is calculated by multiplying total capital by the *cost of capital* as developed in this chapter. The EVA calculation is expressed as follows where equity includes preferred stock.

$$EVA = EBIT(1 - T) - (dept + equity)(cost\ of\ capital\ \%)$$

$EBIT(1 - T)$ is operating income *after tax,* which is then reduced by the charge for all capital used.

EVA is a very important concept in management today. It's worth your while to review the broad implications of the idea now that you have a better understanding of the cost of capital.

SOURCE: sternstewart.com

CONCEPT CONNECTIONS

QUESTIONS

1. Compare the cost of capital concept with the idea of the required return on a stock investment made by an individual. Relate both ideas to the risk of the investment. How would a very risky investment/project be handled in the capital budgeting/cost of capital context?

2. Define the idea of capital structure and capital components. Why is capital structure important to the cost of capital concept? In many capital structure discussions, preferred stock is lumped in with either debt or common equity. With respect to the cost of capital, however, it's treated separately. Why?

3. You are a new financial analyst working for a company that's more than 100 years old. The CFO has asked you and a young member of the accounting staff to work together in reviewing the firm's capital structure for the purpose of recalculating its cost of capital. As you both leave the CFO's office, your accounting colleague says this job is really going to be easy because he already has the information. In preparing the latest

annual report, he worked on the capital section of the balance sheet and has the values of debt, preferred stock, and equity at his fingertips. He says the two of you can summarize these into a report in five minutes and then go out for a beer. How do you react and why? Is the fact that the firm is quite old relevant? Why?

4. The investor's return and the company's cost are opposite sides of the same coin—almost, but not quite. Explain.

5. There's an issue of historical versus market value with respect to both the cost of capital components and the amounts of those components used in developing weights. We're willing to accept an approximation for the weights, but not for the cost/returns. Why?

6. A number of investment projects are under consideration at your company. You've calculated the cost of capital based on market values and rates, and analyzed the projects using IRR and NPV. Several projects are marginally acceptable. While watching the news last night, you learned that most economists predict a rise in interest rates over the next year. Should you modify your analysis in light of this information? Why?

7. Establishing the cost of equity is the most arbitrary and difficult part of developing a firm's cost of capital. Outline the reasons behind this problem and the approaches available to make the best of it.

8. Retained earnings are generated by the firm's internal operations and are immediately reinvested to earn more money for the company and its shareholders. Therefore, such funds have zero cost to the company. Is this statement true or false? Explain.

9. Define the marginal cost of capital (MCC) and explain in words why it predictably undergoes a step-function increase (breaks) as more capital is raised during a budget period.

10. After the break in the MCC caused by using up retained earnings, the schedule can be expected to remain flat indefinitely. Is that statement right or wrong? If wrong, explain what can be expected to happen to the MCC and why.

11. Why is it appropriate to define the WACC as the highest step on the MCC under the IOS? Is anything lost by using this definition?

BUSINESS ANALYSIS

1. You're the newly hired CFO of a small construction company. The privately held firm is capitalized with $2 million in owner's equity and $3 million in variable rate bank loans. The construction business is quite risky, so returns of 20% to 25% are normally demanded on equity investments. The bank is currently charging 14% on the firm's loans, but interest rates are expected to rise in the near future. Your boss, the owner, started his career as a carpenter and has an excellent grasp of day-to-day operations. However, he knows little about finance. Business has been good lately, and several expansion projects are under consideration. A cash flow projection has been made for each. You're satisfied that these estimates are reasonable.

The owner has called you in and confessed to being confused about the projects. He instinctively feels that some are financially marginal and may not be beneficial to the company, but he doesn't know how to demonstrate this or how to choose among the projects that are financially viable.

Assuming the owner understands the concept of return on investment, write a brief memo explaining the ideas of IRR and cost of capital and how they can solve his problem. Don't get into the detailed mechanics of the calculations, but do use the figures given above to

make a rough estimate of the company's cost of capital and use the result in your memo.

2. You're the CFO of a small company that is considering a new venture. The president and several other members of management are very excited about the idea for reasons related to engineering and marketing rather than profitability. You've analyzed the proposal using capital budgeting techniques and found that it fails both IRR and NPV tests with a cost of capital based on market returns. The problem is that interest rates have risen steeply in the last year, so the cost of capital seems unusually high.

You've presented your results to the management team, who are very disappointed. In fact, they'd like to find a way to discredit your analysis so they can justify going ahead with the project. You've explained your analysis and everything seems well understood except for one point. The group insists that the use of returns currently available to investors as a basis for the cost of capital components doesn't make sense. The vice president of marketing put his objection as follows. "Two years ago we borrowed $1 million at 10%. We haven't paid it back, and we're still making interest payments of $100,000 every year. Clearly, our cost of debt is 10%

and not the 14% you want to use. If you'd use our 'real' cost of debt, as well as of equity and preferred stock, the project would easily qualify financially." How do you respond?

(The appropriate response is relatively short. It's worth noting that this kind of thing happens all the time in corporations. Marketing and engineering people often get carried away with "neat" projects that don't make sense financially. The CFO has to watch the bottom line and it's not unusual to be seen as a "wet blanket" who wants to spoil the others' fun!)

3. The engineering department at Digitech Inc. wants to buy a new state-of-the-art computer. The proposed machine is faster than the one now being used, but whether the extra speed is worth the expense is questionable given the nature of the firm's applications. The chief engineer (who has an MBA and a reasonable understanding of financial principles) has put together an enormously detailed capital budgeting proposal for the acquisition of the new machine, which concludes that it's a great deal. You're a financial analyst for the firm and have been assigned to review the engineering proposal. Your review has highlighted two problems. First, the cost savings projected as a result of using the new machine seem rather optimistic. Second, the analysis uses an unrealistically low cost of capital.

With respect to the second point, the engineering proposal contains the following exhibit documenting the development of the cost of capital used.

> **Digitech's capital structure is 60% debt and 40% equity**
>
> **The computer manufacturer is offering financing at 8% as a sales incentive**
>
> Cost of capital = 8% × .6 = 4.8%
> After tax = 4.8% × (1 − T)
> = 4.8% × .6 = 2.9%

You've checked the market and found that Digitech's bonds are currently selling to yield 14%, and the stock is returning about 20%.

How would you proceed? That is, explain the chief engineer's error(s) and indicate the correct calculations.

4. Whitefish Inc. operates a fleet of 15 fishing boats in the North Atlantic Ocean. Fishing has been good in the last few years as has the market for product, so the firm can sell all the fish it can catch. Charlie Bass, the vice president for operations, has worked up a capital budgeting proposal for the acquisition of new boats. Each boat is viewed as an individual project identical to the others, and shows an IRR of 22%. The firm's cost of capital has been correctly calculated at 14% before the retained earnings break and 15% after that point. Charlie argues that the capital budgeting figures show that the firm should acquire as many new boats as it possibly can, financing them with whatever means it finds available. You are Whitefish's CFO. Support or criticize Charlie's position. How should the appropriate number of new boats be determined? Does acquiring a large number of new boats present any problems or risks that aren't immediately apparent from the financial figures?

PROBLEMS

WACC Calculations: Concept Connection Example 13-1 (page 552)

1. Blazingame Inc.'s capital components have the following market values:

Debt	$35,180,000
Preferred stock	17,500,000
Common equity	48,350,000

Calculate the firm's capital structure and show the weights that would be used for a weighted average cost of capital (WACC) computation.

2. The Aztec Corporation has the following capital components and costs. Calculate Aztec's WACC.

Component	Value	Cost
Debt	$23,625	12.0%
Preferred stock	4,350	13.5
Common equity	52,275	19.2

3. Willerton Industries Inc. has the following balances in its capital accounts as of 12/31/X3:

Long-term debt	$65,000,000
Preferred stock	15,000,000
Common stock	40,000,000
Paid in excess	15,000,000
Retained earnings	37,500,000

Calculate Willerton's capital structure based on book values.

Market Value Based Capital Structure: Concept Connection Example 13-2 (page 555)

4. Referring to Willerton Industries of the previous problem, the company's long-term debt is comprised of 20-year $1,000 face value bonds issued 7 years ago at an 8% coupon rate. The bonds are now selling to yield 6%. Willerton's preferred is from a single issue of $100 par value, 9% preferred stock that is now selling to yield 8%. Willerton has 4 million shares of common stock outstanding at a current market price of $31. Calculate Willerton's market value based capital structure.

5. Again referring to Willerton of the two previous problems, assume the firm's cost of retained earnings is 11% and its marginal tax rate is 40%. Calculate its WACC using its book value based capital structure ignoring flotation costs. Make the same calculation using the market value based capital structure. How significant is the difference?

6. A relatively young firm has capital components valued at book and market and market component costs as follows. No new securities have been issued since the firm was originally capitalized.

	Value		
Component	Market	Book	Cost
Debt	$42,830	$40,000	8.5%
Preferred stock	10,650	10,000	10.6
Common equity	65,740	32,000	25.3

a. Calculate the firm's capital structures and WACCs based on both book and market values, and compare the two.

b. What appears to have happened to interest rates since the company was started?

c. Does the firm seem to be successful? Why?

d. What would be the implication of using a WACC based on book as opposed to market values? In other words, what kind of mistakes might management make by using the book values?

7. Five years ago Hemingway Inc. issued 6,000 30-year bonds with par values of $1,000 at a coupon rate of 8%. The bonds are now selling to yield 5%. The company also has 15,000 shares of preferred stock outstanding that pay a dividend of $6.50 per share. These are currently selling to yield 10%. Its common stock is selling at $21, and 200,000 shares are outstanding. Calculate Hemingway's market value based capital structure.

8. The Wall Company has 142,500 shares of common stock outstanding that are currently selling at $28.63. It has 4,530 bonds outstanding that won't mature for 20 years. They were issued at a par value of $1,000 paying a coupon rate of 6%. Comparable bonds now yield 9%. Wall's $100 par value preferred stock was issued at 8% and is now yielding 11%; 7,500 shares are outstanding. Develop Wall's market value based capital structure.

9. The market price of Albertson Ltd.'s common stock is $5.50, and 100,000 shares are outstanding. The firm's books show common equity accounts totaling $400,000. There are 5,000 preferred shares outstanding that originally sold for their par value of $50, pay an annual dividend of $3, and are currently selling to yield an 8% return. Also, 200 bonds are outstanding that were issued 5 years ago at their $1,000 face values for 30-year terms, pay a coupon rate of 7%, and are currently

selling to yield 10%. Develop Albertson's capital structure based on both book and market values. Are they significantly different? If so comment on the implications.

Cost of Debt: Concept Connection Example 13-3 (page 557)

10. Asbury Corp. issued 30-year bonds 11 years ago with a coupon rate of 9.5%. Those bonds are now selling to yield 7%. The firm also issued some 20-year bonds 2 years ago with an 8% coupon rate. The two bond issues are rated equally by Standard and Poors and Moody's. Asbury's marginal tax rate is 38%.
    a. What is Asbury's after-tax cost of debt?
    b. What is the current selling price of the 20-year bonds?

11. The Dentite Corporation's bonds are currently selling to yield new buyers a 12% return on their investment. Dentite's marginal tax rate including both federal and state taxes is 38%. What is the firm's after-tax cost of debt?

12. Kleig Inc.'s bonds are selling to yield 9%. The firm plans to sell new bonds to the general public and will therefore incur flotation costs of 6%. The company's marginal tax rate is 42%.
    a. What is Kleig's cost of debt with respect to the new bonds? (*Hint:* Adjust the cost of debt formula to include flotation costs.)
    b. Suppose Kleig also borrows directly from a bank at 12%.
        1. What is its cost of debt with respect to such bank loans? (*Hint:* Would bank loans be subject to flotation costs?)
        2. If total borrowing is 60% through bonds and 40% from the bank, what is Kleig's overall cost of debt? (*Hint:* Think weighted average.)

Cost of Preferred Stock: Concept Connection Example 13-4 (page 558)

13. Harris Inc.'s preferred stock was issued five years ago to yield 9%. Investors buying those shares on the secondary market today are getting a 14% return. Harris generally pays flotation costs of 12% on new securities issues. What is Harris's cost of preferred financing?

14. Fuller, Inc., issued $100, 8% preferred stock five years ago. The shares are currently selling for $84.50. Assuming Fuller has to pay flotation costs of 10%, what is Fuller's cost of preferred stock?

15. A few years ago, Hendersen Corp. issued preferred stock paying 8% of its par value of $50. The issue is currently selling for $38. Preferred stock flotation costs are 15% of the proceeds of the sale. What is Hendersen's cost of preferred stock?

16. New buyers of Simmonds Inc. stock expect a return of about 22%. The firm pays flotation costs of 9% when it issues new securities. What is Simmonds' cost of equity (*Hint:* This problem is very simple since we don't have to estimate the investors' return. See page 551.)
    a. from retained earnings?
    b. from new stock?

Cost of Retained Earnings—Constant Growth (Gordon) Model: Concept Connection Example 13-6 (page 561)

17. Klints Inc. paid an annual dividend of $1.45 last year. The firm's stock sells for $29.50 per share, and the company is expected to grow at about 4% per year into the foreseeable future. Estimate Klints' cost of retained earnings.

Cost of Retained Earnings and New Common Stock: Concept Connection Examples 13-6 and 13-8 (pages 561 and 562)

18. The Pepperpot Company's stock is selling for $52. Its last dividend was $4.50, and the firm is expected to grow at 7% indefinitely. Flotation costs associated with the sale of common stock are 10% of the proceeds raised. Estimate Pepperpot's cost of equity from retained earnings and from the sale of new stock.

Cost of Retained Earnings—SML: Concept Connection Example 13-5 (page 560)

19. The Longlife Insurance Company has a beta of .8. The average stock currently returns 15% and short-term Treasury bills are offering 6%. Estimate Longlife's cost of retained earnings.

Cost of Retained Earnings—Risk Premium: Concept Connection Example 13-7 (page 562)

20. The Longlife Insurance Company of the preceding problem has several bonds outstanding that are currently selling to yield 9%. What does this imply about the cost of the firm's equity?

21. Hammell Industries has been using 10% as its cost of retained earnings for a number of years. Management has decided to revisit this decision based on recent changes in financial markets. An average stock is currently earning 8%, treasury bills yield 3.5%, and shares of Hammell's stock are selling for $29.44. The firm just paid a dividend of $1.50, and anticipates growing at 5% for the foreseeable future. Hammell's CFO recently asked an investment banker about issuing bonds and was told the market was demanding a 6.5% coupon rate on similar issues. Hammell stock has a beta of 1.4. Recommend a cost of retained earnings for Hammell.

22. Suppose Hammell of the previous problem needs to issue new stock to raise additional equity capital. What is its cost of new equity if flotation costs are 12%?

The MCC: Concept Connection Example 13-9 (page 564)

23. Whitley Motors Inc. has the following capital.

   Debt: The firm issued 900 25-year bonds 5 years ago which were sold at a par value of $1,000. The bonds carry a coupon rate of 7%, but are currently selling to yield new buyers 10%.

   Preferred stock: 3,500 shares of 8% preferred were sold 12 years ago at a par value of $50. They're now priced to yield 11%.

   Equity: The firm got started with the sale of 10,000 shares of common stock at $100 per share. Since that time earnings of $800,000 have been retained. The stock is now selling for $89. Whitley's business plan for next year projects net income of $300,000, half of which will be retained.

   The firm's marginal tax rate is 38% including federal and state obligations. It pays flotation costs of 8% on all new stock issues. Whitley is expected to grow at a rate of 3.5% indefinitely and recently paid an annual dividend of $4.

   Develop Whitley's WACC before and after the retained earnings break and indicate how much capital will have been raised when the break occurs.

24. The Longenes Company uses a target capital structure when calculating the cost of capital. The target structure and current component costs based on market conditions follow:

Component	Mix	Cost*
Debt	25%	8%
Preferred stock	10	12
Common equity	65	20

*The costs of debt and preferred stock are already adjusted for taxes and/or flotation costs. The cost of equity is unadjusted.

The firm expects to earn $20 million next year and plans to invest $18 million in new capital projects. It generally pays dividends equal to 60% of earnings. Flotation costs are 10% for common and preferred stock.

a. What is Longenes's initial WACC?

b. Where is the retained earnings breakpoint in the MCC? (Round to the nearest $.1 million.)

c. What is the new WACC after the break? (Adjust the entire cost of equity for flotation costs.)

d. Longenes can borrow up to $4 million at a net cost of 8% as shown. After that the net cost of debt rises to 12%. What is the new WACC after the increase in the cost of debt? (See "Other Breaks in the MCC Schedule," page 565.)

e. Where is the second break in the MCC? That is, how much total capital has been raised when the second increase in WACC occurs?

f. Sketch Longenes's MCC.

Cost of Capital Comprehensive Example: Concept Connection Example 13-10 (page 567) and Combining the MCC and the IOS (page 565)

25. Taunton Construction Inc.'s capital situation is described as follows:

Debt: The firm issued 10,000 25-year bonds 10 years ago at their par value of $1,000. The bonds carry a coupon rate of 14% and are now selling to yield 10%.

Preferred stock: 30,000 shares of preferred stock were sold 6 years ago at a par value of $50. The shares pay a dividend of $6 per year. Similar preferred issues are now yielding 9%.

Equity: Taunton was initially financed by selling 2 million shares of common stock at $12. Accumulated retained earnings are now $5 million. The stock is currently selling at $13.25.

Taunton's *target capital structure* is as follows:

Debt	30%
Preferred stock	5
Common equity	65
	100%

Other information:

- Taunton's marginal tax rate (state and federal) is 40%.
- Flotation costs average 12% for common and preferred stock.
- Short-term Treasury bills currently yield 7.5%.
- The market is returning 12.5%.
- Taunton's beta is 1.2.
- The firm is expected to grow at 6% indefinitely.
- The last annual dividend paid was $1.00 per share.
- Taunton expects to earn $5 million next year.
- The firm can borrow an additional $2 million at rates similar to the market return on its old debt. Beyond that, lenders are expected to demand returns in the neighborhood of 14%.
- Taunton has the following capital budgeting projects under consideration in the coming year. These represent its investment opportunity schedule (IOS).

Project	IRR	Capital Required	Cumulative Capital Required
A	15%	$3 million	$3 million
B	14	2 million	5 million
C	13	2 million	7 million
D	12	2 million	9 million
E	11	2 million	11 million

a. Calculate the firm's capital structure based on book and market values, and compare with the target capital structure. Is the target structure a reasonable approximation of the market value based structure? Is the book structure very far off?

b. Calculate the cost of debt based on the market return on the company's existing bonds.

c. Calculate the cost of preferred stock based on the market return on the company's existing preferred stock.

d. Calculate the cost of retained earnings using three approaches: CAPM, dividend growth, and risk premium. Reconcile the results into a single estimate.

e. Estimate the cost of equity raised through the sale of new stock using the dividend growth approach.

f. Calculate the WACC by using equity from retained earnings based on your component cost estimates and the target capital structure.

g. Where is the first breakpoint in the MCC (the point where retained earnings run out)? Calculate to the nearest $.1 million.

h. Calculate the WACC after the first breakpoint.

i. Where is the second breakpoint in the MCC (the point at which the cost of debt increases)? Why does this second break exist? Calculate to the nearest $.1 million.

j. Calculate the WACC after the second break.

k. Plot Taunton's MCC.

l. Plot Taunton's IOS on the same axes as the MCC. Which projects should be accepted, and which should be rejected? Do any of those rejected have IRRs above the initial WACC? If so, explain in words why they're being rejected.

m. What is *the* WACC for the planning period?

n. Suppose project E is self-funding in that it comes with a source of its own debt financing. A loan is offered through an equipment manufacturer at 9%. The cost of the loan is

$$9\% \times (1 - T) = 5.4\%$$

Should project E be accepted under such conditions?

26. Newrock Manufacturing Inc. has the following target capital structure:

Debt	25%
Preferred	20
Equity	55

Investment bankers have advised the CFO that the company could raise up to $5 million in new debt financing by issuing bonds at a 6.0% coupon rate; beyond that amount, new debt would require a 7.0% coupon. Newrock's 8.5% preferred stock, issued at a par value of $100, currently sells for $112.50. There are 3 million shares of common stock outstanding on which the firm paid an annual dividend of $2.00 recently. The stock currently trades at $36.00 per share. Next year's net income is projected at $14 million, and management expects 6% growth in the foreseeable future. Flotation costs are 6% on debt and 11% on common and preferred stock. The marginal tax rate is 40%.

a. Calculate the WACC using the target capital structure and the cost of retained earnings for the equity component.

b. Plot Newrock's MCC, identifying the levels of funding at which the first two breaks occur, and calculate the WACCs after each break.

c. Newrock has identified the following capital projects for next year:

Project	Investment	IRR
A	$4.0 million	11.0%
B	3.6 million	10.5
C	8.6 million	13.2
D	2.0 million	8.7
E	5.5 million	9.5
F	5.0 million	7.2
G	4.1 million	10.5
H	6.4 million	8.0

Projects A and B are mutually exclusive, as are Projects C and H. Plot the IOS and the MCC and determine the ideal size of next year's capital program.

PART

4

Long-Term Financing Issues

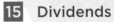

14 CHAPTER

Capital Structure and Leverage

Chapter Outline

Background
- The Central Issue
- Risk in the Context of Leverage
- Leverage and Risk—Two Kinds of Each
- Our Approach to Leverage

Financial Leverage
- The Effect of Financial Leverage
- Financial Leverage and Financial Risk
- Putting the Ideas Together—The Effect on Stock Price
- The Degree of Financial Leverage (DFL)—A Measurement
- EBIT–EPS Analysis

Operating Leverage
- Terminology and Definitions
- Breakeven Analysis
- Breakeven Diagrams
- The Effect of Operating Leverage
- The Degree of Operating Leverage (DOL)—A Measurement
- Comparing Operating and Financial Leverage
- The Compounding Effect of Operating and Financial Leverage

Capital Structure Theory
- Background—The Value of the Firm
- The Early Theory by Modigliani and Miller
- Relaxing the Assumptions—More Insights
- An Insight into Mergers and Acquisitions

We introduced the idea of capital structure in Chapter 13 as a necessary underpinning to the cost of capital concept. In this chapter, we'll discover there's a great deal more to capital structure than calculating the WACC. In fact, its management is one of the most important things financial executives do.

Used properly, capital structure management can be an effective approach to improving financial performance. It can turn good results into better ones, and can even raise the price of a company's stock.

However, the technique has to be used with caution because its benefits come at a price. The cost of improving performance with capital structure can be increased risk. And risk, as we've already learned, is a serious problem. In this chapter, we'll learn all about the benefits and the costs of managing results through capital structure.

14.1   Background

In Chapter 13, we said capital structure describes the mix of debt, preferred stock, and equity a firm employs. In this chapter, we'll simplify that definition by assuming preferred stock is essentially a form of debt.[1] Hence, from here on when we refer to capital structure, we'll mean the mix of just two components, debt and equity, within capital.

"Leverage" is a general term that refers to an ability to multiply the effect of some effort. The term comes from physics where a lever is used to multiply force. **Financial leverage** refers to using borrowed money to multiply the effectiveness of the equity invested in a business enterprise.

The borrowed money with which financial leverage is concerned is the debt in a company's capital structure. Hence, the terms "financial leverage" and "capital structure" are somewhat synonymous. To be leveraged means to have debt. To be unleveraged means to operate with only equity capital.

The idea is quantified by the percentage of debt within total capital (debt + equity). Thus, 10% financial leverage implies a capital structure that's 10% debt and 90% equity.

> **Financial leverage** refers to debt in the capital structure. It **multiplies** the **effectiveness** of equity but adds risk.

14.1a   The Central Issue

The study of capital structure revolves around a central question: Can the use of debt (leverage) increase the value of a firm's equity? Stated slightly differently: Can it increase stock price?

We need to be sure we understand exactly what this question means. To illustrate, think about a firm with $1 million in equity capital and no debt. Then suppose it borrows $.25 million, buys up a quarter of its own stock, and retires the shares. In effect it has traded a quarter of its equity for debt. The procedure is called a **capital restructuring**.

Intuitively, the process shouldn't affect the price of the shares still outstanding. Three quarters of the original shares now represent three quarters of the former equity, so nothing should have changed on a per-share basis.

> **Capital restructuring** involves changing leverage by **shifting the mix** of debt and equity.

But in fact, adding financial leverage in the manner we've just described often increases the price of the remaining shares and the value of the firm. However, the effect isn't consistent, and there are circumstances under which adding leverage decreases stock price and a firm's value.

In other words, there's a relationship between capital structure and stock price, but it's neither precise nor totally understood. Study in the field attempts to explain the

> Under certain conditions, **changing leverage** increases stock price. An **optimal capital structure** maximizes stock price.

---

1. This assumption is based on the fact that preferred stock dividends are fixed in amount, and in that respect are more like interest payments than like common stock dividends. You can think of debt and preferred stock as offering investors returns that are more or less constant regardless of how the company is doing financially. Equity, on the other hand, offers a return that tends to vary with the business's performance.

nature of the relationship and predict when additional financial leverage will increase or decrease price and value.

In particular, we want to discover whether there's an *optimal capital structure* that maximizes stock price, all other things held constant.

After covering a little more background, we'll look at an example to see just how leverage works.

14.1b   Risk in the Context of Leverage

In earlier chapters, we learned that risk and return are related and have a great deal to do with determining stock prices. Here again, we'll find that risk plays an important role in setting values. In fact, leverage influences stock price because it alters the risk/return relationship in an equity investment. We'll understand that better as we go along.

Measures of Performance   We'll often refer to EBIT, ROE, and EPS in this chapter, so it's worthwhile to review their meaning.

EBIT, earnings before interest and taxes, is also called "operating income." It's the lowest line on the income statement that's independent of financing. In other words, because EBIT is above interest expense, it is unaffected by whether the firm is leveraged.

ROE and EPS are return on equity and earnings per share, respectively. They're defined as follows:

$$\text{ROE} = \frac{\text{net income}}{\text{equity}} \qquad \text{EPS} = \frac{\text{net income}}{\text{number of shares}}$$

ROE and EPS are *overall* measures of business performance in that they include both the results of operations and the effects of financing. Both measures are important to investors when they consider buying a company's stock, but EPS is especially significant. It is usually taken as an indication of the future earning power of the firm and is therefore a major determinant of the stock's market price.

EBIT, ROE, and EPS were treated in Chapters 2 and 3, on pages 30 and 98–99. It's not a bad idea to review those pages now.

Redefining Risk for Leverage-Related Issues   We're used to thinking of risk in finance as *variation* in the return on an investment. In this chapter, we'll narrow our focus and think of risk as variation in financial performance measured by variation in ROE and EPS. This notion is separable into two pieces, business risk and financial risk.

Business Risk   Business risk is variation in a firm's operating performance as measured by EBIT. It arises from variations in revenues, costs, and expenses. Hence, **business risk** is *defined* as variation in EBIT itself.[2]

Operation income (EBIT) is **unaffected by financial leverage**.

Investors regard **EPS** as an important indicator of **future profitability**.

Leverage-related risk is **variation in ROE and EPS**.

Business risk is the **variation in EBIT**.

---

2. Be careful not to confuse the business risk we're talking about here with the broader concept of business-specific risk from Chapter 9. Business-specific risk includes variation in EBIT as well as other things tied to a specific company or industry. For example, concern over the possibility of federal regulation of an industry could depress stock prices even though financial results are unchanged. Federal regulation or the threat of it would then be an element of business-specific risk, but not business risk as we're defining it here.

Financial Risk   In an unleveraged firm (one with no debt), the variation in ROE and EPS is identical to the variation in EBIT. In a leveraged firm, the variation in ROE and EPS is always *greater than* the variation in EBIT. Further, the more leverage the firm uses, the larger is the incremental variation.

This leads to the definition of *financial risk* as the *additional* variation in ROE and EPS that arises as a result of using financial leverage (debt). The idea is illustrated in Figure 14-1. The left column shows that business operations produce EBIT, to which we add financing to produce ROE and EPS. In other words, EBIT measures operations, but ROE and EPS measure *overall* performance, which is a combination of operations and financing.

The second and third columns show the sources of variation in the measures and how that variation is defined as risk. It's important to notice that business risk flows down into ROE and EPS by itself. **Financial risk** is *added* only if there is debt financing.

> **Financial risk** is the **additional** variation in ROE and EPS brought about by **financial leverage**.

14.1c   Leverage and Risk—Two Kinds of Each

From what we said in the last section, it's clear that financial leverage is associated with, and indeed causes, financial risk. We've also defined business risk as the variation in EBIT. It turns out there's another type of leverage that has an influence on business risk which is similar to the influence financial leverage has on financial risk. This concept is called *operating leverage.*

Operating leverage is related to a company's **cost structure** rather than to its capital structure. Cost structure describes the relative amounts of *fixed* and *variable* cost in productive and administrative processes.

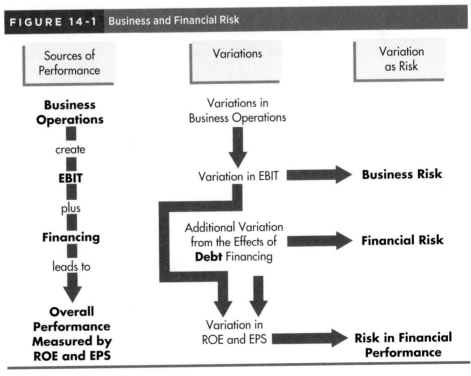

FIGURE 14-1   Business and Financial Risk

© Cengage Learning

When the term "leverage" is used by itself, it generally refers to financial leverage, which is the more important concept. We'll discuss operating leverage, and relate it to financial leverage later in this chapter.

14.1d   Our Approach to Leverage

In the remainder of this chapter, we'll take an in-depth look at leverage. We'll begin by examining how financial leverage works in practical, real-world terms. Then we'll have an equally pragmatic look at operating leverage. After examining both, we'll make a comparison between them and look at how they interact.

Then we'll spend some time studying capital structure theory. We'll do that without much mathematics, but when we're done we'll have a good grasp of the approach taken by sophisticated scholars. We'll also see that the theoretical results are essentially the same as those we arrived at intuitively, but for somewhat different reasons.

14.2   Financial Leverage

Now that we've developed the appropriate background, we can begin an investigation into just why leverage does what it does. We'll begin with an intuitive explanation.

14.2a   The Effect of Financial Leverage

The underlying reason that leverage may increase stock prices is that under certain conditions it improves financial performance measured in terms of ROE and EPS.

However, it sometimes makes performance worse and always increases risk. Hence, it's not immediately clear when leverage will be a benefit and when it won't.

To understand how leverage works, we'll examine the financial results of a rising young company, the Arizona Balloon Corporation, ABC for short, which sells hot air balloon rides in the Arizona desert. We'll look at how ABC performs under three assumptions about its use of leverage. We'll examine a case with no debt, one with 50% debt, and a highly leveraged situation with 80% debt.

Each scenario is represented by a column in Table 14-1. The capital structures are shown at the top of each column along with the number of shares of stock outstanding. Moving from left to right, the share numbers are calculated by assuming borrowed money is used to retire stock that can be bought at its book value of $10 per share.

The issue we want to explore is what happens to financial performance as we vary leverage while holding the level of operating income (EBIT) constant. In other words, given some level of EBIT, are we better off with more or less leverage?

To answer that question, we'll assume EBIT of $200,000, as displayed toward the middle of each column. The next four lines complete the income statement. Interest is 10% of debt, and taxes are figured at a 40% rate.

Return on equity (ROE) and earnings per share (EPS) are displayed next. These are the performance measures in which we're most interested.

The Good News About Financial Leverage   The important thing to observe in the table is the progression of ROE and EPS as we move to the right. As leverage increases, both measures go up dramatically.

TABLE 14-1	Effect of Increasing Financial Leverage When the Return on Capital Employed Exceeds the After-Tax Cost of Debt

Leverage Analysis
Arizona Balloon Corporation
($000)

	Leverage Scenarios		
	1	2	3
	0% Debt	50% Debt	80% Debt
Capital			
Debt	$ —	$ 500	$ 800
Equity	1,000	500	200
Total	$ 1,000	$ 1,000	$ 1,000
Shares @ $10	100,000	50,000	20,000
Revenue	$ 1,000	$ 1,000	$ 1,000
Cost/Expense	800	800	800
EBIT	$ 200	$ 200	$ 200
Interest (10%)	—	50	80
EBT	$ 200	$ 150	$ 120
Tax (40%)	80	60	48
Net income	$ 120	$ 90	$ 72
ROE	12%	18%	36%
EPS	$ 1.20	$ 1.80	$ 3.60

© Cengage Learning

Notice why this happens in terms of computations. ROE and EPS are calculated by dividing net income by equity and the number of shares, respectively.

As debt is added, net income declines because of increasing interest charges. However, equity and the number of shares outstanding also shrink as debt replaces equity in the capital structure and shares are retired. In this case, equity and shares are shrinking proportionately faster than earnings, so the ratios increase.

This is the good news about leverage. If basic **profitability** is good, a dollar-for-dollar replacement of equity with debt improves financial performance as measured by ROE and EPS.[3] Then if investors react positively to the increases, they may bid up the price of ABC's stock.

The Return on Capital Versus the Cost of Debt

The benefit of leverage illustrated in Table 14-1 makes sense because ABC's operating income (EBIT) represents an after-tax return on capital that exceeds its cost of debt. In other words, the company makes more with borrowed money than it pays for the privilege of borrowing.

The after-tax return on capital can be measured by a ratio called "the return on capital employed (ROCE)." The **ROCE** looks at the profitability of **operations**

---

3. A moderating effect that's not included in the illustration is that interest rates generally go up at high levels of debt. That means the interest cost might really be somewhat higher in the third column than the amount shown. However, the effect is unlikely to reverse the trend of increasing ROE and EPS shown.

without regard to how the firm is financed, but does so after tax. This amounts to calculating what the after-tax earnings on EBIT would be if there were no deductible interest, and then dividing by total capital. EBIT after tax is simply EBIT multiplied by $(1 - T)$ where T is the tax rate.

The resulting number is comparable to the return on assets, the return on equity, or the after-tax cost of debt. The computation is given by Equation 14.1.

$$(14.1) \qquad \text{ROCE} = \frac{\text{EBIT}(1 - T)}{\text{debt} + \text{equity}}$$

Calculating Equation 14.1 for any of the columns in Table 14-1 yields 12%. This says that ABC is able to earn 12% after tax on any capital it uses.

If you're a little confused by the ROCE concept, concentrate on column 1, where there's no debt or interest and ROCE equals ROE, at 12%.

Now notice that ABC's after-tax cost of debt is

$$k_d(1 - T) = 10\%(1 - .4) = 6\%$$

where k_d is the interest rate and T is the tax rate. This is half of what the business earns on capital, so it makes sense to use borrowed money.

Whenever a firm can earn an **ROCE** that **exceeds** its after-tax borrowing rate, it *seems* to make sense to use as much borrowed money as possible. In this case, every dollar borrowed frees up a dollar of equity and earns ABC's owners the 6% difference.

We'll learn shortly that other things affect the advisability of borrowing, but it's a basic truth that recorded financial results improve as equity is traded evenly for debt if the ROCE exceeds the after-tax cost of debt.

When the **ROCE exceeds** the after-tax **cost of debt**, more leverage **improves ROE and EPS**.

The Other Side of the Coin—The Bad News About Leverage

Unfortunately, leverage works in two directions. When a company is earning an ROCE that's *less* than the after-tax cost of debt, leverage makes results worse! To see that, we'll reconstruct Table 14-1 assuming bad weather causes a downturn in ABC's balloon business. The result is displayed in Table 14-2.

Assume revenues and earnings fall off to the point where the ROCE is just 4.8% (see the ROE in the first column of Table 14-2). That's less than the 6% cost of debt.

Now look at the progression from column to column as the firm moves from equity into debt. ROE and EPS *decrease* with increasing leverage. That's because the firm is earning less on capital (4.8%) than it's paying for the use of borrowed funds (6%).

When **ROCE is less than** the after-tax **cost of debt**, more leverage makes **ROE and EPS worse**.

This is another basic truth about leverage. Results are worse when **ROCE is less than** the after-tax **cost of debt**. This can cause investors to bid the price of the firm's stock down. Clearly it doesn't make much sense to increase leverage intentionally in this situation, and financial managers don't do it unless something else makes borrowing unavoidable.

Managing Through Leverage

The foregoing suggests that under certain conditions management may be able to manipulate financial results and stock price by changing the firm's capital structure. This is indeed true, but it has to be done with some caution.

It takes time to change capital structure, but operating results can turn around overnight. That means a firm can expand leverage during good times and then be caught by an unexpected business downturn. When that happens, there may be a precipitous drop in ROE and EPS as well as in stock price.

from the **CFO**

TABLE 14-2	Effect of Increasing Financial Leverage When the After-Tax Cost of Debt Exceeds the Return on Capital Employed

Leverage Analysis
Arizona Balloon Corporation
($000)

	Leverage Scenarios		
	1	2	3
	0% Debt	50% Debt	80% Debt
Capital			
Debt	$ —	$ 500	$ 800
Equity	1,000	500	200
Total	$ 1,000	$ 1,000	$ 1,000
Shares @ $10	100,000	50,000	20,000
Revenue	$ 800	$ 800	$ 800
Cost/Expense	720	720	720
EBIT	$ 80	$ 80	$ 80
Interest (10%)	—	50	80
EBT	$ 80	$ 30	—
Tax (40%)	32	12	—
Net income	$ 48	$ 18	—
ROE	4.8%	3.6%	0%
EPS	$ .48	$ .36	$ 0.00

© Cengage Learning

The following example illustrates the management of EPS:

CONCEPT CONNECTION   **EXAMPLE 14-1**

Managing EPS Through Leverage

Selected financial information for the Albany Corporation follows:

Albany Corporation at $10M Debt
($000 except per-share amounts)

EBIT	$23,700	Debt	$ 10,000
Interest (@ 12%)	1,200	Equity	90,000
EBT	$22,500	Capital	$ 100,000
Tax (@ 40%)	9,000	Number of shares	= 9,000,000
Net income	$ 13,500		

stock price = $10 per share

$$ROE = \frac{\text{net income}}{\text{equity}} = \frac{\$13,500}{\$90,000} = 15\%$$

$$EPS = \frac{\text{net income}}{\text{number of shares}} = \frac{\$13,500}{9,000,000} = \$1.50$$

Notice that Albany's total capital is $100 million. It pays 12% interest on debt of $10 million, and its combined state and federal tax rate is 40%. The company's stock is selling at its book value of $10 per share. The treasurer feels debt can be traded for equity without immediately affecting the price of the stock or the rate at which the firm can borrow.

Management believes it is in the best interest of the company and its stockholders to move the firm's EPS from its current level up to $2 per share. However, no opportunities are available to increase operating profit (EBIT) above the current level of $23.7 million.

Will borrowing more money and retiring stock raise Albany's EPS, and if so, what capital structure will achieve an EPS of $2?

SOLUTION: EPS will increase if the ROCE exceeds the after-tax cost of debt. Calculate ROCE by writing Equation 14.1 and substituting from the problem ($ million).

$$\text{ROCE} = \frac{\text{EBIT}(1 - T)}{\text{debt} + \text{equity}}$$

$$= \frac{\$23.7M(1 - .4)}{\$100.0M} = \frac{\$14.2M}{\$100.0M}$$

$$= 14.2\%$$

The after-tax cost of debt is the interest rate paid times 1 minus the tax rate.

$$k_d(1 - T) = 12\%(1 - .4) = 7.2\% < 14.2\%$$

Hence, trading equity for debt will improve EPS.

The second part of the question asks us to find the capital structure that results in an EPS of $2.00. Conceptually the easiest way to do that is trial and error. Simply choose a series of debt levels and recompute the financial results until a value is found that yields EPS = $2.00.

Let's begin with an arbitrary $20 million increase in debt to $30 million. Because Albany's stock is selling for its book value of $10, every $10 borrowed will retire one share of stock and reduce equity by the same $10. Hence, the new equity will be $70 million. The revised interest expense is ($30 million × .12 =) $3.6 million. From there the calculations are straightforward.

Albany Corporation at $30 Million Debt
($000 except per-share amounts)

EBIT	$23,700	Debt	$	30,000
Interest (@ 12%)	3,600	Equity		70,000
EBT	$20,100	Capital	$	100,000
Tax (@ 40%)	8,040	Number of shares	=	7,000,000
Net income	$12,060			

$$\text{ROE} = \frac{\text{net income}}{\text{equity}} = \frac{\$12,060}{\$70,000} = 17.2\%$$

$$\text{EPS} = \frac{\text{net income}}{\text{number of shares}} = \frac{\$12,060}{7,000,000 \text{ shares}} = \$1.72$$

The resulting EPS of $1.72 is less than the $2.00 target. This implies that more than $30 million in debt will be required. As an exercise, show that $45 million is very close to the right level.

An Alternate Approach (optional)

An algebraic approach is available which is computationally more efficient even though it's mathematically a bit complex. We're going to present the technique here to demonstrate an important analytical tool for solving financial problems. The idea is to write ratios and/or parts of financial statements as equations which can be used to solve for unknown financial quantities. Those not mathematically inclined can skip to the next section without loss of continuity.

In this case, we'll use the definition of some ratios, the income statement from EBIT to net income, the relation between debt and interest, and the definition of capital to construct an equation that will lead us to the exact level of debt we need.

We'll begin by noticing that there's a simple relationship between EPS, ROE, and book value per share.

$$\text{EPS} = \text{ROE} \times \text{book value per share.}$$

Convince yourself that this is true by substituting the definitions of these ratios found on pages 98–100.

Since Albany's stock is selling at its book value of $10.00, retiring shares won't change that value, so we can write

(a) $$\text{EPS} = \text{ROE(\$10)} = \frac{\text{net income}}{\text{equity}}(\$10.00)$$

Next consider the bottom part of Albany's income statement. Net income can be written as

$$\text{net income} = (\text{EBIT} - \text{I})(1 - \text{T})$$

where I is interest and T is the tax rate. (EBIT − I) is earnings before tax (EBT), which is adjusted to earnings after tax by multiplying by (1 − T).

Interest is debt times the interest rate, k_d, so we can write

$$\text{I} = k_d \text{ (debt)}$$

Substituting this into the expression for net income yields

$$\text{net income} = [\text{EBIT} - (k_d)(\text{debt})]\, (1 - \text{T})$$

Further, total capital is debt plus equity, so

$$\text{equity} = \text{total capital} - \text{debt}$$

Substituting these expressions for net income and equity into (a), yields

$$\text{EPS} = \frac{[\text{EBIT} - (k_d)(\text{debt})](1 - \text{T})}{\text{total capital} - \text{debt}}(\$10.00)$$

Everything in this equation except debt is available in the problem. If we treat debt as the unknown and set EPS equal to $2.00, we have a single equation in a single unknown, the solution to which is the value of debt at which EPS is exactly $2.00. Substituting we have

$$\$2.00 = \frac{[\$23,700,000 - (.12)(\text{debt})](1 - .4)}{\$100,000,000 - \text{debt}}(\$10.00)$$

from which

$$\text{debt} = \$45,156,250$$

Hence, the capital structure that produces a $2.00 EPS is roughly 45% debt–55% equity.

14.2b   Financial Leverage and Financial Risk

Tables 14-1 and 14-2 show that financial leverage is a two-edged sword. It multiplies good results into great results, but it also multiplies bad results into terrible results. This means when business conditions change, performance measured by ROE or EPS makes wider swings for more leveraged organizations than for those with relatively less debt. The *incremental* variation in results is what we've called *financial risk*.

We can illustrate the idea with Arizona Balloon Corporation using Tables 14-1 and 14-2. The first table represents relatively good times, while the second reflects harder times and lower earnings. Within each table, there's a no-leverage situation in the first column and a high-leverage case in the third column.

To see the effect of financial leverage on risk, we'll compare the changes in ROE in the first and third columns, respectively, between the two tables. The analysis is shown in Table 14-3. Focus on the first three lines of Table 14-3. The column on the left shows that the change in ROE from good times to bad times is just 7.2% when there's no leverage. On the other hand, the column on the right shows that change to be 36.0% when there's a high degree of leverage.

Because there's no financial leverage in column 1 of Tables 14-1 and 14-2, the difference in those ROEs represents the variability of the basic business's results. In other words, that change is due to *business risk*.[4]

The difference in the column 3 ROEs represents the *sum* of the variabilities arising from operations and from financing. The incremental variability, the difference between the two differences, is a result of *financial risk*. This difference is shown on the fourth line of Table 14-3.

In ABC's case, business risk accounts for a swing of 7.2% in ROE. The financial risk associated with 80% leverage, however, accounts for a swing of $(36.0\% - 7.2\% =)$ 28.8% in ROE. In other words, at 80% debt, financial risk is $(28.8\%/7.2\% =)$ four times as large as business risk. The result makes sense, because 80% debt represents a high degree of leverage.

To check your understanding, show that the financial risk associated with 50% debt (column 2) is equal to business risk.

A good way to think of these ideas is to say that leverage magnifies changes in operating income (EBIT) into larger changes in ROE and EPS. Further, the more leverage there is, the larger is the magnification.

Financial risk is the **increased variability** in financial results that comes from **additional leverage**.

TABLE 14-3 Financial Leverage and Risk		
	ROE	
	Column 1 No Debt	Column 3 80% Debt
Good times (Table 14-1)	12.0%	36.0%
Bad times (Table 14-2)	4.8	0.0
Difference	7.2%	36.0%
Incremental difference in ROE due to financial leverage	$= 36.0\% - 7.2\% = 28.8\%$	

© Cengage Learning

---

4. We generally measure business risk at EBIT, but when there's no financial leverage, the result is the same at ROE.

14.2c   Putting the Ideas Together—The Effect on Stock Price

Our study of the Arizona Balloon Corporation has demonstrated two important effects of leverage.

Leverage **enhances performance** while it **adds risk**, pushing stock prices in **opposite directions**.

1. During periods of reasonably good performance, leverage enhances results in terms of ROE and EPS.
2. Leverage adds variability to financial performance when operating results change. This means performance is riskier with more leverage.

Both phenomena become more pronounced as the level of leverage increases.

These effects drive stock prices in **opposite directions**. The first, enhanced performance under favorable conditions makes the expected return on a stock investment higher. That makes the stock more desirable to investors, which causes them to bid up its price.

In ABC's case, for example, suppose everyone expects prosperity consistent with Table 14-1 next year, believing the chances of a recession are very remote. Then ABC's expected EPS with no leverage is $1.20 from the first column. That expectation can be increased to $1.80 by moving to the leverage position in column 2. If no one is too worried about poor economic conditions, the higher expected performance is just accepted at its face value.

The second effect makes a stock investment riskier, and we know from the principle of risk aversion (Chapter 9, page 409) that investors don't like that. Hence, the second effect tends to drive investors away, lowering the price.

The key question is which effect dominates and when?

When **leverage is low**, a little **more** has a **positive effect** on investors, but at **high** debt levels **concerns about risk dominate**, and the **effect of more is negative**.

Real Investor Behavior and the Optimal Capital Structure   It turns out that at low to moderate levels of debt, investors value the positive effects of leverage a great deal and virtually ignore concerns about increased risk. This is especially true if the economic outlook is good. Hence, increases in leverage tend to raise stock prices when leverage is low or moderate.

As leverage increases, however, concerns about risk and poor performance begin to overwhelm the benefits of enhanced return in people's minds. Thus, at higher levels, further increases in leverage have a negative effect on stock price.

As leverage increases, its effect goes from **positive to negative**, which results in an **optimum capital structure**.

In other words, as leverage increases from nothing to very high levels (all other things held constant), stock price increases, reaches a maximum, and then decreases. The idea is shown graphically in Figure 14-2. The maximum point on the graph is conceptually important. It corresponds to the **optimal capital structure**. By definition, this is the capital structure (percent debt, level of leverage) that maximizes stock price.

As a practical matter, the optimum capital structure **cannot be precisely located**.

Finding the Optimum—A Practical Problem   No one doubts that the response pattern of stock price to leverage is generally as pictured in Figure 14-2 or that there is indeed some optimal level of debt that produces a maximum price. The problem is that no one has a way to determine exactly where the maximum is for a particular company at a particular time.

The appropriate level of leverage tends to vary with the nature of a company's business as well as with the economic climate. A firm whose basic business is relatively

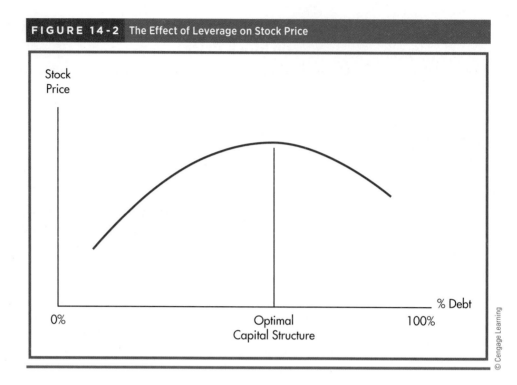

FIGURE 14-2 The Effect of Leverage on Stock Price

volatile would be expected to use less leverage than a company in a stable business. That's because a high level of business risk compounded by a high level of leverage produces an extremely risky company.

With respect to economic climate, investors are more sensitive to risk when the outlook is poor than when it's good. The optimal level of leverage therefore should be lower in bad times because investors are repelled by increasing risk sooner.

Unfortunately, these ideas aren't particularly quantifiable, so we aren't able to locate the optimum along the horizontal axis of Figure 14-2 with any accuracy.

That doesn't mean capital structure thinking is useless. However, it is more of a general guide than a precise set of instructions for managing a company. The accepted wisdom is more or less as follows:

1. *A firm with good profit prospects and little or no debt is probably missing an opportunity by not using borrowed money if interest rates are reasonable.*
2. *For most businesses, the optimal capital structure is somewhere between 30% and 50% debt.*
3. *Debt levels above 60% create excessive risk and should be avoided.*

Keep in mind that these are rough guidelines with lots of exceptions, and not hard rules.

The Target Capital Structure We referred to a *target capital structure* during our discussion of the cost of capital in Chapter 13. We said the target structure is one that management prefers over any other and attempts to maintain as it raises money. We're now in a position to better appreciate that idea.

A firm's **target capital structure** is management's estimate of the optimal capital structure.

The **target capital structure** is just an approximation of the **optimal capital structure**. It is management's best guess at a level of leverage that maximizes the firm's stock price.

You may recall that, in Chapter 13, we weren't concerned about stating target and actual capital structures with a great deal of precision. The reason should be apparent now. We can't find the optimal structure with a high degree of accuracy, so it doesn't make much sense to get too detailed about a guess at it.

The Effect of Leverage When Stocks Aren't Trading at Book Value

There's an important detail that shouldn't be missed in what we've been doing. We've presented illustrations of changes in leverage in which equity is replaced by debt. They have all involved changes in the number of shares of stock outstanding that are proportionate to the changes in equity.

That proportionality is ensured by assuming the stock can be purchased for retirement at a market price equal to its book value. When that isn't the case, things can be somewhat more complex. The relationship between ROE and EPS can be shown to be

$$\text{EPS} = \text{ROE} \times (\text{book value per share})$$

When stock is purchased for retirement at book value, the book value per share of the remaining shares stays the same. And the transaction has essentially the same effect on EPS that it does on ROE. However, when stock is purchased for retirement at a price different from its book value, the book value of the remaining shares changes. Therefore, a transaction can have different effects on ROE and EPS. Our results generally hold for ROE, but may not for EPS.

This phenomenon adds to the general imprecision of the ideas with which we've been working. The important point is the general direction in which leverage drives stock price, not the exact amount of the effect.

INSIGHTS | Real Applications

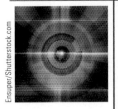

Ensuper/Shutterstock.com

AOL and Time Warner: The Perils of Leverage

On December 9, 2009, Time Warner Inc. divested AOL, through a spinoff heralding the final chapter in the long tale of what may have been the most disastrous merger ever. The spinoff, leaves AOL and Time Warner as two separate corporate entities, each free to pursue its own interests and strategies.

In 2001, America Online (AOL), likely the world's best-known Internet provider at the time, and Time Warner, a media giant with interests in publishing and the film industry, merged in a $147 billion deal that was billed as a marriage of "old media" and "new media." The general expectation was that the combination would be a phenomenal success as the companies took advantage of one another's market power and expertise.

Unfortunately, the "media marriage" initially produced little but red ink. Within months of the ceremony, America Online's business went into a steep slump, and the stock of the combined company, originally named AOL Time Warner, plummeted, wiping out more than $100 billion in market value. To make matters worse, Time Warner's print publishing business suffered a significant unrelated decline in advertising revenue after the September 11th terrorist attacks. The eventual failure of the merger has been blamed on a number of factors including disparate corporate cultures, changing technology, and the personalities and styles of the people at the top.

But another reason the company suffered as badly as it did in the stock market may have been excessive leverage. The combined company reported long-term debt as of September 30, 2002, of $28.2 billion, up from $22.8 billion at the end of 2001. At first glance, that doesn't seem excessive relative to its assets of $161 billion at the end of 2002's third quarter. Indeed, few analysts would argue that debt of about ($28/$161 =) 17% of assets is too much.

But a closer look at the balance sheet was likely to have led investors to a different conclusion. The problem was that more than half of the assets reported represented intangibles, which are generally of little real value. Over half of the total assets figure, about $82 billion, was goodwill, an intangible representing the excess of

the prices paid to acquire companies over the fair market value of the assets actually brought on board.

Other intangibles accounted for about $45 billion more of the balance sheet's value. If investors refused to give these assets full credit in their thinking, they were left with only about $34 billion in "hard" assets like cash, receivables, equipment, and property. Under those assumptions, the $28 billion debt represents 82% of assets, a very big number in most industries, implying that AOL Time Warner was a highly leveraged, very risky company.

In early 2003, the firm took most of the goodwill off of its balance sheet, reporting a $99 billion loss on the transaction. The move was mandated by new accounting rules and made the company's debt load more obvious.

The combined business struggled to pay down its debt and make the combination work, but after eight years, management finally gave up, admitted it wasn't going to happen, and announced the "divorce."

SOURCE: WSJ.com, "AOL Posts a $98.7 Billion Loss on New Goodwill Write-Down," January 30, 2003; AOL Web site, 3rd quarter 2002 10-Q, Thomson One Financials, June 2000; and "Time Warner Inc., completes spin-off of AOL Inc.," December 10, 2009.

14.2d The Degree of Financial Leverage (DFL)— A Measurement

Financial leverage magnifies changes in EBIT into larger changes in ROE and EPS. It is of interest to know just how large that magnification is at any particular level of leverage.

For example, suppose a firm anticipates a 20% drop in EBIT. If the company has no debt, ROE and EPS will also drop by 20%. But what drop should be expected if the firm's capital is 30% or 40% debt? Clearly the question is important if management is interested in the effect that changes in ROE and EPS may have on investors.

It's possible to answer the question using a concept called the *degree of financial leverage,* abbreviated *DFL.* The DFL lets us quantify the effectiveness of leverage by relating *relative* changes in EPS and EBIT at any level of leverage.[5]

The idea is expressed as follows

(14.2)
$$DFL = \frac{\%\Delta EPS}{\%\Delta EBIT}$$

where %ΔEPS and %ΔEBIT mean the relative changes in EPS and EBIT, respectively.

The best way to visualize the meaning of the DFL is to rewrite Equation 14.2 by multiplying through by %ΔEBIT.

(14.2a)
$$\%\Delta EPS = DFL \times \%\Delta EBIT$$

The **DFL** relates relative changes in **EBIT** to relative **changes in EPS**.

This expression says that relative changes in EBIT are multiplied by the DFL to arrive at relative changes in EPS. For example, if a firm's DFL is 1.5 and EBIT changes by 20%, EPS will change by (1.5 $\times$ 20% =) 30%.

If financial statements are available, the DFL can be calculated by assuming a small change in EBIT, working through to the resulting change in EPS, and substituting the relative changes into Equation 14.2. However, that approach is rather tedious. An easier method is available by using the following formula.

(14.3)
$$DFL = \frac{EBIT}{EBIT - I}$$

where I is interest.

The derivation of Equation 14.3 is a little involved, so we'll just accept the result.

CONCEPT CONNECTION   EXAMPLE 14-2

Forecasting Results Through the DFL

Selected income statement and capital information for the Moberly Manufacturing Company follow ($000):

		Capital	
Revenue	$5,580	Debt	$ 1,000
Cost/Expense	4,200	Equity	7,000
EBIT	$ 1,380	Total	$8,000

---

5. A relative change is a percentage change. For example, a 5% change in the number 20 is a change of 1 unit, because 1 is 5% of 20. An increase to 21 is a positive 5% change. A decrease to 19 is a negative 5% change.

In general, a relative change in a number is the change divided by the number itself, expressed as a percentage. If we represent the change in the number N as ΔN, the relative change in N is expressed as

$$\%\Delta N = \frac{\Delta N}{N} \times 100$$

If N is 20 and ΔN is 1, we have

$$\%\Delta N \times \frac{1}{20} \times 100 = 5\%$$

Currently 700,000 shares of common stock are outstanding. The firm pays 15% interest on its debt and anticipates that it can borrow as much as it reasonably needs at that rate. The income tax rate is 40%.

Moberly is interested in boosting the price of its stock. To do that, management is considering restructuring capital to 50% debt in the hope that the increased EPS will have a positive effect on price. However, the economic outlook is shaky, and the company's CFO thinks there's a good chance that a deterioration in business conditions will reduce EBIT next year. At the moment, Moberly's stock sells for its book value of $10 per share.

Estimate the effect of the proposed restructuring on EPS. Then use the degree of financial leverage to assess the increase in risk that will come along with it.

SOLUTION: First we'll calculate the proposed capital structure and display it alongside the current structure. Because equity can be traded at its book value, the restructuring is a straightforward exchange of equity for debt with a proportionate reduction in the number of shares outstanding.

	Current	Proposed
Capital		
Debt	$ 1,000	$ 4,000
Equity	7,000	4,000
Total	$ 8,000	$ 8,000
Shares outstanding	700,000	400,000

Next calculate projected net income and EPS at the current level of business for both capital structures.

	Current	Proposed
EBIT	$1,380	$1,380
Interest (15% of debt)	150	600
EBT	$1,230	$ 780
Tax (@ 40%)	492	312
Net income	$ 738	$ 468
EPS	$1.054	$ 1.170

It's easy to see that if business conditions remain unchanged, the proposed structure will yield a higher EPS.

Next use Equation 14.3 to calculate the DFL under each structure.

$$DFL_{cur} = \frac{EBIT}{EBIT - I} = \frac{\$1,380}{\$1,380 - \$150} = 1.12$$

$$DFL_{prop} = \frac{EBIT}{EBIT - I} = \frac{\$1,380}{\$1,380 - \$600} = 1.77$$

Now we can see why the CFO is concerned. EPS will be much more volatile under the proposed structure than it is currently. To illustrate, suppose business deteriorates and EBIT declines by 30%; that's not unusual. We can use Equation 14.2a to see what will happen under both the current and proposed structures.

Under the current structure, EPS will decline by a percentage calculated as follows.

$$\%\Delta EPS_{cur} = DFL_{cur} \times \%\Delta EBIT$$
$$= 1.12 \times 30\% = 33.6\%$$

But under the proposed structure the percentage decline will be

$$\%\Delta EPS_{prop} = DFL_{prop} \times \%\Delta EBIT$$
$$= 1.77 \times 30\% = 53.1\%$$

Now apply these percentage declines to the projected EPSs to see what they'll become under both structures if the business deterioration does occur.

Current: $1.054(1 − .336) = $.70
Proposed: $1.170(1 − .531) = $.55

The implication is that if the proposed capital structure is adopted *and* a substantial downturn occurs, the resulting EPS will be lower than the EPS under the old structure. Clearly, adopting the proposal adds substantial risk.

The impact of the proposed restructuring on stock prices is arguable. We can't say with certainty whether or not the positive effect of the EPS increase will overcome the negative effect of increased risk. It all depends on the current perceptions of investors.

The uncertainty can be expressed in terms of the graph in Figure 14-2 (page 594). The question revolves around just where Moberly currently is on the graph and whether the restructuring will carry it past the peak. We can't say for sure. However, using the DFL to analyze the risk increase gives management a much better feel for the trade-offs involved than it would get if only the EPS impact were considered.

It's unfortunate that the DFL concept isn't used a great deal in practice. In the Moberly problem, many analysts would have stopped after calculating the two EPSs under good conditions. They'd have understood that risk was increased, but wouldn't have tried to quantify the increase for the benefit of the decision maker. We're certain our current readers will rectify that situation in a few years.

14.2e   EBIT–EPS Analysis

We've learned that financial leverage can enhance results at normal levels of operating profit, but makes those results more volatile at the same time. If that knowledge is to do any good, managers need to be able to use it to make intelligent choices about the amount of leverage their companies should employ given a set of expectations about future business.

This means managers need a way of quantifying and analyzing the trade-off between results and risk implied by moving from one level of leverage to another. EBIT–EPS analysis provides a graphic portrayal of the trade-off that makes the choice relatively straightforward.

We'll illustrate with an example using the financial figures from the Arizona Balloon Corporation, assuming management expects the relatively good year reflected in Table 14-1 and that the choice is between the leverage scenarios of columns 1 and 2 only (page 587).

The EBIT–EPS technique involves graphing EPS as a linear function of EBIT for two or more levels of leverage. Examination of the resulting chart can provide some insight into the best choice of a firm's debt–equity mix given management's expectations about future profitability. Glance at Figure 14-3 within Example 14-3 to get an idea of the appearance of the result.

CONCEPT CONNECTION   EXAMPLE 14-3

EBIT–EPS Analysis

Graph the relationship between EBIT and EPS for the Arizona Balloon Corporation using the financial information in Table 14-1. Graph one line for the all-equity case of column 1 and another for the 50–50 scenario of column 2. Find the value of EPS at which Arizona would be indifferent between the two options.

SOLUTION: Beginning with the all-equity case, the table shows an EPS of $1.20 at an EBIT of $200,000, which provides one point on the EBIT–EPS graph for zero leverage. Since EPS is a linear function of EBIT, we need only one other point to draw the graph. We'll arbitrarily choose EBIT of $400,000 and calculate EPS as follows:

EBIT	$400,000
Interest (10%)	—
EBT	$400,000
Tax (40%)	160,000
Net income	$240,000
Number of shares	100,000
EPS	$ 2.40

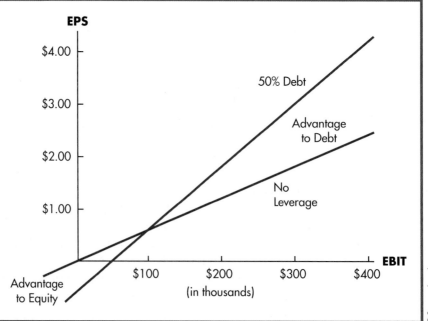

Ensuper/Shutterstock.com

FIGURE 14-3

EBIT–EPS Analysis for Arizona Balloon Corporation from Table 14-1, Columns 1 and 2

© Cengage Learning

These points determine the line labeled "No Leverage" in Figure 14-3.

For the 50% debt scenario, column 2 of Table 14-1 shows an EPS of $1.80 at an EBIT of $200,000. A calculation like the one we've just done (using $50,000 in interest and 500,000 shares of stock) gives a second point at which EPS is $4.20 when EBIT is $400,000. These points determine the line labeled "50% Debt" in the diagram.

The two lines represent EPS at various levels of operating profit under their respective assumptions about leverage. Notice that they cross one another, making different choices of leverage superior on either side of the intersection. We prefer the higher EPS of the upper line anywhere other than at the intersection, where we're indifferent between the two choices.

It's important to be able to find the indifference point. In general the formula of an EPS–EBIT line is the financial computation of EPS from EBIT stated in algebraic form.

EBIT–EPS analysis portrays the results of **leverage** and helps to decide **how much** to use.

$$EPS = \frac{(EBIT - I)(1 - T)}{\text{number of shares}}$$

$$\text{where: } I = \text{interest}$$
$$T = \text{tax rate}$$

Compare the equation to the steps in the partial income statement above. In the numerator, $(EBIT - I)$ is earnings before tax (EBT), which is adjusted to earnings after tax by multiplying by $(1 - T)$. That, divided by the number of shares outstanding, is EPS.

We can find the indifference point by equating the EPS for the no-leverage line with that for the 50% leverage line.

No Leverage	50% Debt
$\dfrac{(EBIT - \$0)(1 - .4)}{100,000}$ =	$\dfrac{(EBIT - \$50,000)(1 - .4)}{50,000}$

Solving yields

$$EBIT_{indif} = \$100,000$$

In other words, the lines cross, and our preference for leverage changes when EBIT passes through $100,000.

Notice how useful the diagram in Figure 14-3 is. It tells management that if EBIT is expected to stay above $100,000, the firm is better off with the higher leverage option. It also gives an indication of how much better off the firm will be for any level of EBIT.

The risk that comes with leverage is reflected by what happens to EPS in the 50% debt case if operating profits fall below $100,000. In that range, ABC will be on the upper line without leverage, but on the lower line with 50% debt.

The analysis doesn't make the leverage decision for ABC's management. But combined with an idea of the likely variability of EBIT, it gives them all they need to make an informed choice. If EBIT is unlikely to fall much below $100,000, higher leverage is appropriate. On the other hand, if big swings are common, little or no leverage may be the wiser decision.

from the
CFO

14.3   Operating Leverage

We mentioned operating leverage briefly in the beginning of the chapter. The concept deals with cost rather than capital, but the functions and effects are similar to those of financial leverage. Operating leverage also has the ability to *combine* with financial leverage to produce alarmingly volatile results. For this reason, we need to be familiar with the workings of operating leverage even though it's not exactly a capital structure issue. We'll begin our study with some background.

14.3a   Terminology and Definitions

The term "operations" refers to a firm's business activities exclusive of long-term financing. In terms of the income statement, those activities involve the items from sales down to operating income (EBIT).

Risk in Operations—Business Risk   A firm's EBIT varies over time for a variety of reasons including ups and downs in sales, changes in cost conditions, and the effectiveness of management. Recall that we've already defined variation in EBIT as **business risk** (page 584).

It's important to realize that every business has some variation in its operating results, but some have more than others. The amount depends to a great extent on the nature of the business. Some industries have stable conditions of demand and cost, while in others things go up and down like roller coasters. Generally, most of the variation in EBIT comes about as a result of changes in the level of sales.

Fixed and Variable Costs and Cost Structure   A business's costs can be separated into two categories, *fixed* and *variable*. A fixed cost doesn't change when the level of sales changes, but a variable cost does.

Fixed costs are things like rent, depreciation, utilities, and management salaries. Variable costs include direct labor, direct materials, and other items that go up and down with volume, like sales commissions. Costs that don't fit neatly into either category can usually be separated into fixed and variable components for purposes of analysis. Ultimately, all costs and expenses can be segregated, at least roughly, into fixed and variable categories. Fixed cost is also called *overhead*.

A firm's **cost structure** is the mix of **fixed** and **variable** costs used in its operating processes. The idea is analogous to the concept of capital structure describing the mix of debt and equity within capital.

Operating Leverage Defined   Given the similar concepts of cost structure and capital structure, operating leverage is defined with respect to cost just as financial leverage is defined with respect to capital. **Operating leverage** refers to the amount of **fixed cost** in the cost structure. Thus, if a firm's costs are largely fixed, it has a great deal of operating leverage.

A good way to get a feel for cost structure and operating leverage is to imagine a factory that can be run in one of two ways, either with (1) a lot of people and a few machines or with (2) a lot of machines and a few people. We tend to describe the first organization as labor intensive or utilizing manual processes and the second as capital intensive or automated.

Variation in EBIT is defined as **business risk**.

Cost structure is the mix of **fixed and variable** costs in a firm's operations.

Operating leverage increases as the proportion of **fixed cost** increases.

People represent variable cost because they can be let go when sales and production decline. Machines, on the other hand, represent fixed cost because they can't be laid off during a downturn. Hence, the automated plant (2) has more operating leverage than the labor intensive plant (1).

14.3b   Breakeven Analysis

Breakeven analysis is widely used to determine the level of activity a firm must achieve to stay in business in the long run. The technique explicitly lays out the effect of sales volume on a firm's use of fixed and variable costs. In doing that, it provides an excellent insight into the nature and effect of operating leverage. We'll develop the breakeven model and then use it to illustrate operating leverage.

Overview of Breakeven   The term "breakeven" means zero profit or loss, generally measured at EBIT (operating income). At breakeven, income (revenue) exactly equals outgo (costs and expenses), and the firm just survives. **Breakeven analysis** is a way of looking at operations to determine the volume, in either units or dollars, a company must sell to achieve this zero-profit, zero-loss situation.

In what follows, we'll use the term "cost" broadly to include items generally referred to as expense. Both costs and expenses can be fixed or variable.

14.3c   Breakeven Diagrams

Fixed and variable costs are represented graphically in the first two panels of Figure 14-4. Cost is plotted along the vertical axis and unit sales (Q for quantity) along the horizontal axis. Fixed cost is constant as sales increase, while variable cost increases proportionately with sales.

The two diagrams are generally combined by plotting variable cost on top of fixed cost. The result is shown in the third panel where the diagonal line represents total cost, the sum of fixed and variable costs.

The *breakeven diagram* is depicted in Figure 14-5. It's formed by overlaying a line representing revenue on the total cost diagram. At any level of sales, revenue is just PQ, price times quantity. A revenue line is shown in Figure 14-5 starting from the origin and extending upward to the right.

> **Breakeven analysis** shows the mix of **fixed and variable** cost and the volume required for **zero profit/loss**.

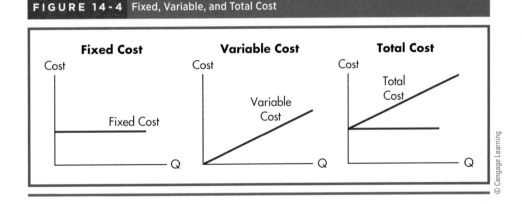

FIGURE 14-4   Fixed, Variable, and Total Cost

© Cengage Learning

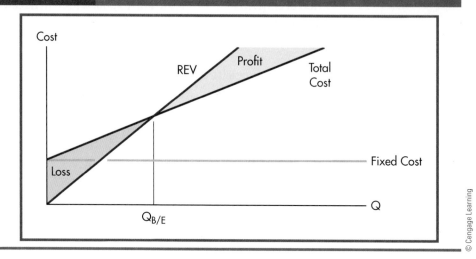

FIGURE 14-5 The Breakeven Diagram

Cost

REV

Profit

Total Cost

Fixed Cost

Loss

Q

$Q_{B/E}$

© Cengage Learning

Breakeven is the level of sales at which revenue equals cost. On the diagram it's the point where the total cost line and the revenue line intersect. The breakeven volume is directly below that point on the horizontal axis, indicated by $Q_{B/E}$ on the diagram.

At any sales volume, the firm's profit or loss is the difference between revenue and total cost. This can be measured by the difference in the heights of those lines above the axis. The shaded area between the two lines to the right of their intersection represents profitable operations, and the shaded area to the left represents losses.

The Contribution Margin Every time a unit is sold, one unit's worth of variable cost is incurred. The amount by which price exceeds that unit variable cost is called the **contribution** made by the sale. Expressed as an equation,

(14.4)
$$C_t = P - V$$

where C_t is the contribution
P is price, and
V is variable cost per unit

The term implies a *contribution* to profit and fixed cost. Notice that the unit contribution is the same anywhere on the breakeven diagram—that is, at any level of sales.

Contribution can be expressed as a percentage of revenue by dividing by the price, P. It's then called the *contribution margin*, which we'll write as C_M. Dividing Equation 14.4 by P, we have:

(14.5)
$$C_M = \frac{P - V}{P}$$

CONCEPT CONNECTION   **EXAMPLE 14-4**

Contribution

Suppose a company can make a unit of product for $7 in variable labor and materials, and sell it for $10. What are the contribution and contribution margin?

SOLUTION: The contribution comes directly from Equation 14.4.

$$C_t = P - V$$
$$= \$10 - \$7$$
$$= \$3$$

The contribution margin comes from Equation 14.5.

$$C_M = \frac{P - V}{P} = \frac{\$3}{\$10} = .3 = 30\%$$

Calculating the Breakeven Sales Level EBIT is revenue minus cost, which can be expressed in terms of price, quantity, and cost as

(14.6) $$EBIT = PQ - VQ - F_c$$

where: P = price per unit,
V = variable cost per unit,
Q = quantity sold, and
F_c = fixed cost.

Notice in this equation that P and V are multiplied by Q to represent revenue (PQ) and total variable cost (VQ), but fixed cost is represented by a single variable, F_c. EBIT is revenue minus both cost components, variable and fixed.

Breakeven occurs where revenue (PQ) equals total cost (VQ + F_c); hence, EBIT = 0. To find that point, rewrite Equation 14.6 with EBIT = 0.

$$0 = PQ - VQ - F_c$$

Then factor out Q, rearrange terms, and solve for the breakeven value of Q, which we've called $Q_{B/E}$.

$$Q(P - V) - F_c = 0$$

(14.7) $$Q_{B/E} = \frac{F_c}{P - V}$$

Notice that the breakeven volume is found by dividing fixed cost by (P − V), which is the contribution per unit sold. In words, the breakeven calculation tells how many units have to be sold to *contribute* enough money to cover (pay for) fixed costs.

The breakeven point stated in terms of dollar sales rather than units is Equation 14.7 multiplied by price, P. If we call $S_{B/E}$ the breakeven dollar sales level, we have

(14.8) $$S_{B/E} = \frac{P(F_c)}{P - V}$$

Breakeven volume is fixed cost divided by contribution.

Dividing the numerator and denominator of Equation 14.8 by P and substituting from Equation 14.5 gives a useful expression.

(14.9)
$$S_{B/E} = \frac{F_c}{(P - V)/P} = \frac{F_c}{C_M}$$

Equation 14.9 says that the breakeven sales level is just fixed cost, F_c, divided by the *contribution margin,* C_M (stated in decimal form).

CONCEPT CONNECTION   **EXAMPLE 14-5**

Breakeven

What is the breakeven sales level in units and dollars for the company in Example 14-4 if the firm has fixed costs of $1,800 per month?

SOLUTION: For the breakeven point in units, write Equation 14.7 and substitute.

$$Q_{B/E} = \frac{F_c}{P - V} = \frac{\$1,800}{\$3} = 600 \text{ units}$$

Because as each unit sells for $10, the breakeven sales level in dollar terms, from Equation 14.8, is just

$$\$10 \times 600 = \$6,000$$

Alternatively, the last result is available from Equation 14.9 by dividing fixed cost by the contribution margin expressed in decimal form.

$$S_{B/E} = \frac{F_c}{(P - V)/P} = \frac{F_c}{C_M} = \frac{\$1,800}{.3} = \$6,000$$

This calculation essentially tells us how many dollars, each of which contributes 30 cents to profit and fixed cost, it takes to make $1,800.

Notice that breakeven volumes in either units or dollars are stated per period of time. In this example, the period is a month because fixed costs were given on a monthly basis.

14.3d   The Effect of Operating Leverage

Breakeven analysis gives us an excellent approach to understanding exactly how operating leverage works. We'll begin by examining the breakeven diagrams for two firms that use different amounts of operating leverage. This is equivalent to saying that they differ with respect to their cost structures, one having relatively more fixed cost than the other. The diagrams are shown in Figure 14-6.

For convenience, we'll assume both firms have the same breakeven volume shown at sales level A in the diagrams. Recall that the diagrams reflect profit or loss in terms of EBIT in the shaded areas on either side of the breakeven points. As output expands, profit grows as we move further to the right of breakeven. On the other hand, if volume falls below the breakeven level, losses grow as we move further to the left.

FIGURE 14-6   Breakeven Diagrams at High and Low Operating Leverage

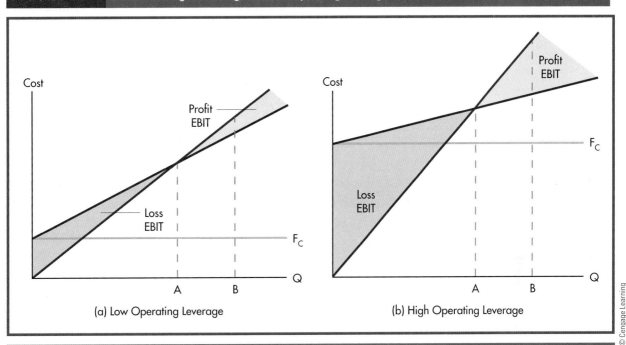

(a) Low Operating Leverage   (b) High Operating Leverage

The Risk Effect   Notice the relative speed with which profit or loss grows as we move away from volume level A in the two diagrams. The high-operating-leverage firm on the right expands profits much faster than the low-leverage firm on the left. However, it also expands losses much faster if output falls below the breakeven at A.

> As volume moves away from breakeven, profit or loss **increases faster** with more **operating leverage**.

This is the essence of operating leverage. Any movement away from point A produces some change in EBIT in the low-leverage company. The same movement away from A will produce a *larger* change in EBIT in the higher-leverage firm. In other words, the increased leverage *magnifies* the change in EBIT that results from a given change in sales volume.

Thus, operating leverage can be said to increase the variation in EBIT as a result of variations in sales. Because variation in EBIT is defined as business risk, it follows that *increased operating leverage increases business risk.*

The effect can be appreciated from the geometry of the diagrams. The high-leverage firm has a smaller variable cost, which makes its total cost line flatter than that of the low-leverage firm. That means it diverges from the revenue line faster.

> Variation in EBIT (business risk) is **larger** with **more operating leverage**.

Stated another way, the high-leverage firm gets a larger contribution from each sale, so it accumulates profits or losses faster as it moves away from the breakeven. Of course, this is true for movement between any two sales levels along the horizontal axis. The trade-off is that the high-leverage firm has more fixed cost to cover before it makes a profit than the low-leverage firm.

The Effect on Expected EBIT   More operating leverage implies higher operating profit at any output above the breakeven. To see this, consider point B in both diagrams of Figure 14-6. The geometry of the diagrams shows that at the same distance above the breakeven output, the higher fixed cost firm will always make more EBIT.

In general, the higher the fixed cost, the higher the profit is at a given point above breakeven. Imagine the F_c line sliding upward in the diagram of Figure 14-6b with the breakeven point staying the same. That would flatten the total cost line and widen the profit triangle.

Hence, if a firm is relatively sure of its output level, it's better off to trade variable costs for fixed. In other words, increasing operating leverage multiplies operating income (EBIT) at output levels that are likely to be high.

What we've said assumes a higher fixed cost is accompanied by a proportionately lower variable cost so the breakeven point stays more or less the same. If that doesn't happen, higher fixed cost doesn't necessarily mean anything.

CONCEPT CONNECTION   EXAMPLE 14-6

Fixed Variable Cost Trade-Off

Suppose the low-leverage firm in Figure 14-6a has fixed costs of $1,000 per period, sells its product for $10, and has variable costs of $8 per unit. Further suppose that the high-leverage firm in Figure 14-6b has fixed costs of $1,500 and also sells product for $10 a unit.

The diagram shows the breakeven volumes for the two firms to be the same. What variable cost per unit must the high-leverage firm have if it is to achieve the same breakeven point as the low-leverage firm? State the trade-off at the breakeven point. Which structure is preferred if there's a choice?

SOLUTION: Compute the breakeven volume for the low-leverage firm (a) by writing Equation 14.7.

$$Q_{B/E-a} = \frac{F_c}{P - V} = \frac{\$1,000}{\$10 - \$8} = 500 \text{ units}$$

This will also be $Q_{B/E-b}$, the breakeven volume for the high-leverage firm.

Now write Equation 14.7 for the high-leverage firm, showing the variable cost per unit as an unknown, V_b. Then substitute the given price and fixed cost and the calculated breakeven volume.

$$Q_{B/E-b} = \frac{F_c}{P - V_b}$$

$$500 \text{ units} = \frac{\$1,500}{\$10 - V_b}$$

Solving for V_b yields

$$V_b = \$7$$

And

$$C_t = \$10 - \$7 = \$3$$

Summarizing, we have the following:

	Low Leverage	High Leverage
Contribution	$2	$3
Fixed cost	$1,000	$1,500

Thus, at the breakeven, a $1 differential in contributions makes up for a $500 difference in fixed cost.

For an expected level of sales somewhat above the breakeven, the preferable structure depends on volatility. If expectations are for relatively stable business, the high fixed cost model gives better operating results. However, if sales are likely to vary a lot, especially below the breakeven point, the low fixed cost structure might be better in the long run.

14.3e   The Degree of Operating Leverage (DOL)—A Measurement

Operating leverage amplifies changes in sales volume into larger changes in EBIT. It can be quantified and measured with an idea called the *degree of operating leverage,* abbreviated DOL. The concept is similar to the DFL we discussed earlier.

The **DOL** relates relative changes in volume **(Q)** to relative **changes in EBIT**.

The DOL is the ratio of the relative change in EBIT to a relative change in sales. We can write this as

(14.10)
$$\text{DOL} = \frac{\%\Delta\text{EBIT}}{\%\Delta\text{Q}}$$

We'll forgo the derivation here, but it can be shown that the DOL can be expressed as follows.

(14.11)
$$\text{DOL} = \frac{Q(P - V)}{Q(P - V) - F_c}$$

where the variables have the meanings we've been using.

CONCEPT CONNECTION   EXAMPLE 14-7

Degree of Operating Leverage (DOL)

The Albergetti Corp. sells its products at an average price of $10. Variable costs are $7 per unit, and fixed costs are $600 per month. Evaluate the degree of operating leverage when sales are 5% and then 50% above the breakeven level.

SOLUTION: First compute the breakeven volume using Equation 14.7.

$$Q_{B/E} = \frac{F_c}{P - V} = \frac{\$600}{\$10 - \$7} = 200 \text{ units}$$

Breakeven plus 5% and 50% implies sales of 210 and 300 units, respectively. Use Equation 14.11 to calculate the DOL at 210 units per month and at 300 units. At 210 units, we have

$$\text{DOL}_{Q=210} = \frac{Q(P - V)}{Q(P - V) - F_c}$$

$$= \frac{210(\$10 - \$7)}{210(\$10 - 7) - \$600}$$

$$= 21$$

At 300 units, we have

$$DOL_{Q=300} = \frac{300(\$10 - \$7)}{300(\$10 - \$7) - \$600}$$

$$= 3$$

Notice that the DOL *decreases* as the output level increases above the breakeven.

As a brief exercise, show that the DOL is infinite (not defined) in Equation 14.11 at the break-even point.

14.3f   Comparing Operating and Financial Leverage

Operating leverage connects sales with EBIT in much the same way that financial leverage connects EBIT with ROE and EPS.

Financial and operating leverage are similar in that **both** can **enhance results** while **increasing variation**.

Recall that financial leverage can improve performance in ROE and EPS, and that it amplifies changes in EBIT into larger relative changes in those ratios. Similarly, operating leverage can enhance EBIT at a given sales level, and expands variations in sales into larger relative variations in EBIT. The idea is illustrated in Figure 14-7.

Another similarity has to do with the nature of operating and financial costs. Financial leverage involves substituting debt for equity in the firm's capital structure, while operating leverage involves substituting fixed cost for variable cost in its cost structure.

Notice, however, that debt is a *fixed* cost method of financing in that it pays a fixed amount of interest to investors regardless of how well the company does. Equity, on the

FIGURE 14-7   The Similar Functions of Operating and Financial Leverage

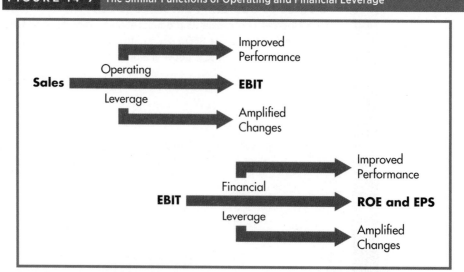

© Cengage Learning

FIGURE 14-8 Risk and Cost Relationships Between Operating and Financial Leverage

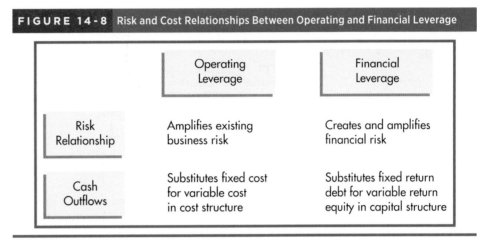

	Operating Leverage	Financial Leverage
Risk Relationship	Amplifies existing business risk	Creates and amplifies financial risk
Cash Outflows	Substitutes fixed cost for variable cost in cost structure	Substitutes fixed return debt for variable return equity in capital structure

© Cengage Learning

other hand, is a *variable* cost form of financing, because the dividends paid to stockholders can be varied or eliminated if the firm isn't doing well. Hence, both forms of leverage involve substituting fixed cash outflows for variable cash outflows.

Finally, there's a similarity but not an exact match between the two kinds of leverage with respect to the two kinds of risk we've defined. Financial risk is the additional variation in ROE and EPS caused by financial leverage, while business risk is variation in EBIT that's enhanced by operating leverage. Both kinds of leverage make their respective risks larger as the levels of leverage increase. However, financial leverage is the sole cause of financial risk, while some business risk would exist even if there were no operating leverage. These last ideas are summarized in Figure 14-8.

Two final points of comparison are worth noting. First, virtually all productive processes involve the use of some equipment that generates fixed cost. Therefore, all firms have some operating leverage. On the other hand, many firms use no debt and therefore have no financial leverage.

Second, financial leverage is more controllable than operating leverage. Technology dictates the minimum and maximum amounts of machinery needed to make most products, so management's choice of an operating leverage level is relatively limited. On the other hand, management can generally choose the amount of debt a firm uses within very broad limits.

14.3g The Compounding Effect of Operating and Financial Leverage

An important result of the existence of two kinds of leverage is that they compound one another. Changes in sales are amplified by operating leverage into larger relative changes in EBIT, which in turn are amplified into still larger relative changes in ROE and EPS by financial leverage. The net effect is quite large because the combined effect of the two kinds of leverage is *multiplicative* rather than additive.

The effects of **financial and operating** leverage **compound** one another.

This means that fairly modest changes in the level of sales can lead to dramatic swings in ROE and EPS in companies that use both operating and financial leverage. The idea is illustrated in Figure 14-9.

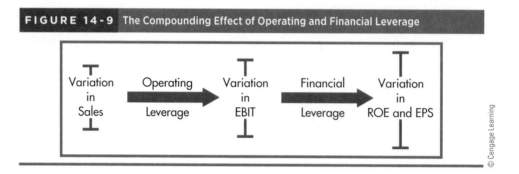

FIGURE 14-9 The Compounding Effect of Operating and Financial Leverage

© Cengage Learning

The **DTL** reflects the combined effect of both kinds of leverage.

The compound effect of operating and financial leverage can be measured by a concept called the *degree of total leverage*, abbreviated DTL. The DTL is simply the product of DOL and DFL.

(14.12)
$$\text{DTL} = \text{DOL} \times \text{DFL}$$

CONCEPT CONNECTION   EXAMPLE 14-8

Degree of Total Leverage

The Allegheny Company is considering replacing a manual production process with a machine. The money to buy the machine will be borrowed. The replacement of people with a machine will alter the firm's cost structure in favor of fixed cost, while the loan will move the capital structure in the direction of more debt. The firm's leverage positions at expected output levels with and without the project are summarized as follows:

	DOL	DFL
Current	2.0	1.5
Proposed	3.5	2.5

The economic outlook is uncertain and some managers fear a decline in sales of as much as 10% in the coming year. Evaluate the effect of the proposed project on risk in financial performance.

SOLUTION: Currently, the degree of total leverage is

$$\text{DTL} = \text{DOL} \times \text{DFL}$$
$$= 2(1.5)$$
$$= 3$$

This means that a 10% decline in sales could result in a 30% decline in EPS. Stated another way, the relative volatility of EPS is three times that of sales.

Under the proposed conditions, the DTL would be much larger.

$$\text{DTL} = \text{DOL} \times \text{DFL}$$
$$= 3.5(2.5)$$
$$= 8.75$$

Here, EPS is almost nine times as volatile as sales, and a 10% drop in volume could produce as much as an 88% decrease in EPS. In other words, EPS could be virtually wiped out. That's likely to affect stock prices a great deal more than a 30% decline.

The conclusion is that the proposal has a great deal more inherent risk than one might think at first glance.[6]

14.4   Capital Structure Theory

During the last 50 years, financial scholars have devoted a great deal of thinking to capital structure. They've essentially been addressing the same question we posed at the beginning of this chapter: Does capital structure affect stock price and the market value of the firm, and if so, is there an optimal structure that maximizes either or both?

The scholarly approach is more mathematical than the work we've been doing, but the results are essentially the same. Structure does affect price and value, and there is an optimum, but there's no way to find it with any precision.

Capital structure theory is one of the more important elements of modern financial thought and has yielded some valuable insights into real-world problems. Hence, it's important that professionals be familiar with the theoretical approach and understand the nature of the results. Fortunately, we can do that without mastering a great deal of mathematics.

14.4a   Background—The Value of the Firm

Theory approaches capital structure by focusing on the market value of the firm and its cost of capital. The assumption is that if market value can be increased by manipulating capital structure, an increase in stock price must follow.

We'll need to become familiar with the terminology and principles used before getting into the theory itself.

Notation   First let's define the notation (symbols) we'll be using. The market value of the firm is the total market value of all of its debt and equity securities represented as follows:

$$V_d = \text{market value of the firm's debt}$$
$$V_e = \text{market value of the firm's stock (equity)}$$
$$V_f = \text{market value of the firm in total}$$

Hence,

(14.13) $$V_f = V_d + V_e$$

---

6. Both of the degree of leverage concepts are a little tricky. The volatility implied by both ratios increases with the addition of debt or fixed cost, but it's even more sensitive to the proximity of breakeven points.

Examine Equation 14.3 (page 597) for the DFL and Equation 14.11 (page 609) for the DOL. Notice that both denominators are zero at breakeven points. In the case of the DOL, the denominator is EBIT, which is zero at the breakeven we've been talking about in this section. For the DFL, the denominator is EBT, which is zero when interest equals operating income.

In the neighborhood of those points, the denominators are very small so the quotients are very large. Hence, we get large *relative* changes in EPS or EBIT, but those changes may not be very large in absolute terms because we're operating at EPS or EBIT levels near zero.

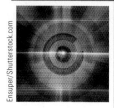

Ensuper/Shutterstock.com

INSIGHTS   Practical Finance

Leverage and Business Strategy

Business strategy involves understanding the factors that define industrial competition. An important issue in strategy is predicting how companies will react to troubled times or competitive challenges. Leverage plays a big part in those predictions.

The more heavily a firm is leveraged, either financially or operationally, the more quickly it loses money when volume decreases. The effect is compounded when both forms of leverage are present. This means leveraged companies react aggressively when something threatens their volume. They cut prices, increase advertising, and offer special promotions quickly in order to keep volume up. That tends to make the industries in which they operate chaotic and less attractive for everyone.

Investors' returns on the firm's securities will be

$$k_d = \text{return on an investment in debt (bonds)}$$
$$\text{and} \quad k_e = \text{return on an investment in equity (stock).}$$

> **Theory begins by assuming a world without taxes or transaction costs**, so investors' returns are exactly component capital costs.

In our study of the cost of capital (Chapter 13), we said that the firm's costs of debt and equity were the investors' returns adjusted for flotation costs and taxes. Theory operates in an abstract world. It assumes away flotation costs and begins by assuming there are no taxes. Therefore, the costs of debt and equity are exactly k_d and k_e, respectively. The cost of capital is then a weighted average of these, which we'll write as

$$k_a = \text{average cost of capital}$$

Value Is Based on Cash Flow, Which Comes from Income   The value of any security is the present value of the cash flows that come from owning it, and all cash flows paid to investors come from earnings. Hence, earnings ultimately determine value.

We'll focus on operating income (EBIT), which is by definition the earnings stream available to either debt or equity investors. To avoid some notational confusion later, we'll refer to operating income as OI rather than EBIT in this section.

Assume OI is completely divided between interest and dividend payments, so we can write

(14.14) $$OI = I + D$$

where: I = total annual interest payment to bondholders and
         D = total annual dividend payment to stockholders.

> **Dividend and interest payments are both perpetuities**, and the firm's market value is the sum of their present values.

Debt is assumed to be perpetual. Whenever principal is paid off, a new amount of equal size is immediately borrowed; hence, I is constant year after year. Because no income is retained, the company doesn't grow, and OI remains constant as well. Then Equation 14.14 implies that dividend payments are also constant. In other words, each stream of annual payments, I and D, is a **perpetuity.**

The values of the firm's debt and equity are then the present values of these perpetuities, (see page 269) and we can write

(14.15)
$$V_d = \frac{I}{k_d}$$

and

(14.16)
$$V_e = \frac{D}{k_e}$$

where k_d and k_e are the costs of debt and equity. Using Equation 14.13, we can also write

(14.17)
$$V_f = \frac{I}{k_d} + \frac{D}{k_e}$$

The nature of the weighted average return is such that the following expression is essentially equivalent to Equation 14.17.

(14.18)
$$V_f = \frac{OI}{k_a}$$

In words, these equations say that the value of the firm is determined by the costs of its debt and equity, and that we can look at them together through the average cost of capital, k_a. Keep in mind that lower rates mean higher values.

Returns drive value in an inverse relationship.

This is an important way of looking at things. It means we can think of **returns** as **driving value**. For example, if something causes investors to require a higher return on an investment in a company's stock, Equation 14.16 says that will drive the value of the firm's equity down. If the return on debt remains the same, the cost of capital, k_a, will also rise and overall value will drop.

Graphic Portrayals   The foregoing means we can look at value by tracking the behavior of the three returns, k_d, k_e, and k_a, as capital structure changes. We're particularly concerned with the behavior of k_a, the average cost of capital, because of its relation to overall value.

Earlier we talked about stock price and value increasing to a maximum as leverage increases. Equation 14.18 tells us that this is equivalent to k_a decreasing to a minimum and then increasing as debt increases. The idea is illustrated in Figure 14-10, where value and stock price, V_f and P_s, achieve a maximum, while k_a reaches a minimum at the same capital structure.

In what follows, we'll find it useful to include k_e and k_d in the bottom graph of portrayals like Figure 14-10 to analyze how changes in the two component costs of capital influence the average cost.

14.4b   The Early Theory by Modigliani and Miller

The theoretical ball got rolling in 1958 when two well-known scholars named Franco Modigliani and Merton Miller published a paper on the effect of capital structure on value.[7] Modigliani and Miller are cited often, and it has become common to refer to them as MM.

---

7. See Franco Modigliani and Merton H. Miller, "The Cost of Capital, Corporation Finance, and the Theory of Investment," *American Economic Review* 48 (June 1958): 261–297.

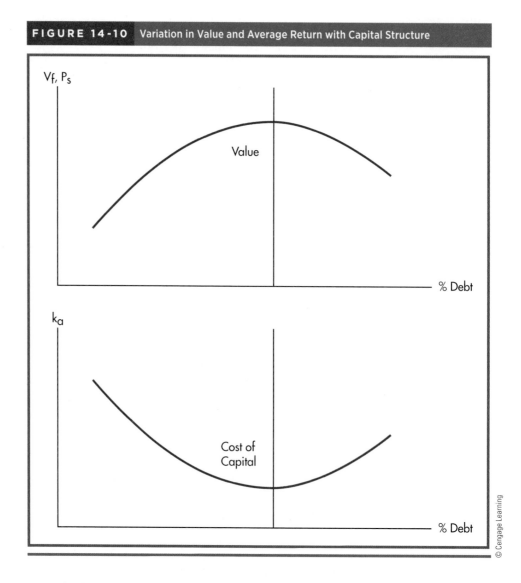

FIGURE 14-10   Variation in Value and Average Return with Capital Structure

Restrictive Assumptions in the Original Model   MM's work was a sophisticated mathematical model of the financial world. It included a number of restrictions on the behavior of firms and individuals that made it less than realistic. Nevertheless, it provided important insights into the effects of capital structure on value. Later work relaxed some of the restrictions and led to the state of the theory as it is today.

For our purposes the most important restrictions were the following:

1. There are no income taxes.

2. Securities trade in perfectly efficient capital markets in which there are no transaction costs.

3. Investors and companies can borrow as much as they want at the same rate. That is,
    a. Rates don't go up as one borrows more money, and
    b. The rate is the same for investors and companies.

The second assumption contains an important subtlety. Among other things, it says that there are no costs associated with bankruptcy. This idea sounds like a contradiction to many students and needs to be explained.

A bankrupt company goes through two processes. First it loses value because of deteriorating business conditions; then it goes into bankruptcy proceedings, which involve either a restructuring of debt or a liquidation of assets.

The assumption of zero bankruptcy cost implies that no legal or administrative fees are incurred in restructuring or liquidating, and if liquidation is required, assets are sold for a value close to what they were worth to the company.

In other words, bankruptcy costs are fees and losses on the sale of used assets. The term does not refer to the loss in value that put the business into a bankruptcy situation in the first place.

The Assumptions and Reality

Clearly, the assumptions of the original MM model were unrealistic. First and most obvious, there are income taxes.

Second, the legal and administrative expenses of bankruptcy are quite large, and assets sold under duress usually bring only a fraction of their original value. In fact, these costs often eat up most of what's left in a bankrupt company.

Third, individuals usually pay higher interest rates than firms pay, and anyone's rates generally go up as more money is borrowed.

In spite of these problems, the MM model made an insightful contribution to thinking on the subject of capital structure and provided a starting point for a great deal more effort.

The Result

MM showed that under the restrictive assumptions we've discussed and several others, the firm's total value is unaffected by capital structure. The result is called the **independence hypothesis**, because it shows value to be independent of structure. It can be described in terms of a firm's cost of debt and equity and its average cost of capital. The ideas are illustrated in Figure 14-11.

The top graph is straightforward. The firm's value is constant with increasing leverage as we move from left to right on the graph. Stock price can also be shown to be unchanging. The bottom graph requires more explanation.

Notice that along the vertical axis, at zero debt, we have only equity capital, so $k_e = k_a$. Also notice that k_d is lower than k_e, reflecting the fact that an investment in debt is somewhat safer than an investment in the same company's equity. The assumption that the firm can borrow at a constant rate is reflected by displaying k_d as a horizontal line for all percentages of debt.

Now consider what happens as the firm replaces equity with debt and moves to the right in the graph. Because the debt is lower in cost, you'd expect the average cost of capital, k_a, to fall as more debt is added to the financing mix. It doesn't, however, because k_e rises as the debt load increases, compensating in the average for the lower cost debt.

Some increase in k_e will always come about when debt is added, because additional debt increases the financial risk on equity holders. As risk increases, equity holders demand higher rates of return. But a constant k_a and the associated constant value

---

*MM initially assumed there were **no costs to bankruptcy**.*

*Under MM's initial set of restrictions, **value** is **independent** of capital structure.*

*As **cheaper debt** is added, the **cost of equity increases** because of increased risk such that the weighted average **cost of capital remains constant**.*

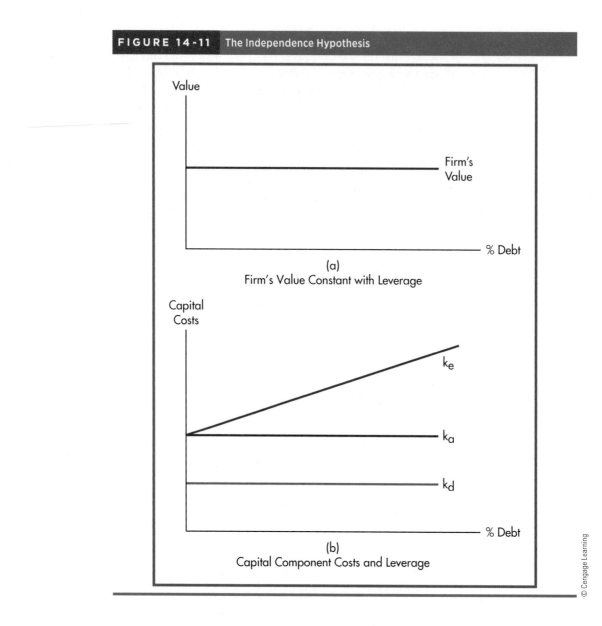

FIGURE 14-11 The Independence Hypothesis

Value

Firm's
Value

% Debt

(a)
Firm's Value Constant with Leverage

Capital
Costs

k_e

k_a

k_d

% Debt

(b)
Capital Component Costs and Leverage

implies that k_e increases *exactly* enough to offset the benefit of the increasing amount of lower cost debt being used.

MM's Result Supports the Operating Income View

MM's result wasn't exactly new. Many people already held what can be called an operating income view that's largely the same.

This position maintains that because the firm's value is the present value of its expected operating income stream, a rational market will implicitly hold the total value of that stream constant no matter how the capital is divided between debt and equity. In a sense, this view says that you can't make something out of nothing. The firm's investment value is whatever it is on the basis of income, and that's that. You can't magically create more value by fooling around with the mix.

However, until MM came along, no one had a very good explanation of how this would happen in the marketplace. That is, no one could satisfactorily explain a *process* that would hold investment value constant as leverage is added or subtracted.

The Arbitrage Concept   MM proposed that a process of **arbitrage**[8] driven by equity investors seeking to *maximize their returns* would hold the value of a firm constant through changes in leverage. The argument is quite complex, but essentially says that if the value of a firm were to go up due to adding leverage, shareholders could get a better return by selling its shares, borrowing some money on their own, and investing in a similar but unleveraged company (the arbitrage is between the leveraged and unleveraged companies). MM's assumption of uniform interest rates comes into play as investors borrow money on their own.

The sell-off would drive the price of the leveraged firm down, while the buying would put upward pressure on the price of the unleveraged firm, driving the two values together. The entire process then holds the value of any firm constant as leverage is increased.

(Don't try to figure out why this should work from what we've said here. We haven't gone into enough detail to do that. It's enough that you get a rough appreciation of the conceptual approach.)

MM were said to have provided *behavioral support* for the operating income argument. In other words, they showed how the behavior of investors in financial markets might hold the total value of a firm constant through changes in capital structure. Keep in mind, however, that to do this they had to assume the absence of taxes, no transaction costs for investing (like commissions), and that everyone could borrow as much as they wanted at the same rate.

Interpreting the Result   It's important to understand what this early result implies about the real world. It doesn't say that a firm's value and its stock price are unaffected by leverage. We know that isn't true. What it does imply is that the *reason* leverage affects value stems from **market imperfections,** like taxes and transaction costs, and not from the basic interaction of investors and companies. That's an important insight into why things are the way they are.

14.4c   Relaxing the Assumptions—More Insights

Things really got interesting when the assumptions that excluded taxes and bankruptcy costs were relaxed. Before we get into the effect of those changes we need to understand an important point about the workings of the tax system.

Financing and the U.S. Tax System   The tax system favors debt over equity financing because interest payments are deductible to the paying company but dividends

---

MM propose that **arbitrage** between leveraged and unleveraged firms will hold **value constant** as debt increases.

The MM result implies that leverage affects value because of **market imperfections**.

---

8. Arbitrage means making a profit by buying and selling the same thing at the same time in two different markets. For example, suppose you noticed that a stock was selling for $45 in New York and $50 in Boston. You could make a profit by placing a buy order in New York and a sell order in Boston at the same time, and delivering the share in Boston that you bought in New York.

TABLE 14-4   The Tax System Favors Debt Financing

	All Equity	50% Debt 50% Equity
Capital		
Debt	$ 0	$ 500
Equity	1,000	500
Total capital	$1,000	$1,000
EBIT	$ 100	$ 100
Interest (10% of debt)	—	50
EBT	$ 100	$ 50
Tax (40% of EBT)	40	20
Net income	$ 60	$ 30
Dividend	60	30
Net retained	$ 0	$ 0
Payments to Investors		
Interest	$ 0	$ 50
Dividends	60	30
Total	$ 60	$ 80

© Cengage Learning

The tax system **favors debt financing** because **interest is tax deductible**, while dividends are not.

are not. We'll illustrate with the two companies depicted in Table 14-4. Assume they're identical except that one is financed entirely with equity and the other is 50% debt financed. Also assume both pay out all after-tax earnings in dividends, the interest rate is 10%, and the tax rate is 40%.

Both companies pay all available earnings to the investors who furnish capital. In the case of the equity-financed company, that means all net income goes to stockholders. However, the other firm pays interest to bondholders and net income to stockholders.

The important point is shown at the bottom of the table. *Total* payments to investors are *higher* for the leveraged company. The difference comes from the fact that the leveraged firm can deduct interest from taxable income and therefore *pays less tax.*

Including Corporate Taxes in the MM Theory

In the presence of taxes, operating income (OI) has to be split between investors and the government. Because value is ultimately based on income received by investors, this lowers the firm's value from what it would be if there were no taxes. However, the amount of the value reduction depends on the firm's use of leverage, because that affects how much tax the government collects.

Let's focus on how much the government gets. The amount depends on the tax rate and the distribution of funds between debt and equity investors.

In the absence of debt, all of OI is taxable. If the tax rate is T, the government gets

(a) $T(OI)$

However, interest is tax deductible, so if there's debt and an amount of interest, I, the government gets only

(b) $$T(OI - I) = T(OI) - TI$$

The difference in what the government gets with and without debt is the difference between a and b, which is TI. Thus, when a firm uses debt financing, the government's take is reduced by TI every year.

Stated conversely, debt results in a yearly perpetuity of TI dollars to be divided among investors that wouldn't be available if debt weren't used. The amount TI is called the **tax shield** associated with debt financing.

The impact of the tax shield on value is simply the present value of the perpetuity TI capitalized at discount rate k_d.

> In the MM model with taxes, **interest** provides a **tax shield** that reduces government's share of the firm's earnings.

(14.19) $$\textbf{PV of tax shield} = \frac{\textbf{TI}}{\textbf{k}_d}$$

This can be written more conveniently by recognizing that interest is just debt times the interest rate.

(14.20) $$I = Bk_d$$

where B = debt. (We use the letter B because debt is in the form of bonds.)

Substituting into Equation 14.19 yields

(14.21) $$\textbf{PV of tax shield} = \frac{\textbf{TI}}{\textbf{k}_d} = \frac{\textbf{TBk}_d}{\textbf{k}_d} = \textbf{TB}$$

> **Value is increased** by the **PV** of the **tax shield**. The **benefit of debt** is the **tax rate** times the **debt** amount.

TB is also referred to as the **benefit of debt.** In words, Equation 14.21 says that *having debt in the capital structure increases a firm's value by the magnitude of that debt times the tax rate.*

For example, suppose an all-equity firm that has a tax rate of 40% and a market value of $2 million restructures by trading $1 million in stock for the same amount in bonds. The implication of the theory with taxes is that the firm's market value will increase by

$$.4 \times \$1M = \$400,000$$

to $2.4 million.

> The benefit of debt accrues **entirely to stockholders** because bond returns are fixed.

Further, the *increment in value will all accrue to the stockholders* because the value of the bonds is fixed by the terms of the bond contract and current interest rates.

This is a very significant conclusion. It says that a firm can increase its value and the wealth of shareholders at a constant rate by trading equity for debt until it is financed virtually 100% with debt (we say virtually because there has to be some equity). The result is represented in Figure 14-12.

> In the MM model with taxes, **value increases** steadily as **leverage is added**.

The top graph shows the market value of the firm increasing from its all-equity value as the addition of debt increases the present value of the tax shield along with leverage. The lower graph shows the behavior of the component and weighted average costs of capital. Notice that with the inclusion of taxes the cost of debt is $k_d(1 - T)$ rather than just k_d.

FIGURE 14-12   MM Theory with Taxes

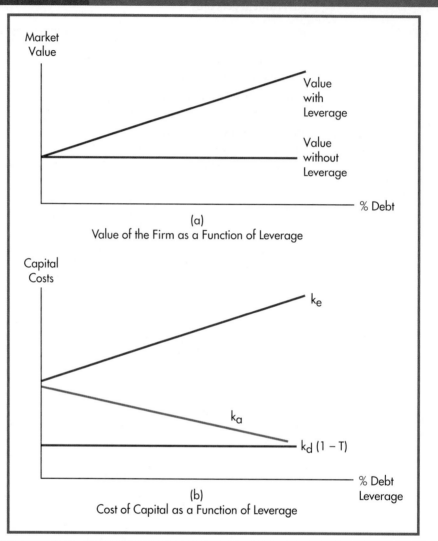

(a)
Value of the Firm as a Function of Leverage

(b)
Cost of Capital as a Function of Leverage

© Cengage Learning

In this representation, the average cost of capital falls with the inclusion of more low-cost debt. The cost of equity increases at the same time, but not fast enough to overcome the effect of the low-cost debt.

Bankruptcy costs eventually make investors **raise required rates**, which **lowers value**.

Including Bankruptcy Costs in the MM Theory

The probability of business failure increases as a firm takes on more debt. As explained earlier, bankruptcy costs are *additional* losses that accrue primarily to stockholders when companies fail. As leverage increases past some point, investors become conscious enough of bankruptcy costs to begin raising their required rates of return. In other words, investors begin to worry that *they* will incur losses due to bankruptcy cost if the firm fails. This happens first to equity investors and later to bondholders. As investor required rates go up, so do the firm's capital costs.

The effect is shown in Figure 14-13b. As we move to the right, critical points are passed after which k_e and then k_d begin to climb. It's important to notice that the average cost of capital, k_a, does not begin to increase as soon as k_e starts upward. That's because it is still being driven downward by the mix change coming from the replacement of high-cost equity with low-cost debt. The minimum value of k_a is reached only after k_e has gone up quite a bit, perhaps reinforced by an increase in k_d.

Now consider the top diagram that shows the firm's value. According to Equations 14.15 through 14.18, increasing required returns have a depressing effect on value as we continue to the right after one or both of the returns begin to rise. However, the growing tax shield continues to add value at the same time.

At first the rate effect isn't strong enough to overcome the tax effect, and the net result of more leverage is still an increase in value. Before long, however, the growing specter of failure overwhelms the tax effect, and value begins to decline with additional leverage. The peak in value coincides with the minimum in k_a.

The **MM model** with taxes and bankruptcy costs concludes that an **optimal capital structure exists**.

Summarizing the Results   In short, the MM model with taxes and bankruptcy costs says that additional leverage increases the value of a firm when total leverage is relatively low. However, a maximum is eventually reached, after which further increases reduce value. Unfortunately, the theory does not provide a method for finding the maximum.

Notice that this result is essentially the same as the one we developed by using an intuitive approach early in the chapter. A little leverage helps, a lot hurts, and it's hard to find the perfect amount.

However, the reasons for the conclusion are different. The MM model attributes the benefit of leverage solely to taxes, while the intuitive approach relies on the impact of improved performance on investors' attitudes and perceptions. Both attribute leverage's negative effects to risk.

14.4d   An Insight into Mergers and Acquisitions

Corporate mergers happen in a number of ways that we'll study in some detail in Chapter 17. For now we just need to understand that in many mergers one company simply buys the stock of another company called the *target*.

To obtain control quickly, the buying company has to purchase most of the shares of the target over a short period of time. That means it can't just buy them in the stock market at the going price, because at any particular time most stockholders aren't interested in selling at that price.

To overcome this difficulty, the acquiring firm offers to buy the target's stock at a *premium* over its current market price. The offer is made to all of the target's stockholders at once and may be extended directly or through the firm's management.

This process means that a corporate buyer usually pays a great deal more for a target company than the pre-merger market value of its stock. Paying twice that value isn't unheard of.

This raises an interesting question. How can any sane acquiring company rationalize paying as much as 50% or 100% over market value for a target company? Are the financial high rollers who do such deals crazy, or do they know something others don't?

One rationale for high acquisition premiums involves capital structure theory and the method of financing the purchase. Target companies are frequently thought to be undervalued because they aren't using much debt. In other words, their capital structures are near the left sides of the graphs in Figure 14-13. The implication is that a restructuring that adds debt might substantially increase their value.

Acquiring firms often raise the money to purchase a target's stock by borrowing. The resulting merged business ends up with a new owner and a great deal more debt than it had before. This seems like a sucker deal for the new owner. *But* if the increase in market value due to adding debt (and moving to the right in Figure 14-13) is greater

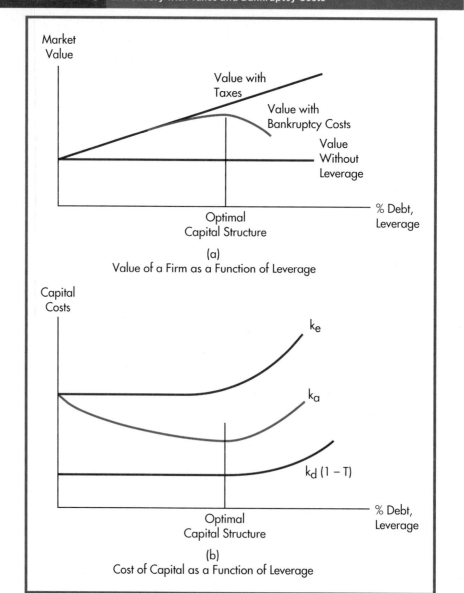

FIGURE 14-13   MM Theory with Taxes and Bankruptcy Costs

Market Value

Value with Taxes

Value with Bankruptcy Costs

Value Without Leverage

% Debt, Leverage

Optimal Capital Structure

(a)
Value of a Firm as a Function of Leverage

Capital Costs

k_e

k_a

$k_d (1 - T)$

% Debt, Leverage

Optimal Capital Structure

(b)
Cost of Capital as a Function of Leverage

than the total premium paid for the stock, everyone can come out a winner, the buyers as well as the old owners.

In other words, the increase in leverage brought about by a merger can *theoretically* produce a value increment that is available to be divided between the new and old owners. If the increment is big enough, and the new owners negotiate wisely enough, they can get rich! On the other hand, if they misjudge the effect of the leverage increase, they can go broke.

The argument certainly has validity, but it tends to be somewhat overblown. Indeed, many acquisitions involve premiums that seem far beyond anything that could be achieved through a leverage-based value increment.

Borrowing to pay a **premium** in an **acquisition** may be theoretically **justified** if value is increasing with leverage.

CONCEPT CONNECTIONS

Basic Concepts and Calculations: Tables 14-1 and 14-2 and Equation 14.1, *pages 587, 589, and 588*

EXAMPLE 14-1   Managing EPS Through Leverage, *page 589*

Basics Plus DFL: Apply Equation 14.3, *page 597*

EXAMPLE 14-2   Forecasting Results Through the DFL, *page 597*

EXAMPLE 14-3   EBIT–EPS Analysis, *page 600*

EXAMPLE 14-4   Contribution, *page 605*

EXAMPLE 14-5   Breakeven, *page 606*

EXAMPLE 14-6   Fixed Variable Cost Trade-Off, *page 608*

EXAMPLE 14-7   Degree of Operating Leverage, *page 609*

EXAMPLE 14-8   Degree of Total Leverage, *page 612*

QUESTIONS

1. The user of leverage might be thought of as taking advantage of the provider. Between stockholders and bondholders, who is the user, and who is the provider? Give a word explanation or illustration that might support this view. What does the used party get in return?

2. The central issue underlying the study of leverage is whether or not it influences stock price and whether there's an optimal structure. But the whole idea seems kind of fuzzy and uncertain. Why are people so interested? (*Hint:* Think of management's goals and of the world of mergers.)

3. Relate business and financial risk as defined in this chapter to the risks described in Chapter 9.

4. Why are ROE and EPS such important measures of performance to investors?

5. Both business risk and financial risk would exist with or without either type of leverage. Leverage just makes them more significant. Are those statements true or false? Explain.

6. Briefly explain the pros and cons of financial leverage. In other words, what are its benefits, and what are the costs that come along with those benefits?

7. Explain in words the ROCE test for the advisability of adding leverage. That is, what is the test really telling us? When will it indicate a company is doing the wrong thing?

8. The risk added by financing is small and insignificant in relation to the inherent risk in most businesses. Is that statement true or false? Discuss.

9. Describe generally how leverage affects stock prices. What forces are at work, driven by what effects?

10. Explain the difference between a fixed and a variable cost. How do these concepts change as the time horizon lengthens? In other words, are the same things fixed over a five-year planning period that are fixed in a typical one-year period? What about a 10-year period? What's the relevant period when we're talking about operating leverage?

11. Why do labor-intensive processes involve less operating leverage than automated processes? What fixed costs are associated with automation? Why can't those costs be eliminated by just selling the machinery?

12. Explain the idea of breakeven analysis in a brief paragraph.

13. Describe the concept of the breakeven point in words by using the concept of contribution and fixed costs. (Short answer.)

14. Summarize the effect of operating leverage on EBIT.

15. The Braithwaite Tool Co. is considering a major modernization and automation of its plant using borrowed funds. Fully discuss a serious financial negative that could result from the project.

16. Explain the idea of bankruptcy costs. Why are they important to investors? When do investors start to worry about them?

17. Briefly describe the result of MM's original restrictive model. Why was it important in spite of its serious restrictions?

18. Briefly summarize the operating income argument that was supported by the original MM result.

19. Outline the arbitrage process proposed by MM that supports the operating income argument. What is the arbitrage between?

20. Explain in words how the tax system favors debt financing.

21. In a short paragraph, describe the result of adding taxes to the MM model.

22. In another short paragraph, describe the effect of adding bankruptcy costs to the MM model with taxes.

23. Compare the implications of the MM model with taxes and bankruptcy costs to the things we discovered by studying the Arizona Balloon Corporation.

BUSINESS ANALYSIS

1. The Armageddon Corp. is in big trouble. Sales are down and profits are off. On top of that, the firm's credit rating has been reduced, so it's facing very high interest rates on anything it borrows in the future. Current long-term borrowing represents 60% of capital but at fixed interest rates, so it won't be affected.

   The firm's major stockholder, the Apocalypse Group, has scheduled a conference with management to discuss the company's problems. Everyone is very nervous about this conference, and the executive team is meeting to decide what to tell Apocalypse.

   Charlie Gladhand, the director of marketing, came into the meeting wearing a wide grin. He explained that he'd read an article about leverage that contained the solution to the company's problem. The article told of several successful firms that had, to the delight of their owners, become more successful by borrowing money. Charlie suggests that Armageddon dazzle the Apocalypse Group by borrowing heavily in the next few days before the conference.

   Critique Charlie's idea.

2. You're interested in investing in the Peters Company, which has shown a remarkable increase in EPS during the last three years. Investigating, you find that the company's debt to equity ratio has increased dramatically over the same period and is now four to one. How does this information affect your feelings about Peters as an investment?

3. You're the CFO of Axelrod Trucking, a privately held firm whose owner, Joe Axelrod, is interested in selling the company and retiring. He therefore wants to pump up its value by any means possible. Joe read an article about leverage in a business magazine the other day and has sent you a memo directing that you restructure the firm's capital to the "optimum" in

order to maximize the company's value. Prepare a brief response to Joe's memo.

4. The Revere Company currently has good earnings and a capital structure that's 20% debt. Its EPS is in the upper quarter of firms in its industry. Top management's compensation is in large part based on the year-end price of the company's stock. It's now October and the president, Harry Upscale, is looking for ways to pump that price before December 31. Harry invests in stocks himself and pays a great deal of attention to EPS when buying and selling. He also understands that leverage can magnify EPS. However, he knows little more than that about finance. Harry has strongly suggested to the treasurer that Revere restructure its capital to 65% debt to enhance EPS and increase stock price.

    You're an analyst in the firm's treasury department. The treasurer has asked you to prepare an analysis of Harry's proposal to help him talk the boss out of the idea. You've calculated the company's current DFL at 2.2, and projected that it would be 5.8 at the proposed leverage level. Draft a memo from the treasurer to Harry tactfully explaining why his idea may not work and might actually have a result opposite to what he wants to achieve.

5. The Appleridge Company is a large manufacturer of capital goods. (The demand for capital goods typically swings up and down a great deal between good and bad economic times.) Business has been good lately and is expected to remain so in the foreseeable future. The firm is currently relatively labor intensive in its processes. The chief engineer, Mike Quickwrench, has suggested a major project to modernize and automate the plant. At the output level planned for next year, the project will reduce total cost by 10%. Mike has presented the idea to the management team in a totally positive light. The other executives are caught up in Mike's enthusiasm and are ready to proceed. You're Appleridge's CFO, and feel that all sides of an issue should be discussed before it is approved. What concerns do you have? How would you present them in a way that keeps you from appearing to be overly negative?

6. The Wycombe Company is doing well and is interested in diversifying, so it has been looking around for an acquisition target. The Albe Company has been found with the help of an investment banker. Albe is quite profitable and is about half the size of Wycombe. This size relationship is reflected in their market values. Both firms are financed entirely by equity. The investment banker has advised that it will be necessary to pay a premium of about 30% over market price to acquire Albe. Wycombe's president is having a hard time with this news and has asked you for advice. Construct and explain an approach to the acquisition that might make the premium easier to rationalize. Would it affect your argument if neither Albe nor Wycombe were particularly profitable? If so, how?

PROBLEMS

Basic Concepts and Calculations: Tables 14-1 and 14-2 and Equation 14.1 (pages 587, 589, and 588)

1. The Connecticut Computer Company has the following selected financial results:

	10% Debt	40% Debt	75% Debt
Debt	$ 10,000		
Equity	90,000		
Total capital	$100,000		
Shares (@ $5)	18,000		
EBIT	$ 18,000		
Interest (15%)	1,500		
EBT	$ 16,500		
Tax (40%)	6,600		
Net income	$ 9,900		
ROE			
EPS			

The company is considering a capital restructuring to increase leverage from its present level of 10% of capital.

   a. Calculate Connecticut's ROE and EPS under its current capital structure.

   b. Restate the financial statement line items shown, the number of shares outstanding, ROE, and EPS if Connecticut borrows money and uses it to retire stock until its capital structure is 40% debt assuming EBIT remains unchanged and the stock continues to sell at its book value. (Develop the second column of the chart shown.)

   c. Recalculate the same figures assuming Connecticut continues to restructure until its capital structure is 75% debt. (Develop the third column of the chart.)

   d. How is increasing leverage affecting financial performance? What overall effect might the changes have on the market price of Connecticut's stock? Why? (Words only. *Hint:* Consider the move from 10% to 40% and that from 40% to 75% separately.)

2. Reconsider the Connecticut Computer Company of the previous problem assuming the firm has experienced some difficulties and its EBIT has fallen to $8,000.

   a. Reconstruct the three-column chart assuming Connecticut's EBIT remains at $8,000.

   b. Interpret the result in terms of stock price and the advisability of restructuring capital under these conditions.

   c. Could these results have been predicted more easily? Use the ROCE concept to come to the same conclusion.

3. Assume Connecticut Computer Company of the last two problems is earning an EBIT of $15,000. Once again, calculate the chart showing the implication of adding more leverage. Verbally rationalize the result.

4. Watson Waterbed Works Inc. has an EBIT of $2.75 million, can borrow at 15% interest, and pays combined state and federal income taxes of 40%. It currently has no debt and is capitalized by equity of $12 million. The firm has 1.5 million shares of common stock outstanding that trade at book value.

   a. Calculate Watson's net income, ROE, and EPS currently and at capital structures that have 20%, 40%, 60%, and 80% debt.

   b. Compare the EPS at the different leverage levels, and the amount of change between levels as leverage increases. What happens to the effect of more debt as leverage increases from a little to a lot?

Managing EPS Through Leverage: Concept Connection Example 14-1 (page 589)

5. The Tannenbaum Tea Company wants to show the stock market an EPS of $3 per share, but doesn't expect to be able to improve profitability over what is reflected in the financial plan for next year. The plan is partially reproduced below.

Tannenbaum Tea Company
Financial Projection 20X1
($000)

EBIT	$18,750	Debt	$ 13,000
Interest (@ 12%)	1,560	Equity	97,000
EBT	$ 17,190	Capital	$110,000
Tax (@ 40%)	6,876		
Net income	$ 10,314	Number of shares =	3,700,000

Tannenbaum's stock sells at book value. Will trading equity for debt help the firm achieve its EPS goal, and if so, what debt level will produce the desired EPS?

Basics Plus DFL: Apply Equation 14.3 (page 597)

6. The Canterbury Coach Corporation has EBIT of $3.62 million and total capital of $20 million, which is 15% debt. The 425,000 shares of stock outstanding sell at book value. The firm pays 12% interest on its debt and is subject to a combined state and federal tax rate of 40%. Canterbury is contemplating a capital restructuring to either 30%, 45%, 60%, or 75% debt.

   a. At the current level of profitability, will more debt enhance results? Why?

   b. Calculate the net income, ROE, EPS, and the DFL at the current and proposed structures, and display your results in a systematic table.

   c. In a short paragraph referring to your table, discuss the trade-off between performance and increased risk (reflected in the DFL) as leverage increases. Do some levels seem to make more sense than others? What business characteristics would make the higher leverage levels less of a problem?

Forecasting Results Through the DFL: Concept Connection Example 14-2 (page 597)

7. Balfour Corp. has the following operating results and capital structure ($000):

Revenue	$6,000	Debt	$ 1,200
Cost/Expense	4,500	Equity	8,800
EBIT	$ 1,500	Total	$10,000

   The firm is contemplating a capital restructuring to 60% debt. Its stock is currently selling for book value at $25 per share. The interest rate is 9% and combined state and federal taxes are 42%.

   a. Calculate EPS under the current and proposed capital structures.

   b. Calculate the DFL under both structures.

   c. Use the DFLs to forecast the resulting EPS under each structure if operating profit falls off by 5%, 10%, or 25%.

   d. Comment on the desirability of the proposed structure versus the current one as a function of the volatility of the business.

   e. Is stock price likely to be increased by a change to the proposed capital structure? Discuss briefly.

8. Algebraically derive:

$$EPS = ROE \times (book\ value\ per\ share)$$

   (*Hint:* Write the definitions of ROE, EPS, and book value, and then start substituting.)

EBIT–EPS Analysis: Concept Connection Example 14-3 (page 600)

9. You're a financial analyst at Pinkerton Interactive Graphic Systems (PIGS), a successful entrant in a new and rapidly growing field. As in most new fields, however, rapid growth is anything but ensured, and PIGS's future performance is uncertain.

   The firm expects to earn operating profits of $4 million next year, up from $1 million last year. To support this enormous growth, the firm plans to raise $15 million in new capital. It already has capital of $5 million that is 40% debt.

   PIGS can raise the new money in any proportion of debt and equity management chooses. The CFO is considering three possibilities: all equity, $8 million debt and $7 million equity, and all debt.

   Interest on the current debt as well as on new borrowing is expected to be 10%, and the company pays state and federal income taxes at a combined rate of 40%. Equity will be raised by selling stock at the current market price of $10, which is equal to its book value.

The CFO has asked you to prepare an analysis to aid management in making the debt/equity decision. You are also to provide a recommendation of your own.

a. Prepare an EBIT–EPS analysis of the situation showing a line for the capital structure that results from each of the three options. (Calculate EPS under each new capital structure at EBIT levels of $1 million, $2 million, and $4 million. Then graph EBIT versus EPS for each option. Refer to Figure 14-3. Show last year's EPS on the graph.)

b. Discuss the effect the options might have on stock price.

c. Make a subjective recommendation under each of the following assumptions about the $4 million operating profit forecast. Support your position with words and references to your EBIT–EPS analysis.

1. The $4 million operating profit projection is a best-case scenario. Anything from $2 million to $4 million has an equal probability of occurring.

2. The $4 million is a fair estimate with about a 60% probability. However, performance better than $4 million is unlikely. Results could range anywhere from zero to $4 million.

3. The $4 million is an easy target. There's an even chance of anything between $4 million and $8 million.

Contribution and Breakeven: Concept Connection Examples 14-4 and 14-5 (pages 605 and 606)

10. Cranberry Wood Products Inc. spends an average of $9.50 in labor and $12.40 in materials on every unit it sells. Sales commissions and shipping amount to another $3.10. All other costs are fixed and add up to $140,000 per month. The average unit sells for $32.00.

a. What are Cranberry's contribution and contribution margin?

b. What is the firm's breakeven point in units?

c. Calculate the dollar breakeven point in two ways.

d. Sketch the breakeven diagram.

Fixed Variable Cost Trade-Off and DOL: Concept Connection Examples 14-6 and 14-7 (pages 608 and 609)

11. Refer to the Cranberry company of the previous problem:

a. Calculate the DOL when sales are 20%, 30%, and 40% above breakeven.

b. Suppose automated equipment is added that increases fixed costs by $20,000 per month. How much will total variable cost have to decrease to keep the breakeven point the same?

c. Calculate the DOL at the same output levels used in part (a)

d. Comment on the differences in DOL with and without the additional equipment.

Problems 12–15 refer to Burl Wood Products (BWP), a manufacturer of high-quality furniture.

12. BWP projects sales of 100,000 units next year at an average price of $50 per unit. Variable costs are estimated at 40% of revenue, and fixed costs will be $2.4 million. BWP has $1 million in bonds outstanding on which it pays 8%, and its marginal tax rate is 40%. There are 100,000 shares of stock outstanding which trade at their book value of $30. Compute BWP's contribution, contribution margin, net income, DOL, and EPS.

13. BWP intends to purchase a machine which will result in a major improvement in product quality along with a small increase in manufacturing efficiency. The machine will cost $1 million which will be borrowed at 9%. The quality improvement is expected to have a significant impact on BWP's competitive position. Indeed, management expects sales to increase by 5% in spite of a

planned 10% price increase. The efficiency improvement combined with the price increase will result in variable costs of 36% of revenue. Fixed cost, however, will rise by 19%.

a. Compute BWP's, new contribution, contribution margin, EAT, DOL, and EPS if it purchases the new machine.

b. If all of BWP's projections come to pass, how will stock price be influenced? What factors should be considered in estimating a stock price change?

14. Calculate BWP's DFL and DTL before and after the acquisition of the new machine.

15. Use the information from the previous two problems. Calculate BWP's breakeven point in units and dollars, with and without the purchase of the new machine.

Degree of Total Leverage (DTL): Concept Connection Example 14-8 (page 612)

16. The Spitfire Model Airplane Company has the following modified income statement ($000) at 100,000 units of production:

Revenue	$10,000
Variable cost	6,500
Fixed cost	2,200
EBIT	$ 1,300
Interest (@ 10%)	500
EBT	$ 800
Tax (@ 40%)	320
Net income	$ 480
Number of shares	20,000

a. What are Spitfire's contribution margin and dollar breakeven point?

b. Calculate Spitfire's current DFL, DOL, and DTL.

c. Calculate the current EPS and estimate what it would become if sales declined by 25%. Use the DTL first and then recalculate the modified income statement. (Assume a negative EBT generates a negative tax.)

17. The Singleton Metal Stamping Company is planning to buy a new computer-controlled stamping machine for $10 million. The purchase will be financed entirely with borrowed money, which will change Singleton's capital structure substantially. It will also change operations by adding $1.5 million in fixed cost and eliminating $2 million in variable cost at the current level of sales. The firm's current financial position is reflected in the following statement ($000):

Revenue	$18,000		
Variable cost	10,000	Debt	$ 5,000
Fixed cost	5,000	Equity	15,000
EBIT	$ 3,000	Total	$ 20,000
Interest (@ 10%)	500		
EBT	$ 2,500	Number of shares	750,000
Tax (@ 40%)	1,000	EPS	$ 2.00
Net income	$ 1,500		

a. Restate the financial statements with the new machine, and calculate the dollar breakeven points with and without it.

b. Calculate the DFL with and without the new machine.

c. Calculate the DOL with and without the new machine. (*Hint:* You don't need Q to use Equation 14.11, because PQ is revenue and VQ is total variable cost.)

    d. Calculate the DTL with and without the new machine.

    e. Comment on the variability of EPS with sales and the source of that variability.

    f. Is it a good idea to buy the new machine if sales are expected to remain near current levels? Give two reasons why or why not. What has to be anticipated for the project to make sense?

18. Schoen Industries pays interest of $3 million each year on bonds with an average coupon rate of 7.5%. The firm has 4.5 million shares of stock outstanding and pays out 100% of earnings in dividends. Earnings per share (EPS) is $3.50. Schoen's cost of equity is 12%. Calculate the firm's total value (the value of its debt plus that of its equity) under the assumptions of Modigliani and Miller's simplest model (i.e., that there are no taxes and no transactions costs in financial markets). (*Hint:* Use Equations 14.15–14.17.)

19. Assume Schoen Industries of the last problem is subject to income tax at a rate of 40%.

    a. Recalculate the value of the firm, assuming there is no tax shield associated with debt, and compare it to the value calculated in the last problem. That is, assume interest is subtracted in calculating earnings, but is not deductible in calculating taxes. How much value has theoretically been lost to investors as a result of taxes? Which investors suffer the loss, stockholders or bondholders?

    b. What is the value of the *tax shield* associated with the firm's debt. What is the *benefit of debt*? Calculate the theoretical value of the firm including the benefit of debt and compare it with the value calculated in the last problem. Who gets the incremental value resulting from the tax shield?

    c. Under what conditions, assuming bankruptcy costs are introduced, are investors likely to receive the full benefit of debt calculated in part b? (Words only.)

THOMSON REUTERS

Go to **www.cengage.com/thomsonone,** select your book, and click on the Thomson ONE button. Enter Thomson ONE—Business School Edition by using the user name and password you created when you registered the serial number on your access card. Select a problem for this chapter, and you'll see an expanded version that includes instructions on how to navigate within the Thomson ONE system, as well as some additional explanation of the presentation format.

20. In this exercise, we will calculate the capital structures of several firms and examine the stability of those structures.

    Enter Thomson ONE for each of the seven companies we have been working with; Sherwin Williams (SHW), Ford (F), Harley-Davidson (HOG), Starbucks (SBUX), Microsoft (MSFT), General Mills (GIS), and Yahoo (YHOO), and locate the five-year balance sheet history. Scroll down to the liabilities and equities section and write down the firm's capital components over the last five years. Then compute the capital structure as of the end of each year.

    a. Are the structures relatively stable over time?

    b. Might stability reflect a target capital structure or could there be other reasons for it?

    c. Which of the firms *might* be applying the ideas presented in this chapter about managing stock price with leverage? Which companies don't seem to be paying much attention to that idea?

    d. Our firms are from different industries but some may have similar capital structures. What characteristic do those firms share that could explain the similarity. (*Hint:* Why do certain companies have little or no debt?)

    e. Do any of the firms seem to have too much debt?

    f. How could a debt-heavy capital structure come about despite management's efforts to maintain a more conservative structure?

21. Now compare each firm's structure with those of its peers. For each firm, enter the Thomson ONE peer analysis module, locate the balance sheet, and scroll down to the liabilities and equity section. Record the firm's capital components and calculate its capital structure.

    Once you have the subject company's figures, make the same calculation for the peer mean balance sheet, which represents an average of the firms in the company's peer set. Comment on the company's capital structure relative to the average structure in its industry.

    Now identify the individual peers. Select one or two firms you recognize, make the same calculation, and compare the resulting capital structure with that of the subject firm. Is there a significant difference? If so, can you hypothesize why?

15 CHAPTER

Dividends

Chapter Outline

Background
- Dividends As a Basis for Value
- Understanding the Dividend Decision

The Dividend Controversy
- Dividend Irrelevance
- Dividend Preference
- Dividend Aversion
- Other Theories and Ideas
- Conclusion

Practical Considerations
- Legal and Contractual Restrictions on Dividends
- Dividend Policy
- The Mechanics of Dividend Payments
- Stock Splits and Dividends

Stock Repurchases (Buybacks)
- Repurchase As an Alternative to a Dividend
- Other Repurchase Issues

In this chapter, we'll concern ourselves with common stock dividends, the payments made by companies to equity investors.[1] Dividends present an interesting puzzle in modern finance. People are basically divided as to dividends' importance to investors and whether their payment has an influence on stock prices. Practitioners tend to think dividends are important to prices, while scholars feel that in theory they shouldn't make much difference. The debate is significant because of the central role dividends occupy in the fabric of finance. To understand the issues, we'll need to review a little background.

15.1 Background

15.1a Dividends As a Basis for Value

Dividends represent a critical piece of the financial system because of their role in determining the value of stocks. Recall that in Chapter 8 we came to the conclusion

---

1. Although payments made to preferred stockholders are also called "dividends," we won't be dealing with them here.

that stock prices depended *entirely* on expected future dividends. We need to review those ideas and revise our focus slightly for the present discussion.

The relationship between dividends and value can be viewed from the perspective of an individual investor or from that of the market as a whole.

The Individual Perspective

Dividends are the basis of value for stocks.

An individual buys a stock because he or she expects an acceptable return from dividends and from the receipts when the shares eventually are sold. Today's price is the present value of those future cash flows discounted at the appropriate rate for an equity investment. If an investor plans to hold a stock for n years, these ideas can be written as follows:

(15.1)
$$P_0 = \frac{D_1}{(1 + k)} + \frac{D_2}{(1 + k)^2} + \cdots + \frac{D_n}{(1 + k)^n} + \frac{P_n}{(1 + k)^n}$$

where: P_0 = today's stock price
         D_i = the dividend in the ith year (i = 1, 2, . . . , n)
         P_n = the selling price of the stock in the nth year
         k = the expected return on equity

This idea was developed in more detail in Chapter 8 in Equation 8.5, page 353.

Since

$$[PVF_{k,i}] = \frac{1}{(1 + k)^i}$$

we can also write

$$P_0 = D_1[PVF_{k,1}] + D_2[PVF_{k,2}] + \cdots + D_n[PVF_{k,n}] + P_n[PVF_{k,n}]$$

which was presented as Equation 8.4 and is more convenient for computation.

The Whole Market View

Valuation can be based on a series of **dividends** and an eventual selling price or an infinite stream of **dividends**.

In Chapter 8, we went on to develop the whole market focus by replacing P_n with the present value of the remaining dividends stretching infinitely into the future. We argued that the buyer in year n would have a model in mind similar to Equation 15.1, and replacing P_n with that model would conceptually push the selling price further into the future. We could apply this mental process as many times as we liked to get the eventual selling price infinitely distant in time, at which point its present value would be zero. Hence, we could work with a model that had an infinite dividend stream rather than a finite stream followed by a price.

Our Current Focus

Both the finite and infinite stream models are valid expressions for valuation. In Chapter 8, we focused on the infinite stream. Here we'll make use of the individual model with a finite time horizon.

Dividends and Ratios

The **dividend payout ratio** states dividends as a fraction of earnings.

Before continuing further, we need to introduce a new financial ratio and review a few we've studied before; first, the new one.

The **dividend payout ratio** is the ratio of dividends paid to earnings. It can be stated in total or per share, is usually called d, and can be expressed as a decimal or a percentage.

$$d = \frac{dividend}{earnings} = \frac{dividend\ per\ share}{EPS}$$

For example, a payout ratio of .4, or 40% would mean the firm pays a cash dividend of 40 cents out of every dollar it earns.

The concept contains a subtlety that's worth pointing out. The dividend is paid in cash, but the earnings figure doesn't represent cash availability. That's because net income (earnings) includes accrual accounting entries for both income and cost. Hence, in any particular year, more or less cash may be available to pay dividends than is implied by earnings.

More significantly, a firm with even a modest payout ratio may have trouble paying the appropriate dividend if it has other substantial cash needs. These might include capital expenditures and debt repayment.

The payout idea is sometimes expressed in reverse form as the **retention ratio,** usually called r, which is the percentage of earnings retained rather than paid out. Clearly d and r are each one minus the other. That is

$$r = 1 - d \ \text{ and } \ d = 1 - r$$

The ratios we need to review are earnings per share and the price earnings ratio, EPS and P/E. Their definitions are self explanatory for our current purposes. Review Chapter 3, pages 99–100 if necessary.

$$\text{earnings per share} = \text{EPS} = \frac{\text{net income}}{\text{number of shares}}$$

$$\text{price earnings ratio} = \text{P/E} = \frac{\text{stock price}}{\text{EPS}}$$

Further, remember from Chapter 8 that the return on a stock investment can be expressed as the sum of its dividend yield and its capital gains yield. Equation 8.3 on page 350 expressed the idea in the context of a one-year investment

(8.3)
$$k = \frac{D_1}{P_0} + \frac{(P_1 - P_0)}{P_0}$$

where D_1 is the dividend and P_0 and P_1 are the stock's prices at the beginning and end of the year. D_1/P_0 is the dividend yield on the investment of P_0 dollars. Also notice that the second term represents the growth in the stock's price as a percentage of the initial investment in it. This is the capital gains yield.

CONCEPT CONNECTION   EXAMPLE 15-1

Dividends and Ratios

The Bokberry Corporation maintains a dividend payout ratio of 40% and recently distributed an annual dividend of $2.50. The firm has a P/E of 19.

a. Calculate Bokberry's EPS and the market price of its stock.

b. How much more dividend income would a stockholder who owns 500 shares have received if Bokberry's payout ratio was 55%?

c. If there are 3.5 million shares of Bokberry stock outstanding, how much equity capital was made available for capital budgeting from retained earnings under the two payout ratios?

SOLUTION:

a. First use the payout ratio to determine Bokberry's EPS.

$$d = \text{dividend per share/EPS}$$
$$.4 = \$2.50/\text{EPS}$$
$$\text{EPS} = \$2.50/.4 = \$6.25$$

Then use EPS and the P/E ratio to find price.

$$\text{P/E} = \text{price/EPS}$$
$$19 = \text{price}/\$6.25$$
$$\text{Price} = 19(\$6.25) = \$118.75$$

b. At a 55% payout ratio, the per-share dividend would be

$$\text{dividend per share} = d \text{ EPS} = .55(\$6.25) = \$3.44$$

for a dividend increase of

$$\$3.44 - \$2.50 = \$0.94$$

Multiply by the number of shares held for the stockholder's additional dividend income.

$$(500)(\$0.94) = \$470$$

c. Total earnings are EPS times the number of shares outstanding.

$$(\$6.25)\ 3{,}500{,}000 = \$21{,}875{,}000$$

Multiply by $(1 - d)$, the retention ratio, for the funds available in each case.

$d = 40\%$:	$\$21{,}875{,}000(.60) = \$13{,}125{,}000$
$d = 55\%$:	$\$21{,}875{,}000(.45) = \underline{\$\ 9{,}843{,}750}$
	Difference $\$\ 3{,}281{,}250$

15.1b   Understanding the Dividend Decision

The dividend decision is simple on the surface. It relates to how much of its earnings a firm should pay out in dividends. The options range from nothing to everything. However, it's important that we understand all the implications involved in the choice because some aren't entirely obvious.

The Discretionary Nature of Dividends   We need to keep in mind the fact that dividends are legally discretionary. A company's board of directors has the authority to determine the amount of every dividend, including whether anything is paid at all.

This is a very significant point. In spite of the importance of dividends in the valuation process, they are never assured. The purchase of a share of common stock includes no guarantee of future dividends, regardless of what has been paid in the past.

The Dividend Decision   A firm's earnings belong to its stockholders. The dividend decision is a choice made by management on behalf of those stockholders about what to do with their earnings. Theoretically, there are only two alternatives. Earnings can be paid out as dividends or retained for reinvestment in the business. Both options benefit stockholders, but in different ways.

The dividend option gives stockholders an immediate cash payment that they can spend or reinvest as they please. Retaining earnings, on the other hand, involves investing the money in business projects that are expected to enhance profitability. Those higher profits should cause the stock price to increase, which means shareowners will hold more valuable financial assets which they will eventually sell at higher prices. It's important to focus on the different characteristics of the benefits created by the two mechanisms.

A dividend gives stockholders *current income* they can spend immediately. Current income is important to some investors because they need to live on it. To others it's less significant because they don't need it immediately and would just reinvest it.

Stock price appreciation, on the other hand, can't be spent without selling the stock, which many people don't want to do right away. Hence, retaining earnings produces *deferred income*.

The **dividend decision** is the choice between paying more or less in *near-term* dividends. That implies trading off between the two stockholder benefits. It is not a question of whether the stockholder gets a dividend or nothing. The issue is whether he or she gets current or deferred income.

> The **dividend decision** is whether to pay **cash dividends** or **retain earnings** for growth, both of which benefit stockholders.

15.2   The Dividend Controversy

The central issue about dividends is whether paying them or paying larger rather than smaller dividends has a positive, negative, or neutral effect on a firm's stock price. The question can also be stated in terms of stockholder preferences. Do shareholders prefer current or deferred income as just described? Presumably, doing what they prefer will make a stock more desirable, and its price will be bid up. In other words, we'd like to know whether it's generally possible for management to partially accomplish the goal of maximizing shareholder wealth by manipulating the firm's dividend-paying policy.

There are three major arguments regarding investors' preferences for or against dividends and several lesser but related theories that tend to tie things together. None of them are entirely right or wrong.

> The **dividend controversy** is whether paying or not paying **dividends affects stock price**.

15.2a   Dividend Irrelevance

The position endorsed by most theorists is that dividends should matter very little to stock price if they matter at all. The reasoning behind this idea can be seen from Equation 15.1. In that equation, suppose early dividends such as D_1 and D_2 are reduced or eliminated, thereby increasing retained earnings. The additional income retained may cause the company to grow faster. That, in turn, will make the eventual selling price of the stock, P_n, higher and may also make later dividends like D_n larger.

The **dividend irrelevance** hypothesis is that the negative impact on P_0 of reducing or eliminating early dividends is offset by the positive effect of an increased selling price in period n as well as larger later dividends. Hence, the current price of the stock, represented by P_0, is more or less independent of changes in the early dividends.

> Under **dividend irrelevance** the value of eliminated dividends is **offset by growth-created value** in the future.

Income Taxes   It's worth noting that the tax system plays a subtle part in the irrelevance theory. Notice that the idea depends on trading short-run dividend income for price appreciation in the longer run. We've described that trade-off in pretax terms with Equation 15.1; however, the tax system can add a complication.

CONCEPT CONNECTION   EXAMPLE 15-2

Dividend Irrelevance and Taxes

Troy Inc. follows a "dividend-only" policy, paying all of its earnings out to shareholders in dividends. Consequently, the firm hasn't grown in years. The payout produces a 10% dividend yield on a $60 stock price. Troy is considering changing to a "growth-only" policy under which it would discontinue dividends entirely and use the cash saved to fund growth, which is also expected to be 10%.

An investor who just bought Troy shares plans to sell them in one year. He is subject to marginal tax rates of 30% on dividends and 20% on capital gains.

   a. Calculate the investor's after-tax income under the dividend-only and growth-only policies.

   b. What growth rate in price (capital gains yield), without dividends, would make the investor indifferent between the two policies on an after-tax basis?

   c. Comment.

SOLUTION:

   a. Dividend-Only Policy (div yield = 10%)

$$
\begin{aligned}
\text{Dividend} = \$60.00(.1) &= \$6.00 \\
\text{Tax @ 30\%} &\quad \underline{1.80} \\
\text{Net} &\quad \$4.20
\end{aligned}
$$

Growth-Only Policy (growth rate = g = 10%)

$$
\begin{aligned}
\text{Selling price} = \$60(1 + g) = \$60(1.1) &= \$66.00 \\
\text{Less cost} &\quad \underline{60.00} \\
\text{Capital gain} &\quad \$\ 6.00 \\
\text{Tax @ 20\%} &\quad \underline{1.20} \\
\text{Net} &\quad \$\ 4.80
\end{aligned}
$$

   b. The capital gain required to yield an after-tax profit of $4.20 under the growth-only policy with a tax rate (T) of 20% is

$$\$4.20/(1 - T) = \$4.20/.8 = \$5.25$$

To achieve that capital gain, the stock would only have to increase in value from $60 to $65.25 in one year. Hence,

$$\$60(1 + g) = \$65.25$$

Solving for g,

$$(1 + g) = \$65.25/\$60 = 1.0875$$
$$g = 1.0875 - 1 = .0875 = 8.75\%$$

   c. This result is very significant. In the absence of taxes, it would take a 10% capital gains yield to offset the loss of a 10% dividend yield. But a lower capital gains tax rate reduces that requirement significantly.

Dividends are taxed as ordinary income, while appreciation is taxed as a capital gain. Most of the time the tax rate on ordinary income is substantially higher than the rate on capital gains. (See pages 47–48 for a discussion of capital gains tax.) Therefore, the difference in the tax rates on those types of income should be included in the offsetting idea. This is conceptually easy to do. To the extent capital gains are taxed at lower rates than ordinary income, it takes a proportionately smaller increase in P_n to offset the value of a near-term dividend reduction than it would if the rates were the same.

Tailoring the Cash Flow Stream   The irrelevance argument clearly makes sense if investors don't have a preference for current income. If they do, we have to reason a little harder.

A preference for current income means people care about the pattern of cash flows from an investment as well as about the present value of the entire stream of payments (the security's price). For example, retirees who need current income from investments to live comfortably will be upset if a stock they hold reduces its dividends, regardless of the fact that the present value of the whole stream doesn't change.

Does this imply that if management reduces or eliminates dividends in the near term, investors who need current income have to get out of the stock? In theory, the answer is no, because an investor in need of cash can always sell some of his or her stock for cash. The portion of the holding that isn't sold appreciates because of the retention of additional earnings, so the value of the original investment can be maintained in spite of the selloff, even though the number of shares owned decreases.

Investors can **tailor** their income stream by selling off shares of a growing stock that doesn't pay dividends.

CONCEPT CONNECTION   EXAMPLE 15-3

Tailoring the Income Stream

Jack and Wendy Winter are retirees who have most of their savings invested in 10,000 shares of Ajax Corporation. Ajax sells for $10 per share and pays a yearly dividend of $.50 per share. The firm hasn't grown for some time. The Winters depend on their Ajax dividends to supplement their retirement income.

This year Ajax discontinued the dividend, but began to grow at 5% per year because of the additional retained earnings. How can the Winters maintain their income and their position in Ajax? Assume there are no costs to buying and selling securities.

SOLUTION: At $10 each, the Winters's 10,000 Ajax shares were originally worth a total of (10,000 × $10 =) $100,000. That's the principal amount of their investment that they want to maintain. At the same time, they have to generate a yearly income stream of (10,000 × $.50 =) $5,000 to replace the dividend that's no longer being paid.

After a year of growth at 5%, Ajax's shares are worth $10.50 each. The Winters can raise $5,000 in cash by selling

$$\frac{\$5,000}{\$10.50} = 476 \text{ shares}$$

At the appreciated price, the remaining (10,000 − 476 =) 9,524 shares are worth

$$\$10.50 \times 9,524 = \$100,002$$

Hence, the gross amount of the Winters's investment is maintained. (The numbers aren't quite exact because we have to deal in whole shares.) As an exercise, calculate the required selloff in the second year.

It's easy to imagine the reverse situation in which a firm's dividend provides more cash than an investor currently needs. In such a case, some of the cash received can be used to buy more stock in the same company. That effectively reduces the dividend and expands the investor's stake in the firm.

Summarizing, it's theoretically possible to *tailor* one's current income from a stock investment in a growing company to any level by buying or selling shares.

Transaction Costs   All this works fine as long as trading in and out of the stock doesn't cost anything. Much of formal economic theory operates in a hypothetical world where this is the case. Capital markets are assumed to be *perfectly efficient,* which among other things implies that securities can be traded without incurring costs. In such a world, people would truly be indifferent to the payment of dividends.

In reality, however, financial markets are burdened with imperfections, including transaction costs such as brokerage commissions. Consider the Winters from Example 15-3. If they have to pay commissions to sell stock, the process of tailoring a current income stream will have a cost. That may make it impossible for them to stay in the Ajax investment.

As a practical matter, if the commission rate is small, selling stock to generate current income can remain a reasonable thing to do. But if the rate is significant, selling off shares can become a prohibitively costly process. Then the discontinuation of the dividend would probably drive the Winters and others like them away from Ajax. If most of the firm's stockholders were affected that way, Ajax's market price would drop.

Clearly, the more significant the transaction costs, the less valid the irrelevance theory becomes.

The View from Within the Company   From the perspective of the firm, dividends represent an outflow of cash that could be used for other things. Specifically, paying dividends reduces retained earnings, which are a source of funds for capital budgeting projects.

Recall that in Chapter 13 (page 563) we dealt with what happens when the firm runs out of retained earnings before it runs out of projects. We concluded that if more equity is needed after retained earnings are exhausted, the company raises it by selling additional stock. This means that a dividend paid may result in the need to sell new stock because it reduces earnings retained.

This doesn't create a problem if the new stock is sold in a perfectly efficient market without incurring flotation costs.[2] In that case, the firm would be internally indifferent between paying and not paying dividends. The cash used for dividends would simply be replaced by selling stock as needed.

However, if there are flotation costs, an expense is associated with selling new stock. Then paying dividends leads to incurring extra cost, and the firm has a definite internal

Transaction costs tend to make tailoring an income stream impractical.

Firms **prefer not paying dividends** if it avoids selling new stock, because **retained earnings cost less** than new equity.

from the
CFO

optimarc/Shutterstock.com

---

2. Recall that flotation costs are the transaction costs associated with issuing new securities.

preference for not paying dividends. This preference is shared by stockholders because more cost ultimately means less earnings.

Needless to say, flotation costs do exist in the real world, and they're quite significant.

15.2b   Dividend Preference

The **dividend preference** theory maintains that generally stockholders prefer receiving dividends to not receiving them. The argument is based on the **uncertainty** of the future. It asserts that stockholders prefer current dividends to future capital gains because something paid today is more certain to be received than something expected in the future. The idea can be put in somewhat cynical terms by saying that stockholders don't trust management to use the cash on hand today to grow the firm into something larger and more valuable later on.

Notice that this is not a time value of money argument. It doesn't say people prefer the dividend today because it's worth more. It says they'd rather have it now to be sure of getting it. The argument is often called the *bird in the hand theory* from the old cliché, "A bird in the hand is worth two in the bush" (because you may not catch either of those in the bush).

The reasoning has one rather substantial flaw. If stockholders are concerned about reinvesting dividend money in a firm because they're afraid it will be lost, why have they invested in that firm in the first place?

15.2c   Dividend Aversion

The **dividend aversion** position asserts that investors generally prefer that companies not pay dividends in order to enhance stock prices later on. The argument is based on capital gains taxes, so its persuasiveness depends on current tax law.

The logic underlying the idea is that dividends are taxed at ordinary income rates, while capital gains are taxed at lower "capital gains rates." Notice that in Equation 15.1 the dividend decision involves trading early dividends for a higher selling price in period n. The current dividend is ordinary income, but the appreciated price represents a capital gain when the stock is sold. Hence, the trade-off between a dividend today and a higher price later has to be modified to reflect the fact that, after taxes, investors usually get to keep more of the appreciation than the dividends. That clearly tends to make the deferred gain more desirable.

Congress makes changes to the tax treatment of capital gains frequently. Most of the time tax rates on capital gains are set lower than the rates on ordinary income to provide an incentive for investing, which in turn stimulates the economy. But that isn't always the case. The issue is politically sensitive because capital gains largely accrue to the wealthy, so favorable rates are a break for the rich. We discussed the capital gains tax situation as of mid-2012 in Chapter 2. (See page 47.)

There are two other less obvious tax benefits associated with capital gains that support a dividend aversion argument. First, taxes on capital gains are deferred until stock is sold. Second, all taxes on capital gains are avoided if stock isn't sold during an investor's lifetime. Then the shares pass to heirs with a tax basis equal to their current market value, so the price appreciation up to that date is never taxed. (This benefit may be eliminated.)

15.2d   Other Theories and Ideas

After all this we're still not sure whether there ought to be a general preference for or against dividends. There are a few other ideas that can help us understand the overall picture.

The Clientele Effect   The clientele argument is that individual investors do have definite dividend preferences because of their needs for more or less current income. These preferences arise because tailoring a cash flow stream by buying and selling stock is expensive and inconvenient.

It's easy to visualize the kinds of people who have various preferences. Retirees living on fixed incomes, for example, are likely to need dividend income to supplement pensions and social security. Young professionals with plenty of disposable income, on the other hand, may be willing to bet on capital gains in the longer run if the expected return is higher. People tend to gravitate toward the type of company that meets their needs. The retirees are likely to prefer companies like public utilities that are stable and tend to pay regular dividends. The young professionals like high-tech start-ups that don't pay dividends at all but may offer huge price appreciation.

Each company develops a *clientele* of investors whose needs match its dividend-paying characteristics, hence, the term **clientele effect.** The most significant implication of the effect is that once a clientele is established, it's unwise to change dividend practices. Such a change would be almost guaranteed to alienate shareholders who invested in the firm at least partially because they liked its dividend policy. It would cause them to migrate away from the stock, creating a general downward pressure on its price.

> The **clientele effect** maintains that investors choose stocks for **dividend policy**, so any **change** in payments is **disruptive**.

The Residual Dividend Theory   The **residual dividend theory** focuses on the firm's internal need for capital. Earlier we mentioned that dividends reduce retained earnings and, therefore, can force the sale of additional stock when a company needs equity capital for projects. Further, we noted that equity from new stock is more expensive than retained earnings because of flotation costs.

Under the residual dividend concept, companies recognize the cost effectiveness of retained earnings and fund the equity portion of all viable projects with earnings before paying any dividends. Anything left over is paid out as a dividend. The term "residual" comes from this *leftover* status of the dividend. See Example 15-4, page 644.

The residual theory has an intuitive appeal, but it isn't the way most companies work. Most managements see a value in dividends and set them aside first rather than last. Further, most companies can come up with a virtually unlimited number of capital projects that look good on paper. As a result, a firm that truly adhered to the residual theory might never pay a dividend.

> Under the **residual** view, dividends are paid from earnings only **after all viable projects are funded**.

from the
CFO

optimarc/Shutterstock.com

The Signaling Effect of Dividends   Rightly or wrongly, financial markets have come to read a great deal of information into the payment or nonpayment of a dividend. Indeed, the dividend is viewed as a way for management to send a message to its shareholders. People seem to have more faith in the message carried by dollars and cents than in spoken words. The phenomenon is called the "signaling or information effect of dividends," and is especially significant when earnings change.

Ensuper/Shutterstock.com

CONCEPT CONNECTION EXAMPLE 15-4

The Residual Dividend Theory

The Aquafine Filters Inc. has a capital structure that's 60% equity and 40% debt. The firm has a list of capital projects with positive NPVs, the initial outlays of which total $45 million. The firm has a P/E of 15 on a stock price of $75. There are 8 million shares outstanding. What will be the per-share dividend this year if Aquafine uses the residual dividend policy?

SOLUTION: Aquafine's earnings are available from its P/E ratio and EPS.

$$P/E = price/EPS$$

Substituting for P/E and price we have

$$15 = \$75/EPS$$
$$EPS = \$75/15 = \$5$$

Earnings (net income) are calculated by substituting into the definition of EPS.

$$EPS = earnings/number\ of\ shares$$
$$\$5 = earnings/8{,}000{,}000$$
$$earnings = \$40{,}000{,}000$$

Sixty percent (60%) of the funding for the $45 million capital plan should come from equity.

$$\$45\ million \times .60 = \$27\ million$$

Hence, the capital plan requires $27 million in equity that can be supplied from earnings, leaving an ($45 − $27 =) $18 million residual available for dividends. So the dividend per share will be

$$\$18\ million/8\ million\ shares = \$2.25\ per\ share.$$

If earnings turn down, the continuation of a regular dividend is viewed as a statement by management that the business is fundamentally sound and that the downturn is temporary. As a result, firms generally continue paying their normal dividends in the face of temporary decreases in earnings. The message to shareholders is, "EPS is off a little, but don't worry about it. Things will be fine. In the long run, we expect to have plenty of money, so here's your regular dividend."

In the same vein, an increase in the dividend is a stronger statement of **management's confidence** in the future. An increase accompanying rising earnings is a statement that the earnings improvement is expected to be permanent, and signifies a generally bright future. An increase in the face of a downturn is a clear attempt to allay stockholders' fears.

On the other hand, a decrease in dividends is taken as terrible news. It generally comes after a sustained reduction in earnings and tells the market that management doesn't expect the company to have the cash it had in the past. Investors usually react negatively and tend to sell off the stock, depressing its price. A decrease without an associated decline in earnings is a more mysterious but nevertheless dark message that isn't well received either.

As a result of all this, managements sometimes maintain or even raise dividends in the face of a downturn in an attempt to forestall negative investor reactions to serious problems. This practice is clearly inappropriate.

Cash dividends signal **management's confidence** in the future.

The signaling effect is very real and makes it difficult to tell what investor preferences for cash dividends really are. For example, suppose a firm has steady earnings but reduces its regular dividend, explaining to stockholders that it needs more money for capital projects. In spite of the explanation, the stock's price drops. Is the drop due to the fact that investors prefer a higher dividend, or is it because they don't quite believe management's explanation and suspect operating problems are coming? It's very difficult to tell.

The Expectations Theory   The *expectations theory* is a refinement of the signaling effect. It says that investors form expectations of what a company's next dividend will be and can become alarmed if those expectations aren't met, even if the dividend actually paid is steady or increasing.

For example, suppose a company whose dividend has been $2.00 per share achieves a substantial improvement in business, and people form the expectation that the next dividend should be $2.20. Then suppose the firm pays $2.10, an increase, but a smaller one than expected. The expectations theory says that investor reaction is likely to be negative because expectations weren't met, and that the stock's price may very well fall.

> **Dividends** that **fail** to **fulfill** stockholders' **expectations** send a **negative message** even if the payment is good.

15.2e   Conclusion

The conclusion is that we don't really have a conclusion. No one knows with certainty whether paying more or less in dividends generally increases or decreases stock prices. Most practicing financial professionals feel dividends have a positive effect on prices. Scholars tend to say that notion can't really be proven.

As a practical matter, the majority of companies do pay dividends. On the average, U.S. companies pay out 30% to 40% of their earnings in dividends.

15.3   Practical Considerations

15.3a   Legal and Contractual Restrictions on Dividends

Companies aren't always entirely free to pay whatever dividends they want. Restrictions are imposed by state law and contractual agreements.

Legal Restrictions   The laws governing corporate dividend practices differ from state to state, but two generalizations are possible.

> Dividends **can't be paid** by an **insolvent** firm and must come from current or prior **earnings**.

First, dividends can't be paid out of contributed capital; they must come from retained earnings. This rule protects creditors. Suppose Able starts a company, investing $1,000 of his own equity money, and convinces Baker to *lend* the firm another $1,000. As soon as the company is set up, Able, being the only shareholder, declares a $2,000 cash dividend which he pays to himself. The company now has no operating money, so it closes. Able has effectively stolen Baker's $1,000. To prevent this abuse, the law requires that firms earn some money before dividends are paid, and that dividends can be paid only to the extent of cumulative past earnings retained.

Second, a firm can't pay dividends if it is insolvent, meaning its liabilities exceed its assets. This rule is also designed to protect creditors. An insolvent company may face bankruptcy proceedings in which its assets may be sold to pay off as many of its liabilities as possible. A company anticipating proceedings could sell its assets and pay a dividend to stockholders with the cash received. This would take the assets out of the hands of the creditors at the last minute and leave them with a loss that should be the stockholders'.

Contractual Restrictions

Debt Contracts Business loans and bond issues usually come with restrictions on the behavior of the borrowing company that are designed to ensure repayment. Such contractual agreements are called **indentures** (bonds) and **covenants** (loans). The restrictions are generally aimed at conserving cash and maintaining prudent, conservative business practices. (See Chapter 7, page 302.)

Loan **indentures** and **covenants** may limit dividend payments to **protect creditors'** interests.

It isn't uncommon for indentures and covenants to restrict or prohibit the payment of common stock dividends under certain conditions. For example, a lender might stipulate that if EBIT falls below two times debt service (the sum of interest and principal payments) in any period, no cash dividends can be paid. This restriction would protect the interests of creditors by preventing cash from being siphoned off to stockholders when it looks like financial troubles might be approaching.

The **cumulative** feature of **preferred stock** limits dividend payments.

Preferred Stock Another common restriction on the payment of common stock dividends is the cumulative feature of **preferred stock** dividends. Recall that preferred stock pays a fixed dividend into the indefinite future, but that the payment isn't quite guaranteed. The **cumulative feature** generally specifies that if one or more preferred dividends are passed, no common stock dividends can be paid until they're caught up cumulatively. (See Chapter 8, page 372.)

15.3b Dividend Policy

Dividend policy refers to the rationale under which a firm determines what it will pay in dividends. The term encompasses both the amount paid and the pattern under which changes in the amount occur over time. First, some definitions:

A **stable dividend** is nondecreasing.

Stability refers to the constancy of dividends over time. A **stable dividend** is constant in amount from period to period but is usually increased occasionally. A dividend with a *stable growth rate* increases by a more or less constant percentage over time.

Recall that a decrease in dividends generally carries a bad signaling effect. Managements therefore try to keep dividends from ever going down. As a result, the term "stable" tends to imply a dividend that can go up or flatten out, but that doesn't decline.

Alternate Policies Three dividend policies are common.

Target Payout Ratio A firm following this policy selects a long-run payout ratio with which it's comfortable. However, it doesn't apply that ratio blindly each year. To do so would result in dividends that fluctuate up and down with earnings. From what we've learned about signaling, that would have a negative effect on the stock's market price. The actual payout ratio is generally somewhat below the target to allow for variations in earnings without forcing a decrease in dividends.

Typical policies include a **target payout ratio**, a **stable dividend**, and **year end extras**.

Stable Dividend per Share A constant dividend is paid regardless of earnings unless business conditions deteriorate so badly that the firm's ability to continue paying comes into doubt. If things go well and the company grows, the dividend is raised from time to time. A stable dividend per share is by far the most common practice.

Small Regular Dividend with a Year-End Extra if Earnings Permit   With this policy, management more or less assures stockholders of the regular dividend, but maintains the ability to either pay or forgo the year-end extra. In theory, this gives the firm the ability to lower its dividend level without a negative informational effect. In other words, the firm attempts to defeat the signaling effect of a reduction by keeping stockholders from counting on the extra payment. Unfortunately, people get used to the extra payment very fast.

INSIGHTS | Practical Finance

The Dividend Aristocrats

Some investors are very focused on dividends. They tend to be people who want their stocks to provide a reliable cash stream but offer better returns and the inflation protection that's not available with fixed-income vehicles like bonds, bank accounts, and certificates of deposit.

But a stock has to do more than just pay dividends to interest a hardcore member of this dividend-focused group. Surprisingly, paying a high dividend yield alone isn't enough. These folks are interested in stocks that have demonstrated a sustained history of *dividend growth.*

Dividend growth investors prefer companies that are members of an elite club known as the **Dividend Aristocrats**. To qualify for Aristocrat status, a company must be one of the S&P 500 and historically has had to have increased its dividend every year for twenty-five (that's **25!**) *consecutive* years. A single slip, a single decrease, or even a single year that's the same as the year before, has kicked an Aristocrat off the list. Needless to say, it's been an exclusive club, and it takes a long time to become a member. The Aristocrats even have their own performance index, which more often than not beats the S&P 500, America's leading broad-based stock market measure. The Aristocrats have returned investors an average of 12.1% per year since 1990, compared with the S&P 500's 9.8%.

But times are tough, and the Aristocrats haven't been immune to 2008's financial crisis or the ensuing recession. Membership in the elite club peaked at 64 in 2001, but stood at only 51 at the end of 2011. Some of the casualties were longtime members and pillars of the corporate world. General Electric (GE), for example, broke a 32-year string of increases in 2009, while pharmaceuticals giant Pfizer snapped a 41-year streak. Indeed, dividends have been broadly lower since the crisis as companies have struggled to conserve cash. The trend raised fears among enthusiasts that club membership could be reduced to as few as 40 if the economy doesn't turn around soon.

Responding to such concerns, Standard and Poor's, the organization that "runs" the club, announced in July of 2012 that the bar would be lowered at least a little. Henceforth, it will only take **20** consecutive years of dividend increases to qualify for membership. The change made fourteen new companies eligible for membership immediately. Some existing members were said to have been against the idea, apparently preferring membership in a dwindling but more exclusive group. But all that's history now, and 20 consecutive years of dividend growth is still pretty impressive!

SOURCES: Elizabeth Stanton, *"The Aristocracy Is Under Siege,"* bloomberg.com (April 2, 2009), updated August 31, 2009; Dan Caplinger, *Dividend Aristocrats Lower the Bar, fool.com,* July 11, 2012.

15.3c   The Mechanics of Dividend Payments

In the work we've done so far, we've treated dividends as annual cash flows. In practice, however, virtually all companies make dividend payments quarterly.[3]

Key Dates   Every quarterly dividend has four key *dates* associated with it.

The Declaration Date   The amount of each quarterly dividend is authorized by the firm's board of directors. A separate authorization occurs every quarter even if the firm's policy is to pay the same amount repeatedly. The date on which the board authorizes the dividend is called the **declaration date**.

The Date of Record   Stocks are **registered securities**, meaning that a list is kept indicating the name of the *owner of record* of every share. When a share is sold, ownership is transferred on the record from the seller to the buyer.[4] When the board authorizes a dividend, it stipulates a **date of record**. The dividend is payable to owners of record as of the date of record.

The Payment Date   The board also stipulates the date on which the dividend check is to be mailed. This is the **payment date**.

The Ex-Dividend Date   When shares are sold, it can take a few days to update the ownership records, so a sale made shortly before the date of record might not be recognized for payment purposes. To allow for a paperwork lag, brokerage firms have agreed to cut off sales *for dividend purposes* two business days prior to the date of record. The cutoff is called the **ex-dividend date**.

Figure 15-1 is a graphic representation of dividend payments and some sample dates. The ex-dividend date is significant with respect to stock market activity. An investor

> Dividends are authorized on the **declaration date** for owners as of the **date of record** and are sent on the **payment date**.

> An investor who buys a stock on or after the **ex-dividend date** does not receive the pending dividend.

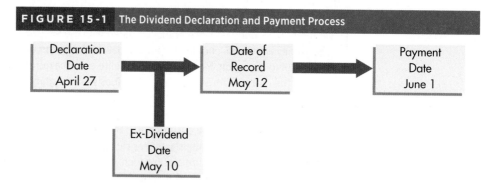

FIGURE 15-1   The Dividend Declaration and Payment Process

Declaration Date — April 27 → Date of Record — May 12 → Payment Date — June 1

Ex-Dividend Date — May 10

The dividend declared on April 27 is payable on June 1 to owners of record as of May 12.

However, to be an owner of record by May 12, an investor must have purchased shares by May 9.

© Cengage Learning

---

3. The annual figures people work with are generally the latest quarterly figure times four.

4. Most large companies use specialized firms called "transfer agents" to do this record keeping chore. See Chapter 8.

who purchases the stock prior to the ex-dividend date receives the next dividend; one who purchases on or after that date does not. In the example, the stock trades without the dividend starting on the morning of May 10.

As ex-dividend dates pass, stocks generally drop in price, reflecting the loss of the dividends to new purchasers. Interestingly, the drop tends to be 20% or 30% less than the full amount of the dividend. The difference is believed to be due to the fact that investors value the dividend after taxes rather than before.

Dividend Reinvestment Plans   Most large companies offer stockholders an optional **dividend reinvestment plan** under which the company keeps the dividends of participating stockholders and gives them additional shares instead.

For example, if a firm paid a $.50 dividend and someone owned 100 shares, his or her dividend check would be for $50. If the stock was selling for $25 at the time, that person would receive two additional shares instead of the money.

Reinvestment plan shares can come from either of two sources, depending on the nature of the plan. In one approach, the undistributed dividends are pooled and used to buy existing shares on the open market. The shares are then distributed back to the participating stockholders. This kind of plan is just a service provided to stockholders and doesn't significantly benefit the company.

In the second kind of plan, the company issues new shares at a price that's usually slightly below market. This approach has two benefits. It avoids the brokerage fees associated with buying existing stock, and it provides the company with a source of new equity capital that's free of flotation costs.

Tax Treatment   It's important to understand the tax treatment of reinvested dividends. In the reinvestment process, stockholders *effectively* receive cash and use it to buy more stock. The company just administers the transaction on their behalf. For this reason, the Internal Revenue Service treats the reinvested dividend as taxable income even though the stockholder never had the cash in hand.

> Large companies offer automatic **dividend reinvestment plans** to shareholders.

CONCEPT CONNECTION   EXAMPLE 15-5

Dividend Reinvestment Plans

The Dinsmore Company has a dividend reinvestment plan in which 40% of its shareholders participate. Management is trying to estimate how much equity it will have available from earnings this year. The firm typically pays out about 30% of earnings in dividends. EPS is expected to be about $6.50. There are 6 million shares of common stock outstanding. How much new equity capital is Dinsmore likely to raise from retained earnings and its reinvestment program?

SOLUTION: Calculate Dinsmore's earnings as the product of EPS and the number of shares outstanding.

$$\text{earnings} = \$6.50 \times 6M = \$39.0M$$

Retained earnings are the retention ratio ($r = 1 - d$) times earnings.

$$\text{retained earnings} = .7 \times \$39.0M = \$27.3M$$

Ensuper/Shutterstock.com

Dividends are earnings less retained earnings.

$$\text{dividends} = \$39.0 - \$27.3 = \$11.7M$$

Reinvestments are dividends times the participation rate.

$$\text{reinvested} = \$11.7M \times .40 = \$4.68M$$

New equity is the sum of retained earnings and reinvested dividends.

$$\text{new equity} = \$27.3M + \$4.68M = \$31.98M$$

15.3d Stock Splits and Dividends

Companies sometimes revise the number of shares of stock they have outstanding with stock splits and stock dividends. These transactions increase the count of shares in the hands of stockholders with no other real effect.

Stock Splits   A **stock split** issues new shares in numbers proportionate to those already outstanding. We'll illustrate the idea with a two-for-one split.

> Stock **splits and dividends** issue new shares to **existing stockholders** in proportion to the number already held.

A firm with 100,000 shares outstanding executes a two-for-one split by issuing an additional share to all current stockholders for every share they already own. After the split there are 200,000 shares outstanding, and all stockholders hold twice as many shares as they held before.

It's important to realize that after a split, every stockholder has the same proportion of outstanding shares he or she had previously. Therefore, the split doesn't result in any change in ownership or control.

> Stock splits and dividends **don't change ownership** or control and have **no real value** to shareholders.

Because there are twice as many shares after the split representing ownership of the same company, each share is worth half as much as it was before. But because each stockholder owns twice as many shares, there's no change in anyone's wealth. In effect, a split doesn't do anything but change the arithmetic involved in keeping track of shares.

A split doesn't have to be two-for-one; it can be made in any proportion. For example, a 1.5-for-1 split implies that shareholders get one new share for every two they already own. A 1.25-for-1 split would give one new share for every four owned. In any case, the effect is the same: The proportionate ownership of the company is unchanged, as is the wealth of stockholders.

Reverse splits are also possible. A company might, for example, call in all of its shares and reissue one new share for every two owned. This would halve the number of shares outstanding and generally double the price.

Stock Dividends   When additional shares are issued as we've just described, and the number of new shares is less than or equal to 20% of the original number of shares outstanding, the procedure is called a **stock dividend** rather than a stock split. For example, a 1.1-for-1 "split," in which 1 new share is received for every 10 owned, is called a "10% stock dividend."

Accounting Treatment of Stock Splits and Stock Dividends   A stock dividend is in reality just a small split. The two transactions are the same conceptually, and neither creates any real economic value. However, their respective accounting treatments differ substantially. Accounting for splits is very simple, while handling stock dividends is more complicated. We'll illustrate with an example after reviewing the standard equity accounts. (See pages 42–43.)

Recall that the equity section of the balance sheet is divided into the following three accounts.

- *Common stock* carries the par value of all outstanding shares.
- *Paid in excess* carries the amount by which the original price of all stock sold exceeded par.
- *Retained earnings* represents the sum of all past earnings that haven't been paid out in dividends.

The equity of Eagle Inc. is presented in Table 15-1. The firm sold 2 million shares of $3 par common stock at $4, and later earned $4 million which was not distributed as dividends.

Accounting for a Split   The impact of a split on the equity accounts is very simple. The number of shares is increased and the par value is reduced proportionately. If Eagle were to split two-for-one, the number of shares would double and par value would halve. The result is illustrated in Table 15-2.

Notice that the dollar amounts in the three accounts are unchanged. The changes appear in the number of shares outstanding, the par value, and the stock's book value per share. Also notice that no reference needs to be made to the current market price of the stock to account for a split.

A **stock split** simply changes **par value** and the **number of shares**. The capital accounts are unaffected.

TABLE 15-1 Eagle Inc. Stockholders' Equity	
Common stock (2 million shares outstanding, $3 par)	$ 6,000,000
Paid in excess	2,000,000
Retained earnings	4,000,000
Total common equity	$12,000,000
Book value per share	$ 6.00

© Cengage Learning

TABLE 15-2 Eagle Inc. Stockholders' Equity After a Two-for-One Stock Split	
Common stock (4 million shares outstanding, $1.50 par)	$ 6,000,000
Paid in excess	2,000,000
Retained earnings	4,000,000
Total common equity	$12,000,000
Book value per share	$ 3.00

© Cengage Learning

Accounting for a Stock Dividend   In a **stock dividend**, new shares are issued but the stock's par value isn't changed. Therefore, the common stock account has to be increased for the par value of the newly issued shares. In addition, the paid in excess account is increased as though the new shares had been sold at a price equal to the market value of the stock just before the stock dividend. The balancing entry reduces retained earnings by the sum of the additions to the common stock and paid in excess accounts.

We'll illustrate with a 10% stock dividend for Eagle Inc. that results in 200,000 new shares. Assume the stock is selling for $10 before the dividend.

The common stock account is increased by the par value of the new shares,

$$200{,}000 \times \$3 = \$600{,}000$$

Because the stock's market price is $10, the excess over par is ($10 − $3 =) $7, so the paid in excess account increases by

$$200{,}000 \times \$7 = \$1{,}400{,}000$$

At the same time, retained earnings is reduced by $2,000,000, the sum of these entries.

Because the additions to the first two accounts are offset by the reduction to retained earnings, total equity doesn't change. Book value per share does change, however, because of the additional shares. The result is shown in Table 15-3.

The entries recording a stock dividend are said to capitalize the market value of the new shares into the two paid-in accounts. They seem to be an attempt to reflect the creation of new market value even though total equity doesn't change. This is misleading, because no new economic value is created by a stock dividend.

Rationale for Stock Splits and Stock Dividends
Because stock splits and dividends don't seem to have any real economic meaning, it's fair to ask why companies do them. The reasons make some sense.

The Trading Range Argument for Splits
Many financial professionals feel that a stock loses its appeal to small investors if the price of a single share gets too high. For example, suppose a share of IBM sold for $20,000. Then no one could invest in the company unless he or she had at least that much money. Most small investors would be out of the market for IBM.

To keep the markets for their equity as broad as possible, companies split their stocks from time to time to keep prices in a **trading range**. Most people feel this is somewhere between $30 and $80.

TABLE 15-3 Eagle Inc. Stockholders' Equity After a 10% Stock Dividend	
Common stock (2.2 million shares outstanding, $3 par)	$ 6,600,000
Paid in excess	3,400,000
Retained earnings	2,000,000
Total common equity	$12,000,000
Book value per share	$ 5.45

It can be argued that keeping the market for a stock broad in this manner puts an upward pressure on price, because it maximizes the number of potential buyers. Whether that's true is debatable. Nevertheless, almost all companies use splits to keep prices in trading ranges. Check any broad stock listing online, and you'll find very few issues trading at prices over $100.

Giving Something That Doesn't Cost Anything   Stock dividends tend to be used as signaling devices. They're often employed when companies want to send a positive message, but for some reason can't give as large a cash dividend as they'd like.

For example, a firm might give a stock dividend in addition to its regular cash dividend if things are going exceptionally well but it needs to conserve cash for investment in projects. Conversely, a stock dividend might be offered if things are going poorly and no money is available for cash dividends, but management wants to make a positive statement by giving stockholders something. The value of such practices is clearly questionable.

> **Stock dividends** are an attempt at signaling.

The Effect on Price and Value   Splits and stock dividends increase shares outstanding without changing the economic value of the underlying company. It's generally accepted by scholars and most professionals that the transactions result in proportionate drops in market price, so stockholders see no real financial gain.

However, there's an underlying sentiment among some investors that something is gained with a split or a stock dividend. This probably comes from the fact that the transactions, especially splits, usually come along when prices are rising. Hence, the split or dividend takes on a positive information effect through a general association with rising prices.

The statistical studies that have been done seem to indicate that there is indeed no free lunch, and that prices do drop proportionately with splits and stock dividends.

A Potential Point of Confusion   It's important not to confuse a stock dividend with the dividend reinvestment plans we talked about in the last section. In a dividend reinvestment, stockholders are actually purchasing additional shares and, because everyone doesn't participate, the proportional ownership of the company changes.

15.4   Stock Repurchases (Buybacks)

From time to time, companies buy up their own stock. There are several reasons for doing this, but the most important is that it's an effective substitute for a dividend.

15.4a   Repurchase As an Alternative to a Dividend

A firm with the cash in hand to pay a dividend can use the money to buy some of its own stock instead. Doing that reduces the number of shares outstanding, thereby increasing the EPS of the remaining shares. If the market attaches the same price/earnings (P/E) ratio to the stock after the repurchase that it did before, the remaining shares will go up in price. As a result, the remaining stockholders will see an appreciation in the value of their shares in lieu of a cash dividend. A numerical example will make the idea clear.

CONCEPT CONNECTION EXAMPLE 15-6

Stock Repurchase

The Johnson Company has after-tax earnings of $5 million and 2,500,000 shares of common stock outstanding that trade at a P/E ratio of 10. The company has $1 million in cash that management would like to distribute to shareholders. Compare the effect of distributing the cash as a dividend with that of using it to repurchase shares.

SOLUTION: First calculate Johnson's EPS and market price.

$$\text{EPS} = \text{net income/number of shares} = \$5,000,000/2,500,000$$
$$= \$2.00 \text{ per share}$$
$$\text{market price} = \text{EPS} \times \text{P/E} = \$2.00 \times 10 = \$20.00$$

If Johnson uses the cash to pay a dividend, the per-share distribution will be

$$\text{dividend} = \$1,000,000/2,500,000 \text{ shares} = \$.40 \text{ per share}$$

If the company uses the $1 million to buy and retire its own shares, it will purchase

$$\$1,000,000/\$20 = 50,000 \text{ shares}$$

After the repurchase, there will be

$$2,500,000 - 50,000 = 2,450,000 \text{ shares}$$

left outstanding. If earnings don't change, EPS will then be

$$\text{EPS} = \$5,000,000/2,450,000 = \$2.04 \text{ per share}$$

Finally, if the P/E remains the same, the market price of the remaining shares will be

$$\text{Market price} = \text{EPS} \times \text{P/E} = \$2.04 \times 10 = \$20.40$$

Under the assumptions in Example 15-6, buying back the shares results in a price appreciation in the remaining shares just equal to the dividend. The company has spent the available cash, and stockholders have received value, but no dividend was paid.

Notice that the repurchase substitutes a potential capital gain for current cash income. Therefore, to spend the value they've received, stockholders would have to sell some of their shares.

> **Repurchasing** shares is an **alternative** to paying a dividend.

Methods of Repurchasing Shares

Stock can be repurchased in three ways. The first and simplest method is to buy the shares on the open market. However, this can be difficult to do quickly and without affecting the market price if a large number of shares are to be acquired.

The second method is to make a **tender offer** to buy shares at a set price from any stockholders interested in selling. In this approach, stockholders are invited to "tender" their shares for purchase at the proposed price, which is generally somewhat above the current market price. If too many shares are tendered, the firm buys a pro rata portion of all those offered.

In the third method, the firm makes a negotiated deal with a large investor who holds a big block of stock. Such investors are frequently institutions such as mutual

Ensuper/Shutterstock.com

funds, pension funds, or insurance companies. This approach can involve some risk, because the price negotiated with a large and powerful investor will generally be above the stock's market price. In essence, the firm is buying one stockholder's shares at a premium with money belonging to all stockholders. It's easy to interpret this as unfair to those who aren't being bought out. Remaining stockholders have been known to sue management over the issue.

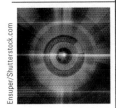

INSIGHTS | Real Applications

Share Repurchases Can Be a Risky Strategy

Share repurchases have become increasingly popular in recent years, but some experts are questioning their wisdom. A repurchase, or buyback as they're alternatively called, is an investment which, in retrospect, can prove to be a smart move or a dumb mistake.

Viewing a repurchase as an investment after, say, a year, involves comparing the repurchase price with the stock's market price after that year and factoring in the dividends saved by retiring the shares. If the stock's price is higher than the price paid a year ago, the investment earned a positive return. But if the price is lower, the return is negative, and the investment was a mistake, perhaps a costly one, for which the CFO and CEO can be faulted.

Another way to look at it is to realize that a repurchase followed by an increase in share price is a transfer of value to continuing shareholders at the expense of those who sold. But if the price decreases after repurchase, value is passed to those who sold at the expense of those who didn't.

The key to a successful repurchase is to buy when the market price of the stock is below its true or *intrinsic* value (see page 352). The problem is that estimating intrinsic values accurately is really tough. In other words a repurchase/buyback is more than just a dividend alternative. It's a strategic move with a grade attached, especially if it's part of a long term buyback problem, which is common lately.

The issue is complicated by the fact that companies like to repurchase stock when they're flush with cash, which generally happens when business is good. But when a company is doing well, the price of its stock is generally high, making a repurchase expensive and risky.

Another problem with repurchases is that they're often used to pump up EPS. But if earnings don't improve after the buyback, the only way to keep EPS from falling may be another repurchase. And another, and another,. . . and so on; that is, the company "has a tiger by the tail" and can't let go!

Hewlett-Packard, a leading hi-tech company with some serious strategic problems of late, is a frequently cited example of how not to do buybacks. Between 2004 and late 2011, the company spent almost $58 billion on stock repurchases. Of that, about $19 billion was spent in 2010 and the first half of 2011 buying shares at average prices of $44 and $38. Unfortunately, by the fall of 2011 the stock was selling at about $24 and then dropped below $18 by the summer of 2012. H-P's cumulative buyback return on investment (ROI) was quoted at −23.3% in October of 2011.

On the other hand, IBM and McDonald's Corp. seem to have gotten it right with buyback ROIs of 19.4% and 19.1% respectively quoted at the same time.

SOURCES: Jason Zweig, "Shareholders, Don't Buy In to Buybacks," *The Wall Street Journal* (October 1, 2011), B1, B2; Maxwell Murphy, "Buying Shares, Buying Trouble," *The Wall Street Journal* (October 12, 2011), B1, B4.

Ensuper/Shutterstock.com

Repurchases are appropriate when a stock is **temporarily undervalued** or the firm has **excess cash**.

15.4b   Other Repurchase Issues

The Opportunistic Repurchase   If a company's stock is undervalued,[5] repurchasing shares can be beneficial to the remaining stockholders. This can happen if the market takes a sudden downturn that's expected to be temporary. Let's consider an example.

CONCEPT CONNECTION   EXAMPLE 15-7

The Opportunistic Repurchase

Catatonic Inc. has 100,000 shares outstanding that sell at their book value of $10. This means the market sees the firm as worth $1 million, the book value of its equity. The firm also has $100,000 in cash available.

The stock market crashed yesterday, losing 30% of its value, and Catatonic shares fell to $7. However, management believes the market will recover quickly and the firm's shares will again sell at book value.

Evaluate the effect of Catatonic using its $100,000 cash to repurchase and retire stock if the market recovers and again values the firm at the book value of its equity. (*Note*: This example is presented to illustrate the effect of buying undervalued stock. The market doesn't price companies on the basis of their book values.)

SOLUTION: At $7 per share, Catatonic will acquire

$$\$100,000/\$7 = 14,286 \text{ shares}$$

leaving

$$100,000 - 14,286 = 85,714$$

shares outstanding.

When the market recovers, the book and market value of the firm's equity will be just $900,000, because $100,000 was spent on stock. Each share will therefore have a market value of

$$\$900,000/85,714 = \$10.50$$

That's $.50 more than before the downturn. Management earned the extra value by taking advantage of the temporary drop in the market at the expense of shareholders who sold at $7.

The situation described in the illustration is exactly what happened during a famous stock market decline in 1987. The market lost approximately 30% of its value in a few weeks and then stabilized. Many corporate managements recognized the situation as a buying opportunity and rushed to repurchase shares. That turned out to be the right thing to do at the time, because the market subsequently recovered. Unfortunately, it's not easy to determine when a stock is *temporarily* undervalued.

---

5.   A security is said to be "undervalued" if it is selling in a financial market for less than its true worth. Clearly, this reflects a difference of opinion about that true worth.

Repurchases to Dispose of Excess Cash   A period of high earnings that isn't expected to be repeated can leave the company with a one-time sum of money. If there aren't sufficient capital investment opportunities available to use up the funds, they should be distributed to stockholders.

Excess cash can be distributed by paying a one-time dividend. However, such a payment can create problems because of the signaling effect. Managers are reluctant to increase and then decrease dividends, because they anticipate a negative information impact from the decrease that more than offsets the positive effect of the extra money paid.

A stock repurchase can be a solution to the dilemma. It effectively distributes the money to the shareholders, but tends not to generate expectations of future distributions the way a dividend might.

Taxes   As we've demonstrated, a stock repurchase creates appreciation in the unredeemed shares. If the firm repurchases its stock occasionally, the appreciation is treated as a capital gain and is not taxed until the stock is sold.

However, if a firm repurchases its stock regularly and predictably, the IRS is likely to take the position that the transactions are effectively dividends. It could then tax the gains received by stockholders as current, ordinary income even though no cash was received.

As a result of this possibility, regular repurchase activity in lieu of dividends is not advisable. There is considerable uncertainty in this area of taxation.

Repurchases to Restructure Capital   It should be clear from our work in Chapter 14 that restructuring capital in the direction of debt involves repurchasing stock. Indeed, capital restructuring is a major reason for repurchases. In a transaction to restructure toward debt, the firm simply borrows money and uses the proceeds of the loan to buy back its stock.

CONCEPT CONNECTIONS

QUESTIONS

1. Dividends are said to be the basis for the value of stocks. If that's true, how do we explain the fact that companies that pay no dividends often have substantial market value? (Such companies are usually relatively young and in high-growth fields.) First explain the phenomenon in terms of the individual valuation model (a stream of dividends followed by a selling price, Equation 15.1). Then reconcile the idea with the whole market model (an infinite stream of dividends). Can you explain cases in which managements claim their companies will never pay dividends? (*Hint*: Does such a claim make sense?)

2. Given the importance of dividends to the well-being of equity investors, why do they put up with the fact that dividends are discretionary?

3. Fully explain the choices implied by the dividend decision. Are the results of the choices known or uncertain?

4. There is said to be a controversy over dividends. What is it, and why is it important?

5. You're an investment advisor and have several well-off older people among your clients. One of these individuals, Charlie Haverty, steadfastly refuses to invest in companies that pay significant dividends. A successful investment counselor advised him to avoid such stocks in 1965, and he's stuck to that view ever since. However, he never really did understand the reasoning behind the advice. How would you advise Charlie today? Include an explanation of why the advisor said what he did in 1965, and whether it was better advice then than it is now.

6. You're a financial analyst for a large mutual fund. You're doing an analysis of the Truebright Apparel Company, which makes stylish cotton clothes for teenagers. The company has recently been under attack by foreign competition and seems to have lost its edge in the fashion market. EPS fell from $2.00 to $1.80 to $1.20 over the past three years. Dividends were held steady at $1.00 per share in spite of the declining earnings for two years. Last year the dividend was raised to $1.50. Why do you think the dividend was maintained and then raised? How would this affect your recommendation?

BUSINESS ANALYSIS

1. You're the treasurer of Super Tech Inc., a high-technology firm in the fast-growing computer business. The management team has recently been trying to decide on a long-term dividend policy. Earnings are good, but the firm has far more investment opportunities than income.

   There's no doubt that the company will need to sell more equity in the near future to fund its growth. Therefore, management wants to do everything possible to maximize stock price, including making the right dividend decision.

   This morning the chief engineer, Susan Mathematica, came into a meeting and professed to have the answer to the firm's problems. She said she's been taking a high-powered finance course at night, and that her instructor assured her that dividends don't matter to stock price. According to Susan, that's because investors are perfectly capable of tailoring their own income stream from any investment. Therefore, she suggests not paying any dividends and using the money for projects.

   How would you respond to Susan's suggestion? Do you think she's missed part of her instructor's message? Is it possible that her suggestion is right, but for the wrong reason? What would you recommend that SuperTech do?

2. The Tanglefern Corporation has traditionally paid out 60% of its earnings in dividends. Recently some marvelous growth opportunities have arisen that involve only a little risk but require a lot of cash. Most of the executive team thinks the firm should do two things to raise the cash needed to take advantage of the opportunities. They want to (1) sell more stock and (2) suspend dividend payments for two to three years. The dividend suspension would be accompanied by an explanation to stockholders of what was going on. You're the company's CFO. Prepare a response to the others' suggestion. Do the two proposed actions taken together create a particular problem?

3. You're a bank officer considering making a loan to a small family-owned company. The firm's principal owner is a hard-working, conservative woman who has built up the company over a number of years. However, two of her grown children are now active

in the company's management. They're both bright and hard working, but have a reputation for taking business risks as well as for extravagant living. You'd like to make the loan, but are concerned about a potential change in the character of the company. How might you make the loan and still protect your bank's investment?

4. Your pal, Fred Flinderbinder, came into class this morning grinning from ear to ear. It seems a stock in which he advised his parents to invest is doing fabulously well. Fred said the firm usually pays a dividend of $2 a share, which is about 4% of its recent $50 market price. Yesterday, however, his folks got a letter that said the cash dividend was being passed, but instead the firm was issuing a stock dividend of 1 share for every 10 owned. Fred calculates that's worth the equivalent of $5 a share, two and a half times the normal cash dividend! Fred has told you all this knowing you're taking finance. He's asked you what you think, obviously expecting praise and approval. What would you say to Fred?

5. Blazingame Mill Works recently sold a tract of land it had owned for 30 years. All expenses and taxes have been paid, and the company has $10 million sitting in the bank as a result of the sale. Because there aren't any pressing investment opportunities available, the board would like to distribute the money to shareholders. Most of the board members are high-income individuals and major stockholders themselves. Discuss the company's options for disposing of the money.

PROBLEMS

Dividends and Ratios: Concept Connection Example 15-1 (page 636)

1. The Argo Pamphlet Company's dividend payout ratio is 35%. It is currently paying an annual dividend of $1.30.
   a. What is Argo's EPS?
   b. What is the market price of Argo's stock if its P/E ratio is 14?
   c. How much current income per share will stockholders lose if Argo cuts its payout ratio to 20% and nothing else changes?
   d. If the change in payout ratio does not affect the stock's price, approximately how many shares would a stockholder who owns 1,000 shares have to sell to make up her loss in current income? Ignore tax effects and transaction costs.

Dividend Irrelevance and Taxes: Concept Connection Example 15-2 (page 639)

2. Richard Ingram just bought 1,000 shares of Sisson Electronics at $40 per share. He plans to hold the stock for one year before selling. Sisson is in the process of selecting a new dividend policy. The firm will either pay out all of its earnings in dividends or retain and reinvest them all. Analysts expect the stock to be worth $45 in one year's time if no dividends are paid and $40 if dividends of $5 per share are distributed. Assume that Richard's marginal tax rate on ordinary income including dividends is 33%, and the capital gains rate is capped at 20%.
   a. How much difference will Sisson's decision make in Richard's after-tax income?
   b. Compare the results of part (a) with the results under the tax code in effect in mid-2012 as described on page 47.
   c. Calculate Richard's pretax and after-tax returns under both of Sisson's possible policies. (Assume the hypothetical tax rates in the problem.)
   d. What after-tax rate of return would make Richard indifferent between the two policies?

Tailoring the Income Stream: Concept Connection Example 15-3 (page 640)

3. Randal Flapjack is a retired short-order cook living on a fixed income in the state of Utopia, where all financial markets are perfectly efficient. Randal has 20,000 shares of the Sugarcooky Corp., which pays an annualized dividend of $1 per share. Sugarcooky sells at a P/E of 10, has maintained

a payout ratio of 50% for many years, and has not grown in some time. Management has recently announced that it will reduce Sugarcooky's payout ratio to 25% but expects earnings to grow at 5% from now on.

   a. What is Sugarcooky's current price?

   b. How much current income is Randal losing as a result of management's action?

   c. If Randal keeps his money in Sugarcooky but needs to maintain his current income, how many shares will he have to sell in the first year?

   d. What will be the value of his remaining shares at the end of a year if the P/E remains the same? Is his investment still growing? Why?

4. Biltmore Industries has grown at an average of 6% per year over its long history. Its stock price is currently $40.00, and its most recent dividend was $2.50. Biltmore just announced that it plans to discontinue dividends for several years to take advantage of some growth opportunities. Analysts expect the stock price to increase by 10% per year for at least the next two years because of this growth. Elmer Bartlett owns 4,000 shares of Biltmore and has counted on their dividend payments to supplement his retirement income. Now it appears that he will have to start selling off his Biltmore stock to replace this lost income. How many shares of stock will Elmer have to sell in each of the next two years to replace his lost dividend income? Ignore taxes and transaction costs.

The Residual Dividend Theory: Concept Connection Example 15-4 (page 644)

5. The Holderall Rope and Yarn Co. has 2 million common shares outstanding. Its capital structure is two-thirds equity. The firm expects earnings of $10 million next year and anticipates capital spending of $12 million on projects. Assume the projects will be funded with money raised in the debt/equity proportions of the existing capital structure. How much will the per-share dividend be next year if the firm adheres to a residual dividend policy?

Dividend Reinvestment Plans: Concept Connection Example 15-5 (page 649)

6. The Montauk Company has a dividend reinvestment plan in which shareholders owning 25% of its common stock participate. Last year the firm's EPS was $4.20, and its payout ratio was 50%. There are 2 million shares of common stock outstanding. How much new capital did Montauk raise through the reinvestment program?

7. Segwick Petroleum Ltd. has a dividend reinvestment plan in which new stock is issued to participating investors. Segwick's payout ratio is 40%, and 30% of stockholders participate in the plan. The firm's ROE is 10%. What percentage increase in flotation-cost-free equity capital does the plan provide?

8. Harrison Hardware anticipates $2 million in net income next year and a 20% participation in the firm's dividend reinvestment plan. Management expects to spend $2.375 million on new capital projects and maintain the current capital structure, which is 64% equity without issuing new stock. What dividend payout ratio has Harrison included in its plan for next year?

Stock Splits: Basics (page 650)

9. You own 1,000 shares of Jennings Corp. stock which is currently selling for $88. Calculate the number of shares you would own and the stock's market price after each of the following stock splits.

   a. A two-for-one stock split

   b. A three-for-one stock split

   c. A three-for-two stock split

   d. A three-for-four reverse stock split

   e. A five-for-three stock split

Accounting for Stock Splits and Dividends: Tables 15-1–15-3 (pages 651–652)

10. The Addington Book Company has the following equity position. The stock is currently selling for $2 per share.

Common stock (8 million shares outstanding, $2 par)	$16,000,000
Paid in excess...	$ 4,000,000
Retained earnings	12,000,000
Total common equity..	$32,000,000
Book value per share..	$ 4.00

   a. What was the average price at which the company originally sold its stock?

   b. Reconstruct the equity statement above to reflect a four-for-one stock split.

   c. Reconstruct the statement to reflect a 12.5% stock dividend.

11. Seinway Corp just declared a 10% stock dividend. Before the dividend the stock sold for $34 per share and the equity section of the firm's balance sheet was as follows:

Common stock (10,000,000 shares, $.50 par)	$ 5,000,000
Paid in excess	56,000,000
Retained earnings	87,500,000
Total	$148,500,000

   Restate the equity accounts and estimate the stock's price after the dividend.

12. Wysoski Enterprises is considering a stock dividend. The firm's capital includes 3 million shares of $1 par value stock issued at an average price of $8. Retained earnings total $20 million. State the equity accounts now and after each of the following possible stock dividends.

   a. Wysoski declared a 5% stock dividend, and the current price of the stock is $15.

   b. Wysoski declared a 10% stock dividend, and the current price of the stock is $20.

   c. Wysoski declared a 15% stock dividend, and the current price of the stock is $23.

13. The Alligator Lock Company is planning a two-for-one stock split. You own 5,000 shares of Alligator's common stock, which is currently selling for $120 a share.

   a. What is the total value of your Alligator stock now, and what will it be after the split?

   b. Alligator's CFO says that the value of the shares will decline less than proportionately with the split because the stock is now out of its trading range. If the decline is 45%, how much will the split make you?

Stock Repurchases: Concept Connection Example 15-6 (page 654)

14. The Featherstone Corp. has $8 million in cash for its next dividend but is considering a repurchase instead. Featherstone has 10 million shares outstanding, currently selling at $40 per share. The P/E is 20 on EPS of $2.

   a. If the dividend is paid, how large will it be per share?

   b. If stock is repurchased, how many shares will remain outstanding, and what will the new EPS be?

   c. If the P/E holds at 20, what will be the new stock price, and how much per share will continuing stockholders have gained? How does that compare with the dividend that could have been paid?

   d. Are there other considerations (words only)?

15. Parnell Bolts Inc. has 20 million common shares outstanding and net income of $30 million. The stock sells at a P/E of 15. The company has $5 million available to pay the next quarterly dividend, but is considering a repurchase instead.

   a. If Parnell pays the cash dividend, what will be its dividend yield on an annualized basis?

   b. How many shares will be redeemed if the repurchase option is chosen and the stock is acquired at market value?

    c. What will be the EPS after the repurchase if earnings remain unchanged?

    d. What will be the new stock price if the P/E remains unchanged?

The Opportunistic Repurchase: Concept Connection Example 15-7 (page 656)

16. Tydek Inc. just lost a major lawsuit, and its stock price dropped by 40% to $6. There are 3.5 million shares outstanding which are currently selling at their book value of $10. The company has $5 million in cash readily available. The CFO feels the decline in price is temporary and the firm's stock is an excellent investment at this time. If Tydek spends the entire $5 million on its own stock and the market-to-book-value ratio returns to its former level, how much more will each remaining share be worth than it was before the temporary price decline?

17. The stock market is generally depressed, and the price of Westin Metals Inc.'s common shares has been below its historic average value for some time. The shares are trading at $35 which represents a P/E of 19 on earnings of $7,000,000. Before the current slump, Westin generally maintained a P/E of at least 24. Despite the general downturn, the firm is doing well, and the CFO is considering an equity repurchase to enhance the position of stockholders who retain their shares when the market recovers. She has identified a piece of real estate the company owns but isn't using, which was purchased 20 years ago for $2,000,000 and can be sold for $9,000,000 today. Using the proceeds of such a sale would make it possible to do the repurchase without impacting dividends or the capital budget. The CFO has asked you to quantify the effect of her plan on stock price and make a recommendation as to whether she should present it to the Board of Directors. Assume it takes two years for the market to recover and that Westin's P/E returns to 24 at that time. Also assume earnings grow at 5% per year until then and the company's marginal tax rate is 37%. Round any number of shares calculations to the nearest 1,000 shares.

PART

5

Operations

The Management of Working Capital

Chapter Outline

Working capital consists of certain balance sheet accounts that arise from routine activities common to most companies. Working capital *management* refers to controlling the balances in the accounts, but more importantly to the way the underlying functions are run. In what follows, we'll gain an understanding of the decisions involved in working capital management and the relationships it creates between finance and other departments.

16.1   Working Capital Basics

The term "working capital" refers to the assets and liabilities required to operate a business on a day-to-day basis. The assets include cash, receivables, and inventories, while the liabilities are generally payables and accruals.

It's important to distinguish these accounts from long-term items such as buildings and equipment on the asset side of the balance sheet and long-term debt and equity on the liabilities side. Long-term assets are held for extended periods (at least a year) and tend to be financed or *supported* with liabilities that don't have to be paid off for similarly long periods of time.

Working capital items, on the other hand, are short term. Most **turn over** continually, meaning that items are held for only a little while. Inventory is a good example. Although firms always have inventory on hand, individual pieces are purchased and sold relatively quickly. The important point is that normal operating activities create and liquidate the elements of working capital on a regular basis.

16.1a   Working Capital, Funding Requirements, and the Current Accounts

The assets associated with short-term operating activities in most companies are cash, accounts receivable, and inventory. Together, they're called *gross working capital*. The word "capital" refers to the idea that funds have to be committed to support these short-term assets, while the word "working" emphasizes the fact that they're associated with the day-to-day operation of the business.

It's important to realize that working capital is an absolute necessity to the operation of virtually all companies. Firms can no more do business without working capital than they can without buildings or equipment.

Working Capital Requires Funds   Providing working capital takes a permanent investment of funds. For example, suppose a company operates with a $10 million inventory. Even though individual inventory items are constantly being bought and sold, approximately $10 million is always required to support the total. In effect, the firm buys an inventory *level* just as it buys a building or a machine.

The same is true of receivables, although it's a little more difficult to visualize. When product is sold on credit, a receivable is created that won't be realized in cash until the customer pays the bill. In the meantime, the receivable represents money the company has recognized from the sale but doesn't have.

Keeping cash in the bank also takes funding. Even though money is constantly flowing in and out of a company's bank account, an average balance has to be maintained to pay bills and conduct business. That money has to come from somewhere

Working capital accounts arise from **day-to-day operations** and include **cash**, **receivables**, **inventory**, **payables**, and **accruals**.

The assets and liabilities in working capital accounts **turn over** regularly.

Maintaining a working capital balance requires a **permanent** commitment of **funds**.

Practical Finance

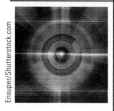

Going Broke Profitably

Can a company that's making a profit and has great prospects for the future fail? That sounds like a trick question, but it isn't. Profitable businesses, especially small ones, fail all the time. All that's necessary is a few mistakes with working capital.

Here's an example. Suppose an entrepreneur has a great idea for a product she wants to sell to a large company nearby. A unit sells for $1,000, costs $500 to make, and requires overhead of about $200. That means in the long run every unit makes $300, and the business looks like it will be solidly profitable.

Flushed with excitement, our entrepreneur leases space, hires workers, and buys a year's inventory. Then she operates for three months, shipping product to a delighted customer who promises to pay in 30 days.

But at the end of that time, the receivable isn't paid and the business is out of cash. Calling the customer, the entrepreneur gets a long story about minor technical problems with the product, a confusing tale about invoices not matching purchase orders, and an assurance of payment after these problems are worked out.

However, after checking around, she finds that the customer is well known for paying bills slowly and using excuses to delay. It also turns out that the customer is in financial difficulty and has been especially bad about paying bills lately.

Notice that at this point the entrepreneur's income statement says she's doing great having made $300 on every unit shipped. But the balance sheet tells a different story. She's got a pile of inventory, a big receivable, and no cash. That means she can't pay the rent or her workers in the fourth month of operation. The new business will fail immediately unless a bank bails it out with a loan until it collects some money.

This entrepreneur's failure comes from two mistakes in working capital management. She bought too much inventory and didn't do a credit check on the customer. Those seemingly small oversights cost her everything. We'll learn how to avoid this kind of disaster in this chapter.

and represents a funding requirement just like inventory or receivables. In effect, the company buys a cash balance in its bank account.

The Short-Term Liabilities—Spontaneous Financing

Operating activities also create payable and accrual liabilities. When inventory is purchased on credit, the payable represents material that can be used (temporarily) without payment. Similarly, labor that's been received but not yet paid is reflected in an accrual. (Review the definition of accruals in Chapter 2, page 40, if necessary.)

These liabilities provide an offset to the funding requirements discussed in the last section. It's important to notice that they come *automatically* with the associated assets and operating activities. In other words, the acts of buying inventory and building product lead directly to the related payables and accruals.

Because of the automatic nature of the **liabilities** arising from operating activities, they're referred to as *spontaneous financing*. They **spontaneously** reduce the need for funds to support gross working capital (cash, receivables, and inventory).

The **liabilities** created by operations **spontaneously** offset the funding required to support the assets.

Working Capital and the Current Accounts   The term "net working capital" refers to the difference between gross working capital and spontaneous financing. *A firm's net working capital reflects the net amount of funds required to support routine operations.*

In Chapter 2, we defined current assets and current liabilities, respectively, as items that are expected to generate or require cash within a year. The elements of working capital make up the bulk of the current accounts in most companies. For that reason, it's customary to define working capital as follows:

$$\text{gross working capital} = \text{current assets}$$
$$\text{net working capital} = \text{current assets} - \text{current liabilities}^1$$

> In practice, **working capital** is the net of **current assets less current liabilities**.

Usage   Common usage isn't particularly consistent in this area. People often use the term "working capital" for "net working capital." In practice, it pays to be sure anyone you're talking with is using the same definition you are.

16.1b   The Objective of Working Capital Management

Good working capital management means running the company effectively with as little money tied up in the current accounts as possible. That involves an important series of cost/benefit trade-offs. The trade-offs arise because it's easier to run a business with more working capital than with less, but it's also more expensive. Let's briefly consider each working capital element to see why.

Inventory: Large inventories keep customers happy because suppliers always have what they want right away. Also, production delays due to running out of materials are minimized by carrying big stocks of parts. However, larger inventories cost more to finance; incur bigger losses from obsolescence, breakage, and theft; and take more storage space than smaller inventories.

Receivables: A large receivables balance means the firm grants credit to customers easily and is willing to wait a long time to be paid. That makes customers happy and tends to increase sales. However, it also means relatively large bad debt losses and big interest charges to finance the receivables balance.

Cash: More rather than less cash in the bank makes it easier to conduct business and minimizes the chance of running short, but it also increases financing costs.

Payables and Accruals: On the liabilities side, more net working capital means smaller payables and accruals balances. That comes from paying vendors and employees quickly, which keeps them happy. However, it also reduces spontaneous financing and thus increases the need for costly external funding.

In general, using more working capital increases sales and improves relations with customers and vendors, but costs extra money. There's no magic prescription for

---

1. There's a minor problem in this definition. Certain items are regularly classified as current that are not related to routine operating activities. For example, when the repayment date for a long-term loan is less than a year away, the loan is normally classified as a current liability. Similarly, a receivable due from the sale of something other than product (like real estate) will be a current asset, but has nothing to do with daily operations. Hence, current assets and liabilities don't quite match the working capital concept. Nevertheless, it's common practice to define working capital in terms of the current accounts, ignoring any imprecision implied.

Working capital management involves **trade-offs** between **easier operation** and the **cost of carrying** short-term assets.

setting the right working capital level. The choice is a matter of policy and involves trade-offs that are often hard to quantify. Therefore, working capital management requires judgment, experience, and an ability to work with others in the organization.

We'll look into the management of each working capital component in detail later in the chapter.

16.1c   Operations—The Cash Conversion Cycle

Current assets can be thought of as going through a series of transformations as a business operates. Cash "becomes" inventory and labor, which combine to become product. When product is sold, a receivable is created, which in turn becomes cash when collected.

The transformation process is conceptually important. In essence, the firm begins with cash, which it turns into things that eventually turn back into cash. This enables it to buy more inventory, which starts the cycle all over again. We referred to the process in our discussion of cash flows in Chapter 3, calling it the cash conversion cycle or the race track diagram (Figure 3-3). We'll repeat part of the diagram here for convenience as Figure 16-1.

The Cash Conversion Time Line   Another way to look at the cash conversion cycle is by laying out its elements on a time line as illustrated in Figure 16-2. In this representation, events occur along the line and processes occupy intervals between the events.

It's important to notice how the two cycles are defined at the bottom of the diagram. A business's **operating cycle** is the period from the acquisition of inventory to the realization of cash from the sale of product. However, the cash conversion cycle is shorter by the period during which the firm holds a payable for the inventory. Cash conversion is the time from the disbursement of cash to pay for materials to the receipt of cash for product sold.

The **operating cycle** is the time from the **acquisition of inventory** until **cash is collected** from product sales.

Notice that Figure 16-2 doesn't show labor. Generally, production labor is continuously added to inventory during the conversion to product process, and is paid relatively quickly. Administrative labor is being performed and paid all the time.

FIGURE 16-1   The Cash Conversion Cycle

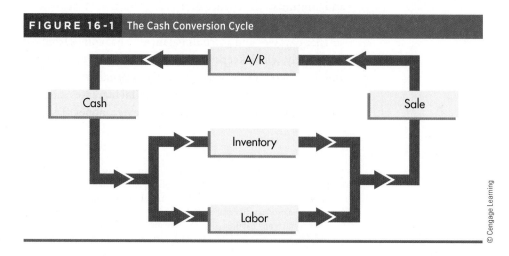

© Cengage Learning

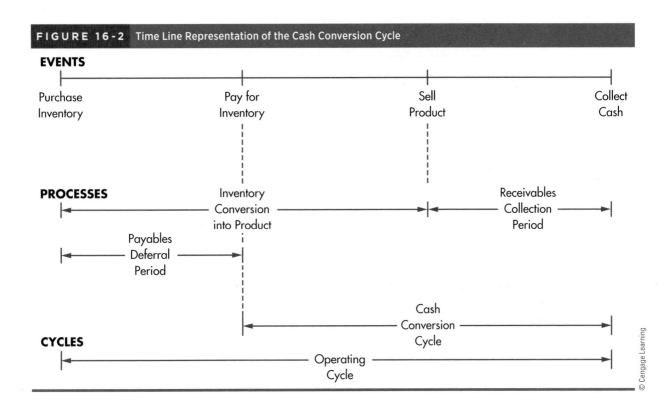

FIGURE 16-2   Time Line Representation of the Cash Conversion Cycle

The cash conversion concept is important because it contributes to our understanding of just how an ongoing business works. It's particularly enlightening in terms of the relationship between physical things and money.

16.1d   Permanent and Temporary Working Capital

A firm's need for working capital varies directly with its sales level. The more it produces and sells, the larger its inventories have to be and generally the more receivables and cash it has to carry.

Some businesses operate at relatively even sales levels year round, and therefore have more or less constant needs for working capital. In *seasonal* businesses, however, sales vary throughout the year, as do working capital needs.

Seasonally variable business gives rise to the ideas of permanent and temporary working capital. Working capital is permanent to the extent that it supports a constant or minimum level of sales. On the other hand, working capital that supports operations above the minimum level doesn't need to be maintained year round and can be viewed as temporary. Temporary working capital can be thought of as supporting peak sales levels. These ideas are portrayed graphically in Figure 16-3.

Temporary working capital supports **seasonal peaks** in business.

16.1e   Financing Net Working Capital

Working capital tends to be **financed separately** with **short-term** debt.

The fact that working capital differs from other assets because of its short-term nature leads to the idea that it may be appropriate to support it separately with short-term

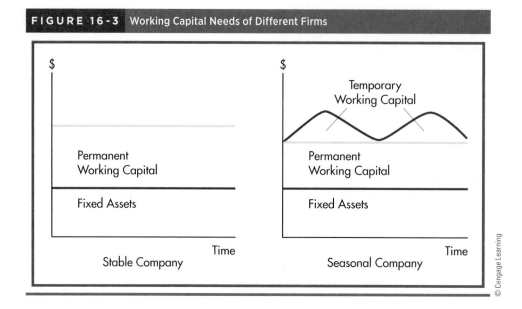

FIGURE 16-3 Working Capital Needs of Different Firms

Stable Company — Time; Fixed Assets; Permanent Working Capital

Seasonal Company — Time; Fixed Assets; Permanent Working Capital; Temporary Working Capital

© Cengage Learning

financing rather than using the firm's general pool of debt and equity capital. The idea arises almost naturally. Let's consider an illustration.

Suppose a merchant who has a store but no money for inventory approaches a bank for a loan to buy merchandise that he'll sell through his store. He promises to repay the loan with money from the sale as soon as the goods are sold. Banks are generally reluctant to lend to very small businesses because they're extremely risky. However, this proposal has some attractive features for the bank.

First, the loan is short term because it will be paid off as soon as the merchandise sells. Banks consider short-term loans safer than those made for longer periods because they don't allow much time for business conditions to deteriorate before repayment is made.

Second, the bank can see exactly where the money to pay off the loan will come from—the proceeds of the sale of the inventory purchased with the borrowed money. This is an important point. The loan is **self-liquidating**. The merchant is not at liberty to do anything else with the sale proceeds until a portion is used to pay off the loan. Such an arrangement is more secure than depending on the business's general profitability for repayment.

Third, the bank can demand that the merchant pledge the inventory itself as security for the loan. Then if the product isn't sold and payment isn't made, it can repossess and sell the inventory. A similar case can be made for a loan based on receivables.

These features enable banks to make working capital loans to businesses that wouldn't qualify for general unsecured loans. The point is that working capital lends itself to short-term financing by offering lenders elements of security that aren't available with loans for other purposes.

The Options Available to Most Companies   Although everyone's situation isn't exactly like the merchant's in our example, most companies have the option of

Self-liquidating debt must be paid off when the **item financed becomes cash** in the borrower's hands.

financing at least some of their working capital needs on a short-term basis. In practice, the loans aren't always tied to specific assets, but they're always short term.

On the other hand, firms can just about always use some of their long-term debt/ equity capital to finance working capital. Therefore, management has a choice between using long-term and short-term funds.

We'll get into the advantages and disadvantages of each option after we review an important financial principle.

The **maturity matching** principle advises that the **term of financing** match the **duration** of the **item supported**.

The Maturity Matching Principle

The **maturity matching** concept says that the maturity date of financing should be roughly matched to the duration of the asset or project being financed. In other words, a loan taken out to finance a project should be repayable at roughly the time of the project's completion. This makes the loan/project combination a *self-liquidating* proposition.

For example, suppose a project requires a $1 million investment today and is expected to pay off $1.2 million in six months. Maturity matching implies that a firm should borrow the $1 million for about six months and use the project's proceeds to pay off the loan. Borrowing for a longer period will leave unused funds drawing interest after the project's end. Borrowing for a shorter period can result in a default.

To illustrate the danger of borrowing short, imagine that a firm borrows $1 million for just three months with the intention of refinancing for the second three months. But suppose conditions change and the lender refuses to refinance after the first three-month period. The firm won't be able to pay off the loan at that time because the project will not yet have generated the expected cash. That can lead to default and potential bankruptcy.

Hence, in principle, it's a good idea to match the duration of short- and intermediate-term projects with the maturity of the financing supporting them. Very long-term projects should be financed with equity, which has an indefinite duration, or with long-term debt lasting 20 to 40 years.

It's also not a good idea to *overfinance* a project. For example, imagine that a new venture requires $6 million to get started, but the owner manages to raise $10 million. Investors will expect a high return on the entire $10 million, but will probably be disappointed because earning opportunities are available for only $6 million.

These guidelines shouldn't be interpreted too literally. Modest overfunding in both time and amount provides conservatism. In our first example, if the $1.2 million is late coming in, borrowing a little long avoids missing the six-month loan repayment date. In the second example, if the start-up is more expensive than anticipated, a slightly larger initial loan might save the trouble and embarrassment of going back to investors a second time.

Permanent working capital can be financed **long or short** term, but **temporary** needs should be supported with **short-term** funds.

Short- and Long-Term Working Capital Financing

Now let's return to the choice between financing working capital with short- or long-term money. It's easy to see that maturity matching doesn't give us a clear prescription in the case of permanent working capital. Although the inventories and receivables financed are clearly short term, they're continuously replaced so the *level* of the working capital assets remains constant. In the context of maturity matching, the situation can be interpreted as appropriate for either short- or long-term financing. Temporary working capital, on the other hand, is more clearly of limited duration and therefore calls for short-term financing.

Firms clearly have a range of reasonable options for financing working capital. They can support it very largely with long-term sources using little or no short-term borrowing, or they can use short-term money extensively. Let's look at why a firm might prefer one or the other.

Financing with **long-term funds** is **safe but expensive**.[2] It's safe because enough money is raised at the outset to cover anticipated working capital needs for a long time, and the firm is unlikely ever to run short. It's expensive because long-term rates of return are generally higher than short-term rates, and raising long-term money usually involves paying flotation costs.

On the other hand, financing with **short-term funds** is **cheap but risky**. It's cheap because short rates are generally lower than long rates, and the transaction costs of raising the money are relatively small. But borrowing short term is risky because every time a new loan is required, the firm has to face a new set of market conditions. For example, if interest rates rise over time, a company borrowing short term will have to pay increasing market rates. These may turn out to be higher than the long-term rate that was available initially.

There's also a possibility that money can become so tight[3] that financing isn't available at any rate. If that happens, the firm may not be able to finance working capital at all, which can seriously affect its survival.

Alternative Policies   The result of all this is that the degree to which a firm uses short-term financing to support working capital is an issue of policy. Two possible options are illustrated graphically in Figure 16-4 for a firm that has both permanent and temporary working capital.

We say a working capital financing policy is **conservative** if long-term funding is used predominantly as illustrated in Figure 16-4(a). Notice that short-term funding supports only the peaks of temporary working capital. When temporary working capital is low and the total funding requirement is below the long-term level, the excess funds are invested in short-term marketable securities. This policy is conservative in that there's very little risk of being unable to fund ups and downs in working capital. However, its cost tends to be fairly high.

A working capital financing policy is **aggressive** if relatively more short-term funding is used as in Figure 16-4(b). Here short-term funds support all of temporary and much of permanent working capital. The policy is aggressive in that some risk is being taken to reduce cost. The illustration makes it easy to see that a sudden rise in short-term rates will substantially increase the firm's interest costs. Further, a drying up of short-term funds could make normal business operations very difficult. These ideas are illustrated in Example 16-1 beginning on the next page.

Long-term financing is **safe but expensive**, while **short-term** money is **cheap but risky**.

The **mix** of short- or long-term working capital financing is a matter of **policy**. Use of **longer-term** funds reflects **conservatism**.

---

2. Long-term funds are capital and may include equity, long-term debt, or preferred stock.

3. "Tight money" means there's little available to borrow, so lenders demand very high rates and may refuse credit to all but the highest-quality borrowers.

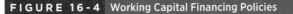

FIGURE 16-4   Working Capital Financing Policies

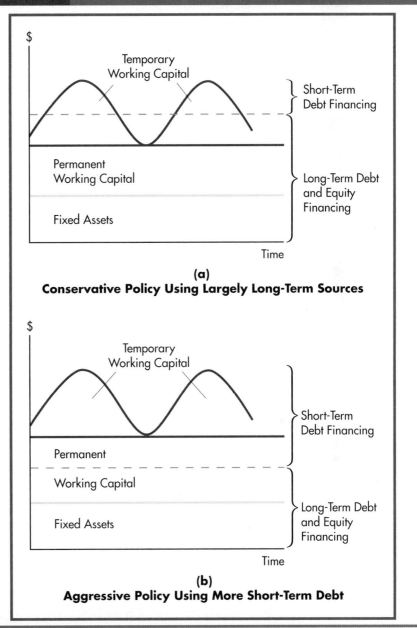

(a)
Conservative Policy Using Largely Long-Term Sources

(b)
Aggressive Policy Using More Short-Term Debt

© Cengage Learning

CONCEPT CONNECTION   EXAMPLE 16-1

Working Capital Financing Policies

The Carolina Card Company makes holiday greeting cards. Most of its manufacturing is done in the four months from July to October so product can be in stores by November. It carries a $2 million base of permanent net working capital all year, which swells to $8 million during those four months. (Temporary working capital varies from zero to $6 million.) Long-term capital costs 18%, and short-term financing is available at 12%. Carolina is considering two financing options.

Conservative: Finance all permanent and half of temporary working capital long term and half of temporary working capital short term.

Aggressive: Finance only half of permanent working capital long term and the other half of permanent along with all of temporary working capital short term.

Calculate the cost of each option. Why might the more expensive conservative option be chosen?

SOLUTION: Applying the policies above results in the following calculations:

Conservative

Permanent for full year	$2M × .18 =	$360,000
Half temporary for 4 months	$3M × .18 × (4/12) =	180,000
Half temporary for 4 months	$3M × .12 × (4/12) =	120,000
Total		$660,000

Aggressive

Half permanent for full year	$1M × .18 =	$ 180,000
Half permanent for full year	$1M × .12 =	120,000
Temporary for 4 months	$6M × .12 × (4/12) =	240,000
Total		$540,000

The CFO might choose the more expensive option if he expected short-term financing to become unavailable or very expensive to small, probably risky companies like Carolina.

16.1f Working Capital Policy

Working capital policy refers to the firm's policies on four subissues.

1. How much working capital is used
2. The extent to which working capital is supported by short- versus long-term financing
3. The nature/source of any short-term financing used
4. How each component of working capital is managed

We've already discussed the first and second of these subissues; we'll consider the third and fourth next.

16.2 Sources of Short-Term Financing

Working capital is the major reason most firms seek short-term loans. It's worth noting explicitly that short-term financing is always debt of one form or another.

We'll divide the sources of short-term financing into the following four categories and review each in some detail:

1. Spontaneous financing consisting of accounts payable and accruals
2. Unsecured bank loans
3. Commercial paper
4. Secured loans, which may be from banks or other sources

16.2a   Spontaneous Financing

Spontaneous financing consists of accounts payable and accruals. We'll consider accruals first.

Accruals   Accruals arise because firms receive services continually, but make payments at fixed intervals. (Review Chapter 2, pages 40–41.) A payroll accrual is relatively easy to understand. Suppose employees working a normal week are paid on Friday afternoon. At any time after the start of work on Monday until paychecks are handed out on Friday, the firm owes its employees for services performed so far that week. The obligation is represented by a balance sheet accrual if the books are closed any time other than Friday.

Accruals are made for any number of other services and obligations such as property taxes, insurance, and rents. Effectively, they're interest-free loans from whomever provides the service.

Accruals, especially for labor, tend to be very short term. In most companies, they're liquidated every week or two on payday. They're also not very controllable. Labor market practices and tax laws dictate when payments have to be made with little or no flexibility. In other words, accruals provide a modest financing advantage, but they're not a policy issue.

> **Payables and accruals** arise in the normal course of business and represent **spontaneous financing**.

Accounts Payable—Trade Credit   Most sales between companies are made on credit. The buying firm receives the goods and is expected to pay for them at a specified later date. Effectively, the selling company *lends* the buyer the purchase price, without interest, from the time the goods are shipped until payment is made. The practice is called extending *trade credit* to the customer.

There's typically no security and very little contractual support for trade credit. The contract between the parties is limited to the terms written on the buyer's purchase order and the seller's invoice.

Trade credit is an attractive source of financing because it's free. However, it typically isn't extended for very long periods of time.

Credit Terms   A vendor's terms of sale specify the number of days after delivery that payment is expected. In most cases, a discount is offered for earlier payment. Typical terms are specified as

2/10, net 30

This expression means that the net amount of the invoice is due within 30 days, but a 2% prompt payment discount may be taken if payment is made in 10 days or less. Any combination of discount period, net period, and discount is possible.

You can also interpret terms like these as meaning the true price of the goods is 98% of the invoiced amount, and 2% is a penalty for not paying quickly.

The Prompt Payment Discount   The early payment discount is typically a very generous offer on the part of the vendor. We'll illustrate with the 2/10, net 30 case.

Because payment is due in 30 days and the discount can be taken within 10, foregoing the discount buys the customer an additional 20 days of trade credit. We can think of this as paying 2% interest for 20 days' use of money. That rate can be converted to an annual figure by multiplying by the number of 20-day periods in a year as follows:[4]

$$\frac{365}{20} \times 2\% = 36.5\%$$

The implication is that by not taking the prompt payment discount, the firm is effectively borrowing at 36.5%, clearly a very high rate. It's apparent that when such a discount is offered, early payment should be made and the discount taken.

Most prompt payment discounts, like the illustration, are quite attractive. Therefore, many companies have simply ordered their payables departments to take all discounts offered. This has prompted some vendors to offer discounts that aren't such a good deal. As an exercise, calculate the approximate interest cost of 1/4/15, net 30. Is it clearly a good idea to take the discount?

Abuses of Trade Credit Terms

On its face, trade credit is purely an accommodation to customers. In fact, however, the practice has become so ingrained in industry that it's come to be expected. In other words, vendors offer credit because they have to rather than because they want to.

In that context, the trade credit relationship can become somewhat adversarial, with customers abusing credit privileges when they can. Paying late, beyond the net date specified in a vendor's invoice, isn't uncommon at all. The practice is called **stretching payables** or **leaning on the trade**. It's probably safe to say that most firms do at least a little stretching if they can. Another common practice involves taking the prompt payment discount after the specified period has elapsed.

Vendors will tolerate a limited amount of abuse because they want to keep the customer's business. But if the practice becomes excessive, the customer is labeled a slow payer and can find itself with problems. Slow-paying customers can be cut off from further shipments until debts are caught up or can be refused product unless payment is made in advance.

In addition, vendors usually report slow payers to a **credit agency** (also known as a credit bureau). Credit agencies prepare **credit reports** on virtually all companies doing business in the country. When new customers approach vendors asking for trade credit, it's customary to consult an agency about the applicant's record. A bad **credit rating** from a credit agency generally prevents a firm from getting trade credit.

---

4. The calculation shown is a simplification in two respects. First, the money made available by not taking the discount isn't the invoiced amount, but 98% of that amount. The extra 2% is interest. That means the cost of the 20 days' use of the funds isn't 2% but (2%/.98 =) 2.04%.

    Second, we should really compound the 20-day rate into a year rather than multiplying it. Because there are (365/20 =) 18.25 20-day periods in a year, the effective interest rate implied by not taking the discount is

    $$[(1.0204)^{18.25} - 1] = .446 = 44.6\%.$$

    Although this is the more technically correct calculation, most people think in terms of the simpler approach.

16.2b   Unsecured Bank Loans

Bank loans are the primary source of short-term financing for most companies, and are the primary business of commercial banks.[5] They come in a variety of forms and may be secured or unsecured.[6]

Promissory Note   A *promissory note* is the traditional bank lending arrangement. A note (contract) is signed promising to repay the amount borrowed at a definite future date along with a specified amount of interest. Sometimes a schedule of several repayments is stipulated. The note also stipulates the nature of supporting collateral[6] if there is any, and any other terms and conditions that may have been agreed upon.

When the agreement is signed, the bank generally credits the amount borrowed directly into the borrowing firm's checking account.

> A **line of credit** is an informal, **revocable borrowing limit** offered by banks.

Line of Credit   A **line of credit** is a relatively informal, nonbinding agreement between the bank and the borrowing firm that specifies the maximum amount that can be borrowed during a particular period, usually a year.

For example, a firm with a $100,000 line of credit could have up to five $20,000 promissory notes outstanding at any time during a year. However, because the agreement is nonbinding, the bank could reduce the line at any time. For example, it could decide that the firm's condition had deteriorated somewhat after $80,000 had been advanced, and refuse to make the last loan. It could not, however, shorten the term of any note that had already been signed. An amount borrowed under a line of credit is said to *take down* the line by that amount.

Under a line of credit agreement, the borrower pays interest only on the amounts actually borrowed.

Credit lines are generally *unsecured,* meaning the loans are not backed by specific assets and the bank relies only on the general creditworthiness of the borrower for repayment.

16.2c   Revolving Credit Agreement

> A **revolving credit agreement** is an **irrevocable** borrowing limit requiring a **commitment fee** on the unused amount.

A **revolving credit agreement** is similar to a line of credit except that the bank guarantees the availability of funds up to a maximum amount during the specified period. In other words, a *revolver* is essentially a *binding* line of credit. It is also generally unsecured.

The bank's commitment to advance funds up to a maximum in a revolver isn't free. The borrower is required to pay a **commitment fee** on the unborrowed balance of the agreement whether it's used or not. Commitment fees are in the neighborhood of one quarter of 1% per year.

The interest rates on revolving credit agreements are generally variable. They're usually specified relative to the bank's **prime rate**, which is the rate it charges its largest and most creditworthy corporate customers. Most banks follow the lead of the

---

5. A *commercial* bank specializes in serving businesses rather than individuals. Although commercial banks do make longer-term loans, about two-thirds of their lending activity entails maturities of less than a year.

6. A secured loan is backed by a specific asset. If the borrower defaults, the bank gets the asset, which it can sell to repay the debt. The supporting asset is called collateral.

major New York banks in setting their prime rates. The interest rate on a smaller firm's revolving debt is likely to be stated as prime plus 2 or 3%.

CONCEPT CONNECTION **EXAMPLE 16-2**

Revolving Credit Agreements

The Arcturus Company has a $10-million revolving credit agreement with its bank at prime plus 2.5% based on a calendar year. Prior to the month of June, it had taken down $4 million that was outstanding for the entire month. On June 15, it took down another $2 million (assume the funds were available on June 16). Prime is 9.5% and the bank's commitment fee is .25% annually. What bank charges will Arcturus incur for the month of June?

SOLUTION: Arcturus's payment will consist of the interest on money actually borrowed and the commitment fee for the unused balance of its revolving credit agreement. Its monthly interest rate is

$$(\text{prime} + 2.5\%)/12 = (9.5\% + 2.5\%)/12 = 1\%$$

and the monthly commitment fee is

$$.25\%/12 = .0208\%$$

In June a loan of $4 million was outstanding for the entire month and an additional $2 million was outstanding for 15 days. Hence, the interest charge is

$$(\$4,000,000 \times .01) + \left(\$2,000,000 \times .01 \times \frac{15}{30}\right) = 50,000$$

The unused balance of the revolver was $6 million for 15 days and $4 million for 15 days. The commitment fee is then

$$\$6,000,000 \times .000208 \times \frac{15}{30} = \$ \ \ 624$$

$$\$4,000,000 \times .000208 \times \frac{15}{30} = \frac{\$ \ \ 416}{\$1,040}$$

Thus, the total payment is $51,040.

Compensating Balances Short-term bank loans often come with a feature that seems outrageously unfair to the borrower, but is actually just a roundabout way of compensating the bank for its services. A **compensating balance** is a minimum percentage of the loan amount that has to be left in the borrower's account and is therefore unavailable for use.

For example, if a firm borrows $100,000 subject to a 20% compensating balance, the bank will deposit $100,000 in the company's account, but only $80,000 can be drawn out and used.

Compensating balances increase the effective interest rate on the loan. Suppose the rate in our example was 12%. That would mean the borrower would pay 12% of $100,000 in interest, but would have actually borrowed only $80,000. In a year, that means the interest would be

$$\frac{\$12,000}{\$80,000} = 15\%$$

A **compensating balance** requires leaving a **portion of the loan on deposit** raising the effective interest rate.

There are two kinds of **compensating balance**. One is the *minimum balance requirement* we've just described. The other is an *average balance requirement,* which may not have as severe an effect. In this arrangement, the average daily balance over a month cannot fall below a specified level. That means the entire loan can be used, but not all the time.

Firms typically maintain positive cash balances in their checking accounts most of the time anyway, so an average balance requirement may not present much of a problem. If that's the case, the effective interest rate on the loan isn't necessarily raised by very much.

Compensating balances are typically between 10% and 20% of amounts loaned.

CONCEPT CONNECTION   EXAMPLE 16-3

Compensating Balances

What is the effective interest rate on a $50,000 loan at 9% for 90 days if a 15% minimum compensating balance requirement is imposed? What is the effective rate if a 15% average compensating balance is required?

SOLUTION: First note that we don't need the loan amount or the term to solve the problem. We can adjust the nominal interest rate directly by dividing by 1 minus the minimum compensating balance requirement stated in decimal form. In this case, the calculation is

$$\text{effective rate} = \frac{9\%}{(1-.15)} = \frac{9\%}{.85} = 10.6\%$$

There isn't an answer to the second question because we can't say by how much the average balance requirement will reduce the borrower's use of the money without knowing what the firm's average balances would have been anyway.

Ensuper/Shutterstock.com

Most banks require that borrowers **clean up** short-term loans once a year.

Clean-Up Requirements   Theoretically, a firm can maintain a balance of short-term debt all the time by borrowing on a new note to pay off each old one as it comes due. Doing that makes it possible to fund long-term projects with short-term money, refinancing the debt again and again throughout the life of the project.

This procedure is rather risky for two reasons. If short-term rates rise, interest expense can increase quickly, putting a strain on the firm's profitability. Worse, if refinancing funds become unavailable, a default on the short-term notes is likely as they come due.

This kind of risk for a borrowing company is also risk for the bank, because a defaulted customer is likely to mean a lending loss. Therefore, banks try to keep customers from falling into the trap of using short-term funds to support long-term projects.

The banks' approach is the clean-up requirement. They simply require that borrowers pay off all unsecured short-term debt periodically and remain out of debt for a specified period. Most clean-up requirements stipulate that borrowers be out of short-term debt for 30 to 45 days once a year.

16.2d Commercial Paper

Commercial paper is short-term borrowing done by the largest corporations.

Commercial paper refers to notes issued by large, strong companies to borrow money from investors for relatively short periods. The paper itself is simply a promise to repay the money borrowed at a given date. Conceptually, commercial paper is simply a very short-term corporate bond, but there are a number of administrative differences.

Buyers and Sellers   Commercial paper is *unsecured* debt issued by a limited number of the nation's largest and strongest companies. It tends to be purchased by other large organizations that have excess funds to invest for short periods. Typically buyers are insurance companies, money market mutual funds, banks, and pension funds. The notes are generally placed with buyers by dealers for a fee.

Maturity and Terms   Commercial paper is actually a debt security of the issuing corporation. However, it can be sold without SEC registration as long as its maturity is under 270 days and the buyers are "sophisticated" investors. Maturities generally range from one to nine months, averaging five or six.

Commercial paper is considered a very safe investment because of its short maturity and the strength of the borrowing organizations. It therefore pays a relatively low interest rate, typically about a half point above the three-month Treasury bill rate. Rather than bearing interest, the notes are generally discounted like Treasury bills. That means the interest is taken out of the price when the note is sold. For example, a six-month, $1 million note paying an annual rate of 6% would sell for approximately ($1M/1.03 =) $970,874.

Commercial paper has one drawback even for the large, strong companies that issue it. The commercial paper market is very rigid and formal. If a company is a little short of cash when a note is due, there's no flexibility in repayment terms. Banks, on the other hand, are generally willing to bend a little to accommodate to business ups and downs.

16.2e   Short-Term Credit Secured by Current Assets

Several common arrangements enable firms to borrow to fund working capital using the value of the current assets themselves to guarantee the loan. The assets that provide such credit security are accounts receivable and inventories. The funding sources are often banks, but can also be other financial institutions.

Borrowing against receivables and inventories tends to be more popular in some industries than in others. It's especially common in seasonal businesses where temporary working capital needs are substantial.

The commitments, rules, and procedures vary considerably between different arrangements. We'll consider receivables financing first and then inventory financing.

Receivables Financing   Under normal circumstances, accounts receivable represent cash that is to be received in the near future. Lending institutions are generally willing to recognize the value of this about-to-be-received money, and will extend credit backed by that value where they otherwise would not. A key lending issue is the collectibility of the receivables, which relates to the creditworthiness of the firm's customers rather than to its own creditworthiness. Two receivables arrangements are common—pledging and factoring.

Pledging Accounts Receivable   **Pledging receivables** involves using their cash value as collateral for a loan. The borrower signs a binding agreement stating that the money collected from pledged receivables will be used to satisfy the loan.

The distinguishing feature of the arrangement is that the receivables continue to belong to the borrowing firm, which receives the cash directly from its customers as it

> Several **short-term financing** arrangements are available in which the **debt is secured by the current asset financed**.

> A borrowing firm can **pledge receivables** by agreeing to use the **cash collected** only to **pay off** the loan.

would in the absence of the pledging agreement. In fact, the company's customers are generally unaware that their obligations have been pledged.

Under a pledging arrangement, if a particular receivable proves uncollectible, the borrowing firm is not relieved of its obligation to the lender. This feature is known as **recourse**. The lender is said *to have recourse* to the borrowing firm for the value of a defaulted receivable.

Pledging can be accomplished in two ways with respect to the receivables offered as security. A lender can provide a *general line of credit* tied to all of the firm's receivables without reviewing individual accounts in detail. In such a case, the lender is unlikely to advance much more than 75% of the receivables balance because of the risk that some accounts may not pay.

In the other approach, the lender reviews each receivable individually, considering the creditworthiness of the customer owing the money. Then funds are advanced only on the basis of acceptable accounts. In this approach, the lender is likely to advance as much as 90% of the balance of accounts accepted.

Under a straight pledging of receivables, the borrowing company continues to do all of its own credit and collection functions. Hence, the lender is relying on the borrower to a great extent for the quality of the assets securing the loan. Some banks offer billing and collection services that the borrower can use for an additional fee.

Pledging receivables is a relatively expensive form of financing. Financing sources generally charge interest at rates 2% to 5% over prime plus an administrative fee of another 1% or 2% of the face value of all the receivables pledged.

> **Uncollectible** accounts remain the **responsibility of the borrower** if the pledging agreement is with **recourse**.

CONCEPT CONNECTION   EXAMPLE 16-4

Pledging Accounts Receivable

The Kilraine Quilt Company has an average receivables balance of $100,000 that turns over once every 45 days. It generally pledges all of its receivables to the Kirkpatrick County Cooperative Finance Company, which advances 75% of the total at 4% over prime plus a 1.5% administrative fee. If prime is 8%, what total interest rate is Kilraine effectively paying for its receivables financing?

SOLUTION: Because the finance company advances 75% of the receivables balance, the average loan outstanding is $75,000. Traditional interest of (8% + 4% =) 12% is charged on this amount.

The administrative fee is 1.5% of all new receivables. The $100,000 balance turns over every 45 days or (360/45 =) eight times a year. That means ($100,000 × 8 =) $800,000 in new receivables is pledged each year. The administrative fee is 1.5% of this total, or ($800,000 × .015 =) $12,000, which can be stated as a percentage of the average loan balance,

$$\frac{\$12,000}{\$75,000} = 16\%$$

Hence, the total financing cost including traditional interest and administration is

$$12\% + 16\% = 28\%$$

a high rate indeed.

Factoring Receivables

Factoring differs from the kinds of short-term financing we've considered so far because it doesn't involve borrowing. **Factoring receivables** means *selling them at a discount* to a financial organization called a *factor,* which can be a commercial bank or a finance company.[7] The cash from the sale of the receivable provides financing to the selling company.

When a receivable is factored, the factor takes possession of the obligation and generally becomes responsible for its collection. In most cases, the customer owing the money is notified to make payment directly to the factor rather than to the selling company. The factor covers its expenses and makes a profit from the difference between the face value of the receivable and what it pays the selling company. This can be in the neighborhood of 10%, depending on the services provided.

Factors generally review the credit standing of the customers whose receivables they buy and don't accept everything offered by the selling firm. Rejected accounts have to be handled by the selling firm on its own.

Companies that factor their receivables generally do so continually. That means a routine procedure is set up under which incoming orders are submitted directly to the factor and funded on an ongoing basis.

The procedures just described are the basic factoring function. In practice, factors offer a wide range of services with respect to receivables. They are willing to virtually take over a firm's credit and collection function. However, it isn't necessary to use everything they offer. Firms can select from a menu of services and tailor an arrangement to suit their needs.

The companies that use the other services offered by factors do so because it can save them money. It can be cheaper to hire an expert to do a specialized administrative function than to gear up and do it yourself. This is especially true for smaller firms.

In general, a factor is willing to do any or all of the following things for the appropriate fees:

1. Perform credit checks on potential customers.
2. Advance cash on accounts it accepts or remit cash after collection.
3. Collect cash from customers.
4. Assume the bad-debt risk when customers don't pay.

Item 2 requires a little explanation. Cash advances can be done in either of two ways. The factor can pay the selling firm for a receivable when it's sold or when the underlying cash is collected from the customer. If payment is made when the receivable is taken over, the factor is out the cash until it collects from the customer. Its fee therefore includes interest despite the fact that the receivable has been purchased and there really isn't a loan outstanding.

If payment to the selling firm is delayed until cash is received from the customer, the factor doesn't charge any interest. Notice that in this arrangement the factor isn't really *financing* the receivable—it's just administering collections.

---

7. The word "customer" can be a little confusing with respect to factoring. The company selling its receivables has customers and is, at the same time, the customer of the factor. We'll use the word to mean the customer of the firm selling the receivable. That's the party actually owing the money that gives the receivable value. We'll call the firm selling the receivable the selling firm.

If the selling firm chooses not to pass the bad-debt risk to the factor, we say the factoring arrangement is done with recourse. In that case, bad debts are charged back to the seller. Of course, factors charge substantially more when there's no recourse to the selling firm.

CONCEPT CONNECTION   EXAMPLE 16-5

Factoring Receivables

Bradley Fabrics Inc. has revenue of $250 million per year all of which is sold on credit. The resulting receivables are factored (sold) without recourse to Frasier Financial Corp for 92% of their face value. The average receivables balance in Frasier's hands is $28 million. The factor advances cash immediately and therefore charges interest on uncollected receivables balances at 7%. There are very few bad debts. Calculate Bradley's cost of factoring and the effective interest rate implied.

SOLUTION: It's important to recognize that factoring is a very expensive form of financing. In this case, Bradley is effectively continuously borrowing the amount that it would have in uncollected receivables if it didn't factor, which averages $28 million.

The factor begins by taking an up-front discount of 8% on everything it handles, which is the entire $250 million.

$$\$250M \times .08 = \$20M$$

On top of that, it charges 7% of the uncollected balance, which is the same $28 million.

$$\$28M \times .07 = 1.96M$$

So the total financing charge is

$$\$20M + \$1.96M = 21.96M.$$

The effective interest rate is the charge divided by the loan.

$$\$21.96M/\$28M = 78.4\%$$

Inventory Financing   Inventory financing uses a firm's inventory as security for short-term loans. The method is popular, but is subject to a number of problems that can make it expensive and difficult to administer.

Financing **secured by inventory** is difficult because specialized or perishable items are **hard to sell**.

A basic problem is the marketability of the inventory in the hands of a lender. Unlike receivables, inventory doesn't turn to cash by itself. It has to be sold, and lenders aren't generally equipped to do that. That means they have to dispose of defaulted inventory at bargain prices, which reduces the amount they can lend on it.

In particular, specialized inventories such as unique or unusual parts have little collateral value because they're difficult for a lender to sell. Perishable goods have a similar problem in that their value is lost by the time a lender can take possession. Other commodity-type inventories are quite marketable and make good loan collateral. Canned foods are a good example.

If an inventory does have an acceptable collateral value, its availability in the event of a default must somehow be guaranteed to the lender. This is difficult, because the borrowing firm is continuously using and replacing inventory in running its business. Several methods that involve varying amounts of administrative attention and cost are used.

Blanket Liens[8]

A blanket lien gives the lender a lien against all inventories held by the borrower. However, the borrower remains in complete physical control of the inventory, and can draw it down to any level without consulting the lender.

For example, suppose a firm borrows $600,000 collateralized by a blanket lien on an inventory of $1 million verified by a bank representative on the date the loan is disbursed. As long as the lender does not inspect the operating facility, nothing prevents the borrower from suspending inventory purchases while continuing to sell the existing stock until its level has reached, say, $200,000. This can easily put the lender in an unsecured position unless it spends an inordinate amount of time and effort monitoring the borrower's activities.

Trust Receipt or Chattel Mortgage Agreement

In this arrangement, financed inventory is identified by serial number and cannot be sold legally without the lender's permission. When the items are sold, the proceeds must be used to repay the lender. The arrangement is legally binding, but the borrower is still in control of the inventory and might sell it without paying the lender. Guaranteeing that the borrower is in compliance requires inspection by representatives of the lender.

Warehousing

Warehousing companies control secured inventories for the **benefit of lenders**.

Under a **warehousing** arrangement, financed inventory is placed in a warehouse and the borrower's access to it is controlled by a third party. When the borrower draws a piece of inventory, paperwork is created that signals the lender to look for repayment of the money lent to finance that inventory. *Warehousing companies* specialize in administering such arrangements.

There are two kinds of warehousing arrangements. A *field warehouse* is a secured area within the borrower's own facility that's accessible only to employees of the warehousing firm. A floor-to-ceiling chain-link fence can be built to segregate open factory space for the purpose. Employees of the warehousing firm make themselves available during designated hours each week.

A *public warehouse* is operated by the warehousing firm at a site physically removed from the borrower's facility. This arrangement provides the lender maximum security because the material is completely out of the borrower's control.

Warehousing gives lenders excellent security, but tends to be expensive because of the administrative cost of operating the warehouse and tracking individual inventory items.

CONCEPT CONNECTION   EXAMPLE 16-6

Inventory Financing

In a typical year, MacDougal Inc., a manufacturing company, has cost of goods sold of $90 million and an inventory turnover of 6X. (See page 93 for inventory turnover ratio calculations.) Homestead Finance Inc. will lend MacDougal 80% of the inventory's value at an interest rate of 9% if the loan is secured by a blanket lien on all inventory. Homestead also insists on a field warehousing system provided by Williams Warehousing Inc. to protect its interests.

---

8. A lien is a legal money claim attached to specific property. The proceeds of the sale of the property must be used to satisfy the lien.

Williams will fence off an area in MacDougal's factory to store material that its employees will dispense for three hours a day. The charge for this service is $200,000 per year plus 1% of the value of materials entering the system. What is the effective cost of inventory financing under Homestead's proposal?

SOLUTION: First calculate the average inventory level using inventory turnover, and then the average loan amount.

$$\text{inventory turnover} = \text{cost of goods sold/inventory}$$
$$6 = \$90M \ / \ \text{inventory}$$
$$\text{inventory} = \$90 \ / \ 6 = \$15M$$

The average loan will be 80% of inventory ($15M × .80 =) $12M.

Entering inventory charge:	
$90M × .01 =	= $0.9M
Base charge:	.2M
Total warehousing charges	$1.1M
Warehousing as a percentage of	
loan = $1.1M/$12M	= 9.2%
Plus interest	= 9.0%
Total effective financing charge	= 18.2%

16.3   Cash Management

Although good cash management can improve financial results, it isn't likely to make a weak business strong. Bad cash management, on the other hand, can make a strong company weak to the point of failure. Especially among small firms, it isn't uncommon for companies to be simultaneously profitable and bankrupt. In other words, a firm that doesn't have the cash to pay its bills and meet its payroll goes out of business, regardless of how good its long-term prospects are. For that reason, it pays to understand how cash oils the gears of business and how firms can get the most out of it.

16.3a   Definitions and Objectives

A firm's *cash* is the money it has on hand in currency and in bank *checking accounts*.[9] The overwhelming bulk of business cash is in checking accounts, because very little commercial activity is transacted in currency.

The Motivation for Holding Cash   Firms have to have cash on hand for three economic and one administrative reason. The economic reasons are transactions

---

9.   A bank checking account is known more formally as a demand deposit. The bank pays money out of the account to third parties on the basis of checks that represent demands of the account owner. In the normal course of business, when buyers and sellers know each other well, checks are accepted as readily as currency. Therefore, the money available in the economy is defined to include checking account balances. The financial definition of cash follows the same principle.

demand, precautionary demand, and speculative demand. The administrative reason for holding cash has to do with compensating banks for the services they perform.

Transactions Demand   Firms need money in the bank to pay bills for the goods and services they use. Payments are made to employees, vendors, utility companies, and taxing authorities, to name just a few. At the same time, most receipts come in the form of checks that are deposited in the bank. The constant flow of money in and out of the bank gives rise to an average account balance that we associate with transactions.

If firms had perfect knowledge of when cash would come in and when it should go out, transactions balances could be kept very low. However, we don't generally have such knowledge, especially with respect to receipts. It's therefore necessary to keep the balance high enough to support routine operations. It's especially important to have enough cash on hand to take advantage of prompt payment discounts offered by vendors.

Precautionary Demand   Sometimes emergencies arise with little warning. For example, suppose a shipment intended for a demanding customer is accidentally damaged on the loading dock, and a new shipment has to be produced immediately. That could require extra labor at overtime rates and the quick acquisition of new raw materials. Firms keep cash on hand to pay for such emergency needs.

Speculative Demand   Firms also keep cash available to take advantage of unexpected opportunities. For example, suppose the price of a particular input drops suddenly, but is expected to go up again quickly. If cash is available, a bargain can be had; if not, it has to be passed up. Firms keep money on hand to take advantage of such opportunities.

Compensating Balances   Banks stay in business by investing the money individuals and companies deposit with them for a return. It is therefore customary for banks to require that depositors receiving certain services maintain minimum *compensating balances* to partially offset the cost of those services. This arrangement is equivalent to charging fees for services. We've already discussed the compensating balances associated with loans. Banks also require them for cashing checks and conducting a variety of transactions.

The four reasons for holding cash aren't entirely additive. Money available for transactions also provides some speculative and precautionary capability, and certainly contributes to meeting compensating balance requirements.

The Objective of Cash Management
The problem with cash in the bank is that it generally doesn't earn a return. Banks don't pay much interest on the balances in most commercial checking accounts.[10] That means companies have to devote a certain

> Firms **hold cash** to make **transactions**, as a **precaution**, for **speculative** opportunities and to maintain **compensating balances**.

---

10. Until recently, banks were prohibited from offering interest-bearing checking accounts to businesses despite the fact that such accounts have been available to consumers for years. The prohibition was part of the Glass–Steagall Act enacted during the Depression of the 1930s and has served no real purpose for years. The law was repealed by a provision of the Dodd–Frank Act in 2010 becoming effective in July 2011. The issue isn't as important as it might seem because checking account rates, which are usually small, are likely to be virtually negligible in the low rate environment of the mid-2010s.

amount of their financial resources to maintaining cash in the bank, but receive little or no return on those resources. For this reason, it's desirable to operate with as little cash as possible.

At the same time, it's clearly easier to run a business with more cash than with less. A firm with a substantial bank balance will never be embarrassed by running out of money. This is described as **liquidity.** An adequately liquid firm will always be able to pay its bills on time, take the appropriate discounts, and take emergencies and opportunities in stride.

Cash management involves striking a balance between these conflicting objectives. Good cash management minimizes the amount of cash in the bank, but at the same time ensures enough is available to operate efficiently. We'll see shortly that there are several relatively standard techniques for doing that.

> Good **cash management** implies maintaining adequate **liquidity** with **minimum cash** in the bank.

16.3b   Marketable Securities

Notice that the precautionary and speculative motives call for having cash on hand that isn't used very often. These demands can be largely satisfied by assets that are only slightly less liquid than cash but earn better a return.

For example, suppose a firm invests some of its cash in short-term Treasury bills and then has an emergency need for funds. Because there's a ready market for government debt, the securities can be sold within a day and the proceeds used to satisfy the emergency need. In the meantime, the Treasury bills pay a modest return on the funds invested. This compromise is known as investing in **marketable securities**. It sacrifices a little liquidity for a modest but significant return.

> **Marketable securities** are **liquid** investments that can be held **instead of cash** and earn a **modest return**.

Marketable securities are short-term obligations of very strong organizations, including Treasury bills and commercial paper. The fact that the securities are short term is important. That insulates them from changes in value due to interest rate fluctuations. The word "marketable" implies that the issues can be sold quickly. Marketable securities are also referred to as *near cash* or *cash equivalents*.

Investing excess cash in marketable securities is a specialized function carried out within the treasury departments of larger firms. People who work in the area develop considerable expertise about the pros and cons of the various investment vehicles available. We won't delve into the operating details here, but the concept of marketable securities and the fact that most large companies invest in them regularly are very important.

16.3c   Check Disbursement and Collection Procedures

The amount of cash companies need is related to the method by which the *financial system* gets money from a paying organization (the *payer*) to the receiving party (the *payee*). Understanding the rudiments of this system is key to understanding cash management.

The Basic Procedure for Transferring Cash   Let's look at the routine procedure through which one party pays another with a check through the banking system. The procedure, called check collection or clearing, is written out below and portrayed graphically in Figure 16-5. In both, typical elapsed time requirements are indicated in parentheses near each step.

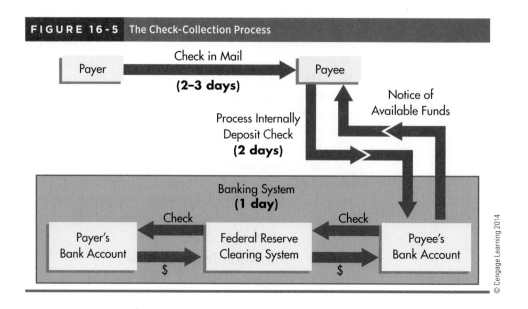

FIGURE 16-5 The Check-Collection Process

© Cengage Learning 2014

1. The payer writes a check on its bank and mails it to the payee. (2–3 days)
2. The payee receives the check, records it, and processes it internally for deposit.
3. The payee then deposits the check in its own bank. (2 days—items 2 and 3)
4. The payee's bank sends the check into the Federal Reserve's interbank *clearing system* at a Federal Reserve office.
5. The clearing system processes the check. This transfers money from the payer's account at its bank into the payee's account at its bank. The funds are now available for the payee's use. (1 day—items 4 and 5)

It's important to pay particular attention to the length of time taken by each step. Money tied up in the process is called **float.** During the time checks are in the mail they're part of *mail float,* when they're being processed at the payee's office they're in *processing float,* and when they're in the Federal Reserve system they're in *transit float.* Collectively, the money in the entire process is called *check-cashing float* or just *float.*

Float is money **tied** up in the **check-clearing process**.

Notice that there are two important geographic variables in the process we've described. The farther the payer is located from the payee, the longer will be the mail float. And if the payee's bank is far from a Federal Reserve office, extra time may be required to get checks into the clearing system. We'll return to these factors later.

Objectives in Managing the Check-Collection Process

The check-collection clearing process normally takes five or six days. During that time, the payee doesn't have the use of the cash even though the payer has written and mailed its check. In fact, funds remain in a payer's account and are technically usable by the payer until the check clears through the banking system.

Payees are interested in **speeding** the check-clearing process, while **payers** want to **slow** it down.

This leads to two important cash management ideas. First, from the perspective of a payee receiving money, speeding up the collection of checks *after they've been mailed* gets cash in faster. Second, from the perspective of a payer, slowing down the payment of checks *after they've been mailed* gives a company use of its cash longer.

All companies are simultaneously payers and payees, so any firm can use both ideas to reduce the funds that need to be committed to cash balances.

16.3d   Accelerating Cash Receipts

In this section, we'll take the point of view of the payee, the party receiving money, and examine approaches to accelerating the receipt of cash.

Lock Box Systems   *Lock box* systems are services provided by banks to accelerate the collection of cash once a check has been mailed to a payee. The idea behind the system is very simple.

Notice that in Figure 16-5, the first step of the payment process involves the payer mailing a check, which is processed and deposited by the payee in the second step. Together, these steps take four to five days. A lock box system reduces this float period by moving the check directly from the payer to the bank, eliminating the stop at the payee's office.

In a lock box system, the payee rents a post office box near its bank. It then orders payers to mail their checks to the post office box rather than to its own headquarters. The bank opens the box several times a day, collects the checks received, and deposits them in the payee's account. This cuts an average of two or three days out of the whole process. The idea is illustrated in Figure 16-6.

After the bank deposits the checks, copies are sent to the payee's office. Its internal processing is based on those copies after the deposit has been made and the clearing process has begun.

> **Lock boxes** are located near customers and **shorten mail** and **processing float**.

Fine-Tuning the Lock Box System   Two geographic details can make lock boxes especially effective. Suppose a payer is on the West Coast and the payee and its primary bank are on the East Coast. That means the payer's checks have to make a time-consuming trip across the country before they're received.

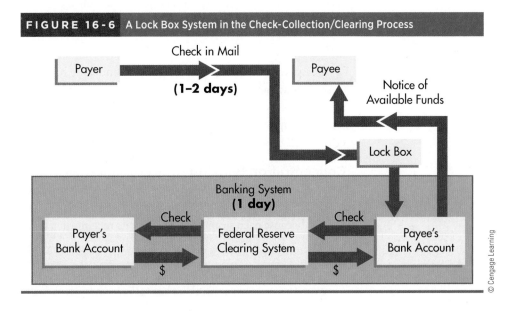

FIGURE 16-6   A Lock Box System in the Check-Collection/Clearing Process

© Cengage Learning

The payee can accelerate the process by establishing a lock box at a bank on the West Coast near the payer, thus eliminating much of the mail float. When funds clear into the West Coast bank, they're electronically transferred to the payee's primary bank on the East Coast.

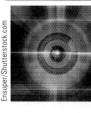

INSIGHTS | Real Applications

Technology Is Speeding Up the Check Clearing Process: "Check 21," the Check Clearing for the 21st Century Act

Technology is allowing the banking system to take big chunks of time and effort out of the check-clearing process. Until 2004, paper checks entering the bank clearing system had to be physically shipped around the country between banks in a laborious, time-consuming process. Most of the shipping was done by plane, which took a lot of flights, since approximately 40 billion checks were processed by the banking system each year.

But that`s changing due to the Check Clearing for the 21st Century Act, known as "Check 21" for short. The act was passed on October 28, 2003, and became effective a year later.

The act allows the banking system to engage in "check truncation." That means that at some point in the clearing process a bank can put the information on a check into electronic form and destroy the paper check. From then on it can be transferred electronically rather than being shipped around the country by air. The process also allows for the creation of a paper "substitute check" if a written copy is necessary somewhere in the system. Substitute checks are legally as good as the originals they represent.

The transition to the Check 21 procedure was gradual after its implementation in 2004, as individual banks weren't compelled to make the change. Some adopted the new system quickly, while others delayed for years. Nevertheless, the vast majority of checks are collected under Check 21 today, which has allowed the Federal Reserve to reduce its check processing infrastructure. In 2003, the Fed had 45 paper check processing locations; by 2010 it had only one.

SOURCE: www.federalreserve.gov/paymentsystems/; www.ffiec.gov/exam/check11/1.htm.

The payee can also speed things up by choosing banks that are close to Federal Reserve branches. That minimizes the time required to get checks from the bank into the central clearing system.

Big companies that receive payments from all over the country maintain lock boxes in all the areas in which their customers are concentrated.

Concentration Banking   Large companies often have a great many *depository*[11] bank accounts spread around the country. This is a result of the multiple lock box systems we described in the last section. It also happens when firms have widespread retail outlets, because each store has to deposit its receipts in a local bank every day.

---

11. A large company's working bank accounts are usually of two kinds for administrative purposes. The depository account receives incoming cash, while outgoing checks are written on the disbursing account.

Holding cash in a number of small accounts tends to be administratively inefficient because of duplicated effort and lack of central control. It also makes it difficult to invest in marketable securities, which tend to be traded in large sums. When cash is separated into a number of small bundles under the control of local divisions, no one has enough to take advantage of short-term investment opportunities.

Concentration banking is a system in which a single *concentration bank* manages the balances in remote accounts to target levels, and *sweeps* excess cash into its own central location. Special documents called *depository transfer checks* are used to move funds from one bank to another within a concentration network. Funds can also be moved electronically.

> **Concentration banks** sweep excess balances in **distant depository** accounts into **central locations** daily.

Wire Transfers

The fastest way of moving money from one bank to another is an electronic wire transfer. The Federal Reserve Wire Network (Fedwire) is available to member banks and their correspondents.

> **Wire transfers** move money electronically.

Wire transfer is quick and secure, but the fees involved make it too expensive for regular use with small sums.

Preauthorized Checks

When there's a very good working relationship between a payer and a payee, preauthorized checks can eliminate mail float entirely. In this arrangement the payer, a customer, gives the payee, a vendor, a number of signed check-like documents in advance. When the vendor (payee) ships product to the customer (payer), it simply deposits a preauthorized check in its bank account. Clearly this arrangement requires a certain amount of trust on the part of the payer.

16.3e   Managing Cash Outflow

We'll look at managing outflows briefly from the perspective of the payer. There are two goals, maintaining control of disbursements and slowing checks in the clearing process.

Control Issues

Most large companies are decentralized, meaning they have operating divisions in locations remote from headquarters. There are benefits to central control of cash, but there are also benefits associated with decentralized control.

In large companies, most agreements with customers and vendors are made at the division level. Because cash payments are a key element in the process of managing such agreements, it makes sense to place disbursing authority in the hands of division management. However, that results in at least one disbursing account at every division, which in turn leads to an undesirable distribution of cash balances around the country.

Zero Balance Accounts (ZBAs)

Zero balance accounts solve this control problem. They are empty disbursement accounts established at the firm's concentration bank for its various divisions. Divisions write checks on their ZBAs that are automatically funded as they're presented for payment. The funds come out of a master account at the concentration bank. In essence, ZBAs are subdivisions of the master account. Although the ZBA never has a positive balance, it has a number and receives statements that enable the division to use it to manage its business just like any other checking account.

Ensuper/Shutterstock.com

Payers sometimes **disburse** checks from **remote banks** to lengthen mail float and **slow** cash outflow.

Remote Disbursing   Look back at Figures 16-5 and 16-6 and take the perspective of the payer. Payers would like to slow the check-collection processes and expand float as much as possible to prolong the time cash remains in their bank accounts.

Remote disbursing is a way to keep checks in the bank clearing system. If a check is written on a bank in a distant city or in a small city that isn't the site of a Federal Reserve branch, it will take a day or two longer to leave the bank and get back to it. This delay has the effect of increasing transit float, keeping money in the payer's account longer. For this reason, it isn't uncommon for checks from large companies located in big cities to be drawn on small banks in out-of-the-way places.

16.3f   Evaluating the Cost of Cash Management Services

To be **effective**, a **cash management** system must lower balances enough to **save more** in interest than it **costs**.

Cash management, especially acceleration of receipts, can reduce the financial resources firms have tied up in their cash accounts. The general implication is that a firm can borrow less money by the amount of the reduction in its cash balance, and pay commensurately less interest. This saving has to be measured against the cost of the cash management system to see if it's worthwhile. The calculations are relatively straightforward.

CONCEPT CONNECTION   EXAMPLE 16-7

Evaluating Lock Box Systems

Kelso Systems Inc. operates primarily on the East Coast, but has a cluster of customers in California that remit about 5,000 checks a year. The average check is for $1,000. West Coast checks currently take an average of eight days from the time they're mailed by customers to clear into Kelso's East Coast account. A California bank has offered Kelso a lock box system for $2,000 a year plus $.20 per check. The system can be expected to reduce the clearing time to six days. Is the bank's proposal a good deal for Kelso if it borrows at 12%?

SOLUTION: The checks represent revenue of $5 million per year. The average amount of West Coast revenue tied up in cash is

$$\frac{8}{365} \times \$5,000,000 = \$109,589$$

The proposal will reduce this to

$$\frac{6}{365} \times \$5,000,000 = \$82,192$$

The difference, $27,397, is the amount of cash freed by the lock box system. If Kelso installs the system, it should be able to borrow an average of this much less money all the time. The interest savings at 12% is

$$\$27,397 \times .12 = \$3,288$$

However, the cost of the system is the annual fee plus the per-check charge.

$$\$2,000 + \$.20(5,000) = \$3,000$$

Hence, the bank's proposal is only marginally worth doing.

Cash management systems are subject to significant economies of scale, so larger companies benefit more clearly from having sophisticated systems than do smaller firms.

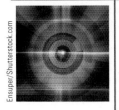

INSIGHTS	Ethics

Ethical Cash Management

Is remote disbursing ethical? Is it in general right to take advantage of mail float to keep cash longer? Isn't the payer who uses the practice essentially stealing a little interest from the recipient on each check?

Is the situation more sensitive to ethical issues if the payer is a financial institution with a "fiduciary" duty to the payee client? A fiduciary relationship is one of trust and confidence in which one party relies on the professional integrity of the other. It usually exists between certain professionals and their clients where money is involved. Banks, brokers, accountants, and lawyers may be fiduciaries.

In other words, is it less appropriate to take advantage of the other party in a transaction when that party is trusting you to look after his or her interests? Most people would say that it is.

Courts have held that remote disbursing is indeed a violation of the trust implied in relationships between parties, like stockbrokers and clients, and have disallowed the practice in that context. In that way, the courts have made something unethical also illegal.

16.3g   Cash Budgeting (Forecasting)

An important part of cash management is planning cash flows in and out of the company on at least a monthly basis. Planning cash is important because running out of money to pay bills and wages is at best embarrassing and at worst can lead to failure. The process is called **cash budgeting** or **cash forecasting** and can be considered part of either financial planning (Chapter 4) or working capital management. In this text, we've included a detailed treatment of cash budgeting in Chapter 4. We'll review some of those ideas briefly for those who may not have covered that chapter. (See pages 159–161.)

Cash budgeting begins with planning exactly when receipts and disbursements will occur for each of the business functions that generate or require cash. Then inflows and outflows are summed to arrive at net figures for each month of the planning period.

Monthly totals are accumulated into a running balance over the forecast period that can be either positive or negative. Positive figures mean the company is building up cash in the bank or paying down debt. Negatives mean more cash is being paid out than taken in, and the firm may have to borrow to meet its obligations.

It's that borrowing need that's crucial. In order to keep operations running smoothly, firms need to know approximately how much they'll need to borrow in the near term so loan arrangements can be made at a bank. Hence, well run businesses forecast cash carefully and often.

Forecasting with Time Lags   Receipts generally come from cash sales, collecting receivables, borrowing, and selling stock. Disbursements include paying for purchases, wages, taxes, and other expenses as well as paying dividends.

Receipts and disbursements usually follow some time after a predictable event like a sale or a purchase. The most problematic item is the collection of accounts receivable—usually a firm's largest inflow.

It's difficult to predict when cash from credit sales will be collected because we rarely know exactly when customers will pay their bills. Some pay within a few days; others stall for months, and a few never pay at all.

As a result of that uncertainty, most planners base receipts forecasts on the firm's collections history, which shows the percent of revenues usually collected in each month after a sale. As illustration is provided in Chapter 4, which we'll summarize here for convenience:

On the average a firm collects revenues according to a *time lagged* pattern such as the following:

Months after sale	1	2	3	Bad Debts
% collected	60%	30%	8%	2%

Applying the pattern to a monthly sales forecast generates a projection of collections. Here's an illustration showing how first quarter sales might be collected.

	Jan	Feb	Mar	Apr	May	Jun
Sales	$500	$600	$700			
Collections from sales made in						
Jan		$300	$150	$ 40		
Feb			360	180	$ 48	
Mar				420	210	$56
Total collections		$300	$510	$640	$258	$56

Payables are handled similarly; however, disbursements are easier to forecast because the date on which a check is written and mailed is under the firm's control.

Cash budgeting procedures are covered in detail in Chapter 4 on pages 159–161 including Concept Connection Example 4-9. End of chapter problems 4-18 and 4-19 on page 178 provide exercises on the material.

16.4   Managing Accounts Receivable

A firm's accounts receivable represent the obligations of customers for future payments that arise when sales are made on credit. The management of receivables is a relatively unique function in finance in that it involves interacting with customers, something usually reserved for the sales department.

16.4a   Objectives and Policy

Higher **receivables** improve **sales and customer relations**, but lead to more **bad debts** and **interest expense**.

In general, companies like to operate with as little tied up in receivables as possible. There are basically two reasons for that preference. First, carrying fewer receivables minimizes the interest cost of supporting the receivable asset. Second, it minimizes bad-debt losses because whenever money is owed, there's a chance that it will never be collected.

There are trade-offs, however. For several reasons that we'll point out shortly, a higher level of receivables generally increases sales and leads to better customer relations.

Managing accounts receivable means striking a balance between these effects. As receivables increase, sales tend to go up, which increases profit. At the same time, interest cost and collection losses increase, which depresses profit.

It's important to notice that the focus of the trade-off is at the EBT level. Managing receivables means finding the point at which *profitability* is maximized as a result of the opposing forces, not the point at which sales are maximized.

The things firms do to influence profitability through receivables management are collectively called **receivables policy** or **credit and collections policy**. Three broad issues are involved.

1. *Credit policy:* How financially strong must a customer be for the firm to sell to it on credit?
2. What *terms of sale* (due dates and discounts) should be offered to credit customers?
3. *Collections policy:* How should customers whose bills aren't paid on time be handled?

Who Is Responsible for Receivables Policy?   Although receivables policy is under the control of financial management in most companies, it has a major effect on sales. Therefore, most policy decisions are joint efforts between financial and sales/ marketing managements. As a practical matter, it's not unusual for this shared area of responsibility to create quite a bit of conflict between the two organizations. We'll understand why this happens as we go along.

16.4b   Determinants of the Receivables Balance

The size of a firm's receivables balance is determined primarily by the level of its credit sales. The more it sells for cash, the smaller will be its receivables and the fewer associated problems it will have. It is axiomatic that everyone prefers to sell for cash when they can. However, industrial custom doesn't permit many interbusiness cash sales, and receivables are substantial for most firms.[12]

Credit Policy   *Credit policy* is the most important decision variable available for influencing the level of receivables. It determines the customers to which a company is willing to make credit sales.

Most firms have *credit departments* staffed by credit specialists. When an order is received from a new customer, or an old customer wants to buy more on credit than it has previously, the credit department has the responsibility of approving or disapproving the request.

To make its decision, the department investigates the creditworthiness of the customer using a number of information sources. These sources include the reports of *credit agencies* (also called *credit bureaus*), the customer's own financial statements, bank references, and the customer's reputation among other vendors.

Receivables policy involves **credit** standards, **terms**, and **collection** procedures.

---

12. The custom is reversed in consumer markets where retailers usually demand cash at the time of sale, either from the customer or from a credit card company.

The primary source of information is usually the report of a credit agency, an organization that keeps files on the financial condition and bill-paying records of vast numbers of companies. For a fee, the credit agency will provide a vendor with a report on any customer or potential customer.

A company's credit policy revolves around how good a risk a customer has to be before it will be extended credit. A typical policy might require that a customer

A firm's **credit policy** is a statement of the **minimum customer quality** it will accept for **credit sales**.

- be in business at least three years,

- have a net worth of three times the amount of credit requested,

- have a current ratio of 2.5:1 or higher, and

- have no adverse comments on its credit report from other vendors.

If the conditions aren't met, the firm will sell to the customer only on a cash basis.

It's important to understand that customers whose credit applications are disapproved generally do not buy from the firm. They either can't because they don't have the cash, or they can find another vendor with a more liberal policy.

Hence, a *tighter* credit policy, meaning higher-quality requirements for credit customers, generally has the effect of reducing sales. On the other hand, a *looser* credit policy accepts lower-quality customers and increases sales. However, some of the incremental customers brought in by a looser policy generally prove unable or unwilling to pay their bills. The result is a *credit loss* (also called a *bad debt loss*) of the value of their receivables. The frequency of bad-debt losses tends to increase substantially as credit policy is relaxed.

Clearly, setting credit policy requires striking a balance between these effects. We want to find the policy that maximizes *profit*. Unfortunately, there's no formula for doing this; it's a matter of judgment and experience.

CONCEPT CONNECTION   EXAMPLE 16-8

Credit and Collections Policy

Nationwide Glass Inc. supplies window glass to the construction industry. A mild recession has depressed building activity, resulting in weak sales for suppliers like Nationwide. The VP of sales has proposed loosening credit standards to increase business. Her proposal projects a revenue increase of $15 million with 5% bad debts. Nationwide's CFO is skeptical on several issues. He feels the sales VP's incremental revenue assumption is much too high. A review of customers who have recently been turned down for credit leads him to believe that incremental revenue would be at most $5 million and that bad debts are likely to run as high as 20%. He also warns that additional collection costs may be as high as $1,000,000. Evaluate the contribution to EBT implied by the two executives' positions. Nationwide's gross margin (see page 30) is 30%.

SOLUTION: There's a subtlety involved in any analysis of bad debts. (Assume there's no bad-debt reserve.) When an account proves uncollectible, the revenue originally recognized on the sale is reversed, resulting in a reduction in EBT of the same amount. That reduction, however, overstates the actual loss associated with the write-off. That's because revenue includes profit, which a seller doesn't actually have until the account is collected even though it's recognized on the income statement at the time of sale.

That means the loss associated with a write-off is just the cost of the product sold plus any direct expenses associated with the sale—rather than the revenue amount.

In general, the financial result of an initiative like the one proposed here is the difference between profits on sales to new customers that do pay—less losses on sales to those that don't. The profit figure is revenue times the gross margin percentage times the percentage of new customers that pay, while the loss is revenue times 1 minus the gross margin percentage times the bad-debt percentage. That is

$$\text{profit on good accounts} = \text{new revenue} \times \text{GM\%} \times (1 - \text{\% bad debts})$$

and

$$\text{loss on bad debts} = \text{new revenue} \times (1 - \text{GM\%}) \times (\text{\% bad debts})$$

Under the assumptions made by Nationwide's VP of sales, the contribution to profit from the 95% of new customers that do pay their bills and the loss on the 5% that turn out to be bad debts would be

Profit	$15,000,000 × .30 × .95 =	$4,275,000
Loss	$15,000,000 × .70 × .05 =	$ 525,000
	Net profit	$3,750,000

The result under the CFO's assumptions is

Profit	$5,000,000 × .30 × .80 =	$1,200,000
Loss	$5,000,000 × .70 × .20 =	$ 700,000
	Gross profit on new sales	$ 500,000
	Less new expenses	$1,000,000
	Net loss	($ 500,000)

The Conflict with Sales over Credit Policy

The job of the sales department is generally to sell as much product as it can. When salespeople's compensation is based on commissions, the task becomes a very personal challenge. The philosophy in most companies is that the salesperson delivers a willing buyer to the credit department, which then approves or disapproves a credit sale.

If the sale is approved, the customer gets product on credit, the salesperson gets his or her commission, and everyone is happy. If the credit sale is disapproved, it is generally lost. That means the salesperson doesn't get a commission and has wasted whatever work has gone into the account. This understandably creates a good deal of resentment on the part of the salesperson toward the credit department, especially if the customer's credit quality was marginal.

But what happens if a credit sale is approved and the customer eventually fails to pay? It's logical to assume that the salesperson in such a case would be charged back his or her commission. *However, most companies don't operate that way. The credit decision is viewed as strictly the responsibility of the credit department, so the blame for a bad-debt loss is laid at its door alone and the salesperson gets to keep the commission.*

This practice can create a counterproductive conflict of interest. Salespeople are generally in close contact with customers and may be aware of things no one else knows about. But if those things are negative, the commission system motivates them not to share the information with the credit department. Credit personnel therefore may harbor some resentment toward salespeople when receivables go sour.

There are often **conflicts** between the **sales** and **credit** departments.

from the
CFO

optimarc/Shutterstock.com

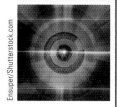

INSIGHTS | Practical Finance

A Practical Management Warning

It's clearly easy to increase sales by easing credit and collections policies, but receivables balances and credit losses go up at the same time. This situation can be dangerous for the senior financial manager. The applause for the increased sales tends to be given to the marketing department, but the blame for a high receivables balance and the associated losses belongs exclusively to the finance department. This can be a political no-win situation for the executive in charge of finance.

In most companies, optimizing collections performance takes a familiarity with customers and their problems that the finance department simply does not have. The best results come only when management directs the sales force to actively participate in identifying and correcting problems.

It's important to make sure the CEO (president, general manager) understands that while receivables are financial, creating them is a joint effort with sales and that problems need to be owned by both organizations.

The Terms of Sale   Recall that credit sales are made on terms that specify the number of days after which the net payment is due and a period during which a prompt payment discount may be taken. For example, terms of 2/10, net 30 mean a 2% discount can be taken if payment is made within 10 days; otherwise, the entire amount is due in 30 days.

Terms can have an effect on receivables in two ways. First, shortening or extending the net period tends to affect the length of time a nondelinquent customer takes to pay its bill. It would therefore seem that shortening the term would reduce the receivables balance. As a practical matter, however, companies don't have a great deal of latitude in making the net period shorter than whatever is customary in the industry.

> The **prompt payment discount** is usually an effective tool for **managing receivables**.

The **prompt payment discount** tends to be a more effective policy variable. A generous discount usually reduces receivables balances because customers pay quickly to save money. As we've said before, however, discounts are expensive for the firm giving them.

Occasionally prompt payment discounts don't help to reduce receivables at all. That happens when a firm's customers are too cash poor to take the discount regardless of how attractive it is. That's often the case when the customers are struggling small businesses. In such situations, increasing the discount in an effort to reduce receivables can backfire and cost money. The reason is that only customers who are already paying promptly take the increased discount.

Collections Policy   A firm's credit department is usually closely connected with its *collections department*. The function of the collections department is to follow up on overdue receivables to get delinquent customers to pay their bills. The process is known as **dunning** the debtor.

> **Dunning** is the process of following up on **overdue** receivables.

The normal procedure begins with mailing a polite reminder that payment is overdue a few days after the net date on the invoice. If payment isn't received, two or three additional *dunning letters* follow using progressively stronger language. After that, phone calls are made first to the customer's payables department and then to responsible executives. If a customer is substantially in arrears, further shipments usually are stopped until some payment is received.

In the majority of cases, unpaid bills are the result of some product or administrative problem. For example, if the product purchased doesn't work as expected, many firms don't pay the bill. In such a case, the collections department gets the customer together with the firm's sales and service personnel to try to straighten out the problem.

Another common problem involves mismatches between the firm's invoice and what the customer's records show as having been ordered and received. If these don't match exactly, many organizations don't pay. In such cases, the collections department works to reconcile the paperwork and get the bill paid.

In other cases, customers don't pay because they don't have the cash or are disreputable and just don't pay bills until they're forced to. When that happens, letters and phone calls don't work and the account is eventually turned over to a **collection agency.** Collection agencies are companies that specialize in dunning and collecting overdue accounts for a percentage of the amounts collected. They use the same techniques as the selling firm, but tend to be more persistent, aggressive, and threatening.

If the agency isn't successful, a lawsuit can be filed against the delinquent customer. The filing can be handled by either the company or the collection agency. If the suit is successful, the firm is awarded a judgment by the court, which still may not be collectible if the customer is missing or bankrupt.

A company's *collections policy* determines how quickly and aggressively it pursues overdue accounts. There's a great deal of difference, for example, between a firm that sends polite letters and calls for several months and one that threatens a lawsuit when a bill is 30 days overdue.

> **Collection agencies** specialize in **pursuing overdue accounts**, and are usually very **aggressive**.

> **Collection policy** is the **manner** and **aggressiveness** with which a firm **pursues payment** from delinquent customers.

Collections and Customer Relations

Overly aggressive collection efforts can damage customer relations. For example, imagine that a particular shipment has become very confused because of malfunctioning product and mistakes in shipping, receiving, and invoicing. Also suppose the customer and the firm's sales and service departments are working reasonably diligently to straighten out the problems. Now imagine that, in the middle of all this, the customer is served with a lawsuit initiated by the collections department for payment of the disputed bill.

Clearly, that would create a tendency for the customer to buy from another vendor in the future. It would also upset the sales department, because it wants to continue selling to the customer. On the other hand, it isn't unusual for salespeople to attempt to placate the collections department in order to sell more commissionable product to a customer they know is a payment risk.

16.5   Inventory Management

Inventory is product held for sale to customers. Its significance and the complexity of managing it vary tremendously between businesses. For example, in retailing operations, inventory management is critically important but relatively simple, while in manufacturing it can be as complex as it is crucial. At the other extreme, most service businesses carry only incidental inventories, so the issue is relatively minor.

It's important to realize that in any business in which inventory is significant, its mismanagement has the potential to ruin the company.

16.5a   Who is Responsible for Inventories?

Unlike cash and receivables, inventory is virtually never the direct responsibility of the finance department. It is usually managed by a functional area such as manufacturing or operations. The executives in charge of those areas generally have broad latitude in choosing inventory levels and management methods.

Finance has an **oversight** responsibility for inventory management.

Finance gets involved in an **oversight** or policing way. If inventory levels become too high, it's the job of financial management to call attention to the fact that things might be run more efficiently. Financial people generally monitor the level of lost or obsolete inventory that has to be written off and ensure that it doesn't become excessive. They also supervise periodic *physical inventories* (counts) that reconcile quantities actually on hand with the firm's records.

In short, although the finance department does not itself manage the typical firm's inventory, it has a responsibility to ensure that those who do manage it act cost effectively.

16.5b   The Benefits and Costs of Carrying Inventory

As might be expected, for firms to which inventory is important, it's easier to operate with more usable inventory than with less. However, carrying the extra material costs money, so there's a trade-off between cost and benefit. The idea behind inventory management is to find a level that's close to optimal in balancing the pluses against the minuses.

The Benefits of Carrying Adequate Inventory

In manufacturing, inventory separates and smooths out the work of different production departments. For example, suppose departments A and B work on product sequentially. If product moves directly out of department A into B, everything runs smoothly as long as there are no delays in A's operation. However, if some defect or accident causes a delay in A, department B will run out of work and be idle until the problem is fixed. Clearly, time and money will be wasted. But if some product is inventoried between the two departments, B can avoid idle time by working on it while department A is fixing its problem.

In any business, carrying more inventory rather than less reduces **stockouts** and **backorders**. A stockout occurs when something the company doesn't have on hand is needed in production or by a customer. The firm is out of stock on the item and places a backorder with its supplier to get it. The term "backorder" implies the order is remedial in the sense that the item is currently needed, and usually implies a request for expedited handling.

In manufacturing, stockouts disrupt operations and cause idle time and missed schedules, which cost money. At the point of sale, stockouts mean customers don't get what they want right away. That causes dissatisfaction and can drive customers to other suppliers, which means lost sales. Too many stockouts can drive customers away permanently.

All in all, carrying more active, usable inventory makes operations run more smoothly, improves customer relations, and increases sales.[13]

The Cost of Carrying Inventory   Keeping inventory on hand takes money. The reasons can be separated into traditional costs of the inventory and potential losses in its value. In general, both increase with the amount of inventory carried.

The following traditional costs are associated with holding inventory:

- *Interest:* Firms have to pay a return on the funds used to acquire inventory just as they do on any other asset.
- *Storage and security:* Inventory takes up space and is often subject to pilfering. Storage space has to be provided along with security to prevent theft.
- *Insurance:* Firms generally buy insurance to protect themselves against large inventory losses due to fire, theft, or natural disaster.
- *Taxes:* Many states and localities levy a tax on the value of inventory.

Several phenomena cause inventory to lose value. In general, the more inventory a firm carries, the more it exposes to a risk of loss from each of the following causes and the higher is its overall loss.

- *Shrinkage:* In spite of security measures, some inventory inevitably disappears. Such vanishing, presumably due to theft, is known as shrinkage.
- *Spoilage:* Many items have a limited shelf life, after which they lose their value partially or entirely. Even when inventory is monitored carefully, some spoilage of perishable items is expected.
- *Breakage:* Inventory in stock can be run over, stepped on, leaked on or into, or broken in any number of ways.
- *Obsolescence:* New products often do jobs better, faster, or cheaper than their predecessors. When that happens, the old products lose value rapidly because no one wants them unless their prices are heavily discounted.

The costs and losses together can be called the **carrying cost** of inventory.

Ordering Costs   The process of ordering and receiving goods generates a different sort of inventory-related expense. The carrying costs we've talked about so far depend on the amount of inventory on hand during a period. *Ordering costs* reflect the expenses of placing orders with suppliers, receiving shipments, and processing materials into inventory. These costs are related to the number of orders placed rather than to the amount of inventory held.

We'll see shortly that ordering costs and carrying costs tend to vary inversely with one another.

16.5c   Inventory Control and Management

Companies develop elaborate systems for tracking and controlling their inventories. The cost of such systems and the people to run them are additional expenses associated

---

13. It should be obvious that carrying extra obsolete or damaged inventory doesn't convey these benefits. Hence, we have to look beyond the dollar inventory figure on the balance sheet to see whether the firm has enough or too much.

with inventory. This kind of cost doesn't necessarily increase with incremental inventory or orders. Rather, it's tied to the number of different pieces carried and the way they're used.

Inventory management refers to the overall way a company oversees its inventory and uses its control system to manage the benefits of carrying inventory against the cost. You can think of the process as defining an acceptable level of operating efficiency in terms of stockouts, backorders, and production problems, and then trying to achieve that level of efficiency with the minimum inventory cost.

There's no single, all-encompassing approach to managing inventory. Success is achieved through frequent reviews, attention to detail, and the use of a variety of mechanized and manual systems. In the rest of this section, we'll review some well-known ideas that address pieces of the inventory management process.

> **Inventory management** refers to the **overall** way a firm **controls inventory** and its cost.

16.5d   The Economic Order Quantity (EOQ) Model

We've defined carrying and ordering costs as being related to inventory in different ways. Carrying costs increase with the amount of inventory held, while ordering costs increase with the number of orders placed to replenish depleted stocks. The total cost of having inventory is the sum of the two. The **economic order quantity (EOQ) model** is an approach to minimizing total inventory cost by recognizing that under certain conditions there's a trade-off between carrying cost and ordering cost.

Imagine that an inventory item is used evenly during the year and is periodically reordered in quantity Q. For the moment we'll ignore time lags in ordering and delivery. We'll assume the item is used steadily until none is left, then is immediately restocked by a delivery of Q units. Figure 16-7 is a plot of the number of units on hand over time under these assumptions.

Notice that inventory in stock decreases steadily along the diagonal lines until it is replenished. Under these conditions, the average quantity on hand is Q/2 units and the number of reorders per year is the annual usage divided by Q.

> The **EOQ** attempts to minimize inventory costs.

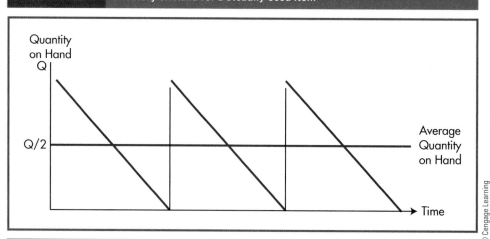

FIGURE 16-7   Inventory on Hand for a Steadily Used Item

© Cengage Learning

The model assumes that carrying costs vary directly with the average inventory balance and that ordering costs are fixed on a per-order basis. If C represents yearly carrying cost per unit, total carrying cost can be written as

(16.1)   **carrying cost = C(Q/2)**

It's clear from Equation 16.1 and the diagram that total carrying cost can be reduced by ordering more frequently in smaller quantities. If Q were smaller, Figure 16-7 would have more sawtoothed peaks, but each would be lower and the average quantity on hand (Q/2) would be lower.

However, ordering more frequently will increase the number of orders placed each year. Because each order costs a fixed amount, this increases total ordering cost. If annual demand is D, the firm places

(16.2)   **N = D/Q**

orders per year. Then if the fixed cost per order is F, total ordering cost will be

(16.3)   **ordering cost = FN = F(D/Q)**

This expression increases as order size decreases as Q is in the denominator.

Total inventory cost, which we'll call TC, is the sum of carrying cost and ordering cost. Adding Equations 16.1 and 16.3 gives

(16.4) $$TC = C\frac{Q}{2} + F\frac{D}{Q}$$

These ideas are represented graphically in Figure 16-8. The diagram shows carrying cost increasing and ordering cost decreasing with order size, Q. Notice that the sum of these costs, total cost, first decreases and then increases as Q gets larger. Hence, it's possible to choose an optimal order size that minimizes the cost of inventory. That value of Q is known as the economic order quantity, abbreviated EOQ. On the diagram, it is directly below the minimum point on the total cost line.

FIGURE 16-8 Inventory Costs and the EOQ

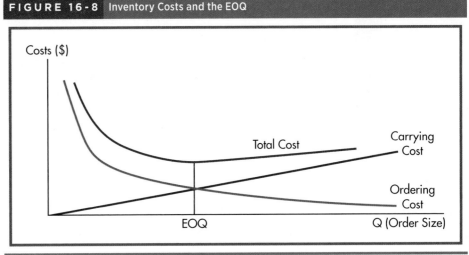

© Cengage Learning

A technique for finding the minimum value of an expression like Equation 16.4 is available using calculus. We'll accept the following result without getting into the math.[14]

(16.5)
$$EOQ = \left[\frac{2FD}{C}\right]^{1/2}$$

CONCEPT CONNECTION   **EXAMPLE 16-9**

Economic Order Quantity (EOQ) Model

The Galbraith Corp. buys a part that costs $5. The carrying cost of inventory is approximately 20% of the part's dollar value per year. It costs $45 to place, process, and receive an order. The firm uses 1,000 of the $5 parts a year. What ordering quantity minimizes inventory costs, and how many orders will be placed each year if that order quantity is used? What inventory costs are incurred for the part with this ordering quantity?

SOLUTION: First note that the unit carrying cost per year is 20% of the part's price, so

$$C = (.2)(\$5) = \$1$$

Next write Equation 16.5 and substitute from the information given.

$$EOQ = \left[\frac{2FD}{C}\right]^{1/2}$$
$$= \left[\frac{2(\$45)(1,000)}{\$1}\right]^{1/2}$$
$$= [90,000]^{1/2}$$
$$= 300 \text{ units}$$

The annual number of reorders is

$$1,000/300 = 3.3333$$

Carrying costs are

$$(300/2) \times \$5 \times .2 = \$150$$

and ordering costs are

$$\$45 \times 3.3333 = \$150$$

Hence, the total inventory cost of the part is $300.

As an exercise, demonstrate that this is a minimum by calculating the cost at several different ordering quantities around 300 units.

Notice from the diagram that the minimum total cost is achieved where the two component cost lines cross one another. That means at the optimal point, carrying cost and ordering cost are equal.

---

14. The mathematically inclined will recognize the EOQ as a straightforward minimization problem with respect to the variable Q. Differentiate with respect to Q and set the result equal to zero to get

$$0 = \frac{C}{2} - \frac{FD}{Q^2}$$

Then solve for Q to get Equation 16.5.

16.5e   Safety Stocks, Reorder Points, and Lead Times

Notice that the inventory arrangement represented in Figure 16-7 assumes a perfectly even and predictable flow of parts out of inventory. It also assumes an instantaneous delivery of parts whenever needed. In reality, usage rates vary and restocking orders don't always arrive on time.

Clearly, these factors can cause the firm to run out of inventory and suffer the problems associated with the stockouts we described earlier. Such outages can be largely avoided by carrying a **safety stock** of inventory for emergencies. A safety stock is simply an additional supply of inventory that is carried all the time to be used when normal working stocks run out.

The EOQ model of Figure 16-7 can be modified conceptually to include safety stocks by placing the sawtoothed lines on top of a safety stock as shown in Figure 16-9.

Safety stock provides a **buffer** against **unexpectedly** rapid use or delayed delivery.

Lead Times and Reorder Points   As a practical matter, a restocking order has to be placed in advance of the time at which it's needed. The advance period, known as an *ordering lead time,* is generally estimated by the item's supplier.

Referring to the leftmost diagonal in Figure 16-9, we see that, as time passes, the quantity on hand diminishes along the diagonal line until the *reorder point* (indicated on the vertical axis) is reached. At that time an order for resupply is placed with the supplier. The reorder point is calculated so that the expected usage during the ordering lead time will bring the stock to its lowest planned level just as the new supply is delivered.

However, if the usage rate increases after an order is placed, the stock will diminish faster than planned and the inventory balance will dip into the safety stock range. That situation is depicted along the second diagonal in the diagram. If there were no safety stock, the increased usage would result in a stockout.

FIGURE 16-9   Pattern of Inventory on Hand Including Safety Stock Showing Reorder Point, Lead Time, and the Effects of High Usage and Delayed Delivery

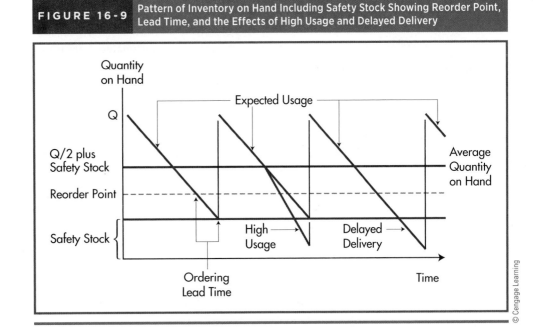

© Cengage Learning

It is also easy to see that a delay in delivery after a reorder will cause a dip into safety stock. This situation is depicted along the third diagonal, and would also result in a stockout if there were no safety stock.

Safety Stock and the EOQ   The inclusion of safety stocks does not change the EOQ. It just increases the total cost of inventory by the carrying cost of the safety stock. In effect, the EOQ model sits on top of a safety stock level as shown in Figure 16-9.

The Right Level of Safety Stock   Choosing a safety stock level involves another cost trade-off. The extra inventory increases carrying cost but avoids losses from production delays and missed sales. These opposing effects have to be balanced in the choice of an appropriate level of safety inventory. The choice can be difficult because the savings aren't visible. They're the result of problems that didn't happen, so they don't appear anywhere on financial statements. The carrying cost, on the other hand, is quite visible and measurable.

It's rarely advisable to carry so much safety inventory that stockouts are avoided entirely. Under most conditions, that would require a huge amount of inventory at an excessive cost. It's generally best to tolerate an occasional outage to keep inventory levels reasonable. In some businesses, backorders are filled quickly and outages don't cause a lot of trouble. In such cases, safety stocks can be minimal.

16.5f   Tracking Inventories—The ABC System

The amount of attention that should be given to controlling inventories of particular items varies with the nature and cost of the item. Some pieces are very expensive, and for that reason alone warrant a great deal of attention. Some items are critical to the firm's processes or to those of customers, and therefore are important whether they cost a lot or not. On the other hand, some items are cheap and easy to get, so spending a lot of effort to control them isn't worthwhile. Common nuts and bolts are a good example.

An **ABC system** segregates items by **value** and places **tighter control** on **higher-cost** pieces.

Most companies recognize this fact and use a variant of the **ABC system** in their inventory control systems. Items designated A are important because of their value or the consequences of running out, and are carefully controlled. They're usually serialized, kept under lock and key, and signed out to a responsible individual when used. C items are cheap and plentiful, kept in a bin accessible to anyone, and reordered when the bin gets low. B items are between As and Cs and are handled accordingly.

Recognizing that inventory items differ in importance enables companies to keep control costs low.

16.5g   Just in Time (JIT) Inventory Systems

In recent years, a manufacturing inventory concept developed by the Japanese has received a lot of publicity. In theory, the **just in time (JIT)** system virtually eliminates factory inventory. Under JIT, suppliers deliver goods to manufacturers just in time (within a few hours) to be used in production. The idea requires a great deal of faith and cooperation between a manufacturer and its suppliers, because a late delivery can stop a factory's entire production line.

JIT eliminates manufacturing inventory by pushing it **back on suppliers**.

Under JIT, the manufacturer is essentially pushing the task of carrying inventory back onto its suppliers. Conceptually, the supplier will push its inventory back onto its suppliers, which do the same to their suppliers. Ultimately, the entire production chain works in a coordinated manner, largely eliminating inventories.

The idea sounds good in theory and does work under certain conditions, but hasn't proven as successful as its proponents originally hoped. In many situations, it doesn't work at all.

JIT works best when the manufacturer is very large and powerful with respect to the supplier and buys most of the supplier's output. In such cases, the supplier is willing to do almost anything to keep the manufacturer's business, including orchestrating JIT deliveries. Even then, the concept works really well only when the supplier is located near enough to the manufacturer that shipping delays aren't a problem. The automobile industry tends to be organized like that and has had great success with JIT. The idea was originally developed by Toyota in Japan.

For smaller companies that don't have any particular clout over suppliers that may be located far away, the idea may not be practical. In such cases, suppliers have little incentive to go to the trouble and expense of making the precise and timely deliveries that JIT requires.

CONCEPT CONNECTION   EXAMPLE 16-10

Just In Time (JIT) Inventory Systems

Wallace Manufacturing Inc. carries an inventory valued at approximately $2 million that's financed at an average cost of 8%. The inventory is subject to 4% shrinkage, taxes and insurance cost 3%, and charges for storage space are $150,000 per year.

The vice president of manufacturing recently attended a JIT seminar and feels the system could save 90% of Wallace's inventory costs. The CFO is less enthusiastic—maintaining that suppliers are unlikely to consistently meet JIT delivery schedules. He maintains that a stock-out of key parts will idle at least 160 workers who earn an average of $45 per hour for about six hours. This doesn't include subjective costs such as the impact of late deliveries on customer satisfaction.

How many missed JIT deliveries per year will it take to consume all of the savings the manufacturing VP attributes to JIT? Does the system seem likely to save money if four suppliers would each have to make three precisely timed deliveries per week?

SOLUTION: Inventory costs estimated as a percentage of the inventory balance are

Interest	8%
Shrinkage	4%
Taxes and Insurance	3%
Total % costs	15%

Cost of carrying $2 million = $2,000,000 × .15 =	$300,000
Cost of storage space	150,000
Total carrying cost	$450,000
Savings at 90%	$405,000

The cost of a missed delivery is estimated as

160 workers $\times$ \$45 per hour $\times$ 6 hours per missed delivery = \$43,200

Breakeven number of delivery misses = \$405,000/\$43,200 = 9.4

The number of JIT deliveries required per year would be

4 suppliers $\times$ 3 deliveries per week $\times$ 52 weeks/yr = 624

Breakeven misses as a percent of deliveries = 9.4 / 624 = .015 = 1.5%

The implication is that the suppliers would have to achieve a 98.5% success rate for the system to save money. Achieving that seems difficult.

CONCEPT CONNECTIONS

QUESTIONS

1. Explain the different circumstances under which firms should use short-term or long-term financing.

2. Because companies always have inventory and accounts receivable, most banks are happy to make long-term loans to support those assets. Either refute or support that statement.

3. Describe the maturity matching principle. What are the risks of not matching maturities? How would you characterize a firm that ignores the principle? Can you think of situations in which it would be advisable for an otherwise prudent firm to deviate from the principle?

4. Working capital spontaneously finances itself because it's being turned over all the time. Is this statement true, false, or a little of both? Exactly what is meant by "spontaneous financing"? Does working capital require funding? Why?

5. Working capital is generally defined as the difference between current assets and current liabilities. Is this definition precisely correct? Why?

6. Support or challenge each of the following statements individually.
   a. Because accounts receivable aren't purchased like inventory or fixed assets, they don't require financing.
   b. Cash represents a pool of available money, so it actually reduces financing needs.

7. How does a firm's operating cycle differ from its cash conversion cycle? Explain fully.

8. You work in the finance department of a manufacturing company. Over lunch, a friend in the engineering department said she'd heard that the firm used a lot of temporary working capital. Because temporary equipment is usually of lower quality than permanent material, she wonders why the company, which is quite prosperous, doesn't buy the best and store it when it isn't needed.

   What misconceptions does your friend have? Write a brief explanation for someone who knows nothing about finance to straighten out her understanding.

9. Why does it make sense to finance net working capital separately from fixed assets?

10. You work in the finance department of HiTech Inc. The firm's owner and CEO, Charlie Dollars, is very profit oriented. He understands that short-term interest rates are quite low at the moment and has suggested that the firm finance all of its working capital needs with short-term loans. The CFO has asked you to prepare a memo for his signature outlining why this may not be the best strategy. In your memo, outline the working capital financing options available to most firms and discuss the trade-offs involved in using long-term versus short-term financing.

11. What are the advantages and disadvantages of stretching payables? If you owned your own business, would you do it? Why or why not?

12. What's the difference between a promissory note, a line of credit, and a revolving credit agreement? Are they mutually exclusive? That is, might one be part of the other?

13. Explain the difference between pledging and factoring receivables. Which is likely to be a more expensive source of financing? Is factoring the same kind of financing as pledging?

14. Factoring may involve interest even though it isn't a loan. How can this come about?

15. What is the biggest problem associated with financing secured by inventory? How is it addressed in practice?

16. Outline the reasons for holding cash and the big cost associated with it. How do these lead to the objective of cash management? How do marketable securities help or hinder achievement of the objective?

17. The Medco Supply Co. operates out of Waco, Texas, and has a number of customers around Portland, Maine. It seems to take a particularly long time for the Portland customers' payment checks to reach Medco. What can the company do to speed things up? Explain how your solution would work.

18. Sally Johnson lives in Baltimore and does business with a large, national brokerage firm. When she sends the broker a check, she mails it to a local address in Baltimore. However, when she receives a check from the broker, it comes from San Francisco. Her sister Joan lives in Los Angeles and uses the same firm. She mails payments to an office a few blocks from her home, but receives checks from an office in Miami. What's going on? Should the Johnson sisters be upset?

19. You're the cash manager for Huge Inc., which has factories and stores all over the country. Each operation has several bank accounts to receive deposits and pay vendors, so the company's cash is spread all over the country under the control of divisional CFOs. It's essential that those divisional executives have control of their cash to run their operations effectively. However, the rather substantial cash total isn't earning anything because it's too dispersed to be invested in marketable securities. Suggest a way to fix this problem and explain how it will work.

20. Every company should take full advantage of the sophisticated cash management services offered by today's banking industry. Right or wrong? Explain.

21. Outline the costs and benefits involved in the trade-off between a tighter versus a looser receivables policy.

22. Inventory management is a shared responsibility between finance and manufacturing just as receivables management involves both sales and finance. Right or wrong? Explain.

23. Because of the advances in computer technology, inventory management is a precise science, and there's

no excuse for not having the optimal quantity on hand at all times. Is that statement true or false? Explain.

24. Does the EOQ model when properly applied prevent stockouts? Does it address stockouts at all? Do you think the EOQ model solves very many of management's inventory problems?

25. The Philipps Lighting Company manufactures decorative light fixtures. Its revenues are about $100 million a year. It purchases inputs from approximately 20 suppliers, most of which are much larger companies located in various parts of the country. Sam Spade, the vice president of manufacturing, is a sophisticated executive who has always been impressed by the latest innovative techniques in management.

Last week Sam came into a meeting of the executive team with a proposal to cut inventory costs to almost nothing. Just in time (JIT) is the wave of the future, he said, and proposed that Philipps enter into negotiations with all of its suppliers to implement the concept immediately.

You're the CFO and tend to be more skeptical about new methods. Prepare a memo to the team, tactfully outlining the problems and risks involved in Sam's proposal.

BUSINESS ANALYSIS

1. You're a supervisor in the treasury department of Big Corp. Recently there has been increasing concern about the firm's rising interest expense. Fred Eyeshade is an analyst in your group who transferred from the accounting department a short time ago. He has suggested that senior management mandate a 50% across-the-board cut in cash, inventory, and receivables along with a doubling of payables to reduce the firm's financing needs for net working capital. Explain why this might not be a good idea with respect to each of these elements of net working capital (four accounts).

2. Things tend to run more smoothly and efficiently with more working capital. With respect to receivables and inventory, explain why this statement isn't absolutely true. In other words, why might a very large inventory or receivables balance not do much good at all?

3. You and your friend Harry have started a business. Harry is a technical whiz, but doesn't know much about business or finance. After several months, you've been approved for a $100,000 bank loan at what seems to be a rather high interest rate, 12%. Harry is especially bothered by the rate. He thinks banks shouldn't get any more than 4 or 5%, but doesn't really know why he feels that way. When you both were about to sign the loan papers, the banker mentioned that a minimum balance of $20,000 would have to remain in the bank. Hearing this, Harry pulled out his calculator and made a calculation at which he became outraged. He then stormed out of the meeting.

Why is Harry so upset? What calculation did he make? Write a short memo explaining banking practices to calm Harry down. Is there a kind of minimum balance requirement that might make Harry's calculation invalid?

4. You're the CFO of the Wachusett Window Company, which sells windows to residential builders. The firm's customers tend to be small, thinly capitalized construction companies that are frequently short of cash. Over the past year, there's been a slump in the housing industry, and Wachusett's sales have slowed. Several months ago, the marketing department initiated a program to attract new customers to counteract the downward sales trend. The VP of marketing and the president agreed that the firm would have to deal with even smaller, newer builders if it were going to keep sales up. At the time, the president overruled your concerns about the credit quality of such customers. He personally approved a number of accounts brought in by the sales department that ordinarily wouldn't have qualified for credit.

More recently, receivables have gone up substantially, and collection efforts have been less successful than usual. Collectors have asked for help from sales representatives in chasing down delinquent customers, but the VP of marketing says they don't have time because "reps have to be out on the street selling."

The president has suddenly become concerned about the receivables increase, and has demanded to know why finance has let it happen. Prepare a memo explaining the processes behind the creation and management of receivables and explain what's behind the increase. Tactfully explain why the blame should not be placed solely on the finance department. Can you argue that finance is completely without fault in this matter?

5. In the situation at Wachusett Window outlined in the last question, do you think a higher prompt payment discount in addition to the new sales program would have kept receivables down? Why?

6. Speculate on the nature of the relationship between the credit and collections department and the sales department at Wachusett Window in the last two questions.

7. Wildebrant Inc. runs out of inventory all the time, both in the factory and at the point of sale. However, the company is profitable, and no one worries about it much. Is this OK? What's probably going on that management doesn't see? Why don't they see it? What would you suggest to fix the problem? How would it work?

PROBLEMS

Definitions (pages 665–667)

1. Scherbert Industries has the following balance sheet accounts as of 12/31/X3 (not a complete balance sheet):

Accounts payable	$ 650,000
Accounts receivable	845,000
Accruals	257,500
Cash	137,200
Common stock	1,200,000
Fixed assets (net)	8,250,000
Inventory	655,000
Long-term debt	3,500,000

Calculate gross and net working capital.

Cash Conversion Cycle: Figure 16-2 (page 669)

2. Southport Inc. has an inventory turnover of 10×, an ACP of 45 days, and turns over its payables once a month. How long are Southport's operating and cash conversion cycles? (Use a 360-day year.)

Working Capital Financing Policies: Concept Connection Example 16-1 (page 673)

3. The Langley Corporation is in a seasonal business. It requires a permanent base of net working capital of $10 million all year long, but that requirement temporarily increases to $20 million during a four-month period each year. Langley has three financing options for net working capital.
   a. Finance the peak level year round with equity, which costs 20%, and invest temporarily unused funds in marketable securities, which earn 6%.
   b. Finance permanent net working capital with equity and temporary net working capital with a short-term loan at 12%.
   c. Finance all net working capital needs with short-term debt at 12.5%.

   Calculate the cost of each option. Which would you choose? Why?

Prompt Payment Discount (page 675)

4. Calculate the effective interest rate implied by the following terms of sale. (Use a 365-day year.)

    2/10, net 30
    1/5, net 15
    .5/10, net 30
    2.5/10, net 25
    1/5, net 20

5. Rocky Inc. can buy its inventory from any of four suppliers, all of which offer essentially the same pricing and quality. Their credit terms, however, vary considerably as follows:

A	2/10, net 30
B	3/5, net 20
C	1/20, net 45
D	3/5, net 90

a. Calculate the implied interest rate associated with each policy.

b. If Rocky buys some material from each vendor, which discounts should it take and which should it forego if it pays 18% for working capital financing? Why?

Revolving Credit Agreements: Concept Connection Example 16-2 (page 678)

6. Thompson Inc. has a $10 million revolving credit agreement with its bank. It pays interest on borrowing at 2% over prime and a .25% commitment fee on available but unused funds. Last month Thompson had borrowings of $5 million for the first half of the month and $10 million for the second half. Calculate its interest charges for the month. The bank's prime rate is 6%.

7. The Conejo Corp. borrows from its bank under an $8 million revolving credit arrangement. It pays a base rate of 9% on its outstanding loan plus a .25% commitment fee on the unused balance. The firm had borrowed $2 million going into April and borrowed an additional $4 million on April 11. No further borrowing or repayment was made during the month. Calculate Conejo's interest charges for April.

8. The Grass Ridge Company has the following current asset accounts:

Cash	$1,900,000
Accounts receivable	4,600,000
Inventory	5,500,000

Its current ratio is 2.5:1. The bank is willing to lend the company enough to finance its working capital needs under a $10 million revolving credit arrangement at a base rate of 12% with a 3/8% commitment fee on the unused balance. If the current accounts stay relatively constant throughout the year, what will Grass Ridge pay the bank for working capital financing?

9. Bridgeport Inc. has a $30 million revolving credit agreement with its bank at prime plus 3.2% based on a calendar year. Prior to the month of April, it had taken down $15 million that was outstanding for the entire month. On April 10, it took down another $5 million. Prime is 8.2%, and the bank's commitment fee is .25% annually. Calculate the charges associated with Bridgeport's revolving credit agreement for the month of April.

Compensating Balances: Concept Connection Example 16-3 (page 679)

10. What is the effective interest rate on a $750,000 loan at 8% for 120 days if a 20% minimum compensating balance is required?

11. Calculate the effective interest rate on loans with the following minimum compensating balance requirements:

	Loan Rate	Compensating Balance
a.	6.5%	20%
b.	12.0%	10%
c.	10.5%	15%
d.	14.0%	25%
e.	8.5%	30%

Pledging Accounts Receivable: Concept Connection Example 16-4 (page 681)

12. Jenkins Appliances has cash flow problems and needs to borrow between $50,000 and $60,000 for approximately sixty (60) days. Because the business is small and relatively new, unsecured loans are very hard to get and are expensive when they are available. The bank has offered such a loan at 25%. Climax Inc., a finance company, has offered an alternative loan if receivables are pledged as collateral. Climax will lend 70% of the average receivables balance for 14% plus an administrative fee of $1,200. Jenkins' average receivables balance is $80,000. Which alternative should Jenkins choose? Calculate using a 360-day year. Assume the bank is willing to lend the same amount as Climax.

13. DeSquam Inc. pledges receivables of $250 million per year to the Sharkskin Finance Company, which advances cash equal to 80% of the face value of the accounts pledged. DeSquam's receivables are usually collected in about 36 days, so 10% of the annual amount advanced is generally outstanding at any time. (Thirty-six days is one-tenth of a year, so receivables "turn over" 10 times a year.) Sharkskin charges 14% interest plus an administrative fee of 1.6% of the amount pledged. What is DeSquam's cost of receivables financing? State the result in dollar terms and as a rate.

14. The York Company has an average receivables balance of $55,000, which turns over once every 30 days. It offers all of its receivables to its bank as collateral for short-term borrowing (pledging). The bank generally accepts 60% of the accounts offered and advances cash equal to 85% of those. Interest is 3% over prime and the bank charges a 1% administrative fee on the gross value of all accounts offered. The prime rate is currently 9.5%. What effective rate is York paying for its receivables financing?

Factoring Receivables: Concept Connection Example 16-5 (page 683)

15. Southern Fabrics Inc. factors all of its receivables. The firm does $150 million in business each year and would have an ACP of 36.5 days if it collected its own receivables. The firm's gross margin is 35%. The factor operates without recourse and pays immediately upon taking over the accounts. It discounts the gross amount factored by 10% and pays Southern immediately. Because the factor doesn't collect from customers until they pay, it charges interest at 10% in the interim.
    a. Calculate the gross cost of factoring to Southern Fabrics if all receivables are collectible.
    b. What interest rate is implied by the arrangement?
    c. Suppose Southern is considering giving up the factoring arrangement and handling its own collections. Should the firm do it if bad-debt losses are expected to average 3% of gross sales and running a collections department will cost about $1.5 million per year? Assume the interest cost of carrying the receivable balance is also 10%.
    d. What is the implied interest rate in the factoring arrangement if the costs in part (c) are taken into account?

Inventory Financing: Concept Connection Example 16-6 (page 684)

16. Central City Bank will lend Williams Inc. 60% of the value of its inventory at 12% if Williams will pledge the inventory as collateral for the loan. The bank also insists that Williams employ a warehousing company to monitor and control the inventoried material. Blyth Warehousing will do the job for an annual fee of $150,000 plus 2% of the value of all the inventory it handles. Williams moves inventory valued at about $15 million through its plant each year at a turnover rate of five times. What will the cost of financing be under this proposal? State the result in both dollar and percentage (of amount borrowed) terms.

17. The Shamrock Company has a raw materials inventory of $20 million, which is completely replaced approximately 10 times a year. The Bridgewater Bank is willing to advance financing of 75% of the value of Shamrock's inventory at an interest rate of 12%. However, it requires a warehousing

system to secure its interests. A warehousing company will install and operate the system for $800,000 a year plus .5% of the value of materials entering the system. What is the effective cost of this financing to Shamrock?

Evaluating Lock Box Systems: Concept Connection
Example 16-7 (page 692)

18. Tambourines Inc. collects $12 million per year from customers in a remote location. The average remittance check is $1,200. A lock box system would shorten the overall float on these receipts from eight days to seven days, but would cost $2,500 per year plus $.20 per check. The relevant interest rate is 9%. Should Tambourines install the system? Use a 360-day year.

19. The Hadley Motor Company is located in Florida but has a number of customers in the Pacific Northwest. Sales to those customers are $30 million a year paid in checks that average about $1,500. The checks take an average of nine days to clear into Hadley's Florida bank. A bank in Oregon will operate a lock box system for Hadley for $8,000 a year plus $.50 per check. The system can be expected to reduce the clearing time to six days.

   a. Is the lock box system worthwhile if Hadley borrows at 13.5%?
   b. What is the minimum number of days of float time the system has to save (to the nearest tenth of a day) to make it worthwhile?

20. Colburn Inc. is considering a lock box system. The firm has analyzed its credit receipts and determined the following:

   > Average time checks are in mail—3 days
   > Average internal check-processing time—3 days
   > Average to clear the banking system—2 days
   > Total credit sales—$180 million
   > Average check—$10,000

   Colburn funds its accounts receivable with short-term debt at 8%. First Bank has indicated that its lock box system will reduce mail float by an average of one day and eliminate internal processing time. The cost of the system is $0.50 for each check processed, plus 0.05% of the gross revenues processed. Should Colburn implement the lock box system? If the charge based on gross revenue remains constant, at what per-check charge would Colburn be indifferent to the lock box arrangement?

21. Bozarth Business Machines (BBM) has analyzed the value of implementing a lock box system. The firm anticipates revenues of $630 million with an average invoice of $1,500. BBM borrows at 12% and has made an arrangement with Old Second Bank to manage a lock box for $.24 per check and 0.06% of total receipts. BBM has estimated that the lock box will save $200,000 annually. How many days does BBM expect the system will save in the collection process?

Credit and Collections Policy: Concept Connection
Example 16-8 (page 696)

22. The Bailey Machine Tool Company thinks it can increase sales by $10 million by loosening its credit standards somewhat. The firm normally experiences bad debts of about 2% of sales, but marketing estimates that the incremental business would be from financially weaker customers who would not pay about 17% of the time. The firm's gross margin is 18% (production-related costs are 82% of revenue).

   a. Should Bailey lower its credit standards to get the new business?
   b. Would your answer change if taking on the new business also involved incremental collection expenses of $150,000 per year?

23. Over the past few years, the marketing department at Goldston & Co. has convinced the finance department to permit credit sales to increasingly marginal customers. Revenue has risen as a result, but bad debts are now at 6% of sales. Finance has suggested that the credit policy be tightened to reduce bad-debt losses. The proposal calls for a more restrictive policy under which sales would fall by 8%, but bad-debt losses would drop to 2.6% of revenue. Under the current policy, Goldston's revenue forecast is $400 million with a contribution margin of 38%. Implementing the new credit policy would have no effect on contribution margin but would require an additional $500,000 in annual fixed costs.

    a. Should Goldston implement Finance's new credit policy?

    b. What nonfinancial considerations should be evaluated?

    c. Should the new policy be implemented if bad debts are expected to drop only to 4% of revenues?

24. The Kranberry Kids Klothing Kompany is in the volatile garment business. The firm has annual revenues of $250 million and operates with a 30% gross margin on sales. Bad-debt losses average 3% of revenues. Kranberry is contemplating an easing of its credit policy in an attempt to increase sales. The loosening would involve accepting a lower-quality customer for credit sales. It is estimated that sales could be increased by $20 million a year in this manner. However, the collections department estimates that bad-debt losses on the new business would run four times the normal level, and that internal collection efforts would cost an additional $1 million a year.

    a. Is the policy change a good idea?

    b. Is it likely that coupling an increased prompt payment discount with the looser guidelines would reduce the bad-debt losses?

    c. Is it possible that the idea in part (b) could have a net negative impact? How?

Economic Order Quantity (EOQ) Model: Concept Connection Example 16-9 (page 704)

25. Sharon's Sweater Shop orders 5,000 sweaters per year from a supplier at a wholesale cost of $65 each. Carrying costs are 22% of cost, and it costs $52 to place and receive an order. How many orders should Sharon place with the supplier each year, and how large should each be?

26. Smithson Hydraulics Inc. carries an inventory of valves that cost $25 each. The firm's inventory carrying cost is approximately 18% of the value of the inventory. It costs $38 to place, process, and receive an order. The firm uses 20,000 valves a year.

    a. What ordering quantity minimizes the inventory costs associated with the valves? (Round to the nearest unit.)

    b. How many orders will be placed each year if the EOQ is used?

    c. What are the valves' carrying and ordering costs if the EOQ is used?

27. Emmons Motors is a distributor of electric motors. The firm projects product demand of 25,000 units next year. It costs $320 to place an order with suppliers. Management has determined that the EOQ is 1,000 units. How much per year does it cost Emmons to carry a unit of inventory?

Just in Time (JIT) Inventory Systems: Concept Connection Example 16-10 (page 707)

28. EverFit Inc. manufactures commercial grade fitness equipment used in spas and health clubs. The firm produces complex resistance exercise machines designed to strengthen specific muscles. EverFit's engineering department designs the equipment and then contracts with metal working shops to produce parts to their specifications. The parts are inventoried at EverFit's factory and assembled for shipment to customers. The $250,000 parts inventory is financed with short-term

debt at 6% interest. Shrinkage and obsolescence cost about 1%, while taxes and insurance run about $10,000 per year.

EverFit has discussed a just in time (JIT) system with its suppliers, all of which are located within 50 miles. The suppliers are small firms that depend on EverFit's business, and are willing to try to deliver parts in accordance with its production schedule.

However, EverFit's CFO is concerned that although their intentions are good, the suppliers won't be able to manage their operations precisely enough to consistently meet customer JIT requirements. Further, he thinks that when a JIT delivery is missed, it will generally be a day and a half before it is finally received. During that time, the assembly staff of 25 people will be idle. Each assembly worker earns about $30 per hour and must be paid for eight hours a day whether working or not.

a. If the measure of the system is saving money, how many JIT failures can the system tolerate and still break even?

b. Comment on the advisability of the JIT idea based on your answer to part a.

c. What qualitative factors might also be concerns?

d. Suggest a way to test the system before making a final decision.

CHAPTER 17

Corporate Restructuring

Chapter Outline

Mergers and Acquisitions
- Basic Definitions, Terminology, and Procedure
- The Antitrust Laws
- The Reasons Behind Mergers
- Holding Companies
- The History of Merger Activity in the United States
- Merger Analysis and the Price Premium
- Defensive Tactics

Other Kinds of Takeovers—LBOs and Proxy Fights
- Leveraged Buyouts (LBOs)
- Proxy Fights

Divestitures
- The Reasons for Divestitures
- Methods of Divesting Operations

Bankruptcy and the Reorganization of Failed Businesses
- Failure and Insolvency
- Bankruptcy—Concept and Objectives
- Bankruptcy Procedures—Reorganization, Restructuring, Liquidation

Corporate restructuring is a broad term that describes a number of the ways in which firms are reorganized. It refers to changes in capital structure (Chapter 14), changes in ownership, merging companies together or breaking them apart (divestitures), modification of asset structures, and certain changes in methods of doing business. In addition, business failure and bankruptcy usually result in some kind of restructuring.

Mergers are the most publicized restructuring activity. They occur when two or more firms combine under one ownership.

In this chapter, we'll have a close look at mergers and then turn our attention to bankruptcy.

17.1 Mergers and Acquisitions

Mergers are an important force in modern business. They've reshaped American industry several times in the last century and continue to have a significant effect on companies and financial markets.

17.1a Basic Definitions, Terminology, and Procedure

The terms "merger," "acquisition," and "consolidation" all mean the *combination* of two (or more) business units under a single controlling ownership. In day-to-day practice, the word "merger" is loosely used to mean any business combination, but technically, each term refers to a particular type of transaction.

A **merger** is a combination of two or more businesses in which all but one legally cease to exist, and the combined organization continues under the original name of the one surviving firm. A **consolidation** occurs when *all* of the combining legal entities dissolve, and a new one with a new name is formed to continue into the future. These ideas are illustrated in Figure 17-1 for combinations involving two firms. The left side illustrates a merger of company B into company A, while the right side shows A and B consolidating into C.

The merger situation is also called an **acquisition**, because the stock of the firm that goes out of existence is usually acquired by the continuing firm. In the left diagram, A is the *acquiring firm* and B is the **target** of the acquisition. The word "**takeover**" is sometimes used to describe the combination, because most of the time company A literally takes over company B. That term tends to have a hostile meaning, implying that A takes over B against the wishes of B's management.[1]

An important subtlety in all this is that the size of combining companies doesn't determine the nature of the combination. As a general rule, A would be larger than B in the merger/acquisition shown on the left and the two would be about the same size in the consolidation shown on the right. However, that isn't a requirement or always the case. There are many examples of smaller firms taking over larger ones.

Relationships   It's important to understand the relationships that come about when firms join together regardless of what the combination is called legally. In one situation, firms combine willingly, more or less as equals, even if there's a difference in their sizes. This is the general situation implied by a consolidation.

In the other situation, one firm dominates the resulting relationship because it *acquires* the other's stock. That's the usual case in an acquisition or merger.

> A **merger** is loosely defined as any **combination** of two or more businesses under **one ownership**.

> In an **acquisition** or **takeover** one firm acquires the stock of another called the **target**.

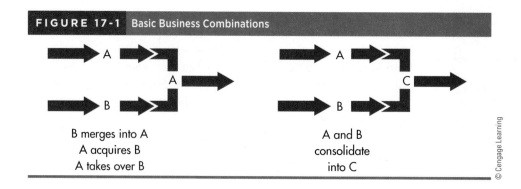

FIGURE 17-1   Basic Business Combinations

B merges into A
A acquires B
A takes over B

A and B
consolidate
into C

© Cengage Learning

---

1. "Takeover" is a fairly general term, simply implying that one group takes control from another. This can occur outside of a merger if one group of stockholders takes over control from another within a single company.

The management of the acquired firm generally works for the management of the acquiring firm after the merger. It's important to note that a merger can be accomplished with the friendly approval of the acquired firm's management or against its wishes.

Stockholders
Any merger or consolidation represents a change in ownership. In the merger shown on the left of Figure 17-1, company B goes out of existence. That means its stockholders give up their shares (in B) for something else, usually either cash or stock in A. In the consolidation shown on the right, the stockholders of both A and B give up their shares for stock in C.

> A **majority** of the **target's stockholders** must accept the price offered by the acquiring company.

No one can force the shareholders of a corporation *as a group* into a business combination. They have to be willing to give up their shares for the price offered in the deal. In the context of an acquisition, this means that a majority of the stockholders of the target (acquired) company must approve the price offered for their shares. (If a majority approves, dissenters may be forced to go along.)

The major issue in the analysis of mergers is the value given for the shares of the companies that go out of existence. For example, consider a merger (left diagram) in which A's stock was selling for $10 a share and B's for $5 just before merger talks began. Negotiations would have to start with an offer of at least $10 or one share of A for every two shares of B. Anything less wouldn't interest B's shareholders.

The Friendly Merger Procedure
In what follows, we'll be primarily concerned with the merger (acquisition) situation shown on the left in Figure 17-1. The merger process generally begins with the would-be acquirer's management contacting the target's management and proposing the deal.

> In a **friendly merger**, the target's management approves of the deal and **cooperates** with the acquiring company.

A **friendly merger** takes place when the management (and board of directors) of the target company agrees that the combination would be a good idea and cooperates with the acquirer. In such a case, negotiations between the two management groups on the price to be paid for the target's stock and other issues proceed until an agreement is reached. After that the proposal is submitted to the stockholders for a vote, with a recommendation by the target's board for approval. The percentage required for approval depends on the corporate charter and state law.

If the stockholders approve the merger, each firm files the appropriate papers with the state in which it's incorporated, cash or new stock certificates are issued to the stockholders of the acquired company, and the deal is consummated.

The Unfriendly Procedure
When a target firm's management and board are opposed to a merger, they refuse to take it to their stockholders. If the acquiring firm doesn't accept the refusal, it can approach the target's stockholders directly. The merger then becomes *hostile* or *unfriendly*. Sometimes the acquiring firm doesn't even try to deal with the target's management, but approaches its stockholders immediately in an effort to take the company's management by surprise.

> In an **unfriendly merger** the target's management resists and may take **defensive** measures to stop the deal.

> An acquiring firm can bypass a target's management by making a **tender offer** directly to shareholders.

In an unfriendly merger, the acquiring firm makes a **tender offer** to the target's shareholders. This is a special kind of a proposal made to buy stock. It offers to pay stockholders a fixed price for shares, but contains a provision stating that if the price isn't accepted on enough shares to gain control of the company, the deal is off. If the tender price is right, enough shares to gain control are offered and the acquiring firm takes over by purchasing them.

While all this is going on, the target company's management is likely to be contesting the proposal with what are known as *defensive measures*. Once an acquisition attempt is under way, these measures usually consist of efforts to convince shareholders not to sell to the acquirer. They generally have a limited effect if the price offered is fairly high. The target's management can also seek a preemptive merger with another acquirer it feels is more desirable. We'll talk more about these tactics later, along with defensive measures that managements can take before an acquirer comes along.

It's important to realize that the hostility in an unfriendly merger is between the managements or boards of directors of the two companies, not the stockholders. To most stockholders, the target company is just an investment. If someone offers a high enough price for their stock, they'll sell without a second thought.

Why Unfriendly Mergers Are Unfriendly

Mergers usually come up when an acquiring company shows an interest in a target. They can be congenial affairs or outright battles between the managements of the two companies.

To understand the difference, recall that most companies are run by professional managers, *theoretically* for the sole benefit of stockholders. In fact, however, managers run companies for their own benefit *as well as* for the good of stockholders. (Recall the agency problems discussed in Chapter 1, pages 17–18.)

There are two basic reasons that a target's management might resist a merger. One is that the deal offered by the acquiring firm doesn't give the target's stockholders enough value. The argument is that the market price of the company's stock is temporarily depressed, and the offer, which is always above the market price, doesn't represent what the stock is really worth. This reason is generally given publicly.

The other reason is more self-serving. After mergers, it's common for the managements of acquired companies to lose a good deal of power and influence. In fact, key executives of target companies often lose their jobs within a short time. This phenomenon is a great incentive to resist being acquired, especially by a company with a history of treating its acquisitions ruthlessly.

Economic Classification of Business Combinations

A common method of classifying mergers[2] describes the relationship between the businesses of the merging firms. This relationship is important because it helps to define the economic impact of the transaction.

Vertical Merger   When a firm acquires one of its suppliers or one of its customers, the merger is said to be **vertical**. The idea is that the companies are at different stages along a vertical production process from raw materials to end product. An automobile manufacturer acquiring a steel mill, or a cereal maker acquiring a grocery distributor, would be an example of a vertical merger.

Horizontal Merger   A merger is said to be **horizontal** if the merging firms are in the same kind of business, usually as competitors. This kind of merger has the effect of reducing competition in the industry. For example, if one maker of personal computers acquired another, the merger would be horizontal.

optimarc/Shutterstock.com

from the
CFO

A target's **management may resist** a merger in its own **self-interest** or because the price offered is too low.

Merger relationships: **vertical**—suppliers and customers; **horizontal**—competitors; **congeneric**—related fields; **conglomerate**—unrelated fields.

---

2. In the rest of this chapter, we'll use the term "merger" loosely to mean either a merger or a consolidation.

Congeneric Merger   In a **congeneric merger**, the combining companies are in related fields rather than in the same business. They also don't generally sell the same product or service. For example, a bank acquiring an insurance company, an airline buying a travel agency, or a newspaper taking over a television broadcasting company would all be congeneric mergers. In a congeneric merger, control of the acquired company may improve the acquirer's competitive position, but it doesn't remove or immediately damage competitors.

Conglomerate Merger   A **conglomerate merger** occurs when the lines of business of the merging companies have nothing to do with one another. If an electronics company acquires a potato chip maker, the merger is conglomerate. A company that is made up of a collection of unrelated businesses is known as *a conglomerate*.

Classification of Mergers as Strategic or Financial   Another way to classify mergers is related to the motivation of the acquirer.

Strategic Mergers   A strategic merger is one that's undertaken to enhance the business position of the acquiring company. For example, a software development company with a broad product line might acquire a smaller developer of a specific type of software, say games. In that way, the acquirer fills out its product line without incurring the risk and expense of starting its own line of games from scratch.

The acquirer may also have recognized a subfield of its business with particularly promising growth prospects. The acquisition enables it to get into the new field quickly and make the most of the opportunity.

Companies often acquire businesses in their own or related fields to grow larger, thereby realizing economies of scale or increased market share/power. Strategic mergers can also be aimed at gaining technical expertise, accessing new distribution channels, enhancing reputation, gaining a presence in a new geographic area (such as another country), or having better access to supplies and raw materials.

Combining similar companies can also lead to more effective use of existing resources and reductions in overhead. (These effects are known as synergies, which we'll describe in detail shortly.)

> **Strategic** mergers **enhance** acquiring firms' **business** positions.

Financial Mergers   Financial mergers are undertaken to make money from the merger itself rather than from the underlying businesses. The classic example is a procedure in which a group of investors (a private equity firm) buys a target company that has several divisions, using largely borrowed funds. It cuts costs in certain divisions, increasing apparent cash flows, and sells those divisions off, paying down the acquisition loans with the proceeds. The acquirer can then be left with a valuable company free of debt.

In other cases, an acquirer simply recognizes and takes advantage of a situation in which the target's market value is, perhaps temporarily, less than it's intrinsic value. That's just finding a bargain, but bargains can be hard to recognize and capture in the merger business.

It's important to notice that in financial mergers the acquiring organization may not have any connection with or expertise in the target's business. Success is based on making money through the operation of financial markets rather than through the operation of the underlying businesses.

> **Financial** mergers make money from the **mergers** themselves.

The Role of Investment Banks   Recall that investment banks are organizations which help companies issue securities (Chapter 5, pages 184, 189–190; Chapter 8, pages 363–369). They function between investors and companies issuing securities by undertaking the sale of the securities to the investing public.

Investment banks are also instrumental in mergers and acquisitions, typically acting as advisors to acquiring companies. They generally assist in establishing a value for the target company and help the acquiring firm raise the money to pay for the target's stock when that's necessary.

Investment banks also advise reluctant targets on defensive measures.

17.1b   The Antitrust Laws

The United States is committed to the maintenance of a *competitive economy* in which most industries consist of at least a few competing firms.

A competitive economy is characterized by opportunity and fair dealing. Opportunity exists because anyone with the right resources can enter any industry and compete with established firms. Fair dealing comes from the notion that consumers are assured of reasonable treatment because no single firm can raise its prices too high without losing business to rivals.

These ideas have been endorsed by the government to a greater extent in the United States than in most other industrialized nations, and are reflected in a body of legislation known as the antitrust laws.[3]

The antitrust laws were enacted between 1890 and the 1930s and have been amended from time to time since then. Their objective is to prohibit certain activities that can reduce the competitive character of the economy.

The Antitrust Laws and Mergers   When the number of firms in an industry shrinks, the remaining firms become more powerful and competition is reduced. When that happens, we say the industry becomes more *concentrated*. Because mergers combine two or more firms into a single unit, they clearly have the potential to increase concentration and reduce competition. As a result, they come under the purview of the **antitrust laws**.

> The **antitrust** laws prohibit mergers that significantly **reduce competition**.

It's fairly obvious that horizontal mergers combining two or more competitors have an anticompetitive effect, but vertical mergers can also be anticompetitive. They can act indirectly, doing things like locking an acquiring firm's competitors out of sources of supply.[4] Conglomerate mergers don't generally have significant anticompetitive effects. Congeneric mergers generally have a mild anticompetitive effect.

The antitrust laws limit the freedom of companies to merge. Proposed mergers over a certain size must be reviewed by the federal government's Justice Department, and/or the Federal Trade Commission (FTC), both of which evaluate whether or not they constitute an excessive reduction in competition.

3. A trust is a group of companies under a single control that acts like a monopoly. Therefore, antitrust means against monopoly or against the excessive concentration of economic power.

4. Suppose two competing firms buy a critical input from a low-cost supplier. Then one firm acquires the supplier and refuses to sell the cheap input to the other. The second firm has to use a more expensive substitute and is forced to raise prices to cover the increased cost. This gives the first firm a price advantage that could drive the second out of business.

If a court decides a merger's effect is too detrimental, the merger will be blocked by the government.

17.1c   The Reasons Behind Mergers

Most mergers don't turn out to be as successful as expected when they're undertaken. That poor record makes it important to take a hard, critical look at why people put companies together in the first place.

Synergies   The most persuasive reason for a merger is that for some reason the merged organization will perform better than the sum of the performances of the unmerged businesses. This means some extra value is available in the combination that can be shared by the owners of the two (or more) merging companies. This phenomenon is called **synergy**. It means that the whole is more than the sum of its parts. Here's an example.

> A **synergy** exists when performance together is better than the sum of separate performances.

Suppose one company makes lawnmowers and another makes snowblowers.[5] The lawnmower factory produces in the winter (for sale in the summer) and is idle in the summer. The snowblower plant produces in the summer (to be ready for the winter) and is idle in the winter. If these companies merge, their similarly manufactured products can be produced in one factory that operates year round, thus saving the cost of the second factory. This saving is a synergy available by combining the two businesses.

Synergies are usually cost-saving opportunities like the one we've just described. Less frequently, they take the form of an enhancement of some kind. For example, suppose a breakfast cereal manufacturer with a recognized brand name acquires the maker of an unknown pancake mix. Marketing the acquired product under the cereal company's name might accelerate its success dramatically because of the recognition and acceptance accorded to the brand name.

Synergies sound good, but in practice have proven difficult to find and harder to implement.

optimarc/Shutterstock.com

from the
CFO

> **External** growth through acquisition is usually much faster than **internal** growth.

Growth   Companies can grow either internally or externally. *Internal growth* occurs when firms get larger by selling more in current businesses or starting new ventures. *External growth* refers to getting larger by acquiring other companies.

External growth is much faster than **internal growth.** A firm can become large in its own industry by acquiring a rival much more quickly than by taking market share from others in competitive battles. Similarly, a company can get into a new industry much more quickly by acquiring a firm already in that business than by starting its own entry from scratch. The quest for rapid growth is therefore a major reason for undertaking acquisitions.

Diversification to Reduce Risk   A company that acquires other firms which aren't in exactly the same business is said to *diversify* itself. It becomes a collection of diverse businesses merged together under one control. Such a firm is generally less

---

5. For the benefit of our southern readers, we should explain that a snowblower is essentially a power snow shovel. It operates like a lawnmower, but instead of cutting grass, it throws snow off sidewalks and driveways. The parts and processes used to manufacture snowblowers are similar to those used to make lawnmowers.

risky than a company in just one business when risk is defined as variation in financial performance.

The reasoning behind this phenomenon is identical to the logic that leads us to diversify a portfolio of stocks (see Chapter 9). Each business unit's performance moves up and down over time, but they don't move entirely together. Variations tend to offset, and the organization's combined performance remains fairly steady.

This kind of stability is sometimes given as a reason to justify mergers. However, it isn't obvious that the logic is appropriate in that context. In fact, a strong counterargument can be summarized as follows.

A firm with **diversified** operations is **more stable** than a company that does a single thing.

When a company acquires another firm, it effectively diversifies the portfolios of its shareholders. The acquiring company becomes a combination of what it was before and the newly acquired business, so its stockholders have an interest in both firms and are exposed to the risks and returns associated with both.

But shareholders don't need or want the firms in which they've invested to do that. Suppose A is thinking about acquiring B. If A's stockholders want to invest in B, they can just sell some shares of A and buy B. In other words, shareholders can diversify their own portfolios. They don't need or want the companies in which they've invested to do it for them.

This logic leads to the conclusion that managements diversify through acquisition to stabilize their own positions rather than their stockholders' interests.

Economies of Scale
Horizontal mergers can lead to a larger company that produces at a lower cost than any of the merging organizations do individually. Scale economies are a variation on the synergy idea.

Guaranteed Sources and Markets
Vertical mergers can lock in a firm's sources of critical supplies or create captive markets for its product.

Acquiring Assets Cheaply
A firm in need of certain assets can sometimes get them by buying a company that already owns them. This can occasionally be cheaper than purchasing the assets alone, either new or used. It usually occurs when the target firm isn't doing well and its stock is selling below book value.

Tax Losses
A firm that's making a profit pays taxes on its earnings, but a firm that's losing money doesn't get a credit for its losses. In such a case, merging the companies saves on total taxes paid. For example, consider the following possible combination of Rich Inc. and Poor Inc.

Acquiring a firm with a **tax loss** can **shelter** the acquirer's **earnings**.

	Rich Inc.	Poor Inc.	Merged
EBT	$2,000	$(1,000)	$1,000
Tax (35%)	700	0	350
Net income	$1,300	$(1,000)	$ 650

Operating independently, Rich pays tax of $700 and Poor pays nothing, for a total of $700. Merged, however, Poor's loss can offset Rich's profit *before* the tax calculation is made, so the combined company pays only $350 in tax. *However,* the IRS won't allow the offset if the primary reason for the merger is tax avoidance. There have to be other demonstrable business reasons behind the combination for the favorable treatment to be allowed.

Ego and Empire   Although it's impossible to prove, powerful people at the top of large organizations sometimes seem to make acquisitions for the sake of making their empires larger. Part of the reason may be that executive pay tends to be more a function of the size of the organization managed than of its success. It is argued that the ego/empire phenomenon has led to a number of acquisitions in which the prices paid for target companies were inflated far above what the firms were reasonably worth.[6] This phenomenon is a windfall for the stockholders of the target at the expense of the acquirer's owners.

> Critics maintain that **empire building** is behind many mergers that don't seem to make sense otherwise.

17.1d   Holding Companies

> **Parent** or **holding companies** own **subsidiaries** as legally separate entities.

Holding company is a general term for a corporation that owns other corporations known as **subsidiaries**. The holding company is also called the **parent** of the subsidiaries, which are legally separate companies. When one firm is acquired by another, it can be integrated into the acquirer's operations or be held as a subsidiary.

The holding company/subsidiary form of organization can be advantageous if it makes sense to keep two or more business operations separate and distinct. For example, it's generally possible to keep the liabilities of different subsidiaries separate, so the failure of one doesn't financially affect the parent or the other subsidiaries.

The holding company organization has another advantage in that it can control a subsidiary without owning all of its stock. An interest as small as 10% can sometimes effectively control a widely held company in which no other single shareholder owns more than 1% or 2%. As a general rule, 25% ownership virtually guarantees control. This means that an "acquiring" company can in some ways control a target without expending the resources necessary to acquire it entirely.

On the other hand, holding companies don't make sense if the benefits of a merger depend on realizing synergies from combined operations.

Businesses acquired in conglomerate mergers are typically held as subsidiaries of a holding company.

17.1e   The History of Merger Activity in the United States

There have been several periods of intense merger activity in the United States in the last 115 years. They're often referred to as *merger waves*.

Wave 1: The Turn of the Century, 1897–1904   The mergers at the turn of the century had a profound effect on the structure of American industry. They were largely horizontal and occurred in primary industries such as mining, metals production, food products, transportation, and energy.

> At the turn of the century a wave of **horizontal** mergers transformed the U.S. into a nation of industrial **giants**.

The first merger wave transformed the country from a nation of small companies to one of industrial giants, which were in many cases virtual monopolies. For example, U.S. Steel was formed by the combination of 785 separate companies led by Carnegie Steel. Other emerging giants included Standard Oil, Eastman Kodak, American Tobacco, and General Electric.

---

6. Richard Roll, "The Hubris Hypothesis of Corporate Takeovers." *Journal of Business*, 59, No. 2 (April 1986): 197–216.

The mergers of the first wave were characterized by large companies absorbing small ones, sometimes by means of unfair and even violent tactics. Large firms often used their power and wealth to force smaller rivals out of business, and then bought the ruined companies at a fraction of their original worth.

Wave 2: The Roaring Twenties, 1916–1929

The second merger wave began during the First World War and ended with the stock market crash of 1929. It was fueled by postwar prosperity and the general boom climate of the 1920s. Mergers in this period also tended to be horizontal and resulted in the concentration of several industries into *oligopolies*.[7]

Wave 3: The Swinging Sixties, 1965–1969

The late 1960s was the era of the **conglomerate merger**. Companies like ITT, Litton Industries, and LTV acquired firms in totally diverse fields that had absolutely nothing to do with one another.

The conglomerate mergers of the 1960s were financial mergers (see page 721) rather than actions driven by operating business considerations. When a large company with a high P/E ratio (see Chapter 3, page 99) acquires a smaller firm with a lower P/E ratio, paying for the target with its own stock, the result can be an increase in the earnings per share (EPS) of the merged company. If the stock market attaches the same P/E to the acquiring firm after the acquisition than it did before, its stock price will rise even though there's no expectation of improved performance by either company. This happened a great deal in the 1960s and led to a large number of business combinations motivated by stock market games rather than by sound economic reasoning.

> Many of the **conglomerate mergers** of the 1960s were **stock market** phenomena without economic substance.

Because so much of this period's merger activity was conglomerate in nature, there was relatively little increase in concentration within industries. That is, the number of firms competing in particular industries didn't change much as a result of mergers. This was a contrast with the first two merger waves in which concentration increased substantially.

An Important Development During the 1970s

Prior to the 1970s, hostile takeovers were viewed as somewhat unethical, and large, reputable companies did not undertake them. If a large firm's merger overture was rejected by a target's board of directors, the effort was generally dropped. Further, reputable investment banks didn't participate in financing hostile takeovers.

> The **hostile takeover** became an acceptable **financial** maneuver during the 1970s.

All of that began to change in 1974 with the acquisition of ESB, the world's largest maker of batteries, by the Toronto-based International Nickel Company (INCO) assisted by Morgan Stanley, perhaps the most prestigious name in investment banking at the time.

That transaction and a few others established the **hostile takeover** as an acceptable financial maneuver.[8]

---

7. An oligopoly is an industry dominated by a few powerful firms (as opposed to a monopoly, an industry in which there's only one seller). The automobile industry is an oligopoly.

8. For a detailed treatment of the important developments of the 1970s, see Patrick A. Gaughan, *Mergers and Acquisitions* (New York: Harper Collins:), 1991.

Wave 4 (1981–1989): Megamergers
Merger activity slacked off during the 1970s but resumed in the early 1980s and remained relatively intense until dropping off again during a brief recession in 1991–92, which marks the end of the wave. The fourth wave was characterized by congeneric mergers and hostile takeovers. It also marks the beginning of a period of very large mergers, often involving industry leaders.

Wave 5 (1992–2000): Globalization
The fifth wave began after the 1991–92 recession. It reflected a new aspect of the globalization of business: a large number of international mergers including several in which the acquisition targets were American companies, which was previously very unusual. The fifth wave ended when merger activity fell off precipitously after the terrorist attacks of September 11, 2001.

Wave 6 (2003–2008): Private Equity
Merger activity surged upward again about two years after September 11, marking the beginning of the sixth wave. This wave was characterized by private equity groups buying up companies for purely financial reasons. Not surprisingly, the wave ended when merger activity ground to a halt during the financial crisis of 2008 and the ensuing recession. (See pages 197–208.) This was due to the unavailability of financing after mid-2008 as well as the psychological impact of the "meltdown."

Merger activity increased after 2009, but as of mid-2012, the increase hasn't been characterized as the beginning of another wave.

The mergers since the 1980s share several distinguishing characteristics, which we'll review briefly. It's important to appreciate that these trends have been ongoing for 30 years.

Size   Very large mergers have become more common, often involving the leading firms in their respective industries. The term "megamerger" is used to refer to such combinations between industry titans. Here are a few examples:

Recent merger activity has been characterized by **very large** combinations frequently involving **industry leaders**.

Companies	Year	Industry	$ Size
Citicorp and Travelers	1998	Financial services	$ 140 billion
MCI and WorldCom	1998	Telecom	$ 37 billion
Daimler-Benz and Chrysler	1998	Automotive	$ 75 billion
America Online and Time Warner	2000	Media and entertainment	$ 350 billion
Hewlett-Packard and Compaq	2001	Computer hardware	$ 25 billion

Global in Nature   Major mergers increasingly involve large corporations from different countries creating powerful companies with global influence. The 1998 acquisition of Chrysler, the number three U.S. automaker, by Germany's Daimler- Benz, manufacturer of Mercedes-Benz, to form DaimlerChrysler AG is a familiar example.[9]

As the volume of international mergers grew from the fourth wave into the fifth and sixth waves, an important change became apparent in the citizenship of the participants. Prior to the fifth wave, most international mergers had a U.S. company on one side of the deal or the other. In subsequent waves, a significant number of deals

---

9. The DaimlerChrysler merger, like many others, failed to produce the synergies and benefits imagined when the deal was put together. As a result, the combination was undone in 2007 with the sale of Chrysler to Cerberus Capital Management, a New York-based private equity firm known for turning troubled companies around.

are completely outside of the United States Further, activity is becoming more distributed around the world, with significant numbers in the U.K., Europe, Canada, Japan, and the Asia–Pacific region.

Horizontal Mergers and the Antitrust Laws   Recall that the best reason for a merger is generally a cost-saving synergy, which is usually accomplished by combining firms that do the same or similar things and eliminating overhead. For example, one factory might take the place of two, or one sales force might carry both companies' products, or one purchasing department might buy all raw materials, etc. That kind of saving usually comes from horizontal mergers, which are generally between competitors, and tend to reduce competition in their industry.

Traditionally, in enforcing the antitrust laws, the Justice Department and its counterpart authorities in other countries scrutinized horizontal mergers carefully and disallowed those that had anticompetitive effects. In the period from 2000 until 2008, however, the U.S. government under a Republican administration took a very relaxed attitude toward antitrust enforcement, and allowed mergers that would probably have been struck down in earlier years.

For example, household appliance maker Whirlpool was permitted to acquire the well-known Maytag Corp. in 2006 even though the combined company was expected to produce approximately half of the dishwashers in the United States and over 70% of the clothes washers and dryers.[10] The transaction clearly took a major player out of the appliance business, reducing its competitiveness. Such a combination was unlikely to have been approved under previous administrations.

The Justice Department's permissive posture during those opening years of the twenty-first century undoubtedly contributed to the high volume of business combinations in the United States.

A big change was expected with the arrival of a Democratic administration early in 2009. Indeed, a major Democratic campaign promise in 2008 had been a far more vigorous and aggressive stance against combinations that might be interpreted as anticompetitive.

As of mid-2012, however, supporters of increased enforcement are somewhat disappointed. Although enforcement is definitely up, many feel that a lot more aggressive action from the Justice Department and the Federal Trade Commission is needed to fulfill the 2008 campaign promises. Of course, proponents of smaller government and fewer regulations governing business are delighted.

Financing   A major contributing factor to the blizzard of mergers after 1980 was the fact that interest rates were held at historically very low levels for a long time. That made debt-financed acquisitions not only feasible but profitable. Further, until 2008, financial institutions were awash with cash and weren't too worried about risk. That made them willing to lend enough money to would-be acquirers to make the deals happen.

---

10. Dennis K. Berman and Jason Singer, "Blizzard of Deals Heralds an Era of Megamergers," *The Wall Street Journal,* (June 27, 2006): A1, A16; www.consumeraffairs.com/news04/2006/03/whirlpool_maytag_approval.html.

Of course all that changed with the financial crisis and the credit drought that followed. As of mid-2012, the Federal Reserve, has held the rate at which it lends to banks at unprecedentedly low levels to stimulate the economy, but that hasn't translated into anything like easy credit for companies.

Hostility   After the attitude change in the 1970s, hostile takeovers became common. The proportion of hostile actions is still small but has increased, especially at the large end of the spectrum. More important, the threat of hostile takeover now pervades corporate life. Few decisions are made at the tops of today's large corporations that don't include consideration of the risk of being taken over.

Raiders   The *corporate raider* emerged as a new kind of player in high finance. A raider is a financier who puts together financing, buys a substantial block of a company's stock (usually at least 15%), and uses the voting rights to force actions aimed at increasing stock price. These can include replacing top management, selling off parts of the company, layoffs, and liquidation of the business. The process can result in the demise of the firm and the loss of jobs.

Defenses   Defensive measures have emerged as a new field because of the prevalence of hostile takeover activity. They are things the management of the target of a hostile takeover can do to avoid losing control. We'll discuss them in some detail later.

Advisors   Investment bankers and lawyers have aggressively expanded their roles as merger advisors, earning substantial fees in the process. Indeed, they're probably responsible for instigating much of the merger activity in the fourth, fifth, and sixth waves. They advise acquiring companies as well as reluctant targets on defensive measures.

Social, Economic, and Political Effects   The large mergers of the latest waves have some disturbing social and economic implications regarding the concentration of power and influence. The megamergers of the later waves have tended to involve major companies, often combining two or more of the top firms within an industry. Beyond the anticompetitive effect of such combinations, it's difficult to argue that they do not concentrate economic power into the hands of a few people who then have an inordinate influence over the direction of society.

A more subtle characteristic of recent large mergers has been a tendency toward congeneric combinations among leading firms in *related* industries. For example, in 1995 the Disney organization, which makes movies (in addition to running theme parks), acquired the American Broadcasting Company (ABC), a major television network. Although these companies didn't compete directly, they both influence the viewing material placed before the public. The merger, therefore, put a great deal of power over public opinion in the hands of the executives in charge of the combined company.

The long-term economic and political implications of megamergers are as yet unclear. On the one hand, it can be argued that the large and powerful companies being created are more efficient than the sum of the unmerged organizations would ever be, and are therefore better able to compete in a global marketplace. On the other hand, the massive accumulation of economic power taking place can be seen as having the potential to change the open and competitive nature of the economy for the worse. We won't know the bottom line for some time.

17.1f   Merger Analysis and the Price Premium

The question of price comes up immediately in any acquisition. In other words, what should an acquiring company be willing to pay for a particular target? The question is answered by a *merger analysis* that attempts to pin down what an acquisition is worth to an acquiring company.

In theory, merger analysis is a straightforward capital budgeting exercise. The price to be paid for the target's stock is the project's initial outlay, while its inflows are the acquirer's estimate of the cash the target will generate in the future. With these inputs, the would-be acquirer does a standard capital budgeting analysis to determine whether the acquisition viewed as a project has a positive NPV at any assumed price.

As in any capital budgeting analysis, two estimating issues are involved. First, the project's cash flows have to be forecast. Second, an appropriate discount rate has to be chosen.

Estimating Merger Cash Flows   Estimating the cash flows associated with a proposed merger should be a straightforward financial planning exercise with respect to the target company, with two exceptions. The first involves making a provision in the analysis for any synergies expected as a result of the acquisition. The second exception requires that the cash flows recognized by the acquiring company be stated net of funds that will need to be reinvested in the business to sustain its competitive position and to provide for whatever growth is expected. These are called **free cash flows,** which we discussed in Chapter 3 (see page 83). We'll demonstrate these ideas in an example shortly.

In practice, however, estimating cash flows in a merger context is quite difficult. Remember all the things we said in earlier chapters about the accuracy of financial plans (Chapter 4) and cash flow estimates (Chapters 11 and 12). Our conclusion was that it's hard to project financial statements because of the inherent uncertainty of the future and because of the biases of the people making the estimates.

These problems are especially acute in a merger. The acquiring company has to do the analysis, but it generally doesn't have easy access to detailed information about either the target's future prospects or its past history. In a friendly merger, the target's management tends to be interested in pumping up the price, so information shared with the potential acquirer is biased optimistically. In an unfriendly merger, management won't share any internal data at all.

It's not unusual for these conditions to lead to terribly inaccurate cash flow estimates. The tendency is to overstate the value of the target. That mistake can turn an acquisition into a financial disaster for the acquiring company, because it pays too much for the acquired firm. Of course, the same transaction is a financial windfall for the stockholders of the target who get an unrealistically high price for their stock.

Merger pricing is a **capital budgeting** exercise, but cash flows are **hard to estimate**, and there's a tendency to **overpay**.

The Appropriate Discount Rate   Because an acquisition is an equity transaction, it should be evaluated using a discount rate that reflects the cost of equity funds. Further, the target's equity rate should be used, not the acquiring firm's. That's because the risk in the project viewed from the perspective of the acquiring firm is inherently that of the target company.

The Value to the Acquirer in Total and per Share   The acquiring firm's analysis leads to an estimated total value for the target company, which is simply the present value of the future cash flows the acquirer is expected to receive from the target after buying its stock. The per-share value is just that total divided by the number of shares of stock the target has outstanding.

This estimated value, in total or per share, is the *most* the acquirer should be willing to pay for the target. Anything less is a bargain for the acquirer and its stockholders; anything more represents a transfer of wealth from the shareholders of the acquirer to those of the target.

Of course, the target's management does the same analysis and comes up with its own estimate of the same figure—which in its eyes is the *least* the company should be worth. Merger negotiations center on agreeing to a single estimate that becomes the price of the acquisition.

It's important to understand that the estimates we're talking about here are very subjective. In other words, they're influenced by the opinions and biases of the estimators. No one knows for sure what the target's future cash flows will be or what interest rate should properly be used to calculate present values. Hence, there's a lot for buyers and sellers to argue over in price negotiations.

The Price Premium   It's important to realize that whether a merger is friendly or hostile, the price offered to the target's shareholders is higher than the stock's market price. To understand this point, consider that any firm's stockholders always have the option of selling their shares at the market price, but at any particular time only a few actually do sell. Most shareholders don't sell on any given day because the market price is less than the value of the stock *to them* at that time.

In an acquisition, the acquiring firm has to offer a price that will cause the owners of a majority of the shares outstanding to sell at once. That price obviously has to be above the current market price. The amount by which the price offered exceeds the target's market price before word of the acquisition gets out is called the *premium*. A major issue in acquisitions is choosing a price that's just high enough to attract a majority of shares but no higher. Anything above that level represents a waste of the acquirer's money.

It should be clear from this that for a merger to make financial sense, the value of the target *to the acquiring firm* must exceed the company's market value at that time.

The Effect on Market Price   The fact that a premium over market price is virtually always paid for the stock of an acquired firm creates a speculative opportunity. If an investor buys the stock of a company that is acquired shortly afterward, he or she is virtually assured a quick profit because of the premium that will be associated with the acquisition.

This opportunity causes the market price of a company's stock to increase rapidly as soon as the fact that the firm is an acquisition target becomes known. Such a firm is said to be **in play.** The phenomenon clearly makes it advisable for the acquiring firm to keep merger negotiations secret.

Most acquisitions are made at **price premiums**, which lead to speculation on **in play** stocks, which drives prices up.

Two other facts are important. First, it is **illegal** *insider trading* for people in any way associated with merger negotiations to make a short-term profit on price increases that come about as a result of the merger. This includes executives of the firms involved as well as peripheral players like the investment bankers and lawyers who advise on the transactions.

Second, an investment strategy has emerged in which people buy the stocks of firms that are likely acquisition targets, without knowledge of specific merger initiatives. Investors using this strategy are hoping that some of the firms whose stocks they buy will be placed in play in the near future.

The Point of Negotiations   If a target company is indeed worth more than its market value to an acquiring company, a gain is available to the extent of the difference between the two values. Merger negotiations involve determining how that gain is to be distributed between the shareholders of the acquiring firm and those of the target.

The target's shareholders get their portion immediately in the form of the price premium paid for their stock. The remainder of the gain becomes incorporated into the value of the acquiring firm, and thereby accrues to its shareholders.

This means that in a friendly merger, the negotiations basically represent the dividing up of the gain between the two shareholder groups. In a hostile merger, the acquiring firm estimates the gain and offers a share of it to the target's stockholders in its tender offer price.

Keep in mind through all this that the gain is very difficult to estimate and particularly easy to overstate.

from the
CFO

optimarc/Shutterstock.com

Calculating a Price and the Problem of Terminal Values   As we've been saying, merger analysis from the acquirer's perspective, is a capital budgeting exercise using the NPV technique, which we studied in Chapter 10 (see page 451). Recall Equation 10.1, the definition of NPV, which we'll repeat here for convenience.

(10.1)
$$NPV = C_0 + C_1[PVF_{k,1}] + C_2[PVF_{k,2}] + \cdots + C_n[PVF_{k,n}]$$

A project's NPV is simply the sum of the present values of all the associated cash flows represented by $C_0, C_1, C_2 \ldots, C_n$. Recall that C_0 is the initial cash outlay required to get the project started. As an outflow, it is represented as a negative number. The subsequent Cs are generally positive and represent the project's cash inflows over the next n years.

In a merger analysis, C_0 is the total amount the acquirer will pay for the target's stock. The subsequent Cs are the sums of the yearly free cash flows expected to be generated by the target plus any synergies management thinks will come from the combination of the companies.

Any project is worth doing only if it has a positive NPV. In a merger context, that means C_0 must be less than the sum of the present values of the other Cs. Hence, that sum is the *most* an acquiring company should be willing to pay for the target's stock. Dividing by the number of shares of stock the target has outstanding gives the maximum per-share price the acquirer should be willing to pay to make the acquisition.

CONCEPT CONNECTION   EXAMPLE 17-1

Basic Merger Analysis

Alpha Corp. is analyzing whether or not it should acquire Beta Corp. Alpha has determined that the appropriate interest rate for the analysis is 12%. Beta has 12,000 shares of stock outstanding, and its cash flows including synergies over the next three years are estimated to be as follows ($000):

Year	1	2	3
Cash flow	$200	$220	$250

Alpha's management is conservative and feels the acquisition should be justified by cash flows projected over no more than three years. Management believes projections beyond that are too risky to be considered reliable. What is the maximum Alpha should pay for a share of Beta's stock?

SOLUTION: The present value of Beta's positive cash flows is calculated as follows:

Year	Cash Flow	$PVF_{12,i}$	Present Value
1	$200,000	.8929	$178,580
2	220,000	.7972	175,384
3	250,000	.7118	177,950
			$531,914

Hence, the maximum Alpha should pay for all of Beta's stock is $531,914. This is the initial outlay (C_0) in the NPV equation that would result in a zero NPV. At that price, Alpha would be indifferent to the acquisition.

Dividing by the number of shares outstanding gives the maximum per share price Alpha should be willing to pay.

$$\text{maximum acquisition price} = \$531,914/12,000 = \$44.33$$

Notice that in Example 17-1, the acquirer's management was financially conservative and based the target's value on only three years of forecast cash flows. Unfortunately, acquirers are often not financially conservative and are willing to value targets based on long-term forecasts. This creates what can be called the *terminal value problem*.

As a merger analysis proceeds, detailed cash flow projections are generally made for a finite number of years, usually three to five. But most acquisitions are envisioned to last forever, and there's a tendency to project a stream of cash flows that goes on indefinitely after the three- to five-year detailed forecast, and to include it in the analysis. This tends to produce results that strongly favor doing the acquisition. The question is, how real are those results? A more realistic (and therefore more complex) example will make these ideas clear.

CONCEPT CONNECTION   EXAMPLE 17-2

Merger Analysis with Terminal Values

The Aldebron Motor Company is considering acquiring Arcturus Gear Works Inc. and has made a three-year projection of the firm's financial statements, including the following revenue and earnings estimate. Period 0 is the current year and not part of the forecast. All dollar figures are in millions, except per share amounts.

	Year			
	0	**1**	**2**	**3**
Revenue	$1,500	$1,650	$1,815	$2,000
Net income	95	106	117	130

Aldebron expects that synergies will net $10 million after tax per year. It also expects that cash equal to depreciation will have to be reinvested to keep Arcturus's plant operating efficiently, and that 60% of the remaining cash generated by operations will need to be invested in growth opportunities. Otherwise, the balance sheet will remain relatively unchanged.

Results beyond three years become increasingly difficult to forecast in any detail, so Aldebron's plan simply assumes a 6% annual growth in all of the target's figures after the third year.

Currently 90-day Treasury bills are yielding 7% and the market returns 12% on an average stock. Arcturus's beta is 1.8, and the firm has 20 million shares of stock outstanding, which closed at $19 a share yesterday.

How much should Aldebron be willing to pay for Arcturus's stock? Discuss the quality of the estimate.

SOLUTION: First we'll compute the appropriate discount rate for present value calculations. Recall that the target's return on equity is the appropriate rate. We'll estimate that using the capital asset pricing model (CAPM) approach (see Chapter 9, page 424). The SML yields the following:

$$k_X = k_{RF} + (k_M - k_{RF})\, b_X$$
$$= 7\% + (12\% - 7\%)\, 1.8$$
$$= 16\%$$

Next we complete the rough cash flow estimate for the target for the first three years, using the information given.

ARCTURUS GEAR WORKS, INC. ESTIMATED CASH FLOWS ($ MILLIONS)

	Year			
	0	**1**	**2**	**3**
Revenue	$1,500	$1,650	$1,815	$2,000
Net income (unmerged)	$ 95	$ 106	$ 117	$ 130
Synergies	10	10	10	10
Net income/cash flow (merged)*	$ 105	$ 116	$ 127	$ 140
Reinvested (60%)	(63)	(70)	(76)	(84)
Free cash flow to Aldebron	$ 42	$ 46	$ 51	$ 56

*We haven't added back depreciation because of our assumption that cash equal to that amount must be reinvested to maintain the plant.

Cash flows after the periods planned in detail are often summarized in a single *terminal value* assumption. We discussed terminal values in Chapter 11, page 495. In this case, Aldebron is assuming that the last year's flow, $56 million, will grow at 6% per year indefinitely. The value of a known payment that will grow at a known rate can be calculated using the constant growth (Gordon) stock valuation model we studied in Chapter 8 (page 356). Recall Equation 8.10.

$$P_0 = \frac{D_0(1 + g)}{k - g}$$

In this application, we'll rewrite the equation, replacing P_0 with the terminal value (TV) we're looking for while D_0 becomes the year 3 cash flow, which we'll call C_3. We've already calculated the discount rate, k, and g is the growth rate assumed after year 3 ($ millions).

$$TV = \frac{C_3(1 + g)}{k - g} = \frac{\$56(1.06)}{.16 - .06}$$

$$= \$594$$

Hence, the cash flow stream in our capital budgeting calculation is as follows ($M):

	Year		
	1	*2*	*3*
Operating cash flow	$46	$51	$ 56
Terminal value			594
Total	$46	$51	$ 650

Notice how large the terminal value is compared to the three annual cash flows. This is not unusual. Next we'll take the present value of the entire stream at the discount rate we calculated earlier. To make a point later on, we'll keep the three-year forecast and the terminal value calculation separate ($ millions).

$$PV = \$46[PVF_{16,1}] + \$51[PVF_{16,2}] + \$56[PVF_{16,3}] + \$594[PVF_{16,3}]$$
$$PV = \$46(.8621) + \$51(.7432) + \$56(.6407) + \$594(.6407)$$
$$PV = \$113 + \$381$$
$$PV = \$494$$

This procedure indicates that Arcturus is worth about $494 million to Aldebron. Notice that approximately three-quarters of this figure comes from the terminal value assumption.

In other words, the absolute maximum that Aldebron should consider paying for Arcturus is $494 million, which, if there are 20 million shares outstanding, is $24.70 per share.

If the stock is currently selling at $19.00, this represents a 30.0% premium over its market price calculated as follows:

$$(\$24.70 - \$19.00)/\$19.00 = 30.0\%$$

The Quality of the Estimate
It's important to understand how arbitrary the valuation process we've just illustrated can be, especially the terminal value calculation. Even though it represents the period about which we know the least (the distant future), the terminal value accounts for fully three quarters of the

from the
CFO

final valuation. That means our results are highly sensitive to the assumptions made about the long-term future. In other words, modest changes in those assumptions can make huge differences in total value.

For example, suppose a more optimistic person did the forecast and decided that an 8% long-term growth rate was more appropriate for Arcturus. Under that assumption the terminal value is $756 million and has a present value of $484 million. The total value of the firm is then

$$PV = \$113 + \$484 = \$597$$

Notice that under this more aggressive but still reasonable assumption, the terminal value represents 81% of the target's final calculated value. The maximum acquisition price is then ($597/20 =) $29.85, which implies a premium of [($29.85 − $19.00)/$19.00 =] 57.1%.

This means an enormous range of values can be calculated for the offering price in an acquisition like this one. Good judgment is called for to avoid basing a multimillion-dollar deal on too high a price.

Although premiums this big have been paid in some large and sophisticated acquisitions, it's hard to believe a company can be worth so much more than its market value.[11] The implication is that something else must be motivating the deal. Many observers have attributed such actions to sheer ego on the part of the executives in charge of the acquiring firms.

Paying for the Acquisition—The Junk Bond Market   Acquiring a company involves giving its stockholders something of value in return for their shares. That something is generally one or a combination of three things: cash, stock in the acquiring firm, or debt of the acquiring firm.

For example, suppose the firms in Example 17-2 agreed to a price of $25 for Arcturus's stock. At the same time suppose Aldebron's stock was selling for $10 a share. The following are a few of the combinations that might be offered for 100 shares of Arcturus:

Cash	Aldebron Stock	Bond
$2,500	—	—
—	250 shares	—
1,000	50	$1,000
1,500	100	—

To the extent that cash is offered, the acquiring firm must either have it or be able to raise it. Investment banks have played an important role in recent merger history by helping companies raise money to pay for acquisitions. In particular, the *junk bond market* was a product of the 1980s that helped acquirers borrow money to pay for acquisitions.

Junk bonds are low-quality bonds that pay high yields because the firms that issue them are risky. Prior to the 1980s, it was virtually impossible for any small, risky company to borrow regardless of the interest rate it offered on its bonds.

Junk bonds are issued by **financially weak** firms and pay high interest rates. They are frequently used to **fund high-risk** acquisitions.

---

11. A number of truly excessive premiums were seen in the 1980s and 90s, some approaching 100% of market value. However, that practice seems to have moderated lately. In the early 2000s, premiums were reported in the neighborhood of 20%. See Berman and Singer, "Blizzard of Deals Heralds an Era of Megamergers," *The Wall Street Journal* (June 27, 2006): A1.

During that period, however, investment banks started pooling risky bonds into funds, claiming that the failure rate of risky companies was only a little higher than that of more reputable firms. Then it was argued that if the failure rate of risky companies is only 1% or 2% higher than that of stable companies, but the pool of their bonds pays 5% or 6% more interest, an investor is better off with a share of the risky pool than with a stable firm's bond.

Investors bought the idea, and suddenly high-risk ventures could borrow substantial sums of money. A prime use of that money was paying for the stock of target companies in risky acquisitions. In other words, the acquiring company would issue junk bonds and use the borrowed money to make acquisitions.

INSIGHTS | Practical Finance

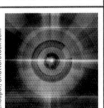
Ensuper/Shutterstock.com

A Classic Case

How a Trendy Soft Drink Gave Cereal Giant Quaker Oats a $1.4 Billion Case of Indigestion

On March 28, 1997, *The Wall Street Journal* carried the modest headline "Quaker Oats to Sell Its Snapple Business." The article announced the end of a story that has become a classic example of overpaying for an acquisition.

Only 2½ years earlier Quaker paid $1.7 billion for Snapple, a leader in "new age" soft drinks. The *WSJ* article reported that the business was being sold for a mere $300 million, a loss of $1.4 *billion*.

The loss amounted to $8.40 per share of Quaker stock. To indicate its magnitude, the newspaper noted that in the same quarter a year earlier, Quaker's earnings were about $0.23 per share. This might suggest that the Snapple disaster wiped out about ($8.40/$.23 =) 36 quarters or nine years of earnings!

Snapple caught on in the early 1990s with sales growing from $95 million in 1991 to $516 million in 1993. This blistering growth caught Quaker's eye and probably fueled the acquisition price of 20 times earnings, which was twice the P/E ratio of other beverage companies. Further, Quaker already marketed Gatorade and probably expected big synergies with Snapple.

But there was trouble from the very beginning that Quaker should have anticipated. First, the long-term growth rate of the beverage industry was only about 3%. That meant Snapple's supernormal growth couldn't last forever. Second, other firms, including Coke and Pepsi, had aggressively entered the new age market. By the time of the acquisition, Snapple's growth had stalled, and its earnings estimates were dropping sharply.

It's hard to imagine how Quaker could have made so great an error. Snapple's 1993 earnings were about $68 million. Quaker could have used the techniques of Example 17-2 to derive the kind of growth rate assumptions that would have been necessary to support an acquisition price of $1.7 billion. For example, if Quaker's required rate of return on the deal was only 15%, Snapple had to have been forecast to grow at about 11% *forever* to justify the price. That was incredibly optimistic when the overall beverage market was growing at just 3% and the competition included market savvy giants like Coke and Pepsi!

So why was Quaker willing to pay so much for Snapple? It's hard to say. A *Business Week* article published about six months earlier had observed that some investors felt it may have had something to do with the "excitement of a splashy deal."

(Quaker was acquired by PepsiCo in 2001.)

SOURCE: *The Wall Street Journal* (28 March 1997); *Business Week* (23 September 1996).

It turned out that the basic premise on which the junk bond market was founded wasn't true. Risky firms failed only slightly more often than higher rated firms *in good economic times.* In bad times, however, they failed a lot more often. A recession came along in the late 1980s, and the junk bond market collapsed.

The junk bond market was pioneered by a leading investment banking firm, Drexel Burnham Lambert. The firm later failed due to allegations of illegal activities related to the junk bond market. In the 1990s and 2000s, high-yield debt reemerged as a source of financing for acquisitions.

The Capital Structure Argument to Justify High Premiums Recall that we came to the conclusion in Chapter 14 (page 587) that capital structure can affect the market price of stock. In particular, we said that replacing equity with debt where there was little or no debt to begin with can sometimes cause the company's stock price to rise.

When the money used to buy out a target's shareholders is raised by borrowing, the result is frequently a more leveraged firm with new owners. If this results in a market value increment, the increment is argued to be a justification for paying a high premium for the acquisition's stock.

Even when this happens, it's hard for a reasonable person to justify premiums in the neighborhood of 50% over market value.

The Effect of Paying Too Much An acquiring company that pays too much for an acquisition with either its stock or cash transfers wealth from its own stockholders to those of the target. This represents a violation of the acquiring management's responsibility to act in the best interest of its stockholders, but isn't likely to cause problems beyond that.

On the other hand, paying too much with borrowed money results in a company that's heavily burdened with debt and the associated interest payments. That can cause the combined firm to perform poorly or fail in the future.

In the context of Example 17-2, if Aldebron borrows $500 million or more to buy Arcturus, and Arcturus's cash flows turn out to be less than expected, there won't be enough money available to service the debt. That can spell bankruptcy.

17.1g Defensive Tactics

A reluctant target's management can use **defensive tactics** to **avoid** being acquired.

Defensive tactics are things management can do to prevent a company from being acquired. They can be divided into two categories, things that can be done after a takeover attempt is under way and things that can be done in anticipation of such an attempt.

Tactics After a Takeover Is Underway After an acquiring firm has announced its intentions, a target's management can take the following actions:

Challenge the Price By this tactic, management attempts to convince the stockholders that the acquirer's price is too low. This usually amounts to arguing that the market has temporarily undervalued the stock, and that the shareholders will do a lot better by holding on until the price rises above the amount offered.

Claim an Antitrust Violation Management can approach the Justice Department and claim the merger is anticompetitive, hoping that the government will intervene.

Issue Debt and Repurchase Shares   This tends to drive up the stock's price, making the price offered by the acquirer less attractive. It also increases the firm's leverage, making the company less desirable from a capital structure point of view.

Seek a White Knight   Some acquirers are particularly unattractive because they have a history of treating the management and employees of acquired companies poorly. A target's management will sometimes try to find an alternate acquirer with a better reputation. Such an alternative suitor is known as a **white knight**.

A **white knight** is an alternate acquirer with a **better reputation** for its treatment of acquired firms.

Greenmail   Mergers are sometimes initiated when a powerful group acquires a substantial but minority interest in a target company. This can signal its intention to acquire a controlling interest later. Managements have eliminated such threats by buying the group's shares at a price in excess of the stock's market value. Essentially management buys off the attacker with the company's money in a process known as paying **greenmail**. Other stockholders have been known to become upset over this practice and sue the board of directors.

Tactics in Anticipation of a Takeover   Several things can be written into a corporation's charter and bylaws that make it difficult to acquire without the cooperation of management.

Staggered Election of Directors   Companies are run by boards of directors which are normally elected annually by stockholders. The annual election of directors implies that if an outside party gains a controlling interest in the firm's stock, it can elect a new board and begin running the firm relatively promptly. However, if the elections of board members are staggered so that only, say, one-third are elected each year, it will take some time for a new controlling interest to take over the board and thereby control the company. That makes the acquisition less attractive.

Approval by a Supermajority   Mergers have to be approved by shareholders owning a majority of the firm's stock. However, the definition of the majority required is written into the corporation's bylaws. Requiring approval by a supermajority, say 80%, of shareholders makes taking control of the company more difficult.

Poison Pills   **Poison pills** are legal devices embedded in corporate bylaws that are designed to make it prohibitively expensive for outsiders to take control without the support of management. Conceptually, the acquirer commits financial suicide by swallowing the target along with its poison pill.

There are any number of poison pill arrangements, but there's also some uncertainty surrounding them. Some ideas can prove to be illegal and therefore aren't binding. Other arrangements can be discriminatory against certain groups of stockholders or can be shown to be an irresponsible squandering of the firm's resources. In such cases, the directors who approve the arrangements can be exposed to personal lawsuits by unhappy stockholders. The following are a few of the more common poison pill arrangements:

Golden parachutes are exorbitant severance packages for a target's management.

Golden Parachutes   *Golden parachutes* are contracts between a company and its senior managers that guarantee exorbitant severance packages if those managers are fired after a takeover. In addition to making the managers rich, the cash drain can debilitate the company.

Accelerated Debt   A firm can include a provision in its debt contracts that requires the principal amounts to become due immediately if the firm is taken over. Most firms don't have the cash available to make such a payment, so a takeover would put them into default. If that happens, the acquirer is forced to come up with enough cash to pay off all of the acquired firm's debt immediately after the acquisition. This is generally distasteful to acquiring firms.

Share Rights Plans (SRPS)   A share rights plan is a complicated arrangement in which current shareholders are given *rights,* which are securities that enable them to buy shares in the merged company at a reduced price after a takeover. That means an acquiring company has to be willing not only to buy the stock of a target, but also to turn over a number of its own shares to the target's stockholders at, say, half price. This doesn't prevent an acquisition, but can make it very expensive.

17.2   Other Kinds of Takeovers—LBOs and Proxy Fights

So far we've associated takeovers with acquisitions of one firm by another. However, changes in ownership and control can occur outside of business combinations.

17.2a   Leveraged Buyouts (LBOs)

In a **leveraged buyout (LBO),** investors **take a company private** by buying its stock with borrowed money.

A **leveraged buyout (LBO)** is a transaction in which a publicly held company's stock is purchased by a group of investors through a negotiated deal or a tender offer. The company is then no longer publicly traded, but becomes a *private* or *closely held* firm owned by the group of investors, who are frequently the firm's management.

The investor group gets the money to buy the stock by contributing a relatively small amount of their own equity and borrowing the rest. The amount borrowed can turn out to be more than 95% of capital—hence, the term "leveraged" buyout. The borrowed funds usually come through *asset-based* financing, meaning the loans are secured by the firm's own assets.

LBOs tend to be very risky because of the high debt burden placed on the firm after the change in ownership. For example, imagine a firm that has no debt and $100 million in equity whose stock is selling at book value. That is, the market value of the stock is also $100 million. Now suppose the management team purchases the stock at book value, contributing $5 million of its own money and borrowing the rest. The firm's capital structure before and after the LBO is as follows ($ millions):

	Before LBO	After LBO
Debt	$ 0	$ 95
Equity	100	5
Capital	$100	$100

It's important to understand that nothing has changed with respect to the operating ability of the company to generate money. However, the post-LBO firm has to pay interest on debt of $95 million, making it a very risky company.

The **result** of an **LBO** is usually a **risky, debt-laden** company.

Notice that the LBO is a *takeover but not a merger.* The company has been taken over by a group of investors, but it hasn't been merged with anything.

Specialized LBO companies help put together LBOs and assist in borrowing the necessary money. The best known of these is Kohlberg, Kravis, & Roberts (KKR), which is famous for its 1988 LBO of RJR Nabisco, a combined tobacco and food products company. Prior to the LBO, the firm's stock was trading at about $55 per share. The deal was finally done at $106 per share for a total of more than $25 billion.

After an LBO is completed, the object is to reduce the debt load as quickly as possible. This can sometimes be accomplished by selling off divisions or assets and using the proceeds to pay down the debt.

LBOs have been criticized as profit-driven financial manipulations that can destroy sound companies. Our numerical illustration gives an indication of what is meant by this accusation. Before the LBO, the company was a conservatively financed firm, presumably with good operating prospects (otherwise the acquiring group wouldn't have been interested). After the LBO, the same firm was in serious danger of collapse under the weight of its debt.

LBOs are less common today than they were in the mid-1980s, presumably because a number have failed as a result of their debt burden.

CONCEPT CONNECTION   **EXAMPLE 17-3**

Leveraged Buyout (LBO)

The management group of Scott Motors Inc. plans a leveraged buyout to take the firm private. The company has 5 million shares of stock outstanding that currently sell at $8 per share. The book value of that equity is $30 million. The firm has long-term debt with a book value of $10 million. Current assets are $10 million. All other assets are fixed and suitable as collateral for a loan. Assume they are saleable at approximately their book values. Liabilities other than debt are $15 million. The group has $15 million in cash, and feels the stock can be acquired if a 25% premium over-market price is offered. Scott pays 10% interest on its existing debt, but will have to pay 12% on new debt because of added risk.

    a. How much does the management group have to borrow?

    b. What percentage of the book value of fixed assets must a lender be willing to advance to make the deal possible?

    c. Compare Scott's capital structures and debt to equity ratios before and after the LBO.

    d. Compare the interest burden under which Scott will operate before and after the LBO.

    e. Comment.

SOLUTION:

    a. To buy the stock the group needs

$$5 \text{ million shares} \times \$8 \text{ per share} \times 1.25 = \$50 \text{ million}$$

It has $15 million of its own money so it must borrow

$$\$50 \text{ million} - \$15 \text{ million} = \$35 \text{ million}$$

Ensuper/Shutterstock.com

b. First develop Scott's pre-LBO balance sheet as follows: Other liabilities, debt, and equity total $55 million, which must also be the value of total assets. Since current assets are $10 million, fixed assets must be $45 million and the pre-LBO balance sheet will be as follows ($ millions):

Current assets	$10	Liabilities	$ 15
Fixed assets	45	Debt	10
		Equity	30
Total assets	$55	Total L&E	$55

Since the borrowing requirement is $35 million, a lender must be willing to advance ($35/$45 =) 77.8% of the book value of assets.

c. During the LBO, the management group will acquire all of Scott's stock for a total of $50 million, $15 million of which will be equity. The post-LBO debt will be the remaining $35 million plus the $10 million already existing, for a total of $45 million.

	Before LBO	After LBO
Debt	$ 10	$45
Equity	$30	$ 15
Debt/equity ratio	1:3	3:1

d. Before the LBO, Scott's annual interest is

$$\$10 \text{ million} \times .10 = \$1 \text{ million}$$

After the LBO, its interest will be

$$
\begin{aligned}
\$10 \text{ million} \times .10 &= \$1.0 \text{ million} \\
+\$35 \text{ million} \times .12 &= \underline{4.2 \text{ million}} \\
&\ \$5.2 \text{ million}
\end{aligned}
$$

e. First, the LBO may not be feasible because the bank may be reluctant to lend almost 80% of the value of fixed assets that may be difficult to sell in the event of default. Beyond that, the LBO makes Scott a very risky company. Its debt to equity ratio increases dramatically, and its interest burden increases more than fivefold. This implies that even a minor business downturn might sink the company.

17.2b   Proxy Fights

A *proxy* is a legal document that gives one person the right to act for another on a certain issue. When corporations elect boards of directors, management usually solicits stockholders for their proxies to use in voting for directors. In other words, management asks stockholders for their proxies to vote for the board members it has proposed. There's generally no opposition, and the proxies are willingly granted by most of the shareholders.

However, sometimes a group of shareholders becomes dissatisfied with management and seeks to gain control of the board. Such a dissident group can also solicit the proxies of the other shareholders for the election of board members. If the dissidents win, they can elect their representatives to the board and take control of the firm.

In a **proxy fight**, opposing groups solicit shareholders' **proxies** for the election of directors.

A **proxy fight** occurs when more than one group simultaneously solicits shareholders' proxies for the election of directors. A takeover is said to occur if the dissident group wins.

Notice that no change in ownership is associated with a proxy fight. The same stockholders own the firm before and after the battle, but the controlling interest on the board changes.

17.3   Divestitures

A **divestiture** is the opposite of an acquisition. A company decides that for some reason it would be better off without a particular business operation, and gets rid of it in one of several ways.

17.3a   The Reasons for Divestitures

There are several reasons for divestitures.

Cash   The most straightforward reason to sell anything is a *need for cash*. A firm can simply sell off a noncritical piece of itself because it needs the money for something else.

After LBOs, firms tend to have huge debt burdens which can sometimes be partially paid down by selling assets or noncritical operations for cash.

Companies **divest** operations to **raise money**, or because of poor **performance** or lack of **strategic fit**.

Acquisition targets sometimes have operations which acquirers don't want but which can't be separated from the things they do want before the merger. It's relatively common to divest unwanted divisions shortly after the acquisition and use the money received to reduce the expense of the original takeover.

Strategic Fit   Sometimes companies have divisions or subsidiaries that don't fit into their long-term plans. This can be especially true if there's been a change in the firm's strategic thinking.

Poor Performance   Certain operations just never become acceptably profitable. Eventually even the most patient of managements will want to get rid of them.

17.3b   Methods of Divesting Operations

There are basically three ways to divest a business unit: sale, spinoff, and liquidation.

Sale for Cash and or Securities   An operation can be sold to another company or to an investor group. The first situation is a friendly acquisition of the operation by the other company. The second is usually an LBO.

A **spinoff** creates a **new company** owned by the same shareholders that can be **separately traded**.

Spinoff   A **spinoff** occurs when two parts of a firm are recognized to be strategically incompatible, but there's no desire to get rid of either. In other words, management believes that it's in the stockholders' best interest to keep both pieces, but it's operationally better to separate them completely. A spinoff is accomplished by setting up the operation to be divested as a separate corporation and giving shareholders of the original company a share of the new firm for every share of the old firm they own.

After the spinoff the two companies are owned by exactly the same shareholders, who are then free to trade the shares separately. After a relatively short time, the ownership is usually no longer identical.

Here's an example. Suppose a stable company begins to acquire and develop a few riskier business divisions. After a few years the firm has two distinct sides, one conservative and one risky. However, many of the original stockholders invested in the company because it was stable, so they're not comfortable with its new risky side. It makes sense to spin off the risky section and let the unhappy stockholders sell their shares in it while maintaining or increasing their holdings in the conservative business.

Liquidation   In a liquidation, the divested business is simply closed down and its assets are sold off piecemeal. Liquidation is generally a last resort to dispose of businesses that have failed badly.

17.4   Bankruptcy and the Reorganization of Failed Businesses

Failure is an unpleasant but real fact of business life. More than 50,000 businesses fail each year, including some very substantial firms. We'll begin our discussion of the subject by defining exactly what business failure means.

17.4a   Failure and Insolvency

Business failure can be defined economically in a long-run sense or in more immediate commercial terms. We're primarily concerned with the commercial concept and its implications, but it's important to understand the economic idea and appreciate the distinction between the two.

A business fails economically if it is unable to provide an adequate return to its owners. For example, suppose a company consistently pays its bills and earns a profit, but never makes more than a 1% or 2% return on the equity invested by its stockholders. After a while, investors will seek to get their capital out of such a company, and it will be closed as a failure.

The economic failure we've just described is an issue between a business and its owners. Commercial failure, on the other hand, is an issue between a business and its *creditors*. A business fails commercially when it can't pay its debts. The condition is described by the term **insolvent**. A firm is said to be *technically insolvent* when it can't meet its short-term obligations as they come due. It is *legally insolvent* if its liabilities exceed its assets.

A **commercial failure** is generally also an economic failure, but a business can be an economic failure without ever failing in the legal or commercial sense.

A firm is **insolvent** and a **commercial failure** if it can't pay its near-term debts.

Potential Actions by Creditors Against an Insolvent Company

Imagine that an insolvent company owes money to a number of creditors. Then suppose one creditor sues and manages to take possession of the firm's producing assets to satisfy its debt.

This would be good for the suing creditor, but would be very bad for everyone else involved. If the insolvent firm loses its production equipment, it probably goes out of business immediately. In most cases, that means all the employees lose their jobs and the firm's stockholders lose their entire investments. Further, because the company no longer has the ability to earn money, none of the other creditors are likely to be paid anything.

In most cases it would be better for the firm to continue in business and use its earnings to pay off its debts slowly. That implies it has to stop doing whatever made it insolvent in the first place if that's possible. The problem is that each creditor is looking out for itself and wants to have its debts satisfied out of the firm's assets before they're paid out to someone else.

17.4b   Bankruptcy—Concept and Objectives

Bankruptcy is a legal proceeding designed to preclude the situation we've just described. When an insolvent firm goes into bankruptcy, the court protects it from lawsuits by its creditors and at the same time determines whether it should be kept running or closed down.

A firm can be insolvent because its business has gone bad to the point of failure or because it has too much debt in an otherwise survivable situation. In the first case, it's better to shut the company down before it loses any more money, and to salvage as many of its assets as possible to pay off its debts. In the second case, the firm may be able to make good on all of its debts if it's given enough time, so it may be appropriate to keep it running if whatever made it insolvent in the first place can be changed. Of course, some situations are combinations of both conditions, a fact that makes the judgment a tough call.

If an insolvent company appears to be worth more as a going concern than the value of its assets, it goes through a *reorganization* under the supervision and protection of the court. This involves a *restructuring* of its debt and a plan to pay everyone off as fairly as possible.

If the court decides that the company is a lost cause, worth more dead than alive, it orders a **liquidation**. In a liquidation, the firm's assets are sold under the court's supervision and the proceeds are used to pay creditors in accordance with a schedule of priorities included in the bankruptcy laws.

In summary, bankruptcy is a federal legal procedure designed to save as much pain and loss as possible when firms fail. A firm isn't *bankrupt* or *in bankruptcy* until the action is filed in court. Until that time it's just insolvent. A bankrupt firm *emerges from* or *comes out* of bankruptcy after a reorganization in which its creditors agree to some settlement of their claims.

17.4c   Bankruptcy Procedures—Reorganization, Restructuring, Liquidation

A *bankruptcy petition* can be initiated by either the insolvent company itself or by its creditors. When the debtor firm itself files the petition, the bankruptcy is said to be *voluntary.* When creditors do the filing, the action is *involuntary.* It takes only a group of three unsecured creditors who are owed a total of $5,000 to place a firm in involuntary bankruptcy. Once either petition is filed, the firm is protected from creditors' further legal actions related to its debts until the bankruptcy is resolved.

Normally, a firm in bankruptcy is permitted to continue in business. To prevent it from doing so would usually cause the kinds of losses described in the last section. However, there may be a concern that the company's management will cause a further deterioration in its financial position during the proceedings. There's also a concern that assets will be removed during this period, leaving an empty shell to satisfy

A bankruptcy proceeding protects a failing firm from creditors until a resolution is reached to close or continue it.

In a liquidation the bankrupt firm's assets are sold and it is shut down.

A trustee oversees the operation of a firm in bankruptcy to **protect** the interests of **creditors**.

creditors. To guard against these dangers, the court may appoint a **trustee** to oversee the company's operation while it's in bankruptcy. When a trustee isn't considered necessary, the bankrupt company continues to own and operate its business, and is called a Debtor in Possession (of its assets).

Reorganization

A **reorganization** is a business plan under which the firm can continue to operate and pay off its debts. Management and the company's stockholders invariably favor reorganization over liquidation, because there's generally little or nothing left for stockholders after a liquidation. Once the bankruptcy petition is filed, management has 120 days to come up with an acceptable reorganization plan.

Reorganization plans are judged on two general criteria, *fairness* and *feasibility*. *Fairness* implies that claims are satisfied in accordance with an order of priorities that's part of the bankruptcy laws. We'll talk about those priorities later. *Feasibility* refers to the likelihood that the plan will actually come true. It's important to realize that a reorganization plan is a business/financial plan just like those we discussed in Chapter 4. As such it's based on a set of assumptions that may or may not be realistic. A court is unlikely to approve a plan that's based on unrealistic assumptions.

To be accepted, a reorganization plan has to be approved by the firm's creditors and its stockholders and by the bankruptcy court. A court-approved plan can be forced on reluctant creditors by the court in a *cramdown*. Once a reorganization plan is accepted, the firm can emerge from bankruptcy and proceed to implement the plan. It's sometimes the responsibility of a court-appointed trustee to oversee the plan's implementation.

> A **reorganization** is a plan under which an insolvent firm **continues to operate** while attempting to pay off its debts.

Debt Restructuring

The heart of most reorganization plans is a **restructuring** of the firm's debt. Keep in mind that insolvent firms are bankrupt because they couldn't pay their debts. Therefore, they aren't likely to be able to work themselves out of their troubles under the debt payment schedules that existed before the bankruptcy petition was filed. What's generally necessary is some kind of a reduction in payments. Restructuring the firm's debt makes such a reduction possible.

Debt restructuring can be accomplished in two ways. The simplest is an *extension* whereby creditors agree to give the firm a longer time to repay its obligations. A temporary deferral of principal and sometimes interest payments is quite common. The second approach is a *composition* in which creditors agree to settle for less than the full amount owed them.

It's important to understand the position of creditors in a bankruptcy case. If they demand immediate payment of the full amounts of their debts, the bankrupt firm will fail and they'll receive only a small fraction of what they're owed. On the other hand, if they accept less in terms of either the amount paid or its timing, they may stand to get a great deal more money in the long run. Therefore, they have an incentive to compromise and make concessions.

A common method of accomplishing a debt restructuring is the conversion of **debt into equity**. Creditors give up their debt claims (loans, bonds, accounts receivable) in return for stock in the bankrupt company. This immediately reduces the debt service burden on the company in trouble and eases its cash flow problems (assuming it doesn't pay dividends on the new equity).

> **Debt restructuring** involves concessions that **lower** an insolvent firm's **payments** so it can continue in business.

> **Extensions, compositions** and **debt to equity** conversions are common approaches to **restructuring**.

After such a conversion, creditors have equity positions in the troubled company. These aren't worth much initially, but if the firm survives and perhaps prospers, in the long run they can be worth more than the debt given up. Notice that in a conversion the original stockholders receive a benefit in terms of the forgiveness of some of their company's debt. In return, their ownership is diluted.

CONCEPT CONNECTION   EXAMPLE 17-4

Debt Restructuring in Bankruptcy

The Adcock Company has 50,000 shares of common stock outstanding at a book value of $40, pays 10% interest on its debt, and is in the following financial situation:

ADCOCK COMPANY SELECTED FINANCIAL INFORMATION ($000)

Income and Cash Flow		Capital	
EBIT	$ 200	Debt	$6,000
Interest	600	Equity	2,000
EBT	$(400)	Total capital	$8,000
Tax	—		
Net income	$(400)		
Depreciation	200		
Principal repayment	(100)		
Cash flow	$(300)		

Notice that although the company has a positive EBIT, it doesn't earn enough to pay its interest let alone repay principal on schedule. Without help of some kind, it will fail shortly. Devise a composition involving a debt for equity conversion that will keep the firm afloat.

SOLUTION: Suppose the creditors (perhaps a number of bondholders) are willing to convert $3 million in debt to equity at the $40 book value of the existing shares. This would require the firm to issue 75,000 new shares, resulting in the following financial situation:

ADCOCK COMPANY SELECTED FINANCIAL INFORMATION
AFTER DEBT TO EQUITY CONVERSION ($000)

Income and Cash Flow		Capital	
EBIT	$ 200	Debt	$3,000
Interest	300	Equity	5,000
EBT	$(100)	Total capital	$8,000
Tax	—		
Net income	$(100)		
Depreciation	200		
Principal repayment	(50)		
Cash flow	$ 50		

Notice that the company now has a slightly positive cash flow and can at least theoretically continue in business indefinitely. *However,* the creditors now own a controlling interest in the firm.

Ethics

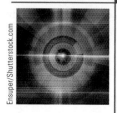

Has Bankruptcy Been Too Easy for Too Long? The Bankruptcy Reform Act of 2005

Many people, especially creditors, have long considered bankruptcy unethical, unfair, and too easy. The issue has been around as long as bankruptcy laws have existed. Here's a quote from the work of the famous French author Honoré de Balzac written more than 179 years ago:

> *"What is a bankrupt, father?" asked Eugenie.*
>
> *"A bankrupt," replied her father, "is guilty of the most dishonourable action that can dishonour a man. . . A bankrupt. . . is a thief whom the law unfortunately takes under its protection. . . A bankrupt is worse than a highwayman. . ."*
>
> Honoré de Balzac, Eugenie Grandet 108 (1833)

Basically, Eugenie's father was saying that people who declare bankruptcy are stealing from those who have loaned them money. Most creditors feel the same way today. They think it's unfair to let debtors off the hook for just obligations they might be able to pay if they tried harder. Creditors have long decried bankruptcies of convenience and popular guide books on how to use court procedures to escape debts. They claim that bankruptcy has become a financial planning tool. In other words, they see bankruptcy as legalized theft from those who extend credit in good faith.

There's undoubtedly an ethical issue in bankruptcy. Is it right to allow people or companies to escape their debts and start over scot-free? Creditors feel it isn't and have lobbied Congress for years to toughen bankruptcy laws.

After several near misses, the creditor lobby succeeded in getting Congress to pass the Bankruptcy Reform Act of 2005. That's shorthand for the Bankruptcy Abuse Prevention and Consumer Protection Act (BAPCPA). The key words in the title are *Abuse Prevention;* the Act keeps bankrupts from abusing court procedures to casually avoid debts. It primarily affects individual rather than corporate bankruptcies.

The law makes it harder to get a liquidation judgment under which the bankrupt party must give up most of his assets but in return has virtually all of his debts wiped away. That was a good deal for bankrupts, since they usually don't have many assets anyway.

The rules now force most bankrupts into reorganization plans under which they have to pay off a good deal of their debt over a several-year period. Only after they've done that will the remaining debt be expunged. This is a more painful process than the quick and easy liquidation.

Consumer advocacy groups vigorously opposed the law, claiming that its biggest proponents were credit card companies that lose money when overextended cardholders escape into bankruptcy. Their point is that the credit card companies create their own problems by issuing millions of cards without doing credit checks. The credit card companies were further accused of advertising deceptively low interest rates and hiding the excessive fees they charge when payments are late or missed. These unethical practices are alleged to trick unsuspecting consumers into running up big bills they can't pay, leading to bankruptcy.

So which argument is right and which is wrong? Was bankruptcy too easy; or is it now too hard? Or have sleazy, unethical lenders made us a nation of credit junkies, sadly over our heads in consumer debt? And do those sleaze-ball lenders deserve to get stuck from time to time? And...did our government do the right thing or the wrong thing by making it tougher to get a "fresh start" through bankruptcy?

Bankruptcy Reform Backfired on Banks in the Financial Crisis

Bankruptcy reform was primarily intended to benefit lenders who claimed the old law made it too easy for debtors to escape legitimate obligations. But the act had an unintended consequence that's made the financial crisis (see pages 197–208) worse for banks and other mortgage lenders.

Prior to the 2005 act, the bankruptcy code generally let people keep their homes under a Chapter 7 liquidation filing. That meant a distressed homeowner could get rid of most of his other debts, like credit cards and car payments, while keeping his home (and mortgage), which left more income for house payments. In many cases, that made it possible to avoid foreclosure.

But the new law makes it much harder to get into Chapter 7, forcing more filers into Chapter 13, which requires that some payment be made on all debts, leaving less money for the mortgage. That means a bankrupt homeowner is more likely to walk away from his house than to struggle to meet his mortgage obligations. That, of course, leaves the bank with a bad loan and a house it may not be able to sell.

Source: Christopher Farrell, "Bankruptcy Reform Bites Back," *Business Week* (October 29, 2007).

Liquidation

Liquidation involves **closing** a troubled firm and selling its assets.

When the court decides that a bankrupt business isn't worth continuing, it orders a **liquidation**, which involves selling off the firm's assets and using the proceeds to pay off as many of its debts as possible. The process is conceptually simple but can be administratively involved.

The liquidation is accomplished by a court-appointed trustee who first looks for and attempts to recover any unauthorized transfers out of the firm around the time of the bankruptcy filing. This is an important step. When business owners anticipate bankruptcy, they frequently try to remove assets from the company. Doing that is illegal because those assets should rightly be used to satisfy creditors' claims. It's the trustee's job to find and recover such articles and payments, which are called *fraudulent transfers*. It's also illegal to make payments to certain preferred creditors without proportionate payments to others. These are called preferences and should also be recovered by the trustee.

Unauthorized **transfers out** of a bankrupt firm can be **recovered** by the trustee.

Next, the trustee supervises the sale of the business's assets, gathering the proceeds into a pool of funds that can be used to satisfy creditor's claims. Finally the trustee distributes the available funds to the various claimants.

It's important to realize that claimants aren't just lenders in the traditional sense. They include vendors who sold to the company on credit, employees who are owed wages, customers who may have put down deposits on merchandise, the government which may be owed taxes, and the people and organizations that are part of the bankruptcy proceeding. This last group includes lawyers and the court itself, which are owed fees for their services. In addition, the company's stockholders are claimants to the extent of whatever is left over after everyone else is satisfied.

Distribution Priorities

The **bankruptcy code** contains **priorities** for the **distribution** of assets among claimants.

The distribution of funds in bankruptcy follows an order of priority laid down by the bankruptcy code. This order is used to determine the sequence of payment in liquidation and as the basis for the fairness judgment in evaluating reorganization plans. Basically the priority rule says that all claimants are not equal in the eyes of the law.

It's important to understand the implications of this rule. The funds available from liquidation usually amount to a fraction of the value of the claims against the company. For example, a firm with total claims of $1 million might end up with a pool of funds from liquidation of $300,000. The priority rule says that the claimants do not all get 30 cents on the dollar for their debt. Some get more and some get less.

Secured creditors are paid out of the proceeds of the sale of pledged assets.

Secured Debt   The first distinction made among claimants is between *secured* and *unsecured creditors*. A **secured creditor's** debt is guaranteed by a specific **asset**. For example, when money is borrowed to buy a car, the loan is generally secured by the automobile itself. That means if the loan isn't paid, the car is sold and the money from the sale must be used to satisfy that debt before any other. Unsecured debts aren't tied to particular assets and just rely on the general creditworthiness of the borrower.

Each secured obligation is paid out of the proceeds of the sale of the related assets before the liquidation pool is established. To the extent that any individual secured debt is more or less than the value of its securing asset, the difference becomes unsecured debt or an addition to the pool, depending on whether the debt or the value of the asset is larger.

Priorities for Payment of Claims   After all secured debts are paid, unsecured claims are paid out of the remaining pool of funds in the following order:

1. Administrative expenses of the bankruptcy proceedings
2. Certain business expenses incurred *after* the bankruptcy petition is filed[12]
3. Certain unpaid wages
4. Certain unpaid contributions to employee benefit plans
5. Certain customer deposits[13]
6. Unpaid taxes
7. Unsecured creditors
8. Preferred stockholders
9. Common stockholders

Clearly, common stockholders receive only the bankrupt firm's residual value after all other obligations have been paid. That's often nothing at all.

Terminology—Bankruptcy Code Chapters 7 and 11

The federal bankruptcy code is divided into chapters. Reorganization is governed by Chapter 11 and liquidation by Chapter 7.

People frequently refer to firms in reorganization proceedings as being "in Chapter 11." When firms voluntarily enter bankruptcy, it's common to say that they've "declared Chapter 11" or "gone into Chapter 11." References to other chapters aren't as common in everyday language.

---

12. The high priority of postfiling expenses is aimed at keeping bankrupt firms in business until the proceedings are resolved. Without it, no one would do business with a firm in bankruptcy without being fully paid in advance.

13. Claims 3 through 5 clearly reflect a legislative intent to protect individuals over companies.

CONCEPT CONNECTIONS

Ensuper/Shutterstock.com

OlegDoroshin/Shutterstock.com

QUESTIONS

1. The Highland Instrument Company has revenues of about $300 million per year. Its management is interested in expanding into a new type of product manufactured primarily by Lowland Gauge Inc., a firm with sales of about $200 million annually. Both firms are publicly held with a broad base of stockholders. That is, no single interest holds a large percentage of the shares of either firm. Describe the types of business combination that might be available for the two firms. Include ideas like merger, consolidation, acquisition, friendly, and hostile. How would Highland's management get started? Do the relative sizes of the two firms have any implications for the kinds of combination that are possible or likely?

2. Hostile acquisitions create animosities between the stockholders of the acquired and acquiring companies. Comment on the truth of this statement.

3. Define vertical, horizontal, congeneric, and conglomerate mergers and describe the economic effects of each.

4. Industry A is dominated by 10 large firms, each with sales of approximately $500 million per year. A proposal to merge two of these firms was approved by the Justice Department as not violating the antitrust laws. Industry B is locally defined and much smaller. It is dominated by three small firms, each selling about $50 million per year. A merger between two of these companies was prohibited under the antitrust laws. Explain the logic under which the merger of two $500 million giants can be allowed while the relatively insignificant merger of two small companies is disallowed.

5. Suppose an industry is dominated by three firms, one of which is twice as large as the other two, which are about the same size. Could a merger of the two smaller firms actually increase competition in the industry?

6. Clarington Corp. has a division that's been performing well but doesn't fit into the company's long-term strategic plans. Describe the methods through which it can divest the operation.

7. The Blivitt Company has been losing money and experiencing serious cash flow problems lately. The main problem is a large debt to the First National Bank that was incurred to purchase a computer that's now obsolete. Bill Blivitt, the firm's owner, has stated his intention to declare bankruptcy to rid the company of the loan. He expects to go in and out of Chapter 11 in a few weeks and emerge essentially as before but without the loan. Write a note to Bill explaining bankruptcy procedures and why this is probably an unrealistic approach on his part.

BUSINESS ANALYSIS

1. The Cranston Company would like to acquire the Lamont Company, but overtures made to management have been emphatically rebuffed. Forty- five percent of Lamont's stock is owned by five investors who were involved in the company's founding and continue to be active in its management. Charlie Hardnose, Cranston's director of corporate development, has suggested a hostile takeover that would bypass Lamont's management. Could this work, and does it seem to be a very good idea in this situation?

2. You're a seasoned financial executive who's recently been hired as the CFO of the Pilaster Corporation. The firm has just finished two years in which its financial performance has been clearly below par. The company isn't in danger of failing, but it's clear that earnings and growth could be much better. The market price of Pilaster's stock reflects this lukewarm performance. It is currently selling for $32, down substantially from its peak of $48 a little over two years ago. (The market has been generally flat in the last two years.)

   Several observers have blamed the lackluster performance on the firm's CEO, Gerald Beanweather, and his top assistants. This team installed some new technological and managerial methods several years ago that haven't worked out well. Recently, they've been talking about returning to the old, time-tested methods that most people feel will bring the firm back to its usual performance levels. In fact, your hiring was part of the turnaround effort.

   It's currently seven o'clock on a cold, bleak Monday morning in February. On the previous evening the CEO's secretary phoned the entire executive team to tell them an emergency meeting was set for this morning. The group is now assembled waiting to hear what's going on.

   At 7:01, Gerry walks into the room, obviously upset. He says that yesterday afternoon he received a call from Harvey Highroller, the CEO of Marble Inc., the leading firm in the industry. Marble is interested in acquiring Pilaster and is willing to offer $37 a share for its stock, a premium of more than 15%. Marble has a history of making both friendly and unfriendly acquisitions.

   a. What kind of combination is Marble currently proposing?

   b. What is likely to happen if Pilaster's management rejects Marble's offer?

   c. Is Marble likely to be successful over management's objections?

   d. Why is Gerry so personally upset?

   e. Should you be personally upset?

   f. Is Marble's offer a good deal for Pilaster's stockholders?

   g. What should Pilaster's management do to avoid acquisition by Marble?

   h. Do you think Marble is likely to be successful in an unfriendly merger attempt over Pilaster's defenses?

   i. If Marble is not successful, what can the Beanweather team do to reduce the chances of a similar attack in the future?

3. The Blue Tag Company and the Pink Label Corporation both make packaging and labeling equipment. The following facts are relevant:

   a. Both firms use similar production and sales methods.

   b. Pink Label has been losing money for years, while Blue Tag has been and is expected to continue to be profitable.

   c. There is a great deal of overhead in label making.

   d. The industry is dominated by the much larger Yellow Marker Co., which is difficult to compete with because of its size advantage.

   The managements of the two companies are considering a merger. What arguments can be made in favor of such a combination?

4. The Phlanders Flange Company has been doing quite well lately and would like to accelerate its growth within the flange industry. Harry Flatiron, the firm's CEO, has become interested in growth through acquisition because of some exciting articles in the business press. In particular, he's interested in a friendly acquisition of the Framingham Flange Factory whose general manager, Jack Daniels (a major stockholder in Framingham), he's known for some time.

   Harry is prone to quick action based on brief analyses that he does himself. In the past, his instincts have been pretty good, and this style has not as yet caused any major mistakes. Harry has taken Framingham's own estimate of its future cash flows and long-term growth rate along with synergies he and Jack have estimated to come up with a projected value for the company. All this has led to a proposal to offer Framingham's stockholders a 60% premium on the price of their stock.

   You're Phlanders's CFO, but Harry has done all this on his own. He's about ready to make a verbal offer to Framingham's management, and has asked you to check over his figures. His arithmetic is correct, but you're very concerned about the validity of his assumptions.

   Prepare a short memo to Harry outlining the risks associated with value estimates in mergers and the consequences of a mistake. Include advice on how to proceed.

5. You're the CFO of the Littleton Lighting Company. Joan Brightway, the president, has approached you and the firm's other senior executives with a proposal to take the company private through an LBO. She says that this is a good time to do it because the economic outlook is shaky and the firm's stock price is depressed, so it will

take less money to acquire control. You agree that the weak outlook has depressed the stock's price, but aren't sure that this doesn't argue against an LBO at this time. You also suspect that some fundamental weakness is developing in the demand for the firm's product.

Certain successful LBOs have received a lot of favorable press lately, and you're concerned that Joan and the other nonfinancial executives may not appreciate the risks involved in the procedure. Prepare a memo outlining what's involved in an LBO and why the maneuver is risky, especially with respect to the business's performance in the immediate future. Make a recommendation on the analyses that should be undertaken prior to going forward.

PROBLEMS

Basic Merger Analysis: Concept Connection Example 17-1 (page 733)

1. The target of an acquisition generates cash flows of $8 million per year with a risk level consistent with a return on equity of 16%.
   a. How much should an acquirer be willing to pay if it won't consider more than five years of future earnings in setting a price?
   b. What is the per-share price if the target has 300,000 shares of common stock outstanding?
   c. Assume the acquirer intends to pay for the acquisition with its own stock, which is currently selling for $36 per share. How many shares must be offered for each share of the target's stock?

2. Grandma's Cookies Inc. is considering acquiring Mother's Baked Goods Inc. After consideration of all benefits, synergies, and tax effects, Grandma (originally a finance major) has estimated that the incremental cash flows from the acquisition will be about $150,000 per year for 15 years. (Grandma is financially conservative and reluctant to base decisions on benefits projected farther into the future.) She has also estimated the project's discount rate, appropriately adjusted for risk, at 12%.

   Mother's is a privately owned firm with 20,000 shares of stock outstanding. Grandma is confident that the owners will sell for $50 a share, but not for less. Should Grandma acquire Mother's?

3. Moser Materials Inc. is considering acquiring Newkirk Products, which produces a number of products that would enhance Moser's product line. Last year, Newkirk reported a $30 million loss. Moser has estimated that Newkirk will break even in the fourth year after acquisition. The improvement in performance will come in four equal steps. Assuming Moser can demonstrate that the acquisition is not simply for tax purposes, calculate the present value of the tax savings that will result during the four-year period at a 12% discount rate. Assume Moser has EBT far exceeding $30 million and is subject to a 40% marginal tax rate.

Merger Analysis with Terminal Values: Concept Connection Example 17-2 (page 734)

4. Harrison Ltd. is considering acquiring Pugs International Inc. Pugs had cash flows of $15 million last year and has 2.5 million shares outstanding which are currently selling at $29 per share. The discount rate for analysis has been correctly estimated at 14%.
   a. How much should Harrison be willing to pay for Pugs in total and per share if the firm is not expected to grow significantly and management insists that acquisitions be justified by no more than 10 years of projected cash flows?
   b. Make the same calculations assuming management will consider an indefinite stream of cash flows.
   c. Make the calculations once again assuming management is very aggressive and is willing to assume Pugs' income will go on forever growing at a rate of 3% per year.
   d. Comment on the results of parts (a), (b), and (c).

5. The Johnson Machine Tool Company is thinking of acquiring Lansing Gear Works Inc. Lansing is a stable company that produces cash flows of $525,000 per year. That figure isn't expected to

change in the near future, and no synergies are expected from the acquisition. Johnson's management has estimated that the appropriate risk-adjusted discount rate for pricing calculations is 15%. Lansing has 200,000 shares of common stock outstanding.

a. What is the most Johnson should be willing to pay for Lansing if management is financially conservative and insists that an acquisition must justify itself within 10 years? State the price in total and per share.

b. How much should Johnson be willing to pay, in total and per share, if management takes a more aggressive position and will consider Lansing's income as continuing forever? (*Hint:* Estimate Lansing's value as a perpetuity starting immediately.)

c. What total and per-share prices are implied if Johnson's executives are financially very aggressive and assume that their management will transform Lansing into a better company that will grow at 3% per year indefinitely?

d. Comment briefly on the differences in your answers to parts (a), (b), and (c).

6. Sourdough Mills has considered acquiring Mrs. Baird's Bakery as an expansion strategy. Mrs. Baird's Bakery generated positive cash flows of $5.3 million last year, and cash flows are expected to increase by 4% per year in the foreseeable future. Mrs. Baird's has 1.3 million shares outstanding, and the appropriate discount rate is 11%.

a. If Sourdough assumes this level of cash flow will continue forever, what is the most that it should pay for each share of Mrs. Baird's Bakery?

b. If Sourdough wants the investment justifiable considering only 5 years of cash flow, what is the most it should pay for the stock?

c. What if it will consider a 10-year planning period?

d. If Mrs. Baird's Bakery stock is currently selling for $35 per share, what would you do if you were Sourdough Mills?

7. Hirschler Motors is considering making a takeover bid for the chain of Richard's Auto Superstores. Richard's has 800,000 shares of stock outstanding, which is trading at $18 per share. Richard's generated $2.5 million in cash last year, and cash flows are expected to increase by 6% per year for at least 10 years. Assume the appropriate discount rate is 12%. What percent premium can Hirschler afford to offer for Richard's stock if management wants to justify the investment over 10 years? 9 years? 8 years?

8. Benson's Markets is a five-store regional supermarket chain that has done very well by using modern management and distribution techniques. Benson competes with Foodland Inc., a larger chain with 10 stores. However, Foodland has not kept pace with technological and merchandising developments, and has been losing money lately. Foodland's owners are interested in retiring and have approached Benson's with a proposal to sell the chain for $50 million.

Within each chain, individual stores perform uniformly. Typical results for an average store in each company are as follows:

Typical Single-Store Results Benson's and Foodland Supermarkets ($000)

	Benson's	Foodland
Revenue	$45,000	$38,000
Cost of product	38,500	33,500
Store overhead: Depreciation	400	300
Other	4,600	4,700
EBT	$ 1,500	$ (500)
Tax	600	—
Net income	$ 900	$ (500)

If Benson were to make the acquisition, it would immediately close three of Foodland's stores that are located close to its own markets and sell the buildings for about $1 million each. The remaining stores would operate at their current loss levels for about two years, during which time they would be upgraded to Benson's operating standards. The upgrades would cost $3 million per store, spread over the first two years. After that, the acquired stores would have about the same operating performance as Benson's other stores. Benson's CFO feels that a discount rate of 12% is appropriate for the risk associated with the proposition. Benson's marginal tax rate is 40%.

a. Calculate the value of the acquisition to Benson's, assuming there is no impact on any of Benson's five original stores. Assume that the incremental cash flow from the acquired stores goes on forever but does not grow. Should Benson pay Foodland's price? If not, does the deal look good enough to negotiate for a better price? What is the most Benson should be willing to pay?

b. (No calculations—just ideas.) Are there reasons beyond the calculations in part (a) that argue in favor of the acquisition? (*Hint:* Think along two lines about the competitive situation. First, what will happen if Benson doesn't buy Foodland? Second, what effect will the acquisition have on Benson's existing stores?)

c. Could the ideas in part (b) be quantified into adjustments to the results in part (a)? Make your own estimate of the impact of such ideas on the price Benson should be willing to pay.

9. Frozen North Outfitters Inc. makes thermal clothing for winter sports and outdoor work. It is considering acquiring Downhill Fashions Corp., which manufactures and sells ski clothing. Downhill is about one-quarter of Frozen's size and manufactures its entire product line in a small rented factory on a mountaintop in Colorado. It costs about $1 million a year in overhead to operate in that factory. Frozen produces its output in a less romantic but more practical southern location. Its factory has at least 50% excess capacity. Frozen's plan is to acquire Downhill and combine production operations in its southern factory, but otherwise run the companies separately.

Downhill's beta is 2.0, Treasury bills currently yield 5%, and the Standard and Poor's 500 Index is yielding 9%. The marginal combined federal and state income tax rate for both firms is 40%. Because Downhill will no longer be maintaining its own production facilities, only a minimal amount of cash will have to be reinvested to keep its equipment current and for future growth. This amount is estimated at $100,000 per year. Selected financial information for Downhill follows:

Revenue	$12,500,000
Net income	1,300,000
Depreciation	600,000

a. Calculate the appropriate discount rate for evaluating the Downhill acquisition.

b. Determine the annual cash flow expected by Frozen from Downhill if the acquisition is made (don't forget to include the synergy).

c. Calculate the value of the acquisition to Frozen assuming the benefits last for (1) 5 years, (2) 10 years, and (3) 15 years.

d. Downhill has 250,000 shares of stock outstanding. Calculate the maximum price Frozen should be willing to pay per share to acquire the firm under the three assumptions in part (c).

e. If Frozen is willing to assume the benefits of the Downhill acquisition will last indefinitely but not grow, what should it be willing to pay per share?

10. In the last problem, assume the cash flow from the Downhill acquisition grows at 10% from its initial value for one year and then grows at 5% indefinitely (starting in the third year). Calculate the value of the firm and the implied stock price under these conditions. Use a terminal value at the beginning of the period of 5% growth. What price premium is implied, in dollars and as a percentage, if Downhill's stock is currently selling at $62? Comment on the range of values in the results of this and the last problem.

11. Lattig Corp. had a $2.0 million cash flow last year and projects that figure to increase by $200,000 per year for the next five years (to $3.0 million). After that, Lattig expects an annual growth rate of 6% forever. Assume the discount rate is 12%.

    a. What percentage of the total present value of Lattig's projected cash flows comes from its terminal value assumption for cash flows after the first five years?

    b. Recalculate the result in part (a) if Lattig raises its terminal value growth rate forecast to 7% and then to 8%.

    c. What other terminal value related issues should be considered by anyone thinking about acquiring Lattig? (Words only.)

Leveraged Buyout (LBO): Concept Connection Example 17-3 (page 741)

12. Integrity Group, an association of venture capitalists, is considering using a leveraged buyout to purchase Schrag Co., a well-established high-tech firm. Schrag has long-term debt with a book value of $15 million and a debt to equity ratio of 1:10. The firm's stock is currently selling at 120% of book value. Integrity Group has $25 million to contribute to the buyout and feels that it will have to offer a 25% premium over the stock's current market price in order to make the deal work. Estimate Schrag's capital structure after the leveraged buyout.

Debt Restructuring in Bankruptcy: Concept Connection Example 17-4 (page 747)

13. Lee & Long, a clothing manufacturer, is considering filing for bankruptcy. The firm has EBIT of $1.4 million and long-term debt of $40 million on which it pays interest at an average rate of 8.5%. It also has fixed assets (gross) totaling $60 million. Depreciation averages 5% of gross fixed assets per year, and the long-term debt matures evenly over the next 20 years.

    a. Calculate Lee & Long's current cash flow.

    b. Assume that Lee & Long's management can convince its creditors to convert 25% of its debt into equity by exchanging their bonds for newly issued stock at book value. Calculate Lee & Long's cash flow after the debt restructure.

14. Garwood Industries has filed for bankruptcy and will probably be liquidated. The firm's balance sheet ($ millions) is shown below:

Current assets	$ 6.5	Current liabilities	$ 8.5
Fixed assets (net)	30.8	Long-term debt	16.5
Total assets	$37.3	Equity	12.3
		Total liabilities and equity	$37.3

The administrative costs of bankruptcy total $1.6 million. Current assets can be sold for 60% of book value and fixed assets for 25% of book value. Twenty percent of the long-term debt is secured. All of the remaining debt is unsecured. Assume there are no additional costs. How many cents on the dollar will unsecured creditors (including trade creditors) receive on the money owed them?

15. The Hamilton Corp. has 35,000 shares of common stock outstanding with a book value of $20 per share. It owes creditors $1.5 million at an interest rate of 12%. Selected financial results are as follows:

Income and Cash Flow		Capital	
EBIT	$ 80,000	Debt	$1,500,000
Interest	180,000	Equity	700,000
EBT	$(100,000)		$2,200,000
Tax	0		
Net income	$(100,000)		
Depreciation	50,000		
Principal repayment	(75,000)		
Cash flow	$(125,000)		

Restructure the financial line items shown assuming a composition in which creditors agree to convert two-thirds of their debt into equity at book value. Assume Hamilton will pay tax at a rate of 15% on income after the restructuring, and that principal repayments are reduced proportionately with debt. Who will control the company, and by how big a margin after the restructuring?

International Finance

Chapter Outline

In the last 60 years, business has become increasingly international.[1] The change has occurred in two distinct ways. First, we do more import/export business with other countries than ever before. In 1960, imports and exports were 3% and 4% of gross domestic product (GDP), respectively. By 2010, imports were about 13% of GDP, while exports were about 9%.

Second, the nature of international business has changed. In 1960, doing business with a foreign country generally just meant importing and exporting goods. Now, international business as often as not implies a **direct investment** in facilities and equipment in another country and the operation of a **full-scale business** there.

---

1. The term "global" is used to describe business's current international character. We'll discuss the broad concept of globalization later in the chapter.

Companies that have divisions and branches in other countries are known as **multinational corporations**, abbreviated **MNCs**.

Financial markets are also increasingly international. Fifty years ago it was very unusual for an investor to buy the stock of a foreign company. Today people make **portfolio investments** in foreign stocks and bonds all the time.

International business is an increasingly large part of commercial activity in the United States. Virtually all companies of any size have some international dealings. It's clearly important, therefore, that we understand the basic financial principles of doing business with companies from other countries. Such business has all of the problems and challenges of operating domestically but includes several additional complications and risks. We'll begin by examining exchange rates in some detail.

18.1 Currency Exchange

Companies operate and expect to be paid in the currency of the countries in which they're located. That means anyone wanting to buy from a firm in another country has to acquire some of that country's currency first.

For example, if a U.S. company that operates department stores wants to buy expensive wool sweaters from a British manufacturer, it has to pay the bill in British pounds, not U.S. dollars. But the American firm has only dollars, not pounds. Clearly, to make the purchase, it has to *exchange* some dollars for pounds. We also say the firm *buys* pounds with dollars.

18.1a The Foreign Exchange Market

The purchase is accomplished in the **foreign exchange market**, which is organized for the purpose of exchanging currencies.[2] The foreign exchange market operates much like other financial markets, but it isn't located in a specific place like a stock exchange. Rather, it's a network of brokers and banks based in financial centers around the world. Most commercial banks are able to access the market and provide exchange services to their clients.

18.1b Exchange Rates

Currencies are traded at an **exchange rate** that, in effect, is the price of each currency in terms of the other. In our illustration, the American firm needs to know how many pounds can be purchased for a dollar. That lets it calculate how many dollars it will need to pay the British firm's price in pounds.

The essence of the foreign exchange market is a table of exchange rates like Table 18-1. (We'll discuss sources of current foreign exchange rates shortly.) The table shows two reciprocal rates for each currency. Rates in the first column are called the *direct quote* and show the number of U.S. dollars required to buy one unit of the foreign currency. Rates in the second column are known as *indirect quotes* and represent

---

2. The term "foreign exchange" is also used as a noun to refer to the foreign currency itself. We say a nation that wants to buy foreign goods needs foreign exchange.

the inverse relationship; that is, how many units of the foreign currency it takes to buy one U.S. dollar. The direct and indirect quotes are reciprocals of one another.

CONCEPT CONNECTION   EXAMPLE 18-1

Exchange Rates

Suppose the American company in our example wants to import 500 sweaters that cost a total of 35,000 pounds, written as £35,000 (where £ is used like the U.S. $). How many pounds will it have to buy?

SOLUTION: Noting that British currency is sometimes listed under U.K. for United Kingdom, the exchange rate table indicates that £1 is worth $1.5740, so the American firm will have to exchange

$$£35,000 \times \$1.5740/\text{pound} = \$55,090$$

to pay for the sweaters. In other words, the cost of the purchase is expected to be $55,090. Alternatively, the £35,000 could be divided by .6353 pounds per dollar to reach the same result (within rounding error).

The Effect of Exchange Rates on Prices and Quantities It's important to notice that the exchange rate is part of the cost of product to a firm importing foreign goods. To illustrate, let's continue the sweater example we began in the last section. The expected cost per sweater at the time of ordering is

$$\$55,090/500 = \$110.18$$

plus shipping and handling. Hence, a reasonable retail price would probably be about $220 (assuming roughly a 100% retail markup).

TABLE 18-1 Exchange Rates—Thursday, August 16, 2012, 18:29 UTC

	Direct Quote ($ per unit of foreign currency)	Indirect Quote (foreign currency units per $)
Argentina (peso)	.2169	4.6095
Australia (dollar)	.9504	1.0522
Brazil (real)	.4948	2.0208
Canada (dollar)	.9866	1.0135
Denmark (krone)	.1661	6.0203
Europe (euro)	1.2366	.8086
Israel (shekel)	.2483	4.0278
Japan (yen)	.01261	79.29
China (yuan)	.1571	6.3673
Mexico (peso)	.0761	13.1460
U.K. (British pound)	1.5740	.6353

SOURCE: www.xe.com/currencytables

But what would happen if the exchange rate was less favorable? Suppose, for example, the direct quote is $2.00 per pound. Then the expected cost of the shipment would be

$$£35,000 \times \$2.0000/\text{pound} = \$70,000$$

a single sweater would cost

$$\$70,000/500 = \$140.00$$

and a reasonable retail price might be about $280.

In other words, the exchange rate has an influence on the domestic prices of imported goods. The more a foreign currency costs, the more expensive that nation's products are when offered to American buyers regardless of their cost in the country of origin.

It's an economic fundamental that when a product is more expensive, people buy less of it. For foreign goods, that means higher prices due to less favorable exchange rates lead to decreased imports. In our illustration, the $2.00 pound implies a $60 higher retail price for a sweater. The American importer might well feel that the product won't sell at such a price and may order fewer than 500 or forgo the order entirely. Conversely, a more favorable exchange rate makes foreign products cheaper in the United States, causing larger quantities to be demanded leading to more imports. We'll come back to this important concept later.

Cross Rates   Given the information in the table, it's possible to develop an exchange rate between any two currencies without going through dollars. These are called **cross rates**.

CONCEPT CONNECTION   **EXAMPLE 18-2**

Cross Rates

Calculate the exchange rate between Brazilian reals and British pounds from the direct quote column of Table 18-1.

SOLUTION: Divide the direct quote for pounds by the direct quote for reals as follows:

$$\frac{1.5740 \text{ dollars per pound}}{.4948 \text{ dollars per real}} = 3.1811 \text{ reals per pound}$$

Alternately, the reciprocal calculation tells us that a real is worth $(1 \div 3.1811 =) £0.3144$.

Exchange Rate Listings   Exchange rate tables are available at a number of Internet Web sites, however, the formats in which they're presented vary somewhat from site to site. Several Web sites display tables of cross rates in which various currencies are listed across the top and down the left side of the table. The column under any particular currency gives either the direct or indirect quote for exchanges between that currency and all the others. The row next to any currency gives the inverse quote.

To find exchange rate listings, set your Web browser to search for *currency* or *foreign exchange* or *exchange rates*. Some sites require a subscription, but listings are available free on others. For a quick look at how all this works, go to **www. bloomberg.com** and click on market data and then on either world currencies or foreign exchange rates to see a cross rate table for eight major currencies. Newspapers, long the primary source of listings, now provide only limited information as of the close of the previous business day.

Terminology—Quoting Exchange Rates

When quoting U.S. dollar exchange rates one at a time, it's standard practice to use the direct quote for the rate for the U.K. pound and the euro, and the indirect quote for everything else. For example, on August 16, 2012, we would have said or written that the pound was selling for $1.5740 and the euro for $1.2366. On the other hand, we would have said the Danish krone was at kr 6.0203 (where kr is used like the U.S. dollar sign, $).

18.1c   Changing Exchange Rates and Exchange Rate Risk

Exchange rates are constantly changing, sometimes quite rapidly and by significant amounts. We'll get into why they change in a little while, but first it's important to understand the implications of the fact that they do change.

Moving exchange rates give rise to **exchange rate risk**, a very important facet of international business. Exchange rate risk means that a firm can make or lose money on an international transaction because of rate movements aside from the business deal itself.

For example, imagine that the American company we've been talking about ordered its 500 sweaters on August 16, 2012, when the exchange rate was $1.5740 per pound. At that time it expected to pay the $55,090 we calculated earlier for the shipment. Also suppose the purchase is part of a contract that calls for payment three months after the order is placed.

When the U.S. firm returns to the foreign exchange market three months after ordering, the pound rate is unlikely to be the same. For the sake of illustration, suppose the direct quote has risen to $2.0000 per pound. That means paying the £35,000 bill will take

$$£35,000 \times \$2.0000/pound = \$70,000.$$

That's $14,910 more than was expected at the time the order was placed. The implication is that the profit made on the U.S. sale of the sweaters will be reduced by $14,910 just due to the fluctuation in the exchange rate.

Of course, the rate could have gone the other way. In that case, more profit than expected would be made. The point is that exchange rate variation throws an element of risk into the American firm's business that wouldn't be there if the sweaters were purchased domestically.

Transactions subject to exchange rate risk as well as the companies that do such transactions are said to have exchange rate *exposure*.

Spot and Forward Rates

The exchange rates we've described so far are *spot rates*, meaning that they're good for immediate, "on the spot" transactions.[3] **Forward rates** are also available for delivery of the currency at some time in the future. They're

Exchange rate risk is the chance of gain or loss from exchange rate movement that occurs **during** a transaction.

Forward rates quote prices for **future delivery** of currencies.

---

3.   Delivery on spot transactions is made within two days.

generally somewhat different from the spot rates reflecting the movement that foreign exchange brokers expect in the future relationship between the two currencies.

For example, Table 18-1 shows that on August 16, 2012, the British pound was available for $1.5740. If, at that time, the pound was expected to become, say, three cents more valuable in the next half year, the six-month forward rate would be quoted at $1.6040. The indirect quote six-month forward quote would show the same thing looking from the pound to the dollar; it would be .6234 pounds per dollar, down from the August 16 value of .6353. In other words, a dollar would be expected to buy slightly fewer pounds in the future.

When a foreign currency is expected to become more valuable in the future, as in this case, the forward currency is said to be selling at a *premium* over the spot currency. In the reverse situation, when a future dollar will buy more of the foreign currency than a present dollar, the forward currency is said to be selling at a *discount.*

The Terminology of Exchange Rate Movements   When a currency becomes or is expected to become more valuable in terms of dollars, we say that it is becoming *stronger* or *rising* or *appreciating* against the dollar. The same idea can also be expressed by saying that the dollar is becoming *weaker* or *falling* or *depreciating* against the foreign currency. In our example, the pound was expected to strengthen against the dollar, which was expected to weaken against the pound.

Hedging with Forward Exchange Rates   As we've said many times, people avoid risk whenever they can, and exchange rate risk is no exception. Most companies prefer to operate without it and are willing to pay a premium to do so.

The forward market provides a way to eliminate foreign exchange risk from international transactions with a process called **hedging**.[4] A firm that knows it will need foreign currency at some time in the future can lock in an exchange rate by contracting with a bank for future delivery at the appropriate forward rate.

Suppose our retailer needs pounds in *six* months rather than three. It can negotiate a six-month *forward contract* for pounds with a bank at the time it places the sweater order. Suppose the six-month forward rate is $1.6040 per pound, as in our example, which is a little more expensive than the spot rate (this isn't always the case; as often as not the forward rate is lower), so the shipment will cost

$$\text{£35,000} \times \text{\$1.6040/pound} = \text{\$56,140}$$

Once the forward contract is written, exchange rate risk is eliminated from the transaction, as £35,000 will be delivered in six months for $56,140. The firm is said to have *covered* its obligation with a *forward market hedge.* Forward contracts can be written between any two currencies, for any amount, and for any length of time—generally up to two years. There is a cost, however, because brokers and banks charge fees for the service.

The forward market enables companies to transfer foreign exchange risk to professionals who are in the business of bearing such risks.

> Exchange rate risk can be eliminated by **hedging** with a forward contract.

---

4. "Hedge" is a general term applied to an arrangement that reduces or avoids risk.

18.1d Supply and Demand—The Source of Exchange Rate Movement

Simply stated, an exchange rate is the price of a unit of foreign currency. For example, Table 18-1 tells us that on August 16, 2012, a British pound cost $1.5740.

We can think of the pound as a commodity offered for sale in a free market. Its price, like that of any commodity, is determined by the interaction of supply and demand, traditionally represented by supply and demand curves like those in Figure 18-1(a). The intersection of the two curves determines the market price of the commodity—in this case, the direct quote exchange rate.

Figure 18-1(b) shows the supply and demand picture from the British side where the dollar is a commodity purchased with pounds. In this view, the intersection is the exchange rate in terms of pounds per dollar, the indirect quote.

FIGURE 18-1   Foreign Exchange: British (U.K.) Pounds and U.S. Dollars

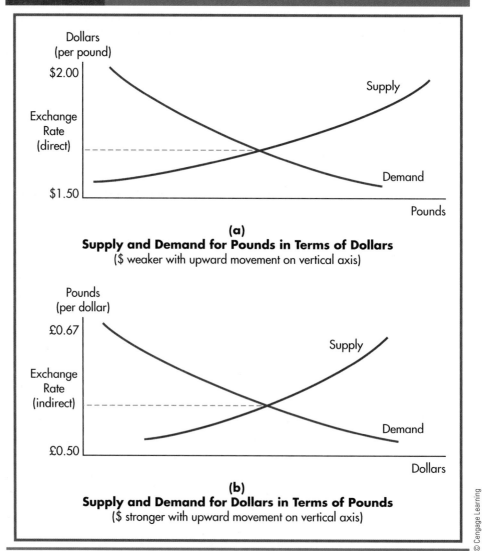

(a)
Supply and Demand for Pounds in Terms of Dollars
($ weaker with upward movement on vertical axis)

(b)
Supply and Demand for Dollars in Terms of Pounds
($ stronger with upward movement on vertical axis)

© Cengage Learning

The Origins of the Supply and Demand for Foreign Exchange

The demand for and the supply of foreign exchange between any two nations stem primarily from trade and the flow of investment capital between those nations. First let's look at trade.

When companies in the United States want to buy things (import) from another country, say Great Britain, they also need to buy the currency to make their purchases. This sets up a demand for pounds. At the same time, British companies that want to buy U.S. goods have to buy dollars with pounds. This sets up a supply of pounds.

Now look at Figure 18-1(a). As the direct exchange rate gets higher on the vertical axis (that is, as a pound becomes more expensive in terms of dollars), British goods get more expensive in the United States. That leads to a reduction in the quantity of those goods demanded by U.S. consumers and consequently to a reduction in the need for pounds. This is reflected by the downward slope of the demand curve in the diagram.

At the same time, moving up on the vertical axis of Figure 18-1(a) means a British pound buys more U.S. dollars. That makes U.S. goods cheaper in Great Britain, so people are willing to buy more of them. British importers therefore would like to buy more dollars with pounds, which increases the available supply of pounds. This is reflected by the upward slope of the supply curve.

Capital flows work in exactly the same way. A strong dollar makes British investments cheaper, so people want more of them, leading to a big demand for pounds. A weaker dollar makes U.S. investments cheap for the British, which leads to a demand for more dollars and a larger supply of pounds.

In summary, the supply and demand curves that establish exchange rates are **derived** from each country's demand for the other country's trade goods and investments.

> The supply/demand for foreign exchange is **derived** from each country's **demand** for the other's **goods** and investments.

Why the Exchange Rate Moves

Movement in exchange rates results from shifts in the supply and demand curves for foreign exchange. Because the curves arise primarily from the demand within each country for the other's products and investments, anything that changes those demands affects the curves for currency. Let's examine several such changeable factors.

> Exchange rates move in response to **changes in the demand for imported goods** within the two countries.

Preferences in Consumption   Anything that makes one country's products more or less desirable to the other's population will move the curves. For example, for many years, Japanese and certain European cars have been perceived as higher quality and more cost-effective than American cars. As a result, Americans buy a large number of foreign cars. This influence tends to shift the demand curve for Japanese and German currencies to the right.

Government Policy   Governments can actively encourage or discourage imports by imposing quotas, charging tariffs and duties, and making import licenses difficult to obtain. Foreign investment can be similarly encouraged or made difficult. For example, some countries prohibit foreign ownership of a majority interest in companies operating within their borders. That makes foreign direct investment less attractive.

Economic Conditions   A number of economic conditions influence the foreign exchange market. Here are a few:

1. In general, more prosperous economies demand more imports than economies undergoing recession.

2. Economies that are growing rapidly have more investment opportunities than those that aren't and therefore attract more foreign investment.

3. Countries in which interest rates are relatively high attract foreign investment because their financial assets offer higher returns than are available in other countries (if the high interest rates aren't accompanied by excessive inflation).

4. Countries with relatively high inflation rates make poor foreign investment targets. During periods of high inflation, a country's currency can lose value at a rate that's greater than the returns offered on most investments. Therefore, the net effect of an investment is likely to be a loss.

Speculation   Changes in exchange rates create speculative opportunities just like changes in the prices of stocks. If a foreign currency is strengthening against the dollar, holding it results in a gain. Hence, some people trade in currencies for profit rather than to do international business. The transactions made by such speculators can be significant in size and sometimes have a noticeable effect on overall demand and supply.

Direct Government Intervention   Governments sometimes buy and sell their own currencies for the express purpose of keeping exchange rates within desirable ranges. We'll discuss the reasons behind this activity shortly.

In the modern world, the factors that cause exchange rate movement change all the time. Hence, the supply and demand curves for foreign exchange are constantly shifting, as is their intersection, the exchange rate.

18.1e   Governments and the International Monetary System

Recall that earlier we said exchange rates influence the domestic prices of imported goods. Let's pursue that idea a little further.

Suppose a nation's currency suddenly strengthens relative to the currencies of other countries. We'll use the U.S. dollar to illustrate, but the results are true for any currency. As a result of a strengthening dollar, two things happen—one good and the other bad. First, imported goods become cheaper, because a dollar buys more foreign exchange and hence more foreign product. That's generally good for consumers, and people like it.

At the same time, however, U.S. exports become more expensive in other countries. That means fewer are sold and the demand placed on U.S. manufacturers for exported product diminishes. The result is a reduction in industrial activity in the United States and eventually a loss of jobs, which, of course, is bad.

Conversely, if the dollar weakens, foreign products become more expensive here, which leads to a general lowering of our standard of living. However, our exports increase because they're cheaper in other nations, and the increased business creates jobs here.

Summarizing, we can say that exchange rates affect the domestic economy through two opposing forces: the cost of imported goods and the employment generated by producing goods for export.

A strong dollar makes **imports cheaper**, but has a negative effect on **employment** because it reduces exports.

Government Influence on Exchange Rates
It's important to recognize that these opposing forces need to be kept in balance. In other words, it isn't good for an economy if the exchange rate goes too far in either direction. Cheap imports aren't worth excessive unemployment, and low unemployment isn't worth a substantially higher cost of living. For that reason, governments occasionally intervene in foreign exchange markets to keep rates within what they feel are reasonable ranges.

Governments accomplish this intervention by buying and selling their own currencies in the foreign exchange market. For example, if the dollar is getting too weak, the U.S. Treasury will buy dollars. This action adds to other demands for dollars and pushes all dollar demand curves to the right in diagrams like Figure 18-1(b). It thus raises the exchange rate for dollars in terms of the other currencies (the indirect quote).

A government's ability to *support* a weakening currency in this way is limited because it has to pay for its purchases of its own money with either gold or foreign exchange already in its possession. Both of these are clearly of limited availability.

Conversely, if a currency is too strong, the government will sell its own currency. This action has the effect of increasing supply and lowering its cost in terms of other currencies.

> **Governments** sometimes **intervene** in foreign exchange markets to keep **exchange rates within desirable limits**.

The International Monetary System
The international monetary system is the set of rules by which countries collectively administer the exchange of currencies. The system in place at the present time, which we've been describing, is known as a **floating exchange rate system**. That means exchange rates are determined essentially by free market forces. Some government intervention does occur, but not much, and it's usually the result of an agreement between several nations to maintain economic stability.

The floating rate system has been in effect since the early 1970s. Between the end of World War II (1945) and that time the world was on a *fixed exchange rate system,* meaning rates were fixed by international treaty and administered by an organization known as the International Monetary Fund (the IMF still exists).

Under the fixed-rate system, market forces tended to push rates around just as they do now, but each country had the responsibility of holding its exchange rate with the U.S. dollar nearly constant. The value of the dollar was fixed in terms of gold at $35 per ounce. Countries maintained the value of their currencies against the dollar by buying and selling in the foreign exchange market as we described in the last section.

As the economic status of nations changed during the post–World War II period, it sometimes became impossible to keep certain exchange rates constant. When that happened, a nation could go through a *revaluation* to officially raise the value of its currency relative to the dollar or a *devaluation* to lower its value. As the West German economy strengthened, it went through two revaluations in the 1960s, while the British pound was devalued in 1967.

By the 1970s, the dollar's tie to gold at $35 per ounce had become unrealistic because the market price of gold had risen to more than $100.[5] At that time the fixed-rate system was abandoned along with the fixed dollar price of gold, and the floating-rate system was established.

> In a **floating exchange rate** system, **market forces** set rates with **little intervention** from governments.

---

5. The price of gold fluctuates a great deal. As of mid-2012, its record high was $1,921 per ounce on September 6, 2011.

Convertibility   Not all currencies are **convertible**. That is, many can't be exchanged in the way we've described in this chapter. For its currency to be convertible, a nation must allow it to be traded on foreign exchange markets and be willing to accept the resulting value. The currencies of Russia and China have traditionally not been convertible, but have moved toward convertibility in recent years.

Nonconvertibility doesn't mean there isn't an exchange rate. If you want to buy a product from a country with a nonconvertible currency, its government will be glad to sell you the currency you need at its official exchange rate. However, the system works only one way. If you have local currency, there is generally no one willing to exchange it for dollars or any other major currency at the exchange rate set by the country's government.

Nonconvertibility is a significant impediment to international business. Suppose a U.S. company establishes a branch in country with a nonconvertible currency and makes a profit doing business there. The profit is in local currency, and because it isn't convertible, it's very difficult to repatriate it back into the company's home country. To get value out of the country, it's generally necessary to buy something made in that country with the money, export it to the home country, and sell it there.

The Balance of Trade   Let's go back to the supply and demand diagrams of Figure 18-1. Unlike the supply and demand diagrams for other commodities, those for foreign exchange represent a reciprocal arrangement. That is, the supply of another nation's currency seen by Americans depends on the demand in that other country for U.S. dollars. In other words, the only place you can get pounds is in Great Britain, and the British have to want to buy U.S. dollars or there won't be any pounds available.

The total money flow between countries includes trade, investing activities, and payments made directly between governments. The latter include loans, loan payments along with interest, and foreign aid.

The net flow between two countries from trade is known as the **balance of trade**. If the United States imports more from another country than we export to it, we say a **trade deficit** exists between the nations from the U.S. perspective. If we export more to a country than we import, we say a *trade surplus* exists.

A consistent trade deficit or surplus with respect to a particular country can continue for a long time if it's offset by other financial flows between the two nations, or if the country with the trade surplus is willing to accumulate a store of the currency of the country with a deficit. When such an accumulation happens, the available pool of the deficit country's money tends to weaken the value of its currency. In Figure 18-1(b), it pushes the supply curve to the right, lowering the indirect exchange rate. That should make the deficit nation's exports cheaper in the surplus nation, thus bringing trade back in balance. However, that tendency toward balance doesn't happen if the surplus nation artificially restricts imports from the deficit nation.

18.2   International Capital Markets

Today it is common for individuals and businesses to make investments in countries other than their own. We've already discussed making a direct investment in facilities in another country and a portfolio investment in the securities of a business from

---

A currency that isn't **convertible** cannot be exchanged for other currencies at **market-determined** rates.

If we **import more** from a country than we export to it, a **trade deficit** exists and our currency accumulates in that country.

another country. A portfolio investment can also be made in bonds issued by another government. These activities require the flow of capital funds among nations, and several institutional practices have arisen to assist in those flows. We'll have a brief look at the Eurodollar market and international bonds after a digression on the status of the American dollar.

18.2a   The Unique Status of the U.S. Dollar

Since World War II, the **U.S. dollar** has been the world's leading currency. In a sense, it functions as **international money**. The dollar has this unique role because people have more confidence in its continuing value than they have in the value of any other currency. This confidence no doubt stems from the United States' unique status as a superpower in both military and economic terms.

The **U.S. dollar** is the world's leading currency and in some ways serves as "**international money**."

In any event, most international businesspeople are willing to take dollars in trade because they're confident that American money can be exchanged for their own currencies at any time and that its value isn't likely to fall suddenly. (The exchange rate is still needed to determine how many dollars something priced in another currency is worth.) In fact, a dollar may be preferable to their own currency, which may not be as stable.

Many international contracts are denominated in dollars even when none of the parties to the contract are American.

A **reserve currency** is widely held by other countries.

Another way to say all this is that the dollar has been the world's leading **reserve currency** for many years. A reserve currency is one that's held by other governments as part of a **foreign exchange reserve,** which serves as a store of value backing the nations's liabilities. The leading reserve currency is generally used to price internationally traded commodities like oil and gold. Oil prices, for example, are quoted in U.S. dollars per barrel around the world. Most of worldwide currency reserves are held in U.S. dollars. Second place belongs to the euro.

Recall that we said governments sometimes intervene in foreign exchange markets to keep exchange rates for their own currencies within acceptable limits. They do that by buying or selling their own currencies using their foreign exchange reserves.

Confidence in the Dollar Is Slipping   Unfortunately, the dollar's status has been under attack recently. The dollar has weakened significantly against other currencies over the past 10 years and shows no sign of recovering in the near term. This has caused the value stored in dollar reserves held by other countries to decline, causing several finance ministers to call for a change to some other reserve currency. The euro was the primary candidate until recently, but its appeal has diminished due to the European debt crisis.

But no one can just declare a change in the leading reserve currency. It has to come through a shift in the collective opinion of other countries when they choose the currencies they hold in reserve, and that isn't likely to happen quickly.

In this regard, the financial crisis of 2008 weakened the rest of the world's confidence in the dollar. That weakening comes from the staggering deficits the U.S. federal government is currently running—i.e., the government spends far more than it takes in every year, and the difference (the deficit) must be borrowed, adding to the cumulative national debt. A large national debt tends to weaken confidence in America's financial stability and therefore confidence in the dollar.

The dramatic increase in deficit spending is related to the money poured into the financial sector to avert collapse in 2008, spending on the wars in Iraq and Afghanistan, and efforts to stimulate the economy.

Although a shift away from the dollar isn't likely in the short run, the long-run drift is definitely in that direction.

A Little More Terminology   A widely traded currency that can be used as a stable, reliable store of value is known as a **hard currency**. A **soft currency**, on the other hand, is one whose value may fall quickly or is difficult to convert to other currencies.

Hard currencies currently include the U.S. dollar, euro, British pound, Canadian and Australian dollars, and the Japanese yen.

> The value of a **hard currency** is stable and reliable.

18.2b   The Eurodollar Market

A **Eurodollar** is U.S. dollar deposited in a bank outside the United States. People deposit money in foreign banks because their interest rates on dollar deposits are somewhat higher than those offered by domestic banks.

The foreign banks create the **Eurodollar market** by lending the Eurodollars to international companies and foreign governments that have a need for American currency. The borrowers use Eurodollars for a variety of things, including payment for U.S. exports, portfolio investments in American stocks and bonds, and as a medium of exchange between parties that don't want to deal in their own currencies.

Eurodollar deposits don't have to be in European banks; they can be anywhere in the world. They're called Eurodollars simply because the practice started in Europe. The deposits are typically made for fixed periods that can range from a single day to approximately five years. They're also rather large, starting at about $500,000.

> A **soft currency** is unreliable in value and may be difficult to convert.

> **Eurodollars** are dollar deposits in **foreign banks** that are loaned to international businesses in the **Eurodollar market**.

18.2c   The International Bond Market

In earlier chapters, we talked about bonds issued by domestic corporations sold in the United States. (Keep in mind that selling a bond means the issuing company is borrowing money from the bond's buyer.) It is possible, however, for companies to borrow internationally by selling bonds outside their own countries. Any bond sold outside the home country of the borrower is called an **international bond**.

The idea of an international bond raises a question about the currency in which the bond's face value is stated. The bond can be *denominated* in the currency of the issuing company's home country, in the currency of the country in which it is sold, or in some third currency.

A bond denominated in the currency of the country in which it is sold, but issued by a foreign borrower, is called a **foreign bond**. For example, a Japanese auto manufacturer like Honda or Toyota might want to open an assembly plant in the United States financed in part by borrowing. It could do that by issuing dollar-denominated bonds in the United States, registering them with the Securities and Exchange Commission (SEC), and selling them through American financial markets. To buyers, the bonds would be just like those of domestic companies except for the headquarters location of the issuing company. Importantly, they would be subject to all of the registration and disclosure requirements of U.S. securities law, which tend to be more stringent than the requirements of other nations.

> An **international bond** is sold outside of the home country of the borrower.

> A bond issued by a foreign company but denominated in **local** currency is a **foreign bond**.

A bond denominated in a currency other than that of the country in which it is sold is called a **Eurobond**. For example, Honda could sell bonds denominated in Japanese yen to Americans in the United States or to people in any other country. Once again, the term "Euro" is historically derived and doesn't imply that the issuing company is European. In fact, most Eurobonds are denominated in American dollars and sold to investors in other countries.

> A **Eurobond** is denominated in a currency other than that of the country in which it is sold.

Eurobonds have several distinguishing features. First, securities regulations in most countries require a much lower level of disclosure for Eurobonds than for domestic or foreign bonds. This significantly lowers the cost of issuing them in comparison with the cost of issuing foreign or domestic bonds.

Second, Eurobonds are issued in *bearer* form, so the owner is not identified. Third, most governments don't withhold income tax on Eurobond interest payments. The second and third features make Eurobonds attractive to some investors, perhaps those who are interested in privacy and/or avoiding their own countries' taxes.

18.3 Political Risk

When capital is invested in another country, especially through direct investment, it becomes subject to the authority of the government of that country. **Political risk** refers to the probability that the value of a firm's investment in a foreign country will be reduced by political actions taken primarily by the country's government.

> **Political risk** is the chance that a foreign government will **expropriate** property or that **terrorists** will destroy it.

Nations have a unique set of powers described as *sovereignty* that aren't shared by companies or lower level government units regardless of their size. In the extreme, a sovereign nation can take human life and seize property located within its borders without compensating the owner. Property taken by a foreign government is said to be **expropriated**.

Expropriation is generally the worst-case scenario contemplated within the idea of political risk. It is relatively rare, but it has happened in a number of less developed countries including Chile, Bolivia, Cuba, Libya, and Iran.

Although not as drastic as expropriation, certain other actions can reduce the value of a foreign venture substantially. They take the form of arbitrarily imposed rules and regulations on operations and ownership. For example, a host country government can:

- Raise taxes of all kinds on the business.
- Limit the amount of profit that can be taken out of the country, either directly or through controls on currency conversion.
- Require that key inputs be purchased from local suppliers at arbitrary prices.
- Limit the prices charged for product sold within the country.
- Require part ownership by citizens of the host country, forcing sale of an interest in the business at an unrealistically low price.

Political risk also includes potential losses due to the actions of politically motivated terrorist groups. In the past, these have included sabotage and bombing of property, as well as the murder and kidnapping for ransom of key executives.

Political risk is quite small in industrialized nations with which the United States is on good terms, such as the Western European countries, Japan, Taiwan, and

Australia. It can be substantial, however, in the Third World nations of Africa, Asia, and South America and in places where the political climate is unstable or free enterprise capitalism is new to the population and the government, like the former Soviet Union and the Eastern Bloc countries.

18.4   Transaction and Translation Risks

Earlier we defined exchange rate risk as the potential gain or loss that arises from changes in the exchange rate between the time an international transaction is contracted and the time it's completed. This idea is also called *transaction risk* because it arises from transactions as they occur. **Transaction gains or losses** have real profit and cash flow impacts because they're *realized* in cash as they happen. For this reason, they're taxable events.

INSIGHTS | Ethics

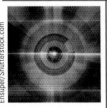

Ensuper/Shutterstock.com

The Foreign Corrupt Practices Act (FCPA)—A Legal/Ethical Dilemma

Corruption in government is a worldwide problem and has been throughout recorded history. Corrupt practices occur in every nation, but they're particularly flagrant in some less developed countries (LDCs), including many in Africa, Asia, and South America.

In international business, the corruption issue typically arises when a government official has control over the selection of a foreign company to perform some work and allows that choice to be influenced by bribes. Virtually all countries have laws against officials taking bribes, but in LDCs they're usually ignored. In fact, in many LDCs, bribery is a common practice that everyone knows about and expects.

In 1977, the U.S. Congress took an ethical position against corruption by passing the Foreign Corrupt Practices Act (FCPA), which makes it illegal for U.S. companies and firms whose securities are traded here to pay bribes to influence decision makers in foreign governments. Companies can be fined and executives jailed for violating the law.

However, the act created a problem for U.S. companies trying to compete against firms from other industrialized nations that didn't have similar laws. If those firms could pay bribes, and U.S. firms couldn't, business would generally be awarded to the non-U.S. companies. Indeed some industrialized countries' policies actually seemed to support bribery. For example, until 2000 France allowed companies to deduct "commissions" paid to secure business from taxable income up to 7.5% of the value of international contracts.

During the 1980s and early '90s, the United States was the only major country with an anti-bribery law like the FCPA. At the time, the law didn't disadvantage U.S. companies too severely because it wasn't actively enforced. However, an international anti-bribery movement was developing through the Organisation for Economic Co-operation and Development (OECD) during those years that eventually led to the OECD Anti-Bribery Convention in 1997. The convention is an agreement in which a number of industrialized nations promised to pass laws in their own countries banning bribes. As of March 2012, 39 countries had ratified it, but not all had actually passed such laws.

Despite the convention, enforcement remained spotty until world attention was drawn to unethical/illegal corporate behavior by the Enron scandal in 2001. The United States passed the Sarbanes—Oxley Act in 2002, and at the same time dusted off the FCPA and began investigating suspected bribery.

Other countries moved in the same direction. Germany, France, and Switzerland actively pursued certain large multinational violators in the mid-2000s, and Great Britain passed a law even more aggressive than the FCPA in 2010. The most visible case so far has been the U.S. and German governments' prosecution of Germany's Siemens AG. It resulted in a settlement in which the firm paid fines to the two governments totaling $1.34 billion.

The United States is still the lead anti-bribery enforcer. As of mid-2011, it had sanctioned or reached settlements with 72 companies and 85 individuals, many times the totals of other countries.

But the FCPA has some serious enforcement problems. Multinational firms complain that the law is vague as to what constitutes an offense because certain payments are permitted to expedite or "grease" the wheels of commerce. It also isn't clear on exactly who is or isn't a foreign government official. On top of that, a firm can be found guilty because of bribes paid by its subcontractors or suppliers or by a company it's acquired even if the illegal payment was made before the acquisition. And, the way the law is written, it's essentially the prosecutor who defines what's right or wrong. In this context, it's important to understand that decisions made by lower level employees in far flung divisions without the knowledge or consent of senior management can create major liabilities for multinational companies.

Further, the penalties for conviction are so severe that individuals and companies accused by the Justice Department are frightened into quick settlements to avoid protracted legal action and potential criminal convictions. That means few cases have gone to trial, so there isn't much case law available to help lawyers and executives interpret the law.

Compliance with the law is proving to be expensive. Some companies have conducted costly internal investigations and reported their own violations to the Justice Department hoping to get lighter fines and avoid criminal prosecution. Firms are also spending money on compliance programs designed to ensure that managers are informed about what they can and can't do under the FCPA. (Penalties tend to be reduced if the offending company has a legitimate compliance program.) Of course multinational firms need expert legal advice to stay out of FCPA trouble, and that's led to a new legal specialty in which top lawyers are earning as much as $2 million per year.

In summary, the businesses community feels somewhat overwhelmed and is saying uncertainty about the law is having a chilling effect on commerce. The government issued a 130 page guidance document in November 2012 which received mixed reviews. Some say it helped, but others claim it didn't do much to clarify the grey areas.

Sources: David Crawford, "French Firm Scrutinized in Global Bribe Probe," *The Wall Street Journal* (May 6, 2008): A1, A8; Dionne Searcey, "U.S. Cracks Down on Corporate Bribes." *The Wall Street Journal*, (May 26, 2009): A1, A4; Dionne Searcey, "In Antibribery Law, Some Fear Inadvertent Chill on Business," *The Wall Street Journal*, (August 6, 2009): A9; Dionne Searcey, "U.K. Law on Bribes Has Firms in a Sweat," *The Wall Street Journal*, (December 28, 2010): B1, B2; Paul Hannon, "Few Nations Are Punishing Bribery," *WSJ.com* (April 21, 2011); John Bussey, "The Rule of Law Finds Its Way Abroad—However Painfully," *The Wall Street Journal*, (June 24, 2011): B1, B9; Joe Palazzolo, "Critics Target Bribery Law," *The Wall Street Journal* (November 11, 2011): B1, B8; Joe Palazzolo, "FCPA INC: The Business of Bribery," *The Wall Street Journal* (October 2, 2012): B1, B4; Joe Palazzolo, "Law's Long Path: Nixon, Carter, Bush" *The Wall Street Journal* (October 2, 2012): B1, B4; Ashby Jones, "The Costs of Compliance Grow" *The Wall Street Journal* (October 2, 2012): B4; Joe Palazzolo and Christopher Matthews, "Bribery Law Dos and Don'ts," *The Wall Street Journal* (November 15, 2012): B1, B2.

Translation gains/losses arise when assets and liabilities held in a foreign country are translated into dollars.

However, exchange rates also generate the risk of another type of gain or loss. **Translation risk** refers to the potential gain or loss that arises from translating the financial statements (especially the balance sheet) of a foreign subsidiary[6] from the local currency into dollars for consolidation with the parent company's financial statements.[7]

For example, suppose a U.S. firm spends $2 million to build a factory in Great Britain when the exchange rate is two dollars to the pound (direct quote $2.00 = £1.00; indirect quote $1.00 = £.50). Immediately after the factory is built, the balance sheet of the British subsidiary shows an asset of £1 million representing the factory and an equity account of the same amount. The parent's balance sheet shows an asset of $2 million representing its investment in the foreign company.

When the parent company closes its *consolidated* books in dollars, the value of the British factory effectively replaces the account carrying the investment in its foreign subsidiary.[8] While the exchange rate remains at two dollars to the pound, the £1 million factory on the British books translates exactly into $2 million, which replaces the $2 million investment account, so there's no problem.

But if the exchange rate changes between the time the factory is built and the consolidated books are closed, the two accounts won't neatly match one another.

CONCEPT CONNECTION   EXAMPLE 18-3

Translation Gains and Losses

Assume that by the time the parent company's books are closed, the dollar has strengthened so that a pound is worth only $1.75 (indirect quote $1.00 = £.57).

Calculate the financial statement impact of the rate movement on the consolidated books. Ignore depreciation on the British books.

SOLUTION: The factory is still valued at £1 million on the British subsidiary's books, which translated at the new rate gives a dollar value of

$$£1,000,000 \times \$1.75/£ = \$1,750,000$$

The parent's investment account still carries a $2 million balance which must now be written down to $1,750,000, implying a loss of $250,000. This is a *translation loss* that has to be recognized in the consolidation procedure.

---

6. Recall that a subsidiary is a company owned by another company which is known as its parent.

7. Three sets of financial statements are used when one company owns another: the parent's, the subsidiary's, and the consolidated sum of the two. The parent's balance sheet carries an asset called *investment in subsidiary* that reflects its ownership of the subsidiary. That account's balance is equal to the balance in the equity account of the subsidiary.

    When the parent's and the subsidiary's balance sheets are consolidated, like assets and liabilities are added together for companywide totals. However, the investment in subsidiary (a debit) on the parent's books is combined with the subsidiary's equity (a credit). Normally, the two accounts are equal in magnitude, so they eliminate one another, and the consolidated books look like one big company.

8. In this simplified example, the subsidiary has only one asset and no liabilities other than equity. Hence, the exchange rate changes on the asset will be mirrored in the equity account.

In other words, because the factory in Great Britain is valued in pounds, and the pound lost value against the dollar, the factory also lost value. And that loss has to be reflected in the company's overall consolidated books. Of course, if the pound had strengthened against the dollar, the firm would have had a translation gain.

The Relevance of Translation Gains and Losses   Notice that a translation gain or loss isn't quite real; it's only on paper. In our example, the U.S. firm still owns the British factory regardless of its value in pounds, so nothing's really changed. As long as the company doesn't sell the factory and attempt to repatriate the proceeds to the United States, the loss isn't *realized* in cash and is something of an abstraction.

Recognizing this, the accounting rules for consolidating international subsidiaries specify that translation gains and losses are not to be included in consolidated income statements. Rather they're shown cumulatively in an account that adds to or offsets stockholders' equity. And because they're not realized, they're not taxable.

18.5   Current Issues in International Trade

As we've already said, there's more international business going on today than ever before. The term "globalization" is used to refer to this rapidly expanding cross-border trade as well as to some unexpected social and political effects that may come along with it. We'll have a look at globalization in this section after beginning with a little background.

18.5a   Background: Free Trade, the Theory of Comparative Advantage, and Protectionism

Countries can take a variety of positions for or against international trade. The two extremes are free trade and protectionism. To illustrate, imagine that there are two countries, A and B, each of which has just two industries, growing wheat and making steel. Assume that there are wheat growers and steel producers in both nations.

Free trade implies that businesses in both countries are at liberty to market their products in the other country as well as in their own.[9] The other extreme is protectionism in which one or both countries pass laws that limit or prohibit the importation of goods and foreign ownership of business.[10] The question we'll ask initially is, why would a country want to limit or prohibit imports?

To understand the motivation, imagine that you're in the steel business in country A when something happens in country B that enables it to produce steel more cheaply than is possible in A. (Perhaps the labor rate is lower in B or it has access to cheaper raw materials.) Under free trade, country B's steel industry will underprice country A's in steel markets in both nations, driving A's steel mills out of business.

---

9. They're also free to make direct investments in the other country and set up business operations there, but we won't get into that in this simple illustration.

10. Import limits usually come in the form of *tariffs,* which are taxes on imported products as they cross the border. Tariffs make imported goods more expensive, which reduces the quantity of foreign products demanded in the importing country.

This is bad news for steel industry stockholders and employees in country A because they stand to lose either their investments or their jobs. Understanding this, they go to their government and ask it to pass laws that "protect" A's steel industry from lower cost imports. A's legislators may pass the laws to maintain popular support or because they're concerned that a loss of jobs will damage A's economy.[11]

A's government may also protect its steel industry for strategic reasons. For example, what if A later goes to war with B? A would be in bad shape if it didn't have a steel industry for weapons production. This kind of strategic concern often prompts governments to protect key industries from foreign competition. Similarly, officials of A's government may limit or prohibit foreign ownership of businesses, because they fear excessive foreign influence and control.

The negative effect of protectionist legislation in country A is that steel will be more expensive there than it might have been. That can be a very big issue, because it leads to higher prices for everything made of steel and will generally lower the standard of living of A's population.

Because of these offsetting positive and negative effects, it isn't clear whether A is better off in the short run with a protectionist or free trade policy. Of course it isn't necessary to take either extreme position, and most nations are somewhere in the middle.

The Theory of Comparative Advantage   Economists and financial scholars are virtually unanimous in their support of free trade. Their position is traceable to a fundamental economic principle called the Theory of Comparative Advantage popularized by a British economist named David Ricardo in the early 1800s.

We can use countries A and B to illustrate the idea behind the theory. Remember that both countries produce wheat and steel. Suppose A is better at growing wheat than it is at making steel, and B is better at making steel than it is at growing wheat. We say that each country has a *comparative advantage* in one product over the other.

The theory says that the overall two-country community will be better off if each nation specializes in what it does best, and buys the other product from the other country. That is, more value will be produced if A just grows wheat and buys its steel from B, while B produces only steel and buys its wheat from A. It can be shown that this is true even if one country is better at both tasks than the other!

The theory of comparative advantage is a powerful argument for free trade in the long run, because it leads to a higher level of aggregate production. In the short run, however, it results in a serious economic burden on people like the steel industry employees in country A whose jobs are displaced. The immediate question is how long does it take to get through the "short run" and reach the happy "long run" situation? Economists define the long run as the time in which all productive inputs are variable. In this context, that's the time it would take for all of A's capital and labor resources to be redeployed from steel into wheat. Realistically that's probably one or two generations, at least 20 and perhaps as many as 40 or 50 years. During that period, the people

---

11. A counter argument is generally made to the second reason stating that the displaced workers should simply go to work in another industry. That, however, can be very difficult and is sometimes impossible.

displaced by the movement of steel production out of A will suffer a great deal of economic pain due to lost jobs and shrinking investment values.

Comparative advantage also has some technical problems. Although it's true that more can be produced under free trade because of the specialization implied, it isn't clear how the additional value will be distributed among the people of countries A and B. Indeed there seems to be some real-world evidence that little of the benefit of free trade filters down to the working classes and that there's a widening of the wealth gap between the very rich and the very poor under free trade.

18.5b　Globalization

Globalization is a broad term that refers to the general movement of the world economy toward free trade as it undergoes a dramatically increasing level of international business. Some observers say that the trend has really been ongoing for at least 200 years, while others maintain that it's only been significant since the end of World War II. In any event, most agree that the process has accelerated in the last 20 or 30 years and that technology is driving it faster all the time.

The question also arises as to whether globalization is a result of government policies favoring free trade or if it's an inevitable result of the capitalist, free enterprise system. But even if globalization is inevitable in the long run, it's clear that government policies are driving its development faster. The most prominent government actions to promote free trade involve forming groups of countries that reduce or eliminate trade barriers among themselves. The best example is the European Union (EU) which consists of 27 member states that have joined together to encourage trade and the movement of labor within itself. The EU has gone so far as to adopt a common currency, the euro.[12] Another important example is the North American Free Trade Association (NAFTA) under which the United States, Canada, and Mexico have eliminated most trade restrictions but not those on labor movement.

Proponents of globalization rely heavily on the comparative advantage argument that more production is available when trade is unrestricted than when it's limited, and that that leads to a better life and a higher standard of living for everyone involved.

Antiglobalization　Although few would argue that the comparative advantage benefits of free trade are not real, not everyone agrees that globalization is a good thing.

In our example involving steel and wheat, production was carried out in the home country, and free trade just meant selling across a national border. In the modern world, however, free trade also means setting up factories in other countries to produce goods that can be sold anywhere. It is this aspect of globalization that's criticized most harshly.

To those who see its dark side, globalization simply means using the cheapest labor available regardless of where it's located. Put another way, critics say it means finding the world's most poverty-stricken countries, paying people subsistence wages to work under horrible conditions, and then making big profits on the products of their labor. This, they say, amounts to exploitation of underdeveloped countries.

---

12. Not all EU members use the euro. The most prominent example is Great Britain.

18.5c Increased Protectionism

The rapid trend toward globalization (page 775) during the 1990s and early 2000s had generated a protectionist backlash before the onset of the financial crisis. It was agreed that globalization produces more product in the long run, but more and more people, including leading economists, were recognizing that the short-run loss of jobs might be too high a price to pay for that benefit.

For example, a March 2007 article in the *Wall Street Journal* described the changed opinions of Princeton economist Alan S. Blinder—who underwent a transformation from hardcore free trader to advocate of measures to protect American jobs from being exported electronically. (He remained opposed to tariffs.) The heart of Dr. Blinder's argument was his estimate that as many as 40 million American jobs could be shipped out of the country during the next 10 to 20 years.

The post-crisis recession intensified the protectionist backlash. That always happens in recessions, because governments try to stimulate their own economies in response to falling output and increasing unemployment. In this case, nations had been implementing restrictive rules since 2009, although most were relatively narrow. The trend continued as the recession lingered into 2012. A June *New York Times* article reported that the World Trade Organization (WTO) "sounded an alarm" in April by reporting that the "Group of 20" economies, the world's largest accounting for the majority of international trade, had implemented 124 new restrictive measures since October of 2011. The article went on to report that in June 2012 the Group of 20 agreed to extend a pact not to protect their own businesses through 2014, but many were reluctant to accept a date that far in the future. At the same time, trade analysts were reporting that the pledge was already being broken.

Although the observed restrictions are not too severe relative to the overall volume of international trade, they represent a "worrisome" and "alarming" trend that isn't slowing down.[13]

18.5d The Migration of Jobs—Outsourcing

When companies move production work to overseas locations, the people who were doing that work at home lose their jobs. This has been happening in the United States since the end of World War II. The work generally flows to the areas of the world with the lowest cost labor. Immediately after the war, work tended to be done in Japan, then it shifted to Taiwan and South Korea, then to the nations of the Pacific Rim. Most recently it has been going to China.

For many years, the exodus was primarily in lower-skilled manufacturing jobs. This did create an unemployment problem in the United States, but it was believed to be manageable in the long run. The argument was that America had to change the nature of its industrial economy. We had to shift from being manufacturers relying on heavy, physical processes for our livelihoods to a nation of more intellectual workers with strengths in research, innovation, design, and information management. Basically the workforce had to be retrained into these knowledge-based careers as manufacturing jobs moved "offshore" to other countries. Clearly this wouldn't work

---

13. Annie Lowrey, "An Increase in Barriers to Trade Is Reported," *The New York Times* (June 23, 2012), B1.

for everyone. It's always been difficult to imagine retraining someone who's worked in a factory for 30 years into, say, computer programming. Nevertheless, the concept was generally accepted as a long-term strategy for the nation as a whole.

But another phenomenon called *outsourcing* was developing at the same time. Outsourcing is related to specialization. Companies have long realized that they don't have to do all of the functions necessary to run their businesses themselves. They can generally get some things done better and cheaper by outside firms that specialize in those functions. For example, most colleges and universities don't run their own dining halls. They hire food service companies to bring their employees on campus to prepare and serve meals.

Traditionally, companies outsourced functions to specialists that were located nearby or at least in the United States, so the outsourced jobs didn't move very far. It was also true that key, knowledge-intensive jobs like design and engineering, weren't outsourced.

It's important to notice that sending manufacturing to low-labor-cost countries constitutes outsourcing production labor. The term *offshore* or *offshoring* was frequently used when referring to the practice.

Outsourcing Knowledge-Based Jobs   An unexpected development related to outsourcing began in the 1990s and is currently causing a great deal of concern with respect to the employment situation in the United States. To understand the phenomenon it's important to appreciate that there are some relatively undeveloped countries in the world in which wages are very low, but segments of the population are very well educated. The primary example is India, which has been sending brilliant engineers, mathematicians, and scholars to the United States and Western Europe for decades.

Starting in the 1990s and continuing today, unprecedented advances in computer and information transfer technology have made it possible to outsource many of the knowledge-based jobs that were expected to become the mainstay of U.S. industry to those countries without physically moving anything.

Here's an example from the health care industry. Suppose you have a medical problem and your doctor orders an X-ray. Your X-ray will generally be read by a radiologist (a physician who specializes in reading X-rays), who sends a report to your doctor. The radiologist doesn't see you in person, and your doctor may never see the X-ray. Today it's possible to outsource the radiologist's function by sending the X-ray to India where it's read by a perfectly competent Indian radiologist who returns his or her report electronically. And because labor of all kinds is cheaper in India, the process is done at a fraction of the U.S. cost. Notice that this practice has the potential to destroy the employment market for radiologists in the United States.

Professional level outsourcing is now happening nationwide. Information technology (IT) services are particularly vulnerable, as are engineering and telephone-based customer support functions. This suddenly widespread phenomenon has led to a middle-class outcry for the government to do something to discourage companies from sending jobs overseas, but as yet no such action has been taken.

18.5e   Labor Migration and Illegal Immigration

Another important aspect of globalization is the movement of labor between countries, usually at the low end of the pay/skill scale. Developed countries often face shortages of people who are willing to do low-end jobs like harvesting crops and cleaning homes and offices. But many people in nearby undeveloped countries are willing to do those jobs for very little money. That creates an incentive for large numbers of workers to migrate into the more developed country.

The developed countries are usually reluctant to admit large numbers of foreign workers and their families, because it can strain the nation's social support infrastructure with respect to things like public education, medical care, and welfare.

One solution is the idea of a guest worker program that allows foreigners to work in developed countries for limited periods of time after which they must leave. Guest worker programs have existed in Europe for some time.

The migration problem is particularly severe in the United States because it has been relatively easy to enter the country and remain here illegally (without official permission) for many years. In 2011, there were an estimated 11.5 million *illegal immigrants* in the United States, most of whom were from Mexico. Critics say that they are taking jobs that should go to Americans, while not paying taxes to support the public services they consume. The other side of the argument is that Americans don't want the majority of the jobs the illegal immigrants do, and that a good portion of American industry has come to depend on them.

In 2012, the nation is seriously divided on the issue. Many are calling for the deportation of illegal immigrants, while others favor letting those who are here stay and eventually earn citizenship.

18.5f   The Balance of Trade with China and Its Inconvertible Currency

Between the end of World War II and the 1980s, China was a rigidly communist country with a backward economy that, despite its enormous population, had relatively little commercial contact with the rest of the world. But in the last 30 or so years, while still a politically authoritarian regime, China has transformed itself into an essentially free market economy that's been growing at a staggering rate.

But much of that growth is due to the Chinese government's currency policy. As of mid-2012, the Chinese government refuses to let its yuan float on international currency markets, instead keeping it grossly undervalued relative to the U.S. dollar. This, coupled with low Chinese labor rates, makes their products very cheap in the United States. Indeed, it's estimated that they have at least a 40% price advantage over U.S. manufacturers. Of course, that's killing U.S. companies competitively. American industry leaders have been crying foul and begging our government to impose a tariff on Chinese imports to level the playing field, but so far their pleas have fallen on deaf ears. In the meantime, the trade deficit with China is more than $280 billion per year.

Strongly advocating free trade, conservatives argue that we shouldn't adopt protectionist policies and that the low prices of Chinese goods currently flooding retail shelves are good for the American people. Opposing interests are promoting legislation that would impose stiff tariffs on Chinese imports if that government doesn't make significant exchange rate adjustments. The issue remains a difficult problem of globalization.

18.5g   European Sovereign Debt Crisis

National (sovereign) governments raise money through taxation and spend it on running themselves and providing various services for their populations. If spending exceeds tax revenues in a year, the shortfall is a *deficit,* which the government must borrow by selling bonds. If deficits are large and persistent, the borrowing accumulates into a national debt, which generates interest that has to be paid out of tax revenues. National debt is also called **sovereign debt** because nations are sovereign entities.

Sovereign debt is money owed by national governments.

If its debt is large, a country can get into a situation in which it has to borrow more every year just to keep going. That means if it can't borrow (sell more bonds), it can't pay for things like the salaries of employees, social security, national defense, unemployment benefits, roads, and interest on its existing debt. When that happens, the country's economy may collapse. Its currency becomes worthless, and its existing bonds lose value.

The European Crisis   The European sovereign debt crisis refers to the fact that at least five countries out of the seventeen that share the euro as a common currency, (the **Eurozone**), are facing that dilemma in mid-2012, and have been for several years.

The **Eurozone** is made up of 17 countries that use the euro.

The problem started with government overspending during the boom years of the early 2000s supported by high tax revenues associated with prosperity. It became a crisis when tax revenues fell off due to the recession that followed the financial crisis of 2008. Countries with big sovereign debts saw their already large annual deficits balloon and had to borrow heavily to stay afloat.

But the recession made lenders take a hard look at the financial positions of the countries whose bonds they were buying. Recognizing their weakness, lenders either stopped buying their bonds or demanded higher interest rates than the borrowing countries could afford. By early 2009, the high-debt countries were essentially shut out of the bond market, cutting off their ability to use deficit financing.

At this point, it's important to understand that Eurozone countries give up an important economic tool when they agree to use a common currency. That tool is control over their own currency and money supply. Economists call it monetary policy, but it boils down to an ability to print money to service the national debt. Without that, all the country has to fight the crisis is fiscal policy, which means cutting spending and raising taxes. That's called **austerity** and isn't guaranteed to work, because it may backfire by slowing commerce, which may deepen the recession.

Austerity means fewer government benefits and higher taxes.

So a Eurozone country in the position we're describing has two choices. It can either exit the zone and resume using its own currency, or it can ask for help from other Eurozone countries or the European Central Bank (ECB). Such help is called a **bailout.**

A **bailout** is outside help to get a country (or a company) out of financial trouble.

But there's another important facet to the problem: IT'S CONTAGIOUS!

Banks and Contagion   Once a nation's financial weakness is recognized, the loss of investor (lender) confidence affects more than the new borrowing we've been discussing. It also extends to the country's existing bonds.

Whenever any bond issuer (borrower) gets in financial trouble there's a possibility that holders of bonds it issued in the past won't receive their interest payments or have their principal returned at maturity. When that happens the resale price (value) of those bonds in financial secondary (page 183) markets is bid down rapidly. That means the value of those bonds must be written down on the books of whomever owns them.

This causes a big problem. Banks tend to invest heavily in government bonds because they're usually very safe. So when government bonds lose value, banks' assets shrink while their liabilities remain unchanged. But banks must maintain certain ratios of assets to liabilities, or they're deemed to have failed. That means a drop in sovereign bond values can bring banks to the brink of failure, which makes them stop lending. And without bank credit, commerce slows and recessions deepen.

On top of that, modern financial institutions are interconnected, meaning one bank failure can lead to other bank failures, sometimes in other countries. Recall the credit default swap (CDS) we discussed in the context of the U.S. financial crisis of 2008 (pages 201–202). A bank that loses money on a defaulted bond may be able to transfer all or some of that loss to another institution, which may be in another country. In that way, it's possible for the failure of certain investments (sovereign bonds) to spread failure across the entire Eurozone. The process is called **(financial) contagion.**

Contagion refers to a country's financial crisis spreading to other countries through the banking system.

Actions to Combat the Crisis
The troubled countries are Greece, Ireland, Italy, Portugal, and Spain. The first to be recognized as a major danger was Greece, which in 2009 revealed that its sovereign debt was much larger than anyone had thought. Previously, its debt had been hidden in a series of opaque financial instruments said to be designed by Wall Street investment bankers. In order to survive, the Greek economy needed a bailout—assistance from other countries in the Eurozone or the European Central Bank (ECB).

The rest of the Eurozone was worried about Greece's financial problems because of contagion and a fear that Greece would exit the Eurozone. Leaders of the large, healthy economies of the zone, mainly Germany and France, were concerned that any country's exit would make the rest of the world lose confidence in the euro. This could lead to its weakening and make people reluctant to invest in European businesses and securities, a negative effect that could last for years.

These concerns made the rest of the zone willing to put money at risk to bail out Greece so it could stay in the zone. However, bailouts were conditioned on Greece's cutting government spending. The idea was that Greece could only return to financial health if it got its spending in line with its income. The term *austerity* was applied to the program, and it did not make the Greek population happy. Nevertheless, several packages were agreed to.

The European Union (the Eurozone plus ten other countries that don't use the euro) and the International Monetary Fund (IMF) paid a total of $320 billion to bail out Greece in 2010 and 2011. Then in March 2012, holders of Greek debt agreed to a restructuring that reduced its burden by roughly half. In December of 2011, the European Central Bank (ECB) made $639 billion in loans available at very low rates to banks that were troubled because of the crisis. Further, a fund called the European Financial Stability Facility was set up to provide emergency lending.

Tensions in the Eurozone   In spite of all this, Greece remains in trouble and is having difficulty living up to the austerity agreement. As of late summer 2012, it looks like more bailouts will be necessary to prevent its exit.

Although most of the attention has fallen on Greece so far, it's not the only country that's in financial trouble. Italy, Spain, Ireland, and Portugal are in similar although not as dire straits. Ireland and Portugal also got some bailout money in 2010 and 2011 respectively. The big concern with respect to the other countries is that while Greece is a small enough economy to at least in theory be saved by bailouts, Italy and Spain are much too big to be rescued by such devices.

While all this has been going on, people in the healthy economies, mainly Germany and France, are getting tired of pouring their tax money into what many perceive as a lost cause. At the same time, the Greeks resent the austerity program they feel is being forced on them.

Many observers have expressed the opinion that the bailout activity was a waste of time and money because it does nothing but postpone Greece's inevitable exit from the Eurozone. Indeed, some financial experts maintain that there's as much as a 75% chance that *at least* one country will exit the zone in the next few years.

It's interesting to notice that the crisis has dragged on so long that financial markets seem to have gotten used to it. A *Wall Street Journal* article in the summer of 2012 observed that market reaction to announcements about the progress of efforts to help Greece, while dramatic at first, have lately been ho-hum.[14]

CONCEPT CONNECTIONS

EXAMPLE 18-1   Exchange Rates, *page 760*

Changing Exchange Rates and Exchange Rate Risk, *page 762*

EXAMPLE 18-2   Cross Rates, *page 761*

EXAMPLE 18-3   Translation Gains and Losses, *page 774*

QUESTIONS

1. Describe the ways in which international business has changed during the last 50 years. Include the concept of an MNC and the different types of foreign investment.

2. After World War II, the United States was the world's dominant economic power. We're still the largest economy, but the rest of the world has caught up significantly. In some areas, we've lost the lead. The production of consumer electronic equipment, for example, is largely done in the Far East. Is this trend good or bad for Americans? Explain.

---

14. Matt Phillips and Jonathan Cheng, "Traders True Out Noise from Europe," *The Wall Street Journal* (July 16, 2012) C1, C2.

3. When you want to buy something from another country, you have to find a seller who's willing to take dollars, but that isn't too hard because the U.S. dollar is widely accepted. Comment on this statement.

4. Exchange transactions between two currencies, neither of which is the U.S. dollar, have to be made by changing one currency into dollars and then changing the dollars into the other currency. This procedure is necessary because the exchange tables are all set up to convert between other currencies and U.S. dollars, the world's leading currency. Are these statements true or false? Why? If false, how does the conversion work?

5. What generates the supply of and the demand for foreign exchange? Why do the supply and demand curves have the shape they do? What makes the supply and demand curves and hence the exchange rate move around?

6. Why might the government be interested in influencing exchange rates from time to time? How would it go about moving the exchange rate?

7. Describe the difference between a floating and a fixed exchange rate system.

8. What is a trade deficit, and why does it hurt us to consistently run a deficit with another country?

9. How and why is the U.S. dollar unique among the world's currencies?

10. A British importer has to pay for U.S. goods, but the exchange rate is temporarily very unfavorable from the British perspective. Describe the Eurodollar market and tell how it might help the importer.

11. Broadly define and describe globalization and its implications.

12. China refuses to allow its currency, the yuan, to float on international currency exchanges. Why is that a problem for the United States?

BUSINESS ANALYSIS

1. You're the treasurer of Warm Wear Inc., which imports wool sweaters from around the world. Kreploc, a company in the country of Slobodia, has a product your marketing department would like to carry and doesn't require payment until 90 days after delivery. Unfortunately, the Slobodian blivit tends to vary in value by as much as 30% over periods as short as three months. This makes you reluctant to do business with Kreploc because of exchange rate risk. The marketing department can't understand why you have any concerns at all. Prepare a brief explanation, including an illustration, of why you're concerned.

2. You're the CFO of the Overseas Sprocket Company, which imports a great deal of product from Europe and the Far East and is continually faced with exchange rate exposure on unfilled contracts. Harry Byrite, the head of purchasing, has a plan to avoid exchange rate losses. He suggests that the firm borrow enough money from the bank to buy a six-month supply of foreign exchange that would be kept in a safety deposit box until used. "We'd never have another unexpected exchange rate loss again," says Harry. Prepare a polite response to Harry's idea. Explain why you do or don't like it, and suggest an alternative if you feel one is appropriate.

3. You're the CFO of the Kraknee Roller Skate Company, which sells roller skates worldwide and also builds and operates roller rinks. Some time ago Archie Speedo, the head of international marketing, proposed selling skates in Russia. Everyone thought he was crazy, but the idea turned out to be very successful. Archie lined up a talented Russian importer, who managed to sell more skates than anyone imagined possible. Now Archie has proposed a new Russian venture. He wants to open and operate a roller rink in Moscow. He says that since the breakup of the Soviet Union, Russians are interested in Western pastimes, and a roller rink in the capital city would make a fortune. Based on his earlier success in Russia, the rest of the executive team is in favor of the idea. You, however, have some concerns. Write a memo explaining how the roller rink proposal differs from exporting skates to Russia, and what problem is likely even if the venture is as commercially successful as the skates. What other risk is involved? Assume the Russian ruble is not convertible.

4. Your friend James is an exchange student from an underdeveloped country. He comes from a privileged family that's influential in the government, but the bulk of the nation's population is very poor despite the fact that the people are frugal and hardworking. James is an idealistic young man who intends to return home after his education and spend his life working to improve the economic condition of his country and its people. You met him for lunch yesterday and noticed

that he was unusually excited. He told you he's taking a theoretical economics course and has been studying Ricardo's Theory of Comparative Advantage, which he now feels is the answer to his people's problems. He intends to return home a staunch advocate of free trade and attempt to get his government to open the

nation's borders to investment by any multinational companies that are interested in doing offshore production there. Write a short paragraph for James discussing globalization and explaining why his government should be cautious as it enters the world of international business.

PROBLEMS

Exchange Rates: Concept Connection Example 18-1 (page 760)

Use the exchange rates in Table 18-1 on page 760 for Problems 1 and 2:

1. A U.S. importer owes vendors the following sums:
   a. 140,560 Canadian dollars
   b. 392,000 Australian dollars
   c. 1,362,000 Mexican pesos
   d. 680,540 British (U.K.) pounds
   e. 14,673 euros

   State each debt in U.S. dollars.

2. A Japanese importer owes a U.S. exporter $450,520.
   a. What is her bill in yen if she pays immediately?
   b. What would the bill be if the importer wanted to lock in an exchange rate today but pay in three months? The dollar is expected to strengthen by 2% against the yen in that time.

3. Go to a currency exchange site on the Internet and look up today's exchange rates for the currencies in Problem 1. Resolve the problem using today's rates. Analyze how the rates have changed since August 16, 2012.

4. The following direct quote exchange rates are found on the spot market today:
   a. euro: $.9347
   b. Israeli shekel: $.2586
   c. British (U.K.) pound: $1.6544
   d. Japanese yen: $.009423

   Calculate the price of a U.S. dollar in terms of each currency, the indirect quote.

5. Bob and Chris received a grant through their University to travel to Germany to do research. The grant awarded them $2,000 for room and board during their stay. It was paid to them in U.S. dollars on May 31 at which time the dollar was worth €.77980. They spent the money in Germany during July when the dollar was worth €.78597.
   a. How many euros were they awarded in May?
   b. Did the change in the euro work to their advantage or disadvantage and by how much?

Changing Exchange Rates and Exchange Rate Risk (page 762)

6. Steve Harris, CFO of Alston Concrete Products, is currently evaluating the purchase of an innovative machine that tests the strength of concrete. The machine is sold only in England and Alston has a price quote at £52,500 from the manufacturer that's good for 60 days. Steve has read that the British pound is expected to strengthen against the dollar by 15% during the next two months. Currently the pound is worth $1.88 U.S. dollars. If Steve believes the currency forecast is accurate, should Alston buy the machine now or wait until just before the price quote expires? How much difference might the decision make in dollars?

7. The Cline family made a trip to Europe in 2012. They paid the following amounts in local currency for hotel, entertainment, and transportation:

England	£ 855
France	€1,462
Germany	€2,753
Denmark	kr6,280

How much did the trip cost in U.S. dollars once they got to Europe? Use the exchange rates in Table 18-1.

8. Suppose a car manufactured in Japan in the mid-1980s, when there were 250 yen to the dollar, cost 2 million yen to produce and was marked up 25% for sale in the United States. Assume the car's cost in yen and markup are the same today, but the exchange rate is 100 yen to the dollar.

   a. What did the car sell for in dollars in the United States in the mid-1980s?

   b. What does it sell for now?

9. The Greenbay Motor Company ordered six German-built engines at €15,000 each when the direct exchange rate was $1.2500 per euro and elected not to cover the obligation with a forward contract. When the bill was due three months later, the rate was $1.1500. Greenbay's marginal tax rate is 40%.

   a. How much was the exchange rate gain or loss on the deal?

   b. What kind of exchange rate gain or loss was it?

   c. What was the tax impact?

Cross Rates: Concept Connection Example 18-2 (page 761)

10. Hampshire Motors Ltd., a British manufacturing company, wants to buy a production machine that isn't available in England. Comparable products are made by an American company and a French firm. The Americans have quoted Hampshire a price of $175,000, while the French want €192,000. How much is each price in British pounds? Calculate a cross rate to state the French quote in pounds. Use the exchange rates in Table 18-1.

Translation Gains and Losses: Concept Connection Example 18-3 (page 774)

11. The Latimore Company invested $8.5 million in a new plant in Italy when the exchange rate was 1.1500 euros to the dollar. At the end of the year, the rate was 1.2000 euros to the dollar. (Indirect quotes.)

   a. Did Latimore make or lose money on the exchange rate movement? If so, how much?

   b. What kind of exchange rate gain or loss was it?

   c. What was the tax impact?

12. Hanover Inc. spent £11.5 million building a factory in England several years ago when the British pound cost $1.5500. The plant operation was set up as a British subsidiary to manufacture Hanover's product for sale and distribution in the United Kingdom and Europe. Hanover closed its consolidated books for the 2012 *fiscal* year on September 16, 2012. (Many companies keep their books on fiscal years that don't coincide with calendar years.) Hanover is subject to a 40% tax rate in the United States and a 45% rate in the United Kingdom.

   a. How much did Hanover make or lose on the value of its English factory due to exchange rate movements in the years since it was built? Use the exchange rates in Table 18-1.

   b. Explain the tax impact of the gain or loss?

   c. Where does the gain or loss show up in Hanover's financial statements? Where doesn't it show up in 2012 or in previous years?

APPENDICES

Appendix B can be found on the text Web site. Go to **www.cengagebrain.com** *and search for this book by its name.*

Appendix A

FINANCIAL TABLES

TABLE A-1	$FVF_{k,n} = (1 + n)^n$												

| | | | | | | **INTEREST RATES** | | | | | | | |
Periods	0.5%	0.67%	0.75%	1%	1.5%	2%	2.5%	3%	3.5%	4%	4.5%	5%	6%	7%
1	1.0050	1.0067	1.0075	1.0100	1.0150	1.0200	1.0250	1.0300	1.0350	1.0400	1.0450	1.0500	1.0600	1.0700
2	1.0100	1.0134	1.0151	1.0201	1.0302	1.0404	1.0506	1.0609	1.0712	1.0816	1.0920	1.1025	1.1236	1.1449
3	1.0151	1.0201	1.0227	1.0303	1.0457	1.0612	1.0769	1.0927	1.1087	1.1249	1.1412	1.1576	1.1910	1.2250
4	1.0202	1.0269	1.0303	1.0406	1.0614	1.0824	1.1038	1.1255	1.1475	1.1699	1.1925	1.2155	1.2625	1.3108
5	1.0253	1.0338	1.0381	1.0510	1.0773	1.1041	1.1314	1.1593	1.1877	1.2167	1.2462	1.2763	1.3382	1.4026
6	1.0304	1.0407	1.0459	1.0615	1.0934	1.1262	1.1597	1.1941	1.2293	1.2653	1.3023	1.3401	1.4185	1.5007
7	1.0355	1.0476	1.0537	1.0721	1.1098	1.1487	1.1887	1.2299	1.2723	1.3159	1.3609	1.4071	1.5036	1.6058
8	1.0407	1.0546	1.0616	1.0829	1.1265	1.1717	1.2184	1.2668	1.3168	1.3686	1.4221	1.4775	1.5938	1.7182
9	1.0459	1.0616	1.0696	1.0937	1.1434	1.1951	1.2489	1.3048	1.3629	1.4233	1.4861	1.5513	1.6895	1.8385
10	1.0511	1.0687	1.0776	1.1046	1.1605	1.2190	1.2801	1.3439	1.4106	1.4802	1.5530	1.6289	1.7908	1.9672
11	1.0564	1.0758	1.0857	1.1157	1.1779	1.2434	1.3121	1.3842	1.4600	1.5395	1.6229	1.7103	1.8983	2.1049
12	1.0617	1.0830	1.0938	1.1268	1.1956	1.2682	1.3449	1.4258	1.5111	1.6010	1.6959	1.7959	2.0122	2.2522
13	1.0670	1.0902	1.1020	1.1381	1.2136	1.2936	1.3785	1.4685	1.5640	1.6651	1.7722	1.8856	2.1329	2.4098
14	1.0723	1.0975	1.1103	1.1495	1.2318	1.3195	1.4130	1.5126	1.6187	1.7317	1.8519	1.9799	2.2609	2.5785
15	1.0777	1.1048	1.1186	1.1610	1.2502	1.3459	1.4483	1.5580	1.6753	1.8009	1.9353	2.0789	2.3966	2.7590
16	1.0831	1.1122	1.1270	1.1726	1.2690	1.3728	1.4845	1.6047	1.7340	1.8730	2.0224	2.1829	2.5404	2.9522
17	1.0885	1.1196	1.1354	1.1843	1.2880	1.4002	1.5216	1.6528	1.7947	1.9479	2.1134	2.2920	2.6928	3.1588
18	1.0939	1.1270	1.1440	1.1961	1.3073	1.4282	1.5597	1.7024	1.8575	2.0258	2.2085	2.4066	2.8543	3.3799
19	1.0994	1.1346	1.1525	1.2081	1.3270	1.4568	1.5987	1.7535	1.9225	2.1068	2.3079	2.5270	3.0256	3.6165
20	1.1049	1.1421	1.1612	1.2202	1.3469	1.4859	1.6386	1.8061	1.9898	2.1911	2.4117	2.6533	3.2071	3.8697
21	1.1104	1.1497	1.1699	1.2324	1.3671	1.5157	1.6796	1.8603	2.0594	2.2788	2.5202	2.7860	3.3996	4.1406
22	1.1160	1.1574	1.1787	1.2447	1.3876	1.5460	1.7216	1.9161	2.1315	2.3699	2.6337	2.9253	3.6035	4.4304
23	1.1216	1.1651	1.1875	1.2572	1.4084	1.5769	1.7646	1.9736	2.2061	2.4647	2.7522	3.0715	3.8197	4.7405
24	1.1272	1.1729	1.1964	1.2697	1.4295	1.6084	1.8087	2.0328	2.2833	2.5633	2.8760	3.2251	4.0489	5.0724
25	1.1328	1.1807	1.2054	1.2824	1.4509	1.6406	1.8539	2.0938	2.3632	2.6658	3.0054	3.3864	4.2919	5.4274
26	1.1385	1.1886	1.2144	1.2953	1.4727	1.6734	1.9003	2.1566	2.4460	2.7725	3.1407	3.5557	4.5494	5.8074
27	1.1442	1.1965	1.2235	1.3082	1.4948	1.7069	1.9478	2.2213	2.5316	2.8834	3.2820	3.7335	4.8223	6.2139
28	1.1499	1.2045	1.2327	1.3213	1.5172	1.7410	1.9965	2.2879	2.6202	2.9987	3.4297	3.9201	5.1117	6.6488
29	1.1556	1.2125	1.2420	1.3345	1.5400	1.7758	2.0464	2.3566	2.7119	3.1187	3.5840	4.1161	5.4184	7.1143
30	1.1614	1.2206	1.2513	1.3478	1.5631	1.8114	2.0976	2.4273	2.8068	3.2434	3.7453	4.3219	5.7435	7.6123
32	1.1730	1.2369	1.2701	1.3749	1.6103	1.8845	2.2038	2.5751	3.0067	3.5081	4.0900	4.7649	6.4534	8.7153
34	1.1848	1.2535	1.2892	1.4026	1.6590	1.9607	2.3153	2.7319	3.2209	3.7943	4.4664	5.2533	7.2510	9.9781
36	1.1967	1.2702	1.3086	1.4308	1.7091	2.0399	2.4325	2.8983	3.4503	4.1039	4.8774	5.7918	8.1473	11.4239
38	1.2087	1.2872	1.3283	1.4595	1.7608	2.1223	2.5557	3.0748	3.6960	4.4388	5.3262	6.3855	9.1543	13.0793
40	1.2208	1.3045	1.3483	1.4889	1.8140	2.2080	2.6851	3.2620	3.9593	4.8010	5.8164	7.0400	10.2857	14.9745
48	1.2705	1.3757	1.4314	1.6122	2.0435	2.5871	3.2715	4.1323	5.2136	6.5705	8.2715	10.4013	16.3939	25.7289
50	1.2832	1.3941	1.4530	1.6446	2.1052	2.6916	3.4371	4.3839	5.5849	7.1067	9.0326	11.4674	18.4202	29.4570
60	1.3489	1.4898	1.5657	1.8167	2.4432	3.2810	4.3998	5.8916	7.8781	10.5196	14.0274	18.6792	32.9877	57.9464
120	1.8194	2.2196	2.4514	3.3004	5.9693	10.7652	19.3581	34.7110	62.0643	110.663	196.768	348.912	1088.19	3357.79
180	2.4541	3.3069	3.8380	5.9958	14.5844	35.3208	85.1718	204.503	488.948	1164.13	2760.15	6517.39	35896.8	*
240	3.3102	4.9268	6.0092	10.8926	35.6328	115.889	374.738	1204.85	3851.98	12246.2	38717.7	*	*	*
300	4.4650	7.3402	9.4084	19.7885	87.0588	380.235	1648.77	7098.51	30346.2	*	*	*	*	*
360	6.0226	10.9357	14.7306	35.9496	212.704	1247.56	7254.23	41821.6	*	*	*	*	*	*

© Cengage Learning

TABLE A-1 Continued

Periods	8%	9%	10%	11%	12%	13%	14%	15%	16%	18%	20%	24%	30%	36%
1	1.0800	1.0900	1.1000	1.1100	1.1200	1.1300	1.1400	1.1500	1.1600	1.1800	1.2000	1.2400	1.3000	1.3600
2	1.1664	1.1881	1.2100	1.2321	1.2544	1.2769	1.2996	1.3225	1.3456	1.3924	1.4400	1.5376	1.6900	1.8496
3	1.2597	1.2950	1.3310	1.3676	1.4049	1.4429	1.4815	1.5209	1.5609	1.6430	1.7280	1.9066	2.1970	2.5155
4	1.3605	1.4116	1.4641	1.5181	1.5735	1.6305	1.6890	1.7490	1.8106	1.9388	2.0736	2.3642	2.8561	3.4210
5	1.4693	1.5386	1.6105	1.6851	1.7623	1.8424	1.9254	2.0114	2.1003	2.2878	2.4883	2.9316	3.7129	4.6526
6	1.5869	1.6771	1.7716	1.8704	1.9738	2.0820	2.1950	2.3131	2.4364	2.6996	2.9860	3.6352	4.8268	6.3275
7	1.7138	1.8280	1.9487	2.0762	2.2107	2.3526	2.5023	2.6600	2.8262	3.1855	3.5832	4.5077	6.2749	8.6054
8	1.8509	1.9926	2.1436	2.3045	2.4760	2.6584	2.8526	3.0590	3.2784	3.7589	4.2998	5.5895	8.1573	11.7034
9	1.9990	2.1719	2.3579	2.5580	2.7731	3.0040	3.2519	3.5179	3.8030	4.4355	5.1598	6.9310	10.6045	15.9166
10	2.1589	2.3674	2.5937	2.8394	3.1058	3.3946	3.7072	4.0456	4.4114	5.2338	6.1917	8.5944	13.7858	21.6466
11	2.3316	2.5804	2.8531	3.1518	3.4785	3.8359	4.2262	4.6524	5.1173	6.1759	7.4301	10.6571	17.9216	29.4393
12	2.5182	2.8127	3.1384	3.4985	3.8960	4.3345	4.8179	5.3503	5.9360	7.2876	8.9161	13.2148	23.2981	40.0375
13	2.7196	3.0658	3.4523	3.8833	4.3635	4.8980	5.4924	6.1528	6.8858	8.5994	10.6993	16.3863	30.2875	54.4510
14	2.9372	3.3417	3.7975	4.3104	4.8871	5.5348	6.2613	7.0757	7.9875	10.1472	12.8392	20.3191	39.3738	74.0534
15	3.1722	3.6425	4.1772	4.7846	5.4736	6.2543	7.1379	8.1371	9.2655	11.9737	15.4070	25.1956	51.1859	100.713
16	3.4259	3.9703	4.5950	5.3109	6.1304	7.0673	8.1372	9.3576	10.7480	14.1290	18.4884	31.2426	66.5417	136.969
17	3.7000	4.3276	5.0545	5.8951	6.8660	7.9861	9.2765	10.7613	12.4677	16.6722	22.1861	38.7408	86.5042	186.278
18	3.9960	4.7171	5.5599	6.5436	7.6900	9.0243	10.5752	12.3755	14.4625	19.6733	26.6233	48.0386	112.455	253.338
19	4.3157	5.1417	6.1159	7.2633	8.6128	10.1974	12.0557	14.2318	16.7765	23.2144	31.9480	59.5679	146.192	344.540
20	4.6610	5.6044	6.7275	8.0623	9.6463	11.5231	13.7435	16.3665	19.4608	27.3930	38.3376	73.8641	190.050	468.574
21	5.0338	6.1088	7.4002	8.9492	10.8038	13.0211	15.6676	18.8215	22.5745	32.3238	46.0051	91.5915	247.065	637.261
22	5.4365	6.6586	8.1403	9.9336	12.1003	14.7138	17.8610	21.6447	26.1864	38.1421	55.2061	113.574	321.184	866.674
23	5.8715	7.2579	8.9543	11.0263	13.5523	16.6266	20.3616	24.8915	30.3762	45.0076	66.2474	140.831	417.539	1178.68
24	6.3412	7.9111	9.8497	12.2392	15.1786	18.7881	23.2122	28.6252	35.2364	53.1090	79.4968	174.631	542.801	1603.00
25	6.8485	8.6231	10.8347	13.5855	17.0001	21.2305	26.4619	32.9190	40.8742	62.6686	95.3962	216.542	705.641	2180.08
26	7.3964	9.3992	11.9182	15.0799	19.0401	23.9905	30.1666	37.8568	47.4141	73.9490	114.475	268.512	917.333	2964.91
27	7.9881	10.2451	13.1100	16.7386	21.3249	27.1093	34.3899	43.5353	55.0004	87.2598	137.371	332.955	1192.53	4032.28
28	8.6271	11.1671	14.4210	18.5799	23.8839	30.6335	39.2045	50.0656	63.8004	102.967	164.845	412.864	1550.29	5483.90
29	9.3173	12.1722	15.8631	20.6237	26.7499	34.6158	44.6931	57.5755	74.0085	121.501	197.814	511.952	2015.38	7458.10
30	10.0627	13.2677	17.4494	22.8923	29.9599	39.1159	50.9502	66.2118	85.8499	143.371	237.376	634.820	2620.00	10143.0
32	11.7371	15.7633	21.1138	28.2056	37.5817	49.9471	66.2148	87.5651	115.520	199.629	341.822	976.099	4427.79	18760.5
34	13.6901	18.7284	25.5477	34.7521	47.1425	63.7774	86.0528	115.805	155.443	277.964	492.224	1500.85	7482.97	34699.5
36	15.9682	22.2512	30.9127	42.8181	59.1356	81.4374	111.834	153.152	209.164	387.037	708.802	2307.71	12646.2	64180.1
38	18.6253	26.4367	37.4043	52.7562	74.1797	103.987	145.340	202.543	281.452	538.910	1020.67	3548.33	21372.1	*
40	21.7245	31.4094	45.2593	65.0009	93.0510	132.782	188.884	267.864	378.721	750.378	1469.77	5455.91	36118.9	*
48	40.2106	62.5852	97.0172	149.797	230.391	352.992	538.807	819.401	1241.61	2820.57	6319.75	30495.9	*	*
50	46.9016	74.3575	117.391	184.565	289.002	450.736	700.233	1083.66	1670.70	3927.36	9100.44	46890.4	*	*
60	101.257	176.031	304.482	524.057	897.597	1530.05	2595.92	4384.00	7370.20	20555.1	56347.5	*	*	*
120	10253.0	30987.0	92709.1	*	*	*	*	*	*	*	*	*	*	*
180	*	*	*	*	*	*	*	*	*	*	*	*	*	*
240	*	*	*	*	*	*	*	*	*	*	*	*	*	*
300	*	*	*	*	*	*	*	*	*	*	*	*	*	*
360	*	*	*	*	*	*	*	*	*	*	*	*	*	*

$^*FVF_{k,n} \geq 100,000$

TABLE A-2 $PVF_{k,n} = (1 + n)^{-n}$

Periods	0.5%	0.67%	0.75%	1%	1.5%	2%	2.5%	3%	3.5%	4%	4.5%	5%	6%	7%
1	0.9950	0.9934	0.9926	0.9901	0.9852	0.9804	0.9756	0.9709	0.9662	0.9615	0.9569	0.9524	0.9434	0.9346
2	0.9901	0.9868	0.9852	0.9803	0.9707	0.9612	0.9518	0.9426	0.9335	0.9246	0.9157	0.9070	0.8900	0.8734
3	0.9851	0.9803	0.9778	0.9706	0.9563	0.9423	0.9286	0.9151	0.9019	0.8890	0.8763	0.8638	0.8396	0.8163
4	0.9802	0.9738	0.9706	0.9610	0.9422	0.9238	0.9060	0.8885	0.8714	0.8548	0.8386	0.8227	0.7921	0.7629
5	0.9754	0.9673	0.9633	0.9515	0.9283	0.9057	0.8839	0.8626	0.8420	0.8219	0.8025	0.7835	0.7473	0.7130
6	0.9705	0.9609	0.9562	0.9420	0.9145	0.8880	0.8623	0.8375	0.8135	0.7903	0.7679	0.7462	0.7050	0.6663
7	0.9657	0.9546	0.9490	0.9327	0.9010	0.8706	0.8413	0.8131	0.7860	0.7599	0.7348	0.7107	0.6651	0.6227
8	0.9609	0.9482	0.9420	0.9235	0.8877	0.8535	0.8207	0.7894	0.7594	0.7307	0.7032	0.6768	0.6274	0.5820
9	0.9561	0.9420	0.9350	0.9143	0.8746	0.8368	0.8007	0.7664	0.7337	0.7026	0.6729	0.6446	0.5919	0.5439
10	0.9513	0.9357	0.9280	0.9053	0.8617	0.8203	0.7812	0.7441	0.7089	0.6756	0.6439	0.6139	0.5584	0.5083
11	0.9466	0.9295	0.9211	0.8963	0.8489	0.8043	0.7621	0.7224	0.6849	0.6496	0.6162	0.5847	0.5268	0.4751
12	0.9419	0.9234	0.9142	0.8874	0.8364	0.7885	0.7436	0.7014	0.6618	0.6246	0.5897	0.5568	0.4970	0.4440
13	0.9372	0.9172	0.9074	0.8787	0.8240	0.7730	0.7254	0.6810	0.6394	0.6006	0.5643	0.5303	0.4688	0.4150
14	0.9326	0.9112	0.9007	0.8700	0.8118	0.7579	0.7077	0.6611	0.6178	0.5775	0.5400	0.5051	0.4423	0.3878
15	0.9279	0.9051	0.8940	0.8613	0.7999	0.7430	0.6905	0.6419	0.5969	0.5553	0.5167	0.4810	0.4173	0.3624
16	0.9233	0.8991	0.8873	0.8528	0.7880	0.7284	0.6736	0.6232	0.5767	0.5339	0.4945	0.4581	0.3936	0.3387
17	0.9187	0.8932	0.8807	0.8444	0.7764	0.7142	0.6572	0.6050	0.5572	0.5134	0.4732	0.4363	0.3714	0.3166
18	0.9141	0.8873	0.8742	0.8360	0.7649	0.7002	0.6412	0.5874	0.5384	0.4936	0.4528	0.4155	0.3503	0.2959
19	0.9096	0.8814	0.8676	0.8277	0.7536	0.6864	0.6255	0.5703	0.5202	0.4746	0.4333	0.3957	0.3305	0.2765
20	0.9051	0.8756	0.8612	0.8195	0.7425	0.6730	0.6103	0.5537	0.5026	0.4564	0.4146	0.3769	0.3118	0.2584
21	0.9006	0.8698	0.8548	0.8114	0.7315	0.6598	0.5954	0.5375	0.4856	0.4388	0.3968	0.3589	0.2942	0.2415
22	0.8961	0.8640	0.8484	0.8034	0.7207	0.6468	0.5809	0.5219	0.4692	0.4220	0.3797	0.3418	0.2775	0.2257
23	0.8916	0.8583	0.8421	0.7954	0.7100	0.6342	0.5667	0.5067	0.4533	0.4057	0.3634	0.3256	0.2618	0.2109
24	0.8872	0.8526	0.8358	0.7876	0.6995	0.6217	0.5529	0.4919	0.4380	0.3901	0.3477	0.3101	0.2470	0.1971
25	0.8828	0.8470	0.8296	0.7798	0.6892	0.6095	0.5394	0.4776	0.4231	0.3751	0.3327	0.2953	0.2330	0.1842
26	0.8784	0.8413	0.8234	0.7720	0.6790	0.5976	0.5262	0.4637	0.4088	0.3607	0.3184	0.2812	0.2198	0.1722
27	0.8740	0.8358	0.8173	0.7644	0.6690	0.5859	0.5134	0.4502	0.3950	0.3468	0.3047	0.2678	0.2074	0.1609
28	0.8697	0.8302	0.8112	0.7568	0.6591	0.5744	0.5009	0.4371	0.3817	0.3335	0.2916	0.2551	0.1956	0.1504
29	0.8653	0.8247	0.8052	0.7493	0.6494	0.5631	0.4887	0.4243	0.3687	0.3207	0.2790	0.2429	0.1846	0.1406
30	0.8610	0.8193	0.7992	0.7419	0.6398	0.5521	0.4767	0.4120	0.3563	0.3083	0.2670	0.2314	0.1741	0.1314
32	0.8525	0.8085	0.7873	0.7273	0.6210	0.5306	0.4538	0.3883	0.3326	0.2851	0.2445	0.2099	0.1550	0.1147
34	0.8440	0.7978	0.7757	0.7130	0.6028	0.5100	0.4319	0.3660	0.3105	0.2636	0.2239	0.1904	0.1379	0.1002
36	0.8356	0.7873	0.7641	0.6989	0.5851	0.4902	0.4111	0.3450	0.2898	0.2437	0.2050	0.1727	0.1227	0.0875
38	0.8274	0.7769	0.7528	0.6852	0.5679	0.4712	0.3913	0.3252	0.2706	0.2253	0.1878	0.1566	0.1092	0.0765
40	0.8191	0.7666	0.7416	0.6717	0.5513	0.4529	0.3724	0.3066	0.2526	0.2083	0.1719	0.1420	0.0972	0.0668
48	0.7871	0.7269	0.6986	0.6203	0.4894	0.3865	0.3057	0.2420	0.1918	0.1522	0.1209	0.0961	0.0610	0.0389
50	0.7793	0.7173	0.6883	0.6080	0.4750	0.3715	0.2909	0.2281	0.1791	0.1407	0.1107	0.0872	0.0543	0.0339
60	0.7414	0.6712	0.6387	0.5504	0.4093	0.3048	0.2273	0.1697	0.1269	0.0951	0.0713	0.0535	0.0303	0.0173
120	0.5496	0.4505	0.4079	0.3030	0.1675	0.0929	0.0517	0.0288	0.0161	0.0090	0.0051	0.0029	0.0009	0.0003
180	0.4075	0.3024	0.2605	0.1668	0.0686	0.0283	0.0117	0.0049	0.0020	0.0009	0.0004	0.0002	0.0000	0.0000
240	0.3021	0.2030	0.1664	0.0918	0.0281	0.0086	0.0027	0.0008	0.0003	0.0001	0.0000	0.0000	0.0000	0.0000
300	0.2240	0.1362	0.1063	0.0505	0.0115	0.0026	0.0006	0.0001	0.0000	0.0000	0.0000	0.0000	0.0000	0.0000
360	0.1660	0.0914	0.0679	0.0278	0.0047	0.0008	0.0001	0.0000	0.0000	0.0000	0.0000	0.0000	0.0000	0.0000

TABLE A-2 *Continued*

Periods	8%	9%	10%	11%	12%	13%	14%	15%	16%	18%	20%	24%	30%	36%
1	0.9259	0.9174	0.9091	0.9009	0.8929	0.8850	0.8772	0.8696	0.8621	0.8475	0.8333	0.8065	0.7692	0.7353
2	0.8573	0.8417	0.8264	0.8116	0.7972	0.7831	0.7695	0.7561	0.7432	0.7182	0.6944	0.6504	0.5917	0.5407
3	0.7938	0.7722	0.7513	0.7312	0.7118	0.6931	0.6750	0.6575	0.6407	0.6086	0.5787	0.5245	0.4552	0.3975
4	0.7350	0.7084	0.6830	0.6587	0.6355	0.6133	0.5921	0.5718	0.5523	0.5158	0.4823	0.4230	0.3501	0.2923
5	0.6806	0.6499	0.6209	0.5935	0.5674	0.5428	0.5194	0.4972	0.4761	0.4371	0.4019	0.3411	0.2693	0.2149
6	0.6302	0.5963	0.5645	0.5346	0.5066	0.4803	0.4556	0.4323	0.4104	0.3704	0.3349	0.2751	0.2072	0.1580
7	0.5835	0.5470	0.5132	0.4817	0.4523	0.4251	0.3996	0.3759	0.3538	0.3139	0.2791	0.2218	0.1594	0.1162
8	0.5403	0.5019	0.4665	0.4339	0.4039	0.3762	0.3506	0.3269	0.3050	0.2660	0.2326	0.1789	0.1226	0.0854
9	0.5002	0.4604	0.4241	0.3909	0.3606	0.3329	0.3075	0.2843	0.2630	0.2255	0.1938	0.1443	0.0943	0.0628
10	0.4632	0.4224	0.3855	0.3522	0.3220	0.2946	0.2697	0.2472	0.2267	0.1911	0.1615	0.1164	0.0725	0.0462
11	0.4289	0.3875	0.3505	0.3173	0.2875	0.2607	0.2366	0.2149	0.1954	0.1619	0.1346	0.0938	0.0558	0.0340
12	0.3971	0.3555	0.3186	0.2858	0.2567	0.2307	0.2076	0.1869	0.1685	0.1372	0.1122	0.0757	0.0429	0.0250
13	0.3677	0.3262	0.2897	0.2575	0.2292	0.2042	0.1821	0.1625	0.1452	0.1163	0.0935	0.0610	0.0330	0.0184
14	0.3405	0.2992	0.2633	0.2320	0.2046	0.1807	0.1597	0.1413	0.1252	0.0985	0.0779	0.0492	0.0254	0.0135
15	0.3152	0.2745	0.2394	0.2090	0.1827	0.1599	0.1401	0.1229	0.1079	0.0835	0.0649	0.0397	0.0195	0.0099
16	0.2919	0.2519	0.2176	0.1883	0.1631	0.1415	0.1229	0.1069	0.0930	0.0708	0.0541	0.0320	0.0150	0.0073
17	0.2703	0.2311	0.1978	0.1696	0.1456	0.1252	0.1078	0.0929	0.0802	0.0600	0.0451	0.0258	0.0116	0.0054
18	0.2502	0.2120	0.1799	0.1528	0.1300	0.1108	0.0946	0.0808	0.0691	0.0508	0.0376	0.0208	0.0089	0.0039
19	0.2317	0.1945	0.1635	0.1377	0.1161	0.0981	0.0829	0.0703	0.0596	0.0431	0.0313	0.0168	0.0068	0.0029
20	0.2145	0.1784	0.1486	0.1240	0.1037	0.0868	0.0728	0.0611	0.0514	0.0365	0.0261	0.0135	0.0053	0.0021
21	0.1987	0.1637	0.1351	0.1117	0.0926	0.0768	0.0638	0.0531	0.0443	0.0309	0.0217	0.0109	0.0040	0.0016
22	0.1839	0.1502	0.1228	0.1007	0.0826	0.0680	0.0560	0.0462	0.0382	0.0262	0.0181	0.0088	0.0031	0.0012
23	0.1703	0.1378	0.1117	0.0907	0.0738	0.0601	0.0491	0.0402	0.0329	0.0222	0.0151	0.0071	0.0024	0.0008
24	0.1577	0.1264	0.1015	0.0817	0.0659	0.0532	0.0431	0.0349	0.0284	0.0188	0.0126	0.0057	0.0018	0.0006
25	0.1460	0.1160	0.0923	0.0736	0.0588	0.0471	0.0378	0.0304	0.0245	0.0160	0.0105	0.0046	0.0014	0.0005
26	0.1352	0.1064	0.0839	0.0663	0.0525	0.0417	0.0331	0.0264	0.0211	0.0135	0.0087	0.0037	0.0011	0.0003
27	0.1252	0.0976	0.0763	0.0597	0.0469	0.0369	0.0291	0.0230	0.0182	0.0115	0.0073	0.0030	0.0008	0.0002
28	0.1159	0.0895	0.0693	0.0538	0.0419	0.0326	0.0255	0.0200	0.0157	0.0097	0.0061	0.0024	0.0006	0.0002
29	0.1073	0.0822	0.0630	0.0485	0.0374	0.0289	0.0224	0.0174	0.0135	0.0082	0.0051	0.0020	0.0005	0.0001
30	0.0994	0.0754	0.0573	0.0437	0.0334	0.0256	0.0196	0.0151	0.0116	0.0070	0.0042	0.0016	0.0004	0.0001
32	0.0852	0.0634	0.0474	0.0355	0.0266	0.0200	0.0151	0.0114	0.0087	0.0050	0.0029	0.0010	0.0002	0.0001
34	0.0730	0.0534	0.0391	0.0288	0.0212	0.0157	0.0116	0.0086	0.0064	0.0036	0.0020	0.0007	0.0001	0.0000
36	0.0626	0.0449	0.0323	0.0234	0.0169	0.0123	0.0089	0.0065	0.0048	0.0026	0.0014	0.0004	0.0001	0.0000
38	0.0537	0.0378	0.0267	0.0190	0.0135	0.0096	0.0069	0.0049	0.0036	0.0019	0.0010	0.0003	0.0000	0.0000
40	0.0460	0.0318	0.0221	0.0154	0.0107	0.0075	0.0053	0.0037	0.0026	0.0013	0.0007	0.0002	0.0000	0.0000
48	0.0249	0.0160	0.0103	0.0067	0.0043	0.0028	0.0019	0.0012	0.0008	0.0004	0.0002	0.0000	0.0000	0.0000
50	0.0213	0.0134	0.0085	0.0054	0.0035	0.0022	0.0014	0.0009	0.0006	0.0003	0.0001	0.0000	0.0000	0.0000
60	0.0099	0.0057	0.0033	0.0019	0.0011	0.0007	0.0004	0.0002	0.0001	0.0000	0.0000	0.0000	0.0000	0.0000
120	0.0001	0.0000	0.0000	0.0000	0.0000	0.0000	0.0000	0.0000	0.0000	0.0000	0.0000	0.0000	0.0000	0.0000
180	0.0000	0.0000	0.0000	0.0000	0.0000	0.0000	0.0000	0.0000	0.0000	0.0000	0.0000	0.0000	0.0000	0.0000
240	0.0000	0.0000	0.0000	0.0000	0.0000	0.0000	0.0000	0.0000	0.0000	0.0000	0.0000	0.0000	0.0000	0.0000
300	0.0000	0.0000	0.0000	0.0000	0.0000	0.0000	0.0000	0.0000	0.0000	0.0000	0.0000	0.0000	0.0000	0.0000
360	0.0000	0.0000	0.0000	0.0000	0.0000	0.0000	0.0000	0.0000	0.0000	0.0000	0.0000	0.0000	0.0000	0.0000

TABLE A-3 $\quad FVFA_{k,n} = \sum_{i=1}^{n}(1 + k)^{n-i}$

INTEREST RATES

Periods	0.5%	0.67%	0.75%	1%	1.5%	2%	2.5%	3%	3.5%	4%	4.5%	5%	6%	7%
1	1.0000	1.0000	1.0000	1.0000	1.0000	1.0000	1.0000	1.0000	1.0000	1.0000	1.0000	1.0000	1.0000	1.0000
2	2.0050	2.0067	2.0075	2.0100	2.0150	2.0200	2.0250	2.0300	2.0350	2.0400	2.0450	2.0500	2.0600	2.0700
3	3.0150	3.0200	3.0226	3.0301	3.0452	3.0604	3.0756	3.0909	3.1062	3.1216	3.1370	3.1525	3.1836	3.2149
4	4.0301	4.0402	4.0452	4.0604	4.0909	4.1216	4.1525	4.1836	4.2149	4.2465	4.2782	4.3101	4.3746	4.4399
5	5.0503	5.0671	5.0756	5.1010	5.1523	5.2040	5.2563	5.3091	5.3625	5.4163	5.4707	5.5256	5.6371	5.7507
6	6.0755	6.1009	6.1136	6.1520	6.2296	6.3081	6.3877	6.4684	6.5502	6.6330	6.7169	6.8019	6.9753	7.1533
7	7.1059	7.1416	7.1595	7.2135	7.3230	7.4343	7.5474	7.6625	7.7794	7.8983	8.0192	8.1420	8.3938	8.6540
8	8.1414	8.1892	8.2132	8.2857	8.4328	8.5830	8.7361	8.8923	9.0517	9.2142	9.3800	9.5491	9.8975	10.2598
9	9.1821	9.2483	9.2748	9.3685	9.5593	9.7546	9.9545	10.1591	10.3685	10.5828	10.8021	11.0266	11.4913	11.9780
10	10.2280	10.3054	10.3443	10.4622	10.7027	10.9497	11.2034	11.4639	11.7314	12.0061	12.2882	12.5779	13.1808	13.8164
11	11.2792	11.3741	11.4219	11.5668	11.8633	12.1687	12.4835	12.8078	13.1420	13.4864	13.8412	14.2068	14.9716	15.7836
12	12.3356	12.4499	12.5076	12.6825	13.0412	13.4121	13.7956	14.1920	14.6020	15.0258	15.4640	15.9171	16.8699	17.8885
13	13.3972	13.5329	13.6014	13.8093	14.2368	14.6803	15.1404	15.6178	16.1130	16.6268	17.1599	17.7130	18.8821	20.1406
14	14.4642	14.6231	14.7034	14.9474	15.4504	15.9739	16.5190	17.0863	17.6770	18.2919	18.9321	19.5986	21.0151	22.5505
15	15.5365	15.7206	15.8137	16.0969	16.6821	17.2934	17.9319	18.5989	19.2957	20.0236	20.7841	21.5786	23.2760	25.1290
16	16.6142	16.8254	16.9323	17.2579	17.9324	18.6393	19.3802	20.1569	20.9710	21.8245	22.7193	23.6575	25.6725	27.8881
17	17.6973	17.9376	18.0593	18.4304	19.2014	20.0121	20.8647	21.7616	22.7050	23.6975	24.7417	25.8404	28.2129	30.8402
18	18.7858	19.0572	19.1947	19.6147	20.4894	21.4123	22.3863	23.4144	24.4997	25.6454	26.8551	28.1324	30.9057	33.9990
19	19.8797	20.1842	20.3387	20.8109	21.7967	22.8406	23.9460	25.1169	26.3572	27.6712	29.0636	30.5390	33.7600	37.3790
20	20.9791	21.3188	21.4912	22.0190	23.1237	24.2974	25.5447	26.8704	28.2797	29.7781	31.3714	33.0660	36.7856	40.9955
21	22.0840	22.4609	22.6524	23.2392	24.4705	25.7833	27.1833	28.6765	30.2695	31.9692	33.7831	35.7193	39.9927	44.8652
22	23.1944	23.6107	23.8223	24.4716	25.8376	27.2990	28.8629	30.5368	32.3289	34.2480	36.3034	38.5052	43.3923	49.0057
23	24.3104	24.7681	25.0010	25.7163	27.2251	28.8450	30.5844	32.4529	34.4604	36.6179	38.9370	41.4305	46.9958	53.4361
24	25.4320	25.9332	26.1885	26.9735	28.6335	30.4219	32.3490	34.4265	36.6665	39.0826	41.6892	44.5020	50.8156	58.1767
25	26.5591	27.1061	27.3849	28.2432	30.0630	32.0303	34.1578	36.4593	38.9499	41.6459	44.5652	47.7271	54.8645	63.2490
26	27.6919	28.2868	28.5903	29.5256	31.5140	33.6709	36.0117	38.5530	41.3131	44.3117	47.5706	51.1135	59.1564	68.6765
27	28.8304	29.4754	29.8047	30.8209	32.9867	35.3443	37.9120	40.7096	43.7591	47.0842	50.7113	54.6691	63.7058	74.4838
28	29.9745	30.6719	31.0282	32.1291	34.4815	37.0512	39.8598	42.9309	46.2906	49.9676	53.9933	58.4026	68.5281	80.6977
29	31.1244	31.8763	32.2609	33.4504	35.9987	38.7922	41.8563	45.2189	48.9108	52.9663	57.4230	62.3227	73.6398	87.3465
30	32.2800	33.0889	33.5029	34.7849	37.5387	40.5681	43.9027	47.5754	51.6227	56.0849	61.0071	66.4388	79.0582	94.4608
32	34.6086	35.5382	36.0148	37.4941	40.6883	44.2270	48.1503	52.5028	57.3345	62.7015	68.6662	75.2988	90.8898	110.218
34	36.9606	38.0203	38.5646	40.2577	43.9331	48.0338	52.6129	57.7302	63.4532	69.8579	77.0303	85.0670	104.184	128.259
36	39.3361	40.5356	41.1527	43.0769	47.2760	51.9944	57.3014	63.2759	70.0076	77.5983	86.1640	95.8363	119.121	148.913
38	41.7354	43.0845	43.7798	45.9527	50.7199	56.1149	62.2273	69.1594	77.0289	85.9703	96.1382	107.710	135.904	172.561
40	44.1588	45.6675	46.4465	48.8864	54.2679	60.4020	67.4026	75.4013	84.5503	95.0255	107.030	120.800	154.762	199.635
48	54.0978	56.3499	57.5207	61.2226	69.5652	79.3535	90.8596	104.408	120.388	139.263	161.588	188.025	256.565	353.270
50	56.6452	59.1104	60.3943	64.4632	73.6828	84.5794	97.4843	112.797	130.998	152.667	178.503	209.348	290.336	406.529
60	69.7700	73.4769	75.4241	81.6697	96.2147	114.052	135.992	163.053	196.517	237.991	289.498	353.584	533.128	813.520
120	163.879	182.946	193.514	230.039	331.288	488.258	734.326	1123.70	1744.69	2741.56	4350.40	6958.24	18119.8	47954.1
180	290.819	346.038	378.406	499.580	905.625	1716.04	3366.87	6783.45	13941.4	29078.2	61314.4	*	*	*
240	462.041	589.020	667.887	989.255	2308.85	5744.44	14949.5	40128.4	*	*	*	*	*	*
300	692.994	951.026	1121.12	1878.85	5737.25	18961.7	65910.7	*	*	*	*	*	*	*
360	1004.52	1490.36	1830.74	3494.96	14113.6	62328.1	*	*	*	*	*	*	*	*

TABLE A-3 *Continued*

Periods	8%	9%	10%	11%	12%	13%	14%	15%	16%	18%	20%	24%	30%	36%
1	1.0000	1.0000	1.0000	1.0000	1.0000	1.0000	1.0000	1.0000	1.0000	1.0000	1.0000	1.0000	1.0000	1.0000
2	2.0800	2.0900	2.1000	2.1100	2.1200	2.1300	2.1400	2.1500	2.1600	2.1800	2.2000	2.2400	2.3000	2.3600
3	3.2464	3.2781	3.3100	3.3421	3.3744	3.4069	3.4396	3.4725	3.5056	3.5724	3.6400	3.7776	3.9900	4.2096
4	4.5061	4.5731	4.6410	4.7097	4.7793	4.8498	4.9211	4.9934	5.0665	5.2154	5.3680	5.6842	6.1870	6.7251
5	5.8666	5.9847	6.1051	6.2278	6.3528	6.4803	6.6101	6.7424	6.8771	7.1542	7.4416	8.0484	9.0431	10.1461
6	7.3359	7.5233	7.7156	7.9129	8.1152	8.3227	8.5355	8.7537	8.9775	9.4420	9.9299	10.9801	12.7560	14.7987
7	8.9228	9.2004	9.4872	9.7833	10.0890	10.4047	10.7305	11.0668	11.4139	12.1415	12.9159	14.6153	17.5828	21.1262
8	10.6366	11.0285	11.4359	11.8594	12.2997	12.7573	13.2328	13.7268	14.2401	15.3270	16.4991	19.1229	23.8577	29.7316
9	12.4876	13.0210	13.5795	14.1640	14.7757	15.4157	16.0853	16.7858	17.5185	19.0859	20.7989	24.7125	32.0150	41.4350
10	14.4866	15.1929	15.9374	16.7220	17.5487	18.4197	19.3373	20.3037	21.3215	23.5213	25.9587	31.6434	42.6195	57.3516
11	16.6455	17.5603	18.5312	19.5614	20.6546	21.8143	23.0445	24.3493	25.7329	28.7551	32.1504	40.2379	56.4053	78.9982
12	18.9771	20.1407	21.3843	22.7132	24.1331	25.6502	27.2707	29.0017	30.8502	34.9311	39.5805	50.8950	74.3270	108.437
13	21.4953	22.9534	24.5227	26.2116	28.0291	29.9847	32.0887	34.3519	36.7862	42.2187	48.4966	64.1097	97.6250	148.475
14	24.2149	26.0192	27.9750	30.0949	32.3926	34.8827	37.5811	40.5047	43.6720	50.8180	59.1959	80.4961	127.913	202.926
15	27.1521	29.3609	31.7725	34.4054	37.2797	40.4175	43.8424	47.5804	51.6595	60.9653	72.0351	100.815	167.286	276.979
16	30.3243	33.0034	35.9497	39.1899	42.7533	46.6717	50.9804	55.7175	60.9250	72.9390	87.4421	126.011	218.472	377.692
17	33.7502	36.9737	40.5447	44.5008	48.8837	53.7391	59.1176	65.0751	71.6730	87.0680	105.931	157.253	285.014	514.661
18	37.4502	41.3013	45.5992	50.3959	55.7497	61.7251	68.3941	75.8364	84.1407	103.740	128.117	195.994	371.518	700.939
19	41.4463	46.0185	51.1591	56.9395	63.4397	70.7494	78.9692	88.2118	98.6032	123.414	154.740	244.033	483.973	954.277
20	45.7620	51.1601	57.2750	64.2028	72.0524	80.9468	91.0249	102.444	115.380	146.628	186.688	303.601	630.165	1298.82
21	50.4229	56.7645	64.0025	72.2651	81.6987	92.4699	104.768	118.810	134.841	174.021	225.026	377.465	820.215	1767.39
22	55.4568	62.8733	71.4027	81.2143	92.5026	105.491	120.436	137.632	157.415	206.345	271.031	469.056	1067.28	2404.65
23	60.8933	69.5319	79.5430	91.1479	104.603	120.205	138.297	159.276	183.601	244.487	326.237	582.630	1388.46	3271.33
24	66.7648	76.7898	88.4973	102.174	118.155	136.831	158.659	184.168	213.978	289.494	392.484	723.461	1806.00	4450.00
25	73.1059	84.7009	98.3471	114.413	133.334	155.620	181.871	212.793	249.214	342.603	471.981	898.092	2348.80	6053.00
26	79.9544	93.3240	109.182	127.999	150.334	176.850	208.333	245.712	290.088	405.272	567.377	1114.63	3054.44	8233.09
27	87.3508	102.723	121.100	143.079	169.374	200.841	238.499	283.569	337.502	479.221	681.853	1383.15	3971.78	11198.0
28	95.3388	112.968	134.210	159.817	190.699	227.950	272.889	327.104	392.503	566.481	819.223	1716.10	5164.31	15230.3
29	103.966	124.135	148.631	178.397	214.583	258.583	312.094	377.170	456.303	669.447	984.068	2128.96	6714.60	20714.2
30	113.283	136.308	164.494	199.021	241.333	293.199	356.787	434.745	530.312	790.948	1181.88	2640.92	8729.99	28172.3
32	134.214	164.037	201.138	247.324	304.848	376.516	465.820	577.100	715.747	1103.50	1704.11	4062.91	14756.0	52109.8
34	158.627	196.982	245.477	306.837	384.521	482.903	607.520	765.365	965.270	1538.69	2456.12	6249.38	24939.9	96384.6
36	187.102	236.125	299.127	380.164	484.463	618.749	791.673	1014.35	1301.03	2144.65	3539.01	9611.28	42150.7	*
38	220.316	282.630	364.043	470.511	609.831	792.211	1031.00	1343.62	1752.82	2988.39	5098.37	14780.5	71237.0	*
40	259.057	337.882	442.593	581.826	767.091	1013.70	1342.03	1779.09	2360.76	4163.21	7343.86	22728.8	*	*
48	490.132	684.280	960.172	1352.70	1911.59	2707.63	3841.48	5456.00	7753.78	15664.3	31593.7	*	*	*
50	573.770	815.084	1163.91	1668.77	2400.02	3459.51	4994.52	7217.72	10435.6	21813.1	45497.2	*	*	*
60	1253.21	1944.79	3034.82	4755.07	7471.64	11761.9	18535.1	29220.0	46057.5	*	*	*	*	*
120	*	*	*	*	*	*	*	*	*	*	*	*	*	*
180	*	*	*	*	*	*	*	*	*	*	*	*	*	*
240	*	*	*	*	*	*	*	*	*	*	*	*	*	*
300	*	*	*	*	*	*	*	*	*	*	*	*	*	*
360	*	*	*	*	*	*	*	*	*	*	*	*	*	*

*$FVFA_{k,n} \geq 100,000$

TABLE A-4	$PVFA_{k,n} = \sum_{i=1}^{n}(1 + k)^{-i}$

INTEREST RATES

Periods	0.5%	0.67%	0.75%	1%	1.5%	2%	2.5%	3%	3.5%	4%	4.5%	5%	6%	7%
1	0.9950	0.9934	0.9926	0.9901	0.9852	0.9804	0.9756	0.9709	0.9662	0.9615	0.9569	0.9524	0.9434	0.9346
2	1.9851	1.9802	1.9777	1.9704	1.9559	1.9416	1.9274	1.9135	1.8997	1.8861	1.8727	1.8594	1.8334	1.8080
3	2.9702	2.9604	2.9556	2.9410	2.9122	2.8839	2.8560	2.8286	2.8016	2.7751	2.7490	2.7232	2.6730	2.6243
4	3.9505	3.9342	3.9261	3.9020	3.8544	3.8077	3.7620	3.7171	3.6731	3.6299	3.5875	3.5460	3.4651	3.3872
5	4.9259	4.9015	4.8894	4.8534	4.7826	4.7135	4.6458	4.5797	4.5151	4.4518	4.3900	4.3295	4.2124	4.1002
6	5.8964	5.8625	5.8456	5.7955	5.6972	5.6014	5.5081	5.4172	5.3286	5.2421	5.1579	5.0757	4.9173	4.7665
7	6.8621	6.8170	6.7946	6.7282	6.5982	6.4720	6.3494	6.2303	6.1145	6.0021	5.8927	5.7864	5.5824	5.3893
8	7.8230	7.7652	7.7366	7.6517	7.4859	7.3255	7.1701	7.0197	6.8740	6.7327	6.5959	6.4632	6.2098	5.9713
9	8.7791	8.7072	8.6716	8.5660	8.3605	8.1622	7.9709	7.7861	7.6077	7.4353	7.2688	7.1078	6.8017	6.5152
10	9.7304	9.6429	9.5996	9.4713	9.2222	8.9826	8.7521	8.5302	8.3166	8.1109	7.9127	7.7217	7.3601	7.0236
11	10.6770	10.5724	10.5207	10.3676	10.0711	9.7868	9.5142	9.2526	9.0016	8.7605	8.5289	8.3064	7.8869	7.4987
12	11.6189	11.4958	11.4349	11.2551	10.9075	10.5753	10.2578	9.9540	9.6633	9.3851	9.1186	8.8633	8.3838	7.9427
13	12.5562	12.4130	12.3423	12.1337	11.7315	11.3484	10.9832	10.6350	10.3027	9.9856	9.6829	9.3936	8.8527	8.3577
14	13.4887	13.3242	13.2430	13.0037	12.5434	12.1062	11.6909	11.2961	10.9205	10.5631	10.2228	9.8986	9.2950	8.7455
15	14.4166	14.2293	14.1370	13.8651	13.3432	12.8493	12.3814	11.9379	11.5174	11.1184	10.7395	10.3797	9.7122	9.1079
16	15.3399	15.1285	15.0243	14.7179	14.1313	13.5777	13.0550	12.5611	12.0941	11.6523	11.2340	10.8378	10.1059	9.4466
17	16.2586	16.0217	15.9050	15.5623	14.9076	14.2919	13.7122	13.1661	12.6513	12.1657	11.7072	11.2741	10.4773	9.7632
18	17.1728	16.9089	16.7792	16.3983	15.6726	14.9920	14.3534	13.7535	13.1897	12.6593	12.1600	11.6896	10.8276	10.0591
19	18.0824	17.7903	17.6468	17.2260	16.4262	15.6785	14.9789	14.3238	13.7098	13.1339	12.5933	12.0853	11.1581	10.3356
20	18.9874	18.6659	18.5080	18.0456	17.1686	16.3514	15.5892	14.8775	14.2124	13.5903	13.0079	12.4622	11.4699	10.5940
21	19.8880	19.5357	19.3628	18.8570	17.9001	17.0112	16.1845	15.4150	14.6980	14.0292	13.4047	12.8212	11.7641	10.8355
22	20.7841	20.3997	20.2112	19.6604	18.6208	17.6580	16.7654	15.9369	15.1671	14.4511	13.7844	13.1630	12.0416	11.0612
23	21.6757	21.2579	21.0533	20.4558	19.3309	18.2922	17.3321	16.4436	15.6204	14.8568	14.1478	13.4886	12.3034	11.2722
24	22.5629	22.1105	21.8891	21.2434	20.0304	18.9139	17.8850	16.9355	16.0584	15.2470	14.4955	13.7986	12.5504	11.4693
25	23.4456	22.9575	22.7188	22.0232	20.7196	19.5235	18.4244	17.4131	16.4815	15.6221	14.8282	14.0939	12.7834	11.6536
26	24.3240	23.7988	23.5422	22.7952	21.3986	20.1210	18.9506	17.8768	16.8904	15.9828	15.1466	14.3752	13.0032	11.8258
27	25.1980	24.6346	24.3595	23.5596	22.0676	20.7069	19.4640	18.3270	17.2854	16.3296	15.4513	14.6430	13.2105	11.9867
28	26.0677	25.4648	25.1707	24.3164	22.7267	21.2813	19.9649	18.7641	17.6670	16.6631	15.7429	14.8981	13.4062	12.1371
29	26.9330	26.2896	25.9759	25.0658	23.3761	21.8444	20.4535	19.1885	18.0358	16.9837	16.0219	15.1411	13.5907	12.2777
30	27.7941	27.1088	26.7751	25.8077	24.0158	22.3965	20.9303	19.6004	18.3920	17.2920	16.2889	15.3725	13.7648	12.4090
32	29.5033	28.7312	28.3557	27.2696	25.2671	23.4683	21.8492	20.3888	19.0689	17.8736	16.7889	15.8027	14.0840	12.6466
34	31.1955	30.3320	29.9128	28.7027	26.4817	24.4986	22.7238	21.1318	19.7007	18.4112	17.2468	16.1929	14.3681	12.8540
36	32.8710	31.9118	31.4468	30.1075	27.6607	25.4888	23.5563	21.8323	20.2905	18.9083	17.6660	16.5469	14.6210	13.0352
38	34.5299	33.4707	32.9581	31.4847	28.8051	26.4406	24.3486	22.4925	20.8411	19.3679	18.0500	16.8679	14.8460	13.1935
40	36.1722	35.0090	34.4469	32.8347	29.9158	27.3555	25.1028	23.1148	21.3551	19.7928	18.4016	17.1591	15.0463	13.3317
48	42.5803	40.9619	40.1848	37.9740	34.0426	30.6731	27.7732	25.2667	23.0912	21.1951	19.5356	18.0772	15.6500	13.7305
50	44.1428	42.4013	41.5664	39.1961	34.9997	31.4236	28.3623	25.7298	23.4556	21.4822	19.7620	18.2559	15.7619	13.8007
60	51.7256	49.3184	48.1734	44.9550	39.3803	34.7609	30.9087	27.6756	24.9447	22.6235	20.6380	18.9293	16.1614	14.0392
120	90.0735	82.4215	78.9417	69.7005	55.4985	45.3554	37.9337	32.3730	28.1111	24.7741	22.1093	19.9427	16.6514	14.2815
180	118.504	104.641	98.5934	83.3217	62.0956	48.5844	39.5304	33.1703	28.5130	24.9785	22.2142	19.9969	16.6662	14.2856
240	139.581	119.554	111.145	90.8194	64.7957	49.5686	39.8933	33.3057	28.5640	24.9980	22.2216	19.9998	16.6667	14.2857
300	155.207	129.565	119.162	94.9466	65.9009	49.8685	39.9757	33.3286	28.5705	24.9998	22.2222	20.0000	16.6667	14.2857
360	166.792	136.283	124.282	97.2183	66.3532	49.9599	39.9945	33.3325	28.5713	25.0000	22.2222	20.0000	16.6667	14.2857

TABLE A-4 *Continued*

Periods	8%	9%	10%	11%	12%	13%	14%	15%	16%	18%	20%	24%	30%	36%
1	0.9259	0.9174	0.9091	0.9009	0.8929	0.8850	0.8772	0.8696	0.8621	0.8475	0.8333	0.8065	0.7692	0.7353
2	1.7833	1.7591	1.7355	1.7125	1.6901	1.6681	1.6467	1.6257	1.6052	1.5656	1.5278	1.4568	1.3609	1.2760
3	2.5771	2.5313	2.4869	2.4437	2.4018	2.3612	2.3216	2.2832	2.2459	2.1743	2.1065	1.9813	1.8161	1.6735
4	3.3121	3.2397	3.1699	3.1024	3.0373	2.9745	2.9137	2.8550	2.7982	2.6901	2.5887	2.4043	2.1662	1.9658
5	3.9927	3.8897	3.7908	3.6959	3.6048	3.5172	3.4331	3.3522	3.2743	3.1272	2.9906	2.7454	2.4356	2.1807
6	4.6229	4.4859	4.3553	4.2305	4.1114	3.9975	3.8887	3.7845	3.6847	3.4976	3.3255	3.0205	2.6427	2.3388
7	5.2064	5.0330	4.8684	4.7122	4.5638	4.4226	4.2883	4.1604	4.0386	3.8115	3.6046	3.2423	2.8021	2.4550
8	5.7466	5.5348	5.3349	5.1461	4.9676	4.7988	4.6389	4.4873	4.3436	4.0776	3.8372	3.4212	2.9247	2.5404
9	6.2469	5.9952	5.7590	5.5370	5.3282	5.1317	4.9464	4.7716	4.6065	4.3030	4.0310	3.5655	3.0190	2.6033
10	6.7101	6.4177	6.1446	5.8892	5.6502	5.4262	5.2161	5.0188	4.8332	4.4941	4.1925	3.6819	3.0915	2.6495
11	7.1390	6.8052	6.4951	6.2065	5.9377	5.6869	5.4527	5.2337	5.0286	4.6560	4.3271	3.7757	3.1473	2.6834
12	7.5361	7.1607	6.8137	6.4924	6.1944	5.9176	5.6603	5.4206	5.1971	4.7932	4.4392	3.8514	3.1903	2.7084
13	7.9038	7.4869	7.1034	6.7499	6.4235	6.1218	5.8424	5.5831	5.3423	4.9095	4.5327	3.9124	3.2233	2.7268
14	8.2442	7.7862	7.3667	6.9819	6.6282	6.3025	6.0021	5.7245	5.4675	5.0081	4.6106	3.9616	3.2487	2.7403
15	8.5595	8.0607	7.6061	7.1909	6.8109	6.4624	6.1422	5.8474	5.5755	5.0916	4.6755	4.0013	3.2682	2.7502
16	8.8514	8.3126	7.8237	7.3792	6.9740	6.6039	6.2651	5.9542	5.6685	5.1624	4.7296	4.0333	3.2832	2.7575
17	9.1216	8.5436	8.0216	7.5488	7.1196	6.7291	6.3729	6.0472	5.7487	5.2223	4.7746	4.0591	3.2948	2.7629
18	9.3719	8.7556	8.2014	7.7016	7.2497	6.8399	6.4674	6.1280	5.8178	5.2732	4.8122	4.0799	3.3037	2.7668
19	9.6036	8.9501	8.3649	7.8393	7.3658	6.9380	6.5504	6.1982	5.8775	5.3162	4.8435	4.0967	3.3105	2.7697
20	9.8181	9.1285	8.5136	7.9633	7.4694	7.0248	6.6231	6.2593	5.9288	5.3527	4.8696	4.1103	3.3158	2.7718
21	10.0168	9.2922	8.6487	8.0751	7.5620	7.1016	6.6870	6.3125	5.9731	5.3837	4.8913	4.1212	3.3198	2.7734
22	10.2007	9.4424	8.7715	8.1757	7.6446	7.1695	6.7429	6.3587	6.0113	5.4099	4.9094	4.1300	3.3230	2.7746
23	10.3711	9.5802	8.8832	8.2664	7.7184	7.2297	6.7921	6.3988	6.0442	5.4321	4.9245	4.1371	3.3254	2.7754
24	10.5288	9.7066	8.9847	8.3481	7.7843	7.2829	6.8351	6.4338	6.0726	5.4509	4.9371	4.1428	3.3272	2.7760
25	10.6748	9.8226	9.0770	8.4217	7.8431	7.3300	6.8729	6.4641	6.0971	5.4669	4.9476	4.1474	3.3286	2.7765
26	10.8100	9.9290	9.1609	8.4881	7.8957	7.3717	6.9061	6.4906	6.1182	5.4804	4.9563	4.1511	3.3297	2.7768
27	10.9352	10.0266	9.2372	8.5478	7.9426	7.4086	6.9352	6.5135	6.1364	5.4919	4.9636	4.1542	3.3305	2.7771
28	11.0511	10.1161	9.3066	8.6016	7.9844	7.4412	6.9607	6.5335	6.1520	5.5016	4.9697	4.1566	3.3312	2.7773
29	11.1584	10.1983	9.3696	8.6501	8.0218	7.4701	6.9830	6.5509	6.1656	5.5098	4.9747	4.1585	3.3317	2.7774
30	11.2578	10.2737	9.4269	8.6938	8.0552	7.4957	7.0027	6.5660	6.1772	5.5168	4.9789	4.1601	3.3321	2.7775
32	11.4350	10.4062	9.5264	8.7686	8.1116	7.5383	7.0350	6.5905	6.1959	5.5277	4.9854	4.1624	3.3326	2.7776
34	11.5869	10.5178	9.6086	8.8293	8.1566	7.5717	7.0599	6.6091	6.2098	5.5356	4.9898	4.1639	3.3329	2.7777
36	11.7172	10.6118	9.6765	8.8786	8.1924	7.5979	7.0790	6.6231	6.2201	5.5412	4.9929	4.1649	3.3331	2.7777
38	11.8289	10.6908	9.7327	8.9186	8.2210	7.6183	7.0937	6.6338	6.2278	5.5452	4.9951	4.1655	3.3332	2.7778
40	11.9246	10.7574	9.7791	8.9511	8.2438	7.6344	7.1050	6.6418	6.2335	5.5482	4.9966	4.1659	3.3332	2.7778
48	12.1891	10.9336	9.8969	9.0302	8.2972	7.6705	7.1296	6.6585	6.2450	5.5536	4.9992	4.1665	3.3333	2.7778
50	12.2335	10.9617	9.9148	9.0417	8.3045	7.6752	7.1327	6.6605	6.2463	5.5541	4.9995	4.1666	3.3333	2.7778
60	12.3766	11.0480	9.9672	9.0736	8.3240	7.6873	7.1401	6.6651	6.2492	5.5553	4.9999	4.1667	3.3333	2.7778
120	12.4988	11.1108	9.9999	9.0909	8.3333	7.6923	7.1429	6.6667	6.2500	5.5556	5.0000	4.1667	3.3333	2.7778
180	12.5000	11.1111	10.0000	9.0909	8.3333	7.6923	7.1429	6.6667	6.2500	5.5556	5.0000	4.1667	3.3333	2.7778
240	12.5000	11.1111	10.0000	9.0909	8.3333	7.6923	7.1429	6.6667	6.2500	5.5556	5.0000	4.1667	3.3333	2.7778
300	12.5000	11.1111	10.0000	9.0909	8.3333	7.6923	7.1429	6.6667	6.2500	5.5556	5.0000	4.1667	3.3333	2.7778
360	12.5000	11.1111	10.0000	9.0909	8.3333	7.6923	7.1429	6.6667	6.2500	5.5556	5.0000	4.1667	3.3333	2.7778

Appendix C

FORMULAS

Chapter 3

Ratios

Liquidity Ratios

$$\text{current ratio} = \frac{\text{current assets}}{\text{current liabilities}}$$

$$\text{quick ratio} = \frac{\text{current assets} - \text{inventory}}{\text{current liabilities}}$$

Asset Management Ratios

$$\text{ACP} = \frac{\text{accounts receivable}}{\text{average daily sales}} = \frac{\text{accounts receivable}}{\text{sales}} \times 360$$

$$\text{inventory turnover} = \frac{\text{cost of goods sold}}{\text{inventory}}$$

$$\text{fixed asset turnover} = \frac{\text{sales}}{\text{fixed assets}}$$

$$\text{total asset turnover} = \frac{\text{sales}}{\text{total assets}}$$

Debt Management Ratios

$$\text{debt ratio} = \frac{\text{long-term debt} + \text{current liabilities}}{\text{total assets}}$$

$$\text{debt to equity ratio} = \text{long-term debt} : \text{equity}$$

$$\text{TIE} = \frac{\text{EBIT}}{\text{interest}}$$

$$\text{cash coverage} = \frac{\text{EBIT} + \text{depreciation}}{\text{interest}}$$

$$\text{fixed charge coverage} = \frac{\text{EBIT} + \text{lease payments}}{\text{interest} + \text{lease payments}}$$

$$\text{EBITDA coverage} = \frac{\text{EBITDA} + \text{lease payments}}{\text{interest} + \text{lease payments} + \text{principal repayment}}$$

Profitability Ratios

$$\text{ROS} = \frac{\text{net income}}{\text{sales}}$$

$$\text{ROA} = \frac{\text{net income}}{\text{total assets}}$$

$$\text{ROE} = \frac{\text{net income}}{\text{equity}}$$

Market Value Ratios

$$\text{P/E ratio} = \frac{\text{stock price}}{\text{EPS}}$$

$$\text{market to book value ratio} = \frac{\text{stock price}}{\text{book value per share}}$$

Du Pont Equation

$$\text{ROA} = \text{ROS} \times \text{total asset turnover}$$

Extended Du Pont Equation

$$\text{ROE} = \text{ROS} \times \text{total asset turnover} \times \text{equity multiplier}$$
$$\text{ROE} = \text{ROA} \times \text{equity multiplier}$$

Free Cash Flow (FCF)

Net Operating Profit (NOPAT)

$$\text{NOPAT} = \text{EBIT} - (\text{T})(\text{EBIT}) = \text{EBIT}\,(1 - \text{T})$$

Operating Cash Flow

$$\text{operating cash flow} = \text{NOPAT} + \text{depreciation}$$

Free Cash Flow (FCF)

$$\begin{aligned}
\text{FCF} = {} & \text{operating cash flow} \\
& - \text{increase in gross fixed assets} \\
& \qquad - \text{increase in current accounts}
\end{aligned}$$

Free Cash Flow to Equity (FCFE)

$$\begin{aligned}
\text{FCFE} = {} & \text{operating cash flow} \\
& - \text{increase in gross fixed assets} \\
& \qquad - \text{increase in current accounts} \\
& \qquad\qquad - (1 - \text{T})\text{interest} - \text{principal reduction}
\end{aligned}$$

Chapter 4

External Funding Requirement (EFR)

$$\begin{aligned}
\text{EFR} = {} & g(\text{assets}_{\text{this year}}) \\
& -g(\text{current liabilities}_{\text{this year}}) \\
& -[(1 - d)\text{ROS}][(1 + g)\,\text{sales}_{\text{this year}}]
\end{aligned}$$

Sustainable Growth Rate

$$g_s = \text{ROE}(1 - d)$$
$$g_s = (1 - d)[\text{ROS} - \text{total asset turnover} \times \text{equity multiplier}]$$
$$g_s = (1 - d) \times \frac{\text{net income}}{\text{sales}} \times \frac{\text{sales}}{\text{assets}} \times \frac{\text{assets}}{\text{equity}}$$

Chapter 5

The Interest Rate Model

$$k = k_{PR} + INFL + DR + LR + MR$$

where k_{PR} = pure interest rate
INFL = inflation adjustment (the average expected inflation rate over the life of the loan)
DR = default risk premium
LR = liquidity risk premium
MR = maturity risk premium

Chapter 6

Time Value of Money

Amounts

$$FV = PV\left[FVF_{k,n}\right]$$
$$PV = FV\left[PVF_{k,n}\right]$$

Annuities

$$FVA = PMT\left[FVFA_{k,n}\right]$$
$$PVA = PMT\left[PVFA_{k,n}\right]$$

Annuities Due

$$FVAd = PMT\left[FVFA_{k,n}\right](1 + k)$$
$$PVAd = PMT\left[PVFA_{k,n}\right](1 + k)$$

Perpetuities

$$PV_p = PMT/k$$

Chapter 7

Bond Pricing

$$P_B = PMT\left[PVFA_{k,n}\right] + FV\left[PVF_{k,n}\right]$$

Bond Likely to Be Called

$$P_B(call) = PMT[PVFA_{k,m}] + CP[PVF_{k,m}]$$

m = periods to call   CP = Call Price = FV + Call Premium

Chapter 8—Stock Valuation

Dividend and Capital Gains Yields – one year holding period

$$k = \frac{D_1}{P_0} + \frac{(P_1 - P_0)}{P_0}$$

Valuation Based on Projected Cash Flows — uneven dividends + price

$$P_0 = D_1[PVF_{k,1}] + D_2[PVF_{k,2}] + \cdots + D_n[PVF_{k,n}] + P_n[PVF_{k,n}]$$

Stock Valuation — Gordon Model (Constant Growth Model)

$$P_0 = \frac{D_0(1 + g)}{k - g} = \frac{D_1}{k - g}$$

Preferred Stock Pricing

$$P_P = \frac{D_P}{k}$$

Chapter 9—Risk and Return

The Security Market Line (SML)

$$k_X = k_{RF} + \overbrace{(k_M - k_{RF})\, b_X}^{\text{Stock X's Risk Premium}}$$

Market Risk
Premium

where:
k_X is the required return on stock X

k_{RF} is the risk-free rate

k_M is the return on the market

b_X is stock X's beta coefficient

Chapter 10—Capital Budgeting

Net Present Value (NPV) – irregular cash flows

$$NPV = C_0 + C_1[PVF_{k,1}] + C_2[PVF_{k,2}] + \cdots + C_n[PVF_{k,n}]$$

Internal Rate of Return (IRR) – irregular cash flows iterative solution required

$$0 = C_0 + \frac{C_1}{(1 + IRR)} + \frac{C_2}{(1 + IRR)^2} + \cdots + \frac{C_n}{(1 + IRR)^n}$$

Net Present Value (NPV) – regular cash flows-annuity

$$NPV = C_0 + C[PVFA_{k,n}]$$

Internal Rate of Return (IRR) – regular cash flows-annuity

$$0 = C_0 + C[PVFA_{IRR,n}]$$

Profitability Index (PI) – irregular cash flows

$$PI = \frac{\dfrac{C_1}{(1 + k)} + \dfrac{C_2}{(1 + k)^2} + \cdots + \dfrac{C_n}{(1 + k)^n}}{C_0}$$

Chapter 13—Cost of Capital

Cost of Debt

$$\text{cost of debt} = k_d(1 - T)$$

Cost of Preferred Stock

$$\text{cost of preferred stock} = \frac{D_p}{(1 - f)P_p} = \frac{k_p}{(1 - f)}$$

Cost of Retained Earnings – CAPM approach

$$k_X = k_{RF} + (k_M - k_{RF})b_X$$

Cost of Retained Earnings – Dividend growth approach

$$\text{cost of RE} = k_e = \frac{D_0(1 + g)}{P_0} + g$$

Cost of Retained Earnings – Risk Premium approach

$$k_e = k_d + rp_e$$

Cost of New Common Stock

$$\text{cost of new equity} = k_e = \frac{D_0(1 + g)}{(1 - f)P_0} + g$$

Chapter 14—Capital Structure and Leverage

Performance Measures

$$\text{ROE} = \frac{\text{net income}}{\text{equity}} \qquad \text{EPS} = \frac{\text{net income}}{\text{number of shares}}$$

Return on Capital Employed (ROCE)

$$\text{ROCE} = \frac{\text{EBIT}(1 - T)}{\text{debt + equity}}$$

Degree of Financial Leverage

$$\%\Delta\text{EPS} = \text{DFL} \times \%\Delta\text{EBIT}$$

$$\text{DFL} = \frac{\text{EBIT}}{\text{EBIT} - I}$$

Break Even Analysis-Contribution

$$C_t = P - V$$

Contribution Margin

$$C_M = \frac{P - V}{P}$$

Break Even Volume

$$Q_{B/E} = \frac{F_c}{P - V}$$

Break Even Sales

$$S_{B/E} = \frac{P(F_c)}{P - V}$$

$$S_{B/E} = \frac{F_c}{(P - V)/P} = \frac{F_c}{C_M}$$

Degree of Operating Leverage

$$DOL = \frac{Q(P - V)}{Q(P - V) - F_c}$$

Capital Structure Theory

Value of debt and equity

$$V_d = \frac{I}{k_d} \qquad V_e = \frac{D}{k_e}$$

Value of the firm

$$V_f = \frac{I}{k_d} + \frac{D}{k_e} \qquad V_f = \frac{OI}{k_a}$$

PV of tax shield

$$\text{PV of tax shield} = \frac{TI}{k_d} = \frac{TBk_d}{k_d} = TB$$

Chapter 16—The Management of Working Capital

Economic Order Quantity

$$EOQ = \left[\frac{2FD}{C}\right]^{1/2}$$

A

ABC System—A system of controlling inventory that recognizes the differing cost and importance of various items. *A* parts are expensive and/or important and are controlled carefully. *C* parts are cheap and plentiful, so little effort is expended to monitor them. *B* parts are between *A*s and *C*s.

Accelerated Depreciation—Any method that shifts depreciation forward in an asset's life. Accelerated methods increase early charges and reduce those that come later, keeping total depreciation constant.

Acquisition—A merger in which one company acquires the stock of another. May be friendly or hostile (unfriendly). See *Merger*.

Agency—A relationship between two parties in which one (the principal) employs the other (the agent) in a decision-making capacity.

Agency Problem—In corporations, managers are the agents of stockholders and are often able to take advantage of the relationship by diverting corporate resources to their own use. Excessive pay is the primary example. The general situation is described as the agency problem. Costs associated with controlling the agency problem are *agency costs*.

Agent—A person authorized to act for another (the principal) in a specific matter.

Amortized Debt (Loan)—A debt in which the principal is repaid over the life of the loan rather than in a lump sum at the end.

Annual Percentage Rate (APR)—Generally 12 times the monthly interest rate on a loan with monthly payments. Also the nominal rate of the loan. For example, a 12% loan with monthly payments generally charges 1% per month, which is effectively 12.68% but is usually quoted as 12% by lenders.

Annual Report—A yearly report on a company's performance prepared by management. An annual report includes financial statements and generally contains verbal discussions of the firm's operations and prospects.

Annuity—A finite series of equal payments at equal intervals of time. In an *ordinary annuity*, the payments occur at the ends of the time periods. In an *annuity due*, they occur at the beginnings.

Antitrust Law—A body of legislation aimed at maintaining the competitive nature of the economy. The antitrust laws can prohibit certain mergers on the basis that they reduce competition.

Audit—A process in which an organization's records, usually financial, are examined to ascertain whether they have been correctly kept and truly reflect the organization's activities. In business, accounting records are usually audited by certified public accountants (CPAs).

Audit Committee—A committee of the board of directors of a corporation charged with reviewing the financial statements and records of the company and more recently the firm's relationship with its auditors.

Average Collection Period (ACP)—A financial ratio that measures how long it takes to collect on credit sales. Also called *days sales outstanding* (DSO).

Average Tax Rate—A taxpayer's total tax bill divided by taxable income. A composite of the various bracket rates to which the taxpayer's income is subject.

B

Backorder—An order to replenish an out-of-stock item, usually on an expedited basis.

Balance of Trade—The difference between imports from and exports to another country. If imports are larger a *trade deficit* exists. If exports are larger there is a *trade surplus*.

Bankruptcy—A federal court procedure to protect a failing firm from its creditors until the best resolution to its problems can be found.

Basic EPS—Earnings after tax divided by the number of shares outstanding during the year.

Bearer Bond—An unregistered bond, owned by the "bearer," the person in possession.

Beta—The measure of market risk in portfolio theory. The degree to which a stock's return moves with the market's return.

Bill—A security associated with very short-term debt.

Black–Scholes Option Pricing Model—A pricing model for stock options, developed by financial scholars Fisher Black and Myron Scholes, that gives results similar to those of stock pricing models.

Board of Directors—The governing body of a corporation, elected by common stockholders.

Bond—A security reflecting a relatively long-term debt relationship between the issuer (borrower) and the buyer (lender).

Bond Indenture—An agreement associated with a bond issue generally restricting the behavior of the borrower in ways that enhance the lender's safety.

Bond Rating—A measure of the likelihood of default on payment of interest or principal. Ratings are prepared by *rating agencies.* The best known agencies are Moody's and Standard and Poor's.

Book Value—For a company, the value of equity, equal to total assets minus total liabilities. Book value can be stated in total or per share. For an asset, book value is the net of original cost minus accumulated depreciation, and is generally referred to as *net book value.*

Bottom-Up Planning—Business planning based on inputs from lower-level management. The process tends to understate achievable performance because people set easily achievable goals for themselves.

Breakeven Analysis—A technique for finding the volume at which a firm breaks even financially—that is, earns zero profit.

Broker—See *Stockbroker.*

Brokerage Firm (House)—A company of stockbrokers generally having the right to trade on an exchange.

Budget—A short-term, financially detailed business plan, usually covering about a calendar quarter.

Business Plan—A document projecting a firm's physical and financial performance into the future. Business plans can be short or long range. Long-range plans are "strategic" and tend to be more verbal than financial. Shorter-term plans are described as "operational," and detail the more routine running of the business.

Business Risk—Variation in a company's financial performance caused by changes in business conditions.

Business-Specific Risk—Variation in the return on a stock investment caused by things that affect specific businesses or industries.

C

Call (Option)—The right to purchase a stock at a specified price over a designated period of time. See *Option.* Compare with *Put Option.*

Call Provision (Feature)—A provision in a bond contract that allows the borrowing organization to "call" in the bond and pay it off early. Calls are generally exercised when interest rates have dropped substantially since the bond's issue. An additional payment known as the *call premium* must usually be made to the investor if the call is exercised. Most call features cannot be exercised during an initial *call protected* period.

Capital—Long-term assets or the money used to support long-term assets and projects. Long-term debt and equity on the balance sheet.

Capital Budgeting—Analysis techniques concerned with justifying money spent on long-term assets and projects.

Capital Component—One of three sources of capital: debt, preferred stock, or equity.

Capital Gain (Loss)—The difference between the sale and purchase prices of an asset held over a period of time.

Capital Gains Yield—The capital gain on a stock divided by the price at which it was purchased.

Capitalization of Earnings—One of several methods of valuing a business. The firm is assumed to be worth the present value of a stream of annual payments, each equal to its current earnings, continuing indefinitely into the future.

Capital Lease—See *Financing Lease*.

Capital Market—A financial market in which longer-term (at least one year) debt and equity securities are traded.

Capital Rationing—In capital budgeting, the process of allocating available capital among projects to maximize total NPV.

Capital Restructuring—Changing a firm's capital structure intentionally by buying and selling stocks and bonds simultaneously.

Capital Structure—The mix of the three capital components (debt, preferred stock, and equity) used by a firm. The *optimal capital structure* is the structure at which stock price is maximized, all other things held equal. Also see *Target Capital Structure*.

CAPM—Capital Asset Pricing Model. A statistical model of the investment world aimed at explaining how required returns are determined in financial markets and thereby how stock prices are set. Also see *SML*.

Cash Budgeting—A forecast of cash flows based on expected receipts and disbursements rather than on projections of income statement and balance sheet accounts.

Cash Flows (Statement of)—One of a firm's financial statements. It details the movement of cash in and out of the company. Constructed from the income statement and balance sheet.

Cash Forecast—A projection of future cash flows over a specified planning period.

Certainty Equivalent–A method of incorporating risk into capital budgeting. A decision maker replaces risky cash flows with lower, guaranteed (certain) amounts that would be considered equivalent. The resulting NPV and IRR are lower but theoretically certain. Calculations are done at the risk free rate rather than the cost of capital.

Chapter 11—The chapter of the bankruptcy code dealing with reorganization. Firms in bankruptcy proceedings are commonly said to be "in Chapter 11."

Chartists—Technical analysts. See *Technical Analysis*.

Chief Financial Officer (CFO)—The executive in charge of the financial function.

Clean-Up Requirement— A banking requirement that borrowers pay off all short-term debt for some period each year. Prevents funding long-term projects with short-term debt.

Clientele Effect—The theory that firms attract equity investors at least in part because of their dividend-paying policies. The firm has a "clientele" of stockholders whose need for current or deferred income matches the firm's dividend practices. The implication is that it isn't a good idea to change dividend policies because such a change is bound to displease most stockholders who hold the stock because they like its past policy.

Closing Price (Close)—The price of a security in the last trade of a business day.

Collateral—An asset backing a loan. In the event of a default, the collateral becomes the property of the lender to satisfy the obligation. Also called *security* for the loan.

Collateralized Debt Obligation (CDO)—A debt security the value of which is based on the cash flows produced by a pool of residential mortgages. The collateral is the homes underlying the mortgages in the pool. Generally purchased by institutional investors. CDOs based on mortgage loans made to marginally qualified borrowers (subprime loans) played a key role in the financial crisis of 2008.

Collection Agency—A firm that specializes in collecting debts, especially overdue receivables, for a percentage of the amount collected.

Commercial Paper—Very short-term debt issued by major companies.

Commitment Fee—A fee charged by a bank to a borrower for guaranteeing that loan funds up to some limit will be available over an agreed term. The fee is charged on unborrowed amounts up to the maximum of the guarantee. See *Revolving credit agreement.*

Common Size Statement—A firm's income statement with every line stated as a percentage of revenue. A balance sheet with every line stated as a percentage of total assets. Used to compare companies of different sizes or to identify performance trends in a single company over time.

Common Stock—The security representing ownership of a corporation. Equity.

Compensating Balance—A portion of a loan that banks require borrowers to leave in their checking accounts. Effectively increases the bank's yield. A minimum balance required to compensate banks for their services.

Compensation Committee—A committee of the board of directors of a corporation charged with reviewing and approving the compensation (pay) of senior executives.

Compound Interest—The concept of earning interest on previously earned interest. A sum earning compound interest grows exponentially over time.

Compounding Period—The period of time after which interest is credited to the depositor's account for purposes of computing subsequent interest.

Concentration Banking—Employing one bank to manage the balances in remote accounts. Balances are generally swept into the concentration bank daily.

Congeneric Merger—A merger between companies in related but not competing businesses.

Conglomerate Merger—A merger between companies in unrelated businesses.

Consolidation—A combination of two or more businesses in which the old legal entities dissolve and a new one with a new name is formed to continue into the future.

Contribution (Margin)—In break even analysis, contribution is the difference between price and variable cost per unit that is "contributed" toward profit and fixed costs. The contribution margin is the contribution expressed as a percentage of price.

Controller—The executive in charge of the accounting function in most companies. The controller generally reports to the CFO.

Conversion Price—The stock price at which a convertible bond can be exchanged for stock. See *Conversion Ratio.*

Conversion Ratio—A ratio set at the time convertible bonds are issued that specifies the number of shares that can be exchanged for each bond.

Convertible Bond—A bond that can be converted into a specified number of shares of stock at the owner's discretion.

Convertible Currency—A currency that can be exchanged for other currencies on foreign exchange markets.

Corporate Governance—The practices senior executives and boards of directors use in running corporations. Recently focused on ethics and the financial relationships between executives and the corporations they serve. See *Agency Problem.*

Corporate Restructuring—A broad term describing a number of ways in which companies are reorganized. Includes capital restructure, mergers, and reorganizations in bankruptcy as well as charges in certain methods of doing business.

Cost—Business spending for items closely associated with production. Contrast with expense.

Cost of Capital—The average rate a firm pays its investors for the use of their funds, adjusted for taxes and administrative expenses. Also called the *WACC* for weighted average cost of capital. Distinguish from the costs of individual capital components that are the adjusted rates paid on debt, preferred stock, and common equity. The component costs are (weighted) averaged to get the WACC.

Cost Structure—The mix of fixed and variable cost used by a firm.

Coupon Rate, Coupon Payment—The interest rate paid by a bond on its face value. The dollar amount of the interest payment, which is usually made semiannually.

Covenants (Restrictive)—Contractual agreements associated with loans that limit the activities of borrowing companies. The limitations are designed to reduce the risk that the firm won't be able to pay the loan's interest and principal.

Credit Agency (Bureau)—An organization that maintains records of the bill-paying histories of most companies and assigns *credit ratings* to firms that indicate how well they've paid their bills in the past. The agency's subscribers can receive *credit reports* on companies with which they're considering doing business.

Creditor—Anyone owed money by a business, including lenders, vendors, employees, or the government.

Cumulative Feature of Preferred Stock—A provision to enhance the safety of preferred stock. If preferred dividends are passed, no common dividends can be paid until preferred dividends are caught up cumulatively.

Cumulative Voting—A method of electing boards of directors in which stockholders can cast all of their votes for a single seat. Enables minority interests to get at least some representation on the board.

Current Assets—Assets expected to become cash in less than one year. Current assets are largely cash, receivables, and inventories.

Current Liabilities—Obligations expected to require cash in less than one year, usually payables and accruals.

Current Ratio—Current assets divided by current liabilities. A financial ratio that measures a firm's liquidity, the ability to pay its bills in the short run.

Current Yield—A bond's annual interest payment divided by its market price.

D

Date of Record—When a dividend is declared, it is paid to owners of record on the transfer agent's books as of the date of record.

Debenture—An unsecured bond, i.e., a bond that is not collateralized by any specific assets but depends only on the general creditworthiness of the borrowing company.

Debt Ratio—Debt divided by total assets. A financial ratio measuring the degree to which the firm uses borrowed money.

Debt to Equity Ratio—The relative amounts of debt and equity in a firm's capital structure.

Decision Tree—A time line representation used in planning projects subject to multiple outcomes. Wherever an event has several outcomes, the time line branches into as many paths, each with a probability. The result is a proliferation of possible paths to completion, each representing an outcome, its financial implication, and its probability. Hence, the decision tree specifies a probability distribution for the project's overall financial outcome.

Declaration Date—The date on which a firm's board of directors declares a dividend.

Deductions—Items of expenditure that the tax code allows taxpayers to deduct from income to arrive at taxable income.

Default—In finance, generally the failure of a borrower to pay interest or repay the principal on a loan. Also the failure to meet other requirements contractually placed on the borrower by the loan agreement.

Default Risk—The risk of loss to a lender from the borrower's failure to pay the full amount due including interest and principal.

Defensive Tactics—Actions taken by the management of a company to resist or avoid being acquired.

Depreciation—The accounting entry allocating the cost of a long-lived asset against income over the asset's life. Depreciation is a *noncash charge,* so net income is generally less than true cash flow by at least the amount of depreciation.

Derivative Security—A security the price of which is derived from the price of another security. The most common example is an option to buy or sell stock. The value of the option is related to the price of the underlying stock. See *Option*.

Designated Market Maker—An official in a stock exchange. The market maker is assigned the stocks of specific companies and is responsible for conducting orderly markets in those securities. Formerly called a *specialist*.

Diluted EPS—Assumes all convertible securities are exchanged for stock (exercised) as of the beginning of the year.

Dilution—The reduction in earnings and book value per share that results from the conversion of convertible securities or the exercise of warrants or employee stock options at prices below market. Fully diluted values for EPS and book value per share reflect the hypothetical conversion or exercise of all convertibles, warrants, and options outstanding.

Direct Investment—In international business, building facilities in another country.

Discount—Generally a reduction in price or value. In finance, a reduction in the present value of a future sum due to the action of interest.

Discounted Cash Flow—Calculations involving the present and future values of money under the action of compound interest. Also called the *time value of money*.

Discount Rate—Interest rate.

Diversification—In finance, selecting a portfolio of different (diverse) investments to limit the overall risk borne by the investor.

Divestiture—Getting rid of a business unit. The reverse of an *acquisition*.

Dividend—The payment made by a corporation to an equity investor (stockholder).

Dividend Decision—The decision by management regarding the portion of earnings paid to shareholders as dividends. The alternative to paying a dividend is to retain the money, investing it in the company for future growth.

Dividend Payout Ratio—The ratio of the annual dividend paid to the year's net income. The ratio can be calculated in total or per share and is usually represented by d in formulas. Also see *retention ratio*.

Dividend Theories: Irrelevance, Preference, and Aversion—Logical arguments that stockholders should be indifferent to, prefer, or be averse to the payment of dividends.

Dividend Yield—A stock's annual dividend divided by its current price.

Double Taxation of Corporate Earnings—The primary financial disadvantage of the corporate form. A corporation's earnings are subject to corporate tax when earned and personal tax when paid to stockholders as dividends.

Dunning—Pursuing a customer for payment of an overdue receivable.

Du Pont Equations—A series of relationships between financial ratios that illustrates the inner workings of businesses and how performance in one area influences performance in others.

E

Earnings Before Interest and Taxes (EBIT)—A measure of a firm's performance without regard to how it is financed. Also known as *operating profit*.

Earnings Dilution—A drop in EPS caused by a sale of stock at a below market price.

Economic Order Quantity (EOQ) Model—A technique for minimizing the sum of inventory ordering and carrying costs.

Economic Value Added (EVA)—A measure of income that recognizes the cost of equity as well as debt. A positive EVA represents a contribution to shareholder wealth over that required by an equity investor, and is viewed as an increment to MVA. EVA is after-tax EBIT less the product of capital and the cost of capital. Also see *Market Value Added (MVA)*.

Effective Annual Rate (EAR)—The annually compounded rate that pays the same interest as a lower rate compounded more frequently.

Efficient Market Hypothesis—The assertion that information travels around the U.S. financial system so fast that stock prices virtually always reflect all available information. The concept implies that technical analysis is useless.

Employee Stock Option—See *Stock Option.*

EPS—Earnings per share. A firm's earnings stated on a per-share outstanding basis. An important measure of business performance in the stock market.

Equity—An ownership interest. In business, the portion of a firm's capital representing funds belonging to its shareholders. An equity investment is an investment in stock. In general, the portion of an asset's value accruing to its legal owner after subtracting the interest of creditors. In home ownership, the house's market value less the value of mortgages and other loans collateralized by the property.

Ethical Investing—Investing only in the securities of companies that meet some ethical criteria in their operations such as being environmentally friendly or not discriminating in hiring or promotion.

Exercise Price—See *Strike Price.*

Euro—A common European currency adopted in January 2002 by most of the members of the European Union.

Eurobond—A bond denominated in a currency other than that of the country in which it is sold.

Eurodollar Market—The debt market created when foreign banks with Eurodollar deposits lend those funds.

Eurodollars—U.S. dollars deposited in banks in other countries.

Exchange—A company that provides a physical marketplace and the administrative capability of transferring stocks from one owner to another.

Exchange Rate—In international finance, the rate at which one currency can be traded for another. *Spot* rates are available for current trades. *Forward* rates are available for currency to be delivered at a specified future time.

Exchange Rate Risk—The risk that international trade dealings will earn less than expected because of movement in exchange rates.

Ex-Dividend Date—The date on which a stock trades without a declared dividend that has yet to be paid. Two days prior to the date of record.

Exemptions (Personal and Dependency)—In personal taxes, an amount by which taxable income can be reduced for each person in a household.

Expectations Theory—With respect to dividends: A dividend that's lower than expected will be taken as a negative by investors even if it is larger than previous dividends. A variation on the signaling effect of dividends. With

respect to interest rates: A theory explaining the shape of the yield curve. The curve slopes up or down depending on whether expectations about future interest and inflation rates are increasing or decreasing.

Expected Return—The return an investor believes is most likely on an investment, understanding that the actual return may be somewhat different in certain investments such as stocks. The mean of the probability distribution of returns.

Expense—An item of expenditure not closely related to production. Contrast with *cost.*

Expropriate—In international business, the seizure of assets held in a foreign country by the government of that country.

F

Factoring Receivables—Selling receivables to a financing source for an amount less than their face value.

FASB—Financial Accounting Standards Board. The body within the accounting profession that sets rules and standards for the form and content of financial statements.

Federal Budget Deficit—The amount by which the government's spending exceeds its income in a year. A surplus implies income is greater. See *National Debt.*

Finance—(noun) The art and science of handling money.

Finance—(verb) To raise money usually to acquire an asset or to do some project.

Financial Analyst—A person who studies the financial results of businesses and makes recommendations on their values as investments.

Financial Assets—Stocks and bonds. More generally, a document giving its owner a claim to certain future cash flows. Stocks base that claim on ownership (equity), while bonds base it on debt. Some, but not all, financial assets are securities.

Financial Economics—A somewhat archaic term for financial theory emphasizing the field's roots in economics.

Financial Instrument—A security or financial asset.

Financial Intermediary—An institution that pools investors' money and invests it on their behalf giving the investors shares of itself. Financial intermediaries transfer money from investors to companies indirectly.

Financial Markets—Markets in which financial assets are traded—for example, the stock market.

Financial Merger—Financial mergers are undertaken to make money from the merger itself rather than from the underlying businesses.

Financial Plan—A projection of a company's financial statements into the future based on a series of assumptions about what the business and the environment will do. Part of a business plan.

Financial Ratios—See *Ratio Analysis*.

Financial Risk—The variation in a firm's financial performance caused by using borrowed money (debt, leverage).

Financial Statements—Reports created from accounting records that summarize a firm's performance in money terms.

Financing Lease—A lease in which the lessee effectively acquires ownership of the leased asset. Also called a *capital lease*. Accounted for by showing the leased asset on the balance sheet offset by a liability representing the obligation to make future lease payments. Compare with *Operating Lease*.

Fixed and Total Asset Turnover—Sales divided by fixed or total assets. Financial ratios that measure the firm's ability to generate revenue using its assets.

Fixed Financial Charge—An expense item that must be paid regardless of how the firm is performing. Essentially, interest and lease payments.

Float—Money tied up in the check-clearing process.

Floor Broker—A broker who buys and sells on the trading floor of a stock exchange.

Flotation Costs—The administrative cost of issuing new securities. Consists largely of commissions and marketing fees, but printing and engraving costs can also be significant.

Forecast—A short-term projection of a company's financial results. For example, most firms do regular cash forecasts to predict their immediate funding needs.

Foreclosure—In real estate/home ownership, a taking of a mortgaged property, usually a home, because the borrower/homeowner has defaulted on the mortgage loan.

Foreign Bond—A bond denominated in the currency of the country in which it is sold, but issued by a foreign borrower.

Foreign Exchange—A general term for the currency of foreign countries.

Foreign Exchange Market—A financial market in which the currencies of different countries are traded.

Free Cash Flow—Cash generated by a business above that needed for asset replacement and growth.

Fundamental Analysis—A systematic process in which a security is valued by estimating the performance of the underlying company and the future cash flows associated with owning the security. These are discounted to arrive at an *intrinsic value* for the security.

Funds—Generally another term for cash.

Future Value—The amount a present sum will grow into at a specified interest rate over a specified period of time.

G

GAAP—Generally accepted accounting principles. The general rules by which financial records are kept.

Going Concern Value—The value of a firm as a profit earning business as opposed to as a collection of assets.

Gordon Model—A mathematical model for valuing stock based on an assumed constant growth rate into the indefinite future.

Greenmail—To avoid an unfriendly acquisition, a firm may buy shares owned by a potential acquirer at a price above the market price of the stock. The above-market payment is *greenmail.*

Gross Margin—Revenue less cost where cost is spending closely associated with production. Stated in dollars or as a percentage of revenue. A fundamental measure of a business's strength.

H

Hedging—A maneuver or contract that eliminates risk from a transaction. In international trade, eliminating exchange rate risk by purchasing a forward contract for delivery of foreign exchange at a specified rate at a specified time.

Holding Company—A company that owns other companies. A *parent* company.

Horizontal Merger—A merger between companies in the same line of business, usually as competitors.

I

Indenture—Contractual agreements associated with bonds that limit the activities of the issuing companies. The limitations are designed to reduce the risk that the firm won't be able to pay the bond's interest and principal.

Independence Hypothesis—In capital structure theory, the original restrictive model by Modigliani and Miller that shows stock price to be independent of capital structure.

In Play—A company is in play when it is the object of an acquisition attempt.

Insider Information—Information about companies that can influence stock price that is available to insiders but not to the general public. It is illegal to make short-term profits using insider information.

Insolvent—A firm is technically insolvent when it can't pay its short-term debts. Legal insolvency implies the firm's liabilities exceed its assets.

Institutional Investor—A business organization that buys and sells securities. Generally a fund of some kind such as a mutual fund or a pension fund that invests the pooled money of its clients; also a bank or investment bank.

Interest—The return on a debt investment. Called *interest rate* when stated as a percentage of the debt on which it is paid.

Interest Rate Risk—The risk of loss to an investor from changes in the price of a bond that arise from changes in the market interest rate. Also called *price risk* and *maturity risk.*

International Bond—A bond sold outside the home country of the issuing organization (borrower).

Intrinsic Value—An underlying or fundamental value. In securities analysis, the price of a security (usually a stock) derived from extensive analysis of the issuing company and its industry. In financial options, the difference between the market price of the underlying stock and the price at which an option on that stock can be exercised (the strike price) if that difference is positive, zero if it is not.

Invest (Investing, Investment)—Using a resource (usually money) to improve the future rather than for current consumption. Investment by companies generally means buying assets to be used in their businesses. Investment by individuals usually means buying financial assets (stocks, bonds, savings accounts) that earn a return.

Investment Bank—An organization that assists companies in issuing securities and selling them to investors.

Investment Grade Bonds—Bonds above a certain quality rating. Moody: Baa; S&P: BBB.

IOS—Investment opportunity schedule. A schedule of capital budgeting projects arranged in decreasing order of IRR.

IPO—Initial public offering. Stock in a new company offered to the public for the first time. Such stock tends to make a volatile, high-risk investment.

IRR—Internal rate of return. A capital budgeting technique that rates projects according to their expected return on invested funds. The higher the return the better.

J

Junk Bonds—Risky bonds issued by financially weak companies that pay high rates of interest. Also called *high-yield bonds*.

Just in Time (JIT)—Just in time inventory systems. In theory, manufacturing parts arrive "just in time" to be used in production, eliminating the need for inventories.

L

LBO—Leveraged buyout. A process in which an investor group buys up a company's stock using a small amount of equity and borrowing the rest of the money required. The debt is often secured by the firm's assets. The investor groups are often the firms' managements, and the company goes from being publicly held to being privately held.

Leaning on the Trade—See *Stretching Payables*.

Lease—An agreement for the use of an asset in return for payments over a specified period. In recent years, long-term leases have been used to acquire assets rather than purchasing them with debt or equity capital. Lease payments then become fixed financial obligations similar to interest.

Leverage (Financial)—The use of borrowed money to multiply financial performance in terms of ROE and EPS.

Leverage (Operating)—The use of fixed as opposed to variable cost in a firm's cost structure.

Leveraged Lease—A three-party leasing arrangement in which a lender extends credit to a lessor to acquire equipment which is then leased to a user. The loan is usually secured by the leased equipment. Sophisticated tax advantages are associated with the technique.

Limited Liability—An advantage of the corporate form. Stockholder liability for the actions of a company is limited to the value of the stock. That is, a suit against the corporation cannot be made against a stockholder simply because he is an owner.

Limited Liability Company (LLC)—A relatively new corporate form combining certain advantages of a corporation (limited liability and the ability to raise money by selling stock) with the tax treatment of a partnership. Avoids double taxation of corporate earnings.

Line of Credit—A relatively informal, nonbinding agreement with a bank as to the maximum amount a firm can borrow during a period of time.

Liquidation—Ending a firm's life by selling off its assets.

Liquidity—With respect to a company, the ability to pay its bills in the short run. With respect to an asset, the readiness with which it can be converted to cash.

Liquidity Preference Theory—A theory of the shape of the yield curve. The curve slopes upward because, all other things being equal, investors prefer shorter, more liquid investments. They must therefore be induced to lend longer with higher rates.

Liquidity Risk—The risk of loss to an investor from the inability to sell a security to another investor at a price close to its true value.

Listed Company—A firm that is traded on an organized exchange is "listed" on that exchange. Unlisted companies are traded, but not on the exchange.

M

Marginal Tax Rate—The rate at which the next dollar of income will be taxed. Generally the taxpayer's bracket rate.

Marketable Securities—Highly liquid short-term debt investments held by companies instead of cash. Marketable securities provide nearly the liquidity of cash but earn a modest return.

Market Capitalization—The total value of a company's stock. The number of shares outstanding times the current price.

Market Risk—Variation on the return on a stock investment caused by things that tend to affect all stocks.

Market Risk Premium—In portfolio theory, the difference between the return on the market and the risk-free rate.

Market Segmentation Theory—A theory of the shape of the yield curve. The debt market is segmented by term, and each segment is independent of the others. Hence, the curve slopes up or down depending on supply and demand conditions in the various market segments.

Market Value Added (MVA)—The excess of market value measured by the product of stock price and the number of shares outstanding over the book value of equity. An indication of the effectiveness of management in contributing to shareholder wealth. Also see *Economic Value Added (EVA)*.

Mark-to-Market—An accounting rule requiring certain financial institutions to value assets on their books at current market prices. The rule contributed to the depth of the financial crisis of 2008.

Maturity—The date on which the principal of a debt is due. Also the time from the present until that date.

Maturity Matching—The idea that the maturity of financing should match the duration of the project being financed.

Maturity Risk—The risk of loss to an investor from changes in the price of a bond that arise from changes in the market interest rate. Also called *price risk* and *interest rate risk*. The term *maturity risk* emphasizes the fact that interest-induced price changes are larger with longer maturities.

MCC Schedule—Marginal cost of capital schedule. A plot of the WACC (weighted average cost of capital) against the total amount of capital to be raised in a planning period. The MCC rises as more capital is raised and the costs of individual components experience step function increases.

Merger—The combination of two or more businesses under one ownership in which all but one legal entity ceases to exist, and the combined organization continues under the name of the surviving firm. When the surviving firm acquires the stock of the other(s), the transaction can be called an acquisition. A merger is *friendly* if it has the approval and support of the acquired *(target)* firm's management. It is *unfriendly* if the target's management resists. The term *merger* tends to be used loosely to refer to any business combination.

Modified Accelerated Cost Recovery System (MACRS)—The system of accelerated depreciation allowed for federal tax computations.

Money Market—A financial market in which short-term (less than one year) debt securities are traded.

Moral Hazard—A condition in which a person can benefit, usually financially, by acting unethically or immorally, i.e., the person is tempted to be less than honest and ethical. A moral hazard exists when executive compensation is heavily based on the market price of the company's stock so that executives may perform illegal or unethical actions to hold the stock price up.

Mortgage Bond—A bond secured by real estate.

Mortgage Loan—A loan secured by real estate. Commonly referred to simply as a *mortgage*.

Multinational Corporation (MNC)—A company with major operations in several countries.

Municipal Bond (Muni)—A bond issued by a government unit below the federal level. The interest on municipal bonds is exempt from federal income tax.

Mutual Fund—An investment vehicle in which investors contribute to a fund that uses their pooled money to invest in stocks, bonds, and other financial assets. The fund owns the assets, while the investors own shares of the fund.

Mutually Exclusive Projects—In capital budgeting, projects that automatically exclude one another. Projects are mutually exclusive either because they're different approaches to doing the same thing or because limited resources preclude doing more than one.

N

Nasdaq (Market)—A major U.S. stock exchange. Formerly known as the *OTC market*. NASDAQ is an acronym for the National Association of Securities Dealers Automated Quotation system. Nasdaq is an electronic exchange on which brokers can trade from anywhere. Other major exchanges have physical locations, requiring a trader's presence on the exchange floor in order to trade.

National Debt—The accumulated total of annual federal budget deficits funded by federal government borrowing.

Nominal Interest Rate—The named or quoted rate usually stated on an annually compounded basis. May be different from the effective rate due to non-annual compounding.

Noncash Charge—An item of cost or expense in the income statement that doesn't require cash. The primary example is depreciation.

Normal Growth—In stock pricing models, growth at a rate less than the rate of return. Growth rates in excess of the rate of return are *supernormal*.

Note—A security reflecting an intermediate-term debt relationship between the issuer and the holder.

NPV—Net present value. A capital budgeting technique that rates projects according to the total present value of all their associated cash flows. The higher the total or net present value, the better.

O

Off Balance Sheet Financing—Acquiring the use of assets without adding debt or equity to the balance sheet. The primary example is an operating lease. Off balance sheet financing avoids the degradation in financial ratios that generally comes with additional debt. The details of off balance sheet financing must be disclosed in the notes to financial statements.

Operating Lease—A lease in which the lessee does not effectively acquire ownership of the leased asset. Accounted for as a stream of expense payments on the income statement. No entry is made on the balance sheet to reflect the acquisition of the asset. The most common form of off balance sheet financing. Compare with *Financing Lease*.

Operating Plan—A short- to intermediate- term business plan addressing a firm's methods and goals over the period covered. Most companies have an annual operating plan.

Operating Profit—See *Earnings Before Interest and Taxes (EBIT)*.

Opportunity Cost—The benefit foregone by using an asset in a particular way. Usually the income or benefit it would produce in its next best use.

Option (Financial)—The contracted right to buy or sell a security at a fixed price within a predetermined period of time, usually three to nine months. Options give speculators the chance to profit on movements in securities'

prices without actually owning those securities. For example, the owner of an option to buy will profit if the underlying security's market price rises substantially above the price specified in the option during the option period.

Option (Real)—See *Real Option*.

Option Price—The price an option holder pays for a contract.

P

Par (Value)—The stated or face value of certain securities, generally bonds and preferred stocks. A bond pays interest on its par value, which is usually $1,000.

Payback Period—A capital budgeting technique that rates projects according to the speed with which they return invested money.

Payment Date—The date on which a dividend check is mailed.

Payout Ratio—The percentage of earnings paid to stockholders in dividends.

P/E Ratio—The ratio of a firm's stock price to its earnings per share (EPS). A measure of the value the stock market places on the company and its future prospects.

Perpetuity—An infinite series of equal payments at equal intervals of time.

Perquisites (Perks)—Privileges and luxuries provided to executives.

Personal Guarantee—Generally, a guarantee made by the owner of a small business when a loan is made to the business. The owner pledges his or her personal credit in addition to that of the company. Personal guarantees circumvent the limited liability feature of the corporate form in the context of lending to small businesses.

Planning Assumption—An assumption about the future on which a business plan is based. The assumption must be reflected in the firm's financial projections by calculating the specific financial statement figures it implies.

Planning Horizon—The time a business plan covers. Typically between a few months and five years.

Pledging Receivables—Borrowing money using receivables as collateral.

Poison Pill—A corporate tactic to avoid being acquired. A poison pill is a clause written into a firm's bylaws that makes it prohibitively expensive for an acquiring firm to take control.

Political Risk—In international business, the chance that the value of a firm's investment in a foreign country will be reduced by political actions of either the foreign government or terrorists.

Portfolio—In finance, a collection of investments.

Portfolio Investment—In international finance, investment in the securities of a foreign company or government.

Portfolio Theory—A body of thought aimed at forming investment portfolios that minimize risk for a given return.

Preemptive Rights—A stockholder's right to maintain her proportionate ownership in a corporation. The stockholder has the right to buy a share of any newly issued stock that is proportionate to her fractional ownership of the company before the new issue. The right is not a matter of law but must be written into the corporation's bylaws.

Preferred Stock—A security that pays a constant dividend forever. A hybrid between debt and common equity.

Present Value—The value today of a sum promised at a specified time in the future given a rate of interest. The amount that would have to be deposited today at the specified interest rate to grow into the promised sum on the specified date.

Price Risk—The risk of loss to an investor from changes in the price of a bond that arise from changes in the market interest rate. Also called *interest rate risk* and *maturity risk*.

Primary Market—A subdivision of financial markets in which securities are sold for the first time. The sale is by the issuing company to investors. Compare with *Secondary Market*.

Prime Rate—The interest rate banks charge their largest and best commercial customers.

Privately Held Company—A company that is not registered with the SEC and whose securities therefore may not be sold to the general public. Also called a *closely held company*.

Profitability Index (PI)—A capital budgeting technique that rates projects according to the ratio of the present value of cash inflows to the present value of cash outflows. Essentially a variation on the NPV technique. The higher the PI the better.

Progressive Tax—An income tax structure in which higher incomes are taxed at higher rates.

Promissory Note—A lending agreement in which the borrower promises to pay principal and interest in accordance with specific terms.

Prospectus—A document disclosing the details of a security and the underlying business to prospective investors.

Proxy—The right to act for another on a specific issue. In finance, the right to cast another's vote in the election of corporate directors. Incumbent directors routinely solicit stockholders' proxies for reelection.

Proxy Fight—A fight for control of a corporation when two or more interests compete for the proxies of shareholders in the election of directors.

Public Company Accounting Oversight Board (PCAOB)—An independent board created by the Sarbanes–Oxley Act to oversee the activities of the public accounting (auditing) industry. Operates under the direction of the SEC.

Publicly Traded Company—A company that is registered with the SEC and whose securities therefore may be sold to the general public.

Pure Interest Rate—The earning power of money. An interest rate without an inflation component or premiums for risk.

Pure Play Company—A firm in a single line of business, as opposed to a firm with divisions in several businesses.

Put (Option)—The right to sell a stock to another at a specified price over a designated period of time. See *Option*. Compare with *Call Option*.

Q

Quick Ratio—Current assets less inventories divided by current liabilities. A financial ratio that measures a firm's liquidity, the ability to pay its bills in the short run, without depending on converting inventory into cash. Also called the *acid test*.

R

Ratio Analysis—A technique of analyzing the strength of a company by forming (financial) ratios out of sets of numbers from the financial statements. Ratios are compared with the competition, recent history, and the firm's plan to assess the quality of its performance.

Real Asset—A tangible object with value derived from the service it provides such as a house or a car. Distinguish from a financial asset, which is a piece of paper giving its owner a claim to future cash flows.

Real Option—The ability to take a course of action that under certain circumstances leads to a benefit. The circumstances that make the action desirable are uncertain, and maintaining the ability to take it requires expenditures before that uncertainty is resolved. Hence, bearing the preliminary cost gives one the option of taking an action in the future that may or may not turn out to be desirable.

Recourse—In secured lending, if the asset collateralizing a loan proves not to have the value anticipated, recourse implies the borrower is still responsible for the debt. The lender is said to have recourse to the borrower. A loan in which the lender bears any risk in the value of the collateral is said to be *nonrecourse*.

Red Herring—A prospectus for the sale of a security not yet approved by the SEC. Stamped with the word *preliminary* in red letters.

Refinancing—Paying off a loan with the proceeds of a new loan generally made at a lower interest rate than the loan being paid off. Homeowners commonly refinance mortgages when interest rates fall.

Registered Securities (Bonds)—Securities with which the issuer or a *transfer agent* keeps a list of the names of

owners. Dividends or interest payments are made to *owners of record* as of specified dates.

Regulation Analyst Certification (Reg AC)—A regulation promulgated by the SEC as a result of the Sarbanes–Oxley Act that requires securities analysts to certify that they actually believe in what they say in their reports and that their pay is not tied to their recommendation.

Reorganization—In bankruptcy, a plan to restructure the failing company so that it may continue in business.

Required Return—The minimum return that keeps an investor in a particular stock. Generally a function of the risk perceived in the investment.

Reserve Currency—In international finance, a significant amount foreign currency held by a nation as a hedge against unforeseen needs. The U.S. dollar is the world's primary reserve currency.

Residual Claim—Stockholders' claim to income and assets is the residual after all other claims are satisfied.

Residual Dividend Theory—The idea that corporations pay dividends with whatever money is left over out of earnings after all projects with a positive NPV are undertaken.

Residual Value—The value of a leased asset at the termination of the lease.

Restructuring (Debt)—A change in a bankrupt firm's debt obligations aimed at allowing it to continue in business. In an *extension*, creditors agree to give the firm longer to pay. In a *composition*, creditors agree to settle for less than the full amount owed.

Retention Ratio—The ratio of annual earnings (net income) not paid out to shareholders as dividends but retained in the business (generally) to support growth. Usually represented in formulas by *r*. Also see *Dividend Payout Ratio*.

Return—The payment to an investor for the use of funds. Usually expressed as a percentage of the investment.

Revolving Credit Agreement—A formal, binding agreement with a bank as to the maximum amount a firm can borrow during a period of time. Interest is paid on the amount borrowed and a commitment fee is paid on the unused balance of the commitment.

Risk (in Finance)—The probability that the return on an investment will be less than expected. The variability of the return on a particular investment. The variance of the probability distribution of return.

Risk-Adjusted Rates—In capital budgeting, a rate used in place of the cost of capital to reflect especially risky projects.

Risk Aversion—The premise that most people prefer lower risk investments when expected returns are about equal.

Risk-Free Rate—The interest rate excluding all risk premiums. The risk-free rate consists of the pure rate and an inflation adjustment. It is approximated by the three-month Treasury bill rate. Written as k_{RF}.

Risk Premium—A component of a rate of interest or return that compensates the investor for bearing some kind of risk.

ROA—Return on assets. Net income divided by total assets. A financial ratio measuring performance concentrating on profitability and asset utilization.

ROE—Return on equity. Net income divided by equity. A financial ratio measuring performance concentrating on profitability, asset utilization, and the use of borrowed money.

ROS—Return on sales. Net income divided by sales revenue. A financial ratio measuring performance, concentrating on profitability.

Run (Bank)—A condition in which large numbers of investors, usually bank depositors, attempt to withdraw their money at the same time. Runs are usually due to panic over reports of the bank's likely failure.

S

Safety Stock—Extra inventory carried to prevent stockouts in the event of heavy use or delayed delivery.

Scenario Analysis—A business planning technique in which the implications of variations in planning assumptions are explored. Also known as "what-if-ing."

Seasoned Issue—An older bond.

Secondary Market—Sales of existing securities between investors. Compare with *Primary Market*.

Secured Debt—Debt backed by specific assets (the security or collateral) that become the property of the lender in the event of default.

Securities Analysis—A systematic approach to valuing securities, especially stocks, by studying an issuing firm's business and industry. The *securities analyst* plays an important role in the financial industry.

Securities and Exchange Commission (SEC)—The federal agency responsible for regulating securities dealings.

Securitization—A process in which loans of a particular class are purchased by an issuing institution and pooled so that their payments create a large periodic cash flow. The issuer then sells to investors securities that carry a legal right to portions of that cash flow.

Security—A financial asset. Commonly a stock or a bond. An asset pledged to guarantee the repayment of a loan. A security is a financial asset that can be traded among investors. Not all financial assets are securities.

Signaling Effect of Dividends—The idea that dividends send a message about management's confidence in the future of the firm—that is, paying a regular or increased dividend signals that the firm is fundamentally sound even if it appears to be having problems. The signaling idea leads to the practice of holding dividends constant or raising them in the face of poor financial performance. Also known as the *information* effect of dividends.

Sinking Fund—An arrangement to guarantee that funds are available to pay off a bond's principal at maturity.

SML—Security market line. The central element of the *CAPM*. The SML purports to explain how the market sets the required return on a stock investment.

Soft Currency—A currency whose value is not stable or reliable and that may be difficult to exchange for other currencies.

Specialist—An out-of-date term for a designated market maker. An official in a stock exchange who is assigned the stocks of specific companies and is responsible for conducting an orderly market in those securities.

Speculation—Assuming known risks in the hope of financial gain, usually with substantial knowledge of the processes that generate gains and losses.

Spinoff—A method of divesting a business unit by setting it up as a separate company and giving its shares to stockholders in proportion to their holdings of the original firm. After the spinoff, stockholders can trade the two stocks separately.

Spontaneous Financing—Financing provided by current liabilities that arise automatically as a result of doing business.

Spread—The difference between two prices or interest rates on which a dealer or a business generally makes money. For example, the difference between the rate a bank pays on deposits and the rate at which it lends. Also the difference between the prices at which a dealer in anything buys and sells; in finance, usually financial assets such as stocks. Economically, the difference between interest rates paid on high- and low-quality bonds.

Stable Dividend—A dividend that may remain constant or increase over time but that does not decrease.

Stand-Alone Project—In capital budgeting, a project with no competition either for the task it is to accomplish or for resources.

Stand-Alone Risk—The risk associated with investing in a stock that's held by itself, outside of a portfolio. Stand-alone risk depends on the volatility of a stock's own return rather than on the effect its inclusion has on the volatility of the return of a portfolio.

Statement of Cash Flows—See *Cash Flows*.

Stock—A financial asset representing a share of ownership of a corporation. Entitles the owner to dividends if any are paid. Common stock ownership also entitles the owner to vote for directors and on certain key proposals.

Stockbroker—A person licensed to assist investors in buying and selling securities for a commission.

Stock Dividend—Essentially a stock split in which the number of new shares issued is less than or equal to 20% of the original number outstanding.

Stock Exchange—A physical place in which stocks are traded by brokers on behalf of their investor clients.

Stock Market—The network of exchanges, brokers, and investors that trade in stocks.

Stock Option (Employee)—A right given to a corporate employee to purchase a designated number of shares of the company's stock at a fixed price over a specified period. If the company's stock price rises above the fixed, optioned price during the period, the employee can make a profit by buying below market and selling at market. Stock options can be given to employees at any level, but large blocks are generally awarded to senior executives as performance incentives. Executive stock options are controversial because they contribute to a tendency by management to maintain a short-run focus on stock price, which may create an incentive to artificially and/or fraudulently pump up the price or take excessive risks with company resources.

Stockout—An inventory shortage.

Stock Repurchase (Buyback)—A company buys, and generally retires, shares of its own stock. Stock may be repurchased to return cash to stock-holders, because it's a bargain at a temporarily depressed price, or to pump up EPS.

Stock Split—A change in the number of shares outstanding by issuing new shares in proportion to those already owned. All stockholders' proportionate ownership is maintained, and no economic value is created. Used to keep stock prices within a desirable trading range.

Strategic Merger—A strategic merger is one that's undertaken to enhance the business position of the acquiring company.

Strategic Plan—A long-term business plan addressing broad issues of what a company's management wants it to become and how it is to do business.

Stretching Payables—Paying invoices after they're due according to the terms of sale. Also called *leaning on the trade*.

Strike Price—The price at which an optioned stock can be bought or sold. Also called the *exercise price* or *striking price*. See *Option*.

S-Type Corporation—A corporate form in the tax code that gives small businesses some of the benefits of both the traditional corporation and the proprietorship. Most notably, S-type corporations escape the double taxation of earnings. S-types are largely being replaced by LLCs.

Subordinated Debt—Debt with a lower priority for the payment of

interest and principal than other (senior) debt.

Subprime Loans—Home mortgage loans made to borrowers who do not qualify for traditional loans. The fundamental cause of the financial crisis of 2008.

Sunk Cost—A cost associated with a project expended prior to making the decision to undertake that project (for example, the cost of research into the idea). Since sunk funds are already spent, they cannot alter future costs or benefits, and should not be included in the analysis leading to a decision.

Sustainable Growth Rate—The rate at which a firm can grow if none of its financial ratios change and it doesn't raise any new equity by selling stock. The growth in equity created by earnings retained.

Synergy—A situation in which two companies operating together under one ownership perform better than the sum of their separate performances. A popular reason given for mergers. The benefits of synergies, however, seem to be very hard to realize.

T

Takeover—The transfer of control over a company from one group to another. The term generally has a hostile implication.

Target Capital Structure—The capital structure that management strives to maintain as new capital is raised.

An estimate of the structure that maximizes stock price.

Target Company—The object of a corporate acquisition or merger. See *Merger*.

Tax Base—The thing that is taxed. Generally income, wealth, or consumption.

Tax Bracket—A range of income over which the tax rate is constant.

Tax Loss Carry Back (Forward)—The allocation of losses in a year to previous or subsequent years for the purpose of calculating taxes in those years. Losses may be carried back 2 years and carried forward 20 years.

Tax Pass–Through—A business organization form in which the business entity does not pay income taxes. Profits are passed-through to owners to be taxed as personal income. There are many pass–throughs forms. The most familiar include LLC, S-Type Corporation, and partnership.

Technical Analysis—An approach to valuing securities by examining past patterns of price and volume. The technique is based on the idea that such patterns repeat themselves.

Temporary Working Capital—Working capital that supports seasonal peaks in business.

Tender Offer—A general offer to stockholders to purchase shares at a specified price, usually for the purpose of acquiring a company.

10-K Report—A supplement to the annual report that public companies must file with the SEC.

Term—The time until a debt security's principal is due to be repaid. Also called the *debt's maturity* or *time until maturity.*

Terms of Sale—The conditions under which a sale is made primarily with respect to payment. Terms include a date on which payment is due and often specify a *prompt payment discount* that may be taken if payment is made within a specified time.

Time Premium—The difference between intrinsic value and the option price.

Time Value of Money—Calculations involving the present and future values of money under the action of compound interest. Also called *discounted cash flow.*

Top-Down Planning—Business planning based on a set of goals forced on the organization by senior management. Top-down planning has a tendency to lead to excessively optimistic plans.

Total Effective Tax Rate (TETR)—The combined income tax rate including federal and state tax. Less than the sum of the two because state tax is deductible from federal tax.

Trade Credit—Credit granted in the normal course of business between companies. That is, vendors don't usually demand immediate payment for their products.

Trading Range—A price range in which stocks are thought to appeal to the widest variety of investors. Typically between $30 and $100. Stock splits function to keep prices within a trading range when the stock is appreciating.

Tranche—The French word for *slice;* in finance, a portion or class of securities that can be split up and sold. Used to describe the securitization process for home mortgages. The term became well known during the financial crisis of 2008.

Transaction Gain or Loss—The difference between the net result of an international transaction and what was initially expected that arises from variation in exchange rates.

Transfer Agent—An organization that keeps records of the owners of a company's securities. When a security is sold by one investor or to another, ownership is transferred on the record by the transfer agent.

Translation Risk—The gain or loss on the value of assets and liabilities held in another country that results from variation in exchange rates. Generally relatively meaningless as long as the foreign operation is not liquidated or sold. Therefore not generally taxable.

Treasurer—The executive in charge of external financing in most companies. The treasurer generally reports to the CFO.

Trustee—With respect to bonds, an organization that ensures compliance with the conditions set forth in the indenture. With respect to bankruptcy, a person who administers the bankrupt organization to ensure funds are properly handled.

V

Valuation—A systematic process to determine the price at which a security should sell in financial markets.

Vertical Merger—A merger between companies when one is a supplier or a customer of the other.

W

WACC—See *Cost of Capital.*

Warehousing—In finance, a method of securing the lender's interest when borrowing is secured by inventories. The inventory is placed in a warehouse operated by a third party. When it is drawn out of the warehouse by the borrower, a pro rata share of payment on the loan is due.

Warrant—A security that grants its owner the right to purchase one or more shares of stock at a designated price over a limited period. Similar to a call option except that a warrant is issued by the company that issued the underlying stock while a call is issued by another investor. Also different in that warrants tend to be exercisable over much longer periods than calls.

What-If-ing—See *Scenario Analysis.*

White Knight—When a firm is an acquisition target by an unattractive suitor, a more desirable acquirer is known as a white knight. (The original suitor may be known for particularly ruthless treatment of acquired companies.)

Widely Held Company—A corporation whose ownership is distributed over a large number of people with no single individual or group having a significant proportion.

Working Capital—The balance sheet accounts associated with day-to-day operating activities. *Gross working capital* is generally defined as current assets and *net working capital* as current assets minus current liabilities.

Y

Yield—Return.

Yield Curve—The relationship between interest rates and the term of debt, generally expressed graphically. A *normal* yield curve is upsloping, reflecting rates that increase with increasing term. An *inverted* curve is downsloping.

YTC—Yield to call. Bond pricing calculations assuming the bond will be called at the end of the protected period.

YTM—Yield to maturity. Bond pricing calculations assuming the bond will pay interest until maturity at which time it will repay its principal (face value).

Z

Zero Coupon Bond—A bond that pays no interest during its life. A "zero" sells for the present value of the principal repayment. However, the IRS imputes interest during the bond's life on which the bondholder must pay tax.